CW00904825

Principles of Economics

Principles of Economics

Belton M. Fleisher
Ohio State University

Edward J. Ray
Ohio State University

Thomas J. Kniesner
University of North Carolina
Chapel Hill

wcb
Wm. C. Brown Publishers
Dubuque, Iowa

Book Team

John D. Stout *Editor*
Kathy Law Laube *Developmental Editor*
Mary K. Sailer *Designer*
Reneé Pins *Art Production Assistant*
Vickie Putman Caughron *Production Editor*
Vicki Krug *Permissions Editor*
Linda M. Galarowicz *Product Manager*

wcb group

Wm. C. Brown *Chairman of the Board*
Mark. C. Falb *President and Chief Executive Officer*

wcb

Wm. C. Brown Publishers, College Division

G. Franklin Lewis *Executive Vice-President, General Manager*
E. F. Jogerst *Vice-President, Cost Analyst*
George Wm. Bergquist *Editor in Chief*
Beverly Kolz *Director of Production*
Chris C. Guzzardo *Vice-President, Director of Marketing*
Bob McLaughlin *National Sales Manager*
Craig S. Marty *Director of Marketing Research*
Marilyn A. Phelps *Manager of Design*
Colleen A. Yonda *Production Editorial Manager*
Faye M. Schilling *Photo Research Manager*

To

Don and David
Beth, Stephanie, Katherine,
and Michael
Grace

Contents

Expanded Contents ix
Preface xxv

Part I

Introduction

1   Scarcity, the Three Questions of Economics, and an Economic System   5

Part II

How Markets Work

2   Demand   *31*
3   The Shape of the Demand Curve   *61*
4   Supply   *77*
5   How Markets Work   *105*
6   Government and Markets   *121*
7   The Competitive Firm and Industry: Supply and Demand in the Long Run   *143*

Part III

Monopoly and Other Market Forms

8   Monopoly   *167*
9   Oligopoly   *189*
10   Monopolistic Competition, Product Differentiation, and Advertising   *205*
11   Government Regulation of Industries   *223*

Part IV

The Market for Inputs

12   Introduction to the Markets for Labor and Other Inputs   *245*
13   Factor Markets   *265*
14   Investment in Human and Physical Capital   *281*
15   The Distribution of Income   *297*
16   Discrimination   *321*

Part V

Government and Markets

17   Market Deficiencies   *339*
18   Government and Markets in Developing Countries   *359*

Part VI

Introduction to Macroeconomics

19   Introduction to Macroeconomics   *379*
20   Employment, Unemployment, and the Aggregate Production of Goods and Services   *413*
21   Aggregate Expenditure on Goods and Services   *437*
22   Money and the Banking System   *463*
23   The Central Bank and Regulation of Money and the Banking System   *479*
24   Money, Credit, and the Rate of Interest   *497*

Part VII

Macroeconomic Policy

25 How the Macroeconomy Works   *519*
26 Aggregate Demand, Aggregate Supply, and the Price
    Level   *537*
27 Fiscal and Monetary Policies   *561*
28 Monetary and Fiscal Policies in Action   *581*
29 Summing Up: Macroeconomic Controversies   *599*

Part VIII

The International Economy

30 Trade among Nations   *621*
31 The Regulation of International Trade   *641*
32 Monetary and Macroeconomic Aspects of International
    Trade   *661*
33 Current Issues in International Trade   *683*

Part IX

Economic Growth and Comparative Systems

34 Economic Growth and Change   *711*
35 Alternative Economic Systems   *723*

Appendix A: Graphs   749
Appendix B: How to Solve Policy Issues   755
References   757
Glossary   765
Index   779

Expanded Contents

Preface xxv

Part I

Introduction

1 Scarcity, the Three Questions of
Economics, and an Economic System   5

Outline   5
Objectives   5
The Three Fundamental Economic Questions   6
  A Thought Quiz   6
Understanding Economic Events with Economic
  Analysis   8
    An Example of Government Policy and Its Impact
    on the Answers to the Three Economic
    Questions: Medical Care   9
Scarcity and an Economic System   10
  What Is an Economic Model?   10
  An Introductory Example: Dealing with Scarcity in
  a Small Economy   11
    The Production Possibilities Frontier (PPF)
    11
  The Production Possibilities Frontier, Opportunity
  Cost, and Economic Efficiency   13
    The Shape of the Production Possibilities
    Frontier   14

Applications of the Production Possibilities
  Frontier and Opportunity Cost   16
    Background   16
    Reckoning with Opportunity Costs: The Case
    of the 55–mph Speed Limit   17
    Opportunity Cost, Comparative Advantage, and
    Specialization   19
The Concept of a Market Economy and the Economy
  of the United States   21
Summary and Conclusions   23
Key Terms   23
Questions for Discussion and Review   23
Appendix *Economics and Your Career*   25
Why Take Economics?   25
Economics as a Major   25
Careers in Economics   25
Prominent Economics Majors and Positions They
  Have Held   26
Policy Issue: You Decide *Who Should Pay for Clean
  Air?*   27
The Action–Initiating Event   27
The Issue   27
Economic Policy Issues   27
Recommendations   27

Part II

How Markets Work

2   Demand   *31*

Outline   *31*
Objectives   *31*
Introduction   *32*
The Demand Relationship   *33*
   Data on Consumer Expenditures in the United
     States   *33*
   Basic Assumptions of the Theory of Demand   *33*
     The Goals of Consumers and How They
       Attempt to Achieve Them   *33*
     Limitations on the Choices Consumers Can
       Make   *35*
   Method of Analysis   *36*
   The Law of Demand and the Demand Curve   *36*
     The Demand Curve, Value, and Marginal
       Utility*   *38*
Demand versus Quantity Demanded   *45*
   Quantity Demanded and Change in Quantity
     Demanded   *45*
   The Demand Curve and Factors that Shift It   *46*
     Income   *46*
     Tastes and Preferences   *47*
     Prices of Related Goods and Services   *47*
     Expectations   *48*
     Time Horizons   *48*
     Time Required for Consumption   *48*
     Population and Income Distribution   *48*
   Summary of Movements Along the Demand Curve
     and Shifts in Demand   *49*
Applications of the Law of Demand   *50*
   The Diffusion of Japanese Cars into the United
     States Market   *50*
   Government Policy and the Theory of Demand
     51
Summary and Conclusions   *52*
Key Terms   *52*
Questions for Discussion and Review   *52*
Appendix *A Closer Look at the Theory of Consumer
   Choice   54*
The Utility Function   *54*
Indifference Curves   *55*
The Budget Constraint: How Much of What You Want
   Can You Get?   *57*
The Geometry and Economics of Consumer Choice
   58
Using Indifference Curve and Budget Constraint
   Diagrams   *59*
Key Terms   *59*

3   The Shape of the Demand Curve   *61*

Outline   *61*
Objectives   *61*
Introduction   *62*
Quantifying the Relationship between Price and
   Quantity Demanded   *62*
   The Slope of the Demand Curve   *62*
   Price Elasticity of Demand   *64*
     Calculating a Price Elasticity of Demand   *64*
     Elasticity, Prices, and Total Consumer
       Spending   *66*
     Estimates of Price Elasticities for the United
       States   *69*
   Why Price Elasticities Vary   *70*
     Ability to Substitute   *70*
     Time Horizons   *70*
     Importance in the Budget   *71*
Other Demand Elasticities   *71*
   Income Elasticity   *71*
   Cross Price Elasticity   *72*
Summary and Conclusions   *73*
Key Terms   *73*
Questions for Discussion and Review   *73*

4   Supply   *77*

Outline   *77*
Objectives   *77*
Introduction   *78*
The Supply Relationship   *78*
   Basic Assumptions of Supply Theory   *78*
     Producers and Their Goals   *78*
     Limitations on Producers   *80*
   Profit, Marginal Cost, and the Law of Supply   *80*
     Method of Analysis   *80*
     An Example   *81*
     Marginal Cost, Profit, and Supply in the Short
       Run   *83*
     Average Cost, Marginal Cost, and Supply   *85*
     Elasticity of Supply   *89*
Factors that Shift Supply   *90*
   Changes in Technology   *91*
   Changes in Labor Skills   *92*
   Changes in Input Prices   *92*
   Changes in Expected Future Prices   *92*
   Time Horizons   *93*

*This section may be skipped without loss of continuity.

Application of the Supply Relationship 95
  The Price and Supply of Oil 95
Summary and Conclusions 98
Key Terms 98
Questions for Discussion and Review 98
Appendix *A Closer Look at a Firm's Costs* 100
An Example: Choosing the Optimal Size of a Pottery
  Firm 100
Key Terms 104

5   How Markets Work   105

Outline 105
Objectives 105
Introduction 106
How the Forces of Supply and Demand Determine
  Price and the Level of Production 107
  The Concept of Market Equilibrium 107
  Forces Working to Establish Equilibrium 108
    Market Price Below Equilibrium 108
    Market Price Above Equilibrium 109
The Effects of Shifts in Supply and Demand on
  Equilibrium Price and Quantity 110
  Background 110
  Permanent Shifts in Supply and Demand 110
    Permanent Shifts in Demand 110
    Permanent Shifts in Supply 111
    Shifts in Both Supply and Demand 112
  Permanent Shifts in Supply and Demand Affect
    Other Markets, Too 114
  The Effects of Temporary Shifts in Supply and
    Demand 115
    Inventories and Transactions Costs 115
    An Example: The Retail Market for Beer 115
    Temporary Changes in Demand Caused by
      One-time-only Customers 116
    More on Inventory Costs and Prices 117
Summary and Conclusions 118
Key Terms 118
Questions for Discussion and Review 118

6   Government and Markets   121

Outline 121
Objectives 121
Introduction 122
Government Intervention and Social Welfare 122
Government Policies to Restrain Market Forces 123
  A Price Ceiling 123

A Case Study of a Price Ceiling: The Gasoline
  Crisis of 1973–74 126
  Gas Rationing as an Alternative to a Price
    Ceiling 127
A Price Floor 129
  Agricultural Price Supports 129
  Agricultural Price Subsidies 132
Government Policies that Work through the Forces of
  Supply and Demand 134
  Policies that Shift Supply Curves 134
    The Payment in Kind (PIK) Program 134
  Policies that Shift Demand Curves 136
    Subsidy: The Case of Food Stamps 137
    Subsidy: The Case of Medicare and Medicaid
      138
  Policies that Shift both Supply and Demand 138
    The Market for Small Cars in the United States
      139
Summary and Conclusions 140
Key Terms 141
Questions for Discussion and Review 141

7   The Competitive Firm and Industry:
     Supply and Demand in the Long Run   143

Outline 143
Objectives 143
Introduction 144
Long-run Supply and Demand in a Competitive
  Industry 145
  Fixed Costs, Variable Costs, and Profit in the Long
    Run 145
    The Industry's Long-run Supply Curve:
      Constant Costs 148
    Increasing Costs in the Long Run 150
  The Theory of the Surviving Firm: Profit
    Maximization with Incomplete Knowledge 152
  Summary: Profit and Economic Rent in the Long
    Run 153
Applications of the Theory of the Competitive
  Industry 154
  Some Complications and Side Effects of
    Regulating Medicinal Drugs 154
  Competition and Economic Efficiency 156
    Economically Efficient Production 157
    Efficiency in Consumption 157
    Efficiency, Marginal Cost, and Equity 158
Summary and Conclusions 160
Key Terms 160
Questions for Discussion and Review 160
Policy Issue: You Decide *Supercows* 162
The Action-Initiating Event 162
The Issue 162
Economic Policy Issues 162

Part III
Monopoly and Other Market Forms

8   Monopoly   *167*

Outline   *167*
Objectives   *167*
Introduction   *168*
Monopoly   *169*
   A Monopolist's Output Decision   *169*
   An Economic Evaluation of Monopoly   *173*
      Monopoly and Survival   *173*
      Monopoly and Efficiency   *174*
      Monopoly Profits, Rents, and the Distribution
        of Income   *176*
      Can Monopoly Be Good?   *178*
   Application: Agricultural Marketing
     Organizations—Equal Opportunity to Compete
     or License to Monopolize?   *180*
   The Sources of Monopoly Power   *182*
Price Discrimination   *182*
   Price Discrimination in Practice   *183*
   Perfect Price Discrimination   *184*
      Price Discrimination in Medicine   *186*
   Price Discrimination When There Are Substantial
     Fixed Costs   *186*
   Price Differentiation versus Price Discrimination
     187
Summary and Conclusions   *187*
Key Terms   *188*
Questions for Discussion and Review   *188*

9   Oligopoly   *189*

Outline   *189*
Objectives   *189*
Introduction   *190*
Price and Output in an Oligopolistic Industry   *191*
   Oligopoly, Concentration, and Collusion   *191*
      OPEC: The Rise (and Decline?) of a Cartel
        193
   Oligopolistic Pricing without Formal Collusion:
     The Problem of Interdependence   *197*
      An Example of Price Leadership with a
        Dominant Firm: The United States Steel
        Corporation   *198*
      Other Pricing Strategies   *199*
An Economic Evaluation of Oligopoly   *202*
Summary and Conclusions   *202*
Key Terms   *203*
Questions for Discussion and Review   *203*

10   Monopolistic Competition, Product
Differentiation, and Advertising   *205*

Outline   *205*
Objectives   *205*
Introduction   *206*
What Is Monopolistic Competition?   *207*
Short-run Monopolistic Competition   *207*
   A Closer Look at a Monopolistically Competitive
     Firm: A Local Clothing Store   *208*
      Price and Output in the Short Run   *209*
Long-run Monopolistic Competition   *210*
   Production Efficiency and Product Variety   *211*
Price Differences within Markets   *212*
   Differences in Costs   *212*
      Aside: Price Differences in Monopoly,
        Competition, and Monopolistic Competition
        213
   Consumer Cooperatives   *213*
Advertising, Information, and Product Differentiation
214
   Informative Advertising and Product Prices   *214*
   Tastes, Preferences, and Product Differentiation
     217
   Advertising, Product Differentiation, and
     Monopoly Power   *219*
   Advertising and Consumer Protection   *219*
   Advertising, Profits, and Prices: Some Evidence
     220
Summary and Conclusions   *221*
Key Terms   *221*
Questions for Discussion and Review   *221*

11   Government Regulation of Industries
223

Outline   *223*
Objectives   *223*
Introduction   *224*
Antitrust Policy   *225*
   A Brief Review of the Social Costs of Monopoly
     225
      Estimates of the Welfare Loss Due to Monopoly
        226
   Antitrust Laws   *227*
   Two Recent Antitrust Cases   *228*
      AT&T   *228*
      The Plywood Industry   *229*

Rate Regulation *229*
   Technical Monopoly and Rate Regulation *229*
   Rate Regulation in Theory *231*
   Rate Regulation in Practice *231*
      Rate Structure *231*
      Summary of the Evidence *233*
   Rate Regulation in Potentially Competitive
      Industries *233*

The Case for Deregulation *235*
   Airline Deregulation *235*
Summary and Conclusions *237*
Key Terms *238*
Questions for Discussion and Review *238*
Policy Issue: You Decide *Drug Resales* *240*
The Action–Initiating Event *240*
The Issue *240*
Economic Policy Issues *240*

Part IV

The Market for Inputs

12 Introduction to the Markets for Labor and Other Inputs *245*

Outline *245*
Objectives *245*
Introduction *246*
Factor Markets and the Distribution of Income *246*
The Demand for Inputs, Using Labor as an Example *247*
   Profit-maximizing Output and Input for a
      Competitive Firm *247*
   The Production Function and the Marginal
      Product of a Factor of Production *249*
   The Value of Labor's Marginal Product *251*
      The Cost of Hiring More Labor *252*
   Events that Shift the Firm's Demand Curve: A
      Change in Product Demand and a Change in the
      Amount of Capital *253*
   The Competitive Industry's Demand for Labor and
      Other Inputs *255*
      The Industry's Demand for Labor *256*
      The Industry's Demand for Other Inputs *256*
The Supply of Labor and Other Inputs *257*
   The Labor–Leisure Decision *257*
      The Demand for Leisure and the Individual's
      Supply of Labor *257*
   Labor Supply to the Firm and Industry *260*
The Supply of Capital Services and Other Nonhuman
   Inputs to Firms and Industries *262*
Summary and Conclusions *263*
Key Terms *263*
Questions for Discussion and Review *263*

13 Factor Markets *265*

Outline *265*
Objectives *265*
Introduction *266*
The Concept of a Factor Market *266*
   Is There a "Market" for Labor? *266*
Short–run Equilibrium in a Single Competitive Labor
   Market *266*
   Review of the Equilibrium Concept *267*
   Shifts in Supply and Demand for Labor *267*
Equilibrium in Interconnected Competitive Labor
   Markets *268*
   Mobility among Labor Markets and the Tendency
      for Wage Equality *268*
      Compensating Wage Differentials *269*
      Economic Efficiency in Markets for Labor and
      Other Factors of Production *270*
Noncompetitive Influences in Factor Markets *271*
   Monopoly in the Product Market *272*
   Monopsony *272*
   Labor Unions *275*
      What Unions Do *275*
      Unions and Wages *278*
      Union Membership *278*
Summary and Conclusions *280*
Key Terms *280*
Questions for Discussion and Review *280*

14   Investment in Human and Physical Capital
      281

Outline *281*
Objectives *281*
Introduction *282*
Physical Capital, Human Capital, Productivity, and
    Income *282*
Introduction to Investment Theory *283*
    Measuring the Value of Capital *283*
        More than One Time Period *284*
        Practical Issues: Selecting an Interest Rate in a
            Present Value Calculation and Accounting for
            Inflation *286*
Investment in Schooling and Training *287*
    The Schooling Investment Decision *288*
    On-the-Job Training and Lifetime Earning Power
        289
        General Training and Lifetime Earning Power
            289
        Specific Training, Lifetime Earning Power, and
            Employment Stability *291*
    The Role of Government: The Equity-Efficiency
        Quandary *293*
Investment in Physical Capital *293*
    Analyzing Government Investment Projects *294*
        The Tellico Dam *294*
Summary and Conclusions *295*
Key Terms *295*
Questions for Discussion and Review *296*

15   The Distribution of Income *297*

Outline *297*
Objectives *297*
Introduction *298*
The Distribution of Wages and Income *298*
    Measures of the Income Distribution *299*
        The Size Distribution of Income in the United
            States and Other Countries *299*
        The Functional Distribution of Income *301*
    Human Capital and the Functional Distribution of
        Income *303*

Income Redistribution *304*
    Why Redistribute Income? *304*
        Measuring Poverty *305*
        Equality of Opportunity or Equality of Results?
            307
    Policies to Redistribute Income *307*
        The Role of Labor Unions *307*
        Minimum Wage Legislation *308*
        Transfer Programs *310*
Summary and Conclusions *318*
Key Terms *318*
Questions for Discussion and Review *318*

16   Discrimination *321*

Outline *321*
Objectives *321*
Introduction *322*
Discrimination in Labor Markets: Race and Sex Wage
    Differences *322*
Economic Analysis of Labor Market Discrimination
    323
    Causes of Labor Market Discrimination *324*
        Employer Discrimination and Profit *324*
        Segregation *324*
        Societal Discrimination *324*
Black–White Wage Differences and Public Policy
    325
    The Effects of Equal Employment Opportunity
        Legislation and Other Antidiscrimination
        Programs on Racial Discrimination *326*
Male–Female Wage Differences and Public Policy
    326
    The Comparable Worth Issue *328*
Discrimination in Housing Markets *329*
    Analytical Issues *329*
    Some Proposed Remedies and Their Effects *330*
        Fair Housing Legislation Perfectly Enforced
            331
        Fair Housing Legislation Imperfectly Enforced
            332
        An Alternative Remedy *333*
Summary and Conclusions *333*
Key Terms *334*
Questions for Discussion and Review *334*
Policy Issue: You Decide *Cutting Labor Costs to Save
    Jobs* *335*
The Action-Initiating Event *335*
The Issue *335*
Economic Policy Issues *335*
Recommendations *335*

Part V

Government and Markets

17   Market Deficiencies   *339*

Outline   *339*
Objectives   *339*
Introduction   *340*
External Economies and Diseconomies   *341*
   The Pollution Problem: Private Costs and Social
    Costs   *341*
   Positive Externalities   *343*
    The Social Benefits of Higher Education   *344*
Public Goods   *345*
Government's Responses to External Diseconomies
  and Public Goods Problems   *346*
   A Closer Look at the Causes of Market
    Deficiencies   *346*
    The Exclusion Problem, Externalities, and
     Transaction Costs   *346*
    The Role of Property Rights   *347*
    Property Rights and Economic Efficiency   *349*
   Possible Solutions to the Pollution Problem   *350*
    Information Difficulties and Limitations on
     Government Policy Implementation   *351*
    Creating a Market for Pollution Rights   *352*
    Government Policy toward Pollution in the
     United States   *353*
    The Politics and International Nature of the
     Pollution Problem   *354*
   Public Goods: National Defense   *355*
    The Free-Rider Problem   *355*
Summary and Conclusions   *356*
Key Terms   *357*
Questions for Discussion and Review   *357*

18   Government and Markets in Developing
   Countries   *359*

Outline   *359*
Objectives   *359*
Introduction   *360*
Economic Conditions in Developing Countries   *362*
   Population Growth and Population Density   *362*
   General Living Conditions in Developed
    Countries and LDCs   *364*
An Analysis of Cheap Food Policies in LDCs   *366*
    Winners and Losers from Cheap Food Policies
     366
    Dependence on Food Imports   *367*
    Long-run Effects   *367*
    Black Markets and Corruption   *367*
Cheap Urban Housing Policies   *368*
   Demand and Supply of Housing in LDCs   *368*
   How Rent Controls Work in the Short Run   *368*
    Winners, Losers, and ''Key Money'' Payments
     368
   The Long-term Decline in the Quality of Standard
    Housing   *369*
Minimum Wages and Price Controls   *369*
   Background: The Perceived Need for Price and
    Wage Controls in Developing Countries   *369*
   The Labor Market in Manufacturing   *370*
    Winners and Losers from Minimum Wage Laws
     and Price Controls   *370*
Cheap Credit   *371*
   Background: The Perceived Need for Government
    Direct Financing of Investment in LDCs   *371*
   The Effects of Subsidized Credit and Loan
    Guarantees   *371*
The Political Difficulties in Adopting Free Market
  Policies in LDCs   *372*
Summary and Conclusions   *373*
Key Term   *373*
Questions for Discussion and Review   *373*
Policy Issue: You Decide *International Cooperation
  on Pollution and Defense Issues*   *374*
The Action-Initiating Event   *374*
The Issue   *374*
Economic Policy Issues   *375*
Recommendations   *375*

Part VI

Introduction to Macroeconomics

19   Introduction to Macroeconomics   *379*

Outline   *379*
Objectives   *379*
An Introduction to the Study of Macroeconomics
380
GNP: A Measure of a Society's Total Production   *381*
   Background   *381*
   The Nominal Value of GNP   *382*
     Consumption   *382*
     Investment   *383*
     Government Spending   *384*
     Net Exports   *385*
   GNP and Economic Well-being   *385*
     The Role of Nonmarket Transactions   *385*
     Leisure Time   *386*
     Illegal Transactions and Barter   *387*
     Intermediate Transactions   *387*
GNP Is Also a Measure of a Society's Total Income
388
   The Circular Flow of Income   *388*
   Data on GNP as a Source of Income   *388*
Other Measures of Production and National Income
390
   Background   *390*
   Calculating Real GNP   *390*
     The Need for a Price Index   *390*
     The CPI and GNP Deflator for the United
     States   *392*
     Price Indexes and Inflation   *393*
     Estimates of Real GNP for the United States
     and Changes in Real GNP   *394*

Interest Rates   *395*
   Real versus Nominal Rates of Interest   *396*
   Real versus Nominal Interest Rates in Recent
   Years   *397*
Unemployment   *397*
   Definition and Measure of Unemployment   *397*
   Why Is Unemployment Such an Important
   Economic Issue?   *398*
Summary and Conclusions   *399*
Key Terms   *399*
Questions for Discussion and Review   *400*
Appendix *Introduction to Supply and Demand*   *401*
The Demand Relationship   *401*
   Basic Assumptions of Demand   *401*
     The Goals of Buyers and How They Attempt to
     Achieve Them   *402*
     Limitations on Choices Buyers Can Make   *402*
   Method of Analysis   *403*
   The Law of Demand and the Demand Curve   *403*
   Shifts in Demand   *404*
The Supply Relationship   *406*
   Basic Assumptions of Supply Theory   *406*
     Suppliers and Their Goals   *407*
   The Law of Supply   *407*
     Method of Analysis   *407*
   Factors that Shift Supply   *408*
     Changes in Technology   *408*
     Changes in Input Prices   *409*
     Changes in Expected Future Prices   *409*
How the Forces of Supply and Demand Determine
Price and the Level of Production   *409*
   The Concept of Equilibrium   *410*
   The Effects of Shifts in Supply and Demand on
   Equilibrium Price and Quantity   *410*
Key Terms   *411*

20 Employment, Unemployment, and the
Aggregate Production of Goods and
Services *413*

Outline *413*
Objectives *413*
Introduction *414*
The Labor Market *415*
    The Demand for Labor *415*
        The Value of Labor's Marginal Product Is a
        Firm's Labor Demand Curve *416*
        A Firm's Demand for Labor, Its Production
        Function, and Its Total Output *420*
        The Aggregate Demand for Labor *420*
    The Supply of Labor *422*
        Factors Underlying an Individual's Labor
        Supply Decision *422*
        The Aggregate Supply of Labor *423*
    The Aggregate Labor Market and the Aggregate
    Quantity of Goods and Services Supplied *424*
        Expectations *424*
        Equilibrium in the Aggregate Labor Market
        424
Unemployment *426*
    What Is Unemployment? *426*
    Varieties of Unemployment and Their Causes
    426
        Frictional Unemployment *426*
        Structural Unemployment *428*
        Cyclical Unemployment *429*
Summary and Conclusions *433*
Key Terms *434*
Questions for Discussion and Review *434*

21 Aggregate Expenditure on Goods and
Services *437*

Outline *437*
Objectives *437*
Introduction *438*
Aggregate Expenditure on Goods and Services:
Background *439*
    The Components of Aggregate Expenditure: A
    Brief Review *439*
    GNP Also Measures Society's Total Income *439*
        A Brief Review *439*
        The Uses of Society's Total Income *439*
An Analysis of Aggregate Expenditure on Goods and
Services *440*
    The Consumption Function *441*
        The Consumption Function Expressed
        Quantitatively *441*
        The Consumption Function Expressed
        Graphically *444*
    Investment *445*
    Government Spending and Net Exports *448*
    Aggregate Expenditure, Aggregate Production,
    and Equilibrium GNP *449*
        Another Look at Equilibrium GNP: Saving,
        Investment, and the Government Deficit
        451
        The National Income Accounts: Measured
        Saving, Measured Investment, the
        Government Deficit, and Measured GNP
        456
Summary and Conclusions *457*
Key Terms *457*
Questions for Discussion and Review *457*
Appendix *A Deeper Look at the Multiplier and
    Graphical Analysis 458*

22   Money and the Banking System   *463*

Outline   *463*
Objectives   *463*
Introduction   *464*
The Role of Money   *465*
   Money as a Medium of Exchange   *465*
      The Advantage of a Monetary Economy Over a
      Barter Economy   *465*
   Money as a Unit of Account   *465*
   Money as a Store of Value   *466*
   Monetary Standards and the Value of Money   *467*
The Banking System and Money   *468*
   The Balance Sheet of a Bank   *469*
   How Banks Create Money   *470*
      Cash Drain and Multiple Deposit Expansion
      473
   The Consolidated Balance Sheet of the Banking
   System   *474*
   The Definitions of Money in the United States
   Economy   *475*
      Are Credit Cards Money?   *476*
Summary and Conclusions   *477*
Key Terms   *477*
Questions for Discussion and Review   *477*

23   The Central Bank and Regulation of
     Money and the Banking System   *479*

Outline   *479*
Objectives   *479*
Introduction   *480*
Keeping Money Scarce: The Role of the Fed   *481*
   The Balance Sheet of the Fed and the Banking
   System   *482*
   The Means of Monetary Control: The Instruments
   of Monetary Policy   *482*
      Open Market Operations and the Quantity of
      Money with No Currency Drain   *483*
      Other Instruments of Monetary Policy   *487*
Preview: The Linkage between Money, Credit, and
National Income   *491*
Summary and Conclusions   *493*
Key Terms   *494*
Questions for Discussion and Review   *494*

24   Money, Credit, and the Rate of Interest
     497

Outline   *497*
Objectives   *497*
Introduction   *498*
   Things to Come   *498*
   Financial Instruments   *499*
   The Decision to Hold Money versus Loan
   Contracts   *500*
The Loan Contract Market   *500*
   Background   *500*
   A Closer Look at the Details of a Loan Contract
   500
   The Model of the Loan Contract Market to Be
   Developed   *501*
   The Demand for Loanable Funds   *501*
      Firms   *501*
      The Government   *503*
      The Aggregate Demand Curve for Loanable
      Funds and the Rate of Interest   *504*
   The Supply of Loanable Funds   *505*
      Households as Suppliers of Loanable Funds
      505
      Banks as Suppliers of Funds   *507*
      The Aggregate Supply of Loanable Funds   *510*
   Equilibrium in the Loan Contract Market   *510*
      The Determination of the Real Interest Rate
      510
      The Structure of Interest Rates   *512*
Summary and Conclusions   *513*
Key Terms   *514*
Questions for Discussion and Review   *514*
Policy Issue: You Decide *Deregulation of the
Banking Industry*   *515*
The Action–Initiating Event   *515*
The Issue   *515*
Economic Policy Issues   *515*
Recommendations   *515*

Part VII

Macroeconomic Policy

25 How the Macroeconomy Works   *519*

Outline   *519*
Objectives   *519*
Introduction   *520*
Full Macroeconomic Equilibrium: Satisfying Three
  Markets Simultaneously   *521*
A Closer Look at Full Macroeconomic Equilibrium
  523
Recessions and Inflationary Episodes   *526*
  Recession: The Effect of a Decline in Planned
    Investment   *526*
    A Leftward Shift in the Demand for Loanable
      Funds   *527*
    A Decline in the Interest Rate   *527*
    Reaction in the Goods and Labor Markets   *529*
    A Decline in Saving: Short-Run
      Macroeconomic Equilibrium in a Recession
      530
    Adjustment toward Full Macroeconomic
      Equilibrium with Flexible Prices   *530*
    Recapitulation   *532*
  An Inflationary Episode Resulting from an
    Increase in Planned Investment   *533*
Summary and Conclusions   *535*
Key Terms   *536*
Questions for Discussion and Review   *536*

26 Aggregate Demand, Aggregate Supply, and
    the Price Level   *537*

Outline   *537*
Objectives   *537*
Introduction   *538*
The Equilibrium Price Level: The Quantity Theory
  539
  The Role of Velocity   *542*
Summarizing Changes in Aggregate Production and
  the Price Level: Aggregate Demand and Supply
  543
  Aggregate Demand   *544*
  Aggregate Supply   *545*
  Equilibrium of Aggregate Demand and Supply
    545
  Aggregate Demand and Supply during a Recession
    545
  Aggregate Demand and Supply during an
    Inflationary Episode   *549*

Macroequilibrium, Recession, and Inflation in a
  Growth Scenario   *552*
    A Brief Historical Note   *554*
    The Rate of Inflation and Unemployment during
      Recessions and Inflationary Episodes   *554*
    Can Workers or Other Suppliers Cause Inflation?
      556
Summary and Conclusions   *559*
Key Terms   *560*
Questions for Discussion and Review   *560*

27 Fiscal and Monetary Policies   *561*

Outline   *561*
Objectives   *561*
Introduction   *562*
Discretionary Fiscal Policy in a Recession   *564*
  Response of the Fiscal Authority to a Decline in
    Investment Demand: An Increase in
    Expenditure   *564*
    Reaction in the Goods Market   *564*
    Reaction in the Credit Market   *564*
  Why Fiscal Policy Works   *566*
  Discretionary Fiscal Policy When Taxes Are
    Adjusted   *566*
Discretionary Fiscal Policy to Prevent an Inflationary
  Episode   *569*
Lags, Politics, and Fiscal Policy   *570*
Nondiscretionary Fiscal Policy   *571*
Recent Fiscal Policy Developments   *571*
Discretionary Monetary Policy in a Recession   *572*
  The Initial Effect in the Loanable Funds Market
    574
  The Effect in the Goods Market   *574*
  Why Monetary Policy Works   *574*
Discretionary Monetary Policy to Prevent Inflation
  575
  The Politics of Discretionary Antiinflation
    Monetary Policy   *576*
Comparing the Short-run and Long-run Effects of
  Fiscal and Monetary Policies   *577*
  Is Discretionary Policy Useless?   *577*
Summary and Conclusions   *578*
Key Terms   *578*
Questions for Discussion and Review   *579*

28 Monetary and Fiscal Policies in Action 581

Outline 581
Objectives 581
Introduction 582
The Great Depression 582
The United States Economy in 1929 and 1930 582
Appropriate Fiscal and Monetary Policies in 1930 583
Actual Fiscal and Monetary Policies in 1930 584
The United States Economy in 1931 and 1932 584
Monetary and Fiscal Policies in 1931 584
Monetary Policy in 1932 585
The Great Inflation: 1965–? 585
The Economic Setting in Late 1965 and Early 1966 585
The War and Increased Government Expenditure 587
How Monetary Policy Could Have Prevented Inflation 587
Monetary Policy in 1965 and 1966 588
The Reversal of the Fed's Monetary Policy 588
The Effects of the Fed's Expansionary Monetary Policy 589
Stagflation: The United States Economy in the 1970s and Early 1980s 589
Money Growth, Inflation, and Unemployment 589
Money Growth, Inflation, and the Interest Rate 595
Summary and Conclusions 596
Questions for Discussion and Review 597

29 Summing Up: Macroeconomic Controversies 599

Outline 599
Objectives 599
Introduction 600
Areas of Agreement and Disagreement among Economists 600
Controversies over Short-run Macroeconomic Policy: Is Fine–tuning Practical? 601
Monetarism and Keynesianism 601
Different Views of How the Economy Works 601
Keynesian and Monetarist Views about How Monetary Policy Affects the Economy 601
Monetarist and Keynesian Explanations for the Recession of the Early 1980s and Continued High Interest Rates through 1985 602
Keynesian and Monetarist Differences of Opinion about the Need to Try to Control the Macroeconomy and the Ability to Do So 603
Differences in Keynesian and Monetarist Policy Recommendations 604
Long-run Considerations and the "Supply Side" 605
Supply-side Economics 605
The Laffer Curve 605
Supply-side, Keynesian, and Monetarist Views of Government Spending Cuts during a Recession 606
The Government Deficit: Does It Matter? 606
Deficits and Presidential Politics 607
The Sources of United States Deficits in the 1980s 608
The Recent Debt Experience of Industrialized Nations 610
The Economic Significance of the Debt 610
Deficits and Business Cycles 610
Structural Deficits 611
"Crowding Out": The Short-run and Long-run Effects of the Deficit 612
Summary and Conclusions 614
Key Terms 615
Questions for Discussion and Review 615
Policy Issue: You Decide *Flat Tax* 616
The Action-Initiating Event 616
The Issue 616
Economic Policy Issues 616
Recommendations 616

Part VIII

The International Economy

30 Trade among Nations   *621*

Outline *621*
Objectives *621*
Introduction *622*
Import and Export Patterns in the United States
  Economy and the World Economy *623*
Imports, Exports, and the Gains from Trade *627*
  The Supply and Demand for Imports and Exports
    627
      The Effect of the World Price on Domestic
        Production and Consumption *628*
      The Equilibrium World Price and the Flow of
        Trade *630*
      Supply, Demand, and International Trade
        Patterns *633*
  Winners and Losers: The Distribution of the Gains
    from Trade *634*
      Winners and Losers in the Importing Country
        634
      Winners and Losers in the Exporting Country
        637
Summary and Conclusions *638*
Key Terms *639*
Questions for Discussion and Review *639*

31 The Regulation of International Trade
    641

Outline *641*
Objectives *641*
Introduction *642*
Why Interfere with a Good Thing? *643*
  Internal Taxes as Substitutes for Tariffs: British
    and United States Experiences *643*
  Income Distribution Considerations *643*
  Strategic Goods and Infant Industries: Bases for
    Import Barriers? *644*
      Strategic Supplies of Steel *645*
      Infant Industries and Technology Transfers
        645
  Import Substitution *646*
Barriers to International Trade *646*
  Tariffs *647*
      United States Tariff History *647*
      A Tariff on Steel Imports from Japan *648*
      Aggregate Economic Losses *649*
      Specific Duties versus ad Valorem Tariffs *650*
  Quotas and Other Nontariff Trade Barriers (NTBs)
    651
      Revenue Needs and the Shift to NTBs *652*
      NTBs and the Tariff Revenue Equivalent *652*
      "Voluntary" Quotas *652*
  The General Agreement on Tariffs and Trade
    (GATT), "Fair" Competition, and Trade
    Restrictions *654*
      The Rules of the Game and "Unfair" Trade
        Practices *654*
  The Trade Expansion Act of 1962 *655*
  Customs Unions *656*
Summary and Conclusions *658*
Key Terms *659*
Questions for Discussion and Review *659*

32   Monetary and Macroeconomic Aspects of
International Trade   *661*

Outline   *661*
Objectives   *661*
Introduction   *662*
Paying for Foreign Trade: Currency's Role   *663*
  The Supply and Demand for Foreign Currency
  664
    Fixed Exchange Rates   *666*
    Flexible Exchange Rates   *667*
The Balance of Payments and the Balance of Trade
669
    Equilibrium and Disequilibrium   *672*
The International Transmission Mechanism   *674*
Macroeconomic Influences on the United States
  Balance of Trade and International Financial Flows
  675
    Inflation and the Trade Balance   *675*
    Macroeconomic Policy, Interest Rates, and
      International Financial Flows   *675*
Summary and Conclusions   *678*
Key Terms   *678*
Questions for Discussion and Review   *678*
Appendix *International Financial Cooperation*   *680*
The International Monetary Fund and the World
  Bank   *680*
Eurodollars and Eurocurrency Banking   *681*
Key Terms   *681*

33   Current Issues in International Trade   *683*

Outline   *683*
Objectives   *683*
Introduction   *684*
Recent United States Economic Performance Relative
  to that of Other Major Industrial Countries   *685*
  Growth, Inflation, and Employment   *685*
  Inflation Rates in Industrial Countries   *687*
  Employment and Unemployment in Advanced
    Economies   *688*
  Monetary and Fiscal Policies in Industrial
    Countries   *689*
    Central Government Deficits Relative to GNP
      690
    Monetary Policy in Major Industrial Countries
      691
The Impact of Changes in World Oil Market   *693*
Export Problems of Small, Developing Economies
694
  Export Prices   *694*
  Trends and Variations in Prices of Primary
    Products Other than Oil   *695*
Trade Imbalance in Developing Economies   *696*
  The Expansion of External Debt in the 1970s and
    1980s   *697*
    Monetary Expansion   *698*
  The Mexican Experience: Domestic Inflation,
    Balance of Trade Deficit, and Overvaluation of
    the Peso   *699*
    Mexican Inflation and the Dollar Value of the
      Peso   *699*
    Overvaluation of the Mexican Peso   *700*
  The External Debt of Developing Nations   *703*
    What Caused the World Debt Crisis?   *704*
Summary and Conclusions   *705*
Key Terms   *706*
Questions for Discussion and Review   *706*
Policy Issue: You Decide *Will Encouraging Workers
  to Cut Their Wages Save Many Jobs Lost to Foreign
  Exports?*   *707*

Part IX

Economic Growth and Comparative Systems

34   Economic Growth and Change   *711*

Outline   *711*
Objectives   *711*
Introduction   *712*
A Review of Scarcity and the Production Possibilities
   Frontier (PPF)   *712*
   Factors that Shift the PPF   *713*
      Labor Productivity in the United States   *714*
   Forces Behind Recent Productivity Growth in the
      United States and Other Industrial Nations   *714*
Adjusting to Economic Change   *718*
   Has the United States Been Deindustrializing?
   718
   A Critical Look at Industrial Policy   *720*
      Japanese Industrial Policy   *720*
Summary and Conclusions   *722*
Key Terms   *722*
Questions for Discussion and Review   *722*

35   Alternative Economic Systems   *723*

Outline   *723*
Objectives   *723*
Introduction   *724*
Basic Issues to Be Addressed by Every Economic
   System   *725*
   The Relative Importance of Market Forces and
      State Planning in Capitalist and Planned,
      Socialist Economies   *726*
   Differences in Performance Criteria for Capitalist
      and Planned Economies   *727*
Characteristics of a Planned, Socialist Economy   *729*
   How Annual Output Plans Are Developed in the
      Soviet Union   *729*
   Incentives   *729*
   Market-Clearing Mechanisms   *730*
      Product Markets Under Price Controls   *730*
      Factor Price Determination and the Allocation
         of Factor Inputs   *731*

Economic Performance of Capitalist and Socialist
   Economic Systems   *733*
   General Measures of Health and Literacy   *735*
      Health and Health Services   *735*
      Communication and Education Services   *735*
   Military Spending and Military Presence   *738*
Summary and Conclusions   *739*
Key Terms   *740*
Questions for Discussion and Review   *740*
Appendix *The Government's Role in Mixed,
   Capitalist Economies   741*
Voting Behavior in a Democracy   *741*
   Self-Interest, Rational Ignorance, and Voting
      Behavior   *741*
Social Choices in a Democracy: Outcomes of the
   Political Process   *742*
   Special Interests and Logrolling   *742*
   Shortsightedness and Obfuscation   *742*
   The Budgetary Process: Separation of Taxes from
      Expenditures   *743*
   Bureaucratic Behavior and the Cost in Output of
      Government Services   *744*
      Labor Costs in Government   *745*
   Some Illustrations of Public Choice   *745*
      Government and Private Costs Compared   *745*
Key Terms   *745*
Policy Issue: You Decide *An Industrialization Plan*
   746
The Action-Initiating Event   *746*
The Issue   *746*
Economic Policy Issues   *747*
Recommendations   *747*

Appendix A: Graphs   749
Appendix B: How to Solve Policy Issues   755
References   757
Glossary   765
Index   779

Preface

What? Still one more principles text?

Yes. The reason we believe that we can contribute something of value to the already crowded field of introductory economics textbooks is that none of the other existing books matches our needs in teaching Principles of Economics. Needless to say, we hope that others perceive some of the needs that we have tried to address. We desired a text that uses a building-block approach, which means that each theoretical tool is developed on the basis of what has gone before, without time- and space-wasting repetition and without theoretical gaps or inconsistencies between microeconomics and macroeconomics. Our goal has been a book that illustrates in every chapter the applicability of economic analysis to important social problems and integrates our knowledge of the economic process with social choices made in a political context. We also wanted a text that would be more effective than any other now available in helping students to understand the role of the United States in the rapidly changing international economy and to appreciate the political-economic problems faced by the world's developing nations. Finally, we believe it is crucial that the beginning student grasp the fundamental interrelationships between the real economy and monetary economy (microeconomics and macroeconomics). This requires developing the "microfoundations" of the determination of unemployment, interest rate, price level, and aggregate production. However, we wanted to avoid the burden of the complex IS-LM analysis that is usually relegated to an appendix in other texts (if it appears at all). Pedagogically, we wished to avoid a text cluttered with "boxed inserts" that, in our judgment, divert students' attention from basic, important issues in economics.

Principles of Economics has been written on the assumption that a few tools, well-learned, provide insights that are unavailable to those who have not studied modern economic analysis. It serves as a summary of basic principles for those who may never enroll in another course beyond the usual two-term introductory sequence and as a foundation for additional courses taken by economics majors and business students. We have strived to keep theoretical analysis simple, yet correct, so that nothing need be "unlearned" by students going on to intermediate or graduate level course work. Numerous applications of economic analysis to policy issues are linked to an analysis of the political process through which social policies are developed. A broad spectrum of policy applications is covered, including health economics, agriculture, technological progress, poverty, the problems of the world's developing nations, current international economic problems, and more. Students' understanding of policy formulation is enhanced by repeated analysis of "winners" and "losers" from alternative policies and how their political power influences actual policy decisions.

▶ Organization

Part I is comprised of a single chapter that introduces the fundamental economic principles of scarcity, the *What, How,* and *For Whom* questions, the production possibilities frontier, opportunity cost, and comparative advantage, with some attention-grabbing applications, including the economics of life and death choices and the 55-mph speed limit. The role of economic theory and the distinction between positive and normative analysis are discussed.

Part II introduces the basic concepts of demand and supply, thereby showing how scarcity affects a market economy. The analysis of a market economy has three elements, or building blocks: demand, supply, and the interaction of demand and supply. These three elements comprise the basic model of how buyers and sellers behave in pursuit of their private goals. Upon this foundation, the text shows how government actions alter the outcome that would prevail if supply and demand operated on their own. Chapter 2 starts out with basic analysis of demand, which is followed by elasticity of demand in chapter 3. Chapter 2 emphasizes a behavioral approach to demand theory, meaning that indifference curve analysis is included in an appendix rather than in the main body of the chapter. The concepts of utility and marginal utility are introduced in the chapter, but the material is presented in a way that permits instructors who prefer to avoid utility analysis entirely to skip this section without loss of continuity. Chapter 4 introduces the basic principles and assumptions of marginal cost and supply. Chapter 5 shows how demand and supply operate in a market economy; chapter 6 shows the impact of government regulations in a mixed economy and how they affect market outcomes. Chapter 7 extends the analysis to the long run, in which the theory of supply is expanded to allow for entry and exit of firms in a competitive industry.

Some instructors may wish that we had introduced the bare bones fundamentals of supply and demand and some applications *before* going on to the underlying fundamentals. Our rationale for rigorously following a building-block approach, taking one basic economic concept at a time, is that we believe it allows *more* time to be spent on interesting applications toward the middle and end of the course. Because each chapter contains several applications to real-world events, students do not get bogged down in dreary analysis. They do see the relevance of what they

are asked to learn at every step. Those instructors who wish to introduce an overview of supply and demand before going on to the underlying concepts can do so by using the appendix to chapter 19 before, or in place of, chapters 2 and 5 (see the Instructor's Manual for more details on chapter sequencing).

Part III introduces departures from the competitive market paradigm. Chapters 8, 9, and 10 introduce the concepts of monopoly, oligopoly, and monopolistic competition, respectively. Chapter 11 emphasizes government regulation of industry, although various aspects of government's role are discussed within each chapter.

Part IV introduces the demand and supply for factors of production, with an emphasis on labor. Our relatively heavy emphasis on labor markets, compared with other texts, reflects our belief that the typical introductory course gives too little attention to the source of nearly 80 percent of our gross national product. Chapter 12 extends the basic tools of demand and supply to the derived demand for labor and labor supply. Chapter 13 extends the analysis to encompass markets for labor and other productive factors. Chapter 14 introduces the concept of investment, with application to human capital. Chapters 15 and 16 introduce the analysis of income distribution and discrimination.

Part V is the final microeconomics section. Chapter 17 extends the discussion of how markets work to promote a deeper knowledge of market performance when externalities are present. Chapter 18, which we believe is unique among existing principles texts, applies basic supply and demand analysis to the problems of developing countries. Not only does this introduce students to problems of the world's less advanced economies, but it also serves as an extremely cogent illustration of the distortions frequently caused by well-intentioned but fundamentally flawed government intervention. The LDC's frequently serve as a powerful illustration of what happens when governments try to repeal the laws of supply and demand.

Part VI is the first macroeconomics section. Chapter 19 defines macroeconomics and introduces GNP and the other principal aggregate economic variables, the price level, interest rate, and unemployment. As mentioned earlier, the appendix to this chapter summarizes the important factors of supply and demand covered in Part II so that instructors can cover either macroeconomics or microeconomics first. In fact, each element of supply, demand, and the equilibrium concept is introduced and defined within the main body of chapter 20, as well, so those instructors who wish to use their course time to cover applied topics more intensively can skip the appendix to chapter 19 without loss of required information in a macro-first course.

Chapter 20 introduces the labor market, a crucial microfoundation of modern macroeconomics. Chapter 21 describes the aggregate expenditure on goods and services that leads to a particular level of GNP in the goods market. The student is continuously reminded that full macroeconomic equilibrium depends on conditions in the labor market, as well, and that equilibrium in the goods market may or may not correspond to "full employment." Chapters 22, 23, and 24 introduce the financial sector and describe the determination of the interest rate, using a loanable funds approach. We believe that we are unique in using the loanable funds approach to link the real and monetary sectors and that this pedagogical device allows the student to learn much more about the mutual interaction of exogenous expenditure components with the interest rate and monetary and fiscal policies than is possible with any other existing text.

In Part VII, we tie the labor, goods, and credit markets together to develop a model of general macroeconomic equilibrium in chapter 25. We use the model to illustrate what happens in each market during recessions and inflationary periods. Chapter 26 emphasizes determination of the price level, using the quantity theory and aggregate demand and supply. Chapters 27, 28, and 29 introduce fiscal and monetary policies in theory and practice. Our approach is unique in that the student does not have to unlearn the partial equilibrium aspects of fiscal policy that hinder understanding of how government expenditure and taxation policies interact with interest rate determination. Chapter 29 summarizes major issues in macroeconomics by comparing Keynesian, monetarist, and supply-side policies.

Part VIII introduces international economics. Chapters 30 and 31 cover "real" trade, using the concepts of supply and demand to analyze imports, exports, and tariff and nontariff trade barriers. Chapter 32 covers monetary and macroeconomic trade issues, including exchange rate determination and the balance of payments. Chapter 33 addresses various current issues in the international economy, including the impact of OPEC on the world's developed and developing nations.

Part IX includes the capstone chapters on economic growth and comparative systems. Once again, the applications of economic tools and empirical issues are stressed. In chapter 34, particular attention is paid to the productivity slowdown in the United States and to the role of "industrial policy" in economic development. Chapter 35 compares the allocation mechanisms of free market and mixed economies with those of planned, socialist economies and emphasizes a comparison of various measures of social and economic welfare between the planned economies and those of the other industrialized nations. This chapter also contains an appendix that deals with the theory of public choice.

▶ Pedagogy

Principles of Economics offers a variety of pedagogical aids for students and teachers. Each chapter opens with a chapter outline, learning objectives, and a prologue/scenario as part of the introduction. The introduction provides a real-world lead-in to the material and relates chapter content to previous and subsequent chapters. A running glossary is presented at the top of each page. The key terms are also listed and page referenced at the end of the chapter. Numerous end-of-chapter questions aid student comprehension of the material.

Each major section of the text concludes with a feature called Policy Issue. These policy puzzles direct students to put themselves in the position of an economic policymaker and formulate decisions regarding the issues presented. An appendix at the back of the book instructs students on how to analyze and work through the policy puzzles.

The careful use of appendices aids students in understanding the use and relevance of economic tools and concepts. The "careers" appendix after chapter 1 shows students the relevance of the subject to their future careers; it contradicts the notion that economics is a dismal science. The supply/demand appendix following chapter 19 provides condensed coverage of basic supply and demand concepts. Instructors can use this appendix to teach macroeconomics without unnecessary detail or to replace chapters 2 and 5 when covering microeconomics (as explained earlier in the preface). Several other chapter-end appendices present mathematical analyses of material contained in the related chapters, allowing a clearer focus on concepts and applications in the body of the chapters.

The text contains numerous direct and rhetorical questions designed to get the student to think more deeply about economic principles and applications discussed. Outlines of answers to these questions are provided in the instructor's manual.

There are numerous applications of such important contemporary topics as public choice analysis, the economics of information, the economics of the allocation of time, and rational expectations. These applications repeatedly stress the political, or "public choice" ramifications of policy formation. At the same time, the authors have carefully avoided taking sides politically, while emphasizing the political limits on economic policymakers.

There is a distinct pedagogical advantage to our use of loanable funds analysis in developing a macroeconomic model of both the real and monetary sectors. Most texts use the loanable funds model in microeconomic analysis of the interest rate, but then drop it in the macro portion of the text. Some texts use the loanable funds theory of interest in describing how monetary policy works but do not integrate this analysis with the goods market and fiscal policy. This gives the appearance of two different theories of the interest rate and macroeconomic policy, which can only leave students confused. Our use of the loanable funds analysis of interest rates, depending only on the tools of supply and demand and combined with the microfoundations of supply and demand for labor, determination of real wage rates, and unemployment, shows how microeconomics applies to an understanding of the complex interrelationships of the macroeconomy. The loanable funds approach illustrates directly how monetary and fiscal policies are *related* means of achieving macroeconomic stability.

The impacts of monetary and fiscal policies on GNP, employment, the interest rate, real investment, and the price level are easily compared. The power of this approach has enabled us to include brief histories of the Great Depression and economic experience in the United States since the 1960s that are superior in depth and scope to any existing principles text. The loanable funds approach is equally well adapted to a Keynesian or monetarist orientation, and the text clearly and succinctly explains the distinctions between modern Keynesians, monetarists, and supply siders in terms of the microeconomic and macroeconomic tools developed.

▶ Teaching and Learning Aids

For the Instructor

Instructor's Manual: Each chapter includes a chapter outline with teaching tips, suggested answers to all end-of-chapter questions, and a set of additional readings from recent magazines and newspapers.

Transparencies: One hundred colorful acetates of selected economic diagrams facilitate instruction and learning.

Test Bank: Approximately 2,000 questions that have been carefully designed using guidelines established by the Joint Council on Economic Education. The questions are also available on complimentary **wcb** TestPak computer diskettes for instructors adopting the book.

Transparency Masters: Fifty transparency masters and the test bank are included in the Instructor's Manual.

QuizPak: A student self-testing program offered free to adopters of *Principles of Economics.* Your students can review course material by quizzing themselves on the microcomputer. All questions in QuizPak are different from those in the Test Bank!

Software: Computer software will be available to help your students learn the principles of micro- and macroeconomics. The computer programs are designed to reinforce key concepts in the book.

For the Student

Student Study Guide: Each chapter contains an overview that summarizes the basic concepts introduced in each text chapter, a vocabulary check that reviews the key terms and definitions in the text, and numerous self-testing items, including true-false and multiple-choice questions and answers. Each chapter also contains at least one exercise and its solution.

StudyPak: An interactive student study guide on the microcomputer available for students to purchase. Students will review study materials selected for a particular text chapter and receive instant feedback. Printed study materials supplement the program to provide maximum coverage of each text chapter.

▶ Highlights

To highlight the significant features of our text, we have summarized some of them below:

1. Can be used in either a micro-first or macro-first sequence of introductory courses.

2. Uses a building-block approach that stresses the applicability of supply and demand analysis throughout.

3. Extensive policy applications to the household, business, health care, and government sectors and to developing nations.

4. Simply presented and current data.

5. A tools-oriented approach to the economist's way of thinking.

6. A unique, loanable funds approach to macroeconomics that facilitates incorporation of real and monetary disturbances in the basic macro model.

7. Stresses the microfoundations of macroeconomics.

8. Three chapters devoted to macroeconomic policy, including a unique historical analysis of two major episodes that continue to influence our lives today and an up-to-date comparison of Keynesian, monetarist, and supply-side policy positions.

9. Macroanalysis that focuses on the three crucial policy variables, inflation, unemployment, and interest rates.

10. Up-to-date analysis of the international economy as it affects the United States and the world's less-developed and -industrialized nations.

11. Fresh applications to the important policy areas of income distribution, externalities, public choice, international trade, and international financial problems.

12. Application of basic economic principles to the problems of developing nations.

13. Emphasis on comparing ideal policies with those that are practicable as determined by the reality of politics and the relationships of government to society.

14. Emphasizes international economic issues (most complete treatment available).

▶ Acknowledgements

We would like to express special thanks to our reviewers, who provided ideas and suggestions of great importance:

Bruce L. Benson, Florida State University; Peter R. Kressler, Glassboro State College; Jerome McElroy, St. Mary's College; Michael G. Ellis, New Mexico State University; Michael Cook, William Jewell College; Richard Hansen, University of Northern Iowa; Randall W. Bennett, Clarkson University; William Shingleton, Ball State University; John Fizel, Pennsylvania State University-Erie; Eleanor C. Snellings, Virginia Commonwealth University; Geoff Carliner, National Bureau of Economic Research; Nancy Jianakoplos, Michigan State University; Timothy J. Perri, Appalachian State University; Mark Berger, University of Kentucky; Abdol Soofi, University of Wisconsin–Platteville; Charles Zech, Villanova University; John Wakeman-Linn, Williams College; Phil Graves, University of Colorado; Jerry Russo, University of Wisconsin–Madison; C. G. Williams, University of South Carolina.

In addition, we express our gratitude to our colleagues Richard Anderson, Lars Sandberg, and Nat Simons at Ohio State and Karen Smith, Helen Tauchen, and Jonathan Veum at the University of North Carolina, who provided many valuable comments that helped improve the text. We would also like to acknowledge the help of Greg Davidson in writing Appendix A.

Kenneth Kopecky graciously released rights to material from an earlier work, and the present text owes much to his influence. We also appreciate the cooperation of David Terry Paul in making publication of this book possible. Sarah Mason provided outstanding typing services.

Principles of Economics

Part I

Introduction

Chapter 1

Scarcity, the Three Questions of Economics, and an Economic System

Outline

I. The three fundamental economic questions 6
    A. A thought quiz 6
II. Understanding economic events with economic analysis 8
    A. An example of government policy and its impact on the answers to the three economic questions: Medical care 9
III. Scarcity and an economic system 10
    A. What is an economic model? 10
    B. An introductory example: Dealing with scarcity in a small economy 11
        1. The production possibilities frontier (PPF) 11
    C. The production possibilities frontier, opportunity cost, and economic efficiency 13
        1. The shape of the production possibilities frontier 14
    D. Applications of the production possibilities frontier and opportunity cost 16
        1. Background 16
        2. Reckoning with opportunity costs: The case of the 55-mph speed limit 17
        3. Opportunity cost, comparative advantage, and specialization 19
IV. The concept of a market economy and the economy of the United States 21
V. Summary and conclusions 23
VI. Key terms 23
VII. Questions for discussion and review 23
VIII. Appendix: Economics and your career 25
    A. Why take economics? 25
    B. Economics as a major 25
    C. Careers in economics 25
    D. Prominent economics majors and positions they have held 26
IX. Policy issue: You decide—Who should pay for clean air? 27
    A. The action-initiating event 27
    B. The issue 27
    C. Economic policy issues 27
    D. Recommendations 27

Objectives

After reading this chapter, the student should be able to:

Explain what scarcity means and why scarcity requires that an economic system answer the three fundamental economic questions.

Distinguish between normative and positive economic issues.

Discuss how the government's policy on medical care affects the answers to the three economic questions.

Explain why economic models are crucial to the study of economics.

Use the concept of the production possibilities frontier to illustrate scarcity, efficiency, opportunity cost, comparative advantage, and economic growth.

Show how specialization leads to economic efficiency.

Use the concepts of opportunity cost and economic efficiency to discuss the formulation of government policies such as the 55-mph speed limit.

Distinguish among various types of economic systems.

Scarcity means that human wants or desires far exceed the capacity of the world's limited resources to satisfy those wants or desires.

*Every economic system must answer the **three fundamental economic questions**: What? How? For whom?*

Opportunity cost is the amount of one good or service that must be given in order to produce a unit of another good or service.

▶ The Three Fundamental Economic Questions

*The most important issue in economics can be summarized in a single sentence. If you understand all of the implications of this one sentence, you understand the essence of economics. A full understanding simply requires successively deeper and deeper analysis of its implications. You'll see as we go along. So let's go. The basic principle of economics concerns **scarcity**, which means that we cannot ever have all we want of every good and service. That is the sentence. While our desires for goods and services are unlimited, our resources—land, raw materials, labor, machinery, energy, and so on that we use to produce goods and services—are limited. Thus, we cannot have everything we want. Without this problem of scarcity, there would be no need for the subject of economics. All of economics really just rests on this idea.*

*The first implication of what you have just learned is that scarcity forces us to choose among alternatives. Because we cannot have everything, scarcity forces society to make choices. Every economic system—whether a free market or government-controlled type—must answer **three fundamental economic questions**: (1) What goods and services will be produced? (2) How will they be produced? (3) For whom will they be produced? If it were not for scarcity, the answers to these questions would be unimportant. Because scarcity does confront us, the answers are crucial to our material well-being and to our social and political decisions. Economics, therefore, is a penetrating and important subject. Let us now think about scarcity in more concrete terms.*

A Thought Quiz

You have had your first lesson in economics. A quick thought quiz will reveal how well you have learned that scarcity forces us to choose among alternatives—*all of the time.*

Consider the following examples in which scarcity forces us to make choices:

1. Last summer you had to choose whether (a) to attend summer school in order to be better prepared for fall courses or to graduate earlier, (b) to take a job to earn money to buy a car, or (c) to join some friends who wanted to visit the national parks of the West.
2. You want to visit a friend at a another college for the weekend. For $300 you could take a round-trip by plane that takes a total of three hours, or you could drive ten hours each way. Should you take the plane or drive your car?
3. You work and go to school. The more you work, the more money you earn and the lower your grades. How many hours a day should you work, and how many hours a day should you study?

These are all simple examples in which scarce time and income force you to make choices. All involve the important concept of **opportunity cost,** which means that when you choose one alternative, you must sacrifice the benefits of choosing something else. Opportunity cost is the most fundamental implication of scarcity. It means that scarcity *forces* us to pay for what we choose. A few items that we value may be considered "free" in the sense that there is no opportunity cost of consuming a bit more. Perhaps taking an additional breath of air is the best example of something without opportunity cost. There are very few others.

In our first example, if you decided to take a summer job, you sacrificed the enjoyment of travel or the benefits of what you would have learned in summer school. In the second example, the opportunity cost of driving to save a large part of the $300 airfare is the seventeen hours you do not get to spend visiting your friend. In the third example, if you choose to work while attending school, the opportunity cost is not only likely to be lower grades but also the future job opportunities you may not receive because your lower grades make it harder to succeed in the job market after graduation.

Opportunity costs confront us in every choice we make in our day-to-day lives. They also force us to make difficult and important decisions when choosing among alternative social policies. Consider this statement and the two possible responses that follow it: No sacrifice is ever too great to save a human life. (1) To knowingly cause or permit a death violates our most basic moral principles. A life is so precious that no cost should be spared if one can be saved. (2) Spending tremendous amounts of money to extend artificially the life of a terminally ill person who is in great pain or exhibits minimal life signs is not always justified. Medical resources used in such efforts can often be used more fruitfully for other patients. In choosing to keep the first patient alive at all cost, one ignores the implications of such a decision for other patients.

Most people do not like to think about this unpleasant subject. However, as adults, we or our political representatives must deal with difficult decisions. One of the most important reasons for studying economics is to help you develop clearer thinking about important social issues. You probably find it difficult to choose between the two statements in the preceding paragraph. Perhaps you are inclined to accept the first argument but find that the second also has some merit. What can you do? Although there is no surefire guide to the right answer, economic analysis will help. It forces us to see that the first statement

fails to recognize that choice is *always* necessary, unpleasant though it may be. In a world with scarcity, opportunity cost forces us to choose among alternatives whether we want to or not. To adhere exclusively to the first statement will not make opportunity cost disappear, although we may try to ignore it. Unfortunately, ignoring opportunity cost will only mean that we disregard the impact of saving one person's life on the life or death of other individuals. While the second statement recognizes that life and death decisions necessarily involve difficult and critical choices, it provides little insight into how to formulate rules society might use to choose who shall live. Let us elaborate.

If you understand the meaning of scarcity, you will realize that the first statement offers *no guide* to decision making in a world of scarcity. Think about it. *All* choices can be framed in a life or death context. At every moment, each of us could help to prolong our own (or someone else's) life by driving more carefully, giving up smoking, eating more healthful foods, or simply donating more of our income to the poor who cannot afford adequate food or medical care. We often choose activities that are enjoyable but that may shorten our own lives. Examples are driving over ten miles per hour, crossing a busy street, eating too many fatty foods, drinking alcoholic beverages, and smoking tobacco. Of course, by choosing to take only actions that prolong our lives, we would give up the pleasures we derive from eating foods that are "bad" for us, driving fast, and puffing on cigarettes. Thus, we return to the three basic economic questions. *What* should be produced—only those goods that prolong life? *For whom*—whose life should be prolonged? *How* should lives be saved? Suppose that all of our resources were devoted to extending life as long as possible. We would ultimately be forced to decide who should live longer and who should not. After all, no one lives forever, but in many cases life can be extended by extraordinary effort and expense. This brings us back to *for whom* again.

Positive economics is the study of
how economic variables are related
to one another.

*A **normative view*** concerns the
ethics of an issue or what is "right"
or "just" versus "wrong" or
"unjust."

Economic analysis helps us to choose among personal and social alternatives by focusing on *positive* issues, which involve what *is* as opposed to what *ought to be.* The most important statement of **positive economics,** to repeat and summarize the "first lesson" stated above is this: *Nothing is free. Economists* do not place price tags on what we desire (including the saving of lives)—*scarcity* does it.

Economics also cannot provide a unique answer to a question such as Who shall live? The answer will always depend in part on the **normative view,** or ethics, of those who must make such decisions. In our life and death example, normative issues involve such questions as, Is it acceptable for someone to choose behavior that may shorten his or her own life (such as smoking cigarettes or eating unhealthfully)? Is it acceptable that some families and individuals have great wealth while others have insufficient resources to purchase life-saving medical care? Notice that the word *should* is usually involved in normative questions: *Should* you take a job while attending school? *Should* you travel by car or by plane to visit your friend at another college?

Most economists emphasize the *economic way of thinking,* which carefully distinguishes between positive and normative issues. The positive part of economic analysis constantly reminds us that our choices deal with scarcity because we cannot make scarcity disappear. Before we can even answer such questions as *should* we tax the rich in order to transfer income to the poor, or *should* we use public funds to support life-prolonging health care for patients who need organ transplants in order to live, we require the answers to the *positive* questions involving the opportunity costs of taking these actions. The costs are not simply measured by the dollars involved but by the *benefits foregone* when dollars are spent one way instead of another. Only when the positive issues are resolved (when the "facts" are known) can we combine our knowledge with our normative beliefs to develop informed opinions on the best choices to make in our personal lives and for society at large.

▶ Understanding Economic Events with Economic Analysis

When you have completed your economics course, you will be better prepared to recognize an economic issue when you hear or read about one. In addition you will have a clearer understanding of how scarcity determines the choices each issue presents. News analyses in the media often discuss economic issues without recognizing them as such. Frequently, the discussions are confusing and unhelpful because they are not organized around the three basic economic questions: What? How? and For Whom? A very helpful guide in sorting through complex issues as reported in the mass media is this: Look for the *for whom* question (how will the gains and losses be distributed). Economic issues involving the most heated public debate *always* involve some group's fear, whether realistic or not, that they will lose out under one or more solutions to the issue in question. For example, if we limit imports of foreign autos, steel, or clothing, consumers of these goods will have to pay higher prices of domestically produced items, while domestic producers (business firms and their employees) of these goods will be able to charge higher prices and receive greater profits and wages. Changes in the way the economy answers *for whom* (for example, who should win, steelworkers or steel consumers) *always* alter the ways in which the *what* and *how* questions are answered (if steelworkers are protected, more domestic steel will be produced and less of other goods). If you remember this hint, it will help you understand the basic issues.

Once you have recognized the three economic questions in debate over an economic issue, you will need some elementary tools of economic analysis to make headway in deciding where you stand. We will describe these tools and show you how to use them in this and following chapters. Before doing so, however, let us discuss another example of how government policy can affect the answers to *what, how,* and *for whom* goods and services are produced.

An Example of Government Policy and Its Impact on the Answers to the Three Economic Questions: Medical Care

In most countries, the United States included, government has intervened in the provision of medical care. The reason for this is the belief held by many that citizens deserve access to health whatever their economic status. Without government provision of some medical services, it is believed that many people would go without adequate medical care. Government policy toward the health care industry is primarily aimed at changing the way the economy answers the *for whom* question. The goal is to create a world in which no one is denied access to medical care because he or she is too poor to pay for it. As a result, certain groups of families and individuals get medical care at little or no monetary cost to them. Examples are the two federal government programs *Medicare,* which pays part of most medical bills for people age sixty-five and older, and *Medicaid,* which helps finance health expenditures for the poor of all ages. The United States is by no means the only country to provide medical care at little or no charge to the elderly and the poor. Most other nations do so, and many do so to a greater extent than the United States.

The main characteristic of programs such as Medicare and Medicaid is that the participants pay less (or nothing) for medical care because many of the costs are paid from general tax revenues or special taxes on wages, such as Social Security taxes. The result is that an eligible beneficiary feels (rightly) that each additional visit to the doctor or hospital costs little or nothing. Of course, this is in keeping with the main goal of the program—to encourage the use of health care and medical services by certain groups (the *what* and *for whom* questions). Unfortunately, there are certain economic side effects to this. The most important is that participants in Medicare and Medicaid have little or no incentive (1) to seek out health care specialists who provide services of a given quality at the lowest cost or (2) to substitute less expensive health care modes for more costly ones when feasible.

Kidney dialysis (placing people whose kidneys do not function on an artificial kidney machine) is a good example of a case in which alternatives are available at very different prices. Under the program in effect in the early 1980s the federal government paid all costs of anyone suffering from complete kidney failure. Kidney patients faced the following choices: (1) hospital treatment at an average cost of $159 per treatment (usually three times a week), or $25,000 a year; (2) clinic treatment at an average cost of $138 per treatment; (3) home treatment, in which family members aid the patient, at an average cost of $97 per treatment, or 30 percent less than in a clinic; and (4) a new approach that does not require a machine but requires the patient to wear a bag of fluid[1]. Because the dollar costs of treatment are not paid by the patients themselves, they have little incentive to save money by using clinic or home care rather than the more expensive hospital mode. This is one reason why the federal government's expenditures for the program have grown very rapidly and now account for a significant share of federal health care expenditures. Clearly, the *what* question (how much kidney dialysis as opposed to other medical and nonmedical goods and services) and the *how* question (which type of care) are being answered much differently because of changes in the answer to the *for whom* question in the case of kidney patients. Serious social issues surround the question of why kidney patients should be singled out for special treatment (instead of, for example, premature babies or heart disease victims). Many physicians fear that rising costs will ultimately force them to make life-or-death decisions regarding kidney patients. An alternative approach would be to provide patients with a fixed payment per month, letting them choose the method of treatment on which to spend the money. Do you think that this would provide increased incentives to reduce costs and thus limit federal expenditures? Explain. Do you favor such a policy? Explain. As you can see, economic decisions resulting from scarcity are often difficult and frequently have critically important consequences. Let us now try to generalize the ways in which scarcity affects an economic system.

*An economic **model** is an abstract, simplified representation of how decision makers interact, how their decisions are affected by the economic environment, and the behavior that results from these decisions.*

▶ Scarcity and an Economic System

Economists and other scientists generally find that the easiest way to grasp the essential features of a subject (such as how an economic system deals with scarcity) is to first construct a **model,** which is a simplified description of how the environment affects behavior. We want you to learn more about what a scientific model is and why a model is an indispensable tool for grasping the essential features of our complex world.

What Is an Economic Model?

When you see the word *model,* you probably think of a model airplane or, perhaps, a model automobile, such as a hobbyist might build in a workshop. These are in fact very good examples. If you were to travel to Wichita, Kansas, and visit a factory of one of the major manufacturers of smaller private airplanes located there, such as Piper or Lear, you would probably be shown a department in which engineers and artists are working on models of various airplane designs that may be built and marketed in the future.

Physically, these models take on several forms. One of them is a miniature version of an airplane that might be built. When you examine such a model, you can instantly see that it is not an exact replication of a real airplane capable of carrying freight or passengers from one place to another. Depending on the stage of development, models by their very nature lack many elements of realism. For example, a model airplane may be completely hollow inside, with no seats, instrument panels, or other equipment. Still, it may be very helpful in studying the patterns of airflows over the wings and fuselage. This crucial stage in aircraft design will probably be conducted in a wind tunnel,

which itself is not an exact replication of the atmosphere in which the plane may someday fly. Despite a lack of realism, the simple airplane model just described will enable researchers to focus on a crucial feature of interest—airflow. Indeed it would be correct to say that *because* the model airplane is incomplete or "unrealistic," it permits aeronautical engineers to focus on one or a few important features that the complexity of the real world would hide.

Models in economics serve much the same purpose as in aircraft design. Economic systems are very complex, and limitations on our time, physical resources, and mental capacity prohibit us from understanding every detail and interrelationship. Economic models help us to overcome these limitations by *abstracting,* or taking out of the complex society in which we live, the *essential* features of the economy. Unessential details are ignored. Models thus permit us to develop basic principles, to use them to understand past events, and to predict whether alternative economic policies will "fly" or "crash." Economic models are almost never *physical* counterparts of the economic system. Because of the nature of the subject matter, economic models are typically constructed verbally, geometrically, or algebraically. Their purpose is to help us to see important features of the economy that the complexity of the real world would otherwise hide. In using words, geometry, and algebra, economists are not all that different from aircraft designers. At crucial stages of their work, aircraft designers also use mathematical equations to describe important relationships such as the forces of lift and drag, which determine airworthiness. They also use drawings to represent, or to model, important features of an aircraft geometrically. But how does all of this help us to understand society?

*An **efficient economy** derives as much benefit as possible from its available resources; in this sense it wastes no resources.*

*A **production possibilities frontier** (PPF) illustrates the alternative output levels for an economy that gets the most it can from its given set of resources and available*

technology. It shows the maximum production possible for each good or service, given the output of all other goods and services.

An Introductory Example: Dealing with Scarcity in a Small Economy

In order to understand how an economic system deals with scarcity, it is first helpful to discuss how a model economy might deal with scarcity. The problems that the economy must solve are similar to those that each of us must deal with in our everyday lives, but on a larger scale. The thought quiz at the beginning of this chapter addresses questions regarding the best ways to spend your time and income. Each choice requires that you give up something you would like in order to obtain more of something else. Now suppose that you are the director of economic affairs for a small country. You are responsible for how your country answers the three fundamental economic questions. Your goal is to make your country an **efficient economy,** which means that its citizens achieve the highest level of well-being possible, given available resources and their productive capabilities.

Your economy, though small, faces the same problems that most other economic systems must deal with. One of the most important economic decisions you must make is related to a question we have already discussed—how much medical care to provide for your citizens. Medical care is desired because it helps people achieve longer and more enjoyable lives. However, scarcity forces you to give up some consumer goods such as clothing, TVs, cars, vacation trips, movies, and so on, if you produce additional medical services. Circumstances are such that the only way people can get consumer goods *and* medical services is to produce them with resources available within the country. (Our economic model is obviously unrealistic in that trade with other countries is assumed to be impossible. Later on, we will deal with

trade among nations in a more complex economic model.) As director of this economic system, your job is to assign individuals to the tasks of producing goods in such a way that they obtain the largest possible output consistent with their limited resources and abilities.

The Production Possibilities Frontier (PPF)

Here is an overview of your problem. Since medical services and consumer goods are both scarce, you want your economy to achieve the largest possible production of consumer goods, given its production of medical services, and the largest possible production of medical services, given its output of consumer goods. In order to achieve your goal, you require information on the economy's capacity to produce medical services and consumer goods. The information you need is contained in your economy's **production possibilities frontier (PPF),** which defines the *maximum* quantities of the consumer goods and medical services that can be produced if no resources are wasted. The PPF is illustrated in figure 1.1. The vertical axis measures production of medical services, and the horizontal axis measures production of consumer goods.

Here are some important features of the small country's PPF. Because their resources are limited, citizens in turn face an upper limit on the amount of medical services they can produce, even if they produce no consumer goods. There is also a maximum amount of consumer goods they can produce, even if they do not produce any medical services. Maximum medical services output is shown as 230 units per month in figure 1.1, and the upper limit on consumer goods is 180 units per month. Of course, the economy is not limited to producing only medical services *or* consumer goods. People can have both. Suppose that

Figure 1.1   Production possibilities frontier for a small economy
The combination of health services and consumer goods along the curve represent the limits on production imposed by scarcity. Therefore, combinations of medical services and consumer goods *outside* the curve cannot be attained. Points A and E, inside the PPF, are inefficient because it is possible to reach points B and F, which represent increased production of at least one of the two goods/services and no less of the other.

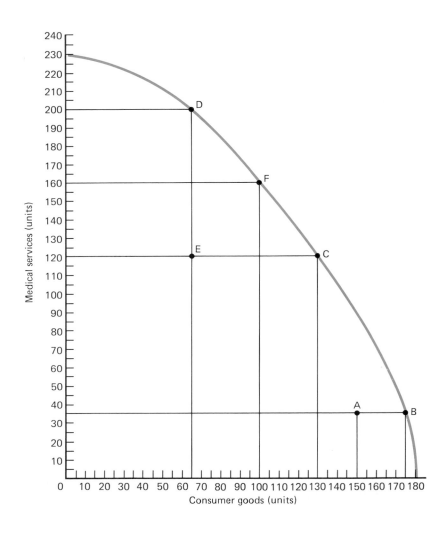

the economy begins with maximum medical services output (230 units in figure 1.1). By giving up 30 units of medical services per month, the country can increase consumer goods production from zero to 65 units per month. This is indicated by point D on the PPF. There are many other possibilities. For instance, by sacrificing 40 *more* units of medical service production per month, *additional* consumer goods can be produced, but only 35 units more (point F on the PPF). Reducing medical services by still another 40 units allows a gain of only 30 more units of consumer goods (point C on the PPF). Reducing medical services output all the way to zero from point C, a 120-unit decline in medical services, would allow consumer goods output to expand to its maximum of 180 units per month.

Economic growth means that society is able to obtain more output and is illustrated by an outward shift of the PPF.

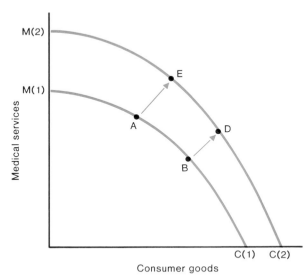

Figure 1.2   Economic growth means that society can produce more goods and services per person and involves an outward shift of the production possibilities frontier
Economic growth could also occur if an inefficient economy, producing at a point *inside* the PPF, became more efficient, moving *toward* or *to* its PPF. For example, a move from point E to point F in figure 1.1 would also be considered economic growth.

At any moment in time, the economy's PPF defines the limits on what can be produced and consumed. (It defines the possible answers to the *what* question.) How is it, then, that the level of consumption that characterizes a typical family or individual is higher now than it was ten, fifty, or one-hundred years ago? The answer is that the economy's PPF is not fixed in one position. Rather, it can shift outward over time. This is known as **economic growth.** An example of economic growth is shown in figure 1.2.

The PPF in figure 1.2 that goes from M(1) on the vertical axis to C(1) on the horizontal axis represents a lower level of potential consumption for the economy, and the PPF connecting M(2) and C(2) represents a higher level. This can easily be seen by noticing that for any point such as A or B on M(1)C(1), a larger output of *both* medical services and consumer goods is possible at points such as E and D on M(2)C(2).

The Production Possibilities Frontier, Opportunity Cost, and Economic Efficiency

If members of your society are to be as well off as possible, it is necessary to produce the maximum amount of consumer goods, given the amount of medical care produced, and vice versa. The production possibilities frontier defines the maximum amounts of medical care and/or consumer goods your economy is capable of producing and the trade-offs it faces. In short, economic efficiency requires that the economy reach its production possibilities frontier.

The PPF tells us something that is of general significance to all economic systems. *When an economy is operating efficiently, it is impossible to obtain more of one good or service without giving up something else.* If society wants more consumer goods, it must make do with fewer medical services. The value of the medical services society must forego in order to produce one more unit of consumer goods is the *opportunity cost* of consumer goods in terms of medical services. Conversely, if more medical services are desired, the opportunity cost is the value of the consumer goods that must be sacrificed. There is probably no economic concept more relevant to our everyday lives than opportunity costs of the choices we make.

In figure 1.1, the opportunity cost that must be paid for the first 65 units of consumer goods is 30 units of medical services. This is the *lowest* possible opportunity cost of obtaining these consumer goods. This follows from the definition of the PPF: The PPF represents the *maximum* quantity of consumer goods that can be obtained, given the amount of medical services produced. For the same reason, the lowest possible opportunity cost of an *additional* 65 units of consumer goods (going from point D on the PPF in figure 1.1 to point C) is an additional 80 units of medical services.

We have seen that the PPF reflects the lowest possible opportunity cost of obtaining any given amount of consumer goods, given its production of medical services. It is also true that if the economy is to reach its production possibilities frontier, opportunity costs must be as low as possible. If your economy is to be efficient, the opportunity cost of producing an additional consumer good (which is the quantity of medical services sacrificed) must be minimized, whatever the desired quantity of consumer good production happens to be. By the same reasoning, the opportunity cost of producing medical services (which is the quantity of consumer goods sacrificed) must also be as low as possible, whatever the amount of medical services desired. In order to reach your goal of achieving economic efficiency for your economy, then, you must minimize the opportuntity costs of producing whatever combination of consumer goods and medical services you or your society chooses.

To see why opportunity costs must be as low as possible if the economy is to reach its production possibilities frontier, suppose you have decided that you want to obtain 35 units of medical services and that you have done this by going to point A in figure 1.1, which is inside the PPF. At point A, you have your desired 35 units of medical services, but you only obtain 150 units of consumer goods. In other words, you have sacrificed 30 units (180–150) of consumer goods to reach point A. Since it is possible to obtain 35 units of medical services by sacrificing only 5 units (180–175) of consumer goods (point B, which is on the PPF), the economy cannot be efficient at point A. When the economy is at point A, more consumption goods are possible (175 units instead of 150 units) while still obtaining the desired 35 units of medical services. If your economy achieves its goal of 35 units of medical services by going to point A, the opportunity cost of medical services is not as low as it can be. When the opportunity cost of the desired level of medical services is made as low as possible, then the output of medical services and consumer goods will be described by a point on the production possibilities frontier of figure 1.1.

Even if you, as economic director, have no opinion concerning *where* on the PPF the economy should be (*what* is produced), you are not doing your job if you make a decision that leads to less production than is possible. That would be wasting resources. You are concerned, in other words, with *how* medical services

and consumer goods are produced so that *opportunity costs are minimized*. If opportunity costs are not made as low as possible, resources are wasted. In general, wasted resources mean that your economy is not efficient. Later on in this chapter, we will examine in greater depth just how you might go about minimizing the opportunity costs of what your society produces. Of course, *where* your economy ends up *on* the PPF is also important. An efficient economy is one that not only produces goods and services somewhere along its PPF but also produces the combination of goods and services that is most desired. How desires for various goods and services determine *what* is produced is a topic we discuss throughout the next several chapters.

Notice that nowhere have we mentioned money in discussing opportunity costs. In everyday life, opportunity costs are often indicated to us through the money (dollar) prices we pay for the goods and services we buy. For example, the dollar cost of buying this book indicates the book's opportunity cost because it measures the value of the other things you could not buy when you spent your limited income on a book rather than other goods or services. Moreover, the opportunity cost of *using* this book includes the time you spend reading it. Right now you are probably acutely aware of the opportunity cost of reading this book. There are many other valuable uses of your time. Each decision you make to do one thing involves a decision not to do something else. The best of the alternatives you choose not to pursue represents the opportunity cost you bear for each chosen course of action. Let us now return to the concept of the PPF and see what else it implies about society's opportunity costs by looking at figure 1.3.

The Shape of the Production Possibilities Frontier

Why do PPFs have the shape indicated in figures 1.1, 1.2, and 1.3? The PPFs we have drawn are not straight lines; rather, they get steeper as the production of consumer goods increases and flatter as the production of medical services increases. The curvature of the PPF means that citizens face *increasing* opportunity costs of producing more of either product.

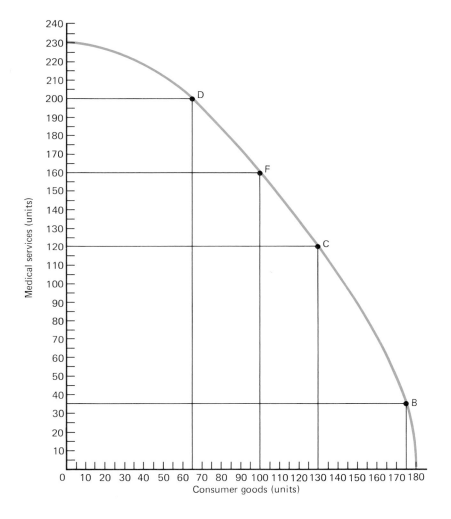

Figure 1.3   The production possibilities frontier and the law of increasing opportunity cost
The opportunity cost of the first 65 units of consumer goods is only 30 units of medical services. However, as more of the economy's resources are devoted to production of consumer goods, the opportunity cost of consumer goods increases. For example, increasing consumer goods production from 65 to 130 units (an additional 65 units) costs 80 units of medical services. Conversely, the opportunity cost of medical services rises as production increases. For example, the first 35 units of medical services require that society sacrifice only 5 units of consumer goods whereas increasing the production of medical services from 120 to 160 units requires giving up 30 units of consumer goods.

Moving *down* the PPF, the *additional* amount of medical services that must be foregone when *additional* consumer goods are produced increases as consumer goods output increases. Let us try to understand this more fully by looking at the numbers along the PPF in figure 1.3. The first 65 units of consumer goods cost only 30 units of medical services; however, increasing the production of consumer goods an additional 65 units, to 130, requires a sacrifice of 80 additional units of medical services. Going in the other direction, the first 35 units of medical services involve giving up only 5 units of consumer goods whereas increasing the production of medical services by 40 units from 160 to 200 requires a sacrifice of 35 units of consumer goods.

One reason why the opportunity cost of a good or service is likely to grow as more of it is produced is that we run out of resources that are best suited for it. If we go back to our example, the more medical services we produce, the more likely it is that we will have to use workers who are relatively better at producing consumer goods. The more specialized the economy becomes in producing either medical services or consumer goods, the more inappropriate the matching of workers to jobs is likely to become. The shape of the PPF in figures 1.1 through 1.3 corresponds to the increasing opportunity costs (difficulty) of having the economy produce more and more of either product. Do not fall into the trap of thinking that the economy is necessarily *less efficient* at the "ends" of the PPF than it is in the middle. Society may *desire* a great deal in terms of medical services and relatively little in the way of consumer goods or vice versa. These can both be efficient places to be on the PPF provided that the desired output is produced at the *lowest possible opportunity cost*.

Applications of the Production Possibilities Frontier and Opportunity Cost

Background

You should now understand why we argued earlier that we cannot ignore the cost of saving lives, even if ethically we abhor avoidable death. The PPF demonstrates graphically how scarcity forces us to make choices because scarcity imposes opportunity costs on us. Perhaps a good definition of heaven would be that it is the only place where scarcity does not exist, where opportunity costs are zero, and where nobody has to study economics. Here on earth, we cannot ignore for long the opportunity costs in choosing more of something we desire. The limitations on our capacity to produce ultimately make us reduce our consumption of another good or service, *whether we intend it or not*. Often government leaders would like to avoid this truth, but they must face up to it daily in choosing among higher military expenditures, taxes, welfare payments, public works, and deficits. Because facing up to opportunity costs is unpleasant, it is not surprising that in political campaigns the candidates often promise voters that they will adopt economic policies to improve economic well-being painlessly.

Here is an example. We are all aware of unemployment in the labor market. While not all unemployment represents economic waste, there are times that unemployment rises above levels that anyone could consider as "normal." When this happens, the economy is operating inside its PPF. The solutions to excessive unemployment, however, are not typically easy (cheap). Moreover, poorly designed policies to reduce unemployment can seriously harm the economy in the long run. Nevertheless, it is tempting for politicians to promise to reduce unemployment by increasing the size of the government sector and thus get from points such as A or E to points such as B or F in figure 1.1. Essentially, they are saying that we can have more output for society by having the government sector do more things. You will learn in your economics courses that such a seemingly costless gain in the output of our economy may be possible, but only under very special circumstances. Nevertheless, politicians are tempted to claim such achievements are attainable more often than is likely to be true. Moreover, we, as voters, often find it easy to believe them because we want to believe that solutions are cheap.

It is true that formulating economic policies is a difficult task and that the existing structure of government taxes, expenditures, and other controls may be less efficient than is possible. Voters, however, should always be skeptical of extravagant promises by politicians to improve the economy and provide benefits with no costs. It is far less painful for policymakers to suggest that their proposals will move us closer to our PPF than to emphasize the opportunity costs involved in moving along the PPF.

To summarize, if private individuals or government policymakers desire to increase the consumption of some good or service, they face two alternatives. Either they must forego consuming some other good or service, or they must find a way to move us closer to the PPF, assuming that current policies lead us to operate inside it. (You face this choice frequently in daily life. For example, if you find a way to use your study time more efficiently by finding a quiet place, without distractions, you will not have to give up a pizza break at ten o'clock the night before a midterm because you will have finished studying by then.) Unfortunately, discovering and adopting economic policies that will truly make our economy more efficient are themselves activities that usually involve opportunity costs. Failure to recognize these limitations is likely to lead to decisions that move *away* from an efficient use of our economy's resources. To make these points more concrete we will use the concept of opportunity cost to discuss the 55-mile-per-hour speed limit.

Reckoning with Opportunity Costs: The Case of the 55-mph Speed Limit

The principle of opportunity cost tells us that there are no free lunches, or that our choices always involve costs of some sort. For example, after oil prices rose sharply in 1973–74, Congress determined that the United States could reduce its gasoline consumption if motorists would reduce their driving speed. As a result, the federal government adopted legislation setting a 55-mph speed limit. Is the 55-mph speed limit good economic policy? Does it contribute to economic efficiency by pushing us closer to our economy's PPF?

Actually, *two* types of opportunity costs are involved in driving at high speeds. One relates to the individual driver and riders in his or her car. The cost of driving faster includes increased gasoline consumption per mile traveled and greater wear and tear on the car's tires and engine. There is also a greater risk of personal injury to the car's driver and passengers from driving faster. The second kind of cost is the increased risk of property damage and personal injury to drivers and passengers in *other* cars.

There is a crucial distinction between these two categories of opportunity costs. The first type involves only the driver of a car and its passengers. They are presumably able to take all of these costs into account in determining the best speed at which to drive. In return for bearing these costs, the driver and passengers reap the *benefit* of reduced travel time. Since time available for working, eating, and leisure activities is perhaps the most basic form of scarcity each of us confronts, the benefits of reduced travel time are substantial. The principal point to recognize with respect to these personal costs and benefits is that the best judge of whether the expected costs of driving faster exceed the benefits is probably those who bear them. This means that as far as saving gasoline or other resources is concerned, there would appear to be no obvious reason for government to interfere with private decisions. (One possible exception is that if injured individuals in the driver's car are eligible for Medicaid, others are paying part of their medical expenses. So, to some extent the driver and his or her passengers may not take all of the relevant costs of speeding into consideration, and they may drive too fast.)

The second type of cost is a different story, however. The driver of a car traveling at a high speed probably places less weight on the risk of injuring other drivers, their cars, and their passengers than do those who may be hurt by the speeder's behavior. Since some of the cost of driving fast is borne by others, a bias is created in favor of fast driving. Thus, there is a reasonably solid basis for speed limits. Is 55 miles per hour the correct speed limit for interstate highways, though? We cannot take the space to discuss all of the information needed to answer this question. We will take a brief look, however. The answer relies on the same basic framework and reasoning involved in our earlier discussion of whether any sacrifice is too great where human life is involved.

Because saving lives is costly, not *all* lives can be saved or prolonged. Choices must be made. Therefore, the question of *how* resources are allocated to prolong life is important. When speed limits are lowered more time is required to drive from one place to another. Over 25 percent more time per mile traveled is required by a driver who must travel at 55 miles per hour instead of 70 miles per hour. Since time is a scarce resource, it has value. Increased travel time is a resource that sales representatives, truckers, and others could use to carry out their business. A reduced speed limit extends the travel time to work for many commuters. Speed limits reduce the distances that can be traveled during a vacation period, thus diminishing the value of leisure and vacation time for many. Society's trade-off between saving lives and time available for activities other than driving is illustrated in figure 1.4.

Economists have conducted studies of how people value their time. These studies are carried out not by interviewing individuals directly but rather by noting the modes of transportation people chose and how these choices depended on the costs in terms of dollars per mile traveled and time per mile traveled. The results of these studies imply that the average person is willing to spend an amount equal to about one-half his or her hourly wage to save one hour of travel time.[2]

Highway safety experts have calculated approximately how many lives are saved annually as a result of the 55-mph speed limit. Thus, it is possible to estimate the dollar cost per life saved. The finding is that it costs society about $2 million per life saved (in terms of average wages earned in 1986).

Is $2 million per life saved too much? Most of us would find it difficult to place a dollar value on our own or on our loved ones' lives, not to mention people we have never met. Still most people would agree that less costly life-saving methods should be chosen over more expensive ones. If the point of the 55-mph speed limit is to save lives, it is fair to ask if this is an efficient way to save lives. Why should we single out

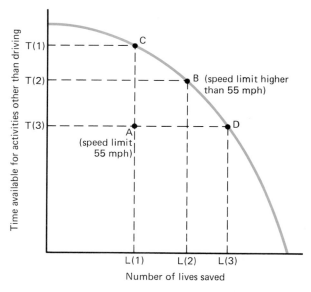

Figure 1.4   Society's trade-off between driving time and lives saved from automobile accidents
This PPF shows that society can choose between saving lives and using time for activities other than driving cars. By lowering the speed limit, we save more lives but we have less time available for other activities. However, there are other means of saving lives that have lower opportunity costs. Because time and lives are extremely valuable to most of us, this is an important social choice. Specifically, when the speed limit is 55 miles per hour, there are other things that can be done to save lives that make better use of our time and save more lives. An example would be to provide every family with a smoke detector. Then the speed limit could be raised while still saving more lives than we do now. This can be illustrated as moving from a point such as A to a point such as B, which is between points C and D on the PPF.

traffic deaths as the appropriate target for government policy? It has been estimated that placing smoke detectors in every home in the United States would save about as many lives per year as the 55-mph speed limit but at much lower cost, only $50,000 to $80,000 per life saved. Perhaps every home in the United States should be required to install smoke detectors. Do you agree?

The preceding discussion may be factually correct, but what would be a less expensive life-saving government policy with respect to automobiles? Here is one possible answer for you to think about. Instead of a 55-mph speed limit, let the federal government issue special license tags in different colors to permit driving up to various speeds on interstate highways. The higher the speed permitted, the higher the annual fee. Suppose that driving in the speed range of up to 70 miles per hour increases the risk of killing someone in another car by one death per year for every 30,000 licensed drivers. (This is based roughly on available statistics.) Suppose that in compensation for this risk, drivers were required to pay into an insurance fund that would compensate anyone injured or the families of anyone killed *plus* enough to save two lives by installation of smoke detectors. If the compensation paid were $1,500,000 per additional death caused by traveling over 55 mph and it cost $160,000 to install enough smoke detectors to save two lives, then anyone who wished to drive at speeds up to 70 mph would be required to pay approximately $55 annually for a license to do so ($55 × 30,000 = $1,650,000). The license revenue would be used to provide compensation to the families of people killed in car crashes and to purchase smoke detectors for the public. Would this essentially make drivers' licenses more of a license to kill than they are now? How would this proposal compare to current efforts to control speeding? Can you suggest what you think is a better alternative?

In the example of the 55-mph speed limit, we saw that there is more than one way to use our time and other resources in order to save lives. Some ways to save lives have lower opportunity costs than others, and in a world of scarcity it makes an important difference which methods are chosen. Before concluding our discussion of opportunity cost and the production possibilities frontier, we will take a closer look at how you, as director of a small economy, can help your economy become efficient by using your labor resources effectively.

Opportunity Cost, Comparative Advantage, and Specialization

Your task is to assign workers to produce either medical services or consumer goods so that production takes place along the production possibilities frontier. (To keep our example simple, we will assume that any worker has sufficient training to produce *some* medical services.) The production possibilities frontier describes the best "menu" from which society can then choose the most preferred combination of consumer goods and medical services.

As we have seen, reaching the production possibilities frontier requires minimizing opportunity costs. We shall see that opportunity costs can be minimized only when workers specialize in production. **Specialization** means that workers do not produce everything they consume; rather, they tend to concentrate their efforts on producing one or a few goods or services. *How* they specialize is of the utmost importance. Opportunity costs will be minimized and the country's maximum potential output, as defined by the PPF, will be obtained only if workers specialize in producing according to their *relative* skills.

A numerical example will show what we mean. Suppose that Larry and Laura are two new workers you must assign to producing either consumer goods or medical services. By carefully examining how Larry and Laura should be assigned, we can derive the basic principle that applies to the other workers as well. Specifically, suppose that Laura can produce at most *either* 50 units of medical services per year *or* 10 units of consumer goods. She can also produce some of both by giving up 50/10, or 5, units of medical services, for each (additional) unit of consumer goods she produces. Suppose that Larry, on the other hand, can produce at most only 40 units of medical services *or* 5 units of consumer goods and must sacrifice 40/5, or 8, units of medical services for each (additional) unit of consumer goods he provides.

Comparative advantage is determined by which producer has the lowest opportunity cost of producing a good or service. Since opportunity cost is measured in terms of the quantity of one good or service that must be sacrificed to produce one more unit of another good or service, everyone has a comparative advantage in producing something.

Table 1.1   Maximum production, opportunity cost, and comparative advantage

Laura's opportunity cost of producing consumer goods is lower than Larry's. The numbers also show that Larry's opportunity cost of producing medical services is lower than Laura's. It costs Larry only 5/40 = 1/8 unit of consumer goods to produce one more unit of medical services, while Laura's opportunity cost of an additional unit of medical services is 10/50 = 1/5 unit of consumer goods.

	Maximum production (units)		Opportunity cost of one more unit of consumer goods		Comparative advantage
	Larry	**Laura**	**Larry**	**Laura**	
Consumer goods	5	10	$\frac{40}{5} = 8$	$\frac{50}{10} = 5$	Laura in consumer goods and Larry in medical services
Medical services	40	50			

To complete our example, we will assume that every worker (besides Laura and Larry) in the economy has already been assigned to produce either consumer goods or medical services in the most efficient manner. We will also assume that society now desires 10 additional units of consumer goods. Given the information we have on Larry and Laura's production opportunity costs, it follows that Laura should produce the 10 additional units of consumer goods society desires. This is true even though by devoting her efforts only to medical services, Laura could produce 50 units, which is 10 more than Larry's capability. The reason is that the *opportunity cost* of producing each additional unit of consumer goods is 8 units of medical services for Larry but only 5 units of medical services for Laura. Because Laura has a lower opportunity cost of producing consumer goods than Larry does, we say that she has a **comparative advantage** in the production of consumer goods and should therefore specialize in producing consumer goods.

A moment's further thought will reveal that Larry has a comparative advantage in producing medical services. From the numbers given above, his opportunity cost of producing a unit of medical services is 5/40, or 1/8, unit of consumer goods. By contrast, Laura's opportunity cost of a unit of medical services is higher, 10/50, or 1/5, unit of consumer goods.

This simple example of opportunity cost, comparative advantage, and specialization is summarized in tables 1.1 and 1.2. It shows that if Larry were to help produce the 10 additional units of consumer goods, Laura would also have to produce 5 units. She would have to sacrifice 25 units of medical services, so society's total additional output would amount to 10 units of consumer goods and 25 of medical services. By contrast, if Laura were to specialize in consumer goods production, she could produce all of the additional 10 units by herself. Even though she would not produce any medical services, total (additional) production of medical services would be 40 units, all produced by Larry. This is a better outcome because it provides more medical services for society, given that society desires 10 additional units of consumer goods. The basic principle is that the economy can reach its production possibilities frontier only when workers produce those goods in which they have a *comparative* advantage, that is, a lower opportunity cost than other workers. In this way we see that the answers to the *what* and *how* questions are clearly intertwined.

A **market economy** *is one in which most goods and services are bought and sold in markets rather than each good and service being produced by each person or family that uses it.*

A **market** *may be an actual location, but in economics it is best thought of as an idealized concept that describes how buyers and sellers of a particular good or service come together.*

A **barter economy** *is one in which money plays an unimportant role and in which goods and services are traded directly.*

Table 1.2	Total production when 10 additional units of consumer goods are desired

If Laura specializes in the production of consumer goods, she will produce the additional 10 units society desires, leaving Larry free to devote all of his efforts to producing 40 units of medical services. This results in greater additional output of medical services than if Larry and Laura both produce consumer goods.

	If Larry produces only consumer goods			If Laura produces all the additional consumer goods desired		
	Larry's production	Laura's production	Total	Larry's production	Laura's production	Total
Consumer goods	5 units	5 units	10 units	0 units	10 units	10 units
Medical services	0 units	25 units	25 units	40 units	0 units	40 units

▶ The Concept of a Market Economy and the Economy of the United States

This chapter has introduced the basic economic problem—scarcity. While people have desires for all types of goods and services, they cannot fully satisfy those desires because of limits to the resources they possess. In the following chapters, we will investigate how scarcity affects a **market economy,** which is a system in which producers and consumers interact to determine the output of goods and services. Market economies are dominant in the United States and most other nations. A **market** should be thought of as the arena in which buyers and sellers interact. Not all markets are formal, visible organizations in the sense that there is a particular geographical location where buyers and sellers come to do business such as in bazaars in the Middle East or at the New York Stock Exchange. These are markets, of course, but so is the labor market. The labor market is an example of a *conceptual* market, which cannot always be pinpointed in terms of a physical location. We have all heard of the labor market. In all likelihood you are either in it now, have been, or soon will be. But have you ever actually *seen* the labor market?

The point is that a market is a convenient analytical device economists use to organize their ideas. Sociologists do something similar when they refer to women's liberation or the civil rights movement. These are important social forces, but they are not things that you can actually touch. What we are saying is that exchanges do occur, even if they are not all in the same place, as in the case of the stock market. The way in which buyers and sellers of houses interact, for example, determines housing prices and how many houses are bought and sold. By developing the concept of a market more fully, we will see the forces that determine the prices and production of goods and services and their effect on the welfare of those individuals involved as buyers and sellers (the answers to the *what* and *for whom* questions).

An important aspect of most market economies is that purchases are made with money. To understand the importance of money we must imagine an economy *without* money, which is called a **barter economy.** In a barter economy, transactions involve trading one good or service for another. Successful trades require *mutual coincidence of want,* which means that if I wished to have my automobile fixed,

Free market economies are those that operate with the least amount of government control over the prices and quantities of goods and services bought and sold; few such economies operate with absolutely no government influence, however.

Controlled economies are characterized by controlled markets, in which prices, and sometimes quantities bought and

sold, are mandated by law or government decree. Some transactions may occur in uncontrolled markets.

I would have to find a mechanic who wanted what I had to trade. If I baked rye bread for a living, the only way I could get a tune-up for my car would be to find a mechanic who just happened to want rye bread. This would be a very cumbersome way of getting something done and suggests why modern economies do not typically use the barter system. It is much simpler to sell the rye bread I produce for money and then use the money to purchase car repairs from any mechanic I might choose.

A market economy is an invaluable means of reducing scarcity because markets permit society to benefit from specialization. We have seen how specialization is crucial to achieving economic efficiency. When we specialize, almost none of us produce all of the goods and services we consume. Indeed, some of us work in jobs that involve goods or services we may never wish to purchase. For example, many famous designers of women's clothing are men; you do not have to like snow sports to work in a ski factory; many workers without pets help manufacture dog, cat, and canary food. If each of us tried to be self-sufficient, scarcity would be much more severe for us because we would not be able to direct our talents and abilities where they are most useful (the answer to the *how* question). We would all have to be Jacks or Jills of all trades. However, in the absence of markets, obtaining the goods and services we want in exchange for those we produce would take so much time and effort that the advantages of specialization would be largely lost. Before analyzing market economies in detail, we must further distinguish among various economic systems.

In this book, our focus is on those economic systems in which governments exert the least direct influence on the prices and quantities of goods bought

and sold (the answer to the *what* question). In no nation are markets totally free of governmental controls. However, the economies of the United States, Canada, Japan, West Germany, and South Korea, among others, are characterized by the predominance of **free markets**—which means *relatively little* governmental intervention in the economy. **Controlled economies** lie at the opposite extreme. Examples are the systems of the Soviet Union, much of Eastern Europe, and the People's Republic of China, where relatively few transactions take place without the explicit approval of some government official. In this sense, government is much more involved in the answer to the *what* question in these countries.

Lying in between these two extremes are the **mixed economies** of such nations as France, Sweden, Great Britain, and Mexico, where government typically owns some major industries that are privately held in free market systems. The United States is sometimes also called a mixed economy because our government does control some industries (for example, mail delivery, some transportation, some utilities, and many schools). Other industries that are frequently owned by the government in mixed economies are basic steel production, petroleum, automobile manufacturing, airlines, and banks. There are various reasons why governments exert ownership over major industries in mixed economies. Some goals of government ownership are the achievement of high employment and high wages, independence from foreign suppliers, and the prestige associated with industrial "power." One of your tasks both as a citizen and as a student of economics will be to decide whether government ownership represents the best way of achieving these goals and, equally important, which economic goals you think it best for society to emphasize.

Mixed economies contain many government-owned industries that are typically privately owned in free market systems.

▶ Summary and Conclusions

This chapter introduced the concept of scarcity and provided an overview of a simple economic system. You should now have a feel for the way an economic system answers the fundamental questions *what, how,* and *for whom*. The following points were emphasized in this chapter.

All economies face limits imposed by scarcity. When these limits are dealt with efficiently, opportunity costs measure the prices that must be paid when choosing among alternative goods and services.

Producing efficiently requires that individuals specialize according to their relative opportunity costs, or comparative advantage.

Opportunity cost and the production possibilities frontier (PPF) help us to understand the economic issues underlying much government policy, including determining the proper speed limit on interstate highways and labor productivity in the United States.

Few economies today are barter economies. In market economies, individuals typically exchange goods and services indirectly by using money. Market economies foster economic efficiency by encouraging specialization.

Market economies may be of the free market type, controlled economies, or mixed economies. The economy of the United States comes closer to a free market economy than most others. Nevertheless, it has many features of a mixed economy.

▶ Key Terms

barter economy *21*
comparative advantage *20*
controlled economies *22*
economic growth *13*
efficient economy *11*
free market economies *22*
market *21*
market economy *21*
mixed economies *23*

model *10*
normative view *8*
opportunity cost *6*
positive economics *8*
production possibilities frontier (PPF) *11*
scarcity *6*
specialization *19*
three fundamental economic questions *6*

▶ Questions for Discussion and Review

1. Define scarcity and positive economics.

2. Some restaurants advertise that after you pay for your meal you can have all the additional helpings you like free of charge. Have they found a way to eliminate scarcity? Is there any cost at all associated with "seconds" and "thirds" in these restaurants? Why do people patronize restaurants that do not price their meals this way?

3. Try to imagine a world in which scarcity did not exist. What would be the importance of answering the *what, how,* and *for whom* questions in such a world? What kind of economic system do you think would be best in this circumstance?

4. In one of the newspaper articles cited in this chapter, a kidney dialysis patient is quoted as saying, "I would not want to be forced into home dialysis just because it gave my doctor a greater profit. The question should be, is it good for the patient." Do you agree with the quotation? Can you imagine a situation in which someone would voluntarily agree to use home dialysis without receiving orders from a doctor or other authority to do so? Would such a situation be good for the patient? Would it be good for society?

5. Make a list of the types of models used in subjects other than economics. How do these models abstract from (ignore) details of the real world to focus on essentials?

6. Your Uncle Sid shows up at your college, takes you to lunch, and pays the bill. Is this really a free lunch? What costs, if any, do you pay for the lunch?

7. Are workers in the United States highly specialized? Do you believe that specialization has helped productivity growth?

8. In figure 1.1, what would happen to the PPF if a new discovery made producers of both medical services and consumer goods more productive?

9. In tables 1.1 and 1.2, how would Larry's and Laura's comparative advantage change if Larry were suddenly able to produce twice as much of both things, but Laura's capabilities did not change? Describe a change that would result in Larry's having a comparative advantage in the production of consumer goods. What would happen to Laura's comparative advantage?

10. In figure 1.2, suppose that workers producing medical services were provided with additional high-tech equipment to work with but that workers in the consumer goods area were not. What would be the effect on the PPF? What would happen to the opportunity cost of medical services? What would be the effect on the opportunity cost of consumer goods?

11. In congressional debates on pollution and environmental policy, one side frequently argues that our environment is too precious to be "sold" in return for higher industrial output. Others argue that the benefits of an improved environment must be weighed against the costs of reducing pollution. What are the costs and benefits they are arguing about? Which side do you support? Why?

12. Suppose that we did not have a market economy and that you had to produce everything you consumed. Make up a "time budget" showing how you would spend your time each week producing everything you need. How much time would you require? Be sure to allow time for eating and sleeping. How many of the goods and services that you now consume would you be able to have? How much time would be left over for leisure?

13. Suppose that you were in charge of organizing an all-volunteer army for the United States government. On the basis of what you have learned about the concept of opportunity cost, what issues would you consider in order to complete your task?

Appendix to Chapter 1

Economics and Your Career

▶ **Why Take Economics?**

Now that you are enrolled in your first or second course in economics, you are probably wondering just how this subject will help you in your future career. Some of you may, in fact, eventually become professional economists, although the probability of this is small. For most students, a course in the principles of economics is not the obvious doorway to a profession that preengineering or premed courses provide for many. Even so, economics can and should be a valuable part of your curriculum.

Economics courses are an important element in a program of liberal education. They offer an understanding of how the economy operates and provide a basis for informed opinions on many public issues. If you are majoring in one of the other social sciences or in business administration, a minor in economics will provide valuable information and training in understanding the social environment in which we live and work.

▶ **Economics As a Major**

There are various opportunities for economics majors. Although employment as a professional economist generally requires a graduate degree, an undergraduate major in economics that emphasizes the quantitative tools of economic theory and statistical applications (econometrics) provides excellent preparation for a career in government, banking, business, organized labor, trade associations, or teaching in the social sciences. Business firms and federal, state, and local government agencies look favorably on economics majors in their quest for bright, clear-thinking trainees capable of moving up the job ladder to positions of managerial responsibility.

An economics major also provides an excellent base for graduate work in law, business administration, public administration, and the health professions, as well as in economics. Admissions committees in these disciplines value economics majors because they know that economics provides sound training in logical thinking, assessment of alternatives, and quantitative skills.

▶ **Careers in Economics**

As we have suggested, taking a few courses or majoring in economics can provide the foundation for a variety of careers. A former advisee of one of the authors of this text who subsequently received a master's degree in public administration is now budget director of the state of Ohio. Two former students whose careers we have followed are professors at major law schools.

Graduate work in economics can lead to either a master's or a Ph.D. degree. Graduates with a master's degree find jobs as economic analysts with many business firms, in the banking industry, and as officials in city, state, and national governments and in international agencies such as the World Bank, International Monetary Fund, and so on. They also have access to teaching positions in high schools and many two-year colleges. Graduates with a Ph.D. frequently are employed by college and university faculties, but many have jobs with major financial institutions and research organizations. It is not uncommon for someone with a Ph.D. in economics to work (as an economist) at the level of vice president of one of the country's largest banks. During the past twenty years the heads of some of our major universities—including the University of California, Carnegie-Mellon University, Northwestern University, Princeton University, and the University of Colorado—have been economists. But so much for abstractions. We can also name names. The following list contains the names of over two dozen prominent people whose college undergraduate or graduate degrees were in economics. Who knows what heights you will attain if you choose economics as your major?

► Prominent Economics Majors and Positions They Have Held

Brock Adams   Representative from Washington and secretary of transportation

Robert O. Anderson   CEO, Atlantic-Richfield Corporation

Roy Anderson   CEO, Lockheed Corporation

Carlos Romero Barcelo   Governor of Puerto Rico

Rose Elizabeth Bird   Chief justice, California supreme court

W. Michael Blumenthal   President, Bendix Corporation, and secretary of the treasury

Thomas A. Donovan   President, Chicago Board of Trade

John Elway   Quarterback, Denver Broncos

Michael Foot   Prominent political leader, British Labor party

Mike Gravel   Senator from Alaska

David Hartman   Host, "Good Morning America"

Brian Holloway   Defensive back, New England Patriots

Alfred Kahn   Chairman, Interstate Commerce Commission

Juanita Kreps   Secretary of commerce and vice president of Duke University

Drew Lewis   Secretary of transportation

Hilla Limann   President of Ghana

F. Ray Marshall   Secretary of labor

Sandra Day O'Connor   Associate justice of the Supreme Court

Merlin Olsen   Professional football player and announcer

Charles Percy   CEO, Bell and Howell Corporation, and senator from Illinois

Sylvia Porter   Syndicated financial columnist

Ronald W. Reagan   President of the United States

George P. Shultz   President, Bechtel Corporation, secretary of state, secretary of the treasury, and secretary of labor

Cyrus P. Vance   Secretary of state

Harold Wilson   Prime minister of Great Britain

Who Should Pay for Clean Air?

▶ The Action-Initiating Event

You are the chief economic adviser to the city council of a medium-sized industrial city. The city council is considering an ordinance requiring that the manufacturing firms in the city cut their air pollution by 50 percent during the next year. The head of the council has asked you to write a memo describing the key economic policy issue(s) that should be discussed by the council before it votes on the ordinance.

▶ The Issue

As you see it, the most important thing to consider here is *not* how the pollution will be curbed; you are reasonably sure that the firms will cooperate if the ordinance is passed and that they are technologically able to curb the pollution. The key issues in your mind involve trade-offs and opportunity costs. Clean air is good for the community, but it will not be free. Some group or groups must ultimately pay one way or another for that clean air. Moreover, the more one group of citizens pays, the less another group or groups will be burdened with the costs of cleaning up the air. Finally, you realize that each of the following groups have something to do with the problem of air pollution in your city: (1) owners of the polluting firms, (2) workers in the polluting firms, (3) the customers who buy the products of the polluting firms, (4) the taxpayers of your city, and (5) the members of the city government itself.

▶ Economic Policy Issues

Who should pay the cost of cleaning up the air in your city? The improvement in air quality that the city council is considering could cause some or all of the manufacturing firms in your city to close and move elsewhere. This would make each of the five groups identified above economically worse off. On the other hand, the people who live in the neighborhoods surrounding the manufacturing plants have been, in a sense, paying for the air pollution for a number of years by having to stay indoors more often, purchasing air conditioners and air purifiers for their homes, and suffering poorer health in the form of more frequent respiratory ailments. Should this continue? To make matters worse, you worry about your city being branded as antibusiness and unable to attract new businesses (and their jobs and tax revenues) to the city in the future—even ones that might not pollute at all, such as computer software companies.

▶ Recommendations

The head of the council wants you to identify in your memo the various groups of people that might be affected by an ordinance severely cutting air pollution. Included in your memo should be an explanation of some of the details of *how* each of the various groups involved might be harmed by the antipollution measures that might be adopted. At the end of the memo you are to outline an amendment to the ordinance being considered such that, should the ordinance pass, the costs of the required cutback in pollution would be *shared* by *all* of the affected groups.

Part II

How Markets Work

Chapter 2

Demand

Outline

  I. Introduction *32*
 II. The demand relationship *33*
    A. Data on consumer expenditures in the United States *33*
    B. Basic assumptions of the theory of demand *33*
      1. The goals of consumers and how they attempt to achieve them *33*
      2. Limitations on the choices consumers can make *35*
    C. Method of analysis *36*
    D. The law of demand and the demand curve *36*
      1. The demand curve, value, and marginal utility *38*
        a. Demand and utility: You *can* get some satisfaction *41*
        b. Marginal utility *41*
 III. Demand versus quantity demanded *45*
    A. Quantity demanded and change in quantity demanded *45*
    B. The demand curve and factors that shift it *46*
      1. Income *46*
      2. Tastes and preferences *47*
      3. Prices of related goods and services *47*
      4. Expectations *48*
      5. Time horizons *48*
      6. Time required for consumption *48*
      7. Population and income distribution *48*
    C. Summary of movements along the demand curve and shifts in demand *49*
 IV. Applications of the law of demand *50*
    A. The diffusion of Japanese cars into the United States market *50*
    B. Government policy and the theory of demand *51*
  V. Summary and conclusions *52*
 VI. Key terms *52*
 VII. Questions for discussion and review *52*
VIII. Appendix: A closer look at the theory of consumer choice *54*
    A. The utility function *54*
    B. Indifference curves *55*
    C. The budget constraint: How much of what you want can you get? *57*
    D. The geometry and economics of consumer choice *58*
      1. Using indifference curve and budget constraint diagrams *59*
    E. Key terms *59*

Objectives

After reading this chapter, the student should be able to:

Discuss the goals of consumers and how they attempt to achieve them.

State the law of demand and discuss how the substitution and income effects support the law of demand.

Show how the demand curve relates to the marginal value of a good or service.

Show how diminishing marginal utility relates to the law of demand.

Distinguish between a change in demand and a change in the quantity demanded.

Distinguish between normal and inferior goods.

List factors that cause a demand curve to shift.

Define the utility function and discuss its properties.

Discuss the properties of indifference curves.

Show how the indifference map and the budget constraint determine consumer choice.

Demand is the relationship between the desire to buy various quantities of a good or service and its price.

Supply is the relationship between the desire to sell various quantities of a good or service and its price.

▶ Introduction

During 1984, the Washington (state) Public Power Commission (WPPS, often called WHOOPS) announced that it could not pay interest or principal on hundreds of millions of dollars of bonds that had been purchased by banks, savings and loan companies, and many individual investors throughout the United States. This was the largest default on government-issued bonds in United States history, and it seriously damaged the credit rating of many state and municipal government agencies. Moreover, many of the individual investors had relied on the supposed safety of these bonds in deciding where to place savings to be used in retirement. Not only did the name of the state of Washington support bondholders' faith in the safety of their funds, but the payments of principal and interest were secured by revenue to be earned from the sale of electricity generated by nuclear power produced in generators financed by WHOOPS bond sales. What went wrong?

The WHOOPS bondholders were victims of two major miscalculations made by the commission. One miscalculation was a serious underestimate of the cost of building and bringing on line nuclear power generating plants. The second was a substantial overestimate of the public's willingness to purchase electricity at ever increasing prices. Historically, electricity consumption had grown steadily each year. Power plant planners had naively projected that this growth would continue indefinitely, so that there would be no problem in selling all the electricity the new nuclear power generators were designed to produce—even if cost overruns developed. What planners failed to consider was the basic economic principle that when the price of a good or service increases, purchasers begin to look for alternative ways to spend their money. This is the

basic principle of demand. Thus, as the costs of all kinds of electricity increased, the public began to conserve on electricity consumption. It soon became apparent that there would be little or no market for nuclear-generated electricity at the price the WPPS would be forced to charge in order to pay off its bonds. The commission's only alternatives were to default or to subsidize paying their bond obligations through raising the price of electricity produced by nonnuclear means. It chose the former course as the politically safer route.

*In this chapter we begin to investigate how scarcity affects a market economy. Our analysis of a market economy has three elements: (1) **demand**, which refers to people's desires to purchase a good or service at various prices—examined in this chapter and chapter 3; (2) **supply**, the desire of firms to sell a good or service at various prices—analyzed in chapter 4; and (3) the interaction of supply and demand, which determines prices and the quantities of goods bought and sold—analyzed in chapters 5 through 11. Together, these three elements comprise our model or summary representation of the economic factors influencing the behavior of buyers and sellers. As a general rule, we will analyze how buyers and sellers behave in pursuit of their private goals. As a second step, we will frequently show how government actions have intentionally or unintentionally altered the outcome that would prevail if supply and demand operated strictly on their own. We will then develop a framework that you can use to help decide for yourself the degree to which you believe that society's goals are better achieved when governmental policies affect the outcomes in a market economy. An understanding of demand and supply analysis can be useful when reading about economic issues in the newspaper or thinking about a government program being debated in Congress.*

Assumptions are statements about the nature of the world that are taken to be true for purposes of developing a model, or theory, such as the theory or model of demand.

▶ The Demand Relationship

Data on Consumer Expenditures in the United States

The *Statistical Abstract of the United States* is an excellent source of data for many of the papers and reports you may be asked to write. It is available in any library, but it is also a book worth owning. Figure 2.1 presents data from two editions showing how United States consumers spent their incomes in 1983 versus 1950. The two largest budget items are food and housing, which together represent over one-third of total consumer spending. Notice also the changes in consumption during this period.[1] In 1983, households spent a much larger fraction of their total expenditures on medical care and housing and a much smaller fraction on food than they did in 1950. In this chapter we will use the theory of consumer demand to discover the economic forces and government policies that have produced some of the changes in expenditure patterns we see in figure 2.1.

Basic Assumptions of the Theory of Demand

Demand refers to desired purchases of a good or service. In economics, we are interested in how the desired purchases of particular goods or services change in response to various influences. Many variables determine how each of us spends his or her income, and probably no two people respond to influences on their demands for goods and services in exactly the same way. Therefore, some simplification is required in order to separate what is important from what can be ignored in understanding demand. In chapter 1, we discussed the importance of *models* in simplifying the development of scientific knowledge. We will now explore a model of how the demand for a good or service is determined. The first part of developing any model is to list its **assumptions,** which are statements that

are accepted as true, or factual, for purposes of the model. As we have said, no model is ever an entirely exact replication of the real world. The assumptions of a model are akin to a rough sketch, or outline, of what it is hoped are the most important characteristics of the world. They are designed to simplify what would otherwise be too complex to understand. Assumptions are the basic building blocks of scientific analysis. To understand how economists analyze the demand for goods and services, we must first learn the basic assumptions upon which the theory of consumer demand is built. There are two general categories of assumptions we must make. One concerns the constraints or limitations placed on a consumer. The other describes consumers' goals and how they try to reach those goals.

The Goals of Consumers and How They Attempt to Achieve Them

1. We assume that individuals plan for a particular amount of time into the future. At the end of that time, be it a week, a month, or a year, they again make consumption decisions. Practically speaking, this assumption means that we will measure the quantities of goods and services people consume by the number of units they buy within a particular period of time. In other words, the theory of consumer demand is based on the concept of flows of goods or services purchased per time period, such as the amount of milk bought per week.
2. We assume that individuals consider the future when making their decisions. Among other things, they will wait for prices to fall or buy now before prices go up. This is not to say that consumers are always correct in their expectations of future price changes. They will make mistakes. Still, their decisions are influenced by expectations of the future.

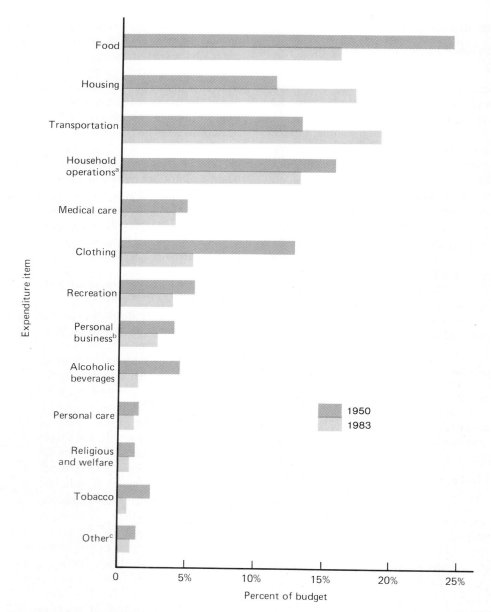

Figure 2.1   Consumer expenditures as a percentage of total budget, 1950 and 1983
[a]Includes furniture, utilities, and cleaning preparations.
[b]Includes brokerage fees, bank service charges, legal fees, and funeral expenses. [c]Includes private education and foreign travel.

From U.S. Bureau of the Census, *Statistical Abstract of the United States,* 1975, (96th edition), p. 382 and 1986, (106th edition), pp. 443–444. Washington, D.C.

3. We assume that consumers know whether or not they would like a particular commodity. By this we simply mean that an individual has tastes and preferences (likes and dislikes) and knows what they are. Economists really have very little to say about the details of individuals' feelings for particular goods and services. For example, some consumers may like yogurt but not bean sprouts, while others have opposite tastes. Economists *do,* however, have some general ideas about the *structure* of an individual's tastes and preferences. This leads us to our next assumption.

4. We assume that people derive satisfaction from consuming a *variety* of goods and services and that *more than one combination* of goods and services can yield a particular amount of happiness. Many people, for example, enjoy drinking Cokes and eating pizza. In addition, it is reasonable to suppose that some individuals get just as much enjoyment from eating a small pizza and drinking a large Coke as they would get from eating a large pizza and drinking a small Coke. Similarly, some people might find it just as much fun to watch two basketball games and play one hour of tennis as to play three hours of tennis and watch only one basketball game.

5. Our final assumption concerning individuals' goals and feelings is that they prefer more to less pleasure from goods and services. This means that when given the choice of two activities that cost the same, say, going to a Woody Allen movie or seeing one of Shakespeare's plays, a person will pick the one that gives the greater enjoyment. The assumption that people wish to have happy and enjoyable lives means that they do their best not to be foolish or wasteful. In addition, they may take the feelings of others into account when making decisions. Clearly, individual economic decisions are influenced by feelings of love, caring, and empathy.

The set of assumptions listed above relate to people's feelings and their attempts to lead satisfying lives. Apart from different tastes, why doesn't everyone have four Rolls Royces, a beach house at Malibu, and an apartment in New York City? The answer lies in our next set of assumptions, which deal with the fact that the choices an individual has available are limited by a number of factors.

Limitations on the Choices Consumers Can Make

1. We assume that no one has unlimited wealth. Our spending power is limited by our earnings from working and the amount of income we receive from stocks, bonds, and other investments, the government, our families, and elsewhere. Because we cannot have everything, we must make choices. For example, if you choose to go to Florida for a couple of weeks in the spring, you might have to eat doughnuts for breakfast for a month to save the money to pay for the trip.

2. We assume that people, as individuals, cannot control the prices they pay for goods and services. While we may look around for the store with the lowest priced beer, once we find it, we must pay that price. We are merely assuming that no one individual has enough buying power to influence, to any great extent, the prices of goods and services. It is important to realize that in making this assumption we do not specify where those prices come from. They may be set by government decree, as in the case of a centrally planned economy such as that of the Soviet Union. They may also be set by market forces, as in most western nations.

3. Finally, we assume that consuming a good or service takes time. In addition to the cost of the airline tickets, a Florida vacation takes time away from other activities. While we are doing one thing, there are limits on the extent to which we can be doing something else. For example, we might accomplish two things at the same time by watching the news during breakfast. However, while eating breakfast, we are not at work or polishing the car.

With these two sets of assumptions in mind, we will now say a few words about the way in which we will analyze the decisions people make concerning how much of a good or service to buy.

Method of Analysis

Remember that the purpose of assumptions in our model of demand is to *simplify*. Even so, we have listed a total of eight assumptions. How can we understand the influence of all of the conditions described by these assumptions at once? The way we will deal with this problem is to examine the forces influencing consumer behavior *one at a time*. That is, we will first assume that all factors affecting demand are fixed or unchanging except for one. We will then proceed to look at the effect of changes in that one variable on the purchases desired by an individual or a set of individuals. This assumption is known as *ceteris paribus,* the Latin phrase for "other things equal." It means that when we analyze the impact of a change in a variable, such as a good's price, on the quantity of the good demanded, we will begin by assuming that *other* variables (such as consumers' incomes), do not change at the same time. *Ceteris paribus* is often abbreviated *cet. par.* Demand theory typically emphasizes the relationship between the price of a good or service and desired purchases. So, in developing the theory of demand, we will first apply the *cet. par.* assumption to those forces affecting demand behavior *other than* the price of the good or service in question. If you review our assumptions of demand theory, you will see that these forces include the individual's time horizon for decision making, expectations of the future, tastes and preferences, income, prices of other goods and services, and the amount of time consumption must take.

It is extremely important to note that by imposing the *cet. par.* method of analysis, we are simply examining, *one at a time,* the factors that influence consumer behavior. We can, and do, look at changes in factors other than price (also one at a time) to discover how they too affect the demand for a commodity. Just how and at what stage of our discussion we consider these other forces depends on the issues we wish to examine. The importance of looking at forces *one by one* is that it enables us to get a much clearer picture of how governmental economic policy and private business practices affect consumption patterns. For example, if the government lowers income taxes and no other influence on consumers changes, we can forecast the likely impact on consumer spending: It will increase.

The Law of Demand and the Demand Curve

The **law of demand** states that, *cet. par.,* (1) price reductions lead individuals to desire more of a good or service, and (2) price increases lead them to desire less of a good or service. This is the result of two effects that reinforce each other when a price changes. They are known as the substitution effect and the income effect of a price change. They are among the most important concepts economists have. The **substitution effect** states that when the price of a good or service falls, *cet. par.,* people have an economic incentive to use more of that particular good or service because it has become less expensive *relative to* all the other goods and services available. To be specific, suppose that rock concert tickets fall in price from $20 to $10, while movie tickets remain $5. Fans then have the incentive to attend more rock concerts while consuming fewer movies and other forms of entertainment. In effect, the reduced price of rock concerts compared to movies will make the concerts a better buy per dollar spent on them and therefore encourage consumers to buy more concert tickets and less of other things.

There is another effect of a price change. When the price of a good or service falls, real purchasing power rises, and people consume more because they are actually wealthier. When we say that someone is poor or wealthy, we do not refer simply to the number of dollars he or she has to spend but to what those dollars will buy. An individual or household's **real income** refers to the quantity of goods or services that its money income can buy. When the price of a good falls, consumers tend to buy more of it in part because their *real income* has increased. Economists call this the **income effect.** Not only can consumers purchase more of a good whose price has fallen, but they can also purchase more of everything else. To see this more clearly, suppose you have an income of $100 per week and you typically spend $21 of your weekly income on beer, which costs $3.00 a six-pack. Now suppose the distributor of your favorite brand lowers the price to $2.50 as part of a sales campaign. It is not hard to see that this is equivalent to an increase in your weekly income of $3.50 (seven six-packs × $0.50). With your fixed income of $100, you can now purchase exactly what you did before and have $3.50 left over. That extra $3.50 can be used to buy a little more of all the things that you like to consume.

Of course, the law of demand holds for a price increase, as well. Just as a falling price, *cet. par.,* causes people to buy more, a rising price causes them to buy less.

It is important to recognize that the law of demand holds for *every* good whether an individual "likes" it or not. To see why this is so, let's take an example in which many people do not like a good very much. At the risk of being sued by the California Prune Advisory Board, we will suppose that prunes are such a good. Many people do not eat prunes "straight" because they do not like the taste. However, of those people who at present do not eat prunes, some probably do not strongly dislike prunes. They simply like other foods better, given what they have to pay for them. These people would probably be willing to try a *few* prunes if they became sufficiently cheap relative to, say, orange juice. All things considered, we would expect to see the total quantity of prunes purchased to increase in response to a decline in the price of prunes, *cet. par.*

Saying that you do not like something is generally equivalent to saying that its price is too high. (Granted, you may feel that you would not eat a prune unless you were paid to do it. But paying you to eat a prune is equivalent to saying that you would not buy prunes unless their price were negative, or less than zero.) If an item becomes cheaper, *cet. par.,* the law of demand predicts that the quantity bought will increase. Similarly, when we say, "I can't afford X," what we mean in terms of the economic way of thinking is "I don't like X well enough to pay the going price for X."

The relationship between the price of a good and the total amount purchased is called **the demand,** or the **demand curve,** for a good. Since the primary focus of social science in general and economics in particular is on group behavior, we are especially interested in the purchases by *all* of the individuals in a market. This is called the *market* demand curve. When the quantity demanded at each price is shown in a table instead of in a graph, the relationship between price and quantity demanded is sometimes called a *demand schedule* instead of a demand curve.

Table 2.1   Market demand schedule for rock concert tickets

Price of rock concert tickets	Quantity of rock concert tickets demanded
$30	2,000
28	4,000
26	6,000
24	8,000
22	10,000
20	12,000
18	14,000
16	16,000
14	18,000
12	20,000
10	22,000
8	24,000
6	26,000
4	28,000
2	30,000

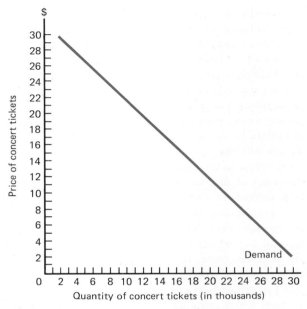

Figure 2.2   The market demand curve for rock concert tickets
The substitution and income effects cause the quantity of rock concert tickets demanded to increase as the price falls and to decline as the price rises.

To explore the demand concept in greater depth, we will use a simple numerical example. A market demand schedule for rock concert tickets is shown in table 2.1. At a price of $30, only 2,000 concert tickets are demanded, but as the the price of tickets falls, the quantity demanded increases. This is because at lower prices, consumers will substitute rock concerts for other forms of entertainment and some people who would not attend concerts at higher prices will attend some at lower prices. Thus, if the price were to fall as low as $2 per ticket, 30,000 tickets would be purchased. The market demand curve for concert tickets is shown in figure 2.2. We measure the price of the particular good concert tickets on the vertical axis and the quantity consumers wish to buy on the horizontal axis. Because *individual* buyers purchase less at high prices, the *market* demand curve for *all* buyers is also a downward-sloping line. For example, at a price of $20 the buyers in figure 2.2 wish to purchase 12,000 tickets. At a lower price, say, $10, they increase their desired purchases to 22,000 tickets. Remember that the demand curve in figure 2.2 is drawn for a given set of the other factors influencing consumer behavior, including income, tastes and preferences, and the prices of other goods. If *any* of these things change, then the demand curve in figure 2.2 will have to be redrawn.

The Demand Curve, Value, and Marginal Utility

The demand curve gives us more information about consumers of a good or service than simply how much they will buy at various prices. It also tells us how much the good or service is worth to them. That is, the demand curve contains information about how highly a good or service is *valued*. To illustrate the relationship between the demand curve and value, we will continue with our example of desired purchases of rock concert tickets. Figure 2.3 represents the demand of an individual consumer for concert tickets. We assume that the concertgoer plans his or her desired concert attendance over a year and can purchase any number of tickets at whatever price happens to prevail in the market. Various possible prices are illustrated in figure 2.3. If the market price is, say,

$10, then $10 worth of other goods must be foregone for each concert ticket purchased. In this sense, the price of a ticket represents its opportunity cost to a concertgoer.

The demand curve for this person tells us that if the market price happens to be $10, then the individual represented will purchase ten tickets. Why are ten tickets and not eight, nine, or eleven tickets desired? We can answer this question by examining the height of the demand curve to the right and to the left of the quantity ten tickets. At any quantity less than ten tickets per year, the height of the demand curve is *greater* than $10, while at any quantity greater than ten, the height of the demand curve is *less* than $10. This tells us that when the individual has fewer than ten concert tickets per year, *the amount of other goods he or she is willing to forego in return for one more ticket is at least $10 worth, while an individual with more than ten tickets would be unwilling to pay as much as $10 for an additional ticket.*

To be more precise, suppose the individual represented in figure 2.3 happened to possess only eight concert tickets for use during the year. The demand curve tells us that this individual is willing to pay up to $11 for the ninth ticket. Since the maximum amount the concertgoer is willing to pay for the additional ticket—$11—is greater than the price of the ticket ($10), this person will feel better off by spending $10 for the ninth ticket and purchasing $10 less of some other goods or services. When the number of concerts is nine each year, the consumer is willing to pay up to $10 for the next (tenth) ticket. Buying this ticket for $10, then, will not make the purchaser feel worse off than if the $10 had been spent on other items.

The demand curve shows that the *most* the consumer is willing to pay for the eleventh ticket in any given year is *less* than $10. In other words, the concertgoer would be worse off, not better off, if forced to pay $10 for even one ticket in addition to ten per year. We conclude that the individual represented in figure 2.3 will not increase the satisfaction, or value, obtained from his or her income by buying any concert tickets in excess of ten per year when tickets sell for $10 each.

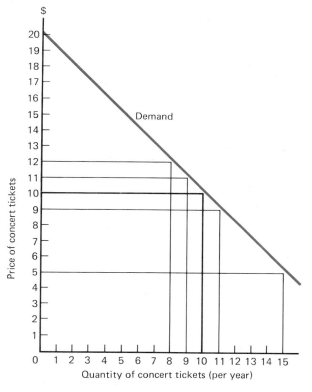

Figure 2.3 Demand for rock concert tickets and the marginal value of rock concert tickets
One of the basic assumptions of the theory of demand is that individuals decide how much of a good or service to purchase so as to achieve the most satisfaction, given their limited incomes or purchasing power. This means that the demand curve tells us how much consumers are willing to pay for a marginal (one more) unit. For example, suppose a typical individual, as represented in this figure, could purchase as many concert tickets as desired at a price of $10 per ticket. The demand curve tells us that this person would purchase ten tickets per year, no more, no less. An eleventh ticket in a given year would simply not be worth $10 to this consumer. By contrast, if the consumer possessed fewer than ten tickets, say, seven or eight, then an additional ticket would be worth *more* than $10 and would therefore be worth buying. If the price of concert tickets should fall to, say, $5, someone who had been buying ten tickets per year would now value additional tickets at more than their price, and the number of tickets demanded per year would increase to fifteen tickets per year.

*The **marginal value** of a good or service is the maximum amount that someone is willing to pay for one more unit.*

A neat way to summarize the relationship between the demand curve and the value of a good or service to an individual is to focus attention on the decision of whether or not to purchase one additional unit. *This is because obtaining the most satisfaction from one's limited income (satisfying assumption 5 on page 35) means not purchasing an additional unit of a good or service if its value is less than its cost.*

Economists refer to one additional unit purchased as a *marginal* unit. For example, for an individual considering whether or not to buy *nine* rather than *eight* tickets, the *marginal* ticket is the *ninth* ticket because it represents *one additional* ticket purchased. Given the definition of a marginal unit, *the demand curve measures the maximum amount that an individual would be willing to pay for just one more unit of a good, which we call the good's **marginal value**. When an individual spends his or her income in the way that provides the most satisfaction, the marginal value of the last unit of any good or service purchased will be equal to its price.* In the example of figure 2.3, the price of concert tickets is $10, and the marginal value of the tenth ticket is $10. Therefore, the consumer purchases ten tickets.*

Perhaps it seems that we are reasoning in a circle when we say that the demand curve measures the marginal value of a good. Haven't we said in the above example that the marginal value of the tenth concert ticket is $10 simply because a consumer is willing to pay $10 for it? We have indeed said this, but the argument is not circular. The reason we can conclude that $10 is the marginal value of the tenth ticket is that our theory, or model, of demand is derived from the *assumption* that individuals try to derive the greatest satisfaction from spending their limited incomes. Therefore, the conclusion that the demand curve represents marginal value is an *implication* derived from the underlying assumption that consumers try to do the best they can.

Why does a good's marginal value decline as indicated by a downward-sloping demand curve? The answer to this important question lies in our assumption that people want to consume a *variety* of goods and services and that they are willing to make *substitutes* to achieve their goals. This implies that as more of one good or service is consumed and less of other goods and services is consumed, the amount that an individual is willing to spend for a marginal (additional) unit usually diminishes (becomes smaller). Also, a decline in a good's price, *cet. par.,* will generally lead to increased purchases. Economists have found that the demand curves for most goods and services do, in fact, tend to slope downward as illustrated in figures 2.2 and 2.3.

The market demand curve, representing the sum of desired purchases of a good or service at each price, reflects the tastes and preferences of each individual who purchases the good or service. Among the good or service's consumers there will be individuals who do not really value it very much. Their low valuation will be reflected by individual demand curves that lie low and to the left: Relatively small quantities will be demanded by these individuals. If an individual's demand curve lies far enough to the left, the quantity demanded of a good or service may well be zero. (For example, in figure 2.3, the individual represented would not purchase any concert tickets if their price rose to $20 or more.) Others might enjoy concerts so much that their demand curves lie high and to the right of the demand curve illustrated in figure 2.3. Such individuals could buy some concert tickets even if they sold for $20 each. This is why we have drawn the *market* demand curve in figure 2.2 showing that the total quantity of concert tickets demanded does not fall to zero at a price of $20.

---

*A question that beginning economics students sometimes ask is "Why should a consumer purchase an additional unit of some item if its marginal value is the same as its price? How does this increase the consumer's well-being?" This question arises because in our example, as well as in the real world, purchases take place in discrete jumps, or lumps. If we can imagine these lumps as being very small (for example, if it were possible to purchase a tiny fraction of a concert ticket and attend only part of a concert with it), then consumers could fine-tune their purchases so that the marginal value of only the very last smidgen of each item purchased equaled its price. In such a case, with very, very small possible adjustments, it would not make any difference to an individual's overall satisfaction whether the last unit of any good were purchased or not. Students who are familiar with differential calculus will recognize that this question does not arise when purchases can be changed by infinitesimally small amounts.

Utility refers to the amount of satisfaction, happiness, or well-being an individual experiences from spending his or her income.

Marginal utility is the increment in satisfaction obtained from greater consumption of a given good, service, or leisure activity, all other consumption held constant.

Demand and Utility: You *Can* Get Some Satisfaction Economists have developed a way of thinking about the relationship between the price of a good or service and its value to purchasers that explicitly introduces the amount of satisfaction consumers derive from the goods and services they purchase. The term used to describe this satisfaction is **utility,** which refers to the well-being we obtain from spending our incomes. One of the most vocal analysts of consumer behavior is Mick Jagger. His point of view should help you understand what we mean by utility. While Jagger was a student at the London School of Economics, he formulated his two best-known conclusions concerning consumer behavior: (1) I can't get no satisfaction, and (2) you can't always get what you want. Jagger's ideas serve as a useful focus for our discussion of utility and demand, where we look more deeply into the basis of the theory of consumer choice. Our purpose is to reinforce your understanding of why the demand curve represents marginal value of a good or service and why marginal value declines as consumption increases.

Notice the double negative in Jagger's first conclusion. You *can't* get *no* satisfaction means that you *can* get *some* satisfaction. At the core of the economist's theory of consumer behavior and choice in the marketplace is the assumption that the individual is always on the lookout for ways to improve his or her level of well-being or utility. Thus, an economist would disagree with Jagger's claim if it is taken to mean that it is impossible to obtain *any* satisfaction. An individual experiences varying degrees of satisfaction over a lifetime, depending upon his or her ability to obtain the things that provide it. Economists definitely agree with Jagger's second statement about consumer behavior: You can't always get what you want. We have already seen that this is the fundamental assumption of economics because *scarcity* means that we cannot get everything we would like. We must make choices.

Marginal Utility The theory of demand tells us how choices are made by consumers. We have seen that the demand curve tells us how much a consumer is willing to pay for one more unit of a good or service (marginal value). The economist's notion of utility simply relates marginal value to the satisfaction that a consumer obtains from spending his or her income on a variety of goods and services. The heart of the matter is Jagger's statement that you can't always get what you want. To see how this applies to the demand for a good, we will develop a simple numerical example, as illustrated in figure 2.4. In this figure, a consumer has $5,000 per year to spend on anything desired, including concert tickets. The consumer's goal is to *maximize utility,* which is nothing more than an economist's way of saying that the consumer wants to obtain the most satisfaction from spending the $5,000 each year.

To begin, let us examine the total satisfaction that a typical consumer might experience from spending the $5,000 on a wide variety of goods and services but *nothing* on concert tickets. For the sake of our example, we will assume that total satisfaction, or utility, can be measured in units called utils, and that if no concert tickets are purchased, the consumer obtains 20,000 utils from spending the $5,000 in the best (utility-maximizing) way on everything else. This is shown by the height of the bars representing no purchases of concert tickets in parts (b) and (c) of figure 2.4.

The question we wish to answer is this: Can the consumer increase total satisfaction by spending some income on concert tickets? As you might have guessed, the answer depends on the **marginal utility** of concert tickets, which refers to the *additional* utility from purchasing one more ticket compared to the marginal utility of other consumption goods. Part (a) of figure 2.4 shows that the marginal utility of the first concert ticket is 38 utils. Remember that a ticket costs $10.

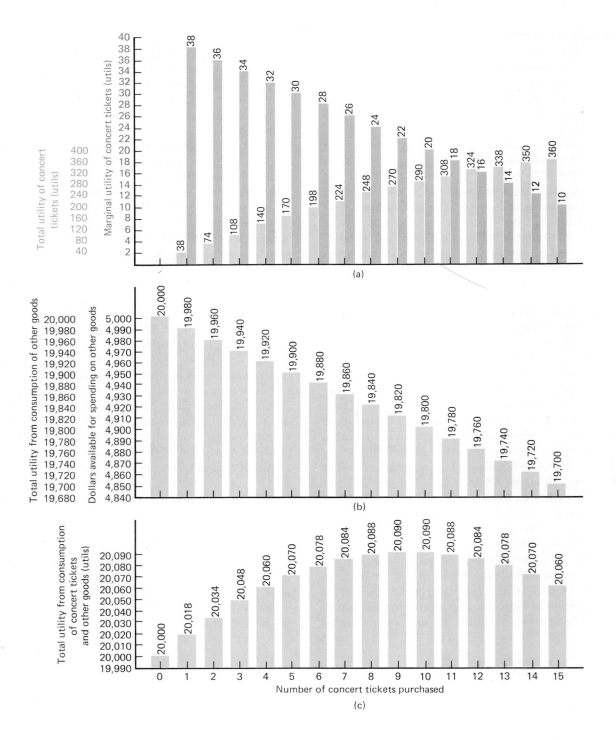

Diminishing marginal utility means that the extra satisfaction obtained from additional consumption, while positive, is smaller the more of the item already consumed.

Figure 2.4 Utility maximization and the demand for concert tickets
In part (a), the marginal utility of the first concert ticket purchased is 38 utils, the second concert ticket is 36 utils, and so on. This represents diminishing marginal utility. The total utility of attending concerts keeps rising, however, as long as the marginal utility is greater than zero.

Part (b) indicates that when no concert tickets are purchased, $5,000 worth of consumption goods yields 20,000 utils of satisfaction. The marginal utility from consuming additional units of other consumption goods is 2 utils per dollar. Each concert ticket costs $10 and has an opportunity cost of 20 utils. Therefore, total utility from all other consumption goods falls by 20 utils for each concert ticket purchased.

In part (c), total utility is the sum of the utils obtained from attending concerts and consuming all other goods. Thus the total utility in this graph is the *sum* of the total utils in parts (b) and (c).

This means that if the consumer buys just one concert ticket, there will only be $4,990 left to spend on other consumer goods. While buying a concert ticket adds 38 utils to total satisfaction, giving up $10 worth of other consumer goods reduces it. We will assume that the $10 spent on the first ticket reduces consumption of each of the other goods by a very small amount—perhaps per year $0.50 less is spent on candy bars, $1.00 less on potatoes, $0.90 less on hamburgers, and so on. We will assume that each dollar's worth of these other goods *not* consumed reduces total utility by 2 utils. That is, the *marginal* utility of a dollar spent on any consumption good other than concert tickets is 2 utils. Therefore, it obviously increases total utility to buy the first concert ticket because the $10 spent on tickets adds 38 utils while the $10 not spent on other items represents an *opportunity cost* of only 20 utils. While the utility derived from these other goods declines to 19,980 utils, *total* utility rises to 20,018 utils. This is shown in parts (a) and (b) of figure 2.4, respectively.

Obviously, buying the first concert ticket increases total utility. What about buying more tickets? The answer to this question and, ultimately, to the question of how many concert tickets will *maximize* utility, depends on the *marginal* utility of the second ticket, third ticket, and so on, compared to the marginal utility of other consumer goods. Assumption 4 on page 35, that people like to consume a *variety* of goods and services, implies that the marginal utility of concert tickets will not stay the same but will decline as the number of concerts attended increases. The same argument implies that the marginal utility of the other goods will *increase* as their consumption *declines*. This is probably the case, but because the reduced consumption of each of the many individual other goods is small when one more concert ticket is purchased, we can safely ignore this subtlety. We will assume that the *marginal* utility of other consumption goods remains the same while the number of concert tickets purchased changes.

More precisely, we say that the typical individual experiences **diminishing marginal utility,** which means that the *increment,* or addition, to satisfaction, although positive, shrinks (diminishes) as more of a given good, service, or leisure activity is consumed. One of your authors recently returned from a vacation in France. During part of his trip he ate dinner at several famous restaurants. Even though he did not eat at all of these restaurants on the same day, he experienced diminishing marginal utility from consuming several fine dinners in close succession. On the first evening, his dinner increased his happiness by a great deal. The second evening was also enjoyable, but not quite as much. By the time he had eaten his fifth fancy dinner, the additional satisfaction he obtained, while positive, was far less than the additional well-being he received from eating the first meal. It is human nature that the more we do of something,

*The **quantity demanded** of a good or service is the particular amount people desire to buy, given its price and other factors influencing demand.*

even something we enjoy, the less *extra* pleasure we obtain from it. This is the essence of diminishing marginal utility.

In our concert example we will assume that the marginal utility of the second ticket is only 36 utils, as indicated in part (a) of figure 2.4. Nevertheless, this is still larger than the 20 utils opportunity cost resulting from the other consumption goods that must be foregone for an additional concert ticket. Thus, purchasing the second concert ticket increases total utility to 20,034 utils, as shown in part (c). If you carry out the addition of utility from consuming more concert tickets and subtraction of utility because "you can't get everything that you want," you will notice that in part (c) of figure 2.4, total utility is never higher than when ten concerts per year are attended (20,090 utils). The marginal utility of the eleventh ticket is 18 utils, and its opportunity cost is 20 utils. Purchasing the eleventh ticket actually lowers *total* utility by 2 utils. Purchasing a twelfth ticket lowers total utility further, to 20,084 utils, and from there on it is all downhill.

The marginal utility of the tenth ticket is 20 utils. Notice that the gain in utility *per dollar* spent on this tenth ticket is 20/10, or 2.0 utils. This is exactly equal to the 2.0 utils *foregone* for each dollar *not spent* on other consumption goods.* If an eleventh ticket were purchased, the marginal utility *per dollar* would be only 18/10, or 1.8 utils, which is *less* than the opportunity cost in terms of foregone utils. We could

carry out this same analysis for *every* good a consumer might choose to buy. The results would be the same. Buying one more unit of a good or service will reduce utility if its marginal utility *per dollar* is less than its opportunity cost in terms of lost utility of the other goods or services that one dollar could have bought. Our analysis of marginal utility and demand therefore leads us to the following conclusion: *When total utility is maximized, the marginal utility per additional dollar spent on any good or service is equal to the marginal utility that could be obtained if that dollar were spent on any other good or service.* If this condition does not hold, then dollars should be reallocated, away from those goods that give less "bang for the buck" and toward those that give more.

Diminishing *marginal utility* implies the diminishing *marginal value* of a good. One way to think of the difference between marginal utility and marginal value is that marginal value represents the most that a consumer is willing to pay for one more unit, whereas marginal utility measures the additional satisfaction that the consumer obtains. We can now see that the assumption that people like to consume a variety of goods and services underlies both diminishing marginal utility and diminishing marginal value of any good, such as concert tickets. This is reflected in the demand curve and its downward slope. When the price of a good or service falls, the marginal utility per additional dollar (marginal utility/price) spent on that good or service (bang for the buck) rises, and a utility-maximizing consumer will reallocate dollars away from other goods toward the purchase of the now lower-priced item. The reverse happens when a good or service's price increases.

---

*If you are puzzled as to why someone would purchase the tenth ticket if the gain in units is no greater than the ticket's opportunity cost in terms of units, see the footnote on p. 40.

*A **change in the quantity demanded** is an increase or decrease in the desired purchases of a good or service because of a change in its price,* cet. par.

*A **change in demand** or a **change (shift) in the demand curve** is a movement of the demand curve to the right (an increase in demand) or left (a decrease in demand). A change in the quantity demanded at every price results when the demand curve shifts to the right or left. Such a shift occurs when there is a change in a factor that affects the demand for a good or service other than the good's or the service's own price.*

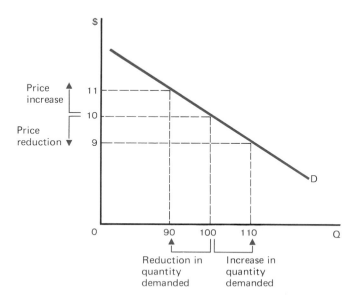

Figure 2.5   Increase and decrease in quantity demanded
An increase in quantity demanded is a southeast movement (downward and to the right) along the demand curve due to a price reduction. A reduction in quantity demanded is a northwest (upward and to the left) movement along the demand curve due to a price increase.

▶ Demand versus Quantity Demanded

Eventually, we wish to use the theory of demand and its key concept, the demand curve, to understand consumer behavior and how it is influenced by economic policy and business practices. To do this, we first need to be completely clear about two things. What do economists mean when they mention the *quantity demanded* versus the *demand* for a good or service? What is the difference between a *change in demand* and a *change in quantity demanded?*

Quantity Demanded and Change in Quantity Demanded

Figure 2.5 reminds us that the **quantity demanded** of a good or service corresponds to a *particular point* on a given demand curve, say Q(0) on the demand curve in figure 2.5. Thus, when there is a change in the amount of a good or service people want to buy *due to a change in its price, other factors held constant,* we say that there has been a **change in the quantity demanded.** Of course, many other things in the economic environment can also change, and these lead to what economists call a **change in demand** or a **change in the demand curve.** When there is a shift in the demand curve, either to the right or left, we are dealing with a change in demand or a change in the demand curve. When the demand curve for a product shifts it will generally change the quantity demanded at any given price. It is very important in thinking about markets to be absolutely clear in your mind whether a change in purchases of a good reflects a shift in demand (a change in the amount consumers are willing to buy at any given price) or whether it reflects a change in the quantity demanded along a given demand curve (consumers are buying more because the price has fallen or less because the price has increased).

*An **inferior good** is one for which the demand curve shifts to the left as purchasers' real incomes rise.*

*A **normal good** is one for which the demand curve shifts to the right as purchasers' real incomes rise.*

The Demand Curve and Factors That Shift It

The demand curve refers to the *whole schedule* illustrating the relationship between price and quantity demanded, *cet. par.* Review the assumptions of the theory of demand listed on pages 33, 35. These assumptions provide us with a list of factors *other than the price of a good or service* that we assume are constant when we derive a demand curve. These other influences on demand include buyers' incomes, their tastes and preferences, and the prices of related goods and services. As long as these other variables affecting buyers' behavior do not change, the demand curve is fixed or unchanging. However, a change in *any* of the other forces will cause a shift in the position of the demand curve. In the next seven subsections we show how changes in several conditions assumed constant when deriving a demand curve will cause a demand curve to shift when they change.

Income

A change in demand refers to a shift in the entire demand curve. For example, suppose consumers of a good or service receive salary increases. The increased income will lead them to purchase more of most of the things they currently buy. This is not necessarily the case for *each and every* good or service consumers might purchase. Consumption of certain goods or services will fall when incomes rise; these goods are known as **inferior goods.** In contrast to inferior goods are **normal goods,** purchases of which *rise* when incomes do. Since we generally expect the consumption of a commodity to increase as income rises, we consider that to be the normal case. An example of an inferior good might be peanut butter and jelly sandwiches. As incomes rise (holding the prices of goods constant), there might be less consumption of peanut butter and jelly sandwiches by most people and more consumption of roast beef sandwiches. Roast beef sandwiches, then, would be a normal good. When a good is normal, its demand curve shifts to the right when income increases. An increase in demand is illustrated in figure 2.6 by a rightward shift in the demand curve from D to D′. At any given price, more

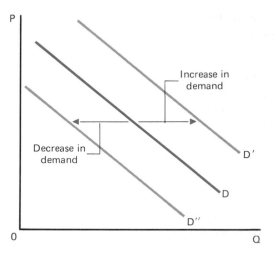

Figure 2.6   Increase and decrease in demand
An increase in demand is a rightward shift in the demand curve. A decrease in demand is a leftward shift in the demand curve. Changes in demand occur if one of the factors held constant when the demand curve was initially drawn (income, for example) changes.

is desired along demand curve D′ than along demand curve D. As you might expect, a salary reduction would reduce demand. This would be denoted by a leftward shift in the demand curve, from D to D″ in figure 2.6. (You may wonder whether demand curves for real-life commodities are straight lines and whether demand shifts are always parallel, as we have drawn them in figure 2.6. Actually, they are not. We have used straight lines and parallel shifts to keep our diagrams simple. The basic principles we learn are the same regardless of whether we make our demand schedules straight or curved and whether the shifts are parallel or not. Remember this is just a model—see chapter 1.)

The effect of income on demand is one of the most important relationships in economics. In the example of the WHOOPS bonds that introduced this chapter, we noted that the planners of the nuclear power plants had forecast a continued rise in sales based on a history of continually rising electricity consumption. This increased consumption was due mainly to a *shift in demand for electricity* as real incomes rose over time.

*Two goods are **complements** if when the price of one good changes,* cet. par., *the demand curve for the other good shifts in the* opposite *direction.*

*Two goods are **substitutes** if when the price of one good changes,* cet. par., *the demand for the other good shifts in the* same *direction.*

It was reinforced by gradually declining electricity prices until the early 1970s, which represented an *increase in the quantity of electricity demanded,* given the demand curve for electric power. What ruined the prospects for selling electricity produced by the eventually canceled plants was a *reduction in the quantity of electricity* demanded *when electricity prices increased.* Had the planners not failed to adequately predict both shifts in the demand for electricity and changes in the quantity demanded along a given demand curve, the WHOOPS disaster could have been avoided.

Tastes and Preferences

If buyers' tastes for one good compared to another should change, the demand curve will be affected. If a certain good or service becomes *more* enjoyable, the demand curve will shift to the right. If it should become *less* desirable, the demand curve will shift to the left. In 1985, the Coca-Cola Company introduced a new, sweeter Coke to regain sales that were being lost to Pepsi. Had consumer tastes shifted toward a sweeter beverage? Millions of dollars were spent researching this question. When the new Coke was introduced, many people preferred it, but a majority of the remaining Coca-Cola fans evidently still preferred the old version, now marketed under the "Classic" label.

Eventually, we will elaborate on some social forces that may cause tastes to change and, with them, demand schedules. For now, try to think of some on your own. For example, why might your feelings toward buying a navy blue suit change in the near future? (Hint: graduation.) How would these new feelings change some of your other demand curves?

It is often tempting to attribute a change in demand to a change in tastes. However, it is difficult to verify whether or not this is true because it is not easy to obtain accurate information about the public's feelings or goals. We must avoid the temptation to conclude that *whenever* purchases change, people's tastes have changed. We must have *reason* to suspect that tastes and preferences have changed *before* demand changes rather than inferring that tastes have changed because demand has changed.

Prices of Related Goods and Services

Frequently, a change in the demand for one good or service reflects a change in the price of some closely related good or service. Suppose, for example, that the price of gasoline rises. Of course, the *quantity of gasoline demanded will decline.* However, people will also eventually desire fewer gas-guzzling large automobiles, and the *demand for such cars will fall.* This, for example, happened in the late 1970s. Such a decline in the demand for large cars does *not* reflect a change in consumer tastes. When the price of gasoline rose rapidly in 1979 and 1980 consumer demand for small fuel-efficient cars increased. That increase in demand for small cars did not simply reflect a change in consumer tastes. Similarly, when gasoline prices fell sharply in the first few months of 1986, the demand for large cars increased. That increase in demand for large cars did not simply reflect a change in consumer tastes.

To describe more precisely how the price of one good affects the demand for another good, it is useful to distinguish between two possibilities. When two goods are typically used together (bread and butter, tape players and cassettes, automobiles and gasoline, or gin and vermouth) such that an increase in the price of one causes a decline in the demand for the other, we call them **complements.** On the other hand, different brands of the same product or even different commodities that can be used for the same or similar purposes are called **substitutes.** Some examples of substitutes are cotton and Dacron, Michelin and Firestone tires, gas ranges and electric ranges, and big luxury cars and small, more fuel-efficient cars. Substitutes display an economic relationship opposite to that of complements. If the price of one substitute rises, the demand for the other will increase because buyers will tend to substitute purchases of the relatively cheaper good for the one that has become relatively more expensive. Can you list other examples of substitutes and complements? What is a complement to a Mazda RX7? What is a substitute for a Mazda RX7? What is a complement to a hot dog? What is a substitute for a hot dog? Would an increase in the price of records increase or decrease the demand for tape cassettes or compact discs? What effect would a decrease in the price of tape cassette players have on the demand for tape cassettes or AM/FM radios?

Expectations

As we noted earlier, the building blocks or assumptions of demand theory provide us with a list of factors that can shift demand curves. This means that if we go through our assumptions once again, we will have an idea of many of the events that will shift demand curves. One possibility is an expectation that prices will change in the near future. For example, if I expect my favorite beer to cost 25 percent more next week, I will increase my demand for it this week (at the current price). Similarly, I will hold off buying a new car if I expect sizable rebates or price cuts to be offered next month. Of course, *how much* I change my demand depends on how eager I am to have the good or service, how storable it is, and how certain I am about future price changes. For example, my freezer may be rather small, so I cannot increase my demand for ice cream by very much right now even if I expect a giant price increase tomorrow unless I also buy a new freezer. Whether or not I want to do that will also depend upon how certain I am about the increase in the price of ice cream and whether I think the price will remain high once it increases.

The two other items from our list of assumptions that can shift demand curves are (1) a change in consumers' time horizons and (2) a change in the amount of time required to consume a good or service.

Time Horizons

As we noted earlier, if the concept of a demand curve is to make sense, we must be discussing a specific time period. I will certainly consume more chocolate cheesecake during a lifetime than during the next week. Moreover, the degree to which I adjust my purchases to a change in price, my income, or other influences will also depend on the time horizon chosen. Suppose that the price of chocolate falls drastically, reducing the price of my favorite chocolate cheesecake from $5 per cake to $2. During the week I first notice that the price has fallen, I may already have

planned my grocery purchases and may increase my consumption of chocolate cheesecake very little if at all. However, over the next several months, I am likely to reduce my purchases of plain cheesecake and substitute the chocolate variety.

In short, if we wish to look at a longer period of time within which consumers are making their choices, the demand curves we draw will differ from those describing a shorter period of consumption.

Time Required for Consumption

Remember that goods and services take time to use. A fancy car is of very little value to me if I have no time to drive it. Similarly, a tennis racket becomes much more valuable if I have the time to play tennis. This means that if, for example, the tennis courts in my neighborhood suddenly get very crowded and I have to wait two or three hours for a court, I will play less tennis. As a result, I will reduce my demand for tennis rackets and tennis balls.

On the other hand, if something can be done much more quickly than before, demand will increase. Suppose, for example, that a new city park with thirty tennis courts is built near my house so that I can almost always get a court to play on without waiting. That change will increase my demand (as reflected in the dollar price I am willing to pay for court fees) for playing tennis and for complementary goods, e.g., tennis rackets and tennis balls. Try to think of some other examples in which willingness to buy something is related to how much time it takes to buy or use it.

Population and Income Distribution

Two additional forces that may shift demand curves are worth noting. They are not part of our assumptions or building blocks of demand theory but rather relate to the fact that demand curves usually describe *groups* of consumers. One is a change in the population. When there are more buyers than before, the demand curve will move to the right of its initial position. With fewer buyers, demand decreases. This may seem like a trivial issue, but it is important if you are a firm selling goods and services. During the 1950s and 1960s at the height of the "baby boom" period, the demand for children's clothes and toys and for teachers, schools, and pediatricians grew rapidly. The

Table 2.2   Factors that change quantity demanded and factors that change demand

Factors that increase quantity demanded (move consumers down their demand curve)	Factors that reduce quantity demanded (move consumers up their demand curve)	Factors that increase demand (shift the demand curve to the right)	Factors that reduce demand (shift the demand curve to the left)
1. A reduction in (current) price	1. An increase in (current) price	1. An increase in the incomes of buyers 2. An increase in the price of a substitute 3. A reduction in the price of a complement	1. A reduction in the incomes of buyers 2. A reduction in the price of a substitute 3. An increase in the price of a complement
		4. A change in preferences that makes the good or service more enjoyable 5. An expectation that price will rise in the near future 6. A reduction in the amount of time required to consume the good or service	4. A change in preference that makes the good or service less enjoyable 5. Expectation that price will fall in the near future 6. An increase in the amount of time necessary to consume the good or service
		7. An increase in consumers' time horizons 8. An increase in the population 9. A redistribution of income toward people who most enjoy consuming the good or service	7. A decrease in consumers' time horizons 8. A reduction in the population 9. A redistribution of income toward people who least enjoy consuming the good or service

rate of growth in demand for each of these things declined in the 1970s and 1980s as the birthrate declined. On the other hand as the population of older people expanded rapidly in the 1970s and 1980s, the demand for retirement homes and medical services increased rapidly.

The other factor that affects market demand is a change in the distribution of income. Not everyone may have exactly the same tastes and preferences. I might love imported beer and have very little use for paperback novels. You may have preferences opposite to mine—a love of paperback novels and a dislike for beer. If something such as a tax takes income from you and gives it to me, this redistribution of income will increase the demand for beer and reduce the demand for paperback novels. Economists call this a *distribution effect*.

Summary of Movements Along the Demand Curve and Shifts in Demand

We have presented many ideas in this section, and some may have seemed complicated. To help make things clearer, table 2.2 provides a summary of the main points of this section. It is a list of factors that change demand or quantity demanded.

Because the concept of a demand curve describes how price changes the quantity of a good or service individuals wish to consume, it can be of great value in understanding human behavior. Many government policies and business practices change the price of a good or service. Once we know the direction of the price change, the demand curve tells us whether consumers will buy more or less of the product. Think of all of the laws we have in the United States that are devoted to increasing the price of what are thought to be undesirable activities like smoking or drinking alcoholic beverages and reducing the price of desirable activities like recreation and getting an education.

Once we identify a force that shifts a demand curve, we have found that consumers change the amount they want to buy at any given price. It is important to realize, however, that we do not know *how much* more or less they will *actually* purchase simply by knowing there has been a rightward or leftward shift in the demand schedule. Why? Because without knowledge of the production side of the market, and therefore the amounts of goods and services available at each price, we do not know what will happen to the market price. Unless we know how shifts in demand affect the price of a particular commodity, we cannot determine how much more or less consumers will actually buy. The point here is to be systematic in explaining why demand may shift so that we may put it with the supply side of the market in chapter 5. It is there that we will achieve our goal of a reasonably complete picture of a market in an economic system and how markets work.

Finally, the *main* purpose of this section is to make it as clear as possible how to *distinguish between a change in quantity demanded and a change in demand.* Changes in quantity demanded are *movements along a demand curve* due to changes in price. Changes in demand are *shifts in the entire demand curve* due to changes in factors other than price. The two are sometimes confused in the media. This leads to a confused discussion of a social issue because causality is attributed to the wrong factor.

For example, after substantial increases in crude oil prices in 1974 and again in 1979–80, news commentators and analysts as well as many government officials often talked or wrote about how to make people conserve energy by various means such as persuading or requiring them to insulate their homes, limit their driving, cut back on heating and air-conditioning, and so on. In other words, they were trying

to get the public to *reduce its demand* for fuel, or shift the demand curve to the left. These discussions frequently seemed to ignore the law of demand: An increase in price leads to a reduction in quantity demanded. As it turned out, given time to adjust, consumers of gasoline, heating oil, and other petroleum products did respond to higher prices by reducing the quantity of petroleum products demanded quite significantly. In the remainder of this chapter and in chapter 3 we will see numerous examples of changes in quantity demanded and changes in demand. Knowing the difference between the two is necessary for clear thinking on economic issues.

▶ Applications of the Law of Demand

The law of demand states, *ceteris paribus,* that there is an inverse (negative) relationship between changes in prices and changes in desired purchases of a good or service. In this section we present a number of applications of demand theory that are designed to help you understand how the United States economy works. They also demonstrate some of the roles played by private business practices and government or public policy.

The Diffusion of Japanese Cars into the United States Market

When Japanese automakers began to sell cars in the United States, why did they first do it on the West Coast? Why not the Midwest or East? And why, even after Japanese car dealerships became widespread, did more Japanese cars appear on the streets of California than on those of Ohio or New Jersey? One possible answer is that California's population includes more people of Japanese background than other states. Another is that Californians are quicker to buy trendy new goods. Here is something else to consider.

California is much closer to Japan than most other states. This means that the delivered cost of a Japanese car will be lower in California (and Oregon and Washington) than in other mainland states. This is

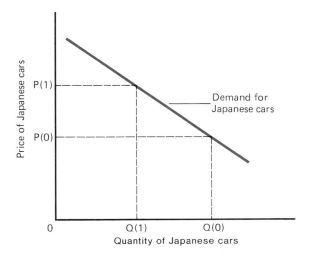

Figure 2.7 The demand for Japanese cars
The law of demand states that the number of Japanese cars demanded will grow smaller as the price rises, *ceteris paribus.*

depicted in figure 2.7, where we see the demand for Japanese automobiles per family in the United States. The vertical axis measures the price "out the door," which includes the cost of shipping from the place of manufacture to the retail dealer. P(0) is the price on the West Coast, and P(1) is the (higher) delivered price of Japanese cars elsewhere in the United States. The law of demand predicts that more Japanese cars will be sold where their price is low relative to that of other cars. This will be on the West Coast. Similarly, sales will be lowest where their price is highest—in the East. So the way that Japanese cars diffused into the United States car market is consistent with what the theory of demand predicts. Purchases were initially higher on the West Coast because the price of Japanese cars was less there (the quantity of Japanese cars demanded on the West Coast would have been greater than elsewhere, given the demand for Japanese cars). Moreover, Japanese car sales may have been higher also because Californians are often eager to try new products and because of the larger population of Japanese and other Asians in the western states. These factors probably resulted in a demand

curve that was farther to the right (a greater demand) than elsewhere in the United States. Our knowledge of the theory of demand helps us to understand the pattern of Japanese car ownership in the United States. Can you think of some examples of European-produced goods that were or are consumed in relatively greater amounts on the East Coast?

Government Policy and the Theory of Demand

You may have heard the comedy album by Father Guido Sarducci (formerly of "Saturday Night Live" on late-night television) on which he reveals his plans for a five-minute university.[2] At his university, students are taught in five minutes all of the things they will remember a few years after college. As you might expect, Father Guido has an economics course. The entire course is just three words, *supply and demand.* We would like to add a few more words to his course. If you remember only a few things from the economics course that you are currently taking, one should be that demand curves slope downward. This is important because many government policies raise the price and thus discourage consumption of goods and services society deems undesirable. Other policies lower the price, thus increasing the consumption of goods and services society deems desirable.

Fines and prison sentences await someone caught selling illegal narcotics in the United States. This raises the cost of supplying narcotics. In this way, the federal government attempts to increase the price of narcotics and reduce drug addiction. Local police attempt to reduce prostitution in a similar way. Bus and train fares are subsidized in most big cities to increase ridership and, in the process, reduce air pollution and congestion. Magazines and books are mailed at postal rates below cost. Subsidized postal rates are intended to encourage reading. See if you can think of some other government policies that might raise the price of goods society deems undesirable and lower the price of goods society deems desirable.

▶ Summary and Conclusions

In this chapter we have begun to sketch a picture of a modern, monetary market economy. The following points were emphasized.

The theory or law of demand helps us to understand how people allocate their limited incomes among the various goods and services available.

There is an inverse or downward-sloping relationship between the price of a good and the quantity demanded.

The income effect of a change in price reflects the influence of the price change on purchasing power.

The substitution effect of a price change reflects the ability to maintain satisfaction by substituting a less expensive good for a more expensive one.

A change in demand occurs when one of the forces held constant in drawing a demand curve changes. A change in demand means that at any given price, consumers will buy more or less, depending upon whether demand has increased or decreased.

The law of demand is derived from the assumption that consumers try to obtain the most satisfaction from their limited incomes.

The law of demand helps us to understand real-world behavior and the effects of government economic policy.

Much economic policy in the United States is designed to increase the price of socially undesirable activities and reduce the price of socially desirable activities.

▶ Key Terms

assumptions *33*
ceteris paribus *36*
change in demand *45*
change in the quantity demanded *45*
complements *47*
demand *32*
demand curve *37*
diminishing marginal utility *43*
income effect *37*
inferior goods *46*

law of demand *36*
marginal utility *41*
marginal value *40*
normal goods *46*
quantity demanded *44*
real income *37*
substitutes *47*
substitution effect *36*
supply *32*
utility *41*

▶ Questions for Discussion and Review

1. Henry Schultz was an economist who pioneered pioneered in estimating actual demand curves (*The Theory and Measurement of Demand,* Chicago: University of Chicago Press, 1937). He estimated the demand curve for sugar in the United States using data for the early part of this century. Roughly, in terms of today's prices, Schultz found that a $0.01 increase in the wholesale price of sugar led to a decline in the quantity of sugar demanded equal to one pound per person per year. The average person in the United States consumed about 100 pounds of sugar per year in the form of table sugar and in home-prepared and commercially prepared foods.

   a. Take a piece of paper (preferably graph paper) and draw the demand curve for sugar that Schultz estimated. Start by plotting one point on your demand curve at the average consumption of sugar (100 pounds per year) and the average price, which you should assume is $0.25 per pound. How much sugar would the average person consume if it were free? At what price would consumption of sugar fall to zero according to this demand curve? Do you think you would stop consuming sugar if its price rose to this level or, perhaps, 25 percent higher to allow for the difference between the wholesale and retail price? How could you redraw the demand curve to reflect your estimate of your demand for sugar at relatively high prices?

  b. Schultz also estimated that per capita sugar consumption was growing at the rate of about 0.1 pound per person per year. Draw another demand curve showing how a passage of fifty years' time would influence sugar demand. Why might sugar demand change this way over time? (Hint: What variable or variables assumed constant in drawing the initial demand curve may have changed?) Today, actual per capita sugar consumption is about seventy pounds per year at a wholesale price of around $0.25 per pound. How does this compare with what you would have expected on the basis of Schultz's estimates? What does this imply for the position of the sugar demand curve? Why do you think the demand curve for sugar has shifted in this direction?

  c. Much of the sugar we consume today is in the form of soft drinks. Many soft drink manufacturers have substituted sweeteners derived from corn for sugar in their products. These corn-based sweeteners are not defined as sugar but serve the same purpose, and they were not generally available until a few years ago. If Henry Schultz were to estimate the demand curve for sugar today, how do you suppose the availability of corn-based sweeteners would affect the demand curve estimate? (Hint: How does the availability of close substitutes affect demand?)

2. Define *ceteris paribus*. What role does the *ceteris paribus* assumption play in consumer demand theory?

3. True or false: Economists misuse the *ceteris paribus* assumption because in the real world everything changes frequently. Justify your answer.

4. State the law of demand. Draw a demand curve for movie tickets. Explain why the substitution effect and the income effect of a price change both make the curve downward sloping.

5. What is the difference between quantity demanded and demand? Support your answer with your graph. What is the difference between a change in demand and a change in quantity demanded? Support your answer with your graph. Which of the following two situations represents a change in quantity demanded? (a) Bad weather kills off much of the peach crop, causing the price of peaches to rise dramatically. Consumers then buy fewer peaches. (b) Consumers hear about some bad weather that has killed off the peach crop. They then buy more peaches because they expect the price of peaches to rise in the near future. Support your answer by drawing demand curves for peaches.

6. What is the difference between a complement and a substitute? Make a table listing substitutes and complements for each of the following: a motel room at the beach, a visit to a psychiatrist, a used car, a stereo, and a date with one of your boyfriends or girlfriends.

7. Draw demand curves for two goods that are substitutes. Suppose that the quantity of the first good demanded increases due to a reduction in its price. What happens to your graph describing the demand curve for the second good?

8. True or false: Those consumers who have a strong preference for a good or service will value it exactly the same as those who do not value it as highly. Defend your answer by using a diagram or diagrams based on figure 2.3.

9. A price change for any good can be separated into a substitution effect and an income effect. Explain how this process works for an inferior good.

10. Suppose that you consume only two goods. Can each of these goods be inferior simultaneously?

*A **utility function** is a mathematical description, either geometric or algebraic, of the link between an individual's utility and his or her consumption of goods and services.*

A Closer Look at the Theory of Consumer Choice

In this appendix, we will take a closer, somewhat more mathematical, look at the economist's concept of utility and how it relates to an individual's demand for a good or service.

▶ The Utility Function

The **utility function** is a mathematical description of the way in which someone's utility is linked to the goods, services, and leisure activities consumed. Those goods, services, and leisure activities are what provide the satisfaction someone seeks, and the pursuit of that satisfaction is a key aspect of the economist's theory of consumer choice. Utility functions can be expressed either algebraically in an equation or geometrically in a diagram. We will use both of these tools to describe an individual's level of satisfaction and how it is linked to the choices he or she makes.

Equation 1 is an algebraic summary of an individual's utility function.

$$u = f \quad \overset{+}{\underset{\text{consumed,}}{(\text{goods}}} \quad \overset{+}{\underset{\text{consumed,}}{\text{services}}} \quad \overset{+}{\underset{\text{activities)}}{\text{leisure}}} \quad (1)$$

Here u is the utility level and f(·) is the utility function. For simplicity, we have summarized an individual's consumption activities into three general categories—goods consumed, services consumed, and leisure activities. The plus (+) signs over the three variables in the utility function indicate that utility *increases* when an individual consumes more goods, services, or leisure, *ceteris paribus*. By this we mean that increasing the consumption of any *one* of the three items providing satisfaction—good, service, or leisure—will increase utility when consumption of the other two items is unchanged.

In chapter 2, we introduced the concept of diminishing marginal utility. In terms of the utility function, diminishing marginal utility refers to the additional utility obtained from consuming more of one good or service *relative* to the utility that must be sacrificed if less of other goods

or services is consumed. The reason for this focus on *relative* marginal utility is the difficulty we would have if we actually wanted to measure *total* utility. Economists generally agree that we do not have the tools to measure the *amount* of utility or happiness an individual actually experiences. That is, an individual's utility cannot in reality be assigned a particular number in the sense that we can measure quarts of beer, pounds of cheese, or tons of steel. This does not mean that you were somehow deceived in the marginal utility example in figure 2.4. If you go back and review that example carefully, you will see that it would have made absolutely no difference to the demand curve for concert tickets if we had said that the total utility obtained from spending $5,000 on all other goods would have been 400 utils, 400,000 utils, or 4 million utils. All that really matters in the example is the *marginal* utility of concert tickets *relative* to (compared to) the marginal utility of the other consumption goods. As long as an additional dollar spent on tickets yields *more* (a relative term) utility than an additional dollar spent on other goods, utility maximization requires spending less on other goods and more on concert tickets.

The fact that we cannot measure total utility in absolute terms means that although we can conclude that someone is better off if he or she has more goods, services, or leisure to consume, we *cannot* say precisely how happy he or she may be or even how much happiness is increased by additional consumption. We *can* say that someone is more or less well off than before, and we can say that the amount that happiness increases with increased consumption of one good *relative* to the increased happiness that would be obtained if consumption of other goods were increased diminishes as consumption of a good grows. The principal implication of our inability to measure how happy a person is, or how much utility he or she derives from consumption, is that there is no meaningful way to compare utility levels among different individuals. Another implication is that we cannot *add up* individuals' happiness to obtain a measure of how happy society is at any moment in time. From time to time, you have probably seen references to such measures of our economy's performance as total income received by all households in a given year. However, it is doubtful that you have ever seen a measure of society's total happiness, utility, or economic well-being. That is because it is generally recognized that no such meaningful measure of overall economic well-being exists.

*An **indifference curve** illustrates combinations of consumption activities to which the individual attaches equal levels of utility.*

A second important property of the utility function—and one we used extensively in chapter 2—is that consumers are willing to make trade-offs among the various items that bring them utility. In particular, they are willing to substitute one good or service for another, and it is possible to find ways in which these substitutions can make a person feel no better off or worse off. A diagram will be useful in illustrating the idea that various combinations of goods and services can offer equal satisfaction to an individual.

▶ Indifference Curves

Suppose you enjoy two leisure activities—playing tennis and watching tennis. Because you like both watching and playing tennis, if you increase the amount that you do of both, you will be happier, and if you decrease the amount of both you will be less happy. This is described in figure 2.A. Point a indicates a particular amount of time spent playing tennis and a particular amount of time spent watching tennis. We have drawn horizontal and vertical dashed lines through point a. The intersection of these two lines creates four regions in the diagram. At any combination of playing and watching tennis in the region labeled A, you are better off than at point a because more time is spent both watching and playing tennis. Combinations in the region labeled C leave you worse off than at point a because you do less of both pleasure-producing activities. This means that if we want to try to find combinations of playing and watching tennis that you like just as well as at point a, we must look in the regions labeled B and D in figure 2.A.

Because consumers are willing to make substitutions, we can find combinations of playing and watching tennis that give someone the same satisfaction as other combinations do. For example, if you spend about five hours a week playing tennis and two hours a week watching tennis, you might find that watching somewhat more tennis and playing somewhat less tennis is just as satisfying. We say that you are *indifferent* to combinations that provide you with equal satisfaction (utility). The geometric representation of combinations of playing and watching tennis to which you attach identical levels of utility is known as an **indifference curve.** Because you find these combinations equally attractive in terms of their satisfaction, you are said to be indifferent to the consumption of any of the combinations.

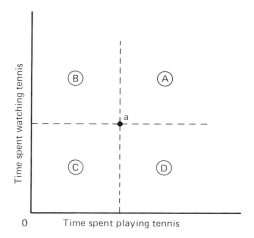

Figure 2.A   Utility of time spent playing and watching tennis
Point *a* describes a particular amount of time spent playing tennis and a particular amount of time spent watching tennis. The four regions of the diagram, A, B, C, and D, are created by drawing a horizontal and a vertical line through point *a*. In region A, the individual will have a higher level of utility because he or she is *both* playing *and* watching more tennis than at point *a*. In region C, the utility level is lower because less tennis is being played and watched. Within both regions B and D, there are likely to be combinations of tennis playing and watching that the individual will find equally attractive to the combination indicated by point *a*.

Figure 2.B illustrates an indifference curve for time spent playing and time spent watching tennis. Notice that it is downward sloping, which indicates it is possible to hold an individual's level of satisfaction constant by increasing the amount of playing tennis and decreasing the amount of watching tennis or vice versa. However, also notice that the trade-offs the individual is willing to make (the slope of the indifference curve) varies with the combination of playing and watching tennis currently being consumed. In figure 2.B, the indifference curve is curved and bowed downward (convex from below). This means that the typical person is not willing always to trade off the same number of hours of watching tennis for an hour of playing tennis.

*An **indifference curve map** is a collection of indifference curves and is a geometric description of a consumer's tastes and preferences (the utility function).*

There is more than one indifference curve. If we take a combination of time spent watching tennis and time spent playing tennis that lies to the northeast (upward and to the right) of combinations along the indifference curve in figure 2.B, the combination lying to the northeast will represent a higher level of satisfaction. Thus, it will lie on another (higher) indifference curve than the one depicted in figure 2.B. Similarly, combinations of time spent watching and time spent playing tennis that lie to the southwest (downward and to the left) of the indifference curve in figure 2.B represent less utility and lie on a lower indifference curve. *Every* combination of time spent watching and time spent playing tennis lies on *some* indifference curve. This means that a consumer can consider one set of activities and decide whether it is more, less, or equally satisfying than any other combination of the two activities. To understand this fully, draw another (downward-sloping and convex) indifference curve that lies above the one shown in figure 2.B and one lying below the curve already shown in the figure. Label the lower indifference curve you have drawn utility level 1. Label the middle one, already printed in the figure, utility level 2, and finally, label the the upper indifference curve you have drawn utility level 3. These utility levels remind us that we can say the highest indifference curve represents being better off than the lower ones. However, the numbers 1, 2, and 3 tell us nothing about how happy one might be along each indifference curve. We might as well have numbered them 101, 102, and 103 so long as the higher indifference curves have larger numbers than the lower ones.

The indifference curves you have drawn, plus the one printed in figure 2.B are three of the many indifference curves that describe all of the conceivable combinations of tennis playing and tennis watching one might experience. The set of all possible indifference curves is known as an **indifference curve map,** which is a complete geometric representation of an individual's tastes and preferences, or the utility function. It looks something like a weather map in that weather maps contain lines called isobars and isotherms, which indicate areas of equal barometric pressure and temperature, respectively. Indifference curves could also be called isoutility lines because they indicate regions of equal utility or satisfaction.

Because the paper these words are printed on has only two dimensions, our indifference curves can depict only two goods or services at a time, even though we all derive satisfaction, or utility, from numerous commodities. Any two of the items that yield utility can be depicted in an indifference curve map such as that in figure 2.B. For example, there is an indifference curve map relating the utility derived from restaurant meals versus home-cooked meals, from

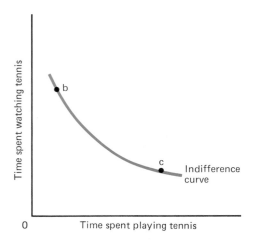

Figure 2.B   An indifference curve for playing and watching tennis

All of the points on the indifference curve represent combinations of time spent playing and watching tennis that the individual finds equally satisfying. The curve is downward sloping because the individual is willing to trade off time spent in one activity for more time in the other activity and remain equally satisfied. It is curved and bowed toward the origin (convex from below) because the individual's willingness to trade off the two activities against each other changes with the combination currently being consumed. Specifically, if the individual is currently at point b, where he or she is watching a lot but only playing a little tennis, the individual will be willing to watch a lot less tennis in exchange for one more hour of playing tennis. At point c, the individual is watching relatively little tennis, so a lot more tennis playing is necessary (compared to point b) to compensate the individual for giving up some tennis watching *and remain equally satisfied.*

A typical individual's willingness to trade off tennis watching for tennis playing depends crucially on where he or she starts out on an indifference curve. For example, at point b in figure 2.B, the individual is spending relatively more time watching than playing tennis. This means that he or she will be willing to give up a relatively large amount of tennis watching for an extra hour of tennis playing. This would not be so at point c, where relatively little tennis is being watched, but a lot is being played. At point c, it takes a lot of additional tennis playing to compensate for losing one hour of tennis watching. We conclude that an individual's willingness to trade off one activity, good, or service, for another depends upon how much of each is being consumed. It is easier to give up something when you have a relatively large amount of it compared to when you have relatively little of it.

*A **budget constraint** is a mathematical description (either algebraic or geometric) of the choices a consumer is able to make in light of his or her available time and income and the prices of goods and services.*

vacations versus motion pictures, or chicken versus beef for dinner. Any of these indifference curve maps would show how an individual is willing to substitute among various goods or services that yield utility.

Now that we have seen how economists describe the way in which various goods and services yield satisfaction to consumers, let us look at the second economic truth enunciated by Mick Jagger—you can't always get what you want.

The Budget Constraint: How Much of What You Want Can You Get?

An individual's tastes and preferences, as represented by the utility function and indifference curve map, are only one aspect of decisions regarding what to consume. If there were no limits on what we can have, we would pig out on goods, services, and leisure activities. If this sounds like hog heaven, you are right. Only in heaven could one have an unlimited amount of everything. Here on earth, scarcity places limits on our ability to consume. The amount of income and time we have available plus the prices we have to pay for goods and services and the time it takes to consume them limit what we can do to make ourselves happy.

Again, a little geometry is helpful in understanding the concept of a **budget constraint,** which is a diagram describing the limitations on a consumer's choices. A budget constraint describes the choices a consumer can make in light of the amount of time and income available to spend and the prices of goods and services in the marketplace. Figure 2.C illustrates a budget constraint for the pounds of hamburger and pounds of chicken that can be purchased when the individual has $20 per month to spend on these two products and the price of chicken is $0.50 per pound and that of hamburger $1.00 per pound. The budget constraint in the figure tells us that if only hamburger is purchased, the individual can buy 20 pounds per month. If only chicken is bought, then 40 pounds a month can be obtained. Given the prices of hamburger and chicken, the opportunity cost of one more pound of hamburger is 2 pounds of chicken because hamburger costs twice as much as chicken. Thus, the budget constraint is a straight line connecting 40 pounds on the vertical axis and 20 pounds on the horizontal axis. The budget constraint is a straight line because the prices of chicken and hamburger are not affected by the amounts any particular individual may purchase.

We could also draw a budget constraint for our previous example of time spent watching tennis and time spent playing tennis. This is so because there is only so much time available for these activities. Suppose, for example, you have a total of ten hours per week available to devote to both

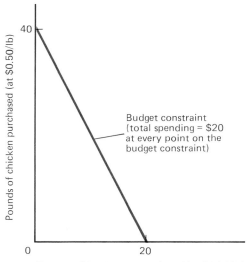

Figure 2.C   A budget constraint for purchasing hamburger and chicken
Chicken costs $0.50 per pound and hamburger costs $1.00 per pound. The individual has $20 per month to spend on chicken and hamburger. The budget constraint depicted here illustrates the combinations of hamburger and chicken the individual is able to purchase. The budget constraint represents the equation $20 = (price of chicken $\times$ pounds purchased + price of hamburger $\times$ pounds purchased).

tennis activities. Suppose further that you have a tennis court in the backyard and a TV in the basement. In this case, every hour spent playing tennis requires giving up one hour watching tennis. However, if you do not have a tennis court in your backyard so that you have to travel a half hour to reach a tennis court and return to your house, every hour you play tennis means that you watch tennis one and a half hours less. On a separate piece of paper draw for yourself such a constraint, describing how an individual's budget of time limits the amount of tennis watching and tennis playing.

The budget constraint shown in figure 2.C and the one you have drawn represent the basic idea of scarcity. It is the limited amount of time and income we have plus the prices we face that require us to make choices. These choices are determined by (1) our economic environment as described by the budget constraint and (2) tastes and preferences described by the utility function and indifference curve map. When we put these two concepts together, we can analyze consumer choice in some detail.

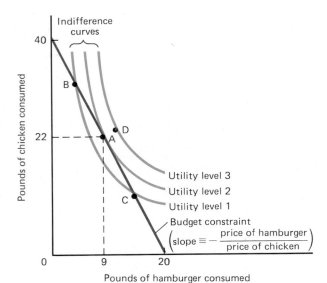

Figure 2.D   The utility-maximizing choice of chicken and hamburger
The budget constraint illustrates the individual's ability to consume chicken and hamburger when they cost $1 and $0.50 per pound, respectively, and a total of $20 per month is available for spending on these two items. The indifference curves illustrate the individual's tastes and preferences for hamburger versus chicken. Maximum utility, given the budget constraint, occurs at point A, where 9 pounds of hamburger and 22 pounds of chicken are consumed per week. Notice that the combinations at B and C are economically feasible (that is, they lie on the budget constraint) but are not chosen because they yield less satisfaction than the combination at A. While the combination of chicken and hamburger at point D is even better, it is not economically feasible because it costs more than $20.

▶ The Geometry and Economics of Consumer Choice

In order to see how the utility function, or indifference map, and the budget constraint determine consumer choice, we need to add the assumption that individuals attempt to maximize their utility. This assumption does not necessarily imply selfishness. Charitable contributions or volunteer work for various causes can easily be included in the utility function.

Figure 2.D brings together an indifference curve map and budget constraint for chicken and hamburger consumption. As in figure 2.C, we assume that the individual has $20 to spend per week and that hamburger and chicken cost $1.00 and $0.50 cents per pound, respectively. In light of the individual's economic environment and preferences for hamburger and chicken, point A is selected as yielding the maximum utility or satisfaction. At point A, the person in the diagram chooses to consume 9 pounds of hamburger and 22 pounds of chicken per week. Notice that the combinations of hamburger and chicken at points B and C are also economically feasible. They are not chosen, however, because they yield a lower level of satisfaction than the combination at point A. What about the blend of chicken and hamburger at point D, which is preferable to the one at point A? The combination at point D is not feasible economically because it would cost more than the amount available to spend, $20.

The utility-maximizing, or optimum, combination of hamburger and chicken occurs where an indifference curve is tangent to or just touches the budget constraint. Other combinations of chicken and hamburger are either too expensive or yield lower levels of satisfaction compared to the one where the indifference curve and budget constraint are tangent. This is a general conclusion that holds for any two goods or services that might be measured along the horizontal and vertical axes. For example, the same would hold true for the utility-maximizing combination of tennis played and tennis watched, or the utility-maximizing combination of restaurant meals and vacations. Thus, Mick Jagger is basically correct when he says that you can't always get what you want. The reason is that scarcity, as reflected in the budget constraint, imposes limits on our ability to obtain all of the goods and services we would like.

At the tangency point A, the slope of the budget constraint is equal to the slope of the indifference curve—that is what tangency means. Remember that the slope of the budget constraint measures the opportunity cost of choosing more hamburger in terms of the amount of chicken that must be given up. On the other hand, the slope of an indifference curve measures an individual's willingness to substitute hamburger for chicken while remaining equally satisfied.

If the slope of the indifference curve and budget constraint are not equal, then consumption can be reorganized so that utility increases without spending any more money. To see this, consider the combination of chicken and hamburger at point B. Here the slope of the budget line is flatter than the slope of the indifference curve. This means that the individual in figure 2.D is *willing* to give up more chicken per extra pound of hamburger than the budget constraint *requires* be given up to purchase the additional chicken. Thus, the individual's utility will be increased if some hamburger is substituted for chicken, and a utility-maximizing individual will move from point B toward point A.

A similar story holds if we start the process at point C. There the market provides the consumer with 2 extra pounds of chicken for each pound of hamburger foregone. However, the consumer requires *less than* 2 pounds of chicken per additional pound of hamburger foregone in order to maintain utility level 1. Thus, if the individual in the diagram moves from point C northwesterly toward point A, utility will rise but no more money will be spent on chicken and hamburger. Only at point A is there no longer any ability to increase utility by reorganizing the consumption bundle.

Using Indifference Curve and Budget Constraint Diagrams

We cannot repeat too often that the diagrams we have used to illustrate budget constraints and indifference curves focus our attention on the consumption of only two items out of the thousands on which we may spend our time and money. Nevertheless, the basic truths illustrated are general because they illustrate the principles of utility-maximizing choice between *any* two goods, services, or uses of time. These diagrams are the economist's way of systematically describing consumer choice. They are extremely useful even though individuals in real life do not use such diagrams to form their actual consumption choices. In reality, we all engage in considerable trial and error in attempting to achieve the most satisfaction from our limited incomes. When we *do* find the best combinations of goods and services to consume, however, diagrams such as figure 2.D describe the consumption bundle we have chosen. Such diagrams allow economists to be systematic and efficient in analyzing how optimal consumption choices will change when factors influencing those choices vary. For example, we are able to predict the impact of a change in income or the price of either chicken or hamburger on the amount purchased even though we may know very little about the actual thought process involved when consumers adjust to such changes.

The value of an economic model, such as that depicted in figure 2.D, is in its ability to describe how changes in the economic environment affect economic behavior. In more advanced courses, we would analyze how changes in income affect the budget constraint and how changes in prices affect its slope. These changes will affect the choices of goods and services consumed and of leisure activities. As a final exercise, think about how the budget line would change in figure 2.D if the price of chicken or hamburger doubled. How would it change if the income available were cut in half?

▶ Key Terms

budget constraint *57*

indifference curve *55*

indifference curve map *56*

utility function *54*

Chapter 3

The Shape of
the Demand Curve

Outline

I. Introduction 62
II. Quantifying the relationship between price and quantity demanded 62
  A. The slope of the demand curve 62
  B. Price elasticity of demand 64
    1. Calculating a price elasticity of demand 64
    2. Elasticity, prices, and total consumer spending 66
    3. Estimates of price elasticities for the United States 69
  C. Why price elasticities vary 70
    1. Ability to substitute 70
    2. Time horizons 70
    3. Importance in the budget 71
III. Other demand elasticities 71
  A. Income elasticity 71
  B. Cross price elasticity 72
IV. Summary and conclusions 73
V. Key terms 73
VI. Questions for discussion and review 73

Objectives

After reading this chapter, the student should be able to:

Calculate the price elasticity of demand.
Describe the relationship between total revenue and price elasticity of demand.
Define the income elasticity of demand and the cross price elasticity of demand.

▶ Introduction

Many college students today own personal computers that cost anywhere from $1,000 to perhaps $5,000 or more. In addition, it is not uncommon for them to purchase software costing another several hundred dollars. Twenty years ago, computers were available, but they were very large and extremely expensive. Few if any individuals purchased computers for home use. Over the years, the price of the "guts" of a computer—its memory—has declined to less than a thousandth of the price per unit of memory that prevailed twenty years ago. This is the main reason why computers cost so much less today than they used to. Moreover, technological improvements have made it possible to manufacture memory circuitry that is small enough to fit into the transportable personal computers that many of us own and use. In short, as the price of computation has declined, *the average consumer and business have spent* more *on purchasing computers.*

By contrast, improved agricultural technology, hybrid seeds, scientific animal breeding, and so on have vastly increased the amount of output a typical farmer can produce. The prices of meat, grains, dairy products, and other commodities have fallen sharply relative to the prices of most other goods and services. As agricultural prices have fallen, many households have decreased their total expenditures on food (after allowing for the effect of inflation on the prices of all goods and services). Even though the quantity *of a good purchased generally increases when its price falls, total expenditure on the good may decline. In this chapter, we will examine more closely the response of the quantity of a good or service demanded to a change in its price.*

▶ Quantifying the Relationship between Price and Quantity Demanded

The demand curves we have discussed up to now are *qualitative* in nature. By this we mean that they indicate the general, inverse relationship between price and quantity demanded. They do *not* give us specific *quantitative* details (how much quantity demanded changes when a commodity's price changes), however. Economists also work with actual demand curves for specific goods and services. The quantitative properties of these demand curves are important, as we have seen, in determining how total purchases of goods and services respond to changes in prices. The responsiveness of quantity demanded to price is a crucial element in the decision making of private businesses, nonprofit institutions, and governments. For example, every year your college's administrators must decide whether or not to increase tuition. An important factor affecting their decision will be whether they expect the total amount of tuition paid to rise or fall. How many students will decide to drop out, and how many will be willing and able to pay the increased cost of attending college? The answer is summarized by the quantitative nature of the demand for a college education.

The Slope of the Demand Curve

One possible quantitative measure of the relationship between price and quantity demanded is the slope or tilt of a demand curve. Take a pencil and draw two demand curves. Make one steep, or nearly vertical, and the other flat, or nearly horizontal. A steep slope means that a given change in price has a rather small effect on the quantity of the good or service demanded. The same change in price produces a large effect on quantity demanded when the demand curve is more nearly horizontal. Figure 3.1 illustrates two

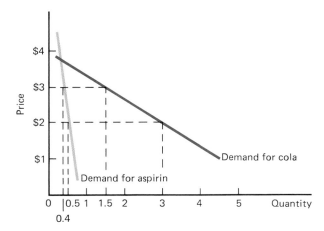

Figure 3.1   The slope of a demand curve and change in quantity demanded
The slope of the demand curve for aspirin is quite steep compared to the slope of the demand curve for cola. This tells us that a $1 price change leads to a much smaller change in the quantity of aspirin demanded than in the quantity of cola demanded.

hypothetical demand curves of a typical college student. The relatively flat demand curve is for cola. At a price of $2 per six-pack, the student purchases three six-packs per month, and a $1 increase in the price of cola would result in a reduction in the quantity demanded of one and a half six-packs per month. This is a fairly sensitive response to a price change compared to the student's demand for aspirin. If the price of aspirin is $2 per bottle of twenty-five tablets, we see that one-half bottle per month is purchased. A $1 increase in price results in a very small decline in the quantity purchased, only one-tenth of a bottle per month. The steep slope of the demand curve for aspirin means that a given change in price has a relatively small effect on the quantity demanded compared with cola.

Comparing the slopes of demand curves often provides interesting and useful information about the responsiveness of quantity demanded to the price of a good or service. One problem with the slope as a measure of the sensitivity of quantity demanded to changes in price, however, is that it does not have the same economic meaning for each and every good. In the example in figure 3.1, a $1 increase in price for the two goods represents the same percentage increase in price. But suppose we wished to compare the demand for cola with the demand for housing. A $1 increase in the price of a house is a much smaller percentage change than the same dollar increase in the price of a six-pack of cola. How should we compare the quantity response to the $1 price rise in cola to the $1 price rise in a house? We could try to use a common unit of measure. There are examples for which quantity changes in common units. For example, we could compare the demand for cola with the demand for beer. We could use gallons to measure the change in the quantity of either beverage demanded as the result of a $1 price change. But we would get bogged down trying to find common units of measure for cola, aspirin, houses, toasters, cars, and so forth.

Even in our cola and beer example, there could be a problem. Suppose that when the prices of gallons of beer and cola are increased by $1 we find that the total quantity demanded in the market for each declines by 1,000 gallons. We might be tempted to conclude that each market is affected equally by the $1 price increase. But if only 2,000 gallons of cola were sold before the price increased while 2 million gallons of beer were sold, the same decline in quantity demanded would represent a dramatic decline of 50 percent in cola sales and a modest 0.05 percent decline in beer sales. Ideally, we would like to have a measure of the responsiveness of changes in quantity

*The **price elasticity of demand** is the percentage change in the quantity of a good demanded divided by the percentage change in its price, from one point to another along a given demand curve. It measures the sensitivity of quantity demanded to a change in price.*

demanded to a price change that can be compared across all commodities and that captures the relative importance of that quantity change in each market.

In order to satisfy these conditions, economists have developed the concept of the **price elasticity of demand,** which measures the sensitivity of quantity demanded to price change as indicated by the percentage change in the quantity demanded by the percentage change in the price of the product. This allows us to compare a vast variety of goods and services much more accurately.

Price Elasticity of Demand

We will use the symbol ϵ_p to represent the price elasticity of demand for a good or service. It tells us the *percentage change* in quantity demanded *per 1 percent change in price*. Price elasticity of demand may be thought of as a standardized measure of the responsiveness of the quantity demanded to its price. Since price and quantity demanded move in opposite directions, ϵ_p is a negative number.

$$\epsilon_p \equiv \frac{\% \text{ change in quantity demanded}}{\% \text{ change in product price}}$$

$$\equiv (\Delta Q/\Delta Y) \times (P/Q)$$

It is important to be able to interpret the numerical value of a price elasticity. For example, if ϵ_p takes on a value of -1.0, this means that a 1 percent change in price causes *exactly* a 1 percent change in quantity demanded in the opposite direction. Economists say that such a demand curve is *unitary elastic.* If ϵ_p takes on a value of less than -1.0 (greater than 1.0 in absolute value), this is known as an *elastic demand* curve. If the demand curve is elastic, buyers are relatively sensitive to price, and a 1 percent change in price causes *more than* a 1 percent change in quantity demanded. To be specific, suppose that ϵ_p equals -4.0. In this case, a 1 percent *increase* in price leads to a 4 percent *reduction* in quantity demanded. Finally, when buyers are relatively *insensitive* to price changes, ϵ_p has a value between -1.0 and zero (less than 1.0 in absolute value), and the demand curve is said to be *inelastic.*

Calculating a Price Elasticity of Demand

Suppose that we have *quantitative* information about a demand curve. In particular, we know the numerical value of its slope. Because economists draw demand curves with the dependent variable, quantity, on the *horizontal* axis, the slope of a demand curve is the change in price divided by the change in quantity demanded. For example, the slope of demand curve D in figure 3.2 is

$$(\$10 - \$11)/(6 - 5),$$

which in numerical terms is $-1/1 = -1$. The slope of demand curve D′, on the other hand, is

$$(\$10 - \$11)/(10 - 5),$$

which in numerical terms is -1 divided by 5, or $-1/5$.

Because we are really after a measure of how price affects quantity demanded, it is more convenient to look at the *reciprocal* of the slope of a demand curve as we usually draw it. The reciprocal of the slope of the demand curve D in figure 3.2 is

$$(6 - 5)/(10 - 11),$$

which is also -1. The reciprocal of the slope of D′ is

$$(10 - 5)/10 - 11),$$

or -5. These calculations demonstrate that between P(0) and P(1), demand curve D′ shows more price sensitivity than demand curve D. The fact that the price sensitivity of the quantity demanded of a product is greater the flatter the demand curve is important. But we want to measure price sensitivity in a way that avoids the units of measurement and relative market impact problems we discussed earlier in this chapter.

As we have seen, a good way to compare demand curves is to calculate the response to a price change in *percentage* terms. How do we calculate the percentage changes in price and quantity demanded? Suppose we go back to our beer and cola example. The change in quantity demanded given the $1 price increase was $-1,000$ in each case. What is the percentage change of quantity demanded? Initially, cola consumption was 2,000 units, and after the price increase it was 1,000 units. Thus, we might calculate

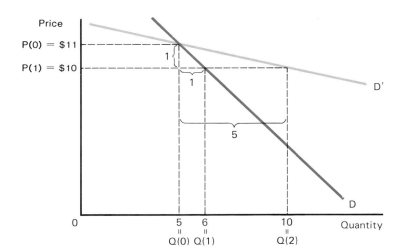

Figure 3.2   Calculating price elasticity of demand
The reciprocal of the slope of a demand curve is the change in quantity demanded divided by the change in price. The elasticity of a demand curve is the *percentage* change in quantity demanded divided by the *percentage* change in price.

The *reciprocal* of the *slope* of demand curve D is $1/-1 = -1$. The *elasticity* of demand curve D is when price varies between $10 and $11 is $(1/5.5)/(-1/10.5) = -1.91$.

The *reciprocal* of the *slope* of demand curve D' is $5/-1 = -5$. The *elasticity* of demand curve D' when price varies between $10 and $11 is $(5/7.5)/(-1/10.5) = -7.0$.

the percentage change as 1,000/1,000, or 100 percent, or we might calculate it as 1,000/2,000, or 50 percent. In order to avoid this uncertainty when price and quantity jump from one value to another, economists usually use the *average* price and *average* quantity in calculating percentage changes when calculating elasticities. (When calculated in this manner, an elasticity is sometimes called an *arc elasticity*.) Using average price and average quantity, the percentage change in quantity and price when the price of cola and beer increases from $5 to $6 is measured as follows.

Percentage change in the quantity of cola demanded:

$$(1,000 - 2,000)/\frac{(2,000 + 1,000)}{2},$$

$$\text{or } \frac{-1,000}{1,500} = -66.67\%.$$

Percentage change in the quantity of beer demanded:

$$(1,999,000 - 2,000,000)/\frac{(1,999,000 + 2,000,000)}{2}$$

$$= -0.05\%.$$

Percentage change in price:

$$(\$6 - \$5)/\frac{(6 + 5)}{2} = 18.13\%.$$

Therefore, in our example, the price elasticity of demand for beer is $-0.05/18.13 = -0.0028$, and the price elasticity of demand for cola is $-66.67/18.13 = -3.677$. Starting with the same set of numbers, calculate the price elasticity of demand for beer and cola when the price decreases from $6 to $5.

What these elasticity calculations show is that even though the price increase for beer and cola from $5 to $6 caused an identical decline in the quantity demanded, the percentage impact on quantity demanded was much more dramatic for the cola market than the beer market. As indicated by our calculation the more dramatic impact of the price increase on the cola market is reflected by the fact that the demand for cola is highly elastic (much greater than 1.0 in absolute value) and that the demand for beer is highly inelastic (very close to zero in value).

As a matter of fact there have been attempts to measure the price elasticity of demand for beer in the United States. In one study using 1956–1959 data, the elasticity of demand was estimated to be -0.9.[1] The same study found that holding price and income constant, the quantity of beer demanded was greater in states with high percentages of German immigrants in the population. Why do you suppose beer demand would be positively related to the percentage of German immigrants in the population?

Total revenue (TR) equals a commodity's price multiplied by the quantity sold; i.e., TR ≡ PQ.

To test your knowledge of how to calculate a demand elasticity, return to figure 3.2. If we use the numerical values in figure 3.2, we see that the percent change in quantity along demand curve D is (6 − 5)/(5 1/2) = 18.2 percent, while the percentage change in price is ($10 − $11)/(10 1/2), or −9.5 percent. Thus the percentage change in quantity divided by the percentage change in price along D is 18.2/−9.5, which equals −1.9. This is the numerical value of ϵ_p for demand curve D in figure 3.2. Prove to yourself that demand curve D′ has an elasticity of −7. These elasticity values for the straight-line demand curves drawn in figure 3.2 hold *only* for the particular prices and quantities shown. To further test your knowledge of elasticity, calculate the elasticity of each demand curve when the price falls from $10 to $9. To get you started, we will provide a hint on how to proceed. Since both demand curves are straight lines, the change in quantity along each curve when the price falls from $10 to $9 will be exactly the same as when the price falls from $11 to $10.

Frequently, price elasticities of demand are written without the minus (−) sign. This is a convenience, but when you see price elasticities of demand reported or discussed as positive numbers, you should always bear in mind that the underlying demand curve does slope downward and to the right.

Elasticity, Prices, and Total Consumer Spending

The price elasticity of demand for a good or service is related to how much is spent on it. We will define the total amount of money consumers spend on a good or service as **total revenue (TR)**. Total revenue is the product of price, P, and quantity demanded, or price times quantity, Q, (P × Q). The concept of a downward-sloping demand curve tells us that when price rises, quantity falls, and when price falls, quantity rises. An increase in price tends to increase total revenue, but the accompanying decline in quantity demanded tends to reduce it. A reduction in price tends to diminish total revenue, but the increase in sales that accompanies a price reduction pushes total revenue upward in the opposite direction. Thus, it is not obvious what happens to total revenue when price

changes. *Quantitative* knowledge of the price elasticity of demand allows us to link changes in price to changes in total consumer spending on a good or service.

If $\epsilon_p = -1$ (demand is unitary elastic), then a price change is *exactly* offset by a change in quantity demanded. In this case, total revenue is *unaffected* by a change in price. Every time price goes up by 1 percent, the quantity demanded goes down by 1 percent. The product of the two, total revenue, stays the same. This is illustrated in part (a) of figure 3.3. Notice that such a demand curve must indeed be a *curve* and not a straight line. A straight-line demand curve eventually crosses both the vertical (price) axis and the horizontal (quantity) axis. Therefore, it has two points where total expenditure is zero. At the point where the demand curve crosses the vertical (price) axis, nothing is purchased. Where the demand curve crosses the horizontal axis, price is equal to zero. Again, total expenditure is zero at this point. Obviously, total expenditure is greater than zero between the points where a straight-line demand curve crosses the two axes. Since total expenditure is *not* the same all along a straight-line demand curve, elasticity cannot equal −1 all along the curve. (Later on, you will see how to calculate elasticity along a straight-line demand curve and show that the elasticity is *different* at *every* point.)

Slightly more complex are the cases where demand is elastic or inelastic. When demand is *elastic*, quantity demanded changes relatively more than price. This leads to an *inverse* relationship between price and total revenue as we see in part (b) of figure 3.3. Increases in price reduce total consumer spending, and reductions in price increase total consumer spending. Finally, the opposite holds when demand is *inelastic*. Because in this case buyers are relatively unresponsive to price, price and total revenue move in the *same* direction. This is illustrated in part (c) of figure 3.3. The relationship between elasticity, price, and total revenue is summarized in table 3.1.

Let us look at some applications of this relationship. Economic studies have shown that the demand for gasoline is price inelastic in the United States. This means that price increases will cause consumers to

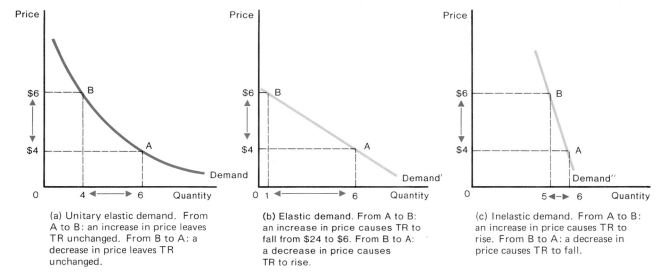

(a) Unitary elastic demand. From A to B: an increase in price leaves TR unchanged. From B to A: a decrease in price leaves TR unchanged.

(b) Elastic demand. From A to B: an increase in price causes TR to fall from $24 to $6. From B to A: a decrease in price causes TR to rise.

(c) Inelastic demand. From A to B: an increase in price causes TR to rise. From B to A: a decrease in price causes TR to fall.

Figure 3.3   The relationship between total consumer spending and price elasticity of demand
In each of the three cases illustrated, the original price and quantity are the same ($4 and 6), and the price rises by the same amount, $2. The area of the rectangle that is bounded by the origin (0), the quantity 6, point A, and the price $4 is total consumer spending at price $4. (Remember that the area of a rectangle is equal to its base times its height, and in this case base is quantity demanded and height is price.) The area of the rectangle bounded by the origin (0), the quantity demanded at the higher price of $6, point B, and the price $6 is total consumer spending at price $6.

Table 3.1   The relationship between price and total consumer spending

Value of price elasticity	Classification	Relationship between price changes and changes in total revenue*
ϵ_p less than −1.0	Elastic demand	$\begin{cases} P\uparrow \rightarrow TR\downarrow \\ P\downarrow \rightarrow TR\uparrow \end{cases}$
ϵ_p equals −1.0	Unitary elastic demand	$\begin{cases} P\uparrow \rightarrow \text{no change in TR} \\ P\downarrow \rightarrow \text{no change in TR} \end{cases}$
ϵ_p greater than −1.0	Inelastic demand	$\begin{cases} P\uparrow \rightarrow TR\uparrow \\ P\downarrow \rightarrow TR\downarrow \end{cases}$

*TR is equal to (P × Q), which is total spending by consumers.

spend greater total amounts on gasoline. Everyone knows that the price of gasoline rose dramatically between 1973 and 1985 because of the activities of OPEC. This, coupled with the inelastic demand for gasoline in the United States, led to increases in the total revenue of gasoline producers and of OPEC. The relationship between price and consumer spending for gasoline also holds if we measure spending in terms of percentage of the budget. This is one of the reasons why figure 2.1 on page 34 shows us that in 1980 consumers were spending a larger fraction of their budget on transportation than they were in 1950. Clearly, the rapid decline in gasoline prices in early 1986 reduced the share of income consumers spent on transportation.

Table 3.2   **Estimated short-term price elasticities of demand for United States consumers[a]**

Product	ϵ_p Value[b]
Inelastic (ϵ_p between 0 and −1.0)	
Automobile repair, greasing, washing, parking, storage, and rental	−0.40
Bank service charges, trust services, and safe deposit box rental	−0.53
Clothing upkeep and laundering	−0.92
Domestic services	−0.66
Electricity (household utility)	−0.13
Flowers, seeds, and potted plants	−0.82
Foreign travel by United States residents	−0.13
Funeral and burial expenses	−0.5
Gas (household utility)	−0.15
Intercity bus	−0.20
Jewelry and watches	−0.41
Kitchen and other household appliances	−0.67
Legal services	−0.37
Legitimate theater and opera	−0.18
Medical care and hospitalization insurance	−0.31
Motion pictures	−0.87
Newspapers and magazines	−0.42
Nondurable toys	−0.30
Ophthalmic products and orthopedic appliances	−0.37
Other educational expenditures[c]	−0.52
Other fuel and ice[d]	−0.73
Other household operation[e]	−0.13
Other professional services[f]	−0.27
Other recreation[g]	−0.57
Radio and television repair	−0.45
Railway (commutation)	−0.72

Source: From Houthakker, H. S., and L. D. Taylor, *Consumer Demand in the United States: Analyses and Projections.* Copyright © 1970 Harvard University Press, Cambridge, MA. Reprinted by permission.

*Less than −1.0 means a "larger" negative number: a 1 percent change in price leads to *more* than a 1 percent change in quantity demanded.

[a]The short-term elasticities presented here indicate how consumers responded to a price change during the first year after it occurred.

[b]ϵ_p is interpreted as the percentage change in quantity demanded caused by a 1 percent change in price, *cet. par.* It is a negative number because demand curves are downward sloping.

Another important item that has increased its share in a typical family's budget is housing. This is also shown clearly in figure 2.1 for the period l950–1983. Much of this increase has been due to rising demand for luxury housing as incomes have risen.[2] However, some is probably due to the fact that the price of housing has risen faster than other prices and that the price elasticity of demand for housing is less than 1 in absolute value (i.e., lies between −1 and 0). The dramatic rise in interest rates on home mortgages beginning in the early 1970s added significantly to home buyers' monthly payments. Economists have estimated the price elasticity of demand for housing, and the weight of evidence indicates that it is in the neighborhood of −0.75.[3] Thus, an increase in price leads to an increase in total expenditure on housing.

Product	ϵ_p Value[b]
Inelastic (ϵ_p between 0 and -1.0)	
Rental value of farm houses	-0.60
Shoes and other footwear	-0.91
Space rental value of owner occupied housing	-0.04
Space rental value of tenant occupied housing	-0.18
Stationery	-0.47
Street and electric railway and local bus	-0.62
Taxicabs	-0.63
Telephone, telegraph, and wireless	-0.30
Tires, tubes, accessories, and parts	-0.86
Tobacco products	-0.46
Toilet articles and preparations	-0.20
Water	-0.20
Wheel goods, durable toys, sports equipment, boats, and pleasure aircraft	-0.88
Unitary elastic (ϵ_p approximately -1.0)	
Furniture	-1.01
Intercity railway travel	-1.14
Religious and welfare expenditures	-1.01
Elastic (ϵ_p less than -1.0)[*]	
China, glassware, tableware, and utensils	-1.54
Other personal business expenditures[h]	-1.94
Purchased meals	-2.27
Shoe cleaning and repairs	-1.31

[c]Includes fees paid to commercial, trade, business, and correspondence schools.

[d]Includes fuel oil and coal.

[e]Includes maintenance services for appliances, postage, and premiums on fire and theft insurance.

[f]Includes services of osteopathic physicians, chiropractors, chiropodists and podiatrists, and private-duty nurses.

[g]Includes photo developing and printing, additions to coin and stamp collections, veterinary services, purchase of pets, and camping fees.

[h]Includes union and professional association dues and spending for classified ads.

Estimates of Price Elasticities for the United States

Hendrik S. Houthakker and Lester D. Taylor have done what is probably the most comprehensive quantitative analysis of price elasticities in the United States. Their findings are summarized in table 3.2. Notice that most of the items have inelastic demand curves. The estimates in table 3.2 are for fairly broadly defined goods and services. For example, think of all of the different items that would be classified as furniture. In addition, the numbers in table 3.2 represent only the response of consumers during the year following the price change. In the next section we will consider some reasons why demand elasticities differ among various goods and services.

Why Price Elasticities Vary

Ability to Substitute

Probably the single most important factor influencing elasticity of demand is the ability to substitute another good or service. It is here that we see more clearly the link between elasticity and how narrowly a good is defined. Consider a very broadly defined item—*food*. It is difficult to think of something you can use instead of food and still stay alive. Thus, food has a relatively inelastic demand curve. Now consider *restaurant food*. Home-cooked meals are a good substitute for restaurant meals, so the demand for restaurant food will be more elastic than the demand for just food. Suppose, however, that we consider a very specific item, *canned tuna fish*. There are many food items a person can consume instead of canned tuna fish. This means that the demand for canned tuna fish will be relatively elastic.

Here is an example that is important to businesses. The demand for a particular *brand* of a product will be more elastic than the demand for the product in general. For example, the demand for automobiles will be less elastic than the demand for a particular model of car. Consider the demand for midsize *Pontiac* cars. One would expect midsize *Chevrolet* cars to be a very good substitute for the *Pontiacs*. Thus, if the price of one of the two makes rises, buyers can readily substitute the relatively cheaper car for the relative more expensive one. Consumers can also substitute a similar model made by Ford, Nissan, or Toyota. This ease of substitution by consumers means that an automobile company will have a rather elastic demand curve for one of its cars compared to the price elasticity of demand for cars in general.

Finally, some goods and services have few good substitutes even though they are fairly narrowly defined. As a result, they have inelastic demand curves. The most obvious example is an addictive substance. In table 3.2, we saw that the demand for tobacco products is inelastic. Cigarette consumers have a difficult time replacing the pleasures of smoking with other kinds of consumption. Imagine how inelastic the demand for heroin must be for a heroin addict.

Time Horizons

A second reason that price elasticities vary among goods and services is that a consumer's time horizon for decision making is not the same for all goods and services. This ties in with the ability to substitute. When time is short, it is difficult to survey the marketplace for alternatives. For example, if you are rushed to the emergency room of your local hospital with a severely cut finger, it is unlikely that you will take the time to shop for a lower price to get your wound tended to if you think the fee is too high. In such an extreme situation your demand curve for emergency medical services will be very inelastic. In general, the longer the decision period, the more adjustments you can make in your behavior to accommodate price changes, and the more elastic your demand for a good or service will be. If you were considering some cosmetic surgery, for example, you would be much more sensitive to price because you have time to search for a good deal.

To cite another example, when OPEC made gasoline much more expensive in the United States, at first there was very little reduction in the amount of gasoline used by United States drivers. Eventually, drivers made many adjustments to reduce the quantity of gasoline they demanded. They carpooled, used public transportation more often, took fewer driving vacations, tuned the engines of their cars more often, and eventually bought cars that used less gasoline per mile. Distance to work became more important in selecting a house or an apartment. Thus, the demand for gasoline became much more elastic with time. When gasoline prices fell dramatically in early 1986, the process was reversed. At first, gasoline consumption increased only slightly. By the middle of 1986, gasoline consumption had risen more sharply in response to decreased gasoline prices.

The short-term price elasticity of demand for gasoline is only about −0.11.[4] This means that consumers respond to a doubling in the price of gas by cutting their gasoline purchases about 11 percent during the next year. When enough time goes by for them to make the long-term adjustments mentioned in the preceding paragraph, the reduction in gasoline consumption is about four times larger.

*The **income elasticity of demand** is the percentage change in the quantity of a good demanded divided by the percentage change in the real income of purchasers of the good.*

In short, do not underestimate the ability of consumers to reduce their dependence on a product if they are given enough time to adjust. In fact, during the gas "gluts" in the early 1980s and between mid-1985 and mid-1986, the price of gasoline fell dramatically. One reason for the gluts and price drop was consumers' cumulative adjustments in their use of gasoline. OPEC ministers understand that too high a price will, in the long term, do them more harm than good.

Importance in the Budget

A third condition influencing elasticity is a good's importance in consumers' budgets. We would expect the demand for chewing gum to be relatively inelastic because no one spends very much on gum. Even if its price were to double, this is simply not a very important economic matter. A doubling of the price of gum would have practically no effect on the real income of the average gum chewer. Therefore, the income effect on gum demand is bound to be very small. Moreover, since it takes time and monetary expenditures to look for and experiment with substitutes for chewing gum, it would probably require a very substantial price increase to lead to much searching for alternative chews. By contrast, gasoline is relatively important in a typical consumer's total expenditures. A doubling of the cost of a gallon of gasoline would put a real dent in his or her wallet—especially if the consumer had to commute twenty or thirty miles to work each day. It would pay the consumer to try to conserve and find substitutes for gasoline. Therefore, the demand for gasoline is probably considerably more elastic than the demand for chewing gum.

Even a commodity that is an unimportant budget item will have a large price elasticity of demand if good substitutes are readily available. Pens do not use up much of a typical consumer's budget. However, as the price of fountain pens has risen and the price of ballpoint and similar pens has fallen, the newer style pens have virtually taken over the market for writing instruments.

All things considered, do you think that if you actually estimated the elasticity of demand for cola and for aspirin, the two goods depicted in figure 3.1, you would find that the elasticity of demand for aspirin is much smaller than that for cola? Why?

▶ Other Demand Elasticities

Price elasticity is only one of the many elasticities economists have developed to describe important economic relationships. In general, an elasticity can be defined to relate the percentage changes between any two variables. In studying demand relationships, two elasticities other than the price elasticity of demand are particularly useful. We will describe them briefly before concluding our discussion of demand elasticities.

Income Elasticity

In chapter 2, we learned that a change in income will in general shift demand curves to the right. So-called normal goods are those that increase in demand when income rises. **Income elasticity of demand** provides a precise quantitative measure of the percentage change in quantity demanded (holding other variables, including price, constant) in response to a 1 percent change in real income. (Remember that *real income* refers to actual quantity of goods and services your dollars will buy.) We will use the term ϵ_y to represent income elasticity of demand. The symbol y denotes *real* income. Income elasticity is calculated in a manner exactly analogous to price elasticity. The formula for ϵ_y is similar to the formula for ϵ_p, with income substituted for price. The formula, or equation, for income elasticity is

$$\epsilon_y \equiv (\Delta Q/\Delta y) \times (\overline{y}/\overline{Q})$$

$$\equiv \frac{\% \text{ change in quantity demanded}}{\% \text{ change in real income}}.$$

Where the $\overline{y}$ and $\overline{Q}$ mean that we use the average values of y and Q in calculating ϵ_y.

The concept of income elasticity can be used to describe various relationships between income and demand. Since normal goods are those that increase in demand when income rises, ϵ_y is positive for all normal goods. Inferior goods are those items that decline in demand when income rises. The value of ϵ_y is negative (less than zero) for inferior goods. Recall our earlier example of peanut butter and jelly sandwiches. Finally, there are two types of normal goods. One type consists of **luxury goods,** for which the percentage change in demand is *larger* than the percent change in income. For example, a 1 percent increase in income might lead to more than a 1 percent rise in the demand for restaurant dinners, *cet. par.* The other type of normal goods has a value of ϵ_y that lies between zero and unity; these normal goods are sometimes called **necessities.** The demand for necessities increases with increases in income but not by as much in percentage terms. Food, clothing, and shelter are often referred to as necessities.

In the previous section we discussed the demand for housing in terms of its price elasticity. Economists have also studied the income elasticity of demand for housing. Recall that the total amount spent on housing has increased by at least half as a share of a typical family's income over the past several decades. One reason for this may have been that housing is a luxury good, with an income elasticity of demand exceeding 1.0. You should be able to see that if a 1 percent increase in income leads to *more* than a 1 percent increase in expenditure on a commodity, then the proportion of income spent on that commodity will increase. However, the weight of evidence gathered by economists is that ϵ_y for housing has a value somewhat less than 1.0. Thus, the increasing share of expenditure on housing in family budgets is more likely to be due to the fact that its price elasticity of demand is smaller than 1.0 in absolute value than because housing is a luxury good for most buyers of housing.

Here are income elasticities that economists have measured for some other major consumer goods: food, 0.28; medical services, 0.22; automobiles, 3.00; beer, 0.93; marijuana, 0.0.[5]

Cross Price Elasticity

Finally, the elasticity concept can be used to link the demand curves for two *different* goods. Recall that earlier, when we discussed factors that shift a demand curve, one of them was a change in the price of another good or service. If we call one good a and the other good b, then a and b are *substitutes* if an increase in the price of one of them leads to a rightward shift in the demand curve for the other. They are *complements* if an increase in the price of one leads to a leftward shift in the demand curve for the other. These relationships can be defined in terms of the **cross price elasticity of demand,** which relates the percentage change in the demand for good a to the percentage change in the price of good b (or the percentage change in the demand for good b with respect to the percentage change in the price of good a). We will use the symbol ϵ_{ab} to denote the cross price elasticity of demand. The formula for cross price elasticity is very similar to the formulas for the other elasticities we have examined:

$$\epsilon_{ab} \equiv (\Delta Q_a / \Delta P_b) \times (\overline{P}_b / \overline{Q}_a)$$

$$\equiv \frac{\% \text{ change in quantity demanded of a}}{\% \text{ change in price of b}} .$$

If ϵ_{ab} is positive (greater than zero), an increase in the price of one good leads to an increase in the demand for the other, and they are substitutes. If ϵ_{ab} is negative, they are complements. If ϵ_{ab} is positive (negative), it is also generally true that ϵ_{ba}, the percentage change in demand for b with respect to the percentage change in the price of a, is positive (negative). Thus if good a is a substitute (complement) for good b, then good b is generally a substitute (complement) for good a.

Recall our discussion of substitutes and complements in chapter 2. We indicated that gasoline and automobiles are complements. Therefore, price increases in gasoline between 1973 and 1985 tended to decrease the quantity of automobiles demanded. American and foreign cars are substitutes. Thus, rapid increases in United States auto prices in the late 1970s tended to increase the quantity demanded of imported automobiles.

▶ Summary and Conclusions

In this chapter we have explored ways to quantify the shape of the demand curve. In terms of the introductory example, the elasticity of demand for personal computers is much larger than that for most agricultural commodities. The following points were emphasized in this chapter.

Elasticity allows us to compare demand relationships for different commodities. The price elasticity of demand tells us whether total revenue increases or decreases when price rises or falls, and it is therefore important to businesses and governments when they decide whether to raise or lower prices of particular goods and services.

As a general rule, the price elasticity of demand is different at different points along a demand curve.

Price elasticity of demand is influenced by substitutability among goods or services, time horizons, and importance of a good or service in consumers' budgets.

Income elasticity of demand tells us whether a good is categorized as normal (either luxury or necessity) or inferior.

Cross price elasticity of demand tells us whether two goods are complements or substitutes.

▶ Key Terms

cross price elasticity of demand *72*

income elasticity of demand *71*

luxury good *72*

necessity *72*

price elasticity of demand *64*

total revenue (TR) *66*

▶ Questions for Discussion and Review

1. What is the difference between the slope of a demand curve and the price elasticity of demand? Why do economists prefer elasticity as a quantitative measure of buyers' sensitivities to price?

2. You own a T-shirt shop. You are currently selling 100 shirts per week at $5 apiece. Below is information on two possible demand curves for your shirts.

Demand curve #1

Price per shirt	*Number of shirts sold per week*
$4.00	120
$4.50	110
$5.00	100
$5.50	93
$6.00	88

Demand curve #2

Price per shirt	*Number of shirts sold per week*
$4.00	132
$4.50	114
$5.00	100
$5.50	90
$6.00	80

Which demand curve for shirts would you rather have?

3. Suppose we know that after the price of a good has risen, consumers increase the total amount they spend on the good. What can we say about the elasticity of demand? Suppose we know that the demand for a good is elastic and that consumers have decreased the total amount they spend on the good after its price changed. Did price rise or fall? Suppose that the price of a good has increased and consumers are not spending any more or less on the good. Does this mean that the demand curve is not downward sloping? Explain carefully.

Figure 3.4   The demand curve for television sets

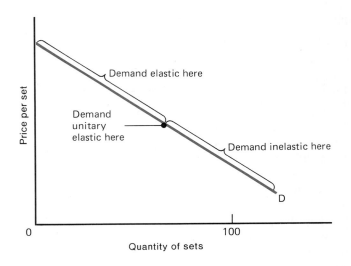

4. Your rich uncle dies. In his will he leaves you a truckload of television sets. Word of this gets out and people who want television sets start calling you up with offers to buy them. You would like to sell some or all of them and get as much money out of your sales as possible. You have 100 sets, and you have decided to charge the same for each set you sell. Figure 3.4 provides some information on the demand curve for your television sets. What price should you charge to achieve your goal of maximizing the revenue from your sales? Explain carefully.

5. The demand curve for narcotics is very price inelastic in the United States. What does this imply about the effectiveness of government policy designed to discourage narcotic use by raising its price? Could such a policy possibly hurt *nonusers* of narcotics? Explain.

6. Obtain estimates of price elasticities of demand in another country. (We suggest you look at the tables in A. Goldberger and T. Gamaletsos, "A Cross-Country Comparison of Consumer Expenditure Patterns," *European Economic Review,* vol. 1, 1970, pp. 357–400. Be sure to look only at the tables of this article; it is much too difficult to read!) Choose five goods and services. Write reasons why each demand is more or less elastic abroad than in the United States.

7. We often observe that commodities taxed by governments have price elasticities of demand that are quite small. Why do you suppose this is so? Explain your answer using a numerical example.

8. In the following graph, which demand curve (I or II) is more elastic?

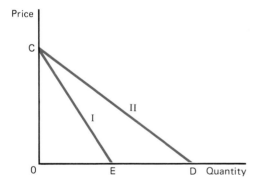

9. Examine the following graph and explain which of the demand curves is more elastic.

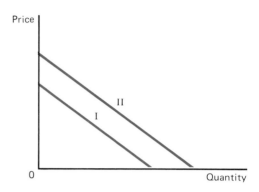

10. Suppose that you are a department store manager and it is your responsibility to determine the sale prices of certain items in your store. You observe that when you decrease the price of French perfume by 20 percent, the quantity demanded increases by 40 percent. Because sales are brisk, you decide to break the monthly sales record and decrease the price another 20 percent. However, you notice now that sales revenue has declined since the last price reduction. What is your explanation for this?

Chapter 4

Supply

Outline

I. Introduction *78*
II. The supply relationship *78*
  A. Basic assumptions of supply theory *78*
    1. Producers and their goals *78*
    2. Limitations on producers *80*
  B. Profit, marginal cost, and the law of supply *80*
    1. Method of analysis *80*
    2. An example *81*
    3. Marginal cost, profit, and supply in the short run *83*
    4. Average cost, marginal cost, and supply *85*
    5. Elasticity of supply *89*
  C. Factors that shift supply *90*
    1. Changes in technology *91*
    2. Changes in labor skills *92*
    3. Changes in input prices *92*
    4. Changes in expected future prices *92*
    5. Time horizons *93*
III. Application of the supply relationship *95*
  A. The price and supply of oil *95*
IV. Summary and conclusions *98*
V. Key terms *98*
VI. Questions for discussion and review *98*
VII. Appendix: A closer look at a firm's costs *100*
  A. An example: Choosing the optimal size of a pottery firm *100*
  B. Key terms *104*

Objectives

After reading this chapter, the student should be able to:

Discuss the goals of producers.
State the law of supply.
Distinguish between fixed and variable costs.
Explain, by using the concepts of marginal revenue and marginal cost, how a competitive firm chooses the profit-maximizing level of output.
Derive the short-run supply curve for a firm.
Discuss the relationships among average variable cost, average total cost, and marginal cost.
Calculate the elasticity of supply.
List factors that cause a supply curve to shift.
Apply supply theory to real-world situations.
Graph a typical firm's average fixed cost, average total cost, average variable cost, and marginal cost curves, indicating the break-even and shutdown points.
Illustrate constant, decreasing, and increasing returns to scale by means of a long-run average total cost curve.

*The **supply** of a good is the quantity offered for sale at each possible price.*

*A **firm** is the basic economic unit that makes production decisions in a market economy just as a household is the basic unit that makes consumption decisions.*

Economic profit is the excess of a firm's revenue over all of its costs of production.

▶ Introduction

In the 1950s, Congress passed legislation severely limiting the price that could be charged for natural gas shipped across state lines. Because of low prices and plentiful supplies, natural gas consumption soared. However, by the 1970s, inflation and diminishing supplies of natural gas made it much more costly to supply. Because natural gas producers were legally restricted from raising their prices, they ceased exploring for new wells, and it became extremely difficult to meet all of the demands for gas to heat homes, fuel electricity-producing generators, and run manufacturing plants. During an extremely cold winter in the late 1970s, the eastern half of the United States was nearly shut down by a major shortage of this crucial fuel. Plants were temporarily closed, workers were laid off, and homes and schools were threatened with no heat during the coldest time of year. Fortunately, business and household users of natural gas were just barely able to get through the winter without a major disruption of family and economic life. However, it was clear that artificially limited prices for natural gas could not be tolerated any longer, and major changes in the laws governing natural gas prices soon followed. In this chapter, we examine how the price that producers can obtain for a good or service influences the quantity they are willing to supply.

▶ The Supply Relationship

The **supply** of a good indicates how much is offered for sale at specified prices. In general, the supply curve for a good or service is the relationship between its own price and the quantity offered for sale, *ceteris paribus. Thus, generally, both demand and supply* shifts are responsible for the changes in consumer expenditures reported in figure 2.1, page 34.

Basic Assumptions of Supply Theory

The building blocks, or assumptions, of supply theory parallel those underlying the demand relationship developed in chapter 2. They can be placed in two categories, one concerning producers' goals and the other concerning constraints on producers' behavior.

Producers and Their Goals

In consumption, or demand, theory the basic consumer unit is an individual. In supply theory, the basic producing unit is a **firm,** which is simply a business entity whose management or owner hires inputs such as labor, machinery, and raw materials in order to provide a good or service. In a market economy this is normally done for profit. **Economic profit** is the difference between a firm's revenue and all of its opportunity costs. As the theory of supply is developed, you will learn that economic profit often differs from the profit an accountant reports on a firm's income statement.

Before going on, we will give you a simple example of the difference between economic profit and accounting profit. Suppose you open a lemonade stand at the state fair and at the end of the season you have sold lemonade for $100 more than the amount you paid for lemons, sugar, rent, and other possible monetary outlays. Your accountant would calculate your profit as equal to your sales revenue less these *explicit* costs. However, this would not reflect your economic profit accurately because it ignores the opportunity cost of your time, which is an *implicit* cost of doing business. It is implicit because it is not reflected in a direct transaction with another party involving an exchange of money for something else. Nevertheless, it is a genuine cost of doing business. Therefore, if you could have earned $500 in wages working in someone else's lemonade stand, you are $400 poorer than you might have been. In other words, the sad economic truth is that you incurred an *economic loss* of $400, not a profit of $100, from your enterprise.

1. We assume that the firm's goal is to earn the largest possible profit. This is the *profit maximization assumption,* and it parallels the assumption that consumers seek to maximize the satisfaction they obtain from allocating their income among alternatives. Profit maximization requires that the firm accomplish three tasks successfully. These tasks lead us to three subsidiary assumptions that are necessary for profit maximization.
   a. The firm must decide *what* goods or services to produce. It cannot maximize its profit if it produces a good or service that cannot be sold at a high enough price to cover costs.
   b. The firm must decide *how* to produce each good at the lowest possible cost. That is, each firm must *minimize its costs* in light of the constraints imposed on it by available technology and its environment. Because a firm's profit is by definition the excess of its revenue over all of its costs, it should be obvious that it is impossible to *maximize* profit unless costs are *minimized*. Cost minimization does *not* mean that the firm is motivated to produce only cheap, low-quality output. Firms have a profit incentive to produce the level of quality that consumers are willing to pay for. Given that level of quality, however, profit maximization requires that costs be as low as possible.
   c. The firm must choose the *quantity* of production that assures it the greatest possible profit.
2. We assume that firms, like consumers, calculate production in terms of *flows* of goods or services offered for sale *per time period*.
3. We assume that firms also consider the *future* in their decisions. This has several important implications that will not be used immediately. It is a good idea to bear in mind, however, that consideration of the future implies that if firms expect prices of inputs or of their product to rise over time, they will have an incentive to speed up their purchases of inputs and slow down their sales of output. (What do you think this implies for the conservation of natural resources?) The assumption that firms consider the future also implies that actions that may increase current profits while damaging prospects for future sales, such as deceiving consumers about product quality, may not be consistent with overall profit maximization. What do you think this implies for consumer protection in a market economy?

Competition defines a type of market that individual firms can enter or leave at will and in which individual firms have no direct control over the price at which they sell their output.

Unrestricted entry means that no factors other than production costs hinder a firm from deciding to produce a good or service.

A price taker is a firm that has no direct control over the price at which it sells its output. All competitive firms are price takers.

Limitations on Producers

Our second set of assumptions of supply theory concern limitations on producers' behavior.

1. From now on, unless we explicitly state the contrary, we will assume that firms *compete* for customers' business with other firms producing the same or a similar product. **Competition** means that any firm is free to produce any good or service it chooses in the pursuit of its profit objective. Competition implies that each firm has **unrestricted entry** into (and out of) an industry; that is, there are no legal or other barriers to prevent a firm from producing a good or service. Competition also imposes limitations on firms. The most important of these restrictions is that every firm acts as a **price taker,** which means that a firm has no discretion over the price that it charges for its output. Competition from other firms assures that if a firm were to charge more than the market price for what it sells, it would lose customers to other firms. If it were to charge less, it would fail to earn the largest possible profit because it would be selling for too little.

2. We assume that a firm's pursuit of profit and minimum costs is limited by available technology. Available technology defines the maximum output that a firm can obtain from the inputs available to it.

Profit, Marginal Cost, and the Law of Supply

Method of Analysis

Once again, as with the theory of demand, we will examine the forces that influence a firm's production decisions *one at a time.* Using the *ceteris paribus* assumption, we will first analyze the relationship between the price of a good or service and the amount firms offer for sale. After deriving this relationship—the supply curve itself—we will expand our understanding of supply by analyzing the effects of *other* forces on *shifts* in the supply curve.

The **law of supply** states that, *ceteris paribus,* price increases lead a firm to supply more of a good or service whereas price reductions lead a firm to supply

less. To see why this should be so, we have to understand something about a firm's production function and the way a firm's *opportunity cost* of supplying its product varies as its output level changes. (You may wish to refresh your memory regarding the definition of opportunity cost in chapter 1.) In this chapter, we will limit our discussion to the **short run,** which is the period of time in which firms adjust their supply decisions without entering or leaving a market. In the short run, a firm views some of its decisions as unchangeable. For example, it may own, or have a long-term lease on, its plant. This means that the costs of maintaining the plant, paying interest on funds borrowed to finance it, or rent on the lease must be paid whether or not the firm produces any output. Thus, in the short run, a firm does not face the option of leaving an industry permanently. Moreover, in the short run, firms outside an industry do not make long-term commitments of plant and equipment or other major costs that entry into the industry would require. It follows that in the short run, the number of firms in an industry is fixed.

Remember, we have assumed that each firm seeks to minimize its production costs. This means that a firm must choose the appropriate scale of operations as measured by the size or quantity of its plant (buildings) and equipment. Since firms do not enter or leave an industry in the short run, the costs of paying for plant and equipment (rental costs, interest on funds borrowed to buy them) are **fixed costs,** or costs that do not vary with output. While this may seem strange to you at first, fixed costs are not opportunity costs of output in the short run because there is nothing the firm can do in the short run to make this component of total costs larger or smaller. Therefore, fixed costs do not influence short-run supply decisions. Accountants treat fixed costs as costs when they calculate a firm's profits. We will follow this accounting convention in calculating a firm's profit.

In the short run, a firm increases or reduces its output by adding or subtracting workers or overtime hours and raw materials to its inputs. These inputs involve **variable costs,** or costs that can be changed as output changes. Adding or discarding plant and equipment is usually very costly. Changes in plant and equipment often take a long time compared to

*The **law of supply** states that the quantity of a good or service a firm desires to sell is greater the higher the price of the good or service, cet. par.*

*The **short run** is the period of time in which firms adjust their output by using more or less inputs but not by entering or leaving the market for a good or service. Over the short run, some of a firm's costs are fixed costs.*

***Fixed costs** are those costs that do not change when a firm adjusts its output.*

***Variable costs** are those costs that change when a firm adjusts its output.*

changing work hours and raw material inputs. Therefore, we assume that changes in plant and equipment are impossible in the short run.

An Example

To understand a firm's decision to supply more or less output, imagine that you are in charge of a firm and your goal is to make your firm as profitable as possible. Let's suppose that you have already chosen the most efficient, lowest cost production methods but that you are not sure whether your firm is producing enough. Because you are a price taker, you need not worry about *selling* output. You can sell all you want at the going market price. Why not increase output until it is physically impossible to produce any more? Wouldn't that lead to profit maximization? Not likely.

To see why increasing production to the limit would not assure an increase in your profit, we have to examine what happens to your opportunity cost and revenue when output changes. *Profit will increase anytime revenue increases more than cost or falls less than cost.* It is easy to see what happens to revenue when a price taker's sales change. If you sell one more unit, revenue increases by an amount equal to the market price. Suppose your firm, the A-1 Balloon Company, produces toy balloons and the market price of balloons is $15 per gross (twelve dozen balloons). Thus, when output and sales expand by one gross, revenue grows by $15. Similarly, if you reduce output, revenue will fall by $15 for each gross that is not sold. The change in revenue that accompanies a change in output and sales is called **marginal revenue** or **incremental revenue**. Marginal revenue defines the *additional* sales revenue a firm derives from a small *addition* (increment) to its production or the *reduction* in sales revenue from a small *reduction* in output. For a price taker, *marginal revenue is equivalent to the price of a unit of output.* The smallest amount of output you think about in your balloon factory is a gross. Therefore, your marginal revenue is the price of a gross of balloons, or $15. Since the market price is not affected by your firm's output (your firm is too small), *marginal* revenue does not change as output changes. We can summarize the relationship between marginal revenue and price for a competitive (price-taking) firm with the following simple expression, in

which MR stands for marginal revenue and P stands for the market price of a good or service sold by the firm:

$$MR \equiv P.$$

Pay careful attention to the use of the symbol $\equiv$ between MR and P rather than the symbol $=$. The symbol $\equiv$ indicates a relationship of *identity,* whereas the symbol $=$ indicates a relationship of *equality.* The identity relationship ($\equiv$) means that the two variables MR and P are *the same thing* for a competitive firm. That is, there is *no* circumstance in which they are *not* equal. As you will see shortly, use of the equality relationship ($=$) signifies that two variables are equal to each other *under certain conditions.* However, if the specified conditions do not hold, then the variables take on different values. Failure to distinguish carefully between an identity relationship and an equality relationship can create a great deal of confusion in understanding important economic relationships.

The relationship between *cost* and output is likely to be different. For a typical firm, output and cost are not likely to increase proportionately with each other. At very low levels of output, it may be difficult to use workers efficiently. As production increases, it becomes possible to take advantage of the opportunity to let workers specialize in particular tasks. Therefore, the cost per unit of output may actually fall as output increases when a firm is not producing very much. However, we can be reasonably sure that the cost of producing additional units of output does not fall indefinitely. If it did, the largest firms would always have lower costs than smaller firms and would take over all of the sales in an industry.

Because most industries have a number of firms, it is safe to assume that costs tend to increase more rapidly than output at the existing level of production for a typical firm. Therefore, we will assume that you are already producing a quantity of balloons such that if you wish to produce more, your cost per unit of output will increase. With your existing balloon factory and equipment, you can increase production by hiring additional workers and purchasing more raw materials. But how do you use the workers? Suppose you are currently running two eight-hour shifts a day.

Marginal, or incremental, revenue is the change in revenue that a firm receives when it produces (and sells) more or less output.

Marginal, or incremental, cost is the change in costs that occurs when a firm produces more or less output.

Table 4.1   Balloon production, input, and cost: An example

Weekly production	Labor (hours worked)	Raw material (pounds of rubber)	Cost of labor and raw materials*			Marginal cost per gross
			Labor	Rubber	Total	
100 gross	210	50.0	$1,050	$50.00	$1,100.00	$11.00
110 gross	220	55.0	1,100	55.00	1,155.00	5.50
120 gross	240	61.0	1,200	61.00	1,261.00	10.60
130 gross	261	67.0	1,305	67.00	1,372.00	11.10
140 gross	286	73.2	1,430	73.20	1,503.20	13.12
150 gross	320	80.5	1,600	80.50	1,680.50	17.73
160 gross	360	88.6	1,800	88.60	1,888.60	20.81

*Labor costs $5 per hour, and rubber costs $1 per pound.

You can increase production in two ways. One is to make each shift larger, adding more workers to each assembly line. For example, you could speed the line up and have more people operating the machinery, checking the balloons for leaks, and placing them in packages. Unfortunately, if you increase your work force by, say, 10 percent, balloon production is likely to grow by less than 10 percent. Why? Because you are crowding more workers around each machine, and they are becoming less productive. Moreover, waste will increase as the assembly line speeds up.

Table 4.1 will clarify the relationship between balloon production and cost. The first column shows balloon production ranging from a low of 100 gross per week up to 160 gross per week. The next two columns show the labor and raw material required to produce each different level of output. The fourth and fifth columns show the costs of these inputs, assuming labor costs $5 per hour and rubber costs $1 per pound. This provides all the information needed to calculate the short-run opportunity cost of balloon production. If you use your calculator, you will see that if you increase balloon production from 120 gross to 130 gross per week (8.3 percent), you must increase your use of labor by 21 hours (8.8 percent) and your use of rubber by 6.0 pounds (9.8 percent). For every increase in production beyond that, output grows by a smaller proportion than the required increase in labor and raw material used. Consequently, total labor and material *costs* also grow more rapidly than output.

The last column of table 4.1 shows what happens to the opportunity cost of producing *additional* output. This cost is called the **marginal cost** or **incremental cost** of balloon production, which is the change in total costs associated with a change in total output. To see how marginal cost is calculated, take any two rows and notice how total labor and raw material cost changes when output changes. For example, if you are currently producing 120 gross balloons per week, increasing output to 130 gross would result in an increased cost of $111.00, or *about $11.10 per additional gross*. Similarly, reducing output from 130 gross to 120 gross per week would provide a cost *reduction* of $11.10 for each gross that production declines. It is clear that marginal cost rises as output increases. *Marginal cost rises with output increases because total labor and material costs rise more than in proportion to increases in production; when production falls, labor and material costs decline in greater proportion.* This is called the **principle of increasing cost.** (Increasing marginal cost for a competitive firm is due to what is often called the principle, or law, of diminishing returns.)

*The **principle of increasing cost** is the assumption that a firm's production costs increase proportionately more rapidly than*   *its output does. This means that marginal cost increases as output increases in the short run.*

Table 4.2   A-1 Balloon Company marginal cost, marginal revenue, profit, and quantity supplied

Weekly production	Marginal revenue per gross (price)[a]	Marginal cost per gross[b]	Variable cost[c]	Fixed cost[d]	Revenue (price × production)	Profit (revenue − total cost)[e]
100 gross		$11.00	$1,100.00	$200	$1,500	$200.00
	$15	5.50				
110 gross			1,155.00	200	1,650	295.00
	15	10.60				
120 gross			1,261.00	200	1,800	339.00
	15	11.10				
130 gross			1,372.00	200	1,950	378.00
	15	13.12				
140 gross			1,503.20	200	2,100	396.80
	15	17.73				
150 gross			1,680.50	200	2,250	369.50
	15	20.81				
160 gross			1,888.60	200	2,400	311.40

[a]Marginal, or incremental, revenue is the *change* in revenue that a firm receives when it produces (and sells) more or less output.
[b]Marginal, or incremental, cost is the *change* in cost that occurs when a firm produces more or less output.
[c]Variable costs are those costs that do change when a firm adjusts its output, either in the short run or the long run.
[d]Fixed costs are those costs that do not change when a firm adjusts its output.
[e]Total cost is variable cost plus fixed cost.

Adding more labor to each of your two production shifts is only one way to increase output. A second possibility is to add another shift. By adding another shift, it may be possible to avoid some of the costs outlined above. However, other costs will arise. For example, by operating three shifts a day, you reduce the time available for maintenance of machinery. This will result in more downtime and wasted wages as workers sit around with nothing to do. Moreover, you will probably have to pay a premium to persuade workers to take the night shift. Therefore, the principle of increasing cost is likely to have an impact on your production decisions no matter what you do. You can reduce its effect on your profits by choosing the cheapest way to increase output, but you cannot avoid it entirely.

Marginal Cost, Profit, and Supply in the Short Run

How will your supply decision depend on the production and cost data shown in table 4.1? To answer this question, we have to see how your *profit* is affected by increases or reductions in output. The profit at each output level is shown in table 4.2. In order to calculate profit, we need information on revenue, or the value of sales, and *total* costs. Table 4.1 contains information only on *variable costs* of production.

Depreciation that occurs whether or not you produce anything and payments on debt and maintenance that must be carried out even if the machinery is not operating are fixed costs, which are not shown in table 4.1. We will show that although fixed costs are subtracted from revenue to calculate profit, profit *maximization* does not depend on fixed costs.

Profit is the difference between a firm's revenue and all of its costs. Even so, in the short run, only variable costs and price are relevant in determining how much the firm will produce or whether it will produce any output at all.

To complete our example, let us assume that fixed costs equal $200 per week. Weekly production, marginal revenue, marginal cost, total cost, and profit are all shown in table 4.2. The data on production, marginal cost, and variable cost come from table 4.1.

Marginal revenue is the market price of $15 per gross, total revenue is price times production, and fixed costs, as noted, equal $200 per week.

To determine the amount of production that maximizes profit, remember that profit increases whenever revenue grows more than or falls less than cost. Variable cost—by definition—grows when output rises and declines when output falls. *Marginal cost depends only on variable costs.* Fixed cost—by definition—does not change with output. Therefore, only variable cost and marginal cost along with price determine the output level at which profit is largest.

In table 4.2, at any output less than 140 gross per week, marginal revenue (price per gross) is greater than marginal cost. Marginal cost rises from $5.50 per gross when output is increased from 100 gross to 110 gross up to $13.12 when output grows from 130 to 140 gross per week. Since marginal revenue is $15 per gross, profit rises as production grows from 100 gross balloons per week up to 140 gross per week. If weekly production grows to 150 gross, however, marginal cost exceeds $15 and profit declines. Table 4.2 shows that you will maximize your profit by choosing an output that is in the neighborhood of 140 gross balloons per week. As you raise your production past 140 gross, marginal cost will exceed $15 per gross so that increasing production adds more to cost than to revenue and profit begins to decline. Therefore, in order to maximize profit when balloons sell for $15 per gross, you must produce approximately 140 gross balloons per week. This leads to the greatest difference between your revenue and costs. This level of output is shown in figure 4.1.

Now that we have thoroughly analyzed how a firm might maximize its profit, we should repeat that our calculation of profit from the *economist's* point of view will not always yield the same figure as measuring profit from an *accountant's* point of view. *Accounting* profit normally is aimed at providing a figure for tax purposes. Some of a firm's opportunity costs may not be deductible for tax purposes. The simplest example would be in the case of a firm owned by a single proprietor. The proprietor has an opportunity cost—what he or she could earn in another firm or industry as a salaried employee. This opportunity cost must be subtracted from revenue to obtain the economist's definition of profit because the proprietor's time is a real

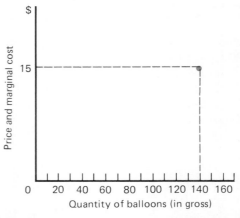

Figure 4.1   A-1 Balloon Company's supply when price is $15 per gross

input into the production process and it has a positive value. However, the accountant would *not* show this cost on the firm's profit and loss statement. The reason is this: If the proprietor claimed the salary he or she could earn elsewhere as a cost for tax purposes, then it would also have to be shown as part of the owner's income for tax purposes. The two items would cancel out, and therefore there is no point in showing them on the firm's profit and loss statement and on the proprietor's income tax forms.

Before going on, it would be a good idea to review what you as a price taker would have to do to find your profit-maximizing output level. If you have precise data as in table 4.2, you will increase or reduce output until marginal cost exactly equals price. Suppose you do not have precise knowledge of your cost data. You can still maximize profit through trial and error. Essentially all you need to do is experiment with higher or lower output levels. If gradually increasing output each week or month leads to higher profit, continue to increase production until profit stops growing. That is the output level at which marginal cost equals price. *To summarize, if marginal revenue exceeds marginal cost, then increasing output will raise profit; if marginal cost exceeds marginal revenue, then reducing output will raise profit; at the level of output where marginal revenue equals marginal cost, profits are maximized.*

The supply curve for the A-1 Balloon Company shows how the quantity of balloons supplied varies as the price rises or falls, *cet. par.* The example described in tables 4.1 and 4.2 provides the information needed to derive the supply curve. If the price of balloons rises to $18 per gross, you will no longer maximize profit by limiting your production to 140 gross per week. While the $3 increase in price will raise the profit from selling 140 gross by $420, to $816.80, your profit will be $819.50 if you increase production to 150 gross per week. Why? Because the marginal cost of producing 10 gross more balloons is $17.73 per gross, while marginal revenue has risen to $18 per gross. Actually, your profit will continue to rise as output grows beyond 150 gross per week because marginal cost remains less than $18 until weekly output grows to between 150 and 160 gross.

To make sure you understand why the quantity of balloons supplied will rise, calculate the *profit* column in table 4.2 with price equal to $18 instead of $15. Next, see what happens to profit and the profit-maximizing output if the price of balloons should *fall* to $14. If you *thoroughly* understand the example, you should see that the analysis still applies. Profit maximization requires that output be *reduced* so long as marginal cost is *greater* than marginal revenue. Thus, if the price declines to $12.50 you should reduce output to a level below 130 gross per week but above 120 gross. If you like, mark the profit-maximizing quantities supplied at $12.50 and $18 on figure 4.1. You now have three points on the A-1 Balloon Company supply curve.

A general rule for deriving the short-run supply curve for any firm should now be apparent. The two additional points we suggested that you mark in figure 4.1 plus the point at the price of $15 already drawn there map out the *marginal cost* of three different output levels, ranging from production of between 120 and 130 gross per week up to between 150 and 160 gross per week. If you were to plot the marginal cost of each output level, you would also be drawing the *short-run supply* curve for the A-1 Balloon Company. *This marginal cost curve is the firm's short-run supply curve, as long as it is producing any output,*

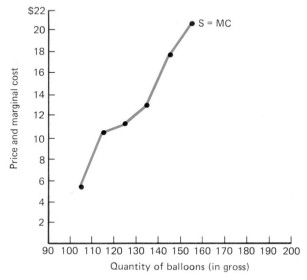

Figure 4.2   Short-run supply curve and marginal cost curve of A-1 Balloon Company
Marginal cost (measured along the vertical axis) comes from the third column of table 4.2.

because it answers the question: How much output will the firm desire to supply at various market prices? As long as the principle of increasing cost applies, the firm's short-run supply curve will be a positively (upward) sloped curve like that shown in figure 4.2 for the A-1 Balloon Company. In other words, the more the firm produces, the higher will be its marginal cost. This profit maximizing relationship between marginal cost and marginal revenue shows why, with a higher price, the firm will be willing to produce and sell more than with a lower price. In the next section we will explain at what price the firm would stop producing balloons rather than produce the output indicated by the marginal cost curve.

Average Cost, Marginal Cost, and Supply

In the preceding section we showed that when a firm maximizes its profit, it chooses a level of output such that marginal cost equals marginal revenue. For competitive (price-taking) firms, marginal revenue is identical to the market price of the good or service

Average cost is the cost a firm incurs per unit of output.

Average variable cost (AVC) is variable cost divided by the quantity of output.

Average total cost (ATC) is total cost divided by the quantity of output.

Table 4.3   A-1 Balloon Company marginal cost, average variable cost, and average total cost

Weekly production	Variable cost	Marginal cost	Average variable cost[a]	Total cost[b]	Average total cost[c]
		$11.00			
100 gross	$1,100.00		$11.00	$1,300.00	$13.00
		5.50			
110 gross	1,155.00		10.50	1,355.00	12.32
		10.60			
120 gross	1,261.00		10.51	1,461.00	12.18
		11.10			
130 gross	1,372.00		10.56	1,572.00	12.09
		13.12			
140 gross	1,503.20		10.74	1,703.20	12.17
		17.73			
150 gross	1,680.50		11.20	1,880.50	12.54
		20.81			
160 gross	1,888.60		11.81	2,088.60	13.05

[a]Average variable cost is variable cost divided by weekly production.
[b]Total cost is variable cost plus fixed cost ($200).
[c]Average total cost is total cost divided by weekly production.

produced. *Therefore, the profit-maximizing output level for a competitive firm satisfies the condition*

$$MC = P,$$

where MC stands for marginal cost and P for price. Notice carefully that we have used the *equality* sign in the relationship describing the competitive firm's profit-maximizing output level. This is because price and marginal cost are not *identically* equal to each other, as are price and marginal revenue for a competitive firm. The variables P and MC are two entirely different variables; *they are equal to each other in value only when the firm has found the profit-maximizing output level*. This is an example of the distinction between an *equality* and an *identity* that we said would be very important in fully understanding crucial economic relationships.

There is something missing from our analysis of how a competitive firm chooses its profit-maximizing level of production. While we have shown what a firm will do to maximize its profit, we have not shown in general that the level of the firm's profit is positive. In our example, the A-1 Balloon Company is earning positive profits and not a loss. However, it would be nice to be able to show in a diagram under what circumstances a firm will actually earn a profit when it chooses a level of output that satisfies the condition

MC = P. In order to do this, we need to introduce an additional measure of cost, **average cost,** which is simply the cost incurred by the firm per unit of output. Actually, two measures of average cost are of interest to us. One of them is found by dividing variable cost by the output produced to obtain **average variable cost** (AVC). The other is defined by dividing the firm's total cost (variable cost plus fixed cost) by the output produced to obtain **average total cost** (ATC). Both cost measures are useful in determining whether the firm is earning a profit and whether it pays to produce anything at all rather than to shut down entirely.

Table 4.3 is based on table 4.2 and shows A-1 Balloon Company's average variable cost and average total cost for levels of weekly production ranging from 100 to 160 gross balloons per week. So that you do not have to flip pages back and forth to see marginal cost (MC), AVC, and ATC, all together, we also show MC in table 4.3, and all three costs are graphed in figure 4.3. Figure 4.3 also has a horizontal line at $15, indicating that A-1 Balloon Company can sell all the output it wants to at $15 per gross. It maximizes profit by going to the point where the horizontal line at $15 crosses the MC curve. It is clear in figure 4.3 that A-1 Balloon Company is earning a profit because the price line lies above the ATC curve. For each unit that it sells, it receives $15, and when it maximizes profit by producing approximately 140 gross balloons, it incurs an average total cost of $12.18 per gross. Although we cannot tell precisely from figure 4.3, let us assume that the profit-maximizing output is exactly 140 gross balloons. A-1 Balloon Company's profit can therefore be calculated as follows: Total revenue ($15 × 140 = $2,100) − total cost ($1,703.20) = $396.80.

Suppose that the market price of balloons were to fall to a level below $15. The price of balloons could, for example, fall below the lowest average total cost at which it is possible to produce them. What should A-1 Balloon Company do? If P is less than ATC, it is impossible to earn a profit. For example, if the market price of balloons should fall to only $11, it would be almost $1 less than the lowest average total cost shown in table 4.3. However, if A-1 Balloon Company produced an output such that MC = P, it would not shut down entirely but produce an output of approximately 120 gross per week.

Table 4.3 and figure 4.3 do not give sufficiently detailed information for us to know exactly where marginal cost actually equals $11. Let us suppose that it is at a level of production equal to 120 gross. Total cost is $1,461 at that output. In other words, if A-1 Balloon Company behaves according to the MC = P rule, it will have a total revenue of $11 x 120 = $1,320 and a total cost of $1,461. Its loss will be $1,461 (total cost) minus $1,320 (total revenue), or $141. Should A-1 Balloon Company produce this level of output? The answer is clearly *yes* because if it were to shut down and not produce anything at all, it would still have to pay its fixed cost of $200 per week. In other words, the MC = P rule still applies because it describes how the firm can *minimize its loss* as long as total variable costs are covered even if the price is too low to allow a profit.

We can readily explain why it would be a good idea for A-1 Balloon Company to continue production (although at a somewhat lower level) if the price should fall from $15 to $11. Note that the average *variable* cost when production equals 120 gross per week is $10.51 per gross. Since the AVC is *less* than price, even when the price is as low as $11 per gross, the firm can earn a surplus over and above the costs

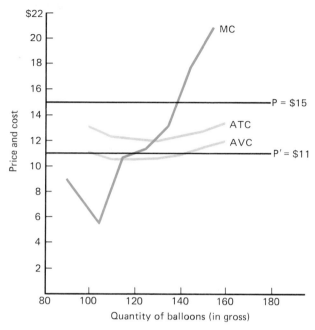

Figure 4.3   Average cost and A-1 Balloon Company's short-run supply curve
Average total cost (ATC) equals total cost divided by output. Average variable cost (AVC) equals variable cost divided by output. Because it is possible to use workers more efficiently as production increases when output is low, both AVC and ATC fall initially. However, the principle of increasing cost implies that they will eventually increase. The marginal cost (MC) curve shows that *additional* cost per *additional* unit of output grows as production increases.

Initially, MC is less than both AVC and ATC. This means that the *additional* cost of producing one more unit is *less than* the average cost of producing each unit. Consequently, *average* cost *falls* over the range of output where average cost is greater than marginal cost. The principle of increasing cost implies that MC must eventually exceed (rise above) both AVC and ATC. When this happens, the *additional* cost of producing one more unit is *greater than* the average cost of producing each unit. Consequently, *average* cost *rises* over the range of output where it is less than marginal cost. Since both AVC and ATC fall while MC is beneath them and rise while MC is above them, MC crosses both AVC and ATC at their lowest points.

As long as the market price (P) is above the lowest point on the ATC curve, the firm will earn a profit by producing a quantity of output such that MC = P. If P is less than ATC but above minimum AVC, the firm's revenue will exceed its variable cost if it produces a quantity of output such that MC = P. This surplus can help pay its fixed cost. Thus the firm will *minimize its loss* in the short run by producing a quantity of output such that MC = P, if P is less than ATC but greater than minimum AVC. However, if P should fall *below* minimum AVC, the firm will minimize its loss by shutting down and not producing anything. *Thus, MC defines the firm's short-run supply curve so long as P exceeds minimum AVC.*

*The **shutdown point** is a firm's minimum (lowest) average variable cost; if the price falls lower than the shutdown point, the firm will not produce anything.*

of labor and raw material when it behaves according to the MC = P rule. This surplus, which is $1,320 (total revenue) less $1,261 (variable cost), or $59, is income that the firm would not receive if it shut down entirely. That is why its loss is only $141 instead of $200 when it continues operations instead of shutting down.[1]

If the market price of balloons were to fall still farther, say, to $10, however, it would no longer pay to continue production. A price of $10 is less than the lowest AVC shown in table 4.3 or figure 4.3. If the price falls below minimum AVC, the firm can no longer earn a surplus over its expenditures on labor and raw material. Therefore, it would minimize its loss by shutting down and not producing anything whenever price falls below the lowest AVC it can achieve. Then its loss would be minimized at $200, its fixed cost. If the firm were to produce any balloons at a price less than minimum AVC, its loss would rise above $200 because it would be spending more on labor and rubber than it would receive from selling its product.

Thus, knowledge of AVC and ATC provides additional information about the firm's short-run supply curve. We can now see that the MC curve is the firm's short-run supply curve *as long as price exceeds minimum AVC.* For prices below minimum AVC, the marginal cost curve does not indicate how much the firm will offer for sale because the firm can minimize its loss by shutting down when the price falls that low. If a firm does not shut down when the price is less than AVC, it must incur all of its fixed cost in addition to variable costs not covered by its sales revenue. This is clearly a higher cost outcome than incurring fixed cost alone. Therefore, it is better to shut down. Because it does not pay a firm to produce anything at a price below its minimum AVC, we call the lowest point on the AVC curve the firm's **shutdown point.**

Before concluding this discussion of a firm's average costs, we should pay some attention to the shape of the AVC and ATC curves and to the geometric relationship between the marginal cost and average cost curves depicted in figure 4.3. First, why do the AVC

and ATC curves have a shape roughly like a bowl—higher at each end and lower in between? One reason why average total cost falls is that fixed cost per unit of output declines as output grows. Moreover, with a fixed amount of plant and equipment but very low output and employment levels, workers are not very effectively used in the production process. Each individual worker has to perform too many different tasks. As employment increases, workers can specialize in performing fewer tasks but doing them better. Gains from specialization as output grows tend to reduce average variable costs and therefore average total costs. This also reduces the marginal cost of producing balloons as output grows initially. Thus, the marginal cost of producing the first 100 gross balloons is higher than the marginal cost of producing the next 20 gross balloons. However, with a fixed amount of equipment, as the number of workers continues to increase, the additional output produced by each additional worker eventually declines. This is indicated by the fact that the marginal cost curve reaches a low point between 100 and 110 gross balloons and then begins to rise. With a fixed amount of plant and equipment, workers will eventually get in one anothers' way, and the principle of increasing cost operates. This means that despite declining fixed cost per unit of output and initial gains from specialization by workers, average costs will eventually increase.

The point at which gains from increased worker specialization and other cost-reducing aspects of increased production become overwhelmed by the principle of increasing cost is most precisely indicated by the marginal cost curve. The point at which the principle of increasing cost overwhelms the cost-reducing effects of increased output is the point at which marginal cost begins to increase.

The geometric relationship between the marginal cost and average cost curves is very interesting, and it illustrates a general pattern that always holds true. Initially, MC is less than both AVC and ATC. This means that the *additional* cost of producing one more unit is *less than* the average cost of producing each unit. Consequently, *average* cost *falls* over the range of output where average cost is greater than marginal cost. The principle of increasing cost implies that average cost must eventually rise and that MC must eventually exceed (rise above) both AVC and ATC. When this happens, the *additional* cost of producing one more unit is *greater than* the average cost of producing each unit. Consequently, *average* cost *rises* over the range of output where it is less than marginal cost. Since both AVC and ATC fall while MC is beneath them and rise while MC is above them, MC crosses both AVC and ATC at their lowest points.

Since we will refer to the relationship between marginal cost and average cost many times, it is important to establish it firmly in your mind. To help, we will state it once again, using symbols.

Relationship between marginal and average cost

When MC < ATC, then ATC is falling.

When MC < AVC, then AVC is falling.

When MC > ATC, then ATC is rising.

When MC > AVC, then AVC is rising.

When MC = ATC, then ATC is at its lowest point.

When MC = AVC, then AVC is at its lowest point.

The relationship between a marginal curve and an average curve applies anytime marginal and average concepts are compared. For example, consider your grades each term. Your marginal performance in college is indicated by the grades you receive each quarter or semester. Your average performance is indicated by the mean (average) grades you receive throughout your college career. Suppose you entered this term with an average grade (in numerical terms) of 3.0 and this term you earn a 4.0. Your *marginal* performance (4.0) is above your *average* performance (3.0), and your overall grade average will rise above 3.0 as a result of this quarter or semester's results. Remember these relationships, and much of what follows will be easier to understand.

Elasticity of Supply

Just as with a demand curve, it is very helpful to have quantitative measures of the steepness of a supply curve. As we learned in our discussion of demand, clear thinking about the economy requires us to distinguish between a change in the quantity supplied and a change or shift in the supply curve. The reason is that we are interested not only in the general, positive relationship between the price of a good or service and the quantity supplied but also in *how much* the quantity supplied responds to a given price increase. Again, the slope of a supply curve provides quantitative information, as it does for a demand curve. However, for the same reason that the slope of a demand curve may provide misleading information about price responsiveness, it is desirable to quantify the supply relationship with an elasticity.

The **elasticity of supply** is defined in the same way as the elasticity of demand. Exactly as with demand, a **change in the quantity supplied** refers to a change in the quantity of a good or service firms wish to sell *due solely* to a change in its price, *cet. par.* This is the percentage change in quantity supplied along a supply curve divided by the percentage change in price. We can develop a formula for the elasticity of supply using the symbol ϵ_s, similar to the various formulas developed for demand elasticities:

$$\epsilon_s \equiv (\Delta Q / \Delta P) \times (\overline{P}/\overline{Q})$$

$$\equiv \frac{\% \text{ change in quantity supplied}}{\% \text{ change in product price}},$$

where Q refers to the quantity *supplied* and $\overline{P}$ and $\overline{Q}$ denote average price and average quantity.

The elasticity of a firm's supply curve tells us how rapidly the firm's marginal cost increases as output grows. Essentially, it reflects how severely the principle of increasing cost limits the firm's ability to expand its output profitably in response to an increase in the price of the good or service it sells. When a firm's supply curve is relatively inelastic, marginal cost grows relatively rapidly in proportion to the growth of output. Of course, if the firm wishes to reduce its

A change in supply of a good or service is a shift in the supply curve that results when a variable other than the price of the good or service changes.

Table 4.4	Estimated price elasticities of supply	

| | Price elasticity | |
Commodity	Short run	Long run
Green lima beans	0.10	1.70
Green snap beans	0.15	∞*
Cabbage	0.36	1.20
Carrots	0.14	1.00
Cucumbers	0.29	2.20
Lettuce	0.03	0.16
Onions	0.34	1.00
Green peas	0.31	4.40
Green peppers	0.07	0.26
Tomatoes	0.16	0.90
Watermelons	0.23	0.48
Beets	0.13	1.00
Cantaloupes	0.02	0.04
Cauliflower	0.14	1.10
Celery	0.14	0.95
Eggplant	0.16	0.34
Kale (Va. only)	0.20	0.23
Spinach	0.20	4.70
Shallots (La. only)	0.12	0.31

Source: From Nerlove, M., and W. Addison, "Statistical Estimation of Long-Run Elasticities of Supply and Demand," in *Journal of Farm Economics,* November. Copyright © 1958 American Agricultural Economics Association. Reprinted by permission.

*According to Nerlove and Addison, this estimate holds only for a limited range of output.

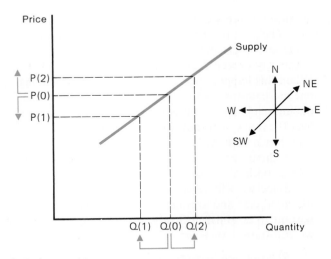

Figure 4.4 Increase and decrease in the quantity supplied of a good or service by an industry
An increase in the quantity supplied is a northeast movement along the supply curve due to a price increase. A reduction in the quantity supplied is a southwest movement along the supply curve due to a price decrease. The industry's supply curve shown in this figure is derived by adding up the quantities each firm offers for sale at each price.

marginal cost, it can do so relatively rapidly with only a small reduction in output if the marginal cost curve is relatively inelastic. If the marginal cost curve is relatively elastic, then marginal cost changes by a relatively small amount in proportion to changes in the quantity produced by a firm. Table 4.4 provides estimates of short-run supply elasticities for different agricultural products, which range from 0.02 for cantaloupes to 0.36 for cabbage. The table also includes long-run supply elasticities, which are always at least as great and often much greater than the short-run supply elasticities. The reasons for the difference between short-run and long-run supply elasticities are explained in the appendix to this chapter and in chapter 7.

Factors that Shift Supply

The distinction between movements along a given supply curve and a change in the supply relationship follows the terminology we developed for the demand curve. When things other than the price change, there results a **change in supply,** or a **shift in the supply curve,** which means that producers wish to sell more or less than before at a given market price. Figure 4.4 represents the short-run supply curve for all of the firms in an industry producing a certain good or service. It is obtained by adding up the amount each firm wants to sell at each price. It summarizes what has been said about the supply curve and reminds us of how a change in price affects the quantity supplied, *cet. par.*

Shifts in supply result from changes in anything that affects the minimum cost a firm must incur to produce a given level of output or, equivalently, the maximum output a firm can produce for a given cost. Thus, an increase in supply results from a change in a firm's environment that permits it to produce a given level of output at a lower cost or to produce more output without spending more on inputs. Any change that affects the opportunity cost of producing a given quantity of output for sale will cause a change in supply. An increase in the minimum opportunity cost of producing a given quantity of output will cause a reduction in supply. Some important factors that frequently result in supply shifts for individual firms or for the market as a whole include the following: (1) changes in technology, (2) changes in the skills of the work force, (3) changes in input prices, and (4) changes in prices of other goods a firm might produce or in expected future prices of the good produced. A fifth factor that would shift an industry's supply curve would be a change in the number of firms in the industry. Changes in supply are illustrated in figure 4.5

Changes in Technology

Improvements in technology have been generally accepted as one of the two most important forces responsible for the improved standard of living we enjoy compared to our great-great-great grandparents, say, 150 years ago. An improvement in technology is described by a change in the production function, which determines how much output firms can obtain for given quantities of inputs. When technology improves, fewer inputs are required, opportunity costs fall (given input prices), and the supply curve shifts downward and to the right as shown in figure 4.5. This represents an increase in supply (a rightward shift) because firms are willing to supply a greater quantity at each price, or equivalently, they will accept a lower price in return for providing a given quantity of output.

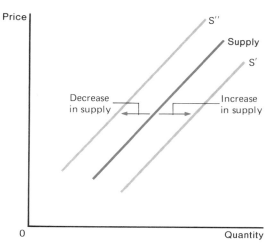

Figure 4.5   Increases and decreases in the supply curve for a good or service
An increase in supply is a rightward shift in the supply curve. A decrease in supply is a leftward shift in the supply curve. Changes in supply occur when one of the factors held constant when the supply curve was initially drawn (for example, technology) change.

A good example of this is pocket calculators. In the early 1960s students purchased slide rules for their math and science courses—pocket calculator technology as we know it today did not exist then. Slide rules cost about $25 and performed only a fraction of the operations that today's calculators can. Moreover, slide rules were much slower and far less accurate. Since calculators were first introduced, technology has improved very rapidly. A pocket calculator that sells for $25 today would have cost $150 or more fifteen years ago. This immense price reduction (occurring over a period of time when inflation increased the prices of most other products) resulted primarily from tremendous improvements in electronics technology.

Another striking example of the effects of changing technology on supply is in stereo equipment. Because of improvements that were almost inconceivable thirty years ago, a modest sum, say, $200, purchases audio equipment today that is by some measures ten times better than $200 worth of "hi-fi" equipment in the 1950s.[2]

Improved technology in both the pocket calculator and stereo industries pushed supply curves to the right. This increase in supply made more product available at all prices and the same amount available at a lower price.

Changes in Labor Skills

Probably the second most important cause of rightward-shifting supply curves in most industries has been improved labor force skills over the years. The average worker today—in industries as diverse as farming, computers, and automobile manufacturing—is much better educated than was the case fifty or one hundred years ago. There are many reasons for the rising level of education, and they will be discussed at greater length in chapter 14. At this point we can say that by and large, increased levels of schooling have made it easier for individuals to acquire greater skill levels in their jobs and have helped raise the productivity of the average worker. This has contributed to our rising standard of living in much the same way as has improved technology.

Changes in Input Prices

In 1973, a war between Israel and her Arab neighbors resulted in an oil boycott that sharply reduced the quantity of petroleum available to most of the world. Subsequently, the Organization of Oil Producing and Exporting Countries (OPEC) found it had substantially strengthened its market power and was able to increase the prices it charged to nations that imported petroleum. The result was a quick and severe leftward shift in the supply of goods and services that use petroleum and its derivatives—fuels, plastics, important chemicals such as synthetic fabrics and rubber, and many others. The higher prices that consumers were required to pay for these products resulted in a lower standard of living for millions of people and in economic adjustments that are still occurring today.[3] What can we expect to happen to many supplies of many goods and services as a result of the oil price decreases that occurred in 1985 and 1986?

Changes in Expected Future Prices

It may not be immediately obvious to you how *future* prices affect *current* supply. This relationship between the present and the future is extremely difficult to predict but important for the way the economy functions and for our economic welfare. When a good can be stored, the opportunity cost of *selling* it today may be greater than what must be given up to *produce* it today. For example, suppose you are a Texas rancher with oil wells on your property. If it costs you $15 to extract a barrel of oil for sale on today's market, you could sell it at a "profit" if today's price were, say, $20 per barrel. However, if you expect oil to sell for $30 per barrel a year from now, and if it costs, say, only $1 to store the oil for a year, your true opportunity cost of selling the oil today is $29, not $15. You would be losing, not profiting, by selling your oil at $20 today. In other words, an increase in the expected future price of oil or other storable commodity will result in a *leftward* shift in the supply of oil this year as producers place more in storage and offer less for current sale.

A moment's thought will show you that this action by suppliers, which is aimed only at increasing their profits, will also benefit consumers a year from now. Why? Because next year, oil buyers will face a *greater* supply than they would have faced if producers had not behaved as we have described. The leftward shift in the supply curve of oil this year cannot lead to higher profits for oil producers until the oil is actually sold.

The relationship between present and future supply has an important application to the problem of conservation of natural resources and to storage of strategically valuable commodities (including petroleum) as protection against short supplies during disasters such as a war. No one has perfect knowledge of our future demand for goods and services. However, business firms have a profit incentive to obtain accurate forecasts of future prices as a guide to how much output to supply today and how much to store for the future. At the present time, the federal government is engaged in a long-term program to purchase crude oil on the world market and place it in a strategic oil reserve. The idea underlying this program seems to be that private industry, left to its own devices, would not have the foresight to store the correct quantity of oil for future emergencies. This may be true. But what is the correct amount to store? What motivation does *today's* government, whose members are unlikely to hold office when and if an emergency need for oil arises, have to provide adequate reserves for the *future*? The costs are paid *now* in terms of government expenditures on other projects that must be foregone in order to finance purchases of oil for storage. These projects or expenditures, which must be foregone in order to purchase oil for storage, might provide more immediate benefit to voters than building a strategic oil reserve for the future. Thus, the benefits to government officials of storing oil will not be received by those who hold office now but will be reaped by others in the *future*.

On the other hand, a private firm that stores oil now can benefit from expected future price increases. Even if its present management or sole proprietor will be retired or dead by then, it will benefit now to the extent that the oil market "believes" that storage is a good idea. This is so because the oil is always *available* for sale and the firm's current assets and net worth will reflect the expected future value of the stored oil.

Time Horizons

Demand and supply are *flow* concepts referring to the quantities of goods bought and sold *over a specific period of time*. If we wish to look at a longer period of time within which production decisions are made (for instance, a month rather than a week), the supply curve will in general lie farther to the right, reflecting the larger quantities produced at each price. For example, our balloon company in tables 4.1 through 4.3 maximizes profit by producing approximately 140 gross balloons per *week*. If we extended the time horizon to a *month*, the profit-maximizing production would be about four times as large.

Extending the time horizon will in general also change the elasticity of supply. The reason is that the longer the period of time during which a firm may adjust to a change in the market price of the product it sells, the more opportunities the firm will have to expand or contract its output. For example, a clothing manufacturer can do relatively little to increase production without purchasing more cloth and, perhaps, hiring more workers. Thus, its ability to increase output if the time horizon is, say, six months is greater than if it is only a week. The same reasoning suggests that if the demand for clothing should fall, a firm that has already contracted to purchase a certain amount

Table 4.5   Factors that change quantity supplied and factors that change supply

Factor that increases quantity supplied (move producers up their supply curves)	Factor that reduces quantity supplied (move producers down their supply curves)	Factors that increase supply (shift the supply curve to the right, or downward)	Factors that reduce supply (shift the supply curve to the left, or upward)
1. An increase in current price	1. A reduction in current price	1. An improvement in technology	1. A deterioration in technology
		2. A reduction in the price of an input	2. An increase in the price of an input
		3. An expectation that price will fall in the future	3. An expectation that price will rise in the future
		4. A decline in the price of other goods a firm is capable of producing	4. An increase in the price of other goods a firm is capable of producing
		5. An increase (lengthening) of producers' time horizons	5. A reduction (shortening) of producers' time horizons

of cloth and hire a given number of workers to cut and sew it into clothing may not choose to reduce output much right away. It may pay the firm to produce the clothes as originally planned this season, even though its plans for a year hence will be to purchase less cloth, lay off some workers, and produce less output.

Before going on, study table 4.5, which contains a list of factors that change the quantity supplied or cause the entire supply curve to increase or decrease. A change in a product's price will result in a change in the quantity supplied in the same direction. A change in other factors, held constant when deriving a given supply curve, will cause supply to increase or decrease. An increase in supply means that producers

are willing to sell more at each price (a rightward shift in supply). Equivalently, an increase in supply means that producers require a lower price than before to induce them to sell a given quantity (a downward shift). The opposite holds true for a decrease in supply. If it is not clear to you how a change in the price of another good or service that a firm could produce shifts supply, work through question 5 at the end of this chapter.

Both the supply and demand concepts are necessary if we are to understand human behavior in the economy and the influence of government policies and business practices on production and consumption. The two concepts are linked in chapter 5, where the theory of demand and supply come together to determine the behavior of prices and output.

▶ Application of the Supply Relationship

The supply relationship—or law of supply—states that, *ceteris paribus,* producers respond to price changes by offering to sell more when the price rises and less when the price falls. The theory also states that, *ceteris paribus,* an increase in costs will shift the supply relationship by causing producers to offer to sell less at any given market price. Examples of supply theory in action occur every day in our economy. Next we describe one of these examples.

The Price and Supply of Oil

As noted earlier, in 1973 the Organization of Petroleum Exporting Countries began a series of sharp increases in oil prices. The increased costs to oil-importing nations had many dramatic effects on consumers and producers of goods that use petroleum as an input. Among those most affected by increases in the price of OPEC oil was the domestic petroleum industry in the United States.

Figure 4.6 shows the effects of an increase in OPEC's price on monthly production of oil in the United States. The supply curve of domestic oil slopes upward. According to figure 4.6, domestic producers can sell all of the oil they want as long as they do not charge more than the price at which United States oil users can purchase petroleum from OPEC. For example, suppose OPEC's pre-1973 price was $3 a barrel. Then, given cost and production conditions determining the United States supply curve, it would have been profitable for domestic producers to supply 9.2 million barrels of oil per day.

Figure 4.6 shows that when OPEC raises its price to, say, $12, it becomes profitable for domestic producers to raise their daily output from 9.2 to 10 million barrels. The increase in domestic production,

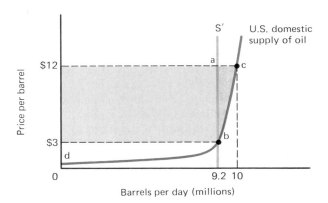

Figure 4.6   The effect of an increase in OPEC's price on domestic production of oil in the United States
The shaded area between the prices $12 and $3 and to the left of the vertical supply curve S′ represents increased rent to producers of the original quantity of oil after the price of oil rises from $3 to $12 and is equal to $82.8 million per day.

The shaded area abc represents rent received by the producers who increase the quantity of oil supplied in response to the price increase from $3 to $12.

800,000 barrels, represents oil that need not be imported from OPEC producers. Thus, in response to an increase in the price that OPEC demands for its oil, the supply curve of domestic oil tells us that United States producers will offer more oil from their wells for sale. The reduced dependence on imported oil that results from United States producers' supply response helps to limit the degree to which OPEC can profit from increasing the price it demands for its oil.

Where does the increase in the quantity of United States oil come from? Your first thought may be that there is only so much oil in the ground and that it is impossible to extract more than we already have. In fact, some people have argued that this is indeed the case—that the supply curve of domestic oil looks more like the vertical curve S′ in figure 4.6 than like the

Economic rent arises from the difference between the price of a good or service and its opportunity cost.

upward-sloping supply curve. The supply curve S' represents a situation in which there is *no* change in the quantity of domestic oil supplied in response to a change in its price. We describe this situation as a case in which the elasticity of supply is zero ($\epsilon_s = 0$). That is, an increase in price brings forth *no* increase in the quantity offered for sale.

There are two reasons why the elasticity of supply of oil is greater than zero. The first reason is that while it may be true that there is a limited amount of oil in the ground, we have not yet discovered all that is there. The higher oil's price, the greater is the reward to someone who discovers oil. Therefore, higher prices stimulate a greater search for new oil fields and more intensive drilling of existing fields. These are long-run considerations, however, which we are not treating in this chapter. Nevertheless, even in the short run (in which the number of oil wells is fixed), much can be done to increase oil output from existing wells. One way to achieve a short-run increase in the quantity of oil supplied, which is the situation depicted in figure 4.6., is to reopen wells that were capped before the OPEC price increases began in late 1973. These wells were not being used because they could not be operated profitably at a price of $3 per barrel. At $12 per barrel, many of these wells were worth reopening in 1974. In between the short-run activity of reopening old, capped wells and the long-run activity of drilling for new wells and exploring for new fields is the application of advanced technology to pumping more oil out of existing wells.

In short, a major reason why the supply of oil is upward sloping ($\epsilon_s > 0$) is that only a fraction of the oil in any well is typically pumped out. Over half the oil is usually left in the ground because the cost of bringing it to the surface is too high. That is, the *marginal cost* of obtaining oil from a given well rises as the quantity extracted grows. When oil's price increases, it pays producers to incur more costs to pump more oil from existing wells.

Many ingenious methods of secondary and tertiary recovery have been devised to squeeze more petroleum from existing wells in response to rising prices. In many areas, production from old wells had nearly vanished until OPEC started to charge more for its

output. For example, in western Pennsylvania, the first oil well in the world was drilled in 1859. As production there became more costly relative to the newer fields in the American Southwest, output in Pennsylvania slowed to a trickle. The sharp increases in world oil prices made production—and drilling—in this area profitable once again.[4]

Public policy toward oil producers after 1973 provides a powerful illustration of the interaction between the private and public sectors in providing the economy's answers to the *what, how,* and *for whom* questions. As we noted, there was debate over how elastic the supply curve of oil is. Just how much more would oil producers supply in response to rising prices? There was much less uncertainty, however, regarding the effect of rising oil prices on oil companies' well-being. A quick look at figure 4.6 will show how United States oil producers, as well as OPEC, were made better off when petroleum prices were increased. At a price of $3, domestic producers provided 9.2 million barrels of oil daily. When the price rose to $12, oil producers were motivated to increase production to 10 million barrels daily. However, the increased price was not required to maintain the initial production of 9.2 barrels, *cet. par.*

The extra revenue that producers received for the quantity of oil they were willing to supply at $3 per barrel is 9.2 million × ($12 − $3), or $82.8 million per day. This revenue, represented by the shaded rectangle to the left of the vertical supply curve S', is called **economic rent**, which is revenue received by the owner of a scarce resource in excess of the amount necessary to induce the owner to offer it for sale. Rent is the amount by which the price of a unit of output exceeds the marginal cost of producing it. It is something like profit. The difference is that economic rent, or rent for short, occurs when someone owns a resource that is superior, or particularly productive. An example is an oil well yielding a great deal of oil with relatively little effort or expense. It is useful to distinguish between rent and profit, even though they are similar concepts. (Economic rent is not the same as the "rent" you pay for your apartment or dormitory room.) We will deal with this distinction in greater detail in chapter 5. For now, it is sufficient to say that while profit disappears in the long run under competitive conditions, rent tends to persist. When the price of oil is $12, the entire area bounded by point d, $12, and point c represents the economic rent received by oil producers.

The increase in oil companies' rents resulted in increased accounting profits when the price of oil rose. Many people heard about this and thought that it was unfair for the oil companies to receive immense benefits while oil users suffered from rising prices. General price controls were established for the whole economy under the Nixon administration in late 1971. These were being phased out in 1973, but public resentment of rising oil company accounting profits provided political pressure to retain oil price controls much longer for the oil (and natural gas) industry than for the rest of the economy. While some price increases were permitted, oil producers were not completely free of price controls until early 1981. (Some controls on natural gas prices persist today.)

While the actual price controls imposed were quite complicated, the essential features of the maximum price legislation applied to domestic oil production are shown in figure 4.7. After OPEC began its series of price increases in 1973, domestic oil prices were allowed to rise, but price controls kept the maximum allowable price for domestic producers below the level charged by OPEC. P(max) represents the legal maximum price for domestic oil that was established. As existing wells became depleted, the cost of bringing additional oil to the surface was rising. This increase in the marginal cost of oil production over time caused the supply of oil to fall, as shown by the leftward shift of the supply curve to S′ in figure 4.7. Thus, despite rising oil prices, domestic production fell after 1973. By 1980, continued leftward shifts of the United States oil supply curve resulted in domestic crude oil production's falling to only three-fourths its 1973 level.[5]

Full decontrol of domestic oil prices did not occur until about February 1981. The effects of price decontrol appear to have been substantial and fast in coming. Oil production in the United States in 1981 was almost equal to that in 1980, compared to a 3 percent decline between 1979 and 1980. In the last seven months of 1981, oil production actually exceeded the levels achieved during the last seven

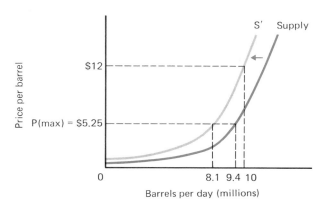

Figure 4.7 The effect of a ceiling price on domestic oil production when supply is declining
As existing oil wells became depleted, the market supply of oil shifted leftward. The quantity supplied at *every* price was falling. Imposition of a *ceiling price*, P(max), meant that the actual quantity supplied fell *more* than it would have if the price had been allowed to rise.

months of 1980. Moreover, the number of oil wells drilled grew by over 25 percent. In other words, allowing the domestic price of oil to rise above P(max) resulted in an increase in the quantity of oil supplied. The effect of price decontrol can be described by means of figure 4.7. Without a price rise, the leftward shift in the supply of oil would have resulted in a *reduction* in the quantity of oil supplied. However, an increase in the price of oil increased the quantity supplied along the new supply curve. For example, a rise in the price of petroleum to $12 dollars per barrel would result in a quantity supplied equal to 10 million barrels per day—more than 9.4 million barrels per day even though the supply of oil had fallen to S′. One effect of increased domestic production was to reduce imports from OPEC, which resulted in less dependence on foreign oil and lower prices charged for imported oil.

What do you think has happened to oil producers' rents as a result of the decline in world oil prices in recent years? Should the federal government now legislate *minimum* prices to protect United States oil producers and their employees from the effects of lower world oil prices?

► Summary and Conclusions

In this chapter, we have developed the theory of short-run supply of a good or service. You should now understand clearly how legal maximum prices limited natural gas production in the introductory example. The following points were emphasized.

By comparison with the law of demand, the law of supply is based on the *firm* as a producing agent rather than on the *individual* or *household* as a consumer.

The driving force of supply behavior is the firm's desire to maximize its profit.

A firm maximizes its profit by increasing output if marginal revenue (MR) exceeds marginal cost (MC) and by reducing output if MC exceeds MR. Firms maximize profits where MR = MC.

For a competitive (price-taking) firm, marginal revenue is identical to market price (MR ≡ P).

A firm's marginal cost curve tells us how much the firm will supply at each price provided price exceeds average variable cost.

A firm's production function and the scarcity of inputs used in production result in a supply curve that is upward sloping on a graph where price is measured on one axis and quantity on the other axis.

An industry's short-run supply curve represents the relationship between marginal cost or price and the quantity produced and sold.

An understanding of the supply relationship helps us to understand economic behavior and the impact of governmental economic policy.

Trying to keep oil producers from receiving increased accounting profits after OPEC raised world oil prices led to a reduction in domestic oil production, to increased imports, and probably to a higher price for imported oil.

► Key Terms

average cost *86*
average total cost (ATC) *86*
average variable cost (AVC) *86*
change in the quantity supplied *89*
change in supply, shift in the supply curve *90*
competition *80*
economic profit *78*
economic rent *96*
elasticity of supply *89*
firm *78*
fixed costs *80*

law of supply *80*
marginal cost, incremental cost *82*
marginal revenue, incremental revenue *81*
price taker *80*
principle of increasing cost *82*
short run *80*
shutdown point *88*
supply *78*
unrestricted entry *80*
variable costs *81*

► Questions for Discussion and Review

1. What is the short run? How long do you think the short run lasts?

2. Define the terms variable cost, marginal cost, and fixed cost.

3. True or false: When a competitive firm maximizes its profit, profit is zero because marginal cost equals marginal revenue. Justify your answer.

4. You have a concession to sell candy apples at the state fair. You buy your candy apples from a local producer at $.50 each and have 100 unsold apples on hand on the last day of the fair. If you don't sell the apples today, state health laws require that you throw them away. You pay the fair management $10 per day rent for your stand (in advance).
   a. What is your opportunity cost of each apple you sell on the last day of the fair?

b. How does the opportunity cost change with the number of apples you sell?

c. Construct your supply curve of apples on the last day of the fair.

d. What is the lowest price you will accept for your apples?

5. A farmer owns 100 acres of land on which he or she can grow either corn or soybeans. The labor, seed, fertilizer, and all other variable costs of raising the two crops are equal, totaling $50 per acre. Each acre yields fifty bushels of crop. Suppose the farmer can obtain firm contracts before he plants to sell all that he grows each year. This spring, he is offered contracts of $5 per bushel for soybeans and $1 per bushel for corn.

a. What is the opportunity cost of growing corn? of soybeans?

b. Construct the farmer's supply curves for corn and soybeans. What variable must you hold constant to construct these supply curves?

c. How many bushels of soybeans will the farmer supply this year? How many bushels of corn will be supplied?

d. Suppose the contract price of corn rises to $6 per bushel. What will happen to the supply curve of soybeans? What will happen to the supply curve of corn? What will happen to quantity of corn supplied?

e. Suppose the variable input costs of both crops double. What will happen to their supply curves? What will happen to the quantity supplied if their prices are as stated at the beginning of this question?

f. When the price of corn is $5 per bushel and the price of soybeans $2 per bushel, calculate the farmer's economic rent, if any, when variable costs equal $50 per acre sown.

6. Suppose you own a shoe factory with a production function relating inputs of labor to daily shoe production as shown below. (Labor and leather are the only variable inputs in shoe production.)

Labor input per day (hours)	Shoe output per day (pairs)
100	50
110	54
121	57
133	59
147	60

Labor is $10 per hour, leather costs $10 per pair of shoes, and the cost of maintaining your plant and equipment is $1,000 per day regardless of how many pairs of shoes you produce. You cannot operate your factory with less than 100 hours of labor per day.

a. Construct a diagram like figure 4.3, with the quantity of shoes on the horizontal axis. Calculate the marginal cost and average variable cost per pair of shoes over the range of output between fifty pairs of shoes per day and sixty pairs per day. Plot these costs on your diagram.

b. What will be the quantity of shoes you will supply if the price of shoes is $50 per pair? What will your profit be? (Calculate profit as total sales revenue less all costs including fixed cost.)

c. Suppose the price of shoes falls to $31 per pair. How many pairs will you offer for sale? Calculate your profit. Should you shut down your factory? What should you do if the price of shoes falls to $29 per pair?

d. Calculate the elasticity of your supply curve over the range of output between 52 and 55.5 pairs of shoes per day and over the range of 58 to 59.5 pairs. Does the elasticity rise or fall as output increases? Why? (Hint: Elasticity of supply has the same formula as elasticity of demand. Review chapter 3 for the formula for elasticity of demand.)

7. How does the elasticity of supply affect the way in which the *what, how,* and *for whom* questions are answered in a market economy? Use the increase in oil prices after 1973 to illustrate your answer. What importance, if any, should supply elasticity have for government policy toward the oil industry and the possibility of price controls on oil?

8. Suppose the government wished to transfer income away from oil producers and give it to consumers. What kind of a tax would have a smaller effect on the quantity of oil supplied—a fixed sum per producer, say, $100,000 per year, or a fixed sum per barrel of oil sold, say, $10 per barrel? Illustrate your answer with a graph.

   Are the statements in questions 9 through 12 true, false, or uncertain? Defend your answers.

9. A competitive firm's short-run supply curve is identical to its marginal cost curve.

10. Whenever marginal cost is increasing, average variable cost is increasing.

11. Whenever marginal cost lies below average total cost, the latter is falling.

12. A competitive firm maximizes profit because marginal cost and price are identical.

A Closer Look at a Firm's Costs

In chapter 4, we examined the costs and supply decisions of the A-1 Balloon Company. In this appendix, we will provide a somewhat more detailed analysis of a firm's costs in the short run and show how it extends to the firm's long-run cost and supply decisions. We will see in chapters 8 through 11 that the number of firms in an industry will often depend on the nature of their costs in the long run. We will also see that whether firms are price takers or end up with some control over the prices at which they sell their output depends on their costs in the long run and, hence, on the number of competing firms in their industry.

▶ **An Example: Choosing the Optimal Size of a Pottery Firm**

Suppose you and a few friends decide to set up a pottery shop near campus. First, you will want to find a good location. Assuming you succeed in leasing an empty store for $400 per month, you can turn your attention to the production process itself. To keep the situation simple, we will assume that your monthly rental cost on the store, $400 per month, is your fixed cost, and the production period we will focus on is a month.

   Because starting the business was your idea, you can be the boss. We will assume that you and your friends could each earn $10 per hour (including tips) by waiting on tables in a local restaurant. This represents the opportunity cost of time for each of you. Obviously, you will have to rent kilns, potter's wheels, and other equipment and purchase materials such as clay, paints, electricity, and so on in order to start production of pots to sell.

   Expenses associated with hiring labor, purchasing material and electricity, and renting machines will vary with the level of production. They therefore make up your variable cost. Total cost equals all of your variable cost plus your fixed cost of $400 per month. Your average total cost

Increasing returns to variable factors (inputs) means that as output increases, with a given set of fixed inputs, marginal cost declines.

Decreasing returns to variable factors (inputs) means that as output increases, with a given set of fixed inputs, marginal cost increases.

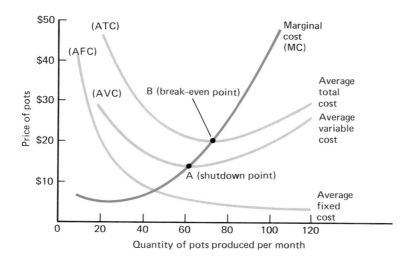

Figure 4.A   Short-run cost conditions for a pottery firm
Average fixed cost (AFC) declines steadily as output increases. Average total cost (ATC) is the sum of AFC and average variable cost (AVC). The minimum point of the ATC curve is above and to the right of the minimum point of the AVC curve. The marginal cost (MC) curve passes through the minimum points of both the AVC and ATC curves. The break-even price and output are indicated by point B and are both greater than the shutdown price and output indicated by point A.

(ATC) is simply equal to your total cost divided by the number of finished pots produced each month. Your average variable cost (AVC) equals total variable cost divided by the number of pots produced each month. Your average fixed cost (AFC) is equal to your fixed cost of $400 divided by your monthly output of pots. Last, but not least, the change in total cost associated with a one-unit increase in output is the marginal cost (MC) of producing pottery. The short-run relationships among ATC, AVC, AFC, and MC are shown in figure 4.A.

Because AFC equals a constant amount, $400, divided by the number of pots produced, AFC declines continuously as output expands. Moreover, we can see that since ATC equals AVC plus AFC, the ATC curve is always above the AVC curve. The U-shape of the ATC, AVC, and MC curves requires some explanation.

When your small shop first begins to produce pots you may have each employee make his or her pots from start to finish; this involves a great deal of starting and stopping of electrical machinery and of work by each employee as employees move from one task to another. However, as production expands, you may find that you can avoid such costly interruptions in machine use and labor time, as well as take better advantage of each worker's talents if you have each worker specialize in one or only a few production tasks. If so, AVC, ATC, and MC will all decrease over some range of production. The resulting declining unit costs per pot reflect what is known as **increasing returns to variable factors (inputs)**.

As output expands further, you will expand your employment of workers, machine rentals, and material purchases. The store you rented will become more crowded. Your workers, who by now are as specialized as they can be, begin to get in one another's way, and your job of coordinating the whole production process becomes more and more complex. Consequently, even though you are not paying any more for your inputs, marginal and—eventually—average costs will stop decreasing and begin to rise as production expands further. The phenomenon of rising marginal and average costs of production as output expands, despite constant input prices, is referred to as **decreasing returns to variable factors (inputs)**.

*The **break-even point** occurs at that price that allows the firm to cover all of its costs exactly but to earn no profit in the short run.*

*A firm's **long run** refers to a period of time over which the firm can alter the amount of inputs that are fixed in the short run.*

*A firm's **short run** refers to a period of time over which the firm cannot alter some of its inputs.*

We saw in chapter 4 that the MC curve intersects both the AVC and ATC curves from below at their minimum points. The minimum points of the AVC curve (point A) and the ATC curve (point B) are the *shutdown point* and **break-even point,** respectively, for your pottery business.

In figure 4.A, we indicate that the break-even point is $19.70, and the associated output is seventy pots. This is the break-even point because total revenue just equals total cost, (including the opportunity cost of your own time—$10 per hour). Point A is the shutdown point because at a price of $14 and output of 60 pots, total revenue will just equal total variable cost, and you will be losing $400 per month (the fixed, rental cost of your property). At any price below $14, total revenue will fall short of total variable cost. If you continue to produce pots under these conditions, your losses will therefore exceed $400 per month. Since you can always reduce your losses to $400 by shutting down production, you will never find it desirable to continue to produce pots at any price below $14. This is why point A is referred to as the shutdown point.

Not only will you shut down production if the market price of pots falls below $14, you will not stay in business if the price remains above $14 but below $19.70 indefinitely. The reason is that at any price below point B but above point A, you are still losing money. It is quite likely that at the end of the year, when your lease is up for renewal, you will not renew it.

Looking on the brighter side, suppose you succeed at selling finished pots at a price well above point B in the short run. Then when your lease expires, you will look for an even bigger location to set up shop. In this example, the **firm's long run** is distinguished from the **firm's short run** by the fact that property rental costs are fixed in the short run and variable in the long run. In our example, your long-run planning horizon would be a year or more. The short run is

a period of time less than one year. (In chapters 4 and 7, we ignore the firm's planning horizon, and the short run refers to a period of time in which the number of firms in an industry is fixed. The long run, in that context, is a period of time long enough to allow for firms to enter or leave an industry.)

Two possible sets of long-run cost relationships for a firm are illustrated in figures 4.B and 4.C The sets of short-run marginal and average total cost curves (SMC and SATC) correspond to different size stores rented to house your pottery firm. In the first case, illustrated in figure 4.B, as sales continue to boom over the years, you find that it makes sense to move to bigger and bigger rental properties to avoid the congestion associated with trying to expand production of pots substantially in a fixed size workshop. To the extent that the moves involved simply permit you to produce more pots at the same minimum average cost over time, the minimum price at which you will operate in the long run is constant. It equals the (identical) break-even price that exists in any short-run planning period. The collection of short-run break-even prices map out the **long-run average total cost (LATC) curve** for your firm. We refer to a firm with a constant LATC curve as one with **constant returns to scale.**

Alternatively, figure 4.C indicates long-run possibilities for both saving costs and increasing costs, depending upon your scale of operation. Suppose there are different kinds of machinery that you might use to make pottery. One machine is efficient if you produce 2,000 pots per year but not if you produce only 1,000 pots per year. Moreover, another machine is efficient if you glaze 5,000 pots per year but not if you glaze only 2,000 pots annually. In other words, when annual production expands, you will not only find it better to rent a larger store, but you will also desire to alter the kind of equipment you rent. You may even want to employ more specialists in production as output expands.

*The **long-run average total cost (LATC) curve** for a firm refers to its average total cost curve when the firm can alter all of its inputs.*

Constant returns to scale for a firm means that the firm's long-run average total cost curve and long-run marginal cost curve are horizontal. Alternatively, increasing

(decreasing) all factor inputs by a constant percentage will cause output to increase (decrease) by the same percentage.

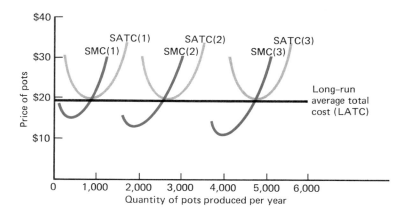

Figure 4.B   Pottery production when the firm has long-run constant cost
The firm's long-run AVC is simply a straight line equal to the common minimum short-run ATC, or break-even price of $19.70, for different size pottery firms. The cost curves SATC(1) and SMC(1) correspond to the initial short-run average total cost and marginal cost curves for your pottery business, which produces 840 pots per year when the price is $19.70. The other sets of cost curves correspond to successively larger businesses, in which minimum SATC occurs at larger scales of operation.

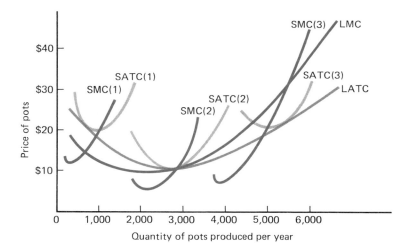

Figure 4.C   Generalized long-run cost possibilities for the pottery firm
The curves LAC and LMC indicate the long-run average total cost curve and long-run marginal cost curve for your pottery firm. The curves SATC(1) and SMC(1) are the cost conditions you began with. Notice that a somewhat different setup could have reduced your minimum short-run ATC to about $19 for 840 pots per year. The curves SATC(2) and SMC(2) and SATC(3) and SMC(3) are alternative setups for production. Note that for each point where SATC equals LATC, the corresponding SMC equals LMC.

Increasing returns to scale for a firm means that the firm's long-run marginal cost curve is downward sloping. Alternatively, increasing

(decreasing) all factor inputs by a constant percentage will increase (decrease) output by a greater percentage.

Decreasing returns to scale for a firm means that the firm's long-run marginal curve is upward sloping. Alternatively, increasing (decreasing) all factor inputs by a constant percentage will increase (decrease) output by a smaller percentage.

To the extent that changes in equipment, kinds of labor employed, and the size of the shop allow you to reduce unit costs as output increases, long-run marginal cost (LMC) and long-run average total cost (LATC) will both decrease as production expands, even if all input prices are fixed. When a firm has decreasing costs in the long run with given input prices, we say that it has **increasing returns to scale.**

Unfortunately, as output expands, monitoring work effort of your employees, coordinating different phases of the production process, keeping informed about every aspect of the business, and communicating changes in market strategy, product design, and so on will become more and more difficult for you. You could hire an administrative staff to help you stay on top of every phase of your pottery empire, but the expense of such help would tend to raise production costs. In effect, there is only one you, and even in the long run it is your entrepreneurial talent that determines how successful the business will remain. In general, for most firms, the limited availability of entrepreneurial talent will determine how much a business can expand before costs begin to rise. In this situation, long-run average total cost and long-run marginal cost will eventually increase when production becomes large enough. The phenomenon of increasing long-run costs, even if factor prices are constant, is referred to as **decreasing returns to scale.**

Figure 4.C illustrates the general possibilities of increasing, constant, and decreasing returns to scale for your pottery firm. The short-run cost curves SATC(1), SMC(1); SATC(2), SMC(2); and SATC(3), SMC(3) correspond to short-run cost conditions for firms of three different sizes.

As illustrated, your initial short-run operation is on the decreasing costs portion of the long-run average cost curve. Consequently, a slightly different production setup could have generated your initial annual output of 840 pots at a price of somewhat less than $19.70, say, $19. Notice that for each output at which short-run average cost and long-run average cost are equal, the corresponding short-run marginal cost must equal long-run marginal cost. In figure 4.B, long-run average cost and long-run marginal cost are the same. Why? In general, a competitive industry in the long run will consist of firms such as the one depicted in figure 4.C, all operating with short-run cost curves like SMC(2) and SATC(2) provided all have access to the same inputs and pay the same prices for these productive factors. Can you explain why this is so?

▶ Key Terms

break-even point *102*

constant returns to scale *102*

decreasing returns to scale *104*

decreasing returns to variable factors (inputs) *101*

firm's long run *102*

firm's short run *102*

increasing returns to scale *104*

increasing returns to variable factors (inputs) *101*

long-run average total cost (LATC) curve *102*

Chapter 5

How Markets Work

Outline

    I. Introduction *106*
   II. How the forces of supply and demand determine price and the level of production *107*
      A. The concept of market equilibrium *107*
      B. Forces working to establish equilibrium *108*
         1. Market price below equilibrium *108*
         2. Market price above equilibrium *109*
  III. The effects of shifts in supply and demand on equilibrium price and quantity *110*
      A. Background *110*
      B. Permanent shifts in supply and demand *110*
         1. Permanent shifts in demand *110*
         2. Permanent shifts in supply *111*
         3. Shifts in both supply and demand *112*
      C. Permanent shifts in supply and demand affect other markets, too *114*
      D. The effects of temporary shifts in supply and demand *115*
         1. Inventories and transaction costs *115*
         2. An example: The retail market for beer *115*
         3. Temporary changes in demand caused by one-time-only customers *116*
         4. More on inventory costs and prices *117*
  IV. Summary and conclusions *118*
   V. Key terms *118*
  VI. Questions for discussion and review *118*

Objectives

After reading this chapter, the student should be able to:

Explain how the forces of supply and demand interact to determine the price of a good or service and the amount of a good or service exchanged.

Show how shifts in supply and demand affect markets for goods and services.

Apply the analysis of supply and demand to explain changes in market prices and differences in prices across markets.

▶ Introduction

A few years ago, the owner of the general store in a small village in the Philippines found himself confronted with an interesting business situation. Heavy rains had wiped out the few roads into and out of the village, and most of the homes and businesses were flooded and filled with mud. Outside help could not reach the village for several days, and the local people were eager to get things back to normal. Because the merchant was the only supplier of pails, shovels, and mops, he realized that he had an unexpected opportunity to profit from raising prices on those items far above their usual levels. He only had a dozen or two each of the pails, shovels, and mops that people wanted, and he figured he could double, or even triple, his normal prices and still sell everything in stock.

Although the merchant had never studied economics, he felt he knew a good opportunity to earn a profit when he saw one. In effect, the floods had caused a temporary increase in demand for cleanup materials, of which he was the only available supplier. So, following what seemed to him to be a perfectly logical course of action, he demanded far higher prices than usual for his goods.

Several days later, when outside help arrived, a grizzly scene awaited the rescuers as they arrived at the general store. The enterprising businessman had been beheaded by someone wielding a machete. Next to the head on the counter of the general store was a note indicating purchases of pails, shovels, and mops along with a sum of money corresponding to the total that would have been required for the purchases before the merchant decided to raise prices.

While the merchant understood the concepts of demand and supply as well as profit, he obviously did not know how to deal with temporary shifts in demand without losing his head. Among other things, this chapter will discuss less hazardous pricing policies.

In chapters 2 through 4 we developed the theories of demand and supply to see how consumers and producers make their decisions. In this chapter we combine supply and demand to see how together they determine the price and the amount of a good or service exchanged. If you master supply and demand analysis, you have at your command the single most important tool in the economist's kit. As always, one of our goals is to demonstrate the help economic analysis provides in understanding social issues. It cannot be said often enough that economic analysis can provide subtle insights into little known or poorly understood effects of government programs.

*The **equilibrium price** is the price at which the quantity demanded of a good or service equals the quantity supplied.*

*The **equilibrium quantity** is the quantity that results from the equilibrium price. It is both a quantity demanded and supplied.*

▶ How the Forces of Supply and Demand Determine Price and the Level of Production

We will begin by considering a market for beer, which is produced by many firms and consumed by many individuals. The first thing we will do is to put its demand curve and its supply curve together in one diagram. As depicted in figure 5.1, the demand curve is, of course, downward sloping and the supply curve upward sloping. When we see supply and demand together in the same picture, our eye is drawn to where they intersect. This is the most important price and quantity in figure 5.1. You will see why once we learn the concept of market equilibrium.

The Concept of Market Equilibrium

In figure 5.1 there is only *one* price at which the amount consumers want to buy exactly matches the amount producers want to sell. This price, $1.00 per bottle in figure 5.1, is called the **equilibrium price,** which occurs at the intersection of the supply and demand schedules. At *any other price,* one of the two parties is "frustrated." Either consumers want to buy more than producers want to sell or producers want to sell more than consumers want to buy. Of course, consumers would be happier if the price were lower than $1.00 and they could still purchase as much as they wanted. Similarly, producers would love to be able to sell 2 million or more bottles of beer at a price higher than $1.00 per bottle. Only at $1.00 per bottle, however, is there a transaction that satisfies both buyers and sellers. The quantity that satisfies both buyers and sellers, 2 million bottles in figure 5.1, is called the **equilibrium quantity.** You should think of

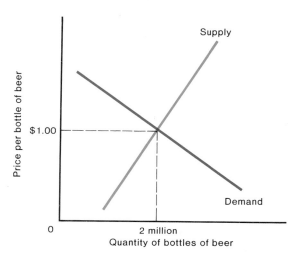

Figure 5.1   Equilibrium price and quantity in a market
In this diagram, $1 per bottle and 2 million bottles of beer are the equilibrium price and equilibrium quantity because quantity supplied equals quantity demanded.

market equilibrium as a "point of rest" where no forces operate to make buyers or sellers change their agreement. If, for some reason, a market is not in equilibrium, the forces of demand and supply will tend to move the market toward equilibrium. In particular, price will remain at $1.00 per bottle and quantity at 2 million bottles until something causes a shift in either supply or demand.

We have just seen how to locate an equilibrium price and quantity in a diagram of a market. This is simple. It is somewhat more difficult to understand the economic forces that cause an equilibrium price and quantity to occur. When we learn this we also learn how factors that change supply or demand change the equilibrium price and quantity in a market.

A shortage, or excess demand, is the amount by which the quantity demanded exceeds the quantity supplied.

Figure 5.2   When price is below equilibrium, quantity supplied is less than quantity demanded
Excess demand will occur when price is below its equilibrium level.

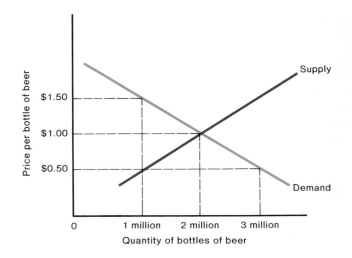

Forces Working to Establish Equilibrium

The easiest way to understand why $1.00 per bottle is the equilibrium price in figure 5.1 is to consider what would happen if the price were either below or above equilibrium.

Market Price Below Equilibrium

Suppose that the price happened to equal $0.50 per bottle in figure 5.2, a price *below* equilibrium. At $0.50 per bottle, the quantity demanded by consumers is 3 million bottles. The quantity offered for sale by producers is 1 million bottles. We see that at a price below equilibrium, consumers would like to buy *more than* the quantity offered for sale. Demand and supply are not in equilibrium. There is a **shortage,** or an **excess demand,** at a price of $0.50 per bottle, which equals 3 million − 1 million, or 2 million bottles. Remember that scarcity and shortages are not the same thing. Most goods and services we value are scarce. A shortage exists only for those scarce goods or services for which there is an excess demand.

What economic forces work to eliminate an excess demand? Remember from chapter 3 that at a price of $0.50 per bottle producers maximize their profits by offering to sell 1 million bottles of beer. However, they will eventually learn that prospective buyers want more than 1 million bottles. Because

$0.50 per bottle is not an equilibrium price, producers can maximize their profits by noticing that the excess demand facing them allows them to charge more and still sell all they wish to sell. Thus, the market price will move from $0.50 toward $1.00. The rising price will create an economic incentive for producers to offer more beer for sale. The quantity offered for sale will then move in the direction of equilibrium, toward 2 million bottles.

This process will continue until equilibrium is reached. Why is this so? When price is below equilibrium there is a natural tendency for buyers to offer a higher price because they cannot get all they want. If the price of beer remains $0.50 per bottle, stores will sell out quickly and customers will complain about the 2 million bottle shortfall between what they want to buy and what sellers are willing to supply. Sellers will soon figure out that they can increase both the price and sales until price equals $1.00 per bottle.

As another example, have you ever tried to purchase a used item that you read about in an ad, perhaps a piece of furniture or some sporting equipment? Suppose that when you met with the seller he or she told you someone else was also interested. One of your first inclinations would probably be to offer more money to make the owner want to sell to you. Similarly, we have all seen ads that say, "best offer takes it." The point here is that, as a buyer, your natural

We now have our first conclusion from the theory of supply and demand. *A permanent or long-term increase in demand leads to higher prices and quantities bought and sold.* You should practice thinking things through in reverse order to make sure you understand the effect of a long-term *reduction* in demand. What would cause a reduction in demand? How do market forces lead producers to cut back their output? When you think this through, you will come to the conclusion that *a permanent reduction in demand leads to lower levels of production and sales as well as reduced prices.* This is our second major conclusion from supply and demand. In both cases, of course, we assume that all else is unchanged.

Permanent Shifts in Supply

In 1973, the price of cereal grains increased noticeably.[1] This made it much more costly to manufacture beer. (Malt and other grain products are key ingredients in the brewing process.) Because it became so much more expensive to produce beer, brewers required a higher price to produce any given quantity. This is reflected in the shift in supply to S′ in figure 5.5. The end result of the increase in the price of a key input, cereal grains, was an increase in the equilibrium price of beer. This is indicated by the movement from P(0) to P(1). The magnitude of the shift in equilibrium quantity from Q(0) to Q(1) depends on both the magnitude of the supply shift and the elasticity of the demand for beer. This, of course, depends on the economic sacrifices beer lovers are willing to make to avoid reducing their beer consumption. This example leads to the conclusion that permanent reductions in supply lead to higher prices and less output bought and sold.

Of course, supply can also increase. In the summer of 1982, the Israeli army besieged West Beirut. Their goal was to capture armed members of the Palestine Liberation Organization (PLO), which they viewed as threatening Israel. Realizing that they might soon be disarmed, PLO members in Beirut sought to sell off their AK-47 automatic rifles. This increase in supply of AK-47s made them a very cheap item in Beirut during July 1982. The blockade also *reduced* the supplies of food, which made *food* very expensive.[2]

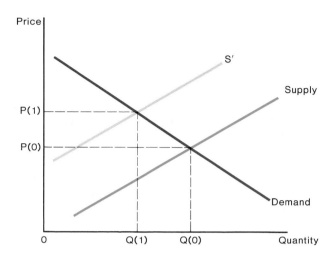

Figure 5.5   The effect of a permanent reduction in supply
A permanent reduction in supply causes the equilibrium price to rise from P(0) to P(1) and the equilibrium quantity to fall from Q(0) to Q(1).

We are now in the position to draw a general conclusion with respect to the impact of permanent changes in supply on equilibrium price and quantity. *Reductions in supply lead to higher prices and less output available. Increases in supply have the opposite effect—lower prices and greater quantities bought and sold.*

The conclusions we have just drawn have another dimension. We can also use our theory to look at differences in supply *across* markets. For example, suppose that two markets are identical except that producers in one have higher production costs; that is, the supply curve in the market with higher costs will be higher and farther to the left than in the other market. In this case, we would expect the market with the higher costs to have a higher equilibrium price. Have you ever stayed in a hotel in New York City? One of the reasons things cost so much there is that labor and land are very expensive in comparison to other cities. Supply and demand analysis is useful in understanding price and quantity differences either over time or across markets. Next we will illustrate the effects of supply and demand shifts.

Shifts in Both Supply and Demand

It is not always possible to predict what happens to equilibrium price and quantity when *both* supply and demand shift. To make this clear let us look at what happened to the world market for sugar during the late 1960s and early 1970s. During this period the major beet sugar growers in the Soviet Union, Europe, and the United States produced very small crops because of external forces, including poor weather conditions.[3] At the same time, expanding world population and rising income levels caused the world demand for sugar to increase. The effect of all of these events on the supply and demand for sugar is illustrated in figure 5.6. The disappointing sugar beet crops moved supply to S'. Even with no change in demand, this severe reduction in supply would have resulted in a sharp price increase. The demand growth, however, pushed prices up even farther, to a level shown by P(1). By the end of 1974, for example, a one-pound box of sugar cost three times as much as it did two years earlier.

What general conclusions can we now draw about equilibrium price and quantity change when *both* supply and demand shift? When supply is reduced and demand is increased, as in the sugar market example, price will clearly rise. When buyers want to buy more than before and sellers want to sell less than before, there is upward pressure on market price from both sides of the market. Whether quantity bought (and sold) goes up or down is another, more complicated issue. It is easy to draw a demand shift in figure 5.6 that is large enough to lead to more sugar's being bought and sold at a higher market price. In general, when supply is reduced and demand increases, we expect the market price to rise. However, two types of information are needed to predict what will happen to equilibrium quantity. They are (1) the relative

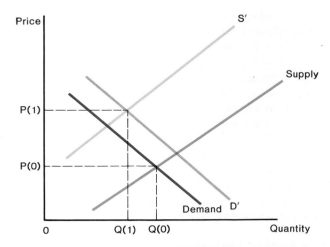

Figure 5.6   The world sugar market during the late 1960s and early 1970s
The reduced supply of sugar and increased demand for sugar pushed sugar prices to a record level.

magnitudes of the supply and demand shifts and (2) *the relative magnitudes of the price elasticity of demand and the elasticity of supply* (ϵ_p and ϵ_s), which reflect the responsiveness of quantity demanded and supplied to price changes. This issue underlies a common misconception in news reports and other casual applications of supply and demand analysis as indicated in the example that follows.

An article in the *Wall Street Journal* points out that San Francisco has a relatively large number of doctors and, therefore, that medical care is quite plentiful in the San Francisco area relative to the United States as a whole.[4] Despite this, doctors' fees are 24 percent higher in San Francisco than the national average. The article then asks the crucial question: Why hasn't the relative abundance of physicians in San Francisco brought with it lower than average fees? Does the *Wall Street Journal* article show that our standard supply and demand analysis does not apply to the medical marketplace? Rather than debate this issue we will simply point out that a high price for medical care along with relatively plentiful medical care available does not contradict supply and demand analysis.

To see this, take a look at figure 5.7. The supply and demand curves represent market conditions for physicians' services in the average United States city. The supply curve labeled S' illustrates the relatively plentiful supply of physicians in San Francisco. Why does S' lie to the right of the typical supply curve? One reason may be that the San Francisco area is a nice place to live. Another reason is that the University of California and Stanford medical schools are located there. If this were all there were to the story, we would expect the price of physician services to be lower in San Francisco, P(1), compared to the United States average, P(0).

The article fails to point out, however, that incomes are higher in the San Francisco area than in the average United States metropolitan area. Thus, we expect the demand for medical care to be higher than average in San Francisco. This is depicted in figure 5.7 by a demand curve for medical care in San Francisco, D', which lies to the right of that for the average United States city. Because of the way in which we have constructed figure 5.7, the difference in demand between San Francisco and the average United States city is large enough to make medical care cost more in San Francisco, (P2). Of course, there may also be other reasons why the price of medical care in San Francisco is relatively high despite the relatively large number of physicians there. To test the hypothesis that both the price and quantity of medical services in San Francisco are higher because

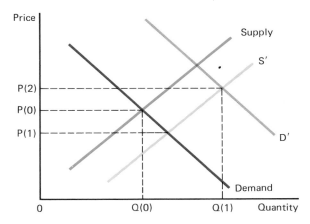

Figure 5.7   The supply and demand for physicians' services in San Francisco versus the average United States city
In San Francisco, the supply of doctors is above the United States average. However, the price of medical care is also above the United States average. One reason for the higher price is the relatively greater demand for medical care by San Franciscans.

the demand curve lies relatively farther to the right of "average" than the supply curve, we might examine the market for medical care in other wealthy cities that are also pleasant places to live. For example, most Beverly Hills residents have high incomes, and there are major medical schools located nearby.

The main point, however, is that high prices along with plentiful output do not contradict supply and demand analysis. Both supply and demand curves can shift over time or differ between areas. The important point is that we must decipher the effects of *both* demand *and* supply changes within a market or differences across markets before we fully understand why equilibrium prices change over time or differ between areas.

Table 5.1   The qualitative effects of permanent supply and demand shifts on market equilibrium prices and quantities

	Supply increases	Supply decreases	Supply unchanged
Demand increases	Q↑ P↑, P↓, or P constant*	Q↑, Q↓, or Q constant* P↑	Q↑ P↑
Demand decreases	Q↑, Q↓, or Q constant* P↓	Q↓ P↑, P↓, or P constant*	Q↓ P↓
Demand unchanged	Q↑ P↓	Q↓ P↑	Q constant P constant

*Depends on whether demand or supply shifts more and on the relative elasticities of demand and supply.

Table 5.1 summarizes what we have learned about how supply and demand shifts or differences affect market prices and quantities bought and sold. When you look at this table be sure to think back to the events responsible for the supply and demand shifts or differences (tables 2.2 and 4.5).

Permanent Shifts in Supply and Demand Affect Other Markets, Too

Markets are interconnected. For example, something that disturbs the equilibrium price of new cars will also affect the equilibrium price of used cars. If the cost of producing new cars were to rise substantially because of a sudden sharp increase in the price of steel, this would increase the equilibrium price of new cars. Since new cars are substitutes for used cars, this price increase would increase the demand for used cars. Ultimately, used cars would cost more. Remember, many goods are either complements or substitutes, and therefore their demands are interrelated.

Think back to our example of the sugar market in the late 1960s and early 1970s. When the price of sugar rose, soft drink makers began substituting corn syrup for some of the sugar in their product. What do

you think this did to the demand for corn syrup? What pressures did it put on the equilibrium price of corn syrup? How do you think it affected the demand for corn? Similarly, how would it have affected consumers' use of sugar substitutes, such as honey and maple syrup? Finally, what do you think happened to the cost of commercially produced sweets as a result of the sugar price increase?

One of the reasons it is important to realize that markets are interconnected is that government policy often tries to affect one dimension of behavior by changing the supply of a complement or a substitute. For example, drug paraphernalia laws seek to reduce the supply of items used in the consumption of drugs. By reducing the supply of these items and increasing their cost to consumers, the hope is that drug use will decline. As you should expect, the effectiveness of drug paraphernalia laws depends on how sensitive the demand for drugs is to a change in the price of drug paraphernalia, or drug complements. One consequence of those laws has been an increase in the multiple use of syringes by drug users. Because the use of unclean syringes has been associated with the spread of hepatitis and AIDS among drug users, New York City officials have begun debating possible repeal of local drug paraphernalia laws.

Transaction costs are expenditures of time, money, and other resources required for a buyer or seller to arrange a transaction.

The Effects of Temporary Shifts in Supply and Demand

Inventories and Transactions Costs

A major implication of supply and demand analysis is that markets, by their very nature, produce forces that move prices and quantities toward their equilibrium values. This means that during the decision-making period underlying the supply and demand curves we draw, quantity demanded will tend to equal quantity supplied. Yet producers and retailers both hold *stocks,* or *inventories.* When we go to a grocery store, a car lot, or a stereo store, we see merchandise just sitting there waiting to be bought. At the end of the day, there are cans of soup on grocery store shelves, speakers and turntables on stereo store shelves, and unsold cars in car lots. Do these examples represent equilibrium in the theory of supply and demand?

The issue here is one of **transaction costs,** which involve the time and effort it takes for buyers and sellers to discover the most favorable terms available. It is expensive in terms of time, gasoline, and telephone bills for a buyer to find the cheapest price for something. Anyone who has shopped for electronics items or bought a car knows this. Similarly, sellers may have to advertise heavily in newspapers or on television to find buyers at what they think is the highest price possible. The main way in which firms discover that the price is *too high* is that not enough customers show up. The fact is that it is costly for buyers and sellers to find each other and then negotiate satisfactory transactions. The simple theory of supply and demand we have developed thus far must be enriched if we are to explain the responses of buyers and sellers to changes in supply or demand over relatively short periods of time, or what we will call the *short term.* Our definition of the short term is that there is *not enough time for buyers and sellers (1) to discover that supply or demand conditions have changed or (2) to make permanent adjustments to those changes.*

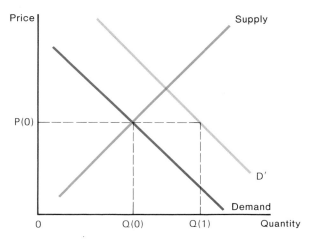

Figure 5.8   The response by suppliers to a temporary increase in demand
The supply curve is the beer retailers' normal supply curve. It reflects their willingness to sell various *average* daily quantities of beer at different prices. Occasionally and perhaps unpredictably, the demand for beer shifts to D'. The marginal cost reflected in the supply curve includes the additional cost of maintaining inventories to reduce the chance of running out of beer when demand is unexpectedly high. Because retailers know that the shift is only temporary, they continue to charge their customers price P(0), while carrying sufficient inventories to sell quantity Q(1). In other words, the beer retailers have a *short-term* supply curve that coincides with the horizontal dotted line at price P(0). *Transitory* shifts in beer demand resulting in quantity demanded anywhere from zero up to Q(1) will not lead to a change in the price of beer.

An Example: The Retail Market for Beer

A concrete example of how transaction costs in the short term enter the theory of supply and demand is the retail market for beer. In figure 5.8, the supply curve reflects the marginal cost of providing an average daily quantity of beer at retail prices in a typical city. The positive slope of the supply curve shows that beer retailers are willing to provide greater quantities of beer per day, on average, if they are paid more

A temporary, or transitory, shift in demand or supply is one that is expected to reverse itself during the period over which buyers and sellers formulate their plans.

per bottle of beer. The reason the supply curve slopes upward is that selling more beer on a regular basis may require staying open longer hours, borrowing funds to finance more stores and inventories, hiring additional help to work late hours at somewhat higher wages, and so on. The retailers are willing to incur these higher marginal costs if the price of beer is high enough. The demand curve represents the normal demand for beer. It shows the average daily amount that beer retailers expect to sell at various prices on an average day. The equilibrium price of beer is $P(0)$, and the equilibrium quantity is $Q(0)$.

Of course, beer retailers know that the demand for beer can fluctuate from day to day, even if the average demand is stable for many weeks at a time. A **temporary, or transitory, shift in demand** is one that is not expected to last very long—one that is due, say, to weather conditions or holidays. Even when beer retailers expect normal business, they will maintain inventories to accommodate an unanticipated, transitory shift in demand to, say, D'.

Because transitory variation in demand cannot be predicted perfectly and because retailers want to avoid the trouble and costs of dealing with disequilibrium that would arise if they ran out of beer, managers of beer stores will generally find it profitable to carry inventories. By doing this, they can keep their regular customers because no one will be disappointed and consider switching to a more reliable beer store. Exactly how large an inventory retail managers decide to carry will depend in part upon how much their customers are willing to pay for the convenience of being able to buy beer whenever they want it. The size of the inventory will also depend upon the cost of storage compared to the cost of obtaining replacement supplies very quickly when needed, the perishability of beer stored in retailers' refrigerators, the interest retailers may have to pay to borrow money to finance their inventories, and so on.

Most sellers hold inventories rather than let the price rise and fall with every transitory change in demand. This is because their customers do not like to feel that they are being gouged, and they do not like to be disappointed by an inability to get what they want. To avoid losing customers, a seller will try to make beer available at relatively steady prices. Consumers will value this degree of certainty about price as well as the availability of beer because it makes shopping easier and cheaper. On average, regular customers are willing to pay a few cents more for the convenience of being able to buy beer at a known price when they want it rather than bearing the transaction costs of searching for the lowest-cost source of supply every time they want to buy a six-pack. You can think of inventories as a shock absorber that smooths out the "bumps" in price that would be caused by shifts in demand were there no inventories.

In our example (refer again to figure 5.8), retailers maintain sufficient inventories to be able to sell, on any single day, the quantity $Q(1)$, while still charging price $P(0)$. This is a service they provide so that their customers will not be frustrated in their desires to purchase beer on short notice. In other words, the beer retailers' *short-term supply curve* is perfectly elastic at price $P(0)$ for sales up to $Q(1)$ on any given day. For sales in excess of $Q(1)$ on any given day, inventories will run out and retailers will have to decide what to do in a disequilibrium situation. This may be difficult for them. (See the story of the Philippine merchant that introduced this chapter.)

Temporary Changes in Demand Caused by One-time-only Customers

In our example of beer retailers, we saw that business firms often find it profitable to maintain the capacity to satisfy transitory changes in demand for their goods or services. Why, then, does price generally rise so much when something suddenly becomes a "hot" item? For example, why were hotel prices in Los Angeles during the 1984 Olympics higher than usual? Again, the answer lies in the response of sellers to transitory shifts in demand. In a case such as this, any long-term relationship between buyers and sellers is either nonexistent or is insufficient to warrant firms' providing the capacity to satisfy a transitory increase in demand. If repeat business is not expected (because the Olympics will not be held in Los Angeles again in the foreseeable future), suppliers view buyers as one-time-only customers. Thus, hotel operators need not be concerned about the effect on their future sales if they charge as much as they can for their rooms during the Olympics. There is little goodwill to be lost from being thought of as a price gouger because the hotel operators probably do not expect to see most of their Olympics visitors again.

Figure 5.9 describes how sellers respond to changes in demand caused by one-time-only customers. The normal demand for hotel rooms is represented by the demand curve. The supply curve reflects the marginal cost of making various quantities of hotel rooms available for occupancy on a normal basis. The equilibrium price of hotel rooms is P(0) and the equilibrium quantity is Q(0). The demand curve D' represents an unusually large demand for the product that is not expected to recur in the foreseeable future. Since the decision has already been made to make Q(0) hotel rooms available, the *short-term* supply curve of hotel rooms is vertical (has zero elasticity) at Q(0). You simply cannot build that many more hotel rooms to accommodate one special event such as the Olympics or a World's fair when you expect business to return to normal after the event is over. Confronted with customers who will not generate much repeat business, producers have the incentive to sell Q(0) for as high a price as possible. That price is whatever buyers are willing to pay for Q(0), or the price where a vertical line through Q(0) (the short-term supply curve) crosses the demand curve D'. This is price P(1) in figure 5.9. Try thinking of additional real-world examples where sellers charge all that the traffic will bear.

More on Inventory Costs and Prices

Examples of how inventories operate and how costs are incurred in maintaining them provide insight into price differences for seemingly similar goods or services. For example, many college communities have food co-ops. These co-ops claim to offer lower prices than conventional food stores run by the national chains. We know that one way to lower prices is to reduce production costs. If a co-op can maintain lower costs, its supply curve will lie below that of a national chain. This will lead to lower food prices in co-ops. How might this occur?

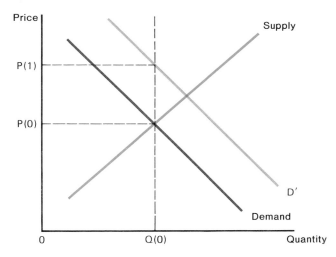

Figure 5.9   The response by suppliers to a temporary increase in demand caused by one-time-only customers
The demand curve represents the normal demand for hotel rooms in a city. The demand curve D' reflects a temporary increase in the demand for hotel rooms by one-time-only customers. Because it would not pay to provide additional capacity to satisfy this once-and-for-all surge in the demand for hotel rooms, the short-term supply curve of hotel rooms is zero elastic (vertical) at the quantity Q(0), and room rates will temporarily rise to P(1) when the transitory shift in demand occurs.

Co-ops often require individuals to place orders and pay for them in advance. This means that the co-op (1) makes only one order per week, (2) has the money up front, and (3) knows *exactly* how much to buy. There is little need to borrow money (and pay interest) to purchase items to put on the shelves, and the costs of storing and maintaining stocks of goods are sharply reduced. The prices of food are reduced because certain costly services, such as large selections and flexible shopping schedules, are not provided for buyers. Another way co-ops lower their costs is to substitute the labor of customers for the labor of employees. In particular, many co-ops require members to pick up and transport the food for dispersal at the co-op center. Similar cost and price reductions occur in food "warehouses," where customers bring their own bags, bag their own groceries, wait in long lines to check out, and pay only in cash.

▶ Summary and Conclusions

In this chapter, we showed how supply and demand analysis can help us understand real-world situations. The following points were emphasized.

Disequilibrium results in excess supply or excess demand.

Excess supply and demand, if there is no intervention in the marketplace, tend to eliminate themselves through price adjustments.

Shifts in supply and demand result in changes in equilibrium prices and quantities.

▶ Key Terms

equilibrium price *107*

equilibrium quantity *107*

excess supply, surplus, glut *109*

permanent shift in demand or supply *110*

shortage, excess demand *108*

temporary, or transitory, shift in demand *116*

transaction costs *115*

▶ Questions for Discussion and Review

1. Listed below are data for a supply and a demand schedule. Find the equilibrium quantity and the equilibrium price. Explain *why* the price and quantity you have found are an equilibrium combination.

Supply		Demand	
P	*Q*	*P*	*Q*
$10	100,000	$10	1,000,000
11	200,000	11	950,000
12	300,000	12	900,000
13	400,000	13	850,000
14	500,000	14	800,000
15	600,000	15	750,000
16	700,000	16	700,000
17	800,000	17	650,000
18	900,000	18	600,000
19	1,000,000	19	550,000
20	1,100,000	20	500,000

2. What is a shortage? Use a supply and demand diagram to explain the concept. What forces in a market work to eliminate a shortage?

3. What is a surplus? Use a supply and demand diagram to explain a surplus. What forces in a market work to eliminate a surplus?

4. Here are two permanent events: (1) consumers have a change in tastes and preferences for a good; and (2) an industry becomes unionized. Using a supply and demand diagram explain how each of these events will affect equilibrium quantity and price. Be sure to explain any assumptions you are using to arrive at your answer.

5. Hotel rooms at the beach cost more in the summer than they do in the winter. Hotel rooms in the Smokey Mountains cost more in the summer and the fall than they do in the winter and spring. These are just two examples of seasonal pricing. Can you give some others? Use supply and demand theory to explain why things have a higher price in the "on" season than during the "off" season. Illustrate your answer with supply and demand diagrams.

6. In 1982, tuna fishermen complained of low incomes because of the low price of tuna fish. They blamed the low price of chicken for part of their troubles. Does this make any economic sense? Support your answer with supply and demand diagrams.

7. Why do firms keep inventories? What role do inventories play in determining price and quantity when there is a short-term shift in demand? Use a diagram to support your answer.

8. What is price gouging? Support your answer graphically. Can price gouging ever be rational behavior on the part of a seller?

9. Suppose that beer and wine are considered to be substitutes. What effect will an increase in demand for grapes have on the price of beer?

10. You read in the newspaper that automobile prices are rising and more and more automobiles continue to be demanded by the American public. Does this suggest that the demand curve for automobiles is upward sloping?

Chapter 6

Government and Markets

Outline

I. Introduction *122*
II. Government intervention and social welfare *122*
III. Government policies to restrain market forces *123*
   A. A price ceiling *123*
      1. A case study of a price ceiling: The gasoline crisis of 1973–74 *126*
         a. Gas rationing as an alternative to a price ceiling *127*
         b. Taxing gasoline purchases as an alternative to a price ceiling *128*
         c. Conflicting policy objectives *129*
         d. Government promotion of economic waste *129*
   B. A price floor *129*
      1. Agricultural price supports *129*
      2. Agricultural price subsidies *132*
IV. Government policies that work through the forces of supply and demand *134*
   A. Policies that shift supply curves *134*
      1. The payment in kind (PIK) program *134*
         a. The ripple effect of PIK and other agricultural programs *136*
   B. Policies that shift demand curves *136*
      1. Subsidy: The case of food stamps *137*
      2. Subsidy: The case of Medicare and Medicaid *138*
   C. Policies that shift both supply and demand *138*
      1. The market for small cars in the United States *139*
V. Summary and conclusions *140*
VI. Key terms *141*
VII. Questions for discussion and review *141*

Objectives

After reading this chapter, the student should be able to:

Give some important examples of how the government intervenes in product markets in the United States.
Identify some of the reasons for this intervention.
Explain how intervention by the government can (a) prevent prices from equalizing quantity supplied with quantity demanded or (b) shift supply and demand to change market outcomes.
Discuss ways in which government intervention creates winners and losers.

▶ Introduction

In fiscal 1983, the federal government provided approximately $28 billion in financial help of all sorts to farmers in the United States. This amounted to approximately $12,000 per farm. In spite of this, the average net income from farming (gross receipts minus production expenses) was only about $9,000 per farm.[1] In September 1985, a number of entertainers, spearheaded by singer Willie Nelson, gathered in Champaign–Urbana, Illinois, to participate in a concert telethon known as Farm Aid. The purpose of the gathering was to try to raise as much as $50 million to help pay off the accumulated debts of farmers, which at the time were over $200 billion.[2] It was a heartwarming experience with much good entertainment by other singers, including Kenny Rogers, interspersed with truly sad stories of the low incomes and financial plight of many farmers.

A number of the speakers at the Farm Aid gathering blamed the federal government for the difficulties faced by small farmers. In this chapter we will examine, among other things, some of the government programs related to the farm sector in the United States. We hope to shed light on how the federal government can spend a great deal of money and still leave many farmers in deep financial difficulty. In some cases we will be quite critical of the federal government. This does not mean we are antigovernment but rather antiwaste. By this we mean that we want the government to achieve the intended goals of a program at a minimum cost to taxpayers. Thus, we take it upon ourselves to point out where government programs have not achieved their desired objectives and, where possible, to suggest ways in which refinements might direct the economic help in the intended direction. In this and other chapters we will, of course, point out situations in which the government is doing an effective job with its programs by achieving the stated goals of the programs.

▶ Government Intervention and Social Welfare

In chapter 5 we analyzed the way in which markets operate. We reviewed the basic elements of supply and demand and their roles in determining market outcomes, in particular the price and quantity of a good or service produced. We also learned how shifting demand and supply conditions lead to new equilibrium prices and quantities in a market. In this chapter we explain how markets work in an economy where government regulations and controls on behavior in the marketplace can shift both supply and demand schedules to alter market outcomes. In other cases government does not shift supply or demand but rather seeks to prevent the market from establishing a particular equilibrium price of quantity in its usual manner. We will provide a number of specific examples to illustrate these two general ways in which the government seeks to affect market outcomes in a mixed economy. In each case we will explain the avenues through which government policies alter market behavior and therefore prices and quantities. A primary focus of this exercise will be to identify the winners and losers involved, with special emphasis on how consumers, as opposed to firms and their stockholders and workers, are affected.

Before getting started it is important to point out that economists have no scientific way to compare one person's economic well-being to that of another. There is no obvious way to make interpersonal comparisons of happiness or satisfaction. The best we can do is to determine whether a given individual or group has been made better off or worse off than before. This allows us to conclude that a government policy helps society as a whole if it makes everyone in society better off or makes some people better off and nobody worse off. Similarly, we can generally conclude that a government policy is bad for society if it hurts everyone or hurts some people and helps no others.

Most economic policy has redistribution effects. This means that it typically makes some individuals better off and others worse off. In this case we cannot

*A **price ceiling** is the highest price at which it is legal to buy or sell a good or service.*

*An **effective maximum price** is a ceiling price that is less than the equilibrium price.*

draw any scientific conclusions concerning the desirability of such economic policy. As we just noted, we cannot compare the well-being of one person to that of another when government policy produces both winners and losers. Objectively, it is impossible to say who should win or lose. This is a normative issue.

Yet in each example we discuss in this chapter we will be able to identify those who win and those who lose as a result of the government policy involved. By identifying who the winners and losers are we will gain some insight into why government intervention takes place and why it takes the particular form that it does. In addition, we will try to look beyond the impact of government policy within a given market to its effects on other parts of the economy. These are the positive issues surrounding the attempt by the government to prevent market forces from working or to shift supply and demand and through them to affect market outcomes.

▶ Government Policies to Restrain Market Forces

Numerous government policies attempt to moderate the effects of supply and demand. They do this by placing floors or ceilings on the prices in a market. In this section we will study some actual attempts by the United States government to restrain the way in which markets work.

A Price Ceiling

In chapters 15 and 16 we will examine the issue of poverty and low incomes in the United States. It does not take much expertise to know that people who are poor have low purchasing power. Thus, government antipoverty policy has sought to increase the purchasing power of the poor. One way to do this is by transferring income from better off families to poor families. This, however, requires taxes and programs that make it obvious that the poor are winners and

the people being taxed are losers. What about another possibility? The poor would have greater purchasing power if they simply paid lower prices for goods and services. Why not simply outlaw high prices? This has occurred in a number of situations where the government has established a **price ceiling,** which is a legal maximum price. For example, the availability of low-cost housing for the poor has been a major concern in most large cities in the United States. One aspect of government policy in this area has been to provide public housing. Between 1960 and 1983, for example, the number of low-income public housing units approximately tripled, to 1.5 million.[3] These units cost money, though, and a number of governments, including the city of New York, have turned to rent controls as a way to try to help the poor obtain affordable housing. Politicians tend to like price controls because they seem to fight poverty without necessitating a tax increase. You can see how politically attractive this might be. Our goal as economic analysts is to discover whether this ability to obtain something for nothing really exists.

To be an **effective maximum price,** a price ceiling must be less than the market equilibrium price. Figure 6.1 reminds us that a price ceiling generally leads to a state of excess demand. There we depict an effective price ceiling of P(max), which in our example is $25. Notice that this is less than the equilibrium price, P(0), which is $50. The excess demand that results is equal to the difference between quantity demanded at the maximum price and quantity supplied, or 1,000.

The price ceiling frustrates consumers in the sense that it creates a shortage. As a result, consumers will spend more time and money searching for a place where they can buy what they want. In the case of rent-controlled apartments, they will take longer to find a place to live. Sometimes people even look at the obituary columns of the newspapers to see who has just died in order to find a landlord with a vacancy. In other words, the transaction costs associated with purchasing a good or service subject to price controls

Discrimination in a product market occurs when a seller requires a higher price from an unfavored group.

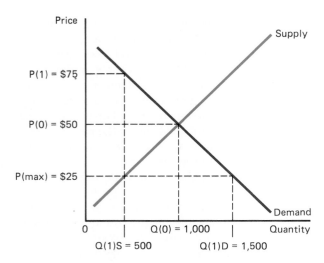

Figure 6.1 An effective price ceiling and excess demand
The equilibrium price and quantity in the absence of
government controls are P(0) and Q(0). By setting a maximum
price at P(max), which is below the market clearing price, the
government induces an excess demand equal to the difference
between the quantity that suppliers are willing to supply at the
controlled price, Q(1)S, and the quantity that consumers want
to buy at the controlled price Q(1)D. Note also that consumers
would be willing to pay P(1) per unit for the restricted supply of
Q(1)S.

could make a cheeseburger have lower quality. You could use a cheaper bun or more filler as opposed to hamburger meat. When there are shortages due to price controls, consumers will also be more willing to accept shoddy merchandise or settle for more costly or less suitable substitutes for the good or service in short supply. When consumers are frustrated by their unfilled demands they may get other consumers who have the necessary "pull" to make purchases for them or try to bribe store owners by offering to pay a price as high as P(1), which is $75 in figure 6.1, "under the table." It is not uncommon to hear of landlords being bribed or requiring large nonrefundable deposits for the keys to a rent-controlled apartment. The point here is that if the price control is initially effective so that suppliers reduce their output to Q(1)S in figure 6.1, buyers are willing to pay much more for this quantity than the control price, P(max). The short supply provides a natural incentive for some frustrated buyers to pay what the good or service is worth to them, P(1).

Of course, sellers have an incentive to take advantage of this situation. They may make their customers purchase other goods they do not really want. It was fairly common during the gas shortage in the United States during the middle 1970s for consumers to have to buy a tune-up or oil change in order to get gasoline. Sellers may engage in **discrimination,** which means treating buyers differently on grounds normally inconsistent with profit maximization, such as race, religion, or ethnic background. During the gas shortage we have been mentioning it was common for attendants to sell to their friends and relatives first. If you were a landlord with a highly prized apartment wouldn't you be more likely to rent it to a relative or at least to someone you know?

Given our knowledge of how markets work, who are the winners and losers when a price ceiling is put into effect? Clearly, those consumers who have an "in" with some store and are able to buy at a price below

increases because buyers want to buy much more than sellers are willing to sell at a price below equilibrium. An example of this occurs when buyers have to wait many hours in long lines. Remember the mile-long lines of cars during the gas shortages of late 1973 and early 1974 in the United States, recall the pictures of people lined up to buy food in Poland during 1982, or remember the scene in the movie *Moscow on the Hudson* when Robin Williams offers to take any size shoes.

Sellers may attempt to circumvent the price ceiling by lowering the quality of their product. For example, think about all of the ways in which you normal come out ahead. For example, the retired and the unemployed may be winners because they have more time to wait. They will be the early birds. Relatives of the sellers will also benefit. Not all consumers are better off, though. Those who want to purchase the good or service but are prevented from doing so are worse off. Similarly, there are winners and losers among firms and their stockholders and workers. Firms who sell less than normal make lower profits for their stockholders and have fewer jobs for their workers. However, firms that circumvent the law and are able to extract prices as high as P(1) in figure 6.1 may end up better off.

An important consideration is what price ceilings do to the social fabric of a city or country. Market forces that tend to move the actual price toward its equilibrium value are often quite powerful. They may cause normally honest citizens to bend or break the law in order to get the goods or the revenue denied them by the ceiling price. Moreover, otherwise honest government officials may be tempted to accept bribes to help consumers or producers get what they want. In short, government intervention in the market process in the form of price ceilings, despite its well-meant motive of keeping prices low, damages a society's respect for its laws. To many, this is an important side effect of price controls.

It is important to recognize that scarcity requires some system for deciding who, among competing buyers, will get the scarce goods and services. A market, and its ability to establish an equilibrium price and quantity, is itself a mechanism for such a decision on the basis of a consumer's ability and willingness to pay money. If the market is not allowed to establish a price and, through it, the allocation of the good or service, then alternative mechanisms must arise. These include willingness to wait in line, discrimination on the part of the sellers, or some kind of government bureaucracy that chooses the lucky recipients of the good or service. One reason government may choose

to interfere with the market-determined allocation of resources is that the winners from government intervention gain a great deal per individual beneficiary, while the losers, although more numerous, do not suffer great *individual* losses. Thus the potential winners are prepared to devote great effort to influence government behavior, while potential losers from government interference in the economy have little incentive as individuals to learn about or to try to influence a particular piece of legislation.

We must also recognize that the system used to allocate goods and services to consumers has an important effect on their behavior outside of the market in question. For example, when willingness to pay money is the criterion used to determine who gets the good or service, consumers compete to earn money by offering their scarce labor resources to those producers who put the highest value on them. Other devices for deciding who among consumers gets a good or service lead to other kinds of competition. These include political lobbying to influence the allocation of the good by the government bureau, searching for a good in short supply, or standing in line. Nonprice allocation mechanisms lead to inefficient uses of resources because time spent standing in line or lobbying is time that could be used to produce something else for consumption. Moreover, sellers who try to sell their good or service under the table and above the control price use resources to avoid getting caught. The government uses resources to try to prevent this from happening and to punish those they catch. These resources could also be used to produce other goods and services that society might want. Included is a more direct attack on poverty, which was the justification for the price controls in the first place. With these ideas in mind, let us apply our understanding of price ceilings as we look at a specific example, the gasoline shortage in the middle 1970s in the United States. We will return to the topic of rent controls in chapter 18.

A Case Study of a Price Ceiling: The Gasoline Crisis of 1973–74

An important example of the effect of a ceiling price comes from the Arab oil embargo of 1973–74. In a very short period of time the embargo sharply reduced the supply of petroleum to the United States and many other western countries. The effect of this on the market for gasoline is shown in figure 6.2. The supply of gasoline moved sharply to the left, and the equilibrium price of gasoline began to rise as the decrease in supply was viewed as permanent. Because the United States economy at this time was under the Nixon administration's "phase four" price controls, the price of gasoline was not allowed to rise to its long-term equilibrium level, P(1) in figure 6.2. It could only rise to an intermediate level, P(2). In particular, the price of a gallon of regular gasoline rose from $0.40 in 1973 to $0.53 in 1974, an increase of almost 33 percent in the space of only one year.[4]

In chapter 5 we saw that the elasticity of demand for gasoline is rather small—about −0.11 over short periods of time when consumers have few options for reducing their consumption. Remember, it takes time for gasoline users to adapt to higher prices by making long-term adjustments, such as buying smaller cars, moving closer to their jobs, taking fewer driving vacations, and so on. A short-term elasticity of −0.11 means that the observed (33 percent) increase in the price of gasoline would reduce the amount demanded by only 3.6 percent. Thus, the price increase required over a short period of time to get to the new equilibrium in the gasoline market would have to have been quite large.

Because the price of gasoline was allowed to rise only to $0.53, P(2) in figure 6.2, this offered little incentive for domestic suppliers to increase their output. The small price increase also did little to discourage domestic consumption of gasoline; it fell only by about 3.8 percent during 1973 to 1974—from 110.5 billion gallons to 106.3 billion gallons.[5] The excess demand for gasoline created by the price restriction, Q(2)D − Q(2)S, caused service stations to close

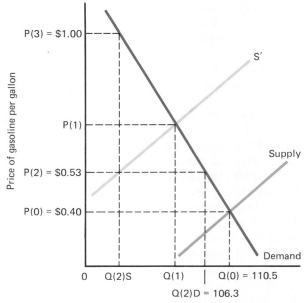

Figure 6.2   The effect of the Arab oil embargo on the price of gasoline in the United States
If the controlled price of gasoline is set at P(2), the equilibrium price of ration coupons would be P(3)–P(2) apiece. The result is a higher total price for gasoline than would be the case without price controls and rationing—P(1).

If the government introduced a tax on consumers of P(3)–P(2) per gallon, consumers would also end up paying P(3) for Q(2)S gallons of gasoline (including the tax).

much earlier than previously, service station operators to refuse to sell to anyone but their regular customers, long lines of cars waiting for gas, and outright violations of the price ceiling. Because drivers were willing to pay prices as high as P(3), perhaps $0.75 to $1.00 per gallon, for the available supply of gasoline, Q(2)S, it was hardly surprising that the price of gasoline at many stations was actually much higher than the legal maximum price. At times, price gouging took place under the table. As mentioned earlier, sometimes consumers were forced to purchase extra services, including tune-ups and oil changes. Drivers

Rationing a good or service means that the right to consume it is allocated by an authority, such as a government, on grounds other than consumers' willingness to pay.

A white market is a legal arrangement for buying and selling ration coupons when a legal maximum price or some other market interference creates an excess demand for a good or service.

A black market is an illegal arrangement for buying and selling a good or service or ration coupons when a legal maximum price or some other market interference creates an excess demand.

were at times asked to buy dolls or rabbit's feet at inflated prices in order to be able to purchase gasoline at P(2), $0.53 per gallon in figure 6.2.

This information is enough for you to identify the winners and losers from the price controls in place during the Arab oil embargo of 1973–74. Construct a table naming the winners and losers. Make sure to show that certain customers and certain producers and their workers were winners and that other customers and other producers and their workers were losers. Of course, your list might change if different policies had been followed in this situation. Let us consider two other policies that might have been used. One is the formal rationing of gasoline through the use of coupons, and the other is a (higher) tax on gasoline purchases. In the course of the discussions that follow you should try to identify who the winners and losers would have been had either of these two policies been pursued. Do the winners gain a lot or a little per individual? How much do individual losers lose?

Gas Rationing as an Alternative to a Price Ceiling

Many public officials and private citizens believed that rationing gasoline was a desirable way to eliminate the excess demand created by the price ceiling. Under **rationing,** a buyer would need a ration coupon along with money to purchase gasoline. In the example in figure 6.2, the government would issue just enough ration coupons for buyers to be able to purchase Q(2)S.

If a so-called **white market** for ration coupons were allowed, consumers could legally buy and sell coupons. Because P(3), which is equal to $1.00, is the price that would make the quantity of gasoline demanded just equal to the amount available, the equilibrium price of ration coupons would be P(3) − P(2), or $0.47, in figure 6.2. Sellers of gasoline coupons would be paid P(3) − P(2), or $0.47 per gallon, for giving up their right to buy gas. Gasoline buyers would eventually pay P(3), or $1.00, in opportunity costs per gallon one way or the other. Either they would purchase coupons or use their own coupons and sacrifice the revenue they could have obtained from selling

them to others. Without a white market in which ration coupons could legally be sold to others, public demand would encourage the creation of an illegal **black market** for gasoline coupons. Why? The answer to this question lies in the fact that a maximum price law does not repeal the economic laws of supply and demand.

Allowing consumers to buy and sell ration coupons amounts to allowing the gasoline market to perform a major part of the government's function: allocating the available supply of gasoline among consumers. Gasoline users who are unwilling to pay the market-clearing price under rationing in figure 6.2, which is P(3), or $1.00, would sell their coupons to those who are willing to pay it. The oil companies, however, would not profit from the excess of P(3) over P(2), which is $0.47 per gallon in figure 6.2, because they would still be receiving only P(2) per gallon of gasoline. Notice that the rationing scheme would redistribute revenue away from the oil companies and to consumers who get ration coupons from the government. But who gets the ration coupons?

How would you give out ration coupons if you were running a gasoline rationing program? Would you issue coupons on a per capita or a per family basis? Would you make the number of coupons people receive proportional to the amount they drive? In this case those who drive the most get the most gasoline. Do you want to let heavy gas users continue to be heavy users? How many coupons go to the poor? Must someone have a driver's license to get coupons? You can see the tough political questions you would have to answer. Think about the winners and losers who might be created by a gasoline rationing system. The point we are trying to make is that it is an inescapable fact that any government intervention will create a new set of winners and losers compared to the outcome established by the forces of supply and demand. Here is another point to think about. We have noted the possibility for sellers to discriminate when there is an effective price ceiling. Under a rationing system, the control of allocation shifts from gasoline sellers to the government; the preferences of the government, including possible discrimination, are substituted for those of gasoline sellers.

These are by no means all of the issues surrounding gas rationing. There are some long-term problems to confront. Rationing offers no incentive for gasoline producers to increase quantities supplied beyond Q(2)S in figure 6.2 by engaging in new exploration or adopting more expensive recovery techniques. If the market were allowed to reach its equilibrium price of P(1), the amount of gasoline supplied would eventually increase to Q(1). Notice that the opportunity cost of gasoline would actually fall because P(1) is less than P(3). Under rationing with a white market, however, producers have no incentive to increase the amount of gasoline they supply beyond Q(2)S. Thus, in the long term, rationing tends to force consumers to pay a higher opportunity cost and get less gasoline than if market forces were allowed to operate unhindered. The producers of gasoline, their stockholders, and workers are, of course, worse off in the long term under rationing. (Remember too that the stockholders of gasoline-producing companies are not necessarily wealthy, even though the corporations in which they hold shares may show large accounting profits.)

The point of this section has been to use our supply and demand framework to develop a scoreboard of winners and losers when rationing is paired with price controls. What can you add to our scoreboard? On the basis of what we have found, how do you feel about gasoline rationing? Would you vote for it or against it?

Taxing Gasoline Purchases as an Alternative to a Price Ceiling   We noted earlier that there was another alternative to allowing the unregulated forces of supply and demand to allocate gasoline in response to the Arab oil embargo. The United States government could have worked through the forces of supply and demand and placed a tax on the gasoline purchases equal to P(3) − P(2), which is $0.47 per gallon in figure 6.2. Research or experimentation would dictate how high to make the tax. The tax would shift the supply curve for gasoline up to pass through the point [Q(2)S, P(3)], which is where P(3) intersects the demand curve for gasoline. (Please draw in this line.) This upward shift in supply reflects a tax imposed on producers of gasoline. Put differently, the supply curve after the oil embargo, S′, indicates how much gasoline firms are willing to supply at various prices of gasoline. That willingness is unchanged by the tax. The tax we are discussing redistributes payments so that part of them go to the federal government instead of all of them going to the oil companies. The new supply curve you have just drawn, which is higher than S′ by the amount P(3) − P(2), or $0.47 per gallon of gasoline, shows what suppliers are willing to offer to the users of gasoline when the tax is in effect. The vertical distance between the supply curve we have asked you to draw in figure 6.2 and the one labeled S′ is the tax paid to the government, which in our example is $0.47 per gallon. You can think of the tax as driving a wedge between the price paid by consumers and the amount collected by firms. Thus, both consumers and the oil companies share the economic burden of the tax.

The effect of this tax on the opportunity cost of gasoline purchases and the quantity would be identical to that of a policy of rationing with a white market for ration coupons. The amount of gasoline demanded would be reduced to Q(2)S in figure 6.2. With the tax, however, the price differential of $0.47, P(3) − P(2), would go to the government rather than to consumers. Who are the winners and losers under such a tax program? Again, oil companies, their stockholders, and workers are worse off because they sell less gasoline at a lower price than if market forces are allowed to create equilibrium price P(1) and equilibrium quantity Q(1). Also worse off are the consumers of gasoline who get less gasoline and pay a higher price. Beneficiaries are those individuals who get to use or receive the tax revenues collected.

Some other facts about the gas tax option are interesting to note. First, the tax is probably easier and cheaper to administer than rationing. However, it would be no more likely to stimulate producers to increase the quantity of gasoline supplied beyond Q(2)S in the long term than a legal maximum price with rationing.

*A **price floor** is the lowest price at which it is legal to buy or sell a good or service.*

Conflicting Policy Objectives   Before leaving this discussion of gasoline pricing, we must note two aspects that nicely illustrate the potential conflicts in goals that can arise with price controls. Conflicts in government policy objectives can lead to further applications of market controls and help to explain how government intervention can perpetuate itself. More simply put, incompatible objectives will easily produce additional policies and controls. The original controls cannot do the "trick" because the trick is undoable. Specifically, price controls were intended to (1) prevent oil producers in the United States from making high profits (windfall profits). Price controls were also supposed to (2) keep gasoline affordable to middle- and lower-income Americans. Yet the government also wanted to (3) promote United States exploration and production of oil and oil substitutes. The question was how to promote expanded domestic exploration and drilling for oil and *at the same time* maintain low prices for oil products. These low prices depressed the oil company profits and earnings necessary for oil companies to want to undertake such projects. Herein lay the conflict.

The United States government's response to this problem was to impose a two-tiered price system: (1) oil produced from existing wells was kept under price controls with a ceiling price of about $5.25 per barrel, and (2) oil produced from wells in areas drilled after 1974 was allowed to sell at the world market price, which at the time (1976–78) averaged about $12 per barrel. Those two types of oil created predictable problems.

The first problem was one of enforcement. How do you distinguish "old" oil from "new" oil? Because the distinction is unrelated to the nature of the oil itself and depends on knowing where the oil came from, you can easily imagine the temptation for individuals to mislabel old oil as new oil. Television's "Sixty Minutes" did a feature on unscrupulous individuals who attempted to earn millions of dollars by mislabeling oil shipments. The indignation of the investigative reporter was certainly justified, but the program never explored the basic absurdity of trying to enforce two different prices for an identical product.

Government Promotion of Economic Waste   It is also important to note that the program of two prices promoted inefficient oil production. Prior to the oil embargo of 1973, the world price of oil was about $3 per barrel, and a number of wells were kept capped because they simply were not profitable to operate at an oil price of $3, or even $6 a barrel. But once the world price of oil went to $12, such wells would have been highly profitable to operate. However, they were "old" oil wells and their output had a ceiling price of $5.25. Obviously, wells in new areas that could not profitably pump oil at a price below $10 per barrel were operating while wells in established areas that could pump oil for $6 per barrel remained capped because of the $5.25 limit on barrels of oil pumped from old wells. In short, some of the nation's oil production was forced away from the lower-cost old fields to the higher-cost, but unconstrained, new fields.

This is a useful example of how price controls that are left in place for any length of time to deal with politically unattractive aspects of market conditions invariably create additional problems. These problems invite additional solutions in the form of more government controls. The web of controls can become complex and economically counterproductive.

A Price Floor

In some cases government policy establishes a legal minimum price known as a **price floor.** If you think about the concept of a minimum price for a second or two, one of the first things that may come to mind is the minimum wage law, which is discussed in chapter 15. Another example of minimum prices occurs in agriculture. Federal policy toward the prices farmers receive in the United States provides an important application of our supply and demand analysis.

Agricultural Price Supports
One feature of farm policy in the United States has been to guarantee growers of certain commodities, most notably many grain and dairy products, that the price will not be allowed to fall below a certain level.

*An **effective minimum price** is a price that is set above the equilibrium price.*

If this price floor is an **effective minimum price**—one above the equilibrium price—then an excess supply of the commodity will result. This is depicted in figure 6.3, which uses the wheat market as an example. If farmers are to receive the minimum price for their wheat, P(min), which is $4.00 per bushel, the excess supply (also called a glut) at that price must be kept off the market. One way to assure that the quantity of wheat Q(1)S − Q(1)D, which is 250 million bushels, is not available for purchasers to buy is either to destroy it or for the government to purchase and store it. The latter procedure is usually adopted. In terms of figure 6.3, the government buys the excess supply at the guaranteed price and stores it. This means that farmers will be paid an amount equal to P(min) × (Q(1)S − Q(1)D), or $1 billion in our example. In addition to this, the government incurs the cost of storing excess commodities, such as wheat. Ultimately, all of these costs will have to be paid by United States taxpayers.

Table 6.1 gives us some detailed information on the general pattern of price supports in United States agriculture during 1983. Notice that the single largest payments go to corn farmers and wheat farmers, almost $7.1 billion and $4.1 billion, respectively. Table 6.1 also shows us that the total value of all price supports was approximately $21.6 billion in 1983. We noted earlier that price supports may lead the government to store large amounts of agricultural commodities. In 1984, the United States government owned approximately 1.5 billion pounds of nonfat dry milk, 152,000 bales of cotton, and 296 million bushels of corn. The total value of all of the commodities owned by the government was about $7.4 billion, most of which was in dairy products ($4.1 billion) and wheat ($1.5 billion).[6]

The issue of who wins and loses is not as obvious as it might seem. Clearly, farmers as a group benefit. Collectively, they sell more at a higher price with the government support than would be possible with free

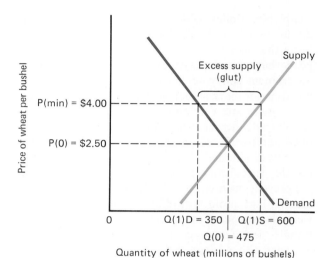

Figure 6.3   The effect of a minimum price on the market for wheat
If the government guarantees wheat growers a minimum price of P(min), then an excess supply (glut) of wheat equal to Q(1)S–Q(1)D will result. In order to assure that farmers receive P(min), the excess supply must either be destroyed or purchased by the government and stored so that it does not enter the market.

market sales. Consider the case of wheat in particular. Consumers pay more for each unit of wheat, have less wheat directly available to them, finance storage costs for excess wheat production at the governmentally imposed price, and ultimately underwrite the government transfer of income to farmers. Consumers are clearly worse off under agricultural price supports.

It is important to realize that most of the economic benefits of agricultural price supports in the United States go to farmers who are the least desperate economically. Because price supports are embodied in the higher prices and outputs for farmers, the gain to any individual farmer will be directly related to the output that can be sold at P(min) in figure

Table 6.1   Commodity credit corporation: Price support granted on 1980 crop, United States and territories[1]

Commodity	Unit	Through Sept. 30, 1983	
		Quantity (millions)	Value (million dollars)
Cotton, upland	Bale	5.0	1,326.6
Cotton, extra-long staple	do		28.4
Seed cotton, upland	Pound		
Seed cotton, extra-long staple	do		
Wheat	Bushel	1,005.3	4,140.6
Corn	do	2,385.2	7,115.4
Honey	Pound	89.2	53.4
Milk and butterfat:			
Butter	Pound	407.2	609.7
Cheese	do	797.0	1,173.2
Dried milk	do	979.7	928.4
Tobacco	do	501.9	1,096.0
Rice, rough	Cwt	68.9	567.3
Grain sorghum	Bushel	390.3	1,161.7
Peanuts, farmers' stock	Pound	539.0	90.5
Oats	Bushel	9.2	12.2
Barley	do	93.0	205.2
Beans, dry edible	Pound		
Rye	Bushel	1.7	3.6
Soybeans	do	396.8	1,985.4
Sugar			
Beets	Pound	3,036.1	567.8
Cane	do	1,101.7	188.5
Special purchase programs[2]		1,705.6	
Total			21,602.9

Source: From U.S. Department of Agriculture, *Agricultural Statistics*, 1984, Table #638, p. 456.

[1]Consists of loans made and acquisitions under commodity loan and purchase programs.

[2]Commodities included in "Special purchase programs" for 1982 crops are wheat flour, corn products, wheat products, rolled oats, vegetable oil products, blended food products, soya flour, feed for government facilities, foundation seeds, sorghum grits, peanut products, milled rice, brown rice, and textured soya rice.

6.3. Wealthy farmers with a great deal of land will be able to produce more at price P(min) than less affluent farmers with small farms. For farms of a given size, farmers fortunate enough to have rich, high-yield soil will be able to produce more output than farmers with land of relatively poor quality. In short, farmers with small acreages of poor quality, who are likely to be the poorest members of the farm sector, receive the least amount of subsidy. Wealthy farmers, with highly productive land, receive the lion's share of the income transfer. It is a cruel irony that the plight of the small farmer and the farmer's difficulties in competing with the "big guys" is so effectively used to generate political backing for a farm support program that ultimately magnifies the difference in wealth distribution between poor and wealthy farmers.

*A **price subsidy** is a government payment to producers or consumers per unit of the good or service sold or purchased.*

Table 6.2   Government payments to farms by value of farm sales: 1975 to 1984

Value of farm sales	Total payments (million dollars)					Average payment per farm (dollars)				
	1975	1980	1982	1983	1984	1975	1980	1982	1983	1984
Total	**807**	**1,286**	**3,492**	**9,295**	**8,430**	**320**	**529**	**1,455**	**3,922**	**3,621**
Less than $2,500	37	23	54	81	30	46	37	94	146	56
$2,500–$4,999	38	24	60	39	32	123	79	201	136	116
$5,000–$9,999	54	51	127	88	108	174	165	420	285	342
$10,000–$19,999	82	59	146	288	233	260	206	527	1,052	865
$20,000–$39,999	140	146	355	569	544	445	521	1,330	2,210	2,200
$40,000–$99,999	230	414	1,065	1,976	1,874	729	1,169	2,986	5,554	5,309
$100,000–$249,999	[1]105	[1]282	1,005	2,949	2,984	[1]1,091	[1]1,700	4,341	12,763	13,004
$250,000–$499,999	[2]64	[2]195	387	1,867	1,583	[2]1,665	[2]2,412	6,160	26,580	20,560
$500,000 and over	57	91	293	1,438	1,044	5,193	3,849	9,829	46,990	33,418

Source: From U.S. Bureau of the Census, *Statistical Abstract of the United States, 1986,* (106th Edition) Washington, D.C., 1985, Table 1146, p. 646.
[1]Farms with sales of $100,000–$199,999.
[2]Farms with sales of $200,000–$499,999.

To get some idea of who receives price support payments, let us first note that approximately 48 percent of farms in 1984 had sales of less than $10,000.[7] Now look at table 6.2. The right side of this table gives the average payment per farm. The average payment per farm for farms with between $0 and $9,999 of annual sales was between $56 and $342 in 1984. This compares to an overall average payment per farm of $3,621. Moreover, the average payment for the very largest farms was almost $33,500 in 1984. Now look at the left side of table 6.2. If we add up the numbers in the column for 1984 we see that total payments were $8.4 billion. Of this, approximately $170 million, or 2 percent, went to the small farms—those 48 percent of all farms with annual sales less than $10,000. In contrast, consider farms with sales of $40,000 or more, or about 30 percent of all farms in 1984.[8] These farms received about $7.5 billion, or 78 percent of the $8.4 billion total.

Agricultural Price Subsidies

One of the difficulties we have noted with agricultural price supports is that the government must store large amounts of grain and dairy products. This adds significant costs to the expenses of running a government price support program. What can the government do to try to reduce some of those storage costs? One thing might be to give the food away to relatively poor countries. The United States does have such a program, known as Food for Peace, which provides more than $1 billion of surplus food commodities to relatively less developed countries. This program is not as popular as one might think, however. Specifically, the countries that are offered free food may not take it because of the detrimental effects on their own farming sectors.[9] Think about it this way: Would *you* like to compete with someone who produces what you do but gives it away?

An alternative means of ensuring a minimum price for an agricultural commodity and avoiding storage costs is illustrated in figure 6.4. In this figure the government guarantees a price P(min), which is $4.00, for sales of Q(1)S, or 600 million bushels of wheat. In this case, farmers sell Q(1)S at price P(1), $1.00 per bushel, and the government pays producers a direct **price subsidy** of P(min) − P(1), or $3.00, for each bushel sold. Which form of aid costs the government more money, price subsidies or price supports?

In each case, total revenue to the producers of the commodity equals P(min) × Q(1)S, or $2.4 billion. If the demand for wheat is inelastic, price and total revenue move in the same direction. In this case, the

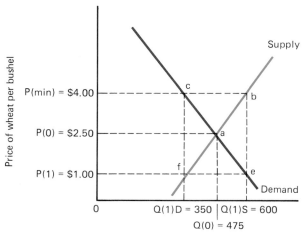

Figure 6.4 Government subsidies versus support purchases of wheat
Support purchases of Q(1)S–Q(1)D to maintain an artificially high price of P(min) will involve direct costs of P(min) × [Q(1)S − Q(1)D], which is represented by the area of the rectangle Q(1) D c b Q(1)S. Direct subsidies to maintain sales of Q(1)S at price P(min) would involve a total subsidy of P(min) − P(1) × Q(1)S, which is represented by the area of the rectangle P(1) P(min) b e. If the demand curve is inelastic, the direct subsidy scheme will involve more direct costs (expenditures). However, the purchase program also involves the indirect costs of storing the commodity purchased by the government.

amount consumers pay for wheat when the price is P(min), which is $4.00, and the quantity purchased is Q(1)D, which is 350 million bushels—$1.4 billion—exceeds their expenditures at the lower price, P(1) × Q(1)S, which is $600 million. Put differently, if the demand for wheat is inelastic, the area of the rectangle 0 P (min) c Q(1)D, which is $1.4 billion, exceeds the area of the rectangle 0 P(1) e Q(1)S, which is $600 million in our example. The main implication of this is that direct payments to farmers would be greater in the case where there is no purchase of the commodity by the government. Government expenditures, when they do not purchase the commodity but rather subsidize the price paid to farmers, are represented by the area of the rectangle P(1) P(min) b e, which is $1.8 billion in figure 6.4.

The area of the rectangle Q(1)D c b Q(1)S, or $1 billion, is the government's expenditures for the commodity when it purchases and stores it. When demand is inelastic, the first rectangle has a greater area than the second because P(1) P(min) c f, or $1.05 billion, exceeds Q(1)D f e Q(1)S, or $250 million. However, if we include the costs of storing the commodity in our calculation, it is possible that the overall cost to the government (the taxpayers) of providing the same economic help to farmers is greater with the government purchase program than with the program of direct price subsidies on sales of Q(1)S. Also keep in mind that under the price subsidy program, consumers purchase a greater quantity of the commodity at a lower price than when the government purchases the commodity and stores it. Moreover, when demand is inelastic, consumers are paying less in total for Q(1)S than for Q(1)D, in this case $600 million versus $1.05 billion.

One example of a direct price subsidy in the United States is the result of the National Wool Act. First passed in 1954, the act deems wool an essential and strategic commodity that is vital to our national defense. Apparently, the argument is that wool is heavily used in military dress uniforms. Thus, it is important that the government ensure the financial health of the wool industry. In 1984, the wool price subsidy program gave wool farmers $115 million. How does this relate to figure 6.4? In 1983, P(1) for wool equaled $0.61 per pound. The price subsidy promised wool farmers was $0.91, so that P(min) for wool was $1.52 a pound. Therefore, the price promised farmers was 2.5 times the price paid by consumers. This led to total payments to wool farmers of $115 million in 1984, which is the dollar value of the area P(1) P(min) b e in figure 6.4 if wool is the product being considered. It has been estimated that since its inception in 1954, the wool subsidy program has cost United States taxpayers approximately $1.5 billion.[10]

Our analysis of policies whereby the government restrains the forces of supply and demand is complete for now. We next turn our attention to some programs that attempt to affect the welfare of various groups in society by changing the supply or demand for a particular good or service.

▶ Government Policies that Work through the Forces of Supply and Demand

At this point, it is important to remind ourselves of how much knowledge we already have. In particular, tables 2.2 (page 49), 4.5 (page 94), and 5.1 (page 114) allow us to think about a large number of policies that the United States federal government and state and local governments use to affect prices and quantities in various markets. Table 2.2, for example, shows us the events that shift demand. Any government policy that changes a variable that underlies a demand curve also shifts the demand curve. The end result is a change in equilibrium price and quantity in a market. Similarly, table 4.5 outlines the factors that underlie supply. If any of them change as a result of government policy, this disturbs the supply curve. Ultimately, equilibrium prices and quantities change, and this changes the answers to the crucial *how, what,* and *for whom* questions that all economies confront. Thus, table 4.5 provides us with another set of ways for policymakers to influence human behavior. Finally, table 5.1 reminds us exactly how policies that affect supply or demand ultimately change long-run quantities and prices.

Policies that Shift Supply Curves

Remember that a supply curve reflects the cost of production. Thus, any government policy that changes the cost of production affects the position of the supply curve. Taxes placed on producers raise the cost of supplying a good or service and shift the supply curve up by increasing the marginal cost of production. Similarly, subsidies to producers lower costs and increase supply. Remember also that the cost of production is related to a firm's technology and input prices. This means that taxes placed on a firm's labor increase the cost of production. Examples include the payroll taxes that firms pay for unemployment compensation and Social Security and workers' compensation insurance premiums for their employees.

Finally, the federal government provides research grants to various organizations, including universities. If the resulting research changes production technology so that firms become more productive, supply will be increased (the marginal cost curve lowered).

A fairly severe form of cost increase (supply reduction) occurs when a particular good or service is outlawed. Such is the case with heroin sales today or abortions two decades or so ago. Doctors who were caught performing abortions were fined or had their licenses revoked. Heroin pushers face jail terms when caught. Such fines or imprisonment of providers can dramatically increase the cost of producing the outlawed good or service, resulting in a substantial reduction in supply. Of course, supply does not totally disappear because some people are still willing to take the risk of getting caught. Even in societies where the death penalty is imposed for certain types of sales (such as Malaysia for large cocaine transactions), supply is not reduced to zero. Where penalties on suppliers are small or not enforced, as in the case of marijuana sales in many United States cities, the reduction in supply can be trivial.

A final factor that shifts supply curves is the number of producers. For example, if government policy encourages foreign suppliers to sell their goods in the United States, supply is increased and prices will fall. Having outlined some of the ways in which the government increases or decreases supply in the United States, let us now turn our attention to an in-depth discussion of a particular program.

The Payment in Kind (PIK) Program

As a follow-up to our earlier discussion of agricultural policies, we now turn to a specific example of government intervention intended to affect the production of an agricultural commodity. Specifically, the third example of government intervention in agricultural markets that we discuss in this chapter involves direct supply restrictions.

During fiscal 1983, the Reagan administration spent approximately $9.4 billion on the "payment in kind" or PIK program. This included $5.9 billion on feed grains, $2.1 billion on wheat, and about $1 billion on cotton.[11] Under the PIK program a farmer pledges not to plant acreage. The farmer then receives government-stored grain, cotton, or rice that he or she can sell in place of the product that would have been grown on the land that the farmer agrees not to plant.

A simplified representation of the PIK program appears in figure 6.5. The original supply curve reflects the supply of an agricultural commodity, such as corn, before the PIK program is instituted. The curve S' represents private farm supply under the PIK program. The reduced supply by farmers is offset by using the government's past purchases of the commodity to make up the difference between $Q(1)$ and $Q(0)$. Put differently, while farmers are actually producing the quantities along the supply curve S', the government gives them back past purchases equal to $Q(0) - Q(1)$. In the case of corn, this gift was worth about $5.4 billion in fiscal 1983. Thus, while S' now describes farms' production, the original supply still describes the availability of the commodity to consumers. You can think of the difference between the two supply curves in figure 6.5 as reflecting the substitution of a government-stored commodity, which is given to the farmers free, for foregone farm output. In effect, the PIK program lets farmers sell some of the same output twice. Specifically, the government purchased their agricultural commodity in the past and then stored it. Under the PIK program, the government gives farmers back some of the commodity it bought and lets the farmers sell the commodity a second time. This is the essential nature of the PIK subsidy, payment in kind.

One of the purposes of this program was to relieve the credit crunch faced by farmers during the 1982–84 period by making it possible for them to maintain the same sales level, $Q(0)$, without having

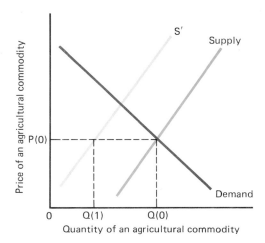

Figure 6.5   The payment in kind (PIK) program
$P(0)$ and $Q(0)$ are the equilibrium price and output without the PIK program. With the program, actual annual supply shrinks to S' and production declines to $Q(1)$. Government commodity transfers to farmers for sale equal $Q(0) - Q(1)$, and land needed to grow $Q(0) - Q(1)$ is set aside by farmers.

to pay for fertilizer, equipment, and all of the other inputs needed to bring output $Q(0) - Q(1)$ to market. Furthermore, government storage costs could be reduced by diminishing the amount of the commodities being stored.

In addition to the $9.4 billion of agricultural commodities farmers received from the PIK program during this period, they also benefited from the reduction in their operating costs. Members of the general public may also benefit from PIK because their annual tax bill can be reduced by the amount of the savings on the government's storage costs for the commodities. The biggest individual winners under PIK, of course, are the wealthier farmers with plentiful amounts of land to set aside. Are there any particular losers that we can identify from the PIK program?

The Ripple Effect of PIK and Other Agricultural Programs   It is relatively easy to see impacts beyond the market we have been discussing. In particular, if you happened to be a producer of fertilizers or farm implements or were a for-hire farm worker during fiscal 1983, you would have found that the PIK program had a direct and undesirable effect on your income. The gain to farmers in terms of cost savings on production translated into direct sales losses to producers of farm production inputs, such as tractor sales and service, as well as to hired hands and seed companies.[12]

Apart from the argument that farm support payments go largely to those farmers who are least in need of financial assistance, there is a widening appreciation of the contribution that farm support programs are making to the systematic destruction of farmland within the United States. Because of government price supports for crops such as wheat, farmers have an incentive to put low-productivity land into production. Much of this land is only profitable because of government price supports. Farmers may also be willing to risk permanent loss of land from farm production through erosion in the hope that they can get paid by PIK type programs to take these lands out of production at some later time. During the dust bowl of the Great Depression, the United States Department of Agriculture estimated United States farm soil to be eroding at a rate of 3.5 billion tons per year. After fifty years of conservation efforts (with conservation program costs rising to $1 billion per year and totaling $18 billion since the New Deal), the rate of soil erosion of United States farmland is now estimated to be 6 billion tons per year.[13]

The international ramifications of the United States program of price supports and storage of agricultural commodities, especially grains, have also received some serious criticism in recent years. Under the terms of a program known as PL480 (Public Law 480), the United States has attempted over the years to make government-stored agricultural output available to consumers in poorer countries. Clearly, that would seem to be an improvement over having excess commodities rot in warehouses. Yet, as we noted earlier, many developing countries now recognize that subsidized grain imports into their countries from the United States have injured their own farm sectors. Farmers in developing countries cannot sell their products if domestic needs can largely be satisfied with cheap grain imports from the United States. In a perverse way, PL480 assistance has sometimes compounded rather than alleviated the economic problems of developing countries.[14]

Policies that Shift Demand Curves

Many government policies in the United States affect consumption by changing demand. Income taxes, which reduce the money people have to spend, reduce the public's demand for goods and services in general. Drug paraphenalia laws raise the price of a drug complement and, in this way, are designed to reduce the demand for drugs. However, because there seem to be rather good substitutes for commercially sold drug paraphenalia, it is unlikely that such laws have much of an impact on drug use. Governments also sometimes try to change people's tastes and preferences and thus their demand for a good or service. There are required cancer warnings on cigarettes, for example. Public advertising campaigns urge us to set our thermostats at 68 degrees in the winter and 78 degrees in the summer. We may feel guilty if we drive over 55 miles per hour or litter the countryside. Probably the most often used policies, though, are subsidies to encourage people to consume certain goods and taxes to discourage them from consuming certain other goods. The effect of these policies on the welfare of the various groups in society depends on the elasticity of the supply curves involved. To see this, we will consider two different subsidy policies, one where supply is relatively elastic and another where supply is relatively inelastic.

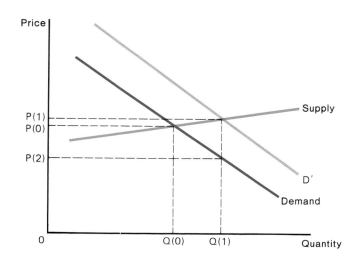

Figure 6.6   The effect of a government subsidy to consumers when supply is relatively elastic
When supply is relatively elastic, anything that increases demand has a relatively small effect on price and a relatively large effect on equilibrium quantity.

Subsidy: The Case of Food Stamps

Remember that a demand curve shows what consumers are willing to buy at various prices. A government program that earmarks transfer payments to people for the consumption of a particular good or service increases their willingness to pay for that good or service. In this way the food-stamp program in the United States increases the demand for food. Consumers have more money, and it is earmarked for food expenditures. This, of course, is the objective of the food-stamp program—to increase the consumption of nutritious food and, in the process, increase the welfare of the people involved. In 1984, for example, there were 20.9 million participants in the food-stamp program, with a federal cost of $10.7 billion.[15] This amounted to approximately $43 per participant per month. In total, about 7 million households received food stamps. About 71 percent of the recipient households were classified as poor by the official government definition.

The supply of agricultural commodities (food) is relatively elastic when farmers are given enough time to expand output over several years. This situation is depicted in figure 6.6. The food-stamp program increases demand to D′, and a new equilibrium price and quantity are established at P(1) and Q(1). Thus, when such a program is applied to a commodity where supply is relatively elastic, there is a fairly large increase in equilibrium quantity without much of a price increase. Food-stamp recipients are better off because they get more food at a lower (net out-of-pocket) price. In figure 6.6, P(2) is the net cost of food to food-stamp recipients. The difference between the shelf price, P(1), and what they actually pay, P(2), is equal to their food-stamp subsidy. Producers (and their workers) are better off because they sell more at a higher price. Remember, producers collect the full market price, P(1). Thus, the food-stamp program increases the welfare of both farmers and food-stamp recipients. Other possible winners are suppliers of nonfood items who benefit from the increased demand by food-stamp recipients who formerly could not afford such items but now can. Who is made worse off? Those who pay higher food prices and higher taxes are worse off. Even though individuals not in the food-stamp program pay higher food prices, the elastic supply of food means that the price increase is rather slight. The people who are taxed to pay for the food-stamp program are also worse off.

Subsidy: The Case of Medicare and Medicaid

Now let us turn our attention to the case where government policy increases demand for a good or service that has a relatively inelastic supply. We keep our eye on the issue of how the effects of such a policy may differ from the case just analyzed—where supply is relatively elastic. The medical care market is one of the most highly regulated in the United States. Think of all of the laws that make it difficult and time-consuming to become a physician or a nurse, or to build and operate a hospital. Moreover, there are government regulations on how much and what type of equipment an existing hospital can buy. These laws and regulations slow the speed at which people enter the medical professions and organizations establish health care facilities. This means that when people demand more health care and the price of health care rises, it takes a long time before health care suppliers can respond by providing more health care services. In basic economic terms, the supply of health care in the United States is relatively inelastic.

In 1985, federal government outlays for Medicare, which is a health insurance program for the elderly in the Social Security system, totaled approximately $66.3 billion. Outlays for Medicaid, which is health insurance for the poor, totaled approximately $23 billion.[16] When Medicare and Medicaid were introduced and then expanded over time, the demand for medical care increased. This type of situation is illustrated in figure 6.7. Notice that the expanded demand elicits very little increase in quantity supplied because of the regulations on the suppliers of medical care but a large increase in price. One result of the relatively inelastic supply of medical care has been the rising cost of medical care with less than the intended improvement in the health of the poor. Medicare and Medicaid have, however, contributed to an increase in the incomes of medical professionals over time in the United States because of the substantial price increases that go with the relatively inelastic supply.

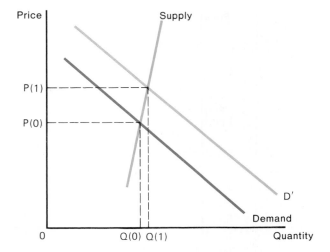

Figure 6.7   The effect of a government subsidy to consumers when supply is relatively inelastic
When supply is relatively inelastic, anything that increases demand has a relatively large effect on price but not much of an effect on equilibrium quantity.

Policies that Shift both Supply and Demand

So far we have discussed government market intervention schemes that have prevented supply and demand forces from clearing markets or have shifted supply or demand curves individually. The purpose of this section is to consider policy actions that simultaneously shift both supply and demand curves. When supply and demand both shift, our ability to predict what will happen to price and quantity depends on our degree of quantitative information concerning the supply and demand shifts and supply and demand elasticities. If all we know is the direction of the shifts in the schedules, then we will be able to predict the direction of the change in the equilibrium price or quantity but not both. To be able to predict the direction of the change in price *and* equilibrium quantity requires more quantitative knowledge. You may wish to review table 5.1 to solidify your understanding of the conclusions we have just summarized.

The Market for Small Cars in the United States

The example we will consider is the result of almost simultaneous decisions by the United States government to move away from controls in one market and toward the establishment of controls in another market. In particular, our discussion is focused on the market for small cars in the United States since 1979. This is illustrated in figure 6.8. Specifically, the decision to remove price controls on oil in the United States in conjunction with rising OPEC prices after the Shah of Iran was deposed in 1979 led American consumers to conclude that small, fuel-efficient cars were a more desirable purchase. The increase in demand for small cars to D′ in figure 6.8 tended to raise both the equilibrium price of small cars and the total number of small-car sales. Unfortunately for United States manufacturers, most of the new car sales went to foreign producers, especially the Japanese. Between 1979 and 1980, for example, the annual number of new passenger cars imported from Japan increased by about 25 percent, from 1.6 million to almost 2 million.[17]

Under pressure from the United States government, the Japanese agreed to limit exports of automobiles to the United States to about 1.8 to 1.9 million units per year. Japan maintained similar restrictions through the mid-1980s. In the simplest sense, this systematic restriction of Japanese automobile sales to the United States can be depicted by a decrease in the supply curve to S′ in figure 6.8. This supply shift alone would tend to increase the equilibrium price of small cars and to put downward pressure on sales of small cars.

Together, the expansion of demand and contraction of supply tended to increase prices of small cars. Thus, removal of oil price controls in the United States, in conjunction with restrictions on Japanese small-car sales in the United States, clearly put upward pressure on small-car prices. On the other hand, the increased demand for small cars tended to increase United States sales. This was happening at the

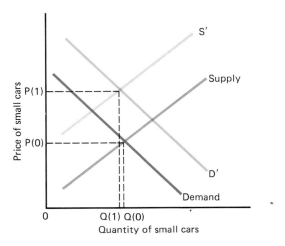

Figure 6.8   The market for small cars in the United States
Demand and supply indicate the original demand and supply curves for small cars in the United States. The equilibrium price and quantity are initially P(0) and Q(0), respectively. Increased oil prices after 1979 raised the domestic price of gasoline. This shifted small car demand to D′. Restrictions on automobile imports into the United States in the early 1980s shifted the supply curve to S′. This leads us to predict a price increase from P(0) to P(1). The change in output is harder to predict because it requires information on the relative magnitudes of the shifts in supply versus demand.

same time that import restrictions tended to reduce sales. Figure 6.8 depicts a net reduction in small-car sales because the decrease in supply of small cars more than offset the increase in demand.

Let us think briefly about some of the winners and losers from the decision to remove oil price controls and at the same time to restrict the sale of Japanese small cars in the United States. Some of the winners include United States auto firms, their stockholders, and workers, who now have greater quantities to produce and sell. The losers include American consumers who have to pay higher prices for small cars and have fewer of them. In chapter 31 we will learn more of the details of how the import quotas affect the Japanese producers and, interestingly, Japanese consumers of small cars. In particular, we will explain why Japan continued to limit car exports to the United States even after President Reagan indicated in March 1985 he would no longer request such limits.

The example just completed gave us some practice in using our supply and demand tools to try to predict what will happen to equilibrium price and quantity when both supply and demand change. When supply is reduced and demand is increased, there is the unambiguous implication that the equilibrium price will rise. Output effects, however, depend on the relative magnitude of the supply and demand shifts and on supply and demand elasticities. Try to think of some government policies that increase both supply and demand and others that decrease both supply and demand. Finally, see if you can think of a government policy that is the mirror image of what went on in the market for small cars—by that we mean a set of policy decisions that simultaneously increases supply and reduces demand for some good or service. One example would be tax laws that encourage firms, including tobacco producers, to expand while at the same time the government is discouraging people from smoking through the widespread use of advertising campaigns.

▶ Summary and Conclusions

The purpose of this chapter has been to explain how government involves itself in the marketplace in the United States in order to alter economic outcomes. We have tried to demonstrate why there was still need for a Farm Aid concert despite a $28 billion agricultural program in the United States. The following main points were emphasized.

One way in which government intervention alters market outcomes is to prevent prices from rising to equate supply and demand or to keep prices from falling to clear a market.

Sometimes government policy works through the forces of supply and demand by changing demand, changing supply, or changing both supply and demand and, through this, equilibrium prices and outputs.

Government policies produce both economic winners and economic losers, and supply and demand analysis is helpful in identifying the groups of winners and losers.

It is important to be able to identify winners and losers because the choice of economic policy often depends upon who the winners and losers will be.

When government policy shifts both supply and demand curves, the qualitative implications of that policy for equilibrium price or quantity (but not both) will be clear; however, information on the relative magnitude of supply and demand shifts is necessary to predict the direction of change in both price and quantity.

▶ Key Terms

black market *127*

discrimination *124*

effective maximum
  price *123*

effective minimum
  price *130*

price ceiling *123*

price floor *129*

price subsidy *132*

rationing *127*

white market *127*

▶ Questions for Discussion and Review

1. What are the two general ways in which governments influence market outcomes? Show how they work with a graph of supply and demand curves. Give some examples of each from the real world that are not cited in this chapter.

2. In what situations is it reasonable to conclude that government policy has improved social welfare? In what situations can positive economic analysis offer no conclusion concerning the effect of a government policy on social welfare? Support your answers graphically.

3. What is a price ceiling or a price control? Explain and depict graphically how one works. What are some of the problems governments have in trying to get price controls to do what they are designed to do?

4. Illustrate and explain how rent ceilings would affect the housing market. Identify the winners and losers from such rent control programs.

5. Suppose that the price of steel rises dramatically because of a severe reduction in the availability of steel from foreign steel makers. Why might the United States government not want to let the price of steel rise dramatically? Name some policies the government might pursue to curb the use of steel. Support your answer graphically.

6. What is a price floor? Give an example of a price floor in the United States. Show graphically how a price floor works.

7. Name a government policy that shifts a demand curve. Be specific. Explain its impact on equilibrium price and quantity. Support your answer graphically. Explain who the winners and the losers are from the policy you have named.

8. Name a government policy that shifts a supply curve. Show how your policy affects equilibrium price and quantity. Explain who the winners and losers are from the policy you have named.

9. Illustrate and explain a government policy that shifts both demand and supply curves and explain how equilibrium price and output would be expected to change. Be sure to use an example that is different from the one cited in this chapter.

10. Suppose that the government, in order to ensure affordability, puts an effective price ceiling on home heating oil. This action of the government creates a black market in home heating oil. After becoming aware of this illegal activity, the government passes legislation that imposes penalties on both the buyers and sellers of home heating oil on the black market. Using a graphical device, compare the white market and black market equilibrium prices of home heating oil.

Chapter 7

The Competitive Firm and Industry

Supply and Demand in the Long Run

Outline

I. Introduction *144*
II. Long-run supply and demand in a competitive industry *145*
  A. Fixed costs, variable costs, and profit in the long run *145*
    1. The industry's long-run supply curve: Constant costs *148*
    2. Increasing costs in the long run *150*
  B. The theory of the surviving firm: Profit maximization with incomplete knowledge *152*
  C. Summary: Profit and economic rent in the long run *153*
III. Applications of the theory of the competitive industry *154*
  A. Some complications and side effects of regulating medicinal drugs *154*
  B. Competition and economic efficiency *156*
    1. Economically efficient production *157*
    2. Efficiency in consumption *157*
    3. Efficiency, marginal cost, and equity *158*
IV. Summary and conclusions *160*
V. Key terms *160*
VI. Questions for discussion and review *160*
VII. Policy issue: You decide—Supercows *162*
  A. The action-initiating event *162*
  B. The issue *162*
  C. Economic policy issues *162*

Objectives

After reading this chapter, the student should be able to:

Derive a competitive industry's long-run supply curve when costs are constant.

Derive a competitive industry's long-run supply curve when costs are increasing.

Explain why profit maximization is necessary for a competitive firm to survive in the long run.

Discuss the possibilities of a competitive firm's earning economic rent or economic profit in the long run.

Explain how competition leads to economic efficiency in production.

Explain how competition leads to economic efficiency in consumption.

Explain why economists often emphasize economic efficiency rather than equity.

▶ Introduction

When Fred and Mary began their computer software business back in 1976 they had no business experience, but they both had a genius for writing software. Throughout the first five years or so, business boomed and the fact that they never quite figured out how to keep the books hardly mattered. They even joked about Fred's modest efforts to study bookkeeping in his spare time. Somehow it did not seem to matter whether their financial records were up to date and accurate or not. They made more money each year than the year before, and the only problem seemed to be that they kept underestimating how much money they were making.

By 1983, both Fred and Mary were prominent members of the community. They were viewed as the local contingent of what appeared to be a national group of whiz kids who were leading the whole country through the computer revolution. The high point came for Fred in the autumn of 1983, when he was elected to the city council.

However, the signs of trouble were not long in coming. By 1984, it was clear to everyone in the industry that there was going to be a serious shakeout in the computer field and that a lot of small companies were already in financial trouble. Atari had entered and left the home computer business. IBM's much-touted PCjr came and went.

In early 1984, it became clear to both Fred and Mary that keeping the books up-to-date was no longer a laughing matter. They had bills to pay, and their sales were becoming less frequent and less lucrative. Fred wished he had worked a little harder on his bookkeeping, and both regretted not having much of a feel for business. In the summer of 1985, Fred had to resign from the city council so that he could work full-time with Mary to try to breathe new life into the business.

How could things have changed so fast? Weren't these the same two people who could do no wrong when it came to writing and selling computer software? Wasn't the country still experiencing a computer revolution, and weren't Fred and Mary both still part of the computer whiz-kid group that was blazing new frontiers? The big picture eluded Fred and Mary. Besides, at the moment they are too busy trying to get the books to balance, maybe to find a buyer for their business, and to come up with some new, hot software package to worry about the big picture.

In this chapter, we will take a look at the big picture—how markets evolve over time. We will explain why firms enter and leave an industry in the long run and why the changes that are taking place in the computer industry are similar to patterns experienced in many other product areas. We will explain why people like Fred and Mary can afford to joke about poor business practices when the market for a product is expanding and why their instinctive fear of going out of business in the long run is justified.

▶ Long-run Supply and Demand in a Competitive Industry

In preceding chapters we developed the theories of demand, supply, and price determination in a market economy, and we showed how these theories apply to current economic problems. The theory of supply developed so far has been based on the behavior of competitive firms in the *short run*. In the short run, firms have fixed costs, usually those associated with their investment in plant and equipment. In this chapter we look at how firms in competitive industries behave in the long run, when all costs are potentially variable. This means that the time horizon over which firms adjust their supply decisions is long enough so that it is worthwhile to adjust *all* inputs, including plant and equipment. It also means that one way in which the amount of a good or service supplied is reduced is to have firms *exit* from an industry and that one way to increase the amount supplied is to have firms *enter* an industry. For example, the number of firms producing personal and business computers and related software increased dramatically during the mid-1970s. However, by the mid-1980s, a number of firms were leaving the industry. That kind of shake-out is common in industries that expand rapidly with a new product, only to settle down later in longer-run equilibrium. We will show how allowing for firm mobility (entry and exit) affects the industry's supply curve and examine the way in which competition deals with firms that cannot or do not minimize costs and maximize profits. In conclusion, we will show how competition generates economic efficiency.

To begin our analysis of the long run, we need to add to the theory of supply developed in chapter 4. In doing this, we will explore how profit affects long-run equilibrium in a competitive industry and how the quantity supplied changes when there is a shift in demand and firm mobility exists.

Fixed Costs, Variable Costs, and Profit in the Long Run

The easiest way to extend the analysis of supply is to return briefly to the example of the A-1 Balloon Company. To do this, we reproduce in table 7.1 some of the information contained in tables 4.2 and 4.3. Remember that profit was defined earlier as total revenue less all of the firm's costs. Also recall that profit is maximized when marginal revenue equals marginal cost.

In the example of the A-1 Balloon Company, fixed costs amount to $200 per week in the short run. Fixed costs include such items as interest payments on money borrowed to finance investment in plant and equipment. In the long run, a firm can avoid these costs only by going out of business and paying off its creditors (or declaring bankruptcy); it may increase fixed costs by increasing purchases of plant and equipment or by entering an industry. Thus, costs that are fixed in the short run are variable in the long run. You may wish to look back at chapter 4 and review the discussion of fixed costs, variable costs, and profit.

Table 7.1   A-1 Balloon Company revenue, costs, and profit

Weekly production	Marginal cost[a]	Total cost[b]	Average total cost[c]	Marginal revenue (price)[d]	Revenue (price × production)	Profit (revenue − total cost)
100 gross		$1,300.00	$13.00		$1,500	$200.00
	$ 5.50			$15		
110 gross		1,355.00	12.32		1,650	295.00
	10.60			15		
120 gross		1,461.00	12.17		1,800	339.00
	11.10			15		
130 gross		1,572.00	12.09		1,950	378.00
	13.12			15		
140 gross		1,703.20	12.17		2,100	396.80
	17.73			15		
150 gross		1,880.50	12.54		2,250	369.50
	20.81			15		
160 gross		2,088.60	13.05		2,400	311.40

[a]Marginal, or incremental, cost is the *change* in a firm's cost that occurs when the firm produces more or less output.

[b]Total cost includes variable cost plus those costs that are fixed in the short run. In the long run, all costs are variable because a firm can choose to enter or leave an industry. When a firm enters an industry, it must incur costs for plant and equipment and other costs that are fixed in the short run. When a firm leaves an industry, it can eliminate these costs.

[c]Average total cost is total cost divided by weekly production.

[d]Marginal, or incremental, revenue is the *change* in the revenue that a firm receives when it produces (and sells) more or less output.

The A-1 Balloon Company is just one of a number of competitive balloon companies operating in the balloon market. It will be easiest to depict A-1 Balloon's situation if we assume all of the remaining balloon manufacturers have production functions identical to A-1 Balloon's and that they pay the same prices for all of their inputs. The revenue data in table 7.1 are based on a price of $15 per gross of balloons. This price is determined by the interaction of *industry* demand and short-run supply, as depicted in part (a) of figure 7.1. The balloon *industry's* short-run supply curve is the *sum* of all *firms'* short-run supply curves. Each firm's short-run supply curve is represented by its marginal cost curve (above minimum average variable cost). For example, A-1 Balloon Company's marginal cost curve is shown in part (c) of figure 7.1.

When each firm in the industry maximizes its profit its marginal cost (MC) equals its marginal revenue (MR). Because competitive firms are price takers, MR is identical to the market price of balloons (P). Part (c) of figure 7.1 shows A-1 Balloon Company maximizing its profit by producing approximately 140 gross per week.

Part (b) of figure 7.1 shows A-1 Balloon Company's total cost and total revenue. Since each firm in the industry is a price taker, it views its total revenue as increasing at a constant rate when its output increases. This is why the total revenue (TR) curve in part (b) of figure 7.1 is a *straight, upward-sloping* line, starting at zero. If output is zero, so is total revenue; as output increases, total revenue increases by the price (P) of each additional gross of balloons sold. Therefore, the value of the *slope* of the total revenue line in part (b) is identical to product price and to marginal revenue. In part (c) of figure 7.1, marginal revenue is always equal to the slope of the total revenue curve in part (b).

The total cost curve in part (b) of figure 7.1 is *not* a straight line starting at zero. First of all, it reflects the fact that even if A-1 Balloon Company decides to produce nothing, in the short run it will incur fixed costs of $200 per week. As output increases, total cost initially rises less than proportionately. However, there is a hump in the total cost curve, which indicates that total cost soon begins to increase proportionately more rapidly than production. After the hump, the total cost increases more and more rapidly as output increases.

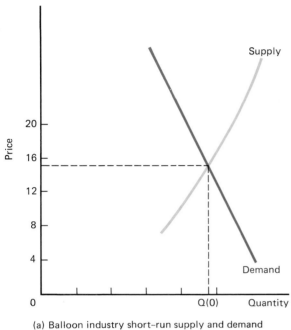

(a) Balloon industry short-run supply and demand

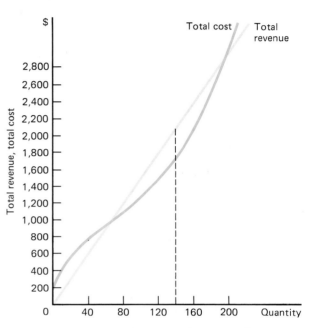

(b) A-1 Balloon Company total revenue and cost

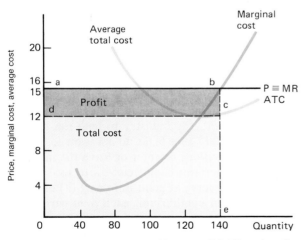

(c) A-1 Balloon Company MR, TR, ATC, TC, and profit

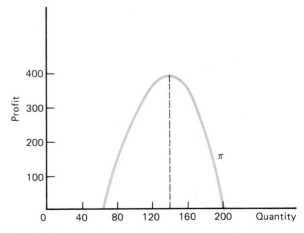

(d) A-1 Balloon Company profit ≡ total revenue minus total cost

Figure 7.1   Revenue, cost, and profit for a competitive industry in the short run

As shown in part (a), the equilibrium price ($15) is determined by the intersection of the industry's supply and demand curves.

As shown in part (b), the equilibrium price for the industry determines the slope of each firm's total revenue curve.

As shown in part (c), when a firm maximizes profit (makes total revenue exceed total cost by the largest amount), then marginal cost equals the price of the product. Total revenue

is defined as the price of the product multiplied by the quantity sold, and total cost is defined as the average total cost multiplied by the quantity of the good produced. Therefore, total revenue is shown in this diagram by the area of the rectangle 0abe, total cost by the area of the rectangle 0dce, and profit by the area of the rectangle abcd.

As shown in part (d), each firm's profit is its total revenue less total cost. Maximum profit occurs where total revenue is farthest above total cost.

*A **constant-cost industry** is one in which production costs per unit of output neither increase nor decrease as industry output changes in the long run, cet. par.*

Long-run equilibrium for an industry means that no firm in the industry has an incentive to change its output and that no firm desires to enter or leave the industry.

This reflects the principle of increasing cost that we discussed in chapter 4. As its output grows, the firm eventually finds it harder to coordinate the use of all of the inputs required for production and, therefore, to keep its costs down.

Just as marginal revenue is the slope of the total revenue curve, marginal cost is the slope of the total cost curve. As we have seen, marginal cost is *not* the same at every output level. Before output reaches the end of the hump in the total cost curve, marginal cost *falls* as output rises. (This does *not* mean that total cost is falling; marginal cost is still greater than zero.) However, at the point where the hump on the total cost curve ends, the principle of increasing cost begins to affect the total cost curve—marginal cost begins to increase and continues to increase for all additional output levels.

Profit (π) is total revenue less total cost. The relationship between profit and output can be seen clearly in part (d) of figure 7.1, where we show the vertical distance between total revenue and total cost from part (b) of the figure. Profit is, of course, zero at the two outputs where total revenue crosses total cost. It is greatest at the output level of approximately 140 gross per week, where total revenue and total cost are farthest apart, that is, where the two curves are parallel. Total revenue and total cost are farthest apart where the *slope* of the total revenue curve equals the *slope* of the total cost curve, that is, where MC = MR ≡ P. This output level is shown in parts (b), (c), and (d) of figure 7.1.

The firm's profit is also shown in part (c). This is possible because part (c) contains information on price, average cost, and the quantity produced and sold. Profit is total revenue less total cost; total revenue is price times quantity; and total cost is average total cost (ATC) times quantity. That is, TR ≡ P × Q, and TC ≡ ATC × Q. Therefore, total revenue is shown in part (c) of figure 7.1 by the area of the rectangle 0abe, total cost by the area of the rectangle 0dce, and total profit by the area of the rectangle abcd.

As parts b, c, and d of figure 7.1 show, the firm's profit is positive. To make sure that you thoroughly understand figure 7.1, redraw it yourself to show a situation in which price (P) has fallen to the point where the maximum profit a firm can earn is zero. (Hint: When price falls, the TR curve in part b becomes flatter.)

The Industry's Long-run Supply Curve: Constant Costs

We can now take the important step of deriving the long-run supply curve for a competitive industry. Figure 7.2 contains the necessary diagrams. In this figure, a competitive industry consists of a number of firms, each of which has *identical* cost conditions as reflected in the total cost curve in part (b) of figure 7.1 and marginal cost in part (c) of figure 7.1. Moreover, we assume that the inputs (labor, equipment, and raw materials) used by this industry do not constitute a significant share of the sales in their respective markets. (For example, the home appliance industry does not dominate the market for steel, paint, electric motors, or the labor used to assemble its products. Producers of children's clothing use only a fraction of all cloth, thread, sewing machines, and apparel workers.) Therefore, this is a **constant-cost industry** because per unit resource costs do not change as the industry expands or contracts production. As we shall see, even though each *firm* faces rising costs as it expands output, the *industry* does not in this case.

We start with the industry in **long-run equilibrium,** which means that firms do not want to change their output decisions or enter or leave the industry. The industry short-run supply curve intersects the industry demand curve at point m in part (a) of figure 7.2. In long-run equilibrium, each *firm* earns zero profit. Remember that at zero profit, each firm's revenue covers *all* of its costs, including the opportunity costs of the resources and managerial talent used to produce its output. If profits were positive, new firms would enter the industry to compete for them in the long run. If firms in the industry were incurring losses,

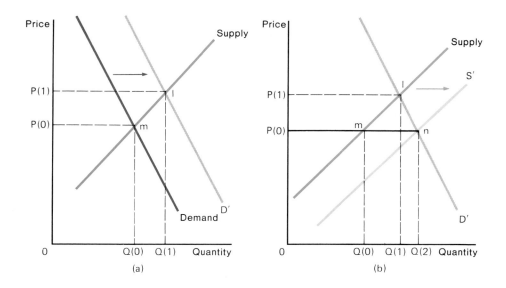

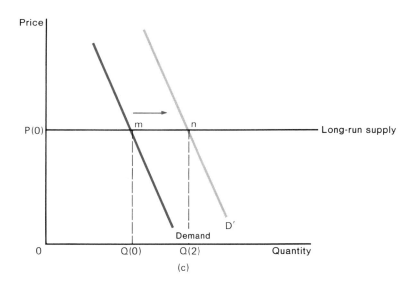

Figure 7.2   A competitive industry's long-run supply curve—constant-cost case

Part (a) shows that an increase in industry demand leads to an increase in price and quantity in the short run as *each* firm increases its production.

Part (b) shows that in the long run, an increase in profits attracts new firms. The short-run supply curve shifts to the right as new firms enter the industry.

In part (c), points m and n are on the *industry's* long-run supply curve. So long as each *firm* has identical costs and input prices do not change, the long-run supply will be *flat*, indicating *constant* long-run cost for the industry. The industry's long-run supply represents the marginal cost of additional output in the long run.

*The **long-run supply (LRS)** of a competitive industry is the relationship between the price of a good or service and the quantity offered for sale when the industry is in long-run equilibrium.*

some of them would leave in the long run. Neither of these situations constitutes long-run equilibrium for the industry, because equilibrium requires that the number of firms in the industry remains constant.

Point m lies on the industry **long-run supply (LRS)** curve, as shown in part (c) of figure 7.2, because the long-run supply curve tells us the quantities supplied by an industry when it is in long-run equilibrium. Equilibrium price is P(0) and equilibrium quantity produced by the industry is Q(0). Total industry output, Q(0), is simply the sum of the amounts produced by each of the firms in the industry.

Now suppose that a change in the economy results in an increase in the demand for the good or service produced by the industry described in figure 7.2. Thus, the demand curve shifts to the right. It intersects the short-run supply curve at point l, indicating a higher price in the short run, P(1). Consequently, each *firm's* marginal revenue increases, and each firm's production increases in the short run. With a constant number of firms in the industry, total industry output increases to Q(1). However, point l is *not* on the industry's long-run supply curve because it does not represent a position of long-run equilibrium for the industry.

We have already seen why point l in part (a) of figure 7.2 cannot represent long-run equilibrium. Profits are now positive and entry will occur. As new firms enter the industry, industry short-run supply (the sum of all the firms' marginal cost curves) increases and price begins to fall. This process continues until the industry short-run supply curve reaches the supply curve S', as shown in part (b). Since the new firms in the industry have exactly the same cost curves as the original firms and since input prices have not changed, S' intersects the demand curve D' at point n, which results in equilibrium price P(0) again. Each firm's profit is equal to its value at the beginning of our example—zero. However, there are now more firms in the industry than before. At point n, the equilibrium price is exactly the same as at the starting point, m, because any higher price will lead to positive profits and further entry of new firms. The quantity supplied is, of course, higher at n than at m. At P(0), each firm

produces the same output as it did before industry demand increased. However, total industry output is now Q(2). Point n also lies on the long-run supply curve, as shown in part (c) of figure 7.2.

When all firms are identical and input prices are constant, long-run supply is a horizontal line. This is because in the case of a constant-cost industry, changes in demand result only in *quantity* changes in the long run but no change in long-run equilibrium price. When a supply curve is flat, we say that it is *infinitely,* or *perfectly,* elastic because no price increase is necessary to obtain an increase in the quantity supplied. An interesting and important implication is that in the long run, consumers do not have to pay a higher price to increase their consumption of a good if it is produced in a constant-cost industry.

The industry's long-run supply curve answers the question of how much an industry will produce at various market prices. The long-run supply curve in part (c) of figure 7.2 shows that any amount will be supplied in the long run so long as the price consumers are willing to pay equals the cost of the product. *The long-run supply curve is the industry's long-run marginal cost curve. It maps out the additional cost of producing additional output for the industry.* This is very important to remember for the applications of the industry's long-run behavior that follow.

Increasing Costs in the Long Run

Is it possible for a long-run supply curve to slope upward, indicating long-run costs that increase as output grows? The answer is yes. There are two assumptions underlying the flat long-run supply curve derived in figure 7.2: (1) Each firm's total cost curve is identical; and (2) input prices do not change as firms purchase more or less inputs. If *either* of these assumptions does not hold, then the long-run supply curve will not be flat.

Suppose, for example, that while the new firms entering the industry all pay the same prices for labor, equipment, and raw materials as existing firms in the industry, the new firms do not have access to all of the same management skills as existing firms. In particular, there may be some innate talents that the managers of the older firms have that the managers of the

*An **endogenous** change in an economic variable is caused by a change from within an industry (or an economy). An endogenous change in an input price is caused by a shift in the demand for the input by the industry experiencing the price change.*

*An **exogenous** change in an economic variable is caused by a change from outside an industry (or an economy). An exogenous change in an input price is caused by a shift in the supply of the input to the industry experiencing the price change.*

new firms will never acquire. Situations such as this will cause *new* firms' costs to be higher than those of *existing* firms. Consequently, entry of new firms will cease *before* the equilibrium price falls back to the level that prevailed at the industry's initial output. Because existing competitive firms can sell all they want to at the going price, they have no incentive to cut prices to drive the less efficient new firms out of business. To summarize, in this case the entry of new firms stops while the price is higher than it was before the demand curve shifted to the right, and the long-run supply curve is the upward-sloping line in figure 7.3. In figure 7.3 the *new* long-run equilibrium price is P(0)′, which is greater than P(0). If after long-run equilibrium is reached, industry demand should subsequently fall, it is these relatively high-cost firms that will be the first to exit the industry.

The second reason the long-run supply curve may slope upward is that the industry is an important user of an input that is produced under conditions of increasing costs. Examples of such inputs might be petroleum, iron ore, or land of a particular quality. For example, petroleum is a basic input into the manufacture of gasoline. An increase in the demand for gasoline will probably place such demands on the petroleum industry that the price of crude oil will rise. This increase in turn raises the price of petroleum to *all* oil users in all industries. As production expands in the gasoline industry, both existing firms and new entrants will have to pay more for this important input. Note that the increase in the price of petroleum we are describing is a necessary condition for output of the petroleum industry to grow. The situation is reversed when the demand for gasoline falls. The rising price of the input, petroleum, reflects the rising opportunity cost of producing it rather than other goods or services. This increase in the price of the input, petroleum in our example, results in the long-run supply curve of gasoline being less elastic than otherwise—that is, upward sloping rather than flat. We say that the increase in the price of this gasoline industry input is **endogenous,** meaning that it is determined by output changes *within* the gasoline industry. It does *not* cause the supply curve of gasoline to shift upward and to the left.

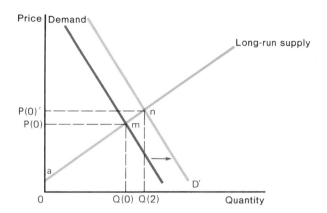

Figure 7.3   A competitive industry's long-run supply curve—increasing-cost case
When "old" firms in an industry have access to special skills or when input prices rise as output grows, the industry's long-run equilibrium price will rise when output increases and fall when output declines.

The increase in the price of petroleum that is endogenous to the gasoline industry, because it results from an expansion of gasoline production, is **exogenous** to other industries using petroleum, meaning that it is determined outside those industries. Thus, the increased price of oil caused by expanded gasoline production will result in a *leftward shift* in the supply curves of the nylon, synthetic rubber, and plastic industries. For example, in the first half of 1976, the United States economy was in recession, which reduced the demand for clothing and, consequently, polyester fiber—a petroleum product. Reduced production of polyester fiber increased the supply of petroleum available to manufacture antifreeze; supplies of antifreeze were much more abundant in the winter of 1976–77 than they had been a year earlier and sold for a lower price. Four years later, another recession reduced the demand for autos and construction, releasing steel and cement for use in oil drilling, which had been restricted because of material costs. During the first three months of 1980, the number of drilling rigs was 26 percent greater than during the first quarter of 1979.[1]

The Theory of the Surviving Firm: Profit Maximization with Incomplete Knowledge

The theory of supply is sometimes criticized because it describes a firm's management as carrying out calculations of cost minimization, marginal cost, marginal revenue, and profit maximization that are rather complex. Were you to conduct a survey of business firms in your community, it would become apparent that many owners and managers have never heard of marginal cost and marginal revenue, let alone tried to equate them. Moreover, many would not admit to trying to maximize their profits. This might make you uncomfortable with our assertion that supply theory is useful in understanding how a market economy works.

Although the theory of supply may not accurately describe thought processes of business managers, firms do behave *as if* they adhere to it. Therefore, we are able to explain and predict their actions, even if we are not describing their exact thoughts. Here is another example of this kind of behavior. You do not have to be a physics professor to win the Indianapolis 500 or the World Cup downhill championship in skiing. (In fact, some would say such a background might be a disadvantage.) However, if you want to understand what it takes to move a racing vehicle fast enough to win without going out of control and to *apply* this knowledge to developing better vehicles or a better track, you will be far more likely to succeed if you do understand the laws of physics. The same statement holds true if you want to design an improved racing ski. Similarly, you do not necessarily need economic analysis to make a fortune in business, but it is an indispensable tool for understanding the way the economic system works and for avoiding bad economic policy. Moreover, understanding the basic structure of our economy and how the economy responds to changing events may at times help in reaching profitable business decisions.

To illustrate the relationship between the theory and practice of profit maximization, let's suppose that you actually do conduct a survey of an industry—say, the balloon industry in the United States—collecting information on the output, costs, revenue, and profits of each firm. (We will assume that the balloon industry is *not* in long-run equilibrium.) Imagine constructing a diagram like the one in part (d) of figure 7.1. You will plot a point for each firm corresponding to that firm's output, measured along the horizontal axis, and its profit, measured along the vertical axis. Since this is a real-world situation, the various balloon manufacturing firms in your sample will not be equally successful in achieving the lowest possible cost of production or in finding the profit-maximizing output level. If they were, the point plotted for each firm would be near the top of the profit curve. What you will observe instead is that you have plotted points all over your diagram. Firms that have not minimized their costs will earn lower profits or even experience losses. Other firms, while minimizing their costs, will be to the right or left of the profit-maximizing output in your diagram.

If you draw a line connecting the points representing the firms that earn the highest profits, given their level of production, this line will look something like the profit (π) curve in part (d) of figure 7.1. That is, *if* a firm produces approximately 140 gross of balloons per month, and *if* it produces them at the lowest possible cost, *then* it will be found at the top of the profit curve. Firms producing more or less earn lower profits, but they will still be on the profit curve in the diagram if they minimize their costs.

Not all of the firms in your survey will be on the profit curve, however. Since the balloon industry is not in long-run equilibrium in this example, it is not necessary to minimize costs to earn *some* profit. Firms that have not minimized their costs will be represented by points above the zero profit line (the horizontal axis in part (d) of figure 7.1) but below the profit curve (π). Still other firms, because they are producing too much or not minimizing costs, will be located below the zero profit line. They are incurring losses—that is, not covering all of their costs of production.

All of the firms represented by points above the zero profit line are doing better than they would do by shutting down or moving to another industry that is in long-run equilibrium. This is true even if a firm is not earning the maximum possible profit. In contrast, the owners of unprofitable firms, represented by points below the zero profit line, are doing worse than they would do by shutting down in the long run. Sooner or later these firms will run out of funds to purchase inputs if they do not change their behavior. They must reduce their costs and adjust output to increase their profits. If they do not, they will eventually disappear from the industry.

As long as the industry is not in long-run equilibrium, firms can survive—avoid losses—even if they do not use the lowest cost production methods or produce the profit-maximizing level of output. However, as we have seen, the opportunity to earn profits will attract additional firms to enter the industry. The resulting decline in the market price of balloons forces the curve to shift downward. When this happens, the opportunities for firms to earn profits, even if they do not produce at the profit-maximizing output level or minimize their costs, become more and more limited. Some firms that could survive under the conditions reflected in figure 7.1 will not be able to do so after new firms add to the competitive pressure on them. If they do not reduce their costs or adjust their output, they will be forced out of the industry.

Finally, as the industry approaches long-run equilibrium, maximum profit approaches zero. Only those firms that do minimize their costs and that do produce the profit-maximizing output quantity can survive. This is because, even doing the best they can, firms cannot earn more than just enough to cover their opportunity costs. The conditions for survival in a competitive industry require that firms somehow minimize their costs and find the output level at which marginal cost equals price. Moreover, even if these surviving firms do not believe that maximizing profit is consistent with their "corporate responsibility" to society, competition will force them to do so.

Summary: Profit and Economic Rent in the Long Run

The main idea underlying the competitive industry's long-run supply curve is this: The long-run supply curve indicates prices and outputs that result when an industry is in long-run equilibrium. Even though the quest for profit is the driving force behind the supply curve, competition is constantly at work to eliminate profit opportunities. Competition assures that the price consumers must pay for a good is exactly equal to the marginal opportunity cost of producing it. When all of the firms in a competitive industry are identical, total revenue for each surviving firm is exactly equal to its total opportunity cost. Thus, in the case of a constant-cost industry, whose long-run supply is derived in figure 7.2, no firm earns a profit in the long run. An increase in demand results in increased output but no change in long-run profits or the price of the good produced.

What can be said about profits and prices when long-run supply is upward sloping, as in figure 7.3? Remember that there are two related reasons why long-run supply may be upward sloping. One reason is that an industry is an important user of an input whose price rises as more is demanded in the long run. In this case, the industry providing that input, for example, the petroleum industry providing oil to the chemical industry, benefits from rising prices when demand for its product grows. Owners of superior (especially productive) sources of supply (oil wells, land, and so on) will receive economic rents when demand

*A **marginal firm** is one that generates no economic rent for its owners in the long run.*

for their product grows. However, the industries *using* such inputs must pay for everything they use. Therefore, an upward-sloping long-run supply curve does not lead to rents in the industries that purchase inputs whose prices rise when more is demanded.

A second reason for an upward-sloping LRS curve is that existing firms may possess better knowledge about the industry than new firms. For example, they may know more about efficient production methods and can therefore achieve lower costs. If this special ability or knowledge is "owned" by a salaried employee, the firm for which the employee works will not earn a profit in the long run. This is because competition among firms for such employees' services will bid up their salaries. Suppose the market price in figure 7.3 is P(0). If the lower cost segment of the industry's long-run supply curve below P(0) reflects the fact that some firms have management with special abilities, competition among firms for these managers' services will assure that these employees' salaries fully reflect the area aP(0)m. None of this rent accrues to the firms themselves because it is paid out to talented managers.

What if some firms' *owners* possess a special talent for the industry? (For example, Yves St. Laurent is a highly talented clothes designer.) Such firms will earn economic rents, which accrue to their owners as remuneration for their specialized talents or abilities.

A **marginal firm** (a firm that does not have a management or talent advantage over other firms in the industry) will earn zero rent in the long run. Are the economic rents received by especially talented owners the same as profits? Not really, because the talented owners can presumably become salaried employees in other firms in that industry, and if they do their salaries will fully reflect the rents they now receive as owners. This shows that the rents talented owners receive for their special talents are a firm's opportunity cost of employing their services. It is important to remember that economic rents are ultimately paid to the *owners* of especially productive *inputs,* be these inputs land, labor, or capital.

▶ Applications of the Theory of the Competitive Industry

The theory of the competitive industry, especially when coupled with the theory of surviving firms, provides valuable insights into the behavior of a majority of industries in our economy, even if their characteristics do not exactly match the assumptions listed at the beginning of chapter 4. One advantage of this theory is that it is relatively simple and readily adapted to the special features of individual industries.

Some Complications and Side Effects of Regulating Medicinal Drugs

In the United States, as in many other countries, the sale of most pharmaceutical products—drugs and medications used to relieve or cure illness and injury—is closely regulated. The federal agency responsible for this regulation in the United States is the Food and Drug Administration (FDA). The original purpose of the federal Food, Drug, and Cosmetic Act was to protect consumers from harm caused by using dangerous or poisonous substances. Since 1962, federal law has required the FDA to assure that drugs are not only safe but also *effectual* in preventing, curing, or alleviating illness.

There is little doubt that unscrupulous firms have in the past sold dangerous drugs to consumers on the basis of advertising they know to be false, such as in the medicine shows of the Old West. Moreover, ignorance of all of the side effects of certain medications—for example thalidomide, which caused serious birth defects in children of mothers who used the tranquilizer during pregnancy—have led to severe hardship and tragedy for many people. We will not dwell on the best way to reduce the risk of injury to consumers that is inevitable whenever new products are introduced. We will deal with a much simpler problem: the impact of regulation on the supply of all new drugs, whether harmful or not.[2]

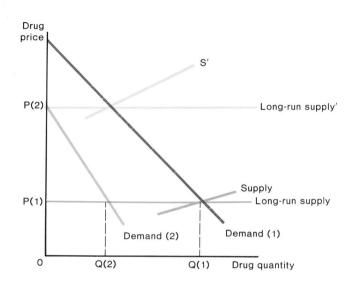

Figure 7.4   Possible effects of an increase in development costs on the pharmaceutical industry
Demand (1) is the demand curve for a drug that is used to treat a common disease. Demand (2) is the demand curve for a drug that is used to treat a rare disease. Demand (2) lies to the left of Demand (1) because so few people demand the drug. An increase in development and testing costs causes Long-run supply to shift up to Long-run supply′. At the new price P(2), no one demands the drug to treat the rare disease, and it is not produced.

Suppose we lived in a world of costless knowledge—one in which information on product safety was not a scarce commodity. In such a world, product safety regulation would simply amount to a rule stating the penalties for selling a dangerous product. But such rules would not be needed because no consumer would ever unintentionally use a dangerous drug or other good in a world where knowledge was free. Unfortunately, the world around us contains many unknowns, not the least of which are the effects of using new drugs. This leads to uncertainty, the risk of unforeseen injury and death, and a demand for protection from such dangers.

In a world of uncertainty and no government-imposed regulation of consumer safety, producers would still find it worthwhile to incur the costs of testing their products. These costs would exist because it is impossible to weed out dangerous products without devoting scarce resources to testing them. Firms would be willing to bear these costs because they would wish to avoid the damaged reputation and costly legal suits that result if a product harms consumers. The purpose of product safety regulation is to require firms to spend more on assuring product safety (and effectiveness) than they would do otherwise.

The effects of safety and effectiveness regulation in the pharmaceutical industry are illustrated in figure 7.4. This figure depicts a competitive industry's long-run supply and demand for a medicinal drug. In the absence of regulation, the curve Demand (1) and the long-run supply curve represent demand and long-run supply for drugs that are useful in treating a common disease or group of diseases. The equilibrium quantity is Q(1), and the equilibrium price is P(1). We will discuss Demand (2) later. The industry described in figure 7.4 is initially in long-run equilibrium. Now suppose the government issues a regulation requiring more extensive testing and research before a drug is marketed. The additional costs for a typical firm are up-front costs, which do not affect the marginal cost of producing a drug once it is on the market. However, these development costs throw the industry into disequilibrium. It will no longer pay firms to develop or market a drug under the initial conditions depicted in figure 7.4. Drugs already on the market will still be sold provided the firms producing them do not have to spend increased costs to keep them on the market. However, new drugs will not be introduced if the market price remains at P(1).

Equity, when describing the way in which society's income or wealth is divided among society's members, refers to the fairness of the division when judged against an ethical standard.

As firms leave this market for more profitable (and perhaps less regulated) markets, the industry's *short-run* supply curve shifts upward until eventually it reaches the supply curve S'. The result is that the market equilibrium price will be forced up to P(2). This price is high enough to compensate the remaining firms for supplying the drug to this market. Thus, an important effect of regulation is to raise the price of drugs. Note that because the price has risen, the total quantity of a drug purchased will fall.

Can we conclude from our analysis that drug safety and effectiveness regulation is bad for society because it raises the price of drugs? To answer this question, we need to know whether patients (and their doctors) systematically underestimate the risks of taking drugs. The answer also depends on a *normative* judgment as to whether patients (and their doctors) should be allowed to decide for themselves how much they are willing to pay for more drug safety and assured effectiveness.

Before you make up your mind on this issue, we must carry our analysis a little further. So far we have shown the effects of regulation when the demand curve—Demand (1)—is for drugs to treat a relatively common disease. Suppose, however, that relatively few people are affected with an illness or that relatively few people develop very serious cases of it. In this situation, the demand curve will lie farther to the left, such as Demand (2) instead of Demand (1). Long-run supply may not intersect the demand curve for the drug at all. This means that as a result of regulation costs, no firms are willing to supply drugs to this market in the long run, and patients must do without them. You may have seen or heard this referred to in the news media as the "orphan" drug problem.

The readings cited in reference 2 argue that one effect of the regulation of drug safety and effectiveness in the United States has indeed been to reduce the number of new drugs introduced. Moreover, some medications that are available in other countries have not been available to patients in the United States because the testing required by other countries is less costly than in the United States; and the FDA does not in general accept the results of tests done abroad. Although benefits accrue to United States drug users in the form of less risk of dangerous side effects, users must also pay costs in terms of higher drug prices. Just how much additional cost is warranted? An even more serious question involves the price in terms of illness or death paid by those with rare diseases who cannot buy drugs that would be available if testing costs were lower. Even drugs that ultimately prove to be worthwhile will be slower in reaching the market with regulation than without. Patients who cannot obtain a particular drug now will suffer pain and perhaps loss of life while testing establishes the safety and beneficial effects of using such a drug for future patients.

Competition and Economic Efficiency

In chapter 1 we emphasized that in a world of scarcity, economic efficiency is a very important measure of an economy's performance. Efficiency is not, of course, the only criterion. Most people are also concerned with **equity,** which refers to how fairly an economy's wealth is distributed among consumers. We shall return to this criterion later in this chapter. An efficient economy operates on its production possibilities frontier (PPF). This means that it is impossible, without increased resources or advances in technology, to produce more of one good or service without producing less of another. If it were possible to obtain more of something without sacrificing anything else, an economy would not be operating efficiently (be on its PPF). The reason is that a costless increase in output of a scarce commodity could make at least one person better off without anyone else sacrificing any of his or her consumption. An efficient economy exploits all such opportunities to increase consumers' well-being.

Market deficiencies are situations in which competitive equilibrium prices do not reflect all of the opportunity costs (or all of the benefits) of producing a good or service.

The following definition of economic efficiency is generally accepted by economists. *When an economy is efficient, it is impossible to make any consumer better off without making another consumer worse off.*

Before we summarize the way in which competitive markets lead to economic efficiency, two warnings should be posted. (1) We do not want to suggest that because competitive markets lead to economic efficiency, the economy of the United States is therefore as efficient as possible. There are industries in which competition as outlined in chapters 2 through 7 does not function well. In addition, some government regulations hinder economic efficiency. We will deal with these features of the United States economy in subsequent chapters. (2) Even competitive markets do not lead to economic efficiency if *firms'* opportunity costs of producing a good or *consumers'* opportunity costs of using it do not coincide with *society's* opportunity's costs. An example of when this occurs involves the matter of pollution, which we treat in chapter 17. Pollution is an important special case of the general economic problem of **market deficiencies,** which result when the market price of a resource fails to measure its opportunity cost accurately. In showing how competition promotes economic efficiency we will focus on two aspects: efficiency in production and efficiency in consumption.

Economically Efficient Production

Efficiency in production is achieved if the economy reaches its PPF. We have seen that a competitive firm cannot survive unless it minimizes its costs. This is an important step toward the economy's reaching its PPF. Specifically, resources not used by one firm or industry are available to increase output elsewhere. Thus, if firms do *not* minimize costs, the economy will be *inside* its PPF, not *on* it. (Refer back to figure 1.1 to review the importance of being on the PPF.)

Efficiency in production—reaching the PPF—requires not only that firms minimize their costs of whatever quantity they produce but also that each firm produce just the right quantity of output relative to other firms in the industry. In other words, we want to be sure that each *industry,* as well as each *firm,* minimizes its costs. To achieve this goal, firms with lower marginal and average costs should produce more output than those with higher costs so as to equalize the *marginal* cost of production across all firms in the industry.

Efficiency in Consumption

We now take a step beyond the question of whether competition leads an economy *to* the PPF and ask whether it also leads it to the "right" place *on* the PPF. In what sense is there an economically efficient *mix* of goods produced, and how do we decide what that mix might be? Remember our definition of economic efficiency. Suppose it is possible to make someone better off without making anyone else worse off by producing more of one good and less of another—by moving from one place on the PPF to another. If this situation holds, then the first place on the PPF is not economically efficient.

Once again, as in the case of production efficiency, competition among firms will lead to efficiency in consumption. If figure 7.5 represents a competitive economy, the quantity produced in industry 1 will tend toward 17 million units in the long run and the quantity produced in industry 2 will tend toward 11 million units because this is where Long-run supply (1) intersects Demand (1) and Long-run supply (2) intersects Demand (2). In general, in competitive equilibrium, the value to consumers of the last unit produced in any industry equals its marginal cost. A dollar's worth of resources moved from one industry to another will cause output to fall by an amount valued by consumers at a dollar in the first industry and output to rise by an amount valued at a dollar in the second. Thus, in competitive equilibrium, no reallocation of resources among competitive industries will increase consumers' welfare.

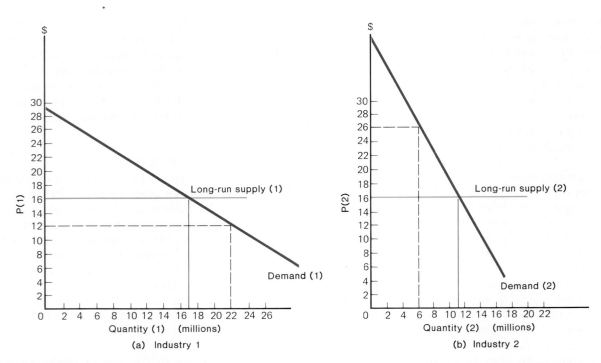

Figure 7.5   Efficient allocation of resources and production between two industries
The prevailing prices in industries 1 and 2 reflect each good's marginal value to every consumer. If transferring a given amount of resources from industry 1 to industry 2 will add more to the value consumers derive from the goods they consume than it subtracts, then consumers will be better off with more of good 2 and less of good 1. When such a transfer no longer increases consumers' well-being, then the allocation of resources between the two industries is economically efficient.

Efficiency, Marginal Cost, and Equity

We have seen that because competition forces firms to minimize their costs and to produce quantities such that $MC = MR \equiv P$, competition promotes economic efficiency. This is true even though firms are assumed to act only in their own interest. Even if firms have no concern for consumers' welfare, they must act *as if* they cared if they want to survive under competitive conditions. Thus, competition fosters economic efficiency. The profit motive, while superficially inconsistent with consumers' goals of maximizing satisfaction, is actually a crucial force helping them to achieve it. Adam Smith first articulated this notion in the *Wealth of Nations* (1776), when he observed that under competitive conditions, profit-seeking entrepreneurs act as if guided by an invisible hand to promote the common good.

As we mentioned earlier, economic efficiency is only one criterion by which most people judge the functioning of an economy. The equity of the distribution of income and wealth is also considered to be an important criterion of economic performance. Indeed, it may well be impractical to achieve a perfectly efficient economy and a satisfactory distribution of wealth in society. There are several reasons for our emphasis on economic efficiency rather than equity.

1. Criteria of economic efficiency are easier to establish than criteria of equity. For example, reasonable people may well disagree on whether it is better to have an equal distribution of income or a distribution that more closely reflects individual abilities and industriousness (assuming these qualities are not equally shared among us).

2. Given basic agreement on the desired distribution of purchasing power, most people would support a movement toward a more efficient economy that would improve the welfare of some individuals as long as it did not reduce the welfare of others.

3. Most people would agree that any programs aimed at redistributing wealth in order to achieve greater equity ought to be implemented with an eye to preserving as much economic efficiency as possible. At several points in this text, we discuss means by which government programs aimed at redistributing wealth might be made more efficient.

4. As a matter of historical record, many economic policies that superficially appear to improve equity (for example, setting maximum allowable prices on petroleum production or minimum prices on agricultural products) promote neither equity nor efficiency, and their pitfalls should be well understood.

5. There are considerable economic gains to be made by most individuals—rich or poor— through policies aimed at improving economic efficiency. It is possible to increase the benefits derived from our limited resources, and this route is a surer way to a higher standard of living than activities that focus mainly on reallocating existing wealth. Think of the economy's total output as a pie to be divided up among all citizens. The conflict between equity and efficiency arises when efforts to give part of society a larger *share* of the pie in the name of greater equity results in the pie's becoming so much smaller (because of economic inefficiency) that the actual size of the piece of pie also shrinks.

As long as scarcity exists, the goal of economic efficiency will remain important. Even the governments of planned economies have recognized that economic inefficiency hinders them in achieving their goals.[3] Thus, in different ways and to varying degrees many nations that do not have predominately free markets have allowed or even introduced a limited degree of private enterprise and competition in order to take advantage of the increased efficiency and production that it promotes. Here are some examples:

Hungary is called "the communist world's economic showcase" largely because consumer goods are more readily available there than in neighboring Eastern European nations. It has been suggested that the reason for this abundance is that private enterprise flourishes in important sectors of the Hungarian economy.[4]

The Soviet Union, bastion of controlled economies, simulates Western competitive pressures—and rewards—in procuring armaments. This may be an important factor in the buildup of Soviet military power vis-à-vis the West.[5]

Communist China is exploring ways to capture the benefits of competition and free markets in fostering the growth of industrial and agricultural productivity.[6]

Despite wars and violent political upheavals in Southeast Asia, the standards of living in those countries that have rejected communism and its economic controls have increased much more rapidly than the standards of living among their communist neighbors.[7]

▶ Summary and Conclusions

In this chapter, we have completed our analysis of the competitive firm and industry. We have tried to make it clear why Fred and Mary, the two computer software entrepreneurs we met at the beginning of this chapter, eventually began to have difficulties surviving in their business and why knowledge of how a competitive industry evolves over time might have helped them avoid some of their problems. Here are the main points we developed in this chapter.

In the long run, all costs are variable and represent a firm's opportunity costs.

The principle of increasing cost need not apply to a competitive *industry* in the long run.

In long-run equilibrium, competitive firms do not earn economic profits.

In the long run, an industry supply curve may be perfectly elastic or upward sloping.

An industry's long-run supply (LRS) curve is also its long-run marginal cost curve.

Competition forces firms to minimize cost and maximize profits (if they are to survive in the long run) by producing where $MC = MR \equiv P$.

Economic rents may persist in the long run.

Factors that shift LRS curves are similar to those that shift supply curves in the short run.

Competition fosters economic efficiency.

▶ Key Terms

constant-cost industry
    148
endogenous *151*
equity *156*
exogenous *151*
long-run equilibrium
    148
long-run supply (LRS)
    150
marginal firm *154*
market deficiencies
    157

▶ Questions for Discussion and Review

1. The following table contains cost information for a competitive firm in a constant-cost industry composed of a large number of firms with identical costs.

Weekly production	Variable cost	Short-run fixed cost
1	$ .25	$1.00
2	.50	1.00
3	.85	1.00
4	1.30	1.00
5	1.85	1.00
6	2.50	1.00
7	3.30	1.00
8	4.25	1.00
9	5.30	1.00
10	6.45	1.00

a. Construct a graph showing total cost curve for this firm.
b. Calculate and plot this firm's marginal cost on a graph.

2. Using the data from question 1, calculate the price that would be high enough to allow each profit-maximizing firm to cover all of its costs but not earn any profit.

3. Using the data from question 1, plot the short-run supply curve for this industry, assuming there are 1,000 identical firms in the industry.

4. Using the data from question 1, plot the industry's long-run supply curve. Assume that the fixed factors happen to be at the levels desired by the firm in the long run.

5. Suppose the industry in question 1 experiences an exogenous change in input prices so that each firm's costs double. Show what happens to the industry's long-run supply curve. What will happen to the industry's total production in the long run? What will happen to a typical firm's output in the long run?

6. In the long run, competition eliminates profits, but not economic rents. Explain.

7. Is the following statement true or false? The law of increasing cost does not apply in the long run. Explain your answer.

8. Suppose you are the president of a large United States corporation that uses a significant quantity of gold in its manufacturing process. Your principal source of supply has been to import the gold from South Africa. What would you decide to do if you were requested by a political action group to stop buying gold from South Africa because of its racial segregation policies that hurt the black population there? How would your feelings about racial segregation and your duties as president of your firm affect your decision? How do you think your decision would be affected if your firm operated in a controlled economy?

9. Some states and localities levy considerably higher business taxes than others. Assume that the tax revenues are spent in ways that have no effect on business costs. Since the taxes themselves are a cost of doing business, can such differential taxes persist without driving competitive firms away in the long run? Can you cite some examples?

10. Suppose the federal government imposes a tax of a fixed amount per unit of output produced on a single competitive industry. Assume there are no imports or exports of this good. Show how the tax affects the equilibrium price and quantity produced assuming (a) perfectly elastic LRS and (b) upward-sloping LRS.

11. Using your answer to question 10, go on to analyze the effect of the tax on economic efficiency, assuming that all of the other industries in the economy are competitive and are *not* taxed. What is more likely to be affected, efficiency in production or efficiency in consumption?

Supercows

▸ The Action-Initiating Event

You are chief of the research staff for the head of the Senate committee on agricultural policy. Your boss is concerned about the rising level of government expenditure on surplus agricultural commodities—particularly milk and other dairy products. Recently, animal breeders at a major university announced a "supercow"—a Holstein bred with the assistance of advanced genetic science that typically produces at least 25,000 pounds of milk per year. This is a 50 percent increase over the current standard.

▸ The Issue

The government currently sets price supports for dairy products and spends billions of dollars annually buying surplus dairy products in the form of dried milk, cheese, and butter. At the same time, the Department of Agriculture funds research grants to many land-grant universities with large agricultural research departments. One result of these grants is ever increasing productivity of United States dairy cows. The constantly increasing efficiency of United States dairy farms is "trapping" dairy farmers into adopting the newest technologies in order to survive, while at the same time increasing production forces down prices—making survival in the dairy business all the more difficult.[1] You are to help formulate a plan that will help get the government out of its conflicting roles—buying up agricultural surplus while at the same time funding research that pushes up agricultural productivity.

▸ Economic Policy Issues

Increased agricultural output per farmer has been a cornerstone of the growing real income and standard of living in the United States—and in other countries of the world. No one could seriously argue in favor of curing the farm problem by wiping out the productivity gains of the last seventy-five years. At the same time, large dairy cooperatives—farmer organizations that buy milk from farmers and market dairy products—appear financially able to finance agricultural research themselves if they believe it will be profitable. Federal support of agricultural research—particularly in the dairy industry—appears to be motivated by the immense political power of the farm bloc rather than by a pressing need for bigger and better cows.

Your recommendation to the agricultural committee must consider the following issues. Urban working people, many of whom are poorer than farmers, pay taxes to support agricultural research while at the same time are forced to pay higher prices for agricultural products than they would without federal price supports. Because of dairy price supports and government purchases of surplus output, a great deal of labor and other resources is devoted to producing output that never benefits consumers. These resources could be used more fruitfully in other industries, where the output would increase the economic well-being of consumers. Federal expenditures on agricultural subsidies paid to farmers and on purchasing surplus commodities constitute a large share of the federal deficit—10 percent or more in some years.

The committee head you are working for would like to develop a more efficient farm program and wants a memo containing your recommendations. At the same time, she is concerned that the political power of the farm bloc is so great that she and other members of Congress will not be reelected if the legislation they adopt represents too sharp a departure from current practice. This fear is made all the more severe by the high rate of bankruptcy and foreclosures on American farms. These financial difficulties are not only creating hardship for many farm families, despite massive federal programs of farm aid, but they also threaten the solvency of hundreds of rural banks and the farm credit system.

"High Efficiency Is 'Trapping' New York State's Dairy Farmers," *New York Times*, 5 Apr. 1982.

Part III

Monopoly and Other Market Forms

Chapter 8

Monopoly

Outline

I. Introduction *168*
II. Monopoly *169*
  A. A monopolist's output decision *169*
  B. An economic evaluation of monopoly *173*
    1. Monopoly and survival *173*
    2. Monopoly and efficiency *174*
    3. Monopoly, profits, rents, and the distribution of income *176*
    4. Can monopoly be good? *178*
      a. Technical monopolies *178*
      b. Innovations, patents, and monopoly power *179*
  C. Application: Agricultural marketing organizations—Equal opportunity to compete or license to monopolize? *180*
  D. The sources of monopoly power *182*
III. Price discrimination *182*
  A. Price discrimination in practice *183*
  B. Perfect price discrimination *184*
    1. Price discrimination in medicine *186*
  C. Price discrimination when there are substantial fixed costs *186*
  D. Price differentiation versus price discrimination *187*
IV. Summary and conclusions *187*
V. Key terms *188*
VI. Questions for discussion and review *188*

Objectives

After reading this chapter, the student should be able to:

Explain how a monopolist chooses its profit-maximizing output level and price.

Compare a monopolist's price, output, and profit with a competitive industry's equilibrium price, output, and profit when costs are similar.

Explain why a monopoly can survive without minimizing costs.

Explain why the existence of monopoly will reduce economic efficiency.

Discuss how the granting of monopoly power can affect the distribution of income.

Discuss under what circumstances monopoly power may result in lower costs.

Discuss how agricultural markets can reflect monopoly power as a result of government policies.

Explain under what conditions a firm is able to use price discrimination.

Compare the economic efficiency of perfect price discrimination with competitive conditions.

▶ Introduction

As Janet listened to her brother-in-law Harry talk over dinner about what a good idea it was for the city to increase the number of authorized cabs in New York for only the second time since World War II, she couldn't help feeling that he had been suckered somehow by the system. About twelve years ago, Janet quit her job as a driver for the Yellow Cab Company and took all of her savings, almost $25,000, to buy a medallion so that she could have her own cab and be her own boss. Janet and her husband had been saving the money for a down payment on a house. But she had always wanted her own cab, and she knew that the number of available medallions was limited and that one had to have a medallion to operate a cab. She expected to be able to earn back the medallion's cost in just a few years. However, she is sure that she is now working harder and making less money than she would be making if she had stayed at her old job.

Shortly after Janet bought the medallion, the city announced that it would be issuing more medallions. Janet realized that with more cabs on the street, she would be earning less than she had originally expected. Not surprising, too, was the fact that the price of a medallion fell sharply. Still, Janet worked hard to put back into the savings account each week everything above what the drivers on payroll at the cab company earned, just as she had promised her husband. With more cabs on the street, the savings did not pile up nearly as quickly as she had hoped. In fact, the only real reason why Janet seemed to be able to earn more than the fleet drivers was because she worked longer hours and had years of experience in where to be at what time to get the best fares.

Now Harry was going on about how taxi fares were a big rip-off and how it was a good thing that the city was going to issue more medallions again because people were getting pretty fed up. Of course, Harry said that he didn't begrudge Janet all the money she must be socking away. Janet couldn't help but wonder why most people felt like Harry did about cabbies. How could people view her as someone who must be making a killing at the public's expense when she knew she was barely making a decent living? Janet saw herself as more of a victim than a profiteer.

In this chapter we will discuss the consequences for market equilibrium that arise when there is only one seller of a product. By referring to such a simple model we will be able to explain what happens when competition does not force profits to zero, even in the long run. In the process we will explain why people like Harry are right to feel cheated when confronted with markets that are not competitive. We will also be able to explain why Janet had to pay so much for a medallion and expected to earn her money back quickly. Finally, by referring to our analysis, we will be able to explain the apparent paradox that while people like Harry are feeling cheated by independent cab drivers, independent drivers like Janet feel as if they are somehow victims, too.

This last point is an important one to understand. One of the reasons it is difficult to find the political will to force markets that have not been competitive to change is that there seem to be very few culprits to apprehend and a great many victims, including the Janets of this world. This chapter contains specific examples similar to the one just described that will help you understand where the profits went.

Monopoly is a market form in which only one seller provides an industry's total production.

Monopoly power is the ability of a firm or group of firms to charge more than the competitive price for the goods or services they sell.

Price searchers are firms that seek the profit-maximizing price for the goods or services they sell.

Until now, we have treated the economy as if it were essentially competitive, with firms as well as consumers accepting market prices as beyond their control. In the competitive world of price takers, firms are free to produce any good or service that they choose and consumers may purchase any product sold by any seller. In this chapter we explore a number of deviations from the competitive market form. Our primary goal is to see what effect departures from narrowly defined price-taking behavior by firms have on prices, output, and efficiency in a market economy. The analysis of these practices is applied to an important industry—agriculture—where many firms that would normally be competitive share in monopoly power granted by the federal government. In chapter 9 we will assess the impact of government policies that regulate monopolistic practices and investigate the effectiveness of antitrust policy and public utility regulation in promoting the economic well-being of the general public.

▶ Monopoly

This chapter deals with **monopoly,** which literally means "one seller." We sometimes use the term *monopoly* more loosely to describe markets with more than one firm, but markets in which firms are not price takers. The essential difference between firms in monopolistic markets and firms in competitive markets treated in previous chapters is the way they view market prices. Competitive firms are price takers and can increase their profits only by lowering their costs or adjusting output in the face of a *given* market price. In contrast, some firms have **monopoly power,** which means that the price at which they sell their output is under their control to some degree.

Using the strict definition of monopoly, there is only one firm in a monopolistic industry. Thus, the firm's demand curve is identical to the industry's demand curve. The firm can produce any amount that might be demanded by purchasers. In this case, the monopolistic firm can clearly raise its price if it offers less for sale. If it wishes to sell more, it must be prepared to accept a lower price. The steepness of the demand curve will determine how great a price increase will result if the firm restricts its output by a certain amount. If the monopoly does not know precisely how steep its demand curve is, it can experiment with various adjustments of its sales to find out. For this reason, firms in a monopoly situation are sometimes called **price searchers** because they must try to discover how much they can sell at various prices. Obviously, the more elastic the demand curve is, the more sales will fall for a given price increase or rise for a given price decrease. Swings in total revenue received will be greater for a monopolist, the more elastic the demand curve. This is in contrast to the behavior of price *takers* in competitive markets. When firms are monopolists, or have a degree of monopoly power over the prices they charge, their output and other decisions will be different than if they were price takers. In this chapter we explore the implications of monopoly power for consumers' welfare in a market economy.

A Monopolist's Output Decision

How does a monopolist's control over the price charged affect the amount offered for sale compared to a competitive industry? In order to answer this question, it is important to bear in mind what we assume is the same for monopolistic and competitive industries and what we assume is different. The *ceteris paribus* principle is still very important when comparing monopolistic and competitive industries.

*A **barrier to entry** is a financial, legal, or technological restriction faced by firms that are outside an industry that did not or do not affect the firm(s) already in the industry.*

To begin, we will compare the output of a monopolistic industry with a competitive industry, *assuming that their costs of production are the same and their motivation to maximize profits is the same.* One feature of a monopolistic industry that is crucially different from a competitive situation is that there must be some barrier, legal, financial, or technological, keeping other firms from competing for customers. The assumption that any firm is able to enter the industry cannot hold if one firm has monopoly power in an industry. Understanding the nature of such **barriers to entry,** which restrict a monopolist's competition from other firms, is crucial to understanding monopoly.

Because a monopolistic firm and industry are identical, a monopoly faces the *industry's demand curve.* It is not a price taker, adjusting to a given market price determined by industry supply and demand. Before going on to see precisely how a monopolist's profit-maximizing output differs from a competitive industry's, we want to emphasize that even a monopolist cannot charge *any* price it chooses and still survive. Consumers do have choices, even when facing a monopolistic seller. The industry's demand curve is downward sloping because at higher prices, buyers will substitute away from the monopolized product and purchase other goods or services. Therefore, the industry demand curve *constrains* the monopolist's profit-seeking behavior. For example, we shall see that much of the United States orange market is monopolized. However, orange growers face competition from grapefruit and apple growers. A copper monopolist will lose customers to sellers of aluminum and even silver as copper's price increases. A monopolist producing nylon is forced to consider the prices charged for other fibers.

A simple numerical example will show how a monopolist determines the profit-maximizing output level. The basic law of profit maximization is the same for both a monopolist and a price taker—the profit-maximizing output is the one for which marginal cost

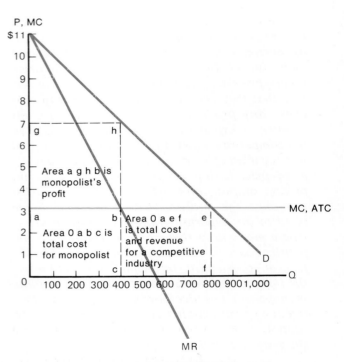

Figure 8.1   Price and output in the long run for a monopolistic industry and for a competitive industry with constant costs
A monopolist's marginal revenue is less than price as shown by the MR curve. Profit maximization occurs where MR = MC. Therefore, the monopolist produces 400 units and charges a price of $7. The monopolist's TR equals $7 × 400, or $2,800, while total cost equals $3 × 400, or $1,200. Monopolistic profit equals $1,600.

For competitive firms, MR ≡ P. Therefore, if this industry were competitive, output would equal 800, price would equal $3, and profit would be zero.

equals marginal revenue (MC = MR). The difference between monopoly and competition exists because marginal revenue is *not* in general equal to price for a monopolist, while MR and P are *identical* for a price-taking firm. Table 8.1 and figure 8.1 show why.

Table 8.1 and figure 8.1 represent the demand and *long-run* supply conditions for an industry. To make the example as simple as possible, we compare a monopolistic and competitive situation for a *constant-cost*

Table 8.1   Industry demand, the monopolist's marginal revenue, and profit-maximizing output

Demand				Long-run supply		Profit
Quantity demanded Q	Price P	Total revenue TR	Marginal revenue per additional unit sold MR	Marginal cost, average cost MC, AC	Total cost TC	π
0	$11.00	$ 0.00			$ 0	$ 0.00
			$10.00	$3.00		
100	10.00	1,000.00			300	700.00
			8.00	3.00		
200	9.00	1,800.00			600	1,200.00
			6.00	3.00		
300	8.00	2,400.00			900	1,500.00
			4.75	3.00		
325	7.75	2,518.75			975	1,543.75
			4.25	3.00		
350	7.50	2,625.00			1,050	1,575.00
			3.75	3.00		
375	7.25	2,718.75			1,125	1,593.75
			3.25	3.00		
400	7.00	2,800.00			1,200	1,600.00
			2.00	3.00		
500	6.00	3,000.00			1,500	1,500.00
			0.00	3.00		
600	5.00	3,000.00			1,800	1,200.00
			−2.00	3.00		
700	4.00	2,800.00			2,100	700.00
			−4.00	3.00		
800	3.00	2,400.00			2,400	0.00
			−6.00	3.00		
900	2.00	1,800.00			2,700	− 900.00
			−8.00	3.00		
1,000	1.00	1,000.00			3,000	−2,000.00

TR is price × quantity sold.

MR is the *change* in TR that occurs when one more or less unit is sold.

TC includes all of the firm's costs for producing a given level of output.

MC is the *change* in TC that occurs when one more or less unit is produced.

π is total revenue less total cost. Profit is maximized (largest) when the firm produces the output such that one more or less unit sold changes TR by exactly the amount that TC changes, or MR = MC. This occurs at 400 units of output. See figure 8.1.

industry in the *long run*. Remember that in the long run all costs are variable costs. Therefore the constant MC of $3 per unit of output in table 8.1 represents *all* of the opportunity costs incurred by either monopolistic or competitive firms in this industry. Every time output increases by one unit, costs grow by $3. When output is reduced, each unit results in $3 costs not incurred.

Since this is a constant-cost industry, MC is constant. This means that each additional unit of output costs $3 and, therefore, the *average* cost of each unit is also $3. That is, the monopolist's average cost curve is not U-shaped but flat and coincides *exactly* with the marginal cost curve. (Notice that this is consistent with the rule that the MC curve crosses the ATC curve at its lowest point. Since there is no single lowest point for ATC, MC never lies beneath it or above it.)

The first four columns of table 8.1 describe the industry's demand curve. In order to increase sales, the monopolist must reduce price. Starting at the highest price shown, $11 per unit, price reductions increase total revenue because the increase in the quantity demanded is sufficiently large to offset the effect of declining price. For example, reducing the price from $10 to $9 would result in an increase in sales from 100 to 200 units. Total revenue would grow by $800. If we divide this additional revenue by the additional 100 units sold, we see that the marginal revenue (MR) *per additional unit sold is $8*. On the supply side, we see that the marginal cost (MC) of each additional unit is only $3. Therefore, reducing price from $10 to $9 will increase the monopolist's profit (π). Following the same chain of reasoning, we find that reducing the price from $9 to $8, and even further, will also increase π. The profit increases that result from price reductions grow smaller and smaller, however. Table 8.1 shows that when the price is dropped from $7.25 to $7.00, MR exceeds MC by only $0.25 and π increases by only $6.25, to its maximum level, $600. (Eventually, price reductions lead to *falling* profits.)

Figure 8.1 allows us to see the values of P, MR, and Q (quantity sold) for each unit of output. If you have followed the discussion to this point, you should be able to calculate that when P equals $7.01, Q equals 399. Therefore, reducing P to $7.00 increases sales to 400 units, with MR equal to $3.01. Reducing price by another cent to $6.99 will raise sales to 401 units, while MR is less than MC. Maximum profit is $1,600, which occurs when P equals $7.00 and Q equals 400 units. Since TR equals price times quantity, the monopolist's profit-maximizing TR is represented by the area of the rectangle 0ghc in figure 8.1. Total cost is average total cost times quantity, ATC x Q, or the area 0abc. Therefore, the monopolist's profit is the difference between the larger and smaller areas, or the rectangle aghb. Why doesn't the monopolist charge the highest price possible? The reason is that although the monopolist *can* charge much more than $7 per unit, doing so would reduce revenue more than cost and result in lower profit. The monopolist is limited in the price it is most profitable to charge because higher prices cause consumers to switch to other goods. Even a monopolist is affected by the principle of substitution!

Suppose the industry described in table 8.1 and figure 8.1 were composed of a number of identical *competitive* firms. Would industry price equal $7 and output equal 400? A quick review of chapter 7 will remind you that the MC, ATC curve in figure 8.1 is the competitive industry's long-run supply curve. Equilibrium for the *competitive* industry is determined by the intersection of the industry's long-run supply and demand curves. Thus, the competitive equilibrium price is only $3. Each competitive firm is a price taker and therefore views P = $3 as a magnitude over which it has no control. For each competitive firm, therefore, MR $\equiv$ P = $3. Once again, a review of chapter 7 will show that the competitive *output* will equal 800 units. If this industry were competitive, price would be $3 instead of $7 and output would equal 800 instead of 400 units.

In general, a monopolist will charge a higher price and sell less output than a competitive industry with the same costs. The ability to charge a higher price creates the possibility for a monopolist to receive an economic profit. Such a profit could not persist in the long run in a competitive industry. In a monopolistic industry, however, a barrier to competition prevents other firms from competing for monopoly profit and driving it down to zero in long-run equilibrium. Therefore, profit may persist in the long run when a monopoly is present.

As a rule, monopoly in one market will affect other markets, even if they are competitive. When the monopolist charges a higher price, the quantity produced will generally be less. The resources that might

Table 8.2   The essential differences between monopolistic and competitive markets

Competition[a]	Monopoly[b]
1. Firms produce where P ≡ MR = MC	1. Firms produce where P > MR = MC
2. Competitive industry produces more	2. Monopolistic industry produces less
3. Competitive firms earn zero economic profit in the long run	3. Monopolistic firms may earn a positive economic profit (called monopoly rent) in the long run

[a]A competitive industry consists of a number of rival producers of the same good or service, all of which are price takers.
[b]A monopolistic industry consists of one seller. The comparison between monopoly and competition in this table assumes that the monopolistic industry's costs of production are identical to those of the competitive industry. Both face the same *industry* demand curve.

have been used to produce more of the monopolized good will flow to the rest of the economy. This will lead to more goods and services being produced in the remaining, competitive industries than these industries would have produced otherwise. In short, the emergence of monopoly production in a competitive environment leads to a higher relative price of the monopolized good or service and smaller output, while the indirect impact on competitively produced goods and services is to reduce their relative price and to increase their output.

The barriers that prevent competing firms from entering a monopolistic industry are frequently created by government regulations. For example, until recently only AT & T was permitted to operate long-distance telephone lines in the United States. Another reason for an entry barrier is exclusive ownership of an essential resource or control over its sale. For example, the DeBeers Company of South Africa controls most of the sources of gem-quality diamonds and thus has been able to monopolize the world market for diamonds used in jewelry.

The differences between monopoly and competition are summarized in table 8.2.

An Economic Evaluation of Monopoly

Monopoly, strictly defined as one firm or seller in an industry, is rare in market economies, particularly in the United States. One reason is that most monopolies are illegal in the United States under terms of the *Sherman Antitrust Act of 1890*. There are, however, exceptions to this act. For example, the *Clayton Antitrust Act of 1914* removes labor unions from the threat of prosecution for violating the Sherman Act. The *Capper–Volstead Act of 1922* exempts agricultural co-ops and permits cooperation among farmers to set prices for their products.

Why do we have laws that restrict monopolistic practices in many industries but that allow them in others? Does monopoly have a bad or a good effect on the economy?

Monopoly and Survival

Perhaps the most important effect of monopoly on an economic system's ability to deal with scarcity is its impact on a firm's ability to survive without minimizing its costs. If more resources are used than the minimum required, then economic efficiency is not attained and consumers are not as well off as they might be given available resources. Until now, we have assumed that monopolistic firms, like competitive firms, try to maximize their profits. This requires minimizing the cost of whatever output is produced. However, we have seen that even if competitive firms do not consciously try to maximize profits, those that survive under competitive conditions will be forced to do so. Competitive firms that do not maximize profits will be forced out of business by those that do minimize their costs and choose profit-maximizing output levels. Why should a monopolist exert all of the effort needed to minimize cost if a profit, although smaller, can be earned without as much trouble? It is probably more realistic to think of monopolists as interested in profits as well as other goals, such as less effort in managing their firms, pleasant colleagues to work with, nicely decorated offices, luxurious working conditions, and so on. Thus, profit alone cannot be used as a measure of monopoly power, and the effect of monopoly power on production costs is a potentially important source of inefficiency in an economic system. Even if a monopolist produces output at minimum cost to maximize profit, economic resources will be misallocated as explained below.

Monopoly and Efficiency

If firms do not minimize their costs, then a necessary condition for economic efficiency is violated and the economy cannot operate on its PPF. There is still another reason, however, why the presence of monopolistic industries is likely to interfere with economic efficiency. If you quickly review the discussion of economic efficiency in chapter 7, you will recall that efficiency results only if resources are allocated *among* industries in accordance with consumers' desires. Remember that a good's market price measures the value that each consumer places on the last unit purchased. It follows that if a market economy has both competitive and monopolistic industries, then the competitive industries will be allocated too many resources and produce too many goods and services, while the monopolistic sector of the economy will produce too few. Monopoly reduces economic efficiency because it distorts the mix of goods and services produced.

Therefore, even if the monopolist maximizes profit, the existence of monopoly will reduce allocative efficiency in the economy.

Figure 8.1 will help you see how monopoly results in an inefficient allocation of resources among industries. Suppose for the sake of simplicity that there are two industries, one competitive and one monopolistic, and that the marginal cost of producing a unit of output is the same in both industries. Both industries are in equilibrium. Therefore, one unit of output costing $3 sells for $7 in the monopolistic industry. If enough resources to produce one unit of output were transferred from the competitive industry to the monopolistic industry, consumers would value the loss of the competitively produced good at $3. However, they would value the gain in monopoly production at $7. Since monopoly results in a "wedge" between P and MC, market forces will not lead to economic efficiency, monopoly production will be too small, and competitive output will be too large.

Figure 8.1 provides a simple measure of the degree to which society would be made better off if a monopolistic industry could be forced to expand its output to the competitive level. To see this, we must remember that the height of the demand curve measures consumers' *marginal value* of the good or service produced by the monopolistic industry. That is, at the monopolistic output of 400 units in figure 8.1, consumers would be willing to pay $7 for an additional unit. It will help to cement this concept in your mind if you take a pencil and draw a vertical line from the quantity 401 on the horizontal axis up to the demand curve in figure 8.1. The height of this line is approximately $7 and represents the amount that a typical consumer would be willing to pay for one extra unit of output. Now draw a similar vertical line from the horizontal axis up to the demand curve for the next unit of output, 402. Notice that the height of the line indicates that consumers would be willing to pay slightly less for unit 402 than for unit 401. If you continue to draw such vertical lines for greater and greater quantities of output, you will notice that consumers are willing to pay less and less for each extra unit. This, of course, is nothing more than the essence of

Consumers' surplus is the maximum amount consumers are willing to pay for a good or service less the amount they have to pay.

the downward-sloping demand curve. The key point here, though, is that there is a *difference* between what consumers are *willing* to pay for additional production of a good or service and its marginal cost. This difference ($4 in figure 8.1) represents the gain in economic well-being that society would obtain from one more unit of the monopolist's output, given that the monpolistic level is currently produced.

Suppose that in figure 8.1, we continue to draw our vertical pencil lines to illustrate the value of each extra unit of production until we reach 800 units. This is the output level of a competitive industry with the demand and cost curves in figure 8.1. By drawing these vertical pencil lines, we will have blackened the area chef. Filling in this area is equivalent to adding up the marginal value of each of the extra units from 400 to 800. In other words, if output were expanded to the competitive level, 800 units in figure 8.1, the additional value to consumers would be represented by the area under the demand curve from point h to point e, or the area chef. The cost of this additional output is the area cbef. This cost represents the value of the goods and services that are currently produced in the competitive sector of the economy with the resources competitive industries obtain because the monopolist produces 400 units of output instead of 800 units. Because MC = P in the competitive sector of the economy, MC also reflects consumers' marginal value of the additional goods and services produced in the competitive sector with the resources flowing to it from the monopolistic sector.

The *net gain* that consumers would receive from having more of the monopolistic good but less of the goods produced in competitive industries is called **consumers' surplus,** which is measured by the area of the triangle bhe. The area of the triangle bhe, then, measures the value consumers would obtain from 400 additional units of the monopolist's good or service if resources sufficient to produce them were transferred to the monopolist from the competitive sector, less the value that consumers would lose by not having the goods produced in the competitive sector of the economy with these resources.

Do not get the idea that there is *no* consumers' surplus under monopoly. Consumers' surplus simply refers to the fact that buyers are willing to pay more for each unit of every good they buy (except the last, or marginal unit) than they have to pay for it. The entire area under a demand curve up to a particular level of output is the total value to consumers from consuming that particular quantity. Consumers' surplus is the difference between this value—what consumers would be *willing* to pay for what they consume—and what they actually have to pay. Consumers' surplus is consumers' gain from buying the quantity of a good or service they choose to purchase. Why buy something if it does not make you better off? Every unit of a good or service makes its purchaser better off than if the money had been spent on something else (except for the last, or marginal unit bought).

In figure 8.1, for example, when the monopolist offers 400 units for sale at $7, consumers are getting consumers' surplus equal to the area of the triangle with base gh and height equal to the portion of the vertical axis from $7 up to where the demand curve cuts it ($11). Notice how much less consumers' surplus is under monopoly than it would be if this industry were competitive. If the industry in figure 8.1 were competitive, output would be 800 units. Consumers' surplus would equal the area of the triangle with a height equal to the distance between the point where the demand curve cuts the vertical axis ($11) and $3 (where the marginal cost curve cuts the vertical axis) and base ae (from the vertical axis to where MC intersects the demand curve). To make absolutely sure that you understand how to measure consumers' surplus, show that under monopoly, consumers' surplus would equal $800, while under competitive market conditions, consumers' surplus would equal $3,200. How much of this increase in consumers' surplus comes from elimination of monopolistic profit and how much from increased output and consumption of the good?

Monopoly Profits, Rents, and the Distribution of Income

Economists view monopoly power as undesirable because it leads to economic inefficiency. Essentially, the *what* and *how* questions are answered differently under monopolistic conditions than when competitive forces prevail. Why, then, do federal laws prohibit monopolistic practices in some instances but allow them in others? One reason, which we will develop later on, is that under certain circumstances a monopolist may be able to achieve lower costs or generate other benefits that would not result from competition. The assumption that monopolistic and competitive firms face the same production or cost conditions cannot always be maintained. However, a more important reason underlying the lack of uniform legal treatment of monopoly involves our old acquaintance, the *for whom* question. As we have seen, monopoly not only affects the allocation of resources, it also influences the allocation of income.

The principal reason why some groups in society are granted legal monopoly power is to permit them to increase their incomes. The source of society's opposition to most forms of monopoly results from the perception that monopolists charge higher prices than competitive firms and therefore earn higher profits. Insofar as monopoly power is associated with relatively large wealth, any profits arising from monopolistic practices are usually viewed as undeserved. However, if monopoly is viewed as evil when it enables the already wealthy to become wealthier, it is consistent to view it as good when it enables the relatively poor to improve their economic well-being.

Economic analysis has nothing to say about the *normative* questions of how much more the poor should receive, how much should be taken away from the rich, or whether farmers or union members are more deserving than other groups. However, economists as social scientists can and do draw attention to the following observations associated with monopoly policy.

1. *Granting monopoly power to particular industries or to particular people may well help the well-to-do more than the poor.* Not all farmers who benefit from preferential treatment under our antitrust laws are poor—some are very rich. Yet all members of a favored group benefit from increased incomes. Not all workers are in poverty, but monopoly power granted to labor unions benefits all members regardless of their income status. Workers who do not, or cannot, become union members do not benefit.

2. *Monopoly power generates economic inefficiency.* Therefore, other means of altering the distribution of income that accomplish desired goals at least as precisely and with less economic inefficiency should be used if they are available. For example, if we want to help the poor, why not use methods that improve their ability to find rewarding jobs or, if they cannot work, give them money? The benefits and problems of a number of alternative means of changing the distribution of income are discussed in chapter 15.

3. *Only those who initially receive the right to participate in a monopoly or their heirs benefit from it.* Members of the favored group who arrive later do not benefit. Suppose, for example, you own a grove of orange trees in California and as the result of a new law you are permitted to join with all of the other California orange growers to restrict total orange production and thereby avoid "ruinous competition" in the orange industry. There is little doubt that *you* and other orange growers *currently in business* will benefit *for a while*. Under competitive conditions, the profit resulting from higher orange prices would attract entry into the orange growing industry, and the profits would disappear if the price fell to its old level. However, since your group has monopoly power, you can control the total number of oranges placed on the market. Therefore, entry will not lower the price of oranges. If new growers do enter the industry, each orchard will be allowed to sell a smaller fraction of

its output, so profit will fall despite the maintenance of a monopoly price. Eventually, monopoly profits will disappear, and farmers will no longer be induced to enter the industry. Thus, if society eventually changes its mind and seeks to abolish the grant of monopoly power, many of the parties that gained initially will not be those that lose when the grant is repealed. This represents a major barrier to change once monopoly power is granted to firms in an industry.

It is, of course, possible to pass additional legislation restricting entry into the industry. For example, it is illegal to grow peanuts, rice, tobacco, or hops commercially in the United States without a permit or "allotment." Permits can be obtained only by purchase from existing permit holders. Thus, in these industries, monopoly profits cannot be reduced by firms entering the industry and the resulting decline in price. Monopoly profits, when accompanied by an effective barrier to entry such as a permit system, become monopoly *rents*. (Remember from chapter 7, an important difference between *rent* and *profit* is that rents do not disappear as a result of new entrants forcing down the market price of a good.) Can a permit system ensure that monopoly power will increase farmers' incomes forever? The answer is no. After the monopoly power is created, anyone who wants to enter the peanut, rice, tobacco, or hops industry must buy a permit from an existing farmer. How much will the new grower have to pay? The equilibrium price of permits will rise so long as farmers can earn more in growing these crops than in other forms of agriculture. The equilibrium price of permits will rise to a level high enough so that the revenues received from growing a protected crop are barely large enough to justify paying for the permits. Thus, only the farmers to whom the permits were *initially* issued (or perhaps their heirs) will benefit from the creation of monopoly power. Those who come later will face costs of entry so high that they will be no better off growing protected crops than other crops.

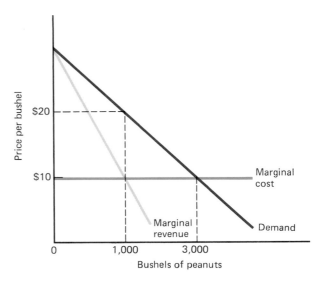

Figure 8.2   Selling peanut allotments
If I own a peanut farm with cost and demand conditions reflected here, my allotment or permit is worth $10 × 1,000, or $10,000 per year to me. If you buy my allotment from me, I will charge you the equivalent of $10,000 per year for it. You will still produce the monopoly output, 1,000, and sell at the monopoly price of $20 per bushel. However, your total costs will be $10,000 for production and $10,000 in permit payments to me. So you will earn zero economic profit.

Referring to figure 8.2, if I own a peanut farm and have a government allotment, I will sell 1,000 bushels of peanuts per year at a price of $20 each and a marginal cost of $10 each. My monopoly rent will be equal to $10,000 per year. Now, if you offer to buy my allotment from me, I will insist on a price of at least $10,000 per year. You will still produce 1,000 bushels per year, which you will sell for $20,000. But your production costs plus allotment payments to me will also equal $20,000. Your monopoly rent is zero. As a matter of simple fact, I will have captured all of the monopoly rent.

*A **technical monopoly** (sometimes called a* natural monopoly*) is a market form in which one firm can provide a good or service at a lower cost than a larger number of firms.*

Economies of scale define a situation in which a firm's average total cost decreases as output increases.

Figure 8.3   Example of a technical monopoly
A bridge is built to connect two sides of a river. Maintenance costs, which are independent of bridge traffic, equal $15 per day. If the bridge is provided for only one crossing, the maintenance cost per crossing (ATC) is $15. Subsequent crossings each day require no *additional* maintenance costs. This cost structure is reflected in the MC and ATC curves.

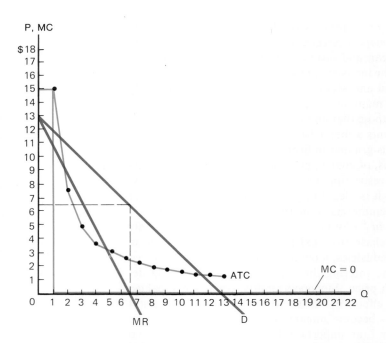

Can Monopoly Be Good?

So far, we have assumed that if a monopolist minimizes its cost of production, it will achieve no lower costs than competitive firms. This is not always true. There are circumstances when a monopoly may achieve *lower* costs than would prevail under competitive conditions. When this is true, a monopoly may promote economic efficiency.

Technical Monopolies   A **technical monopoly** results in an industry in which the cost of producing the first unit of output is higher than that of producing any additional output (over the range of output that satisfies user demand). Each firm in an industry such as this would have to incur the high cost of the first unit; therefore, increasing the number of firms would result in higher total industry costs for a given level of production. Fewer resources are required to produce a given quantity of output if only one firm produces the good rather than several firms. Consequently, a cost saving results. In the case of a technical monopoly, it is incorrect to assume constant costs for the

industry because even in the long run, average total cost is not constant; on the contrary, average total cost declines continuously over the range of output that satisfies demand for the good. When average total cost declines as output increases, we say that a firm experiences **economies of scale.**

A very simple technical monopoly is illustrated in figure 8.3 In this example, a bridge is built to connect two communities on opposite sides of a river. A demand to use this bridge exists because business and pleasure travelers between the two towns can save time and transportation costs by avoiding longer, alternate routes between the two towns. Only one bridge is required to accommodate all traffic that would use it, even at a zero toll. The bridge is a technical monopoly because once the bridge is in place, the cost of providing bridge services (i.e., one crossing equals one unit of bridge services) is independent of the amount of traffic. Figure 8.3 shows that the resources required to maintain the bridge cost $15 per day. Thus, if more than one person crosses the bridge, the marginal cost of each crossing is zero. Not only is one

*An **innovation** is the application of a new production technique or the development of a new product by a firm.*

*A **property right** is the legal entitlement to use or sell an asset, such as land, a good or service, or an invention.*

bridge sufficient to supply the market for bridge services, but if there were two or more bridges competing with each other, the cost of bridge services would be higher. For example, a second bridge would also involve a maintenance cost of $15 per day. Thus, if there were two bridges, the cost of bridge services would be $30 per day even if only one person crossed each bridge daily. This would be twice the minimum expenditure necessary to accommodate two or more people crossing the river and would therefore be inefficient. We will return to this example in chapter 9 when we discuss whether granting monopoly power will lead to economic efficiency when there is a technical monopoly.

Certain aspects of providing utility services (gas, electricity, telephone) with current technology are similar to the situation depicted in figure 8.3. In any area to be served, the cost of setting up the grid of trenches, pipes, or poles to bring utility service to each block is largely independent of the number of houses or people served. A block with small lots and twenty houses will be little more expensive to serve than one with large lots and only ten houses.

Innovations, Patents, and Monopoly Power   In addition to technical monopolies, there is another case in which monopoly may result in lower costs. One of the principal causes of a rising standard of living has been new products and new methods of production resulting from **innovations,** which are new inventions, new products, or new techniques of production that a firm adopts in anticipation of making a profit. Firms have an incentive to lower their costs relative to other firms and to offer improved products in order to increase their profits. Therefore, individuals and firms have an incentive to invest time and money in research on new products and technology.

A firm's goal when it engages in innovation is to secure for itself a degree of monopoly power that will shield it from the competition of other firms. That is, a new method of production will allow a firm to produce at a lower cost than firms that have not adopted the innovation. An improved product means that the

innovating firm can charge a higher price than its rivals. However, if competing firms are able to quickly copy an innovating firm's cost-saving techniques or its new products, then the goal of monopoly profits will prove ephemeral. The incentive for innovation will be reduced or eliminated if an innovating firm expects to bear costs but not to reap returns. Can you imagine a world without electronic computers, cheap ballpoint pens, self-developing photographs, or photocopying machines? None of these products were in general use forty years ago, and all of them were introduced by firms that hoped to reap monopoly profits from their innovations.

The creation and adoption of economic innovations is one case in which the conflict between consumers' desires to obtain the greatest satisfaction from their limited incomes and firms' desires to obtain the largest possible profits is not necessarily resolved efficiently by competition in the marketplace. Competition results in consumers' being able to purchase goods at their lowest cost so that consumers benefit the maximum amount from innovations when they are introduced. Unfortunately, there would be *very few* innovations leading to cost reductions or new products if firms expected all of their profits from innovations to be quickly eliminated by competition from their rivals.

The *patent system* protects the developer of a new product or technique from competition (for seventeen years in the United States) in order to encourage innovations that ultimately benefit society at large. Essentially, a patent creates a **property right,** which means that ownership is established just as a bill of sale or deed establishes ownership of a car or piece of land. This property right provides monopoly power that protects the inventor for a specified time period from the risk that someone else will use his or her idea without paying for it. Patent protection is seldom perfect, but it probably helps foster innovation. When Eastman Kodak Company marketed its version of a camera that develops its own pictures, it was immediately sued by Polaroid for patent infringement. Kodak no doubt expected to pay some compensation to Polaroid when it released its new camera but not as much as Polaroid would have demanded if Kodak had initially asked to purchase the rights to manufacture the camera that it eventually placed on the market. The Kodak–Polaroid dispute ended with Kodak's withdrawing its camera from the market. It demonstrates that the patent system can provide protection to inventors and innovators who invest their own resources in developing new products or production techniques.

Application: Agricultural Marketing Organizations—Equal Opportunity to Compete or License to Monopolize?

We turn now to an example of monopoly practices in the United States agriculture industry. Additional examples will be provided in chapter 11. When you read this discussion of a market in which monopoly power has raised market prices above competitive levels, you should look for the conditions that allow monopolization to occur in an industry that would normally be highly competitive. You should also try to decide whether the grant of monopoly power has been sufficient to allow the favored firms to restrict output and achieve a permanent increase in their incomes. For each of the cases discussed below it is worth noting that demand curves for agricultural products tend to be relatively inelastic. Programs that artificially raise agricultural product prices are also likely to increase total farm income. Moreover, the general rationale for farm support programs is to raise farm incomes.

We have already seen that special legislation exempts farmer *cooperative associations* from the Sherman Antitrust Act.[1] Cooperatives, as distinct from corporations, do not earn "profits." Their "surpluses," above what is needed to finance current operations, are all paid out to members as dividends. The exemptions granted to cooperatives from antitrust regulation have been interpreted to apply to a range of firms that do not necessarily match the strict definition of cooperative enterprises envisioned when the

protection from antitrust regulation was initially granted. Some of these cooperatives are very large. Despite this favorable treatment, agricultural cooperatives have achieved significant monopoly power in the marketing of only a few crops.[2] A discussion of the reasons for the development of agricultural marketing organizations will help to provide an understanding of the role that monopoly power plays in our economic system.

Probably the main reason why Congress saw fit to exempt agricultural cooperatives from the antitrust restrictions that govern most other industries was that farmers were viewed as helpless in negotiating with shippers and processors of their output. By joining together in a cooperative effort, growers in a local market would be able to negotiate their mutual interest, it was thought. In recent years, however, cooperatives have begun to merge across local markets. Some of them have become very large businesses indeed.[3]

Exempting cooperatives from the Sherman Act is not the only way in which Congress has provided economic aid to agriculture. For some commodities, most notably milk and grains, Congress legislates minimum, or target, market prices that are generally higher than the equilibrium prices that would prevail in a free market for these commodities. As we learned in chapter 6, an effective minimum price has led to excess supplies in these markets. The dairy industry has benefited from both minimum price legislation and exemption from antitrust legislation. Thus, the federal government purchases many surplus commodities produced by dairy cooperatives that have been given important monopoly rights.

As mentioned earlier, other agricultural commodities have received protection from antitrust regulation. These include sugar, rice, peanuts, oranges, lemons, raisins, hops, and tobacco. The same laws of supply and demand that apply to dairy and grain markets apply to these agricultural products, too. Therefore, if prices are set above market equilibrium levels, gluts will result. The presence of these excess supplies will frustrate efforts to maintain prices at monopolistic levels. How can such gluts be controlled?

With fruit crops, the principal means used to control excess supplies is the *marketing order*. Federal, and some state, laws permit the majority of growers in an area to vote for a marketing order, which the government then issues to establish a marketing organization for that area. Such marketing boards may also establish minimum prices for their respective areas. In order for similar procedures to be effective in grain markets, marketing orders would have to cover very large areas because most grains can be grown throughout a large part of the United States and transportation costs between markets are not prohibitive. This would be relatively difficult to carry out and might well attract public and official opposition. However, climatic conditions limit the areas in which sugar, hops, rice, peanuts, citrus fruits, nuts, grapes, lettuce, and tobacco are grown commercially. Thus, the Navel Orange Administrative Committee, which controls marketing in Arizona and California, has been called "the OPEC of oranges." (Oranges that are grown in Florida and California ripen at different times in the two states. Therefore, these two areas do not compete in marketing fresh produce.)

What agricultural businesses and marketing orders cannot do without additional crop-by-crop legislation is to limit entry into the market. Therefore, as we have already seen, market power exists to set and enforce minimum prices in many agricultural markets, but growers probably cannot earn monopoly rents in the long run. Entry of new growers will increase total production, requiring the destruction of a larger and larger share of output. Consequently, monopoly rents will tend to be eliminated. Special legislation *does* apply, however, to rice, peanut, hop, and tobacco growers, as we have already mentioned. Since permits, or allotments, must be purchased from existing growers to enter these industries, legislation creates a barrier to entry.

The dairy industry is also a special case. Federal laws support the dairy cooperatives in setting minimum prices for fresh milk through marketing orders. Much of the resulting glut of fresh milk is converted into butter, cheese, and dry milk, which the government purchases so that it does not have to be destroyed. Some of this has been given away to poor developing countries or to the poor in the United States, but a rapidly growing quantity is simply stored. Efforts to enforce output restrictions on dairy farmers are frequently attempted, but they have met with little success. In 1981, the federal government purchased almost $2 billion of "surplus" dairy products. This was seventeen times the amount spent only five years earlier and about 11 percent of all dairy product sales in 1981.

Our brief survey of the power to exert a degree of monopoly control in what would, without protective legislation, be a competitive industry illustrates the conditions that are necessary to establish a price above competitive market levels. It also draws our attention to the need for more than output restrictions if monopoly rents are to be maintained for farmers. Either entry must be limited through a permit system or government must purchase agricultural "surplus" goods and keep them off the market. Even with such controls, our earlier discussion of monopoly rents points out that in the long run the resulting rents will be converted into farmers' costs. This will occur as land or allotments change hands and their prices rise to reflect the value of the monopoly rents they yield. Only those farmers who are in the industry when price and entry controls are first imposed or increased will benefit economically. It should come as no surprise, therefore, that farmers do not appear to earn large profits. They generally complain that at best revenues barely cover their costs. Indeed, it has been proposed that the ultimate solution to the farmer's plight would be to make it illegal for farmers to sell their output below the cost of producing it.[4] Do you think this would solve farmers' economic problems?

The Sources of Monopoly Power

Our discussion of agriculture illustrates the difficulties that must be overcome for monopoly power to result in an effective transfer of wealth from consumers to producers. After you have read more about attempts to monopolize important industries in chapter 11, you will see that at least one of two fundamental conditions is necessary for a monopoly to be effective. (1) Ownership or control of a basic resource must reside in the hands of one seller or in the hands of a sufficiently small number of sellers so that cooperation and restriction of entry is practical. The resource owned could be intangible, such as a patent on a basic production process or a crop allotment, or it might be a basic raw material, such as oil. This is the condition that we shall see gave OPEC at least temporary monopoly power over world oil markets. It also supported one of the few effective monopolies that has existed in the United States without government protection in some form. The United States Steel Corporation once controlled a very high proportion of high quality domestic iron ore deposits. This enabled it to exert a strong monopolistic influence on iron and steel production in the United States from the year it was formed, 1901, through the end of World War I and perhaps longer.[5] (2) If a monopolist or group of firms does not control a fundamental resource, it must possess other means to control output and/or restrict entry. Such control may involve government's purchase of excess supplies or the use of force. The former possibility arises when a group such as farmers has political clout. The latter technique is common in industries dominated by organized crime, such as illegal gambling and drug trafficking.

▶ Price Discrimination

Before concluding our discussion of monopolistic firms, we need to investigate an important set of circumstances in which a firm is able to charge different prices to various buyers of the same good or service. One reason a firm may be able to do this is that the firm has some degree of monopoly power. The practice of charging different buyers different prices is known as **price discrimination.** In this section we will examine the economic implications of price discrimination and the conditions under which it may exist. There are numerous interesting examples of price discrimination. First, however, we need a little background discussion.

Figure 8.4 illustrates what happens to a monopolist's revenue and to consumers' surplus when the monopolist is able to charge two different prices for a given level of output, Q(0). In the absence of price discrimination, the monopolist in figure 8.4 sells output level Q(0) at price P(0). Suppose now that the monopolist can divide its buyers into two easily identified groups that the monopolist knows are willing to pay different prices for the good or service it produces. One group of buyers is willing to pay the higher price P(1) and to purchase half of the total output of Q(0) at this price. The other group will purchase half of the output Q(0) only if it is able to purchase it at the price P(0). Under this simple form of price discrimination, the monopolist's revenue is increased by the area of the rectangle aedf, which is also the increase in the monopolist's profit. Under the two-price system shown in figure 8.4, consumers' surplus has been reduced by the monopolist's revenue gain and is now equal to the sum of the two triangles ebd and fdc.

A common condition under which price discrimination can exist is some degree of monopoly power. If a significant number of producers of identical or nearly identical products compete with one another for sales, then producers will drive the price to a common level for all customers—equal to marginal cost. Moreover, price discrimination requires that the two groups of buyers in the preceding example must find it difficult or impossible to resell the product among themselves. Otherwise, those who are able to buy it cheaply would profit by selling it to the others at a price less than they could buy it for from the discriminating monopolist.

Price Discrimination in Practice

How will monopolists justify price discrimination to the public or to the government? Will they say that they are simply charging higher prices to wealthier buyers who are willing to pay more for the product? Not likely. They are more likely to say that they are giving discounts to low-income people such as the elderly and students. At this point, a number of examples of price discrimination may occur to you. One example is student subscriptions to newspapers and magazines. While publishers operate in a highly competitive industry, copyrights tend to create newspapers and magazines that are not perfect substitutes for one another, and many are quite distinct from their rivals. Moreover, it is difficult for a student who buys the *Wall Street Journal* or *Sports Illustrated* at half price to resell it to the general public at the newsstand price. The time and trouble of going to the local drugstore each day to try to resell a newspaper or magazine is generally greater than the potential profit.

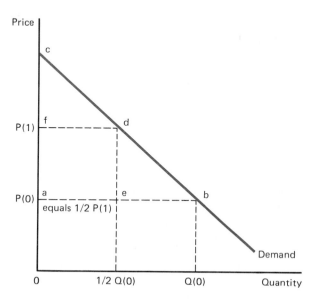

Figure 8.4 Price discrimination, monopoly revenue, and consumers' surplus

When there is no price discrimination, the monopolist sells all its output, Q(0), at a common price, P(0), which is what consumers are willing to pay for the last or marginal unit of output. However, if the monopolist can sell some of its output, say, half of it, at a higher price P(1), the monopolist will be better off. The demand curve shows that consumers are willing to pay a price equal to P(1) for the quantity 1/2 Q(0) and a price equal to P(0) for an additional quantity of output up to the quantity Q(0). In this case, known as price discrimination, the monopolist's revenue is increased by the area of the rectangle aedf. Consumers' surplus is reduced to the sum of the two triangles ebd and fdc.

Perfect price discrimination exists
when a firm is able to charge the
most consumers will pay (all the
traffic will bear) for each unit of
output separately.

At times in the past—when regulation created many monopoly-like market situations in the transportation industry—the airlines offered half-price tickets for available seats to members of the armed forces and to students. These discount seats could not easily be resold to full-fare business travelers. Local (monopolistic) transportation systems often issue bus or subway passes at a discount to senior citizens. Each pass may have the owner's picture on it so that a full-fare passenger cannot easily repurchase a seat from an elderly person on the subway at something between half and full fare. The common element in each of these examples is that a monopolist can increase total revenue and profit by selling the same product to different groups of consumers by charging them different prices. The ability to separate markets or groups of buyers for its product augments the monopolist's market power and, therefore, its monopoly profits.

In separating markets, the monopolist will equate the common marginal cost of supply of the product in each market to the marginal revenue associated with each group's demand curve. Remember, the more elastic demand is, that is, the more price sensitive consumers are, the closer the marginal revenue curve for a product will be to the demand curve. So, by equating a common marginal cost to marginal revenue in each market, the discriminating monopolist will set a lower price in the market with the more elastic demand curve and a higher price in the market with the less elastic demand curve. Students get subscription discounts because their demand for the *Wall Street Journal* is more elastic than the demand by business executives.

Perfect Price Discrimination

A more elaborate form of price discrimination is depicted in figure 8.5. What could be called **perfect price discrimination** is the situation where the monopolist is able to charge the maximum possible price (what the traffic will bear) for each *separate* unit of the good or service. In this way, the monopolist is able to capture the marginal value of each and every unit by getting the most that consumers will pay for each unit

separately. This requires that each seller offer a unique product or, at least, that information about the products of competing sellers is so poor that the sellers appear to be monopolists to uninformed consumers. It also requires negotiating the price of each and every unit separately and offering the consumer an all-or-nothing deal. The consumer either pays the full value of the product or will not obtain the product at all. Obviously, this situation cannot persist if buyers can resell the product among themselves.

What are some examples of markets that approach perfect price discrimination? There are probably none that exactly match figure 8.5. After all, why bother to buy something that yields you *no* extra satisfaction compared to other goods or services you could have purchased? However, a Middle East bazaar in, say, Cairo or Jerusalem is an approximation. Here each of the shopkeepers will negotiate separately for a given item with every customer who comes into the shop. In this way, it may be possible to charge a price approaching the marginal value to each consumer for a particular item. Obviously, well-informed consumers (locals, or natives) will be able to shop around—or threaten to do so—unless they obtain a price at or near the cost of production. Tourists, who have less time and knowledge about available alternatives, however, are more likely to be taken by price discrimination and end up paying a price that significantly exceeds what a product actually costs to produce. The next time you go to the supermarket to select your breakfast cereal from among the myriad competing products, think about how much harder it would be to be sure you were not paying too much if each grocer sold a mixture contained in a brown bag without any label indicating brand or contents. Under such circumstances, how long do you think it would take before some enterprising and profit-seeking manufacturer introduced an identifiable product that could be obtained in many stores in a large number of locations? What conditions would militate against the manufacturer's finding stores to sell this product? What conditions would contribute to its speedy acceptance by stores and their customers? We will have more to say about brand names and advertising in chapter 10.

Chapter 9

Oligopoly

Outline

I. Introduction *190*
II. Price and output in an oligopolistic industry *191*
   A. Oligopoly, concentration, and collusion *191*
      1. OPEC: The rise (and decline?) of a cartel *193*
   B. Oligopolistic pricing without formal collusion: The problem of interdependence *197*
      1. An example of price leadership with a dominant firm: The United States Steel Corporation *198*
      2. Other pricing strategies *199*
         a. The game theoretic approach *199*
         b. The kinked demand curve hypothesis *201*
III. An economic evaluation of oligopoly *202*
IV. Summary and conclusions *202*
V. Key terms *203*
VI. Questions for discussion and review *203*

Objectives

After reading this chapter, the student should be able to:

Explain why a concentration ratio is only a crude measure of monopoly power.

Discuss various forms of collusion that might exist in an oligopolistic industry.

Discuss what conditions in an industry make collusion more likely to occur and what conditions make effective collusion more difficult.

Discuss how OPEC was able to charge prices above the competitive price for oil.

Explain why OPEC had difficulty maintaining its monopoly power over the long term.

Discusss how a game theoretic approach can be used to explain oligopolistic interdependence.

Discuss the kinked demand curve hypothesis and its drawbacks.

Discuss the possible price and output outcomes in an oligopolistic industry.

▶ Introduction

Alma and her husband, Joe, ran a small pizza shop in lower Manhattan. For years, local residents had dropped into the pizzeria from the time it opened at 11 A.M. until it closed at 3:00 A.M. Everybody agreed that Alma and Joe's pizza had a really good homemade taste that brought to mind images of southern Italy. The prices were right, too, so that even people with low-income budgets could afford a meal out now and again.

Then, in the early 1980s, a major national chain announced it was going after the lucrative New York pizza market, where until then small "mom and pop" operations like Alma and Joe's had always been the rule. Soon, a shiny, modern restaurant featuring weekly specials, coupons, and slick new furniture opened up just a couple of blocks from Alma and Joe's. Although their product didn't quite have the Old World flavor of Alma and Joe's pizza, the chain outlet's product wasn't bad, and if you used coupons, you could save a dollar or two. The service was quicker, too, so it didn't take an hour from the time you ordered your pizza until you finished eating.

Joe and Alma saw their business gradually shrinking. They had hoped to sell their pizzeria in a few years and retire to Florida with the money they received. However, a year after the chain opened, they simply closed up shop and sold their equipment to a second-hand dealer. Instead of retiring to Florida, they had to move in with their oldest daughter and her husband. They wrote a letter to their congressman, complaining that the national chain had forced them out of business by selling pizzas at below cost, hoping to profit with higher prices later. Their congressman, although influential, was informed by the Federal Trade Commission that it had investigated the practices of the chain for over a year and had found no evidence that the chain was trying to monopolize the pizza market. It was, simply, a very well-run business. Alma, Joe, and their daughter and son-in-law were never convinced by this explanation.

*In chapter 8, we dealt with monopolies, which strictly speaking means there is only one seller in an industry. Besides the public utilities industries (electricity, natural gas, and some local telephone services), few markets are served by one seller. Given the potential profitability of attaining a monopoly position, the quest for monopoly power ought to be one of the most important activities of business firms in a market economy. Some industries contain relatively few firms. Do these firms possess monopoly power? Are there circumstances in which firms in an industry that is not strictly monopolistic can raise prices above competitive levels by restricting sales? If so, how do they do it? In this chapter, we analyze the behavior and market performance of **oligopolies**, which are industries with few sellers. An oligopolistic industry may also have a number of small firms as well as a few large firms that account for most of its sales. The brewing industry in the United States is probably a good example. A few major firms sell most of the beer in the United States, but many states have at least one or two small breweries catering to local tastes and markets.*

When a few firms' sales make up a significant share of the industry total, each major firm's output decisions will affect the sales of its major competitors. Such firms are therefore likely to consider the reactions of their rivals to any change in the prices they charge and the output they sell. This means that oligopolies are characterized by **mutual interdependence of price and output decisions** *and that oligopolistic firms are not, in general, price takers. On the other hand, the rivalry among firms for sales and profits limits the power of any one firm to charge the monopoly price. As you might suspect, the analysis of the price and output strategies of oligopolistic industries is not as clear-cut as that for competitive and monopolistic industries. The price charged and output produced in an oligopolistic industry can fall anywhere between the competitive and monopolistic extremes, depending on circumstances. In the following sections, we investigate what some of these circumstances are and how they affect oligopolistic market outcomes.*

▶ Price and Output in an Oligopolistic Industry

Oligopoly, Concentration, and Collusion

Table 9.1 contains a list of some United States manufacturing industries in which a relatively small number of firms account for most of industry output. Many economists measure this concentration of production with a **concentration ratio,** which in table 9.1 is the percentage of industry shipments (roughly equivalent to industry sales) accounted for by (a) the four largest firms in the industry and (b) the eight largest firms.

Table 9.1   **United States manufacturing industries with relatively few firms**

Industry	Concentration ratio*	
	(a)	**(b)**
Motor vehicles	93	99
Blast furnaces and steel mills	45	65
Motor vehicle parts and accessories	62	70
Aircraft	59	81
Petroleum refining	30	53
Photographic equipment and supplies	72	86
Electronic computing equipment	44	55
Construction machinery	47	55
Tires and inner tubes	70	88
Guided missiles and space vehicles	64	94
Toilet preparations	40	56
Organic fibers, noncellulosic	78	90
Soaps and detergents	59	71

Source: From *Statistical Abstract of the United States, 1981,* Table 1427, p. 793. Department of Commerce—Bureau of the Census.

*Percentage of total domestic industry shipments accounted for by (a) four largest and (b) eight largest United States firms in 1977.

*A **shared monopoly** is an industry in which a group of firms establish the monopoly price and share the monopoly rents.*

Collusion is cooperation by the firms in an industry in order to create or exert monopoly power.

*A **cartel** is a group of firms that collude.*

Concentration is a very crude measure of monopoly power. One reason is that concentration ratios ignore the *extent* of markets. Although *nationwide* concentration ratios may be low in some industries, individual firms may be the principal or only supplier in a *local market* (beer and oil distributors in a small community, for example). Can a firm such as this exploit monopoly power? In contrast, other industries, such as automobiles, that are dominated by only two or three firms nationally, face foreign competition that severely limits the monopoly power of United States producers.

Economists generally agree that when a few companies produce a large share of a market's sales, they can potentially act as a **shared monopoly,** which means that they set the monopolistic price and divide the monopolistic profit among themselves. The means used to establish a shared monopoly is called **collusion,** which means cooperating formally (through a written agreement or contract) or informally to restrict sales, raise prices, and share sales and profit. However, very powerful forces may limit the exploitation of monopoly market power in oligopolistic industries. Collusion to exploit monopoly power is illegal in the United States under terms of the *Sherman Antitrust Act of 1890,* which is discussed in detail in chapter 11. However, as noted in chapter 8, there are exceptions to the Sherman Act. For example, the *Clayton Antitrust Act of 1914* removed labor unions from the threat of prosecution for violating the Sherman Act. As also noted in chapter 8, the *Capper–Volstead Act of 1922* exempts agricultural co-ops from the Sherman Act and permits collusion among farmers to set prices for their products.

If members of an oligopoly in the United States wish to collude, which is to act as a **cartel,** they will have to find a way to circumvent the laws against collusion if they are not in a protected industry. One way to do this is to maintain as much secrecy as possible and hope they are not caught. Illegal collusion does take place, and the antitrust division of the United States Department of Justice occasionally prosecutes

firms and their executives—and wins convictions—when secret collusion is discovered. In 1979, for example, Brink's Incorporated and Wells Fargo Armored Service Corporation pleaded no contest to charges that they conspired to fix prices and divide the market for armored car services between them. They paid fines of $625,000 and $375,000, respectively. In the late 1960s, Westinghouse was convicted, along with other manufacturers of electrical equipment, of fixing the prices of its products. Not only were there substantial fines, but several senior executives received prison terms. Most states also have anticollusion legislation, and antitrust prosecutions sometimes occur at the state level, too. In 1977, three major grocery chains in the Cleveland area (Fisher Foods, Stop-N-Shop, and Pick-N-Pay) were convicted of collusion to fix prices. They were fined $2 million and required to refund $20 million to their customers, and their executives received suspended prison sentences.[1]

Collusion need not be formal, however. One possible practice is **price leadership,** which means that one firm (the leader) sets the price and others follow suit without any formal communication taking place. Informal collusion may allow firms to escape prosecution for explicit agreement to restrain trade. Probably the most widely recognized case of price leadership in the United States economy involved the cigarette industry between 1923 and 1941. During this period, the American Tobacco Company (Lucky Strike) and Liggett and Myers (Chesterfield), led by R. J. Reynolds (Camel) changed their prices in a virtual lockstep relationship. Moreover, these "big three" tobacco firms earned a return on capital that was approximately twice the average of United States manufacturing firms.[2]

Under a system of perfect collusion (formal or informal), a cartel would charge the monopolistic price as shown in figure 8.1, page 170, with each firm limiting its output to some mutually acceptable share of total industry sales. Each firm would share in the cartel's monopolistic profits.

Price leadership is a form of collusion, usually informal, in which one firm assumes the responsibility for setting the industry price; other firms follow.

Enforcement of a market-sharing agreement is crucial if an oligopoly wishes to act as a monopoly would. While each member of a cartel may agree in principle to restrict output so that all may gain from selling at the monopoly price, another force works to encourage cheating. Each firm can increase its own profit by selling more at the monopoly price. When the number of firms in an industry is small, enforcement of formal or informal collusion is an easier and more profitable task than when a large number of firms must communicate, and agree, with others. When the number of firms is small, deviation of a single firm from an agreement to limit output will have a large proportionate impact on industry output and price and be relatively easy to detect. If there are only two or three firms, it is easier to discover if one of them is selling more than its share. The other firms may be able to keep the cheater in line by threatening to break the agreement, letting price fall to its competitive level. When the number of firms is large, however, cheating by a single firm has a small effect on total production and market price, while the costs of monitoring each firm's output are relatively large. Thus enforcement of market-sharing arrangements is likely to grow less effective as the number of firms increases. If each firm cheats, then all will suffer as output grows and prices fall toward the competitive level.

What number of firms is small enough to produce a cartel that can effectively monopolize an industry? There is no simple answer to this question. Although agreement and enforcement of cartel rules are more difficult when the number of firms is large, many other factors influence the likelihood that a cartel will operate as a monopoly would. For example, government antitrust efforts are most frequently aimed at industries where concentration is high, raising the potential *costs* (penalties) of collusion. Even without government antitrust efforts, there is no assurance that even two firms in an industry will develop a successful cartel. Each firm may feel that it has so much to gain by increasing sales that effective competition prevails. Factors that militate against effective collusion (other than vigorous antitrust activities on the part of government) include differences among firms in their production costs and most profitable scale of output. Changes in market conditions, which require adjustments of price and quantities, also make effective collusion more difficult.

To summarize, as in other economic situations, *costs* and *benefits* determine the likelihood of effective collusion in an oligopoly. Factors that increase the benefits of collusion are (1) a relatively inelastic demand for the industry's product and (2) effective barriers to entry so that profits are not reduced by entry of new firms. Conditions that raise the costs of collusion are all associated with how easy it is to enforce a cartel agreement and to detect cheating. The following factors are among those that raise such costs: (1) effective enforcement of antitrust laws, (2) a large number of firms in the industry (low concentration ratio), (3) a large number of customers in the industry, (4) differences among firms in their costs and optimal output, and (5) changes in industry demand and cost conditions. Many of the conditions that determine the potential success of a cartel in monopolizing an industry and the difficulties of maintaining monopoly power when conflicting interests among cartel members arise are illustrated in the recent history of the Organization of Petroleum Exporting Countries (OPEC).

OPEC: The Rise (and Decline?) of a Cartel

In 1973, the Arab oil-producing countries withheld petroleum shipments to the United States and its allies in retaliation for their support of Israel in its war with Egypt. When the embargo was lifted, OPEC, led by Saudi Arabia, was able to raise petroleum prices to levels that were unimaginably high by previous standards. At first oil prices doubled, then tripled, and continued upward, so that by 1981, OPEC oil was priced *twenty times higher* than in 1971.[3]

Although the tremendous acceleration in oil prices followed the war between Israel and Egypt, the reasons why OPEC was able to sustain the increase are more fundamentally economic in nature. If higher oil

Table 9.2   Crude oil imports into the United States by country of origin

	1970	1972	1973	1978	1979	1980	1981	1982	1983	1984
Total imports (Millions of barrels)	483	811	1,184	2,320	2,380	1,911	1,605	1,417	1,283	1,317
Imports as a percent of total use	12.0	18.9	26.0	42.2	37.7	37.0	34.0	28.0	28.0	30.0
Country of origin	Percentage of United States imports coming from each country									
OPEC countries	**46.0**	**58.6**	**64.7**	**81.5**	**78.4**	**73.4**	**66.5**	**49.7**	**44.4**	**44.1**
Saudi Arabia	3.1	7.9	14.2	17.9	20.6	23.9	25.3	15.2	9.6	9.0
Nigeria	3.5	11.0	13.9	14.3	16.4	15.9	13.9	14.6	9.0	6.0
Venezuela	20.2	11.5	10.6	2.8	4.5	2.9	3.3	4.4	4.9	7.4
Non-OPEC countries	**54.0**	**41.4**	**35.3**	**18.5**	**21.6**	**24.6**	**33.5**	**42.8**	**46.7**	**46.0**
Canada	50.7	38.4	30.8	3.9	4.2	3.8	3.7	6.1	8.2	9.9
Mexico	0.0	0.0	0.0	5.0	6.7	9.6	10.7	18.5	23.0	19.2
United Kingdom	0.0	0.0	0.0	2.7	3.0	3.3	8.4	12.7	11.0	11.0

Source: From *Statistical Abstract of the United States, 1981*, Table 1005, p. 584 and Table 1316, p. 733; 1982/83, Table 986, p. 578 and Table 1290, p. 724. Department of Commerce—Bureau of the Census: and 1986, Table 1247, p. 701, Table 1245, p. 700, Table 972, p. 564.

prices benefited the oil-exporting countries, why had prices not been raised earlier? Part of the answer can be seen in table 9.2. Prior to 1970, United States dependence on oil imports was increasing, but it was not very high. This situation was not to last. The ratio of imported oil to total use grew by half between 1970 and 1972, and in 1973 it was more than twice as high as in 1972. In 1973, imported crude oil amounted to over one-fourth of the quantity used in the United States. By 1978, the ratio had grown to more than 42 percent. The sources of these imports were highly concentrated, with four countries accounting for over two-thirds of all imports.

Given the uneven world distribution of petroleum reserves, when OPEC began to raise its prices, the United States had little short-run flexibility for securing cheaper domestic and non-OPEC foreign oil. Canada, its principal non-OPEC supplier, worried about exhausting its own reserves and becoming dependent on imports itself. Therefore, Canada decided to sharply reduce its exports to the United States after

1973. Other non-OPEC countries were such small producers that they could easily profit by charging whatever price OPEC set. If they had wanted to undercut OPEC's prices, they would not have been able to meet the world demand for their oil. OPEC, in turn, relied on Saudi Arabia to take primary responsibility for maintaining prices by limiting its output. Saudi Arabia's share of world oil reserves outside the Soviet Union is so large that it alone can send world oil prices plummeting by a relatively small proportionate increase in its willingness to export. Saudi Arabia's power was enhanced by Iran's political problems of the late 1970s, which resulted in a severe decline in its oil production and exports. Last, but very important, in the list of factors enhancing OPEC's ability to restrict world oil output was the existence of maximum price legislation covering oil produced in the United States. We showed in chapter 4 how maximum prices reduced the United States' ability to replace OPEC oil with domestically produced oil when prices rose.

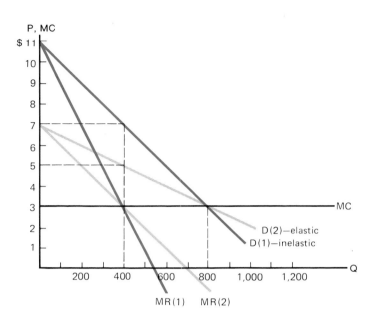

Figure 9.1 Relatively elastic demand, relatively inelastic demand, marginal revenue, and monopoly price
Demand curve D(1) is less elastic than D(2). In a competitive industry, both demands would lead to an equilibrium price of $3 and output of 800. In a monopoly, the equilibrium price would equal $7 with demand curve D(1) but only $5 with demand curve D(2).

Collusion among world oil producers outside the United States is not restricted by any enforceable laws. Therefore, there is no effective legal barrier to collusion among OPEC countries. Moreover, the ownership of oil fields by private individuals or firms outside the United States is the exception rather than the rule. This substantially reduces the number of parties that must communicate and cooperate with one another to maintain the cartel. The representatives of only a handful of governments need meet periodically in order to discuss their price and production strategies. In addition, Saudi Arabia's dominant position in the non-Soviet world oil market, which led to its role as the de facto leader of OPEC, gives it considerable power to enforce OPEC's output decisions if it chooses to do so. Entry of competing oil suppliers is limited by the existence of known petroleum reserves.

The monopoly price that OPEC could charge was much higher than the competitive price of oil for two reasons: (1) There were few good substitutes for OPEC oil, and (2) oil itself is a product for which users cannot quickly find good substitutes when its price rises. This means that the *elasticity of demand* for oil

is low, and the monopoly price will be much higher than the competitive price. The reason why a low elasticity of demand leads to a relatively high monopoly price is simple enough. When buyers have few alternatives, a monopoly will lose fewer sales by raising its price a given amount, and it will maximize its profit by taking advantage of the situation. Figure 9.1 demonstrates this. In this figure, demand curve D(2) is more elastic than D(1) but would result in the same equilibrium price as D(1) if this were a *competitive* industry. Under monopolistic conditions, however, the seller would charge customers $7 ($4 above the competitive price) if D(1) were the demand curve but only $5 ($2 above the competitive price) if D(2) were the industry demand curve.

The best available estimates of the elasticity of demand for gasoline, one of the principal products of crude oil, is about -0.1 over the short term.[4] That is, a doubling (100 percent increase) of the price of gasoline results in only a 10 percent decline in consumption in, say, the first year after the price increase. This is fairly small when compared to most demand elasticities for which we have estimates—you may wish to review table 3.2, pages 68–69, to refresh your memory. The elasticity of demand for petroleum and its products is considerably larger, however, after users have had a chance to adapt by buying smaller cars, insulating their houses and buildings, switching to alternative fuels, and so on.[5] This has proved to be an extremely important factor adversely affecting OPEC's ability to maintain its high monopoly price over the long term, as we shall see.

If OPEC were to maintain its prices and effective output restrictions at the levels reached in, say, 1980, the factors that contributed to its success over the preceding seven years would have had to continue to support its monopoly power. This was not to be, however. There are two sets of reasons why OPEC has found it more difficult to maintain its effective monopoly power over the long run. One set of reasons is systematically related to the effects of monopoly on price—forces are set in motion to produce and use substitutes for any product whose price rises relative to other prices. This applies to any cartel and to any product, not just OPEC. The other set of reasons consists of unrelated events. It was fortuitous for OPEC that price controls existed in the United States when the 1973 oil embargo began. It was historical chance that led to the downfall of the Shah of Iran in the late 1970s. However, the United States price controls were eventually removed; Iran's oil production recovered, and Iran's need for revenue to finance imports and its war with Iraq dictated selling as much oil as possible.

The long-term effects of OPEC's initial success in raising world oil prices have been dramatic. Remember that demand and supply elasticities increase as consumers' and producers' time horizons become longer. As it became clear that OPEC's price increases were not going to disappear quickly, incentives to conserve energy and to explore for new sources of supply became very strong. We began to use oil and other energy resources much more sparingly than we did in the early 1970s. Moreover, there was a tremendous increase in exploration for new sources of oil around the world and exploitation of known reserves that were previously too costly to operate profitably.

As a result, the United States has tapped oil reservoirs in the frozen Arctic and under the oceans off its shores. Mexico has discovered oil reserves that may eventually prove larger than Saudi Arabia's. Coal, gas, nuclear power, and solar power have been substituted for petroleum.

In short, OPEC's initial success in raising world oil prices also initiated forces that eventually undermined the cartel. A weakening OPEC was further damaged by the world wide recession in 1981–82 and the resulting drop in industrial demand for oil. Even as the world economy recovered from the recession, however, OPEC was unable to recover its former strength. Figure 9.2 shows that between the peak of OPEC power in 1980 and early 1986, world oil prices have declined approximately *60 percent* relative to the prices of most other goods, and the incomes of oil-exporting nations have suffered. Adding to OPEC's difficulties, the world's major oil-exporting nations have learned to depend on oil revenues to support massive government expenditures on various social and economic development projects. Thus, as domestic political pressure to expand these social expenditures heats up and as world oil prices have softened, enforcement of output restrictions among OPEC and non-OPEC exporters has become increasingly difficult. As a result of all of these forces, OPEC oil prices declined dramatically to less than $15 per barrel in early 1986.

Couldn't OPEC have anticipated the long-term effects of very large price increases and modified its behavior accordingly? One reason it did not do so may be that there is a wide dispersion of time horizons among OPEC members. Those with relatively small reserves of petroleum may have decided it was best to charge all the market would bear in the short term. Those with larger reserves would have taken a long-term view. This hypothesis is consistent with the observed behavior of Saudi Arabia. Between 1974 and 1981, Saudi Arabia seems to have been less inclined than other OPEC countries to go for the largest price increases. It apparently correctly anticipated the long-term effects on its market of maximizing profits over

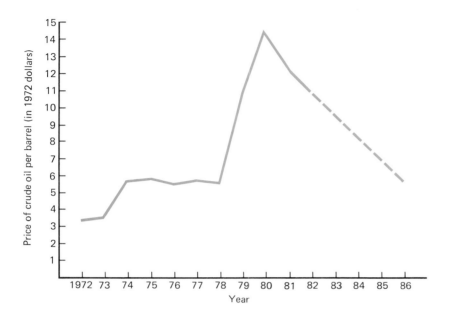

Figure 9.2   The world price of crude oil in dollars per barrel, expressed in terms of the purchasing power of the dollar in 1972
From *Statistical Abstract of the United States*, 1985, p. 479 (price of crude oil) and 475 (Consumer Price Index). The 1986 figure in the graph was estimated by the authors on the basis of newspaper reports.

the short term and tried to moderate the behavior of the other members of OPEC in the interests of long-term gains. Evidently, Saudi Arabia was unable or unwilling to compensate those countries with short time horizons in return for moderating their demands for higher oil prices. Presumably, Saudi Arabia could have persuaded these countries to go along with its long-term interests by providing financial aid to their governments or some other payment. Its failure to do so underlines the fact that cartel agreements, like labor-management agreements, are partly political decisions. Thus, outcomes may depend on political considerations within the participating organizations that conflict with long-term profitability. When there appeared to be no consensus on limiting output in February 1986, Saudi Arabia indicated that it would not go it alone by limiting its output to prop up other members' prices and profits. Briefly, in March of 1986, the market price of oil fell to just over $10 per barrel. Later in the year, cartel members agreed to cooperate with one another and oil prices rebounded somewhat.

Oligopolistic Pricing without Formal Collusion: The Problem of Interdependence

Our discussion of OPEC illustrates the benefits to a cartel of formal collusion and the difficulties of maintaining effective monopoly power even when formal collusion is not prohibited by law. Where collusion to restrict output formally is illegal, firms have an incentive to engage in informal means of gaining monopoly profits. We have already noted that price leadership may enable the dominant firm in an industry to set a price that, when adopted by the other firms, will lead to economic profits for the industry. Evidently, in the case of the United States cigarette industry, price leadership during the 1920s and 1930s allowed the big three tobacco companies to set higher than competitive prices without attracting entry of new firms to compete for their substantial monopoly profits. The process by which one firm might become the price leader and the circumstances under which its leadership would result in an effective cartel are not always clear, however.

An Example of Price Leadership with a Dominant Firm: The United States Steel Corporation

We mentioned in chapter 8 that one of the surest ways to gain monopoly control of an industry is to own most or all of a resource essential to that industry. We noted that an outstanding example of this type of monopoly power was exhibited by the United States Steel Corporation during the first twenty years of this century.[6] Through a series of mergers between 1898 and 1901, the Federal Steel Corporation and the Carnegie Steel Company joined other firms to become the United States Steel Corporation. The new corporation owned or controlled three-fourths of the high-grade iron ore deposits in the United States and also possessed superior technological capabilities in various steel production processes. Competing steel companies in the United States suffered a cost disadvantage because of United States Steel's technological and resource advantages.

Despite its advantages, United States Steel never completely dominated the market for pig iron or steel. However, between 1902 and 1910, the famous "Gary dinners," hosted by United States Steel board chairman Judge Elbert Gary, probably served as a meeting place for the executives of colluding steel firms to negotiate over market shares and pricing strategy. In 1910, Congress began investigating United States Steel's behavior, and a case was filed against the corporation alleging violations of antitrust provisions of the Sherman Antitrust Act in the United States district court in New Jersey. United States Steel knew it was under the gun, and the Gary dinners ceased. (In 1920, the Supreme Court in a very convoluted argument found that there was no evidence of overt collusion to fix prices or share the steel market between United States Steel and its competitors.)

However, all was not lost for the erstwhile monopoly. Instead, United States Steel took advantage of its dominant position by becoming an informal price leader. Because its costs were lower than those of other steel firms, it was able to set prices well above competitive levels without losing all of its business to its rivals. The competing steel firms were able to stay in business mainly because "big steel" established a substantial margin between its costs and the prices it charged.

In this type of "dominant firm" price leadership situation, the dominant firm sets a price that maximizes its monopoly profit, knowing that a fringe of more-or-less competitive rivals will take advantage of the higher price to increase their production. The competitive fringe does reduce the dominant firm's market share but does not eliminate it so long as the dominant firm retains a cost advantage. That United States Steel was able to retain such an advantage is reflected in the price of its common stock. Between 1900 and 1913, the price of United States Steel Corporation common stock rose by 169 percent, while the average stock price of the United States steel industry common stock, excluding United States Steel, rose by only 40 percent.

There is a striking parallel between the United States steel industry in the early part of this century and OPEC during the 1970s. Despite the lack of overt collusion in the steel industry, United States Steel played a role parallel to that of Saudi Arabia—dominating the industry with superior production capabilities. The other side of the coin is the parallel development of forces undermining the dominant firm's monopoly power. Exploration for iron ore sources around the world led to discoveries that reduced United States Steel's control over the domestic market. Technological knowledge became more widespread as other firms learned to adopt advanced equipment and manufacturing processes. As a result, United States Steel experienced a steady decline in its share of the market for steel products. Its nearly two-thirds market share in 1902 had fallen to just half of the market by 1914 and to less than 40 percent by 1929. At the same time, its arch rival, Bethlehem Steel, with less than 1 percent of the market in 1905, saw its share grow to over 13 percent over the same period. It takes only casual reading of today's newspapers to reveal that any dominance of the United States market for steel by the United States Steel Corporation or any of its domestic rivals has long since vanished. With the development of electric arc furnaces that can use scrap iron instead of iron ore, control of ore deposits has become much less important.

*The **game theoretic approach** to price setting in oligopoly analyzes firm behavior in terms of achieving the best outcome in a game played against the other firms in the industry.*

Firm 1's price policies

	Increase	No change	Decrease
Increase	1's profit and 2's profit both increase by $500,000	1's profit +$350,000 2's profit −$100,000	1's profit +$100,000 2's profit −$1,000,000
No change	1's profit −$100,000 2's profit +$350,000	No change in profit	1's profit +$200,000 2's profit −$400,000
Decrease	1's profit −$1,000,000 2's profit +$100,000	1's profit −$400,000 2's profit +$200,000	1's profit and 2's profit both fall by $80,000

Firm 2's price policies

Figure 9.3   The effect of alternative pricing policies on the profits of firm 1 and firm 2
Firms 1 and 2 are trying to adopt a pricing policy that will lead to the largest profit, but they are uncertain as to what their rival's pricing policy will be. If both firms adopt a *minimax* strategy, they will choose the pricing policy that leads to the least disastrous outcome. This would mean reducing their prices toward the competitive level as indicated by the $80,000 profit decline shown in the lower right-hand cell of the diagram.

However, if firms can signal among themselves by setting prices temporarily at some particular level, then the advantages of a minimax strategy are not as great because the disastrous losses for a firm that raises its price while its competitor lowers price can be quickly averted. If one firm raises its price and by so doing can signal its rival to raise price, they will be able to share a monopolistic profit, earning $500,000 more profit each, as indicated by the upper left-hand cell of the diagram.

Furthermore, the development of continuous-casting production techniques to reduce energy casts of steel production gave both Japan and West Germany clear cost advantages over the United States by the late 1970s.

Other Pricing Strategies
Economists have developed additional hypotheses about firms' behavior when formal collusion is ruled out, but they have not been generally accepted as providing useful descriptions of price and output decisions in oligopolies.

The Game Theoretic Approach   One of the more promising attacks on the price and output problem in oligopoly has been the **game theoretic approach,** which treats the oligopolist's pricing problem as one of strategic behavior against an opponent under conditions of uncertainty. The game theoretic approach is based on ideas from the "theory of games," a pathbreaking analysis of how the behavior of players in such games as chess can be applied to economic problems.[7]

A simple illustration of the game theoretic approach to an oligopolist's price decision is shown in figure 9.3. Figure 9.3 is what is called a *payoff matrix* from the point of view of. two identical firms in an oligopoly. (An oligopoly with only two firms is called a *duopoly*.) Even though only two firms are depicted in figure 9.3, their problem in choosing a profit-maximizing price characterizes any number of firms whose profit-maximizing price decisions depend on what their rivals do. You might think of firm 1 as a single firm and firm 2 as representing the actions of a set of rivals to firm 1 within the oligopoly. We will assume that firms 1 and 2 produce an identical good and have identical costs. They are currently charging a price that lies between the monopolistic price that would maximize the sum of their profits and the competitive price that would assure them of revenue barely sufficient to cover all of their opportunity costs. We also assume that each firm's cost curves are such that either firm could produce enough output to satisfy the entire industry's demand and earn a profit. Each firm

*The **minimax strategy** is one rule that a firm may follow in pursuing a game theoretic approach to setting its price; it means choosing a price that minimizes the probability of a very bad outcome in terms of profit.*

is faced with the following choices: (1) raise its price toward the monopolistic price, hoping that its rival will follow and thus increase their joint profits; (2) do nothing, hoping that its rival will raise its price, leading to more business and profits for itself and less for its rival; (3) lower its price in an effort to gain a larger share of the industry's sales and increase its profits by doing so.

Each box, or cell, in figure 9.3 shows what happens to both firms' profits under alternative pricing policies. In the upper left-hand cell, for example, we see that if both firms raise their price toward the monopolistic level, their profits will *both* increase by $500,000. Going down one cell, we see that if firm 1 does raise its price but firm 2 does not, then firm 1 will lose many of its customers, and its profits will fall by $100,000, while firm 2 will increase its profits by $350,000. The lower left-hand cell shows that if firm 1 increases its price while firm 2 lowers its price, firm 1 will experience a disastrous profit decline of $1 million, while firm 2's profit will increase by $100,000. The three boxes in the second column show what happens to firm 1 and firm 2's profits when firm 2 increases, does not change, and lowers its price while firm 1 adopts a no-change policy. The boxes in the third column show what happens to both firms' profits under the three different policies for firm 2 if firm 1 lowers its price.

What to do? Each firm would like to obtain its share of the monopoly profit that comes from both firms raising their prices, but they would both like to avoid the disaster that would occur to the firm that raises its price while the other firm lowers price. A safe strategy for both firms to follow, even though it will not lead to the highest possible profit, is to adopt a price policy that minimizes the risk of a truly disastrous outcome. From firm 1's point of view, a price increase could conceivably lead to a $1 million decline in its profit—the worst possible outcome. Leaving price unchanged would still leave it open to a possible profit decline of $400,000, while lowering price would limit a possible profit decline to only $80,000. Similarly, the *best of the bad* possible results is obtained

by firm 2 if it lowers price. You can verify this by going across each row of cells from left to right and observing what happens to firm 2's profits.

In the theory of games approach to oligopoly behavior, it is often argued that firms will follow a **minimax strategy,** which means choosing the action that will lead to the least harmful bad outcome—the best of the bad. That would mean that both firms 1 and 2 would lower their prices in the situation described by figure 9.3. Price would move toward the competitive level, and both firms would experience a decline in profit of $80,000.

At first glance, the game theoretic approach with the minimax strategy might appear to solve the indeterminacy of the oligopolistic pricing problem and sidestep the difficulty of mutual dependence of pricing and output decisions. Unfortunately, the minimax strategy is based on the assumption that once a firm chooses a price, there is no turning back. Suppose, however, that if firm 2 decides to raise its price, but firm 1 does not, then firm 2 can quickly rescind its decision and lower its price to a more competitive level. If such a quick response is possible, then the cost of a mistaken guess as to its rival's behavior will not be very large. Under these circumstances, it would be reasonable for each firm in an oligopoly to raise its price initially, aiming to maximize its share of the industry's monopoly profits. Economists have developed repeated game models that do allow firms to respond to each other's actions over time. Depending upon what one assumes firms know about political payoffs, the possibility of collusion, and so forth, many outcomes other than the competitive solution are possible. Therefore, the game theoretic approach does not seem to take us much beyond the point of knowing that in oligopoly, the range of possible price outcomes lies somewhere between the monopolistic price and the competitive price.[8] It is to be hoped that the efforts of economists working in this fascinating area will provide us with a clearer understanding of the conditions under which market equilibrium conditions will approximate the competitive solution or diverge from it substantially.

*The **kinked demand curve hypothesis** is a description of oligopoly behavior that says that if a firm raises its price, it will lose a large amount of sales but that if it lowers its price, it will gain very few sales.*

The Kinked Demand Curve Hypothesis   Another approach to the oligopoly pricing problem is designed to explain a supposed fact—that prices charged in oligopolistic industries are "rigid," that is, that they do not change in response to shifting demand or cost conditions as one might expect in a competitive industry. This observation led to the development of the **kinked demand curve hypothesis,** as illustrated in figure 9.4. In this approach, each firm is assumed to believe that if it raises its price above P(1), each of its rivals will keep its price unchanged in hope of gaining customers. However, if it lowers its price below P(1), all of the other firms in the industry will also lower their prices in order to avoid losing sales. Consequently, each firm believes that if it raises its price, its demand curve will be very elastic because few if any industry customers will buy its output at a price above that charged by its competitors. On the other hand, each firm believes that if it lowers its price, its demand curve will be much less elastic—essentially its share of the industry demand curve—because it will not attract any additional sales at other firms' expense.

It is true as a proposition of mathematics that if a curve like the demand curve in figure 9.4 has a kink in it, the corresponding marginal curve has a break in it, jumping from one position to another. This is indicated by the dashed vertical line in figure 9.4. A moment's thought will show why the MR curve jumps as it does. If all of the rivals of a firm kept their prices the same when the oligopolist in figure 9.4 raised price above P(1), then the firm's demand curve would be *elastic* (elasticity of demand would be considerably greater than 1.0 in absolute value), and MR would be positive to the left of the "kink." If all of the firm's rivals matched any reduction in price below P(1), then the oligopolist's demand curve would be much *less* elastic to the right of the kink. When the demand curve becomes less elastic, MR becomes much less. Remember that if the elasticity of demand is *less than 1,* then marginal revenue is *negative.* Thus, to the right of the kink, MR might well fall below the horizontal axis. Because MR depends on demand elasticity and because elasticity changes abruptly at the kink in the demand curve, the MR curve has to "jump" to get from left of the kink in the demand curve to right of the kink.

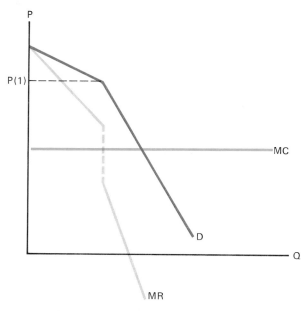

Figure 9.4   The kinked oligopoly demand curve hypothesis
The kinked demand curve hypothesis describes a situation in which if one oligopolist raises price, its rivals will not raise theirs, but if one lowers its price, all the others will follow. Therefore, from the point of view of each firm in an oligopoly, the demand curve has a kink at the current market price. This results in a discontinuity of the marginal revenue curve (the vertical dashed line) so that if the demand curve shifts up or down within a certain range, a profit-maximizing firm will not adjust its price. Similarly, if cost conditions should change, firms will not necessarily change their prices.

Because of the break in the marginal revenue curve, if costs should change, the MR and MC curves will not necessarily cross at a different quantity, and the firm will not change its price. Similarly, only a "large" change in demand will result in an increase or decrease in the price charged. To be sure you understand why a kinked demand curve would lead to no price change unless there were a large increase in demand, take a piece of paper and copy figure 9.4. Now shift the MC curve up or down slightly, along the MR curve. What happens to the quantity at which MC and MR intersect? What happens to the price charged?

There are two problems with the kinked demand curve hypothesis. One problem is that it provides no information on what determines the price at which the kink occurs. How do oligopolists get where they are in the first place? The other problem with the kinked demand curve as a general description of oligopolistic behavior is that there have been serious challenges to the validity of the idea that prices in oligopolistic industries do not change as frequently as in those with lower concentration ratios. In a study that has yet to be refuted, George J. Stigler and James K. Kindahl have shown that when actual transaction prices (as opposed to published list prices) are examined, there is considerable variability in the prices charged for goods produced in industries with relatively high concentration ratios.[9]

▶ An Economic Evaluation of Oligopoly

We have seen that the price and output results of oligopoly cannot be predicted unambiguously, as in the cases of monopoly and competition, because firms' decisions are based on conjectures of what their rivals' responses may be. However, the price and quantity outcomes of "pure" competition and monopoly establish bounds for the likely outcome in oligopoly. As with monopoly, in comparing the prices charged for the products of oligopolistic industries with the competitive standard, we must consider whether the *ceteris paribus* assumption holds. In particular, production costs in oligopoly may not be the same as they would be if the industry consisted of a larger number of smaller firms. For example, if larger firm size is associated with mass production economies, then a certain degree of monopoly power may not result in a higher price and smaller quantities for consumers. On the other hand, if oligopolies are protected from the competition of new entrants by a barrier to entry, then they may not be forced to minimize their costs, and consumers will be worse off than with a more competitive industry structure.

▶ Summary and Conclusions

Many major industries in the United States are oligopolies in the sense that they have fairly high concentration ratios. Here are some of the important points that you should remember about oligopolies.

A barrier to entry is necessary if oligopolists are to receive economic profits or rents in the long run.

Mutual interdependence of pricing and output decisions is characteristic of oligopolies.

In order to obtain monopoly profits or rents, some form of collusion among the firms in an oligopolistic industry is necessary.

Firms in an oligopoly frequently have an incentive to cheat on a formal or informal cartel agreement to achieve a larger share of industry sales and profits.

Conditions that work in favor of an effective cartel are those that increase the benefits of achieving monopoly control over output, including an inelastic demand for the product, an effective barrier to entry, and a relatively small number of firms (high concentration ratio).

Conditions that work against forming or maintaining an effective collusive agreement are those that raise the costs of collusion, including vigorous antitrust enforcement, a low concentration ratio, significant differences in each firm's profit-maximizing output and price (because of cost differences), changes in cost and technology conditions in the industry, and a larger number of customers (which makes it more difficult to observe cheating).

Price and output in an oligopolistic industry may match the market outcomes of a competitive industry, a monopolistic industry, or fall somewhere in between the competitive and monopolistic extremes.

▶ Key Terms

cartel *192*

collusion *192*

concentration ratio *191*

game theoretic
  approach *199*

kinked demand curve
  hypothesis *201*

minimax strategy *200*

mutual interdependence
  of price and output
  decisions *191*

oligopoly *190*

price leadership *193*

shared monopoly *192*

▶ Questions for Discussion and Review

1. In discussing OPEC's effect on world oil prices, we noted that the elasticity of demand for oil is very small over the short term. Show that when a monopolist is maximizing profit, the elasticity of demand for its product must be less than -1.0 (in the neighborhood of the monopolistic price). Show why this is true. Was OPEC maximizing its profit before 1972? In 1980? Use the theory of monopoly to explain your answer.

   State whether the statements in questions 2 through 6 are true, false, or uncertain, and defend your answer.

2. The industry concentration ratio is the ratio of a firm's sales to the total sales of the industry.

3. In the kinked demand curve model of oligopoly, an increase in the variable costs of the firm will always change the profit-maximizing level of output for the firm.

4. In the kinked demand curve model, an increase in demand will always lead to an increase in the price charged by the firm.

5. The main problem with a cartel arrangement is each member's incentive to cheat.

6. Under the minimax strategy of game theory, the cost to a firm of incorrectly guessing the rival firm's strategy is negligible.

7. State the assumptions of the oligopolistic model.

8. Explain the concept of mutual interdependence.

9. Some oligopolistic firms charge a price below the profit-maximizing price level. What economic strategy are these firms implementing?

10. Is the excess capacity of existing firms in an industry an effective deterrent to entry by new firms? Explain.

Chapter 10

Monopolistic Competition, Product Differentiation, and Advertising

Outline

I. Introduction *206*
II. What is monopolistic competition? *207*
III. Short-run monopolistic competition *207*
    A. A closer look at a monopolistically competitive firm: A local clothing store *208*
        1. Price and output in the short run *209*
IV. Long-run monopolistic competition *210*
    A. Production efficiency and product variety *211*
V. Price differences within markets *212*
    A. Differences in costs *212*
        1. Aside: Price differences in monopoly, competition, and monopolistic competition *213*
    B. Consumer cooperatives *213*
VI. Advertising, information, and product differentiation *214*
    A. Informative advertising and product prices *214*
    B. Tastes, preferences, and product differentiation *217*
    C. Advertising, product differentiation, and monopoly power *219*
    D. Advertising and consumer protection *219*
    E. Advertising, profits, and prices: Some evidence *220*
VII. Summary and conclusions *221*
VIII. Key terms *221*
IX. Questions for discussion and review *221*

Objectives

After reading this chapter, the student should be able to:

Describe an industry with monopolistic competition.

Compare and contrast outcomes in a market with monopolistic competition to markets with competitive firms or a monopoly producer.

Explain price differences for the same good or service in a particular geographic area.

Analyze the way in which advertising affects prices and economic profit.

Identify the link between monopoly power and product differentiation.

▶ Introduction

In the early 1980s, the Coca-Cola Company took a detailed look at who was buying its diet drink known as Tab. It discovered that Tab was largely drunk by women. In an attempt to capture some of men's desires for svelte bodies, Coca-Cola introduced a new diet drink, Diet Coke, with an advertising campaign aimed at the male consumer.

At roughly the same time, the Coca-Cola Company observed that in blind taste tests more consumers preferred Pepsi-Cola to Coke, primarily because Pepsi-Cola was sweeter. In response to these test results, Coca-Cola introduced a new drink in 1985. At the time it was called New Coke. The Coca-Cola Company intended to replace its traditional formula with New Coke. Instead of success, Coca-Cola received numerous complaints from customers who had been thoroughly satisfied with traditional Coke as their soft drink. As a result, Coca-Cola not only kept its new formula but it also returned its original formula to the market under the name, Coca-Cola Classic.

At about the same time all of this was taking place, the Coca-Cola Company also began to market Cherry Coke. All of these new soft drinks made it difficult for soda fountains to figure out what to put in their limited space. Similarly, there were too many drinks for the typical Coke machine to hold.

Many of you would say that it is difficult to tell the difference between Tab and Diet Coke or to taste a difference between New Coke and Coca-Cola Classic. If this were not bad enough, the Coca-Cola Company eventually came out with caffeine-free Diet Coke and caffeine-free regular Coke. All of these products, while slightly different from one another, have many similarities, not only to themselves but also to the analogous products sold by Pepsi.

The focus of this chapter is on these kinds of products, items with trademarks and brand names that make distinctions but items that are not all that different among producers. These types of products typically involve much advertising to remind the consumer of the subtle differences among them, and one of the focal points of this chapter is the economic role of advertising. Virtually every business college program offers a marketing major. What are these people up to anyway?

Monopolistic competition is a market form in which firms produce differentiated products and therefore are not price takers. However, there are also few or no barriers preventing firms from producing quite similar products in a monopolistically competitive industry.

▶ What Is Monopolistic Competition?

Chapters 7 through 9 emphasize the effects of monopoly and collusive practices on price, production, profit, and economic rent. We have been careful to compare outcomes in a monopolistic setting to those in a market made up of price takers (a competitive industry). We now turn our attention to markets that exhibit some characteristics of both monopoly and competition. The name economists have applied to this form of market structure is **monopolistic competition.** In monopolistic competition each firm is somewhat like a monopoly in that customers view a firm's output as somewhat different from that of other firms and, perhaps, even unique. For example, there is only one *Time* magazine or Bayer aspirin. In a monopolistically competitive industry, however, there are typically no output restrictions or barriers to entry. This is the competitive aspect of this type of industry. So, while there may indeed be only one producer of *Time* magazine or Bayer aspirin, it is possible to produce an alternative brand of aspirin or a *Newsweek* magazine. Of course, even though experts emphasize that "all aspirin is alike," many consumers still prefer the Bayer brand to the generic aspirin sold at the drugstore, even at a higher price.

Other examples of monopolistic competition are laundry detergents and deodorants. Deodorants are differentiated by their scent, package shape, and medium for transferring the deodorant and antiperspirant material to the body. You may be surprised to learn that the Food and Drug Administration has approved only one formula of active ingredients for deodorants. Thus, the *only* way in which deodorants differ in the United States is according to whether they appeal to your male versus female instincts, whether they go on wet or dry, and what kind of container they are held in.

▶ Short-run Monopolistic Competition

Our models of a competitive industry and a monopoly industry represent polar cases. Under competitive market conditions, the individual firm is a sensible but somewhat passive player in the marketplace. In equilibrium, the competitive firm chooses the sales volume that maximizes its profits, with product price viewed as given and outside of its control. There are no sophisticated strategies involved. By knowing overall market conditions, each producer in a competitive market can pretty much ignore what competitors down the street are doing. The main thing one must do in a competitive industry is tend to one's own business and keep an eye out for short-term profit opportunities elsewhere in the economy.

In a monopoly market, a firm needs to consider both price and output effects on profitability. However, again no complex strategies are involved. Just by tending to its own business—in particular, equating marginal revenue with marginal cost—the monopolist can maximize profits. There is no competitor down the street, so to speak, to consider when a monopolist makes output and pricing decisions.

Most businesses are neither as small nor as insignificant relative to the market they serve as the typical competitive price-taking firm. Most businesses are also not as powerful and in as complete control as a monopoly. A noted expert on industrial organization, F. M. Scherer, feels that 5 to 10 percent of gross national product in the United States is produced under conditions approaching pure monopoly and another 5 to 10 percent under conditions approximating competition. The remainder of economic activity in the private sector falls in between monopoly and competition. While oligopoly tends to be the most economically significant market structure in terms of gross national product produced, monopolistic competition characterizes the overwhelming majority of firms in the United States economy.[1]

A Closer Look at a Monopolistically Competitive Firm: A Local Clothing Store

Suppose that we open a small clothing store specializing in the sale of sportswear. The first thing we have to do is to decide what goods to sell and what prices to charge. The so-called brand names we will carry and the mix of products we want to sell will be somewhat similar but far from identical to the mix of clothing sold by other stores in town. The quality of clothes we will carry and the ambiance of our store will also not be identical to other stores. Thus, we cannot simply adopt the same price schedule as other suppliers. The other stores in our town will obviously compete with us for customers and sales, but they will not sell identical products. Our personnel and their ability to serve customer needs will not be identical to those of our nearest competitors. Our parking facilities, dressing rooms, clothing displays, and location will be somewhat different from those of other stores.

Yet we will not be so different from other clothing stores that we can ignore the possibility of losing customers by charging relatively high prices or of gaining customers by charging relatively low prices or improving our customer services. In short, we will not be able to act as a monopolist and ignore the likelihood that new stores, or existing stores, compete with us for sales to the same customers. We have just argued that our clothing store does not seem to fit either the economist's idea of a competitive firm or of a monopolistic firm. Can our clothing store possibly be thought of as part of an oligopolistic industry?

There are two important characteristics of an oligopolistic industry. First, there are a limited number of firms in the market. Second, there are barriers to entering an oligopolistic industry. As a result, every firm in an oligopoly faces actual or potential competition for sales from other firms. Actual or potential competitive threats to sales will certainly be present in the case of our small clothing store. However, recall that in an oligopoly the number of sellers is small and each seller is very much aware of the other firms'

sales and prices. Each seller in an oligopoly anticipates the price, quantity, and quality of output of the other firms and tries to plan an appropriate profit-maximizing strategy. In fact, oligopoly firms will collude if the benefits in terms of profits to be shared are large enough and the cost of forming and operating a cartel is low enough. This means that oligopoly firms may act as a joint monopoly when market conditions permit and legal restraints fail or are absent, as has been the case with OPEC in the past. If our business is located in a small town with only a few retail clothing outlets, then we might behave something like an oligopolistic firm. Our ability to "manipulate" the local clothing market will obviously be restricted by the ability of consumers to travel to other towns to buy clothing directly or to purchase clothing through the mail. There is also the possibility that chain stores and other retail outlets will enter into a fight for our sales. Thus, the more easily consumers can switch to other suppliers or the lower are the barriers to entering the retail clothing business, the less likely it is that we will be able to organize a cartel. It is also less likely that we will be able to develop a retailing strategy in anticipation of any strategies by existing or potential competitors.

Where, then, does our small clothing store fit with respect to the types of industry known as competitive, monopolistic, and oligopolistic? It does not seem to be in a competitive environment. Our products are not identical to those of other stores, and we probably have some price-setting latitude that does not exist under exact competitive conditions. Our store will not have the power of a pure monopoly, however. Other retail stores supply similar goods and services and could take customers away from us if we try to maintain monopoly-level prices for very long. Furthermore, as suggested earlier, in an oligopoly a few firms interact with one another in a market with some limitation on the entry of new suppliers. Our clothing store will probably face a good deal of competition for sales, particularly in the long run, because barriers to entering the retail clothing industry are not likely to be very significant or effective. A market for retail

Table 10.1   The essential differences among competition, monopoly, oligopoly, and monopolistic competition

	Competition	Monopoly	Oligopoly	Monopolistic competition
Number of firms in industry	Numerous	One	Few; may band together as a cartel to act as one firm	Numerous; however, a group of firms may have the legal right to act as one for marketing purposes
Barriers to entry	None	Always present in the case of monopoly; strictly defined as one firm	Some barrier likely; keeps number of firms small	None
Economic rent in long-run equilibrium	Possible, but none for marginal firms	Possible	Possible	Possible, but none for marginal firms
Product differentiation within the industry	None	Only one product	Possible, but not necessary	Typical

clothing or any other market with the type of characteristics we have been discussing best fits the market structure of monopolistic competition. Table 10.1 summarizes how monopolistic competition differs from the basic competitive, monopoly, and oligopoly situations.

Price and Output in the Short Run

In order to clarify how economists analyze a monopolistically competitive industry, we will first focus on the short-term behavior of an individual firm. Figure 10.1 illustrates the short-term pricing and output decisions of a single firm producing a product in a monopolistically competitive industry. The demand curve facing the firm is not the industry demand curve but rather the demand for that particular firm's version of the product. This might be one particular type of deodorant, soap, or toothpaste. In the case of our clothing store, we might sell one brand of leather gloves that are similar but not identical to those sold by other clothing stores in town. The industry demand curve might usefully be thought of as the demand for gloves by consumers, including knit gloves,

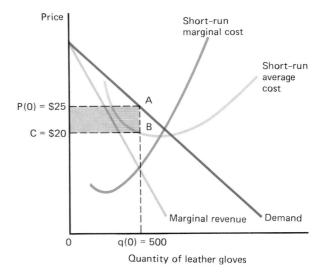

Figure 10.1   Short-run monopolistic competition
With the demand curve and cost conditions illustrated here, the monopolistically competitive firm will equate marginal revenue with marginal cost. Price per unit will be P(0), and output will be q(0). Short-run profit will be equal to the shaded area CBAP(0) ($2,500).

leather gloves, and even mittens. Apart from muffs or pockets, there are no good substitutes for gloves. Therefore, the demand curve facing the retail glove industry is somewhat inelastic. However, the demand for the gloves our little firm sells will be fairly elastic because a number of other stores are selling similar, if not identical, gloves. In short, the demand curve facing a single monopolistically competitive firm should be more elastic than the demand curve facing the industry, although the demand curve for the monopolistically competitive firm will not be horizontal (perfectly elastic). Put differently, in a competitive industry the firms are so-called price takers and face horizontal or perfectly elastic demand curves to go with a downward-sloping industry demand. In a monopolistically competitive industry both the industry and individual firms' demand schedules are downward sloping.

As illustrated in figure 10.1, the individual firm will equate marginal revenue with marginal cost to maximize profit in the short term. Price will be set equal to P(0), which is $25, and output will be equal to q(0), which is 500 in our example. Total profit, $2,500, is identified by the shaded area in figure 10.1. In the short term, then, our monopolistically competitive clothing firm looks similar to a monopolist. It is important to realize, however, that demand conditions could be such that our clothing firm suffers economic losses in the short run. How would figure 10.1 look if the monopolistically competitive firm depicted were losing money? In particular, what would the position of the demand curve be with respect to the short-run average cost curve?

▶ Long-run Monopolistic Competition

The unique features of monopolistic competition are apparent when we look at long-run equilibrium. Suppose short-run market conditions are those described by figure 10.1. In this case, where the firm is making short-run economic profits, we would expect our clothing store's competitors to try to expand their sales of close substitutes for our items, including the leather gloves we sell. They will do this to try to capture some of the profits we enjoy in the short run. The entry of new competitors will change the elasticity and location of the demand curve we face for our leather gloves. Because substitutes will never be exact, our long-run demand curve will be fairly elastic but not perfectly elastic (horizontal).

Figure 10.2 illustrates a long-run demand curve for a single monopolistically competitive firm and its associated marginal revenue, long-run marginal cost, and long-run average cost curves. We can maximize our store's profits by equating marginal revenue with long-run marginal cost, once long-run demand conditions are established. The unusual feature of long-run equilibrium in a monopolistically competitive industry is that there is no economic (excess) profit because producers of near substitutes can freely enter our market and bid customers away from us. Thus, the long-run equilibrium price will just be equal to long-run average cost. In figure 10.2, there is no long-run economic profit (economic rent) for the monopolistically competitive firm because the long-run average cost curve just touches, or is tangent to, the demand curve. (There may be economic rent for firms with access to superior resources, as for some competitive firms. See pages 153–54.)

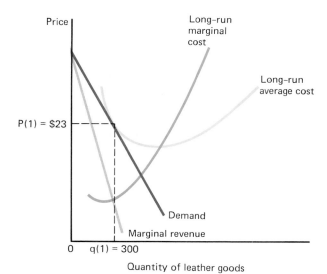

Figure 10.2   Long-run monopolistic competition
In the long run, the individual firm continues to equate
marginal revenue with marginal cost, selling q(1) units of
output at a price equal to P(1). Because price equals long-run
average cost, no long-run profit (rent) is being earned. But
output is not produced at the minimum point on the firm's
long-run average cost curve.

Finally, notice that the competition for our
clothing store's products reduces the demand and
marginal revenue schedules compared to those our
store faced when it was making profits (in figure 10.1).
If cost conditions do not change between the long run
and the short run, our store will have a lower price
and less output in the long run than in the short run.
Suppose, however, that in addition to demand's being
reduced because of competition for profits, demand
becomes substantially more elastic in the long run. In

this case, not only will price be lower in the long run
than in the short run but also quantity may actually
be higher in the long run. It is important to recognize
that the outcomes we have been describing depend on
identical short-run and long-run cost conditions.
Shortly we will examine some reasons why a monopolistically competitive firm's costs may change in the
long run. Before proceeding, however, we would like
you to redraw figures 10.1 and 10.2 and analyze the
way in which production, price, and profits change as
the industry adjusts to its long-run equilibrium situation.

Production Efficiency and Product Variety

Recall that in a competitive industry the market forces
firms toward zero economic profit and each industry
toward minimum long-run average cost of production
in the long run. When a long-run competitive equilibrium price is established, output will be produced
efficiently. In a competitive industry, where there are
completely identical products, the goal of profit maximization and the ability of firms to enter the industry
assure efficient production of goods and services in the
long run. As described in figure 10.2, the monopolistically competitive industry also has firms with zero
economic profit in long-run equilibrium. However, this
does not correspond exactly to a competitive industry.
Output and price are not at the minimum point on
the monopolistically competitive firm's long-run average cost curve. Goods and services will not be produced at minimum per unit cost as long as firms face
downward-sloping demand curves in the long run.
Should we be concerned by the apparent loss of production efficiency associated with a monopolistically
competitive industry?

Remember a key distinction between long-run equilibrium in a competitive market and long-run equilibrium in a monopolistically competitive market. Every firm's product is the same in a competitive market. In contrast, products are different, though similar, in a monopolistically competitive market. While laundry soap is laundry soap, hair spray is hair spray, toothpaste is toothpaste, and deodorant is deodorant, it is not hard to notice the differences that firms try to establish among their products. In our example of competition among retailers selling gloves, there would be a competitive situation only if all clothing stores marketed identical gloves. To the extent that consumers like diversity in glove styles, fabric, and color, sellers will respond by producing similar but not identical kinds of gloves. The loss of long-run efficiency is the price we, as consumers, pay for such variety. It is the cost of having deodorants that go on dry, deodorants in roll-on containers, as well as deodorants in spray cans. It is the cost of being able to choose a liquid versus a powder with which to wash our clothes. It is our ability to have toothpaste in a pump as well as in a metal or a plastic tube, and to have it be a gel or paste, mint flavored, and with or without fluoride. Thus, we might amend the old saying to read as follows: "Variety is the spice of life, and it is not free."

Of course, a major concern of ours is whether or not price differences that emerge from the alternative products we have just been mentioning reflect differences in the products themselves. Is it possible that the prices for the same or very similar products differ because consumers are "manipulated" by sellers into seeing differences that do not really exist? In particular, could consumer preferences for variety be the wasteful by-product of slick Madison Avenue advertising campaigns? Without advertising, could price differences even exist for the same or very similar products under conditions of monopolistic competition? We will suggest answers to these and other important questions in the remainder of this chapter.

▶ Price Differences within Markets

Within any city, the prices of many goods and services vary from place to place. In particular, you may have noticed that the price of food, cosmetics, and other personal items may differ by neighborhood. Two neighborhoods known for relatively high prices are the campus area and the inner city. Because college students and poor people frequently lack cars and find it difficult to travel to other parts of the city, it is tempting to conclude that they are exploited by the merchants in their areas. Does this immobility of buyers give firms in campus or inner-city areas monopoly power?

The answer is that consumer immobility does not automatically allow abusive monopoly practices. Remember that every market has two sides. Suppose that buyers indeed have very few choices of firms from which to purchase a particular item. Suppose that this leads to abnormally high prices and profits for the local merchants. If new firms can enter and compete for these profits, this process should move prices and profits toward a competitive level. Only if there are barriers to entry in neighborhoods such as those we have been discussing will prices and profits remain high. To our knowledge, these barriers have not been well documented. This leads us to examine another possible reason for relatively high prices in low-income and college neighborhoods.

Differences in Costs

The cost of providing retail services can vary greatly from neighborhood to neighborhood. The cost is typically higher in those areas where higher prices are found. The type of services provided in these areas may also contribute to firms' higher operating costs. In particular, buyers in low-income neighborhoods often obtain credit from local merchants when such credit is unobtainable through normal channels such as charge accounts in large department stores and bank credit cards. Merchants who provide credit bear the cost of discovering which customers are good risks. One of the ways they do this is by suffering losses when they cannot collect what is owed them and when they cannot collect payment on bad checks. Most important, however, is that the cost of providing a particular good or service will be higher in the areas we have been describing. Insurance premiums will be higher in order to cover the greater risk of loss due to violence and fire and the higher incidences of shoplifting and burglary. Higher population densities may contribute to higher rents for space of a given quality.

The higher prices charged by retailers, especially food stores, in some inner-city areas have led to consumer complaints and political pressure to lower prices. However, if high costs are the reason for high prices, firms will tend to withdraw from high-cost areas rather than operate there at a loss. The result of this is that in some major cities consumers are left with almost no retail food stores in their neighborhoods and with inadequate means of transportation to reach distant shopping centers.[2]

Aside: Price Differences in Monopoly, Competition, and Monopolistic Competition

Before moving on, there is a related and important point to be added here. Not all price differences among firms are evidence of monopolistic competition. They can occur in any market structure and may simply reflect cost differences as well as the level of affluence and taste patterns of consumers. Suppose we were considering the price of oranges in different grocery stores. For the sake of argument let us assume that the oranges are identical and produced under competitive conditions. We have been describing the situation where there are differences in costs of providing oranges for sale in different locations. In this case, we would expect the prices of identical oranges to differ from one place to another. Thus, as long as transportation and transaction costs exist, there will not be a single price for oranges, even in long-run equilibrium. Now here is the clever part. If identical items sold in

different locations can have different prices at the same point in time, goods that are similar, but not identical, can also vary in price from place to place. Consequently, price differences for the same good or service can be observed in competitive markets, monopoly market structures, and everything in between.

Consumer Cooperatives

On the other hand, not all price differences truly reflect actual cost differences. Take the case where consumers have banded together to form cooperatives in order to obtain goods and services at lower prices. Such cooperatives are often able to sell to members of the cooperative at lower prices than their "for-profit" competitors. Why the quotation marks around for-profit? One of the things cooperatives do is to rely on membership fees instead of borrowed money to finance their inventories. They also use volunteer services by the members instead of paid labor. In some instances, customers must preorder and prepay for purchases, and business hours of the cooperative are rather limited. Therefore, the opportunity cost to customers of cooperatives is not always fully reflected in the market prices they charge for their goods and services.

The point is that the ability of consumer cooperatives to sell products at prices below those charged by local merchants does not prove that the market is not competitive for those items. Rather, some of the costs of bringing the goods to market may be absorbed by the members of the cooperative directly (such as through volunteer clerk or distribution services) and thus are not reflected in the shelf prices of the merchandise. What *would* be some evidence of noncompetitive pricing? It might include proof that the price differentials between a cooperative and a neighboring private store exceeded differences in the quality of goods and services provided and the full costs of providing those goods and services. That kind of evidence would be difficult to assemble.

▶ Advertising, Information, and Product Differentiation

One reason firms advertise is that customers are not always aware of sellers' locations and prices. Customers are more likely to patronize establishments that help them find what they want. However, advertising is also a cost that must be reflected in the prices firms charge. Nevertheless, because buyers may have more important things to do than search for a store, the full cost of goods and services, including search costs, may actually be reduced by advertising. Think about it this way. Would you enjoy driving around town for two hours next Friday night just to find out what movies are playing? In this section, we examine the issue of advertising in some detail. We identify situations in which advertising actually reduces the full cost of a good or service and situations in which advertising seems to be economically inefficient or wasteful. It is especially important to keep these two situations straight. As with most institutions in society, there are some good and bad aspects of advertising to consider.

Informative Advertising and Product Prices

Advertising that reduces buyers' costs of finding a good or service promotes competition among firms. Specifically, informative advertising increases the elasticity of demand for each firm's product(s) as buyers become more aware of the substitutes available to them. If a particular firm seeks to avoid the increased competition that advertising can create, it may lose customers to firms that do provide product information through advertisements. Because advertising is costly, firms must choose among various means of attracting customers who possess rather incomplete knowledge of their consumption alternatives.

Perhaps we can paint a clearer picture of the forces governing advertising expenditures by considering the market for apartments near a large university. If there were no advertising, consumers'

information costs of renting an apartment would be very high, as would landlords' costs of renting apartments. Renters would face the alternatives of an extended and costly search or of taking an easy-to-find apartment at what might turn out to be an unusually high rent. It would be worthwhile for landlords to pay some costs of advertising. This might enable them to reduce their expected vacancy rates given the rent they plan to charge or perhaps to charge higher rents given the vacancy rates they anticipate. Prospective tenants might find it worthwhile to pay somewhat higher rents, on average, if they could find satisfactory apartments more easily through advertising and reduce their chances of being grossly overcharged. Thus, equilibrium apartment rents might actually be lowered by advertising because vacancy rates would probably be lower. Because the time an apartment is vacant represents a cost of providing apartment services, the cost savings associated with lower vacancy rates could more than pay for the extra advertising expenditures. This means that landlords should find that, up to a limit set by prospective tenants' willingness to pay for information, the cost of advertising can be regained in higher apartment rents or lower apartment vacancy rates.

As you might expect, the amount of information provided through advertising tends to reflect the forces of supply and demand. Firms are willing to incur advertising expenses that enable them to achieve greater sales and lower production costs. The latter may result from the ability to use their buildings and equipment more productively. Remember that consumers typically have a choice between paying a higher price for advertised products and using their own resources to search for cheaper unadvertised alternatives. This means that informative advertising can be viewed as an integral part of a market economy in which information is itself produced by the use of valuable resources.

Figure 10.3 illustrates an example of the beneficial effects advertising can have on competition by informing potential buyers of alternative consumption possibilities. Suppose you are considering buying a

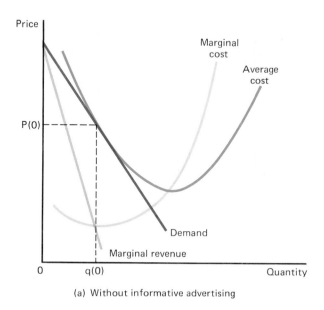

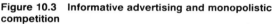

(a) Without informative advertising

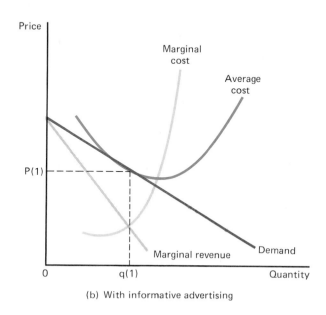

(b) With informative advertising

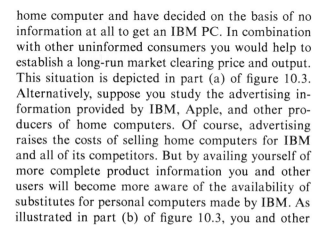

Figure 10.3   Informative advertising and monopolistic competition
Without informative advertising, long-run equilibrium price and output are P(0) and q(0). With informative advertising, marginal cost and average cost increase, while marginal revenue and demand become flatter. The equilibrium price with informative advertising is P(1), which is lower than the equilibrium price without informative advertising, P(0).

home computer and have decided on the basis of no information at all to get an IBM PC. In combination with other uninformed consumers you would help to establish a long-run market clearing price and output. This situation is depicted in part (a) of figure 10.3. Alternatively, suppose you study the advertising information provided by IBM, Apple, and other producers of home computers. Of course, advertising raises the costs of selling home computers for IBM and all of its competitors. But by availing yourself of more complete product information you and other users will become more aware of the availability of substitutes for personal computers made by IBM. As illustrated in part (b) of figure 10.3, you and other

consumers will create a flatter or more elastic long-run demand curve for personal computers produced by IBM and other manufacturers. Thus, even if advertising increases costs of the product, the market price you pay for a personal computer can be lower with informative advertising than without informative advertising.

When economists identify the potential benefits of advertising, they have in mind the possibility we have been discussing. We live in a world in which information about products is incomplete and expensive (or at least not costless) to obtain. Advertising that transmits useful information about products can be an important contributor to efficient information

Figure 10.4 Courtesy of American
Association of Advertising Agencies.

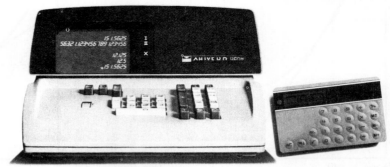

A SIMPLE LESSON IN ECONOMICS FOR ANYONE WHO BELIEVES ADVERTISING RAISES PRICES.

1965 Calculator — Over $2,000.00   1984 Calculator — Under $10.00

In the beginning there was the calculator.

It was a new idea. It had never been advertised. And it cost a fortune.

Then the people who sold calculators started to advertise them. That was hardly a new idea. But it, too, cost a fortune.

Now, you might think all that expensive advertising would drive the price of a calculator to incalculable heights.

But no. What happened was exactly the opposite.

It doesn't make sense. How can something as costly as advertising end up saving you money?

It's really quite simple. Advertising spreads news. When it spread the news of the calculator, people started to buy.

As more calculators were sold, more were produced. As more were produced, the cost of producing them came down. And because advertising creates competition, their quality and sophistication went up.

So today, using an electronic calculator is almost cheaper than counting on your fingers. And advertising helped make it happen — just as it has for countless other products.

In fact, with a little effort you could probably figure out precisely how much money advertising has saved you over the years.

But don't try it without a calculator.

ADVERTISING.
ANOTHER WORD FOR FREEDOM OF CHOICE.
American Association of Advertising Agencies

gathering and to individual and social welfare. This is certainly what people working in the advertising industry believe. To see this more clearly take a look at the ad from the American Association of Advertising Agencies presented as figure 10.4. Do you agree with all of the points the association is making in this figure?

Let us make matters somewhat more concrete. Figure 10.5 illustrates the breakdown in advertising expenditures by major media between 1970 and 1984. Notice that the most rapid expenditure growth has been in newspaper and television advertising. We also see that more than half of the money spent on advertising is national, as opposed to local, in focus. The

Product differentiation is the creation of brand names or superficial distinctions among products that are either identical or very similar.

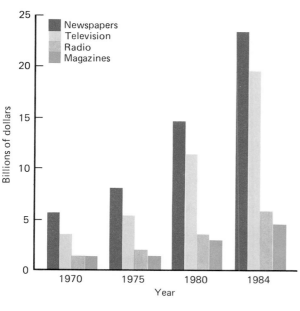

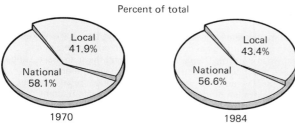

Figure 10.5   Advertising expenditures by selected media, 1970–1984
From *Statistical Abstract of the United States,* 1986 edition, p. 552.

share of national advertising in total advertising expenditures has declined in recent years but was still almost 57 percent in 1984.

Both local and national advertising frequently seem directed at convincing consumers that closely related goods or services are quite different in quality from one another. (We even see doctors and lawyers locally advertising their services these days.[3]) This has led some observers to question the value of advertising in our society. The issue is whether advertising expenditures simply serve to inform consumers about alternative consumption possibilities or actually seek to alter consumer preferences.

Tastes, Preferences, and Product Differentiation

Anyone who reads newspapers and magazines or watches television is aware that much advertising conveys neither knowledge of prices nor specific information about the locations of sellers. Such advertising can hardly be called informative. Rather, much (though not necessarily most) advertising seeks to persuade buyers that one brand of a commodity is somehow preferable to another. When different brands and models of the same good or service exist, such advertising is called **product differentiation.** Critics of the free enterprise system feel that there is a tendency to "waste" resources on advertising that suggests "artificial" differences among product brands and tries to persuade consumers to buy more of some products than they might otherwise. We take this criticism most seriously when it refers to heavily advertised products that are generally agreed to be of little objectively measurable value. Examples include foods with empty calories or goods that harm physical health, such as cigarettes or other tobacco products.

Advertising that seeks to create product distinctions is not only criticized for being wasteful and helping firms acquire monopoly power but also for manipulating buyers' preferences. In our discussions of economic efficiency we have been assuming that consumer preferences are determined by forces independent of the economic system itself. Suppose, however, that consumer preferences can be shaped by the process of producing and marketing goods and services. In this case, firms' tendencies to satisfy consumers is no longer a sound foundation for the argument that competition among firms promotes an economically efficient mix of goods and services in a society.

Having identified some of the basic arguments against product differentiation in advertising, let us now dig more deeply into the issue. It is extremely important that we distinguish the positive and normative issues here. The key positive issue we will address is whether advertising that deals with nonprice characteristics of a product creates barriers to entry that give firms monopoly power. The key normative

(a) Price and output without manipulative advertising

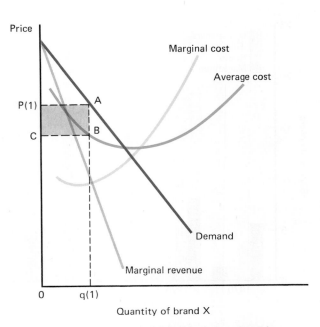

(b) Price and output with manipulative advertising

Figure 10.6   Advertising and monopoly power
In this figure, demand, marginal revenue, marginal cost and average cost are for a monopolistic competitor in long-run equilibrium. As shown in part (a), in the absence of manipulative advertising, profits are zero and equilibrium price and output are P(0) and q(0), respectively. Because advertising that manipulates consumers into believing brand X is unique is not costless, marginal cost and average cost increase, as shown in part (b). The demand curve and the marginal revenue curve also become steeper (less elastic) when there is manipulative advertising. The new equilibrium price is higher, and equilibrium output is less. Economic profits become positive and equal the shaded area shown in part (b).

question we confront is whether it is socially acceptable for firms to "create" a want or desire for a product. The answer to this normative question depends in part on the answer to the positive question that precedes it. Specifically, do advertising and brand-name promotions in fact deprive consumers and producers of alternative forms of production and consumption?

Suppose that advertising expenditures can indeed manipulate consumer preferences by convincing consumers that brand X is more necessary than they previously thought. This is illustrated in figure 10.6,

where the demand curve for brand X becomes less elastic with advertising. As a result, economic profits can emerge, and society can be made worse off. Unproductive advertising expenses will increase, and consumers will pay a higher price for less output.

Advertising and brand-name promotion of the type we have been discussing are costly. Their costs will be reflected in the higher prices of advertised brand-name goods purchased by consumers. On the other hand, new firms will feel that they can profit from catering to consumers' desires for the same quality at a lower price. For example, we observe an increased availability in recent years of low-priced generic brands. This suggests that advertising and product differentiation do not totally prevent competitive forces from meeting basic consumer desires.

Why might people not switch to lower-cost non-brand goods?[4] The proliferation and persistence of many kinds of product differentiation in advertising can be understood only if we realize that human wants and motivations are complex. People often buy goods to satisfy very subtle desires. An automobile, for example, can be a prestige symbol and an aid to attracting pleasant companions, as well as a means of transportation. In the case of a real estate agent, the size and value of his or her car indicates some degree of success to potential clients. Who wants to buy a house from someone who drives a beat up Volkswagen? Many of the human motivations to which advertising and product differentiation appeal are strong and persistent. It does not take a great deal of insight or sensitivity to recognize the erotic implications of much alcohol and cigarette advertising and most perfume and cologne advertising. Automobile advertising is often not aimed at the demand for transportation but rather at the desire for prestige.

Presumably, cigarette smokers, automobile buyers, and others who rise to the advertiser's lures have the option of changing their buying habits if they do not experience the satisfaction they want from their purchases. They may also change their buying habits if they discover that the bad characteristics of a commodity or particular brand outweigh its desirable characteristics. For example, in recent years automobile sales have been rather lackluster. Possible reasons are that with downsizing and fuel economy considerations, automobiles now provide "only" transportation. Buying a new model every three years or so no longer provides the thrill it once did. In the case of cigarettes, knowledge that smoking may lead to lung cancer or heart disease seems to have reduced demand, even though it has not totally eliminated it.

Advertising, Product Differentiation, and Monopoly Power

Now let us return to the question of whether advertising, by creating barriers to entry, gives firms what amounts to monopoly power. A successful brand name, new product, or variation on an existing good or service can allow a firm to charge a higher price without losing all of its customers. This means that it may be possible to earn economic profits for a while. However, the talent and other resources needed to mount advertising campaigns and to develop rival products are available to all unless legal copyrights or patents are involved. Of course, the dividing line between legal and illegal product copying is often hotly contested.[5] For example, designer jeans are no longer the exclusive products they once were. Rival advertising campaigns and the introduction of further new twists on old product ideas will therefore tend to eliminate excess profits that result from advertising or product differentiation.

Advertising and Consumer Protection

Some would argue that advertising simply caters to human motivations. This does not mean that we must approve of all promotional techniques indiscriminately. Should we, for example, tolerate advertisers who knowingly make false claims? Trying to persuade potential buyers to purchase a good that will harm them or that will not perform as claimed is similar to stealing consumers' money outright. Just as we have laws against theft and fraud, there are government regulations to discourage dishonesty in advertising.[6] If you think about it for a moment, where repeat buyers are involved, advertisers themselves have much to gain by preserving public trust in their claims. (Recall the discussion of the problems of one-time buyers in chapter 5.) If rampant dishonesty in advertising were to destroy the credibility of all advertisers, firms would lose a valuable tool with which to communicate to their customers. Specialists in the advertising industry would risk losing much of their clientele. Interestingly, when the Federal Trade Commission moved in 1982 to reduce the strictness of its rules on the prior substantiation of advertising claims, advertisers themselves objected. They argued that if the government withdrew the requirement that advertisers have prior proof for their claims, the advertising industry would be seriously harmed.[7]

There are many fascinating questions regarding the ethics of advertising and its impact on consumer well-being. One of them involves the need to make informed judgments. Suppose, for example, you believe that it is acceptable to advertise cigarettes to adults who can decide for themselves whether the perceived benefits outweigh the health risks. But should such advertisements be seen or heard by teenagers? Should young children be exposed to advertisements that encourage them to eat heavily sugared breakfast cereals? What, if any, protection is needed for consumers who may not have developed the capacity to choose what is best for themselves? Who should provide this protection—their families or government agencies?

Advertising, Profits, and Prices: Some Evidence

This chapter contains much discussion of the role of advertising. At this point it seems useful to summarize some of the key implications concerning advertising and its effect on prices and profits. In general, we have grouped advertising into two types—informative and manipulative. The distinction is important because informative advertising can actually lower consumer prices whereas manipulative advertising raises prices and produces economic profits.

What type of products tend to rely on informative advertising as opposed to manipulative advertising? Although any generalization can be dangerous, products characterized by informative advertising tend to be big ticket durable goods, such as furniture or houses. These are items for which individuals spend

a lot of money, and price differences can be substantial. Advertising surrounding durable goods such as refrigerators or washers also tends to be informative. It typically conveys information concerning the location of sellers and the price of the item and usually appears in the print media. This advertising, as we have seen, tends to increase elasticity of demand for a product, and although the advertising costs money, prices and profits can actually be reduced.

What we have been calling manipulative advertising tends to be associated with relatively low-priced convenience goods, such as toothpaste, wine, beer, soft drinks, laundry detergent, and deodorant. Such advertising oftentimes tries to establish brand loyalty and reduce demand elasticity, thereby raising prices and profits. Advertising of this type rarely carries ingredient or price information. It is typically persuasive and appears most often on television.[8]

Is there any evidence that the type of advertising we have been calling informative lowers prices and profits whereas the type of advertising we have been calling manipulative raises prices and profits? Often the distinction is between advertising done by manufacturers, which tends to be more manipulative, and advertising done by retailers, which tends to be more informative. There does, in fact, seem to be a positive relationship between profits and advertising of convenience goods and a negative relationship between profits and advertising of durable goods.[9] There is also evidence of a strong positive relationship between advertising and profits for manufacturers and a weak negative relationship between advertising and profits in retail and service trades, such as advertising by auto dealers or drugstores.[10] Finally, there have been a number of interesting studies of the effects of advertising restrictions on the prices of goods and services. For example, Lee Benham studied the effects of legal restrictions on the advertising of eyeglasses and eye examinations. He found that the average price of eyeglasses is more than twice as much in states where advertising is prohibited as it is in states where advertising of eyeglasses is totally unrestricted.[11] Studies of the effects of prohibiting retail drug advertising reveal a similar pattern. Restrictions on such advertising seem to raise prices from 4 to 9 percent.[12]

▶ Summary and Conclusions

In this chapter we examined industries that produce somewhat differentiated products even though they have no formal restrictions or barriers to entry. A newsworthy example of product differentiation was contained in our discussion of soft drinks in the introduction. The following points were emphasized in this chapter.

A monopolistically competitive firm faces a downward-sloping demand curve and can make economic profits in the short term.

In the long term, entry (by profit-seeking firms) causes monopolistically competitive firms to earn zero economic profits.

Because of the downward-sloping demand curve, monopolistic competition does not force firms to minimize the average cost of their production in the long run, even though their economic profits have been forced to zero. This means that monopolistic competition is not quite as efficient as the competitive industries we have studied.

The loss in productive efficiency relative to competition is the price society must pay for the product variety that appears in a monopolistically competitive industry.

Price differences for the same product within a given market can be the result of cost differences or monopoly power.

Advertising expenditures are motivated in part by attempts to inform consumers and sometimes by attempts to influence their tastes for a product. Informative advertising can actually decrease a product's price even though it raises production costs. Manipulative advertising is designed to reduce the elasticity of demand for a product and can raise prices and create economic profits.

Evidence suggests that advertising we characterize as manipulative tends to be associated with higher prices and profits, and advertising we characterize as informative is associated with lower profits and prices. For example, advertising by manufacturers is associated with higher profits and advertising by retailers with lower profits.

▶ Key Terms

monopolistic competition *207*

product differentiation *217*

▶ Questions for Discussion and Review

1. State whether the following statements are true, false, or uncertain, and write a short paragraph supporting your position.
   a. Advertising cannot harm people because no one is forced to purchase unwanted goods.
   b. Product differentiation leads to waste and economic inefficiency.

2. State whether each of the following industries is competitive, monopolistic, oligopolistic, or monopolistically competitive and explain why. (Hint: Use the information in table 10.1.) The industries are wheat growing, orange growing in Florida, orange growing in California, diamonds for jewelry, gasoline manufacturing, crude oil, automobile manufacturing, and men's casual wear (jeans, shirts, jackets).

3. Look up the following newspaper articles in your library: Walter E. Williams, "Taxes, Taxis, and the Poor," *New York Times,* 8 Jan. 1983, p. 23; and "Australian Venture Preparing to Mine Argyle Diamonds," *New York Times,* 10 Jan. 1983, p. D4. On the basis of the information contained in these articles answer the following questions about the New York City taxicab market and the world diamond market.
   a. Would you classify these markets as monopolistic, oligopolistic, or monopolistically competitive?
   b. Are these markets characterized by higher prices than would prevail in a market of price takers?
   c. Are there barriers to entry in these markets? If so, what are they? What role, if any, does government play?

d. Do the firms in these markets earn monopoly rents? How are the rents, if any, shared among the firms? What is your evidence?

e. Does monopoly power promote economic well-being in either market? If so, who benefits? Does anyone lose?

4. In 1975, the Federal Trade Commission prohibited General Motors from advertising that *Road and Track Magazine* had cited the Chevrolet Vega as "the best handling passenger car." The reason was GM did not have scientific evidence that the Vega was indeed the best handling passenger car. Did this prohibition serve consumer interests? Write a one-page essay defending your answer.

5. Compare and contrast the long-run equilibrium positions of firms under monopolistic and perfect competition.

6. Explain why monopolistic competitors will have excess capacity in the long run.

7. On the basis of the assumption of excess capacity, why would two monopolistic competitors have any economic incentive to merge?

8. The purpose of advertising is to increase the demand for the advertiser's product. Therefore, it is reasonable that a firm with a given set of cost curves should continually increase expenditures for advertising in order to maximize profits. Is this statement true or false? Justify your answer.

9. Illustrate and explain why the purpose of advertising is to increase demand for a firm's output and not to make demand more inelastic.

10. Monopolistic competitors exert a degree of monopoly power over the markets they serve. Explain how coupons allow supermarkets to practice price discrimination.

Chapter 11

Government Regulation of Industries

Outline

I. Introduction *224*
II. Antitrust policy *225*
   A. A brief review of the social costs of monopoly *225*
      1. Estimates of the welfare loss due to monopoly *226*
   B. Antitrust laws *227*
   C. Two recent antitrust cases *228*
      1. AT&T *228*
      2. The plywood industry *229*
III. Rate regulation *229*
   A. Technical monopoly and rate regulation *229*
   B. Rate regulation in theory *231*
   C. Rate regulation in practice *231*
      1. Rate structure *231*
      2. Summary of the evidence *233*
   D. Rate regulation in potentially competitive industries *233*
IV. The case for deregulation *235*
   A. Airline deregulation *235*
V. Summary and conclusions *237*
VI. Key terms *238*
VII. Questions for discussion and review *238*
VIII. Policy issue: You decide—Drug resales *240*
   A. The action-initiating event *240*
   B. The issue *240*
   C. Economic policy issues *240*

Objectives

After reading this chapter, the student should be able to:

Discuss some of the social costs of monopoly.

Explain the logic behind government policy designed to promote competition among firms.

Explain the logic behind government policy to affect firms' prices directly.

Discuss some recent actions taken by the United States government to deregulate certain industries.

▶ Introduction

In 1969, the federal government sued IBM Corporation on the grounds that it was engaging in monopolistic practices. The government argued that IBM had introduced selected computers with inordinately low prices in sectors of the computing industry where IBM's competitors appeared to be on the verge of success. Moreover, the government maintained that IBM had announced nonexistent software so as to forestall orders for competitors' existing products.[1] One of the key issues in the government's case, which was designed to punish IBM for what it perceived as monopolistic behavior and restructure the firm so as to promote greater competition in the computer industry, was the extent of IBM's share of the computer market. The government (the plaintiff in the case) argued that IBM had 80 percent of the mainframe (large hardware) market. Defense (IBM) witnesses emphasized that to consider only mainframes was too narrow a definition of the market and that computing equipment in general should be considered, including peripherals and personal computers. When viewed

this way, IBM's revenues in 1979 were only about 35 percent of the total computer market. Moreover, witnesses testifying on behalf of IBM argued that the real economic issue was whether IBM could raise prices or hold back innovation.[2]

In January of 1982, after thirteen years of prosecution, the government withdrew its suit against IBM. The assistant attorney general in charge of the case decided that the government's position was weak and that it had only a small chance of winning.[3] The Justice Department's decision to drop the IBM case disturbed many industrial organization experts because it was reached after four or five months of studying evidence that had been presented over the course of thirteen years. Moreover, even if the government had only a small chance of winning its case, the opinion of the court was only a few months away. Thus, the cost of waiting for the outcome seemed to be low, and there was no obvious benefit from preventing the proceedings from reaching a conclusion. In this chapter we will discuss additional examples of how the government has acted when there is potential monopoly power in an industry.

Antitrust laws permit the
government to sue, and thus
penalize, firms that try to prevent
other firms from competing in the
production and sale of a product or
service.

▸ Antitrust Policy

A firm or group of firms may effectively be a monopoly if it can keep other firms from setting up production. **Antitrust laws** are aimed at removing power
such as this. In order to understand the logic and effectiveness of antitrust laws in the United States, it
is helpful to briefly review what we learned previously
concerning price and production under monopoly as
compared to competition. We will also examine in
more detail the social costs of monopoly. Once we understand these issues more thoroughly, we can turn
our attention to why antitrust laws exist and what their
expected and actual effects on firms are.

A Brief Review of the Social Costs of Monopoly

Figure 11.1 reminds us of the differences in price and
quantity produced under monopoly conditions compared to competition in the situation where there are
constant (marginal and average) costs of production.
Figure 11.1 is essentially a generalization of figure
8.1. Ask almost anyone what the main difference is
between monopoly and competition, and he or she will
probably give you a correct answer. Most people will
say monopolists produce less and sell at higher prices
than a competitive industry. Clearly, then, consumers

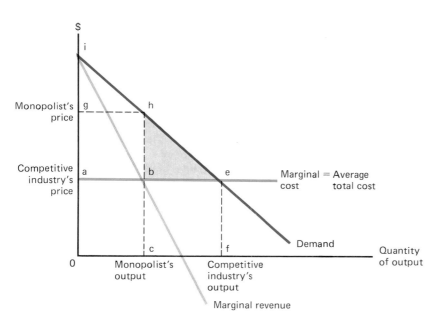

**Figure 11.1   Price, quantity, and
consumers' surplus under monopoly
and competition when production has
a constant marginal cost**
Not only do consumers pay a higher
price for less output under monopoly as
compared to competitive conditions, but
they also suffer a loss of consumers'
surplus. The shaded area of the diagram
illustrates this so-called deadweight loss
from monopoly. It is called this because
it is *not* captured by the monopolist; it
simply evaporates instead of contributing
to the well-being of consumers—as it
does when the industry is competitive.

*The **deadweight loss of monopoly** is the consumers' surplus that is lost in excess of the consumers' surplus that becomes monopoly profits.*

are worse off under a monopoly than under a competitive industry. Similarly, the owners of monopolies or cartels are better off because of the excess economic profits that exist under monopolistic compared to competitive conditions. Is this transfer of income from consumers to the owners of monopolies the only reason for antitrust laws? No.

There is an additional economic justification for antitrust legislation. It is related to the loss of consumers' surplus as the monopoly or cartel restricts output in comparison to competition. We know that consumers' surplus is the (extra) economic benefit buyers get from a good or service over and above the price they have to pay. Remember also that the demand curve in figure 11.1 illustrates the value of an additional unit to consumers and that consumers will pay the same price for all of the units they buy. In this case, only the marginal, or last, unit purchased is worth to consumers what they pay for it. All of the other units consumers buy, up to that last one, are actually worth more to consumers than they have to pay. This creates consumers' surplus. Of course, consumers' surplus will be lower when the number of units purchased is less. Thus when monopolies or cartels restrict production and raise the price of a product, they also eliminate part of consumers' surplus.

In chapter 8 we learned that the way to measure consumers' surplus is to evaluate the area under the demand curve associated with the price consumers pay and the quantity of the product they purchase. When the industry in figure 11.1 is competitive, consumers' surplus is measured by the area of the triangle aie. However, when the industry is effectively a monopoly, consumers' surplus is only the triangle gih. What

happens to the consumers' surplus that is lost under monopoly conditions? This loss is the area of the rectangle aghb plus the triangle bhe. The rectangle aghb becomes monopoly profits. Thus, part of consumers' surplus is captured by the monopolist or the group of firms (cartel) that behaves jointly as a monopolist. What happens to the triangle bhe, though? It has simply vanished.

The point here is that part of the consumers' surplus that is lost if an industry is monopolized goes to no one. It can be thought of as a loss to society in general because of the economically inefficient amount of production when an industry is a monopoly compared to the output that would be produced in a competitive industry with a similar cost structure. This loss of consumers' surplus that just disappears is called the **deadweight loss of monopoly.** The triangle bhe is a measure of society's cost of allowing monopoly production. This lost value is important because it means that society has a special benefit from antitrust laws. In particular, if the industry in figure 11.1 is at first a monopoly and then is forced to become competitive, society as a whole benefits. Society could more than compensate the owners of the monopoly for their lost profits and still have money (resources) left over. This is an additional justification for antitrust laws—the fact that society is a net beneficiary from competitive as compared to monopoly production.

Estimates of the Welfare Loss Due to Monopoly
It is sometimes said that theory without evidence is simply fantasy. We are about to remedy this situation. A number of economists have attempted to calculate for the United States the dollar value of the shaded

triangle in figure 11.1. A reasonable estimate seems to be in the range of 2 to 3 percent of GNP.[4] This may not seem very large, but remember that in 1986, GNP in the United States was over $4 trillion. If we take 2 to 3 percent of this number, we get something like $80 billion to $120 billion! This is about $325 per person or about $750 per family. Again, this may not seem like very much, but remember it is a deadweight loss. Wouldn't you like to have an extra $325? Suppose you are still not convinced that monopoly leads to significant economic losses for the United States. Consider it this way: $80 to $120 billion is enough to give between 8 million and 12 million poor families $10,000 apiece and not cost anyone else a dime!

At this point you should be asking yourself why anyone opposes antitrust laws if we can all benefit from the extra output and associated consumers' surplus. The answer basically relates to the politics of the situation. Specifically, the owners of a monopoly or a cartel and the workers employed in that monopoly or cartel see themselves as losers from antitrust enforcement because it is typically unaccompanied by arrangements to fully compensate them for any lost income. Why don't we simply add such required compensation to the antitrust laws and eliminate the political opposition? Things are not so straightforward. If you were a manager or a stockholder in a monopoly or a firm in a cartel, would you believe that the political process could adequately compensate you for your losses? Moreover, would you trust economists to devise a set of taxes and transfer payments that would indeed make you no worse off? This leads us to a discussion of antitrust policy in the United States in terms of the difference between ideal outcomes and actual outcomes.

Antitrust Laws

The Sherman Antitrust Act of 1890 is the principal antitrust law in the United States. In particular, it seeks to eliminate (1) collusive restraint of trade and (2) monopolization of an industry. The typical way the Sherman Act is applied in the latter situation is for the government to sue a firm (or firms) in court for damages and a restructuring of the firm (or firms). It is common for antitrust cases to be drawn out processes, with trials that last up to three years. One case had 1,200 witnesses.[5]

In order to prove illegal monopolization by an individual firm, the court must be convinced of two things. The first is that the firm has substantial market power. Second, there must be evidence of an intent to monopolize. In addressing the issue of market power, the courts have looked at many things, including the existence of patents, product differentiation, and the cost of capital. However, the market share of the accused firm is what the courts look at most carefully when deciding if there is substantial market power.[6] A key aspect of an antitrust case, then, is the definition of the relevant product market.

One of this book's authors is currently a monopoly supplier of the introductory economics course at 12:30 P.M. on Tuesdays and Thursdays at his university. If that were the entire market for introductory economics courses, he might be guilty of an antitrust violation. However, the relevant market includes introductory economics courses at other times at his university and at other colleges and universities across the country. On the basis of that definition of the market for introductory economics courses, this author provides a trivial percentage of total production.

What have the courts generally decided is too large a market share? There seems to be a feeling among industrial organization experts that if a firm has less than 60 percent of total production, it will not have an antitrust problem. A firm with 60 to 75 percent of the relevant market is risking an antitrust suit. A firm with a market share greater than 75 percent is almost certain to be sued.[7]

Thus far we have discussed only situations where a firm's possible monopolization of an industry is the issue. It is also true, as we earlier noted, that the Sherman Act seeks to restrict collusion by firms attempting to fix the price of a good or service above its competitive level. In recent years, the Justice Department has initiated about twenty criminal prosecutions per year for price fixing.[8] What constitutes price fixing in the eyes of the government? Overt collusion, whereby firms create a single agency to sell their output, is clearly price fixing. Other attempts by firms to collude and raise the industry's price are more subtle, or at least more covert. The Justice Department has, for example, prosecuted industry trade associations that help firms to exchange detailed cost and pricing information or encourage firms to hold down production.[9] Finally, firms can attempt to "rig" bids. By this we mean firms may collude in a way that, while seeming to be competitive, predetermines which of their group will be the lowest bidder on a project. They may also set up an industrywide pricing scheme that effectively delivers the same monopolistic price to all of the buyers in the country no matter where they are located relative to the firm that is actually selling the output.

Two Recent Antitrust Cases

AT&T

Interestingly, at about the same time the Department of Justice was dropping the antitrust case against IBM (early 1982), it was settling an antitrust suit against AT&T. The gist of the case was that AT&T had been permitted to be a monopoly supplier of local telephone services, telephone equipment, and long-distance telephone services. While we argued in chapter 8 that local telephone services probably fit the definition of a technical monopoly quite well, it is not the case that telephone equipment or long distance calls need be produced by only one firm to minimize industry average costs. It is possible for many companies to make telephone equipment that will work and be compatible with that produced by AT&T prior to 1982. Moreover, there is room for other companies to have their own microwaves and to make use of communications satellites in transmitting long-distance telephone calls.

The objective of the suit against AT&T was to take away the three-part monopoly that the government had given it (local service, equipment, and long-distance service) and to restructure the telephone communications industry. In particular, AT&T was split into portions representing its technical monopoly and its potentially competitive segments. AT&T had to shed its regional phone companies, which continue to be regulated for price and service by state public utilities commissions. AT&T kept its equipment manufacturing and long-distance service operations. These, however, are now both subject to competition from other firms. Ads stressing AT&T's advantages over their competition did not appear prior to 1982, when AT&T had its three-part monopoly. Why?

Among consumers, who are the winners and the losers from the AT&T antitrust case? Those portions of the telephone communications industry that could be competitive, but were not when AT&T was a three-part monopoly, have had lower prices in recent years. Walk through a shopping mall and count the number of stores that now sell telephone equipment, much of which is relatively inexpensive. Similarly, the users of long-distance service have benefited by the new competition. Open a magazine such as *Newsweek* or *Time* and you will see numerous advertisements for inexpensive long-distance telephone service. On the other hand, following the AT&T breakup, local telephone companies have tried to get permission to impose hefty rate increases from the state regulatory agencies that determine the price of local telephone service.

The changes in the telephone communications industry we have been discussing are important because they seem to have promoted greater efficiency.

By this we mean that society now can use fewer of its scarce resources per unit of output and increase its consumers' surplus. Whether you as an individual consumer of telephone services have benefited from the AT&T breakup depends on your use of long-distance relative to local phone service and whether you are someone who prefers to buy a telephone rather than rent one from your local telephone company. Can you name some other winners and losers from the AT&T antitrust decision?[10]

The Plywood Industry

An especially interesting case of price fixing occurred in the plywood industry during the late 1970s. The collusive behavior was precipitated by a rapid growth in plywood production in the South during the 1960s. This growth was caused by new technology that permitted plywood to be made out of southern pines. Formerly, such lumber was unusable in plywood production. In the absence of any collusion on the part of plywood firms, southern producers would have been able to supply plywood to many parts of the country at lower prices than the long-established plywood producers in the Pacific Northwest. For example, it was estimated that because of lower transporation costs, southern plywood firms could deliver their product to Chicago at a price approximately 10 percent less than the price charged by firms in the Northwest. To eliminate any negative consequences for industry profits, southern plywood firms agreed to price their output at the higher (Northwest) price. It was as though southern plywood had been shipped from Portland, Oregon. But how did they handle consumers in the South who were willing to come to the mill and pick up their plywood purchases? Those customers were quoted prices that still included the cost of shipping the plywood from Portland. Only if southern customers actually picked up their plywood from a mill in the northwestern part of the country would the plywood firms subtract shipping costs. In this case, the purchasers in the South would have had to pay their own shipping costs, so the price was effectively the same. The Federal Trade Commission eventually ruled this practice by the plywood industry an illegal restraint of price competition.[11]

▶ Rate Regulation

A second major way in which government may affect firms is through **rate regulation,** which means that a government agency must approve price and output decisions. Independent commissions at both the state and federal levels are the primary regulatory agencies in the United States. In general, the federal commissions have regulated certain services that cross state lines, such as air and truck transportation, communications, and the shipment of natural gas through pipelines. These organizations have included the Interstate Commerce Commission (ICC), the Civil Aeronautics Board (CAB), and the Federal Communications Commission (FCC). At the state level, public utilities commissions regulate the operation of telephone, electric, and natural gas companies. In general, the issue of whether interstate commerce is involved determines whether an industry is a candidate for rate regulation by the state or by the federal government.

The typical justification for rate regulation is that the firm being regulated is a technical monopoly. Later in this chapter we will address situations where rate regulation has been applied to potentially competitive industries and the consequences for the firms and consumers involved. For now, let us try to understand the logic behind what could be termed "ideal" rate regulation of a technical monopoly.

Technical Monopoly and Rate Regulation

Figure 11.2 reminds us of the key features of a technical monopoly. In particular, a technical monopoly is an industry in which there are high fixed (capital) costs that lead to a falling average cost curve over a large range of output. These fixed costs are typically the expenses of setting up a service network. Once the gas mains or electric lines are networked around a city, for example, additional houses can be serviced at low and relatively constant cost. This results in the average total cost curve shown in figure 11.2. With this type of cost structure, one firm will dominate production.

Figure 11.2   Price, output, and profit of a technical monopoly before and after rate regulation
The key feature of a technical monopoly is its falling average cost over a large range of output due, to a great extent, to the large fixed costs of establishing a service network. The unregulated profit-maximizing technical monopolist will produce output level Q(1), charge price P(1), and have excess (economic) profits equal to the shaded rectangle. Rate regulation typically tries to eliminate these profits by requiring the firm to charge a price equal to P(2), where the average cost curve crosses demand. At price and quantity P(2) and Q(2), respectively, excess profits are eliminated but the technical monopoly still makes a so-called normal profit in that its total revenue covers the full costs (direct plus opportunity costs) of its inputs.

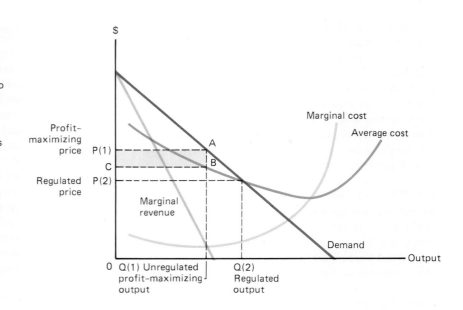

In the situation illustrated in figure 11.2, the firm will maximize profit by producing output level Q(1) and charging price P(1). Prove to yourself that if there were two profit-maximizing firms in figure 11.2, each with the average cost curve illustrated and each producing one-half Q(1), then the average cost per unit of output would be higher than 0C, the average cost of a single firm. Costs would clearly be higher with multiple producers than with a technical monopoly that produces Q(1) and sells it at P(1) per unit.

The unregulated profit-maximizing technical monopoly in figure 11.2 is making economic or excess profits equal to the shaded rectangle. Typically, rate regulation tries to eliminate the technical monopolist's excess or economic profits. This would occur if AT&T were required to charge price P(2). While it is easy for us to draw such an outcome in a diagram, what are the practical issues and problems of trying to regulate technical monopolies in this way?

Rate Regulation in Theory

Regulatory commissions influence both the level and the structure of prices for the various services that technical monopolies provide. The general idea is to try to set the price of a service so that the monopoly receives enough revenue to pay its full costs of operation, including the opportunity cost or "fair return" on the physical capital it owns. We can think of rate regulation as an attempt to balance the interests of consumers against those of stockholders. Specifically, consumers clearly prefer more of the service at a lower price while stockholders prefer higher prices and greater profits.

Rate Regulation in Practice

The key issue in rate regulation as it is practiced is what is allowed into the average total cost curve in figure 11.2. There are bitter controversies over certain components. Let us be more specific. A consumer interest group may argue that certain expenses are unnecessary or that certain workers are overpaid in terms of their salary or perks. However, operating expenses, actual payments to people and firms for the goods and services they provide the monopoly as inputs, are not the most controversial components of allowable costs. A somewhat more controversial component of average total cost is the opportunity cost of capital.

The opportunity cost of capital is a controversial issue for a number of reasons. Establishing the economic value of the investment, as well as what is a reasonable rate of return on that investment, is not as simple as you might think. For example, is the proper base for evaluating the investment the original cost of the plant and equipment, which may have been purchased many years ago, or is it the cost of replacing the plant and equipment with currently available new (and improved) items? What percentage return would you allow the stockholders of the firm to receive on their investment? Should they receive the average on all stocks in recent years? Perhaps they should receive something less because if the firm is a monopoly it is less likely to go out of business because of the absence of competition. These decisions are open to argument at public utilities commission hearings.

In essence, rate regulation decisions can boil down to a situation in which the regulatory commission is simultaneously confronted by (1) a public utility, which typically says that a substantial price increase is needed to provide the quantity and quality of service consumers want, and by (2) a consumer interest group, which typically says that the costs are padded and that a far smaller price increase is appropriate. Despite the fact that the public utilities commission may try to set price at a level where fair (normal) but not excessive (economic) profits will be earned by the regulated firm, the proceedings (as well as the eventual decision) may basically reflect the relative political power of the parties involved.

Rate Structure

A more subtle dimension of rate regulation involves the structure of prices. That is, the rate a firm charges for its service may vary according to the time of day or the identity of the buyer of the product. This has been the case, for example, with local telephone and electric services. One of the most difficult aspects of running a local public utility is what economists call the **peak load problem,** which means that the firm must have the capacity to serve customers who often bunch their demand at a certain time of the day. This can force the firm to have a large amount of equipment, which it only uses for a small fraction of the total day. In particular, much of the machinery needed to produce electricity at 2:00 P.M. will lie idle at 2:00 A.M. Still, the local public utility has to install equipment to meet the peak demand period of the day. This uneven usage of productive capacity is expensive and economically inefficient. To try to alleviate it somewhat firms often charge prices based on the time of the day that customers use the service, which is known as **time-of-day pricing.**

An economically efficient way to deal with the peak load problem is for the firm to charge lower prices in off-peak hours of the day. This encourages consumers to move their usage of electricity or other services to evening or night from the daytime. Another issue in rate regulation, then, is whether the commission will allow the utility to charge by the time of day. For example, telephone and electric companies often charge a higher price during peak times. In particular, long-distance phone calls have historically cost callers more during so-called business hours than during the evening or late at night. Many local electric companies charge households higher prices for their daytime than their nighttime electric use. Sometimes electric companies are permitted to restrict the amount of electricity they send to your house during periods of especially high demand if they give you a lower overall electricity price. In these ways, the quantity of electric and telephone services are "smoothed out," and the economic inefficiencies that go with idle equipment are reduced.

Of course, if a public utility has the ability to charge differential prices it may also price discriminate in ways discussed in chapter 8. Specifically, it is common for a telephone company to charge business firms, who may have a relatively low elasticity of demand for phone services, a higher price than it charges residential homes for the same service. In the past, it was not uncommon for electric companies to charge a relatively high price for the first "block" of electricity and then lower the rate the more electricity the customer used. The logic behind this is that there are few or no substitutes for basic electricity uses such as lighting. However, heat could come from gas, wood, or oil. Thus, the price of additional electricity had to be lower to prevent such across-energy substitutions.

Is the price discrimination we have just identified good or bad for society? Clearly, there is no scientific answer to this question. However, the winners and losers from price discrimination are relatively easy to identify. A firm's stockholders will receive higher profits if the firm can increase its total revenue (for a given level of output) by price discrimination. Compared to a situation of no price discrimination, those customers who pay higher prices are worse off and those who pay lower prices are better off. One tricky dimension of price discrimination is that it is possible that a monopoly can cover its total costs only if it price discriminates. In this case, the service will not be provided at all unless differential prices can be charged. In such situations, the public utilities commission will have to take into account not only the equity issues surrounding rate structure but also the need of the firm to charge prices that vary by time of day or identity of the consumer in order to provide the service at all.

Summary of the Evidence

Douglas Greer has surveyed the economic literature on the impact of rate regulation on prices and concludes that prices have been 6 to 10 percent lower for electric power and local telephone service as the result of rate regulation.[12] He has also considered the issue that rate regulation can actually cost consumers money by making potentially competitive industries noncompetitive. It has been estimated that in recent years rate regulation cost the customers of the railroad, trucking, and water transportation industries $4 billion to $9 billion per year by actually increasing the prices in those industries above competitive levels. More dramatically, rate regulation of airfares tended to inflate them as much as 25 percent during the early 1970s. This meant that consumers paid $1.4 to $1.8 billion dollars more per year for air travel than they would have if air travel had been unregulated.

Rate Regulation in Potentially Competitive Industries

A key policy issue is whether rate regulation has been applied in an "economically proper" way. While there is a cost to consumers of not regulating a technical monopoly, there is also a cost to consumers of economically inappropriate regulation. By this we mean that consumers may be made worse off if industries that could be competitive are subjected to regulation as though they were technical monopolies. In the latter case, the regulatory function could serve as a way to fix prices above what the firms could charge if they were to remain unregulated. Regulation is a tricky business. Not only can one do damage by not taking the appropriate action to regulate prices, but one can also do damage by regulating where it is not needed.

The Interstate Commerce Commission (ICC) was the first federal organization to regulate prices and production. It was created to resolve growing controversies between railroads and shippers. In fact, many of the federal regulatory agencies developed to mediate disputes among several important economic groups. For example, the Federal Communications Commission (FCC) evolved to resolve disputes among users of the broadcast spectrum. Over time, regulatory agencies have grown to be independent quasi-judicial bodies that have developed their own set of administrative laws.[13]

Throughout this chapter we have been discussing the primary justification for rate regulation, the desire to force a technical monopoly to earn minimal profits. Most of the industries that have been affected by federal economic regulation, however, do not fit the description of a technical monopoly. It is difficult to make the case, for example, that air transportation, banking, energy, and interstate trucking are technical monopolies. What, then, is the logic behind regulating prices and production levels in potentially competitive industries?

One argument has been that firms sometimes go out of business and this inconveniences their former customers. Thus, the argument goes, rate regulation is needed to prevent such inconvenience. This strikes us as a somewhat odd argument for rate regulation. After all, the reason competition leads to economic efficiency is that firms exit (or enter) an industry on the basis of the presence of economic losses (or profits). We, as a society, pay for such economic efficiency with the "confusion" that accompanies the necessary reordering of the number and location of producers.

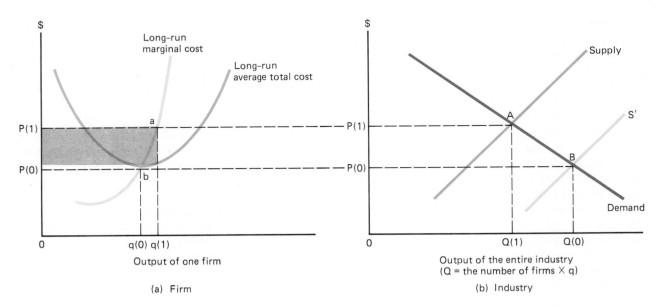

(a) Firm

(b) Industry

Figure 11.3   Regulation in a potentially competitive industry
In the typical competitive industry, if price is above minimum average total cost, say, at P(1), individual firms are making economic (excess) profits. This causes new firms to enter the industry, which shifts the industry supply curve to the right (increases it). Firms continue to enter and increase market supply until economic profits are eliminated. This occurs at market supply curve S′ and price P(0). This process would be reversed, of course, if price had initially been below P(0). Economic regulation of such a potentially competitive industry has tended to eliminate such fluctuations in price and production by setting price floors so that price cannot fall to P(0) and by limiting entry so that total output cannot rise to Q(0).

Another version of the argument that competition inconveniences customers is related to the price fluctuations that accompany output fluctuations in a competitive industry. Thus, it is claimed, the government needs to stabilize prices because it is bad for consumers, and of course producers, when prices fluctuate. These ideas can be seen more clearly in figure 11.3.

Suppose that, initially, the industry described in figure 11.3 is in equilibrium at point A. In this situation, the individual firms are each supplying q(1) units and earning excess, or economic, profits equal to the area of the shaded rectangle in part (a) of the figure. In the typical potentially competitive industry,

this situation would not last. Economic profits are a signal for new firms to enter the industry. Eventually, new firms will increase the industry supply to S′. At this point, excess profits will be eliminated, price will have been competed down to P(0), and each individual firm will be producing q(0) units. This is a long-run competitive equilibrium situation. Firms are still making normal profits because total revenue exactly equals long-run total cost, which includes the opportunity costs of all resources used in production. This process would be reversed had we begun in a situation where firms were confronting a price below P(0), so that economic losses were being made initially. In this case, firms would then leave the industry and eventually price would rise to P(0).

A useful way to view economic regulation of a potentially competitive industry is as an attempt to eliminate the fluctuations in price and production mentioned in the preceding paragraph. How is this achieved? Return to figure 11.3. Now suppose that price is initially P(1) and that not only is a price floor set at P(1) but that new firms are also prohibited from entering the industry. In this case, regulation makes price stay at P(1) and industry output stay at Q(1). Of course, such regulation also eliminates any "inconvenient" price and quantity fluctuations. We have just summarized how the typical regulatory agency tended to operate until recently. It set rates and decided whether to approve applications for new firms to enter the industry or for existing firms to expand.

▶ The Case for Deregulation

In this section we will probe more deeply into the issue that there are costs to society from enforcing economic regulation where it might not be appropriate. The feeling that economic regulation had been misapplied to potentially competitive industries led to a political movement for deregulation in the United States during the late 1970s. Specifically, laws were passed that either partially or totally deregulated the energy, transportation, communications, and financial services industries.[14] We must be careful to realize that even if full deregulation is socially desirable, as in the case of a competitive industry, this is a long-run situation. In other words, existing firms will suffer short-run economic losses. As a result, most deregulation efforts in the United States have been organized so that the deregulation is phased in over time. In terms of figure 11.3, the move to permit entry, and ultimately increase supply to S', also reduces the economic profits to the individual firms in the industry. (See the left-hand side of the diagram.) Recent deregulation efforts have been designed so that this will not take place suddenly but rather slowly, so that the

lost economic profits do not occur all at once. In particular, price restrictions and entry restrictions have been removed slowly rather than overnight.

Although limited space does not permit us to discuss in detail all of the industries in which deregulation has recently been attempted in the United States, we will provide a summary of some of the key issues surrounding deregulation in air travel. We will pay special attention to whether deregulation has worked the way we would expect from figure 11.3. Specifically, has deregulation actually increased the production of goods and services, lowered prices, and reduced the profitability of firms? Once we analyze whether deregulation has produced the anticipated economic results in the case of air travel, we will discuss recent attempts to set in motion forces to reregulate the airline industry.

Airline Deregulation

It is difficult to use the technical monopoly argument to justify the regulation of air travel. Labor and capital are quite mobile across airlines, and there is the potential for new airlines to develop when excess (economic) profits persist. Competition from other transportation modes serves to hold down airline prices. For example, cars, buses, and in some cases trains serve as alternative modes for travel. Airlines must take this into account when establishing availability and price of routes.

The Civil Aeronautics Board (CAB) was formed in 1938 and extensively regulated United States airlines until the late 1970s. Specifically, the CAB allocated interstate routes and controlled airfares on those routes. The regulation of this industry was so strict that basically no new major airlines were allowed to enter the interstate market between 1938 and the late 1970s.[15]

Figure 11.4   Courtesy Delta Air Lines, Inc.

Data suggest that these actions substantially inflated interstate airline fares. Perhaps the best way to see this is to compare the fares on certain *inter*state routes to those on unregulated *intra*state routes of equivalent length before deregulation. For example, in 1975 the cost of traveling from Chicago to Minneapolis was more than twice that of flying from Los Angeles to San Francisco, although the mileage is identical. As another example, the same ratio of prices held for the Las Vegas to Los Angeles route as for the Dallas to Houston route. The two routes are of equivalent distance, but the Dallas to Houston fare was less than half the Las Vegas to Los Angeles fare. Estimates are that in the period 1969–1974, CAB regulation inflated airfares paid by consumers by $1.4 to $1.8 billion dollars per year.[16]

In 1978, Congress passed the Airline Deregulation Act, which provided for gradual deregulation of domestic air travel. The act produced an eventual elimination of the fare and regulatory powers of the CAB, along with the ultimate disappearance of the agency itself in 1984.

Is there reason to believe that airline route and fare competition have increased significantly since these deregulation efforts? Crude evidence in favor of this hypothesis is contained in the advertisement in figure 11.4, where we see one-way fares as low as $29 in 1986. Let us be more scientific, however, and look at some data for the airline industry in the three years following deregulation, 1978–1981. (This allows us to eliminate any effects of the 1982–1983 recession. We also avoid confusing the effects of deregulation with any impact of the air traffic controllers strike that so greatly disrupted the airline industry during the early 1980s.) Based on the additional data we are about to present, the answer to our question at the beginning of this paragraph is clearly yes.

The number of airlines certified in the United States more than doubled, from thirty-six to eighty-six, during 1978–1981. The market share of local, intrastate, and new airlines increased by almost one half, to a total of 16 percent. Moreover, the percentage of domestic markets with four or more carriers grew from 13 percent to 73 percent in only three years. In April 1982, 77 percent of domestic coach traffic traveled on discount fares compared to 46 percent in April 1978. Finally, while operating expenses per available seat mile increased by 73 percent during 1976–1981 (in part because of rising oil prices), airline revenues per available seat mile rose by only 58 percent during the same period.[17]

These data give us reason to believe that airline deregulation has worked much as expected. Prices have declined, and service availability has improved in the major market areas. It is important to remember, however, that service has not improved everywhere and the airlines formerly protected by rate and entry regulation have lower profits and fewer employees. Newspaper accounts of the market for airline pilots suggest that new nonunion airlines formed during the period just following deregulation were able to attract fully qualified pilots at salaries ranging from one-third to one-half of those paid to pilots in established, formerly regulated airlines.[18] Still, it is important to keep in mind that the social benefits of deregulation should outweigh these losses. This means that it is possible for the winners from deregulation to compensate the workers and stockholders fully for any economic losses and still leave society as a whole better off. However, this transfer of the fruits of deregulation has not actually occurred to any great degree. The result has been numerous complaints and calls for reregulation by heads of well-established airlines and unions such as the Airline Pilots' Association.

▶ Summary and Conclusions

In this chapter we have explored the many ways in which government intervention in markets can in theory alleviate economic inefficiencies caused by elements of monopoly power. We have also seen some of the many ways in which regulation of markets can actually interfere with the forces of competition and reduce overall economic well-being. Here are some of the important points developed in this chapter.

In addition to causing consumers to pay higher prices, monopolies cause a deadweight loss of consumers' surplus. These are the key reasons for antitrust laws.

The government enforces antitrust laws suing the offending firm or firms in court for damages and a restructuring of their economic activities. Commonly, antitrust cases take a relatively long time to settle and are usually complex.

Rate regulation is another public policy toward firms. In this case, the government regulates the price and output policy of the producers in an industry.

In some cases, potentially competitive industries have also been subject to economic regulation that prevents new firms from entering the industry and fixed prices at a level that exceeds the typical firm's long-run minimum average total cost. Recent attempts at deregulation in such industries seek to reduce industry prices and profits and increase availability of services to consumers.

In every case of economic regulation there will be both winners and losers. When regulation prompts economic efficiency the winners could compensate losers and still remain better off. However, such compensation is seldom assured.

▶ Key Terms

antitrust laws *225*

deadweight loss of
  monopoly *226*

peak load problem *232*

rate regulation *229*

time-of-day pricing
  232

▶ Questions for Discussion and Review

1. Antitrust laws exist to remove monopoly power because it is considered bad for society. This conclusion is based on the premise that the output of the monopolist is something that is "good" for society. Consider the following situation: The output of a particular firm is something that is considered bad for society, such as the production of heroin or some other addictive and debilitating substance. In this case, should the argument be reversed concerning antitrust laws? In particular, should the government have protrust laws? In other words, should the government prevent competition so that heroin or services such as prostitution are produced by a monopoly firm like the Mafia? Justify your answer.

2. Read Robert E. Taylor, "Congress Is Moving to Protect Localities from Costly Antitrust Suits by Business," *Wall Street Journal,* 13 Sept. 1984, p. 31. Write a one-page essay describing whether such suits are simply private sector antitrust policy against local governments.

Specifically, are the cases discussed in the article examples in which a government has "victimized" consumers by being a monopoly and the private sector has tried to function in the same way that the government has? Use a graph in your discussion.

3. Consider a competitive industry with a linear demand curve and a monopoly industry with the same demand curve. Suppose production costs are zero. That is, both industries receive all of their inputs free from the government so that it essentially costs them nothing to produce their output. In this case, will antitrust laws still be needed? Analyze graphically.

4. Show graphically that if a monopolist is maximizing its profit, then it is producing an output at which the demand for its product or service is elastic (the price elasticity of demand has an absolute value that exceeds 1.0). If we observe a monopoly producing a product for which the estimated demand schedule is inelastic, can we then conclude that the monopolist is not maximizing its profits?

5. Show that if the demand for the output of a monopoly increases, the monopoly may actually lower its price along with producing more output. Does this mean that if the demand for a monopolist's good or service increases substantially, the socially detrimental effects of monopoly disappear? Analyze graphically.

6. Consider a monopoly industry and an otherwise identical competitive industry. Both have identical linear demand curves and identical horizontal marginal (equal to average) cost schedules. Show that the deadweight loss due to monopoly is equal to ½[P(Monopoly) − P(Competitive)] × [Q(Competitive) − Q(monopoly)]. Support your answer graphically. One problem with this formula is that an industry will either be competitive or monopolistic. We will typically never observe an industry change from being competitive to monopolistic so that the deadweight loss can be calculated in this fashion. See if you can express this formula for the monopolist's deadweight loss in a way that uses only observable economic concepts. In other words, see if you can reexpress this equation in a way that uses only phenomena that we would observe for a monopolist currently in business and from which we could infer the deadweight loss that this monopoly is creating.

7. Suppose that instead of having antitrust laws, we simply levy large taxes on a monopoly, making its marginal and average total costs increase substantially. Does this eliminate the deadweight loss of monopoly? Support your answer graphically.

8. In this chapter we saw that the typical public policy toward a technical monopoly is rate regulation. Under rate regulation the technical monopolist is typically required to charge a price equal to its average cost of production and produce the associated output level (where demand crosses average cost). Why have antitrust laws at all? Why not simply require all monopolies, technical or otherwise, to produce where price equals marginal cost? Discuss the practicality of such a policy compared to existing antitrust enforcement.

9. Suppose that a potentially competitive industry that has been subjected to economic regulation in the past becomes deregulated. What do we expect to happen to its output price, number of firms, and quantity of output supplied to consumers? If we do not observe output prices falling after deregulation, can we conclude that deregulation has not worked very well? Support your answer graphically.

10. Public utilities are regulated by state and local commissions that determine the fair rate of return on investment in plant and equipment for each firm. What effect might this regulation have on the quantity of plant and equipment each utility employs?

Drug Resales

▶ The Action-Initiating Event

You are an economic adviser to an important senator who is concerned about the high price of medical drugs. He asks you to find out whether there have been any recent attempts by the drug industry itself to lower the cost of medicinal drugs.

▶ The Issue

In the course of your research you discover a scheme known as drug diversion.[1] This is the situation in which one firm, such as a drug retailer, buys excess drugs from a firm that bought them from the manufacturer but did not use them. One estimate of drug diversion is that it has grown to a $600 million per year business involving more than 1,000 hospitals.[2]

An example of drug diversion is a major drugstore chain purchasing unused drugs from a hospital, medical clinic, or international relief group that overbought drugs. Because drug companies frequently give discounts to hospitals, medical clinics, and international relief groups, it may prove cheaper for a drugstore chain to purchase medicinal drugs from these organizations rather than from the manufacturer itself. You explain the issue of drug diversion to the senator, who then asks you for advice on whether Congress should encourage or discourage drug diversion.

▶ Economic Policy Issues

On the one hand, you can see some clear economic benefits to the consumer from drug diversion. In particular, if drugstores can purchase medicinal drugs more cheaply, some of these savings can be passed on to consumers. Moreover, if hospitals do indeed have excess drugs, isn't it better to get them to consumers as opposed to storing them until they lose their effectiveness and have to be destroyed?

On the other hand, there are some potential problems with drug diversion. One difficulty is that the drugs may be counterfeit because the manufacturer is not the source of supply. It is also possible that the hospitals have not taken good care of the drugs they store, so the drugstore chains are purchasing less than completely effective drugs. These issues seem to suggest a conflict. Certain parts of the drug industry (the drugstore chains) are attempting to lower their costs, while the drug manufacturers would like to maintain their profits; finally, consumers would like to be sure that the drugs they purchase are of high quality.

In writing a memo to the senator on drug diversion you will need to address the following questions. Why do drug manufacturers sell at lower prices to certain customers such as hospitals? Who are the economic winners and losers from drug diversion? If Congress were to outlaw drug diversion, what should hospitals and other organizations do with excess drugs? Is it feasible to have drug diversion without low-quality or counterfeit drugs reaching the drugstore chains?

The senator wants to understand the various implications of drug diversion before his next press conference. While he would like to favor policy to lower consumers' expenditures on medicinal drugs, he is also concerned about drug quality and wants to be fair to the drug manufacturers.

References

1. Walt Bogdanich and Hank Gilman, "Gray Market, Sale of Drugs Bought from Hospitals Raises Worries about Safety," *Wall Street Journal*, 6 Aug. 1985.
2. Ibid.

Part IV

The Market for Inputs

Chapter 12

Introduction to the Markets for Labor and Other Inputs

Outline

I. Introduction *246*
II. Factor markets and the distribution of income *246*
III. The demand for inputs, using labor as an example *247*
   A. Profit-maximizing output and input for a competitive firm *247*
   B. The production function and the marginal product of a factor of production *249*
   C. The value of labor's marginal product *251*
      1. The cost of hiring more labor *252*
   D. Events that shift the firm's demand curve: A change in product demand and a change in the amount of capital *253*
   E. The competitive industry's demand for labor and other inputs *255*
      1. The industry's demand for labor *256*
      2. The industry's demand for other inputs *256*
IV. The supply of labor and other inputs *257*
   A. The labor-leisure decision *257*
      1. The demand for leisure and the individual's supply of labor *257*
   B. Labor supply to the firm and industry *260*
V. The supply of capital services and other nonhuman inputs to firms and industries *262*
VI. Summary and conclusions *263*
VII. Key terms *263*
VIII. Questions for discussion and review *263*

Objectives

After reading this chapter, the student should be able to:

Use the concept of the value of the marginal product of labor to explain how a competitive firm's labor demand curve is derived.

Describe a competitive industry's demand for labor and other inputs and list the events that cause it to shift.

Explain what factors affect the economy's demand for labor and capital.

Describe the factors that affect an individual's labor supply decision.

Describe the labor supply curve faced by a typical firm or industry.

Describe the supply curve for capital services and other nonlabor inputs faced by a typical firm.

Human capital describes society's labor resources.

Physical capital consists of society's nonlabor resources.

The term capital is often used as a short expression for physical capital and for the services of physical capital used in production.

The term labor is frequently used to refer to the services of human capital used in production.

▶ Introduction

Here are some questions worth answering.

The United States today has about 3 million corporations and between 8 million and 9 million unemployed workers. Why doesn't each corporation simply hire a few more workers and eliminate unemployment?

During the early 1980s, Congress was very concerned about the large number of illegal aliens who crossed the southwestern border of the United States to work in jobs in Arizona, California, New Mexico, and Texas. One of the reasons for this was that Mexican nationals could obtain higher real incomes by working for American firms than by working for Mexican employers in their own country. How can it be that the same identical worker is worth more to an American firm than to a Mexican firm?

Finally, at some point reasonably soon you will look for your first job or consider switching to a new job from the one you have now. You will spend some time and effort trying to find the employer who will offer you the highest wage. Why do you think that one employer will be willing to pay more than another? You are the same person, yet you expect your labor to be more highly paid by one firm than another. Why might this be the case?

The questions we have raised can be answered after you learn more about the demand and supply of labor and other inputs that firms use in production.

▶ Factor Markets and the Distribution of Income

You may never have thought of it this way, but when we work for a living, we are using or selling to an employer the services of our capacity to work. The employer, in turn, uses these services to produce goods or services that it is hoped will yield a profit. Essentially, every individual and household in society receives its earned income from the sale of the services of two kinds of *assets,* which is another name for the ways in which we hold our wealth. Economists use the term **human capital,** or *human assets,* to define our capacity to produce goods and services with our labor. The term **physical capital** defines all nonhuman assets, such as buildings, equipment, improved land, and so on. Usually, when economists want to refer quickly to physical capital, they shorten the term to **capital,** *and when they want to quickly describe some aspect of human capital, they often use the term* **labor** for short. A more general term describing the services of human and nonhuman assets that are used to produce goods and services is **factors of production** or **productive factors.** When factors of production are sold to business firms, they yield the income which, in turn, permits households to purchase the goods and services they want.

Of course, many sales of productive factors are indirect. General Motors, for example, may purchase sheet steel from the United States Steel Corporation, which in turn purchases ore, ingots, coal, and equipment from other firms. All of these firms, however, have proprietors, shareholders, and/or creditors. The firms' income in excess of the cost of material is distributed to their workers (wages), to their creditors (interest), to their proprietors ("profits"), and to their

Factors of production, or productive factors, include the services of labor and capital.

Factor payments are the amounts firms spend to purchase the services of productive factors.

Derived demands for inputs are so called because they depend on the demand for the goods and services the inputs are used to produce.

A factor demand curve relates the quantity of the factor demanded to its price.

shareholders (dividends) as **factor payments.** Ultimately, all of the factor payments to for-profit business firms wind up as household income. Thus, in free market economies, if we are to fully understand the production and consumption process, we must learn about the markets for factors of production, in which the prices of productive factors are determined, along with the quantities traded.

In chapters 12 through 16, we will show how factor markets represent the other side of the coin of markets for goods and services and how they determine wages and other forms of income. Our general approach is applicable to the markets for all kinds of productive factors, but we will emphasize markets for labor. One reason for this emphasis is that wages and salaries constitute three-fourths or more of our total income in the United States and comparable amounts in other nations.

▶ The Demand for Inputs, Using Labor as an Example

A firm demands inputs because it requires them to produce output and earn a profit. Since a firm's demand for productive factors is *derived* from the market demand for whatever the firm produces, factor demands are called **derived demands.** If you quickly review the list of assumptions underlying the theory of supply in chapter 4, you will see that if the price of an input changes, the firm's supply curve will shift. The firm will produce more if, say, wage rates fall because it will increase its profit to do so. Obviously, if the firm is to produce more it will need more factors of production. The relationship between the quantity of each factor demanded and its price is the firm's **factor demand curve.** Factor demand curves are drawn,

just as other demand (and supply) curves, *holding constant* variables other than the factor's price. For example, the *ceteris paribus* assumption tells us that anything that changes the price a firm can charge or the demand for the good or service produced by an industry will shift all of the associated factor demand curves.

Profit-maximizing Output and Input for a Competitive Firm

To illustrate the mirror-image relationship between a firm's output and input decisions, we will examine the simple case in which the only input a firm needs to adjust when it changes its output is labor. A good example of this occurs during the Christmas season, when many stores hire temporary workers for the holidays. Other examples occur during recessions, when many firms temporarily lay off some employees, and during boom periods, when many workers put in overtime hours.

Figure 12.1 depicts a situation of equilibrium for a typical competitive firm and its industry. The equilibrium price is determined by industry supply and demand as shown in part (b) of figure 12.1. Since competitive firms are price takers, each firm takes the market price as given and adjusts its output accordingly to maximize profit. Remember that when a firm maximizes profit, it will produce the output level that assures marginal cost (MC) is equal to marginal revenue (MR). Since price is marginal revenue from the price-taking firm's point of view, the profit-maximizing output for each competitive firm occurs at the point where

$$MC = MR \equiv P.$$

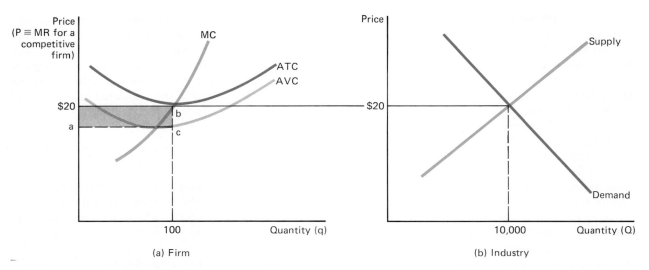

From Belton M. Fleisher/Thomas J. Kniesner, *LABOR ECONOMICS: Theory, Evidence, and Policy*, 3rd ed., © 1984, pp. 47, 48, 57. Reprinted by permission of Prentice-Hall, Inc., Englewood Cliffs, New Jersey.

Figure 12.1   Equilibrium price and output in a competitive industry
In a competitive industry, each firm takes the industry price $20 as given and chooses its profit-maximizing output 100 so that MC = MR ≡ P.

The firm in part (a) of figure 12.1 has only one input—labor—accounting for its variable cost and marginal cost. Suppose that circumstances change so that the firm can now hire labor at a lower wage rate than before—say, $8 per hour instead of $10. If the average cost of a unit of output had been $20 and wages made up half of these costs, then the average cost of producing the profit-maximizing quantity shown in part (a) of figure 12.1 will now be only $18. This reduction in costs is reflected in the downward shift of the average and marginal cost curves (AVC and MC) shown in figure 12.2. As a result, the firm's profit-maximizing output grows from 100 to 125. But how is the firm to increase its output? The only way in the short run is to use more labor. Figure 12.3 depicts the firm's adjustment of its labor input when the wage rate falls from $10 to $8; the quantity of labor

demanded grows from 20 to 25. A decline in the wage rate results in a change in the firm's cost curves and a movement along its labor demand curve. The firm's labor demand curve slopes downward and to the right just like all of the other demand curves we have seen. To make sure you understand how a change in the price of an input affects both the quantity of the input used and the amount of output produced by a firm, show what would happen to the firm's cost curves and the amount of labor hired if the wage rate were to increase. In a slightly different context, think of a bakery producing bread. A good wheat harvest will lower the price of wheat, allowing the baker to purchase flour at a lower price. What will be the initial reaction of the baker regarding the amount of bread to bake and the amount of flour to purchase? What will happen to the the number of workers the baker wants to hire?

A production function defines the maximum output that can be obtained from all possible quantities of productive factors.

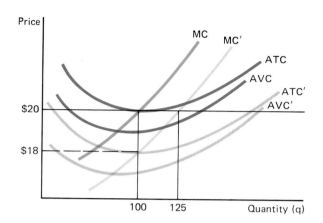

Figure 12.2   The firm's adjustment when a lower wage rate reduces its costs and the quantity of capital is fixed
When the wage rate declines, AVC and MC decline because labor is the input responsible for variable cost. Assuming that labor makes up half of total cost, a decline in the wage rate from $10 to $8 per hour will reduce the average cost of producing 100 units from $20 to $18.
From Belton M. Fleisher/Thomas J. Kniesner, *LABOR ECONOMICS: Theory, Evidence, & Policy,* 3rd ed., © 1984, pp. 47, 48, 57. Reprinted by permission of Prentice-Hall, Inc., Englewood Cliffs, New Jersey.

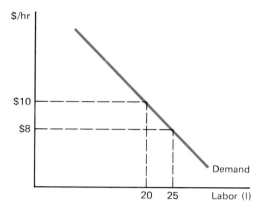

Figure 12.3   The firm's labor demand curve when the quantity of capital is fixed
When the wage rate declines, the firm uses more labor to produce increased output, leading to a downward-sloping labor demand curve.

The Production Function and the Marginal Product of a Factor of Production

At the heart of the firm's output decision and input demands is what economists call the **production function,** which is the technical relationship that shows how the firm's output is related to its use of inputs. A firm, such as an automobile maker, uses many inputs in its production process. Glass, steel, electricity, and the labor of various managerial and production workers are only a few of the inputs used in making a car. We can simplify the issue, however, by looking at the general relationship between a firm's output and its labor input, assuming that all of the other inputs used in the production process are unchanging. This is illustrated in figure 12.4. The curve illustrates how a typical firm's output varies with the labor it uses, measured as the total number of workers (l). The other inputs used in the production process are assumed to be unchanging when drawing figure 12.4 so that we can focus on the relationship between the quantity of output and the quantity of labor.

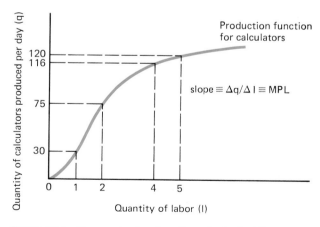

Figure 12.4   The production function of a typical firm
A firm's production function illustrates how its output increases by using more labor, assuming that other inputs do not change. The slope of the production function illustrates the marginal product of labor (mpl), which is the extra output produced by adding an additional unit of labor to the production process.

*The **marginal product of labor** (mpl) is the additional output obtained (or foregone) from using one more (or less) unit of labor with a given amount of capital. (The marginal product of capital is defined as the additional output obtained from using one more unit of capital with a given amount of labor.)*

A simple example will help to show how a firm decides how much labor to employ. Suppose you decide to enter the calculator business. Since you are just beginning, your firm does just one thing. It assembles pocket calculators, using parts—integrated circuits, keyboards, displays, and cases—purchased from other companies. When you set up your firm, you purchase the equipment you and your workers will need to assemble any number of calculators up to 500 per day. Obviously, the output of your calculator-assembly firm is zero before you hire any workers. You do not assemble any calculators if you do not hire any assemblers. The number of calculators your company assembles increases with the number of workers you hire. If you were to hire one worker, your firm's total output would be 30 calculators assembled per day. This quantity of output is not only your total output, it is also the *additional output* you have produced by hiring your first worker. Should you hire a second worker? Your decision will depend upon how much *additional output* in terms of the number of calculators per day he or she can assemble. In general, the *extra* output produced whenever another worker is added is called the **marginal product of labor (mpl).**

As we have done before, we will use the Greek letter *delta* (Δ) to indicate a change in a variable. Because mpl is defined as the *change* in output due to a *change* in the amount of labor used, we use the following expression:

$$\text{mpl} \equiv \Delta q / \Delta l.$$

In this expression for mpl, please note that we have used the symbol $\equiv$ (the identity symbol) rather than $=$ (the equality symbol). This is to remind you that mpl is *defined* to equal $\Delta q / \Delta l$ *in all places and at all times.* This is in contrast to an *equality* relationship in which two variables are equal to each other *only when certain conditions hold.*

Returning to our example, how much does output grow when you hire additional workers? When you hire the second employee, does the quantity of calculators assembled per day double? Hiring a second worker *could* actually *more* than double your calculator output, perhaps to something like 75 units per day. The reason is that with a second worker your employees can now be used more efficiently. Instead of one person's assembling all the parts to make one calculator, the two workers can specialize in performing a smaller set of tasks. This way, each worker becomes more efficient in assembling a part of a calculator than he or she would be in doing everything, which requires using a larger number of tools, starting and stopping to lay down and pick up different parts, and so on. At some point, however, the gains from additional worker specialization will taper off, and the marginal product of labor will start to diminish. You will reach the situation where additional workers increase the number of calculators assembled but *by progressively less and less.* By the time you hire a fifth worker, the *additional* number of calculators assembled drops to only 4 units per day (total output grows from 116 to 120). This decline in the marginal product of labor stems in part from the fact that you have only a certain amount of equipment for your workers to use. (Remember, this example of the marginal product of labor is *ceteris paribus.*)

While our example may be somewhat contrived for the purposes of demonstration, it is in general true. *At a given level of other inputs, additional labor is productive, but the marginal product of labor eventually diminishes.* Table 12.1 summarizes the data for this example. Think about the concept of the marginal product of labor as you look at these numbers. Then take a look at figure 12.5, which illustrates the two most important general concepts introduced thus far—a typical firm's marginal product of labor is positive and diminishing.

*The **value of the marginal product of labor (vmpl)** is the marginal product of labor multiplied by the price of the good or service the labor is used to produce.*

Table 12.1	The marginal product of labor in producing calculators	
Number of workers	**Total production of calculators per day**	**Marginal product of labor ($\Delta q/\Delta l$)**
0	0	—
		30 calculators
1	30	
		45
2	75	
		25
3	100	
		16
4	116	
		4
5	120	
		1
6	121	

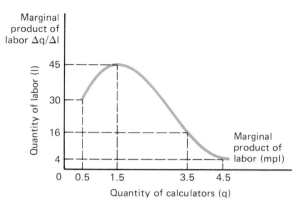

Figure 12.5   The marginal product of labor for a typical firm
The marginal product of labor ($\Delta q/\Delta l$), denotes the extra output (Δq) produced as the firm increases its labor input by one additional worker. The mpl for a typical firm is positive and diminishing—additional workers add to total output, but the increment shrinks as the firm's labor force grows, *cet. par.* From Belton M. Fleisher/Thomas J. Kniesner, *LABOR ECONOMICS: Theory, Evidence, & Policy,* 3rd ed., © 1984, pp. 47, 48, 57. Reprinted by permission of Prentice-Hall, Inc., Englewood Cliffs, New Jersey.

The marginal product of labor plays a crucial role in the basic economic decision that any firm makes—how much to produce and how much labor to use in the process. The most important thing to realize is that the amount of output a firm will produce and, therefore, the number of workers it wants to hire depends upon the profit it will receive from the sale of its product. A firm will find it profitable to hire more labor and produce more output as long as the additional labor and output increase its profit.

The Value of Labor's Marginal Product

In order to earn the most profit, a firm should increase its production as long as doing so increases its profit. We have seen that, *cet. par.*, it takes more labor to produce more output. Therefore, a firm will continue to hire additional labor as long as the additional output it produces can be sold for at least as much as it costs to hire the labor.

To see how this fact relates to the firm's demand for labor, we must remember that this is a competitive firm, and therefore it is a price taker. When a firm is a price taker, the additional revenue it realizes from hiring an extra worker is known as the **value of the marginal product of labor (vmpl).** Vmpl is simply the marginal product of labor times the price of the firm's output. Symbolically, the value of the marginal product of labor can be defined by the following expression:

$$vmpl \equiv P \times mpl \equiv P \times \Delta q/\Delta l,$$

where P is the market price of the product the firm sells.

Assuming that your calculator firm faces competition from many other calculator manufacturers, with a market price of $5 per calculator, the value of the first worker's marginal product in table 12.1 is $150 per day. At the price of $5 per calculator, the

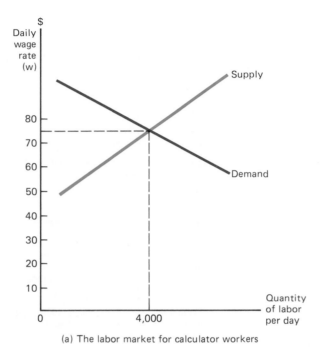

(a) The labor market for calculator workers

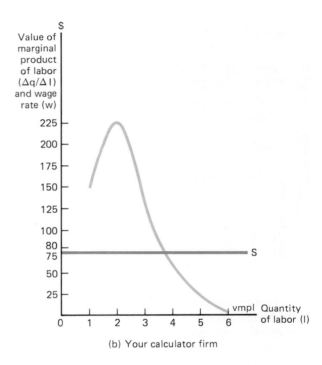

(b) Your calculator firm

Figure 12.6   The vmpl curve is also the firm's labor demand curve
Your calculator firm can hire all of the labor it wants at $75 per day. Calculators sell for $5 each. Therefore, hiring the fourth worker yields a value of marginal product of $80, which is $5 more than it costs to hire the third worker. Hiring a fifth worker, however, adds only $20 to revenue. Therefore, profit is maximized by hiring four workers.

value to the firm of adding, say, a fourth worker is $80. Notice that the value of labor's marginal product is positive but eventually shrinks because of the diminishing marginal product of labor.

Because a competitive (price-taking) firm's product price is a constant, vmpl has the same general shape as the the mpl curve in figure 12.5. The vmpl curve is illustrated in part (b) of figure 12.6. The curve showing the value of labor's marginal product tells a story similar to that told by the mpl curve. Additional units of labor have positive economic value to the firm, but that economic value eventually shrinks as the size of the firm's labor force grows.

The Cost of Hiring More Labor

Now that we understand the value to the firm of an additional worker, we need to consider the firm's *cost* of hiring more labor. This enables us to identify two important things: (1) the amount of labor the firm will choose, and (2) how the firm will respond if the wage rate changes.

In order to complete our analysis of the firm's demand for labor, we will assume that the firm is a price taker in the market for labor, just as it is in the market where it sells its output. This means that a typical firm has no direct effect on the wage rate it must offer. The wage a competitive firm must pay is determined in the labor market, where *all* of the buyers and sellers of labor interact. Figure 12.6, part (a), shows that in the calculator labor market, the supply and demand for workers intersect to determine an equilibrium daily rate of pay of $75. The horizontal line in part (b) of figure 12.6 illustrates that the firm may hire as much or as little labor as it wants at the going wage, which we will assume is $75 for an eight-hour day. The firm will keep hiring as long as additional units of labor more than pay for themselves. It will stop hiring when it notices that the *next* unit of labor will add more to total cost than to sales revenue. This is the point where profit is greatest. In part (b) of figure 12.6, the profit-maximizing quantity of labor is four workers. When the firm has a work force smaller than this amount, the value of additional labor exceeds the cost of additional labor. This reverses itself at four workers. The fifth worker costs $75 but adds only $20 to the firm's revenue. That is, the value of marginal product of the fifth worker is less than the wage rate, what the worker costs to hire.

As a general rule, the firm will earn the most profit by hiring workers up to the point that the value of labor's marginal product equals (or slightly exceeds) the wage rate. In our example, we have shown that the vmpl of the last worker hired is the same as the wage rate. The important point to recognize is that the firm *reduces* its profit by hiring an additional worker if the worker's vmpl is not *at least as great* as the wage rate the worker must be paid. Symbolically, we can express what the firm does when it earns the most profit it can as

vmpl = w,

where w represents the wage rate at which the firm can hire all the labor it wants. Notice that we have used the *equality* sign (=) in the above expression. This is because the value of the marginal product of labor is *not the same thing as* the wage rate. They are *equal* to each other when, and only when, the firm hires just that quantity of labor that leads to the largest profit. To repeat, we use the equal sign as a streamlined way of describing what the firm does when

it hires the profit-maximizing quantity of labor. Since workers come in "lumps" (a firm cannot usually hire a small fraction of a worker), the actual vmpl of the last worker hired may be slightly greater than his or her wage; it cannot be less if the firm is a profit maximizer.

A firm's labor demand curve traces out its profit-maximizing labor force at the various wage rates it might have to pay. Profit is highest when the wage rate of the last worker hired is no greater than the value of marginal product of labor. Therefore, the vmpl curve is also the firm's labor demand curve. It is downward sloping, just as the demand curves for goods and services are. It takes a lower wage for a firm to want to hire more workers because additional workers add progressively less and less to the value of the firm's total output, *cet. par.*

To reenforce your knowledge of why the value of labor's marginal product is also a firm's labor demand curve, look at part (b) of figure 12.6 once again and answer the following questions: How many workers would be hired if the wage rate fell to $15 per day? How many would be hired if the wage rate rose to $120 per day? Your answers should be five and three, respectively. If these were not your answers, review the concept of the value of labor's marginal product and how the firm chooses its work force.

Events that Shift the Firm's Demand Curve: A Change in Product Demand and a Change in the Amount of Capital

The labor demand curves depicted in figure 12.1 and part (b) of figure 12.6 are derived *holding constant all variables except the wage rate that affect the firm's employment and output decisions.* If any of these other variables change, the firm's labor demand curve will shift. In this section, we will discuss three important variables that affect the position of the firm's demand for labor: (1) the price of the good or service that the firm produces, (2) the quantity of capital the firm uses in production, and (3) the technology available to the firm.

Suppose that a change in industry demand leads to a higher price for the good or service sold by a firm. A look at figure 12.1 shows that the higher price will cause the firm to increase its output. In order to produce more, the firm must hire more labor. Therefore, an increase in the price of the good or service produced by a firm will cause it to demand more labor at any given wage rate. In other words, its labor demand curve will shift to the right. In figure 12.7, we illustrate the relationship between an increase in the price of output and the firm's demand curve for labor. Obviously, a *reduction* in the price of the good or service produced by the firm will lead to a *leftward shift* in vmpl and the labor demand curve. To make sure you understand how a change in the price of a firm's product affects its demand for inputs, suppose the price of calculators increases to $20 each. Redraw part (b) of figure 12.6 on a separate piece of paper and show what happens to the amount of labor employed by the firm.

A second variable that affects a firm's demand for labor is the amount of physical capital it uses in production. However, the impact of a change in the amount of capital on the demand curve for labor is a bit harder to pin down than the effect of a change in the price of the firm's product. The reason for this uncertainty is that the relationship between a change in the quantity of capital and the firm's demand for labor depends on the reason for the change in the quantity of capital. Suppose robots that can be used in automobile manufacturing suddenly become much lower in price and automobile manufacturers adopt them to perform certain tasks. Is this good news or bad news for automobile workers? Your initial response will probably be to say it is bad news, and labor unions act in ways that suggest they believe this is true. However, the answer is uncertain. On the one hand, it is true that more robots and fewer workers will be required to produce each automobile, and this *substitution* of capital for labor will lead to a *leftward* shift, or decline, in the firm's demand for labor.

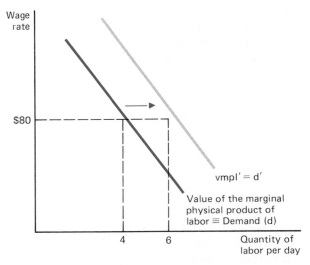

Figure 12.7   A shift in labor demand caused by a change in the price of the good or service produced by a firm
An increase in the price of the good or service produced by a firm will increase vmpl ≡ P × mpl ≡ P × Δq/Δl. This means that the labor demand curve will shift to the right. A decline in the price of the good or service produced will shift the labor demand curve to the left. When the labor demand curve shifts, the quantity of labor demanded at each wage rate changes in the same direction.

On the other hand, however, the automobile manufacturers decided to use more robots because they are now cheaper, and this means that the cost of producing automobiles has fallen and more automobiles will be produced. Thus, this *scale* effect will work in the opposite direction of the substitution effect described earlier, tending to shift the firm's labor demand curve to the right. In the end, whether the labor demand curve shifts right or left depends on the relative importance of the firm's substitution of capital for labor and the firm's need for more labor to increase production.

A change in the price of capital is only one reason why a firm's use of capital might change. The amount of capital a firm uses might also change because of a change in the wage paid to labor. Going back to figure 12.6, we see that in response to a change in the wage rate, the firm will change the quantity of labor demanded in the opposite direction. However, this is not the end of the story as far as the firm's input decisions are concerned. If the firm expects the change in the wage rate to persist for a long time, the firm will probably begin to think of changing its method of production. For example, an increase in the wage rate that is expected to persist will lead the firm to explore ways in which it can substitute capital for labor in order to keep its costs as low as possible in the long run. An increase in the wage rate you must pay workers to assemble calculators might induce you, for instance, to adopt robots for some tasks associated with assembling calculators if their price has not changed. As another example, substantial increases in the wage rates of farm workers led to the development and use of tomato-picking machinery and even new varieties of tomatoes better adapted to mechanical harvesting.

When such long-run adjustments occur, a firm's labor demand curve will shift to the left. In other words, the decline in the amount of labor demanded when the wage rate rises will be even larger if the firm adjusts its use of capital, too. If the wage rate should *decline,* a firm will eventually find that it is cheaper to produce its output using less capital and more labor per unit of output. This means that the quantity of labor demanded at each wage rate will increase; that is, the labor demand curve will shift to the right.

To summarize, when a firm adjusts the quantity of capital as a result of a change in the wage rate perceived to be a long-run change, the labor demand curve will eventually shift to the left when the wage rate has risen and to the right when the wage rate has fallen. Both of these shifts *increase* the *change* in the quantity of labor demanded because of a wage rate change. Simply put, the long-run demand for labor will be more elastic than the short-run demand for labor.

This brings us to a third variable influencing the firm's demand curve for labor—technology. In discussing the concept of the value of the marginal product of labor and the fact that it also serves as the firm's labor demand curve, we are holding constant the level of the firm's other inputs, including machinery and energy (such as electricity). We are also holding constant the firm's technology. One key reason why workers are better off today than they were fifty or one hundred years ago is that technology has not in fact been constant. In other words, a typical firm's *production function* is not the same today as it was in the past.

Suppose, for example, that your calculator firm discovers a new technology for assembling computers, such as a laser soldering gun that makes installation of integrated circuits quicker and easier. The firm can profit by using this new technology because it will lower its costs. Calculator assemblers will become more productive because a given number of them can now assemble more calculators in a day than before. The change in technology we are describing also means that the marginal product of labor shifts rightward and upward because there is more additional output per extra unit of labor. The result of an improvement in labor productivity is to increase the value of labor's marginal product and the number of workers a firm will hire at any given wage. Will a firm be able to sell all the additional output it produces if every other firm also benefits from the same increase in technology?

The Competitive Industry's Demand for Labor and Other Inputs

In this section we will explore two issues: (1) What does the demand curve for labor of a competitive *industry* look like, and (2) can we apply knowledge of the demand for labor to the demand for other inputs, in particular the services of capital? Both of these questions are relatively easy to answer.

The Industry's Demand for Labor

The industry's demand for labor is downward sloping and looks very much like the labor demand curve of a typical firm. Of course, the quantity of labor demanded by the industry represents the sum of the amount each firm in the industry demands. Many interesting and important questions about labor markets can be answered with information about an industry's labor demand curve. We will discuss some of these questions in chapter 13.

One of the most important features of an industry's labor demand curve is its *elasticity*. The elasticity of an industry's labor demand curve is exactly the same concept as the elasticity of demand for any good or service. It measures the percentage change in the quantity of labor demanded per percentage change in the wage rate. When a labor demand curve is highly elastic, a small increase in the wage rate will lead to a relatively large increase in the quantity of labor demanded. What determines whether an industry's labor demand curve is relatively elastic or relatively inelastic? Economists have focused on several determinants of the elasticity of demand for labor and other inputs. We will list three of them here. These three determinants of the elasticity of demand for labor and other inputs are called Marshall's rules, after the famous economist Alfred Marshall, who first formulated them.

1. The elasticity of demand for labor or any other input is larger, the larger is the elasticity of demand for the output produced by the input. This reinforces our knowledge that the demand for labor and other inputs is a *derived* demand. That is, it depends on the demand for final output. For example, the elasticity of demand for labor in fast-food restaurants is relatively high. This is because consumers are relatively willing to substitute food eaten at home for food eaten in fast-food restaurants. By contrast, the elasticity of demand for labor in the food-processing industry is smaller than the elasticity of demand for labor in fast-food restaurants. People do not cut back much on their food consumption when the price of food increases.

2. The elasticity of demand for labor will be higher, the easier it is to substitute other inputs for labor in production. For example, it has proven relatively easy to substitute machinery for labor in textile manufacturing. As wages have risen generally, textile mills have become very highly automated.

3. It is also usually true that the elasticity of demand for labor or any other input is greater, the greater is the share of the cost of the input in total production cost. For example, electricians do not make up a very large part of the total cost of building a skyscraper. Therefore, an increase in electricians' wages will not drive up the total cost of high-rise buildings very much, and the number of skyscrapers built will consequently not depend to a great extent on electricians' wage rates. Therefore, an increase in electricians' wage rates will not have as proportionately great an impact on the quantity of their labor demanded as, say, an equal proportionate increase in the wage rate of barbers and hairdressers, whose wages make up a large share of the total cost of hair care services, will have on the quantity of *their* labor demanded.

The Industry's Demand for Other Inputs

The answer to the second question we asked on page 255 is quite simple. The theory of the demand for labor *does* tell us all we need to know about the demand for other inputs as well. In our calculator firm example, we could just as well have calculated the marginal product curve for electronic testing equipment, holding constant the quantity of labor employed. If we had done so, we would have derived the firm's demand curve for the services of this type of physical capital. In general, a firm's demand curve for the services of capital is the value of marginal product curve for capital. The industry's demand curve is related to that of a typical firm in the same way as the industry labor demand and firm labor demand curves are related. To summarize, everything we have learned about the demand for labor carries over to the demand for other inputs.

Nonmarket activities are the production of goods and services at home that are not sold for a price on a market.

Nonlabor income is income someone receives that is independent of the amount that person works.

▶ The Supply of Labor and Other Inputs

In the first part of this chapter, we explored the demand for the *services* of labor and capital. We now examine the supply side of factor markets. We have emphasized the word *services* because clear thinking about factor markets requires that we clearly distinguish between the *services* of labor and capital—an hour of labor or the use of a machine for a fixed period of time—from the objects, or assets, that provide these services. Individual human beings (human assets) provide labor services, and physical assets—farms, mines, machines, computers, and buildings, to name a few—provide capital services.

The supply of productive factors has two dimensions: (1) the decisions to supply labor or capital services from a fixed population of human beings and a fixed stock of physical capital, and (2) decisions that affect the size and the skill level of the human population and the quantity and quality of physical capital. In this chapter we shall be concerned mainly with the first dimension of factor supplies. In chapter 14, longer-run decisions involving *investment* in capital assets and in improving the quality (skills) of the labor force will be analyzed in depth.

The Labor-Leisure Decision

In examining the supply of labor, we will proceed in a manner similar to our discussion of the demand for labor. First, we describe the decision an individual makes concerning how much labor to supply. Next, we relate this to the supply of labor to firms and industries.

The Demand for Leisure and the Individual's Supply of Labor

Whether or not someone desires a job in the labor market depends upon a number of things. One consideration is whether that person wants to spend all available time in **nonmarket activities,** which include going to school, cooking, shoveling snow, taking care of children, painting the house, fixing the car, and watching television. Thus, someone's decision to supply labor (seek a job) depends upon whether that person desires (demands) 100 percent of his or her time for nonmarket activities. In other words, the amount of labor an individual *supplies* is the mirror image of his or her *demand* for time to use in nonmarket activities. We will use the term *leisure* to encompass all of an individual's nonmarket activities even though there is much more to time spent outside the labor market than just recreation or having fun, as indicated by the examples just mentioned.

What determines individuals' demands for leisure? Three obvious candidates are (1) our tastes for the goods we can purchase with our earnings versus our tastes for spending time in leisure activities, (2) our income or spending power if we do not work for pay, and (3) our opportunity cost of not working for pay. The opportunity cost of leisure time is, of course, a person's wage rate, the amount that can be earned per hour of work. The wage rate is the opportunity cost of time spent in nonmarket activities because it is also the purchasing power an individual gives up by working one hour less for pay and taking one hour more to cut the grass, for example. As you should expect, an individual is more likely to desire a job and seek employment in the labor market the higher his or her wage rate, *cet. par.* At higher and higher wages the cost of not working increases (the benefit of working grows), and at some point the person receives an offer he or she cannot refuse.

A closer look at the individual's supply of labor or demand for leisure reveals a close similarity to the demand for ordinary goods and services, but there is an interesting difference between leisure demand and other demand curves we have seen. While everyone can change his or her income by working more or less, there is still a limit on the amount earned or spent. This limit is related to one's **nonlabor income,** which is income from sources other than a job, and the total amount of time available. Therefore, if we hold constant an individual's tastes for market goods versus leisure, the amount of time available, and nonlabor income, we can derive the demand curve for leisure time, which is the mirror image of the supply curve of market work.

Figure 12.8   Income-leisure possibilities for an individual
The individual represented in this diagram receives $100 per week income from sources other than working. The two upward-sloping lines show this person's possibilities for various combinations of weekly income and leisure. The steeper line represents an hourly wage rate of $6 per hour and the other an hourly wage rate of $5 per hour. One possibility for this person if the wage rate is $5 per hour is to work 50 hours per week (and enjoy 118 hours of leisure time), for wage income of $250 and total income of $350 per week. If the wage rate should increase to $6 per hour, this person could continue to work 50 hours per week and receive a total income of $400, or reduce the amount worked to only 41⅔ hours (increasing leisure time to 126⅓ hours) while still receiving a total income of $350 weekly.

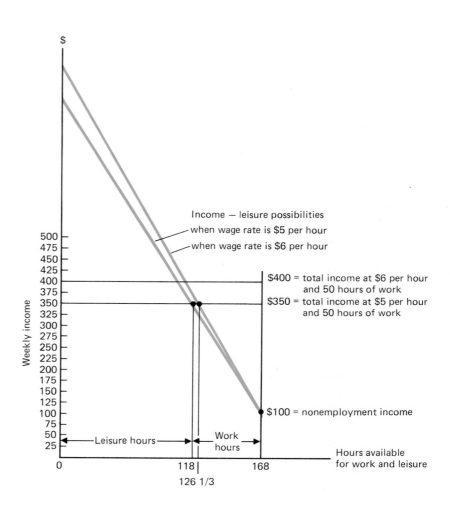

Figure 12.8 illustrates the choices between leisure and income an individual faces. We will use a week as our basic unit of time over which labor-leisure decisions are made. Each week contains 24 × 7 = 168 hours that must be allocated to either leisure activities or working for pay. Suppose someone with a wage rate of $5 per hour and nonemployment income of $100 per week has been working 50 hours per week and allocating 118 hours weekly to leisure activities. Then income, as we usually measure it, is 50 × $5 + $100 = $350 per week. What happens to the number of leisure hours demanded and to the

number of hours worked if the worker unexpectedly receives a raise to $6 per hour? Although the worker is clearly better off, the opportunity cost of an hour of leisure time has risen, too. These two forces have opposite effects on the labor-leisure decision.

On one hand, the increase in the opportunity cost of leisure time leads in the direction of working more. On the other hand, the worker can earn the same income as before by working only 41⅔ hours per week (8⅓ hours less). If the incentive to take advantage of the higher wage rate is more important to the individual than the desire to take it easier because more

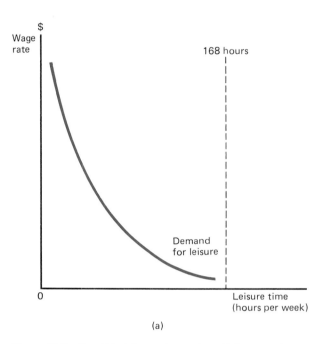

Figure 12.9   Possible leisure demand and labor supply curves for an individual
When the wage rate increases, the quantity of leisure demanded will rise and the quantity of labor supplied by an individual will fall if the income effect dominates the substitution effect.

income can be earned with the same or even less effort, then the individual's leisure demand curve will be downward sloping, as shown in part (a) of figure 12.9. The labor supply curve will be upward sloping, as shown in part (b). However, the possibility exists that these "normal" demand and supply conditions could be reversed by a strong income effect or preference for leisure time.

Although an increase in the wage rate may lead an individual to work either more hours or fewer hours, there is another important aspect of labor supply decisions. This involves the possibility of not working at all. How is the decision to enter the labor market affected by the wage one expects to earn? Here we are concerned with an either-or choice between two activities. The decision is not *how much* time to offer the labor market but whether to offer any at all.

If you think about it, this decision is similar to the choice between working for one firm or another firm. The decision will be based on the relative wage rates and working conditions offered by each firm. We can think of the household as a kind of "firm" where one "produces" child rearing, home-cooked meals, laundry services, and so on. If the rewards of working outside the household improve relative to the family's desire to have the services produced by, say, the mother in the home, there will be an incentive for her to enter the labor market. In other words, the **labor force participation** decision, which is the choice between home and market work, can only be affected in one way by a change in the wage rate. An increase in wages, *cet. par.,* will lead some individuals to enter the labor market, at least part-time. An increase in the wage rate will never cause someone who is already working to leave the labor market entirely.

Labor Supply to the Firm and Industry

We can now *aggregate* individuals' labor supply decisions and derive the labor supply curve faced by a firm and by the various groups of firms that make up industries. This is not very difficult. We have already discussed how an individual's labor force participation decision can be viewed similarly to the choice between working for one firm or another. If one firm pays a higher wage rate than others do and its working conditions (fringe benefits, working environment, safety, attitudes of supervisors toward employees, opportunities for advancement, and so on) are the same, workers will seek jobs there.

Suppose a firm wishes to expand its output and therefore the amount of labor it hires. If it wishes to do so quickly, it will probably have to offer a premium to hire workers away from jobs they already have. A wage increase may also attract some new workers to enter the labor force, seeking jobs with the best-paying firms. Over time, however, there are always some workers who leave their old jobs because they are unhappy or because they want to move from one neighborhood or one part of the country to another. There is a continuous flow of older workers leaving the labor force (going into retirement), young workers entering the labor force for the first time, and mothers reentering the labor market after their children reach a certain age. All of these workers will seek the best jobs they can find. Given a long enough period of time adjustment, the wage premium that an expanding firm must pay need not be very large. In other words, it is reasonable to assume that most firms are *price takers* in the labor market.

Being a price taker in the labor market means the same thing as in the product market, except that we are talking about a firm's *purchases* of an input instead of its *sales* of its product. A firm that is a price taker in the labor market faces a labor supply curve like that shown in figure 12.10. The infinitely elastic (horizontal) labor supply curve in figure 12.10 tells

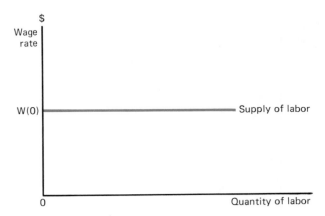

Figure 12.10 A firm's labor supply curve
Given a sufficient period of time, a typical firm is a price taker in the labor market, meaning that it can expand its employment without having to raise the wage rates it pays and that if it pays less than its competitors it will not be able to maintain its work force.

us that in the long run, a growing firm will not be forced to pay a higher wage rate than its rivals. At the going wage, w(0), the firm can eventually hire all of the labor it desires. A further implication is that if a firm pays a wage rate less than its competitors, it will find its labor force disappearing as its employees find jobs elsewhere.

A similar analysis applies to the labor supply curve for an industry. Unless the production process of an industry requires workers with very special talents, there is no reason, over the long term, why its firms should have to pay more than firms in other industries to attract workers of a given quality. What kind of special talents might make an exception to this rule? Suppose a construction boom in our major cities increases the demand for structural iron workers who work high above the ground helping build the steel frameworks of skyscrapers. This occupation is not

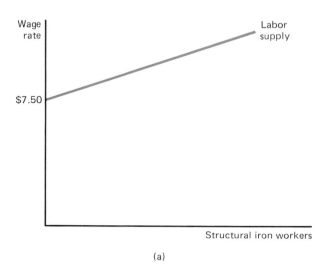

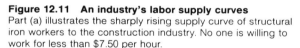

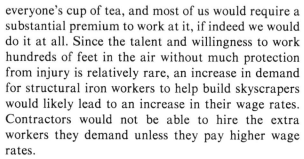

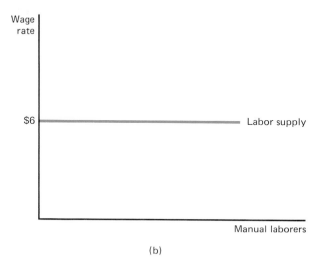

(a)

(b)

Figure 12.11 An industry's labor supply curves
Part (a) illustrates the sharply rising supply curve of structural iron workers to the construction industry. No one is willing to work for less than $7.50 per hour.

Part (b) illustrates the highly elastic supply of manual labor available to the construction industry. The industry can hire as many workers as desired at a wage rate of $6 per hour.

everyone's cup of tea, and most of us would require a substantial premium to work at it, if indeed we would do it at all. Since the talent and willingness to work hundreds of feet in the air without much protection from injury is relatively rare, an increase in demand for structural iron workers to help build skyscrapers would likely lead to an increase in their wage rates. Contractors would not be able to hire the extra workers they demand unless they pay higher wage rates.

When wage rates rise, some workers will be willing to give up their relatively safe jobs to accept employment working on skyscrapers. Those who already have jobs building skyscrapers will benefit from the wage increase. They will be paid more than is necessary to attract them to work on skyscrapers and will therefore be receiving *rent*. You may wish to review the discussions of economic rent in chapters 4 and 7.

For workers with special talents or training, the labor supply curve to an industry may well be upward sloping, even for adjustments that take place over a long period of time. But what about the labor supply of workers who perform less exotic tasks? Going back to our construction industry example, the demand for new skyscrapers will increase the derived demand for manual laborers in the building industry as well as for office personnel such as secretaries, accountants, purchasing agents, employment office staff, and so on. These blue-collar and white-collar jobs do not require highly specialized talents, and employees are likely to be hired from among those who have jobs in other industries and new labor force entrants and reentrants. In the long run, the supply curve for these workers is likely to be highly elastic. The two possibilities for an industry's labor supply curve are illustrated in figure 12.11.

The Supply of Capital Services and Other Nonhuman Inputs to Firms and Industries

Physical capital, like human capital, is owned by individuals (or households), who decide where and how much to offer to the market. In deciding where and how much to work, individuals are not only interested in obtaining the largest monetary return for their services. They are, of course, also concerned with their working environment—how it affects their health, the pleasantness or unpleasantness of the job, and so on. Even so, it is a reasonable assumption that the labor supply curves faced by most firms and industries are extremely elastic over the long term, as illustrated in figure 12.10 and part b of figure 12.11. The owners of physical capital presumably desire to reap the largest *monetary return* from their assets. Bearing in mind the *ceteris paribus* assumption, the services of physical capital should always find their way to the highest bidder.

What conditions are held constant when we say that the services of physical capital will be sold to the firms willing to pay the highest price? One key consideration is how well the firms maintain their physical capital. Firms that are careless about maintaining capital equipment in good working order will experience more wear and tear to their machines in production. Such firms will find that they have to repair or replace equipment more often. Even with constant machine prices, careless firms will have to spend more on capital per units of output than will the average firm. Holding constant the wear and tear on the physical capital it uses, any firm willing to pay the market price should be able to do so as a price taker. That is, the supply curve of physical capital facing individual firms is likely to be highly elastic. The same statement applies to an industry.

Let us return to our construction industry example. If contractors need more cranes, jackhammers, bulldozers, and other equipment to build more

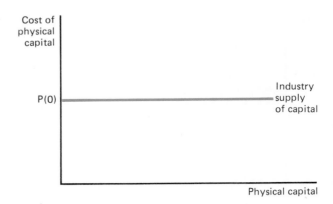

Figure 12.12   The supply of capital to firms and industries
As long as the firms producing physical capital are in constant-cost industries, the supply curves of physical capital to firms and industries are infinitely elastic (horizontal).

skyscrapers, we would expect them to face highly elastic supply curves for these items. Once again, we are speaking of a period of time that is sufficiently long so that the firms *supplying* capital goods have time to expand their production. If the industries that produce capital goods are constant-cost industries (as defined in chapter 7), then the supply curve of capital to firms and industries will be infinitely elastic, as illustrated in figure 12.12.

Figure 12.12 illustrates the relationship between the quantity of physical capital services supplied to an industry, measured along the horizontal axis, and the price of physical capital services measured on the vertical axis. The supply curve is horizontal, indicating that as the quantity supplied grows, the price will not rise. If the firms in the industry do not pay P(0), the market price, they will not be able to purchase these inputs. We have not provided a separate diagram for the firm and industry supply curves since they are both infinitely elastic (horizontal), as in figure 12.12.

▶ Summary and Conclusions

In this chapter we have examined the demand and supply sides of factor markets. The demand and supply conditions in factor markets determine not only the prices of inputs firms use but also the incomes earned by society's households and individuals. In answer to one of the questions asked at the beginning of this chapter, you should now understand that Mexican nationals are paid more by American firms than Mexican employers because their value of marginal product is higher in the United States. We shall see that government policies designed to alter the answer to the *for whom* question—the distribution of income—all affect and are affected by the markets for factors of production. The following main points were emphasized in this chapter.

Factors of production can be classified as either labor (human capital) or capital (physical capital).

A firm's profit-maximizing output decision also determines its cost-minimizing and profit-maximizing demand for inputs.

The derived demand for a factor is the value of marginal product curve for the factor.

Important causes of rising productivity of labor have been an increasing quantity of physical capital and improvements in technology.

An individual's supply of labor is the mirror image of the demand for leisure time.

Both labor and capital tend to flow to the firm and market that will pay the highest price, *cet. par.*

If no restraints impede the flow of labor and capital to firms willing to pay the highest price, firms are price takers in factor markets.

The supply curves of factors to industries are likely to be highly elastic when enough time is allowed for adjustments to changing factor prices to take place.

▶ Key Terms

capital *246*
derived demands *247*
factor demand curve *247*
factor payments *247*
factors of production, productive factors *247*
human capital *246*
labor *246*
labor force participation *259*
marginal product of labor (mpl) *250*
nonlabor income *257*
nonmarket activities *257*
physical capital *246*
production function *249*
value of the marginal product of labor (vmpl) *251*

▶ Questions for Discussion and Review

1. Explain the relationship between the law of increasing cost and the firm's demand for labor.

2. Illustrate and explain what effect each of the following situations would have on the firm's demand curve for labor.
   a. An increase in demand for the firm's product.
   b. A decrease in the marginal productivity of labor.
   c. A new, more efficient technology that substantially changes the production function of the firm.

3. If a firm's total revenue increases by $100 at the same time its labor force increases by one employee and its output increases by two units, what wage rate should the firm pay in order to maximize profits?

4. If an industry's demand curve for labor is relatively elastic, will a decrease in wage rates reduce total costs? Explain.

5. Determine the effect of each of the following situations on the elasticity of demand for labor.
   a. Exactly 85 percent of yearly budget expenditures by the local school board is for personnel compensation.
   b. The price elasticity of demand for electricity is 0.5.
   c. The elasticity of supply of automated car wash machines is 4.5.

6. Suppose that professional manicurists organize their ranks and agree to decrease their weekly labor supply by reducing the amount of hours they work. All of the manicurists believe that this strategy will increase their wages. Do you agree?

Tell whether the statements in questions 7 through 10 are true, false, or uncertain, and defend your answers.

7. The wage rate can be considered the opportunity cost of leisure activities.

8. An increase in the wage rate will cause a firm to reduce its profit-maximizing level of output.

9. A decline in the wage rate in the short run will force the average fixed cost curve to shift downward.

10. The greater affordability of office computers will result in a decrease in demand for bookkeepers.

Chapter 13

Factor Markets

Outline

I. Introduction *266*
II. The concept of a factor market *266*
   A. Is there a "market" for labor? *266*
III. Short-run equilibrium in a single competitive labor market *266*
   A. Review of the equilibrium concept *267*
   B. Shifts in supply and demand for labor *267*
IV. Equilibrium in interconnected competitive labor markets *268*
   A. Mobility among labor markets and the tendency for wage equality *268*
      1. Compensating wage differentials *269*
   B. Economic efficiency in markets for labor and other factors of production *270*
V. Noncompetitive influences in factor markets *271*
   A. Monopoly in the product market *272*
   B. Monopsony *272*
   C. Labor unions *275*
      1. What unions do *275*
         a. Collective bargaining and strikes *276*
         b. Influence on the supply and demand for labor *277*
      2. Unions and wages *278*
      3. Union membership *278*
VI. Summary and conclusions *280*
VII. Key terms *280*
VIII. Questions for discussion and review *280*

Objectives

After reading this chapter, the student should be able to:

Describe short-run equilibrium in a competitive labor market.

List causes of shifts in factor supply and demand curves.

Explain how mobility among labor markets tends to lead to wage equality.

List reasons for inequalities in wage rates.

Discuss the implications of economic efficiency in factor markets.

Describe the monopolist's demand for inputs.

Describe how a monopsonist determines the profit-maximizing wage rate and employment level.

Discuss the goals of labor unions and how they go about achieving them.

Discuss union membership in the United States from 1930 to the present and some of the reasons for its rise and decline.

▶ Introduction

A recent newspaper story told of repairmen who received twelve hours' pay for only ten minutes' work.[1] What happened? Were they holding a gun to their boss's head? Why would any employer be willing to pay one and a half days' wages for only one-sixth hour of work? Was there something special about those ten minutes?

The workers in the news story are known as "glow boys" because they clean and repair the insides of nuclear reactors. They work only ten minutes because at that point they have reached a dangerous level of exposure to radiation. These men know that they are increasing the risk of death from cancer as a result of radiation exposure. They also know that if they get cancer in the future they cannot sue the nuclear power plants. Then why do they do this work? The answer is that the pay is too good to pass up.

In this chapter we will see how a labor market establishes pay differentials for a given set of workers on the basis of the characteristics of their workplace and the components of the pay package, including fringe benefits. We will see that jobs that are more dangerous or have relatively low fringe benefits will have relatively high wage rates. Keep this in mind when you are looking for your next job. If you find an employer who seems to have an especially high rate of pay, think about other aspects of the work or the workplace that might be inferior to other jobs in the same industry. Be sure to ask yourself what you might be giving up in order to get a relatively high salary in comparison to salaries paid by other employers. For example, perhaps other employers have higher fringe benefits or a better medical plan, or perhaps they offer more potential for advancement as a way of offsetting a lower starting salary.

▶ The Concept of a Factor Market

We can now apply the analysis of chapter 12 to see how the supply and demand for productive factors interact to determine their prices and the quantities exchanged in factor markets. The markets for physical capital operate in a similar way to the markets for goods and services discusssed in chapters 2 through 11. Therefore, in this chapter we will focus on the operation of labor markets, with only brief reference to markets for nonhuman factors of production.

Is There a "Market" for Labor?

What does it mean to define a labor market? Labor isn't a commodity like wheat or iron ore. Nevertheless, the *services* of labor are exchanged for earnings every day. Since labor supply and demand interact to determine wages and employment, it is just as valid to talk about a labor market as a wheat market. Some labor markets actually come closer to the concept of a well-defined geographical location than do the markets for other inputs. For example, dockworkers are typically hired on a daily basis at a particular location in a seaport. Hiring halls are common for unskilled and semiskilled workers in construction and the building trades. By contrast, the markets for professional athletes involve nationwide and sometimes international networks of information regarding player talents and availability.

▶ Short-run Equilibrium in a Single Competitive Labor Market

To begin our analysis of factor markets, we will first see how supply and demand interact to determine employment and wages in a single labor market. We will analyze the case where there is only one type of labor and where the number of firms is fixed. This labor market, depicted in figure 13.1, is just one of many

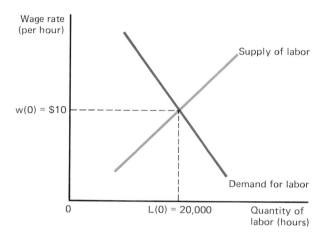

Figure 13.1   Equilibrium in a single competitive labor market
This intersection of labor demand and supply determines the equilibrium wage rate and level of employment.

labor markets in the economy. The short-run labor supply curve is upward sloping, indicating that it is necessary to increase wage rates, *ceteris paribus,* to induce workers to move into this market from elsewhere in the economy. Some individuals may enter the labor market as wages rise or leave the market as wages decline. The labor demand curve in this market is, of course, downward sloping. It represents the total hours of labor that employers seek to hire at each wage rate.

Review of the Equilibrium Concept

The labor market "clears" where supply and demand intersect, at the equilibrium wage rate w(0), $10 per hour in figure 13.1, and equilibrium quantity of employment L(0), 20,000 hours in figure 13.1. If the wage rate were higher than $10 per hour, there would be an excess supply of labor. Employers would notice the relatively plentiful quantity of workers, and ultimately the wage would fall toward $10 per hour. If

the wage rate were below $10 per hour, there would be an excess demand for labor (a shortage of labor). Employers, experiencing this shortage, would bid the wage rates up toward $10.[2]

It is important to recognize that *all* labor markets have *some* unemployment. Does this mean that excess supply is the rule in labor markets? The answer is no. *All* labor markets *always* have some people looking for work and some employers who have unfilled job vacancies. The scarcity of information about workers and jobs is a particularly important influence on labor market equilibrium. Therefore, there is an *equilibrium amount of unemployment and an equilibrium number of job vacancies* at the same time that both the wage rate and employment are at their equilibrium values.

Shifts in Supply and Demand for Labor

Shifts in supply and demand have the same qualitative effects in labor markets as in other markets. By this we mean events that increase demand increase equilibrium prices and quantities. Events that increase supply decrease equilibrium prices and increase equilibrium quantitites. Chapter 12 suggests a list of specific events that can shift labor demand curves. Events that may shift the supply curve to a labor market include the following:

An increase or decrease in the equilibrium wage rate in other labor markets.

A change in workers' nonlabor income.

A change in tastes or attitudes toward "leisure" time versus income.

The demand curve for labor may be shifted by any of the following events.

A change in the demand for final output will cause the derived demand for inputs to shift in the same direction.

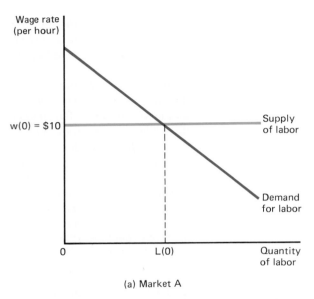
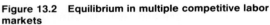
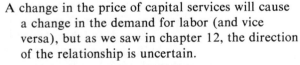

(a) Market A

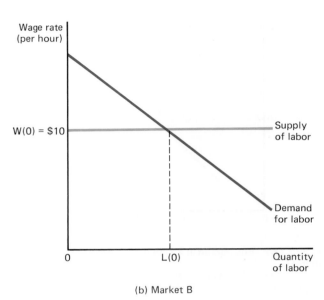

(b) Market B

Figure 13.2   Equilibrium in multiple competitive labor markets
When the same kind of labor is employed in more than one market, worker and firm mobility lead to wage equality.

A change in the price of capital services will cause a change in the demand for labor (and vice versa), but as we saw in chapter 12, the direction of the relationship is uncertain.

A change in technology that allows more output to be produced with a given quantity of factor inputs may cause the demand for labor (and other inputs) to shift either to the right or the left. Historical evidence suggests that technological progress has, on average, *increased* the demand for labor.

To summarize, increases in demand, holding the supply curve constant, result in rising wage rates and employment, while *rightward* shifts in labor supply, holding the demand curve constant, reduce wages and increase employment. This is, of course, familiar ground (see chapter 5). You should have no trouble in figuring out (1) the labor market effects of events that shift demand *and* supply in the *same* direction and (2) the labor market effects of events that increase one curve and decrease the other.

▶ Equilibrium in Interconnected Competitive Labor Markets

We will now examine equilibrium in interconnected labor markets when all employers and employees are price takers. You might think, for example, of the numerous metropolitan areas in the United States as constituting a set of interrelated labor markets. Figure 13.2 illustrates equilibrium in two labor markets that use the same type of workers. For example, markets A and B in figure 13.2 might represent two cities chosen at random.

Mobility among Labor Markets and the Tendency for Wage Equality

As we saw in chapter 12, the fact that workers attempt to find the highest paying jobs means that labor flows toward higher wage rate labor markets and away from lower ones in the long run. This labor mobility promotes wage equality among labor markets. In the short run, an increase in labor demand in one market

*Compensating wage differentials
are pay differences that offset
unequal working conditions in jobs
held by identical workers.*

results in increased wage rates in that market. However, in the long run, labor will move to firms that pay more. Figure 13.2 illustrates long-run multimarket equilibrium, which means that wage differentials between labor markets are eliminated for similar workers.

In the *long run,* a shift in labor demand in either market A or market B in figure 13.2 will cause the quantity of labor employed to change (in the same direction) but not the wage rate. To show this, we have drawn the labor supply curves for markets A and B as infinitely elastic (horizontal). The equilibrium wage rate, $w(0) = \$10$, will be the same in markets A and B, which employ identical kinds of workers. The wage $w(0)$ is determined in the *economy-wide* labor market by the interaction of the economy-wide demand and supply for labor. The infinitely elastic labor supply curves in figure 13.2 do not mean that employment can grow without limit in either market, however. What they indicate is that as long as every labor market employs only a fraction of the total labor force, we can treat each market's labor supply curve *as if* it were horizontal in the long run. This is just a way of illustrating the tendency of worker (and firm) mobility to promote wage equality across labor markets.

As you might expect, labor markets do not adjust instantaneously to eliminate wage differentials. We can, and do, observe regional wage disparities for a given occupation. The principal reason is that it is costly for a worker to quit a job and move to another part of the country (or another country altogether). Not only are there the direct costs of transportation, finding new housing, and so on, but other family members are also frequently involved. If two spouses are employed, the benefits from one spouse's move may be offset by the need for the other spouse to find a new job. Children may be unhappy to leave their old schoolmates, and parents must also face the problem of adjusting to a new social environment. There are reasons why the *short-run* labor supply curve for a labor market is likely to be upward sloping as in figure 13.1. Despite these forces mitigating against speedy labor market adjustments, wage equality does tend to emerge eventually.[3]

Compensating Wage Differentials

The analysis of supply and demand in connected competitive labor markets implies a long-run tendency toward wage equality for identical workers. However, we often see significant wage differences among workers who have similar schooling, training, and skills but who (a) live in different geographical areas, (b) are of different races or sex, or (c) have jobs in different industries or occupations. These wage differentials may be due to one or more of the following forces: (1) labor markets are not in long-run equilibrium; (2) labor market equilibrium is influenced by noncompetitive forces; and (3) the *ceteris paribus* assumption does not hold.

If labor or other markets do not approach equilibrium fast enough to make the theory of competitive markets a good predictor of prices and quantities, then this theory is not very helpful in understanding economic behavior. Therefore, we will look to the second and third factors in the preceding paragraph to find possible explanations of wage inequality for seemingly similar workers. Let us begin by examining more closely the "other factors" that need to be equal for wages to reach exact equality across connected competitive labor markets.

Our analysis predicts wage equality in competitive equilibrium only for identical workers. If workers are the same, what "other factors" are there that might explain different wage rates? The answer is that even if workers are identical, their *jobs* need not be. Various aspects of jobs and working conditions can certainly differ among employers who hire similar workers. When jobs differ in their fringe benefits and other favorable or unfavorable employment conditions, we tend to observe offsetting differences in wage rates, which are called **compensating wage differentials.** For example, other things equal, a worker in a job with an excellent employer-paid pension plan would expect to receive a lower hourly rate of pay as measured by his or her "cash" wage compared to someone without the benefit of such a pension plan. The same applies to employer-provided insurance, transportation, meals, and so on. In competitive equilibrium, it is the full cost of employing a given type of labor (including fringe benefits and workplace amenities) that is equated across employees.

There are less obvious differences among jobs that also account for much wage inequality. Some jobs require workers to be constantly alert. For example, air traffic controllers have little opportunity to relax or slow down the pace of work. In other jobs, it may be possible to arrive late to work some days and make up the lost time by performing tasks after hours or at home (teachers grading exams or computer programmers who can access their hardware via a telephone hookup). Some jobs have to be performed in dangerous or uncomfortable locations (mining or building construction work). For example, a welder might find employment in a reasonably comfortable factory located in or near a pleasant town; however, welding jobs also must be performed in building offshore oil rigs in the North Sea or on the Alaska pipeline. Why would a worker accept a job in a dangerous location or one where the climate is unpleasantly hot or cold when other jobs are available? The answer is to earn more money. Other things equal (including worker skills), we would expect unpleasant or dangerous jobs to pay more to compensate workers for taking them. This is the essence of the pay differential for "glow boys" discussed at the beginning of this chapter.

While there are many examples of workers who have been unknowingly harmed by workplace hazards, particularly in the chemical industries and in jobs associated with radioactive materials, there are others in which unusual risks or unpleasant working conditions are recognized and for which compensating wage differentials are paid. For example, occupations whose members are known to have an unusually high risk of death, such as "glow boys" or human cannonballs, pay more than average.[4] Employees of the oil firms operating in Alaska and on offshore drilling rigs earn substantially more than their counterparts in safer, more pleasant jobs.

Economic Efficiency in Markets for Labor and Other Factors of Production

In several earlier chapters we discussed the benefits of economic efficiency and the degree to which efficiency is achieved in markets for goods and services. In chapter 12 we saw how factor markets are tied directly to the production of goods and services. Therefore, economic efficiency in markets for goods and services also implies efficiency in factor markets. Let us see how.

Remember that when the allocation of resources is economically efficient, no one in society can be made better off without making someone else worse off. The key to understanding efficiency in factor markets is the relationship between the price of factor services and the factor's value of marginal product. When a firm maximizes profit, it must minimize its costs and produce a certain quantity of product. How much of each factor will be used when its costs are minimized and a profit-maximizing output level achieved? Each competitive (price-taking) firm will hire each factor of production that it uses up to the point where the price of each unit of a factor service equals the value of marginal product of that factor. With labor, for example, profit maximization implies that

$$w = vmpl$$

for every competitive firm. Thus, in long-run equilibrium, each factor's value of marginal product is the same in every factor market. The meaning of this equality for economic efficiency is illustrated in figure 13.3, using labor as an example.

The horizontal axes measure the quantity of labor hired in terms of days of service, and the vertical axes measure the value of marginal product and wages *per day* in markets A and B. The equilibrium wage rate is $80 for one eight-hour day. Consequently, in long-run equilibrium, the wage will tend to be $80 per day in each market employing this type of labor. This is also the value of marginal product of labor.

Employment in market A will equal 300 units of labor per day. In market B, 100 units will be hired. Let us see why this is economically efficient. Suppose

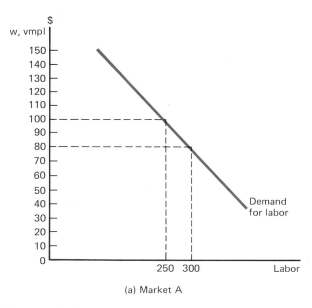

(a) Market A

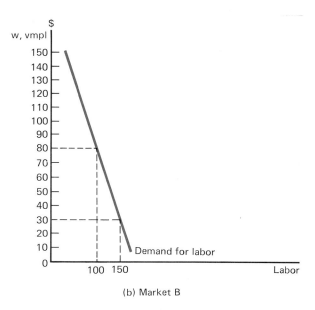

(b) Market B

Figure 13.3   Economic efficiency in factor markets
In long-run competitive equilibrium, the price of each factor of production and its value of marginal product are equal in every market. Therefore, a reallocation of factor services from one market to another cannot raise the value of society's output. This means that the allocation of productive factors is economically efficient.

that instead of these equilibrium quantities, employment in markets A and B were 250 and 150, respectively. An additional unit of labor would produce additional output worth $100 per day in market A, while removing a unit of labor from market B would result in a loss of output valued at only $30 per day. Transferring one unit of labor from market B to market A would result in a net $70 increase in the value of society's total output. This additional $70 worth of output could be used to make some people better off at no cost to any others. Thus, the allocation of labor is not economically efficient when employment is 250 in market A and 150 in market B. When the long-run equilibrium employment levels are reached in each market, no further reallocation of labor among markets would raise the total value of output because the output gain in one market would be lost in the other. As a result, employment of 300 days of labor in market A and 100 days of labor in market B would be economically efficient.

▶ **Noncompetitive Influences in Factor Markets**

So far we have assumed that firms are price takers in both product and factor markets. If a firm is not a price taker in the market for its product, it will in general produce less and therefore require fewer inputs. Firms that are price takers in product markets may not necessarily be price takers in one or more input markets, though. Workers may attempt to improve their economic position through collective bargaining with employers so that individual workers do not compete with one another for work opportunities. In the remainder of this chapter, we will examine each of these three noncompetitive conditions to see how each affects the equilibrium price of a productive factor and the quantity employed.

Monopoly in the Product Market

Since factor demands are *derived* demands, anything that affects the product market will also affect input markets. Suppose a firm that purchases inputs competitively is nevertheless a *product market* monopolist. In chapter 8 we saw that when a monopolist maximizes profit, it must do what a competitive firm does—minimize its costs and produce a level of output such that marginal cost equals marginal revenue. One basic difference between a monopoly and a competitive firm is the way in which marginal revenue is perceived. For competitive firms, which are price takers, marginal revenue is the market price of the good or service produced. Monopolists, however, do influence the prices at which products are sold. A monopolist faces a downward-sloping product demand curve. Thus, a monopolist's marginal revenue is generally *less* than the price it charges for its output. In the factor market, then, a monopolist will stop hiring when *marginal revenue product* (marginal revenue multiplied by marginal product) equals the price of a factor.

Because marginal revenue is less than product price, a profit-maximizing monopolist will produce *less* output and receive a higher price for it than an *otherwise identical* competitive industry. This means that a monopolist requires a *smaller* quantity of each input at any given factor price. Other things equal, monopolists will purchase less of each input than competitive industries. This is because they simply produce less.

However, recall that monopolists do not have the same pressure to minimize costs as competitive firms do. If monopolists decide to take some of their monopolistic profits in the form of not worrying too much about whether their costs are minimized, then they may use as much, or more, of each input as a competitive industry. The owners of a monopolistic firm may be happier with lots of employees or a large and fancy office building than with increased profits. This is especially true if the existence of large profits is likely to make the government take antitrust action. Moreover, the additional employees or office building will not be subject to income tax, as profits are.

Monopsony

The word **monopsony** means that a market has only one *buyer*, as contrasted with one *seller* in the case of monopoly. A monopsony can affect either a product market or an input market. However, the study of monopsony has concentrated almost exclusively on labor markets. At first this may seem surprising since most of us live in areas where there are numerous employers. However, a moment's thought will reveal the appeal of the monopsony concept. In the short run, we are all somewhat at the mercy of our employers. If your boss says you must work late this week or forget any bonus, you can quit, but the cost to you will probably be substantial. This means that, in the short run, many employers can reduce their employees' wages or take away fringe benefits without losing all of their workers. In other words, a firm may face an upward-sloping labor supply curve in the short run. This gives it some degree of *monopsony power* over its workers.

Monopsony power is not limited to labor markets. From time to time, we read that a major manufacturer in financial difficulty insists that its suppliers accept lower prices for the materials they supply. A giant firm in the automobile industry, for example, can force its suppliers to reduce prices, at least in the short run, because it takes time for materials suppliers to find alternative markets for their products. In the long run, if these suppliers are unable to cover all of their costs, they will go out of business; but in the short run, their major customer may act like a monopsonist.

We are more concerned here, however, with *long-run* monopsony power—a situation in which a firm has persistent control over what it pays its workers or suppliers of other inputs. The impact of monopsony on a labor market is illustrated in table 13.1 and figure 13.4. The conditions that describe cost and revenue when a monopsonist maximizes profit are the same as for monopolists and competitive firms: Marginal cost equals marginal revenue. The difference between monopsony and other market forms lies in the relationship between marginal cost and factor price.

Table 13.1   Labor supply and marginal labor cost for a monopsonist

Quantity (workers)	Labor supply Hourly wage rate	Total cost of labor (per hour)	Marginal cost of labor (per hour)
1	$5.00	$ 5	$ 5
2	5.50	11	6
3	6.00	18	7
4	6.50	26	8
5	7.00	35	9
6	7.50	45	10
7	8.00	56	11
8	8.50	68	12
9	9.00	81	13
10	9.50	95	14

In table 13.1, the monopsonist is, of course, the sole user of labor in the labor market. It recognizes that it faces an upward-sloping supply curve of labor. This means that if an additional worker is hired, the firm must raise the wage rate it pays *all* of its workers. As table 13.1 shows, the total cost of labor (per hour of work) is simply the hourly rate of pay multiplied by the number of employees. The *marginal* cost of labor, shown in the last column, is the *additional* cost per hour of labor that results when one more worker is hired. Both the labor supply schedule and the marginal cost of labor are illustrated in figure 13.4.

Suppose the monopsonist wishes to increase employment from five to six workers. The wage rate necessary to induce five workers to seek jobs is $7.00 per hour and the total hourly cost of labor is $35. However, if employment is to rise to six workers, the firm must pay $7.50 per hour to all of its workers. This implies a total hourly cost of labor of 6 × $7.50 = $45. Since $45 − $35 = $10, the marginal cost of hiring the sixth worker is $10 per hour, clearly greater than the wage rate of $7.50. The difference, $10 − $7.50 = $2.50, is simply the additional $0.50 per hour that each of the original five workers receives.

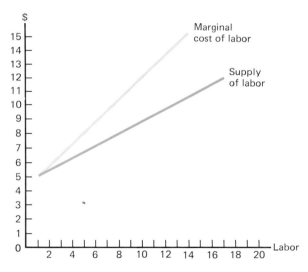

Figure 13.4   The labor supply and marginal labor cost curves of a monopsonist
When a monopsonist wishes to hire more labor, it is necessary to raise the wage rate offered. Since all workers receive the wage increase, the marginal cost of hiring an additional worker equals the wage rate plus the increased wages paid to all previously employed workers. Consequently, the marginal cost of labor is greater than the wage rate.

**Figure 13.5   Equilibrium wage and
employment when a firm is a
monopsonist**
When a monopsonist maximizes profit,
MCL = vmpl. This means that
employment will be less and the wage
rate lower than if employers were price
takers in the labor market. The
monopsony wage w(M) is less than the
competitive wage w(C) and the
monopsony employment L(M) is less
than competitive employment L(C).

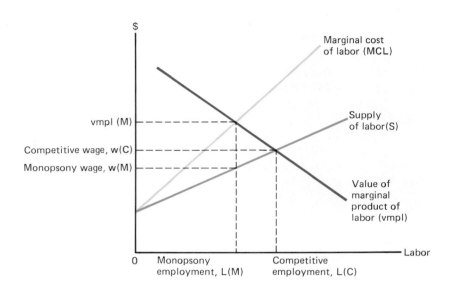

The curves representing the monopsonist's marginal cost of labor (MCL) and labor supply (S) are shown in figure 13.5, along with the monopsonist's value of marginal product of labor curve (vmpl). We assume that the monopsonist is a price taker in its product market. In other words, the vmpl curve corresponds to the demand for labor by a firm that is competitive in its market for output. Notice that the monopsonist's MCL curve intersects the vmpl curve *to the left* of where the labor supply curve crosses vmpl. If this firm were a price taker in the labor market, it would hire L(C) workers and pay a wage of w(C). However, the monopsonist maximizes profit where MCL = vmpl. This means hiring fewer workers, L(M) rather than L(C), and paying a lower wage rate, w(M) instead of w(C). Notice that by reducing employment, the monopsonist not only lowers the wage it must pay its workers, but it also pays a wage below vmpl. This gap between the wage it pays and the value of labor's marginal product results in a profit (or rent) for the monopsonist that is similar to

the profit (or rent) a product market monopolist receives. Compared to the situation in a competitive labor market, workers are worse off and the employer better off under monopsony. This brings us to a crucial issue.

How important is monopsony in United States labor markets? It is tempting at times to attribute many problems of low-income workers to exploitation by monopsonistic employers. A closer look, however, leads most labor economists to conclude that monopsony is not a major source of poverty or low incomes in the United States. The principal reason is that most workers live in areas where there are numerous employers. Thus any *persistent* tendency to pay workers less than they are worth (as measured by vmpl) results in workers shifting toward more rewarding jobs. Moreover, employers have an incentive to seek out pockets of low-cost labor that might be subject to monopsonistic exploitation. In other words, competition by new employers for low-cost labor can offset a tendency by existing employers to take advantage of any monopsony power.[5]

In modern market economies with relatively cheap communications and transportation between labor markets, monopsony is most likely to be found in markets where legal barriers to competition among employers exist. For example, at one time, organized athletic leagues were able to legally restrict competition among teams for star players. Such barriers are fewer today than they were earlier. Players in professional baseball and football leagues have engaged in strikes and other campaigns to reduce the market power of team owners.[6] Large government employers, including the federal government, may have some degree of monopsony power. They frequently employ such a large fraction of the labor force in a geographical area, for example in Washington, D.C., that they can reduce wage rates without losing many workers for a while. By the same token, if they wish to increase employment significantly, they must increase wage rates.[7] It is doubtful, however, that even large government employers can maintain their labor forces unless they pay a competitive wage in the long run.

Labor Unions

The most widely recognized noncompetitive element in factor markets occurs in labor markets where labor unions are present. In the remainder of this chapter, we will take a close look at unions—their goals, the methods they use to achieve them, their influence on wages and working conditions, and some causes of the ebb and flow of union membership in the United States economy.

What Unions Do

Unions are organizations of workers who elect leaders to represent them in bargaining with employers and who employ lobbyists to obtain legislation favorable to their cause. Most workers have the option of joining a union or not joining and, in the long run, seeking union or nonunion jobs. Joining a union is costly. It requires the payment of dues and initiation fees, and members may lose some freedom as to when and where they work (for instance, when there is a strike). As a result, a union must be successful in increasing its members' economic well-being in order to survive. Workers are interested in many aspects of their jobs, including employment security, paid vacations, sick leave, general working conditions, and so on. Unions seek to improve all of these for their members, as well as to obtain higher wage rates. Unions face a trade-off in attempting to achieve all of these goals. Higher wage rates may be obtained at the expense of fewer rest breaks, for example. In other words, they all have monetary equivalents. Therefore, we will use the hourly rate of pay as a simple measure of the degree to which unions may improve the economic well-being of their members.

Unions have several tools they can use to increase wage rates for their members. The best-known tools, of course, are collective bargaining and the strike. When most people are asked, "What wage goal does a union hope to achieve in collective bargaining," a frequent answer is "To obtain the highest possible wage rate." This simplistic view of a union's goal fails to consider that unions, like all other economic agents, are limited in their ability to achieve their ends. Unions are limited in terms of the gains they can obtain for their members by the *demand for labor*. A union's success in obtaining higher wages for its members is offset by employers' decisions to cut back on employment as labor costs increase.

A union's members will be happy to receive higher wages, but they will be angry when some of them lose their jobs. Moreover, workers who are unable to obtain union jobs will seek employment in nonunion firms. These firms, with lower labor costs, are likely to take business away from unionized firms, and this will make it more difficult for unions to increase wage rates in the future. Therefore, unions must always

Collective bargaining is the process by which a union represents the interests of its members as a group in negotiating pay and working conditions with an employer or group of employers.

A lockout is the employer's counterpart to a strike whereby workers are not allowed inside an establishment without a valid contract with a union.

consider the *disemployment effects* of wage increases in setting their goals. Reduced employment not only makes future collective bargaining successes more difficult but also leads to a smaller union. Since union members pay dues that support the salaries of union leaders, the leadership is likely to prefer a larger union to a smaller one.

Given the trade-off between higher wage rates for its members and jobs, a union will try to strike a balance between the two, and the elasticity of labor demand plays a crucial role in the long-run viability of a union. In general, unions will have a difficult time in industries or occupations where the demand for labor is relatively elastic because a wage increase leads to a relatively large loss of employment. Entire unions have been known to vanish—for example, the air traffic controllers' union in the early 1980s. On the other hand, certain public employees' unions, such as those representing police officers and fire fighters, have grown quite powerful because of a relatively inelastic demand for the services of the labor they represent. In chapter 12, we learned Marshall's rules, which identify three industry characteristics related to the elasticity of demand for labor. Think about how they help us understand union successes and failures by identifying situations where the demand for labor is inelastic or elastic. In the case of the air traffic controllers, demand was elastic because plenty of substitutes, such as military controllers, were available (the second rule discussed). A plentiful supply of trainees was also available. Thus, when the unionized controllers tried to strike for higher pay, they learned the hard way how very elastic the demand for their services was.

Collective Bargaining and Strikes   The most widely used procedure for obtaining higher wage rates is **collective bargaining,** which means that unions represent their members as a group in negotiating wages and working conditions. The reason that collective bargaining is a powerful tool for a union is that it poses a threat to employers: Either they sacrifice some profit for higher labor costs or face the prospect of sharply reduced revenues during a strike.

Strikes are also costly for unions. The most obvious cost is the lost earnings of its members. If the union has accumulated a strike fund, it may be used to pay strike benefits to offset members' lost earnings, but such funds are limited and generally run out if strikes persist. In some states, striking workers may be able to collect unemployment benefits for a number of weeks. This reduces the cost of a strike to unions. If a strike is long enough, a union also risks the possibility that employers will find nonunion workers to replace union members, leaving the union out in the cold. While former union members may be able to find jobs with their old employers if they are willing to do without their union representation, the union leaders will have nothing to do if they have no one to represent.

Employers need not be entirely passive in the collective bargaining process. Their strategy may occasionally involve calling a union's bluff by assuming a rigid bargaining stance and "forcing" a union to strike in order not to appear weak-willed. An employer can also initiate a work stoppage by refusing to let employees work if a contract has not been agreed to; this is called a **lockout.**

Work stoppages due to strikes and lockouts arise in great part from imperfect knowledge, in particular, how far each side can push the other in collective bargaining. In a relatively stable economic and political environment, unions and employers should learn each others' limits and behavior patterns. Strikes should therefore be relatively infrequent. In fact, although strikes and lockouts are events that receive considerable publicity in the news media when they occur, they are generally unimportant when measured against the total amount of work performed in the United States. For example, in 1983, only *0.08 percent* (eight ten-thousandths) of total estimated working time in the United States was lost in work stoppages of more than one day involving more than 1,000 workers. In the preceding decade, the average amount of time lost was less than 0.1 percent of total time worked.[8] These figures suggest that in most cases the perceptions of the parties involved in a labor negotiation are not all that far off.

Featherbedding refers to a practice, usually provided in a contract with a union, that forces an employer to pay for more labor than the employer would like to hire.

Influence on the Supply and Demand for Labor   We noted earlier that the labor demand curve is an important constraint that unions face in obtaining higher wage rates for their members. Suppose figure 13.1 represents a labor market without a union. Now suppose a union enters the scene and seeks to raise the wage rates of its members. When collective bargaining is the sole means of gaining a wage increase, the higher wage obtained will be greater than $w(0)$, the equilibrium wage in this market. The result will be an excess supply of labor. Some union members may lose their jobs. Others will be able to find only part-time work. Another possibility is a general reduction in work hours below the amount the union's members desire.

The union may avoid an excess supply of labor if at the same time that it bargains for a wage increase, it can take actions that move the labor supply curve to the left or move the labor demand curve to the right. Indeed, shifting labor supply to the left or labor demand to the right will raise the equilibrium wage rate without collective bargaining. This can be an alternative means of achieving the union's goal of raising the wages of its members. Thus, one of the things that unions do to improve their members' economic well-being is likely to involve trying to influence labor demand and supply in relevant labor markets.

What are some activities that affect labor supply and demand in favor of union members? One way to discover the answer is to examine the types of legislation supported by unions. Among them you will see that unions favor restrictions on immigration, which move labor supply curves to the left or at least slow down the speed with which they shift to the right.[9]

If we define what we mean by a labor union broadly enough to include all organizations that represent the economic interests of a group of workers, then union efforts to influence labor supply become even more important. The reason is that many professional and trade organizations, such as state and local bar associations in the legal profession, medical associations, beauticians' and hairdressers' groups, morticians' societies, and the like have as a principal goal maintaining or improving the economic status of their constituents. Since it is often impractical or unappealing for many "professionals" to engage in collective bargaining, they must resort to less obvious strategies to influence labor supply if they are to succeed.

Probably the most important means professional organizations use to influence the markets for their services is to obtain legislation prohibiting nonlicensed practitioners from competing for clients. Obtaining a license usually involves specialized training or schooling and passing one or more examinations. Thus, the supply of labor to an occupation can be limited by increasing the training or schooling required and by raising the minimum score needed to pass a licensing examination. These restrictions are usually advocated in the "public interest" rather than in terms of a desire to increase the fees that members of a trade can charge. For example, protection from quack doctors, incompetent lawyers, or beauticians who damage their clients' hair is touted. However, the requirement that practitioners be licensed goes much farther than requiring that information about their qualifications and background be freely available.

Unions frequently favor protection from imported substitutes for the goods their members produce and thus advocate tariffs and import quotas. This raises the demand for goods produced by union workers in this country and hence the *derived* demand for labor. You may have noticed that unions often express considerable concern over the safety of consumers, particularly when laws that would provide health and safety benefits also involve the hiring of additional workers. Examples are regulations requiring (1) projectionists in movie theaters where films are shown automatically and may catch on fire if not watched continuously, (2) fire fighters on locomotives that operate with diesel engines, (3) a third pilot (or "navigator") on airliners designed to be flown by two people, and so on. The term **featherbedding** is used to describe a situation in which a negotiated union contract requires employers to hire more labor than they believe is needed to perform a task.

*A **threat effect** is the effect of unions on the pay received by* nonunion *workers whose employers pay them more than the competitive wage to forestall their joining a union.*

Unions and Wages

We have seen that unions can raise the wage rates of their members by negotiating a rate of pay higher than the market wage that would otherwise prevail, by increasing the demand for union labor, and by reducing the supply of labor that competes with union workers. These activities can have two effects on wages. One is to increase union members' pay directly. The other is to influence the pay of nonunion workers.

How can a union affect nonunion wage rates? As union wage rates rise, unionized employers are likely to reduce the amount of labor they use. Workers who lose, or fail to obtain, jobs in the unionized sector of the economy must either drop out of the labor force or compete for jobs elsewhere. To the extent they seek jobs with nonunion employers, they will drive down wages for nonunion workers. However, there are forces that work to increase wages in the nonunion sector of the economy. One of these is just the opposite of the depressing effect of the flow of workers from the union to the nonunion sector of the economy. In particular, when wage rates increase in union jobs, nonunion workers may be induced to leave their jobs in order to seek higher-paying work in the union sector. This may be worthwhile, even if they are unemployed while waiting to be hired by unionized firms. This flow of workers away from nonunion jobs reduces the supply of labor there and puts upward pressure on the wage rates of the remaining nonunion workers.

There is another way in which labor unions may indirectly raise the wage rates of nonunion workers. Many employers fear unionization not only because they wish to avoid paying higher wage rates but also because the process of collective bargaining is itself costly. Firms may have to hire specialists who are paid simply to negotiate with the union rather than to contribute more directly to production. Moreover, collective bargaining agreements often limit employers' flexibility in assigning workers to various tasks. As a result, employers find it more difficult to minimize their production costs given the wage rates they must pay. Consequently, employers may feel that it is worthwhile to offer their workers a higher rate of pay simply to discourage them from joining a union. This indirect impact on nonunion wage rates is called a **threat effect.**

As you can see, when we compare the wage rates received by union members with those paid to nonunion workers, we may obtain a very crude estimate of how successful unions have been in achieving the goal of improved economic well-being for their members. The question that we would like to answer is "How high are the wage rates union workers receive compared to the wages they would have received if there were no union?" What we are able to observe, however, are the wage rates received by union workers relative to the wages that workers in nonunion jobs are paid. Since nonunion wages are probably affected by unions, too, economists must resort to some fairly complex statistical studies to make sure the *ceteris paribus* assumption holds in measuring the effects of unions on relative wages.

The results of a large number of studies of the impact of unions on wage rates yield estimates varying from a *negative* effect all the way up to a doubling of wage rates compared to their nonunion levels. Moreover, the estimated effect of unions on wage rates varies across industries and occupations and over time. Nevertheless, the great majority of measured relative wage effects fall in the range of 0 to 25 percent.[10]

Union Membership

Table 13.2 shows the fraction of the United States civilian labor force who were union members during various years from 1930 through 1984. The first year in the table, 1930, marks the beginning of the end of an important era for labor unions in the United States. Before 1932, labor unions operated without the protection of legislation that currently defines the rules now governing collective bargaining and other union activities. The Great Depression of the 1930s made it extremely difficult for unions to attract members, and 1933 is one of the historical low points of union membership in the United States.

However, the *Norris-LaGuardia Act of 1932* negated the so-called "yellow-dog contract," which was an agreement between an employer and an employee

*An **unfair labor practice** is an illegal action on the part of labor or management to frustrate the opposition in an organizing or collective-bargaining dispute.*

Table 13.2 **Union membership as a percentage of the civilian labor force, 1930–1984**

Year	Union membership
1930	7%
1933	5
1940	16
1945	22
1950	22
1953	26
1960	24
1970	23
1978	20
1983	20.1
1984	18.8

Source: From *Historical Statistics of the United States, Colonial Times to 1970,* Series D–949 and *Statistical Abstract of the United States, 1984,* Table 726, p. 439, and 1986, Table 713, p. 424.

in which the latter promised not to join a union. The act also severely limited employers' use of the courts to obtain injunctions against union-organizing activities and collective bargaining. Later, in 1935, the *Wagner Act* ushered in what most labor market specialists mark as the beginning of the modern era of labor-management relations in the United States.

The Wagner Act established the *National Labor Relations Board* and defined **unfair labor practices,** including employers' locking out workers in anticipation of a strike or firing workers who try to organize a union. The Wagner Act gave clear legal sanction to the rights of workers to organize, bargain, and strike. Thus, despite the persistence of depressed labor market conditions and high unemployment, union membership as a fraction of the labor force was over three times as high in 1940 as in 1933.

Union membership as a fraction of the labor force peaked in 1953. Economists offer several reasons for the decline of union membership since 1953. One contributing factor may have been that the *Taft-Hartley Act of 1947* redefined some of the rules governing union activities, making it somewhat more costly for unions to organize workers than it had been. However, basic changes in the economy also made it

more difficult for unions to achieve the successes they enjoyed during the 1940s and early 1950s. In particular, unions have traditionally found it easier to organize workers in various craft occupations and goods-related industries (mining, construction, and manufacturing) than in service-related industries (wholesale and retail trade, finance, and other services). One reason is that wages constitute a larger fraction of total costs in service industries than in other industries. This means that a given increase in wages causes a relatively large increase in total costs and hence the price charged customers. As a result, when unions win a wage increase in the service industries, a firm is more likely to experience a loss of business and thus reduce employment more severely than is the case in goods-related industries. This is the result of Marshall's rule regarding the share of labor in the total cost of production, which we learned in chapter 12. Successful union attempts to raise wages will reduce employment and therefore union membership most in industries in which the demand for labor is highly elastic.

Unfortunately for union interests, employment in goods-related industries began to grow more slowly than in the service-related industries after World War II. In addition, the immense increase in the participation of married women in the labor force militated against growing union membership. Women are more likely than men to work part-time and to drop out of the labor force occasionally. Both of these factors reduce the benefits women expect to enjoy from any given wage increase won by a union. As a result, they are less likely to want to pay the costs of dues and strikes that union membership entails.

In concluding our discussion of union membership, we should note that not all changes in the economic and political environment have worked against union growth. One area of the economy that has grown relatively rapidly and in which unions have won many new members is in the public sector. From 1956 to 1980, the number of government employees holding membership in unions or employee associations grew from 915,000 to 5,031,000.[11]

▸ Summary and Conclusions

In this chapter we have explored the interaction of supply and demand in factor markets, with emphasis on markets for labor. The following main points were emphasized.

The forces of supply and demand operate on labor markets much as they do for other factors of production and for goods and services.

Mobility of factors among markets leads to equality of factor prices across markets and to an economically efficient allocation of inputs among firms, industries, and geographical areas.

Monopoly in product markets and monopsony in input markets are noncompetitive influences that may affect factor prices and lead to an inefficient allocation of factors across markets.

Labor unions are organizations that seek to better the interests of their members by raising wages and other benefits above the levels that would otherwise prevail. Unions attempt to achieve their goals through collective bargaining and activities that affect labor supply and demand.

Unions are limited in the extent to which they are successful in gaining wage increases for their members by employers' demand for labor.

▸ Key Terms

collective bargaining
  276
compensating wage
  differentials 269
featherbedding 277

lockout 276
monopsony 272
threat effect 278
unfair labor practices
  279

▸ Questions for Discussion and Review

Are the statements in questions 1 through 5 true, false, or uncertain? Defend your answers.

1. A competitive firm should be cautious about the amount of labor it hires because the firm may force an increase in wage rates.
2. The demand for labor is a derived demand in the sense that the demand depends on the worker's ability to produce (productivity).
3. Labor unions have no interest in affecting the elasticity of demand for the final product that labor produces. However, labor unions do have an interest in the elasticity of demand for labor.
4. The monopsonist's demand curve for labor is downward sloping regardless of the elasticity of demand for its output.
5. The wage rate in a competitive labor market is equal to the revenue a firm would lose if one worker quit his or her job with the firm.
6. List and explain some methods to counteract the power of a monopsony.
7. Explain why labor unions have a strong interest in the following:
   a. The elasticity of demand for members' labor.
   b. The elasticity of demand for the final product that the members produce.
   c. Improving productivity for all of their members.
   d. Tough immigration laws.
8. Compare and contrast the profit-maximizing levels of employment and the wage rates for a competitive firm and a monopolist.
9. Illustrate and explain the effects that minimum wage legislation has on a monopsonist.
10. According to the theory of equalizing differences, will we always observe higher wages in less desirable occupations?

Chapter 14

Investment in Human and Physical Capital

Outline

I. Introduction *282*
II. Physical capital, human capital, productivity, and income *282*
III. Introduction to investment theory *283*
    A. Measuring the value of capital *283*
        1. More than one time period *284*
        2. Practical issues: Selecting an interest rate in a present value calculation and accounting for inflation *286*
IV. Investment in schooling and training *287*
    A. The schooling investment decision *288*
    B. On-the-job training and lifetime earning power *289*
        1. General training and lifetime earning power *289*
        2. Specific training, lifetime earning power, and employment stability *291*
    C. The role of government: The equity-efficiency quandary *293*
V. Investment in physical capital *293*
    A. Analyzing government investment projects *294*
        1. The Tellico Dam *294*
VI. Summary and conclusions *295*
VII. Key terms *295*
VIII. Questions for discussion and review *296*

Objectives

After reading this chapter, the student should be able to:

Explain the general theory of investment in capital, both human and physical.

Use the theory of investment to help understand the accumulation of schooling and training by individuals.

Use the theory of investment to help understand private firms' investments in human and physical capital.

Use the theory of investment to help understand government policy decisions involving present costs and future benefits.

▶ Introduction

Some of us smoke. Some of us drink alcohol. Some of us eat fatty foods. Why do we do this? After all, medical research indicates that these activities may shorten our lives and adversely affect the health of any children we may choose to have. The answer must lie in the fact that some of us get pleasure from smoking, drinking, or eating food high in cholesterol.

You may not have thought of good health as a type of investment, but it clearly is because improving one's health involves present costs and future benefits. Most people do not like visiting a doctor or dentist (and paying for it), taking blood pressure medication or other pills, and avoiding certain "fun" foods (such as ice cream). Smoking and drinking can be highly addictive and not easy habits to kick. These are some of the costs of good health, though. The benefits lie in the fact that avoiding tobacco, alcohol, and foods high in cholesterol pays off in the future by reducing the risk of heart attack or stroke, for example. Such improvements in health lead to higher lifetime happiness both directly through feeling good and indirectly through higher earning power. Better health also has important intergenerational consequences. Your mother's health and how well she took care of herself when pregnant with you may have important lifetime consequences for you.

Think about how many of the things you do today will affect your well-being later in life. Of course, health is not the only example of this. Other activities that involve present costs and future payoffs include going to school or getting trained on the job. In this chapter we focus on the individual's choices of schooling and training and how they relate to future economic well-being. This will provide us with a partial explanation of why some people in society may have very high incomes while others live in poverty.

▶ Physical Capital, Human Capital, Productivity, and Income

We know from our analysis of the labor market in chapter 13 that an increase in labor demand leads to an increase in the wage rate. Thus, if we want to know why wages may rise over time or why some people earn more than others during the course of their lives, we need to think about the forces determining the demand for labor in the long run. An outward shift in the demand for an industry's or an economy's output will result in a similar shift in the derived demand for inputs, both labor and physical capital. This will ultimately lead to higher wages and payments to the owners of that capital. What factors tend to raise wages and incomes over time?

In chapters 12 and 13 we noted that improvements in technology are an important cause of real wage rate increases over time. One of the basic reasons why our standard of living has grown is that households have saved part of their incomes, and these savings have been used to purchase new capital equipment. This has expanded our productive capacity and, with it, wages and incomes. In particular, as the amount of capital per worker grows, so does workers' marginal productivity. (Remember that the marginal product of labor is the additional output that results when another unit of labor is employed.) When the value of labor's marginal product—the amount the additional output sells for—increases, employers demand more labor at any given wage. This rightward shift in the labor demand curve ultimately leads to higher wages. Moreover, purchases of additional capital equipment today will generate higher future incomes for the owners of that capital.

It is not always true, however, that increases in society's physical capital stock have beneficial effects on the incomes of *both* workers and the owners of the capital. We saw in chapter 12 that increases in physical capital can sometimes harm workers. For example, automation that involves the use of robots can displace workers from their jobs. Workers who retain their jobs, perhaps those supervising an assembly line of robots in an auto plant, are more productive. The people who lose their jobs must find work in other industries or may be retrained to make and repair robots. As productivity rises as a result of automation, incomes and the demand for goods and services throughout the economy rise. This is accompanied by a general increase in the demand for labor. There is no question that the adjustments we have just described can create severe difficulties for individual workers. However, without them the high standard of living we share today would be impossible.

Improvements in technology and growth in the amount of nonhuman, or physical, capital per worker are only two sources of growth in productivity, wages, and incomes. There are some other sources too. In particular, part of the explanation for why wage rates vary among individuals at any moment and a principal reason why wages grow over time has to do with the amount of human capital per worker. On average, people who have acquired greater schooling and training are more productive. Because of the skills these people have acquired, employers are willing to pay them more.

▶ Introduction to Investment Theory

Before we analyze investments in human and physical capital, we need to develop some basic concepts of the theory of investment and capital itself. Remember that capital, in economics, is something that provides a flow of value (a return) over an extended period of time. Machinery, buildings, land, livestock, and human beings all fall into this category.

Measuring the Value of Capital

Because capital is a productive resource that yields a flow of value—a return—over time, capital derives its worth from the value placed on the return it yields. You have to invest in order to obtain these returns, however. Specifically, you must sacrifice something of value in the present to purchase capital, which yields its return in the future. This connection between *present* and *future* is the essence of capital and investment theory. But how do we know whether investing in capital is worthwhile? The answer to this question depends upon the opportunity costs and returns involved.

A simple example will help us understand how the value of capital and its opportunity costs together determine whether an investment is economically worthwhile. Suppose that someone offers to sell you a remarkable piece of physical capital—a tree that, once planted, requires no care. At the end of one year, it bears 1,100 one-dollar bills and then dies. There is absolutely no risk that the tree will die prematurely or will not bear "fruit." How much would you be willing to pay for this tree?

Suppose that the tree sold for $1,000. Is this the tree's opportunity cost? No. It is only part of the cost. To measure the tree's full opportunity cost, we need more information on what else you could do with the $1,000, or if you do not have $1,000, how much it would cost you to borrow it. Let us assume for the sake of discussion that if you did not buy the tree you could put $1,000 in a passbook (savings) account that pays 5 percent interest per year. This means that after one year you could withdraw your $1,000 deposit plus interest, for a total withdrawal of $1,050. Because $1,050 is less than $1,100, investing in (buying) the tree would increase your financial wealth. If you had borrowed the $1,000 at 5 percent interest to purchase the tree, it would still "pay" to buy the tree. In particular, at the end of the year you could repay the $1,000 loan, pay the $50 interest, and still have $50 left over as a profit from your investment.

Compound interest is the interest paid on interest payments that have been accumulated in the past.

Present value (PV) is a single number that measures the economic value of a financial asset or capital good yielding a stream of returns (benefits) over its lifetime.

The rate of interest at which you borrow (or lend) is a crucial part of any investment decision. Suppose that the rate of interest in the preceding example happened to be 10 percent instead of 5 percent. In this case, you would have $1,100 at the end of one year if you had put your $1,000 in the bank, or you would have to repay the bank $1,100 at the end of the year if you had borrowed the money. Either way, investing in the tree would no longer be profitable—it would be a break-even proposition. Clearly, if the interest rate were to rise above 10 percent, you would lose money by buying the tree. You would do better either by placing your $1,000 in the bank or by not borrowing the money in the first place.

More than One Time Period

More typically, an investment opportunity has returns that occur over several years. In this case, it is necessary to keep in mind that interest compounds when a deposit is left in a bank for an extended period and the interest is not withdrawn. **Compound interest** means that interest is paid on the original deposit plus any interest accrued to that point. Similarly, if interest payments are not made on a loan every year, you have to pay interest on the interest when you eventually repay your debt.

To see how compound interest affects an investment decision, we will return to the example of our tree that yields $1,100 and then dies. Suppose now that the crop of dollar bills matures after two years instead of after one year. What is your alternative to investing in the tree now? If you deposited $1,000 in the bank and left it there at a 5 percent interest rate for two years, you could then withdraw the following amount: $1,000 plus $50 interest for leaving it in the bank for the first year, plus $50 interest for the second year, plus 5 percent of the first year's interest, which has become part of the deposit in the second year. All of this amounts to $1,000 $\times$ $(1.05)^2$ = $1,102.50.

What does tying up your money for an additional year do to the opportunity cost of the tree? It increases it to $1,102.50. While the tree was a profitable investment at a 5 percent interest rate over a one-year period, it is no longer worthwhile if it takes two years to obtain $1,100. You would do better by putting the $1,000 in the bank. Buying the tree lowers your wealth by $2.50 compared to the alternative of putting your $1,000 in a savings account. Similarly, if you had to borrow in order to buy the tree, you would end up repaying the bank $1,102.50.

Here is an extremely important point. *The farther into the future a return on investment occurs, the less that return is worth today.* In our example, a tree that yields $1,100 after one year is a worthwhile investment if the interest rate is 5 percent per year (or even higher, up to 10 percent). However, it is a losing proposition if the return does not occur until the end of two years. This is one of the most important principles in the theory of investment. We can use it to derive what is known as **present value (PV),** which measures the value of an asset yielding a stream of benefits (returns) now and in the future. If the present value of an asset exceeds its cost, then it will increase one's wealth to buy the asset. The opposite is true if present value is less than cost.

It will help you grasp the concept of present value if you remember that when you buy an asset, you are purchasing a set of returns received over time. The value of the asset is the present value of these returns. If you know the present value, you will know how much money you would now have to place in a savings account (at a given rate of interest) to obtain returns from the savings account that are economically equivalent to the returns from the asset. Therefore, if you can purchase an asset for less than its present value, it will increase your wealth to do so.

Let us see how the concept of present value works when applied to the money-bearing tree. At an interest rate of 5 percent how much would you have to deposit in a savings account to produce a yield equivalent to 1,100 dollar bills paid to you one year from now? The answer is $1,100 ÷ 1.05 = $1,047.62. This is the present value of $1,100 received one year from today when the interest rate is 5 percent. Because you can purchase the tree for $1,000, your wealth will be increased by $47.62 in present value terms if you buy the tree.

Now work through our money tree example when the 1,100 dollar bills mature on the tree at the end of two years. In this case, the present value of the $1,100 is $1,100 ÷ (1.05 × 1.05), or $1,100 ÷ (1.05)² = $997.73. With a deposit of $997.73, interest credited after one year is $49.89. If this is left in the account, then the interest at the end of the second year is $1,047.62 × .05 = $52.38. The total that can be withdrawn at the end of two years is $1,100. Because in this example it would cost $1,000 for the tree and you need only deposit $997.73 in the savings account to receive $1,100 two years from now, you would be worse off by $2.27 in present value terms if you bought the tree. To make sure you understand the concept of present value, work through the example assuming that you have to borrow the money to buy the tree. Assume that repayment is required after the tree bears its "fruit" and that the interest rate is 5 percent per year.

As we said earlier, most assets yield returns over a number of years, not just in one year. What is the present value of physical or human capital when its returns occur in each of a number of years? It is the sum of the present values of each year's return. For example, if the money tree in our example bears 1,100 dollar bills at the end of each year for three successive years and the interest rate is 5 percent, the tree's present value would be

$$[\$1,100 \div 1.05] + [\$1,100 \div (1.05)^2] +$$
$$[\$1,100 \div (1.05)^3] = \$1,047.62 + \$997.73 +$$
$$\$950.22 = \$2,995.57.$$

The present value of an asset is less than the simple sum of its returns as long as the interest rate exceeds zero. For example, the bonuses of star professional athletes and winnings in state lotteries are usually reported as the simple sum of payments to be spread out over a number of years. Sometimes this delay makes good sense because of income tax considerations. Nevertheless, the present value of such payments is less than their simple sum. The money that the lottery payer needs to put in an interest-bearing account in order to pay winners their annual prize amounts each year is less than the simple sum of the payments.

It is also important to remember that the present value of an asset depends on the rate of interest. For example, while the present value of three annual payments of $1,100 at 5 percent interest is $2,995.54, at a 10 percent rate of interest, the present value is only $2,735.54. In general, the present value of an asset whose annual returns (R) accrue over a number of years in the future can be calculated with the following formula

$$PV = R(1) \div (1 + i) + R(2) \div (1 + i)^2 +$$
$$R(3) \div (1 + i)^3 \ldots + R(n) \div (1 + i)^n,$$

where the numbers 1 through n denote the number of years from today the returns are received and i is the rate of interest. Keep in mind that it will always increase your wealth to invest in capital when its present value is greater than the amount it costs to buy it.

Practical Issues: Selecting an Interest Rate in a Present Value Calculation and Accounting for Inflation

In order to apply our concept of present value in discussing the economic benefits from investments we need to address two additional points. In particular, when implementing the concept of present value, what interest rate do you use and how do you adjust for inflation? Because the main objective in a present value calculation is to determine whether or not you are making a profit in an economic sense, the interest rate should reflect the opportunity cost of the funds used in the investment. This is more straightforward in the case of households or firms than it is with investments by the government. Let us elaborate. Households frequently have to borrow the money to invest in physical or human capital. The interest paid on the borrowed funds is the opportunity cost, and this is the interest rate that goes into the present value calculation. What about the situation in which households do not borrow the money? Such households will be taking the money out of another financial asset, perhaps a money market or savings account. In this case, the interest rate to use in the present value calculation is the rate of return on the money had it remained in a household's savings or money market account. The interest rate for a business firm's present value calculation is determined similarly. In particular, did the firm have to borrow (sell bonds) to finance the investment, or did the firm have to withdraw the money from another project with a particular return associated with it? Market interest rates will reflect the opportunity cost of funds.

What about the interest rate used in government investment projects? Here, when we attempt to apply the concept of the opportunity cost to the funds, the situation is not so straightforward. In many cases it is not obvious where the funds are coming from when the government invests. If the investment is the direct result of funds the government has borrowed, then the interest rate paid for those funds is the opportunity cost of the money. However, suppose the money is obtained from taxes. In this case, the opportunity cost is related to who bears the burden of the tax. If the tax is largely on the business sector and displaces private investment, then the opportunity cost of the funds (the appropriate interest rate to use in the present value calculation) is what firms could have earned with the money had they invested it in the private sector. If the tax is largely on households, then the interest rate to be used in the present value calculation by the government should largely reflect the rate of return to personal saving. When the tax falls on both households and firms, it has been suggested that the interest rate used in the present value formula be some weighted average of the rate of return on business investment and personal saving.

This brings us to the second topic of this section: How does one adjust the value of an asset for the fact that payments received in the future may buy less because of inflation? Fortunately, the answer here is quite simple. Inflation is automatically entered into the calculation when we select the interest rate to use in determining the present value of a stream of payments. Generally, market interest rates, such as those on savings accounts or those that borrowers pay to lenders when a bond is issued, already incorporate the fact that lenders expect to be repaid with dollars that may purchase less in the future because of inflation.

Thus, the interest rates you see advertised in the financial section of the newspaper reflect expectations of inflation. Using the interest rates we have already discussed in this section appropriately accounts for the possibility that future benefits will purchase less because of inflation. Market interest rates will rise when inflation is expected to increase and fall when inflation is expected to decrease. Therefore, no additional adjustments are needed.

Table 14.1   Years of school completed, by age, 1940–1983

	Percent not high school graduates		Percent with four years of high school or more		Median years of school completed*
	Total	**With less than five years of school**	**Total**	**College, four years or more**	
Age 25 years and over					
1940	75.5%	13.7%	24.5%	4.6%	8.6 yr
1950	65.7	11.1	34.3	6.2	9.3
1960	58.9	8.3	41.1	7.7	10.5
1970	47.7	5.5	52.3	10.7	12.1
1983	27.9	3.0	72.1	18.8	12.6
Age 25–29 years					
1940	61.9%	5.9%	38.1%	5.9%	10.3 yr
1950	49.5	4.7	52.8	7.7	12.0
1960	39.3	2.8	60.7	11.1	12.3
1970	26.2	1.7	73.8	16.3	12.6
1983	14.0	0.9	86.0	22.5	12.8

Source: From U.S. Bureau of the Census, *Statistical Abstract of the United States, 1985* (105th edition), p. 134.

*Level of schooling such that 50 percent of the population has more and 50 percent has less.

▶ Investment in Schooling and Training

From the point of view of labor markets, schooling is a very important form of human capital investment. By schooling we generally mean attending formal classes at a primary school, secondary school, junior or community college, technical college, four-year college, or university. Some occupations, such as engineering, medicine, and law, require students to enroll in specific programs and obtain specific advanced degrees. Others require the general skills obtained by completing high school or college. Table 14.1 presents data on how schooling levels increased in the United States between 1940 and 1983. Among adults twenty-five years of age and older, the percentage not completing high school fell by about two-thirds, from 75.5 percent in 1940 to 27.9 percent in 1983. Within that same group, the percentage of individuals with four or more years of college increased fourfold, from 4.6 percent in 1940 to 18.8 percent in 1983. Among younger adults, those twenty-five to twenty-nine years old, the percentage not completing high school fell from 61.9 percent in 1940 to 14 percent in 1983. Finally, college completion among young adults more than tripled, from 5.9 percent in 1940 to 22.5 percent in 1983.

Investment in schooling is not the only form of human capital that contributes to the typical individual's labor market success. Training is also part of the set of skills required in an occupation. Training is just as important as schooling in terms of the amount a typical worker invests in human capital over his or her lifetime.[1] Training is a more elusive concept than schooling, however. It is probably fair to say that most training is informal, occurring on the job. Virtually all occupations require some sort of internship or hands-on experience before workers are fully qualified. For the sake of simplicity, we will focus our attention on analyzing the economics of the schooling investment decision and discuss the implication of on-the-job training for lifetime earnings and employment stability.

The Schooling Investment Decision

An analysis of an investment decision must begin by identifying the costs and returns involved. Two important characteristics distinguish investment in human capital from investment in physical capital. (1) The costs of investing in human capital are frequently not paid in cash but involve the opportunity cost of a person's time. (2) The returns cannot be permanently transferred or sold by the initial investor to another person. This would involve slavery or indentured servitude. While you can work for a firm, selling your labor power by the day, the month, or even the year, in the United States, you have the right to quit.

From the individual's point of view, even so-called free schooling is costly. The reason is that the decision to acquire more schooling is also usually a decision to defer entry into the labor force on a full-time basis. Thus the costs of schooling include the earnings foregone by not taking a full-time job. Outlays for books and tuition are also investment costs. The returns to schooling occur mainly in the future in the form of higher earnings and access to more satisfying jobs.

We can capture the essential features of the decision to invest in schooling by making three simplifications that help us avoid complicated calculations. (1) We assume that a typical college education occurs instantaneously. (2) We assume that after college a graduate works forever. (This is acceptable

arithmetically because after forty years or so, the present value of the return to schooling is very small. For example, at a 10 percent interest rate, the present value of $10,000 received forty years from now is only $221.) (3) We assume that while in college a student earns an amount exactly equal to the so-called direct cost of schooling—books, materials, and tuition. Practically speaking, this means we ignore the direct costs of schooling and focus on the indirect or opportunity costs of attending college, taking them to be the amount a student would have earned as a high school graduate who works full time.

In 1979, for example, a typical male high school graduate earned $13,300 per year while a typical male with four years of college earned $19,100.[2] Using the three assumptions listed above, a typical male's opportunity cost of four years of college in 1979 was about $53,200 (4 × $13,300). The annual returns consisted of the increased income that a college graduate earned compared to a high school graduate, $5,800 ($19,100 − $13,300). The present value of $5,800 per year can easily be calculated by means of our second assumption. Specifically, when the return (R) to an asset is the same amount each year and is received forever, its present value (PV) is simply $PV = R/i$, where i is the interest rate. Let us use an interest rate of 5 percent to make our present value calculation because 5 percent per year is approximately what someone could readily earn on a perfectly safe financial asset, such as a savings account. All of this information suggests $116,000 as an estimate of the present value of the returns for a typical male who in 1979 invested in a college education. Because this exceeds the estimated opportunity cost of a college education by $62,800, a typical male would have significantly increased his wealth by attending four years of college. A similar set of calculations for women is more complex because women college graduates are more likely to work full time than women high school graduates.[3]

General training *increases a*
worker's labor market productivity
by the same amount in a large
number of jobs and firms.

Specific training *increases a*
worker's labor market productivity
primarily in the job and firm where
he or she is currently employed.

On-the-job Training and Lifetime Earning Power

Most of us expect to earn more in real terms as we grow older. Why? If the only investment in human capital we ever made were schooling, then our lifetime productivity on the job would be more or less established upon graduation. In the absence of any depreciation due to aging and declining health, our productivity at work would be constant over our lives. This suggests that in a competitive labor market a worker's real wage would remain largely constant from the time he or she left school until retirement (except for the effects of any technological change). If there were declining productivity due to failing health or the effects of aging, then the typical worker's real wage would be constant for some time and then decline in his or her later years. Instead, most of us (correctly) expect our real wage to rise as we get older and accumulate more labor market experience. To understand why the typical worker's wages grow with age and experience, we need to understand investment in on-the-job training. When discussing on-the-job training, we must make the distinction between **general training,** which is valuable in many jobs and with various employers, and **specific training,** which is useful only in the job and firm where the training takes place.

What are some examples of general and specific training? Most skilled craft worker jobs require some type of apprenticeship before a person becomes, say, a master carpenter or a so-called journeyman plumber. These are examples of general training because the skills obtained allow one to work as a carpenter or plumber in many different firms. Internships are primarily general training. Medical interns (now called residents) receive on-the-job training that is useful in a variety of hospital and other settings in the health care sector. The same holds true for internships in law or government. When young lawyers join a law firm

they must first learn who the judges are and where certain legal papers have to be filed. They also become acquainted with other attorneys, both in local government offices and in the law firms around town. This knowledge enhances their productivity for their legal clients and is useful if they go to work for another law firm in the area.

Probably the best way to think of specific training is as the "ropes to skip" and "ropes to know" in a particular organization. For example, knowing your supervisors' and coworkers' likes and dislikes, abilities, and quirks will make you a more productive worker. However, this knowledge is of little use in other firms because different people will be there. A similar story holds for learning your employer's particular accounting or computing systems. Learning the peculiarities of an organization requires effort that pays off within that organization but has very little value in other organizations.

Of course, we recognize that most on-the-job training has both general and specific components. Rarely is on-the-job training useful in *every* firm in the industry or useful in only *one* firm in the industry. In fact, the distinction between general and specific training is one of degree. Is the training useful in very few firms, or is it useful in nearly all of the firms in the industry?

General Training and Lifetime Earning Power

Figure 14.1 illustrates how general training gives an upward tilt to the lifetime earnings profile. In the absence of any on-the-job training, the horizontal line through point A is the value of a worker's productivity. This will also be the wage paid each year of this person's working life in a competitive labor market. General on-the-job training makes a worker less productive during the early part of the work life and more productive later on. During the training period, a worker is learning (investing) and is therefore producing less output than someone who is spending all

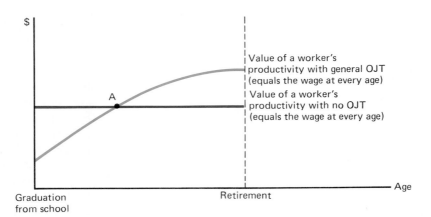

Figure 14.1   General training and the age-wage profile
In a competitive labor market, a worker's wage equals the value of labor's marginal product. When there is no on-the-job training (OJT), and no depreciation of skills due to aging or declining health, a worker receives the same wage in each year (unless there is overall productivity growth in the economy).

General training gives a "tilt" to the wage-earnings profile. During training, a worker is less productive than an untrained worker. After training, productivity eventually exceeds that of an untrained worker. Under general training, a worker still receives a wage equal to the value of his or her marginal product in each year.

of the time on the job actually working. The payoff to this training is the greater labor market productivity after the training is completed.

The present value of the area between the horizontal line and the upward-sloping line to the left of point A in figure 14.1 is the cost of general on-the-job training (OJT). The present value of the area between the two lines to the right of point A is the payoff from such training. Who pays these costs and receives these benefits? Because general on-the-job training is valuable in different jobs, the worker typically pays the costs and reaps the benefits. Physicians who wish to become specialists, for example, earn much less while serving as residents in hospitals than they would receive in private practice without specializing.

Now let us consider the case in which the firm tries to pay the costs and reap the economic benefits of on-the-job training. How might the firm try to do this? One way is for the firm to pay workers a wage equal to the value of labor's productivity without OJT, the horizontal line in figure 14.1. In this case, the firm would be overpaying workers during the training period and underpaying them later. This situation could not endure for very long in a competitive labor market.

Why? The reason is that once a worker reached point A, he or she would quit and go to work for another firm. Because general training can be applied to many jobs, a worker's value to every firm is the upward-sloping line to the right of point A. Thus, a firm would have lots of trainees but relatively few trained workers because the workers would be able to increase their wages by moving to a new job after the training period. The firm that provided the training would be stuck with training costs but reap few of the economic benefits from the training. This is why firms do not typically pay for workers' general training. The United States military has sometimes ignored this fact and has had difficulty retaining its experienced personnel. Specifically, men and women are induced to enlist in exchange for vocational training of a general nature. During the training period, they are paid more than they are worth to the military. After training, the military attempts to recoup its investment by paying its members less than they are worth in the private market. As you might expect, there is a relatively high turnover rate of trained workers into areas such as aircraft maintenance and piloting, computer programming, and electronics.

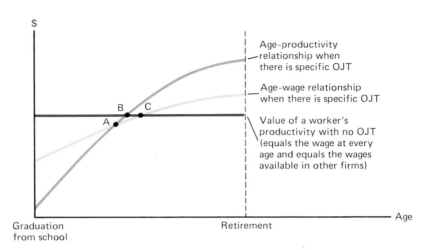

$

Age-productivity
relationship when
there is specific OJT

Age-wage relationship
when there is specific OJT

Value of a worker's
productivity with no OJT
(equals the wage at every
age and equals the wages
available in other firms)

Graduation
from school

Retirement

Age

Figure 14.2   Specific training and the age-wage profile
When specific on-the-job training (OJT) is present, a worker's
wage in a given year need not equal the value of labor's
marginal product, even in a competitive labor market. Workers
will typically be "overpaid" during their early years with the firm
(paid more than the value of marginal product) and
"underpaid" during their later years with the firm (paid less
than the value of marginal product). This switchover occurs at
the age associated with point A. Why doesn't a worker quit his
or her job at this age and seek alternative employment? The
answer is that the worker is still being paid more than the next
best job would pay because specific training has no portability.
This is also the reason why firms would be willing to "overpay"
workers in the early years. The later underpayment is the firm's
return to its investment in a worker's specific human capital.

Under what circumstances might a firm invest in (pay for) a worker's general on-the-job training? The answer is that there must be some mechanism for preventing the worker from quitting once the value of his or her services exceeds the value of an untrained worker (after point A in figure 14.1) or for making the worker pay back the training costs if he or she does quit. The military academies provide general education, basically engineering degrees, to their students. These graduates then owe the military a number of years of service, which is viewed as the military's return on its payment for general training. Private firms will sometimes pay for general OJT or even MBA degrees if the recipient promises to remain with the firm for a specified number of years or repay the cost of the training or tuition.[4]

The issue of who pays for human capital investment and who owns the returns has become hotly contested in recent years. One case arises when a spouse provides financial support for the education and training of a husband (or wife) and is later divorced before the returns from that investment are realized. The state legislatures and courts have come to feel that a divorced spouse who provided financial support during a husband's (or wife's) training should receive some return on, or at least repayment of, that implicit investment. In the course of calculating those costs, returns, and the divorced spouse's share, the issue of present value is important.[5]

Specific Training, Lifetime Earning Power, and Employment Stability

Specific training reinforces the effect of general training on lifetime earning power. Figure 14.2 shows us that specific training also gives a tilt to the age-wage relationship. During the training period, a worker's wages are relatively low and rise as the training begins to have its labor market productivity-enhancing effects. One aspect of specific training, however, is that the wage need not equal the value of the worker's productivity in any given year if specific training is present. This has important implications for understanding labor market discrimination and employment stability.

Because specific training is not valuable in alternative firms, the costs and benefits will typically be shared by the worker and the employer. Let us see how this occurs and why its effects are to enhance the stability of employment. In figure 14.2, a worker who is younger than the age associated with point A is being paid more than the value of labor's marginal product. The present value of this "overpayment" is the employer's cost of specific on-the-job training. The worker is also paying part of the cost of the specific on-the-job training because the wage is less than that paid to someone with no specific training (the worker whose wage productivity profile is the horizontal line in figure 14.2). Moreover, the benefits of specific training are also being shared. Notice that eventually the value of a worker's labor market productivity rises to where it exceeds the wages being paid. This is the firm's payoff for its investment in a worker's specific training. Moreover, the wage rate paid to the worker also exceeds what he or she would obtain in the absence of any specific training. However, those wages are less than the worker's value to the particular firm in which the worker is employed. This (positive) difference between the wage a worker is paid by the firm where the training is received and the worker's next best available wage explains why the worker does not quit after age C, even though he or she is paid less than the value of his or her labor market productivity.

There are a number of key points to remember here. First, specific training means that (even in a competitive labor market) a worker may not be paid the value of labor's marginal product during any given year. Thus, a gap between productivity and pay does not necessarily indicate some kind of exploitation or discrimination. It may simply be part of a long-term situation wherein the present value of the total wages paid to a worker equals the present value of labor's marginal productivity. These present values are what balance out in a competitive labor market—not necessarily the wage and productivity in any given year of employment. Second, when workers and firms share the costs and benefits of specific training, the employment relationship is more stable. Workers are less likely to quit and firms are less likely to lay off workers when there is a substantial investment in specific training. The reason is that both parties have something to lose. The worker will lose a chance at the payoff to specific training if he or she quits, and the firm will lose a chance at its payoff to specific training if it fires a worker.[6] This is one of the reasons why workers with more specific training (professionals and managerial workers) tend to have lower unemployment rates than unskilled workers. Individuals who invest more in on-the-job training are not only going to receive higher earning power over their lifetimes, but they are also going to have more stable employment (less unemployment). Therefore, on-the-job training is an important factor underlying earning power differences and differences in job stability among individuals.

We can view the employment relationship as a kind of "marriage" between a worker and an employer. This suggests that there may be some parallels between the dynamics of the family and the dynamics of the workplace. For example, we would expect that the more capital a husband and wife accumulate that is specific to their marital union, the less likely it is that they will divorce. Examples of such capital may be memories and own children. Indeed, we find that the likelihood of divorce falls with years married and number of own children.[7]

*The **equity-efficiency quandary** occurs when a society must choose between promoting an efficient economy and improving the fairness with which income or wealth is divided among its members.*

Durable consumer goods are equipment that provide services to a household over a number of years.

The Role of Government: The Equity-Efficiency Quandary

Think of all of the ways in which the United States government affects the amount that individuals invest in schooling, health, and training. Financial support of low-cost or tuition-free public schools is just one example. The Job Training and Partnership Act provides financial incentives for employers to train workers. When influencing the human capital investment decisions of individuals, the government faces an important dilemma. Should it target its funds at those individuals from whom the payoff from investment (present value) is highest? Or should it provide its investment funds to those individuals who would normally have the lowest incomes in society?

By targeting investment funds to individuals with the greatest present values, society gets the most out of its limited resources. This produces economic efficiency, but it also widens the disparity of incomes among society's members. On the other hand, if society targets its investment funds toward individuals with the lowest incomes in society, the payoff from its investment will typically be lower, but it will have an equalizing effect on the distribution of income. In this sense, society sacrifices efficiency for equity. The trade-off we have just been describing has been termed the **equity-efficiency quandary.**

How does society solve this quandary? In the United States, the government does some of each. While most available scholarships are based on need, some are based on a student's ability. Government money funds such prestigious institutions as the University of Michigan and the University of California at Berkeley, as well as a range of educational institutions that may educate less able students. See if you can think of some examples in the area of investment in schooling or training where the government promotes both equity and efficiency.

▶ Investment in Physical Capital

As in the case of human capital, households, firms, and the government invest in physical capital, too. What are some of the individual components of this investment in physical capital, and how important is each in total investment in physical capital in the United States?

In 1984, the business sector invested $426 billion in nonresidential structures and equipment. In 1984, the United States economy also produced a total of $154 billion in residential structures. At the same time, the household sector in the United States purchased $319 billion worth of what are known as **durable consumer goods;** these include things such as motor vehicle parts ($150 billion) and furniture and household equipment ($117 billion) that yield a stream of services to a household over a period of time. Because of this, durable consumer goods are a type of physical capital. It is not so easy to get a handle on government investment in physical capital. This is because published data typically categorize government expenditures by function rather than by whether it is a consumption versus an investment item. To get some idea, however, we note that in 1984 governments at all levels purchased $747 billion worth of goods and services. Without doing a line-by-line analysis of all of the governments' budgets, it is impossible to tell how much of this was investment (for example, military hardware or computer systems) versus current consumption (salaries of government employees).[8]

While households, firms, and governments all invest in physical capital, we will focus our attention here on investments by government. There are several reasons for not dwelling on the analysis of physical capital investments by firms and households. One is that the basic economic issues involved are comparatively straightforward and have already been addressed in our discussion of investment in human capital. Specifically, the investment decision by a firm will involve a comparison of the present value of the production generated by a capital good, for example, a computer to be purchased by an accounting firm, with the price of the item.[9] Similarly, households will compare the purchase price of, say, a house, car, or personal computer with the present value of the services it yields over its useful life.

The case of government investment in physical capital is somewhat different. Here we have the political debates over what to include in the costs and the benefits of the investments. The interest rate used to calculate present value is also sometimes a political issue. Troublesome distributional questions and issues of the "greater good" come into play, too. Finally, some well-documented investment decisions not only allow us to consider the investment decision on the basis of the facts available before it was made but also permit us to perform an "economic autopsy" to see whether the present value of benefits versus costs worked out in the way the planners had anticipated.[10] As an example, we will consider government investment in physical capital for flood control.

Analyzing Government Investment Projects

The comparison of the present value of economic costs and benefits stemming from public expenditure decisions is known as **cost-benefit analysis.** Cost-benefit analysis may be used as a tool to decide whether a project in the planning stage would be worthwhile or to determine whether an investment actually made has been worthwhile. In the former case, cost-benefit analysis can be used to rank public investment projects by the greatest net benefit or to decide to accept or reject a single project. It can also help policymakers to establish the economically appropriate scale for a project.[11]

A variation on cost-benefit analysis is something known as **cost-effectiveness analysis,** which occurs when a given level of investment spending has already

been established and analysts compare projects' net benefits to decide which to select. Alternatively, we might have the situation where a number of projects have identical benefits and the projects will be ranked by how little they cost.

It is important to point out that cost-benefit and cost-effectiveness analyses typically focus on economic issues rather than on equity or normative issues, such as whether a project raises the income of the poor relative to the wealthy.[12] One of the reasons for this is that tax and transfer programs are viewed as more direct and appropriate approaches to income redistribution. Still, government investments do have income redistribution effects, and the analyst may try to work them into the cost-benefit calculation.

The Tellico Dam

The objectives of the Tellico Dam project, initially proposed in 1963 for the Little Tennessee River, included recreation, flood control, and electric power generation. This is an interesting example of a government decision to invest in physical capital because it demonstrates (1) how the benefits and costs can be viewed differently depending upon the groups involved and (2) how politics and public investment decisions are intertwined, especially when the environment is involved.

The construction of the Tellico Dam actually began in 1967. However, in 1969, Congress passed the National Environmental Policy Act, which required that investment projects such as this file statements of their environmental impact. As a result, construction of the dam stopped during 1971–1973. Next came the 1973 amendment to the Endangered Species Act, which was supposed to prevent federal agencies from jeopardizing an endangered species in its natural habitat. In late 1973, the snail darter, a four-inch minnow, was discovered in the region of the Tellico Dam. Environmentalists argued that the full operation (closing) of the dam would kill off the snail darter. This led to further delays in completion of the Tellico Dam project while the issue was fought in the courts and in Congress.

The Tellico Dam dispute was ultimately heard by the Endangered Species Committee, a cabinet-level organization set up by Congress to decide cases dealing with disputes involving public investment projects and endangered species. The committee looked at numerous sets of cost-benefit calculations. Edward Gramlich notes that three were especially important.[13] One was the cost-benefit calculation of the Tennessee Valley Authority, the organization responsible for constructing the dam. A second set of cost-benefit calculations was made by the staff of the Endangered Species Committee. The committee staff also considered an alternative to completion of the dam project—partial completion of the dam in a way that would not disturb the snail darter.

Gramlich argues convincingly that the committee's calculations were more economically accurate and that the net economic benefits of finishing the dam project (closing the almost completed dam) were rather small. In particular, they were estimated to be in the neighborhood of +$1.7 million to -$0.7 million (1978 dollars). This compares to a total construction cost of $50 million.[14] By comparison, the committee staff also estimated that there were negative net benefits, -$1.2 million, associated with the partial completion option designed to save the snail darter.

These numbers suggest that it was economically more efficient to complete (close) the dam. As a point of fact, the Endangered Species Committee ruled *not* to close the dam and to accept the partial completion option. However, Congress and President Carter overruled their decision, and the dam was completed in 1979. An attempt was to be made to relocate the snail darter in a nearby river.

The Tellico Dam project and the associated cost-benefit calculations illustrate the way in which politics and economics are intertwined. They also emphasize the importance of the distributional issues (workers' and firms' economic benefits versus environmental costs) that play an important role in government decisions to invest in physical capital.

▶ Summary and Conclusions

In this chapter we have analyzed investment in physical and human capital. The following major conclusions were developed.

Investments in human and physical capital are important to understanding the level and distribution of income.

Because investment in capital involves present costs and future returns, these must be compared in present value terms.

Investment in human capital takes many forms, including schooling and on-the-job training.

The concept of general training helps us to understand why earnings rise over the typical individual's lifetime. The concept of specific training helps us to understand why employment stability differs among individuals.

When allocating funds for investment, the government must decide how it will balance equity versus economic efficiency.

Government investment decisions are based not only on economic efficiency considerations but also on many related normative issues.

▶ Key Terms

compound interest *284*

cost-benefit analysis *294*

cost-effectiveness analysis *294*

durable consumer goods *293*

equity-efficiency quandary *293*

general training *289*

present value (PV) *284*

specific training *289*

▶ Questions for Discussion and Review

Are the statements in questions 1 through 5 true, false, or uncertain? Defend your answers.

1. Present value is inversely related to the rate of interest and the length of maturity of an investment.

2. If the present value of some capital equipment exceeds its purchase price, then buying the equipment will increase your wealth.

3. A lottery that pays the winner $10,000 per year forever has a greater present value than a lottery that pays $20,000 per year for ten years. Assume the rate of interest is 10 percent.

4. In order to estimate completely the opportunity costs of attending college, you should include the explicit costs of clothing, health care, and food while you are attending school.

5. Firms are more likely to lay off workers with specific on-the-job training than unskilled workers because the higher salaries of trained workers will yield higher cost savings.

6. Suppose that you win the state lottery, which pays $50,000 per year for twenty years. Are your winnings worth $1 million? Explain.

7. Describe the trade-off facing the government when it decides to whom funds should be provided for investment in education and/or training.

8. Describe the difference between cost-benefit analysis and cost-effectiveness analysis.

9. What effect, if any, do scholarships, fellowships, and low-cost loans have on the decision to attend college?

10. In terms of cost-benefit analysis, why do you think that academically prestigious schools have the highest tuition rates?

Chapter 15

The Distribution of Income

Outline

I. Introduction *298*
II. The distribution of wages and income *298*
   A. Measures of the income distribution *299*
      1. The size distribution of income in the United States and other countries *299*
      2. The functional distribution of income *301*
   B. Human capital and the functional distribution of income *303*
III. Income redistribution *304*
   A. Why redistribute income? *304*
      1. Measuring poverty *305*
      2. Equality of opportunity or equality of results? *307*
   B. Policies to redistribute income *307*
      1. The role of labor unions *307*
      2. Minimum wage legislation *308*
      3. Transfer programs *310*
         a. Income maintenance programs *310*
         b. Progressive income taxation, a "flat" tax, and the supply side *311*
IV. Summary and conclusions *318*
V. Key terms *318*
VI. Questions for discussion and review *318*

Objectives

After reading this chapter, the student should be able to:

Describe the methods used to measure the distribution of income.

Compare the United States' income distribution with income distributions in other nations.

Describe the functional distribution of income.

Explain the role human capital plays in the functional distribution of income.

Discuss ways in which poverty is measured.

Discuss laws and institutions that redistribute income, such as labor unions, minimum wage legislation, income maintenance programs, and income taxation.

Income distribution is a quantitative summary of how society's total income (production) is divided among the members of society.

▶ Introduction

It should come as no surprise to you that not every individual, or even every family, in the United States has the same income. Data from the Statistical Abstract of the United States *tell us that in 1984 about 14 percent of all families had money incomes of under $10,000. Approximately 25 percent had money incomes of less than $15,000. On the other hand, approximately 34 percent of all families had money incomes of $35,000 or more and approximately 16 percent received more than $50,000. Thus, a significant proportion of families can be thought of as well-off and others— approximately 63 million families in 1984—as poor.*

In 1984, the Catholic bishops in the United States issued a 120-page Pastoral Letter on Catholic Social Teaching and the United States Economy. Here is what the Catholic bishops had to say about income equality and inequality in the United States.

> Catholic social teaching does not suggest that absolute equality in the distribution of income and wealth is required. Some degree of inequality is not only acceptable, but may be desirable for economic and social reasons. However, gross inequalities are morally unjustifiable, particularly when millions lack even the basic necessities of life. In our judgment, the distribution of income and wealth in the United States is so inequitable that it violates this minimum standard of distributive justice.

Clearly, the degree to which our inequality in income in the United States is acceptable or unacceptable is a moral or normative issue. There is, however, a way to view it as a more scientific or positive issue. Specifically, we live in an imperfect world. At last count, there were over a hundred countries in the world. Perhaps a more reasonable way to look at the degree of income inequality in the United States is to put it in a global context. In other words, as we go through this chapter, keep an eye out for what we have to say concerning how the amount of income inequality in the United States compares to that in other countries. On the basis of that comparison, see if your feelings change and whether the clergymen who wrote the letter excerpted above might feel differently had they, too, read this chapter.

▶ The Distribution of Wages and Income

Our emphasis in the preceding three chapters has been on the input side of the marketplace. In this chapter and the next we will emphasize the forces determining individual and family incomes, with particular emphasis on labor earnings. Income from the sale of labor services accounts for about 80 percent of all income in the United States. For this reason, knowledge of why workers earn different wage rates is fundamental to understanding income inequality. We begin by examining the **income distribution,** which is a measure of how the total amount of income in an economy is divided up. There is more than one way to measure the distribution of earnings or incomes in the United States and other countries. Society's total income can be thought of as being shared among individuals, families, or various groups. These groups can be made up of individuals who are in the same occupation or are members of the same race. We can look at how income varies among people who live in the same area, who are relatively poor, who are relatively wealthy, and so on. We can also think of income as being divided, or distributed, into categories such as wages, interest, rent, and profit.

The analysis of the labor market developed in chapters 12 through 14 provides the framework for understanding why wage rates differ among workers. Labor supply and demand and investments in human capital all contribute to an individual's earning power. They also give us important insights into poverty and the effects of race and sex discrimination in labor markets on incomes. In addition, they help us examine the issue of income redistribution and the actual effects of policies aimed at transferring income or wealth.

*The **size distribution of income** is a quantitative summary of the percentage of society's income received by various groups of individuals.*

Measures of the Income Distribution

Economists frequently describe in two ways how income is shared among society's members: (1) the distribution according to amount received and (2) the distribution according to source of income. Remember that whenever business firms produce goods and services, they must use productive factors, or inputs. The payments for all of these inputs generate wages, salaries, "rent," interest, and profits, which add up to society's total income. (Rent as measured in government statistics refers to payments for the use of land and buildings. Some economic rent is probably included in these figures, but there is also economic rent in wages and salaries, as we pointed out in chapter 13. Profit as measured in government statistics includes both economic profit and the return to firms' owners for supplying physical capital and managerial talent.) Since society's output is produced with the inputs that generate its income, the distribution of income amounts to the distribution of the goods and services an economy produces. Besides transfers of income from others, then, two conditions determine an individual's income: the quantity of productive factors owned by the individual and their value. Keep in mind that a reasonably fair or equitable distribution of income can be important to the long-term survival of an economic system. Once you have seen the facts we present, see if you think the income distribution in the United States is reasonably "fair."

The Size Distribution of Income in the United States and Other Countries

We will first examine the distribution of income by amount received. If income were equally distributed—everyone is receiving the same amount—this would be revealed by what is known as the **size distribution of income,** which indicates the income received by each individual, family, or group. Exact equality means that everyone's share of society's total income would be the same. For example, if there were 1,000,000 recipients, each person's share would be 1/1,000,000, or 0.0001 percent. There is no nation in which the size distribution of income exhibits even nearly complete equality.

There are several ways to measure the degree of inequality in the size distribution of income. One simple procedure is to focus on the poorest and richest individuals or households. For example, the lowest 20 percent of income recipients can be classified into one group and the highest 20 percent of income recipients into another group. If the income distribution were completely equal, then the bottom 20 percent of recipients and the top 20 percent would each receive one-fifth of society's total, or aggregate, income. The larger the share received by the top 20 percent compared to the bottom 20 percent, the more unequal is the income distribution.

To illustrate, suppose that five households receive an aggregate income of $100,000. If the income were equally distributed, each household would receive $20,000, or 20 percent of the total. Now suppose that income is unequally distributed as follows: Household 1 receives $2,500, 2 receives $5,000, 3 receives $10,000, 4 receives $15,000, and 5 receives $67,500. In this case, the lowest one-fifth of households would receive $2,500/$100,000 = 2.5 percent of total income, while the top one-fifth would receive $67,500/$100,000 = 67.5 percent.

Figure 15.1 shows the income shares received by the highest 20 percent and the lowest 40 percent of the income recipients in the United States and several other countries. Some of these countries, such as the United States, have predominately uncontrolled market economies, others have controlled economies, and still others have mixed economic systems.

A number of interesting features of the income distributions are described in figure 15.1. In every country listed, the top group receives a much larger share of income than those at the bottom. In *no* country is income even approximately equally distributed. Moreover, income shares do not vary sharply from year to year in the United States. It is important to note that the United States falls somewhere in the middle of the countries in terms of inequality. The socialist economies of Poland and Hungary have a smaller share of aggregate income accruing to the top 20 percent and a larger share accruing to the bottom 40 percent as opposed to the situation in the United

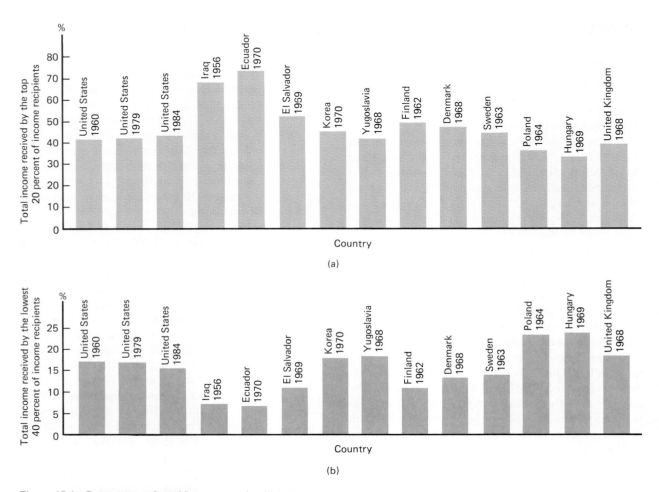

Figure 15.1   Percentage of total income received by the top 20 percent of income recipients and by the lowest 40 percent of income recipients.
From United States—*Statistical Abstract of the United States,* 1981, Table 730, Department of Economics—Bureau of the Census, p. 438. Other Countries—H. B. Chenery et al., *Redistribution with Growth,* Oxford University Press, Oxford, England, 1974, pp. 8–9.

*The **functional distribution of income** is a quantitative summary of the percentage of society's total income paid to the owners of various inputs that are used to produce goods and services.*

States. However, in Yugoslavia, the income distribution is much like that of the United States. The mixed economies in figure 15.1 are Denmark, Sweden, and Finland. What is the degree of income inequality in these nations compared to the United States? In which countries does income appear to be most unequally distributed?

The Functional Distribution of Income

Another way to view the distribution of income is by type of productive factor owned, or source of income. For example, if I receive $20,000 per year in salary and $5,000 per year in interest payments from corporate bonds, then 80 percent of my total income comes from selling my labor services. The remainder is classified as interest in official government statistics. We have seen that all income can be traced back to payments for productive inputs and transfers from one person or household to another. When we view the economy as a whole, transfers cancel out, so all of society's income is attributable to factor payments of one kind or another.

What factor of production corresponds to the interest payment of $5,000 I have received in the above example? The corporation from which I purchased my bonds used the money to buy labor, physical capital inputs, and perhaps some raw materials. The payments for labor inputs appear in the income distribution data as wages; the payments for raw materials are other firms' revenues, and the firms that sold these raw materials have themselves paid for inputs such as labor and physical capital. In addition to the sums a firm pays for the labor and raw materials it purchases, it must pay interest to its creditors; the remainder of the firm's revenue is profit. The revenue a firm generates from selling its output is based on the productivity of the inputs it uses. Therefore, the

interest I receive on my corporate bonds can only be paid because *factors other than labor* used by the firm also contribute to total output. In short, the interest I receive is derived from the contribution of physical capital to the firm's output and total revenue.

Imagine that the economy is one giant firm, and subtract all of the sales that one firm makes to another firm. We are left with a grand total of what can be called "final" sales of goods and services. Corresponding to this grand total is the distribution of the revenue from all final sales. Since we have "netted out" all of the payments that one firm makes to another firm, we are left with payments to labor and nonlabor factors of production, or to human versus nonhuman (physical) capital. The distribution of these payments between labor and capital is called the **functional distribution of income.** Because labor power is the only factor of production owned by everyone, the forces affecting the functional distribution of income are particularly important in determining the economic well-being of most households.

The functional distribution of income between labor and other factors is fairly easy to calculate because most business firms keep accurate records of their expenditures. The major difficulty lies with the self-employed: people who work for themselves. Suppose you owned your own automobile agency. Each year your accountant would tell you by how much your revenue exceeded your expenses. What part of this "profit" would be payment for your labor and what part a return on your investment in inventories, buildings, and so on? The answer to this question must be obtained indirectly. For example, if you knew how much you could earn by working for someone else, you could subtract this opportunity cost from your accounting "profit" to determine the return on your *nonlabor* contribution to your business. To avoid this

Figure 15.2   Employee compensation as a share of income in the United States and other countries
From United States—*Statistical Abstract of the United States,* 1986, Table 729, Department of Commerce–Bureau of the Census, p. 436. Other Countries—*National Account Statistics; Analysis of Main Aggregates,* 1982, United Nations.

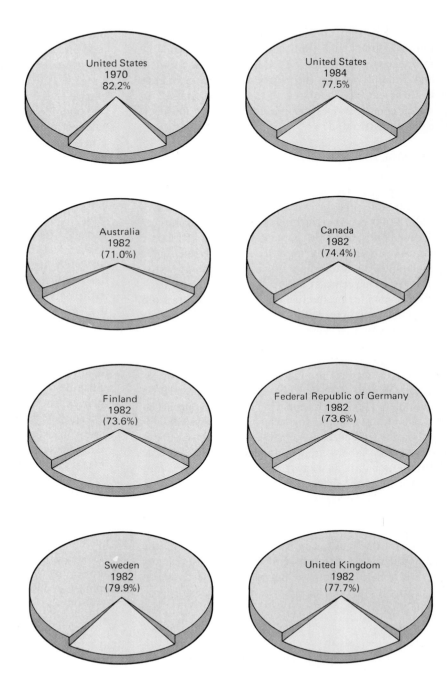

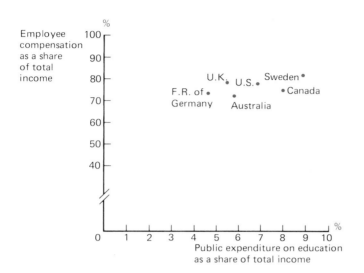

Employee compensation as a share of total income

Figure 15.3   The share of employee compensation in income and public expenditures on education
The share of wages and salaries in GNP is positively related to the amount spent on education.
From Figures 15.1, 15.2 and *Statistical Abstract of the United States,* 1986, Table 1471, p. 841.

difficulty, figure 15.2 presents data on the functional distribution of income in the United States for incorporated businesses only. Since nonincorporated proprietors account for only a small fraction of all output produced in the United States, omitting proprietors' income does not create a serious problem in estimating the functional distribution of income.

Figure 15.2 emphasizes the importance of the rewards to labor in total income. Notice that in the United States four out of five dollars of society's income is the result of selling labor services. We can go a long way toward understanding the causes of income inequality in the United States and other countries if we understand the determinants of labor's earning power. We have explored these determinants in chapters 12 through 14, and much of the remainder of this chapter deals with society's efforts to alter the distribution of income. These efforts must also be based on an understanding of the underlying determinants of factor payments if they are to achieve their goals.

Human Capital and the Functional Distribution of Income

We have just seen that the returns on human capital are a very important component of the typical person's income, and that is true not only in the United States but also around the world. In countries where more is spent on schooling, workers acquire more and better schooling and consequently earn more. Moreover, countries that spend more on schooling tend to have a larger share of their total income represented by labor earnings. To provide a picture of this relationship between schooling and the functional distribution of income, we have taken the information in figure 15.2 and plotted it in figure 15.3 along with educational expenditure information. Each dot represents information on a country's share of earnings and the amount spent on public schooling. The fact that the dots lie roughly on an upward-sloping line shows the positive relationship between schooling and labor's share in total income.

Schooling is also important in explaining income differences among individuals. Of course, many other factors play a role in determining the size distribution of income. Imagine constructing a graph something like figure 15.3 in which every adult would be represented by a point. The vertical axis would measure each individual's annual income and the horizontal axis would measure his or her years of schooling completed. (Adults who choose not to work at all or who cannot work would be excluded.) Needless to say, everyone who had completed the same amount of schooling would not receive the same income. Famous movie stars and athletes, for example, would be found near the top of the graph, given their schooling. Some people might have acquired vast amounts of physical capital in the form of land, oil wells, or commercial real estate. Others might have had very bad luck or, perhaps, physical or mental handicaps that lower their incomes. Nevertheless, the dots would be scattered around a line sloping upward from left to right. As schooling increases, so do personal incomes, on the average.

Using complex statistical techniques, economists have studied a large number of factors that contribute to personal differences in incomes. Of the conditions over which an individual has control, it is probably fair to say that none has a greater influence on income than the amount, quality, and type of schooling acquired. As we pointed out in chapter 14, another important component of human capital comes from the training workers acquire after leaving school. The study of the relationship between human capital investments and income is important for both positive and normative questions in economics. Policies aimed at changing who receives how much income cannot be effective unless we know how income is determined in the first place.

▶ Income Redistribution

We have emphasized the importance of how an economic system answers the *for whom* question. The answer determines who is rich and who is poor. Moreover, debate over whether the distribution of income is fair and, if it is not, how to correct inequities probably constitutes the single most time-consuming activity of legislative bodies, particularly at the state and federal levels. The remainder of this chapter deals with several topics related to income redistribution policies, primarily in the United States.

Why Redistribute Income?

Given scarcity, there are essentially two ways in which an individual's standard of living can be increased. One is for the individual to become more productive, expanding society's production possibilities frontier and thereby raising everyone's earnings. The second is via transfer of income from someone else.

Every human society in some way supports its poor. The generosity of such support has varied immensely, of course, with available resources and with social mores. Today, there is much variation among nations as well as within the United States in the extent of public and private transfers to lower-income individuals. When an economy is growing at a relatively fast pace and when this growth in resources or productivity is shared more or less equally, individual incomes will tend to grow as well. This reduces pressures for income redistribution. If the size of the total economic pie is growing, you do not need a bigger proportion of the pie to get a bigger slice. However, even in the most favorable circumstances, health problems or bad luck will cause some people to fall behind in their ability to support themselves. One reason for income redistribution is to aid these victims of misfortune.

When an economy's productive capacity is not growing very rapidly, income transfers are seen as a more important means whereby those in the low ranges of the income distribution can improve their lot. Political and social pressures for redistribution policies may be stronger in this case, but so will the resistance of those who must pay, because their losses are less likely to be recouped when the economy is growing only slowly.

Even in a fast-growing economy, there may be groups who perceive themselves, and who may be so perceived by others, as being treated unfairly. Let us consider a specific case where market forces have lowered incomes in some industry (steel) or for some occupation (steelworkers) while others in society have benefited (users of steel). An argument has been made, for example, for policies that protect or compensate steel firms and the members of steelworkers' unions when imports reduce domestic steel sales and therefore steelworkers' job opportunities. This argument is also part of the public discussion of policies aimed at maintaining the prices of farm products. Another example involves the very important debate over the extent to which classes of individuals have suffered unfairly from discrimination in the labor market and elsewhere. This has led to programs designed to enhance the earning power of blacks and women and sometimes to compensate them for past injustices. We will analyze discrimination and programs to combat its effects in detail in chapter 16.

Income redistribution occurs for many reasons and takes a multitude of forms. Not all beneficiaries are poor, and they may not even be worse off than those who pay for the transfers they receive. We will take a closer look at income redistribution, focusing on a few of the most important issues that policymakers have confronted in altering the distribution of income and wealth in the United States.

Measuring Poverty

When income redistribution is mentioned, your first thought is probably one of programs aimed at helping the unfortunate poor. Who is in poverty, and what policies can help them? We noted in our analysis of human capital that over the long term, schooling and other activities that enhance earning power are the most reliable means of avoiding poverty for most people. Nevertheless, even the best-laid plans do not always yield their intended results. If we wish to aid some or all who are poor by maintaining their incomes directly, we first must decide at what level their incomes are to be supported.

In very constrained circumstances—being stranded on a lifeboat in the Pacific Ocean, for example—it may be impossible to keep everyone from perishing from lack of food and shelter. It is the case in some very poor economies today that maintaining incomes above the poverty line means providing enough money, or goods, to survive and little more. In advanced economies such as the United States, however, the measurement of poverty is more arbitrary. It often involves defining a socially acceptable or socially preferred minimum income rather than measuring one that is biologically necessary for survival.

Income maintenance programs that provide payments to the poor can be measured against an official definition of poverty to judge their adequacy in reducing poverty. An official definition of poverty can also be used to identify the members of society whose incomes have temporarily or permanently fallen to a level that calls for corrective action (income transfers). Despite the fact that poverty has been officially defined in the United States, the definition is controversial. Nonfarm families and individuals are classified as in or out of poverty in terms of their cash income. This can miss many sources of income that

*The **poverty level of income** is the official government figure used to determine whether or not a particular family is poor.*

Table 15.1   Poverty level income for a nonfarm family of four and percent of population below poverty level, United States

Poverty level income for family of four			Poverty level as a percent of median income for four-person nonfarm family[b]	Percent of the population below poverty level
Year	Current dollars[a]	1972 dollars[a]		
1965	$ 3,223	$4,275	40.6%	17.3%
1970	3,968	4.276	35.2	12.6
1975	5,500	4,274	34.5	12.3
1980	8,414	4,272	34.3	13.0
1984	10,609	4,273	34.2	14.4

Source: From *Statistical Abstract of the United States, 1981*, Table 746, p. 446 and *Statistical Abstract of the United States, 1986*, pp. 446 and 457, Department of Commerce—Bureau of the Census.
[a]Current dollars refers to the actual dollar amount of the income level below which a family was defined to be in poverty. 1972 dollars refers to the purchasing power of the poverty level income in terms of how much a dollar would buy in 1972.
[b]Data for 1980 and 1984 reveal poverty level income as a percent of median income of all four-person families.

are not represented by a current cash flow. For example, many elderly people own their own homes. The value of the housing services they receive is not included in their cash income.[1]

The official **poverty level of income** in the United States is the income level used to separate in-poverty and out-of-poverty families for statistical and public policy purposes. Table 15.1 presents data on the poverty level of income for a family of four in 1965, 1970, 1975, 1980, and 1984.

Several variables are used to establish the poverty level of income. One is an estimate of the goods and services needed to maintain an acceptable standard of living for an individual, depending on age and sex. Another is family size and composition. Still another is whether the family lives on a farm (farm families can supplement their money incomes with home-grown food). Finally, the purchasing power of the dollar must be considered.

As the third column of table 15.1 shows, the official definition of poverty in terms of the quantity of goods and services that can be purchased was basically the same in 1984 as in 1965. The last column shows that the fraction of the United States population living in poverty was significantly smaller in 1984

than in 1965. There are two reasons for the decline of the fraction of the population below the poverty line during this period. One is the overall growth in the general level of incomes. The fourth column of table 15.1 shows that the poverty level income amounted to almost 41 percent of the median income for four-person nonfarm families in 1965, but only about 34 percent of the median in 1984. The facts that the poverty income did not change in terms of purchasing power and the purchasing power of the average family's income was growing pulled many families above the poverty line. The second cause of the decline in the proportion of individuals below the poverty line was probably the growth in coverage and generosity of income transfer programs during the period. These are programs such as *Aid to Families with Dependent Children (AFDC)* and Social Security, which are designed to maintain the income level of poor families and individuals above some minimum level. Finally, it is important to note the increase in poverty between 1980 and 1984. How much of this increase was temporary because of the severe recession of the early 1980s and would therefore eventually subside as the economy recovered and how much is permanent because of government budget cuts is a hotly debated topic.

Equality of Opportunity or Equality of Results?

In the remaining sections of this chapter we survey some of the programs that have been adopted or proposed to redistribute income in the United States. Apart from issues of war and peace, it is unlikely that any other government activities will have a greater effect on our welfare over the remainder of our lifetimes. Therefore, it is vital that both voters and policymakers thoroughly understand the basic issues of income redistribution.

The basic philosophy of a nation's income redistribution strategy is important. What is the fundamental goal toward which we strive—*equality of opportunity* or *equality of results?* This is an issue each of us must decide on the basis of ethical considerations (a normative question) and on the basis of how we believe altering the answer to the *for whom* question affects *what, how,* and *how much* is produced (all positive questions).

Assuring equality of opportunity means providing equal access to human capital investment opportunities and to the labor markets in which human capital services are traded for income. We have already discussed the role of public education financing in determining equal opportunity to attend school. Antidiscrimination policies constitute a cornerstone of the framework of rules governing fair play in labor markets. However, even if there were *complete* equality of opportunity, incomes would still not all be equal. Interpersonal differences in inherited wealth, luck, motivation, willingness to take risks, and ability would result in a substantial dispersion of wage rates and incomes. While there is probably wide agreement that people whose incomes fall below a socially acceptable level should be helped to maintain their standard of living, just how high that level should be is the subject of intense debate. What is directly transferred to the poor must be taken away from others through taxation. This reduces incentives to strive for wealth and achievement. It is probably one reason why no country we know of, even those countries with socialistic goals, has achieved equality of *results* in the income distribution.

Policies to Redistribute Income

Probably few, if any, government programs—from criminal justice to public works to the military—are completely neutral with respect to the income distribution. We will survey the nature and impact of some policies and proposals that have major distributional effects or that have received considerable attention in policy debates. We will not discuss programs that are covered in other chapters, such as farm price supports, unemployment compensation, and antidiscrimination programs.

The Role of Labor Unions

Although labor unions are not government agencies, the fact that workers have special legal rights to organize and bargain collectively means that their activities have received special government sanction. The government's regulation of labor union activities is one of its tools in affecting the distribution of income. In the United States in general, workers have the legal right to form unions and to bargain collectively with employers over wage rates and working conditions under rules established by the Wagner Act of 1935. The rationale is similar to that supporting agricultural cooperatives and marketing organizations. Without unions, it is argued, workers would be at a competitive disadvantage in the marketplace and subject to exploitation by employers. We have seen that a number of organizations in addition to labor unions, strictly defined, attempt to maintain or raise the labor incomes of their members. These are professional organizations such as associations of lawyers, doctors, accountants, hairdressers, and so on. Most of our discussion about unions applies to these organizations as well.

Unions can and have raised wage rates, but how has this affected the incomes of union workers? What have been the effects on nonunion workers? What are the effects on the real income of the general public? The answers to these questions tell us, to a great extent, the effects of unions on the distribution of economic well-being. Union members' income gains, if any, must come from somewhere. There are four possible sources.

1. Unions may increase economic efficiency—equivalent to pushing the economy's production possibility frontier outward. Although monopoly elements in an economy, which unions resemble, generally *reduce* efficiency, some economists claim that unions often "pay for themselves" by acting as a *collective voice* for their members.[2] These economists argue that by better representing their members' desires for nonwage aspects of jobs—safety, pleasant working environment, fringe benefits, and so on—unions reduce labor turnover. Whenever workers quit, employers must engage in costly searches for and training of new workers. To the extent that unions help reduce these costs, *ceteris paribus,* there may be a net gain in production, not a loss in production as the standard monopoly inefficiency argument claims. Economists disagree on the importance of this possible source of union gains.

2. Union members may derive income gains at the expense of owners of physical capital. In other words, there could be a transfer from those who receive dividends, interest, and profits to union members. This is a relatively unlikely source of union gains, however, because in the long run owners of physical capital are free to transfer their investments to industries where the return is highest. Thus, if unions in a particular labor market are especially successful in extracting wage gains, they may lose out in the long run as physical capital—and jobs—move elsewhere.[3]

3. Union income gains may be derived from consumers of goods and services produced with union labor. To the extent that consumers cannot find good substitutes for higher-priced union products, their real incomes are lowered and unions' power to achieve wage gains is enhanced. Indeed, unions frequently attempt to reduce consumers' willingness to purchase nonunion goods. Examples are the movements to "look for the union label" and to boycott nonunion lettuce and table grapes.

4. Wage and income gains by union workers may come at the expense of lower wages and incomes for nonunion workers. When a union wins a wage increase, workers in other jobs may seek union jobs. If they are successful in sharing union jobs, the result will be a dilution of union *income* gains. However, it is possible that the reduction in the quantity of union labor demanded will be so great that workers from a unionized industry will be forced to seek employment in nonunion jobs. This will force down wages and incomes there. Both kinds of shifts probably have occurred, and their *net* effect is uncertain. Moreover, there is no assurance that wage earners who gain are located at a lower position in the income distribution than those who lose.

As you can see, the channels through which unions can affect the income distribution are complex. Union wage gains do not automatically result in income gains. Moreover, the individuals whose incomes are reduced are not necessarily initially better off than union members who may gain. It should not surprise you that we have relatively imprecise knowledge of the exact magnitude of income redistribution caused by labor unions. However, most economists who have studied unions agree that they have not been *the* major source of income redistribution in the United States.[4]

Minimum Wage Legislation

Legal minimum wage rates have been established in most states for many jobs. The logic underlying the use of a minimum wage rate to redistribute income is based on two assumptions: (1) An increase in a worker's wage rate will raise his or her income, and (2) low wage rates result in low family incomes. Whether these assumptions hold up to the facts determines whether minimum wage legislation has the potential to reduce poverty.

To assess the impact of minimum wage rates on low-income families, we need to address four issues. The first is directly related to the demand for labor.

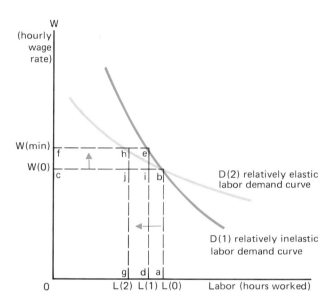

Figure 15.4 The effect of a minimum wage rate on employment and earnings
An effective minimum wage (one that is higher than the market equilibrium wage, W(0) will increase workers' *total* income only if the elasticity of the labor demand curve is smaller than 1 in absolute value. Then the rectangle illustrating the increase in income arising from the increase in the wage rate will be larger than the rectangle illustrating the loss in income arising from the decline in employment. Demand curve D(1) is relatively inelastic, while demand curve D(2) is relatively elastic.

The impact of imposing an *effective* minimum wage rate (one that is above the market wage in the absence of the minimum) is shown in figure 15.4. Since the derived demand for labor is a negatively sloped curve, increasing the wage rate employers must pay from W(0) to W(min) reduces the quantity of labor demanded. What happens to workers' earnings depends on the elasticity of labor demand. Demand curve D(2) is more elastic than D(1). At the wage rate W(0), workers earn W(0) × L(0) dollars per time period. This is represented by the area 0abc. If the demand curve is relatively inelastic, such as D(1), the

quantity of labor demanded falls to L(1) and earnings become the area 0def. Whether this represents greater earnings or less total earnings depends on whether the area cief (the effect of the increased wage) is greater than or less than the area dabi (the effect of reduced work hours). The more elastic the demand curve, the more hours worked fall. When labor demand is relatively elastic, the negative influence on earnings (gabj) will be larger than the positive influence (cjhf), and earnings of the average low-wage worker may actually fall as a result of increasing the minimum wage. If so, *ceteris paribus,* this would tend to reduce labor's share in the functional distribution of income.

The results of a number of studies suggest that the earnings of low-wage workers are often reduced when minimum wage rates increase.[5] The effect of minimum wages on employment and work hours may take many forms. For example, employers may open later and close earlier; restaurant workers may have to perform food preparation tasks while customers are in the establishment rather than before; mechanization may be used to replace some labor, and so on.[6]

The next three issues that must be addressed to determine the effectiveness of minimum wages in reducing poverty are these: Who gets the minimum wage jobs? Are they the same workers who would have been employed at lower wages? Are they, in fact, low-income individuals or members of low-income families? In recent years, we have learned much about the answers to these questions, particularly the last one. Workers who actually obtain minimum wage jobs may replace less capable workers. For example, raising the wage in figure 15.4 from W(0) to W(min) may attract well-educated married women into the labor force, women who take jobs that might otherwise have gone to disadvantaged male adults or to teenagers with little work experience. In other words, those who lose their jobs when minimum wages rise are frequently the least advantaged and cannot compete at the higher

*A **categorical welfare program** uses personal and family characteristics to determine who in the low-income population is eligible for financial support.*

wages with those who replace them. Moreover, minimum wage recipients who keep their jobs are more likely than not to be married women or teenagers whose family incomes are well above the poverty line.[7]

Does the minimum wage, then, constitute an effective tool to redistribute income toward the poor? Here is a passage from a report issued by a specially appointed government commission.

> Inasmuch as there is not a strong correlation between individual earnings and family income, with large numbers of minimum wage workers found in households in all income levels, the message from the body of empirical evidence is that the minimum wage has had *small* "beneficial" effects on the distribution of income. There are, however, other mechanisms that would be more effective in providing income support for individuals and families such as direct federal government transfer payments or some variant of a negative income tax.[8]

Transfer Programs

All of the income redistribution policies described so far are targeted only indirectly at incomes. Their direct effects are aimed at hiring policies or wage rates. We now turn to programs that are aimed directly at income. As such, they focus on promoting equality of results. Some of these programs are designed specifically to maintain incomes above some specified level. They come under the general title of "welfare" or, more technically, "income maintenance programs," and include Aid to Families of Dependent Children (AFDC), the federal food stamp program, and various general welfare programs operated by states. Subsidized housing for families and individuals whose incomes fall below specified levels are also basically income maintenance programs. Another means of altering the income distribution involves transfers from the higher end of the distribution to the middle and lower end via government taxation.

Income Maintenance Programs   The three major goals of an income maintenance program are (1) to provide a socially acceptable minimum standard of living, (2) to minimize the economic inefficiency caused by the program, and (3) to accomplish these

goals within a politically acceptable time limit. All taxation and income maintenance programs affect work incentives. This can be a major source of economic inefficiency, and much debate has centered on trade-offs among these three goals.

To see how these three goals conflict, we will describe two income maintenance programs in some detail. One is an existing part of the transfer programs operating in the United States—AFDC. The other has been proposed from time to time under the banner of welfare reform. AFDC is a **categorical welfare program,** which means that only certain categories of people are eligible to receive support. To receive AFDC, a person must be a member of a family with children in which one parent is absent, or if both parents (or stepparents) are present, one must be unemployed. Thus, not all low-income people are eligible for AFDC support. Other categorical income maintenance programs include unemployment insurance, workers' compensation insurance, Social Security disability insurance for people who are unable to work, and the Black Lung disability program for those afflicted with this occupational disease.

Those who are eligible for AFDC receive a basic payment determined by (1) family size, (2) the maximum payment in their state, and (3) the amount of income they earn or receive from other sources. Historically, a family's AFDC payments have been reduced by about $0.67 for every dollar of income earned. To see how work incentives are affected, compare two individuals who are alike in every respect except that one is eligible to receive AFDC and the other is not. Suppose that both have wage rates of $4 per hour, that apart from AFDC neither receives income from any source other than earnings, and that the maximum AFDC payment to the eligible person is $400 per month. Thus, every time the eligible individual works an hour, his or her AFDC payment is reduced by $2.68. That is, the AFDC recipient's net pay is only about $1.32 per hour before payment of income and Social Security taxes. (We will ignore income and Social Security taxes to keep our illustration simple.)

If the *eligible* individual works 150 hours during any month, earnings equal $600 and the AFDC payment is reduced to *zero*. (To see this, multiply 150

*A **progressive income tax** has a rate schedule whereby the higher one's taxable income, the higher is the percentage of an additional dollar of taxable income that must be paid in taxes.*

*The **marginal tax rate** is the percentage of an additional dollar of taxable income that must be paid in taxes.*

hours by $2.68, the "take back" rate, to obtain approximately $400, the maximum AFDC benefit amount.) The individual who is not eligible will also earn $600 by working 150 hours. Now consider what will happen if the person who is eligible for AFDC decides to reduce his or her work effort by 25 hours per month. *Earnings* fall by $100, but *income* actually received falls by only $33 because his or her effective wage rate is only $1.32 per hour. Thus, $67 is gained in the form of an AFDC payment. By contrast if the noneligible person works 25 hours less, *both* earnings *and* income fall by $100. It would be surprising indeed if both people decided to work an equal number of hours.

AFDC is not the only existing income maintenance program that reduces work incentives. Unemployment compensation, food stamps, and other such programs also raise income levels for those who do not work relative to the amount they would earn at a job. In Western European countries, unemployment compensation is often so high that income is not raised at all by acceptance of a job. It has been suggested that the resulting work disincentives are creating serious problems in Western European economies.[9]

We should recognize that one purpose of the AFDC program is to enable mothers to work less so that they may care for their children. That is why the payments are limited to families with children under eighteen years of age. However, if it were decided that work incentives should be increased, one way to accomplish this would be to reduce the implicit penalty, or tax, on work by reducing the "take back" rate of $0.67 per dollar earned in our example. An extreme case will illustrate this. Suppose that in our example the individual who is eligible for AFDC received $400 per month with no reduction for any amount earned. The opportunity cost of the decision to cut back on work hours would then be $4.00, not $1.32, per hour. On the one hand, work incentives would be greater. On the other hand, with a zero "take back" rate someone working 125 hours per month would receive $400 per month from AFDC instead of only $67 when the "take back" rate is 67 percent. The point is that there is a trade-off between work incentives and the amount of AFDC support the government (the rest of society) pays. With no take back, the amount spent

by the government could be reduced by decreasing the size of the basic grant below $400, but this would conflict with the goal of providing an acceptable standard of living for those who do not work or who work relatively few hours.

One means of resolving the conflict among the three goals of an income maintenance program is to maintain both high benefit levels and high take back rates but to try to force all AFDC recipients to work at least a specified number of hours if work is available.[10] This procedure, known as workfare, is not without its costs, however, because it requires that government intrude to a greater extent in the private lives of welfare recipients. Balancing income redistribution policies to achieve each of these goals is a fundamental problem facing all democratic societies.

Progressive Income Taxation, a "Flat" Tax, and the Supply Side   All income redistribution schemes affect work incentives in one way or another because they change the rewards for working. In recent years, much attention has been paid to the "supply-side" impact of our **progressive income tax,** which takes a higher fraction of taxable income the higher the taxpayer's taxable income happens to be. (A key word here is *taxable* because exemptions, deductions, and other loopholes often create a sizable gap between income received and the income upon which taxes are paid.) To gain some insight into the way our tax system can discourage work effort, consider the situation of a married woman contemplating reentering the labor force after her children begin high school. Suppose her husband has taxable income of $40,000 per year. This places the family in a fairly high income tax bracket. What is relevant to the wife's decision to work is the tax rate applicable to the additional income earned by the family—its **marginal tax rate.** Because of progressive tax rates and the Social Security tax, the first dollar earned by the wife upon reentering the labor force would be taxed at a rate of around 50 percent. Since her family would have to replace her services in the home by working more around the house, eating out, and so on, from a financial standpoint it would be somewhat surprising if the wife decided to reenter the labor force after weighing the costs and benefits.[11]

*A **flat tax** would tax all eligible income at the same rate.*

Figure 15.5 The flat-rate income tax proposal by economist Robert Hall and political scientist Alvin Rabushka. The flat tax rate would simplify tax forms and apply the same tax rate to everyone.

HALL-RABUSHKA SIMPLIFIED FLAT-RATE TAX FORM

Form 1	Individual Compensation Tax	1984

Your first name and initial of joint return (also give spouse's name and initial)　　　Last name　　　Your social security number

Present home address (Number and street, including apartment number or rural route)　　　Spouse's social security no

City, town or post office State and ZIP code　　　Your occupation ►
　　　Spouse's occupation ►

1 Compensation as reported by employer **1**
2 Other wage income, including pensions **2**
3 Total compensation *(line 1 plus line 2)* **3**
4 Personal allowance . . . .
　(a) ☐ $6800 for married filing jointly . . . . **4(a)**
　(b) ☐ $4160 for single . . . . **4(b)**
　(c) ☐ $6130 for single head of household . . . . **4(c)**
5 Number of dependents, not including spouse **5**
6 Personal allowances for dependents *(line 5 multiplied by $820)* . . **6**
7 Total personal allowances *(line 4 plus line 6)* **7**
8 Taxable compensation *(line 3 less line 7)* **8**
9 Tax *(19% of line 8)* **9**
10 Tax withheld by employer **10**
11 Tax due *(line 9 less line 10, if positive)* **11**
12 Refund due *(line 10 less line 9, if positive)* **12**

As originally proposed, a **flat tax** on incomes would replace our present progressive tax system with a single rate on all incomes and eliminate most deductions for expenses not directly related to producing income (such as interest payments on owner-occupied homes and charitable donations). Figure 15.5 illustrates the income tax return form that would be used if the flat-rate income tax proposed by economist Robert Hall and political scientist Alvin Rabushka were adopted. Compare it to the 1985 federal income tax return in figure 15.6. Would your tax bill be higher or lower under this particular flat tax than under the existing system? Try filling out both forms to find the answer.

The woman in the situation described above is discouraged from working by the current progressive income tax and thus pays no taxes. By lowering the family's marginal tax rate, the flat tax would encourage the wife to work and to earn income, thus paying *some* taxes. The amount of taxes paid by the family under a flat tax would not necessarily fall, but the income of the family would rise. Supporters of a flat tax claim that the increased output for the economy, and the incomes earned by those who produce it, would be so large that the reduction in *marginal* tax rates for those in today's upper-income brackets would not reduce total taxes collected. Those who are now in the lower tax brackets would also pay no more tax under the flat tax. In other words, the economy's production possibilities frontier would be pushed outward through increased efficiency, enabling us to have more private consumption without sacrificing government expenditures. Whether this would actually occur is an empirical question that will continue to be debated both in and out of Congress. In mid-1986 Congress was considering a bill that would reduce the number of income tax brackets from the fifteen listed in figure 15.6 to only two. This would make the United States income tax structure more like the flat tax system described in figure 15.5.

Form 1040 Department of the Treasury—Internal Revenue Service
U.S. Individual Income Tax Return 1985 (3)

For the year January 1-December 31, 1985, or other tax year beginning _____, 1985, ending _____, 19____   OMB No. 1545-0074

Use IRS label. Otherwise, please print or type.	Your first name and initial (if joint return, also give spouse's name and initial)	Last name	Your social security number
	Present home address (number and street, including apartment number, or rural route)		Spouse's social security number
	City, town or post office, state, and ZIP code	Your occupation	
		Spouse's occupation	

Presidential Election Campaign ▶ Do you want $1 to go to this fund? — Yes ☐ No ☐
If joint return, does your spouse want $1 to go to this fund? — Yes ☐ No ☐
Note: Checking "Yes" will not change your tax or reduce your refund.

For Privacy Act and Paperwork Reduction Act Notice, see Instructions.

Filing Status
Check only one box.
1. ☐ Single
2. ☐ Married filing joint return (even if only one had income)
3. ☐ Married filing separate return. Enter spouse's social security no. above and full name here. _____
4. ☐ Head of household (with qualifying person). (See page 5 of Instructions.) If the qualifying person is your unmarried child but not your dependent, write child's name here. _____
5. ☐ Qualifying widow(er) with dependent child (year spouse died ▶ 19____). (See page 6 of Instructions.)

Exemptions
Always check the box labeled Yourself. Check other boxes if they apply.

6a ☐ Yourself   ☐ 65 or over   ☐ Blind — Enter number of boxes checked on 6a and b ▶
b ☐ Spouse   ☐ 65 or over   ☐ Blind
c First names of your dependent children who lived with you _____ — Enter number of children listed on 6c ▶
d First names of your dependent children who did not live with you (see page 6). _____
(If pre-1985 agreement, check here ▶ ☐) — Enter number of children listed on 6d ▶

e Other dependents:

(1) Name	(2) Relationship	(3) Number of months lived in your home	(4) Did dependent have income of $1,040 or more?	(5) Did you provide more than one-half of dependent's support?

Enter number of other dependents ▶

f Total number of exemptions claimed (also complete line 36). — Add numbers entered in boxes above ▶

Income
Please attach Copy B of your Forms W-2, W-2G, and W-2P here.
If you do not have a W-2, see page 4 of Instructions.

Please attach check or money order here.

7	Wages, salaries, tips, etc. (Attach Form(s) W-2.)	7
8	Interest income (also attach Schedule B if over $400)	8
9a	Dividends (also attach Schedule B if over $400) _____, 9b Exclusion _____	
c	Subtract line 9b from line 9a and enter the result	9c
10	Taxable refunds of state and local income taxes, if any, from the worksheet on page 9 of Instructions	10
11	Alimony received	11
12	Business income or (loss) (attach Schedule C)	12
13	Capital gain or (loss) (attach Schedule D)	13
14	40% of capital gain distributions not reported on line 13 (see page 9 of Instructions)	14
15	Other gains or (losses) (attach Form 4797)	15
16	Fully taxable pensions, IRA distributions, and annuities not reported on line 17 (see page 9)	16
17a	Other pensions and annuities, including rollovers. Total received [17a]	
b	Taxable amount, if any, from the worksheet on page 10 of Instructions	17b
18	Rents, royalties, partnerships, estates, trusts, etc. (attach Schedule E)	18
19	Farm income or (loss) (attach Schedule F)	19
20a	Unemployment compensation (insurance). Total received [20a]	
b	Taxable amount, if any, from the worksheet on page 10 of Instructions	20b
21a	Social security benefits (see page 10). Total received [21a]	
b	Taxable amount, if any, from worksheet on page 11. Tax-exempt interest _____	21b
22	Other income (list type and amount—see page 11 of Instructions) _____	22
23	Add lines 7 through 22. This is your **total income** ▶	23

Adjustments to Income
(See Instructions on page 11.)

24	Moving expense (attach Form 3903 or 3903F)	24
25	Employee business expenses (attach Form 2106)	25
26	IRA deduction, from the worksheet on page 12	26
27	Keogh retirement plan deduction	27
28	Penalty on early withdrawal of savings	28
29	Alimony paid (recipient's last name _____ and social security no. _____)	29
30	Deduction for a married couple when both work (attach Schedule W)	30
31	Add lines 24 through 30. These are your **total adjustments** ▶	31

Adjusted Gross Income

32 Subtract line 31 from line 23. This is your **adjusted gross income.** If this line is less than $11,000 and a child lived with you, see "Earned Income Credit" (line 59) on page 16 of Instructions. If you want IRS to figure your tax, see page 13 of Instructions. ▶ | 32

Figure 15.6   Federal individual income tax return for 1985
From Department of the Treasury—Internal Revenue Service.

Figure 15.6　Continued

Form 1040 (1985)　　　　　　　　　　　　　　　　　　　　　　　　　　　　　　Page **2**

Tax Compu-tation (See Instructions on page 13.)	33　Amount from line 32 (adjusted gross income)	33
	34a　If you itemize, attach Schedule A (Form 1040) and enter the amount from Schedule A, line 26. **Caution:** If you have unearned income and can be claimed as a dependent on your parents' return, check here ▶ ☐ and see page 13 of Instructions. Also see page 13 if you are married filing a separate return and your spouse itemizes deductions, or you are a dual-status alien.	34a
	b　If you do not itemize but you made charitable contributions, enter your cash contributions here. (If you gave $3,000 or more to any one organization, see page 14.)　34b	
	c　Enter your noncash contributions (you must attach Form 8283 if over $500)　34c	
	d　Add lines 34b and 34c. Enter the total　34d	
	e　Divide the amount on line 34d by 2. Enter the result here	34e
	35　Subtract line 34a or line 34e, whichever applies, from line 33	35
	36　Multiply $1,040 by the total number of exemptions claimed on line 6f (see page 14)	36
	37　**Taxable income.** Subtract line 36 from line 35. Enter the result (but not less than zero)	37
	38　Enter tax here. Check if from ☐ Tax Table, ☐ Tax Rate Schedule X, Y, or Z, or ☐ Schedule G	38
	39　Additional taxes. (See page 14 of Instructions.) Enter here and check if from ☐ Form 4970, ☐ Form 4972, or ☐ Form 5544	39
	40　Add lines 38 and 39. Enter the total　▶	40
Credits (See Instructions on page 14.)	41　Credit for child and dependent care expenses (attach Form 2441)　41	
	42　Credit for the elderly and the permanently and totally disabled (attach Schedule R)　42	
	43　Residential energy credit (attach Form 5695)　43	
	44　Partial credit for political contributions for which you have receipts　44	
	45　Add lines 41 through 44. These are your total personal credits	45
	46　Subtract line 45 from line 40. Enter the result (but not less than zero)	46
	47　Foreign tax credit (attach Form 1116)　47	
	48　General business credit. Check if from ☐ Form 3800, ☐ Form 3468, ☐ Form 5884, ☐ Form 6478　48	
	49　Add lines 47 and 48. These are your total business and other credits	49
	50　Subtract line 49 from line 46. Enter the result (but not less than zero)　▶	50
Other Taxes (Including Advance EIC Payments)	51　Self-employment tax (attach Schedule SE)	51
	52　Alternative minimum tax (attach Form 6251)	52
	53　Tax from recapture of investment credit (attach Form 4255)	53
	54　Social security tax on tip income not reported to employer (attach Form 4137)	54
	55　Tax on an IRA (attach Form 5329)	55
	56　Add lines 50 through 55. This is your **total tax**　▶	56
Payments Attach Forms W-2, W-2G, and W-2P to front	57　Federal income tax withheld　57	
	58　1985 estimated tax payments and amount applied from 1984 return　58	
	59　Earned income credit (see page 16)　59	
	60　Amount paid with Form 4868　60	
	61　Excess social security tax and RRTA tax withheld (two or more employers)　61	
	62　Credit for Federal tax on gasoline and special fuels (attach Form 4136)　62	
	63　Regulated Investment Company credit (attach Form 2439)　63	
	64　Add lines 57 through 63. These are your **total payments**　▶	64
Refund or Amount You Owe	65　If line 64 is larger than line 56, enter amount **OVERPAID**　▶	65
	66　Amount of line 65 to be **REFUNDED TO YOU**　▶	66
	67　Amount of line 65 to be applied to your 1986 estimated tax　▶　67	
	68　If line 56 is larger than line 64, enter **AMOUNT YOU OWE.** Attach check or money order for full amount payable to "Internal Revenue Service." Write your social security number and "1985 Form 1040" on it　▶	68
	Check ▶ ☐ if Form 2210 (2210F) is attached. See page 17　**Penalty: $**	
Please Sign Here	Under penalties of perjury, I declare that I have examined this return and accompanying schedules and statements, and to the best of my knowledge and belief, they are true, correct, and complete. Declaration of preparer (other than taxpayer) is based on all information of which preparer has any knowledge ▶ Your signature　Date　▶ Spouse's signature (if filing jointly, BOTH must sign)	
Paid Preparer's Use Only	Preparer's signature ▶　Date　Check if self-employed ☐　Preparer's social security no. Firm's name (or yours, if self-employed) and address ▶　E.I. No.　ZIP code	

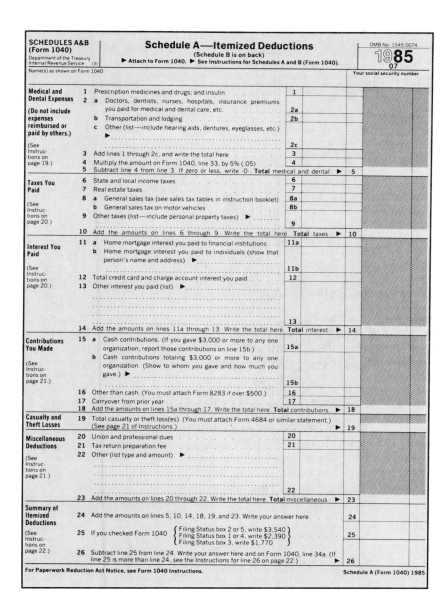

Figure 15.6 Continued

Figure 15.6   Continued

Schedules A&B (Form 1040) 1985 **Schedule B—Interest and Dividend Income**   08   OMB No. 1545-0074   Page **2**

Name(s) as shown on Form 1040 (Do not enter name and social security number if shown on other side.) | Your social security number

**Part I
Interest
Income**

(See Instructions on pages 8 and 22.)

Also complete Part III.

If you received more than $400 in interest income, you must complete Part I and list ALL interest received. If you received interest as a nominee for another, or you received or paid accrued interest on securities transferred between interest payment dates, see page 22.

Interest income	Amount
1 Interest income from seller-financed mortgages. (See Instructions and show name of payer.) ▶ **1**	
2 Other interest income (list name of payer) ▶	
....	
....	
....	
....	
.... **2**	
....	
....	
....	
....	
3 Add the amounts on lines 1 and 2. Write the total here and on Form 1040, line 8 ▶ **3**	

**Part II
Dividend
Income**

(See Instructions on pages 8 and 22.)

Also complete Part III.

If you received more than $400 in gross dividends and other distributions on stock, or you are electing to exclude qualified reinvested dividends from a public utility, complete Part II. If you received dividends as a nominee for another, see page 23.

Dividend income	Amount
4 Dividend income (list name of payer—include on line 4 capital gain distributions, nontaxable distributions, etc.) ▶	
....	
....	
....	
....	
.... **4**	
....	
....	
....	
....	
5 Add the amounts on line 4. Write the total here . . . **5**	
6 Capital gain distributions. Enter here and on line 15, Schedule D. * **6**	
7 Nontaxable distributions. (See Schedule D Instructions for adjustment to basis.) **7**	
8 Exclusion of qualified reinvested dividends from a public utility. (See page 23 of Instructions.) **8**	
9 Add the amounts on lines 6, 7, and 8. Write the total here . . . **9**	
10 Subtract line 9 from line 5. Write the result here and on Form 1040, line 9a ▶ **10**	

If you received capital gain distributions for the year and you do not need Schedule D to report any other gains or losses, do not file that schedule. Instead, enter 40% of your capital gain distributions on Form 1040, line 14.

**Part III
Foreign
Accounts
and
Foreign
Trusts**

(See Instructions on page 23.)

If you received more than $400 of interest or dividends, OR if you had a foreign account or were a grantor of, or a transferor to, a foreign trust, you must answer both questions in Part III. | Yes | No

11 At any time during the tax year, did you have an interest in or a signature or other authority over a financial account in a foreign country (such as a bank account, securities account, or other financial account)? (See page 23 of the Instructions for exceptions and filing requirements for Form TD F 90-22.1.)   .   .   .   .

If "Yes," write the name of the foreign country ▶ ....

12 Were you the grantor of, or transferor to, a foreign trust which existed during the current tax year, whether or not you have any beneficial interest in it? If "Yes," you may have to file Forms 3520, 3520-A, or 926.

For Paperwork Reduction Act Notice, see Form 1040 Instructions.   Schedule B (Form 1040) 1985

Figure 15.6   Continued

1985 Tax Rate Schedules
Your zero bracket amount has been built into these Tax Rate Schedules.

Caution: You must use the Tax Table instead of these Tax Rate Schedules if your taxable income is less than $50,000 unless you use **Schedule G,** Income Averaging, to figure your tax. In that case, even if your taxable income is less than $50,000, use the rate schedules on this page to figure your tax.

Schedule X
Single Taxpayers
Use this Schedule if you checked **Filing Status Box 1** on Form 1040—

Over—	But not over—	Enter on Form 1040, line 38	of the amount over—
$0	$2,390	—0—	
2,390	3,540	.......11%	$2,390
3,540	4,580	$126.50 + 12%	3,540
4,580	6,760	251.30 + 14%	4,580
6,760	8,850	556.50 + 15%	6,760
8,850	11,240	870.00 + 16%	8,850
11,240	13,430	1,252.40 + 18%	11,240
13,430	15,610	1,646.60 + 20%	13,430
15,610	18,940	2,082.60 + 23%	15,610
18,940	24,460	2,848.50 + 26%	18,940
24,460	29,970	4,283.70 + 30%	24,460
29,970	35,490	5,936.70 + 34%	29,970
35,490	43,190	7,813.50 + 38%	35,490
43,190	57,550	10,739.50 + 42%	43,190
57,550	85,130	16,770.70 + 48%	57,550
85,130	....	30,009.10 + 50%	85,130

Schedule Z
Unmarried Heads of Household
(including certain married persons who live apart—see page 5 of the instructions)

Use this schedule if you checked **Filing Status Box 4** on Form 1040—

Over—	But not over—	Enter on Form 1040, line 38	of the amount over—
$0	$2,390	—0—	
2,390	4,580	.......11%	$2,390
4,580	6,760	$240.90 + 12%	4,580
6,760	9,050	502.50 + 14%	6,760
9,050	12,280	823.10 + 17%	9,050
12,280	15,610	1,372.20 + 18%	12,280
15,610	18,940	1,971.60 + 20%	15,610
18,940	24,460	2,637.60 + 24%	18,940
24,460	29,970	3,962.40 + 28%	24,460
29,970	35,490	5,505.20 + 32%	29,970
35,490	46,520	7,271.60 + 35%	35,490
46,520	63,070	11,132.10 + 42%	46,520
63,070	85,130	18,083.10 + 45%	63,070
85,130	112,720	28,010.10 + 48%	85,130
112,720	....	41,253.30 + 50%	112,720

Schedule Y
Married Taxpayers and Qualifying Widows and Widowers

Married Filing Joint Returns and Qualifying Widows and Widowers

Use this schedule if you checked **Filing Status Box 2 or 5** on Form 1040—

Over—	But not over—	Enter on Form 1040, line 38	of the amount over—
$0	$3,540	—0—	
3,540	5,720	.......11%	$3,540
5,720	7,910	$239.80 + 12%	5,720
7,910	12,390	502.60 + 14%	7,910
12,390	16,650	1,129.80 + 16%	12,390
16,650	21,020	1,811.40 + 18%	16,650
21,020	25,600	2,598.00 + 22%	21,020
25,600	31,120	3,605.60 + 25%	25,600
31,120	36,630	4,985.60 + 28%	31,120
36,630	47,670	6,528.40 + 33%	36,630
47,670	62,450	10,171.60 + 38%	47,670
62,450	89,090	15,788.00 + 42%	62,450
89,090	113,860	26,976.80 + 45%	89,090
113,860	169,020	38,123.30 + 49%	113,860
169,020	....	65,151.70 + 50%	169,020

Married Filing Separate Returns

Use this schedule if you checked **Filing Status Box 3** on Form 1040—

Over—	But not over—	Enter on Form 1040, line 38	of the amount over—
$0	$1,770	—0—	
1,770	2,860	.......11%	$1,770
2,860	3,955	$119.90 + 12%	2,860
3,955	6,195	251.30 + 14%	3,955
6,195	8,325	564.90 + 16%	6,195
8,325	10,510	905.70 + 18%	8,325
10,510	12,800	1,299.00 + 22%	10,510
12,800	15,560	1,802.80 + 25%	12,800
15,560	18,315	2,492.80 + 28%	15,560
18,315	23,835	3,264.20 + 33%	18,315
23,835	31,225	5,085.80 + 38%	23,835
31,225	44,545	7,894.00 + 42%	31,225
44,545	56,930	13,488.40 + 45%	44,545
56,930	84,510	19,061.65 + 49%	56,930
84,510	....	32,575.85 + 50%	84,510

Page 40

▶ Summary and Conclusions

In this chapter we discussed how labor markets affect the distribution of income and analyzed various government policies that affect labor markets and the distribution of income. In light of what you have learned, how do you feel now about the statement of the Catholic bishops cited at the beginning of this chapter? We emphasized the following points in this chapter.

Income distribution can be measured according to the amounts people receive (the size distribution) and according to the source of income (the functional distribution).

The distribution of income depends on the prices of factors of production, the quantities of factors owned, and transfers of income among individuals.

Income redistribution efforts can be divided into those that promote equality of opportunity and those that seek to promote equality of results.

Income redistribution activities do not always benefit the poor and may harm some poor people.

Government policies to redistribute income almost always affect labor market outcomes.

▶ Key Terms

categorical welfare program *310*

flat tax *312*

functional distribution of income *301*

income distribution *298*

marginal tax rate *311*

poverty level of income *306*

progressive income tax *311*

size distribution of income *299*

▶ Questions for Discussion and Review

1. Are the following statements true, false, or uncertain? Defend your answers.
   a. A minimum wage will cause employment to fall and thereby make workers worse off than if there were no minimum wage.
   b. The United States has one of the most unequal income distributions in the world.

2. Figure 15.1 shows that the share of the lowest 40 percent of income recipients in aggregate income is much higher in the United States than in Iraq or Ecuador. List three factors you think might be important reasons for this difference.

3. In 1929, employee compensation amounted to 59 percent of total incomes received in the United States. By 1970, this fraction had risen to 75.4 percent. (These data are not exactly comparable to those in figure 15.2.) List three reasons you think are important in explaining this trend. How does your answer to this question relate to your answer to the previous question?

4. Make a list of every government policy discussed so far in this text that affects the distribution of income. Show how each policy affects the supply or demand for labor and other productive factors. State how each policy affects equality of opportunity or equality of outcome. Decide whether each policy raises the income of persons in the lower, middle, or upper part of the income distribution. Give each policy a grade from A to F for each of the following properties: (1) equity (are people in equal circumstances treated equally by the policy?) and (2) effect on economic efficiency (how does each policy affect the economy's production possibilities frontier and the allocation of production among industries?).

5. There are many different methods for measuring personal income. One method is to consider an individual's gross income. Another method is to adjust gross income for taxes and transfer payments. What difference, if any, would these two measures have on the resulting distribution of income?

6. Explain the concepts of equality of opportunity and equality of results.

7. Income distribution does not always occur at a national or statewide level. Can you think of some methods that colleges and universities use to redistribute income among their students?

8. What evidence is presented in this chapter to support the hypothesis that minimum wage legislation does not always help the poor?

9. What are some of the key problems with using a progressive income tax to redistribute income?

10. Considering what you have learned up to this point about economic theory, does it make any economic sense for the government to pursue redistribution programs that promise higher economic welfare for everybody? Explain.

Chapter 16

Discrimination

Outline

I. Introduction *322*
II. Discrimination in labor markets: Race and sex wage differences *322*
III. Economic analysis of labor market discrimination *323*
   A. Causes of labor market discrimination *324*
     1. Employer discrimination and profit *324*
     2. Segregation *324*
     3. Societal discrimination *324*
IV. Black-white wage differences and public policy *325*
   A. The effects of equal employment opportunity legislation and other antidiscrimination programs on racial discrimination *326*
V. Male-female wage differences and public policy *326*
   A. The comparable worth issue *328*
VI. Discrimination in housing markets *329*
   A. Analytical issues *329*
   B. Some proposed remedies and their effects *330*
     1. Fair housing legislation perfectly enforced *331*
     2. Fair housing legislation imperfectly enforced *332*
     3. An alternative remedy *333*
VII. Summary and conclusions *333*
VIII. Key terms *334*
IX. Questions for discussion and review *334*
X. Policy issue: You decide—Cutting labor costs to save jobs *335*
   A. The action-initiating event *335*
   B. The issue *335*
   C. Economic issues *335*
   D. Recommendations *335*

Objectives

After reading this chapter, the student should be able to:

Define and give examples of simple labor market discrimination, societal discrimination, and secondary discrimination.

Discuss the causes of labor market discrimination.

Identify the likely causes of black-white wage differences and the role government antidiscrimination programs have played in reducing the differences.

Identify the likely causes of male-female wage differences.

Discuss the issue of comparable worth legislation.

Explain why discrimination exists in housing markets, and describe some remedies.

Discrimination occurs when an individual or a group of individuals must pay or receive a price for a good or service that differs from the price charged or paid to others who are alike in every respect except some personal characteristic unrelated to the cost or productivity of the good or service provided.

▶ Introduction

The grandparents of one of the authors of this book came to the United States from Italy during the late 1800s. They had two children, the author's mother and her brother. While the author's mother and her brother seemed to be about equally intelligent, their parents encouraged the daughter to take secretarial training in high school. When she graduated, she began to work as a secretary in a chemical plant. Her brother, however, was encouraged by their parents to take college preparatory courses in high school. As a result, he went on to college and ultimately to graduate school at MIT. He now has a much higher annual income than his sister, the author's mother.

There is more to the story. While working at the chemical plant as a secretary, the author's mother met his father, who was a truck driver. Of course, his mother earned a lower salary than his father, in part because her work may have been less valuable to the company, in part because his father belonged to a union and she did not, and in part because she had a cleaner, more pleasant job, which tends to pay less. Why didn't she become a truck driver? She did not want to and probably could not have done so. In 1938, there were few women members of the Teamsters Union.

The point of this story is that the author's mother had a lower wage because she was in a lower-wage occupation, even though she had finished high school and her husband had not. Her lower wage was partly the result of her choice of occupation and partly the result of a lack of access to certain better-paying jobs.

How much of the earnings differential between the author's mother and her brother and between his mother and father could be termed unfair or discriminatory? We hope to make the answers to these questions clear during the course of this chapter.

*In this chapter we take a close look at the problem of **discrimination**, which refers to a situation in which individuals are treated differently in the labor market or in markets for goods and services (such as housing) because of their race, religion, national origin, sex, or other characteristics not intrinsically related to their ability to work or to pay for the goods and services they wish to consume. Discrimination in the labor market can lower wages and income for an unfavored group of workers, and discrimination in product markets may lower real income, or purchasing power, because it can raise the prices paid by an unfavored group of consumers. Therefore, an understanding of discrimination, its causes, and policies to combat it is essential in studying the distribution of income and economic well-being.*

▶ Discrimination in Labor Markets: Race and Sex Wage Differences

We saw in chapter 15 that there are many causes of low incomes, among them individual misfortune and a low level of labor productivity. One aspect of the income distribution that has caused much concern is a tendency for women and for blacks of both sexes to earn consistently lower wages than men and whites. Figure 16.1 shows that the chances of being below the poverty line are over three times larger in families with a black householder (head of household) than in families with a white householder. Almost 40 percent of all people in families headed by a woman are below the poverty line.

Labor market discrimination occurs when members of a particular race, sex, or other group receive lower pay even though they have the same investment in human capital as others do.

Societal discrimination occurs when members of a particular race, sex, or other group receive less favorable treatment from government, firms, or their families regarding opportunities for investing in human capital.

Secondary discrimination occurs when members of a particular race, sex, or other group are discouraged from investing in human capital because of labor market discrimination.

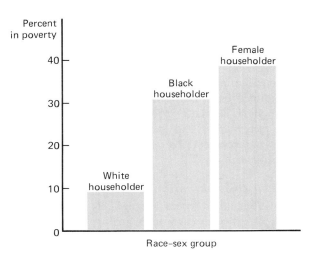

Figure 16.1   Percentage of people in families below the poverty line, by race and sex of householder, 1984
From *Statistical Abstract of the United States*, 1986, Table 767, p. 451.

Does this income gap arise because women and blacks are simply less productive than men and white workers or because women and blacks receive less favorable treatment from employers even though they are as productive as other workers? If they are less productive, is this because blacks and women invest less in human capital? If so, do they have the same opportunities to improve their skills as whites and men do? It is important to answer these questions if we are to know whether sex and race differences in wages and incomes arise from discrimination or some other cause. In this section we deal mainly with discrimination in the labor market on the basis of race and sex because, as the data in figure 16.1 show, the income gap for blacks and women is so large.

▶ Economic Analysis of Labor Market Discrimination

One of the most important things we hope you have learned in studying economics is that effective government policies require a thorough understanding of the underlying causes of whatever it is we may want to change. This basic principle applies to the problem of discrimination just as it does to other aspects of the economy. To begin with, we need to define what we mean by labor market discrimination and find a way to distinguish between it and other possible factors as causes of low incomes. Next we must understand how discrimination works in order to choose the best policy or policies to combat its effects.

Discrimination is a complex process that has many possible roots. It will help to classify discrimination according to the way in which it affects labor market earning power and investment in human capital. Labor market discrimination can be divided into three categories: (1) Simple **labor market discrimination** occurs when workers with given schooling, training, and other labor market characteristics are paid less because the demand curve for their services lies below the demand curve for other individuals who have identical qualifications but who are of a different race or the opposite sex. (2) **Societal discrimination** occurs when a group such as blacks or women does not have access to the same opportunities for schooling or training as do whites or men. (3) **Secondary discrimination** occurs when members of such a group invest less in their human capital because the payoff just is not there. For example, a black or a woman may not even try to attend medical school if hospitals will not employ blacks or women. The second and third forms of discrimination can lead to a crowding of minority workers into low-status, low-wage jobs.

Causes of Labor Market Discrimination

Most people have preconceived ideas about what discrimination is and how it works. Probably the most serious misconception is to confuse *prejudice* or *distaste* with *discrimination*. You, as an individual, may strongly dislike people with hair a different color from yours. However, your dislike cannot result in simple labor market discrimination against, say, blondes for reasons we will soon see.

Employer Discrimination and Profit

Suppose you absolutely refused to employ a blonde worker because of your dislike for such hair. This would not economically harm blondes in the long run because there are numerous other (unprejudiced) employers who would hire them. The only person who could possibly be harmed by your distaste for blondes is *you,* because you may have to forego employing some good workers to exercise your taste for dark hair. This example illustrates why, in an economy with competitive forces, such as that of the United States, simple labor market discrimination is unlikely to be the *only* factor explaining race or sex differences in income.

Segregation

Employers who are prejudiced against blacks and women will sacrifice profit opportunities if they are willing to pay more to whites or to men who perform at the same level of productivity as blacks or women. If white or male *employees* demand higher pay when they are required to work with others of the opposite sex or a different race, or if customers refuse to do business with members of a minority group, the cost-minimizing employers will *segregate* their labor forces if legally permitted to do so. However, workplace segregation *alone* does not necessarily result in labor market discrimination. Automobiles produced by all-white or all-male labor would be indistinguishable from those produced by blacks or women with the same skills and would sell for the same price. Therefore, the profit motive would lead competing employers to bid up the wages of underpaid blacks and women, eliminating discriminatory wage differences in the long term. The point here is that in markets where some degree of competition is present, as in most free market and mixed economies, there are powerful forces working *against* simple labor market discrimination.

Societal Discrimination

Segregated labor forces are unlikely to be equally productive if blacks or women acquire fewer skills on the job than do whites or men. Societal or secondary discrimination may also result in less, different, or lower-quality schooling. For instance, separate schooling probably provided inferior education for blacks; in some families young women have been encouraged to enroll in home economics rather than computer courses or encouraged to enter the labor force or marry immediately after high school. If, as a result, the basic skills or the quality of management for all-black or all-women work forces suffered, this would lead to lower productivity and lower wages for blacks and women regardless of whether or not they were segregated in the workplace. The result would be labor market discrimination. What we would actually observe in the labor market is a mixture of segregated and integrated labor forces in which blacks and women hold different types of jobs than whites and men. In both cases blacks and women would earn less than whites and men.

Once again, a warning is necessary. When we observe men and women or blacks and whites holding different jobs and earning, on the average, different incomes, this does not in itself mean that labor market discrimination is the explanation. Other causes of lower income, such as less schooling or training must

women or men on both jobs, but women prefer sewing to cutting, for whatever reason. In either case, implementing a comparable worth rule would require that someone (probably under the supervision of a government official) determine whether or not both jobs have the same value to an employer. There are two problems involved: (1) Where would the information about the value of a job be obtained? (2) Should the wage of cutters be lowered or the wage of sewing machine operators be raised to satisfy the law? The answer to the first question is usually provided by the labor market. That is, the two wage rates represent the *value* to a firm from adding one more hour of a cutter's labor or one more hour of a sewing machine operator's labor because these are the amounts a firm is willing to pay for each, respectively. It would be no easy task for an outside observer to decide whether the wage of sewing machine operators would equal the wage of cutters if employment in the two occupations were equal. Even the employers might not know the answer to this question.

Anyone trying to answer the second question would have to face the following additional problem. If it were decided that a comparable worth law required that firms must lower the cutters' wage to equal $W(1)$, the wage of sewing machine operators in figure 16.2, cutters would be angry. Moreover, firms would experience a *shortage* of cutters. If a regulation were issued to raise the sewing machine operators' wage to the level of $W(2)$, the cutters' wage, firms would lay off some sewing machine operators or cut back on their work hours. Thus, sewing machine operators would not necessarily benefit from the regulation because average incomes might fall. Moreover, if hours per employed worker did not change, the laid-off sewing machine operators would definitely be worse off than if their wage had remained at $W(1)$ in figure 16.2. Much needs to be considered before the concept of a comparable worth law is put into practice.

▶ Discrimination in Housing Markets

We now turn to discrimination in a market where incomes are spent rather than earned. As we pointed out earlier, if members of some group are discriminated against in a product market, they cannot purchase certain goods or services unless they are willing to pay a higher price than others must pay. This means that their real income is lowered, just as if they received lower wage rates for their work effort. If discrimination against these people occurs in both the labor and product markets, the impact on their economic well-being is magnified. Again, in studying discrimination we should bear in mind the following questions.

What is the basic source of discrimination?

Is discrimination caused or made worse by the profit motive?

What market forces turn a *desire* to discriminate into *actual* discrimination, which means that actual economic harm is done to members of the unfavored group?

What can government do to alleviate the effects of discrimination?

Analytical Issues

Discrimination in United States housing markets has affected many different minority groups. However, blacks have been the largest single group victimized by housing discrimination. Therefore, in our discussion of discrimination in housing markets, we will divide the population into two groups, blacks and whites. We will assume that a significant number of blacks would prefer to live in predominately white neighborhoods. (The remainder would prefer to live in predominantly black neighborhoods.) The reason for this preference may have nothing to do with race. Rather, it may be based on a desire to live in an area with nicer homes, good public services, and a low crime rate. If blacks have lower incomes on average than whites, it may be difficult for blacks to find "nice" neighborhoods that do not have a majority of whites living in them. We will also assume that blacks are hindered in achieving their desired housing goals because a large number of whites in *every* white neighborhood prefer a segregated environment.

The assumption that white *home owners* have a widespread desire to live only with whites is crucial to the result that blacks are harmed by a desire to discriminate against them in the housing market. Suppose, by contrast, that white home owners could not care less about the color of their neighbors but that *home builders* desired to discriminate against blacks. In order to carry out this desire, a home builder would have to be prepared to sell houses to blacks only if they were willing to pay *more* than whites. If *all* home builders discriminated against blacks, the result would be an equilibrium in the housing market in which blacks paid higher prices for housing of a given quality than whites. On *average,* however, home builders would receive just enough revenue to cover their costs in a competitive housing industry. (You may wish to review chapter 7 to verify this conclusion.) This means that the price blacks would pay for a house would be greater than the cost of providing it, while the price paid by whites would be less.

If home builders carried out their desire to discriminate, a difference in the price of houses would result, and this would represent actual discrimination against blacks in the housing market. Could this price differential persist, however? Not if, as we have assumed, white *home owners* had no preference regarding the race of their neighbors. If white home owners were "color blind," the profit motive would lead to the elimination of the housing premium that blacks would have to pay. Any white person would be able to purchase a house from a home builder at a lower price than blacks would have to pay and eventually sell it to a black family, for a profit, at a price somewhat lower than that charged by discriminating

home builders. In other words, an industry of housing brokers would emerge in response to the profit potential created by home builders' desire to discriminate against blacks. Since blacks would no longer have an incentive to buy directly from home builders, home builders would end up selling houses only to whites. In equilibrium, the price of these houses would have to cover their cost of production, and the difference in the price of housing to blacks and whites would be sharply reduced, if not entirely eliminated. (Since brokerage has a cost, the price of housing to blacks would include the brokers' business costs.)

Studies of racial discrimination in housing are hampered by the lack of data on whether blacks must pay a premium to live in a predominately white neighborhood. The few studies that exist imply that blacks do pay such a premium.[11] The main point of our analysis is this: Racial discrimination in housing has its roots in a widespread desire of whites to live in segregated neighborhoods. Therefore, antidiscrimination efforts must recognize this underlying cause if they are to be successful in achieving economic fairness for blacks who wish to live in integrated neighborhoods. (Remember, we are not saying that *all* blacks want to live in such neighborhoods, just that some do.)

Some Proposed Remedies and Their Effects

One possible way to eliminate racial discrimination in housing would be to "help the market along" by legally permitting blacks to pay more than whites for the same housing. Our analysis suggests that competitive market forces would eventually eliminate or sharply reduce the premium paid by blacks for housing of given quality. However, that solution has some obvious ethical drawbacks. A common alternative has been "fair housing" legislation, which makes it illegal to discriminate in the sale of housing on the basis of race, religion, sex, and sometimes other personal attributes. We will now explore the likely impact of such policies on the supply of housing, the actual prices paid by whites and blacks, and the extent of discrimination in the housing market.

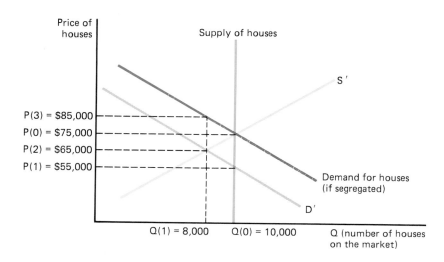

Figure 16.3 The market for housing with a perfectly enforced fair housing law
A fair housing law causes the market demand for housing to fall to D'. In the long run, the quantity of housing falls to Q(1) and the price falls to P(2). White buyers, however, are willing to pay P(3) for segregated housing.

Fair Housing Legislation Perfectly Enforced

A perfectly enforced fair housing law requires that enforcers have perfect knowledge of the prices paid by blacks and whites for identical housing. Moreover, two houses are seldom exactly alike, and advertised prices typically differ from selling prices. Therefore, perfect enforcement of fair housing legislation is a fairly strong assumption. Later, we will explore the impact of fair housing legislation when enforcement is less than complete.

Figure 16.3 depicts the effects of a fair housing law on the housing market. The initial supply curve in figure 16.3 represents the supply of existing housing in a community that has recently adopted fair housing legislation. At the time the law is passed, Q(0) houses exist (10,000 houses in our example). The market demand for this housing, if segregated, leads to an equilibrium price of P(0), or $75,000, per house. Under the fair housing law, blacks are allowed to buy houses in the community. However, they are a minority, and the white majority prefer segregation in our example. Therefore, as a result of integration, the demand curve for housing falls to D', and the equilibrium price of a house declines to P(1), which is $55,000.

The effect of the law in the *short run* is to inflict a loss equal to P(0) − P(1), or $20,000, on home owners and on home builders who had been holding new homes for sale in the community. As the price of houses falls, home builders will no longer find it profitable to construct new homes in this community and will tend to move to other communities (or even to other lines of work). This tendency is reflected in the long-run supply curve S' in figure 16.3. The positive slope of S' shows the extent to which the quantity of housing available declines as the price of houses falls.

The steepness of S' depends to a considerable extent on the geographical coverage of the fair housing law. If the law applies only locally, new houses can easily be built in nearby communities, and S' will tend to be fairly elastic (flat). Both producers and consumers of white-only housing will quickly move to nearby communities. However, if the law is regional or statewide, then the movement of both buyers and sellers of houses to communities outside the covered area will be relatively costly. The supply curve will be relatively inelastic (steep), and the demand curve will not shift downward so much. The law will be more effective in promoting integrated housing.

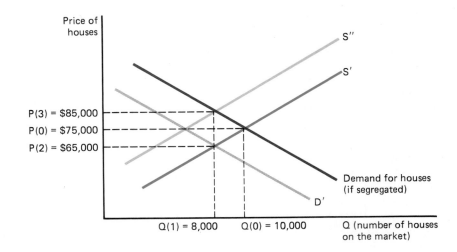

Figure 16.4   Imperfect enforcement of a fair housing law
When a fair housing law is imperfectly enforced, the vertical distance between S′ and S″ represents the amount per house that may be paid to circumvent the law.

In the long run, the price of housing, which is now fully integrated, falls to P(2), or $65,000, and the quantity available falls to Q(1), or 8,000 houses. Successful enforcement of the fair housing law alters the equilibrium price of housing for both whites and blacks, as well as the quantity of housing. Whites would have been willing to pay a price equal to P(3), or $85,000, for the quantity of housing Q(1), or 8,000 houses, if it were segregated. The satisfaction whites derive from housing is reduced. On the other hand, blacks benefit from the successful enforcement of the fair housing law. Previously, if they could buy housing in an integrated neighborhood, they had to pay a price greater than P(0), or $75,000 in our example. Now they can purchase integrated housing at price P(2), which is $65,000. The successful enforcement of fair housing, then, eliminates segregation and the effects of housing discrimination against blacks. These benefits come at the cost of reducing the satisfaction derived by whites who want segregated housing in our example, and the benefits may also reduce the profits or economic rents earned by builders who had supplied housing to the segregated community.

Fair Housing Legislation Imperfectly Enforced
Fair housing legislation may not be perfectly enforced, however. There are a number of reasons for this. One is simply that it is costly to uncover violations. Moreover, whites who want segregation and, perhaps, home builders lose out from such regulation and may take steps to emasculate fair housing legislation. The effects of the forces working against enforcement are depicted in figure 16.4.

In figure 16.4, whites who prefer segregated housing are willing to pay as much as P(3), or $85,000, for the quantity of housing currently available if it is segregated. The gap between P(3) and the current price of housing P(2), or $65,000, represents a gain that can be obtained by anyone who can supply segregated housing to whites. Anyone who may benefit from segregation—builders, home owners, or white home buyers who want segregated housing—has an incentive to pay as much as P(3) − P(2) per house ($20,000 in our example) in legal fees, bribes, lobbyists' salaries, and so on, to help avoid the fair housing law.

Suppose these costs are paid by builders or by home owners and that they are successful in avoiding enforcement of the law. The demand curve for housing is raised back to what it was with housing segregation. However, the costs paid to avoid enforcement of the law are added to the other costs of providing segregated housing. In other words, the supply curve of segregated housing becomes S'' because additional costs of P(3) − P(2), or $20,000, have been added to the basic cost of building a home in order to make sure the fair housing law is not enforced. If this happens, lobbyists, lawyers, and perhaps corrupt public officials receive the "discrimination premium" of P(3) − P(2), blacks are unable to purchase integrated housing or must pay a higher price to do so, and whites are able to obtain segregated housing at the price P(3), which is $85,000 in our example.

An Alternative Remedy

Given that the root cause of housing discrimination and segregation is the desire on the part of many whites to live in segregated communities, there are policies that may reduce the negative impact of housing discrimination on black families who wish to live in integrated neighborhoods. One solution would be for the government to subsidize the cost of housing in integrated communities. For example, home owners in neighborhoods with a certain percentage of blacks (or other minority groups) might receive a property tax rebate paid for by higher taxes in neighborhoods where most or all housing is occupied by whites. This would give whites a financial incentive to move into neighborhoods with a significant number of black families. It is to be hoped that once such a movement started, whites would lose some of their prejudices against integrated neighborhoods so that additional integration would occur.

▶ Summary and Conclusions

In this chapter, we have analyzed some of the causes and effects of discrimination in labor and housing markets. You should now understand more about the earning power differences between the author's mother and his uncle and between his mother and father that were described in the introductory example. The following major points were emphasized in this chapter.

Labor market discrimination may affect earnings directly and may also reduce incentives to invest in human capital.

The wages of blacks have risen relative to whites since 1964; however, there is no general agreement on whether this has been due to a reduction in market discrimination or in societal discrimination.

It is much more difficult to estimate the effects of discrimination on the male-female wage gap than on the white-black wage gap.

Comparable worth legislation is an attempt to substitute the judgment of "experts" for the principal task performed by labor markets.

Discrimination in product markets can lower the real income of a minority group that is discriminated against.

An imperfectly enforced fair housing law may raise the price of housing without reducing actual discrimination.

Public policy to reduce or eliminate the adverse effects of discrimination must be based on an understanding of the underlying cause of discrimination and how it operates through labor or product markets.

▶ Key Terms

Civil Rights Act of
 1964 *326*

comparable worth
 legislation *328*

discrimination *322*

Equal Employment
 Opportunities
 Commission (EEOC)
 326

labor market
 discrimination *323*

secondary
 discrimination *323*

societal discrimination
 323

▶ Questions for Discussion and Review

Are the statements in questions 1 through 5 true, false,
or uncertain? Defend your answers.

1. Because of labor market discrimination, women
 typically earn only about 60 percent as much as
 men.

2. Since discrimination against certain racial
 groups is only a statement of tastes and
 preferences, discrimination is economically
 efficient.

3. Comparable worth legislation will force
 employers to raise wages of employees who are
 the most valuable to the firm.

4. Less consumer discrimination in the product
 market will occur with manufactured products
 than with personal services.

5. An economically efficient method of eliminating
 sex discrimination is to require that a firm's
 labor force reflect the male-female ratio of the
 surrounding community.

6. Since the mid-1960s the ratio of the wage rates
 of blacks to the wage rates of whites has risen
 more for young people than for older workers.
 If the cause has been a decline in racial
 discrimination in labor markets, what kind of
 discrimination is most likely to have been
 reduced or eliminated—simple, societal, or
 secondary?

7. Explain the three categories of labor market
 discrimination.

8. From the substitution effect in demand theory,
 we know that consumers substitute more of a
 relatively less expensive good into their
 consumption bundle when faced with a change
 in relative prices. With this in mind, what effect
 would higher market wages for females have on
 their labor force participation rates and their
 decision to have children?

9. On the basis of evidence presented in this
 chapter, does sex discrimination in the labor
 market appear to be prevalent for females who
 have never married versus females who have
 married, *ceteris paribus?*

10. Cases involving housing discrimination do not
 always concern race. Recently, many
 condominiums, apartment cooperatives, and
 mobile home parks have prohibited families
 with children. Is there any economic reasoning
 behind these rules or is this simply
 discrimination?

Cutting Labor Costs to Save Jobs

▶ The Action-Initiating Event

A firm and a union are involved in a labor negotiation. At the core of their discussion lies the fact that the firm is in danger of closing because of high labor costs compared to new, nonunion firms. Management and the union have hired you as an informal arbitrator to advise them on the possibility of cutting labor costs.

▶ The Issue

The difficulty that you face is that while cutting workers' wages will keep the firm competitive, workers do not take kindly to income losses and may not agree to any proposal involving a pay cut. You are worried that the workers do not understand the magnitude of the situation and the fact that if a pay cut is not forthcoming, the firm will go out of business. In this case, all of the workers will lose their jobs. How can labor costs be cut if workers are unwilling, or at least strongly resistant, to any reductions in their wage rates?

Recently, some firms and unions have agreed to a plan known as a two-tiered pay structure.[1] Under such an arrangement, existing workers keep their current level of wages and promised pay raises while future employees are hired at a lower wage rate, despite the fact that they may perform the same duties as existing workers. You decide to advise management and labor to consider such a plan, but you want them to understand the economic issues involved.

▶ Economic Issues

On the one hand, you want management and labor to realize that they will both lose out if the firm closes. Thus, a two-tiered pay scheme may achieve the objective central to both parties, keeping the firm in business. On the other hand, you wonder if the firm can indeed hire new workers at a lower wage rate, and how these new workers will feel about performing the same activities for lower pay than other people working alongside them. You also want current workers to consider carefully the long-run implications of a labor force increasingly made up of workers who are paid less than they are.

▶ Recommendations

In making your report to management and the union you will want to consider the following questions. What is the wage rate that will be offered to new employees in the lower tier of the two-tiered wage plan? More specifically, what economic forces need to be considered when this wage rate is set? Can we expect the new employees to have the same productivity and commitment to job as the current employees, who will receive a higher wage? Should the existing employees be concerned about allowing the firm to hire potential future replacements for them at a lower rate of pay? In this regard, should the labor union seek a contract with a clause in it that tries to protect existing employees from being fired and replaced by newly hired workers who receive a lower rate of pay? Finally, what issues does the union have to think about in terms of any internal political problems that it might have when some workers are paid lower wages but pay the same dues and belong to the same union as workers in the upper tier?

Both management and labor want to understand the potential economic benefits and economic costs to each of them from going to a two-tiered wage plan. While they would like to have the firm stay in business and continue to employ the present workers, they are worried about the potentially negative long-run implications of adopting such a pay plan.

Reference

1. For background reading, see Roy J. Harris, Jr., "More Concerns Set Two-Tier Pacts with Unions Penalizing New Hires," *Wall Street Journal*, 15 Dec. 1983, p. 33; and David Wessel, "Split Personality: Two-Tier Pay Spreads but the Pioneer Firms Encounter Problems," *Wall Street Journal*, 14 Oct. 1985, p. 1.

Part V

Government and Markets

Chapter 17

Market Deficiencies

Outline

I. Introduction *340*
II. External economies and diseconomies *341*
   A. The pollution problem: Private costs and social costs *341*
   B. Positive externalities *343*
      1. The social benefits of higher education *344*
         a. Reassessing social benefits *345*
III. Public goods *345*
IV. Government's responses to external diseconomies and public goods problems *346*
   A. A closer look at the causes of market deficiencies *346*
      1. The exclusion problem, externalities, and transaction costs *346*
      2. The role of property rights *347*
         a. Copying computer software: Lowering costs or theft of property? *348*
         b. Saving the world's whales *348*
      3. Property rights and economic efficiency *349*
         a. The political economy of property rights *349*
   B. Possible solutions to the pollution problem *350*
      1. Information difficulties and limitations on government policy implementation *351*
      2. Creating a market for pollution rights *352*
      3. Government policy toward pollution in the United States *353*
      4. The politics and international nature of the pollution problem *354*
   C. Public goods: National defense *355*
      1. The free-rider problem *355*
         a. International free riding *356*
V. Summary and conclusions *356*
VI. Key terms *357*
VII. Questions for discussion and review *357*

Objectives

After reading this chapter, the student should be able to:

Explain when pollution is an external diseconomy and what solutions lead to economic efficiency.

Give examples of external economies.

Define and give examples of public goods.

Discuss when government should intervene to alleviate market deficiencies.

Discuss the importance of property rights in achieving economic efficiency.

Explain how a pollution tax might be used to achieve economic efficiency and what some of the difficulties would be in implementing such a plan.

Discuss who the winners and losers are from pollution control policy in the United States.

Explain how the aggregate demand for a public good is determined.

Discuss the political economy of property rights.

Market failure is the provision of a good or service in a quantity that is not economically efficient.

► Introduction

Jim and Mary Smith had always wanted to visit the American Southwest—particularly the Grand Canyon. Now that two of their three children were fifteen and seventeen years old, they wanted to take the whole family to visit this area before the children went off to college. They knew that the next ten years would be difficult for them financially, college tuition and expenses being so high, but a raft trip down the Colorado River had been their longtime dream.

Therefore, Jim and Mary arranged for the family to spend two weeks floating down the Colorado with professional guides. The family was thrilled when they embarked on their rubber rafts in northern Arizona, and the trip started out better than they had ever hoped it would. However, after they had been on the river a day and a half, they began to notice small airplanes flying overhead with greater and greater frequency. By the time they reached some of the most isolated and beautiful canyon areas, the airplanes were flying every couple of minutes and often dropping down well below the canyon rim. Instead of quiet beauty, the Smiths experienced noise not unlike that around their home, which was only ten miles from a major airport. Their guides told them that the small planes were carrying sightseers who did not want to spend the time or effort to hike, ride, or float down the river. In the past ten years, they were told, the number of flights had increased tenfold and were still on the rise. The Smiths enjoyed their raft trip down the Colorado very much, but they felt, after they returned home, that much of the special experience they had expected was destroyed because of the encroaching airplane noise.

In 1985, the National Park Service began hearings that it hoped would lead to strict regulation of tourist flights over and into the Grand Canyon. There was great controversy over the proposed regulations. Representatives of the travel industry argued that the proposed regulations would deprive the elderly and infirm of their right to see the Grand Canyon, which is, of course, the property of all Americans. Conservation groups argued that the right to visit the canyon does not extend to infringements of noise and the sight of airplanes on the enjoyment of those who desire to experience the area in its natural state. In this chapter, we will explore the economic issues that lead to the type of conflict that currently rages over who has the right to visit the Grand Canyon and how.

In this chapter, we summarize and extend the discussions of how markets work to analyze market performance and market malfunctions. We will discuss **market failure**, which occurs when the price and quantity outcomes in markets do not lead to economic efficiency. (Reminder: Economic efficiency requires that marginal cost equal price in all markets and that buyers—firms and households—pay all of the opportunity costs of the goods, services, and productive resources they purchase.) We will explore the situations in which unregulated markets do not provide economically efficient answers to the basic economic questions of what and how goods shall be produced.

We will analyze some important social problems, one of which is pollution. Another problem occurs when markets fail to provide a good or service, the cost of which is less than the value of that good or service to society. Since markets seldom actually fail to work at all in the situations we will examine, we will generally use the term market deficiency to describe them instead. We will also explore possible solutions to these situations. Perhaps the most important lesson to be learned is that when markets work well, they work very well indeed, and the substitutes for the cost and benefit information provided by market prices are almost always fundamentally flawed.

*An **external diseconomy, external cost,** or **negative externality** results when part of the cost of producing or consuming a good or service is paid for by a firm or household other than the one that produces or consumes it.*

*An **external economy, external benefit,** or **positive externality** results when part of the benefit of producing or consuming a good or service accrues to a firm or household other than that which produces or consumes it.*

▶ External Economies and Diseconomies

A market deficiency of great current importance is the pollution of our environment. Smoky or smoggy air, rivers loaded with chemicals, and seawater coated with crude oil are some obvious and common examples. In 1980, nearly $56 billion was spent on pollution abatement and control in the United States.[1] (See figure 17.1.) This, of course, does *not* include the costs to society that are caused by pollution that has yet to be eliminated. Pollution occurs around the world, in market economies and controlled economies alike. It is not confined to advanced industrialized nations, although its form tends to change with economic development. For example, water contaminated with human and animal wastes is a major problem in developing countries, whereas smoke and chemical pollution characterizes industrialized economies. To understand the best way to control pollution and still obtain the most from our scarce resources, it is necessary to understand the economic causes of pollution. What we learn from this analysis is that, in general, the economically efficient cure for pollution is to reduce it, not to eliminate it. We will also learn that reducing pollution raises *measured* costs and prices while reducing other costs, many of which are *hidden* and thus unmeasured.

In the terminology of economics, pollution occurs as a result of an **external diseconomy, external cost,** or **negative externality,** which means that part of the cost of producing or consuming a good is not borne by the producer or consumer. For example, a factory belching smoke inflicts costs on nearby residents without paying them for the right to do so. When your roommate studies late and keeps the radio blaring so that you cannot sleep, you are partly paying for your roommate's grades. It is also possible to have an **external economy, external benefit,** or **positive externality,** which is the opposite of a negative externality. If your roommate is so punctual that you can set your watch by the time he or she leaves for class in the morning, you receive a benefit that you do not have to pay for directly. Have you ever walked by a shop

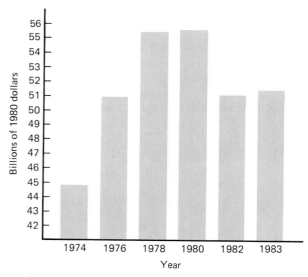

Total expenditure on pollution abatement and control in the United States, 1974–1983

Figure 17.1   Total expenditures on pollution abatement and control in the United States, 1974–1983
From U.S. Department of Commerce, *Statistical Abstract of the United States*, 1985, Table 353.

selling coffee roasted on the premises? The delicious aroma is something most people enjoy but do not pay for. These "free" services are simple examples of external economies.

The Pollution Problem: Private Costs and Social Costs

Suppose there is a small laundry in a large midwestern city. Historically, its least-cost method of drying clothes has been to hang them on a clothesline and use unpaid factors of production—sunshine and clean air—to finish the job. Many other laundry firms in the city operate in much the same way, and all tend to earn zero economic profits. In other words, the owners of the laundry firms tend to do no better and no worse than they would in their next best alternative lines of work.

*The **free-rider problem** occurs because of the ability of a user of a good or service to avoid paying for it when the user cannot easily be excluded from the benefits.*

*The **marginal private cost**, or internal cost, of a good or service is the opportunity cost that the producer or user must pay to produce or use one more unit.*

*The **marginal social cost** of a good or service includes both the private and external costs (if any) of producing one more unit.*

One day, however, a large steel plant begins operation in the city. That afternoon, when the owner of the laundry goes out to take in the wash hung out to dry in the morning, it is covered with soot from the steel mill. Discovering the cause of the problem, the launderer realizes that the only feasible solution is to replace the backyard clothesline with a modern electric or gas dryer. Dryers get the clothes just as dry as the clothesline—but they are considerably more costly to operate. As a result of the steel mill, then, it now costs more to produce clean laundry. This is an *external cost* or *external diseconomy* of the steel production. It is a cost that is not borne by the steel firm itself. Rather, it is paid by the laundries and their customers.

Can anything be done to alleviate the local laundry industry's plight? A good solution from the laundries' point of view would be to persuade the steel firm to reduce its emissions at its own expense. The problem with this approach is twofold: (1) The profit-seeking steel firm has no incentive to reduce its emissions on its own since production costs would increase without any positive effect on revenues; and (2) even if the steel firm were altruistic and wanted to restore clean air for the laundries, it would be prevented from doing so by the force of competition. In a competitive environment, the steel firm will tend to produce steel at the lowest possible cost (not considering external costs) and earn no economic profit. If a single firm unilaterally imposes additional costs on itself, competing steel firms in other communities or countries will still be producing steel at a lower cost, and the steel firm that reduces its pollution will eventually be forced out of business.

Another possibility is for the laundry firms to band together and offer to pay the steel firm for installing antipollution devices in its smoke stacks. For example, one of the laundry owners might call a meeting to propose that each firm contribute $100 per year, a

sum lower than the costs of electric clothes dryers, to pay the steel firm for installing antipollution devices. But this possibility presents at least two major complications: (1) It is costly in terms of time and effort to organize a group of business leaders to discuss the best course of action and to present the proposal to the steel mill; and (2) individually, each laundry owner has a strong incentive to understate how much he or she would be willing to pay to get the steel firm to reduce its pollution. The first complication constitutes a *transaction cost* of negotiating a solution to the pollution problem. The second complication is crucial. Since it is physically impractical, if not impossible, to provide clean air *only* to those laundry owners who pay for it, each individual has an incentive to let the others bear the costs. This aspect of the situation, called the **free-rider problem,** arises when it is impractical to exclude anyone from using resources for which they have not paid.

Figure 17.2 illustrates the pollution problem caused when every firm in the steel industry uses the atmosphere to dump its smoke particles free of charge. The demand curve for steel (D) represents the value the rest of the economy derives from using various amounts of steel. The **marginal private cost** or **internal cost,** of producing steel (the MPC curve) reflects only those costs steel firms actually pay. It is the steel industry's supply curve. The marginal private cost schedule represents the costs that steel producers recognize in making their output decisions. The **marginal social cost** of steel production (the MSC curve) is the *sum* of the marginal private cost and the marginal external cost of producing steel. In the example of figure 17.2, the marginal external cost of producing a ton of steel is the vertical distance between the MSC and MPC curves, or $70. The external cost is an opportunity cost of steel production, but it is borne by *other* firms, such as those in the laundry business and by individuals whose standards of living

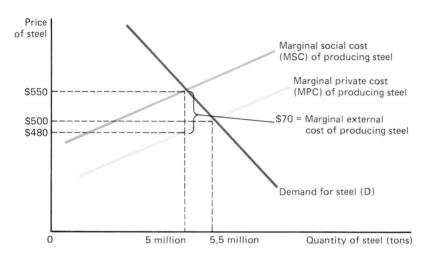

Figure 17.2   Private and social costs of steel production
Marginal social cost (MSC) equals marginal private cost (MPC) plus the marginal external cost of producing a ton of steel. The marginal external cost of a ton of steel is $70. If the steel firms consider only private costs, they will produce 5.5 million tons and charge a price of $500 = MPC. However, if the steel producers must consider *total* costs, including those external to the firm, then the marginal social cost schedule, along with steel demand, determines the quantity of steel produced, which would be 5 million tons, and its price, which would be $550 per ton. Less steel is produced, at a higher price, when *all* costs must be paid by buyers and sellers.

and/or quality of life are lowered by pollution. If all resources required to produce steel, including the clean air now being used, were paid for by the steel firms, all steel production costs would be internal costs, and marginal social cost would equal marginal private cost. Since the marginal private cost schedule is the steel industry's supply curve in our example, output is 5.5 million tons per year and steel users pay $500 per ton of steel. If steel users paid the marginal social cost of producing steel, the price of steel would be $550 per ton, and they would demand only 5 million tons per year.

Positive Externalities

Just as external costs create an economic problem with pollution, the *external benefits* of some goods and services also lead to market deficiencies. One example, some would argue, is education. In addition to the income redistribution aspect of publicly supported schooling (discussed in chapter 15), there are probably benefits to society at large arising from maintaining a literate electorate that can inform itself on social and political issues. Additional benefits from education follow from the discussion of employment and educational attainment in chapter 15. Increased education raises employment prospects, earned incomes, and taxes paid and perhaps reduces crime.

A generally accepted example involving external benefits in the medical area is epidemic prevention. Smallpox has been largely eliminated as a result of vaccinating almost everyone against this dread disease. When an individual is vaccinated, others benefit because one source of potential contagion is eliminated. Thus, each *individual* has too small an incentive to be vaccinated because health benefits to others are probably not weighed as heavily as private benefits. Since the sum of private benefits from a group of individuals being vaccinated is less than the value to society of the reduced risk of an epidemic, too few people will get vaccinations. The sum of the benefits to a group of individuals that results from vaccinations understates the total benefit gained in terms of community health.

The Social Benefits of Higher Education

When you finish your undergraduate education, you can look forward to lifetime earnings that are higher than the earnings of others who have acquired less education. Furthermore, what you choose for a major will also influence how much you will probably earn. If the increased earnings from your education were the whole story, there would be a good reason for you to pay all of the costs of your education. Whether you or your parents paid for your schooling would be of interest to you, but from society's point of view it would be a private, family matter. You or your family would pay for your education, and you would reap the personal and financial benefits. How well your schooling investment paid off would depend on how wisely you spent your time in school. The labor market in an advanced economy like the United States provides adequate signals on how best to invest resources in schooling from the point of view of individual costs and returns.

However, there may be more involved in obtaining a college education than the personal benefits of higher earnings and self-satisfaction. In a democracy, education serves two purposes that benefit society at large and that are not fully reflected in the private gains to the educated individual. First, better-educated voters are more likely to make more intelligent decisions at the polls. Better-educated politicians are probably better able to serve their constituencies and the general public. All of us are affected by the quality of public policy decisions whether we like it or not. For example, if you as an individual choose to ignore the history of United States involvement in Vietnam, it is not likely to affect your potential earnings. However, if all of the college students in America ignore this important part of history over the next twenty years, it will increase the probability that a future generation will endure the same tragic conditions experienced in the late 1960s and 1970s. Clearly, society has a stake in having an educated population, and the benefits go beyond the private returns to educational investments.

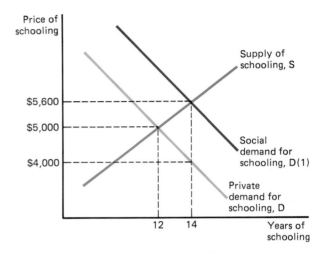

Figure 17.3   Externalities and information problems
D, D(1), and S represent the private demand, social demand, and the marginal social cost of education. Individuals would choose twelve years of education at a price of $5,000 per year. The socially optimal amount of education would be fourteen years at a price of $5,600 per year. The public subsidy of education would be equal to $1,600 per person per year of schooling. With a subsidy of $1,600, a typical individual would be willing to go to school for fourteen years.

In addition to generating an informed electorate, the educational system transfers an appreciation for our system of law, sense of justice, and regard for individual liberties from one generation to the next. That training is an important part of the glue that holds our society together. In effect, widespread access and participation in postsecondary education is an important source of societal stability in a democracy.

In figure 17.3, the supply curve represents the marginal social cost of providing various amounts of education to an individual. The demand curve D represents a typical individual's demand for education, based on the expected private benefits. The demand curve D(1) represents the sum of the private demand for education and the additional benefit to society at large. A price of $5,600 per year of schooling and

*A **public good** (or service), if provided for one user, is, by its nature, provided for many users at no additional cost.*

*The **exclusion principle** refers to the possibility, at a reasonable cost, of preventing people from using a good or service if they do not pay for it.*

fourteen years of schooling are the economically efficient price and quantity of education for an individual. If only the private benefits are considered, a typical individual will obtain only twelve years of schooling and pay a price equal to $5,000 per year.

Reassessing Social Benefits   Prior to the college campus demonstrations that began modestly in 1963 with the free-speech movement and peaked with the killing of the Kent State students protesting the Cambodian invasion by United States troops in the spring of 1970, a typical young adult might have received an amount of education equal to fourteen years. The difference between $4,000, which represents the marginal private benefit of the fourteenth year of schooling, and $5,600 would have been paid by direct government subsidies to education of $1,600 per student per year or reduced-interest loans financed or guaranteed by the government, which lowered a student's annual cost of education by $1,600.

However, when taxpayers watching the evening news saw college students burning United States flags, torching buildings, and throwing rocks at police on campuses across America, some of them began to doubt seriously the value of education in making students intelligent citizens. In terms of figure 17.3, taxpayers reassessed the difference between the demand curves D(1) and D and decided that it was much smaller than they had originally supposed it to be. Not surprisingly, politicians got the message, and aid to education tapered off significantly. Federal aid to higher education fell from $3.5 billion in 1968 to $2.5 billion in 1969 and $2.6 billion in 1970.

The main point is that it is difficult to estimate the true external benefits of education. This is partly because the benefits are highly intangible and difficult to measure and partly because they are spread so widely. Since the market is not equipped to price these external benefits appropriately, policymakers have no adequate guide to measuring them. Consequently, the level of public support for education will always be the product of political moods as well as economic and scientific measurements.

▶ Public Goods

There is another situation in which the quantity of a good or service may be too small in a free market economy. In this type of market deficiency, a firm will not provide a good or service, although consumers' benefits from it exceed its cost. This brings us to the classic rationale for government. Why wouldn't a firm provide a good or service that provides benefits greater than costs? The answer is that in order to earn enough revenue to cover its costs, a firm must be able to charge consumers for using it. The main reason consumers will pay is that they can be excluded from using a good or service if they refuse to pay. Most commodities fall into this category. You are breaking the law and committing theft, for example, if you try to enjoy the benefits of a T-bone steak without passing by the cashier and paying on the way out of the supermarket.

Goods and services are called **public goods** when users cannot easily be excluded from using them and when the goods made available for one user become available to many without further cost. When users cannot easily be excluded from using a good if they do not pay, we say that the **exclusion principle** does not apply. Perhaps the purest example of a public good is national defense because once a country's borders are protected from foreign invasion, every resident inside the borders is equally protected, whether or not a fee is paid. A private firm could not easily collect an appropriate fee from each citizen reflecting how much each would be willing to pay for military protection. The free-rider effect would lead everyone to understate the amount he or she would be willing to pay. The result would be that without coercion, few would be likely to pay anything. An alternative is to grant some agency—a government—the right to coerce payment in the form of taxation. But the problem of determining what the socially optimal level of defense should be cannot be resolved by simply giving the government the power to coerce people to pay for it.

It would be impractical to provide police protection on a strictly fee-for-service basis. When a police officer arrests the driver of a speeding auto, who would pay—all of those who *might* have been hurt if the speeder were allowed to continue driving? In the case of fire protection, should the fire fighter be prohibited from putting out a fire in a house or building that does not display a sticker showing its fire protection fees are paid? What if the fire spreads to neighboring protected property? These two services have significant public good characteristics.

Some economists place technical monopolies, discussed in chapter 8, in the category of public goods. This is a matter of definition. The difference between a technical monopoly and a public good, in our definition, is whether the exclusion principle applies. In our technical monopoly example of a bridge, potential users *can* be excluded if they do not pay. However, since the marginal social cost of each crossing is zero, the market would not in general promote economic efficiency. This is because a firm could not cover its costs if it charged the economically efficient price (zero). Radio and television broadcasts do not require significant additional costs to be received by additional radio or television sets; however, exclusion of nonsubscribers from pay programs is possible through electronic scrambling techniques. National defense and police protection are not the only commodities with the characteristics of a public good. However, there are few that fit the mold quite as well. Generally, it comes down to a matter of judgment whether a particular good or service would be provided in a market economy without government intervention and, if it would be provided, whether it would be provided efficiently (that is, in the "correct" quantity). Even in the case of national defense, it is conceivable that one person could be so wealthy that it would pay that individual to provide military protection for all. The individual's benefit might be large enough to cover all costs. Thus, a government with the right to levy taxes would not be required to provide defense.

▶ Government's Responses to External Diseconomies and Public Goods Problems

A Closer Look at the Causes of Market Deficiencies

We have surveyed a variety of situations that lead to inefficiencies in the marketplace. It will help you to understand what government can do to help overcome these inefficiencies if we take a closer look at their fundamental causes.

The Exclusion Problem, Externalities, and Transaction Costs

While economists may at times disagree over how to categorize the several causes of inefficiencies we have discussed, there is general agreement that if a provider of a good or service cannot exclude users who do not pay, then government intervention is normally required if the good is to be provided at all. The degree and level of government intervention depends on the size of the group that benefits. National defense clearly implies national government involvement, while policing city streets suggests local government involvement. This does not necessarily mean that *government* must produce or provide the good, however. Other corrective actions may make it possible for markets to work. In most markets, where the exclusion problem does not arise, consumers must reveal their demand for a product—the amount they are willing to pay for one more unit—or they cannot have the product. Thus, a seller can appropriate this value per unit sold, and it becomes revenue that covers the firm's costs. The exclusion problem occurs when a provider cannot collect the cost of a good or service from its users for one practical reason—the cost of executing a transaction or excluding nonpayers. This was clear in our illustration of the pollution problem. Given present technology, it would be impractical and costly to prevent those who do not pay from enjoying or using clean air. Under some circumstances, such as travel to the moon, or even in a high-flying plane, it pays to provide oxygen to individuals or small groups. Some allergy sufferers wear air filtration devices during the pollen season. But for most of us to use a special apparatus in our everyday lives to breathe clean air would be far more costly than other, less precise techniques for ensuring that we have clean air.

The existence of neither external costs nor benefits *necessarily* requires government intervention to reduce market distortions. As the parties involved become fewer in number, the transaction costs diminish. For example, suppose that you are burning leaves in your backyard and your neighbors complain. In return for your neighbors' consideration of *your* dislike of smoke when *they* burn *their* leaves, you will probably agree to bag your leaves for the trash or shred them and spread the mulch on your garden. Your desire to maintain your neighbors' friendship and goodwill helps to internalize the external costs you inflict on others when you burn your leaves, and your neighbors will probably behave similarly toward you.

The same idea applies to external benefits. When only a few parties are involved, negotiation is relatively inexpensive, and the exclusion problem is not likely to arise. A classic example of external benefits is the relationship between beekeepers and farmers. The beekeepers need blossoms to produce honey, and farmers need the bees to pollinate blossoms so their crops will grow. Despite these externalities, the transaction cost problem does not seriously interfere with a well-organized market in bee services. This is because bees tend to return to their hives, and the hives can be moved around from farm to farm. An investigation of the Washington state bee industry has shown that farmers whose crops are poor honey producers must, and do, pay beekeepers to move the hives into their fields. However, farmers who grow clover and other heavy honey-producing crops are paid by beekeepers for the privilege of locating the hives in their fields.[2]

The Role of Property Rights

One essential function of government is to provide the framework within which low-cost transactions can occur. A well-defined institutional framework is necessary for a market economy. One element of a well-defined institutional setting is the legal definition of property rights. As we saw in chapter 8, a property right defines who can legally charge a fee or price for use of a good or service. No firm will survive if, after hiring labor and purchasing equipment and materials, it cannot sell its output for a price that will cover its opportunity costs. If the firm's right to sell its output is not clearly defined and enforced by government, then it must incur significant additional costs to protect itself. The resources used in this way cannot be used to produce goods and services. Thus, the T-bone steak you want for dinner is the property of the supermarket until you buy it. The right of the grocer to demand payment from you is defined in law and enforced by a government agency. Without this right, the supermarket would have to spend much more on security personnel and enforcement, and the price of the steak and the other goods the supermarket sells would be much higher. Without the legal institution of property rights, so many resources would be required to carry out transactions that the net gains from specialization would be greatly diminished. Our standard of living depends crucially on the right to hold and exchange property (including our labor services).

Those of you who have studied the history of civilization will have learned that commercial law defining property rights emerged along with growing wealth and that without these laws economic growth would have been seriously curtailed. The reason for this is that specialization—benefiting from comparative advantage—leads *away* from self-sufficiency. Because trade is required to obtain the benefits of specialization, the establishment of property rights and a growing standard of living are inseparable partners.

The exclusion problem arises when property rights have not been established or are poorly defined. Does it follow that market inefficiencies associated with externalities and public goods can be overcome by the creation of property rights? The answer to this question depends on the value of the resources involved and on available technology for excluding those who do not pay. Establishing property rights *may* lead to a substantial reduction in transaction costs. This means that an appropriate change in the legal framework may eliminate a particular pollution problem or transform a public good into one that markets provide efficiently. However, one reason a property right has not been established may be the obviously prohibitive cost of enforcing it. Thus, simply to pass a law giving individuals the right to a specified volume of air free of all dust, smoke, and objectionable odors would probably not result in a more efficient market where every individual would breathe purer air. The current debate over no-smoking areas in offices and public places illustrates this difficulty forcefully.

In some cases when creating property rights will result in reduced transaction costs, the gains are apparent to all, and a property right will evolve as a result of the political process. It is important to recognize that while a change in the legal framework governing property rights may create *potential* gains for all affected parties, not everyone involved will *necessarily* gain from the creation of a property right. Someone who is currently using a resource free of charge may fear losing that ability if property rights are established and will therefore object. For example, the steel producer in our pollution illustration would probably object if the right to use the fresh air and hence a right to charge for pollution were assigned to the laundries. The steel manufacturer would argue that the right to use the air ought to be assigned to the steel firm, along with the right to charge the laundry owners for any clean air they might use in their businesses. On their side, the laundries would resist being forced to purchase the right to use the outdoor air from the steel firm. Thus, the *for whom* question can, and often does, interfere with the creation of property

rights that might lower transaction costs sufficiently to allow the marketplace to work where it now does not function well or at all.

Copying Computer Software: Lowering Costs or Theft of Property?   Another area in which technological progress has led to new problems with property rights is in the computer industry. The development of the home computer has led to immense growth in the production of programs, or software, necessary to use the computers. However, the computers can also be used to copy programs, thus short-circuiting the market and depriving software developers of returns to their efforts. Indeed, software producers themselves are partially to blame, for they have developed programs that decipher the secret codes used to protect against copying.

Major producers have estimated that copying reduces industry revenues by a substantial fraction, possibly 50 percent or more. If this is true, then it is likely that the development of new programs will be seriously curtailed. Even the decoding programs can be copied. Computer programs are protected by copyright law. However, relatively high legal costs and concern over public image have discouraged producers from prosecuting individuals, computer clubs, and educational institutions that illegally copy their products. Can you think of a government action that would promote the protection of property rights in this market? Can you think of other markets with similar problems?

Saving the World's Whales   Few issues create as much political, economic, and emotional conflict as the battle to save the world's whales from extinction. Why are they endangered? They are not, like the desert pupfish or the snail darter, the last surviving members of species whose habitat has been reduced by geological evolution. Instead, the answer to this question has to do with their economic value. Many nations, particularly Japan and the Soviet Union, have great commercial whaling industries that harvest whales for industrial and human use. However, this in itself does not explain why the catch is so large that many claim the whales' survival is seriously threatened. After all, no one has suggested that cattle, hogs, and chickens, Americans' principal sources of protein, are about to enter the endangered species list.

The answer, as you might expect by now, lies in the issue of property rights. Who owns the whale? The nations of the world exert control over fishing and exploration rights in the oceans within various distances of their shores—generally 200 miles. But they cannot control the fish and other animal life that live in the sea. Given migratory patterns and the various physical problems involved, it would be impractical to close off fish ranges with fences, as ranchers do with cattle, or to use branding irons to mark each country's herds of sea life. Consequently, any individual whaler, or nation, that tries to reduce its catch to conserve the whale or fish population generates an external benefit by making more available for others to harvest. Conservation does not pay when the benefits cannot be internalized, or appropriated, by those who restrict their harvests today. Their harvests in the future will not benefit, and as a result, whale conservation is not practiced to the extent that it would be if whales did not swim about freely in the sea.

What do you think would happen if all of the world's whaling rights were assigned to one nation? What would have to be done to obtain agreement to establish such a property right?

Property Rights and Economic Efficiency

We have shown that market deficiencies are frequently associated with failure to establish property rights that assign benefits and costs to specific parties in economic transactions. One reason for a lack of property rights is that changes in the economic and social environment have transformed a previously free resource into a scarce commodity. Another reason is more basic: The costs of defining and enforcing property rights may be greater than the current benefits. This would be the case, for example, if we tried to assign everyone in society his or her "own" clean air.

The Political Economy of Property Rights   Ideally, a fundamental function of government is to define and enforce property rights where doing so would allow markets to promote economic efficiency. Unfortunately, governments are not disinterested parties whose only concern is to promote the economic well-being of the general public. Government officials have other, more personal objectives, too. Thus, there is frequently a conflict between the state and individual economic well-being with respect to the assignment of property rights. This conflict is emphasized in nations that reject private property as the principal basis of economic organization, as in socialist systems, but it is also present in market economies. Establishing and enforcing property rights generally provides individuals with greater incentives to economize and to choose among alternatives in an economically efficient manner. However, it also reduces the political and economic power of those who run the government. In short, politics is not the servant of economics; rather, they are closely intertwined.

Classical economists such as Adam Smith appreciated the extent to which economics and politics interact. They understood that institutions like the courts and the legal system in general both influence economic circumstances and are influenced by them. In a sense, the legal environment determines the rules and regulations by which individuals and groups can participate in the economy. Defining who has property rights to resources, what constitutes legal transactions, which commodities can be produced and consumed, and what coalitions (cartels) among buyers and sellers will be permitted, clearly has a tremendous impact on who the likely winners and losers will be in the economy. So it should not surprise us to find that economic agents will use their political influence, personal wealth, and guile to influence the political system to define rules of the game favorable to their economic interests.

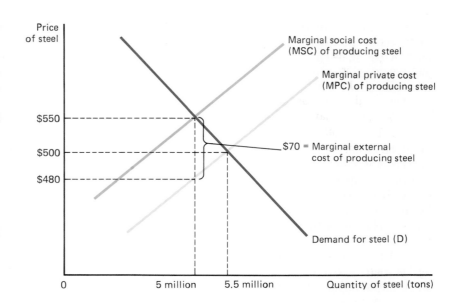

Figure 17.4   Steel production and air pollution
In a competitive economy without government intervention, the equilibrium price of steel would be determined by the intersection of the steel demand curve and the marginal private cost curve for steel, at $500 per ton. A quantity of 5.5 million tons of steel would be produced and purchased each year. Economic efficiency would require a price of $550, determined by the intersection of the marginal social cost curve of steel and the steel demand curve. The economically efficient production of steel is only 5 million tons per year. From a social standpoint, the competitive market produces too much steel. Imposing a tax on steel production equal to $70 per ton would internalize the difference between marginal social costs and marginal private costs and generate the appropriate price and output combination.

Possible Solutions to the Pollution Problem

The leading example of a negative externality is pollution. We will now explore whether it is possible to achieve economic efficiency when there is a negative externality if the government can somehow simulate a market evaluation of the benefits and costs of reducing pollution.

Refer back to figure 17.2 on page 343. If it were possible to measure the marginal external cost of producing a ton of steel, an all-knowing government could achieve an economically efficient solution to the pollution problem quite simply. It could levy a tax on steel producers of $70 per ton, which is exactly equal to the difference between marginal social cost and marginal private cost. This would, in effect, make the marginal social cost (MSC) curve the steel producers' marginal private cost (MPC) curve. By paying the tax, the steel producers would essentially be purchasing the clean air they use to make their steel. The

proceeds of the tax could be distributed to those harmed by pollution to offset the costs inflicted on them. One way to do this would be to grant an income tax credit to all those harmed by pollution.

By imposing a tax on steel firms equal to the external costs of steel production, the government could cause the supply curve of steel to shift from the marginal private cost curve to the marginal social cost curve in figure 17.4. Equilibrium output would fall to 5 million tons of steel per year and price would rise to $550 per ton. As we noted earlier, steel firms would not be forced to eliminate air pollution entirely. This point may seem surprising since the traditional response to pollution is that none is acceptable. Pollution abatement is simply one use of scarce resources. When a scarce resource is used to produce a given output, it cannot, to that extent, be used to produce something else. The question, then, is not whether any air should be "used" (polluted) in the process of steel production but rather how much.

Consider momentarily the use of another resource, coal. If coal is used to make coke for steel production, the same coal cannot be used to fire electric power generators. Does this mean that no coal should be used to make steel? Of course not. The economic problem of air pollution arises because of *exclusion difficulties,* as we have seen. That is, it is not practical to exclude individuals or business firms from using the clean air if they do not pay for it. By contrast, there are well-defined property rights regarding coal, and similar market distortions do not occur in the allocation of coal among alternative uses. In terms of efficient allocation of the economy's scarce resources, clean air is a scarce resource that has alternative uses. One possible use is to produce steel; other uses include drying clothes and providing oxygen for us to breathe. An efficient pollution policy is one that prices clean air so it will be allocated among all its competing uses in accordance with the opportunity costs involved. In general, this policy will not entail legislation prohibiting the use of air in steel production (or any other activity) simply because it is costly (for example, it may create pollution) to do so.

By raising the cost and price of steel, a pollution tax transfers the cost of pollution from the general public to users and producers of steel. Consumers of steel products will have to pay higher prices. Producers of steel and steel products will probably have to reduce their output levels; some firms at the margin of profitability may have to leave the industry entirely. It is important to note that by establishing a price on a resource that previously appeared to be free, government intervention will always cause some market prices to increase. This means that purchasers of certain products—those that pollute—will be induced to switch expenditures to other products. Moreover, producers in areas that are less worried about pollution—perhaps in foreign countries—will be able to increase their sales relative to producers in regions that tax pollution to a greater extent.

Before we go on to discuss the problems involved in implementing antipollution policy, we should point out that there is an even better way to attack pollution than to impose a simple tax per unit of output. It is to attack more directly the external costs of a polluting activity such as steel production. Specifically, the government could tax the effluents (sulfur dioxide, particulate matter, and so on) directly by charging so much per ton of each that is emitted. The technological knowledge is now available to measure these effluents relatively inexpensively. Taxing pollution as such would provide steel producers, for example, with an appropriate incentive to substitute antipollution devices for dumping their waste products into the clean air. This would reduce pollution in two ways: (1) Effluents per ton of steel would decline, and (2) steel production would fall. Since an effluents tax gives producers the incentive to minimize the cost of pollution reduction, those steel producers who find it easiest (cheapest) to reduce pollution will account for a disproportionate amount of the industry's pollution reduction. They will also increase their market share relative to firms whose costs are increased more when they try to reduce the amount they pollute. As a result, the effect of taxing pollution on steel production and its market price will be less than if steel as such is taxed.

Information Difficulties and Limitations on Government Policy Implementation

How much does a ton of a given pollutant cost society? That is, how much should pollution be taxed? Because of the exclusion problem, individuals do not reveal how much pollution actually costs them or, equivalently, how much they would be willing to pay to reduce it. Conceivably, the government could hire engineers to estimate pollution's social cost. However, even with expert estimates, much would no doubt depend on battles fought in the political arena. Producer groups would argue that the experts have estimated too large a marginal social cost, while environmental groups would argue the opposite. Given these difficulties, it should still be possible for government to promote an approximate market solution to the pollution problem. Figure 17.5 illustrates this possible solution, using sulfur dioxide pollution as an example.

Creating a Market for Pollution Rights

The information gathered through research and filtered through the political process is depicted by the supply curve S in figure 17.5. It is a representation of the marginal cost of sulfur dioxide pollution to society, sulfur dioxide's marginal social cost. The demand curves D(1) and D(2) represent two possible relationships between the price that firms must pay for the right to dispose of sulfur dioxide in the atmosphere and the amount of sulfur dioxide they emit from their smokestacks. This supply-demand framework need not be limited to the sulfur dioxide generated in any particular industry, such as steel production. Each pollutant, including sulfur dioxide, particulate matter, and carbon monoxide, would have a separate marginal social cost schedule such as the supply curve S in figure 17.5. Each of the industries generating each type of pollution would have a demand for pollution licenses. Added together, these demands would constitute the total demand for each type of pollution right.

Since pollution is a by-product of the production of steel and other goods, growth of output will shift the demand for pollution to the right. A decline in the price of pollution-preventing equipment will lead to a leftward shift of the demand for pollution because it will be cheaper to prevent pollution with improved devices. The supply curve S shifts if the factors underlying the marginal social cost of pollution change. Consider how the supply curve would shift, for example, if sulfur dioxide suddenly became recognized as a carcinogen.

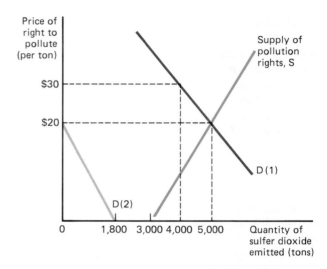

Figure 17.5   Creating a market for pollution rights
The supply curve S represents the marginal social cost of sulfur dioxide pollution as determined by experts and the political process. The demand curves D(1) and D(2) represent two possible demand curves for the right to emit sulfur dioxide into the atmosphere. If the demand for sulfur dioxide pollution rights were D(1), the equilibrium price of the right to dump each ton of sulfur dioxide into the atmosphere would be $20 and the economically efficient amount of sulfur dioxide pollution would be 5,000 tons per year. If the demand curve were D(2), then there would be no charge for emitting sulfur dioxide, and the quantity of sulfur dioxide emitted into the atmosphere would be 1,800 tons per year, where D(2) crosses the horizontal axis.

Suppose the demand by firms for the right to emit sulfur dioxide into the atmosphere were described by demand curve D(1) in figure 17.5. Once the government specified the supply curve S, it would be a matter of trial and error to discover that the equilibrium price of licenses to emit sulfur dioxide would be $20 per ton. For example, the government might auction off the rights to dump 4,000 tons of sulfur dioxide. It would observe that polluters would be willing to pay $30 per ton for this quantity. Since this is more than the price indicated by the supply curve that society demands for the right to dispose of 4,000 tons of sulfur dioxide per year, the government would then offer a greater quantity of licenses to pollute. Eventually, it would be discovered that if licenses to emit 5,000 tons of sulfur dioxide were made available, the maximum price polluters would be willing to pay would be $20 per ton. Since $20 per ton is the amount society demands for this quantity of pollution, 5,000 tons of sulfur dioxide per year would be the economically efficient quantity of sulfur dioxide pollution.

If the demand for the right to emit sulfur dioxide were described by the curve D(2) in figure 17.5, polluters would not be willing to pay anything for pollution rights if more than 1,800 tons per year were allowed. The supply curve S tells us that the cost of sulfur dioxide pollution is inconsequential if less than 3,000 tons per year are emitted. In this case, the equilibrium price of pollution rights is zero. Licenses should be given away, and 1,800 tons of sulfur dioxide would be emitted. The simulated market for pollution rights would show that in this particular case, for this particular pollutant, fresh air is a free good.

Government Policy toward Pollution in the United States

Despite the feasibility of simulating a market for rights to pollute, government policy in the United States has not typically taken this direction. There are a few exceptions. For example, we do not prohibit disposing of sewage or trash. Rather, most households and business firms pay to have these forms of pollution transported away and dumped via pipes or trucks.

For other forms of air and water pollution, however, immense quantities of time and resources have been spent to regulate the quantities of pollutants permitted with little or no explicit reference to the social costs of the various forms of pollution or to the benefits of allowing business firms or households to create some pollution. The major legislation governing current United States policy is the *National Environmental Policy Act of 1969 (NEPA)*. Under

the general provisions of this act, the Environmental Protection Agency administers a host of regulations issued under terms of eight additional acts, including Clean Air, Clean Water, and Safe Drinking Water. There is little doubt that without regulation, too much pollution of the types regulated by these laws would be created. However, it is difficult if not impossible to evaluate whether the quantities of pollutants that result under the system of rules governing environmental quality in the United States are greater or less than the amounts that would be economically efficient.

To the extent that the government successfully implements a program to price pollution from, say, steel production, the relative price of steel and steel-using products like automobiles will be higher. So while consumers in general will benefit from cleaner air, steel and automobile producers and their shareholders, along with car buyers, suppliers of coal-mining equipment, steel and coal haulers, and so on, will disproportionately bear the costs of pollution abatement. Employers and workers in states like Michigan, Ohio, and Indiana will experience lower profits, wages, and perhaps employment than would be the case without pollution controls, whereas Americans in general will benefit from being able to breathe cleaner air. In short, while the benefits are widely and more or less uniformly distributed, the costs of reducing pollution are concentrated among specific firms, industries, consumer and employee groups, and regions. Those groups have a strong incentive to lobby government to shift the costs of pollution abatement away from themselves.

Domestic consumers of automobiles and other durable consumer goods made with steel, such as refrigerators, washers, and dryers, can reduce the burden on themselves by buying more foreign cars and other durables. Even producers of products made with steel in the United States can minimize the upward pressure on their prices by importing steel from Japan and West Germany or by switching to domestic products, such as aluminum, plastic, and fiberglass, that may not cause as much pollution. Thus, domestic producers of steel substitutes and foreign producers of steel in countries that do not have as stringent antipollution regulations win from United States efforts to reduce pollution caused by steel manufacturing.

Inevitably, United States producers of steel and automobiles and other goods made with steel will use their political clout to have import restrictions adopted by Congress. To the extent that they succeed, domestic consumers will bear a larger share of the costs for pollution control. In early 1985, it was estimated that steel import restrictions in the United States in conjunction with Japan's "voluntary" agreement to limit automobile exports to the United States added about $500 to the average price of an automobile in the United States. In addition, states like Michigan, Indiana, and Ohio have pressed the federal government, particularly since 1979, to provide job-training programs to retrain underemployed steelworkers and autoworkers. These programs are funded out of general tax revenues.

The Politics and International Nature of the Pollution Problem

There are two additional elements of the pollution control story. First, the political scandal about both the use of EPA funds and EPA enforcement policies, particularly with respect to toxic waste dumps, in the first years of the Reagan administration, highlighted the susceptibility of such programs to both political manipulation and corruption. Once economic power and the ability to make and break fortunes is removed from the marketplace and moved into the political arena, efforts to corrupt the system will follow.

The second consequence of pollution control in the United States that is often ignored is what happens when production of commodities that create pollution shifts to other parts of the world with less restrictive regulations. For example, throughout the 1970s and 1980s, a number of developing countries like Brazil, South Korea, and Taiwan began exporting steel to the United States. The success of these countries in selling cheap steel benefited United States consumers by keeping down prices of domestic durable goods and shifting the pollution problem to other countries. Observers have viewed this shift of basic industry production to "third world" countries as potentially beneficial to the United States and other industrialized nations. In a sense we have been exporting our "dirty" industries to the rest of the world. Of course, the other side is that we have also exported jobs and income to the third world countries that have imported our pollution problems.

For the longer term, we will also have to recognize that polluting the atmosphere is an ongoing threat to our environment, even if we have removed the location of the source several thousand miles from our shores. Governments in developing nations desperate to promote industrialization may be willing to take environmental risks that we no longer tolerate in the United States or other advanced industrialized nations. For some decades to come, their willingness to bear such risks may help us to reduce local environmental costs in our country and aid us in maintaining or increasing our standard of living. One would hope we can do better in the longer run. In a sense, the nuclear accident in Chernobyl in May 1986 reflected risks that the Soviet Union was willing to take with nuclear power given the fact that they need not bear all of the costs and the inability of other nations to do much about it.

There are other aspects of jurisdictional considerations in pollution problems. States like Ohio and Pennsylvania have traditionally been producers of coal and still have tremendous potential to meet a substantial share of United States and European energy needs. To promote coal exports, the Carter administration began pushing for federal support of harbor improvements in the late 1970s. Unfortunately, these coal deposits are high in sulfur content, which causes acid rain and severe environmental damage affecting the northeastern United States and Canada. Congress has debated the question of who should bear the costs of acid rain damage in the United States. In addition, the Canadian government has demanded that the United States assume responsibility for acid rain damage in Canada. This has been an important source of friction between Canada and the United States in recent years.

Obviously, there are potential winners and losers in the dispute over acid rain. Workers and their employers in the coal-mining industry and in industries that rely on coal as an important energy source benefit from being able to exploit our coal resources as inexpensively as possible. So do suppliers of coal-mining equipment, coal transport haulers, and consumers who are able to purchase cheaper electricity, products made of steel, and products that require a great deal of energy to manufacture. Losers from acid rain pollution include the general public living in affected areas in the United States and Canada. In arguing against controls over acid rain, those who benefit from being able to pollute will emphasize the increased costs of products they produce and the number of jobs that will be lost. Those who are harmed by pollution have the somewhat more difficult task of attributing environmental degradation and health problems to acid rain in particular rather than to some other set of causes. They must also develop a persuasive evaluation of the costs of these damages. Such cost estimates are probably always more imprecise and difficult to support than the costs associated with potential job losses and decreased purchasing power. Both sides, of course, are tempted to exaggerate to prove their case.

The industrial losses of pollution abatement are often direct, localized, and specific because production activity is so concentrated geographically. However, the environmental losses of nonabatement are often not only geographically disperse but also cumulative; that is, they occur gradually and cumulatively over time. Diffuse impacts in time and place are always more difficult to measure than concentrated ones.

Regardless of how the political system determines who should bear the costs of environmental degradation attributable to acid rain, it is important to bear in mind that it is the *external cost* that has placed the issue in the political arena. Because markets are unable to deal efficiently with this particular problem, politicians have little guidance from the marketplace in deciding how to decide between opposing sides.

Public Goods: National Defense

The distinguishing feature of a *public good* is that consumption of the good by one individual does not diminish its availability to other consumers. In effect, the marginal cost of providing the good or service to additional individuals is zero. Furthermore, it is often difficult to exclude consumers from access to a public good they have not paid for. Consider national defense. Once a particular level of national defense has been developed, the psychological and practical value of having a given degree of military security is available for all citizens to enjoy. Your sense of personal safety and protection from foreign attack is independent of my satisfaction, and the fact that you have that particular degree of satisfaction in no way reduces the value of national defense to me.

By contrast, consider consuming a pitcher of beer. The more you drink, the less is left for me to consume. Suppose the pitcher of beer costs $3 and we agree to share the costs. Even though I would be willing to pay $2 for two-thirds pitcher of beer, I might try to trick you by offering to pay $1 with the intention of drinking two-thirds of the pitcher. But since you are going to pay $2 you will make sure that you drink two-thirds and I only get one-third. By understating how much beer I want, I end up with one-third when I really wanted two-thirds. So I end up outsmarting myself. If I understate the amount of beer I am willing to pay for, I end up with less than I want to consume. As a general principle, the marketplace forces us to reveal how much we value a commodity at the margin. That is, the value of the last unit purchased equals the amount we must pay. If we do not reveal our preferences by plunking down hard cash, we are *excluded,* meaning that we cannot legally obtain goods and services that are provided through markets.

The Free-Rider Problem

The economics of the consumption of public goods is much different from that of drinking beer. Since your satisfaction from a given level of national defense in no way reduces my satisfaction from the same level of national defense, I *can* benefit by understating how much national defense is worth to me. Suppose that you and everyone else except me agree to pay $100 each for national defense. National defense gives me at least $100 satisfaction, but by lying and claiming that I do not care about defense spending, I get away without paying anything to support it. Yet I can enjoy close to $100 worth of satisfaction from the military strength that everyone else but me paid $100 each to buy. I can behave as a *free rider,* consuming the benefits of defense without paying for it.

Obviously, you and others who pay the defense bill will resent my cheating and try to prevent it. One way to exclude me would be to put me in a rowboat with the words *dummy target* on the side in the middle of an ocean in the hope that someone would take a shot at me.

International Free Riding   If the story ended with free-riding problems in one country, we could simply conclude that the quantity of defense provided is too low by some unspecified amount. However, the free-rider problem does not end at national borders. United States defense spending obviously provides some degree of national security to Canada, Europe, and other areas. Those affected areas have a strong incentive to ride free on United States military expenditures and to understate the value to themselves of military protection.

It is quite possible that a fortress America, or isolationist philosophy in the United States, would generate much lower levels of military expenditures in the United States. To some extent, such a tendency in the United States may be fostered by the perception that other countries are not shouldering their fair share of the defense burden. Congress has perceived that other countries' populations have benefited from higher consumption levels than would have been possible if they had not chosen to ride free on United States military spending. United States citizens, on the other hand, are losers in such a relationship. The public goods nature of defense spending is responsible for these perceptions, whether they are true or not.

▶ Summary and Conclusions

In this chapter we extended our discussion of deficiencies and distortions in the market economy. Problems like those of the Smiths arise because society has not fully specified property rights to fresh air, unspoiled scenery, and freedom from noise pollution. Consequently, many of these economic problems are dealt with in the political arena as well as in the marketplace. The topics considered were problems of externalities, public goods, and property rights. The following main points were emphasized.

Markets fail to generate economic efficiency when private and social costs differ.

Externalities lead to a gap between the marginal social cost and the marginal private cost of producing goods and services only when an exclusion problem exists.

An economically efficient solution to a pollution problem would in general not totally eliminate pollution.

Unless an exclusion problem exists, technical monopolies will not lead to a public goods problem.

Creating a property right is a means of reducing or eliminating an exclusion problem.

Transaction costs may hinder the enforcement of property rights as a cure for exclusion problems.

Government remedies are generally flawed because there is no reliable source other than the marketplace to provide accurate estimates of costs and benefits of alternative actions.

Winners and losers from alternative policies will attempt to influence the form and nature of government remedies for externalities and public goods problems.

Groups and individuals harmed by pollution generally have an incentive to overstate the amount they are harmed because there is usually no direct linkage between pollution reduction and the amount those harmed by pollution must pay to eliminate it.

The free-rider problem generally leads to underprovision of public goods.

Government itself is not a disinterested party in remedying public goods and externality problems. This further complicates the interaction between government and the economy.

▶ Key Terms

exclusion principle *345*

external diseconomy, external cost, or negative externality *341*

external economy, external benefit, or positive externality *341*

free-rider problem *342*

marginal private cost, internal cost *342*

marginal social cost *342*

market failure *340*

public goods *345*

▶ Questions for Discussion and Review

1. A pollution tax of exactly the correct amount would shift the polluters' marginal private cost of production to coincide with the marginal social cost of production (see figure 17.2). Suppose a private individual could sue producers for damage resulting from the polluters' methods of production. How would the effects of such a system compare with those of the pollution tax approach?

2. Suppose you participated in a public debate on the proper level of environmental protection. Your opponent states that it is immoral to place a dollar price on clean air and therefore your proposal to license pollution is to be rejected. What arguments would you use to defend your position?

3. Illustrate and explain the difference in the way that individual demands are summed to get an aggregate demand curve for private and public goods.

4. Illustrate and explain how a monopolist could actually reduce pollution by a previously competitive industry.

5. Illustrate and explain whether a competitive firm producing chemicals with a process that creates water pollution is likely to produce too much or too little output from society's standpoint.

6. Does a private market always provide too little of a public good? Explain your answer with reference to a specific example.

7. Is a song a public good? Explain.

8. Explain why inventions can be thought of as public goods and therefore why governments would grant patents to inventors to deal with public goods problems.

9. Illustrate and explain how a new production technique for removing sulfur from coal would change the socially optimal level of coal production.

10. Are the following statements true, false, or uncertain? Defend your answers.
   a. When external costs or benefits exist, market outcomes are not economically efficient.
   b. The economic problem of pollution arises because of a discrepancy between social and private costs.
   c. Since vaccinations against communicable diseases create external benefits, only government should provide them.
   d. Assigning property rights to the world's fishing grounds would solve the problem of overuse of our fish resources.
   e. The optimal quantity of pollution is never zero.

11. State whether each of the following is an internal (private) or external cost.
    a. You buy a barbeque grill from a department store and pay $19.95 for it.
    b. You purchase a sack of charcoal at the supermarket for $2.98.
    c. You cook hamburgers on your grill, but while lighting the charcoal on your deck, you scorch the deck of the apartment above yours.
    d. The local steel mill, which employs 80 percent of your town's labor force, produces smoke that darkens the paint on your town's buildings.

12. Which of the following is an example of the exclusion problem?
    a. It is necessary to drop a token in the turnstyle before boarding the subway train.
    b. The local Fourth of July fireworks display can be seen all over town.
    c. Your new dish antenna receives movies being transmitted to your local television system, but the signal is scrambled so that you cannot enjoy the movies.

13. Identify whether each of the following goods involves (1) technical monopoly, (2) an external benefit, or (3) an external cost.
    a. As an extremely wealthy resident of a small subdivision, you hire a private police force to patrol the streets to deter burglaries and kidnapping.
    b. You install an underground conduit to bring electricity to your house. The minimum size conduit available can carry enough electricity to serve you and all your neighbors.
    c. You install a giant stereo system that provides music "services" to all of your neighbors day and night.

14. Imagine that you are the director of a controlled economy and that you wish to determine the economically efficient amount of military defense. A unit of defense, consisting of one soldier and one gun plus ammunition, costs $10,000 per year. The minimum-size defense system for your country requires an army of 10,000. (Less than that would result in completely ineffective protection.) Your country has 10 million inhabitants. Through a detailed consumer survey, you have determined that an average citizen's marginal value of military protecton is as follows:

Amount of protection (in units of defense)	Marginal value of protection (per year)
10,000	$150.00
11,000	50.00
12,000	10.00
13,000	5.00
14,000	1.00
15,000	0.75
16,000	0.55
17,000	0.35
18,000	0.25
19,000	0.20
20,000	0.18

What size army will you choose? Draw a graph illustrating your answer.

15. Under current law, the revenues received by the United States Forest Service are treated the same as taxes. The costs of reforestation and forest maintenance are appropriated by Congress as part of the normal budget process. What effect do you think these policies have on the conservation of publicly owned forests? How do you think the owner of a private forest would behave in comparison?

Chapter 18

Government and Markets in Developing Countries

Outline

I. Introduction *360*
II. Economic conditions in developing countries *362*
   A. Population growth and population density *362*
   B. General living conditions in developed countries and LDCs *364*
III. An analysis of cheap food policies in LDCs *366*
   A. Winners and losers from cheap food policies *366*
   B. Dependence on food imports *367*
   C. Long-run effects *367*
      1. Black markets and corruption *367*
IV. Cheap urban housing policies *368*
   A. Demand and supply of housing in LDCs *368*
   B. How rent controls work in the short run *368*
      1. Winners, losers, and "key money" payments *368*
   C. The long-term decline in the quality of standard housing *369*
V. Minimum wages and price controls *369*
   A. Background: The perceived need for price and wage controls in developing countries *369*
   B. The labor market in manufacturing *370*
      1. Winners and losers from minimum wage laws and price controls *370*
VI. Cheap credit *371*
   A. Background: The perceived need for government direct financing of investment in LDCs *371*
   B. The effect of subsidized credit and loan guarantees *371*
VII. The political difficulties of adopting free market policies in LDCs *372*
VIII. Summary and conclusions *373*
IX. Key term *373*
X. Questions for discussion and review *373*
XI. Policy issue: You decide—International cooperation on pollution and defense issues *374*
   A. The action-initiating event *374*
   B. The issues *374*
   C. Economic policy issues *375*
   D. Recommendations *375*

Objectives

After reading this chapter, the student should be able to:

Describe the economic conditions that prevail in most developing countries.

Describe the short-run and long-run effects of cheap food policies in less-developed countries: Who are the winners and losers?

Describe the short-run and long-run effects of cheap urban housing policies in less-developed countries: Who are the winners and losers?

Discuss the effects of minimum wages and price controls used in less-developed countries.

Discuss the effects of subsidized credit used in less-developed countries.

Discuss the political difficulties in adopting free market policies in less-developed countries.

▶ Introduction

While Alfredo waited outside the office of the minister of finance, he thought about the circumstances that had brought him to this moment. He had left home to study economics and finance in the United States only ten years earlier. He returned with his Ph.D. and in short order had risen through the ranks to his present position as first deputy assistant to the minister of finance. Throughout his school years, Alfredo and his friends had joked about the bungling government bureaucracy and the need for sweeping economic reforms. The housing authority was a joke. Yes, rent controls kept housing cheap if you could find it. But the housing that was available was generally poor in quality, and apartments were almost impossible to get. Everyone knew that housing officials had to be bribed and/or side payments made to landlords to obtain decent housing.

The food program was as bad or worse than the housing program. The government kept food prices low by fixing prices at below market-clearing levels and even sold food in the cities at prices that were less than the prices at which the food had to be imported by the National Government Food Bureau. Every year the government lost money importing food and selling it at prices below costs to the people. There was widespread smuggling of food into the country that sold on the black market for prices well above the official rates. Nobody liked going to the black market to buy food from government agents and private entrepreneurs, but everyone knew that the best food could be obtained there.

Employment policies included minimum wages that had the effect of attracting workers to the cities from the rural areas in the hope of getting high-paying city jobs. But it did not take a genius to observe that jobs were scarce in the city. Estimates of the urban unemployment rate ran as high as 40 percent. Job conditions were poor. Health and safety standards were largely ignored by all concerned.

The government's investment promotion program was in a shambles. The major policy tool was to provide cheap loans to manufacturers to encourage investments. The program cost the government millions of dollars each year, and the loans usually went to people with political connections. Kickback payments to government officials for loan approvals were widespread. At the same time, farmers were unable to get government or private loans to invest in what seemed like very good investment projects.

Alfredo's studies in the United States had served to reenforce his intuition that the whole mix of programs should be scrapped, and he could hardly believe it when the new government rushed to embrace the ideas that he and his friends had brought with them into the government two years ago. Quickly, rent controls, food subsidies, minimum wage laws, and cheap credit programs were terminated, and the country became a model for the effectiveness with which free market forces could be unleashed to promote economic prosperity.

However, in the last few months, the military had made several attempts to overthrow the civilian government, the National Workers' Union had forced businesses to close for the day more than once, and food riots in the capital city had resulted in many deaths and arrests. Most of Alfredo's bright, young friends had been fired, and his own job security was uncertain. In his meeting he would have to try to explain to the minister why the program changes that were introduced and that seemed obviously right only two years earlier had resulted in the current state of economic stagnation and political crisis. It would take all of Alfredo's ability to explain to the minister what had happened and how the government might proceed from now on. Almost too quickly to be believed, everything seemed to be on the line.

In this chapter we will explore the conditions that led to the various programs that Alfredo and his friends ridiculed. We will explain how they

Less-developed countries (LDCs), also known as developing countries, are characterized by economies that generate low per capita incomes and generally have not achieved the high level of industrialization that is typical of the world's developed nations.

worked and led to the abuses he observed. We will also discuss the effects that economic reform can have and provide some insight into why the reform movement may have failed.

In this chapter we will look at examples of market intervention by governments in many poorer nations of the world, which are commonly referred to as **less-developed countries (LDCs) or developing countries**. There are two reasons for focusing on LDCs. One is that they contain a very large share of the world's population, and the obstacles they face in achieving higher standards of living affect billions of people. The second reason is that most of the types of government intervention in the markets of advanced nations such as the United States are also found in LDCs, but their impact there is magnified. Therefore, LDCs constitute an example for the advanced nations of the world, providing a picture of what could happen if market intervention in, say, the United States were extended to a larger number of industries and markets and affected a larger fraction of the population.

One reason why many types of intervention affect LDCs is that so many individuals are poor and so many business firms find it difficult to borrow funds needed to finance their growth. If government decides, say, to maintain nationwide food consumption at a given level, a larger proportion of the population in an LDC will fall below that level than in a country with higher per capita income. If government policies aim to support manufacturing industries that have difficulty competing in world markets, inherently a larger fraction of industries in LDCs find it difficult to compete. The forms of intervention we will discuss in this chapter are (1) cheap food policies, (2) rent controls and subsidies to urban housing, (3) minimum wage laws and price controls in manufacturing, and (4) subsidies to investment in the industrial sector.

In order to understand why such programs emerge in developing countries, we will compare and contrast population trends, health conditions, the mix of agricultural and manufacturing production activities, financial market conditions, and general economic well-being for representative industrialized and developing countries. We will discuss the short-run and long-run economic effects of each of the four types of market intervention listed above. We will then analyze who the winners and losers are when government intervenes in these markets and the long-run effects of each program on the allocation of resources. In addition, we will explain why market alternatives to government intervention are evidently more difficult to implement in LDCs than in advanced economies.

Before discussing government intervention in the economies of LDCs, we should discuss one major characteristic of underdeveloped economies that is often seriously misunderstood. We have defined economic development in terms of two criteria: (1) per capita income and (2) the level of industrialization. Industrialization *refers to the proportion of a country's total production that comes from its "modern" sectors, which usually is taken to mean manufacturing industries as opposed to agriculture. However, there is nothing fundamental in economics that precludes primarily agricultural economies from being well-to-do. After all, no one would refer to the states of Iowa, Illinois, and Kansas in the United States as underdeveloped or poor because a large fraction of their labor force is employed in agriculture.

Given enough physical capital, a well-educated labor force, and modern techniques, agriculture can provide a road to economic well-being that is as direct as "industrialization" or even more so. It is true that most modern, developed economies are also largely industrial in their output and employment. For this reason, many LDCs have sought to emulate the pattern of industrialization observed in developed economies in the pursuit of higher per capita income. We should always remember, however, that it is higher per capita economic well-being that makes a sensible economic goal for a country—not some particular type of industrial structure for its own sake.[1]

Economic Conditions in Developing Countries

Population Growth and Population Density

Figure 18.1 illustrates data on population and its growth for regions of the world and for particular developed and less-developed countries. The graphs show that world population growth has averaged 1.8 percent per year.[2] This rate has not changed much since at least 1970. However, the pressure of population growth has not been evenly distributed around the world or among developed and developing countries. North America and Europe, which are more industrialized, have experienced population growth rates that are well below the overall average and only 20 to 40 percent as large as the growth rates in less-developed economic regions such as Latin America, Africa, and parts of Asia. In eastern Asia, where population density (people per square mile) is greatest, population growth is 40 to 80 percent faster than in North America and three to four times faster than in Europe.

Figure 18.1 shows that in recent years the United Kingdom and the Federal Republic of Germany have experienced virtually no population growth and that the United States, Canada, and Japan have grown at the slow pace of only 1 percent per year. At the other extreme, developing countries such as Bangladesh, Brazil, Chile, Egypt, India, Mexico, the Philippines, and Turkey have experienced annual population growth rates that are two to three times larger. In part, the high population growth rates in developing countries have resulted from improvements in medical care that have reduced mortality rates in both developing and developed nations since World War II. However, birthrates in developing countries have remained extremely high, while they have declined rapidly in developed countries, particularly in the last twenty years. More extensive use of birth control techniques could alleviate the population pressure in poorer countries, but such practices often conflict with accepted cultural and religious practices.

American students often have difficulty comprehending economic and social conditions in less-developed parts of the world. Perhaps the simplest way to appreciate the crowding effect of population pressure in countries like Bangladesh, India, and the Philippines would be to consider how life might be different in the United States if instead of 238 million people there were 2.19 billion people, matching the population density of India, or 6.58 billion people, matching the population density of Bangladesh. This would amount to putting the entire world population within the borders of the United States and then increasing it further by another third! With those figures in mind, one can begin to appreciate the problems of food, housing, health care, transportation, and communication that plague many developing nations.

Before moving on to other aspects of comparative economic conditions in developed countries and LDCs, consider the implications of the population growth figures in figure 18.1. Again, if we use the United States as a benchmark, we can obtain a clearer perspective of the economic problems associated with rapid population growth within the developing countries. During the period 1947–1961, the United States experienced a "baby boom," during which the annual population growth rate averaged 1.73 percent. That burst in population growth created tremendous pressures within the society for housing, health care, educational facilities, welfare programs, and so on. As the baby boom generation entered the work force during the late 1960s and early 1970s, the overall unemployment rate rose and worker productivity gains declined. Some have argued that the economy struggled with higher unemployment, inflation, and lower economic growth in part because of the difficulty of absorbing so many new workers. Consider how much greater the short- and long-term impact of the baby boom phenomenon would have been on the United States economy if that spurt in population growth had been over 25 percent more rapid, as it is in the developing countries of Brazil, India, and Turkey. Consider how the United States might have been affected by a jump in population that was 66 percent faster, as it is in Egypt, or 72 percent faster, as it is in Bangladesh.

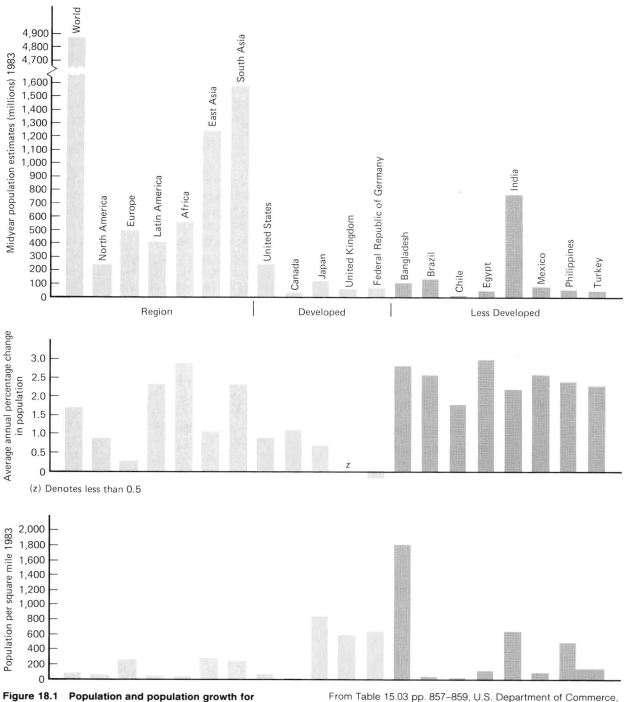

Figure 18.1   Population and population growth for developed and developing countries (z denotes less than 0.5 percent).

From Table 15.03 pp. 857–859, U.S. Department of Commerce, *Statistical Abstract of the United States,* 1984 (104th edition), *Statistical Abstract of the United States,* 1986 (106th edition), pp. 834–835, Tables 1463, 1466.

General Living Conditions in Developed Countries and LDCs

Figure 18.2 illustrates differences in various measures of living conditions and social welfare in a number of countries. This figure shows that life expectancy at birth averages around seventy-five years in developed countries compared to only fifty-nine years in our sample of LDCs. The average difference of sixteen years is partly attributable to an infant mortality rate in LDCs that is an average of almost nine times larger than in developed nations. Both high infant mortality rates and higher death rates among the adult population are related to low-income levels and the frequently inadequate supplies of food and therefore inadequate nutrition experienced in LDCs. We shall see later on that government policies often exacerbate food shortages in LDCs. They are also affected by the relatively poor quality of medical care generally available. Apart from quality differences, medical care facilities are simply much fewer in LDCs than in the developed regions of the world. Imagine how inaccessible hospital care would seem if the availability of hospital beds were half as great relative to population as it presently is in the United States. This is the case in Egypt and Turkey. In Mexico, their availability is only one-fourth as great as in the United States, while in Bangladesh, there are only one twenty-fifth the number of hospital beds per person as in the United States. What would be your chance of seeing a doctor or scheduling elective surgery (if you could afford it), if on average the number of people per doctor in the United States were six times greater than it is, as reflected by the LDC average of 3,288 people per physician rather than 549 people?

Other contrasts between the living and social conditions in LDCs and the developed nations—the United States in particular—are equally stark. The illiteracy rate in each of the developed countries in figure 18.2 is only 0.5 percent. By contrast, the illiteracy rate in the sample of LDCs ranges from 5.6 percent in Chile to 66.9 percent in Bangladesh. The developed countries have between 52 and 76 telephones per 100 population. By contrast, the availability of telephones in LDCs ranges from one per *1,000* people in Bangladesh to 9 per 100 in Mexico. There are more than eight times as many telephones per person in the United States as in Mexico. Copies of daily newspapers per 1,000 population in the United States are forty-five times more plentiful than in Bangladesh and thirteen times more than in India. What does this suggest about the quality of information on product prices, job opportunities, and investment possibilities within developing countries? How easy is it likely to be to collect reliable economic information on how the economy is doing or how well a government program is working under such circumstances? What is the likelihood that national economic policies will be responsive to the "will of the people" when a third or more of the population cannot read or write and when newspapers, telephones, radios, and television sets are curiosities for most people rather than everyday sources of information?

Moreover, the prospects for change in the underlying conditions in LDCs are not great. Expenditures on public education relative to overall economic activity (which is low to start with) average only half as much in the LDCs noted in figure 18.2 as in the developed countries.

With the background information presented in figures 18.1 and 18.2, it should be no surprise that overall economic well-being is much lower in LDCs than in developed nations. Average per capita income in 1980 was nine times greater in typical advanced countries than in an average developing nation.[3] Clearly, the economic environment in which government policies toward markets are formed and carried out is much less forgiving in developing countries than in the economically advanced regions of the world.

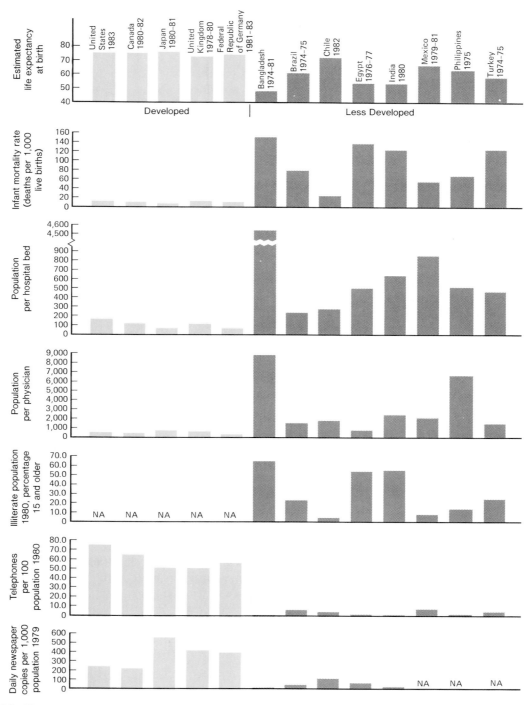

Figure 18.2   Measures of social welfare for developed and developing countries.

From *Statistical Abstract of the United States*, 1986 (106th edition), Tables 1471, 1478, 1469, and 1468, pp. 839–845.

▶ An Analysis of Cheap Food Policies in LDCs

Surely, one would not be surprised to learn that economic conditions in developing countries often tempt governments to impose price controls and other restrictions that are intended to keep the price of food artificially low. Whether motivated more by altruism or simply a way to buy political stability, such programs never work quite the way they are intended to work. This is illustrated in figure 18.3, which is a useful tool in our discussion of who the winners and losers are and what the short-run and long-run economic effects of cheap food policies are likely to be. The demand and supply curves represent the short-run demand and supply for food in a typical LDC. Ruling out the possibility of imported food for the moment, the market equilibrium price and quantity of food are P(0) and Q(0), respectively. The government's decision to intervene in the domestic food market is presumably based on the decision by policymakers that the free market equilibrium price is unacceptably high. For example, the government may feel that free market food prices will be much higher than many people can afford. There may be a real risk of violent attacks against the government. In recent years, popular uprisings over rising prices in countries as diverse as Poland and Chile suggest that government fears are not unfounded. If the government imposes a maximum price for food of P(2), the quantity of domestically produced food supplied will fall to Q(S), resulting in a shortage of Q(D) − Q(S).

Winners and Losers from Cheap Food Policies

Who wins and who loses? Clearly, domestic farmers are worse off as a group if they cannot sell their products illegally in a black market. The decline in the quantity supplied will include cutbacks by farmers who hope the program will not last and who store some

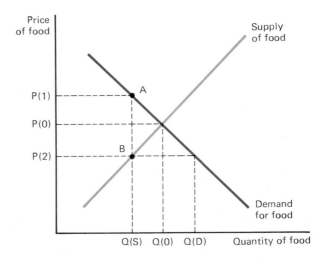

Figure 18.3   The effect of cheap food policies in LDCs
The diagram shows the short-run domestic demand and supply of food in a developing country. P(0) and Q(0) are the equilibrium price and quantity of food. P(2) is the legal maximum price of food, and Q(S) is the quantity of food supplied at the ceiling price. Without food imports, the area P(2) P(1) AB represents potential black market profits to food providers. Q(D) − Q(S) is the quantity of food imports required to maintain the price of food at P(2).

of their produce to sell later. However, storing crops is costly and involves a loss in current income that cannot be recaptured relative to free market conditions. Some farmers may find that they cannot afford to remain in farming. They will simply stop farming and look for other work.

Consumers as a group are not necessarily better off. Those consumers who can buy as much food as they could in the free market situation are obviously better off. However, since there is a shortage of food, some consumers must be obtaining less food after the price controls are imposed.

As a result of the shortage, consumers are willing to pay a price equal to P(1) in figure 18.3 for the limited supply Q(S). It is not unlikely that a black market in food will arise. Whoever controls the final distribution of food for sale to consumers will make a lot of money, as illustrated by the area P(2) P(1) A B in figure 18.3. The ultimate winners in a program of controlled food prices are more likely to be middlemen who legally or illegally profit from food shortages than the consumers who are the supposed beneficiaries. To the extent that imports are either not available or quite expensive, a government committed to this cheap food policy will be at least partly responsible for (1) declining domestic agricultural production, (2) reduced domestic food consumption, and (3) the development or worsening of nutritional deficiencies among the domestic population. Thus, we should not be surprised if a country committed to a cheap food policy also has a low standard of living.

Dependence on Food Imports

If the government decides to discourage private profiteering by importing enough food to satisfy domestic demand at the official price, it will have to import $Q(D) - Q(S)$ units of food at a world market price. The price of imported food is likely to be higher than the government-imposed ceiling price (or food will likely have been imported to begin with). Therefore, the government will end up losing money by importing food and reselling it to the general public. Where does the money come from to support these losses? We will return to a consideration of how the government finances its cheap food program later in this chapter since the method chosen to fund such programs will affect our assessment of who the winners and losers turn out to be.

Long-run Effects

Now let us consider the long-term consequences of the government's cheap food policy. First, as the program continues, fewer and fewer farmers find that they are able to survive in agriculture. The level of output and the living standard of rural inhabitants decline, and families migrate to urban areas in search of jobs. One of the remarkable statistics of many developing nations is that the proportion of population living in urban areas approaches that of industrial countries even though a far larger proportion of the jobs are in rural areas.[4] Cheap food policies make agricultural production unprofitable, driving farmers off the land to urban centers, where jobs are scarce. The government's food program gets bigger, and losses on import purchases expand.

The second long-term effect of government policies regarding cheap food is increasing dependence on imported food. Over time, the gap between the quantity of food demanded and the quantity supplied will increase along with the population shift to urban areas. The dependence of the economy on food imports relative to domestic production will increase as the need to feed the urban poor grows.

Black Markets and Corruption

A third effect often seen is that the government's ability to maintain the integrity and efficiency of the food price control program deteriorates. Scoundrels within the government sector as well as in the private sector will find ways to alter invoices on imports, smuggle food into the country, reduce food quality, and discover other means to make huge profits on illegal food sales and adulteration through black market operations. Legal restrictions on economic activity always create profitable business opportunities for those willing to work outside the law. Moreover, otherwise decent people unable to obtain food legally because of the controls may feel compelled to turn to extralegal means to meet their needs. In such circumstances, general respect for the rule of law under a democratic government often deteriorates.

▶ Cheap Urban Housing Policies

Demand and Supply of Housing in LDCs

Disturbances in one major sector of an economy are likely to affect other major markets, too. We have just seen how cheap food policies lead to a shift of the population toward urban areas despite a lack of job opportunities there. As a result, urban unemployment among unskilled workers is frequently substantial. The food problems of the urban poor are likely to be compounded by a housing problem.

How Rent Controls Work in the Short Run

Figure 18.4 illustrates the short-run implications of subsidized housing programs. The demand and supply curves represent the demand and supply for standard housing units (housing units of a given quality) in an urban area. Market equilibrium price and quantity are represented by P(0) and Q(0), respectively. In many developing countries, governments deal with the embarrassment of high housing costs by simply imposing price controls. As illustrated, if the government imposes a ceiling price, or rent, on housing equal to P(2), the quantity of housing supplied will shrink to Q(S). The short-run reduction in available housing will occur as owners decide not to rent properties for housing purposes because of the artificially low price of P(2). Perhaps they will rent buildings for other uses, such as storage, expand their own housing consumption, or simply board up or knock down existing structures and use their land for other purposes.

Winners, Losers, and ''Key Money'' Payments

How does cheap housing get allocated? Who wins and who loses? Clearly, the owners of housing are likely to be worse off as a group unless they can rent housing on a black market. Either they will continue to rent

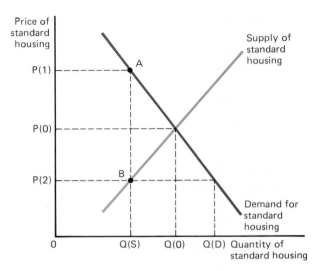

Figure 18.4   The effects of subsidized urban housing
The diagram shows the demand and supply of standard housing units in an urban area. P(0) and Q(0) are the market-determined equilibrium price and quantity. If a price ceiling equal to P(2) is imposed, a housing shortage equal to Q(D) − Q(S) results. The area P(2) P(1) AB represents the ''key money'' paid for subsidized housing.

housing at substantially reduced rental rates, or they will shift their assets into other uses. Renters who are able to obtain standard housing at the controlled price, P(2) in figure 18.4, who used to have to pay P(0), are clearly better off as a result of rent controls. However, fewer units of housing are available. Because of the shortage—Q(D) − Q(S)—renters are likely to have to pay more than P(2) or else switch to substandard housing accommodations. Those who cannot obtain standard housing at the controlled price are clearly worse off because their changed housing consumption patterns are in response to reduced housing options and not the result of a change in their housing preferences.

How does the limited available supply of standard housing units get distributed among consumers, given the shortage that emerges at the ceiling price? The market-clearing price for the quantity of housing offered is P(1), substantially more than the ceiling price. In figure 18.4, the area P(2) P(1) A B represents the amount of black market profit to be gained by whoever controls the availability of standard housing. The big winners in this case could include corrupt government officials who make certain that rent control apartments go to individuals willing to make side payments equal to as much as P(1) − P(2) per unit of time. Alternatively, individuals lucky enough to live in the housing when the rent controls were imposed might illegally rent their apartments to someone else for a side payment equal to P(1) − P(2). Side payments of this sort for rent control housing are often called "key money." In Cairo, Egypt, a city of 11 million in 1984, rent control apartments along the Nile rented for the equivalent of about $30 per month. However, "key money" prices on those apartments were rumored to be as high as $200,000 to $300,000. Those figures pertain to a housing market in a country where the basic unskilled laborer wage rate was equivalent to $1 per day. Consider our earlier discussion of consumer surplus in chapter 8 and trace how "key money" reduces consumer surplus and redistributes it to property owners and/or corrupt government officials. Compare total consumer surplus with price ceilings to consumer surplus without rent controls in figure 18.4.

The Long-term Decline in the Quality of Standard Housing

As rent controls persist through time, the stock of available housing of standard quality shrinks in part as the result of owners' deciding to neglect unprofitable housing units and let them deteriorate into slums.

It is common in cities in which rent controls are not extended to new housing (presumably in an attempt to revive the urban housing market) to find whole areas of rent control housing deteriorating into the worst possible slums while new and extremely expensive housing rises nearby. Sometimes governments attempt to sustain the quality and quantity of housing in the urban areas despite the imposition of rent controls by directly financing housing construction. However, if private investors find that activity to be unprofitable, it will be unprofitable for the government, too. Where does the government get the money to finance the construction and maintenance of unprofitable housing? We will return to this question later. Again, the distribution of winners and losers from government market intervention programs will be affected by the methods used to finance those programs.

▶ Minimum Wages and Price Controls

Background: The Perceived Need for Price and Wage Controls in Developing Countries

We have seen that programs undertaken by governments to alleviate scarcities of food and housing have ironically more often led to rising prices and reduced quantities available. Thus, there is a political appeal to imposing price ceilings in general on all goods and services consumed by lower-income consumers and imposing a floor on the wages they earn. Politicians often opt for minimum wage laws to assure that workers will earn enough. We will now briefly examine the effects on employment of simultaneously imposing maximum prices and minimum wage rates.

The Labor Market in Manufacturing

Figure 18.5 illustrates the short-term demand and supply of labor in manufacturing. The market equilibrium wage and level of employment are W(0) and L(0), respectively. Price controls are generally imposed because the government believes that the market-determined equilibrium price of manufactured goods would be too high. The reduction in prices of manufacturers' goods causes their demand for labor to shift leftward to D'.

The demand for labor decreases in response to price controls as some businesses close down and others cut back production in response to reduced profits. That policy alone would reduce both employment and wages. Can you explain in your own words why the forced decrease in the price of manufactures would reduce the demand for labor and any other relevant factors of production?

The imposition of a minimum wage law is usually based on the government's judgment that the market-determined equilibrium wage rate would be unacceptably low. By imposing a minimum wage of W(M) the government squeezes business profits further. This encourages businesses to use less labor in production. The new equilibrium level of employment occurs at L(D).

Winners and Losers from Minimum Wage Laws and Price Controls

Who wins and who loses as a result of these government programs? In the very short run, the government may be able to produce data that reveal the not very surprising fact that when prices are fixed, inflation is substantially reduced. Workers who were employed before both the wage and price controls were imposed clearly are better off at the higher wage W(M) than they were at the lower market wage W(0). Moreover, some producers are likely to profit from black market sales at prices well above price ceilings. Finally, government officials assigned to enforce maximum prices and minimum wages might be able to extract bribes for ignoring black market transactions in both product and labor markets.

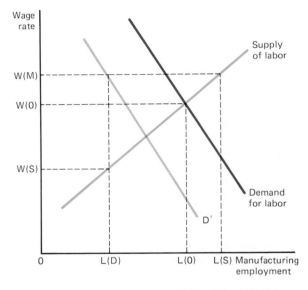

Figure 18.5   The effects of minimum wage rates and maximum prices in manufacturing in LDCs
The diagram shows the short-run demand and supply of labor in manufacturing. The equilibrium wage rate and employment are W(0) and L(0), respectively. W(M) is the legal minimum wage rate. A maximum price on manufactured goods shifts the demand for labor leftward to D'. Thus, the quantity of labor demanded is L(D), and unemployment equals L(S) − L(D).

To the extent that price controls are effective, consumers who either cannot buy goods that they purchased before the controls were imposed or who must now buy the same goods illegally at much higher black market prices are clearly worse off. Some consumers will benefit if they can now purchase as much as before at lower prices.

Workers who lose their jobs because of the controls are clearly worse off. As illustrated in figure 18.5, L(0) − L(D) workers have lost their jobs. Producers who will not, or cannot, sell their products on the black market are clearly worse off. Even the gains to workers who remain employed may be exaggerated. As indicated in figure 18.5, the L(D) employed workers would be willing to work under existing conditions for a wage equal to W(S), which is considerably below W(M).

Employers understand that fact and may be able to extort payments from workers who are eager to work. They may also take advantage of the excess supply of labor by reducing health and safety standards in the workplace.

In the long run, some businesses will close for good, and the economy will stagnate. Resources that used to go toward productive economic activity will be diverted to efforts to circumvent government regulations. Market signals about the appropriate allocation of society's limited resources will be distorted. The willingness of the private sector to invest in the economy will be shakier than ever. As general economic well-being declines, the problems that led the government to impose wage and price controls are likely to be worse than they were when the controls were instituted. Referring to figure 18.5, can you detect how the share of income going to labor is changed by price fixing and minimum wage legislation? On the basis of the diagram, can you demonstrate that policies aimed at helping workers as a group could actually reduce total labor income?

▶ Cheap Credit

Background: The Perceived Need for Government Direct Financing of Investment in LDCs

The policies we will discuss in this section are partly related to the belief that in LDCs, private individuals and households are so poor that they consume practically all of their incomes just to survive. Consequently, there is little left over for saving that could finance investment in capital needed to promote economic growth. As a result, there is often the sense that government must take the lead in long-term investment activity in LDCs whether or not tax revenues are adequate to finance those investments. The lack of tax revenues to pay for investment projects desired by the governments of LDCs is made more severe by the need to finance food imports and subsidized public housing, which we discussed earlier. Not only do the direct expenditures by governments on food imports

and housing subsidies use up tax revenues, but these programs require labor and other resources to administer. The additional program costs associated with policing the potential corruption and waste associated with nonmarket allocations of resources can also be substantial.

One policy commonly adopted in developing countries to reduce the burden of financing capital formation faced by the government is for the government to subsidize private loans and to provide loan guarantees, particularly in the manufacturing sector. Such loans work to the benefit of existing and potential producers of manufactured goods. One can be sure that substituting government decisions for market signals will lead to bad loans, invite corruption, and generally induce a misallocation of investable funds both in the short run and the long run. Another consequence of government-subsidized credit to manufacturing is an associated credit squeeze in agriculture.

The Effects of Subsidized Credit and Loan Guarantees

Figure 18.6 illustrates the demand and supply of credit to the agricultural sector. As indicated, before the government intervenes in the credit market, the equilibrium cost of credit in agriculture is R(0) and the equilibrium amount of money borrowed is C(0). Once loans to manufacturing are subsidized, the demand for credit in manufacturing increases. The increased reward to lenders for supplying credit to manufacturers causes the supply of credit to agriculture to shift leftward to S′. As illustrated, the cost of credit in agriculture increases from R(0) to R(1), while the quantity of funds borrowed falls from C(0) to C(1). Clearly, the agricultural sector is worse off since the cost of credit has increased. As a consequence, agriculture becomes less profitable, and the pace of migration from rural to urban areas accelerates. Developing countries find that their traditionally strong agricultural sectors are in decline and that the urban problems discussed earlier increase further.

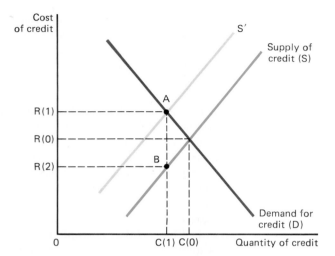

Figure 18.6   The agricultural credit squeeze
The curves D and S represent the demand and supply of credit to the agricultural sector. Credit subsidies to manufacturing industries shift the supply of credit to agriculture leftward to S'. This raises the equilibrium cost of credit in agriculture from R(0) to R(1) and reduces the quantity of credit used in agriculture to C(1) from C(0). The area R(2) R(1) AB is a measure of the added cost of credit to agriculture resulting from credit subsidies to manufacturing.

▶ The Political Difficulties of Adopting Free Market Policies in LDCs

To many students of economics it seems self-evident that a return to free markets would reduce the policy-induced problems we have discussed in this chapter. Fortunately, there is a mood in many policy circles to attempt to move back toward greater reliance on market signals in determining the course of economic development among the poorer nations. However, the political problems involved are easy to underestimate. Consider the difficulty that politicians in the United States face in withstanding special interests in the automobile and steel industries to protect them from foreign competition and the losses in terms of profits and jobs that might be involved.

In the presidential election of 1984 the theme of the Democratic party was partly one of protecting individuals from the cruel realities of the marketplace. Ronald Reagan was portrayed as a tyrant who cared little for the less fortunate. Imagine how much more volatile the debate would be and how much more violent conditions might become for a government in a developing country faced with all of the social and economic problems we have discussed should it decide to move quickly toward a free market policy.

It is more the result of practical political considerations than a lack of understanding of economics that explains why developing countries are moving slowly, if at all, in the direction of depending on market forces to promote economic development. The economic soundness of such a shift may be clear, but the political risks involved are often substantial. Moreover, as we indicated in each of the examples discussed in this chapter, government officials often share in the profit-making illegal activities that are the inevitable by-product of market controls. Such officials may control the domestic political agenda, and they have no interest in reducing their own profits by deregulating markets.

Recall the discussion in chapter 8 regarding who captures monopoly rents. We indicated that the initial owners of monopoly power usually extract all of the rents. Subsequent owners of monopoly enterprises often earn zero profits in the long run. Breaking up such monopoly activities seems often to create victims with little evidence of gains. One can easily imagine that after price ceilings, rent controls, minimum wage laws, and subsidized credit programs have persisted for a long time in developing countries, well-intentioned efforts to reduce market controls quickly will create victims and hardship in all directions. Even if a government attempting to govern responsibly could survive such a transition, it might not be willing to accept the hardship that a policy of market deregulation would impose on people who already have very little going for them.

▶ Summary and Conclusions

In this chapter we have analyzed some frequent cases of market intervention by governments of developing countries. We have tried to show how the problems encountered by Alfredo in the story introducing this chapter arise from a complex mix of economic and political problems facing the leaders of the world's less-developed countries. The following main points were emphasized.

LDCs, by definition, have lower levels of income and other measures of social and economic well-being than the industrialized nations of the world.

Population pressures in the LDCs are far more severe than in industrialized nations.

Governments of LDCs often find it politically expedient to impose maximum prices and minimum wages, but the effects on resource allocation tend to be even more severe than in advanced, industrialized nations.

Government policies in LDCs often penalize agriculture, forcing population shifts to already densely populated urban areas and thus exacerbating housing shortages and unemployment.

Government interference with credit markets tends to accentuate the deterioration of agriculture and the artificial emphasis on urban growth in LDCs.

Political realities make it difficult to switch quickly from interventionist policies toward free market resource allocation in LDCs.

▶ Key Term

Less-developed countries (LDCs) or developing countries *361*

▶ Questions for Discussion and Review

1. Explain carefully why it might be difficult politically to drop food subsidy and rent control programs in developing countries. Who would the winners and losers be from such a change?

2. Illustrate and explain how cheap food programs increase a developing country's dependence on food imports.

3. Illustrate and explain why government-financed housing that is subject to rent controls is likely to be unprofitable and to drain government revenues.

4. Illustrate and explain why wage and price controls often lead to higher rates of inflation after the controls are removed than existed before the controls were put in place.

5. Illustrate and explain how loan subsidies and loan guarantees affect the cost and availability of credit in the manufacturing sector targeted for those programs.

6. In light of the discussion of illiteracy rates and the availability of communication and information networks in this chapter, what problems face policymakers in developing countries that would be of less concern in industrialized countries? Is there any advantage to policymakers in developing economies associated with the poor quality of information and communication capabilities?

7. Illustrate and explain how price controls can contribute to the profits of corrupt government officials.

8. Why do you suppose that population growth rates are systematically higher in LDCs than in industrialized economies?

9. Suppose that instead of rent controls the government subsidized private construction of standard housing. Who would gain and who would lose as the result of such a policy?

International Cooperation on Pollution and Defense Issues

▶ The Action-Initiating Event

The upcoming economic summit meeting of free world government leaders will afford the president the opportunity to demonstrate international leadership in two areas that have continued to plague him on the domestic political front. Political opponents of the administration continue to hound the president to take a definitive stand on the acid rain issue. Whether it is fair or not, there seems to be a public perception that the administration has failed to deal adequately with environmental issues. The Canadians are bound to deliver one of their regular harangues about acid rain at the summit. This time, the president wants to be ready with a specific set of proposals that will demonstrate concern and understanding for the Canadian point of view and project the president as a leader of vision with respect to the international scope of pollution problems.

The second issue is the defense budget. The president has become convinced that the only way to get cooperation from Congress in reducing federal budgets is to indicate some willingness to reduce anticipated defense spending. Obviously, the administration does not want to proceed in a way that could be interpreted as bending to the will of Congress. If the allies would finally agree to increase their own defense expenditures, the president could use that change as a basis for scaling back our defense spending. The problem is figuring out how to raise the issue with our allies without creating suspicion that we are reneging on our mutual defense commitments.

▶ The Issues

Several aspects of the acid rain issue must be kept in mind in formulating a position that the president can take to the summit. First, the domestic politics of dealing with the acid rain issue are very sticky. Apparently, a lot of people in Congress from states that do not rely heavily on the production of steel and automobiles for jobs and state revenues are willing to cripple those industries just to make themselves look good on the environmental front. They are actually talking about imposing pollution taxes on all users of high-sulfur coal to reduce the acid rain problem. Of course, that action would add to the costs of domestic producers and reduce their already questionable ability to compete for sales in the United States against the Japanese and others. The administration cannot support that position without risking a huge loss of voter support in the industrial Midwest in the next elections.

The second element to consider in the formulation of the acid rain position at the summit is the adverse effect that the problem is creating for our relations with Canada and the time that discussion of acid rain takes away from consideration of other important international issues. Obviously, the Canadians have an interest in seeing the steel and automobile industries maintain their North American market shares, and the Canadian public would benefit from the reduction in acid rain that controls would generate. The president feels that any proposal to reduce acid rain pollution would have to involve some form of United States and Canadian cooperation. To the extent that pollution abatement benefits the Canadians they should provide some of the financing. Any agreement that could shift some of the costs of pollution controls away from producers in the Midwest would be a political gain for the administration.

The final element of the acid rain issue that should be addressed is also an international one. While there is a great deal of concern in the White House about imports taking sales and jobs away from United States producers of steel and automobiles, there is also an appreciation of the fact that the local pollution problem can be reduced if we import the products of heavy-polluting industries from other countries. With all of the talk about the external debt problems of third world countries we are wondering if some kind of restriction on imports of steel and automobiles from Western Europe and Japan combined with special import rights for developing countries could be used to modestly reduce domestic pollution and make us look good internationally.

With respect to national defense there are two principal concerns. First, the president wants to break the stalemate with Congress without appearing to be backing down on his commitment to a strong national defense. The only way to do that is by having some change in the current status of spending by the allies and/or the Eastern Bloc countries that could be used to defend a reduction in anticipated defense spending that just happens to accommodate Congress's demand for cuts in projected defense spending. We could go to the summit and tell our allies that they must pick up more of the tab for their own security, but there is a danger that such a posture would simply trade a domestic problem for an international problem.

The second element of the defense issue is whether we can make a sensible case to our allies that they should pay more of the cost of their own defense security without sounding like we are going back to a "Fortress America" policy of isolationism. The president is convinced that our allies are getting a lot more defense than they are paying for and that the American taxpayer is getting less than he or she is paying for. Can you think of an argument that explains how our allies could be benefiting at our expense, an argument that does not just sound like sour grapes? We need an argument in defense of shared financing of our mutual security that does not draw attention to the administration's current problems with Congress.

▶ Economic Policy Issues

Although there is a certain amount of folly in asking an economist for input on politically sensitive issues of the sort already described, there do seem to be a number of legitimate economic factors to be taken into account. Your job is to provide a general analysis of how the cost of acid rain pollution might be allocated and to indicate who the winners and losers from different policy options would be. Does the notion of expecting the Canadians to bear some of the costs of pollution abatement make any economic sense? Does the idea of shifting steel and automobile sales away from industrial competitors make any economic sense?

With respect to the national defense issue, is there anything to the president's notion that from the standpoint of our joint well-being the United States is paying too large a share of the defense bill and our allies are paying too little? Is it possible that under the present arrangement the United States is spending too much on defense and yet the overall defense position of our allies is underfunded? That would be a handy argument to be able to use at the summit.

▶ Recommendations

You are to provide written answers to the specific questions that have been raised. The positions that have been outlined look pretty solid politically, but the administration wants to make sure the economic aspects of both positions can be presented sensibly. As you know, the president is willing to change strategies if the present one can be shown to be badly flawed. You are to prepare an economic position paper that details the most efficient ways of dealing with the problem of acid rain and allocating mutual defense expenditures among the allies without regard to political factors. Please provide a sense of whether or not the politicians are getting carried away with their own cleverness and lousing up the policy picture.

Part VI

Introduction to Macroeconomics

Chapter 19

Introduction to Macroeconomics

Outline

I. An introduction to the study of macroeconomics *380*
II. GNP: A measure of a society's total production *381*
  A. Background *381*
  B. The nominal value of GNP *382*
    1. Consumption *382*
    2. Investment *383*
    3. Government spending *384*
    4. Net exports *385*
  C. GNP and economic well-being *385*
    1. The role of nonmarket transactions *385*
      a. Labor force participation of women *386*
    2. Leisure time *386*
    3. Illegal transactions and barter *387*
    4. Intermediate transactions *387*
III. GNP is also a measure of a society's total income *388*
  A. The circular flow of income *388*
  B. Data on GNP as a source of income *388*
IV. Other measures of production and national income *390*
  A. Background *390*
  B. Calculating real GNP *390*
    1. The need for a price index *390*
    2. The CPI and GNP Deflator for the United States *392*
    3. Price indexes and inflation *393*
      a. Why worry about inflation? *394*
    4. Estimates of real GNP for the United States and changes in real GNP *394*
V. Interest rates *395*
  A. Real versus nominal rates of interest *396*
  B. Real versus nominal interest rates in recent years *397*
VI. Unemployment *397*
  A. Definition and measure of unemployment *397*
  B. Why is unemployment such an important economic issue? *398*
VII. Summary and conclusions *399*
VIII. Key terms *399*
IX. Questions for discussion and review *400*
X. Appendix: Introduction to supply and demand *401*
  A. The demand relationship *401*
    1. Basic assumptions of demand *401*
      a. The goals of buyers and how they attempt to achieve them *402*
      b. Limitations on choices buyers can make *402*
    2. Method of analysis *403*
    3. The law of demand and the demand curve *403*
    4. Shifts in demand *404*
  B. The supply relationship *406*
    1. Basic assumptions of supply theory *406*
      a. Suppliers and their goals *407*
    2. The law of supply *407*
      a. Method of analysis *407*
    3. Factors that shift supply *408*
      a. Changes in technology *408*
      b. Changes in input prices *409*
      c. Changes in expected future prices *409*
  C. How the forces of supply and demand determine price and the level of production *409*
    1. The concept of equilibrium *410*
    2. The effects of shifts in supply and demand on equilibrium price and quantity *410*
  D. Key terms *411*

Objectives

After reading this chapter, the student should be able to:

Define macroeconomics and relate it to aggregate economics.

Define GNP and differentiate between nominal GNP and real GNP.

Explain the components of GNP, including consumption, investment, government spending, and net exports.

Describe the relationship between GNP and economic well-being.

Explain the circular flow of income.

Calculate and interpret price indexes.

Explain the relationship between GNP and the business cycle.

Define unemployment and explain its impact on economic issues.

Explain the types of interest rates and indicate how they are related to inflation.

Macroeconomics analyzes the behavior of an entire economy.

Aggregate economics is a synonym for macroeconomics that reminds us that in order to be manageable, *macroeconomic analysis must summarize the workings of an entire economy as the behavior of a few aggregate measures of economic performance including the inflation and unemployment rates.*

Gross national product (GNP) measures the total value of all final goods and services the economy produces during a year.

▶ An Introduction to the Study of Macroeconomics

On an early morning in February 1984 an Iowa farmer and his family stood and watched in numbed silence as federal agents auctioned off their farm equipment, house, and land to repay federal loans on which the farmer had defaulted. Some neighbors faced with the same grim prospects swore they would not participate in the sale and even talked abut using force to stop the auction. The farmer and his wife had worked the land for years, as had his father and grandfather before them. He had imagined that his children and their children would work the same land and share many of the same experiences that made the farm stand for everything he was and everything he ever hoped to be.

All of that was gone now. The farm, the equipment, the friends and neighbors, all the things that told this family who they were and what they should do, were gone. How could so much disappear so quickly?

Like many other farm families during the late 1970s, they borrowed substantial amounts of money to improve their land and buy new equipment. Interest rates were high, but prices were continuing to rise rapidly so the debts they acquired seemed easily manageable. Then the recession of 1981–1982 came; prices stopped rising rapidly. Farmland prices plunged, but interest rates remained high. The farmer could not meet his debt payments, and he could not get any new loans to keep the farm going. Why did land values decline by one-third to one-half of their 1980 value in only a few years? Why did crop
prices stop rising at the double-digit rates experienced in 1979 and 1980? Why did interest rates stay so high that the farmer could not refinance his debt?

The next eleven chapters of this book will help explain the changes in prices, land values, and interest rates in the United States economy that ultimately spelled financial ruin for the farm family we have described, as well as for many others. These changes were beyond the farmer's control. Nevertheless, they had a profound effect on his life and the lives of many others. Millions of similar stories can be told about auto workers in Detroit, steelworkers in Pennsylvania, coal miners in West Virginia, and other workers in other places in America whose lives were dramatically affected by the changes that have occurred in the United States economy in the last few years. In more or less dramatic fashion, government actions regarding these changes will affect each of our lives. The purpose of the chapters that follow is to explain as clearly as we can how the aggregate economy works and how economic policies affect each of us.

Macroeconomics deals with economywide problems such as inflation and unemployment. The Great Depression of the 1930s, the inflationary spiral of the 1970s, and the high unemployment of the early 1980s are examples of the important events that we will study in macroeconomics. In order to understand macroeconomics, it is necessary to simplify our view of the economic system quite a bit. One of the most important parts of this simplification is to add up— or aggregate—the inputs and outputs of thousands of firms and the expenditures of millions of households. The result of this adding up is a small

Intermediate goods are goods purchased by a firm to use in further production.

Current prices are the prices of goods and services actually in effect during the year in question.

Nominal GNP is the observed value of GNP during a given time period, say, a year, because goods and services are evaluated at current prices.

Real GNP is the value of the economy's total production adjusted to ignore changes in the prices of goods and services over time.

number of aggregate variables *that summarize much of what goes on in our economic system. One of these aggregate variables, for example, is total consumption, which is the expenditures by all of the economy's households on most of the goods and services they use in their everyday lives.*

Because of this process of adding up crucial economic variables, perhaps a better name for macroeconomics would be aggregate economics, *because it deals with the summation of all markets into a few aggregate measures of the economy's performance. For the sake of simplicity, we will say that the aggregate economy can be represented by three very large markets: (1) the market for currently produced goods and services, (2) the market for financial instruments such as money and bonds, and (3) the labor market.*

Newspaper and magazine accounts of the macroeconomy's performance frequently mention inflation, unemployment, interest rates, and economic growth. We will clarify the meaning and measurement of these variables, which describe an economy's aggregate performance. We will examine what has happened to measures of macroeconomic performance both in recent years and over time and summarize important trends or relationships that our macroeconomic analysis must be able to explain.

This chapter, part of chapter 20, and chapters 22 and 23 present basic facts and institutional details needed to understand the macroeconomy. Part of chapter 20 and chapters 21, 24, 25, 26, and 27 present a basic theoretical analysis of the aggregate economy. Chapters 28 and 29 deal with macroeconomic policies and controversies that affect all of us.

▶ GNP: A Measure of a Society's Total Production

Background

Probably the most widely known measure of macroeconomic performance is the measure of aggregate production known as **gross national product (GNP),** which is the total market value of the *final* goods and services produced in the United States *during a given year.* (A closely related measure is gross domestic product, GDP. This measure is frequently used in international comparisons of aggregate economic performance. We will occasionally use it in later chapters dealing with the international economy and macroeconomic issues in countries other than the United States. When you see this term, you should think of it as equivalent to GNP.) The word *final* indicates that **intermediate goods,** which are goods purchased by a firm for further production, are not included in GNP. Purchases of goods produced in previous years are not part of GNP either because they were counted in an earlier year's GNP.

The federal government first calculates GNP in terms of **current prices,** which are the prices in effect during the year under consideration. This value of GNP is known as the **nominal GNP.** *Nominal* means that total production is calculated at prices currently prevailing in the economy. It is important to distinguish between the nominal value of GNP and the **real value of GNP,** which is the value of GNP calculated in such a way that it does not reflect changes in the prices of goods and services over time. We will soon see that the price level and the rate of inflation are what link the nominal and real values of GNP.

Consumption refers to households' expenditures on goods and services to be used primarily during the year in question.

Nondurable consumer goods are goods used up by households in the year they are purchased.

Durable consumer goods are pieces of equipment that provide services to households over a number of years.

The Nominal Value of GNP

The nominal value of GNP is a measure of the economy's total production of goods and services in a particular time period. These data are taken from the *Economic Report of the President,*[1] which contains an extensive listing of the economic variables that describe the performance of the United States macroeconomy over time. If you are interested in such data, this publication is well worth buying. For selected values of macroeconomic data, the *Statistical Abstract of the United States* is a useful source of information.

Except for the depression era of the 1930s, nominal GNP has risen steadily, as shown in table 19.1. This table also contains data on personal consumption expenditures, investment by firms, exports (less imports) of goods and services, and the purchases of goods and services by the various government agencies in the United States. Together, these items represent the total value of all the goods and services produced in the United States economy and are, therefore, the basic components of GNP.

Table 19.1 shows that GNP consists of expenditures on several categories of goods and services, which are called consumption (C), investment (I), government (G), and net exports of goods and services to foreign countries (X). Because GNP is the sum of total expenditures for various items, we will use the symbol E to represent it. GNP can be expressed symbolically as

$$E \equiv C + I + G + X.$$

This identity will prove to be valuable when we build a model of how the macroeconomy works. For now let us store it in our memory banks and elaborate somewhat on each of the basic components of gross national product.

Consumption
Consumption (C) in table 19.1 includes those goods and services bought by households during the year being considered. Examples include clothing and food. Consumption expenditures include both **nondurable**

and **durable consumer goods.** An ordinary nondurable consumer good, such as bread, is purchased and used up within a relatively short period of time. In contrast, a durable consumer good provides service over an extended period of time. For example, a car is usually expected to provide transportation for a number of years. Cars, refrigerators, and television sets are all examples of consumer durables. Strictly speaking, when we buy a car we really intend to use only a fraction of its total services during the year. Unless it is a real lemon, the car will give us use over its lifetime of, say, five years. Thus, the purchase price of the car, paid this year, exceeds the consumption value attached to the use of the car this year. To the extent that GNP lumps all consumption expenditures together, including the purchases of consumer *durable goods,* changes in GNP over time misrepresent changes in society's current consumption. (Purchases of new houses are *not* included in the consumer durable goods group; they are treated as investment expenditures. The reason for this is that there is a flow of benefits from a house to its users over a long period of years. These *annual* benefits, which are measured by rent in the case of people who do not own their own homes, are included in consumption. Thus GNP also includes the estimated rental value of owner-occupied homes.)

As an example, suppose a new discovery permits the manufacture of robots that can do all household chores. (This discovery also permits the robots to be produced with no reduction in the production of any other good.) These robots cost $25,000 each and last for twenty-five years, so their one-year consumption benefits are about $1,000. However, measured GNP will reflect the $25,000 purchase price. By including the total value of consumer durables purchased, GNP overstates the increase in consumption occurring in the year the robots are purchased. GNP calculations generally ignore the consumption value of consumer durables in the years *after* they are purchased, thus understating the consumption from consumer durables in these years. (As mentioned above, there is an exception. GNP includes the estimated rental value of the services received by people who own their homes.)

Investment occurs when businesses add to their collection of physical capital (plant and equipment) and inventories. It also includes the purchases of new dwellings, even if by individuals or families.

Table 19.1   Gross national product, expenditure components, 1929–85 (billions of current dollars)

Year	Gross national product (E)	Personal consumption expenditures (C)	Gross private domestic investment (I)	Government purchases of goods and services (G)	Net exports of goods and services (X)
1929	103.4	77.3	16.2	8.8	1.1
1933	55.8	45.8	1.4	8.2	0.4
1939	90.9	67.0	9.3	13.5	1.2
1940	100.0	71.0	13.1	14.2	1.8
1945	212.4	119.5	10.6	74.6	− 0.5
1950	286.5	192.0	53.8	38.5	2.2
1955	400.0	253.7	68.4	75.0	3.0
1960	506.5	324.9	75.9	100.3	5.5
1965	691.1	430.4	113.5	138.4	8.8
1970	992.7	621.7	144.2	220.1	6.7
1971	1077.6	672.2	166.4	234.9	4.1
1972	1185.9	737.1	195.0	253.1	0.7
1973	1326.4	812.0	229.8	270.4	14.2
1974	1434.2	888.1	228.7	304.1	13.4
1975	1549.2	976.4	206.1	339.9	26.8
1976	1718.0	1084.3	257.9	362.1	13.8
1977	1918.0	1204.4	324.1	393.8	−04.0
1978	2163.9	1346.5	386.6	431.9	−01.1
1979	2417.8	1507.2	423.0	474.4	13.2
1980	2633.1	1667.2	402.3	538.4	25.2
1981	2937.7	1843.2	471.5	596.9	26.1
1982	3073.0	1991.9	414.5	649.2	17.4
1983	3309.5	2158.6	471.3	690.2	−10.6
1984	3774.7	2423.0	674.0	736.8	−59.2
1985	3992.5	2581.9	670.4	814.6	−74.4

Source: From *Economic Report of the President*, 1986, Table B–1, pp. 252–253.

Definitions: E is the market value of (final) goods and services produced by the United States economy.

C is the market value of goods and services purchased by individuals and nonprofit institutions, the value of food, clothing, housing, and financial services received by them in kind and the rental value of owner-occupied housing. It does not include purchases of dwellings.

I is net acquisitions of fixed capital goods by private businesses and nonprofit institutions, net increases in inventories, and all private new dwellings.

G is net expenditures on goods and services by federal, state, and local governments.

X is sales to foreign countries less purchases from foreign countries.

Investment

Investment (I) consists of the economy's addition to capital during a year. Thus, the investment category of GNP basically represents purchases of *newly produced* goods that will be used as inputs into firms' production of other goods. We cannot emphasize too strongly that the economist's definition of *investment* does not match the everyday meaning of the word. In economics, investment does *not* include purchases of *existing* goods such as buildings constructed in earlier years or used machinery. It does *not* refer to items

such as stocks and bonds issued by companies to finance their operations. (We shall discuss the role of these items, which are called financial assets, in chapters 22, 23, and 24.) Investment, in the language of economics, refers only to the part of *currently produced* GNP that consists of goods purchased by business firms and households for use over a period of years. Investment includes the construction of *new* buildings, production of *new* capital goods (machines), and purchases of machines, buildings, and equipment that replace old ones.

Government spending is the total dollar value of the purchases of goods and services by all government units—federal, state, and local.

Transfer payments are the opposite of taxes: payments from government to individuals or firms to raise their incomes.

The investment component of GNP includes firms' expenditures on building their inventories of goods. For example, suppose you buy a six-pack of your favorite soft drink from a supermarket. This is counted as consumption in GNP. However, in order to make sure that you can buy soft drinks whenever you want them, your favorite supermarket carries an inventory, or stock, of various brands on its shelves and in its warehouse. If the supermarket increases the value of soft drinks it has on hand from, say, $100,000 to $110,000, it must purchase $10,000 worth of soft drinks from bottlers. This represents an increase in the sale of final goods and services ($10,000 worth of soft drinks), but it is clearly not consumption, because the goods are being held for future use. Therefore, purchases of currently produced goods that go to increase inventories count as part of the investment component of GNP.

It is important to bear in mind that if one firm purchases an *existing* capital good (such as a used machine) from another firm, this is *not* investment in the GNP sense. The reason is that the seller of the used capital is *disinvesting* and the buyer is investing. When these activities are aggregated (added up) in the calculation of GNP, they cancel each other because they do not represent the *production* of investment goods during the year.

Given what you now know about the components of investment, does an increase in investment *necessarily* mean that society is better off? Why? (Remember that investment is defined as the purchase of a *currently produced durable good*. It does *not* include the purchase of previously produced goods or financial assets such as stocks and bonds. Here is an instance where an economic definition differs from everyday usage.)

Government Spending

The next major part of GNP you need to be aware of is **government spending (G)**, the expenditures for goods and services by government at all levels—federal, state, and local. The government spending portion of GNP runs the gamut from expenditures for FBI

agents' salaries to the purchase of chemicals for your town's sewage-treatment plant. The government spending portion of GNP does *not* include a very important component of government *outlays*. *Transfers* to the private sector are direct payments that are not purchases of goods and services. They are called **transfer payments** because they *transfer* spending power from those individuals and households that pay taxes to other individuals or households (who may or may not pay taxes). Transfers are usually aimed at raising the incomes of certain groups that society chooses to aid. They support expenditures by their recipients, which are reflected in GNP when the expenditures are used to purchase currently produced goods and services.

Table 19.1 shows us that government spending has grown quite dramatically in the last forty years. If you compute the percentage of GNP accounted for by government spending in 1940 compared to 1980 or beyond, you will find an almost 50 percent increase in the relative size of the government sector. Government spending on currently produced goods and services was about 14 percent of GNP in 1940, and it grew to about 20 percent of GNP by 1980. As government spending has become an increasingly larger fraction of total GNP, other components of GNP must have fallen in relative importance. Has government spending increased across the board, or has it been concentrated at a particular level of government? Let us dig a little more deeply into these issues.

The relative importance of government spending in GNP has been matched almost point for point by a reduction in the share of personal consumption expenditures. The relative shares of net exports and gross private investment have changed little over the time that the government sector has grown. What appears to have happened is a substitution of *collective* consumption for *private* consumption by individuals. An even more interesting issue involves which level of government is responsible for the relative growth of the government sector. If you were to look at more detailed data from the *Economic Report of the President,*[2] you would see that most of the increase in government spending has come from state and local

Net exports represent the dollar value of a country's exports minus the dollar value of its imports.

governments. While politicians may blame the federal government for the increase in the size of government, purchases of goods and services at the federal level have not grown much more rapidly than GNP during the last forty years. For example, the federal government's purchases of goods and services amounted to about 6 percent of GNP in 1940 and to about 7.5 percent of GNP in 1980. In contrast, the expenditures by state and local governments accounted for approximately 8 percent of GNP in 1940 but had risen to about 13 percent by 1980. Evidently, citizens are demanding more public services from their state and local governments, to the extent their demands are reflected in their votes for tax and bond issues and for their legislative representatives.

Net Exports

When you buy an imported product, you are increasing the GNP of *another* country. The reason is that GNP includes **net exports (X),** the difference between goods and services exported and goods and services imported. When foreigners purchase goods and services from us, they contribute to *our* GNP. Note that in some years, X is negative in table 19.1. When a country has positive net exports, it has produced more goods and services for foreign customers than foreigners have produced for it. More goods and services flow out of the country than flow in. Often you read in the newspapers that a *trade deficit* is a bad thing. A trade deficit for the United States means that the value of goods and services foreigners sent us exceeded the value of goods and services we sent to them.

To make sure that you understand how the components of GNP make up the total, go through a couple of the rows of table 19.1 and actually calculate GNP. For example, in 1983, total gross national product of $3.309 trillion was the sum of personal consumption expenditure of $2.158 trillion + gross private domestic investment of $.471 trillion + government purchases of goods and services of $.69 trillion − net *imports* of $.01 trillion (why is there a minus sign here, and why have we relabeled net exports net imports?).

GNP and Economic Well-being

The news media often treat GNP as a measure of a society's economic well-being and an increase in GNP as an improvement in the welfare of a society. How valid is this? To understand the issue we must pay more attention to what is and is not included in aggregate production as measured by GNP. Remember that GNP is defined as the market value of the final goods and services produced during a given time period. Economic well-being, however, depends on many goods and services produced *outside* the market sector of the economy—mainly in households. Moreover, some production creates "bads," in the form of pollution, that detract from our welfare. In other words, not all production leads to consumption of items we value, and much of what we value economically is not measured in GNP statistics. In the next few sections we will discuss in greater detail some of the deviations of economic well-being from official measures of GNP.

The Role of Nonmarket Transactions

GNP measures the *market* value of goods and services produced. Market prices provide a convenient way to evaluate the production of diverse activities. Given the large number of different goods and services produced, it is an especially convenient way to calculate a grand total for production. As you might expect, some problems exist because of GNP's emphasis on market values. Problems occur whenever activities that clearly relate to society's well-being take place outside of any obvious market.

For the most part, GNP excludes nonmarket transactions. This does not create major difficulties for measuring changes in society's output and well-being as long as the *ratio* of market to nonmarket production remains reasonably constant. *Serious problems in the use of GNP to measure changes in society's economic welfare will occur, however, if there are changes in the relative proportion of market to nonmarket transactions.* There is no consensus on the actual size of nonmarket transactions relative to GNP in the United States. Estimates range from 3 percent to 60 percent of GNP.[3]

Labor Force Participation of Women   To understand the role of nonmarket transactions more clearly, consider the changes in measured GNP that occur when married women enter the labor force in greater proportions, as they have been doing in the United States since the early 1900s. Prior to entering the labor force, the typical married woman spent at least part of her time in household activities such as shopping and cooking. Each of these activities contributed to the economic welfare of her family. Without this effort toward maintaining a clean, safe, and pleasant home environment, her family's well-being would have been substantially lower.

Suppose that we place a price tag of $100 per week on the value of the services that the homemaker rendered to her family. GNP places a zero value on these services that occur in the home, because they are outside the market system. It is important to realize that GNP basically ignores the services of individuals in home production of any sort. You do not have to be a full-time housewife or househusband. Every time you change the oil in your car or wash the windows of your house or apartment rather than pay someone else to do it, you have implicitly lowered the GNP of the United States.

Suppose that a homemaker decides to accept employment as, say, an installer with the telephone company. She now begins to receive a salary of $200 per week. In the process, her family probably uses part of her weekly income to purchase goods and services in the marketplace. Some will be substitutes for things the homemaker had previously been doing at home. In particular, the household may now buy more meals in restaurants and begin to use a laundry service. Suppose that these substitutes cost a total of $100 per week. The actual change in the welfare of our homemaker's family as a result of her new job (ignoring taxes) is really the *difference* between her current wage income and the value of the services she formerly produced as a homemaker. Her family is better off by $100 ($200 − $100) per week. GNP, on the other hand, calculates a welfare gain equal to the full $200 per week because it ignores the homemaker's contribution to her family's well-being.

As we said, GNP's emphasis on *market* value can overstate the change in society's well-being if people decide to do things differently. This issue is quite important whenever many people, as in this case, are simultaneously reducing the extent of their nonmarket activities and increasing their participation in market production. GNP is calculated as if market-employed women suddenly appeared as productive citizens on the economic scene. No allowance is made for previous contributions in their homes. When more women begin to participate in the labor force, then, the true increase in society's economic welfare is *less* than the amount measured by GNP. How would you suggest changing the way GNP is calculated so that it correctly evaluates the change in society's well-being as more and more married women enter the labor force?

Leisure Time

The treatment of leisure time is another example of how GNP misrepresents actual changes in economic welfare. Every year includes a fixed number of hours (approximately 8,760). Each individual divides these hours between work and other activities, including eating, sleeping, and recreation. The hours commonly referred to as *work* are purchased by firms in order to produce market goods and services. The hours not sold in labor markets are used by individuals in leisure activities and household production. We have just seen that household production is undervalued in GNP. GNP also attributes no value to the leisure time of its citizens.

This issue has a number of important economic implications. Let us briefly mention one. The average workweek in the United States was approximately fifty to sixty hours near the turn of the century and has fallen to under forty hours today. At the same time, GNP has risen fairly steadily. The increase in GNP does not account for this almost one-third reduction in the average workweek. How would you go about changing the way GNP is calculated so that it reflects the benefits of greater leisure time? What value would you place on an hour of leisure?

Illegal Transactions and Barter

Gross national product also ignores the value of goods and services exchanged in illegal markets. Whether this causes GNP to overstate or to understate the value of society's well-being depends on your point of view. Here is an example. The "underworld's" revenue from its gambling operations or its sales of cocaine is not included in GNP unless it is reported to the Internal Revenue Service. To the extent that society is worse off when more of these things occur, society's well-being is overstated by GNP.

Incomes and earnings in the United States are taxed under a progressive tax system, which means that tax rates increase with the level of income or earnings. One of the results of this has been that as earnings have risen over time, people have turned to forms of payment that avoid taxes. Recent news accounts note the exchange of services for services, or a return to a form of barter system. An example is a plumber who agrees to fix the toilet of an auto mechanic who in turn tunes up the plumber's car. While the goods that go into the repair of the toilet do get counted in GNP, the exchange of labor services does not. If these transactions are omitted from income tax returns (which is illegal), GNP does not measure them and it thereby undervalues production and society's economic well-being.

Intermediate Transactions

A firm usually does not make each and every component of its final product by itself. As we noted, a firm typically purchases goods from other firms in what are called intermediate transactions. These transactions are a key part of specialization. Specifically, a firm usually finds it advantageous not to make all the inputs that go into its final products. For example, a hospital usually finds it cost effective to buy medicines from drug companies rather than making them itself. What does this imply about the relationship between economic well-being, intermediate transactions, and the computed value of GNP? We will see that we are dealing with two issues here. The first is the fact that GNP *ignores* intermediate transactions. The second is whether that practice is desirable.

Suppose that we ignored the distinction between final and intermediate goods. In this case the economy's total production would be measured by the value of every single item that is bought and sold in a marketplace. Let us call this figure GNP'. Because GNP' counts *both* intermediate and final goods, GNP' can vary even though there is *no* net change in the economic well-being of society. This is best seen with a simple example.

Consider a person who purchases an $8,000 car and intends to use it on pleasure trips over the course of the year. The $8,000 spent represents the value of a final good produced, the automobile. Now suppose that the company that made the car had to purchase $3,000 worth of steel from a steel manufacturer and $500 worth of paint from a paint supplier. These two transactions are *intermediate* in the sense that the car company had to buy these two goods to make its finished product, the car. If we add together the car, steel, and paint purchases, the total value of all of these transactions equals $11,500. This sum is included in our *fictional* measure of society's output, GNP'.

Now suppose the car, steel, and paint companies merge into one large corporation. The inputs that the car company had previously been purchasing from the steel and paint companies will no longer appear as market transactions because the transfer of inputs now takes place *within* the new corporation. As a result of this change in corporate structure, the $3,500 worth of intermediate transactions disappears. In computing GNP', we are left with a total figure that is $8,000, the value of the car sold to the final buyer. Because GNP' falls by $3,500, it seems as though the formation of the large corporation reduces society's total welfare. In fact, economic welfare really remains unchanged because the car buyer still purchases exactly the same car at a price of $8,000. Because GNP includes only final goods and services and excludes all intermediate goods, we avoid such problems. In this way, we do not misinterpret data on changes in the total amount of output taking place when the industrial structure of the economy changes.

*The **circular flow of GNP** (circular flow of income) refers to the flow of money back and forth between the buyers and sellers of society's output*

and means that GNP can be calculated in either of two ways—as the flow of payments for the products of society or as the payments for the inputs used to make society's output.

*The **Proprietors' income** is the income earned by the self-employed from their business activities.*

▶ GNP Is Also a Measure of a Society's Total Income

The Circular Flow of Income

Gross national product should be thought of as a set of exchanges between *producers* of goods and services and *purchasers* of goods and services. Remember that purchasers include households, business firms, and governments. Thus, the sum of those purchases (GNP) is a measure of total production by society. In the process of producing goods and services, however, producers purchase numerous inputs. They range from the services of workers to machinery and natural resources. Inputs used by producers also include the interest paid to people who lend them money and dividends paid to stockholders. The point of this is that we can also think of GNP as the sum of the expenditures on the inputs required to create it. This is illustrated in figure 19.1

To keep things simple, only exchanges between households and business firms are shown in figure 19.1. The inner circle of the figure shows us that business firms sell goods and services to households and receive payments for those goods and services in exchange. The outer circle reminds us that, at the same time, households are selling inputs to the firms, including the services of labor and money lent. In exchange, firms pay for these inputs through the wages and fringe benefits they pay workers and the dividends they pay out to stockholders. A simple principal of accounting is that all revenues must be accounted for. The total sales of goods and services by a firm must *exactly* balance the payments it makes in the course of producing that output. The two will balance if firms are careful in listing *all* payments, explicit and implicit. Some of the firm's expenditures are implicit because they are *opportunity costs,* which means that the owners of the firm must give up something, even if it is not a cash payment. For example, an implicit cost is depreciation. Firms may pay for machinery in one year and use it in a later year. If using the machinery makes it less productive in future years, then there is an implicit cost that is not explicitly accounted for by a cash payment during the year the cost is incurred.

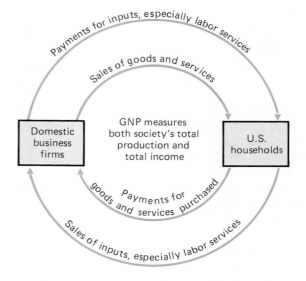

Figure 19.1   The circular flow of payments and purchases between households and firms
Households purchase goods and services from business firms. The total amount spent by households is the largest single component of GNP—Personal Consumption Expenditures. In the course of producing goods and services for sale, firms purchase the services of labor and other inputs, pay taxes to the government, and distribute profits to the people that own the firms. The sum of these also measures GNP, which can be thought of as society's total income. For this reason, GNP is sometimes loosely referred to as *national income.*

The flow of revenues back and forth between firms and households illustrated in figure 19.1 is known as the **circular flow of GNP** or **circular flow of income.** Because of this circular flow, GNP is sometimes casually referred to as national income, although as we shall see, the phrase "National Income" also refers to another, related measure of society's total production.

Data on GNP as a Source of Income

Figure 19.1 emphasizes that total expenditure on GNP is matched by income. In fact, GNP can be measured by adding up individuals and households' incomes as well as by expenditures on production. Business income, such as profit, is attributed to the people who own the business or shares in a corporation. Table 19.2 gives you an idea of the various ways

Rental income is the income produced by renting out machinery or buildings for use in production or consumption.

Corporate profits represent the income people receive from dividends paid to them on the stocks they own and earnings retained by the corporation for reinvestment.

Indirect business taxes are those taxes paid by firms on the basis of the value of production taking place.

Table 19.2   Gross national product as sources of income, 1929–85 (billions of dollars)

Year	Gross national product (Y)	Compensation of employees	Proprietors' income	Rental income	Corporate profits	Interest	Depreciation	Indirect business taxes
1929	103.4	51.1	15.0	4.9	9.0	4.7	9.7	7.7
1933	55.8	29.5	5.9	2.2	−1.7	4.1	7.4	7.8
1939	90.9	48.1	11.8	2.6	5.3	3.6	8.8	9.9
1940	100.0	52.1	13.0	2.7	8.6	3.3	9.1	10.5
1945	212.4	123.1	31.8	4.6	19.0	2.2	12.2	20.0
1950	286.5	154.8	38.7	7.1	33.9	3.0	23.5	24.2
1955	400.0	224.9	42.9	11.3	45.5	5.9	34.8	33.4
1960	506.5	294.9	47.2	14.5	47.6	11.4	46.3	47.4
1965	691.1	396.5	56.9	18.0	80.0	21.0	56.0	65.4
1970	992.7	612.0	66.2	19.4	71.4	41.4	88.1	98.4
1971	1077.6	652.2	69.4	20.2	83.2	46.5	96.5	108.1
1972	1185.9	718.0	76.9	21.0	96.6	51.2	106.4	116.4
1973	1326.4	801.3	93.8	22.6	108.3	60.2	116.5	126.4
1974	1434.2	877.5	88.7	23.5	94.9	76.1	136.0	134.9
1975	1549.2	931.4	90.0	23.0	110.5	84.5	159.3	147.5
1976	1718.0	1036.3	94.1	23.5	138.1	87.2	175.0	159.6
1977	1918.3	1152.3	103.5	24.8	167.3	102.5	195.2	174.3
1978	2163.9	1301.1	118.5	26.2	192.1	121.7	222.5	187.5
1979	2417.8	1458.1	132.1	27.9	194.8	153.8	256.0	199.9
1980	2633.1	1598.6	116.3	31.5	181.6	187.7	293.2	224.4
1981	2937.7	1767.6	129.7	41.4	190.6	235.7	330.1	263.7
1982	3073.0	1865.7	109.0	49.9	164.8	261.1	359.2	258.3
1983	3309.5	1990.1	128.6	54.8	226.3	247.2	377.4	285.8
1984	3774.7	2221.3	233.7	10.8	273.3	300.2	418.9	310.6
1985	3992.5	2372.7	242.4	14.0	299.0	287.7	438.2	328.5

Source: From *Economic Report of the President,* 1986, Tables B–1, B–19, and B–21, pp. 276–279.
Notes: 1. Row totals will not exactly equal GNP because of measurement error (statistical discrepancy) and the subsidies less surplus of government enterprises.
2. The category labeled "Indirect business taxes" includes business transfer payments.

in which GNP is measured as income of members of United States society. The income in table 19.2 is paid out to individuals and households and is used by them to purchase the goods and services produced. A few categories require some elaboration. **Proprietors' income** is the income of the self-employed. **Rental income** is what people receive when they let firms or households use the machinery or buildings they own, and **corporate profits** are divided between dividends corporations pay their stockholders and earnings retained for reinvestment in the corporation. As we noted, depreciation refers to the implicit costs of wearing out equipment in the course of production. The final category in table 19.2, **indirect business**

taxes, represents excise and sales taxes paid by firms and is included in the costs of the goods produced. To make sure that you see how GNP calculated in table 19.2 compares to GNP calculated in table 19.1, go across the row for 1985. Prove to yourself that the sum of employee compensation of $2.372 trillion + proprietors' income of $.242 trillion + rental income of $.014 trillion + corporate profits of $.299 trillion + interest payments of $.287 trillion + depreciation of $.438 trillion + indirect business taxes of $.328 trillion = GNP of $3.992 trillion. (Note that there will always be a slight statistical discrepancy because these data come from different sources.)

*A **price index** is a number that indicates the ratio of the cost of purchasing or producing a given bundle of goods and services relative to some base year, multiplied by 100.*

*The **consumer price index** (CPI) for the United States is a number that represents the cost of purchasing a representative group of goods and services relative to some time in the past.*

*The **base year** is the date at which a cost of living index is set equal to 100 for the purpose of comparison with other years.*

▶ Other Measures of Production and National Income

Background

Most of the time, GNP is the measure of society's production and income that is referred to in newspapers and other media discussions of the macroeconomy. For this reason, we will use GNP throughout most of our analysis of macroeconomics. However, sometimes more refined measures of income or production are needed to study how our economic well-being or total production has changed over time. For this reason, macroeconomists have developed additional measures of national production and income. So that you will know what these concepts measure, we have listed them, along with their definitions and recent magnitudes, in table 19.3. Notice that one of these measures, which is closely related to gross national product, is called National Income. As a rule, when the term *national income* is used it is a loose reference to GNP; however, in technical discussions, if this *particular* measure of society's production and income is meant, it is usually spelled with capital letters: as National Income rather than national income.

Calculating Real GNP

Our discussions have centered on the nominal, or monetary, value of gross national product. We have seen that except for the years of the Great Depression, there has been a continual increase in nominal GNP. Inflation is one factor behind this trend. Remember that each year's GNP in table 19.1 is calculated at the prices in effect during the year in question. As a result, rising prices lead to larger nominal values of GNP even if the quantity of goods and services produced is unchanged. For example, an economy may produce ten units of a good in one year at a price of $1 apiece. Suppose that in the following year ten units are again produced but at a higher price, say, $2 apiece. The nominal value of GNP in the first year is $10; in the second year it is $20.

The increase in the monetary value of GNP from year to year sometimes creates a misleading impression of the growth in society's production and economic welfare. In the preceding example society's

Table 19.3   Relation of GNP to other measures of aggregate production and income, 1985 (billions of dollars)

Gross national product	3573.5
Less: Capital consumption allowances (depreciation)	438.2
Equals: **Net national product**	3554.3
Less: Indirect business taxes	328.5
Business transfer payments	19.3
Statistical discrepancy	0.7
Plus: Net subsidies of government enterprises	9.9
Equals: **National Income**	3215.6
Less: Corporate profits	299.0
Net interest	287.7
Contributions for social insurance	354.9
Wage accruals less disbursements	−0.2
Plus: Government transfer payments to persons	465.2
Personal interest income	456.5
Personal dividend income	78.9
Business transfer payments	19.3
Equals: **Personal income**	3294.2
Less: Personal tax payments	493.1
Equals: Disposable personal income	2801.1

Source: From *Economic Report of the President*, 1986, Tables B–21, B–22, B–25.

production has remained unchanged. In each year its citizens have ten units of output to satisfy their economic wants. Our economic welfare is basically dictated by our consumption of the goods and services themselves—not by their price tags. Of course we all like it when prices are lower, but the real source of our happiness lies in our ability to purchase the goods and services we want.

The Need for a Price Index

A crucial ingredient in determining real GNP is a **price index,** which indicates the cost of purchasing or producing a given set of goods and services at some time compared to the cost at another time. Probably the best-known price index constructed by the United States government is the **consumer price index (CPI).**

The consumer price index is constructed by calculating how much it costs to purchase a fixed bundle, or *market basket,* of goods and services at different times relative to a particular date. The choice of the date, or year, with which to compare the cost of goods and services at other times is arbitrary. The date that is chosen is called the **base year.** The value of a price index in the base year is always set at 100. For example, suppose the cost of a market basket of goods

*The **GNP deflator** is a special index number that expresses the average price of current GNP in terms of prices that prevailed in a base year.*

Table 19.4   How price indexes are calculated

Suppose that the economy consists of firms and households that produce and consume only two goods, steak and pizza. Between the base year, 1987, and the current year, 1988, the price of pizza rises from $1.00 to $1.50, while the price of steak doubles from $2.00 to $4.00. Because the price of steak has risen *relatively* more than the price of pizza, consumers decide to purchase fewer steaks and more pizzas. This can be seen in the 1988 quantities in the section showing how the GNP deflator is calculated.

The consumer price index depends on how much the quantities purchased in the base year cost in the base year and in the current year. The ratio of the cost in the current year (1988) divided by the cost in the base year, multiplied by 100, is the consumer price index.

The GNP deflator is calculated by using a somewhat different procedure. The base-year prices are used to calculate how much it would have cost to purchase the current year's actual purchases if prices had not changed. Then the amount that it actually costs to purchase the current year's quantities is divided by the amount that it would have cost had prices not changed. The resulting ratio, multiplied by 100, is the GNP deflator.

Consumer price index

	Base-year quantity of pizza	Price of pizza	Base-year quantity of steak	Price of steak	Cost of living	Consumer price index*
1987 (base year)	25	$1.00	35	$2.00	$ 95.00	100
1988	25	$1.50	35	$4.00	$177.50	187

GNP deflator

	Quantity of pizza	Base-year price of pizza	Quantity of steak	Base-year price of steak	Quantities valued in		
					Base-year prices	Current prices	GNP deflator**
1987 (base year)	25	$1.00	35	$2.00	$95	$ 95	100
1988	30	$1.00	33	$2.00	$96	$177	184

*Consumer price index ≡ (base-year quantities valued in current-year prices/base-year quantities valued in base-year prices) × 100.

**GNP deflator ≡ (Current quantities valued in current-year prices/current quantities valued in base-year prices) × 100.

was actually $150 in the base year. If, nine years later, the same quantities of these goods still cost $150, the price index would equal 100, because $150 is 100 percent of $150. However, if nine years later, the market basket of goods cost $225, the price index that year would be 150, because $225 is 1.5 (150 percent) times $150. The price index tells us that a representative bundle of goods cost 1.5 times as much in the second year as it did during the base year ($150 × 1.5 = $225). The upper part of table 19.4 contains an example of how the consumer price index is calculated in a simple economy where there are only two goods— steak and pizza.

Another commonly used price index is called the implicit GNP deflator, or **GNP deflator,** for short. The GNP deflator is based on the prices of *all* the goods and services included in GNP, not just the consumption goods component. In computing the GNP deflator, the value of goods and services purchased in

the current year is measured by using the prices that prevailed during the base year. The result is called real GNP, or GNP measured in terms of base-year prices. If the nominal GNP for the current year is divided by the real value of the current year's GNP, the result is the GNP deflator. The GNP deflator is sometimes called the *implicit* deflator because it is the price index that is *implied* in calculating real GNP. An example of how you might calculate the GNP deflator is shown in the lower part of table 19.4. Notice in the table that the amount prices have risen as measured by the CPI (87 percent) is greater than the price increase measured by the GNP deflator (84 percent). This is generally the case because the GNP deflator takes into consideration the effect on purchases when the prices of some goods increase *relatively* more than other goods.

Table 19.5   Some important measures of the macroeconomy's performance, 1929–85

Year	Consumer price index (CPI)[a](base 1967)	Annual rate of inflation	Real GNP (base 1972) (billions of dollars)	Civilian unemployment rate[a]	Prime interest rate[a]	GNP deflator (base 1967)
1929	51.3	− 2.53%	$ 315.7	3.2%	5½–6%	43.0
1933	38.8	3.35	222.1	24.9	1½–4	33.4
1939	41.6	0.96	319.8	17.2	1.5	36.7
1940	42.0	5.0	344.1	14.6	1.5	37.3
1945	53.9	2.28	560.4	1.9	1.5	50.8
1950	72.1	0.98	534.8	5.3	2.07	68.2
1955	80.2	− 0.37	657.5	4.4	3.16	77.3
1960	88.7	1.60	732.2	5.5	4.82	87.8
1965	94.5	1.72	929.3	4.5	4.54	94.3
1970	116.3	5.92	1085.6	4.9	7.91	114.9
1971	121.3	4.30	1122.4	5.9	5.72	123.7
1972	125.3	3.30	1185.9	5.6	5.25	129.5
1973	133.1	6.23	1254.3	4.9	8.03	137.9
1974	147.7	10.97	1246.3	5.6	10.81	150.4
1975	161.2	9.14	1231.6	8.5	7.86	165.1
1976	170.5	5.77	1298.2	7.7	6.84	175.8
1977	181.5	6.45	1369.7	7.1	6.83	187.5
1978	195.4	7.66	1438.6	6.1	9.06	201.1
1979	217.4	11.26	1479.4	5.8	12.67	218.9
1980	246.8	13.52	1474.0	7.1	15.3	238.7
1981	272.4	10.37	1502.6	7.6	18.87	261.8
1982	289.1	6.13	1485.4	9.5	14.86	278.5
1983	298.4	3.22	1534.8	9.5	10.79	289.1
1984	311.1	4.0	1543.4	7.4	12.04	301.1
1985	322.2	3.8	1548.8	7.1	9.93	311.1

Source: From *Economic Report of the President*, 1986.

[a]The CPI, Unemployment Rate, and Prime Interest Rate are annual averages.

Definitions: The CPI is a measure of the average cost of a *market basket* of goods and services purchased by a typical family expressed in terms of 1967. The value of the CPI in 1967 is 100 in this table.

—The Rate of Inflation is the percentage change in the CPI between years.

—Real GNP is the value of GNP measured in terms of the prices that prevailed in 1972.

—The civilian unemployment rate is the number of people in the labor force who were actively seeking work or were on layoff expressed as a percentage of the total labor force.

—The prime interest rate is an interest rate banks stated they charged their most credit-worthy customers for loans.

—The GNP deflator measures the average cost of current GNP in terms of 1967 prices.

The CPI and GNP Deflator for the United States

Table 19.5 gives us some values of the consumer price index and GNP deflator since 1929. The CPI tells us that consumer goods are roughly three times more expensive today than they were in 1967. How much has the price level gone up, using the GNP deflator as a measure? How much more expensive are goods and services today than in 1940?

The numbers in table 19.5 do not tell us the particular items that have contributed most to the increase in the general price level in the last twenty years or so. If you were to get a copy of the *Economic Report of the President* and look at the individual categories of goods and services, you would find that three items have had especially large price increases since 1967. They are gasoline, home heating fuel, and houses. Each of these now costs nearly four times more than it did in 1967.

*The **rate of inflation** is the
percentage change in the general
price level and is typically measured
by the percentage change in the CPI
between two years.*

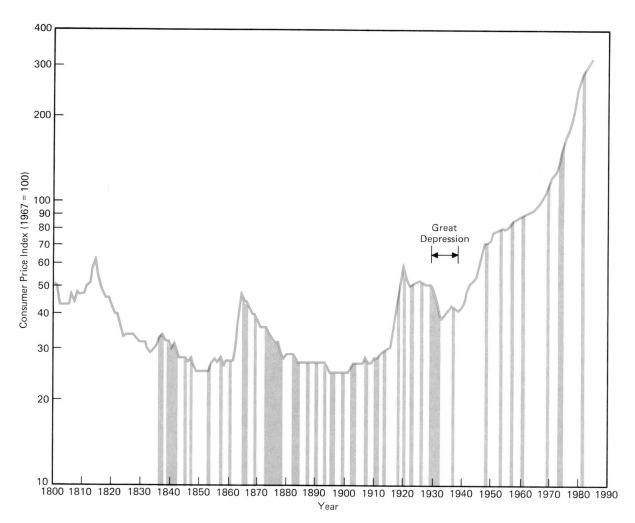

**Figure 19.2   The consumer price index for the United
States: 1800–1985 (1967 = 100)**
The United States has experienced many periods of inflation
and declining prices (deflation) in its history. However, the past
fifty years' inflation is unprecedented. Recessions and
depressions, as measured by the National Bureau of Economic
Research, are indicated by the vertical shaded areas.

From *Historical Statistics of the United States*, Series E
135–166, pp. 210–211, 1970; *Economic Report of the President*,
Table B-52, p. 221; *Journal of Economic Literature*, "Recent
Works on Business Cycles in Historical Perspective: A Review
of Theories and Evidence," Victor Zarnowitz, Vol. XXIII, (June,
1985), pp. 527–528; and *Economic Report of the President*,
1986, Table B-55, p. 315.

Price Indexes and Inflation

One interesting aspect of price indexes is that they
can be used to tell us the **rate of inflation,** which is the
percentage change in the general price level for one
year. The second column of table 19.5 gives us the
annual rate of inflation from year to year in the United
States since 1929, based on the CPI. Figure 19.2

shows the CPI for the United States since the year
1800. One of the most interesting features of figure
19.2 is that there has been much more inflation in the
last fifty years than during any comparable period in
the history of the United States. (This inflationary
tendency characterizes many other industrialized nations, too.)

Indexing is a means of adjusting nominal payments by referring to a price index so that their real value is unaffected by the rate of inflation.

A **recession** *is a period of time when real GNP declines for two or more consecutive quarters.*

A **depression** *is a very severe recession, a period of time when a very severe decline in real GNP is occurring.*

Why Worry about Inflation?   What difference does it make if the general price level is constant or grows at an annual rate of 5 percent, 15 percent, or even 500 percent, as it has in some foreign countries? If wages are increased to account for inflation, workers would do just as well under one rate of inflation as under another. Income from other sources such as rent, interest, and dividends can—and generally does—get adjusted by the forces of supply and demand to offset inflation. Government transfer payments such as Social Security and welfare are adjusted by legislation to offset inflation. So, why is double-digit inflation such a hot political item?

One problem with inflation is that the adjustments we just mentioned are not instantaneous. While the various sectors of the economy are adjusting from one rate of inflation to another, important changes can and do occur in *real* economic variables. Money (nominal) wage rates may lag behind the price level because a union contract is renewed only every two or three years and does not have a cost of living clause. In this case the *real* wage rate will fall when the rate of inflation increases. In addition, suppose that business firms or workers simply take time to adjust to a new rate of inflation. This means they will also suffer a loss of purchasing power when inflation raises the prices they must pay faster than their sales revenues or incomes are rising. Finally, creditors will also suffer and debtors gain if the rate of inflation increases and debts are *unexpectedly* repaid in dollars worth less than when they were borrowed.

In general, people whose *incomes* are fixed in nominal (money) terms are harmed by *unforeseen* accelerations in inflation. Those people whose *payments* are fixed in nominal terms benefit. These are not the only difficulties caused by inflation. Business decisions are difficult in an environment of unstable prices. Such decisions are much simpler when planning for the future can be based on accurate predictions of the wage and price levels.

The effects of unanticipated inflation can be lessened through a general scheme of **indexing,** which

means tying all financial arrangements to the rate of inflation so that payments and receipts are adjusted proportionately. Prices and payments can be contractually or legislatively tied to the general rate of inflation. This would be similar to the way wage rates in many union contracts are currently tied to the consumer price index. If there were a "perfect" price index, or set of price indexes, indexing could basically eliminate any real effects of unanticipated inflation. However, we have already seen that our two most commonly used indexes do not give the same measure of the rate of inflation. Practically speaking, the chances are slim that "perfect" indexing will ever be possible. This means we can safely proceed under the assumption that unanticipated changes in the rate of inflation will continue to have significant real economic effects. As such, lowering the rate of inflation will continue to be politically and economically important in the United States and other noncommunist economies.

Estimates of Real GNP for the United States and Changes in Real GNP

Bearing in mind that price indexes are imperfect, let us see how real GNP has grown over the years. The data in table 19.5 and figure 19.3 show that real GNP is over five times as high today as it was in 1929. Changes in real GNP from year to year are an important measure of how well the macroeconomy is doing. In particular, they tell us whether or not production is growing. When real GNP is declining, economists say that we are in a **recession.** Officially, the beginning and ending of recessions are determined by a nonprofit private corporation, the National Bureau of Economic Research, in Cambridge, Massachusetts. This bureau defines a recession as two consecutive quarters of decline in real GNP (negative growth rate for real GNP), although there have been cases where one quarter was deemed sufficient (1980). Many economists, however, will speak of a recession when the growth rate of real GNP slows sharply, even though the rate of GNP growth is still positive. This is called a *growth recession.*

*The **business cycle** is the pattern of recession followed by recovery that characterizes the United States and other market economies.*

*The **interest rate** is the percentage of a dollar that a borrower must pay a lender per year for each $1 borrowed.*

*The **prime interest rate** is the standard or base rate of interest that banks charge borrowers for one-year loans.*

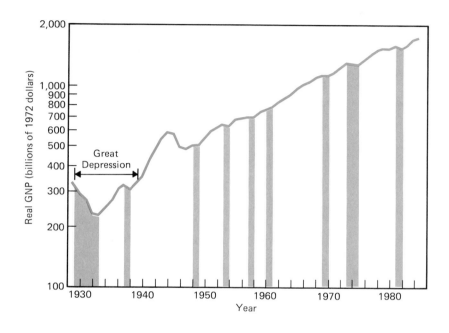

Figure 19.3   Real GNP in the United States, 1929–1984, in 1972 dollars
Real GNP has grown, with many ups and downs in between, so that it is several times higher today than it was in 1929. From *Economic Report of the President,* Table B-2, p. 164; *Economic Indicators,* p. 2; U.S. Department of Commerce (Bureau of Economics Analysis), *The National Income and Product Accounts of the United States,* 1929–1974, statistical tables; and *Economic Report of the President,* 1986, B-2, p. 254.

A very severe form of recession, that is, a very severe decline in real GNP, is called a **depression.** Major recessions and depressions of record are marked off in figure 19.3. Table 19.5 and figure 19.3 remind us of the substantial decline in real GNP that occurred during the Great Depression. Real GNP fell by 2.2 percent between 1932 and 1933. This is one of the largest reductions in output ever experienced in the United States. There was another recession severe enough to be labeled a depression in 1937–38, and we have had two relatively severe recessions in the postwar period. One was in the middle 1970s and the other in the early 1980s. Between 1974 and 1975 real GNP fell by 1.1 percent. Between 1981 and 1982 it fell by almost 2 percent, a quite severe recession by United States standards. It will be our goal in subsequent chapters to try to understand why real GNP sometimes rises and sometimes falls. The pattern of increases and decreases in real GNP is known as the **business cycle.**

▶ Interest Rates

The easiest way to think of an **interest rate** is as the cost of credit. It is the number of cents per year that borrowers have to pay lenders for each dollar they borrow. Interest rates are a key economic variable in the macroeconomy because of their influence on investment decisions. The way in which government policy influences interest rates and thus investment, production, and unemployment is discussed in chapters 24 and 27–29.

Probably the best-known interest rate—the one you will often read about in the newspapers or hear about on television—is the **prime interest rate,** which is the standard or base rate of interest that is charged on loans of a predetermined risk level. Loans with greater than standard risk will be charged rates above the prime (prime plus); loans with lower than standard risk will be given discounts from the prime (prime minus). You should think of the prime rate of interest as a reference point indicating the general level of interest rates on all types of loans. Changes in the prime rate tend to foreshadow similar changes in other key interest rates, such as the rate of interest charged on thirty-year home mortgage loans or four-year car loans.

Refer back to table 19.5 for data on the prime interest rate. Notice that when inflation rates are low, such as in the 1940s, the interest rate (as measured by the prime rate) is also low. However, when inflation is relatively high, such as in 1974 or from 1979 to 1981, interest rates follow suit.

Real versus Nominal Rates of Interest

In discussing macroeconomic concepts, we have been careful to distinguish between nominal and real values. For example, we discussed the difference between nominal GNP and real GNP. There is a similar distinction in the case of interest rates. The interest rate displayed in table 19.5 is a **nominal interest rate,** because it indicates the total price of credit borrowers pay lenders *unadjusted* for inflation. In considering the cost of credit and the return from lending, borrowers and lenders care about the real purchasing power of the interest payments. Lenders will account for the fact that the return on the credit is in reality lower when there is inflation. For example, suppose that you are considering lending $1,000 for one year at a 10 percent nominal rate of interest. This is what the borrower will pay you for the privilege of having $1,000 of credit for a year. Of course, it will make a big difference to you if the $100 interest you receive at the end of the year can purchase a lot or a little next year. Suppose the rate of inflation is zero. This means that your $100 interest payment could purchase the same amount of goods and services as $100 could now. However, if the rate of inflation is 10 percent, then your $100 interest payment is really worth only $90 in terms of its current purchasing power.

To account for the influence of inflation on the purchasing power of interest payments, economists have developed the concept of the **real interest rate,** which is the nominal interest rate adjusted for the rate of inflation that borrowers and lenders *expect* to prevail when they engage in credit transactions. Formally, we can write the expression for the real interest rate as

$$r \equiv i - \dot{P}.$$

In this expression, r represents the real rate of interest, which is equal to the nominal rate of interest (i) minus the expected rate of inflation $\dot{P}$. An example of a nominal rate of interest, i, would be the prime interest rate quoted in table 19.5.

We can view the relationship between the real and nominal interest rates slightly differently by rearranging the identity to read

$$i \equiv r + \dot{P}.$$

This shows us that the market rate of interest equals the real rate of interest plus the rate of inflation. Lenders expect a real return (r) plus an adjustment for the inflation rate to offset the fact that money repaid in the future has less purchasing power the higher the rate of inflation. It is important to note that for a short-term loan such as a three-month treasury security, the expected rate of inflation will generally equal the inflation experienced in recent years. For longer-term loans, the average inflation rate *expected* to be in effect during the loan period may differ among lenders and between borrowers and lenders much more than for short-term loans because predictions of inflation far into the future are very uncertain. To make sure that you understand the concept of the real interest rate, go back to table 19.5 and calculate the real prime rate of interest for the years 1975, 1976, 1980, and 1983. In which year was the real prime rate highest? In which year was the real prime rate lowest? When was the nominal prime rate highest and lowest? Are these the same years in which the real rate was highest and lowest? Was the real prime rate always positive (greater than zero)?

Real versus Nominal Interest Rates in Recent Years

Think of an interest rate as the rental payment on the use of borrowed money, where this rental payment reflects not only the risk to the lender but also the real return that must be earned to make lenders willing to lend. The importance of this is that the nominal rate of interest seems to vary largely because of changes in the (expected) rate of inflation rather than because of changes in the real rate of interest.

These facts underlie the positive relationship between market interest rates and the rate of inflation. Consider the prime rate of interest. We can then use the actual inflation rate as a reasonable approximation of the expected inflation rate because the prime interest rate usually applies to relatively short-term loans. If you review the inflation rates and prime interest rates in table 19.5, you will see that the prime rate minus the inflation rate, which is the real prime rate, does not vary all that much. Of course, there is some variation with unexpected swings in the rate of inflation. For example, in 1974 the prime rate was 10.8 percent. The rate of inflation was unexpectedly high—nearly 11 percent. This means that in 1974 the real prime rate of interest was negative, −.16, approximately −0.2 percent. By the late 1970s, lenders had

come to expect possible high inflation, so the real prime rate returned to a more typical long-run value. In 1980, when inflation was 13.5 percent, the nominal prime interest rate was 15.3 percent. These two figures yield a real prime rate of about 1.8 percent in 1979.

▶ Unemployment

Unemployment in the United States for the period 1890–1984 is shown in figure 19.4. Unemployment has been a quite serious economic problem in the United States at various times in history. Obvious examples are the early 1920s, the Great Depression, and more recently, the early 1980s, especially 1982. Let us see where these figures come from, what they mean, and what unemployment data tell us about economic policy to reduce unemployment.

Definition and Measure of Unemployment

The total number of unemployed people is determined by how people respond to a set of questions in the **Current Population Survey, (CPS),** which is a monthly survey of about 60,000 households by the United States Census Bureau. The CPS is chosen to

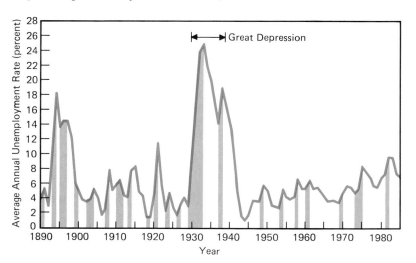

Figure 19.4 Unemployment rates for the United States, 1890–1985
Fluctuations in the unemployment rate coincide with the business cycle. Recessions and depressions are indicated by the vertical shaded areas. From *Historical Statistics of the United States, Economic Indicators.*

*The **unemployed** are people who did not work during the week before the CPS, but were available for work that week and (1) made specific efforts to find a job within the four weeks prior to the survey, (2) were waiting to be called back to jobs from which they had been laid off, or (3) were waiting to report to a new job within the next month.*

*The **unemployment rate** is the percentage of the labor force classified as unemployed.*

*The **labor force** is the sum of employed plus unemployed people in the population.*

provide reliable estimates of the characteristics of the nation as a whole, including the labor force status of individuals who are sixteen years of age or older. Someone is classified as **unemployed** if he or she has no job, wants one, and has tried to find one recently (generally within the previous four weeks). People waiting to start a new job or to be called back to an old one are also classified as unemployed by the CPS. The **unemployment rate** is the number of unemployed people expressed as a percentage of the labor force. The **labor force** is the total number of people employed or unemployed. In other words, the labor force consists of all people age sixteen and over who are either working, seeking work, or are on layoff from a job to which they expect to be recalled.

The definition of unemployment is an attempt to include only people who are actively willing and able to work and to exclude those who would prefer not to work or who are unable to work. In practice, this distinction is not as easy as it might seem. It has been claimed that in some cases the official definition includes too many people and in other cases too few.

Two categories of individuals are often cited as possible candidates for inclusion in the unemployed category. They are (1) people who are working part-time because they could not find full-time jobs and (2) people who have given up looking for work and have dropped out of the labor force because they believe that no jobs are available. On the other hand, it may be argued that the unemployment rate is an overstatement because it includes (1) part-time job seekers, (2) students attending school, (3) voluntary job quitters, and (4) workers on indefinite layoff who are not actively searching for new jobs.

Let us get some idea of the magnitude of a few of these categories. In December 1982 over twelve million people were unemployed.[4] At the same time, two million people said they were involuntarily working part-time schedules. Finally, the Bureau of Labor Statistics reported that in December 1982 over 1.8 million workers had given up trying to find jobs because they believed none were available. We will discuss unemployment in greater detail in chapter 20.

Why Is Unemployment Such an Important Economic Issue?

One obvious reason why we are concerned with unemployment is that much of the time spent looking for a job or waiting to be recalled might instead be used to increase our production of goods and services if only unemployment could be alleviated. As we shall show in chapter 20, however, not all unemployment is simply wasted time. Some unemployment is necessary if workers are to find the jobs that suit them best and in which they are most productive.

An equally important problem with unemployment is that in many instances it is a cause of poverty. Many of the unemployed live in families in which other members work extra hours to compensate for their unemployment. Moreover, many unemployed people receive unemployment insurance payments. However, unemployment is clearly linked to economic hardship for many families and individuals. Here are some facts. In 1981 families in which both the husband and wife worked had a median income of $31,600. Median family income was only $23,000 when either the husband or the wife was unemployed for one to twenty-six weeks. The median income of families in which either the husband or the wife was unemployed for more than half a year was less than $18,000.[5]

Financial losses of the unemployed are not their only costs associated with being out of work. In 1982 the media reported many stories of the anxiety and emotional distress felt by people who had lost their jobs or who feared that they might lose their jobs. The unemployment experience also seems to be associated with bad health, the decline of job skills, numerous psychological problems, and even increases in crime rates.[6]

Unemployment means lost national output. For example, according to recent estimates, each percentage point of unemployment in 1982 reduced GNP by an average of 2 to 2.5 percent ($75 billion). In later chapters we will examine in some detail the link between the business cycle and unemployment. We will also try to understand the reasons for the severe decline in output and severe increases in unemployment in the 1930s and early 1980s.

▶ Summary and Conclusions

In this chapter we introduced the concept of the macroeconomy and explained the key measures of its performance. You have seen how inflation, recession, and increases in the real interest rate contributed to the personal tragedy of the farm family we described in the introduction. In the following chapters we will show how all of the unfortunate events that they experienced occurred. The following points were covered in this chapter.

Gross national product (GNP) measures the total market value of final goods and services produced in the United States during a year.

The nominal value of GNP refers to total production measured in current prices, and the real value of GNP adjusts for the fact that prices may be higher today than in the past.

Real GNP is an important measure of the economy's performance. Reductions in real GNP from year to year are what economists call a recession. A depression is a very severe decline in real GNP from year to year.

The ups and downs in real GNP experienced by economies are what economists call a business cycle.

An economy's economic growth is measured by examining the changes in real GNP over a long period of time, for example, ten to twenty years.

GNP is also a measure of society's income. This stems from the fact that total production has a cost, and when all input costs are tallied, they equal the total value of production.

The rate of interest is the cost of credit—it is the number of cents per dollar per year that borrowers pay to lenders for each dollar they borrow.

Nominal interest rates are related to the rate of inflation. When inflation is relatively high, so are nominal interest rates. When inflation is relatively low, so are nominal interest rates.

The unemployment rate is basically the percentage of the labor force that does not have jobs but wants them.

Unemployment is a major economic problem because it is associated with reduced incomes among the unemployed and lost real GNP.

▶ Key Terms

aggregate economics 380
base year 390
business cycle 395
circular flow of GNP (circular flow of income) 388
consumer price index (CPI) 390
consumption (C) 382
corporate profits 389
Current Population Survey (CPS) 397
current prices 381
depression 394
durable consumer goods 382
government spending (G) 384
gross national product (GNP) 380
GNP deflator 391
indexing 394
indirect business taxes 389

interest rate 395
intermediate goods 381
investment (I) 383
labor force 398
macroeconomics 380
net exports (X) 385
nominal GNP 381
nominal interest rate 396
nondurable consumer goods 382
price index 390
prime interest rate 395
proprietors' income 388
rate of inflation 393
real interest rate 396
real value of GNP 381
recession 394
rental income 389
transfer payments 384
unemployed 398
unemployment rate 398

▶ Questions for Discussion and Review

1. You are given the following series for the consumer price index. The base year for this series is 1967 (that is, 1967 = 100). Suppose you need to calculate real wages in 1972 dollars. Show how you would adjust this series of index numbers to reflect a 1972 base.

Year	CPI
1968	110
1969	112
1970	118
1971	125
1972	129
1973	135

2. For a research project, you need a real investment series expressed in 1980 dollars. However, every reliable source of data has a base year of 1972 for this series of numbers. Describe how you could obtain the series that you need for your project.

3. Define macroeconomics. Give four examples of macroeconomic problems.

4. What is gross national product? What is the difference between nominal and real GNP?

5. How does GNP incorporate the value of consumer durables? Suppose that a person buys a $100,000 house. How does this affect the measured value of GNP? Be complete.

6. Evaluate this statement: it seems rather strange to call inventories a form of investment.

7. Discuss the following. When net exports are negative, this means that the value of goods and services foreigners send to us exceeds the value of goods and services we send to them. Thus, trade deficits are good.

8. Is the following true or false? Government spending has grown dramatically as a fraction of GNP since World War II. This has been the result of a large growth in the federal government. Support your answer with facts.

9. A new steel mill costing $10 million is built. It produces $1 million of steel this year. It creates pollution that costs people who live near the steel mill $100,000 to clean up. How much does all of this change GNP? Explain carefully. Does your answer overstate or understate the effect of the steel mill on society's economic well-being? Explain and draw a numerical conclusion.

10. Do you feel that the value of household production should be incorporated into GNP? Why? Suppose that the government decides it will indeed incorporate the value of home production into GNP. How would you recommend it make such a calculation?

11. The value of certain illegal transactions such as drug sales, prostitution, and gambling are not currently included in GNP. Discuss the pros and cons for including such transactions in GNP. How would you go about gathering the data to do such calculations?

12. Real GNP per capita is sometimes used as a simple measure of intercountry differences in well-being. Here is a topic for a short term paper. Go to your university library or the main library in your town and get some data for real GNP per capita in other countries. In your paper, discuss how real GNP in the United States stacks up against other western countries. Be sure your paper discusses the pitfalls of using real GNP per capita as a measure of the average person's well-being in a country. Focus on what real GNP per capita does or does not say about how well off a country's citizens are.

13. In 1944 nominal GNP was $210.6 billion. In 1947 it was $233.1 billion. The value of the GNP deflator is 37 for 1944 and 49.6 for 1947. Calculate real GNP in 1944 and in 1947. What was the dollar change in real GNP between the two years? Was there a relatively large

Demand is the relationship between the desire to buy various quantities of a good or service and its price.

Supply is the relationship between the desire to sell various quantities of a good or service and its price.

percentage change in real GNP between the two years? What do you think played a major role in the change in real GNP between 1944 and 1947? Support your answer with data presented in the chapter if you can.

14. Bob Dylan said, "Everybody's got to be someplace." Many people in the United States live in houses that they own. Others rent houses or apartments. For people who own their own homes, their house payments are constant for a relatively long period of time. They are zero when their houses are paid off. Find out how owner-occupied housing is accounted for in the consumer price index. Discuss recent changes in the consumer price index's treatment of owner-occupied housing.

15. If you were to look at data presented in the *Economic Report of the President,* you would find that historically the interest rate for thirty-year residential mortgage loans is noticeably higher than the prime rate of interest. What factors do you think contribute to making the interest rate on mortgages exceed the prime rate? Be complete. In 1979–81 this relationship changed. The prime rate was substantially higher than the interest rate charged for home mortgages. Speculate on some reasons for this twist in the structure of interest rates.

16. It is sometimes argued that the unemployment rate does not take account of people who are part-time workers but would like to be full-time workers and individuals who have given up looking for jobs. How would you go about changing the way unemployment is measured to include either or both of these groups? Do you think either of the two groups ought to be included in an official definition of unemployment? Justify your answer.

Appendix to Chapter 19

Introduction to Supply and Demand

If you have taken an economics course in the past, you undoubtedly are well-acquainted with the concepts of supply and demand and know how they interact with each other in markets for goods and services. However, if you are just beginning your study of economics, then learning about these simple but invaluable tools will make your study much more rewarding. Indeed, you cannot study economics without them.

Our analysis of a market economy has three elements: (1) **demand,** which refers to people's desire to purchase a good or service; (2) **supply,** the desire of firms to sell a good or service, and (3) the interaction of supply and demand, which determines prices and the quantities of goods bought and sold. Together, these three elements comprise a model or summary representation of the economic factors influencing the behavior of buyers and sellers. As a general rule, we will analyze how buyers and sellers behave in pursuit of their individual goals. As a second step, we will frequently show how government actions have intentionally or unintentionally altered the outcome that would prevail if supply and demand operated strictly on their own. We will then develop a framework that you can use to help decide for yourself the degree to which you believe that society's goals are better achieved when governmental policies affect the outcomes in a market economy. An understanding of demand and supply analysis can be useful when reading about economic issues in the newspaper or thinking about a government program being debated in Congress.

▶ The Demand Relationship

Basic Assumptions of Demand

Any scientific analysis has building blocks. To understand how economists analyze the demand for goods and services, we must first learn the basic assumptions or postulates upon which the theory of demand is built. There are two general

Ceteris paribus means that all but one factor influencing some form of economic behavior (such as demand) are assumed not to change.

categories of assumptions we must make. The first describes buyers' goals and how they try to reach those goals. The second concerns the constraints or limitations placed on a buyer.

The Goals of Buyers and How They Attempt to Achieve Them

1. We assume that individuals and firms plan for a particular amount of time into the future. At the end of that time, be it a week, a month, or a year, they again make purchase decisions. Practically speaking, this assumption means that we will measure the quantities of goods and services buyers use by the number of units they buy within a particular period of time. In other words, the theory of demand is based on the concept of the flow of goods or services purchased per time period, such as the amount of milk bought per week.

2. We assume that firms and individuals consider the future when making their decisions. Among other things, they will wait for prices to fall or buy now before prices go up. This is not to say that buyers are always correct in their expectations of future price changes. They will make mistakes. Still, their decisions are influenced by expectations of the future.

3. We assume that buyers know whether or not they would like a particular commodity. By this we simply mean that an individual buyer has tastes and preferences (likes and dislikes) and knows what they are. Economists really have very little to say about the details of preferences for particular goods and services. For example, you may like yogurt but not bean sprouts. Economists *do,* however, have some general ideas about the *structure* of tastes and preferences. This leads us to our next assumption.

4. We assume that people derive satisfaction from consuming a *variety* of goods and services and that *more than one combination* of goods and services can yield a particular amount of happiness. For example, you might enjoy drinking Cokes and eating pizza. In addition, you might get just as much enjoyment from eating a small pizza and drinking a large Coke as you would get from eating a large pizza and drinking a small Coke. Similarly, you might find it just as much fun to watch two basketball games and play one hour of tennis as to play three hours of tennis and watch only one basketball game.

5. Our final assumption concerning individuals' goals and feelings is that they prefer more to less pleasure from goods and services. This means that when given the choice of two activities that cost the same, say, going to a Woody Allen movie or seeing one of Shakespeare's plays, a person will pick the one that gives the greater enjoyment. The assumption that people wish to have happy and enjoyable lives means that they do their best not to be foolish or wasteful. In addition, they may take the feelings of others into account when making decisions. Clearly, individual economic decisions are influenced by feelings of love, caring, and empathy.

The set of assumptions introduced in this section relate to people's preferences and their attempts to lead satisfying lives. Apart from different tastes, why doesn't everyone have four Rolls Royces, a beach house at Malibu, and an apartment in midtown Manhattan? The answer lies in our next set of assumptions, which deal with the fact that the choices an individual has available are limited by a number of factors.

Limitations on Choices Buyers Can Make

1. We assume that no one has unlimited wealth. Your spending power is limited by your earnings from working and the amount of income you receive from stocks, bonds, and other investments, the government, and your family, or elsewhere. Because you cannot have everything, you must make choices. For example, if you choose to go to Florida for a couple of weeks in the spring, you might have to skip lunch for a month to save the money to pay for the trip.

2. We assume that buyers cannot control the prices they pay for goods and services. While you may look around for the store with the lowest-priced beer, once you find it, you must pay that price. We are merely assuming that no one has enough buying power to influence, to any great extent, the prices of goods and services. It is important to realize that in making this assumption we do not specify where those prices come from. They may be set by government decree, as in the case of a centrally planned economy such as that of the Soviet Union. They may also be set by market forces, as in most western nations.

*The **law of demand** states that there is a negative relationship between desired purchases and the price of a good or service,* cet. par.

*The **substitution effect** refers to the tendency for desired purchases of a good or service to rise when its price falls and to fall when its price rises relative to other prices,* cet. par.

*The **income effect** refers to the tendency of people to demand more of a good or service when their purchasing power rises and to demand less when their purchasing power falls.*

3. Finally, we assume that consuming a good or service takes time. In addition to the cost of the airline tickets, a Florida vacation takes time away from other activities. While we are doing one thing, there are limits on the extent to which we can be doing something else. For example, we might accomplish two things at the same time by watching the news during breakfast. However, while eating breakfast, we are not at work or polishing the car.

With these two sets of assumptions in mind, we will now say a few words about the way in which we will analyze the decisions people make concerning how much of a good or service to buy.

Method of Analysis

Throughout our analysis we will examine the forces influencing demand behavior *one at a time.* That is, we will first assume that all factors affecting demand are fixed or unchanging except for one. We will then proceed to look at the effect of changes in that one variable on the purchases desired by an individual or a set of individuals. This assumption is known as *ceteris paribus,* the Latin phrase for "other things equal." It means that when we analyze the impact of a change in a variable, such as a good's price, on the quantity of the good demanded, we will begin by assuming that *other* variables (such as buyers' incomes), do not change at the same time. *Ceteris paribus* is often abbreviated *cet. par.* Demand theory typically emphasizes the relationship between the price of a good or service and the quantity of that good or service buyers desire to purchase. So, in developing the theory of demand, we will first apply the *cet. par.* assumption to those forces affecting demand behavior *other than* the price of the good or service in question. If you review our list of building blocks of demand theory, you will see that these forces include the individual's time horizon for decision making, expectations of the future, tastes and preferences, income, prices of other goods and services, and the amount of time consumption must take.

It is extremely important to note that by imposing the *cet. par.* method of analysis, we are simply examining, *one at a time,* the factors that influence buyers' behavior. We can, and do, look at changes in factors other than price (also one at a time) to discover how they too affect the demand for a commodity. Just how and at what stage of our discussion we consider these other forces depends on the issues we wish to examine. Thus, as you will soon see, we develop the theory of demand by first determining how an individual buyer responds if the price of a particular good

changes. We then proceed to analyze how changes in certain other variables—the amount of money available to spend, preferences, and so on—influence the amount of a good or service demanded. The importance of looking at forces *one by one* is that it enables us to get a much clearer picture of how governmental economic policy and private business practices affect consumption patterns.

The Law of Demand and the Demand Curve

The **law of demand** states that, *cet. par.,* (1) price reductions lead buyers to desire more of a good or service; and (2) price increases lead them to desire less of a good or service. This is the result of two effects that reinforce each other when a price changes. They are known as the substitution effect and the income effect of a price change. They are among the most important concepts economists have. The **substitution effect** states that when the price of a good or service falls, *cet. par.,* people have an economic incentive to use more of that particular good or service because it has become less expensive *relative to* all the other goods and services available. To be specific, suppose that rock concert tickets fall in price from $20 to $10, while movie tickets remain $5. Fans then have the incentive to attend more rock concerts while consuming fewer movies and other forms of entertainment. In effect, the reduced price of rock concerts compared to movies will make the concerts a better buy per dollar spent on them and therefore encourage buyers to purchase more concert tickets and less of other things. This desire to substitute rock concerts for other forms of entertainment is one of the reasons why rock fans attend more rock and roll concerts when ticket prices are reduced.

There is another effect of a price change yet to be considered. When the price of a good or service falls, real purchasing power rises, and people consume more because they feel wealthier. Economists call this the **income effect.** Not only can people purchase more of a good whose price has fallen, but they can also purchase more of everything else. To understand this more clearly, suppose that you have an income of $100 per week and you typically spend $21 of your weekly income on beer, which costs $3.00 a six-pack. Now suppose the distributor of your favorite brand lowers the price to $2.50 as part of a sales campaign. It is not hard to see that this is equivalent to an increase in your weekly income of $3.50 (7 six-packs × $0.50). With your fixed income of $100, you can now purchase exactly what you did before and still have $3.50 left over. That extra $3.50 can be used to buy a little more of all the things that you like

*A **demand curve** for a good or service is a geometric representation of the law of demand. It is sometimes called a demand schedule.*

Figure 19.A   Buyers' demand curve for a good or service
The substitution and income effects cause the quantity demanded to increase as price falls and to decline as price rises.

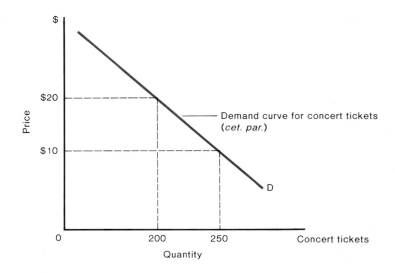

to consume. The overall increase in your consumption as a result of that freed up $3.50 in spending power is the income effect of the $0.50 fall in the price of beer.

As we said earlier, the income effect of a price change is reinforced by the substitution effect. Thus, when the price of something falls, there are two reasons to buy more of it. One reason is greater purchasing power (the income effect), and the other is a lower price relative to the prices of all other goods (substitution effect). Of course, the law of demand holds for a price increase as well. Just as a falling price, *cet. par.,* causes people to buy more, a rising price causes them to buy less.

It is important to recognize that the law of demand holds for *every* good or service whether a buyer "likes" it or not. To see why this is so, let's take an extreme example, in which you would not choose to consume any of a good, even if it were free. At the risk of being sued by the California Prune Advisory Board, suppose that prunes are such a good. Even if you would not eat a prune if it were free, we conjecture that if you were paid enough, you would be willing to eat at least one prune. Paying you to eat prunes is equivalent to having you pay a *negative* price for prunes. If our conjecture is true, there exists *some* price at which you would consume prunes even if it is not a *positive* price. You can probably think of other examples of some goods or services that you do not buy now because you do not like them very much. However, saying that you do not like something is generally equivalent to saying that its price is too high. If it became sufficiently cheaper, *cet. par.,* the law of demand predicts you will buy it.

Because the primary focus of social science in general and economics in particular is on group behavior, we are especially interested in the purchases by *all* of the buyers in a market. The relationship between the price of a good and the total amount purchased by all those who buy it is called demand, or, the **demand curve,** for a good. A demand curve for concert tickets is shown in figure 19.A. We measure the price of the particular good, concert tickets, on the vertical axis and the quantity buyers wish to purchase on the horizontal axis. Because individual buyers purchase less at high prices, the demand curve for all buyers is a downward-sloping line. The downward-sloping demand curve reminds us that the buyers of a good or service want more of it if price falls and less of it if price rises. For example, at a price of $20 the buyers in figure 19.A wish to purchase 200 tickets. At a lower price, say, $10, they increase their desired purchases to 250 tickets.

Shifts in Demand

Figure 19.B reminds us that the *quantity demanded* of a good or service corresponds to a *particular point* on a given demand curve, say, price $10 and quantity 100 on the demand curve in figure 19.B. Thus, when there is a change in the amount of a good or service people want to buy *because of a change in its price, other factors held constant,* we say that there has been a *change in the quantity demanded.* Of course, many other things in the economic environment can also change, and these lead to what economists call *a change in demand or a change in the demand curve.* When there

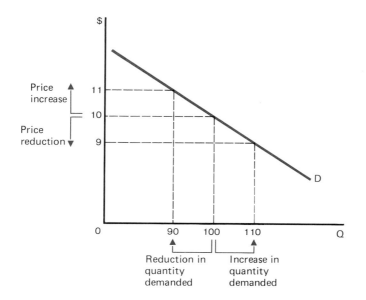

Figure 19.B   Increases and decreases in the quantity demanded of a good or service
An increase in quantity demanded is a southeast movement along the demand curve due to a price reduction. A reduction in quantity demanded is a northwest movement along the demand curve due to a price increase.

is a shift in the demand curve, either to the right or left, we are dealing with a change in demand or a change in the demand curve. When the demand curve for a product shifts, it will also generally change the quantity demanded at any given price. It is very important in thinking about markets to be absolutely clear in your mind whether a change in quantity demanded results from a change in price, given the position of a good's demand curve, or whether it results from a shift in the position of the curve. Among the most important factors that shift demand curves are (1) increases or decreases in buyers' incomes, (2) changes in tastes and preferences, (3) changes in the prices of related goods, and (4) changes in expectations about future events.

For example, suppose consumers of a good or service receive salary increases. The increased income will lead them to purchase more of most of the things they currently buy. Moreover, as wealth increases even with prices unchanged, people often will substitute more expensive and/or higher quality products for less expensive and/or lower quality ones in consumption. An increase in demand is illustrated in figure 19.C by a rightward shift in the demand curve from D to D'. At any given price, more is desired along demand curve D' than along demand curve D. As you might expect, a salary reduction would reduce demand. This would be denoted by a leftward shift in the demand curve from D to D'' in figure 19.C.

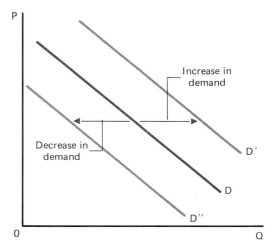

Figure 19.C   Increases and decreases in the demand for a good or service
An increase in demand is a rightward shift in the demand curve. A decrease in demand is a leftward shift in the demand curve. Changes in demand occur if one of the factors held constant when the demand curve was initially drawn (for example, income) changes.

Another possible reason for demand to shift is a change in tastes or preferences of buyers. For example, if buyers' tastes for one good compared to another should change, the demand curve will be affected. If a certain good or service becomes *more* enjoyable, the demand curve will shift to the right. If it should become *less* desirable, the demand curve will shift to the left. Eventually, we will elaborate on some social forces that might cause tastes to change, and with them, demand schedules. For now, try to think of some on your own. For example, why might your feelings toward buying a navy blue suit change in the near future? (Hint: graduation.) How would these new feelings change some of your other demand curves?

It is often tempting to attribute a change in demand to a change in tastes. However, it is difficult to verify whether or not this is true because it is not easy to obtain accurate information about the public's feelings or goals. We must avoid the temptation to conclude that *whenever* purchases change, people's tastes have changed. We must have *reason* to suspect that tastes and preferences have changed *before* demand changes rather than inferring that tastes have changed because demand has changed.

Frequently, a change in the demand for one good reflects a change in the price of some closely related good or service. Suppose, for example, that the price of gasoline rises. Of course, the *quantity of gasoline demanded will decline*. However, people will also eventually desire fewer automobiles, and the *demand for cars* will fall. This, for example, happened in the late 1970s. Such a decline in the demand for cars does *not* reflect a change in people's tastes. When the price of gasoline rose rapidly in 1979 and 1980 people's demand for small fuel-efficient cars increased. That increase in demand for small cars did not simply reflect a change in people's tastes.

An increase in the price of one good may cause the demand for some related goods to increase, too. When two goods are typically used together (bread and butter, tape players and cassettes, automobiles and gasoline, or gin and vermouth), an increase in the price of one causes a decline in the demand for the other. However, if two goods can both be used for the same purpose, we say they can be *substituted* for each other, and an increase in the price of one will cause an *increase in demand* for the other. Some examples of substitutes are cotton and Dacron, Michelin and Firestone tires, gas ranges and electric ranges, or big luxury cars and small, more fuel-efficient cars.

Expectations play a crucial role in macroeconomics, and we will see that changes in expectations about the future can be a very important cause of changes in demand. For example, if I expect my favorite beer to cost 25 percent more next week, I will increase my demand for it this week (at the current price). Similarly, I will hold off buying a new car if I expect sizable rebates or price cuts to be offered next month. Of course, *how much* I change my demand depends on how anxious I am to have the good or service, how storable it is, and how certain I am about future price changes. For example, my freezer may be rather small, so I cannot increase my demand for ice cream by very much right now even if I expect a giant price increase tomorrow unless I also buy a new freezer. Whether or not I want to do that will also depend upon how certain I am about the increase in the price of ice cream and whether I think the price will remain high once it increases.

▶ The Supply Relationship

The preceding section introduced the principle of demand, which comprises the first half of the theory describing how prices are determined in a market economy. This section introduces the other half, the principle of supply. How markets work with both supply and demand is discussed in the next section. In the preceding section we explained the relationship between the quantity demanded of a product and price. In order to determine the price that buyers would have to pay to purchase various amounts of a product, we have to understand the principle of supply.

The *supply* of a good tells us how much is offered for sale at specified prices. In general, the supply of a good or service is the relationship between its price and the quantity offered for sale, *ceteris paribus*.

Basic Assumptions of Supply Theory

The building blocks, or assumptions, of supply theory parallel those underlying the demand relationship. They can be placed in two categories, one concerning suppliers' goals and the other concerning constraints on suppliers' behavior. The limitations suppliers—particularly business firms—face in achieving their goals will be analyzed in detail later. Therefore, we will only discuss suppliers' goals in detail here.

A firm is the basic economic unit that makes production decisions in a market economy, just as the household is the basic unit that makes consumption decisions.

Economic profit is the excess of a firm's revenue over all its costs of production.

The law of supply states that the quantity of a good or service firms desire to sell is greater the higher the price of the good or service, cet. par.

Suppliers and Their Goals   Any individual, household, or business firm is a potential supplier of a good or service. Most frequently, however, we will be concerned with business firms as producers and suppliers. A **firm** is simply a business entity whose management or owner hires inputs such as labor, machinery, and raw materials in order to provide a good or service. In a market economy this is normally done for profit. **Economic profit** is the difference between a firm's revenue and all its opportunity costs.

1. We assume that the firm's goal is to earn the largest possible profit. This is the *profit maximization assumption,* and it parallels the assumption that buyers seek to maximize the satisfaction they obtain from allocating their income among alternatives. Profit maximization requires that the firm accomplish three tasks successfully. These tasks lead us to three subsidiary assumptions that are necessary for profit maximization.
   a. The firm must decide *what* goods or services to produce. It cannot maximize its profit if it produces a good or service that cannot be sold at a high enough price to cover costs.
   b. The firm must decide *how* to produce each good at the lowest possible cost. That is, each firm must *minimize its costs* in light of the constraints imposed on it by available technology and its environment. Because a firm's profit is by definition the excess of its revenue over all of its costs, it should be obvious that it is impossible to *maximize* profit unless costs are *minimized.* Cost minimization does *not* mean that the firm is motivated to produce only cheap, low-quality output. Firms have a profit incentive to produce the level of quality that consumers are willing to pay for. Given that level of quality, however, profit maximization requires that costs be as low as possible.
   c. The firm must choose the *quantity* of production that assures it the greatest possible profit.
2. Firms, like consumers, are also assumed to calculate production in terms of *flows* of goods or services offered for sale *per time period.*

3. Firms also consider the *future* in their decisions. This has several important implications that will not be used immediately. It is a good idea to bear in mind, however, that consideration of the future implies that if firms expect prices of inputs or of their product to rise over time, they will have an incentive to speed up their purchases of inputs and slow down their sales of output. (What do you think this implies for the conservation of natural resources?) The assumption that firms consider the future also implies that actions that may increase current profits while damaging prospects for future sales, such as deceiving consumers about product quality, may not be consistent with overall profit maximization. What do you think this implies for consumer protection in a market economy?

The Law of Supply

Method of Analysis

Once again, as in the theory of demand, we will examine the forces that influence suppliers' decisions *one at a time.* Using the *ceteris paribus* assumption, we will first analyze the relationship between the price of a good or service and the amount offered for sale. After deriving this relationship—the supply curve itself—we will expand our understanding of supply by analyzing the effects of *other* forces on *shifts* in the supply curve.

The **law of supply** states that, *ceteris paribus,* price increases lead suppliers to supply more of a good or service, whereas price reductions lead them to supply less. To see why this should be so, we have to understand something about the way a supplier's *opportunity cost* of supplying its product varies as its output level changes. (You may wish to refresh your memory regarding the definition of opportunity cost in chapter 1.) Basically, we assume that the opportunity cost of producing more of a good eventually increases for a firm. This means that as a general rule, no individual supplier can produce all of a good or service that is demanded. However, suppliers are willing to increase their output if consumers are willing to pay a higher price. Moreover, as the price of a good or service increases, suppliers that had not found it profitable to supply the good or service

*A **change in supply** of a good or service or a shift in the supply curve is a movement of the supply curve that results when a variable other than price of the good or service changes.*

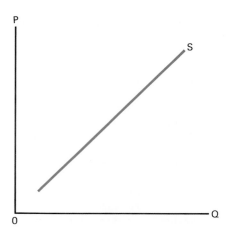

Figure 19.D   The supply curve
The law of supply states that as a good's price increases, firms will produce more of it, and additional firms will offer it for sale.

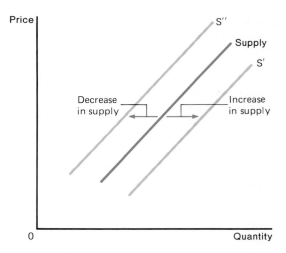

Figure 19.E   Increases and decreases in the supply for a good or service
An increase in supply is a rightward shift in the supply curve. A decrease in supply is a leftward shift in the supply curve. Changes in supply occur if one of the factors held constant when the supply curve was initially drawn (for example, technology) changes.

previously may decide that it is worthwhile to do so in light of the increased revenue they can earn. For these two reasons, the quantity of a good or service supplied increases as its price rises. This relationship is illustrated in figure 19.D.

Factors that Shift Supply

The distinction between movements along a given supply curve and a change in the supply relationship follows the terminology we developed for the demand curve. When things other than price change, there results a **change in supply** or a **shift in the supply curve,** which means that suppliers wish to sell more or less than before at a given market price. Figure 19.D summarizes what has been said about the supply curve and reminds us of how a change in price affects the quantity supplied, *cet. par.*

Shifts in supply result from changes in anything that affects the quantity supplied except the good's price. Any change that affects the opportunity cost of producing a given quantity of output for sale will cause a change in supply. Some important factors that frequently result in supply shifts include the following: (1) changes in technology, (2) changes in input prices, and (3) changes in prices of other goods a firm might produce or in expected future prices of the good produced. A fourth factor that would shift an industry's supply curve would be a change in the number of firms in the industry. Changes in supply are illustrated in figure 19.E.

Changes in Technology   Improvements in technology have been generally accepted as the single most important force responsible for the improved standard of living we enjoy compared to our great-great-great grandparents, say, 150 years ago. An improvement in technology means an increase in the amount of output firms can obtain for given quantities of inputs. When technology improves, fewer inputs are required, opportunity costs fall (given input prices), and the supply curve shifts downward and to the right as shown in figure 19.E. This represents an increase in supply (a rightward shift) because more is offered for sale at each price, or, equivalently, suppliers will accept a lower price in return for providing a given quantity.

A good example of this is pocket calculators. In the early 1960s students purchased slide rules for their math and science courses—pocket calculator technology as we know it today did not exist then. Slide rules cost about $25 and performed only a fraction of the operations that today's calculators can. Moreover, slide rules were much slower and far less accurate. Since the introduction of pocket calculators, technology has improved very rapidly. A pocket calculator that sells for $25 today would have cost $150 or more fifteen years ago. This immense price reduction (occurring over a period of time when inflation increased the prices of most other products) resulted from tremendous improvements in electronics technology.

Another striking example of the effects of changing technology on supply is in stereo equipment. Because of improvements that were almost inconceivable thirty years ago, a modest sum, say, $200, purchases audio equipment today that is by some measures ten times better than $200 worth of "hi-fi" equipment in the 1950s.

Improved technology in both the pocket calculator and stereo industries pushed supply curves to the right. This increase in supply made more product available at all prices and the same amount available at a lower price.

Changes in Input Prices   In 1973 a war between Israel and its Arab neighbors resulted in an oil boycott that sharply reduced the quantity of petroleum available to most of the world. Subsequently, the Organization of Oil Producing and Exporting Countries (OPEC) found it had substantially strengthened its market power and was able to increase the prices it charged to nations that imported petroleum. The result was a quick and severe leftward shift in the supply of goods and services that use petroleum and its derivatives—fuels, plastics, important chemicals such as synthetic fabrics and rubber, and many others. The higher prices that consumers were required to pay for these products resulted in a lower standard of living for millions of people and in economic adjustments that continued into the early 1980s. What can we expect to happen to many supplies as a result of the oil price decreases that occurred in 1985 and 1986?

Changes in Expected Future Prices   It may not be immediately obvious to you how *future* prices affect *current* supply. This relationship between the present and the future is extremely difficult to predict but important for the way the economy functions and for our economic welfare. When a good can be stored, the opportunity cost of *selling* it today may be greater than what must be given up to *produce* it today. For example, suppose you were a Texas rancher with oil wells on your property. If it costs you $15 to extract a barrel of oil for sale on today's market, you could sell it at a "profit" if today's price were, say, $20 per barrel. However, if you expect oil to sell for $30 per barrel a year from now, and if it costs, say, only $1 to store the oil for a year, your true opportunity cost of selling the oil today is $29, not $15. You would be losing, not profiting, by selling your oil at $20 today. In other words, an increase in the expected

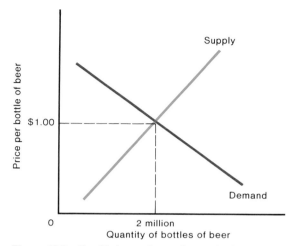

Figure 19.F   Equilibrium price and quantity in a market for beer
The equilibrium price is $1 per bottle and the equilibrium quantity is two million bottles, where quantity supplied equals quantity demanded.

future price of oil or other storable commodity will result in a *leftward* shift in the supply of oil this year as producers place more in storage and offer less for current sale.

We have seen how the market price of a good or service affects the quantities demanded and supplied. But what determines the price? Both the supply and demand concepts are necessary if we are to understand how prices and quantities are determined. Supply and demand are the tools that provide immense insight into human behavior in the economy and the influence of government policies and business practices on production and consumption. They are linked together in the next section.

▶ How the Forces of Supply and Demand Determine Price and the Level of Production

We will begin by considering a market for beer, which is produced by many firms and consumed by many individuals. The first thing we will do is to put the beer demand curve and the beer supply curve together in one diagram. As depicted in figure 19.F, the demand curve is, of course, downward sloping and the supply curve upward sloping. When we see supply and demand together in the same picture, our eye is drawn to where they intersect. This is the most important price and quantity in figure 19.F. You will see why once we learn the concept of market equilibrium.

The **equilibrium price** *is the price at which the quantity of a good or service demanded equals the quantity supplied.*

The **equilibrium quantity** *is the quantity that results from the equilibrium price. It is both a quantity demanded and supplied.*

An **excess demand,** *or shortage, is the amount by which the quantity demanded exceeds the quantity supplied.*

The Concept of Equilibrium

In figure 19.F there is only *one* price at which the amount consumers want to buy exactly matches the amount producers want to sell. This price, $1 in figure 19.F, is called the **equilibrium price,** which occurs at the intersection of the supply and demand schedules. At *any other price,* one of the two parties is frustrated. Either buyers want to buy more than sellers want to sell or sellers want to sell more than buyers want to buy. Of course, buyers would be happier if the price were lower than $1 and they could still purchase as much as they wanted. Similarly, sellers would love to be able to sell two million or more bottles of beer at a price higher than $1 per bottle. Only at $1 per bottle, however, is there a transaction that satisfies both buyers and sellers. The quantity that satisfies both buyers and sellers, two million bottles, is called the **equilibrium quantity.** You should think of market equilibrium as a "point of rest" where no forces operate to make buyers or sellers change their agreement. In particular, price will remain at $1 and quantity at two million bottles until something causes a shift in either supply or demand.

We have just seen how to locate an equilibrium price and quantity in a diagram of a market. This is simple. What is crucially important, however, is to understand *why* the equilibrium price turns out to be the price that actually prevails in a market. Why is it, for example, that the price of a good or service does not get stuck below or above equilibrium? The answer is that unless equilibrium prevails, it is in the interest of both buyers and sellers to take actions that push the market price toward its equilibrium value.

For example, suppose the price of beer in figure 19.F were $0.75. Frustrated buyers would not be able to purchase all the beer they would like. An **excess demand, or shortage,** would exist. Sellers would notice lines forming in front of their stores early in the morning, before they opened. Some thirsty beer lovers might offer to pay a premium if only shopkeepers would sell them a six-pack or two. Profit-maximizing sellers, realizing that they could sell all they like at a higher price, would start raising their prices. (In other words, when there is a shortage, individual sellers *do* have some control over the prices they charge.) The upward trend in price would increase the quantity offered for sale

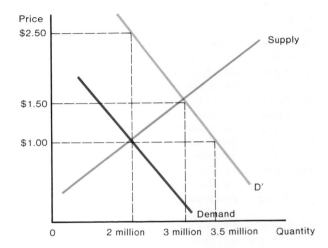

Figure 19.G   The effect of a long-term increase in demand
A permanent increase in demand from D to D′ causes the equilibrium price to increase from $1 to $1.50 and the equilibrium quantity to increase from two million to three million.

and reduce the quantity demanded. This adjustment process would go on until the equilibrium price of $1 was reached.

You should be able to work through the adjustment process when the market price is greater than the equilibrium price. When this happens an **excess supply, or glut,** exists and sellers cannot find buyers for all the goods or services offered for sale.

The Effects of Shifts in Supply and Demand on Equilibrium Price and Quantity

Probably *the* major use of supply and demand theory is to predict how changes in demand or supply conditions affect prices and sales of a good or service. Consider the market for beer again as represented in figure 19.G. Initially, supply and demand are denoted by S and D. Now suppose that demand shifts to D′. Perhaps beer is found to have an anticholesterol agent in it that reduces the risk of heart disease. Equilibrium will not be restored until the price rises

*An **excess supply**, or **glut**, is the excess of the quantity supplied over the quantity demanded.*

Table 19.A **The qualitative effects of permanent supply and demand shifts on market equilibrium prices and quantities.**

	Supply increases	Supply decreases	Supply unchanged
Demand increases	Q↑ P↑, P↓, or P constant*	Q↑, Q↓, or Q constant* P↑	Q↑ P↑
Demand decreases	Q↑, Q↓, or Q constant* P↓	Q↓ P↑, P↓, or P constant*	Q↓ P↓
Demand unchanged	Q↑ P↓	Q↓ P↑	Q constant P constant

*Depends on whether demand or supply shifts more and on the relative steepness of demand and supply.

to $1.50 per bottle and quantity reaches three million bottles. At the old equilibrium price a shortage now exists. More beer is demanded than is supplied. This excess of demand over supply—3.5 million − 2 million bottles of beer—created when demand shifted to D′, leads to upward pressure on the price of beer. This in turn leads producers to expand their production.

Notice that the new equilibrium quantity, three million bottles, is more than the quantity originally demanded but less than buyers would buy had price *not* changed. The market in a sense serves as an auctioneer who matches buyers and sellers. When the auctioneer senses an increase in the amount buyers want to buy, the auction price is raised. The rising price mitigates the increased amount buyers want to buy.

We now have our first conclusion from the theory of supply and demand. *An increase in demand leads to higher prices and quantities bought and sold.* You should practice thinking things through in reverse order to make sure you understand the effect of a long-term *reduction* in demand. What would cause a reduction in demand? How do changes in supply and demand lead producers to cut back their output? When you think this through, you will come to the conclusion that *a reduction in demand leads to lower*

levels of production and sales as well as reduced prices. This is our second major conclusion from supply and demand. In both cases, of course, we assume that "all else is unchanged."

Table 19.A summarizes how shifts in supply and demand affect equilibrium price and quantity. After you have studied table 19.A carefully, you will be ready to go on to see how these basic economic concepts are applied in later chapters.

▶ **Key Terms**

ceteris paribus 402
change in supply, shift in the supply curve 408
demand 401
demand curve 404
economic profit 407
equilibrium price 410
equilibrium quantity 410
excess demand, or shortage 410

excess supply, or glut *410*
firm *407*
income effect *403*
law of demand *403*
law of supply *407*
substitution effect *403*
supply *401*

Chapter 20

Employment, Unemployment, and the Aggregate Production of Goods and Services

Outline

I. Introduction *414*
II. The labor market *415*
   A. The demand for labor *415*
      1. The value of labor's marginal product is a firm's labor demand curve *416*
         a. Events that shift a firm's labor demand curve *419*
      2. A firm's demand for labor, its production function, and its total output *420*
      3. The aggregate demand for labor *420*
   B. The supply of labor *422*
      1. Factors underlying an individual's labor supply decision *422*
      2. The aggregate supply of labor *423*
   C. The aggregate labor market and the aggregate quantity of goods and services supplied *424*
      1. Expectations *424*
      2. Equilibrium in the aggregate labor market *424*
III. Unemployment *426*
   A. What is unemployment? *426*
   B. Varieties of unemployment and their causes *426*
      1. Frictional unemployment *426*
         a. Policies to reduce frictional unemployment *427*
      2. Structural unemployment *428*
         a. Policies to reduce structural unemployment *429*
      3. Cyclical unemployment *429*
         a. Why are workers laid off during recessions? *430*
         b. Normal versus cyclical unemployment and government policy *433*
IV. Summary and conclusions *433*
V. Key terms *434*
VI. Questions for discussion and review *434*

Objectives

After reading this chapter, the student should be able to:

Explain how a firm's demand curve for labor is derived, and explain how the concepts of the production function, the marginal product of labor, and the value of the marginal product of labor are used.

Relate the aggregate demand for labor to the aggregate value of marginal product of labor.

Describe factors that affect an individual's labor supply decision.

Discuss the shape of the aggregate supply of labor curve and factors that will cause it to shift.

Explain how equilibrium is achieved in the labor market and how expectations affect the aggregate labor market.

Distinguish between frictional, structural, and cyclical unemployment, and discuss policies designed to reduce each.

▶ Introduction

Jo worked in the textile mill in her hometown for nearly ten years. By 1980, she was a supervisor earning more than $12,000 a year. She and her husband had a nice home, a boat, and new car, and she belonged to a strong union local. But by 1983, all that had changed. Jo lost her job in 1982 when the mill closed. Many people were looking for work. In the nation as a whole, the unemployment rate reached 10.8 percent, a rate that had only been exceeded during the depression of the 1930s.

When the economy picked up in 1983, the textile mill stayed closed and Jo got a job for about $7,000 a year as a night manager in an all-night convenience store. She didn't like that because her children were not getting enough supervision. By 1984, as the economy began to expand rapidly and unemployment dropped to 7.3 percent, Jo quit and took a job as a taxi driver. Unfortunately, the taxicab business went bankrupt, so she is unemployed again. However, she is presently looking into several jobs. She and her husband have had to sell their boat, the car is falling apart, and they have difficulty meeting their mortgage payments. Her old union local has dwindled to 50 percent of its former membership, and no new textile mills are on the horizon.

Jo can't figure out how or why things changed for the worse. She is the same woman who used to go to work every day and make more than $12,000 a year, isn't she? Why can't she make that kind of money some other way? Why, she wonders, couldn't she even keep a crummy job that paid less than she had been making before? In order to answer such questions, we have to understand how labor markets work and how they are affected by overall economic conditions.

In this chapter we set in place the first stone in our foundation of macroeconomic analysis. In particular, we examine the link between the input and output sides of the macroeconomy. Among other things, we focus on how firms' individual economic decisions lead them to produce a particular aggregate level of output for society (real GNP) and to hire a particular amount of labor. We also examine the forces that motivate households to provide the labor that firms use to produce society's goods and services. One of our primary goals will be to see how the interactions between buyers and sellers of labor (firms and individuals) influence wages, employment, and unemployment. If you have had a previous course in economics, much of the material in this chapter through page 425 will be familiar. Here we review the discussion of labor demand and supply to refresh your memory before we move on to a discussion of unemployment.

A worker who becomes unemployed suffers more than just an economic loss. During the severe recession of 1980–82, television and newspapers carried chilling accounts of the loss of self-esteem and of the pain and suffering experienced by the unemployed. Such feelings stem not only from lost income but also from uncertainty and anger. Unemployment is one of the most misunderstood economic concepts. Some, perhaps most, unemployment is a normal consequence of a large industrial economy such as ours. This means that government policy must be carefully constructed to take account of this. We will consider various government policies designed to reduce unemployment and, most important, begin to develop the macroeconomic model we will use to analyze recessions, inflation, and government policies to reverse them. The links we establish in this chapter between unemployment, employment, output, and prices play crucial roles in our discussions in chapters 25 through 29 of business cycles and macroeconomic policy.

*The **demand for labor** is the relationship that defines the quantity of labor a firm would like to hire.*

*The **supply of labor** is the relationship that defines the amount of labor offered to firms by individuals.*

*The **marginal product of labor (mpl)** measures the additional output a firm produces when it hires an additional unit of labor, all other inputs such as machinery held constant.*

▶ The Labor Market

A firm's desire to purchase labor is called its **demand for labor.** The amount a firm is willing to pay for some labor depends upon how much the firm receives for the good or service that labor helps to produce. Because of this dependence on the demand for a firm's product, the demand for labor (and other inputs) is called a *derived demand.* Although we concentrate on the demand for labor in this chapter, the ideas we develop can also be applied to the firm's demand for other inputs into its production process, such as machinery. We shall see that the amount of labor that a firm actually hires depends not only upon its demand but also on the willingness of individuals to offer their services, which is called the **supply of labor.**

The Demand for Labor

A simple example will help to see how a firm decides how much labor to employ. Suppose you decide to enter the calculator business. Since you are just beginning, your firm does just one thing. It assembles pocket calculators, using parts—integrated circuits, keyboards, displays, and cases—purchased from other companies. When you set up your firm, you purchase the equipment you and your workers will need to assemble any number of calculators up to 500 per day. Obviously, the output of your calculator-assembly firm is zero before you hire any workers. You do not assemble any calculators if you do not hire any assemblers. The number of calculators your company assembles increases with the number of workers you hire. If you hire one worker, your firm's total output would be thirty calculators assembled per day. This quantity of output is not only your total output, it is also the *additional output* you have produced by hiring your first worker. Should you hire a second worker? Your decision will depend upon how much additional output in terms of the number of calculators per day he or she can assemble. In general, the *extra* output produced whenever another worker is added is called the **marginal product of labor (mpl).**

Sometimes it is easier to use symbols for an expression like the marginal product of labor. When we are dealing with an economic concept that involves a *change* in one variable with respect to a *change* in another, we use the Greek letter delta (Δ) to indicate a change in a variable. Because mpl is defined as the *change* in output due to a change in the amount of labor used, we use the following expression:

$$\text{mpl} \equiv \Delta q / \Delta l.$$

In this expression for mpl, please note that we have used the symbol $\equiv$ (the identity symbol) rather than $=$ (the equality symbol). This is to remind you that mpl is *defined* to equal $\Delta q / \Delta l$ *in all places and at all times.* This is in contrast to an *equality* relationship in which two variables are equal to each other *only when certain conditions hold.* We will come back to the distinction between an equality and an identity later because it is very useful in understanding important economic relationships.

In calculating the marginal product of labor, you must be very careful to measure *only* the additional output produced by adding exactly one worker. For example, if at the same time you hired an additional worker, you also purchased more equipment for use in assembling computers, part of the additional output would be due to using more equipment, too. In other words, the marginal product of labor is the additional output gained by hiring an additional worker, *ceteris paribus,* or *holding constant* the amount of equipment your workers use. Remember, by imposing the *ceteris paribus (cet. par.)* method of analysis, we are simply examining, *one at a time,* the factors that influence a firm's behavior. We can, and do, look at changes in many factors (also one at a time) to discover how they too affect the demand for labor.

A price taker is a buyer or seller that has no direct influence over the market price of a good or service.

Competitive firms are price takers in the market for the good or service they produce and in the markets for the inputs that they use.

Returning to our example, how much does output grow when you hire additional workers? When you hire the second employee, does the quantity of calculators assembled per day double? Hiring a second worker *could* actually *more* than double your calculator output, perhaps to something like seventy-five units per day. The reason is that with a second worker your employees can now be used more efficiently. Instead of one person's assembling all the parts to make one calculator, the two workers can specialize in performing a smaller set of tasks. This way, each worker becomes more efficient in assembling a part of a calculator than he or she would be when doing everything. Doing everything requires using a larger number of tools, starting and stopping to lay down and pick up different parts, and so on. At some point, however, the gains from additional worker specialization will taper off, and the marginal product of labor will start to diminish. You will reach the situation where additional workers increase the number of calculators assembled but *by progressively less and less.* By the time you hire a fifth worker, the *additional* number of calculators assembled drops to only four units per day. This decline in the marginal product of labor stems in part from the fact that you have only a certain amount of equipment for your workers to use. (Remember, this example of the marginal product of labor is *ceteris paribus.*)

While our example may be somewhat contrived for the purposes of demonstration, the basic principal is extremely important. *At a given level of other inputs, additional labor is productive, but the marginal product of labor eventually diminishes.* This basic principle is illustrated with numbers in table 20.1 and graphically in figure 20.1.

Put yourself in the position of the owner or manager of a firm trying to decide whether to add more workers. Perhaps business has been good and you are tempted to start a second shift, hoping that the extra

Table 20.1   The marginal product of labor in assembling pocket calculators

The marginal product of labor is the number of additional calculators assembled per day when an additional worker is hired. While marginal product is positive in this example, it becomes smaller and continues to decline after the second worker is employed.

Number of workers	Number of calculators assembled per day	Marginal product of labor ($\Delta q/\Delta l$) (in number of calculators)
0	0	
1	30	30
2	75	45
3	105	30
4	116	11
5	120	4
6	123	3

sales will more than repay the cost and effort of hiring new workers and managing them. The marginal product of labor will play a crucial role in your decision. Whether or not adding the new workers will increase your profit will depend in a very important way on the marginal product of labor.

The Value of Labor's Marginal Product Is a Firm's Labor Demand Curve

In order to show that adding more workers may or may not increase profit, we need to know what happens to the price of your firm's product as output grows. We will assume that your firm is what economists call a **price taker,** which means that the price for which its output sells is influenced only by the combined output of all similar firms, *not* by the output of your firm alone. Your firm is simply too small to affect the market price of calculators. Because firms that are price takers must *compete* with each other for customers, they are often called **competitive firms.**

*The **value of the marginal product of labor (vmpl)** is the increase in a competitive firm's sales revenue resulting from the sale of the extra output produced when an additional worker is hired.*

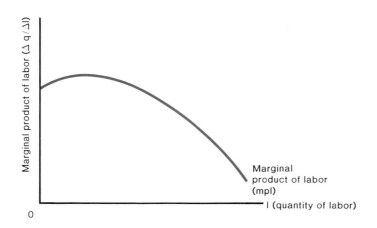

Figure 20.1   The marginal product of labor for a typical firm
The marginal product of labor ($\Delta q/\Delta l$) denotes the extra output (Δq) produced as a firm increases its labor input by one additional worker. The mpl for a typical firm is positive and diminishing—additional workers add to total output, but the increment shrinks as the firm's labor force grows, *cet. par.*

When a competitive firm hires an extra worker, it receives additional revenue, called the **value of the marginal product of labor (vmpl),** which is simply the marginal product of labor times the price of the firm's output. If we denote the market price for the firm's output as p, then the value of the marginal product of labor is

$$vmpl \equiv p \times mpl \equiv p \times \Delta q/\Delta l.$$

To be precise, we should recognize that a firm is concerned with the goods and services that can be purchased with the revenue it receives. Therefore, the firm's market price, p, used in the calculation of vmpl should be thought of as the *real price* at which it can sell its output. A simple way to calculate the real price faced by a firm is to divide the nominal (dollar) price at which it sells its product by a price index such as the Consumer Price Index (CPI) or GNP deflator. (You would set the price index equal to 1.0 in the base year rather than 100. Thus, if 1987 were the base year and your firm sold calculators at $5 each in 1987, the *real price* would equal $5. If calculators still sold for $5 in 1988 but the price index doubled, you would divide $5 by 2.0 to obtain a real price of only $2.50.)

Here and elsewhere in this chapter we will use the symbol p to denote the real price at which the firm sells its output and the symbol P to denote the CPI or GNP deflator.

Assuming that your calculator firm faces competition from many other calculator manufacturers, with a market price of $5 per calculator, the value of the first worker's marginal product in table 20.1 is $150 per day. At the price of $5.00 per calculator, the value to the firm of adding, say, a fourth worker is $55. Notice that the value of labor's marginal product is positive but eventually shrinks because of the diminishing marginal product of labor.

Because the value of marginal product is marginal product times price of output, vmpl has the same general shape as the the mpl curve in figure 20.1. The vmpl curve is illustrated in figure 20.2. The curve showing the value of labor's marginal product tells a story similar to that told by the mpl curve. Additional units of labor have positive value to the firm, but the firm benefits less and less from additional labor as the size of the firm's labor force grows.

*The **real wage (W/P)** is equal to the nominal (or paycheck) wage (W) divided by the aggregate price level (P); the real wage expresses a worker's pay in terms of its ability to purchase goods and services.*

*The **nominal**, or **paycheck**, **wage (W)** is the pay a worker receives measured in dollars per hour.*

Figure 20.2   The value of labor's marginal product curve is also a firm's labor demand curve
The value of labor's marginal product (vmpl ≡ p × Δq/Δl) is the extra revenue a firm gets from selling the additional output generated by hiring one more worker. In order to earn the largest profit, a competitive firm chooses its labor input so that the last unit hired just pays for itself. This is where vmpl equals the (constant) real wage the firm must pay to attract workers.

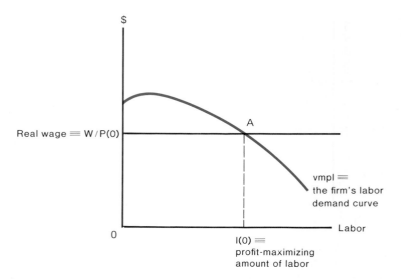

In order to decide whether to hire additional workers, you also need to know what it will *cost*. We will assume that your firm is also a price taker in the labor market. This means that your hiring decisions have no direct effect on the **real wage (W/P)** you must offer, which is the **nominal, or paycheck, wage (W)** you pay, taking purchasing power into account. Workers, as well as firms, are concerned with how many goods and services they can buy with their earnings. Suppose, for example, you are a wage earner and your nominal wage increases by 10 percent between 1987 and 1988. How much better off are you? The answer depends on the price level next year versus today. If the price level (P) is the same in both 1987 and 1988, then you will be able to purchase 10 percent more next year with your salary. However, if the price level rises by 10 percent, you will be no better off. Should the price level rise by *more than* 10 percent, then your real wage will actually *fall*. Firms and workers will take inflation into account when deciding how much labor to buy or sell.

The horizontal line in figure 20.2 illustrates that the firm may hire as much labor as it wants at the going real wage, W/P (0). If you, as owner of the computer firm illustrated in table 20.1, are making a decision about whether to hire more workers, you will keep hiring as long as additional units of labor pay for themselves by adding more to revenue than to cost. You will stop hiring when you decide that one more unit of labor will add more to total cost than to revenue. This is the point where profit is greatest. In figure 20.2, if your work force is smaller than l(0), the value of additional workers exceeds their cost. Additional workers beyond l(0) worker cost more than they are worth because their wage rate exceeds the value of their marginal product. Thus, l(0) is the profit-maximizing amount of labor to hire in figure 20.2. This is marked by point A.

Suppose that your calculator firm shown in table 20.1 can hire all the workers it wants at $50 per day. If you can sell your calculators for $5 each, how many workers will you hire? If you answered four, you are correct. The fourth worker yields a value of marginal product equal to $55 but costs only $50 to hire. The fifth worker must also be paid $50 per day but yields a value of marginal product of only $5 x 4, or $20. If your answer was not four workers, we suggest you review the material in this section before you read on.

Symbolically, a firm earns the most profit by hiring workers up to the point that

$$vmpl = W/P(0).$$

A firm's labor demand curve [d(1)] is a graph illustrating the firm's desired labor force at various possible real wage rates.

Notice that we have used the *equality* sign (=) in this expression. This is because vmpl is *not the same thing as* W/P(0). They are *equal* to each other when, and only when, the firm hires just that quantity of labor that leads to the largest profit.

We have just seen how a firm chooses the size of its work force at the going real wage. If any of the conditions that determine the firm's choice change, then the choice of number of workers will change. For example, suppose your firm is so profitable that you decide to purchase additional equipment. With more machinery and tools, the marginal product of your workers will increase, and their value of marginal product will also rise. Given the wage rate, it will now be profitable to enlarge your labor force. Suppose, on the other hand, that increased foreign competition forces you to sell your calculators at $4.50 instead of $5 each. Because the demand for labor is a *derived demand,* this will reduce the value of marginal product of labor, and you will desire to reduce the number of workers hired. Using the numbers in table 20.1, calculate how much your employment and output will decline if the price of calculators falls from $5 to $4.50.

What happens to employment if the real wage rate changes? The answer to this question is given by a **firm's labor demand curve [d(l)].** We can think of this as a curve tracing out the firm's profit-maximizing labor force at the various real wage rates it might have to pay. Because the profit-maximizing competitive firm hires the amount of labor denoted by the vmpl curve at a given real wage, *the vmpl curve is also the firm's labor demand curve.*

To reinforce your understanding of the firm's labor demand curve, assume that you can hire all the labor you want at $50 per day and that calculators sell for $10 each. How many workers will you hire? How many will you hire at $35 per day? How many at $25 per day? Your answers should be four, five, and six workers, respectively. If these were not your answers, review the concept of the value of labor's marginal product and how the firm chooses its work force.

Events that Shift a Firm's Labor Demand Curve   A firm's labor demand curve is downward sloping. This means that as labor becomes more expensive, the *quantity of labor demanded* by the firm declines. A firm adjusts to higher labor costs by becoming more capital intensive (using more machinery relative to labor) and cutting back on its level of production. Perhaps this seems paradoxical, though. If employment falls as real wage rates rise, then why hasn't employment in the United States diminished nearly to zero as real wage rates have grown over time? There is no doubt that even the lowest-paid workers today earn more per hour in terms of their purchasing power than workers did in 1900. Still, there are many more jobs in our economy today than there were at the turn of the century. The solution to this puzzle lies in remembering what we are holding constant (*ceteris paribus*) when we draw the labor demand curve in figure 20.2. In discussing the concept of the value of the marginal product of labor and the fact that it also serves as a firm's labor demand curve, we are *holding constant* the level of the firm's other inputs, such as machinery and energy. We are also holding constant the firm's technology. One key reason why workers are better off today than they were fifty or a hundred years ago is that technology has not in fact been constant. Increased use of machinery and energy sources and improved technology have led to an *increase in demand* (a rightward shift in the demand curve) for labor.

Suppose, for example, that you discover a new technology for assembling calculators, a technology that allows you to use labor more productively and lower your costs per calculator significantly. The change in technology means that the marginal product of labor shifts outward in figure 20.1 because there is more additional output per extra unit of labor. Similarly, the curve illustrating the firm's vmpl must be redrawn in figure 20.2 to reflect the fact that an additional worker will now be more valuable because of his or her greater marginal product. The result is to increase the value of labor's marginal product and the number of workers your firm will hire at any given wage.

*The **production function** quantifies the relationship between a firm's output and its inputs.*

*The **aggregate demand for labor** [D(L)] illustrates the total number of workers that society's firms wish to hire at various real wage rates.*

As a matter of historical record, the effects of improved technology have resulted in increased demand for labor. This has resulted in *both* higher wage rates and employment over time in the United States. For example, in the early part of this century, over a third of our labor force was required to produce food and other agricultural products for themselves and the rest of the nation. Vastly improved agricultural technology and investment in machinery now permit all of our food to be produced by less than 3 percent of today's labor force. Farmers and agricultural workers today have a far higher standard of living than they did seventy-five years ago. Workers no longer needed in agriculture have moved to jobs in other industries where they, too, earn much more than they would if they were still employed in menial jobs on the farm. Another way to see the effect of additional inputs and technology is to compare wages internationally. Those nations with the highest standards of living, such as the United States, the countries of Western Europe, and the industrialized nations of Asia, use a great deal of machinery, energy, and advanced technology. The poorest nations, those in Africa and parts of Asia and South America, use relatively small quantities of machinery and energy per worker and have not been able to adopt advanced technologies. They would like to do so to reduce the abject poverty of the majority of their populations.

A Firm's Demand for Labor, Its Production Function, and Its Total Output

We started off our discussion of a firm's demand for labor by focusing on the *marginal,* or *extra,* output obtained by hiring each additional worker. It will be very important as we develop our macromodel to relate employment to *total* output as well. This is a very simple step beyond our discussion of the marginal product of labor. At the heart of a firm's demand for labor is what economists call the **production function,** which is the technical relationship that shows how the firm's output is related to its input use. The term *production function* is derived from the mathematical definition of a *function.* A function is simply a relationship between one variable, such as the amount of

output *produced,* and other variables that determine it. In the case of the production function, the amounts of labor and other inputs, such as machinery and raw materials, determine the amount of output a firm produces. A firm, such as an automobile maker, uses many inputs in its production process. Glass, steel, electricity, and the labor of various managerial and production workers are only a few of the inputs used in making a car.

We can simplify the production function by looking at the general relationship between a firm's output and its labor input alone, assuming that all of the other inputs used in production are unchanging. In the example of your calculator firm, the production function is illustrated by the first two columns of table 20.1—the relationship between employment and the production of calculators. A production function is illustrated in figure 20.3. The curve illustrates how a typical firm's output varies with the labor it uses, measured as the total number of workers (l). Notice that the marginal product of labor, mpl, is nothing more than the *slope* of the production function. Figure 20.3 illustrates the relationship between the firm's production function, its demand for labor, employment, and output. We will return to the production function later.

The Aggregate Demand for Labor

So far we have discussed the demand for labor of an individual firm. The focus of this chapter, however, is on the *aggregate* or *economywide* labor market. As a result, we are most interested in the **aggregate demand for labor [D(L)],** which is the *total* number of workers that all the economy's firms seek to hire.

Think of each firm in the economy adding one more worker. The benefit to society of one more worker's services in each firm is the real value of the additional GNP produced, which is the real aggregate value of marginal product of labor. Remember that when we calculate a variable such as real GNP, the price of each good or service is divided by the GNP deflator (P). When we use the GNP deflator, we must first divide it by 100. This is necessary because of the custom of setting price indexes equal to 100 in the

in figure 20.6. Notice that in figure 20.6 we have explicitly noted the important role of the *expected* price level in determining labor supply and demand. Only at the *expected* real wage rate $W/P^e(0)$ is the amount of employment firms desire exactly equal to the amount individuals seek. For now, we will assume that the price level has been constant for a while, so that firms' and workers' price expectations are both identical and correct. This means that the current price level is what firms and workers expected it to be and so is the real wage rate. Because workers are supplying the amount of labor they desire when there is labor market equilibrium, the employment level where supply equals demand in figure 20.6 is called equilibrium normal employment.

In the upper part of figure 20.6 we have drawn an aggregate production function for the economy, which relates the aggregate output of goods and services (real GNP) to aggregate employment. The aggregate production function in figure 20.6 illustrates how the economy's total output of goods and services varies with total employment in the economy. When there is equilibrium in the aggregate labor market, there is a normal employment level equal to $L^n(0)$. At the normal employment level, society produces real GNP equal to $Y(0)$ as shown in the upper part of figure 20.6. It is important to remember that along with equilibrium normal employment of labor comes a particular aggregate output of goods and services (real GNP). This is the aggregate quantity of goods and services supplied by the economy's firms. In the remainder of this chapter we examine how labor market equilibrium relates to observed unemployment. Events that disturb labor market equilibrium may move employment away from its normal level and are associated with fluctuations in unemployment and in the aggregate quantity of goods and services produced.

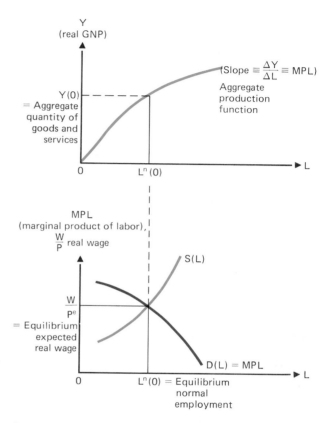

Figure 20.6   The aggregate labor market and the aggregate quantity of real GNP supplied
When there is aggregate labor market equilibrium, the amount of labor firms want to hire equals the number of people who want jobs. Labor market equilibrium is contingent on all the factors that underlie the aggregate labor supply and demand schedules plus the expected price level, P^e, used to calculate real wages. When the aggregate labor market is in equilibrium and the actual price level is equal to what firms and workers expected, employment is at its equilibrium normal level, $L^n(0)$. This level of employment leads to a particular aggregate level of goods and services supplied by firms.

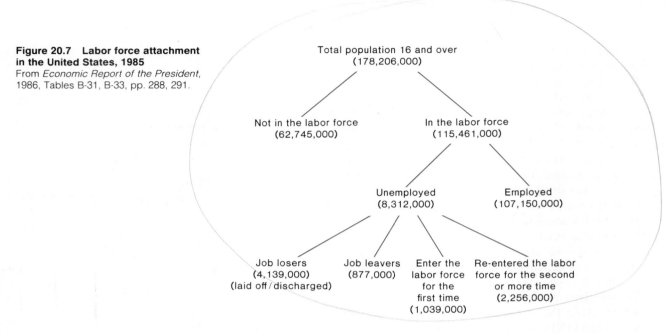

Figure 20.7 Labor force attachment in the United States, 1985
From *Economic Report of the President*, 1986, Tables B-31, B-33, pp. 288, 291.

▶ Unemployment

What Is Unemployment?

In chapter 19 we saw that the federal government uses the Current Population Survey to determine whether or not an individual is unemployed. Alternatives to being unemployed include being employed or out of the labor force. These possibilities are summarized in figure 20.7, which illustrates how the Current Population Survey categorizes people according to their labor force attachment. Keep in mind that the official definition of unemployment makes no reference to the wage rate that would lead someone to accept a job offer. A perfect definition of unemployment might take account of whether an unemployed worker is willing to work for a "reasonable" wage or whether an unemployed worker is looking for an "unrealistic" job in light of current opportunities.

Our objectives in this chapter include trying to understand how the flow of workers into and out of unemployment is related to economic well-being and how much unemployment is "normal" as opposed to

"excessive." We will develop some subcategories of unemployment and classify different types of unemployment by their root economic causes. We will see that a portion of unemployment is due to relatively low aggregate demand for output and another portion is due to shifts in the regional or industrial structure of the economy. Still another portion stems from the fact that it takes time for new workers and other job seekers to find employment. By understanding the various components of total unemployment, we will get a much clearer understanding of government policies to reduce unemployment and its detrimental effects on economic welfare.

Varieties of Unemployment and Their Causes

Frictional Unemployment

Figure 20.7 suggests that unemployment would still exist even if there were no recessions or the economy never underwent any changes in its regional or industrial structure. Why? Every month some people

Frictional unemployment occurs because it takes time for newly unemployed workers to find jobs even though there are enough jobs to go around.

leave school, others return to the labor force after having children, and still others come out of retirement. In each of these situations an individual must seek information concerning job opportunities. During the process of discovering what jobs are available, a person is classified as unemployed. Moreover, there will always be experienced workers who feel that they could get better jobs than their last or current jobs. In the process of looking around for better jobs they may be unemployed.

Information is scarce concerning what jobs are available. As a result, some, perhaps many, labor force participants must *necessarily* be unemployed as a way of obtaining good or better jobs. The twenty-one-year-old who spends the summer after graduating from college looking for her first job or the forty-five-year-old assembly line worker who tells his boss to "take this job and shove it; I ain't working here no more" are two examples of what economists call **frictional unemployment.** Employers also play a direct role in creating frictional unemployment. Firms continually seek to improve the quality of their labor forces by testing out new employees and then laying off or firing those they find unacceptable.

Labor market "frictions" occur because both workers and firms have less than perfect knowledge of job opportunities and available employees. The pool of unemployed workers is regularly replenished because it takes time for jobs and workers to find each other. Frictional unemployment is a *normal* situation in a modern industrial society. Workers and firms simply cannot find each other instantaneously. This is not to say, of course, that our economy generates what could be called an acceptable, or ideal, amount of frictional unemployment. Similarly, this is not to say that economic policy cannot or should not reduce the typical period that a frictionally unemployed worker searches for a job.

Policies to Reduce Frictional Unemployment The primary way government policy in the United States attempts to reduce frictional unemployment is by funding the Employment Service. The Employment Service is your state employment agency, which is a joint federal-state venture with 20,000 to 30,000 employees who run branch offices. These branch offices are where you can go to check the jobs listed by employers who tell the service they have vacancies. The goal behind the Employment Service is to make it easier for workers and employers to find one another. The Employment Service is designed to make information more readily available, and in this way help an unemployed worker find a job more quickly. The intended result is a reduction in the unemployment rate.

There are also a number of government programs that *indirectly* affect frictional unemployment by providing income support to the unemployed or by encouraging workers to enter or leave the labor force. For example, the goal of the unemployment insurance system is to provide needed financial support to workers who are unemployed. Unemployment compensation is sometimes made available to workers who have quit their previous jobs. This financial support enables workers to be more careful and take longer in finding their next jobs. The result is an increase in frictional unemployment. The unemployment compensation payments are paid for by a system of taxes on employers. In many states taxes are structured so as to increase the use of layoffs by firms during off seasons. In this way the unemployment insurance system contributes to frictional unemployment.[1] It is important to recognize the trade-off inherent in the unemployment compensation system in particular and programs to help people with low incomes in general when discussing economic policy. The trade-off is that the valuable economic support provided to the unemployed also increases the unemployment rate somewhat.

Structural unemployment arises from the job losses people suffer when firms move out of a region, the skill requirements of the work force change, or when there is a minimum wage rate.

Frictional unemployment is beyond the scope of government policy to a certain extent. The age and the sex mix of the population both have much to do with the number of people who are entering or reentering the labor force. The number of people who are entering the labor force for the first time is strongly related to the number of students graduating or leaving school, and this is largely the result of how many people are sixteen to twenty-two years of age or so. The same situation describes the relative number of women who have decided to return to work after rearing their children. For example, in 1950 only about 30 percent of women twenty years old and over were in the labor force; today the figure is about 50 percent. Many economists feel that demographic factors are the primary reason that frictional unemployment varies over time.

Structural Unemployment

Structural unemployment occurs when major changes in the industrial, occupational, or regional structure of the economy cause a substantial decline in the job opportunities in a particular labor market or among a particular group of workers. Examples include the unemployment caused when many steel mills closed in Youngstown, Ohio, when the federal government deemphasized the space program, and when automatic elevators replaced elevator operators. In short, structural unemployment results from a mismatch of workers' skills and the available jobs either because the jobs and workers are in different parts of the country or workers' skills are not "right" for today's job market.

Since changes in the industrial and occupational structures of the economy occur quite often, why don't workers and firms make adjustments to prevent structural unemployment? First of all, structural unemployment does not *always* happen when firms move

out of an area or when there is a technological innovation such as robotics. Most economists note how well firms and workers adjust, even to rather major changes in the economy. Still, workers and firms may adjust too slowly to changing economic conditions to prevent structural unemployment. Reacting to a changing economic environment is costly. Workers may have to relocate or retrain, or firms may have to install new equipment or alter their old plants to take account of changes in their available work forces. Neither firms nor workers will necessarily take such steps unless the changes in their economic environment seem to be reasonably permanent, or at least permanent enough to justify the substantial expenses involved. Neither workers nor firms have perfect information. If you are a worker, for example, it takes time to decide whether or not job opportunities have declined permanently or whether job opportunities will eventually return. Similarly, the decision to move to another part of the country will not be made in haste. In addition to the economic costs of moving, there are psychological costs of adjustment to a new environment and changed surroundings.[2]

The interdependence of the aggregate supply and demand for labor can also produce structural unemployment. When the labor force adjusts to changing demand conditions—perhaps by moving out of an economically declining community—this often further reduces the demand for labor. For example, when people move out of an area, they stop buying goods and services there. The demand for labor in food stores, auto repair shops, and hospitals, to name a few places, is reduced. Moreover, firms may keep wages high rather than lowering them and spreading available employment around because they (1) fear social disapproval, (2) confront unions with contracts that prohibit wage reductions, or (3) are subject to state or federal minimum wage rates that prohibit offering more employment opportunities at lower wages.

Cyclical unemployment results when workers are laid off because the aggregate demand for output declines and firms cut back on production.

Policies to Reduce Structural Unemployment   Examples of the structurally unemployed include many teenagers as well as adults experiencing long-term unemployment in industries such as meat packing, automobiles, steel, rubber, and textiles. Policies to reduce structural unemployment must consider the special problem faced by these workers. A problem in the teenage labor market is the relative lack of *career-ladder* employment opportunities. There is much economic support available to young people who go on to get postsecondary educations in publicly subsidized colleges and universities and scholarships. Similar financial support has not typically been given to young people in the United States who choose to enter the labor force after high school. Moreover, employers may not offer much on-the-job training to teenagers for various reasons, including minimum wage legislation. Minimum wage laws discourage employers from hiring unskilled workers at very low wages while compensating them further in other ways—including providing training. To the extent that this is prevented by minimum wage laws in the United States, such laws contribute to our extremely high teenage unemployment rate.

Reducing the instability of employment and the high unemployment of youths requires more career-oriented employment and training opportunities. A variety of programs in the United States are designed to accomplish this. The two most important are probably the Job Training and Partnership Act of 1982 (JTPA) and the Targeted Jobs Tax Credit (TJTC). The JTPA is a major federal initiative designed to reduce structural unemployment among youths and adults. It is different from previous federal employment training programs because of its greater involvement with private industry and vocational training institutions. Under JTPA, federal funds are targeted to individuals identified in the law as being substantially in need, including economically disadvantaged youths.[3]

The JTPA also attempts to alleviate long-term unemployment experienced by adults. It creates state-administered programs of employment and training assistance for (1) workers who have become unemployed as a result of plant closures, (2) laid-off workers who are unlikely to return to their previous industry or occupation, and (3) individuals experiencing long-term unemployment in occupations with limited employment opportunities.[4] The JTPA helps states to establish a wide variety of employment and training activities, including job search assistance, job training, employment counseling, and relocation assistance. It is too soon to judge whether the JTPA has had its hoped-for effect on structural unemployment.

Cyclical Unemployment

Much of the concern with unemployment in general stems from the Great Depression of the 1930s or the severe recession of 1981–82. It would be fair to say that most economists and policymakers still associate unemployment with the economy's periodic reduction in the rate of growth of aggregate demand for output and the derived demand for labor. Such fluctuations in business activity (the business cycle) result in a parallel movement in the overall unemployment rate, called **cyclical unemployment.**

Our understanding of cyclical unemployment is improved if we know the process by which people become unemployed. The data underlying figure 20.7 permit us to classify the unemployed into one of five groups: (1) people who are laid off but can expect to return to their previous jobs, (2) people who have lost jobs to which they cannot expect to return, (3) people who have quit their jobs, (4) people who are returning to the labor force after a period of neither working nor looking for work (reentrants), and (5) people who have never worked at full-time jobs before but are now seeking employment (new entrants).

Full employment occurs when there is no cyclical unemployment.

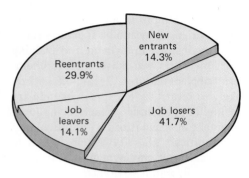

Full-employment year
1978

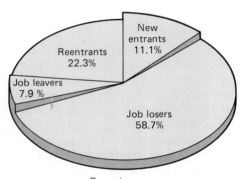

Recession year
1982

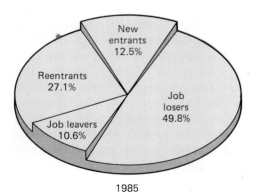

1985

Figure 20.8   The distribution of unemployment by reason
Note: data relate to people sixteen years old and over.
From *Economic Report of the President,* 1986, Table B-33,
p. 291.

Figure 20.8 shows us that the distribution of the unemployed among these categories is quite sensitive to the business cycle. We see this by comparing 1982, when the economy was in a recession, to 1978, when there was approximately **full employment,** and by definition, no cyclical unemployment. Remember that while full employment means that there was basically no cyclical unemployment, there was still frictional and structural unemployment. The unemployment rate was 6.1 percent in 1978. In contrast, 1982 was a year of relatively severe recession by U.S. standards. The unemployment rate hit 10.8 percent (twelve million people) during December of 1982. This was higher than at any other date since the Great Depression.

Figure 20.8 helps us to see that the relative number of people who have lost their jobs, either temporarily or permanently, rises noticeably during a recession. During 1978–82, this fraction rose from 42 percent to approximately 59 percent of the total unemployed. The total number of job losers more than doubled. Figure 20.8 also suggests a significant decline in employment opportunities for the unemployed during the 1981–82 recession. The share of unemployment traceable to workers voluntarily leaving their jobs declined from 14 percent in 1978 to 8 percent in 1982. Finally, the relative number of labor force entrants and reentrants declined from over 44 percent in 1978 to 33 percent of the total unemployed during the 1981–82 recession.

Why Are Workers Laid Off During Recessions?   It is not immediately obvious why cyclical unemployment occurs. Why don't firms smooth out production so that it remains fairly constant over the business cycle? Or why don't workers accept lower wages during recessions to maintain employment opportunities?

Suppose that firms could predict future fluctuations in economic activity and that goods and services could be stored for future sale at low cost. If this were true, a *temporary* reduction in aggregate demand for goods and services due to the business cycle would not necessarily result in a decline in the demand for labor. Firms would find it profitable to continue production

*The **normal unemployment rate** (u) is the unemployment rate when the labor market is in equilibrium; it is the percentage of the labor force that is frictionally or structurally unemployed.*

at a constant level. Realistically, of course, these conditions do not hold. Firms do not know how long a given recession will last or probably even how it will affect their particular product line. Services and many goods (perishables) cannot be stored at low cost. The result is that the demand for labor will shift in the same direction as the demand for output over the business cycle. This means that during recessions, firms will want to reduce either the real wage rate or the amount of labor they hire.

Figure 20.9 will help us understand the interrelationship between the demand for output, the demand for labor, real wage rates, layoffs, and cyclical unemployment. The labor market is initially in equilibrium at point A where the aggregate labor supply curve intersects the aggregate labor demand curve. At point A employment is at its normal level, and the expected real wage is at its equilibrium value. There is no cyclical unemployment when the labor market is in equilibrium. However, there *is* still normal unemployment, so that the unemployment rate is u^n, which is known as the **normal unemployment rate.**

Suppose that a downturn in economic activity reduces the demand for labor. Remember that the labor demand curve, $D(L)$, represents the aggregate marginal product of labor. How can the demand curve shift if the aggregate production function and the marginal product of labor have not changed? The answer is that the demand for labor is a *derived* demand. If firms cannot sell all the output they produce when they hire labor up to the point where the expected real wage equals the aggregate marginal product of labor, then the aggregate demand curve for labor will shift leftward.

If the expected real wage were to fall when aggregate labor demand declines, equilibrium could be reestablished at point B in figure 20.9, and *no* cyclical unemployment would be created. While *employment* would be reduced, no new *unemployment* would result. How can this be? The answer is that the reduced demand for labor and the employment opportunities that go with it reduce the real return on an hour of work enough so that workers leave the labor force. At the (lower) real wage rate, $W/P^e(1)$, labor market work is no longer as attractive relative to the alternatives available outside the labor market. The exit

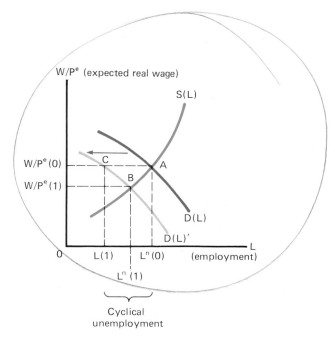

Figure 20.9   Recession, the demand for labor, and cyclical unemployment
Point A illustrates initial equilibrium in the aggregate labor market. There is no cyclical unemployment at point A because there are enough jobs to go around. Of course, there is still normal unemployment at A because new workers and labor force reentrants do not immediately find work and workers do not immediately retrain or migrate when the occupational or regional structure of labor markets changes.
During a recession the demand for labor is reduced to, say, $D(L)'$. If the real wage is flexible, it will fall and equilibrium is reestablished at point B, where there is reduced employment but not cyclical unemployment (everyone who wants a job can eventually get one). If wages are rigid at, say, $W/P^e(0)$, then cyclical unemployment results. More people want jobs, $L^n(0)$, than there are jobs available, $L(1)$.

of some individuals from the labor force results in *less employment* but *no cyclical unemployment.*

Cyclical unemployment is generated when real wages do not fall to their new equilibrium level. Why might this happen? Specifically, why don't firms and workers agree to reduce real wage rates rather than keeping them rigid? One possibility is that unions and their collective bargaining agreements prevent real wage reductions and require layoffs as the adjustment firms must make to a recession. As long as less than half the labor force of a firm is laid off, a majority vote by workers might tend to prefer *some layoffs* to reduced wages for *everyone.*

Real wages *do* get reduced in the United States, even under collective bargaining, during severe recessions. Newspapers and magazines carried numerous stories of "give backs" by industrial unions, such as the United Steelworkers, during the early 1980s.[5] More important, layoffs, as opposed to wage reductions, also occur in industries and occupations that are not covered by union collective bargaining agreements. The negative relationship between cyclical unemployment and aggregate economic activity is not just a creature of the past forty years, the time in history when unions have been most plentiful in the United States. And about 80 percent of workers are currently *not* covered by collective bargaining agreements. Thus, while unionism may seem an obvious reason for wage rigidity, forces more fundamental to labor markets must be responsible for cyclical unemployment.

Two reasons are frequently offered for employers' unwillingness to lower their real wages during a recession. The first relates to employers' credibility and their ability to attract new employees in the long term. Economists have recently come to view the employment relationship as a contract (sometimes written, other times unwritten) specifying the terms of employment over a relatively long time. Although lowering the real wage to take advantage of depressed labor market conditions might be profitable for the firm in the short term, long-term profitability of a firm could be severely harmed if its workers had expected stable or increasing real wages as part of their bargain with an employer. For example, workers often expect their employers to provide not only employment and training opportunities but also some degree of protection, or insurance, against a fluctuating real income. In return, employees agree to accept a stream of wage payments that is lower than it would be if real wages were allowed to fluctuate over the business cycle. In this sense workers often "purchase" what could be called income insurance. Keep in mind that such income insurance is not free; it is paid for in terms of a lower average rate of pay. Therefore, employees seldom choose complete freedom from the risk of a fluctuating income. Thus, during times of extremely

low demand for output (severe recessions), the employment relationship still permits firms to lay off some workers.

This leads us to another question. Why don't these implicit income-insurance contracts permit wage reductions when the demand for labor falls below a critical level? After all, when a worker is laid off his or her income is dramatically reduced. Wouldn't employment at a reduced wage be better than no employment? Not necessarily. When a worker is laid off, income is not reduced to zero because unemployment compensation and other forms of transfer (welfare) payments take effect. Moreover, many workers prefer to stay home and do domestic chores or care for their children rather than accept a drastically reduced wage. Therefore, if the real wage were cut by enough to make firms willing to keep employment at its normal level, L^n in figure 20.9, when aggregate demand was reduced to $D(L)'$, some workers would simply leave the labor force. Notice how the quantity of labor that workers supply is reduced from point A to point B when the aggregate demand for labor is reduced and real wages are allowed to fall. Thus, firms may lay off workers during a recession because they know their employees would not want to work at the wage the firms would be willing to pay them.

There is a second possible reason for layoffs as opposed to wage cuts when the demand for labor declines. Workers may want to be sure that firms are not trying to "fool" them into accepting lower pay for no good reason. A firm will always be better off if workers agree to accept lower pay. However, when employment is reduced so is production, and the firm loses some of its profits. Thus, by refusing to accept lower wage rates and forcing the firm to lay off workers instead, workers are keeping the firm "honest." Employers will only lay off workers when they really have to, because they share in lost income along with their employees.

Before concluding this section on layoffs, we should note that the opposite often occurs during short periods of unusually high labor demand. Written or unwritten agreements between employees and employers often call for the employees to work overtime when asked to do so. Sometimes an overtime premium is paid for this additional work, and at other times it is not. The main point is that if employers treat employees fairly during periods of reduced demand for output, employees are expected to refrain from "holding up" their employers—demanding sharply higher wage rates—when a firm experiences a temporarily high demand for its output.

In addition, employees are often glad to have temporary extra work, because it allows them to compensate for the days when they are laid off.

Normal versus Cyclical Unemployment and Government Policy   We noted that *normal unemployment* is that portion of total unemployment that results from the fact that it takes time (1) for workers who have just quit, or entered, or reentered the labor force to find jobs and (2) for workers to relocate in another firm, industry, or occupation because the structure of the labor market has changed. As such, the normal unemployment rate characterizes the economy in the *absence* of macroeconomic "shocks." Thus, cyclical unemployment, which is the result of the business cycle, is *not* part of the economy's normal unemployment. Currently, economists suspect that the normal rate of unemployment is in the range of 6 to 7 percent.[6]

Cyclical unemployment is the result of relatively rigid real wages in the face of a decline in the demand for labor during a recession. This means that government policies that make real wages less rigid or "smooth out" the aggregate demand for output will reduce cyclical unemployment. Unemployment compensation helps to make real wages more rigid because workers know that they have income available outside of their jobs. This brings us back to one of the trade-offs that policymakers face when attempting to reduce cyclical unemployment. Unemployment compensation provides valuable assistance to the needy. However, it also may contribute to increased unemployment. As yet, no policymaker has developed a socially popular way to fine-tune our unemployment compensation program in a way that increases wage flexibility and thus reduces cyclical unemployment.

▶ Summary and Conclusions

This chapter sets in place the first stone in our foundation of macroeconomic analysis. We can now understand the experience of the unemployed textile worker that introduced this chapter in terms of structural and cyclical unemployment. By analyzing the supply and demand for labor we see how the interaction between firms and individuals in the aggregate labor market leads to a particular (1) real wage, (2) level of employment, (3) aggregate production of goods and services, and (4) unemployment rate. These links play crucial roles in our later discussions of the commodity and loan contract markets in chapters 21 and 24 and our analysis of recession and inflationary episodes in chapters 25 through 29. The key points in this chapter include the following.

Diminishing marginal productivity of labor means that firms will only hire more labor if the real wage rate falls, *cet. par.* As a result, the aggregate demand for labor is downward sloping.

Higher real wages induce more individuals to seek employment by making the opportunity cost of nonmarket activities more expensive. As a result, the aggregate supply of labor is upward sloping.

Equilibrium in the aggregate labor market occurs where supply equals demand. At equilibrium, the expected real wage equals the actual real wage and employment is at a level acceptable to all firms and households.

The equilibrium level of employment implies a particular aggregate quantity of goods and services supplied by the economy's firms.

Economists classify unemployment according to whether it is caused by frictional, structural, or cyclical factors. The purpose of this classification is to emphasize the need for different types of economic policy to reduce unemployment.

Frictional unemployment and structural unemployment are part of what economists call normal unemployment. This is not to say that they are "good" for society but rather that they are an unavoidable part of a modern industrial economy in a democratic country.

Cyclical unemployment results when the demand for labor declines but real wages do not. Economists are just beginning to understand why real wages may not adjust sufficiently to prevent substantial cyclical unemployment. One possibility is that workers prefer a job "package" that contains relatively rigid real wage rates and fluctuations in employment to one that permits real wage rates to vary but stabilizes employment.

When there is no cyclical unemployment, the economy is said to be at full employment. Full employment takes account of the fact that there will still be unemployment even if there are enough jobs to go around.

▶ Key Terms

aggregate demand for labor [D(L)] *420*

aggregate supply of labor [S(L)] *423*

competitive firms *416*

cyclical unemployment *429*

demand for labor *415*

equilibrium in the aggregate labor market *424*

expected real wage (W/Pᵉ) *424*

firm's labor demand curve [d(l)] *419*

frictional unemployment *427*

full employment *430*

marginal product of labor (mpl) *415*

nominal, or paycheck, wage (W) *418*

nonlabor income *423*

nonmarket activities *422*

normal employment (Lⁿ) *424*

normal unemployment rate *431*

production function *420*

price taker *416*

real wage (W/P) *418*

structural unemployment *428*

supply of labor *415*

value of the marginal product of labor (vmpl) *417*

▶ Questions for Discussion and Review

1. What is the marginal product of labor? What are the two key properties of marginal product of labor? What is the difference between the marginal product of labor and the value of labor's marginal product?

2. Explain why the value of labor's marginal product is also the competitive firm's labor demand curve. Support your answer graphically.

3. Pete's Pizzeria of Piscataway makes (what else?) pizzas. Pete has a fixed capital input (ovens, etc.) and purchases only one additional input, the labor of pizza makers. There are many similar pizza shops in Piscataway so that Pete sells pizzas and purchases labor under competitive conditions. You have the following information about Pete's operation.

l	q	mpl	vmpl
0	0		
1	15	15	75
2		22	
3	67		150
4	90		
5	108		
6		15	
7	135		
8			
9	150	6	
10	153	3	15

where	
l	≡ number of pizza makers
q	≡ number of pizzas made per day
mpl	≡ marginal product of labor
vmpl	≡ value of the marginal product of labor

a. How many pizzas are made when six pizza makers are employed? Explain.

b. What is the marginal product (mpl) of the seventh pizza maker? Explain.

c. What is the price of a pizza in Piscataway? Explain.

d. What is the value of marginal product of the eighth pizza maker? Explain.

e. Suppose that the competitive daily wage for pizza makers is $90? How many pizza makers will Pete hire so as to maximize his profit? Explain.

4. Listed below are an economy's aggregate labor demand and supply schedules.

Aggregate labor demand schedule		Aggregate labor supply schedule	
Daily real wage (dollars)	Employ- ment (000's)	Daily real wage (dollars)	Employ- ment (000's)
60	0	0	0
55	500	5	500
50	1,000	10	1,000
45	1,500	15	1,500
40	2,000	20	2,000
35	2,500	25	2,500
30	3,000	30	3,000
25	3,500	35	3,500
20	4,000	40	4,000
15	4,500	45	4,500
10	5,000	50	5,000
5	5,500	55	5,500

What is the equilibrium real wage? What is equilibrium employment? Explain how you arrived at your answer.

5. Describe the set of government policies that would be required to make frictional unemployment disappear. Why do you think that the United States government has not totally eliminated frictional unemployment?

6. Why is structural unemployment a part of normal unemployment? Explain why there would be much less structural unemployment if adjustments to economic change were *free*.

7. Economists say that frictional and structural unemployment are part of normal unemployment. Explain. Is cyclical unemployment also part of normal unemployment? Explain. Does it make sense to classify some unemployment as normal? Discuss.

8. Explain why cyclical unemployment results if the demand for labor declines but real wages do not. Support your answer graphically. Describe some economic policies that would make real wages more "flexible." Why do you think the government has not adopted all of your suggestions?

9. Some economists feel that the rigid real wages leading to cyclical unemployment are the result of worker preference. Put differently, economists suspect that workers might prefer relatively constant real wages and the threat of unemployment to a job "package" that would have stable employment but more variable rates of pay. This amounts to assuming that workers themselves are responsible for cyclical unemployment. Evaluate and discuss. Why do *you* think cyclical unemployment exists?

10. Suppose that the teenage labor market is in equilibrium at the legislated minimum wage rate. If a recession occurs in the economy, what is the likely effect on this market?

Chapter 21

Aggregate Expenditure on Goods and Services

Outline

I. Introduction *438*
II. Aggregate expenditure on goods and services: Background *439*
   A. The components of aggregate expenditure: A brief review *439*
   B. GNP also measures society's total income *439*
     1. A brief review *439*
     2. The uses of society's total income *439*
III. An analysis of aggregate expenditure on goods and services *440*
   A. The consumption function *441*
     1. The consumption function expressed quantitatively *441*
     2. The consumption function expressed graphically *444*
   B. Investment *445*
   C. Government spending and net exports *448*
   D. Aggregate expenditure, aggregate production, and equilibrium GNP *449*
     1. Another look at equilibrium GNP: Saving, investment, and the government deficit *451*
      a. The multiplier *453*
      b. A final look at equilibrium GNP *454*
     2. The national income accounts: Measured saving, measured investment, the government deficit, and measured GNP *456*
IV. Summary and conclusions *457*
V. Key terms *457*
VI. Questions for discussion and review *457*
VII. Appendix: A deeper look at the multiplier and graphical analysis *458*

Objectives

After reading this chapter, the student should be able to:

Identify the four components of aggregate expenditure.
Identify the three uses of society's total income.
Distinguish between endogenous and exogenous consumption and the factors that influence each.
Explain the significance of the consumption function's various components, such as its slope and the vertical intercept.
Discuss the factors underlying the level of investment.
Explain the relationship between planned aggregate expenditure, the 45° line, and GNP.
Describe algebraically and graphically the relationship between planned investment, planned saving, and the government deficit at equilibrium GNP.
Use the multiplier to determine the change in equilibrium GNP that results from a given change in planned expenditures.

▶ Introduction

A well-known economist who served as an economic adviser to policymakers in developing countries related the following experience in one emerging African nation during the 1960s. When he first arrived in the country, he visited the Ministry of Planning and asked to see any available data that might give him a picture of recent and current economic conditions there. He was stunned by the wealth of data available both in terms of the number of years covered and the amount of detail on various sectors of the economy. Experience had taught him that such data were hard, if not impossible, to find in most developing countries.

The solution to the mystery became apparent when he discovered that for the previous ten years the country's measured total production was always equal to 1 percent of that in the United States. Further investigation revealed that bureaucrats in the planning office in the capital city had no idea what was actually going on in the economy. Under pressure from their superiors to produce numbers, they simply took United States data and created what they thought were "good" numbers for their country.

Clearly, numbers are not very useful for appraising how an economy is developing over time if they are pure inventions. How can intelligent government policies be developed if the government itself is ignorant about conditions in the economy?

Even if one wanted to conscientiously collect data for a particular economy and had a well-trained staff to perform the task, there still would be a number of questions to answer before the job could begin: What kind of data should be collected? How should data on household, business, and government activities be grouped? Are some measures more useful than others? How can data be added up to provide useful information about the economy? Once the data are collected, how can they be used to help understand the way past economic conditions affect those of today and to forecast the economic scene in the near future? What macroeconomic theory enables one to make sense of various measures of aggregate economic activity? These are some of the questions we will look into in this chapter.

▶ Aggregate Expenditure on Goods and Services: Background

In this chapter we set in place the second stone in the foundation of macroeconomic analysis. In particular, we describe aggregate expenditure on goods and services and how this leads to a particular level of gross national product. Keep in mind that this chapter really deals with only *one* aspect of the macroeconomy, aggregate *expenditure* on goods and services. In chapters 25 and 26 we put things together into a complete representation of the aggregate economy.

The Components of Aggregate Expenditure: A Brief Review

We will begin by briefly reviewing the components of society's aggregate expenditure on goods and services. In chapter 19 we saw that one way to categorize these components is according to which group is doing the spending. We saw that aggregate expenditure is composed of personal consumption expenditures by individuals (C), investments by firms (I), purchases of goods and services by the various government agencies in the United States (G), and net exports of goods and services to foreign consumers (X). Added up they equal the total aggregate expenditure for goods and services (E). This relationship can be described simply as

$$E = C + I + G + X.$$

You should assume in our discussions of aggregate expenditure and gross national product that we are concerned with *real* values. This means that aggregate expenditure on GNP in any year will be expressed in terms of the prices that prevailed during the base year for calculating real gross national product.

GNP Also Measures Society's Total Income

A Brief Review

In chapter 19 we saw that real GNP is *always* equal to the real value of the income people receive from the sale of their labor and other productive resources to firms. This is illustrated in the circular flow diagram of figure 19.1. All those goods and services produced in an economy do not just appear out of thin air. To create them, firms use resources such as labor, land, energy, and physical capital. Whenever producers decide how many final goods and services to make, they must also decide what inputs to purchase. When firms purchase productive resources, this generates income to the owners of those resources—the individuals in society. We have been using the symbol Y to represent the total income paid out to the owners of society's productive resources. At this point we suggest you review table 19.2 for data on how the production of GNP in the United States creates different categories of payments or income for the owners of society's various productive resources.

The Uses of Society's Total Income

The income people receive is used in three general ways: to purchase consumer goods and services (C), to save (S), and to pay taxes to the government (T). At this point, one difference between macroeconomics and microeconomics becomes clear. If we were concerned with microeconomics, for instance, we would be discussing the various types of taxes individuals pay, including sales taxes, property taxes, and taxes on earnings and nonlabor income. We would also be discussing the particular components of consumption, such as food versus housing. We are now interested in the macroeconomy, however, so we concern ourselves only with aggregate or total consumption, saving, and taxes paid to the government.

Saving is the difference between total income and the amount spent on the consumption of goods and services or paid to the government in taxes.

Full-employment GNP requires that there is equilibrium in the aggregate market for goods and services and full employment in the aggregate labor market at the same time.

The consumption function is a schedule, or equation, indicating society's total intended consumption expenditures at various levels of aggregate income.

The portion of people's income that is not paid in taxes or used to purchase consumption goods and services is **saving.** Saving may entail adding to a bank account, buying a stock or bond portfolio, or contributing to a pension fund. In our discussion saving does not refer to any particular form of adding to one's wealth.

Figure 21.1 contains a simple numerical example that illustrates the relationship between income, consumption, saving, and taxes. Suppose that the aggregate real income received by households is $200 billion and that they are required to pay taxes of $20 billion. If the households decide to spend $130 billion on consumption of goods and services, then we know that saving, the remainder, must equal $50 billion. If households had instead spent more on consumption of goods and services, they would, of course, have saved less. This relationship between income, taxes, consumption, and saving can be illustrated by using the following equation:

$$Y = C + S + T.$$

▸ An Analysis of Aggregate Expenditure on Goods and Services

In developing our analysis of aggregate expenditure on goods and services, we draw upon our understanding of its components—consumption, investment, government spending, and net exports. One of the major points to bear in mind as we analyze aggregate expenditure is that our macroeconomic model is concerned with *planned* or *intended* behavior. By this we mean that we wish to understand the various forces that lead households to *choose* one level of consumption over another and investors to *choose* a certain quantity of spending on investment goods. Thus, we need to detail the forces underlying consumption and investment *plans*, along with what drives government spending and net exports to their particular levels. We will see that only when all expenditure plans are actually realized will the aggregate market for goods and services be in equilibrium. Whether full

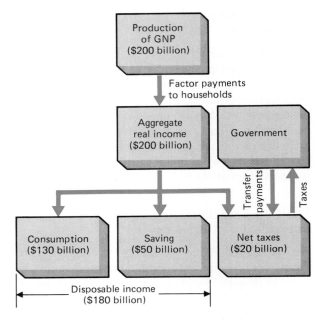

Figure 21.1   The relationship between GNP, total income, disposable income, consumption, and saving
Production of GNP equals $200 billion, which generates factor payments to households of $200 billion (wages, profit, interest, rent, etc.). Households also receive transfer payments from the government and pay taxes to the government. *Net* taxes equal the taxes households pay to the government less the transfer payments they receive from the government. The income households receive from factor payments less *net* taxes equals their *disposable income.* Net taxes equals $20 billion, and households allocate their disposable income of $180 billion to consumption ($130 billion) and saving ($50 billion).
    The relationship between total income, net taxes, consumption, and saving can also be illustrated using the equation

$$\begin{array}{rcccc} Y &=& C &+& S &+& T \\ 200 &=& 130 && 50 && 20. \end{array}$$

employment in the labor market will prevail when the goods and services market is in equilibrium—leading to **full-employment GNP**—is another question. It is answered in chapter 25. In this chapter, we are concerned *only* with the circumstances that lead to equilibrium in the aggregate market for goods and services.

Endogenous consumption is that part of planned consumption that depends on GNP.

Exogenous consumption is that part of planned consumption that depends on factors other than GNP.

Disposable income (YD) is the total income consumers have to spend after their taxes (T) are paid, so that $YD \equiv Y - T$.

The Consumption Function

The cornerstone of the aggregate expenditure relationship is the **consumption function,** which illustrates the relationship between planned consumption and society's total income (GNP). It is called the consumption function because it is a relationship between the variable *consumption* and another set of variables that determine how much households desire to consume in any given year.

Economists who analyze macroeconomic issues have found it very useful to distinguish between two categories of factors that affect household consumption behavior. One category includes only one variable—the income that households receive. The other category includes all of the factors *other* than household income that affect consumption, such as basic subsistence needs, expectations about the future, the desire to save income now so that more may be consumed later, and so on. We have seen that GNP, which determines the income of households, depends itself on the level of planned consumption expenditure. For this reason, that part of consumption that depends on household income is called **endogenous consumption.** The word *endogenous* is used because it refers to that part of consumption that originates *in* the circular flow between GNP and income. That part of consumption that depends on factors other than income and GNP is determined *outside* the circular flow and is therefore called **exogenous consumption.** To summarize, we divide planned consumption into two parts: endogenous consumption and exogenous consumption. Using the symbol $\overset{*}{C}$ to denote total planned consumption, we say that

$\overset{*}{C} \equiv$ (planned) endogenous consumption
$+$ (planned) exogenous consumption.

The income *available* for consumption, which is the amount households have left over after paying their taxes, is called **disposable income (YD),** as indicated in figure 21.1. (We shall ignore the fact that in the official national income statistics as shown in

chapter 19, *depreciation* of plant and equipment must also be subtracted from GNP to derive disposable income.) If you take another look at table 19.3 on page 390, you will see that disposable income (or disposable personal income as it is officially named) includes *government transfer payments,* which include Social Security, Aid to Families with Dependent Children, and similar payments that add to the spending power of individuals and families over and above what they earn. You should think of government transfer payments as taxes in reverse, or negative taxes. In figure 21.1, we have simply subtracted government transfer payments from the taxes the public pays the government to obtain *net taxes* of $20 billion. For example, if taxes paid were $35 billion and transfers paid by the government to households were $15 billion, then net taxes paid by households to the government would be $20 billion. Since taxes paid to the government typically exceed transfer payments from the government, net taxes are usually positive. What households have left to save or consume after net taxes are subtracted from their incomes is disposable income.

A good way to remember how GNP, net taxes, disposable income, and consumption are related is this. A change in GNP (national income) will change disposable income and endogenous consumption but not exogenous consumption. Variables *other* than a change in GNP will change exogenous consumption but not endogenous consumption. A change in taxes that does *not* itself result from a change in GNP will cause exogenous consumption to change. If tax policy does not change, then exogenous consumption will change only when forces other than GNP or taxes change.

The Consumption Function Expressed Quantitatively

We will now put some meat on the bare bones of the exogenous and endogenous consumption concepts. Table 21.1 contains a numerical example of the relationship between GNP, taxes, disposable income

Table 21.1   A numerical example of the consumption function

GNP (Y)	Net Taxes (T)	Disposable income (YD) ≡ (Y − T)	Exogenous consumption (a constant)	Endogenous consumption (depends on Y)	Total consumption (C)		Saving (S) ≡ (YD − C)	
			(billions of dollars)					
						$\Delta C/\Delta Y$ (MPC)		$\Delta S/\Delta Y$ (MPS)
25	20	5	10	15	25		−20	
						0.6		0.4
60	20	40	10	36	46		−6	
						0.6		0.4
75	20	55	10	45	55		0	
						0.6		0.4
80	20	60	10	48	58		2	
						0.6		0.4
100	20	80	10	60	70		10	
						0.6		0.4
120	20	100	10	72	82		18	
						0.6		0.4
125	20	105	10	75	85		20	
						0.6		0.4
150	20	130	10	90	100		30	
						0.6		0.4
200	20	180	10	120	130		50	
						0.6		0.4
300	20	280	10	180	190		90	

Exogenous consumption is $10 billion annually. Endogenous consumption equals GNP × 0.6. Total consumption is exogenous consumption plus endogenous consumption, and saving is disposable income (YD) less total consumption. When GNP falls below $75 billion, total consumption exceeds disposable income, and households *dissave*, or draw down their savings to maintain their standard of living. As GNP rises above $75 billion, saving becomes positive. Notice that whenever GNP rises or falls, disposable income changes by the same amount because we have assumed taxes are fixed.

Both endogenous and total consumption change by exactly 60 percent of the amount that GNP and YD change, and saving changes by exactly 40 percent of any change in GNP and YD. The *change* in consumption per dollar *change* in GNP can be expressed symbolically as $\Delta C/\Delta Y$ and is called the **marginal propensity to consume (MPC)**. Similarly, the *change* in saving per dollar *change* in GNP is expressed symbolically as $\Delta S/\Delta Y$ and is called the **marginal propensity to save (MPS).** For example, when GNP goes from $150 billion to $200 billion, YD also increases by $50 billion, and consumption increases by $50 billion × 0.6, or $30 billion, going from $100 billion to $130 billion. Saving goes up by $50 billion × 0.4, or $20 billion, from $30 billion to $50 billion.

Factors that influence exogenous consumption
basic consumption needs
expectations about the future
tastes and preferences
accumulated savings
access to borrowed funds
net taxes that don't depend on GNP

Factor that influences endogenous consumption
GNP

Dissaving occurs when people consume more than their disposable income.

(YD), exogenous consumption, endogenous consumption, total consumption, and saving. In this example, we assume that net taxes are fixed at $20 billion annually and that exogenous consumption is fixed at $10 billion per year. Endogenous consumption, as defined, depends on the level of total income, or GNP. To be precise, endogenous consumption equals 60 percent of GNP, so when GNP and disposable income change, total consumption changes by exactly 60 percent as much. Notice that when GNP equals $200 billion, total consumption equals $130 billion, as in figure 21.1. What figure 21.1 does not show is that total consumption consists of $120 billion endogenous consumption and $10 billion exogenous consumption.

The general nature of the consumption function will be easier to understand if we use some simple algebra. In our algebraic representation of the consumption function, we will use the symbol A to represent exogenous consumption. In table 21.1, A equals $10 billion. Where does A come from; why and how is it determined? The list at the bottom of table 21.1 indicates that exogenous consumption depends on basic consumption needs, expectations about the future, tastes and preferences, accumulated savings, access to borrowed funds, and, *very important,* taxes and transfer payments that do not change with the level of GNP. If a household's disposable income were temporarily to fall to zero, it would not eliminate consumption entirely, for to do so would make it impossible to survive. The consumption that would persist even if disposable income were zero is part of exogenous consumption. The funds to purchase consumption goods might come from savings accounts, borrowed funds, or private charity. When people spend more than their disposable income, we say they are **dissaving.**

To elaborate somewhat, when consumers anticipate inflation, they will spend now to "beat" the price increases. This was the case in the late 1970s and early 1980s. Later, in 1982–83, consumption became "sluggish" because inflation expectations slacked off as a result of the relatively low inflation rates and falling prices.[1] Suppose your job prospects are especially bright and you expect to be promoted soon. You are likely to increase the amount you consume out of your current income. This is equivalent to an exogenous increase in your consumption function. Tastes can also affect exogenous consumption by influencing the amount of expenditure an individual or household views as "necessary" for basic subsistence. Comparing two individuals whose incomes temporarily fall to zero, one of them might be more willing to draw down savings or to borrow from friends or relatives to maintain a given standard of living than the other one. The first individual would have a higher level of exogenous consumption (value of A) than the second.

Endogenous consumption depends on GNP and variables, such as disposable income, that change when GNP changes. In the simple example in table 21.1, taxes do not change with people's incomes. Therefore, disposable income changes only when GNP changes. (We will treat taxes more realistically later on, after we establish the basic nature of the consumption function and how it relates to the aggregate goods market.) Notice that whenever GNP and disposable income change, we have assumed that endogenous consumption changes by a constant 60 percent as much. To formulate the consumption function in terms of an equation, we will use the symbol b to indicate the amount by which endogenous consumption changes whenever GNP or disposable income change by a given amount. As we show in table

*The **marginal propensity to consume (MPC)** is the additional aggregate consumption spending that occurs out of each additional dollar of disposable income; MPC is a fraction (b) between 0 and 1.*

*The **45° line** exactly divides the right angle created by the two axes of the consumption function graph. Along this line, whatever expenditure*

components are measured along the vertical axis exactly equal GNP, which is measured along the horizontal axis.

21.1, this fraction, b, is known as the **marginal propensity to consume (MPC).** It tells us the *change* in consumption when consumers receive an *additional* dollar of disposable income. (Remember that with net taxes fixed, disposable income changes by exactly the same amount that GNP changes.) We will use the symbol Δ to denote a *change* in consumption and a *change* in income. Thus, b, the marginal propensity to consume, can be denoted as $\Delta \overset{*}{C}/\Delta Y$. The asterisk (*) indicates that we are referring to *planned* consumption. In table 21.1, the marginal propensity to consume equals 0.6.

We can summarize everything we have said about consumption and the consumption function with the following simple expression for the consumption function:

$$\overset{*}{C} = A + bY,$$

where b ≡ MPC = 0.6 in our example and A = $10 billion. To see how this formula for the consumption function works, simply plug in some of the numbers from table 21.1. When GNP is only $25 billion, endogenous consumption equals 0.6 x $25 billion, or $15 billion, so total consumption equals $10 billion plus $15 billion, or $25 billion, as shown in the total consumption column of table 21.1. Verify for yourself that when GNP equals $100 billion, total consumption equals $70 billion, according both to the equation above and table 21.1.

The Consumption Function Expressed Graphically

Figure 21.2 illustrates the consumption function graphically. The horizontal axis is gross national product (households' total income), which is measured in billions of real dollars. The vertical axis is planned consumption and net taxes, also measured in billions of real dollars. One way to think of the consumption function is as a computer program. This program first takes aggregate income before net taxes (real GNP), then calculates the net taxes consumers must pay, and thus also calculates their disposable income (YD). The program then considers consumers' tastes and preferences and determines an amount they desire to spend on goods and services. It is the first

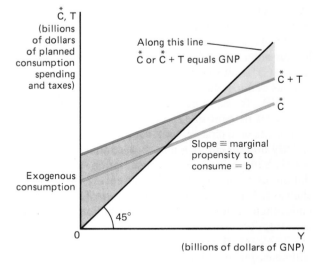

Figure 21.2   The consumption function
The consumption function illustrates how real income (GNP) influences society's consumption spending. The slope of the consumption function is the marginal propensity to consume (b). The point where the consumption function crosses the vertical axis measures the quantity of exogenous consumption.

The upper line, marked $\overset{*}{C}$ + T, represents planned consumption plus taxes. Where the $\overset{*}{C}$ + T line crosses the 45° line, planned consumption plus taxes equals disposable income. In other words, at this point, planned saving is zero. To the right of this point, planned saving is positive, and to the left, planned saving is negative (there is planned dissaving).

and last statements in this computer program that we see in the line marked $\overset{*}{C}$ in figure 21.2. The upper line in the figure measures planned consumption plus net taxes that people are required to pay out of the income they receive. It is labeled $\overset{*}{C}$ + T. We will discuss this line later.

There is a special line in figure 21.2 that is the same distance from the horizontal axis as from the vertical axis. Because it runs through the middle of the right (90°) angle created by the horizontal axis and the vertical axis, this line is known as the **45° line.** At all points along the 45° line, the variables measured along the vertical axis are *exactly* equal to real GNP. How does the consumption function ($\overset{*}{C}$) relate to the two axes and the 45° line?

Figure 21.2 illustrates that the consumption function has two components. The first component, the marginal propensity to consume, is represented in the diagram by the slope of the line labeled $\overset{*}{C}$. We have already seen that the marginal propensity to consume is the fraction b, the change in planned consumption for every dollar change in disposable income. The fact that the $\overset{*}{C}$ line is flatter than the 45° line reminds us that consumers do not plan to spend all of each additional dollar of disposable income on consumption goods. Some of it they plan to save. In other words, while b is greater than 0, it is less than 1. The second component of the consumption function is exogenous consumption. In figure 21.2, exogenous consumption is measured as the amount consumed when GNP equals zero. (In table 21.1, consumption would equal $10 billion, even if GNP dropped to zero.) It is measured by the height of the consumption function where it crosses the vertical axis, because at this point, GNP equals zero.

Given that exogenous consumption is positive, while the slope of the consumption function is less than the slope of the 45° line, the consumption function *must* cross the 45° line at some point. At this point, planned consumption (measured along the vertical axis) is exactly equal to GNP (measured along the horizontal axis of figure 21.2). In table 21.1 this point occurs at GNP equal to $25 billion.

Now we can explain why the line labeled $\overset{*}{C}$ + T is also shown in figure 21.2. From what we have said already, it should be clear that where the $\overset{*}{C}$ + T line crosses the 45° line, planned consumption *plus net taxes* equals GNP. It will help to say the same thing algebraically, as follows: the point at which the $\overset{*}{C}$ + T line crosses the 45° line can be expressed as

$$Y = \overset{*}{C} + T.$$

However, we have already seen that saving is defined as the portion of households' disposable incomes that is not consumed. In other words, planned saving is GNP minus net taxes minus planned consumption, or

$$\overset{*}{S} \equiv Y - T - \overset{*}{C}.$$

Therefore, when planned consumption plus net taxes equals GNP, planned saving must be zero. In table 21.1, this occurs at GNP equal to $75 billion. You can see this algebraically if you substitute the first equation in this paragraph for Y in the second expression.

In figure 21.2, the shaded area to the right of the intersection of the $\overset{*}{C}$ + T line indicates that planned saving is positive and grows larger as GNP increases. The shaded area to the left of this point indicates planned dissaving (negative saving).

Figure 21.2 is a basic representation of aggregate consumption that *models* the observed behavior of United States consumers. Figure 21.3, by comparison, plots out *actual data* on aggregate consumption and disposable (after net tax) income for 1929 to 1985. Notice the similarity with figure 21.1. In 1933, when aggregate disposable income was quite low, people were dissaving. More recently people have been saving about 9 percent of their aggregate disposable income. For example, in 1981 real aggregate disposable income was $1.04 trillion and real aggregate consumption expenditure was about $948 billion. On a *per capita* basis, real disposable income in 1981 was about $4,538 (measured in 1972 prices) and real consumption expenditure was about $4,123 (also measured in 1972 prices).[2] If you were to calculate the marginal propensity to consume in recent years from the slope of the consumption function in figure 21.2, you would see that consumers actually spent about 80 to 90 percent of an additional dollar of income after net taxes.

Investment

In chapter 19 we saw that investment includes spending by firms for their buildings, equipment, and inventories. As we discuss the role played by investment in aggregate expenditure, it is important to keep a number of things in mind. First, investment has both planned and unplanned components. Firms "draw down" on their inventories when their sales exceed what they had anticipated. They build up their inventories unexpectedly when sales fall short. Second, purchases of plant and equipment may be the result of either capacity expansion or the need to replace equipment because of wear and tear from past usage. The most important point, however, is that current investment is largely *independent* of firms' *current* sales. Let us explain this more fully and identify the economic variables that have the greatest impact on aggregate investment.

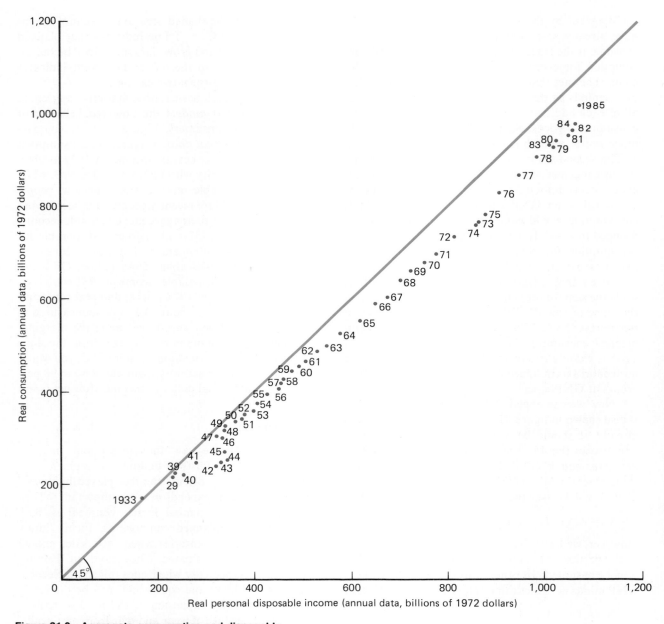

**Figure 21.3   Aggregate consumption and disposable
income in the United States, 1929–1985**
From *Economic Report of the President*, 1983, Table B-24 and
1986, Table B-26, p. 283.

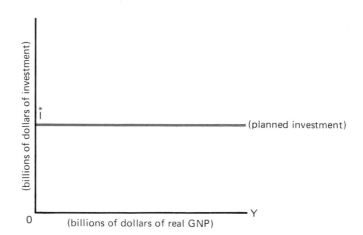

Figure 21.4 Planned investment
Investment largely depends upon (1) the interest rate at which firms borrow to finance growth of their productive capacity, (2) expectations of future output growth, and (3) past levels of production. Thus, intended investment tends to be unaffected by short-term changes in production (real GNP). $\overset{*}{I}$ represents the level of investment that firms plan to make during the current period.

The interest rate is very important in determining firms' investment decisions. High interest rates make it expensive to borrow funds for investment. Sometimes, however, the investor does not have to borrow funds. In this case, the investor uses his or her own funds to purchase investment goods. However, these funds could have been lent to others at the prevailing interest rate. This means that an opportunity cost is incurred—the interest that could have been earned on the money that financed the investment. Thus, it really does not matter whether a firm has to borrow from a lending institution such as a bank or borrow implicitly from itself. In either case, there is an interest cost of investing, and that cost rises with the interest rate. This means that the "backend" of investment—the future payoff—becomes less profitable. Thus, investment will be lower the higher the cost of credit (the interest rate). Conversely, lower interest rates encourage greater investment.

The profitability of investment is also related to the rules for taxing the return on an investment. Examples are depreciation allowances and tax rates on capital gains. The goal of the Economic Recovery Tax Act of 1981 (ERTA) is to make investment more profitable in general and especially more profitable in specific areas such as research and development. The hope is that by encouraging investment, ERTA will promote increased production (economic growth).[3]

Another factor to consider is that investment takes time and pays off in the future. As a result, today's investment is heavily influenced by a firm's anticipations of what sales are likely to be over a period of years. Thus, many economists would say that expected *future* growth in production, not current production, plays the major role in determining new investment.

Finally, we know that a part of current investment is the replacement of worn-out buildings and machinery. In fact, one-half to three-fourths of total investment in recent years falls into the category of replacement or depreciation. Thus, a good deal of current investment depends upon how rapidly machines and other equipment become obsolete and how they were used *in the past*. This means that *past* production, but not necessarily current production, also plays an important role in determining current *investment*.

One of the main implications of this section is that it is appropriate to treat planned investment as independent of *current* production (real GNP). Intended investment can be shown as the horizontal line labeled $\overset{*}{I}$ in figure 21.4. The fact that the line representing intended investment is horizontal means that aggregate investment does not change if current output (real GNP) changes.

Figure 21.5   Planned aggregate investment and government spending
Planned aggregate investment and government expenditures are each largely independent of current real GNP. Thus, they can be represented by the horizontal lines Î and G, respectively. We can designate their sum by the horizontal line that hits the vertical axis at the height Î + G.

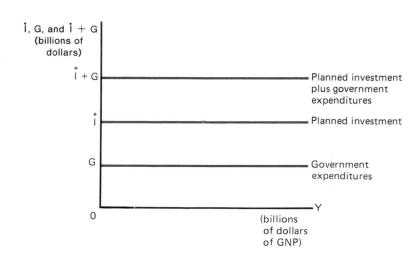

To summarize, planned investment depends on such factors as taxation policy, the rate of interest, past production, and expected future production. Investment should be viewed as *exogenous* with respect to current real GNP, just as part of consumption expenditure is. This does *not* mean investment never changes. If, for example, the interest rate were to fall, then intended investment would change from Î in figure 21.4 to some higher level, say, Î'. If the government reduced taxes on business profits, or if investors expected future sales to grow sharply, then planned investment would also be likely to increase.

Government Spending and Net Exports

We will only briefly discuss the two remaining components of aggregate expenditure, government spending on goods and services and net exports. These topics are treated at greater length in other chapters.

In completing our model of aggregate expenditure on goods and services, we will assume for now that the trade sector of the aggregate economy is "in balance" so that imports equal exports, or net exports

(X) equal zero. Government spending on goods and services, like investment, will be treated as exogenous, or independent, of real GNP. (By government spending we refer only to spending on goods and services. Government also spends on transfer payments, but this form of government expenditure is already accounted for by our calculation of net taxes.) We will assume that government spending is for the most part determined by past budget decisions that are updated relatively slowly.

Government spending is shown by the horizontal line in figure 21.5. This figure also shows us that it is easy to illustrate the sum of planned investment plus government spending. The line labeled Î + G indicates aggregate investment plus government spending. The technique of adding components of aggregate demand will soon prove useful. It is important to reemphasize that while planned investment, government spending, and their sum are exogenous (not dependent on the current level of GNP) in figure 21.5, this does not mean that they never change. For example, governments can and do change the level of their expenditures on public works, such as highway construction and new buildings.

*Planned aggregate expenditure (Ė)
is the sum of aggregate planned
consumption by households (Ĉ),
investment planned by firms (Î),
and government spending (G)—
as well as net exports (X),
assumed to equal 0 in this chapter.*

*Equilibrium real GNP occurs
when the aggregate real quantity
of goods and services produced
exactly equals planned aggregate
expenditure.*

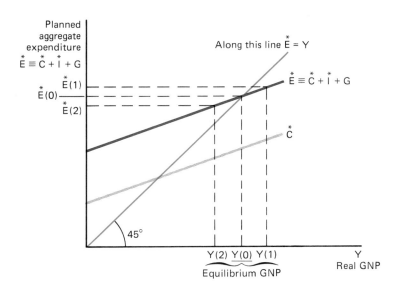

**Figure 21.6   Equilibrium real gross
national product**
Ė represents planned aggregate
expenditure, Ĉ + Î + G. The point at
which Ė crosses the 45° line shows
where planned aggregate expenditure
equals GNP. Since producers are able to
sell all they produce at this level of GNP
and consumers, investors, and the
government can purchase all the goods
and services they desire, Y(0) represents
equilibrium GNP, which is equal to Ė(0),
planned aggregate expenditure on GNP.

If GNP produced equals Y(1), then
planned aggregate expenditure, Ė(1),
will be less than Y(1), and firms will have
to reduce their production. If GNP
produced equals Y(2), then planned
aggregate expenditure, Ė(2), will be
more than Y(2), and firms will increase
their production.

Aggregate Expenditure, Aggregate Production, and Equilibrium GNP

Planned aggregate expenditure (Ė) is simply the sum of planned expenditures by firms, households, and the government. It is defined as planned consumption plus planned investment plus government spending, or

$$\overset{*}{E} \equiv \overset{*}{C} + \overset{*}{I} + G.$$

At this point you may be asking yourself why there is no asterisk (*) over G. Remember that firms' or consumers' planned behavior may not be realized, so that firms, for example, may end up investing more or less than intended. However, we are assuming that the government always spends what it planned to spend, so that actual and desired spending typically coincide. Thus, there is no need to put an asterisk over G.

Planned aggregate expenditure, Ė, can be depicted in a graph that starts out with the basic consumption function illustrated in figure 21.2 and then adding to it planned investment and government expenditure, as illustrated in figure 21.5. Since figure 21.5 shows that planned investment plus government expenditure does not vary with GNP, the shape of the

aggregate expenditure line, Ė, in figure 21.6 is exactly the same as the consumption function. However, the Ė line lies above Ĉ by the amount of Î + G. Remember that the 45° line plots out all the points where whatever is measured along the vertical axis equals what is measured along the horizontal axis. Therefore, at the point where the planned aggregate expenditure line, Ė, crosses the 45° line, Ė = GNP. This means that at the level of GNP at which planned aggregate expenditure crosses the 45° line, firms sell exactly the quantity of goods and services (GNP) that they have produced, and all consumers, investors, and the government are able to carry out their expenditure plans. In short, Y(0) is called **equilibrium real GNP** because firms sell all they had planned to sell and buyers' plans also are exactly realized. Ė(0), which is equal to Y(0), represents equilibrium planned expenditure.

The common sense of this is that if firms decide to produce one dollar more than Y(0), the additional income generated will lead to *less* than an additional dollar of planned expenditure. This is because planned consumption rises by less than $1 for each $1 increase in disposable income. Planned saving also increases, but there is no direct effect of the increased planned saving on planned investment or government spending. Therefore, planned expenditure rises only as much as planned consumption increases. If firms decide to produce one dollar less than $Y(0)$, the reduction in income received by households will induce them to reduce their planned consumption spending by *less* than one dollar. Planned saving also falls, but planned investment and government spending do not respond directly to reduced planned saving.

Of all production levels firms might choose, only one, which we have called $Y(0)$, exactly matches the total quantity of goods and services that households, firms, and the government want to buy. If the decisions of firms lead them to produce at $Y(0)$, then the quantity they produce will just match aggregate expenditure. This is illustrated numerically in figure 21.7, which is nothing more than a review of the circular flow of GNP we first illustrated in chapter 19. Figure 21.7 shows how the situation depicted in figure 21.1 would turn out to be one of equilibrium in the aggregate market for goods and services. The level of planned consumption generated by aggregate real income of $200 billion equals $130 billion. Government expenditure on goods and services exactly equals net taxes ($20 billion). Therefore, if planned investment happens to equal $50 billion, then planned expenditure will be $200 billion, exactly the amount of GNP produced.

Returning to figure 21.6, suppose that firms choose to produce a level of real GNP, call it $Y(1)$, that is greater than planned aggregate expenditure. This leads to a situation where firms cannot sell all they have produced and therefore cut back on their production. Real GNP falls, and some workers will lose their jobs.

The story is reversed if firms' decisions lead them to produce at a real GNP level that is less than planned aggregate expenditure, call it $Y(2)$. In this case, society demands more goods and services than firms have produced. Production and/or prices will increase as buyers bid for the items they desire and firms try to meet sales that exceed their projections.

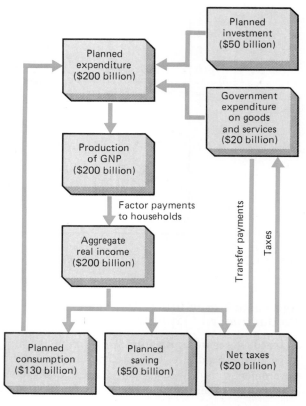

Figure 21.7   A numerical example of equilibrium GNP
With net taxes equal to government expenditures, GNP = $200 billion will be an equilibrium level of GNP if planned investment happens to equal $50 billion. Only then will planned aggregate expenditure, $\dot{E}$, exactly equal $200 billion, the amount of GNP produced.

In summary, given planned investment, government expenditure, net taxes, and the consumption function, there is only *one* level of real GNP that is an equilibrium. At equilibrium real GNP, firms sell what they had planned and buyers purchase exactly what they had planned. The aggregate market for goods and services is at a point of rest, so to speak. Equilibrium means that GNP will not change unless there is a change in one of the exogenous factors underlying planned aggregate expenditure. Should any of these factors change, planned investment for instance, so will equilibrium GNP. In chapter 25 we

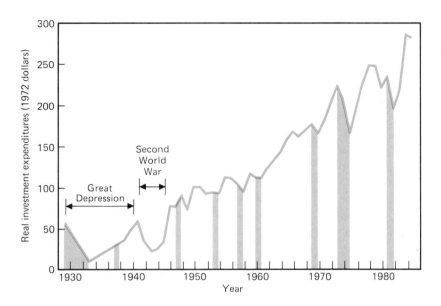

Figure 21.8   Swings in investment and business cycles in the United States, 1929–1985
From *Economic Report of the President*, 1986, Table B-16, p. 271.

discuss changes in investment and how they affect the macroeconomy, and in chapter 28 we look carefully at the role of investment spending during the Great Depression. For now let us give you some startling facts. Between 1929 and 1933 real aggregate investment (in 1972 dollars) fell from $55.8 billion to $8.4 billion, a decline of 85 percent. Not until 1941 did real investment again reach its 1929 levels. This severe reduction in investment between 1929 and 1933 contributed to the decline in aggregate expenditure that led to the period of substantial idle productive capacity and unemployment known as the Great Depression. The large swings in investment and their association with business cycles in the United States is illustrated in figure 21.8

Another Look at Equilibrium GNP: Saving, Investment, and the Government Deficit

In developing a full view of macroeconomic equilibrium, it will be very helpful to look at equilibrium in the aggregate market for goods and services from another perspective. In this view, the cornerstone of our analysis remains the relationship between the production of GNP and aggregate income. To review

briefly, remember that there are three ways for this income to be used: planned consumption, planned saving, and net tax payments. Remember, too, that planned aggregate expenditure has three components: consumption, investment, and government spending. Finally, remember that in equilibrium, planned production equals planned expenditure on GNP. This means that in equilibrium, planned spending on goods and services in the aggregate ($\overset{*}{E}$) is equal to the income people receive from producing these goods and services, which we have labeled Y(0).

As we have seen, planned aggregate expenditure is defined as planned consumption plus planned investment plus government expenditure, or

$$\overset{*}{E} \equiv \overset{*}{C} + \overset{*}{I} + G.$$

Similarly, income can be broken down into its three components of planned consumption, planned saving, and net taxes paid so that

$$Y \equiv \overset{*}{C} + \overset{*}{S} + T.$$

(We do not use the asterisk (*) over the Y, because we assume that producers always carry out their production plans exactly.) When there is equilibrium GNP, production equals planned aggregate expenditure, or

$$\overset{*}{E} = Y(0).$$

This is the same as saying that planned consumption plus planned investment plus government expenditure equals planned consumption plus planned saving plus net taxes, or

$$\overset{*}{C} + \overset{*}{I} + G = \overset{*}{C} + \overset{*}{S} + T.$$

Note that we have used the equality sign ($=$) in the preceding two expressions. This is because planned production and planned expenditure are *not* the same variable. They are *equal* to each other *only* when the aggregate market for goods and services is in equilibrium.

We can gain further insight into equilibrium GNP by noting that planned consumption ($\overset{*}{C}$) appears on both sides of the equation. Thus, we can subtract it from both sides. If we also subtract net taxes (T) from both sides, we see that in equilibrium, planned saving must equal planned investment plus the difference between government spending and net taxes, or

$$\overset{*}{I} + (G - T) = \overset{*}{S}.$$

If government spending (G) exceeds net taxes (T), then G − T is positive, and we say there is a *government deficit*. If the opposite holds true, then there is a *government surplus. We conclude that equilibrium GNP can be described as the level of GNP where investment plus the government deficit equals society's intended saving.*

Now, to clinch your understanding of this important relationship between planned investment, the government deficit, and planned saving, go back and review figure 21.7. There we have assumed that the government's budget is balanced, so that G − T = 0. Consequently, equilibrium in the aggregate market

for goods and services requires that planned investment equal planned saving. In figure 21.7, planned investment and planned saving are both $50 billion, and equilibrium prevails.

Another way to think about the relationship between planned saving, planned investment, the government deficit, and equilibrium GNP is this. When people save or pay taxes, they are withdrawing funds from the flow of GNP-income-consumption-GNP that is illustrated in figure 21.7. Sometimes, saving and taxes are therefore called "leakages" from the flow of income and expenditure described in our model of the goods and services market. On the other hand, the government and investors "inject" funds back into income-expenditure flow. Therefore, equilibrium in the aggregate market for goods and services requires that "injections" into the flow of expenditure and income equal "leakages" out of the flow. In this terminology, net taxes constitute a leakage, too, whereas government expenditure is an injection. Another comparison that may help you understand equilibrium GNP is to think of it as similar to the level of water in a lake. If the water level does not rise or fall, we can say that the lake is in equilibrium. But what does this require? An equilibrium lake level results when the amount of water flowing in (injections) is exactly equal to the amount that flows (leaks) out or evaporates.

It should be clear that if the level of government spending or planned investment were to change, the situation depicted in figure 21.7 would no longer be one of equilibrium. That is, if either government expenditure or planned investment were to increase, the equilibrium level of GNP would no longer be $200 billion because planned expenditure would exceed that amount. Similarly, if either planned investment or government spending were to fall, firms would be unable to sell all their output if they produced GNP worth $200 billion. In both these situations, the equilibrium level of GNP would change. In the next section we will see exactly how equilibrium GNP relates to the level of planned investment and government expenditure. This relationship is called the *multiplier,* for reasons that you will soon understand.

The Multiplier   To begin, we will work through a simple numerical example showing just how much equilibrium GNP would change if planned investment or government spending were to change in figure 21.7. For instance, suppose planned investment increases *permanently* by $10 billion per year, to $60 billion. This will upset the equilibrium flow of income, consumption, investment, government spending, and taxes. Planned investment plus the government deficit will now exceed planned saving by exactly $10 billion, and there will be excess planned expenditure. GNP will begin to rise. Increased GNP leads to increased disposable income and, hence, an increase in planned consumption expenditure. When more consumption goods are produced, a further increase in GNP and disposable income results, leading to a further, somewhat smaller increase in planned consumption expenditure. This chain of increased consumption expenditure, increased income, and further increased planned consumption continues until the goods market is once again in equilibrium. (Can you explain why each subsequent increase in planned consumption is smaller than the last?) Equilibrium will be restored only when planned saving is once again equal to planned investment plus the government deficit. An increase in GNP can eventually restore equilibrium because planned saving rises as GNP increases. The aggregate market for goods and services will return to equilibrium when planned saving has risen by exactly $10 billion, which was the initial increase in planned investment.

We can calculate exactly the amount GNP must increase before planned saving increases by $10 billion by referring back to table 21.1 on page 442. In table 21.1, we see that for every dollar increase in GNP, planned saving increases by $0.40. This relationship between changes in planned saving and changes in GNP is called the **marginal propensity to save (MPS)**. Because an increase in disposable income must be either saved or consumed, the marginal propensity to save is nothing more than one minus the marginal propensity to consume (the fraction b). Symbolically,

$$\text{MPS} \equiv 1 - \text{MPC} \equiv 1 - b.$$

Using our knowledge that the marginal propensity to consume in the numerical example in table 21.1 is 0.6, we see that the marginal propensity to save is 0.4. Thus, planned saving will rise by $10 billion when GNP increases by $25 billion ($25 billion x 0.4 = $10 billion). Only at this new equilibrium level of GNP will leakages from the circular income-expenditure flow once again equal injections.

Notice that the increase in GNP needed to restore equilibrium in the aggregate market for goods and services is much larger than the initial increase in planned investment. It is, in fact, 2.5 times as large. The change in GNP divided by the initial change in planned investment equals 2.5. This ratio is **the multiplier** we mentioned at the end of the preceding section. A little simple arithmetic will show you that *the multiplier equals the reciprocal of the marginal propensity to save, or 1/MPS*. Symbolically, in terms of our example,

$$\text{the multiplier} \equiv \Delta Y(0)/\Delta I = 1/\text{MPS} = 2.5.$$

The multiplier relationship is also useful for analyzing the influence of government policy on planned expenditure. For example, if government expenditure in figure 21.7 rose by $10 billion, *cet. par.* equilibrium GNP would increase to $225 billion. This effect of an increase in government expenditure on equilibrium GNP is exactly the same as the effect of a $10 billion increase in planned investment in the preceding example. Can you explain why? What do you think would happen if the increase in GNP required to restore equilibrium were greater than the economy's productive capacity? Can you explain what would happen to equilibrium GNP if planned investment or government expenditure were to *decline* by $10 billion?

Interestingly, a reduction in net taxes will also raise planned expenditure, but by a somewhat smaller amount than an equal increase in government expenditure. For example, suppose that in figure 21.7, net taxes fall by $10 billion with government expenditure unchanged. This means that the government deficit (G − T) rises by $10 billion, and planned investment plus the deficit will now exceed planned saving by $10 billion. The aggregate goods and services market will no longer be in equilibrium, and equilibrium will be restored only when planned saving increases by $10 billion.

The difference between the multiplier effect of a $10 billion increase in government expenditure and a $10 billion decrease in taxes lies in their initial impact on total expenditure and saving. Whereas the increase in government expenditure has no *direct* impact on saving and increases total expenditure on GNP by $10 billion, the reduction in taxes has two *direct* impacts. One is to increase exogenous consumption by $10 billion multiplied by the MPC (0.6), and the other is directly to increase planned saving by $10 billion multiplied by the MPS (0.4).

Now, we know that planned saving must increase by $10 billion before equilibrium GNP is restored. Since the direct impact of a tax reduction is to increase planned saving by $4 billion, GNP need increase only by enough to get planned saving the rest of the way to $10 billion. How much does GNP have to increase to raise planned saving an additional $6 billion? The marginal propensity to save tells all. If GNP increases by $15 billion, planned saving will increase by $15 billion x 0.4, or $6 billion. Prove to yourself that this is correct. Notice that $15 billion equals $25 billion (the increase in equilibrium GNP when either government expenditure or planned investment increases by $10 billion) multiplied by 0.6—the marginal propensity to consume! In other words, the multiplier effect of a *reduction* in taxes is

$$-(\Delta Y(0)/\Delta T) = b/MPS.$$

(Remember that ΔT is a *negative* quantity when taxes are *reduced*.) Since the marginal propensity to consume, b, is less than 1, this tax multiplier is smaller than the multiplier effect of an increase in government expenditure or planned investment. What will happen to equilibrium GNP if government transfer payments increase by $10 billion?

A Final Look at Equilibrium GNP   We can now take a brief, final look at equilibrium GNP that will graphically illustrate what equilibrium looks like in terms of planned saving, planned investment, and the government deficit. To begin, we need to show more formally how planned saving is related to GNP. The relationship between planned saving and GNP is called the **saving function,** and it is a kind of mirror image of the consumption function.

To derive the saving function, review table 21.1 on page 442 once again. Notice, for example, that when GNP rises from $100 billion to $120 billion, planned saving rises from $10 billion to $18 billion, or by $8 billion. If GNP were to fall from $100 billion to $25 billion, planned saving would fall from $10 billion to −$20 billion. In other words, at this very low level of GNP, there would be *dissaving*. Notice that the change in planned saving divided by the change in GNP is always $\Delta S/\Delta Y \equiv MPS = 0.4$. This logic shows us that if GNP were to fall to zero from $25 billion, planned saving would drop even further, by $25 billion x 0.4, or $10 billion, to −$30 billion. In other words, there would be dissaving of $30 billion. (Of course, GNP never actually falls to zero. The saving function tells us, mathematically, what planned saving would be under these imaginary circumstances.) We have already seen that if GNP were to fall to zero, planned consumption would remain positive. We called this *exogenous consumption* and denoted it by the symbol A. Similarly, when GNP equals zero, the quantity of planned saving is called *exogenous saving*. In the example in table 21.1, exogenous saving is negative. This follows from the fact that exogenous consumption is positive and consumption equals disposable income less saving. The saving function tells us that planned saving equals exogenous saving plus endogenous saving, just as the consumption function tells us that planned consumption equals exogenous consumption plus endogenous consumption. Symbolically, we can write the saving function as

$$\overset{*}{S} = -A' + (1 - b)Y,$$

where $-A'$ stands for exogenous saving (which is negative) and $(1 - b)Y$ is endogenous saving, or the marginal propensity to save multiplied by GNP. In terms of the table 21.1 example, $-A' = -\$30$ billion and $1 - b = 0.4$.

We will now illustrate equilibrium GNP with a diagram that contains the saving function. The horizontal line in figure 21.9 depicts planned investment plus the government deficit, and the upward-sloping line labeled $\overset{*}{S}$ is the saving function. The point at which the saving function intersects the horizontal line that represents planned investment plus the government deficit marks equilibrium GNP.

What happens when planned saving exceeds planned investment plus the deficit? This is equivalent to an excess of production over planned aggregate expenditure. To see this, we need simply restate the relationship between planned expenditure and production when production is greater than planned expenditure:

$$Y > \overset{*}{E},$$

or,

$$\overset{*}{C} + \overset{*}{S} + T > \overset{*}{C} + \overset{*}{I} + G.$$

When production rises above planned expenditure, we see that planned consumption plus planned saving plus net taxes will exceed the sum of planned consumption, planned investment, and government spending. This boils down to planned saving exceeding planned investment plus the government deficit, or

$$\overset{*}{S} > \overset{*}{I} + (G - T).$$

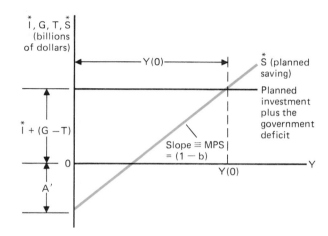

Figure 21.9   Aggregate expenditure in terms of planned saving, planned investment, and the government deficit
Equilibrium GNP, Y(0), occurs at the point where the saving function (the planned saving line) crosses the line representing planned investment plus the government deficit.
   If planned saving exceeds planned investment plus the government deficit, then production exceeds Y(0), and GNP and employment will fall. If planned saving is less than planned investment plus the government deficit, then production is less than Y(0), and production, employment, and/or the price level will increase.

Using the same analysis, we can see that when planned saving is *less* than planned investment plus the government deficit, we have planned expenditure *greater* than aggregate production, and business firms will be able to sell more than they have produced.

To summarize, when planned saving exceeds planned investment plus the government deficit, then production exceeds Y(0), and GNP and employment will tend to fall because firms will not be able to sell all they have produced. When planned saving is less than planned investment plus the deficit, production will be less than firms can sell, and production, employment, and/or the price level will increase.

The National Income Accounts: Measured Saving, Measured Investment, the Government Deficit, and Measured GNP

The national income accounts published by the United States government contain separate entries for aggregate investment, saving, government spending, taxes, and transfer payments. Can we compare all of these numbers published in the national income accounts to determine the state of equilibrium or disequilibrium in the aggregate market for goods and services? The answer is no.

The reason that the national income accounts do not provide direct information on the state of equilibrium or disequilibrium in the aggregate market for goods and services arises from the way the accounts are constructed. In the GNP accounts, measured saving is *always* equal to measured investment plus the government deficit (and net exports, which we have temporarily ignored in this chapter). In other words, the national income or GNP accounts do not identify the *planned* behavior of business firms and households in our economy. They simply measure the purchases and sales that have actually taken place. A numerical example may be useful.

Consider a fictitious country with national income accounts constructed in the same way as in the United States. This fictitious country has planned aggregate expenditure equal to $125 billion, but aggregate production is only $110 billion. Thus there is excess aggregate expenditure of $15 billion. Let us suppose that this occurs because $\overset{*}{S} = \$25$ billion while $\overset{*}{I} = \$30$ billion and $G - T = \$10$ billion. Despite this excess, we will assume that everyone is successful in carrying out planned purchases because firms carry inventories of goods that were produced in previous years. The national income accounts in our fictitious country will show that *measured* investment equals $15 billion, even though *planned* investment equals $30 billion. The reason is that investment is defined to include both the production of new investment goods *and* the change in the firms' inventories.

In our example, producers' inventories will fall by $15 billion because firms sell $125 billion worth of goods and services but produce output worth only $110 billion.

A reduction in inventories is treated as negative investment in the national income accounts. Although *we* know that this inventory reduction is contrary to the intentions of the producers in the economy, the accounts do not make any distinction between planned and actual behavior. The national income accounts in our example will report $30 billion worth of goods sold as investment goods and $15 billion worth of goods subtracted from inventories. In terms of the national income accounts, *measured* investment is $30 billion − $15 billion = $15 billion. This is how measured investment plus the government deficit equals $25 billion, which is also *measured saving*.

Similar situations will occur when planned aggregate expenditure is less than GNP. The difference is that in the case of excess aggregate production, additions to inventories, while unplanned, will be treated as a positive act of investment in the national income accounts. Measured saving will again be precisely equal to measured investment plus the government deficit. To summarize the point of this section, *GNP figures on investment, saving, government deficit (and net exports) tell us nothing about the state of disequilibrium in the aggregate market for goods and services.* These items *always* balance in the national income accounts.

Can you work through an example, using the same level of planned expenditure and production, but assuming that households and firms are *unable* to purchase goods and services in excess of actual production? What would the GNP accounts look like? Whose *measured* behavior (consumption, investment, etc.) would represent actual plans and whose would represent disequilibrium—a deviation of actual from intended expenditures or production?

▶ Summary and Conclusions

This chapter develops the concept of equilibrium in the aggregate market for goods and services. It is not an analysis of the entire macroeconomy; rather, it deals with only *one* of its aggregate markets. Nevertheless, you should now have a clearer picture of the frustration faced by the visiting economic expert in the introduction to this chapter. In order to analyze how the aggregate goods and services market works, accurate data on gross national product and its components are absolutely essential. The following points were discussed.

Consumption is a key component of aggregate expenditure. Consumption is generally less than total income because consumers pay taxes and save.

Equilibrium in the aggregate market for goods and services occurs when planned aggregate expenditure by consumers, firms, and the government coincides with the aggregate quantity of goods and services produced.

When discussing government policy in later chapters it will be convenient to have an alternative way of describing equilibrium aggregate expenditure for goods and services. This is that equilibrium planned aggregate expenditure is the level of aggregate income at which planned saving equals planned investment plus the government deficit.

The equilibrium level of GNP can be expressed as the product of the multiplier and an expression containing the exogenous components of planned expenditure.

When society produces fewer goods and services than consumers, firms, and the government seek to buy, this leads to increases in production, employment, and/or the price level as buyers seek to purchase more goods and services and firms try to meet their demands.

When firms produce more goods and services than society seeks to purchase, this leads to reduced production and employment as firms cut back on their production.

The national income accounts of the United States contain information on actual expenditures and production. They do not contain information that directly tells us what planned expenditure or production was in a year.

▶ Key Terms

consumption function *441*

disposable income (YD) *441*

dissaving *443*

endogenous consumption *441*

equilibrium real GNP *449*

exogenous consumption *441*

45° line *444*

full-employment GNP *440*

marginal propensity to consume (MPC) *444*

marginal propensity to save (MPS) *453*

the multiplier, exogenous expenditure multiplier *453*

planned aggregate expenditure ($\overset{*}{E}$) *449*

saving *440*

saving function *454*

▶ Questions for Discussion and Review

1. What are the components of expenditure?
2. What determines the amount of investment firms make? Is it reasonable to treat investment as independent of *current* output (real GNP)? Through what avenues does government policy influence investment? Is the following statement consistent with our treatment of investment as exogenous:
   Investment depends, in part, on last year's GNP. Explain.
3. Explain the concept of equilibrium real GNP. Describe equilibrium real GNP in a diagram.

4. Suppose that there is a country with
$$\overset{*}{C} = 10 + 0.9(Y - T)$$
$$T = 10$$
$$\overset{*}{I} = 25$$
$$G = 10$$
where the numbers represent billions of dollars. Show that the equilibrium aggregate expenditure on goods and services is $360 billion.

5. Take the data in question 4 and use it to derive a saving function. On the basis of this expression, what is the value for the marginal propensity to save?

6. A hypothetical country's macroeconomy is described by the following information
$$\overset{*}{S} = -10 + 0.1(Y - T)$$
$$\overset{*}{I} = 25$$
$$T = 10$$
$$G = 10$$
Solve for its equilibrium GNP. Show that the aggregate market for goods and services in this economy is *identical* to that in question 4.

7. During the Great Depression saving was thought to be "bad" because it held down aggregate expenditure. Newspaper articles often say that saving is "good" for the macroeconomy. Can it be true that saving is both good *and* bad for the macroeconomy? Discuss.

8. True or false? The macroeconomy is always in equilibrium because the national income accounts show that saving *always* equals investment. Explain your answer carefully.

9. Using the hypothetical model in question 4, solve for the exogenous spending multiplier. What is the tax multiplier equal to in this model?

10. Using the same model as in question 4, let taxes depend on income ($T = tY$ where t is a constant). Now solve for the exogenous spending multiplier. How does this compare with the exogenous spending multiplier in your answer to question 9?

A Deeper Look at the Multiplier and Graphical Analysis

We can develop a deeper understanding of the multiplier by using the equilibrium relationship between planned saving and planned investment plus the government deficit. This will provide additional insight into how changes in planned investment, government spending, or net taxes affect GNP, employment, and unemployment.

First, we will derive the saving function somewhat more rigorously than we did in chapter 21. Recall that saving is defined as what remains after net taxes are paid and planned consumption expenditure is carried out, or

$$\overset{*}{S} \equiv Y - T - \overset{*}{C}.$$

We also need to remember that planned consumption consists of exogenous consumption plus endogenous consumption as described by the consumption function

$$\overset{*}{C} = A + bY.$$

If we substitute the consumption function in the definition of saving above, we can derive the saving function as follows. By substituting the consumption function for $\overset{*}{C}$ in the preceding definition of saving, we obtain

$$\overset{*}{S} = Y - T - A - bY.$$

When we combine the two terms that have Y in them, we obtain the saving function,

$$\overset{*}{S} = -A - T + (1 - b)Y,$$

which says that planned saving depends on GNP, (Y), exogenous consumption multiplied by -1, and net taxes. Remember, in our simple model of the aggregate goods market, taxes are exogenous; that is, taxes do not change with the level of GNP. Because both A (exogenous consumption) and T are independent of the level of GNP, it will simplify things if we combine them into a new term, A', where

$$A' = A + T,$$

so that the saving function can be written as

$$\overset{*}{S} = -A' + (1 - b)Y,$$

which is the saving function specified in chapter 21.

The next step in our in-depth analysis of the multiplier is to substitute the saving function in the equation for equilibrium GNP, which tells us that in equilibrium, planned saving must equal planned investment plus the government deficit:

$$\underbrace{\overset{*}{I} + (G - T)}_{\substack{\text{planned investment} \\ \text{plus govt. deficit}}} = \underbrace{-A' + (1 - b)Y.}_{\text{planned saving}}$$

We can now show how rewriting the equation for equilibrium GNP leads the way to a deeper understanding of how planned investment and government spending affect equilibrium GNP. We need only solve the above equation for Y. First, we move the one term with Y in it, $(1 - b)Y$, to the left-hand side of the equation, then we place all of the other terms on the right-hand side and multiply both sides of the equation by -1. Then, we divide through by $1 - b$. This gives us the following equation describing equilibrium gross national product:

$$Y = [A' + \overset{*}{I} + (G - T)]/(1 - b).$$

Now, recall that $A' = A + T$. Therefore, the expression above can be further simplified to

$$Y = [A + \overset{*}{I} + G]/(1 - b) = Y(0), \text{ or}$$

equilibrium GNP =

$$\frac{\substack{\text{exogenous} \\ \text{consumption}} + \substack{\text{planned} \\ \text{investment}} + \substack{\text{government} \\ \text{spending}}}{\text{marginal propensity to save}}.$$

To further simplify the above expression for equilibrium GNP, we can use the expression Y (0) to denote equilibrium GNP and EX to stand for all of the *exogenous* variables, G, $\overset{*}{I}$, and A. Then we can rewrite it simply as

$$Y(0) = EX/(1 - b).$$

This equation says that equilibrium GNP depends on two major variables. The first major variable, which we have named EX, includes all of the components of exogenous expenditures on GNP—exogenous consumption, planned investment, and government spending. The second major variable is the marginal propensity to save. More precisely, equilibrium GNP equals EX multiplied by the ratio $1/(1 - b)$, which as we have already seen, is the multiplier.

To make sure that you understand the multiplier equation, we will show how it applies to the numerical example in table 21.1 and figure 21.7. We have claimed that the level of GNP in figure 21.7 is an equilibrium value, because

planned saving equals planned investment plus the government deficit. If this is true, then we should be able to show that the level of GNP, $200 billion, equals EX times the multiplier. From table 21.1 and figure 21.7, we see that exogenous consumption equals $10 billion and planned investment plus government spending equals $70 billion, yielding a total value for EX equal to $80 billion. The MPC equals 0.6, the MPS—$(1 - \text{MPC})$—equals 0.4, so the multiplier, $1/0.4$, equals 2.5. EX $\times$ the multiplier is $80 billion $\times 2.5 = 200$ billion, which is the level of GNP shown in figure 21.7. Thus, figure 21.7 does represent equilibrium in the aggregate market for goods and services.

There is nothing mysterious about the conclusion that equilibrium GNP depends on exogenous expenditure and the multiplier. It is just an *alternative* way of describing the situation in which society's planned expenditure on goods and services exactly matches aggregate production.

Figure 21.9 also shows how equilibrium GNP relates to exogenous expenditure and the multiplier. To see this, take the following steps. (1) First note that the point at which the saving function cuts the vertical axis lies below the zero line by the amount $A' = A + T$. This is the quantity that appears (with a minus sign in front of it) as the first, bracketed term of the saving function on p. 455. (2) Now add this quantity to planned investment plus the government deficit. The result is the quantity EX in the multiplier equation. That is, the distance from the point that the saving function intersects the vertical axis up to the horizontal line representing planned investment plus the government deficit equals EX. You may wish to mark the distance EX on your copy of figure 21.9. (3) Next note that the slope of the saving function, which is the MPS, $(1 - b)$, can be expressed as the ratio of the two quantities EX and Y(0). Therefore, the multiplier, $1/(1 - b)$ equals $Y(0)/EX$. (4) Finally, you can see that the multiplier equation on p. 453 is equivalent to

$$Y(0) = EX \times Y(0)/EX.$$

To show how the multiplier works from a somewhat different perspective, figure 21.A presents a numerical example. The data in this example are somewhat different from those in table 21.1 and figure 21.7. Figure 21.A shows how a *change* in exogenous expenditure, such as an increase in planned investment, affects production *over time* as the economy gradually approaches the new equilibrium level of GNP. When the new equilibrium is finally attained, the change in GNP compared to the original equilibrium GNP equals the change in exogenous expenditure multiplied by the multiplier.

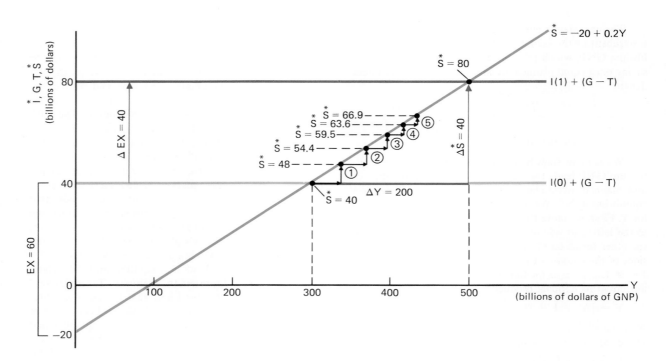

	ΔEX	ΔY	$\Delta\overset{*}{C}$	$\Delta\overset{*}{S}$	$\Delta\overset{*}{E}$ = ΔEX + ΔC	
Start	40	0	0	0	40	
1st round	40	40	32	8	72	
2nd round	40	72	57.6	14.4	97.6	
3rd round	40	97.6	78.1	19.5	118.1	(all changes measured
4th round	40	118.1	94.5	23.6	134.5	in comparison to their
5th round	40	134.5	107.6	26.9	147.6	initial equilibrium
6th round	40	147.6	118.1	29.5	158.1	values)
7th round	40	158.1	126.5	31.6	166.5	
8th round	40	166.5	133.2	33.3	173.2	
9th round	40	173.6	138.6	34.6	178.6	
•	•	•	•	•	•	
•	•	•	•	•	•	
•	•	•	•	•	•	
Final round (new equilibrium)	40	200.0	60.0	40.0	200.0	

Figure 21.A   The multiplier

In this example, the saving function tells us that planned saving equals −$20 billion plus 0.2 times GNP, or

$$\dot{S} = -20 + 0.2 \text{ GNP}.$$

Planned investment plus the government deficit equals $40 billion. Therefore, the quantity EX equals $40 billion plus $20 billion, or $60 billion. Using the multiplier formula tells us that equilibrium GNP, Y(0), must be $60 × 1/0.2 = $60 × 5 = $300 billion.

Now suppose that a $40 billion increase in planned investment raises the value of EX from $40 billion to $80 billion. The multiplier formula tells us that the resulting *change* in equilibrium GNP will be

$$\Delta Y = \Delta EX \times 5 = \$40 \times 5 = \$200.$$

The new equilibrium GNP will be $500 billion.

It is helpful in understanding how the economy reaches the new level of GNP to think of the changes in planned expenditure as occurring in "rounds" or steps as follows. To start, as shown in the diagram, planned investment expenditure increases by $40 billion, resulting in an increase in planned aggregate expenditure, $\dot{E}$, of the same amount. This increase in exogenous expenditure means that firms could have sold $40 billion more output than they have produced. Thus, in the first round, they increase their production, Y, by $40 billion. Because income has risen by $40 billion, planned saving and consumption now increase. Since the MPS is 0.2, we know that the MPC is 0.8. Therefore, in the first round, there is an increase in planned consumption equal to 0.8 × $40 billion, or $32 billion. There is increased planned saving of 0.2 × $40 billion, or $8 billion. While planned saving has risen to $48 billion, this is still less than the new amount of planned investment plus the government deficit ($80 billion).

Now you should be able to see how consumption expenditure and saving increase in the second and subsequent rounds. Firms had not expected to be able to sell $32 billion additional output, so they have unfilled orders for their output at the end of the first round. Responding to this excess of desired expenditure over production, firms increase production by $32 billion, which leads to $32 billion increased income and, in the second round, a *further* increase of 0.8 × $32 billion = $25.6 billion *more* planned consumption and $6.4 billion *additional* planned saving. Planned saving has now risen by a total of $14.4 billion, to $54.4 billion.

The amount that planned saving increases during each round is shown graphically up through the 5th round. As you can see, at each step, planned consumption and planned saving increase by smaller and smaller amounts as GNP, planned consumption, and planned saving approach their new equilibrium values. By the ninth round, planned saving has risen $34.6 billion over its original value, to $74.6 billion. This is 86.5 percent of the amount that planned saving must rise to reach its new equilibrium value of $80 billion. In equilibrium, planned saving will have increased by exactly the amount that planned investment has risen. Once again, planned aggregate expenditure will equal aggregate production.

Chapter 22

Money and the Banking System

Outline

I. Introduction *464*
II. The role of money *465*
   A. Money as a medium of exchange *465*
      1. The advantage of a monetary economy over a barter economy *465*
   B. Money as a unit of account *465*
   C. Money as a store of value *466*
   D. Monetary standards and the value of money *467*
III. The banking system and money *468*
   A. The balance sheet of a bank *469*
   B. How banks create money *470*
      1. Cash drain and multiple deposit expansion *473*
   C. The consolidated balance sheet of the banking system *474*
   D. The definitions of money in the United States economy *475*
      1. Are credit cards money? *476*
IV. Summary and conclusions *477*
V. Key terms *477*
VI. Questions for discussion and review *477*

Objectives

After reading this chapter, the student should be able to:

List and discuss the three functions of money.
Compare a commodity standard with a paper standard of money.
Describe how the banking system creates money through the process of multiple deposit expansion.
Give three official government definitions of money.
Explain why credit cards are not money.

*The **financial sector** consists of the economy's money and credit markets.*

Credit markets are markets in which loans of various time lengths are arranged between borrowers and lenders.

*A **bank** is a financial institution that accepts deposits and makes loans.*

*A **depository institution** accepts deposits from the general public and from other banks.*

▶ Introduction

There are two common sayings about how banks work. The first is that "a bank will only lend you money if you don't need it." Whether or not that saying strikes you as having an element of truth, it does make one wonder what role banks play in the economy when they lend money and why people borrow money. Could a bank really lend money if nobody needed it, and why would anyone borrow money if he or she did not need it? Why do we need money in a modern economy, and what role does the banking system play in meeting that need?

The second saying, which is sometimes attributed to the famous economist John Maynard Keynes, is that "if you owe a bank a dollar, the bank owns you; but if you owe a bank a million dollars, you own the bank." We cannot really judge the truthfulness of this observation unless we have some understanding of how banks work. What is it that a bank has to sell? How does a bank produce the services it offers, and do profit-maximizing banks work like other profit-seeking businesses?

*Complementing the macroeconomy's real sector is its **financial sector**, which includes the money and credit markets. **Credit markets** are where corporate bonds, stocks, United States Treasury bills, and other forms of debt are bought and sold. In this chapter we focus on money—what it is, its function in the economy, how it is produced, and its relationship to the real (non-financial) sector of the economy. The banking system plays a crucial role in the interactions between money, finance, and the markets for goods and services. Therefore, a fundamental task of this chapter is to spell out the place of banks in the macroeconomy. While almost everyone has a good idea of what a bank is, a definition is in order. Briefly, we shall refer to a **bank** as any institution that accepts deposits and makes loans. As savings and loan associations and credit unions fit this definition, we shall refer to them as banks, too. Because banks accept deposits, they are also called **depository institutions**.*

Money consists mainly of checking account balances owned by business firms and individuals (not those owned by banks and the government) plus paper money and coins (currency) outside banks' vaults.

A medium of exchange is something that is widely accepted by people in return for the sale of commodities or services or as payment for a loan.

A unit of account is the way in which an economy's prices are expressed (such as in dollars or yen).

▶ The Role of Money

The best way to understand the nature of money is to learn what functions it performs. We analyze these functions of money in the next few sections. Later we will outline the specific definitions of money in the United States economy, but for now, it is sufficient to know that in the United States and in most modern economies, **money** primarily consists of checking accounts, paper currency ("folding money"), and coins owned by the general public.

Money as a Medium of Exchange

If we were forced to choose the most important role of money, it would probably be its function as a **medium of exchange,** which is anything that members of society are commonly willing to accept in return for goods and services or in payment of debts. Money, by this definition, may include gold, silver, personal checks, or paper currency printed by a government agency. Various commodities other than gold and silver have also been used as money. For example, at various times and places, cattle, tobacco, stones, and seashells have all been used as money. Some of these commodities are used as money in primitive economies even today.

The Advantage of a Monetary Economy Over a Barter Economy

We saw in chapter 1 that modern, market economies are also monetary economies. It is inconceivable that the tremendous advantages of specialization could be obtained in a barter economy because in barter situations every transaction requires a mutual coincidence of wants. Without money, we would all have to produce much of what we consume, and our standard of living would be much closer to bare subsistence.

The essential difference between an item used in a barter exchange and a monetary transaction is whether it is valued for its intrinsic characteristics or simply because it can readily be exchanged in further transactions at a known value. Thus, if I trade my cow for your goat in today's economy, this does not mean that cattle are money. However, if you were to accept my cow simply because you and others find cows to be a convenient and efficient means of executing transactions, not because you want to own my cow as such, then cows would be a medium of exchange—money, in short.

With the money from the goods you buy, sellers pay their employees and suppliers, who in turn buy whatever *they* want. Only one party in each transaction must consider the quantity and quality of the particular goods or services bought. The other party is perfectly willing to accept money. With money, markets work smoothly and efficiently. Without it, in a barter economy, much time and material resources are required before anyone can exchange one commodity for another.

Money as a Unit of Account

When a society has adopted a currency as a medium of exchange, it is natural to use it also as the country's **unit of account,** the measure in which prices are denominated. Thus, in the United States, the dollar is not only the official currency, but prices are also stated in terms of dollars and cents. Curiosities and anachronisms occur, however. For example, prices in United States stock markets are denominated in *eighths* of a dollar, even though there is no combination of coins worth exactly 12 1/2 cents. This practice probably has historical roots in early Spanish coins called "pieces of eight" that could be cut into eight "bits" to make

Hyperinflation is an extremely rapid and continuous increase in the price level.

*A **store of value*** is any means of keeping wealth over time.

*A **monetary standard*** defines the basis of an economy's money.

transactions. Thus, the colloquial expression "two bits" for a quarter dollar is an informal unit of account in the United States. In the United Kingdom, before the pound was decimalized it consisted of twenty shillings, each containing twelve pence. Nevertheless, fashionable stores, high-class lawyers, and doctors to the rich quoted prices in *guineas*. In modern times, there has been no such thing as a guinea coin or note, and if you bought a coat for 100 guineas, you would write a check for 105 pounds because a guinea equaled twenty-one shillings.

An official currency may cease being used as a medium of exchange and a unit of account when legal price controls destroy its usefulness. For example, in occupied Germany at the end of World War II, price ceilings were so low and rigid that currency became useless in making transactions. For small purchases, cigarettes were much more useful. They were quite scarce and easily carried about, so it was easy to substitute cigarettes for currency and to measure prices in cigarettes rather than deutsch marks. Larger transactions were consummated with cognac. Milton Friedman, the Nobel Prize-winning economist and a historian of money, refers to cognac as "by all odds the most liquid currency of which we have record."[1]

Another example of a change in a monetary system, also from Germany, dates back to the almost unimaginable inflation following World War I. Between August 1922 and November 1923, the German price level increased by over *10,000,000,000 percent*. The German currency of the time became useless as a medium of exchange because its value was declining so rapidly. As a result, the United States dollar became the measure of prices until stability was restored.[2] Such extremely inflationary periods are called **hyperinflations.** The impact of hyperinflation on the German economy was very severe because transactions became difficult and the benefits of specialization in production were diminished. The resulting economic devastation was so great that it inspired Germany during World War II to try to sabotage the British economy by introducing counterfeit five-pound notes designed to cause hyperinflation in Great

Britain. One description of the impact of hyperinflation in Germany in the 1920s can be loosely quoted as follows: "We used to go shopping with our money in our pockets and our groceries in our wheelbarrow. Now, we go shopping with our money in our wheelbarrow and return home with our groceries in our pockets."

Money as a Store of Value

The principal purpose for adopting some kind of money as a medium of exchange is to achieve substantially lower costs of everyday transactions. There are two reasons why money achieves this goal. One, as we have seen, is that barter is generally very time-consuming. The second reason is that at the time at which a commodity is demanded, a purchaser may not have a good or service available for sale. Money allows purchases and income to be separated. When you place money in a drawer or put it in a checking account today so that you can spend it in the future, say, on a vacation or for your education, money serves as a **store of value.**

Of course, many commodities in addition to money serve as stores of value. Any asset that does not rot or wear out quickly can be a store of value and a means of transmitting purchasing power from one date to another. At different times in history, depending on economic conditions—particularly the expected rate of inflation and interest rates—money has been a relatively good or poor store of value. Some of the most important macroeconomic relationships we will discuss in later chapters relate to this issue. For example, the rapid rise in the prices of houses and of farmland in the United States in the late 1970s was to a considerable extent due to a switch from money to "real" assets as a store of value. This was a period of high inflation and low interest rates (restricted by law). Consequently, money depreciated in spending power as prices of goods rose, and lending money to others was unrewarding because of legal ceilings on interest rates. During the early 1980s, interest rates were deregulated and rose rapidly, while inflation was reduced greatly. Consequently, farmland and house prices declined dramatically.

Monetary Standards and the Value of Money

Whatever custom or law that determines a society's money is called its **monetary standard.** The standard that is adopted is of fundamental importance in determining how the financial sector of the economy relates to the nonfinancial (real) sector. When stones, cattle, tobacco, gold, silver, or some other commodity is used as money, we say that society has adopted a **commodity standard of money.**

It should be apparent why commodity monetary standards were adopted early in the economic history of the world. No central authority is needed to maintain a monetary system in which a commodity serves as the medium of exchange, unit of account, and store of wealth. Money under a commodity standard is produced as an ordinary economic activity. Any commodity will do as long as it serves as a satisfactory medium of exchange. Because of this, it should also be fairly obvious why such exotic standards as stones, tobacco, and cattle have never achieved wide popularity as monetary standards. Can you imagine using a cow to buy a candy bar from a vending machine? How many boulders would you have to carry to your bursar's office to pay your tuition? Could tobacco or some other readily reproducible commodity serve as money for long without strict limitations on the amount farmers could plant and harvest? Could such restrictions be efficiently enforced without martial law?

Gold and silver have had nearly universal appeal as monetary standards because of the ease of making them into coins, their high value per unit of weight, and the relative difficulty of producing more. This means that a precious metal fulfills the functions of money very efficiently compared to most other commodities. Why do you suppose that diamonds have not been a popular monetary standard?

Even though no modern society today uses money based on a commodity standard, nearly all modern monetary systems have evolved from systems based on commodities. This is reflected in the names of various currency units. For example, the *pound* and the *peso* both refer to a given weight of gold or silver. The term *dollar* dates back to Spanish and American coins made from silver. Modern economies have adopted monetary systems based on a **paper standard,** which means that the money society uses has no intrinsic value and that the government determines how much money is in circulation. Today's monetary systems use **fiat money,** from the Latin word *fiat* meaning "let it be." This means that money is whatever a government says it is.

What determines paper money's value, then? We have already seen that a government edict is not sufficient to give money value. The examples from Germany show that if one monetary standard ceases to be a useful medium of exchange, society will adopt another, regardless of what government officials say. Money's value, like any other commodity's, is based on its scarcity relative to society's desire for it, that is, on supply and demand. We have seen that without money, everyone's standard of living would be much lower than is attainable given available resources. Thus, the higher standard of living attainable in a monetary economy gives rise to the demand for money. Government's role in determining the value of fiat money is to make sure that people have *faith* that the money they accept today will be accepted later by others. This faith in the value of a particular currency is essential to maintain the demand for it.

With a commodity standard, such as gold, faith in the value of money is based on the well-known difficulty of creating more of it. To maintain faith in a paper standard, it must be clear that the government will not supply (produce) an unlimited amount. As with any other commodity, money's value will plummet toward zero if it ceases to become scarce. Because a dollar bill's value as a piece of paper (its commodity value) is far less than its exchange value as money, it is tempting for a government to print a lot of it to purchase goods and services or to buy political support. This is the principal danger with a paper standard. (Commodity standards are not immune from a practice called *debasing the currency,* which occurs when the government adds "base" materials, such as lead, to precious metals, such as gold, in its coinage as a means of increasing the amount it

Reserves consist of assets banks retain to pay their depositors when they wish to withdraw from their accounts. In today's banking system, reserves include a bank's cash on hand and demand deposits it holds in other banks. The most important component of commercial banks' reserves are deposits they hold with the central bank—the Fed in the United States.

The central bank is a nation's monetary authority and is responsible for determining the quantity of money under a paper monetary standard.

can spend.) As we will see in later chapters, the temptation for government to sacrifice the long-term benefits of maintaining the public's faith in the value of money for short-term political gains is a fundamental cause of macroeconomic difficulties—particularly inflation. In the remainder of this chapter we will see how the government and the banking system interact to determine the quantity of money under a paper standard.

► The Banking System and Money

The banking system is of fundamental importance in the production of paper money. Modern banks have arisen from two historical roots. One is early business firms (depository institutions) that accepted deposits of commodity money—particularly gold and silver—for safekeeping. The other root is wealthy families and firms that lent money to merchants and landowners who borrowed to finance their ventures or their consumption needs. Early depository institutions also soon developed into lending institutions. After all, depositors seldom withdrew their accounts all at once. In the meantime the firm holding the gold or silver could profit by lending part of the assets it held to eager borrowers willing to pay interest. It only needed to keep a *fraction* of its deposits as **reserves,** which are assets retained to pay customers who wish to withdraw their deposits. We shall soon see that an important feature of banks today is that they could not pay cash if all—or even a large number—of their depositors wanted to withdraw their deposits at the same time.

The banking systems of modern economies consist of two parts. The first part includes all of the banks that are the institutions most of us deal with in our everyday activities of depositing funds, borrowing

money, and so on. The second part consists of the **central bank,** which is responsible for regulating the commercial banks and controlling the quantity of money in the economy. The central bank is usually a branch of government or a semigovernmental institution. In the United States, the central bank is called the **Federal Reserve System,** or the **Fed** for short. We will study the role of the Fed in detail in chapter 23. In this chapter, we will deal mainly with the role of the banks other than Fed in the financial sector of the economy. When we use the term *bank,* we mean one of these banks unless we specifically refer to the Fed.

The crucial role of banks today is their ability to create money by adding to their depositors' checking accounts. Of course, banks do not credit our accounts because they enjoy playing Santa Claus. They do so only when we give them something of value in return. Either we must deposit funds, or we must give the bank a promise to repay at a future date the amounts it credits to our checking accounts, along with an additional payment of interest for the service it has provided. We will call this promise to repay a loan a **loan contract,** which is merely another expression for an IOU. The interest payments banks receive on the loan contracts they accept represent their principal source of revenue.

A loan contract is only one example of a **financial instrument,** which is a financial obligation between two parties. In general, financial instruments represent liabilities of governments, firms, or individuals to other governments, firms, or individuals. Another example of a financial instrument is a checking or savings account. When we deposit funds in a bank, a claim is created on the bank's assets, but this is not a loan contract in the sense usually meant by a loan. If we purchase stock in a new business firm, we buy still another type of financial instrument.

The **Federal Reserve System**, or Fed for short, is the central bank of the United States.

A **loan contract** is an agreement created when one party borrows from another. The financial instrument specifies a repayment schedule along with interest owed to the lender.

A **financial instrument** is an asset for one party and a liability for another party.

Demand deposits include any bank account from which the owner may demand immediate payment to the owner or to a third party by means of a check, telephone call, or telegram.

The Balance Sheet of a Bank

In order to see how banks create money, we need to examine a simplified version of the balance sheet of a typical bank. Remember that banks are institutions that make loans and accept deposits. In particular, we shall be concerned with a particular type of deposit called a demand deposit. **Demand deposits** are accounts that the owners may redeem *anytime* without financial penalty. Checking accounts are the most widely used form of demand deposits, but accounts that can be transferred by telegram or electronic systems also qualify. In recent years, savings and loan companies, savings banks, and other financial firms such as credit unions have received the legal right to establish demand deposit accounts. They are all banks by our definition and are therefore part of the banking system.

A simplified balance sheet for a bank is shown in table 22.1. Those of you who have taken an accounting course will know that a bank's balance sheet is similar to that of any business or individual in that it is based on the **basic accounting identity:**

Net worth ≡ assets − liabilities.

Simply put, what you are worth is defined as what you own less what you owe. This applies to banks, too.

We are primarily interested in the *composition* of a bank's assets and liabilities, which differs from other types of firms. In particular, a substantial component of banks' assets consists of loan contracts, and a substantial fraction of their liabilities consists of deposits. Over three-fourths of United States banks' assets consists of various kinds of loan contracts, and approximately the same fraction of their liabilities consists of checking accounts and other deposits.[3] Table 22.1, following accounting convention, lists all assets on the left-hand side of the balance sheet. Liabilities and net worth are listed on the right-hand side. The accounting identity assures that when we add up the items on the right side they always *exactly equal* the sum of all the items on the left.

We can now use the bank's balance sheet to become more precise in defining and measuring the quantity of money in our economy. Since money consists primarily of checking accounts plus currency and coins outside of banks' vaults, it follows that the demand deposit liabilities of each bank make up an important component of the quantity of money.

There is no reason in principle why *any* liability of a bank could not be used as money. As a matter of fact, it was not until 1913 that the right to issue paper currency was granted solely to agencies of the federal government. Before that time, authorized banks not only issued checking account liabilities but also their own notes, which circulated just as dollar and larger-denomination bills (Federal Reserve notes) do today.[4]

Table 22.1   A simplified balance sheet for a bank

Assets	Liabilities and net worth[a]
Loan contracts	Demand deposits
Reserves (checking account balances of the bank at the central bank, vault cash)	Time deposits[b] (some savings accounts, certificates of deposit, and similar accounts)
Physical assets (buildings and equipment)	IOU's payable to others (accrued payroll, taxes, borrowed funds)
	Net worth (stockholders' or owners' equity)

[a]Net worth is defined as assets minus liabilities.
[b]Time deposits cannot be withdrawn before a specified date without incurring a penalty.

*The **basic accounting identity** describes the structure of all balance sheets; it says that net worth is defined as the difference between assets and liabilities.*

Table 22.2	First FRK Bank balance sheet

First day of business

Assets		Liabilities and net worth
Office furniture	$25	Liabilities (none)
Cash (reserves)	25	Net worth $50

Second day of business

Loan contract	$10	Liabilities
Office furniture	25	Demand deposit $10
Cash (reserves)	25	Net worth $50

How Banks Create Money

To illustrate how a bank's liabilities form part of the nation's money stock, let us suppose that your authors were to use the royalties they receive from sales of this text to establish a bank. (In reality, it is necessary to obtain permission of state and sometimes federal regulatory agencies to open a bank.) Their goal is, of course, to earn profits. The balance sheet of the First FRK Bank on the first day of business is shown in table 22.2. Your authors have used their first royalty payment of $50 in cash to purchase $25 worth of office furniture and have retained $25 in cash for use as reserves. Just after lunch on the second business day, the bank's first and only customer asks to borrow $10. After checking the borrower's references and credit history, FRK agrees to accept the customer's loan contract (the customer's promissory note or IOU) for $10. The loan is completed by creating a checking account for the borrower and crediting it with $10. As a result of the bank's activities on its second business day, its assets and liabilities have both increased by $10.

Remember that the principal component of the money supply consists of demand deposits. By lending $10 to its first customer and creating a checking account (demand deposit) for the same amount, *the First FRK Bank has created a $10 increase in the economy's money supply.* Moreover, this transaction will lead to a chain of events that increases the money supply even more. To see how this happens, we will make the simplifying assumption that the entire banking system consists of two banks: the First FRK Bank and the Other Bank. Table 22.3 shows the balance sheets of the First FRK Bank and the Other Bank immediately following FRK's transaction creating the new $10 checking account outlined in the preceding paragraph. Since the Other Bank is a long-established bank, we will only show *changes* in its balance sheet in table 22.3, starting from the point at which FRK's first customer spends the borrowed money.

When FRK's customer spends the borrowed $10, the customer writes a check for $10. The payee deposits the check in an account with the Other Bank. In step 2 of table 22.3, we see that this results in changes for both FRK's balance sheet and that of the Other Bank. Upon receiving the deposit, the Other Bank presents the check to FRK for payment. FRK pays the Other Bank from its cash reserves, which fall to $15; at the same time, FRK charges (debits) its customer's checking account for $10, so that FRK's demand deposit liabilities fall back to zero. (In the banking system that now exists in the United States, FRK would have deposited most of its initial $25 in reserves with the Fed. The Other Bank would have sent the FRK customer's check to the Fed for collection, and the Fed would have paid the Other Bank by subtracting $10 from FRK's reserve account.) The Other Bank's assets have increased by $10 in cash. This cash is considered reserves by the Other Bank. We see that the money supply is still $10 higher than before the entire process started but that the new checking account balance of $10 is now located in the

Table 22.3   Multiple deposit expansion and the money supply

Balance sheet of First FRK Bank

Step 1—FRK lends $10 to its first customer

Assets		Liabilities and net worth	
Office furniture	$25	Liabilities	
Cash (reserves)	$25	Demand deposit	$10
Loan contract	$10		
		Net worth	$50

Balance sheet of First FRK Bank

Step 2—FRK's customer spends the borrowed money

Assets		Liabilities and net worth	
Office furniture	$25	Liabilities	
Cash (reserves)	$15	Demand deposit	$ 0
Loan contract	$10		
		Net worth	$50

Change in balance sheet of Other Bank

Assets		Liabilities and net worth	
Cash (reserves)	$10	Liabilities	
		Demand deposits	$10
		Net worth	$ 0

Change in balance sheet of Other Bank

Step 3—Other Bank uses its new reserves to lend $8 to a customer

Assets		Liabilities and net worth	
Cash (reserves)	$10	Liabilities	
Loan contracts	$ 8	Demand deposits	$18
		Net worth	$ 0

Balance sheet of First FRK Bank

Step 4—Other Bank's customer spends the borrowed money

Assets		Liabilities and net worth	
Office furniture	$25	Liabilities	
Cash (reserves)	$23	Demand deposit	$ 8
Loan contract	10		
		Net worth	$50

Change in balance sheet of Other Bank

Assets		Liabilities and net worth	
Cash	$ 2	Liabilities	
Loan contracts	$ 8	Demand deposits	$10
		Net worth	$ 0

Multiple deposit expansion means that when the banking system's reserves increase, the quantity of checking account liabilities can be increased by a larger amount.

The *money multiplier* is the ratio of the change in the quantity of money that results from a change in banks' reserves.

Other Bank rather than in the First FRK Bank, where it originated. At the same time, $10 in reserves has been transferred from FRK to the Other Bank.

The *increase* in the Other Bank's cash (reserves) of $10 now places it in a position where it can purchase a loan contract. It would like to do so because the interest it will collect will increase its profits. However, the Other Bank is unlikely to lend $10 to one of its customers. The reason is that the Other Bank fully expects the new checking account balance to be spent and that when this happens, the check may find its way to FRK. Moreover, the Other Bank is likely to want to be sure that it always has enough cash on hand to meet the demands of its customers for currency when they request it. Therefore the Other Bank lends only $8 as a result of the $10 increase in its reserves. This loan occurs in step 3 of table 22.3.

Compared to its situation before step 2, the Other Bank now has both assets and liabilities that are $18 greater. These changes consist of (1) an increase in cash assets of $10, (2) an increase in loan contracts of $8, and (3) an increase in demand deposits of $18. For the *banking system as a whole*, checking account liabilities have risen by $18 compared to the beginning of our example. The essential point of step 3 is that the initial increase in the money supply of $10 created by the First FRK Bank has led to an *additional* increase of $8 created by the Other Bank! Nor is this the end of the story.

In step 4 of table 22.3, we see that the Other Bank's customer has spent the borrowed money and the check has indeed been deposited in the First FRK Bank. FRK has collected its check from the Other Bank, so that its cash reserves are now $23, while its demand deposit liabilities are only $8. Therefore, FRK can buy new loan contracts, paying for them with new checking accounts or increases in existing checking accounts. This means that the money supply will continue to rise.

The process we have described in steps 1 through 4 of table 22.3 is called **multiple deposit expansion,** which means that an increase in banks' reserves will lead to an increase in banks' deposits and in the money supply that is a multiple (greater than 1) of the initial increase in reserves. The ratio of the additional quantity of money that results to an increase in reserves is called the **money multiplier.** We will have more to say about multiple deposit expansion and the money multiplier in chapter 23. Obviously, multiple deposit expansion must come to an end, or the money supply would grow without limit. Two factors limit multiple deposit expansion. The basic limit in the United States economy is that banks are required by regulations to maintain a certain ratio of reserves to their deposit liabilities; this means that, given their reserves, they cannot continue to buy loan contracts forever. In chapter 23, we will examine the way in which these reserve requirements operate. However, even in the absence of specific reserve requirements, it is unlikely that the banking system would generate an unlimited amount of money on its own. The reason for this is implicit in our description of the multiple deposit expansion process in steps 1 through 4 of table 22.3. It is that individual banks will always wish to retain their ability to honor their customers' (depositors') demands for cash withdrawals and the demands for payment that are created when a depositor writes a check that is deposited in another bank. The amount of reserves each bank desires will depend on the amount of deposits it has. Thus, even if they were not required to do so, banks would maintain their reserve balances at a certain fraction of their outstanding deposit liabilities. This means that, given their reserves, banks will limit the amount of loans they issue and the new money balances they create. To do otherwise would result in the risk that they would be unable to meet obligations to their customers (depositors) and to other banks. The need to retain the confidence of the public forces banks to limit the deposits they create, even though buying loan contracts is their principal source of income.

Cash Drain and Multiple Deposit Expansion

Our analysis of multiple deposit expansion has dealt only with one form of money—checking accounts. We have already noted, however, that another principal component of the money stock is currency held by the public. The desire of the public to hold currency affects the relationship between the addition of new reserves to the banking system and the amount of new money that is eventually created. The reason is that cash held by the public cannot be used at the same time by banks as reserves. Because the public's demand for cash, in addition to checking account money, reduces the size of the money multiplier, the relationship between the amount of money held by the public and its demand for cash results in what is called a **cash drain.**

A numerical example will help you see how cash drain reduces the money multiplier. Suppose that the public desires to hold 30 percent of its money in the form of cash. Thus, at step 2 of table 22.3, instead of $10 being deposited in the Other Bank, only $7 is deposited. The remainder, $3, is held as cash. The new reserves of the Other Bank are only 70 percent as large as they would be if there were no cash drain. Thus, it will make new loans of only $5.60 (80 percent of $7) instead of $8. The money supply has grown by $15.60 instead of $18 (the original FRK loan of $10 plus the Other Bank's new loan of $5.60). At the beginning of step 4 in table 22.3, the First FRK Bank receives a new deposit of only $3.92 (70 percent of $5.60) instead of $8. Thus, in step 4 of table 22.3, the First FRK Bank has reserves of only $18.92 instead of $23. Instead of excess reserves of $21.40, it has only $18.14. (Be sure you can calculate FRK's excess reserves.) If FRK uses all of its excess reserves to buy

new loan contracts, it can purchase only about $18 worth instead of over $21 worth. It is obvious that at each succeeding step, the amount of loans and new money created will be smaller than if there were no cash drain and that the money multiplier is reduced.*

---

*The money multiplier with cash drain is more complex than the simple money multiplier defined in the text. Let the public's desired currency holdings be determined as follows:

$$C = k(C + D),$$

where C represents currency holdings, D represents checking account money, and k is the fraction of its total money balances the public desires to hold as cash. We have already seen that checking account deposits are related to banks' reserves by the relationship

$$D = R/r,$$

where r represents the required reserve ratio and R represents bank reserves. We assume that banks will always increase their loans if they have excess reserves. By substituting the second expression for D into the first expression and combining terms, we derive the relationship

$$C = (R/r) \times k/(1 - k).$$

The next step is to define the ratio of the total money supply to the sum of currency plus bank reserves. (This sum is called the *monetary base,* which is discussed in the text on page 487.) This ratio is

$$(C + D)/(C + R).$$

When two preceding expressions for C and D are substituted into this ratio and the result is simplified, we derive the equation

$$(C + D)/(C + R) = 1/[k(1 - r) + r],$$

which is the money multiplier when there is a currency drain. When r and k are both fractions, this multiplier is clearly smaller than 1/r, the money multiplier when there is no currency drain. For example, if r = 0.1, the money multiplier without a currency drain is simply 1/0.1 = 10. However, if k = 0.3, the multiplier given by the formula we have developed here is only 1/(.3 × .9 + .1) = 2.7. The way to understand the formula is to think of the Fed as changing the monetary base when it engages in an open market operation, not simply bank reserves.

M1 includes all deposits (except those of the United States Treasury) in the banking system's consolidated balance sheet on which checks can *be written plus currency and traveler's checks in the hands of the nonbank public.*

Table 22.4   Consolidated balance sheet (millions of dollars) of the banking system, December 1985

The banking system[a]				
Assets			**Liabilities and net worth**	
1. Loan contracts			1. Deposits	
a. Non-United States government obligations[b]	1,614.6		a. Demand deposits	536.4
			b. Savings accounts	450.0
b. United States government obligations	249.9		c. Certificates of deposit and other time deposits[c]	777.1
2. Cash	211.6		2. Total liabilities	1,763.5
3. Other assets	189.4		3. Net worth	502.0
4. Total assets	2,265.5			

Source: From *Federal Reserve Bulletin*, March 1986. Column totals may not be exact due to rounding.

[a]Domestically chartered commercial banks.

[b]Includes obligations of states and subdivisions and commercial, industrial, and real estate loans.

[c]Certificates of deposit (CDs) are a special type of time deposit whereby the depositor agrees not to withdraw the funds during a specified time period, usually ninety days or more; a time deposit is a deposit that earns a fixed rate of interest over a specified time period with a substantial interest penalty for early withdrawal.

The Consolidated Balance Sheet of the Banking System

Table 22.3 presents a simplified picture of how individual banks interact to create new money balances through multiple deposit expansion. Now that we have seen how this process works, it will be easier to analyze the economy's financial sector if we view the banking system as a whole. Macroeconomics is aggregate economic analysis, and from now on, we will refer to the *aggregated,* or *consolidated,* balance sheet of the economy's banks in discussing the financial sector. In other words, we will treat the entire banking system as if it were one gigantic bank with a balance sheet of its own.

Consolidation involves *adding up* (aggregating) all of the individual banks' assets, liabilities, and net worths, but *not including* the assets of one bank that are liabilities of other banks in the system. For example, in table 22.3, we might have shown an intermediate step between steps 1 and 2, step 1a. At step 1a, FRK's customer would have spent the $10 it borrowed, and the check would have just been deposited

in the Other Bank. If the Other Bank were to *immediately* credit its depositor's account for $10 but were to delay a day in presenting the check to FRK for payment, the Other Bank's assets would not show an increase in cash of $10. Rather, its assets would show an increase in uncollected checks of $10, and the $10 in cash would still be shown on the books of FRK. At the same time, FRK would also have a *liability* in the form of a $10 demand deposit that would be eliminated as soon as it paid the Other Bank. If we were to *consolidate* the FRK and Other Banks' balance sheets at step 1a, the Other Bank's $10 uncollected check and FRK's $10 demand deposit would be eliminated. The consolidated balance sheet would show only the cash (reserve) assets of the two banks and the $10 demand deposit that is recorded as a liability of the Other Bank in step 2.

The consolidated balance sheet of the banking system contains only assets that are *not* claims of one bank on another bank within the system. Similarly, the liabilities in the consolidated balance sheet of the banking system consist only of obligations payable to individuals, firms, and governments *outside* the

M2 includes M1 plus "small" certificates of deposit, savings accounts, money market mutual fund accounts, and certain other

bank obligations that banks' depositors treat as readily available to carry out transactions.

M3 includes M2 plus "large" CD's and other deposits that are relatively liquid but are inconvenient to use in day-to-day transactions.

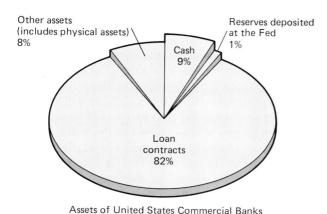

Assets of United States Commercial Banks

Figure 22.1   Assets of United States commercial banks
From *Federal Reserve Bulletin*, December 1985, Table 1-25.

banking system. Items inside the system cancel out. The consolidated balance sheet of the United States banking system is shown in table 22.4 and summarized in figure 22.1.

Figure 22.1 shows us that about 82 percent of the banking system's assets consist of *earning assets*— loan contracts on which the banks receive interest payments. In the banking system's assets, cash amounts to about 9 percent of the total and to only 12 percent of deposit liabilities. Obviously, if all depositors tried to withdraw the amounts credited to their checking accounts, savings accounts, and certificates of deposits all at once, there would not be nearly enough funds to pay them. Of course, individual depositors have no reason to cash in as long as they believe their deposits can either be converted to currency or used to carry out transactions as desired. A monetary system works as long as people believe it will work. In the next chapter, we will see how the banking system's ability to purchase loan contracts and create money balances is regulated in the United States.

The Definitions of Money in the United States Economy

We are now able to define money more precisely. We have seen that in most modern economies money consists of demand deposits plus paper currency and coin. In the United States there are three official government definitions of what constitutes our money supply, two of which are commonly used in media discussions of economic issues. The reason for multiple definitions is that savings accounts and other deposits are *substitutes* for checking accounts and currency in satisfying needs for the means to pay for transactions. Some economists prefer the government's narrowest definition of money, which excludes savings accounts and other deposits that are not available on demand. Others find the broader definitions more useful.

M1 includes all currency held by the general public, traveler's checks, and all bank deposits held by the general public on which checks can be written.

M2 includes M1 plus money market fund shares, savings accounts, and time deposits (certificates of deposit) up to $100,000, also called "small" time deposits, plus other highly liquid assets.

M3 which is a far less commonly used definition than M1 or M2, includes M2 plus "large" time deposits.[5]

Time deposits in excess of $100,000 are not included in M2 because they usually involve severe restrictions on when their owners can claim payment. Therefore, they are not very close substitutes for demand deposits and small savings and time deposits. Currency and deposits owned by the Fed, the banking system, or the federal government are *not* part of the money supply.

Money consists mainly of items that are liabilities on the banking system's consolidated balance sheet. One important item, however, is not a liability of privately held banks. This is currency, which consists mainly of Federal Reserve notes. **Federal Reserve notes** are our paper money, generally in $1, $5, $10, $20, $50, and $100 bills. Legally, Federal Reserve notes are liabilities of the Fed and are issued by the twelve Federal Reserve Banks in quantities sufficient to satisfy the public's demand for this form of money. However, suppose you went to your local Federal Reserve Bank and demanded payment for, say, a $20 bill. You might, if you persisted, receive the Fed's check for $20, which you could deposit in a checking or savings account at your bank. Traveler's checks issued by nonbanks such as American Express are not liabilities of either the banking system or the Fed. Coins are minted by the U.S. Treasury and do not constitute a claim on any financial institution.

Are Credit Cards Money?

Many of us carry "plastic money" in the form of at least one major credit card. Even if we pay the full balance every month, credit cards such as VISA, MasterCard, American Express, and Diner's Club are great conveniences because we can make purchases without having to worry about having enough cash in our wallets. Are credit cards money? You now have enough information to answer this question.

Suppose the First FRK Bank were to issue credit cards to its customers. These cards would allow their holders to purchase goods and services from participating firms without cash or writing a check. To see how a credit card purchase would affect the bank's balance sheet depicted in table 22.2, we will analyze what happens when someone uses a card to purchase a $25 dinner at a restaurant. When the credit card is presented to the waiter, a voucher is prepared that, when signed by the customer, creates a loan contract liability for $25 between the customer and the First FRK Bank. The restaurant presents a copy of the voucher to the bank, and the bank makes the following entries in its books: (1) increase the bank's loan contract assets by $25 to reflect the credit provided to the purchaser of the meal; (2) increase the bank's liabilities by $25 (less a service charge retained by the bank) to reflect an addition to the restaurant's checking account with the bank. The second entry will be reflected as an increase in the checking account liabilities of the consolidated balance sheet of the banking system. Thus, M1, M2, and M3 will rise by the amount the restaurant receives. Clearly, credit cards are not money themselves, but when they are used to make purchases, money is created. When the First FRK Bank credits the restaurant's checking account for $25 less the service charge, the money supply increases by the same amount. What happens to the money supply when the customer receives a statement for $25 at the end of the month and pays the balance in full?

▶ Summary and Conclusions

In this chapter we learned what banks have to sell, how they earn their profits, and why a bank may not be willing to lend you money when you really need it. We outlined the structure of the banking system and its relationship to the supply of checking account money. The basic features of a paper monetary standard and a banking system in which reserves amount to only a fraction of banks' outstanding checking and savings account liabilities characterize all modern economies today. The following main points were emphasized.

Money serves as a medium of exchange, unit of account, and store of value.

Under a paper standard, money is a liability of the banking system.

The banking system creates money when it satisfies the public's desire to finance purchases of goods and services with borrowed funds.

▶ Key Terms

bank *464*

basic accounting identity *469*

cash drain *473*

central bank *468*

commodity standard of money *467*

credit markets *464*

demand deposits *469*

depository institutions *464*

Federal Reserve System (Fed) *468*

Federal Reserve notes *476*

fiat money *467*

financial instrument *468*

financial sector *464*

hyperinflations *466*

loan contract *468*

M1, M2, M3 *475*

medium of exchange *465*

monetary standard *467*

money *465*

money multiplier *472*

multiple deposit expansion *472*

paper standard *467*

reserves *468*

store of value *466*

unit of account *465*

▶ Questions for Discussion and Review

Are the statements in questions 1 through 5 true, false, or uncertain? Defend your answers.

1. The United States dollar is not "backed" by anything of intrinsic value.
2. Money is both an asset and a liability.
3. Writing a check and depositing it in your money market fund account increases M2.
4. Increasing the amount of money that you carry in your wallet will affect a banking system's ability to expand deposits.
5. If you close out your checking account and take the balance in dollar bills, your actions reduce the quantity of money.
6. Can an item fulfill money's role as a medium of exchange if it is not also a store of value? Cite historical examples to defend your answer.
7. If only one bank were chartered to do business in a country, how would this affect the deposit expansion process?
8. Do people ever have more money than they want? Explain.
9. Suppose a traveler takes $10,000 from a cookie jar and purchases traveler's checks. How does this affect M1, M2, and M3?
10. Suppose the Federal Reserve paid market rates of interest on bank reserves held at the Fed. How would this affect the size of the money supply?

Chapter 23

The Central Bank and Regulation of Money and the Banking System

Outline

I. Introduction *480*
II. Keeping money scarce: The role of the Fed *481*
  A. The balance sheet of the Fed and the banking system *482*
  B. The means of monetary control: The instruments of monetary policy *482*
    1. Open market operations and the quantity of money with no currency drain *483*
      a. The impact of currency drain *486*
    2. Other instruments of monetary policy *487*
      a. The required reserve ratio *487*
      b. The discount rate *488*
      c. Direct credit controls, interest rate regulations, and moral suasion *488*
      d. Deposit insurance and bank bailouts *489*
      e. Deregulation of the banking system: Increased competition and increased risk *490*
III. Preview: The linkage between money, credit, and national income *491*
IV. Summary and conclusions *493*
V. Key terms *494*
VI. Questions for discussion and review *494*

Objectives

After reading this chapter, the student should be able to:

Describe the structure of the Federal Reserve System.

Explain how each of the three major instruments of monetary policy (open market operations, changing the reserve requirement, and changing the discount rate) are used by the Fed to expand or contract the money supply.

Explain how direct credit controls, interest rate restrictions, and moral suasion can affect the money supply.

Describe the role of the Federal Deposit Insurance Corporation.

Discuss recent attempts to deregulate banking.

*A nation's **monetary authority** is usually its central bank, which is responsible for determining the quantity of money under a paper monetary standard.*

▶ Introduction

When the Johnson family moved to a quiet suburb in Ohio in 1980, they put their modest savings in a neighborhood savings and loan association. They think it was owned by a Cleveland-based bank that is federally insured. After a couple of years, ownership of the savings and loan association changed hands, but the Johnsons didn't give it much thought. In fact, it was purchased by a firm that insured through a state fund rather than with the Federal Deposit Insurance Corporation.

In February 1985 something called ESM Investment Securities Corporation in Florida went bankrupt, and by March 1985 all Ohio savings and loan associations that were insured by the Ohio state deposit insurance fund were closed to depositors by order of the governor. The Johnson family had $5,000 in one of those savings and loans, and both Dick and Mary Johnson's monthly paychecks had been automatically deposited just before it closed its doors.

Checks that they had written to pay the mortgage, utilities, and other monthly bills were all returned unpaid. The Johnsons borrowed money from their parents and friends to buy groceries. For three agonizing months, the Johnson family waited to learn if they would ever see their money again, if they would be evicted from their home, if their car would be repossessed, and how long they could keep borrowing from friends and relatives to survive. Finally, an out-of-town savings and loan association with federal deposit insurance took over the bank in which the Johnson family had its money, and life returned to normal.

During the course of that financial and emotional roller-coaster ride, Dick and Mary Johnson learned a lot more than they had ever thought they would care to know about how banks earn profits and how safe deposits are under federal and state insurance programs. How much do you know about the bank in which you keep your money? Can what happened to the Johnson family happen to you? How effectively are bank deposits protected by federal insurance programs that became effective in the mid-1930s? During the Great Depression (before federal deposit insurance became effective) there were 4,000 bank suspensions in 1933 alone, and over 8,000 banks were closed at least temporarily between 1930 and 1933, before President Roosevelt ordered all banks closed, just as the governor of Ohio did in 1985. In 1985, bank failures in the United States hit a post-Great Depression high of 120.[1] While this is a much smaller figure than that reached in 1933, many people began to wonder whether anything like Great Depression levels of bank failures could happen again. We will explore this question, among others, in this chapter, where we study the role of the Fed in regulating the banking system and the money supply.

*In chapter 22 we saw that the United States and most of the world's economies employ a paper standard of money. Under a paper standard, the quantity of reserves is not determined by the cost of producing a commodity such as gold or silver. Rather, the banking system's reserves, which limit the quantity of money that banks can supply, are determined by a nation's monetary authority. A nation's **monetary authority** is the government agency responsible for controlling the banking system's ability to create money. The monetary authority in most countries today is its central bank. Actually, a nation's central bank need not be an official government agency, but most of them are. For example, the Bank of England, Great Britain's central bank, was originally a privately owned firm. Nationalization of the Bank of England essentially formalized the functions it had customarily assumed over the years. Some other countries' central banks are the Australian National Bank, the Bank of Japan, and the German Federal Bank. In chapter 22 we noted that the central bank in the United States is the Federal Reserve System, frequently referred to as the Fed. In this chapter, we shall explore the role of the Fed in the financial sector of the United States economy.*

*The **Depository Institutions Deregulation and Monetary Control Act of 1980** extends control of the Fed to all depository*

institutions and provides for greater competition among banks and for eventual decontrol of most interest rates they charge and pay.

*The Fed's **monetary policy** determines how much money circulates in the United States economy.*

Table 23.1   Balance sheet of the Fed, March 1986 (millions of dollars)

The Fed			
Assets		**Liabilities and net worth**	
1. Gold certificates[a]	$11,090	1. Federal Reserve Notes (paper money)	$177,189
2. Coins	570	2. Deposits	
3. Loan contracts		a. Banking system	30,782
a. Banking system obligations	818	b. United States Treasury	3,280
b. United States government		c. Foreign governments	274
obligations (government bonds)	176,620	d. Other	511
4. Other assets[b]	34,035	3. Other liabilities[c]	7,119
5. Total assets	223,133	4. Total liabilities	219,155
		5. Net worth	3,978

Source: From *Federal Reserve Bulletin*, June 1986. Column totals may not be exact due to rounding.

[a]Can be turned over to the United States Treasury in exchange for gold.

[b]Includes Special Drawing Rights (SDRs), which are an account the United States government has with the International Monetary Fund (IMF) as an official reserve to finance balance of payments deficits.

[c]Includes deferred availability cash items and accrued dividends.

▶ **Keeping Money Scarce: The Role of the Fed**

The United States' central bank is not located in a single place, although its headquarters are in Washington, D.C. The Federal Reserve *System* includes twelve Federal Reserve District Banks. Each Federal Reserve District is named for the city that is the home of its principal Federal Reserve Branch Bank. These cities are Boston, New York, Philadelphia, Cleveland, Richmond, Atlanta, Chicago, St. Louis, Minneapolis, Kansas City, Dallas, and San Francisco. Overseeing the district banks is a board of governors, the members of which are appointed by the president of the United States. The members of the board serve fourteen-year terms, which are staggered so that every two years someone's term expires.

Also included in the Federal Reserve System are a large number of commercial banks, which are called *member banks*. (Commercial banks are institutions that accept deposits and make loans but are not savings and loan institutions, mutual banks, or credit unions.) The member banks own common stock of the

Fed and must subscribe to certain rules and regulations that until recently were more stringent than those governing nonmember banks. Only about half of the commercial banks in the United States are member banks. They tend to be larger than nonmember banks and account for about three-quarters of all deposits of member and nonmember banks combined. Under the **Depository Institutions Deregulation and Monetary Control Act of 1980,** Congress has mandated that nonmember banks are subject to most of the same controls by the Fed as are member banks. At the same time, many services that the Fed used to perform only for member banks are now provided for all banks, savings and loan associations, and credit unions. These services include check clearing, wire transfer of funds, and access to borrowing from the Fed.

The Fed's activities that determine the supply of money constitute its **monetary policy.** In order to understand how the Fed carries out its monetary policy, we need to see how the Fed's balance sheet ties into that of the consolidated balance sheet of the banking system, which is shown in table 22.4. The Fed's balance sheet is shown in table 23.1.

The Balance Sheet of the Fed and the Banking System

The principal connection between the Fed's balance sheet and the consolidated balance sheet of the commercial banking system is through the reserve accounts the commercial banks keep with the Fed. These accounts are deposit liabilities of the Fed and assets of the commercial banks. The commercial banking system's reserves include its cash on hand and its reserve accounts with the Fed. In chapter 22, we noted that the First FRK Bank began business with a certain amount of reserves. In today's financial world, the First FRK Bank would have deposited most of its reserves with the Fed and kept only a small portion as cash on hand to meet its customers' daily demands for currency.

The FRK's reserve account with the Fed would be very similar to a checking account that any of us might hold with a commercial bank, such as FRK. The First FRK Bank would be able to draw upon its reserves to meet the demands of its customers to withdraw their funds or the demands of other banks to honor checks that FRK's customers have written and that have been deposited in accounts elsewhere. As we shall see, the Fed controls the money supply essentially by controlling the banking system's reserves and by requiring a certain ratio of reserves to the commercial banks' deposit liabilities.

One aspect of the Fed's balance sheet may surprise you. Nearly three-quarters of the Fed's assets consist of loan contracts that are obligations of the United States government—bonds and notes used to finance the federal deficit. Notice also that less than 6 percent of the Fed's assets consist of gold certificates, which are claims on the government's stock of gold. As we have said, and as you can see, gold has virtually nothing to do with the quantity of money in circulation in the United States. Table 23.1 shows us that our money is essentially backed by whatever the Fed has as an asset, very little of which is gold.

The Means of Monetary Control: The Instruments of Monetary Policy

We can now take a closer look at the **instruments of monetary policy,** which are the means used by the Fed to control the quantity of money. As we suggested, the most powerful means of limiting the money supply is to control the amount of reserves in the banking system or the quantity of reserves banks must hold for each dollar they have as checking account and savings account liabilities. In other words, the Fed has the power to control the size of the reserve accounts commercial banks hold with it. We will see how shortly. The Fed also has the power to rule that for every dollar in the deposit accounts of commercial banks' customers, the commercial banks must themselves keep a certain fraction of a dollar as cash in their vaults or in their reserve accounts with the Fed. For example, if a commercial bank's customers have deposits worth, say, $1 billion, the Fed can require the commercial bank to hold reserves of 10 percent of this amount, or $100 million.

The amount of reserves banks are required to hold relative to their checking account and savings account liabilities is determined by the **required reserve ratio.** The United States has a **fractional reserve system,** which means that this ratio is less than 100 percent. For every dollar commercial banks owe their customers in the form of checking or savings accounts, they are required to keep less than a dollar in reserves.

In order to satisfy their reserve requirements, individual banks must maintain minimum balances in their accounts with the Fed. The Fed can alter either the required reserve ratio or the amount of reserves available as a means of monetary control. If the Fed wants to reduce the quantity of money, or reduce its rate of growth, it need only reduce the quantity of reserves available to the banks, or its rate of growth. Alternately, the Fed can increase the required reserve ratio, which also reduces banks' ability to lend, given the quantity of reserves available.

*The **Federal Open Market Committee (FOMC)** is the part of the Fed that controls bank reserves.*

__Excess reserves__ are banks' deposits at the Fed and other reserves in excess of their required amount.

__Open market operations__ are the purchases and sales of government bonds by the Fed on the open market (the market for government bonds).

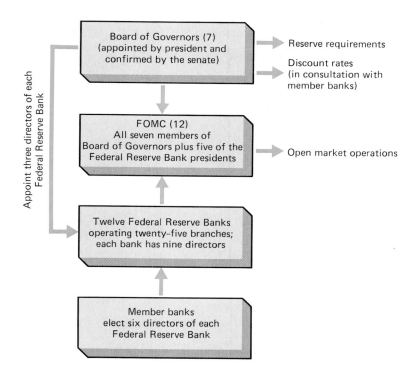

Figure 23.1   The Federal Reserve System

The question of whether the quantity of reserves available to the banking system is too large or too small is determined by a part of the Fed called the **Federal Open Market Committee (FOMC),** which consists of the entire Board of Governors, the president of the Federal Reserve Bank of New York, and four chairpersons of the other Federal Reserve Banks, who serve on a rotating basis. The FOMC is the agency most directly concerned with the short-run management of the money supply and meets approximately every six weeks to determine monetary policy. The relationship of the FOMC to the Board of Governors and the member banks is illustrated in Figure 23.1

For example, suppose the banking system's demand deposit liabilities total $1 billion and the required reserve ratio is 10 percent. As a result, banks' required reserves equal $100 million. If actual reserves held as deposits with the Fed equal $100 million, then the banking system has no **excess reserves,** which are reserves over and above the legally required amount. Let us suppose the FOMC decides it would be desirable to change the quantity of money in circulation. In order to achieve its goal, the Fed will most likely act to change the quantity of reserves available. Just how does it accomplish this task?

Open Market Operations and the Quantity of Money with No Currency Drain

The means that the FOMC is most likely to use to change the quantity of reserves is called an **open market operation,** in which employees of the Fed are directed to buy or sell United States government bonds

Table 23.2   Open market operations and multiple deposit expansion

	Balance sheet of the First FRK Bank (FRK)		
Step 1—the Fed buys a $10,000 bond from the FRK	**Assets**		**Liabilities and net worth**
	United States Govt. bonds	−$10,000	Demand deposits +$10,000
	Reserve account at the Fed	+$10,000	
	Loan contracts	+$10,000	
Step 2—the customer of the FRK who received the new $10,000 loan contract spends the money	**Balance sheet of the First FRK Bank**		
	Assets		**Liabilities and net worth**
	Reserve account at the Fed	−$10,000	Demand deposits −$10,000
	Balance sheet of other banks in the banking system		
	Assets		**Liabilities and net worth**
	Reserve account at the Fed	+$10,000	Demand deposits +$10,000
Step 3—the banking system eliminates its $9,000 of excess reserves by issuing new loan contracts	**Balance sheet of other banks in the banking system**		
	Assets		**Liabilities and net worth**
	Loan contracts	+$9,000	Demand deposits +$9,000
Step 4—the borrowers of the money write checks, which are then deposited in the FRK	**Balance sheet of other banks in the banking system**		
	Assets		**Liabilities and net worth**
	Reserve account at the Fed	−$9,000	Demand deposits −$9,000
	Balance sheet of the First FRK Bank		
	Reserve account at the Fed	+$9,000	Demand deposits +$9,000

on the open market, that is, the market for United States government bonds. Let us see how when the Fed purchases bonds on the open market this affects banks' reserves and the money supply when all of the additional money created is held by the public in the form of checking accounts. Suppose the First FRK Bank owns United States government bonds worth $100,000 and decides to sell a $10,000 bond to the Fed. The Fed pays by crediting FRK's account at the Fed for $10,000. The result is that FRK's balance sheet will show the changes indicated by step 1 in table

23.2 and figure 23.2—the assets side of the balance sheet shows *plus* $10,000 in reserves and *minus* $10,000 in United States government bonds. This is a very important change for the First FRK Bank, even though *total* assets are unchanged.

The easiest way to see how the Fed's open market operation affects the money supply is to assume that the First FRK Bank, like the banking system as a whole, had no excess reserves before the Fed took action. (Banks may actually hold excess reserves—reserves over and above their requirements—to

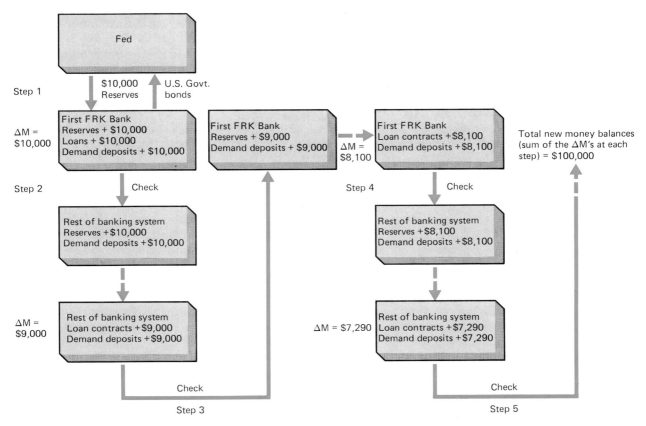

Figure 23.2   An open market operation and multiple deposit expansion
The arrows show how the initial purchase of government bonds worth $10,000 by the Fed leads to an increase in reserves, demand deposits, and new loans by the First FRK Bank. Subsequently, the $10,000 in new loans leads to increased reserves for the rest of the banking system and new loans of $9,000. Each new loan raises the money supply (ΔM). By the time the fourth step has been completed, the money supply has been increased by $10,000 + $9,000 + $8,100 + $7,290 = $34,390. When the process is complete, the money supply will have increased by $100,000.

accommodate unforeseen demands for cash by their customers. However, they must forego the interest revenue on the loan contracts they might have otherwise purchased.) With no excess reserves, the First FRK Bank is unable to increase the amount of credit supplied to its customers, because it is not allowed to add to its demand deposit liabilities. With the $10,000 in excess reserves it receives through sale of the bond,

the bank is now in a position to buy more loan contracts and to create new demand deposits. Since the First FRK Bank would like to increase its profits whenever possible, it lends $10,000 to a customer. Thus, the almost immediate effect of the Fed's purchase of a $10,000 bond from the First FRK Bank is to indirectly increase the quantity of money by $10,000.

As we saw in chapter 22, our story is by no means over. A borrower who gave the First FRK Bank a $10,000 loan contract in return for an addition to its checking account did so to use the money for purchases. Let us review the process of multiple deposit expansion as we follow the $10,000 in new reserves and new money through the banking system. Suppose that the $10,000 in purchases financed by the initial loan created by FRK in step 1 of table 23.2 ends up deposited with other banks in the system as indicated by step 2. After receiving the new deposits, these banks present checks worth $10,000 for payment. The Fed helps them collect from the First FRK Bank by acting as a *clearinghouse* for checks, *subtracting* $10,000 from the First FRK Bank's account at the Fed, and adding the same amount to the accounts of the other banks at the Fed. In other words, FRK's reserves are reduced by $10,000, while the reserves of the other banks are increased by the same amount. Assuming they originally had no excess reserves and that the required reserve ratio is 10 percent, these banks now have excess reserves of $9,000. They need retain only $1,000 in reserve against the $10,000 in new demand deposits and are free to buy loan contracts and create new demand deposits totaling $9,000 (step 3 in table 23.2).

The story continues. The borrowers of the $9,000 also write checks totaling this amount, and the money is deposited in the First FRK Bank (step 4). The First FRK Bank needs to hold only $900 in reserves, and in the next set of transactions (which *you* should write in the balance sheet), it lends $8,100. So far, the money supply has increased by $27,100, which is equal to the $10,000 created in step 1, plus the $9,000 created in step 3, plus the new $8,100 just noted. If you were to carry out the succeeding chain of transactions, you would see that the initial open market operation of purchasing a $10,000 bond from the First FRK Bank will lead to a *total* increase in the money supply of $100,000. This is because *when there is no*

currency drain, the *money multiplier,* which determines how much the total quantity of money changes as a result of a change in excess reserves, is given by the formula

money multiplier = total new money/change in reserves = 1/required reserve ratio.

Because the required reserve ratio is 0.1 (10 percent), the money multiplier in this case is $1/0.1 = 10$. The Fed's purchase of the $10,000 bond from the First FRK Bank leads to the creation of $100,000 of new money for the economy. After demand deposits have grown by $100,000, the additional reserves the banking system is required to deposit with the Fed will total $10,000, exactly equal to the Fed's initial purchase of the government bond on the open market.

The Impact of Currency Drain   In practice, the money multiplier will probably be smaller than the amount shown in the formula given above. The reason is that the public is likely to increase its holding of currency as the money supply grows. The public obtains currency by withdrawing it from its bank accounts. When the banks pay out this currency, they must draw down their cash reserves. In other words, some of the additional reserves created by the Fed's open market operation "leaks" into the public's currency holdings, limiting banks' ability to purchase new loan contracts and expand deposits. In practice, part of the initial $10,000 in new reserves created by the Fed in the preceding example ends up as currency held by the public instead of bank reserves. The *sum* of new bank reserves and additional currency held by the public will equal the initial $10,000 the Fed injected into the banking system. Suppose, as in our example of currency drain in chapter 22, the public desires to hold 30 percent of its total money balances in the form of cash. Then, when the monetary expansion induced by the Fed's open market operation is complete, the money supply will not have risen by $100,000. Instead, it will have grown by only $27,028.

*The **monetary base** is the raw material from which banks create deposit liabilities and is equal to the sum of banks' reserves, currency in their vaults, and currency in the hands of the public.*

Of this total, 30 percent, or $8,108 will be held as cash by the public. The difference between the public's increased cash holdings and the initial increase in reserves of $10,000, or $1,892, will remain as increased bank reserves. As a consequence, banks will have increased their loans by $18,920 (ten times their increase in reserves). The increase in checking account money plus the increase in the public's holding of cash equals the $27,028 increase in the money supply. (See footnote on page 473.)

However, the actual story is likely to be still more complex. The increased money supply may cause the public to wish to transfer funds from checking accounts to savings accounts. The immediate impact is to reduce M1 but leave M2 and M3 unchanged. (Why?) Since required reserve ratios are generally lower for banks' savings account liabilities than for their checking account liabilities, this action by the public leads to a money multiplier that is larger than it otherwise would be. The main point to remember is that excess reserves encourage banks to increase the quantity of money by a multiple greater than one. Currency drain tends to make this multiple closer to one than it would otherwise be, but transfers from checking accounts to savings accounts may make the multiple larger when M2 is used to measure the quantity of money.

There is another side of the "coin" of cash drain. Cash held by the public, if deposited with banks, becomes bank reserves. The sum of bank reserves and currency, either held by banks in their vaults or held by the general public, is known as the **monetary base** because it represents the basic raw material for creating money. The Fed, when it purchases bonds, either by increasing bank reserves or by paying in cash, increases the monetary base and lays the groundwork for an increase in the money supply. However, when the public desires to increase its cash holdings, it allocates part of the monetary base toward a form that cannot be used by banks to increase checking account money further.

It would be a good idea for you to work through the example illustrated in figure 23.2 and table 23.2 and show that if the Fed were to *sell* United States government bonds on the open market, the money supply would *fall* by a multiple of the initial decline in excess reserves. In a sense, money is destroyed. To see this, think about how banks meet their reserve requirements when the Fed sells United States government bonds on the open market. What happens to banks' outstanding loans and to demand deposits?

Other Instruments of Monetary Policy

Buying and selling government bonds on the open market is the Fed's most frequently used instrument of monetary policy. We also noted that the Fed sometimes changes, albeit rarely, required reserve ratios. There are still other instruments of monetary policy that the Fed uses either in conjunction with its open market operations or sometimes as substitutes for them. We will consider these other tools of monetary policy briefly in the next sections.

The Required Reserve Ratio   In the example of an expansionary open market operation illustrated in table 23.2 and figure 23.2, the Fed purchased government bonds to expand the money supply. The required reserve ratio was 10 percent. Suppose now that the Fed decides to reverse its policy and wishes to reduce the money supply. We have already seen that the most likely course of action will be a contractionary open market policy, which involves *selling* government bonds to the public or to the banking system directly. However, another possibility is for the Fed to *increase* the required reserve ratio. Suppose the banking system is "loaned up," in that it has no excess reserves, that the money supply is $1 billion in checking accounts, and that reserves equal $100 million (10 percent of outstanding checking accounts), exactly what the Fed requires.

*The **discount rate** is the interest rate banks must pay when they borrow from the Fed. The term **discount** refers to the payment of the interest charge in advance so that the actual loan is the net of the total interest payment.*

Direct credit controls allow the Fed to tell banks how much they can lend and to whom.

If the Fed wants to reduce the money supply by $100 million, it can sell $10 million worth of government securities, or it can achieve the same result by raising the required reserve ratio to 11.1 percent. With $1 billion in checking accounts, increasing the required reserve ratio to 11.1 percent will increase required reserves from $100 million to $111.1 million. Banks will be deficient in meeting this requirement by $11.1 million and will have to start a process of reducing their outstanding loans. As loans come up for renewal, the banks will simply refuse to renew them. When the loans are paid off, the banks' demand deposits will decline and so will their required reserves. Finally, when $100 million in loans has been paid off, demand deposits will have fallen by $100 million, and required reserves will be .111 × $900 million, or $100 million. Since $100 million equals the actual reserves of the banking system, there will be no more pressure to reduce outstanding loans, and the decline in the money supply will come to an end.

The Discount Rate   In the discussion of open market operations and the reserve requirement, we asked you to work through the transactions involved in a *contraction* of the money supply. A contraction results from a sale of government bonds by the Fed on the open market. We have also seen that a contraction can be the result of an increase in the required reserve ratio. Still another possible cause of declining reserves is an increase in the public's desire to hold money in the form of currency rather than checking accounts. If banks have no excess reserves, then their reserves will fall below the legally required minimum. What happens then?

When banks' reserves fall below the required level, banks will reduce the value of loan contracts they hold. As loans are repaid, the banking system's checking account liabilities will fall, and banks will eventually be able to meet their reserve requirements. But this takes time. What is a bank to do while its reserve balances are legally too low? (A bank can actually lose its charter if deficient reserves are a persistent problem.) One possibility is for a bank to *borrow* reserves from the Fed, using its loan contract assets (earning assests) as security. Of course, the Fed charges banks for these loans. The interest rate the Fed charges banks when they borrow reserves is called the **discount rate.** By raising the discount rate, the Fed increases banks' costs for allowing their checking account liabilities to remain above the legally permissible level. This discourages them from allowing their borrowers to repay their loans slowly and from making new loans. By lowering the discount rate, the Fed can encourage banks to borrow reserves to meet their obligations and even to expand the amount of money in the economy.

Financial analysts often place considerable importance on announcements by the Fed that it is changing the discount rate. This is because the Fed sometimes changes the discount rate as a means of announcing to the general public its intentions regarding the money supply. This can be a quicker way to inform the public of the Fed's intentions than waiting for the news of changes in open market operations and their effects on the money supply to filter down through detailed statistical summaries in the news media.

Direct Credit Controls, Interest Rate Regulations, and Moral Suasion   Banking is a regulated industry, and the Fed is one of its principal regulatory agencies. (Other regulators include various state banking agencies, the Comptroller of the Currency, and the Federal Deposit Insurance Corporation.) From time to time, Congress has authorized the Fed to impose **direct credit controls** on the banking system, which involve restricting the banks' right to supply credit to certain classes of borrowers. For instance, credit may be limited to large businesses that want to purchase trucks as opposed to small businesses or consumers who want to purchase cars. Direct credit controls are difficult to justify in a market economy. They almost always lead to various distortions in what is produced and consumed. Direct credit controls could conceivably be used to restrict the overall ability of the banking system to expand the money supply, but the direct control of credit is a much less effective tool than open market operations.

The Fed also has an instrument of monetary control known as **moral suasion,** which has been called the Fed's "open mouth" policy, as opposed to its open market policy, because it involves persuading banks to behave in a way that pleases the Fed. An implied threat may be that if banks fail to please the Fed, it may restrict their access to the "discount window" (bankers' jargon for the process of borrowing reserves). The channels through which moral suasion can affect the quantity of money are similar to those through which direct credit controls operate.

Deposit Insurance and Bank Bailouts   The most troublesome feature of a fractional reserve monetary system is its susceptibility to **bank runs,** which occur when depositors lose faith in a bank's ability to meet its deposit obligations. As we have seen, reserves are never sufficient to convert all deposits into cash under a fractional reserve banking system. One of the major factors that caused the Great Depression was a one-third decline in the quantity of money between 1930 and 1933. This drop was partly caused by bank runs, which led to bank failures.

A review of the multiple deposit expansion process will show you how a decline in the public's confidence in the banking system leads to a fall in the quantity of money. Suppose depositors begin to cash in their deposits. Banks lose reserves as a result and

must call in their loans—demanding repayment as soon as they legally can. This reduces the quantity of money. If bank reserves fall to zero, banks will be unable to meet their depositors' demands. Panic may then set in, spreading throughout the banking system. Under the worst circumstances, everyone wants to cash in, banks fail, and depositors may lose part or all of the wealth represented by their deposits.

The Fed has always had the power to provide reserves to avoid a financial panic, but it failed to exercise that power during the Great Depression. (We will say more about this in chapter 28.) The **Federal Deposit Insurance Corporation (FDIC)** was created by an act of Congress in 1933 for the purpose of insuring "small" deposits in participating banks. As of 1984, the definition of a small deposit was one not in excess of $100,000. The Federal Savings and Loan Insurance Corporation (FSLIC) performs a similar service for savings and loan institutions.

Since the mid-1930s, the FDIC and FSLIC have guaranteed that most depositors need not fear banks' inability to honor their deposit liabilities. If a bank is about to fail, the FDIC (or FSLIC) first tries to find a financially solvent bank to take over the failing bank's assets and liabilities so that no depositors, large or small, need suffer a loss. If a bank does fail, the FDIC steps in and operates it until a purchaser is found. The bank's stockholders will probably lose their equity, but most deposits are guaranteed. Therefore, depositors have little incentive to start a run on the bank. Since the FDIC was established, bank runs have been uncommon in the United States. However, in the early 1980s, several major banks found themselves in serious difficulty. Some large regional banks and savings and loan institutions became insolvent, and depositors began to withdraw their balances in bank runs that most financial analysts had thought disappeared with the 1930s. The run on banks in Ohio in the spring of 1985, referred to in the introduction, stemmed from the fact that the savings and loan institutions involved were members of a private, state-based insurance program. Their deposits were not guaranteed by official federal and state agencies.

Perhaps the most startling of the bank difficulties of this period was the de facto bankruptcy of one of the nation's largest banks, Continental Illinois National Bank of Chicago. Continental was heavily involved in loans to the United States petroleum industry. When oil prices began to decline in the early 1980s, many of these borrowers defaulted, and Continental saw its net worth plummet toward zero. A bank run ensued, and many observers feared that panic would spread to the rest of the banking system if Continental were not protected from actually declaring bankruptcy. The FDIC could not find any bank willing to take over Continental's assets and liabilities without substantial guarantees against financial loss. In other words, potential merger partners viewed Continental's net worth as negative. The FDIC faced the difficult choice of intervention to save the bank from bankruptcy, protecting its large depositors and possibly its stockholders, or letting events take their natural course toward actual bankruptcy.

Economists and financial analysts engaged in intense debate over the wisdom of intervention to bail out Continental. Proponents of intervention felt it was essential to protect the banking system from possible massive runs and collapse. Opponents believed a bank failure was necessary to signal large uninsured depositors and stockholders that they should be more careful by not placing deposits in, and buying the stock of, banks with careless management. While the bank was "saved," along with the accounts of both small and large depositors, stockholders lost practically all of their equity in Continental because the value of their stock was reduced to nearly zero. Nevertheless, those who opposed intervention felt that large depositors were not punished enough for failing to exercise discretion in placing funds with a potentially very risky bank.[2]

Until 1980, the FDIC also enforced interest rate ceilings set by the Fed on checking accounts (no interest allowed) and savings accounts. However, the Depository Institutions Deregulation and Monetary Control Act of 1980 established the Depository Institution Deregulation Committee to phase out most interest ceilings by 1986. As a result, most individuals now receive interest payments on their checking accounts and rates determined by the market on other accounts.

Deregulation of the Banking System: Increased Competition and Increased Risk   In recent years, many aspects of banking have been increasingly deregulated under the Depository Institutions Deregulation and Monetary Control Act of 1980. The rationale for banking deregulation is that by fostering increased competition among financial institutions of all types, borrowers will benefit from greater access to funds and depositors will receive higher interest rates. We have already mentioned several provisions of the act as it affects required reserves and services available to banks. To a certain extent, the act is misnamed because some of its provisions actually *increase* banking regulation by subjecting nonmember banks, savings and loan associations, and other depository institutions to the same controls that the Fed exercises over member banks.

One provision of the act grants permission for all depository institutions to offer NOW (negotiable order of withdrawal) accounts throughout the United States.

These are essentially interest-bearing checking accounts. Providing them has eliminated the most significant difference distinguishing commercial banks (those that have always offered conventional checking accounts and a full range of loan services to individuals and businesses), savings banks, savings and loan associations, and credit unions. The act has set up machinery to phase out most interest rate ceilings on bank deposits and restricted the power of states to place ceilings on the interest rates banks are allowed to charge their customers (usury laws).

Under provisions of the act, banks are now freer to compete for deposits by paying higher interest rates. They are permitted to venture into riskier markets, seeking loan contracts yielding higher returns. As we saw in the discussion of the Continental Illinois bailout, deregulation has created serious questions regarding the degree to which the Fed and the FDIC should bail out banks and protect large depositors from the risk of making bad loans.[3]

Before deregulation, people seeking high returns on their funds were frequently forced to bypass the banking system and lend directly to borrowers. These lenders had a strong incentive to assess the risk of default because they would bear the full cost of a borrower's failure to pay interest or repay principal. Suppose now that a major United States bank has attracted large deposits by offering high interest based on relatively risky loans to foreign governments and businesses. (See chapter 33 for a discussion of the international debt problem and its effect on United States banks.) Depositors seeking these interest rates are likely to worry much less about the riskiness of these loans if they believe banks will be bailed out should default appear imminent.

Unfortunately, such bailouts are not costless. If the Fed or the FDIC uses moral suasion to force a solvent bank to lend money to other banks or to borrowers in difficulty in order to avoid their default, these funds are not available for less risky loans. As a result, some potential borrowers must do without. An alternative would be to pay off small depositors if a bank should fail, letting the bank's large depositors and its stockholders bear the penalty of making a business error in search of higher returns. This is an issue that will occupy much space in the economic news during the next several years.

▸ Preview: The Linkage between Money, Credit, and National Income

As the Johnson family in the introduction to this chapter learned very unfortunately, when the Fed or members of the banking system do anything to disrupt the normal relationship between the supply of money and the rest of the economy, the consequences can be quite serious. In the following chapters on the macroeconomy, we will explore the crucial linkages between the monetary system and the goods-producing sector. The principal connection is through credit markets. Banks are among the most important purchasers of loan contracts from households and business firms. The money balances created through this channel are used to purchase consumer durable goods and finance business investments. Thus, they are a crucial link in the relationship between aggregate expenditure on goods and services and aggregate production. Some important aggregate measures of the money stock, the monetary base, and bank-financed credit are contained in table 23.3 and illustrated in figure 23.3.

Table 23.3   Money stock, monetary base, and bank loans and investments, 1959–85 (billions of dollars)

Year	M1[a] (annual average)	M2[b] (annual average)	Monetary base[c] (figures for December of each year)	Bank loans and purchases of United States Treasury and other securities (figures for December of each year)
1959	$140.9	$ 297.7	$ 44.3	$ 188.7
1960	141.9	312.3	44.5	197.4
1961	146.5	335.5	45.7	212.8
1962	149.2	362.8	47.1	231.2
1963	154.7	393.4	49.4	250.2
1964	161.9	425.1	51.9	272.3
1965	169.5	459.5	54.7	300.1
1966	173.7	481.3	56.8	316.1
1967	185.1	526.6	60.5	352.0
1968	199.4	569.4	64.8	390.2
1969	205.8	591.3	67.9	401.7
1970	216.5	628.8	72.0	435.5
1971	230.6	713.6	77.1	485.7
1972	251.9	806.4	84.2	572.6
1973	265.8	863.2	90.3	647.8
1974	277.4	911.2	98.3	713.6
1975	291.0	1,026.9	104.5	745.2
1976	310.4	1,171.2	112.0	804.2
1977	335.5	1,297.7	121.4	891.5
1978	363.2	1,403.9	132.2	1,013.5
1979	389.0	1,518.9	142.5	1,135.9
1980	414.5	1,656.2	155.0	1,239.6
1981	440.9	1,822.7	162.7	1,316.3
1982	478.5	1,999.1	175.1	1,412.4
1983	528.0	2,188.8	185,485	1,553.0
1984	558.5	2,371.7	199,032	1,716.8
1985	624.7	2,563.6	216,935	1,895.5

Source: From *Economic Report of the President, 1986,* Tables B-64, B-66, B-67, pp. 327, 330, 333.

[a]M1 includes all demand deposits in the banking system (except those of the United States Treasury) upon which checks can be written or that can be transferred by telephone or electronic means, plus currency and travelers' checks in the hands of the nonbank public.

[b]M2 includes M1 plus "small" (under $100,000) certificates of deposit, savings accounts, money market mutual funds, and certain other bank obligations that depositors treat as readily available to carry out transactions.

[c]Monetary base is the sum of the bank's reserves, currency in their vaults, and currency in the hands of the public.

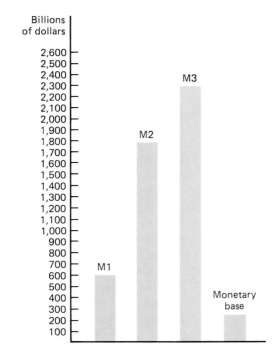

Important Monetary Aggregates for the United States, June, 1985

Figure 23.3   Important monetary aggregates for the United States, June, 1985
From *Federal Reserve Bulletin*, December 1985, Tables 1-20, 1-21.

Table 23.4	How the Fed controls the money supply
Action by the Fed	**Effect on the money supply**
Buy government bonds from banks or the public	Increases total bank reserves, which causes deposit expansion and an increase in the money supply
Sell government bonds to banks or the public	Reduces total bank reserves, which causes deposit contraction and a decrease in the money supply
Lower the reserve requirement (the required reserve ratio)	Decreases banks' *required* reserves, which causes deposit expansion and an increase in the money supply
Raise the reserve requirement (the required reserve ratio)	Increases banks' *required* reserves, which causes deposit contraction and a decrease in the money supply
Lower the discount rate	Encourages banks to borrow reserves from the Fed, which causes deposit expansion and an increase in the money supply
Raise the discount rate	Discourages banks from borrowing reserves from the Fed, which causes deposit contraction and a decrease in the money supply
Direct credit controls	Prevents certain types of lending by banks, which restricts the money supply
Moral suasion	Restricts (encourages) lending by banks, which restricts (increases) the money supply
Interest rate restrictions	Lowers the attractiveness of certain deposit liabilities, which discourages deposit expansion and restricts the money supply
Deposit insurance (by the FDIC)	Encourages people to use bank deposits instead of cash, which tends to increase the money supply

▶ Summary and Conclusions

In this chapter we showed how the Fed, the central bank of the United States, regulates the quantity of money in our economy. We also described the role of the Federal Deposit Insurance Corporation. Although the institutional details describe the economy of the United States, the basic features of a paper monetary standard and fractional reserve banking characterize all modern market economies today. A complete listing of how the Fed can affect the money supply is given in table 23.4.

▶ Key Terms

bank runs *489*

Depository Institutions Deregulation and Monetary Control Act of 1980 *481*

direct credit controls *488*

discount rate *488*

excess reserves *483*

Federal Deposit Insurance Corporation (FDIC) *489*

Federal Open Market Committee (FOMC) *483*

fractional reserve system *482*

instruments of monetary policy *482*

monetary authority *480*

monetary base *487*

monetary policy *481*

moral suasion *489*

open market operation *483*

required reserve ratio *482*

▶ Questions for Discussion and Review

Are the statements in questions 1 through 3 true, false, or uncertain? Defend your answers.

1. The Fed, through an open market operation, buys a bond from John Smith for $10,000. Smith decides to keep $1,000 as mad money and deposit the rest in his checking account. With a required reserve ratio of 10 percent, the banking system can create $90,000 in new money through multiple deposit expansion.

2. To ensure that the poor have access to credit, the Fed should impose interest rate ceilings on lenders below current market rates.

3. If a bank buys a loan contract, the money stock increases, but if the Fed buys a government bond, the money stock does not increase.

4. After the deregulation of interest rates that banks pay on deposit accounts, many banking services such as checking accounts were no longer free of charge to the customer. Why?

5. Some institutions, such as Merrill Lynch and Sears, offer financial services similar to those of banks but are not subject to the same regulations as banks. Why?

6. The stated intention of Federal deposit insurance is to insure depositors against the loss of their funds should the depository institution fail. What incentives do managers of financial institutions have as a result of this insurance?

7. Show how the following transactions initially affect the banking system's assets, liabilities, and the quantity of money as measured by M1 and M2. Use balance sheets such as those in tables 22.1, 22.2, 22.4, and 23.2 to illustrate your answers.

   a. A business firm pays off a $100,000 bank loan by writing a check.
   b. The Fed buys $1 million worth of government bonds from the United States Treasury.
   c. The United States Treasury sells a $1,000 bond to a private citizen and uses the proceeds to buy office equipment. The citizen pays for the bond by withdrawing $1,000 from a savings account.
   d. The Treasury pays off $1 million of the national debt by redeeming (buying back) bonds from the public. It pays for these bonds by writing checks on its account with the Fed. The public deposits the $1 million in savings accounts.
   e. Suppose that in the transaction in part d, the Treasury pays by collecting $1 million in taxes from the public. The taxes are paid by drawing down checking accounts.
   f. One bank borrows $1 million in reserves from another bank (*not* from the Fed).

   Why does the question specify the *initial* effects of the transactions on the quantity of money? Is there a further impact? If so, how large is it? Show how each of the transactions affects the monetary base and the amount of loan contracts held by banks.

8. Suppose that there was no central bank, that open market operations were never carried out, and that there were no reserve requirements. Would the money supply grow without limit under a paper standard? What might comprise the monetary base? What could cause the monetary base to change? How could currency be issued? Would it help you to answer this question if there were paper currency issued by the government's treasury? Hint: How would banks' profit motive lead them to act?

9. Suppose the federal government decided to pay off the entire government debt. This would mean that the Fed's open market operations as we now know them would no longer be feasible. What means might the Fed adopt to control the quantity of money?

10. Assume there are no excess reserves. Use the balance sheets of the Fed and the banking system to show the way an open market sale of government bonds reduces the monetary base and the quantity of money.

Chapter 24

Money, Credit, and the Rate of Interest

Outline

I. Introduction *498*
   A. Things to come *498*
   B. Financial instruments *499*
   C. The decision to hold money versus loan contracts *500*
II. The loan contract market *500*
   A. Background *500*
   B. A closer look at the details of a loan contract *500*
   C. The model of the loan contract market to be developed *501*
   D. The demand for loanable funds *501*
      1. Firms *501*
         a. Firms' demand for loanable funds *502*
      2. The government *503*
         a. Monetizing the budget deficit *503*
         b. Financing the budget deficit in the loan contract market *503*
         c. The government's demand for loanable funds *504*
      3. The aggregate demand curve for loanable funds and the rate of interest *504*
   E. The supply of loanable funds *505*
      1. Households as suppliers of loanable funds *505*
         a. The household's financial wealth *505*
         b. The household's saving decision *505*
         c. The rate of interest and the household's supply of loanable funds *506*
         d. Households' supply curve of loanable funds *507*
      2. Banks as suppliers of funds *507*
         a. The rate of interest and banks' supply of loanable funds *508*
         b. Banks' supply of loanable funds schedule *509*
      3. The aggregate supply of loanable funds *510*
   F. Equilibrium in the loan contract market *510*
      1. The determination of the real interest rate *510*
      2. The structure of interest rates *512*
III. Summary and conclusions *513*
IV. Key terms *514*
V. Questions for discussion and review *514*
VI. Policy issue: You decide—Deregulation of the banking industry *515*
   A. The action-initiating event *515*
   B. The issue *515*
   C. Economic policy issues *515*
   D. Recommendations *515*

Objectives

After reading this chapter, the student should be able to:

Discuss the roles of the lender and the borrower in a loan contract.

Explain why firms' demand for loanable funds is downward sloping.

Explain how the government's demand for loanable funds is related to its budget deficit.

Describe the aggregate demand for loanable funds and what factors cause it to shift.

Explain what factors affect households' decisions to save and how households allocate their financial assets between money and loan contracts.

Describe why banks add to the supply of loanable funds and the role the real interest rate plays in this decision.

List factors that shift the supply of loanable funds.

Use households' and banks' supplies of loanable funds to derive the aggregate supply of loanable funds.

Explain how equilibrium in the loan contract market determines the real interest rate.

Discuss factors that affect the structure of interest rates.

▶ Introduction

In 1979, real GNP in the United States grew 2.8 percent. In 1980, it declined *by 0.8 percent. In 1978, unemployment was 5.8 percent of the labor force and grew to 7.0 percent in 1979. Although these figures were both high by historical standards, the CPI increased 11.3 percent in 1978 and 13.5 percent in 1979. These data were typical of the "stagflation" that plagued the United States economy in the 1970s. Such conditions boded ill for the reelection of the Carter administration in November 1980.*

Throughout 1978–79 economists forecast a recession that did not materialize. The political calculation had been that a recession in 1978 and/or 1979 would precede an economic expansion in 1980. In the early stages of an economic expansion, real GNP grows at a faster rate, inflation falls, and so does unemployment. Such conditions obviously would be favorable to a president seeking reelection.

In October 1979 the Fed announced a major change in its monetary policy. Instead of trying to achieve an ideal interest rate, it claimed it would focus primarily on achieving a desirable rate of growth of the quantity of money as measured by M1 and M2. This change was well-received by many economists. However, the promised change in policy goals was not achieved. Over the next twelve months, the money supply in the United States grew first at the slowest rate in twenty-five years and then at the fastest rate in many years. The economy experienced the shortest recession and then the shortest recovery in recorded business cycle history. The Fed was accused of trying to manipulate the economy to reelect a president. Whether this accusation was true or not, the timing of Fed policy was such that the economy sank into a minirecession in mid-1980.

In this chapter, we will take a closer look at the connection between the financial sector of the economy and the goods sector. We will explore how government policies can affect interest rates and inflation. We will begin to explore how monetary policy may be used to affect macroeconomic conditions.

Things to Come

In chapter 21 we noted that it is impossible to understand how the macroeconomy works by analyzing the goods and services sector alone. Full understanding requires incorporating the connections between the market for goods and services and the financial sector of the economy.

In this chapter we develop a simple, yet realistic, model of the supply and demand for financial assets such as bank deposits, corporate bonds, and United States Treasury securities. This clarifies a number of important economic issues. Among them are the economic variables that influence the behavior of buyers and sellers of financial assets, including the price level. We will also concern ourselves with the concept of equilibrium in financial markets and how it results in a particular interest rate or set of interest rates. In this chapter we reiterate the importance of the difference between the nominal and the real rate of interest. An important objective of this chapter is to link the financial and nonfinancial sectors of the economy. In particular, we show how the analysis we develop helps us to understand how government policy affects interest rates and thus affects investment and aggregate expenditure for goods and services.

Table 24.1   Some credit market instruments held by households, 1960–1983

| | Billions of dollars | | | | Percent of total | | | |
	1960	1970	1981	1983	1960	1970	1981	1983
Total credit market instruments[a]	**$150**	**$262**	**$646**	**$868.1**	**100%**	**100%**	**100%**	**100%**
United States government securities	$ 73.8	$ 93.9	$313.4	$425.0	49	36	49	49
State and local government obligations	30.8	48.4	89.1	160.0	21	18	13	18
Corporate and foreign bonds	10.0	53.1	76.5	58.6	7	20	12	7
Mortgages	33.4	60.5	130.2	184.3	23	23	20	21

Source: From *Statistical Abstract of the United States: 1982–83* (103d edition), U.S. Bureau of the Census, 1982, Table 814 and 1985, Table 810, p. 488.
[a]These are loans made by households in various forms to institutions and people.

Financial Instruments

There are many financial markets in a modern economy such as that of the United States. If you turn to the business section of your city's newspaper, you will see numerous ads for financial instruments, which as we saw in chapter 22, are the various ways you can hold your financial wealth. One possibility is to hold it as money. Another possibility is to hold your wealth in a loan contract. In exchange for lending money to some borrower, you will receive interest payments plus a promise that your money will be repaid by the end of the loan period. The best way to think of a loan contract is as a bond, such as one issued by a large corporation (General Motors or Sears) or the federal government. At first glance, the term *loan contract* seems a very cumbersome name for a bond. The reason we will use it is that it is a more general expression, which also includes other forms of loans, such as a mortgage to finance a construction project or funds that a bank may lend an individual to start a small business.

Table 24.1 presents data on the total dollar value of credit market instruments held by United States households in recent years. (Banks and other institutions hold financial instruments, too. Their behavior in the loan contract market will be discussed later.) Between 1960 and 1983, households increased the nominal dollar value of the credit market instruments they held by almost 600 percent. During the same period, consumer prices rose by about 300 percent. Based on these data, what happened to the real holdings of credit market instruments by households? Table 24.1 also tells us that the dollar value of corporate and foreign bonds holdings by households in 1983 was almost *six times* what it was in 1960. Of course, corporate bonds are not the only credit market instruments owned by households. In fact, the largest single category in 1983 was United States government securities. Keep in mind that the data in table 24.1 ignore the assets held as reserves by private pension funds. In 1983, United States pension funds' reserves totaled almost $1 trillion. These are a form of loan contract held by individuals in a group sense and include the types of loans listed in table 24.1. Loan contracts held as pension fund reserves were nine times larger in 1983 than in 1960.

*The **loan contract, financial,** or **credit market** is where borrowers and lenders of money arrange the terms of loans.*

__Loanable funds__ consist of money borrowed and lent in the credit market.

The Decision to Hold Money versus Loan Contracts

It is important to point out that money and loan contracts are linked in the individual's decision to hold financial wealth. In particular, if we know someone's spending behavior in the market for currently produced goods and services and his or her behavior in the loan contract market, then we *automatically* know his or her behavior in the money market.

To better understand this, a simple example is helpful. Suppose that a person with an after-tax income of $1,000 this month decides to buy $750 worth of consumption goods and $150 worth of bonds. This means that $100 is left over ($1,000 − $900) to be kept as an addition to this person's money balances. This behavior concerning how much money to be held (the additional $100) can be immediately inferred once we know the behavior of the individual in the goods and services market (purchases of $750) and the loan contract market ($150 lent out). The point is that although we will focus on the loan contract market in this chapter, we are also implicitly examining people's decisions concerning how much money they wish to hold.

▶ The Loan Contract Market

Background

In a modern economy such as that of the United States, some individuals would like to purchase goods and services now but lack the necessary dollars to pay the sellers of those goods and services. Of course, at the same time there are other individuals with a completely different problem. They would prefer *not* to use all of their dollars currently available to purchase goods and services. These are not necessarily people who are rich or who don't know what to do with their money. Instead, they are individuals who would like to purchase more goods in the future compared to today. The market for **loan contracts** is also called the **financial or credit market,** which brings these individuals together. The loan contract market is the "place"

where the two types of people "meet" to transfer their money. Money is transferred from those who have more than they want for current uses to those who want more than they now have. A loan contract arranges such a reallocation of spending power.

It is important that we define loan contract precisely. A loan contract is basically a piece of paper that obligates someone to repay money borrowed from someone else. Two parties are obviously involved in any loan contract transaction—the borrower of current dollars and the lender of current dollars. Those of you who go on to law school will study the detailed legal language of a loan contract. When all the details are stripped away, though, a loan contract is simply an exchange of today's dollars for a promise of future dollars.

A Closer Look at the Details of a Loan Contract

To understand the commitments involved in a loan contract, we can examine what is involved from the viewpoints of the two parties involved. In our analysis, the *demander* in the loan contract market is the *borrower*. The demander (or borrower) wishes to receive a certain number of dollars from the lender; these dollars are known as **loanable funds.** In exchange, the demander (or borrower) of loanable funds gives the lender an IOU. This IOU is the loan contract in which the borrower promises to pay back the money borrowed plus interest. The loan contract specifies very clearly the future dates when these payments are to be made. The *demander* of loanable funds, then, *supplies* a loan contract and, as a result, gains *current dollars*. At the same time, the loan contract obligates the demander to return *future dollars* to the lender. The demander of loanable funds is willing to go into debt today because of the potential benefits he or she expects from putting borrowed dollars to good use.

The dollar commitments made by the *supplier* of loanable funds, the *lender,* are mirror images of the dollar commitments made by the demander of loanable funds. The supplier of loanable funds parts with current dollars and in return acquires ownership of the demander's IOU. Because the IOU represents a claim over a specified sequence of payments of future dollars, the supplier of loanable funds has basically traded current money for the money the demander is obliged to pay back in the future.

At the outset it is important to correct any impression that the lender is a loser in the deal. Remember that interest is paid on a loan contract. The rate of interest, and typically not altruistic feelings, is what motivates the lender to willingly part with current dollars. Also keep in mind that it is the *real* interest rate that concerns borrowers and lenders, not the observed or nominal interest rate. If this distinction is unclear, review the definitions of these terms in chapter 19, pages 396–97. Later we will discuss the precise role played by the rate of interest in the decisions of borrowers and lenders in the loan contract market.

The Model of the Loan Contract Market to Be Developed

Two points should be made concerning how our model of the loan contract market relates to the financial markets currently in existence in the United States economy. First, the financial markets in a large modern economy develop according to the principle of specialization. This means that many different types of IOUs are traded. Each IOU pays its own specified rate of interest. Thus, at any time many different interest rates are in effect in the economy. To keep things manageable, our model of the loan contract market will ignore this complexity and simply use the concept of a loan contract or IOU as a generic term. The rate of interest paid on this representative loan contract will be the economy's average interest rate. The second point is that our model is not concerned with the total volume of outstanding loan contracts that have been bought and sold in the *past*. Our model is concerned only with how *new* issues of loan contracts are created in the economy and how this process relates to the determination of aggregate economic activity.

The Demand for Loanable Funds

Firms

Business firms demand loanable funds by selling corporate bonds, by selling their stock, and by borrowing from banks. Firms also borrow loanable funds in another way. Sometimes firms retain earnings, which are profits that go undistributed to stockholders. Because households own the firms in society, retained earnings or business saving is simply another component of firms' demand for loanable funds. The basic reason firms demand loanable funds is to finance investments. Consider, for example, the case of a builder who wants to start an investment project such as the construction of a new building. The contractor is faced with a dilemma. On the one hand, he or she has to buy materials such as bricks, concrete, electrical wiring, and so on from producers who make and sell these products. Construction workers will only be willing to supply their labor services if they receive the current market wage. These and the other expenditures require dollars *now*. However, the builder will not realize any profits from renting space in the building to be constructed until it is completed, which means that profits will be realized in the future. Our builder might try to pay for the goods and services currently supplied by promising future dollars. The fact that this is not the way things actually happen suggests that construction workers and materials suppliers tend not to be interested in producing investment goods unless they are paid in *current* dollars.

We will simply assume that to satisfy the need for current dollars, our builder can enter the loan contract market and exchange an IOU for current dollars. What is the value of the loan contract the builder will demand? It is exactly the same as the value of the current goods and services he or she wishes to buy for the investment project.

Figure 24.1 Firms' demand for loanable funds
Lower interest rates make additional investments profitable because the interest rate is the cost of the credit necessary to finance investment. As a result, the quantity of funds firms wish to borrow increases as the interest rate falls. Thus, the amount of money firms wish to borrow at any particular interest rate is equal to the amount they plan to invest ($\overset{*}{\text{I}}$).

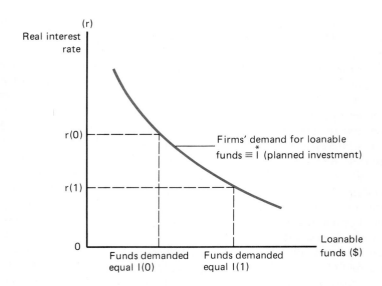

Firms' Demand for Loanable Funds   We assume that a firm's decision to demand loanable funds will reflect its decision to purchase investment goods and that firms borrow for no other reason. This means that firms' demand for loanable funds schedule in figure 24.1 has a negative slope. As the interest rate falls, the amount of funds firms wish to borrow rises. The inverse relationship between the real interest rate (r) and firms' demand for funds stems from the effect of the interest rate on the profitability of investments they might make. There are always more investment projects that will be profitable when the interest rate declines.

The interest rate provides investors with a way of calculating the economic value of potential investment projects, each of which generates a stream of payoffs at various dates in the future. Because a higher interest rate reduces the profitability of investment projects, firms' demand for funds to finance these investments is downward sloping. An investment decision involves present costs and future returns to firms from the services of the additional capital. The rate of interest is what allows a proper economic comparison of these present costs and future returns. As such, it plays a key role in the investment decision.

The total dollars needed to complete *all* the projects deemed profitable at the prevailing interest rate is also the total dollar value of investment goods demanded. When the interest rate is r(0) in figure 24.1, this quantity equals $\overset{*}{\text{I}}$ (0). To finance this investment, investors will try to borrow an equivalent amount of money in the loanable funds market. Although additional investment projects are available, investors will reject them because the cost involved exceeds the value of their returns.

Suppose the interest rate is lower, say, r(1) in figure 24.1. This makes each investment project more profitable. Some projects that were unprofitable at interest rate r(0) become winning ventures at the lower interest rate, r(1). To finance the purchase of this larger quantity of investment goods, investors increase the amount of funds they wish to borrow. Thus, the dollar value of the loans firms desire at interest rate r(1) is $\overset{*}{I}(1)$, which is greater than $\overset{*}{I}(0)$. Remember that we are concerned with the *real value* of loanable funds demanded. This means that we are evaluating the funds that firms wish to borrow at prices that prevailed during some base period (year).

The Government

We know that the federal government purchases goods and services from producers in the economy and provides income support to certain poor, sick, and elderly members of society. One way it pays for these is with revenue collected through taxes. When government expenditure exceeds the tax revenue it collects, we say that the government runs a *deficit*. Only once since 1960 has the federal government in the United States not been in a deficit situation where its total tax revenue (T) fell short of its total expenditure (G). Prior to 1960, budget *surpluses,* the situation where tax revenue exceeds government expenditures, were not uncommon.[1] Let us represent the budget deficit by (G − T), the real value of the difference between the government's expenditure and its tax revenue. The size of the government deficit is a source of great controversy in debates over macroeconomic policy. We will have much more to say about the government deficit in the following chapters—particularly chapters 27–29. For now, we will explore how the government finances a deficit.

Monetizing the Budget Deficit   There are two basic ways the federal government can deal with a budget deficit. First, the United States Treasury can borrow

directly from the Fed. This is equivalent to the federal government's simply printing the money necessary to finance the deficit. When firms demand cash before turning over their goods to a government buyer, the government could simply produce the exact number of dollar bills required to pay for the goods.

Many Latin American governments use their ability to borrow from their central banks or to print money as a "magical" source of financing for their budget deficits. In chapter 28 we analyze the link between inflation and the rapid expansion of the money supply. For now, we turn our attention to another, more commonly used method of financing budget deficits in modern Western economies.

Financing the Budget Deficit in the Loan Contract Market   Suppose that the Treasury does not borrow directly from the Fed when faced with a budget deficit. This means that the government behaves like a private investor in the loan contract market. When government expenditures exceed tax revenues, then, the government enters the loanable funds market as a borrower, seeking enough dollars to finance its budget deficits from the private sector of the economy. In exchange for the loans it receives, the government issues new loan contracts (government bonds) and promises to pay back its debt with future dollars plus interest.

Households and the commercial banking system are perfectly willing to part with their dollars in exchange for the loan contracts the government provides for one basic reason. The federal government can *never* go bankrupt. As a last resort it can always raise taxes or print new money to pay its debt. This means that government IOUs have the lowest risk of all loan contracts and therefore usually pay a lower rate of interest than the bonds of private borrowers. Remember, though, that in our simple model of the aggregate loan contract market we are dealing with a single (average) interest rate.

*The **aggregate demand for loanable funds (DLF)** is a schedule illustrating the total amount of loanable funds borrowers seek to borrow at various real interest rates.*

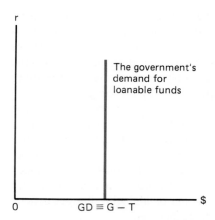

Figure 24.2   The government's demand for loanable funds
The government demands loanable funds equal to its budget deficit and pays whatever interest rate is necessary.

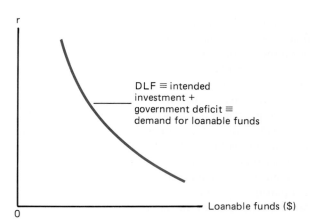

Figure 24.3   The aggregate demand curve for loanable funds
The aggregate demand for loanable funds (DLF) comes from two sources: private investors and the government.

The Government's Demand for Loanable Funds
Figure 24.2 illustrates the real value of the loanable funds demanded by the government. We have drawn the government's demand curve as a vertical line. This implies that the government will finance its entire deficit, $G - T$, in the loan contract market regardless of the interest rate it must pay. The government's need for dollars to finance any deficit is so immediate that it accepts the prevailing rate of interest in the loan contract market.

Exactly how does this happen in practice? Currently, all government securities are auctioned off to the highest bidders. The difference between the face value of the security and the price paid by the lender is the implicit interest rate on the loan contract. For example, suppose that the government wants to borrow $100,000 for one year. It might auction off a security that is a promise to pay the lender $100,000 one year from today. If the winning bidder offers $90,000 for this security, then the implicit rate of interest paid by the government is about 11 percent. The interest rate is higher the lower the amount paid for the promise that the government will pay the lender a fixed $100,000 one year from now.

The Aggregate Demand Curve for Loanable Funds and the Rate of Interest

The **aggregate demand for loanable funds (DLF)** has the two components just discussed: the demand for funds stemming from investment by firms in the private sector of the economy and the government's demand due to any budget deficit. These two sources of demand for loanable funds produce the aggregate demand curve for loanable funds shown in figure 24.3. The real rate of interest is measured on the vertical axis and the total real dollars of loanable funds on the horizontal axis. To obtain the points for the aggregate demand for loanable funds, we have simply added the amount the government wishes to borrow (its budget deficit) to the amount demanded by private investors at the various rates of interest. By considering the various possible real rates of interest, we can plot the aggregate demand for loanable funds schedule, DLF in figure 24.3, from the information in figures 24.1 and 24.2. The demand for loanable funds schedule takes the shape of the demand for loanable funds by investors. In our model, private investors are the only borrowers who are sensitive to changes in the real rate of interest. Thus, the market demand for loanable funds is simply the investors' demand for loanable funds moved to the right or left by an amount equal to the government deficit or surplus.

The aggregate demand for loanable funds shows us how borrowers *as a group* respond to changes in the rate of interest. It is important to realize that the DLF schedule is drawn holding constant the other factors that influence the demand for credit. Should anything that determines investment or the government deficit change (other than the real interest rate), this will disturb the aggregate demand for loanable funds. What are some examples?

Think about factors that would change the individual components of the demand for loanable funds. First, anything that reduces the government deficit, such as a reduction in government expenditures or an increase in taxes, shifts the demand for loanable funds schedule to the left. The opposite holds if the political process generates a larger government deficit through increased government expenditures, reduced taxes, or both. Finally, anything that affects the profitability of investment will also shift the demand for loanable funds schedule. Suppose, for example, firms suddenly hit upon a new technology that makes all investments more profitable. This means that at any given interest rate, firms will desire to invest more and therefore demand more loanable funds.

The Supply of Loanable Funds

Households as Suppliers of Loanable Funds

The Household's Financial Wealth   At the beginning of a given period of time—say, a month—a household will possess a certain level of financial wealth. One way households hold their wealth is in money, which is largely checkable deposits at banks plus currency issued by the government. A second way households hold their wealth is in loan contracts—bonds issued by private firms, foreign countries, or the United States government.

The Household's Saving Decision   Households own productive resources that they ultimately sell to producers of goods and services in exchange for income. All households then face two basic decisions. One is that they must decide how many currently produced goods and services to consume. How many chicken dinners, light bulbs, and vacation trips will they buy?

We know from the discussion in chapter 21 that once a household has made its consumption purchases and paid its taxes, the remainder is its saving. This brings us to a second basic economic decision households make. How will they allocate saving between the two financial assets we are discussing, money and loan contracts? Money is useful to have on hand because it facilitates purchases. However, it pays relatively little or no interest. Holding your wealth in bonds will earn relatively high interest, but then you cannot use it to buy that new car. There are costs and benefits to holding money versus lending it out. The decisions of how much to consume and how to allocate saving are the basic economic choices faced by households on a day-to-day basis. Many complex factors are involved in a household's financial decisions, but two generalizations are reasonable.

1. Day-to-day fluctuations in the rate of interest seem to play no role in how much households save versus consume. Economists disagree over the long-term impact of a permanent change in the return people expect to receive on the amount they save. However, they tend to agree that over short periods of time, other factors are much more important determinants of saving behavior. If the interest rate is not what determines the total amount of saving, then what is? We already have an answer to this question from chapter 21. The saving function discussed there showed us that *total aggregate saving is largely based on aggregate disposable income.* But if the real interest rate does not affect aggregate saving, what role does it play in households' financial decisions?

2. The rate of interest is crucial in determining the *distribution* of households' wealth *between* money and loan contracts. Households will place more and more of their wealth into interest-bearing financial instruments—loan contracts—as the real rate of interest rises. Higher interest rates induce households to increase the amount of money they lend (loan contracts they buy) and also induce them to reduce the amount of money they desire to hold.

For example, suppose we have a household with financial wealth at the beginning of this month that includes $100 in the form of a checking account deposit and $300 worth of loan contracts. These loan contracts may, for example, be held as shares in a mutual fund that purchases corporate and government bonds. Suppose further that the household intends to sell $200 of labor services to an employer this month. The household intends to spend $100 of its earnings on consumption goods, including food and recreation. Its tax bill is $50. These data mean that our hypothetical household is saving $50 ($200 − $150), the portion of its income not consumed or paid out in taxes. This $50 in saving will allow the household to consume more in the future.

The household's next choice concerns the form in which it will hold its $50 saving. The answer depends on the real rate of interest at the time the decision is made, because the interest rate is the opportunity cost of holding financial wealth in currency or in a checking account. Remember, the alternative is to lend the money out and receive an interest payment in return. While a household values dollars in its checking account to facilitate purchases of goods and services, unfortunately it must give up something for that privilege. To hold dollars, the household has to give up the interest it could have earned had it held its savings in loan contracts as opposed to cash or a checking account. The higher the interest rate, the higher is the cost attached to holding money in cash or in a checking account and the greater is the incentive to turn these dollars into interest-bearing loan contracts. (We are discussing the very basic case where the household owns a checking account that pays no interest. In reality, many checking accounts, such as NOW accounts and money market accounts do pay interest. However, the interest that can be earned on loan contracts is higher. The opportunity cost of holding money in a NOW-type checking account is the *difference* between the interest rate paid in the loan contract market and that paid on the NOW account.)

The Rate of Interest and the Household's Supply of Loanable Funds   Let us dig a little deeper into the relationships between the interest rate and the quantity of funds that households supply to the loan contract market. Suppose that within the context of the example we have been developing the interest rate is very low. This means that the opportunity cost of holding money (currency and checking accounts) is also low. The result is that the household in our example decides to save its $50 by placing $10 in its checking account and $40 in a mutual fund that purchases corporate bonds. Thus, the household exactly uses up the $50 it planned to save. Keep in mind that at the low rate of interest we are discussing, the household's supply of loanable funds is less than its current total saving. The low rate of interest makes adding to its checking account a relatively attractive option. By putting some of its saving in a checking account, the household is thereby lending less money ($40) than the maximum it could if it had placed all its saving in a loan contract ($50).

If the real rate of interest rises, a checking account becomes a more expensive asset to hold because total interest rises with the interest rate. Eventually, the interest rate can increase to the point where the household considers the *initial* $100 in its checking account as just the right amount. This means that it will not add any of its intended saving to its checking account. At that particular interest rate, the household's planned saving ($50) will precisely equal the amount it supplies to the loanable funds market ($50).

As the interest rate rises further, the household will reevaluate the benefits it receives from its initial $100 checking account balance. Higher and higher rates of interest mean that the costs of holding a checking account rise relative to the benefits. The financially astute household will therefore decide to keep less than the initial $100 in its checking account. As the interest rate continues to rise, the household will move more and more of its financial wealth out of its checking account and into the loan contract market. At relatively high interest rates, then, households may purchase *more* loan contracts than their saving alone can finance. The balance comes from reducing their holdings of cash and checking account balances.

Households' Supply Curve of Loanable Funds   Figure 24.4 illustrates households' supply of loanable funds. The vertical axis indicates the real rate of interest, r, and the horizontal axis measures the real value of the money households supply to the loanable funds market. (Remember that the real value of funds supplied to the bond market is the amount of money households lend expressed in terms of the base period's prices for currently produced goods and services.)

Based on our discussion, the households' supply curve of loanable funds in figure 24.4 is drawn with a positive slope. Before proceeding, it is important to point out that households do not *only* supply loanable funds (save). Many households borrow to finance purchases of houses, cars, farms, mobile homes, and so on (dissave). However, households are *net* savers.

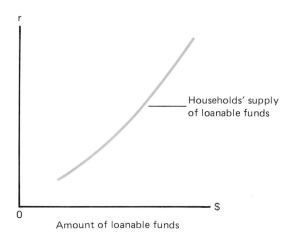

Figure 24.4   Households' supply of loanable funds
Households offer more funds to the loanable funds (credit) market as the real interest rate rises. At higher and higher interest rates the opportunity cost of holding money rises and loan contracts become a financially more attractive way to hold wealth.

For example, in 1983 the average United States family had an average net worth (assets − liabilities) of $66,050.[2] Thus, the supply of loanable funds by households in figure 24.4 should be thought of as the amount households offer to lend *in excess of* any funds they borrow.

Banks As Suppliers of Funds

The banking system is a second major supplier of loanable funds in the economy. Because we studied the banking system and money creation in detail in chapters 22 and 23, we need only review briefly the money creation process and how it is a source of loanable funds. The key point to remember is that as long as banks have sufficient reserves, they can supply (write) loans without first receiving dollars from other sources. Banks can do this by creating new checkable deposits.

Table 24.2   A bank's loan operation

The bank supplies loanable funds by purchasing a loan contract and creating a new checking account balance

Assets	Liabilities
+$100,000 loan contract	+$100,000 checking account

Consider a simple example. A potential borrower comes into a bank wishing to finance a construction project. He or she enters into negotiations with the loan officer, and the loan officer views the investment project as a profitable one for the bank. As a result, the bank agrees to supply loanable funds (buy the borrower's loan contract). To fulfill its part of the transaction, the bank gives our investor the loan in the form of a new checking account. The borrower now has dollars that can be used to buy the goods and services necessary to complete the construction project.

Table 24.2 reminds us how the banking system conducts a loan operation. When a borrower buys a $100,000 loan contract, the bank takes the $100,000 loan contract and adds it to its assets. At the same time, the bank increases its liabilities by crediting the borrower with a *new* $100,000 checking account (or increasing the balance in the borrower's existing account). *The crucial issue illustrated in table 24.2 is that the commercial bank did not depend on household saving to make this transaction.* The loan occurred entirely within the banking system through the creation of new money in the form of a checking account balance.

Another way to state what we have just learned about the banking system's supply of loanable funds is that the checking account balances created by the loan activities of banks add to the value of society's money supply (M). To see this more clearly let us use the symbol P to represent the current price level *relative* to the base period price level. P might, for example, be the consumer price index or the GNP deflator. Finally, let us use the symbol Δ to signify a change, so that we have

$$\text{banks' supply of loanable funds} \equiv \Delta M/P.$$

Banks' supply of loanable funds is an addition to the real stock of money in the economy.

The Rate of Interest and Banks' Supply of Loanable Funds   Banks' reserve position is probably the main factor determining the amount of loanable funds banks supply to the economy. However, higher interest rates may induce the banking system to expand the amount of loanable funds it offers. The reason for this is that banks suffer an opportunity cost whenever they hold reserves in excess of the amount required by the Fed.

Remember that without excess reserves banks would find it difficult to satisfy both the desires of the public (for example, a sudden, unexpected withdrawal from checking accounts) *and* the Fed's reserve requirements. If a bank were to have no excess reserves when it cashed a customer's check, it would be placed in the position of holding less than its required reserves. This is a result of fractional reserve banking. To return its reserves to the required level, a bank would have to do something fairly costly, such as borrow from the Fed, call in a loan contract early, or sell off an earning asset. The point is that excess reserves are a valuable source of flexibility for a bank.

The opportunity cost of holding excess reserves is the interest income banks *could have* earned had they supplied loanable funds to the full extent permitted by the reserve requirements of the Fed. As the real rate of interest rises, this opportunity cost also increases. In an attempt to obtain profits, the banking system has an incentive to reduce its excess reserves and to supply more loanable funds to the public whenever the interest rate rises.

Banks' Supply of Loanable Funds Schedule   Figure 24.5 depicts the supply of loanable funds by the banking system. The real rate of interest is measured on the vertical axis, and the real quantity of loanable funds supplied by banks is measured on the horizontal axis. The upward slope indicates that higher rates of interest induce banks to offer greater amounts of loanable funds to their customers.

Two events can shift banks' real supply of loanable funds: (1) a change in the price level and (2) a change in banks' excess reserves. The first event is worth discussing in order to explain how the rate of inflation and the real rate of interest are related. The second event gives us the avenue through which monetary policy affects credit markets, saving, investment, and economic activity in general.

Banks supply loanable funds by creating *new* checking account money. A change in the price level of goods and services (P) alters the quantity of goods and services that can be purchased with a given amount of money. In terms of the expression $\Delta M/P$, an increase or decrease in P will change the denominator. Since banks' supply of loanable funds is the real value of the *change* in the money stock resulting from their loan activities, a change in the price level changes the real value of this additional money supplied. A higher price level shifts the banks' supply of loanable funds to the left because a given amount of money created has a lower real value at a higher price level. Similarly, a reduction in the price level shifts the banks' real supply of loanable funds to the right.

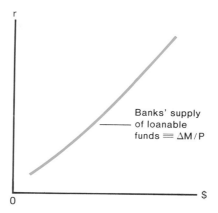

Figure 24.5   Banks' supply of loanable funds
The banking system supplies more loanable funds at higher real interest rates. At higher interest rates the opportunity cost of holding excess reserves rises. This leads banks to reduce their excess reserves and supply more loanable funds.

In this case, a given amount of new checking account money has a greater purchasing power and a greater real value.

It is also important to remember that the supply curve of loanable funds by banks depicted in figure 24.5 illustrates their willingness to turn a *given* amount of excess reserves into loans at various interest rates; that is, the curve is valid for a particular level of excess reserves. Should monetary policy change those excess reserves, banks' supply of loanable funds would shift. More excess reserves means that banks will offer greater amounts of loanable funds to borrowers at any given interest rate and the supply curve will shift to the right. Monetary policy that reduces banks' excess reserves will result in a leftward shift in the supply schedule in figure 24.5. At any given interest rate, banks will supply less loanable funds should monetary policy reduce their excess reserves.

*The **aggregate supply of loanable funds (SLF)** is a schedule illustrating the total amount of loanable funds lenders offer at various real interest rates.*

*The **equilibrium interest rate** is the real interest rate that equates the aggregate supply and demand for loanable funds; at the equilibrium interest rate borrowers want to borrow exactly the amount of funds that lenders want to lend.*

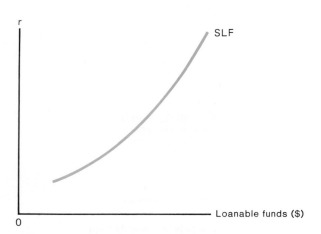

Figure 24.6   The aggregate supply curve of loanable funds
SLF is the sum of households' net supply and banks' supply of funds to the loan contract market. It is positively sloped because both banks and households are willing to lend more at higher real interest rates.

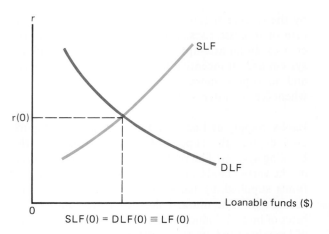

Figure 24.7   Equilibrium in the aggregate loan contract market
The equilibrium interest rate, r(0), is the price of credit where the amount of money borrowers wish to borrow exactly matches the amount lenders offer to lend. Anything that disturbs the demand curve (the demand for investment projects, for example) or the supply curve (banks' excess reserves or households' saving, for example) will lead to a new equilibrium real rate of interest.

The Aggregate Supply of Loanable Funds

The total supply of loanable funds to the credit market stems from the supply of funds by households and the banking system and is known as the **aggregate supply of loanable funds (SLF)**. It represents the *real value* of the total dollars supplied to the loan contract (credit) market by banks and households.

Figure 24.6 illustrates the market supply curve for new loan contracts with respect to the real rate of interest. To derive points on SLF, we first choose a particular value of the real rate of interest. We then look at the total funds offered by households at the rate of interest in figure 24.4 and at the total loanable funds offered by banks at the rate of interest in figure 24.5. The sum of these two numbers is plotted in figure 24.6 against the real rate of interest we chose. Repeating this exercise for various interest rates traces out the SLF in figure 24.6. Because both banks' and households' supply of loanable funds schedules are upward sloping with respect to the interest rate, so is the aggregate supply of loanable funds.

Equilibrium in the Loan Contract Market

The Determination of the Real Interest Rate

The loan contract market performs two extremely important functions for the aggregate economy. First, it is where scarce funds available for lending are allocated among different borrowers. Second, the interaction of borrowers and lenders in the loan contract market leads to the current real interest rate.

Figure 24.7 contains both the aggregate supply and demand schedules for loanable funds. The intersection of these two curves shows us that at interest rate r(0), the real value of new loan contracts demanded in the economy equals the amount supplied. The **equilibrium interest rate** is r(0) because no other rate of interest can satisfy both the desired plans of borrowers and lenders in the aggregate loan contract market.

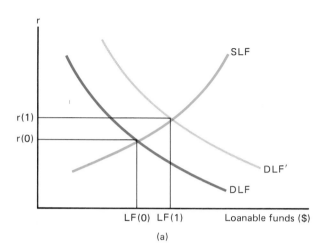

(a)

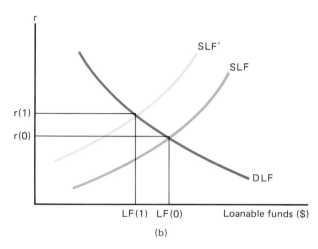

(b)

Figure 24.8 Shifts in the demand and supply of loanable funds
In part (a) an increase in planned investment or in the government deficit has shifted the demand for loanable funds to the right. The result is an increase in the rate of interest and an increase in the quantity of money borrowed.

In part (b) an increase in the desire of households to add to their cash balances or a decline in the willingness of banks to make new loans has shifted the supply of loanable funds to the left. The result is an increase in the rate of interest and a reduction in the quantity of money lent.

When the interest rate is above equilibrium, the quantity of loanable funds offered by lenders exceeds the quantity of funds borrowers wish to borrow. In a sense, borrowers are in the driver's seat. Money for investment projects is more than readily available. However, some lenders will not be able to find borrowers with whom they can satisfactorily negotiate loan contracts. As lenders begin to realize the extent of the market's disequilibrium, downward pressure will be exerted on the real interest rate. This pressure ceases when the loan contract market finally reaches its equilibrium interest rate, r(0).

The opposite effects are felt in the aggregate loanable funds market when the interest rate is below equilibrium. In this case, *suppliers* of loanable funds are in the driver's seat. Borrowers are unable to find all the funds they want, but lenders have no trouble getting loan contracts that meet their approval. Eventually, some potential borrowers will fear that they might get caught short in their total borrowing and start to compete with one another by bidding up the interest rate. The excess demand for loanable funds at the lower interest rate will generate upward pressure on the market rate of interest until the aggregate loanable funds market settles into an equilibrium at real interest rate r(0).

When either the demand or supply of loanable funds shifts, the equilibrium interest rate will also change. Shifts in the demand and supply of loanable funds are illustrated in figure 24.8. In part (a), an increase in planned investment or in the government deficit has shifted the demand for loanable funds to the right. The result is an increase in the rate of interest and an increase in the quantity of loanable funds borrowed and lent. In part (b) of figure 24.8, an increase in the desire of households to add to their cash balances or a reduction in the willingness of banks to lend money has shifted the supply of loanable funds to the left. The result is, again, an increase in the rate of interest but a *reduction* in the quantity of loanable funds borrowed and lent.

The **structure of interest rates** refers to the variation in interest rates across loans by the type of borrower and the term of the loan (loan period).

Table 24.3   Selected nominal interest rates, 1960–1986

	1960	1965	1970	1975	1978	1980	1982	1983	1986
United States Treasury securities									
1-year Treasury bill	3.41	4.06	6.48	6.28	7.74	10.89	11.07	8.80	6.65
3-year maturity	3.98	4.22	7.29	7.49	8.29	11.55	12.92	10.45	7.27
10-year maturity	4.12	4.28	7.35	7.99	8.41	11.46	13.00	11.10	7.71
High-grade (Aaa) corporate bonds	4.41	4.49	8.04	8.83	8.73	11.94	13.79	12.04	9.09

Source: From *Statistical Abstract of the United States: 1982–83* (103d edition), U.S. Bureau of the Census, 1982; *Economic Indicators*, January 1983, and *Statistical Abstract of the United States*, 1985, Table 850, p. 515.

The equilibrium interest rate r(0) satisfies all suppliers and demanders in the loanable funds market. Table 24.3 illustrates selected nominal interest rates in the United States for 1960 through 1986. In chapter 19 we saw that nominal interest rates and the rate of inflation tend to move together. For example, the interest rates for 1960 in table 24.3 are in the range of 3 to 4 percent. In 1960, the rate of inflation was 1.6 percent. In 1970, when the rates of interest were 6 to 8 percent, the rate of inflation was 5.9 percent. A generally positive relationship between interest and inflation rates continued in the 1980s. In 1980, the inflation rate was 14.5 percent and the interest rates were 11 to 12 percent. After inflation fears subsided considerably, interest rates fell to an average of about 7.5 percent in 1986.

It is important to reemphasize the distinction between the nominal, or so-called market, interest rate and the real rate of interest. The interest rates in table 24.3 are the total price of credit borrowers pay lenders *unadjusted* for inflation. When borrowers and lenders consider the cost of credit and return from lending, they care about the real purchasing power of the interest payments. Both will take account of the fact

that at a given nominal interest rate, the real interest rate is lower the greater the rate of inflation expected to prevail. Thus, at higher rates of inflation borrowers insist on higher nominal interest rates to offset the reduced purchasing power of the dollars they will receive in the future when goods and services cost more.

The Structure of Interest Rates

A number of factors underlie the **structure of interest rates,** which is the variation in interest rates depending upon the type of borrower and the duration of the loan contract as listed in table 24.3. Notice that for the three different types of United States Treasury securities listed, generally the longer the term of the loan, the higher the rate of interest. Second, corporate bonds have a rate of interest that is higher than that on United States Treasury securities. Thus, we see that interest rates in a given year vary by the term of the loan contract (number of years) and who the borrower is.

A key factor underlying the rate of interest a borrower must pay is the risk to the lender that the loan will not be repaid. We have already discussed the unlikelihood of the United States government's going bankrupt. This means that United States Treasury securities have lower default risk than corporate bonds because a given corporation is more likely to go bankrupt and not pay its loan obligations. This is one of the reasons why the United States Treasury securities listed in table 24.3 generally bear lower interest rates than high-quality (Aaa) corporate bonds.

Another aspect of risk is that the farther into the future you consider, the more dramatically the economy may change. Who is to know, for example, whether there will be extremely high inflation or taxes on interest earnings five to ten years from now? As a lender, I will require a higher compensation to tie up my money for ten years than if I will be repaid at the end of this year. Because many things can happen in my personal life in ten years—for example, death or a new baby, just to name two—I must receive relatively high compensation to be willing to tie up my funds in a ten-year bond. The riskier the loan (from the perspective of the lender), the higher the rate of interest on the loan. This is what underlies the fact that long-term United States securities pay higher interest rates than one-year Treasury bills and that United States Treasury securities generally pay lower rates of interest than corporate bonds.

▶ Summary and Conclusions

It is impossible to understand how the macroeconomy works without taking careful account of the financial sector. In this chapter we have seen how the Fed's decisions on whether to use its powerful policy tools to control the money supply or the interest rate can have a crucial influence on the course of the macroeconomy and the fortunes of politicians in office during periods of prosperity or recession. We discussed the economic factors that underlie the supply and demand of loanable funds and developed the concept of equilibrium in the aggregate loanable funds market. The following points were emphasized.

Knowledge of the individual's behavior in the market for goods and services and the market for loan contracts implies the amount of money he or she will choose to hold.

The loan contract market brings together two different groups—those who would like to divert expenditure into the future and those who would like to move their expenditure from the future into the present.

The aggregate demand for loanable funds is downward sloping. At higher real interest rates borrowers wish to borrow less money, and at lower interest rates they wish to borrow more.

The aggregate supply of loanable funds is the sum of the net supply of funds by households and the banking system. The aggregate supply of loanable funds is positively sloped with respect to the real interest rate.

The loan contract market performs two important functions for the aggregate economy: (1) it is where scarce funds available for loans are allocated among various borrowers, and (2) the interactions of borrowers and lenders in the aggregate loan contract market determine the real interest rate.

From the standpoint of the aggregate economy, the real interest rate is what matters to borrowers and lenders.

The longer the term of a loan, typically the higher the rate of interest on the loan, *cet. par.*

The greater the risk of default on a loan, typically the higher the rate of interest on the loan, *cet. par.*

▶ Key Terms

aggregate demand for
  loanable funds (DLF)
  504

aggregate supply of
  loanable funds (SLF)
  510

equilibrium interest
  rate *510*

loan contract, financial,
  or credit market *500*

loanable funds *500*

structure of interest
  rates *512*

▶ Questions for Discussion and Review

1. Lenders are rich people and borrowers are poor people. Discuss and evaluate this statement. In the course of answering be sure to discuss the motives underlying the respective behavior of borrowers and lenders.

2. What are the basic properties of a loan contract; that is, what are the respective economic motivations of the borrower and the lender?

3. The lenders in a loan contract are the winners because they get back more money than they lent. Evaluate this statement.

4. The lenders in a loan contract are the losers because they are repaid with money that will buy less because of inflation. Evaluate this statement.

5. What are the sources of the market demand for loanable funds? Which of them is sensitive to the rate of interest? Why are some of the demanders of loanable funds not influenced by the rate of interest?

6. Make a list of events that would shift the demand for loanable funds. Next to your list indicate the direction in which each event would shift the aggregate demand for loanable funds. Next to that indicate a government policy, if any, that would produce the event you have listed.

7. Who are the two major suppliers of loanable funds? Why is each of them willing to supply more loanable funds the higher the real rate of interest?

8. Explain and graphically describe the equilibrium point in the loan contract market. Now suppose that a (usury) law is introduced placing a ceiling on the rate of interest that is below the equilibrium value r(0). How do you take account of the usury law in your diagram? If the law is effectively enforced, what will the market rate of interest and the amount of loanable funds borrowed and lent be? Who are the winners from the usury law? Who are the losers?

9. The rate of inflation is 10 percent per year. You open a newspaper and see that long-term government bonds in the United States pay an annual rate of interest of 15 percent. Is this a high or a low rate of interest? Explain carefully. Would your answer be any different if the rate of inflation were 14 percent? Explain.

10. A recent newscast reported that high interest rates are bad because borrowers cannot afford them. Another newscast reported that low interest rates are bad because lenders cannot make any money. Is any particular rate of interest good for society? Discuss carefully.

11. In the early 1980s there was a great deal of concern over large government deficits. It was felt that these deficits raised the interest rate and, in the process, crowded out private investment. Analyze this conclusion within the context of the model of the loanable funds market developed in this chapter. Support your answer graphically.

12. Considering the supply and demand framework of the loanable funds market, what is the relationship between real interest rates and bond prices?

Deregulation of the Banking Industry

▶ The Action-Initiating Event

The House Subcommittee on Money and Banking has begun hearings with a view toward stopping and perhaps reversing the deregulation of financial institutions begun in 1980. The committee is being lobbied heavily by representatives of savings and loan institutions and commercial banks. The political judgment is that the committee is evenly split on the issue. There will be an attempt to draft legislation within the committee for House consideration after the next recess. Apparently, the committee is considering raising reserve requirements on all types of deposits, eliminating branch banking, and imposing ceilings on all lending and deposit interest rates.

▶ The Issue

The economics of the situation seem fairly straightforward. Deregulation of the banking industry has cut into local savings and loan bank monopolies and those of commercial banks in general at a time when savings and loans are still trying to recover from losses caused by long-term mortgages with rates of interest well below the current interest rates they must pay to retain existing deposits and acquire new ones. In addition, many commercial banks of all sizes are facing default on a significant portion of their loans to developing nations. Moreover, the substantial number of bank failures throughout the 1980s has made the public afraid for the safety of their deposits. Consequently, the President needs to take a strong position on this issue going into the upcoming national elections.

▶ Economic Policy Issues

I have been asked by the President to solicit your opinion on a number of substantive issues. First, to what extent would protection of local bank monopolies against competition from new banks entering their local markets help avoid bank failures? How would protecting them against competition affect interest rates? What would be the effect of reregulation of banks on consumer debt, the housing market, and business investment plans? Can you propose alternative schemes to assist banks that would address their problems more directly, with fewer potential adverse affects on the economy? Should the administration take a promarket approach and let weak institutions fail? If so, is there any danger of a 1930s-style financial collapse?

▶ Recommendations

In brief, I would like you to consider a wide range of policy options, from doing nothing to returning to the pre-1980 regulatory conditions in which banks had local monopolies (i.e., were protected against competition from other banks entering their local markets by state regulations) and in which both deposit and lending interest rates were limited by law. First, I need your assessment of the economic pros and cons of alternative policy options and your estimate of what would be best for the country. Second, I need your judgments regarding who the potential winners and losers would be for the alternatives you consider. The office of the President will then try to make a political judgment about the feasibility of supporting the various options you outline, considering the upcoming elections. We want to maintain a posture of leadership by getting out front on this issue. But we do not want to set the administration up as an easy target for the opposition in the next campaign.

economy is in recession, *and cyclical unemployment is positive. When the economy is in short-run macroequilibrium at a level above full macroequilibrium, the unemployment rate is less than its normal value, and an* inflationary episode *is inevitable.*

Since the end of World War II, the United States has experienced six severe recessions and four mild recessions. During the severe recessions, GNP declined by an average of 3.3 percent, while the unemployment rate increased by an average of 3.8 percentage points. In the mild recessions, GNP declined on average by 1.7 percent and unemployment increased by an average of 2.3 percentage points. Each contraction of economic activity was followed by an expansion, in which GNP growth was greater than average and the unemployment rate declined.[1] In chapter 28, we review in detail the inflationary episode that started in the mid-1960s, some effects of which continue to the present time.

We will focus particularly on the role of interest rate and price level adjustments in pushing the economy toward macroequilibrium. Once you understand how the macroeconomy behaves when it is "disturbed," it will be relatively easy to understand how various government policies influence unemployment and inflation. This subject will be investigated in chapter 27.

A model of the economy with only three markets may seem simplistic given the vast number of markets in the actual economy. Even with only three markets, you will see that keeping track of everything at the same time can get a little tough. In a macroeconomic setting, events happen simultaneously in all markets. A change in demand in the goods market will affect the credit market and the labor market. What happens in the credit and labor markets will feed back into the goods sector. Because of this cause-and-effect cycle, we must keep careful account of supply and demand conditions in all markets *simultaneously. This task is made much easier by simplifying our macroeconomic model to contain only three aggregate markets.*

▶ **Full Macroeconomic Equilibrium: Satisfying Three Markets Simultaneously**

First, we will review equilibrium in each of the separate aggregate markets we have studied in chapters 19 through 24. These are the markets for labor, goods and services, and credit. During this review, remember that only when equilibrium prevails in *each* market *at the same time* can we say that the entire macroeconomy is in equilibrium.

1. The aggregate labor market is in equilibrium when the quantity of labor demanded equals the quantity of labor that the population wishes to supply. Moreover, when full macroeconomic equilibrium prevails, there is full employment in the labor market (cyclical unemployment equals zero), and the total unemployment rate is at its so-called normal level. The real wage rate will equal the marginal product of labor. The real wage is equal to the real wage workers expect to be paid because no one is surprised by an unexpected change in the price level.

   Equilibrium in the aggregate labor market determines not only the real wage rate, the level of employment, and the level of unemployment but also the aggregate quantity of goods and services produced. Figure 25.1 shows how the aggregate supply of labor and aggregate demand for labor interact to determine the equilibrium real wage rate and equilibrium employment, $L(0)$. Employment determines aggregate production, GNP, through the aggregate production function. We have seen that this is called *full-employment GNP*. (You may wish to review pages 424–25 to remind yourself of how employment determines GNP through the aggregate production function.) In 1986, employment averaged more than 108 million and GNP was close to $4 trillion.

2. The aggregate market for currently produced goods and services is in equilibrium when *planned expenditure equals production.* In chapter 21, we learned that the aggregate

Figure 25.1   The aggregate labor market and the quantity of real GNP supplied
Equilibrium employment and the real wage rate are determined by the aggregate supply and demand for labor.

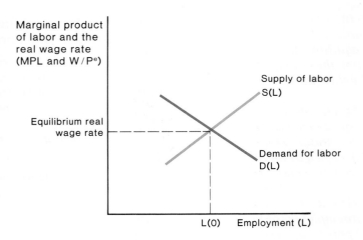

Figure 25.2   The aggregate market for goods and services
The aggregate market for goods and services is in equilibrium when planned saving equals planned investment plus the government deficit. The market for goods and services and the labor market must *both* reach equilibrium at the *same* value of gross national product.

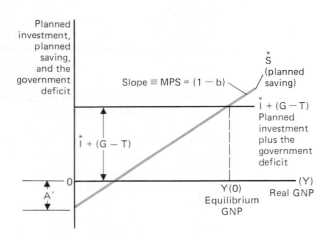

market for goods and services is in equilibrium when planned investment plus the government deficit equals planned aggregate saving or when

$$\overset{*}{I} + (G - T) = \overset{*}{S}.$$

In figure 25.2, we see that planned investment plus the government deficit does not rise as GNP rises. Planned saving, however,

does increase with GNP. Therefore, there is one, and only one, value of GNP at which the previous equation holds. At this level of GNP, $Y(0)$, planned saving equals planned investment plus the government deficit, and aggregate planned expenditure on goods and services exactly equals the quantity firms have produced. In full macroeconomic equilibrium (and *only* then), the level of GNP will equal the amount produced when the labor force is fully employed. That is, in full macroeconomic equilibrium cyclical unemployment will not exist.

3. The aggregate credit market is in equilibrium when the quantity of loanable funds demanded by borrowers equals the quantity supplied. Remember that the aggregate supply of loanable funds includes the new money balances (measured in real dollars) provided by banks' desired purchases of new loan contracts. The demand for loanable funds is created by planned investment expenditures and borrowing by the government to finance its own deficit. Figure 25.3 summarizes equilibrium in the credit market. Equilibrium in the market for loan contracts requires that the real interest rate be at exactly the level that makes the quantity of loanable funds demanded equal to the quantity supplied.

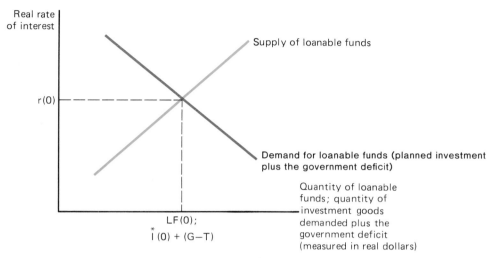

Figure 25.3   The aggregate market for loanable funds
The demand for funds comes from the demand by borrowers to purchase investment goods (I) and from the government to finance its deficit (G − T). At the equilibrium real interest rate, the quantity of funds demanded exactly equals the quantity supplied. Full macroeconomic equilibrium requires that

$\dot{I}$ + (G − T) in this diagram equal planned investment plus the government deficit in figure 25.2. In other words, equilibrium in the credit market and equilibrium in the market for goods and services must both occur at the same time, and the value of GNP, Y(0), must be the same in both figures 25.1 and 25.2.

Remember that the quantity of loanable funds demanded is, by assumption, equal to investment plus the government deficit. Therefore, the rate of interest is a crucial variable linking the credit market to the market for goods and services. In full macroeconomic equilibrium, the rate of interest must be at precisely the level that assures that planned investment plus the government deficit equals planned saving at the *full-employment level of GNP*. This assures that the goods and services market equilibrium as depicted in figure 25.2 is the same as implied by figure 25.1.

In full macroeconomic equilibrium, inflation is zero. The price level is stable and is not expected to change. Therefore, the real and nominal rates of interest are equal because the real rate of interest is the nominal rate minus the inflation rate.

▶ A Closer Look at Full Macroeconomic Equilibrium

To understand how the macroeconomy works and the means government policymakers may use to prevent recessions or inflations, it is helpful to combine as many macroeconomic variables as possible into one diagram. Figure 25.4 depicts full macroeconomic equilibrium with GNP = $200 billion. Part (a) of this figure is a flowchart representation of macroequilibrium, showing how the aggregate labor, goods, and credit markets are interrelated. For convenience, we depict a situation in which government expenditure is equal to taxes so that the government deficit is zero. However, the representation of macroequilibrium would be just as valid if, for example, the government deficit were positive or negative (a surplus). To make sure you understand part (a) of figure 25.4, redraw it on a piece of paper with a government deficit of $10

Figure 25.4 Full macroequilibrium
This figure depicts full macroequilibrium because $\dot{S} = \hat{I} + (G - T)$ at $Y(0)$, the level of GNP that assures full employment equilibrium in the aggregate labor market.

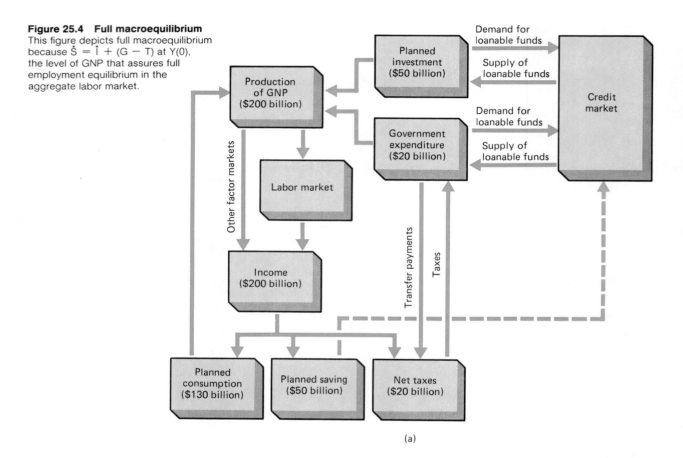

(a)

billion. (Will you lower taxes or raise expenditure?) Now adjust planned investment so as to maintain macroeconomic equilibrium. (Do you have to raise planned investment or lower it? Could you also adjust planned consumption and saving to maintain macroeconomic equilibrium?)

Figure 25.4, part (b) describes macroeconomic equilibrium geometrically in terms of supply and demand in the aggregate credit market and on the market for goods and services. We can combine these two markets in one diagram because the real value of loanable funds, the real value of investment expenditure and the government deficit, and the real value of saving all have the same unit of measurement (real dollars). This means that they can all be measured along the horizontal axis.

Remember, figure 25.2 shows that equilibrium in the goods market occurs at the level of GNP where planned saving equals planned investment plus the

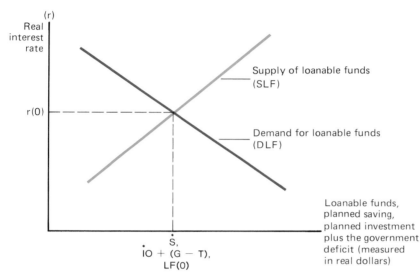

Supply of loanable funds
(SLF)

Demand for loanable funds
(DLF)

Loanable funds,
planned saving,
planned investment
plus the government
deficit (measured
in real dollars)

S,
İO + (G − T),
LF(0)

These symbols show that the quantity
of loanable funds demanded and
supplied, investment plus the
government deficit, and planned saving,
are all equal to each other.

(b)

government deficit. Along the horizontal axis of part (b) of figure 25.4, we have marked the level of planned saving that occurs when GNP is at its *full-employment level*. The DLF curve marks off the quantities of loanable funds demanded to finance new investment projects at various interest rates plus the amount the government needs to borrow to finance its deficit. The DLF curve crosses the SLF curve (which represents the quantity of loanable funds supplied at various interest rates) at just the point that assures

planned investment plus the government deficit equals planned saving. Thus, in part (b) of figure 25.4, we depict a situation in which planned saving equals planned investment plus the government deficit, assuring equilibrium in both the loan contract market and the market for goods and services *at the full-employment level of GNP*. We know the labor market is at full employment because the level of planned saving marked by Š has been specified to be the amount of saving that households desire when the labor market is in full-employment equilibrium. This corresponds to the level of employment shown in figure 25.1. Therefore, figure 25.4 describes full macroeconomic equilibrium.

We can now use figure 25.4 to show what happens when the economy heads toward a recession or an inflationary episode. Will the economy ever return to full macroequilibrium after it begins to move away, or will it get "stuck" in a short-run equilibrium at less than full employment or with permanent inflation? The answer to this question is crucial in understanding how the macroeconomy works and how government policies can help or hurt macroeconomic performance.

▸ Recessions and Inflationary Episodes

We will now analyze how the macroeconomy responds to exogenous changes in some of the variables that affect the full equilibrium levels of employment, GNP, the real interest rate, and the price level. Economists who specialize in studying macroeconomic adjustments generally agree that the major events affecting macroequilibrium involve changes in investors' optimism about the profitability of investment projects and changes in government expenditure, taxation, and monetary policy. In the remainder of this chapter and in chapter 26, we will explore the impact of changes in planned investment and planned saving during a recession and during an inflationary episode. Changes in government expenditure, taxation, and monetary policy will be treated in depth in chapters 27–29.

Our analysis of recessions and inflationary episodes is based on figure 25.4. Starting from an initial position of full macroeconomic equilibrium, we will assume a change in the economic behavior of some

group. In response to this shock, a new intersection of supply and demand for loanable funds will produce a new equilibrium real interest rate. Once we know the value of this new rate of interest, we can compare planned saving with planned investment plus the government deficit, which monitors the state of disequilibrium in the goods market. The goods market will then adjust to achieve a state of *short-run* equilibrium in which planned expenditure equals production but GNP is less than its full-employment level. We will then note which conditions of *full* macroeconomic equilibrium are *not* satisfied. Thus, we will be able to predict whether, and how, the cycle of adjustment will continue until the economy regains full macroequilibrium.

Recession: The Effect of a Decline in Planned Investment

Recall that *today's* planned investment depends on investors' expectations about the *future* stream of profits, or returns, from new investment projects. Suppose investors observe that a major decline in the birthrate twenty years ago will result in fewer young adults marrying, forming households, buying new cars, and so on. This forecasted change in expenditures on consumer durable goods leads to a more pessimistic view of the returns on investing in new plants and equipment to produce lumber products, automobiles, household appliances, and other goods. This decline in investment leads to further reductions in planned investment in the industries producing capital goods in the economy. In other words, since the *future* no longer appears as profitable as it once did, investors will respond *today* by reducing their current rate of planned expenditure. The economy's probable initial reactions to this change are outlined below.

A Leftward Shift in the Demand for Loanable Funds

The assumed change in investors' expectations can be represented graphically on the basis of figure 25.4 part (b). In figure 25.5, part (a), the lines DLF and SLF represent macroeconomic conditions *prior* to the change in investment expectations. Full macroeconomic equilibrium prevails with real interest rate r(0). To remind you what is going on in the goods and labor markets, we have reproduced figures 25.2 and 20.9 in figure 25.5, parts (b) and (c), respectively. In part (b) you can see that the full-employment level of GNP is Y(0), where planned saving equals planned investment plus the government deficit. In the labor market, part (c) of figure 25.5, full employment occurs at expected real wage $W/P^e(0)$, with employment equal to $L^n(0)$.

In part (a) of figure 25.5, we can depict the effects of reduced investor optimism about the future by noting that a reduction in planned investment shifts the demand curve for loanable funds leftward to DLF'. Given the change in investor expectations, DLF' tells us how many dollars are now demanded when borrowers are confronted with various interest rates. Planned investment at *each* rate of interest is now *less* than it was. Thus, at interest rate r(0) investors intend to spend less than previously. This decline in the demand for loanable funds due to a reduction in planned investment is indicated by the arrow pointing leftward in the loanable funds market diagram.

A Decline in the Interest Rate

With the new demand for loanable funds, the interest rate r(0) no longer equates the demand and supply for loanable funds. At interest rate r(0), the loanable funds market is in a state of excess supply. Suppliers of loanable funds (households and banks) will then compete for the reduced number of loan contracts offered to them by bidding down the interest rate until the loanable funds market is again in equilibrium, at interest rate r(1) in figure 25.5, part (a). This decline in the interest rate, which closes the gap between the quantity of loanable funds demanded and supplied, is indicated by the downward-pointing arrow.

Viewed from the supply side of the credit market, the lower rate of interest induces households to devote *more* of their saving to acquiring additional money balances (and hence less to the purchase of loan contracts) because the opportunity cost attached to holding money has gone down. The lower interest rate also induces banks to purchase smaller amounts of loan contracts. Viewed from the demand side of the loanable funds market, the decline in the rate of interest to r(1) *partially* offsets the effects of the reduction in the demand for loanable funds. In part (a) of figure 25.5, the lower interest rate r(1) has induced investors to move down along their *new* loanable funds demand curve. Thus, they wind up purchasing *more* investment goods than they would have purchased at the old interest rate r(0) given their current pessimism about the future. However, they still do not want to purchase as many investment goods as they did before they became pessimistic and when full macroeconomic equilibrium prevailed. Along DLF', planned investment plus the government deficit now equals $\overset{**}{I}(1) + (G - T)$, which is also the quantity of loanable funds demanded. (The two asterisks, **, over the symbol I indicate that the planned investment schedule has shifted to a different position compared to the initial planned investment schedule, which is marked with one asterisk, *.)

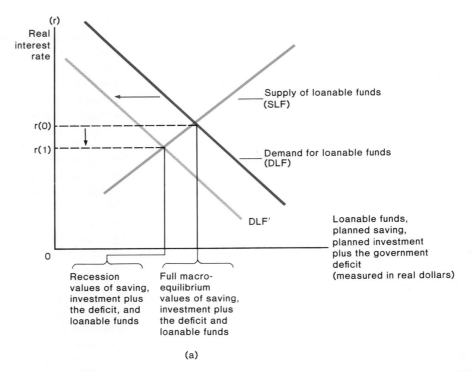

(a)

Figure 25.5   A decrease in planned investment leading to short-run macroeconomic equilibrium in a recession
In part (a) planned investment and the demand for loanable funds have declined. This leads to a decline in real GNP and in the real rate of interest. As GNP falls, planned saving falls as well.

In part (b) equilibrium in the market for goods and services has changed. GNP is now lower than its full macroequilibrium value because planned investment has declined.

In part (c) we note that during a recession the demand for labor is reduced to $D(L)'$. If the real wage rate is "stuck" at $W/P^e(0)$, then cyclical unemployment results. More people want jobs, $L^n(0)$, than there are jobs available, $L(1)$.

You might wonder how the decline in the interest rate in part (a) of figure 25.5 increases the quantity of planned investment, since we started by assuming that investor expectations had declined to a point where investors want to invest less (and hence demand less loanable funds). The answer lies in the process by which the interest rate determines the quantity of investment goods demanded. Although investors may believe that future returns on investment projects have declined, they may nonetheless *revise* their decision concerning any particular investment project *if in the meantime* the interest rate has also declined.

Why? Because lower rates of interest reduce the cost of paying for investment projects. Thus, when the interest rate falls, investors' initially pessimistic view is offset *somewhat* by the prospect of lower investment costs. This reasoning underlies the movement *along* the new demand for loanable funds from $r(0)$ to interest rate $r(1)$. While investors may view the future as less rosy, it can still be reasonable to invest if the interest rate also falls. The result is that the decline in the interest rate has offset somewhat, but not fully, the decline in investment due to pessimistic expectations about the future.

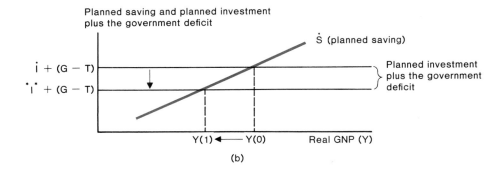

Planned saving and planned investment
plus the government deficit

$\dot{S}$ (planned saving)

$\dot{I} + (G - T)$

$\dot{I}^{*} + (G - T)$

Planned investment
plus the government
deficit

Y(1) ← Y(0)   Real GNP (Y)

(b)

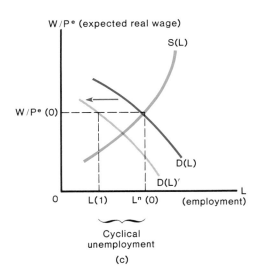

W/P^{e} (expected real wage)

S(L)

W/P^{e} (0)

D(L)

D(L)'

0   L(1) L^{n} (0)   L
(employment)

Cyclical
unemployment

(c)

A major event in recent times that reduced investor optimism was the increase in world oil prices that occurred in two stages during the middle and late 1970s. We will analyze the impact of the oil-price "shock" on the United States and world economies in greater detail in chapters 28 and 33. However, we can note here that following both major increases in world oil prices, unemployment rose and GNP growth slowed. In addition, there was a decline in real interest rates in the United States following both episodes. *One* reason for this decline was probably the reduced demand for loanable funds during the recessions that followed the oil-price shocks.

Reaction in the Goods and Labor Markets

The interest rate performs the extremely important function of *cushioning* the shocks produced by sudden changes in macroeconomic variables such as aggregate investment. The loanable funds market returns to equilibrium at interest rate r(1). In the macroeconomic setting, however, we must also consider what is taking place in the goods and labor markets. Despite the cushioning effect of the decline in the rate of interest from r(0) to r(1), the goods and labor markets are no longer in full-employment equilibrium. The reduced level of planned investment plus the government deficit, $\overset{**}{I}$ (1) + (G − T), is *less* than planned saving when GNP is at its full-employment level. At the full-employment level of production, the goods market is now in a state of *excess production*. Since the goods market is in disequilibrium at a level of GNP equal to $Y(0)$, full macroeconomic equilibrium no longer exists. Business firms cannot sell all they would like if they hire enough workers to preserve full employment in the labor market.

A Decline in Saving: Short-Run Macroeconomic Equilibrium in a Recession

A glance at part (b) of figure 25.5 shows us that the aggregate market for goods and services will not remain in a state of excess production. As aggregate production, employment, and income decline, so does planned saving. As you can see in the figure, as planned investment, an *exogenous* component of planned expenditure, declines, the resulting fall in GNP leads to a lower level of planned saving. The goods market reaches a new short-run equilibrium in which production equals planned expenditure, with GNP reduced to $Y(1)$. At this lower level of GNP, planned saving once again equals planned investment plus the government deficit. The economy is now in a recession, with higher than normal unemployment. Notice that if the interest rate had not fallen to $r(1)$, the line representing planned investment plus the government deficit in part (b) of figure 25.5 would be even lower than $\overset{**}{I} + (G - T)$ and GNP would have fallen still farther. Moreover, as we shall shortly see, the equilibrium that occurs at GNP equal to $Y(1)$ will probably not persist because further macroeconomic changes are likely to cause the interest rate to fall even lower than $r(1)$.

Figure 25.5, part (c) shows that in the labor market, the decline in firms' ability to sell their output has caused the aggregate labor demand curve to shift leftward from $D(L)$ to $D(L)'$. In other words, declining production in the goods market leads to smaller desired employment in the labor market. We saw in chapter 20 that in the short run, the real wage rate remains "stuck" at $W/P^e(0)$, so employment falls to $L(1)$, and cyclical unemployment equal to $L^n(0) - L(1)$ results.

The *multiplier* concept tells us exactly how much GNP will fall to reach its lower, short-run equilibrium level provided planned investment remains at its lower level, $\overset{**}{I}$. Since the multiplier relates all of the exogenous components of planned expenditure to the equilibrium level of GNP, the *change* in equilibrium GNP is equal to the *change* in exogenous planned expenditure (the change in planned investment in this case) times the multiplier. It may help you to remember how the multiplier works if we recall the numerical example of chapter 21. In that example, the MPC is 0.6, the MPS is 0.4, and the multiplier, 1/MPS, equals 2.5. Therefore, if planned investment $\overset{**}{I}(1)$ is now $10 billion less than the *initial* level of planned investment $\overset{*}{I}(0)$, the new short-run macroeconomic equilibrium level of GNP $Y(1)$ will be $25 billion less than $Y(0)$. Algebraically,

$$\Delta Y \equiv Y(0) - Y(1) = \Delta I \times 1/\text{MPS},$$
$$\$25 \qquad\qquad\quad = \$10 \times 1/0.4 \text{ (in billions)},$$

where as usual, the symbol Δ indicates the *change* in a variable. (Can you show that the decline in planned saving is *exactly* equal to the decline in planned investment? Hint: The decline in planned saving equals the MPS multiplied by the decline in GNP.)

Adjustment toward Full Macroeconomic Equilibrium with Flexible Prices

In chapter 27, we shall discuss the different types of government policies that can be used to combat a recession. The rationale behind these policies can be better understood, however, if we first discuss how a market economy *might* regain a new position of full-employment macroeconomic equilibrium when it is in a recession.

In figure 25.5, we have seen that firms have cut back on their production so that short-run equilibrium exists in the goods and credit markets at interest rate $r(1)$ and a level of GNP equal to $Y(1)$. Both firms and workers, however, will become increasingly distressed as sales and job opportunities remain below their full-employment levels. Unemployment compensation does not last forever. Firms' profits decline.

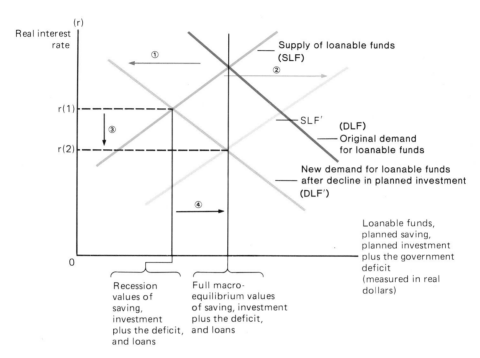

Figure 25.6   A decline in the price level leading to an increase in the real value of the supply of loanable funds
When the economy is in recession, prices and wages will eventually decline. As prices fall, a given nominal (money) value of loans will purchase more investment goods. Therefore, the supply curve of loans, measured in *real* dollars, shifts rightward as prices fall. This leads to a movement down along DLF′ and an *increase* in planned investment, which eventually rises back to the level of planned investment before the recession began. It is the decline in the interest rate, not optimistic expectations, that returns the economy to full employment.

As their discomfort increases, business firms will become more aggressively competitive with their rivals and begin to cut prices on a wider and wider range of their products in an attempt to recapture lost customers. Firms will also place increasing pressure on their employees to accept wage cuts, or "givebacks," to help firms survive and to reduce employees' risk of further layoffs.

Declining Prices and the Supply Curve of Loanable Funds   The way in which declining prices may eventually lead back to full macroeconomic equilibrium is through their effect on the *real value* of the supply of loanable funds originating in the banking system. In our discussion of the credit market, we showed that the *real value* of the banking system's supply of loanable funds is $\Delta M/P$, the change in the *real* money supply. If the denominator, P, of $\Delta M/P$ falls, the value of the fraction must rise. Thus, a decline in the prices of goods and services leads to an increase in the *real value* of the banking system's supply of loanable funds.

Since the aggregate supply of loanable funds is the sum of the households' supply and the banks' supply ($\Delta M/P$), the aggregate supply of loanable funds shifts to the right when the price level declines. This rightward shift in the supply curve of loanable funds is depicted in figure 25.6. At each and every rate of interest, the *real value* of new loans will be larger when the price level declines.

As the supply of loanable funds shifts rightward from the position occupied by SLF in figure 25.6, downward pressure is placed on the rate of interest in the loanable funds market. Downward adjustment of prices in the aggregate market for goods and services will persist as long as firms are unable to sell all the output they would like to sell under conditions of full employment. Eventually workers will adjust their expectations of future prices downward. This is a very important part of the macroeconomic adjustment process. Remember that when workers accept jobs, they do so in the *expectation* that every hour will yield a certain level of *real* earnings. If they expect the price level that prevails when they spend their earnings to be lower than it has been in the recent past, then they will be willing to accept lower *nominal* wage rates. Thus, the downward trend in prices and wages will continue as long as the economy is not in full macro-equilibrium.

A Further Decline in the Interest Rate with Wage-Price Flexibility and Self-Correction in the Goods and Labor Markets   As long as there is wage-price flexibility, there will be self-correction in the goods and labor markets. As suppliers of loanable funds compete with one another for loan contracts, the rate of interest will continue to decline. This reduction in the rate of interest will affect expenditures on investment goods. A lower interest rate lowers the cost of investment projects, thereby inducing increased investment. As investment rises, so does real GNP. This increase in production shifts the aggregate demand for labor to the right and raises employment. As incomes increase, planned consumption and saving also grow. *This downward trend in prices and wages and the upward spiral of investment, income, consumption, and saving continues until full macroeconomic equilibrium is restored.*

In figure 25.6 we show that at full macroeconomic equilibrium, planned investment plus the government deficit returns to the level that had prevailed originally. Investors' views of the future are still more pessimistic than they used to be. However, a decline in the interest rate has encouraged them to restore investment expenditure to its original level.

Recapitulation

Let us retrace the events that have occurred, following the arrows in figures 25.5 and 25.6. (1) The initial macroeconomic shock was a decline in business firms' planned investments at the interest rate r(0), shown by a *leftward shift* in the DLF curve indicated by the leftward-pointing arrows in each diagram. (2) This was followed by a *decline* in the rate of interest to r(1) and excess production in the aggregate market for goods and services. A decline in planned saving brought about short-run macroeconomic equilibrium in a recession at a lower level of real income Y(1) in figure 25.5, with higher than normal unemployment. A *decline* in prices and wages led to a *rightward* shift in the supply of loanable funds to SLF' in figure 25.6, indicated by the arrow labeled 2, and a further *decline* in the interest rate to r(2) in figure 25.6, indicated by the arrow labeled 3. Even though the DLF curve had shifted to the left, the rightward shift in the SLF curve caused a movement *down* along the new DLF curve associated with the decline in the interest rate from r(1) to r(2) in figure 25.6. The decline in the interest rate caused an increase in planned investment, indicated by the arrow labeled 4, which led to higher GNP. Increased production of GNP led to a greater demand for labor and higher employment, income, and planned saving. Finally, full macroeconomic equilibrium was restored. This new full-employment equilibrium is depicted in figure 25.6 by the intersection of DLF' and SLF' at interest rate r(2).

Planned investment plus the government deficit once again equals planned saving at the full-employment level of GNP. Buyers and sellers in all markets are now simultaneously satisfied, and the economy is in a position of full macroequilibrium. The crucial variables that allowed the economy to reattain full-employment equilibrium are *the price and wage levels* and the *rate of interest.*

It is important to note that although both the price level and the *money* wage rate have fallen, the *real* wage rate in the new, full-employment equilibrium is *exactly the same* as before the recession. This is because the aggregate demand for labor, derived from aggregate production in the goods market, has been restored to its full-employment level. Full equilibrium requires the same real wage and employment level as before the recession began. In full-employment equilibrium, both employers and employees have learned to accept a new, lower price level and *money* wage level as permanent. Therefore, the expected *change* in the price level is again zero.

An Inflationary Episode Resulting from an Increase in Planned Investment

Now that we have examined the adjustments that occur in the macroeconomy as it cycles from full equilibrium through a recession and back to full equilibrium, we can summarize a movement through an inflationary episode quite easily. To begin, we assume that an event takes place that causes investors to become more optimistic about the future. Suppose, for example, that the discovery of a new electronic principle revolutionizes all forms of manufacturing and communications. All firms now desire to invest in new equipment to take advantage of the new processes made profitable by this discovery. The result is that planned investment at *every* rate of interest is greater than before.

Using figure 25.5 as a guide, construct a diagram with the DLF and SLF curves showing the economy at full-employment macroequilibrium. Then construct a DLF' curve, showing a *rightward* shift in the demand for loanable funds corresponding to investors' more optimistic view of the future. If you have drawn your diagram correctly, there will be an *excess demand* for loanable funds at the original equilibrium rate of interest, r(0), after DLF increases to DLF'. However, the credit market will quickly move to a new (higher) equilibrium interest rate, r(1), as investors compete among themselves for available dollars to borrow.

The *rise* in the interest rate has two immediate effects. (1) Suppliers of loanable funds now find it desirable to economize on their cash balances and reserves, and they increase the quantity of loan contracts they are willing to purchase. (2) Some potential borrowers drop out of the market in the face of the higher interest rate. Despite the higher returns they anticipate on investment projects, the increased interest rate raises their costs and turns some attractive projects into losers. Nevertheless, at the new short-run equilibrium rate of interest, r(1), the quantity of loanable funds supplied and demanded will be higher than the original full equilibrium quantity.

Even though the credit market is now in equilibrium, there is a problem in the aggregate market for currently produced goods and services. In particular, planned expenditure now exceeds production. Business firms are pleased that their sales are growing and ask their employees to work extra hours; they also hire additional help as they attempt to expand production. As production and incomes increase, so does planned saving. As saving grows, the goods market approaches a short-run equilibrium with higher than normal production. In the labor market, employment is greater than normal, and the unemployment rate falls below its normal level.

In the labor market, employment rises in part because workers agree to put in longer hours temporarily when their employers ask them to do so. Of course, overtime work often requires that employers agree to pay extra money per hour. New employees may be hired, too, but they are unlikely to be as productive as a firm's experienced workers. Thus, labor costs per unit of output begin to rise. Employers, facing excess demand for their products, will begin to charge higher prices. Despite the fact that the price level is beginning to rise, workers do not yet expect inflation to continue. Moreover, past experience has shown that it is wise to accept additional work during periods of high demand to build up savings for a rainy day. Therefore, the population is willing to supply more labor for a while without demanding major wage increases. Thus, *short-run* macroeconomic equilibrium can be achieved at a level *above* full employment, with higher output sustained by above-normal employment and overtime hours.

It won't be long, however, before bottlenecks begin to appear in various markets in the economy. Certain raw materials will become more costly to obtain. Some industries have limited flexibility to expand output to meet higher than expected demand. The resulting potential shortages will lead to price hikes that purchasers view as increased costs of supplies. Thus, the initial increase in aggregate expenditure on goods and services will be followed by increased production costs for many firms. These cost increases, along with increased labor costs, will lead to further price increases, and gradually the economy will enter an inflationary phase, with rising prices becoming the rule.

As the price level increases, workers begin to notice that their real wages are not as high as they thought they were going to be. As inflation becomes the norm, employers find that they are unable to retain their workers unless they grant major wage increases. Members of unions with cost of living allowances begin to receive automatic wage hikes. New collective bargaining agreements now call for larger wage increases than in the past. The economy is now in the middle of an inflationary episode.

The inflationary, upward spiral of prices is likely to move the economy relatively quickly back to full macroequilibrium compared to the relatively slow speed of adjustment during a recession. When prices are rising, workers will be relatively quick to demand compensatory wage increases that lead to further price increases. While contracts with labor unions set floors on wage rates, they do not establish ceilings. Since businesses are enjoying increased prosperity, they may not be as cautious about raising their prices as they are about lowering them during a recession.

As the price level increases, there is an important impact in the loanable funds market. As the price level (P) rises, $\Delta M/P$ declines. An increase in the price of goods and services shifts the banking system's supply of loanable funds, $\Delta M/P$, to the left. Draw the leftward shift of the aggregate supply of loanable funds in your diagram. Prices will continue to rise, and SLF will continue shifting to the left as long as production remains above its full-equilibrium level. Thus, the process continues until SLF' crosses DLF' at r(2), the interest rate that is high enough to restore equality between planned aggregate expenditure and the aggregate production of goods and services. When this occurs, both planned investment and planned saving have fallen back to the levels observed in the initial full macroeconomic equilibrium. A higher interest rate has offset increased investor optimism. Planned investment plus the government deficit once again equals planned saving at GNP equal to Y(0), the full macroeconomic equilibrium value of GNP.

Once full macroequilibrium has been regained, inflation ceases. At the new, higher price level, a typical firm no longer experiences either increasing costs or excess demand. Borrowers can satisfy their demands for loanable funds at the new, higher interest rate. In the labor market, the quantity of labor demanded will have declined back to its normal, full-employment level and the unemployment rate will have risen back to its normal value. The real wage rate will also have returned to its preinflation value, with both the nominal wage rate (W) and the price level (P) higher than before. Neither firms nor workers have any reason to anticipate further inflation. Although the price level, the nominal wage level, and the interest rate are higher at the new full macroequilibrium than before the initial increase in planned investment, they are *no longer increasing.*

Let us briefly retrace the events that have occurred, following the arrows that you have drawn in your diagram. If you did not draw in arrows indicating shifts in the curves, you should do so as we go along. (1) The initial macroeconomic shock was an increase in business firms' planned investments at the interest rate r(0), shown by a *rightward shift* in the DLF curve. (2) This was followed by an *increase* in the rate of interest and excess planned expenditure in the aggregate market for goods and services. An increase in planned saving brought about short-run macroeconomic equilibrium in an inflationary episode, with less than normal unemployment. An *increase* in prices and wages led to a *leftward* shift in the supply of loanable funds, leading to a further *increase* in the interest rate and a movement *upward* along the new DLF curve. The increase in the interest rate caused a decline in planned investment, which led to lower GNP, income, employment, and planned saving. Finally, full macroeconomic equilibrium was restored. Once again, the crucial factors that allowed the economy to reattain full-employment equilibrium were *the price and wage level adjustments* and the *rate of interest.*

▶ Summary and Conclusions

In this chapter, we saw how the macroeconomic adjustment process generates powerful forces that even President Nixon could not overrule with laws governing legal maximum wages and prices in the 1970s. We have used a macroeconomic model to trace the impact of changes in planned investment, the money supply, the quantity of capital, and the cost of labor on GNP, unemployment, the price level, and the rate of interest. The following points were emphasized.

In the *short run*, a decline in planned investment (or any other component of exogenous expenditure) will cause a decline in the equilibrium level of GNP and in employment. This leads to short-run equilibrium in a recession.

In the *long run*, a decline in the price level and a further decline in the rate of interest are capable of restoring full-employment macroeconomic equilibrium. Once the economy reaches a new full macroequilibrium, however, unemployment and real income end up unchanged from their initial equilibrium values.

In the *short run*, an increase in planned investment (or any other component of exogenous expenditure) will cause an increase in the equilibrium level of GNP and in employment. This leads to an inflationary episode.

An *increase* in planned investment has a positive initial impact on the price level, the rate of interest, and real GNP, and it has a negative effect on the unemployment rate in the short run. Once the economy reaches a new full macroequilibrium, however, unemployment and real income are unchanged from their initial equilibrium values. The nominal wage rate, the price level, and the interest rate have all increased.

▶ Key Terms

full macroeconomic   short-run
  equilibrium *520*   macroeconomic
                               equilibrium *520*

▶ Questions for Discussion and Review

Are the statements in questions 1 to 4 true, false, or uncertain? Defend your answers.

1. In short-run recessionary macroequilibrium, all macroeconomic variables are unchanging, by definition.

2. In comparing one position of full macroeconomic equilibrium to another, the price level generally is unchanged.

3. The interest rate is the principal variable promoting short-run macroequilibrium when planned investment changes.

4. An important difference between short-run and full macroeconomic equilibrium is the behavior of the price level.

5. Assume that the marginal propensity to consume is 0.8, taxes are zero, exogenous consumption is $100, planned investment is $1,000, the government deficit is $50, and net exports are zero. (All these data refer to a one-year time period and are in billions of dollars.) Calculate aggregate expenditure for goods and services. Suppose that households' desire to save equals $1,200 when the economy is at the full-employment level of national income. What do you think will happen to the price level and the interest rate in the future? What conditions must be held constant to make your forecast? What change in net exports would bring about full macroequilibrium immediately?

6. Explain why a flexible price level is crucial to achievement of full macroeconomic equilibrium.

7. How would a decline in the marginal propensity to save affect full macroequilibrium? (You can use the data in question 5 to answer this question.) What would be the long-term impact on economic growth?

8. Suppose the government decided to repeal the income tax on corporation profits. Assuming that this tax is essentially a tax on the returns on investments, how would macroeconomic equilibrium be affected in the short run? How would full equilibrium be different compared to before the tax was repealed? What effect would this policy have on economic growth?

Chapter 26

Aggregate Demand, Aggregate Supply, and the Price Level

Outline

I. Introduction 538
II. The equilibrium price level: The quantity theory 539
   A. The role of velocity 542
III. Summarizing changes in aggregate production and the price level: Aggregate demand and supply 543
   A. Aggregate demand 544
   B. Aggregate supply 545
   C. Equilibrium of aggregate demand and supply 545
   D. Aggregate demand and supply during a recession 545
   E. Aggregate demand and supply during an inflationary episode 549
IV. Macroequilibrium, recession, and inflation in a growth scenario 552
   A. A brief historical note 554
   B. The rate of inflation and unemployment during recessions and inflationary episodes 554
   C. Can workers or other suppliers cause inflation? 556
V. Summary and conclusions 559
VI. Key terms 560
VII. Questions for discussion and review 560

Objectives

After reading this chapter, the student should be able to:

State the quantity equation and what each variable represents.

Explain how the quantity equation leads to the quantity theory of nominal GNP.

Explain the linkage between the money supply and the price level.

Explain why the aggregate demand curve slopes downward and what factors are held constant when constructing it.

Explain why the short-run aggregate supply curve slopes upward and what factors are held constant when constructing it.

Describe factors that would cause the aggregate demand curve or the aggregate supply curve to shift.

Explain why the long-run aggregate supply curve is vertical.

Use aggregate demand and supply to describe a recession and an inflationary episode.

Use aggregate demand and supply to describe recession and inflation in a growth scenario.

Describe the relationship between unemployment and the rate of inflation in the short run and in the long run.

Distinguish between demand-induced inflation and cost-push inflation.

▶ Introduction

At the beginning of chapter 25 we discussed the political concerns that contributed to President Nixon's decision to impose wage and price controls on the United States economy in August 1971. There is one key element in that decision that we did not explain. Why did an economically conservative president decide that conditions warranted such drastic and uncharacteristic actions by his administration? After all, while an inflation of nearly 6 percent per year along with an unemployment rate of 6 percent might seem disappointing, the experience of the late 1970s and early 1980s was not much better, and neither Democrats nor Republicans have pushed for similar controls.

The ability of Democrats to make political gains by calling for controls in 1971 and the administration's decision to proceed in that direction can be understood best by placing the issues in historical perspective. In the first two decades following World War II, economists and political leaders developed a general consensus on how the macroeconomy works. On the basis of the experience of the Great Depression of the 1930s, the economic research of John Maynard Keynes and others, and early postwar experience, it seemed clear at the time that during economic downturns prices either remained fairly constant or declined. On the other hand, when the economy was at or near full employment, inflation tended to be the major macroeconomic problem—not unemployment.

Therefore, the disturbing picture that emerged in 1971 was that both inflation and unemployment were high by recent historical standards and that both were rising. In a sense, it appeared that the conventional economic story did not correspond to the facts. No wonder unconventional policy initiatives seemed plausable and popular. This chapter explains why the strange events of the early 1970s occurred.

In chapter 25 we saw that full macroeconomic equilibrium involves full employment in the labor market, an interest rate that equates the quantity of loanable funds demanded and supplied, and planned expenditure equal to the production of GNP in the aggregate market for goods and services. We also saw that the price level is a key variable in restoring macroeconomic equilibrium during recessions and inflationary episodes. What we did not learn, however, is what determines the actual price level that exists when macroeconomic equilibrium prevails. Why does a typical market basket of goods cost, say, $100 rather than $0.10 or $1 million? In this chapter, we will answer this question. We will develop two sets of tools that enable us to deal with the forces underlying changes in the average price of goods and services. These tools—the quantity theory of nominal GNP and aggregate demand and supply curves—provide another way of summarizing inflationary episodes and recessions. They also provide additional insights into the causes of macroeconomic disequilibrium, as well as suggestions for some possible cures.

*The **quantity equation** expresses the quantity of money as proportional to nominal GNP.*

Velocity (V) tells us the constant of proportionality in the quantity equation: 1/V is the constant of proportionality between nominal GNP and the quantity of money required to sustain it.

▶ The Equilibrium Price Level: The Quantity Theory

As we have seen, when the economy is in macro-equilibrium, the price level is stable. However, we have not pinned down the reason that macroeconomic equilibrium occurs at the *particular* price level corresponding to equilibrium in the goods, labor, and credit markets. One simple view that is accepted by many economists explains the average price of goods and services in terms of the amount of money available to spend on them. This view states simply that if the number of dollar bills (or pound or lira or peso notes) increases but the quantity of goods and services produced stays the same, then there will be "too much money chasing too few goods" and prices will rise. Similarly, if the quantity of money in circulation falls, *ceteris paribus,* the price level will decline.

To understand the importance of the quantity of money in explaining the price level, remember that one of the variables held constant in deriving our model of macroeconomic equilibrium is the quantity of banks' reserves. Banks' reserves determine their willingness to lend funds to borrowers and thereby increase the money supply. In the explanation of the price level we have just described, the average price of goods and services is determined by the *total quantity* of money balances in the economy and by the *quantity of goods and services* on which those money balances can be spent. In an economy with a large amount of reserves, banks will furnish a great deal of money and the price level will be relatively high compared to an economy in which reserves and the amount of money in circulation is smaller but the quantity of goods and services is the same.

We will now state this theory of the price level more precisely. If you multiply the price level, P, by the real value of GNP, Y, the result is the *money or nominal value of GNP.* In the theory of the price level we have just described, the economy's quantity of money is related to nominal GNP by what is called the **quantity equation,** which is expressed

$$MV = PY.$$

In the quantity equation, M is the quantity of money, P is the price level, Y is real GNP, and PY is nominal GNP. The variable V is extremely important in the quantity equation and is called the **velocity of money.** The velocity of money is nothing more than a number relating the nominal value of GNP (PY) to the quantity of money. It is called velocity because it reflects the "speed" with which money circulates in the economy. For example, suppose PY equals $1 trillion and V equals 4. Then the quantity of money required to sustain this level of nominal GNP is $250 billion because each dollar "changes hands" an average of four times during the year.

The quantity equation is the basis of what is called the *quantity theory of nominal GNP,* or the quantity theory for short. Economists who accept the quantity theory tend to believe that V is constant or changes slowly and predictably. Economists who accept the quantity theory with few, if any, qualifications are called *monetarists.* Monetarists believe that at full employment, current changes in the money supply are the best predictor of changes in nominal GNP—PY in the quantity equation—six months into the future.

(Their views will be contrasted with alternative views of the macroeconomy in chapter 29.) According to the quantity theory, if the quantity of money is not equal to the amount needed to sustain the current level of nominal GNP, nominal GNP will change. The quantity equation makes it clear how much money is needed to sustain any given amount of nominal GNP. To find out how much money is needed, we simply solve the previous equation for the quantity of money M, obtaining

$$M = (PY)/V.$$

Using the preceding numerical example, if nominal GNP is \$1 trillion and velocity is 4, then \$250 billion is required to support aggregate expenditure. If the actual money supply is greater or less than the amount specified by this equation and if V is a constant, then the quantity theory says that either P or Y will be forced to adjust.

Why is it that the quantity theory is an explanation of the price level rather than the level of real GNP? The reason is that economists who accept the quantity theory believe that in the long run the production of real GNP is determined by "real" variables, which are the economy's available resources—its labor, capital equipment, technology, and so on. They also believe that upward or downward adjustment of the price level will lead the economy to the full-employment level of GNP. Full-employment GNP, they believe, is not determined by the quantity of money or the velocity of money. Therefore, when full-employment GNP is represented by the variable Y in the quantity equation, it is treated as a constant. That is, full-employment GNP is treated as *exogenous*—not determined by the quantity equation itself but by other variables. With V also a constant, it follows that the price level, P, is proportional to the quantity of money. This can be seen by rearranging the terms of the quantity equation, placing P alone on the left-hand side. We then have the following equation that describes how the quantity of money is related to the price level:

$$P = (V/Y)M.$$

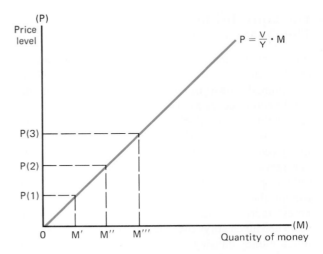

Figure 26.1   The relationship between the price level and the quantity of money according to the quantity theory
The straight-line relationship between the price level and the quantity of money indicates that the price level is directly proportional to the quantity of money, as indicated by the price-level equation we have just derived from the quantity equation. If velocity should increase, holding Y constant, the slope of the price line would increase, too. If real GNP should increase, the slope of the line would decrease.

This equation says that, given velocity and real GNP, the price level is proportional to the quantity of money. Notice that an increase in velocity (the "speed" at which money changes hands), given real GNP and the quantity of money, will increase the equilibrium price level. An increase in real GNP, given velocity and the quantity of money, will reduce the price level.

Figure 26.1 illustrates the relationship between the price level and the quantity of money as described by the quantity theory. In figure 26.1, velocity, V, and real GNP, Y, are assumed to be constant. Therefore, an increase in the quantity of money from an amount such as M′ to an amount such as M″ will cause the price level to increase from P(1) to P(2). The straight-line relationship between the price level and the quantity of money indicates that the price level is directly proportional to the quantity of money, as indicated by the price-level equation we have just derived from the quantity equation. If velocity should increase, holding

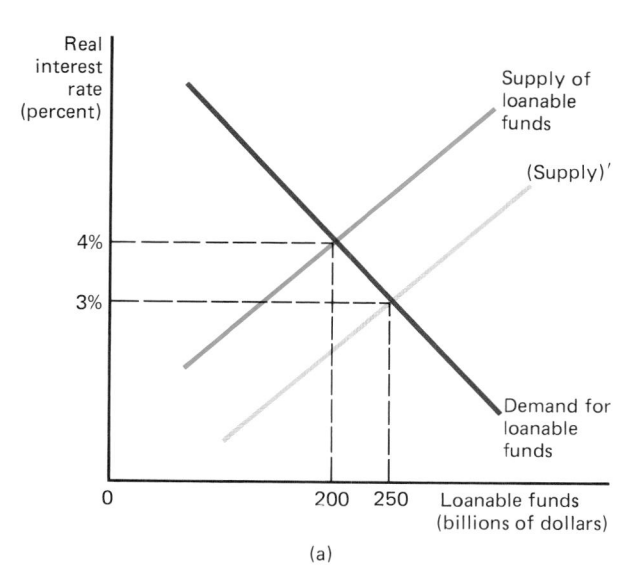

(a)

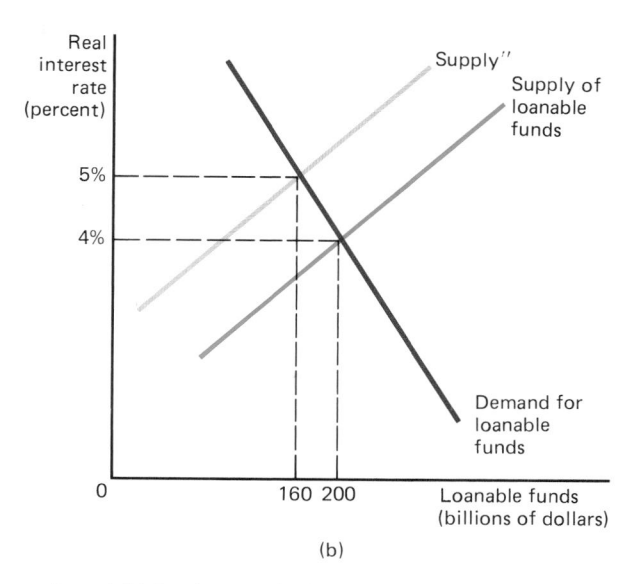

(b)

Figure 26.2   Money supply and the loanable funds market
In part (a) the increase in the money supply shifts the supply of loanable funds to the right. The real interest rate falls from 4 percent to 3 percent, and loans rise from $200 billion to $250 billion. At full employment the increased demand for goods and services of $50 billion pushes the price level up.

In part (b) the decrease in the money supply shifts the supply of loanable funds to the left. The real interest rate rises to 5 percent, and loans decrease by $40 billion. At full employment the decrease in demand for goods and services of $40 billion exerts downward pressure on the price level.

Y constant, the slope of the price line would increase, too. If real GNP should increase, the slope of the line would decrease. Be sure you can explain why.

Just how does an increase in M lead to an increase in P? What is the *linkage* between the quantity of money and the price level? The connection can be seen if we work through the effects of a change in the quantity of money on the loan contract and goods markets. Assume that the economy is currently at full-employment equilibrium and that something happens to increase the quantity of banks' reserves. Banks respond by increasing the aggregate supply of loanable funds. Since more loanable funds are available, the interest rate declines, investors borrow more, and the money supply (M) increases. With the economy at full employment, the rightward shift in the supply of loanable funds has led to higher levels of planned expenditure and production of GNP than are consistent with stable prices. An inflationary episode results.

When the economy returns to macroequilibrium, real GNP will be unchanged but the price level will have gone up. The quantity equation tells us that the price level will have increased by the same proportion that M increased. Figure 26.2, part (a), illustrates the rightward shift in the loanable funds supply curve and the increase in the quantity of loanable funds borrowed in response to the reduced real interest rate.

The same logic tells us how a decrease in the quantity of money will shift the aggregate supply of loanable funds to the left. This will lead to an increase in the rate of interest, a reduction in planned investment, and a recession. However, there is no effect on the *full-employment* level of GNP. The recession will ultimately result in declining prices that lead the economy back to full employment. The quantity theory tells us that when full employment is restored, the price level will have fallen by the same proportion that M decreased. Part (b) of figure 26.2 illustrates the leftward shift in the loanable funds curve caused by a contraction of the money supply. As a result, the real interest rate increases and the quantity of funds borrowed declines. It is important to note that the reduction of the interest rate in part (a) and the increase in part (b) are both temporary. Be sure you can explain why the interest rate returns to 4 percent when full macroequilibrium is restored.

As illustrated, the increase in the money supply creates $50 billion of new planned expenditure that induced price increases at full employment. The decline in the money supply reduces the supply of loanable funds in part (b) and, therefore, the planned expenditure on goods and services by $40 billion. At full employment, the decline in planned expenditure on goods and services puts downward pressure on prices.

The Role of Velocity

The heart of the quantity theory is the assumption that velocity, V, is constant or changes only slowly and predictably over time. If you were to divide the nominal values of GNP reported in chapter 19 by the values of M2 reported in chapter 23 you would see that the ratio has varied in the narrow range of 1.55 to 1.67. This means that an average dollar of M2 changes hands 1½ to 1⅔ times per year. This measure of V has exhibited little long-run change and represents a relatively stable relationship between M2 and PY. Velocity as measured with M1 has varied over a considerably wider range. (Economists are not in general agreement regarding whether M1 or M2 is the better measure of the quantity of money to use when calculating velocity, but popular attention remains focused on M1. In recent years, deregulation of the banking system has resulted in interest's being paid on demand deposits and checking privileges allowed with savings accounts and money market funds. The usefulness of most components of M2 balances for transactions resulting from these changes suggests that M2 may be a good measure of the quantity

of money when we want to calculate velocity in discussions of the quantity theory and the price level.) Remember, the quantity equation says that

$$V = PY/M.$$

An average dollar in our supply of M1 currently "changes hands" about six times per year.

The value of velocity does change gradually over time. It is determined in the long run by the technology of carrying out transactions, by the expected riskiness of holding assets in nonmonetary forms such as loan contracts, and by the rate of interest. An improvement in the technology of conducting our everyday business, such as the increased use of electronic funds transfer systems, would reduce our need to hold cash for transaction purposes. This would reduce the quantity of money balances required to sustain a given level of nominal GNP and increase velocity. An increase in the rate of interest would also increase velocity because the opportunity cost of holding wealth in the form of checking accounts or currency rather than loan contracts would be higher.

Economists who accept the quantity theory base their belief on the idea that velocity is relatively constant and predictable over long periods of time. However, they do recognize that temporary changes in the public's expectations about future events may cause rather sharp fluctuations in V for short time periods. For example, if households and firms should suddenly turn pessimistic about the likelihood of selling goods and services in the near future, they might seek safety in holding larger money balances. This would result in a reduction in the velocity of money until the public regained its confidence.

We will have more to say about economists who disagree with the quantity theory (most of whom are known as *Keynesians*) in chapter 29. Briefly, however, they believe that velocity, V, is very sensitive to changes in interest rates and to the public's perceptions of current and future economic events. In their view, a change in M is equally, or more, likely to result in a change in V (in the opposite direction) than

*The **aggregate demand and supply curves** describe the relationship between the price level and the quantities of real GNP demanded and supplied, respectively.*

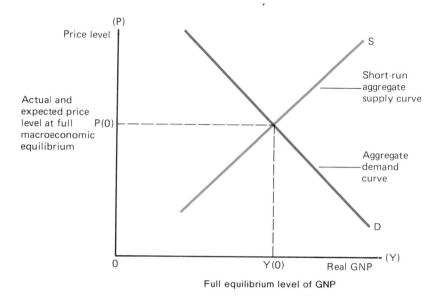

Figure 26.3   Aggregate demand and short-run aggregate supply
The aggregate demand and supply curves show how the quantities of GNP demanded and supplied change along with the price level. Several variables are assumed constant in deriving aggregate demand and supply, including the expected price level. A change in any of these variables results in a shift of either the aggregate demand curve or the aggregate supply curve.

a proportional change in the price level. For example, if an increase in the quantity of money simply leads the public to enlarge checking account balances, this will not result in increased planned investment, GNP, or the price level.

To summarize, the reason that the quantity theory provides an explanation of the price level in the long run is the belief that in the long run real GNP (Y) is determined by the economy's available resources and technology. Velocity (V), however, is believed to be determined mainly by the technology of executing transactions and to a lesser extent by the opportunity cost of holding money versus other assets. That is, the values of V and Y are *exogenously* determined by forces that the quantity of money does not affect. Therefore, the quantity equation tells us that when the monetary authority determines M, it also indirectly determines P, the only *endogenous* variable of the quantity equation in the long run.

▶ Summarizing Changes in Aggregate Production and the Price Level: Aggregate Demand and Supply

A more elaborate framework for analyzing the price level involves developing the concepts of demand and supply curves in the aggregate market for goods and services. We have already seen how production of goods and services and the price level change during recessions and inflationary episodes. We have also seen how the quantity theory of nominal GNP offers an explanation of what determines the price level when macroeconomic equilibrium prevails. Many students find it easier to remember how all of the pieces of the macroeconomy fit together when they are summarized in terms of demand and supply curves for GNP. Such curves are depicted in figure 26.3. The curves relating the price level and the level of real GNP shown in the figure are called the **aggregate demand** and **supply curves** because they describe how the

*The **short-run aggregate supply curve** shows what happens to the price level and real GNP during inflationary episodes and recessions.*

*The **long-run aggregate supply curve** is a vertical line relating the price level to the full macroeconomic equilibrium value of real GNP.*

quantities of GNP demanded and supplied are related to the price level during recessions and inflationary episodes.

After deriving the aggregate demand curve, we will derive the **short-run aggregate supply curve,** which describes the aggregate supply of GNP during recessions and inflationary episodes. We will then show how their intersection describes the equilibrium price level and the production of goods and services. Finally, we will derive the **long-run aggregate supply curve,** which shows how the price level and the quantity of GNP supplied are related when the economy is in full macroequilibrium.

All of the conditions that were assumed constant when we discussed the aggregate labor market, the aggregate market for goods and services, and the credit market are assumed constant as we derive the aggregate demand and supply curves. Among other things, we assumed that the economy has a given stock of physical capital and a fixed population and that the aggregate supply curve of labor is given. We shall see that a change in any of these variables results in a *shift* in aggregate supply. Another very important variable that is assumed constant when we derive the aggregate supply curve is the *expected price level.* We shall see that if the expected price level changes, the short-run aggregate supply curve shifts in the same direction (up or down).

Another set of conditions is assumed constant when we derive the aggregate demand curve for GNP. First, we assume that investors' desire to purchase investment goods is given. This means that the relationship between the quantity of investment goods demanded and the rate of interest does not change. If it does, the aggregate demand for GNP will shift. If, for example, investors become more optimistic about

the future and wish to purchase more investment goods at any given interest rate, then the aggregate demand for GNP will shift. Second, we assume that the levels of government expenditure and taxation are given. A change in either of these variables will cause a shift in aggregate demand.

Finally, we have seen that an increase in the quantity of money (or any other change that increases banks' or other lenders' willingness to lend funds) will result in an increase in aggregate expenditure. This is equivalent to saying that an increase in the quantity of money causes a rightward shift in *aggregate demand* for GNP. The reason is that a rightward shift in the supply of loanable funds, *cet. par.,* will lead to a fall in the rate of interest. The lower interest rate increases the quantity of investment goods demanded, which increases the quantity of GNP demanded *at every price level.* Of course, a reduction in the quantity of money following a leftward shift in the supply of loanable funds will accompany a decline in the aggregate demand for GNP. Less GNP will be demanded *at every price level.* We will return to our earlier example of the relationship between changes in the money supply and changes in the price level after we illustrate aggregate demand and aggregate supply.

Aggregate Demand

The aggregate demand curve in figure 26.3 slopes downward and to the right. The reason is that planned expenditure on goods and services (real GNP) falls as the price level increases and grows larger as the price level declines. To see why, we need only review the macroeconomic adjustments that take place during recessions and inflationary episodes. As the price level declines, a given amount of dollars will purchase more goods. Thus, a decline in the price level shifts the aggregate supply of loanable funds (measured in *real* dollars) to the right, as described in figures 25.5 and 25.6 on pages 152 and 155. This causes a decline in the rate of interest. As the interest rate falls, planned investment expenditures increase. This raises the level of total expenditure on GNP. In other words, the quantity of real GNP *demanded* rises as the price level falls, and it declines when the price level rises.

Aggregate Supply

The aggregate supply curve in figure 26.3 slopes upward and to the right. Once again, a quick review of macroeconomic adjustments during recessions and inflationary episodes will show why. During a recession firms reduce production (and employment) to avoid accumulating unsold goods. As excess productive capacity persists, firms start to lower their prices in an attempt to regain lost sales. Thus, during recessions, we observe a decline in the price level and in the quantity of GNP supplied. During an inflationary episode, by contrast, the price level tends to increase as firms produce larger quantities of output for sale. Workers supply the additional labor needed to produce this output because in the short run they are glad to have the extra work and typical employer-employee relationships call for working overtime when asked to. Moreover, workers are usually surprised by the decline in the purchasing power of their wages at the beginning of an inflationary episode. At first they are not likely to perceive price increases. When they do notice the beginnings of inflation, they do not immediately view an increase in the price level as a permanent change. (Remember our assumption that the

expected price level is constant.) Because workers expect prices to return to "normal" in the near future, they do not anticipate permanent decline in their *real* wage rates. Thus, in the *short run,* there is a positive relationship between the quantity of goods and services supplied and the price level.

Equilibrium of Aggregate Demand and Supply

Just as with other demand and supply curves we have dealt with, there is only one price level and quantity of GNP at which the aggregate demand and supply curves cross. If the price level is higher than P(0) in figure 26.3, the quantity of GNP demanded will be less than the quantity supplied. If the price level is less than P(0), there will be excess demand for GNP. Given all the conditions we assumed constant in deriving the aggregate demand and supply curves, there is one, and only one, equilibrium price level and quantity of real GNP. In figure 26.3, we have drawn the aggregate demand and supply curves when full macroeconomic equilibrium prevails. It is easy to use the aggregate demand and supply curves to summarize the changes that take place in the macroeconomy during a recession or an inflationary episode. By tracing the macroeconomic adjustments that occur during such episodes, we will also be able to derive the *long-run aggregate supply curve.*

Aggregate Demand and Supply during a Recession

Remember that the macroeconomic "shock" that starts the economy into a recession was assumed to be a decline in investors' optimism about the returns on future investment projects. This means that the planned investment component of the demand for

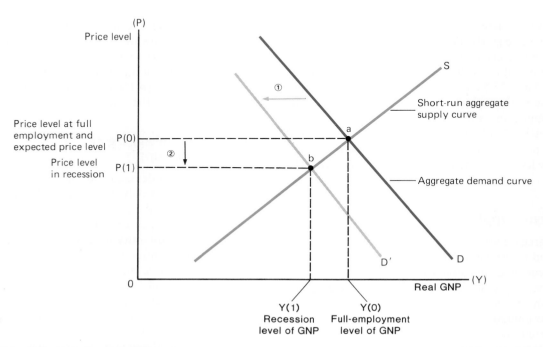

Figure 26.4 Aggregate demand and short-run aggregate supply in a recession
A recession begins with a leftward shift in the aggregate demand curve. The intersection of aggregate demand and aggregate supply moves from point a to point b. The economy moves into a recession as GNP falls from Y(0) to Y(1) and the price level falls from P(0) to P(1).

loans shifts to the left. At every rate of interest, fewer investment goods are demanded. This change causes a leftward shift in the aggregate demand curve, as shown by the arrow numbered 1 in figure 26.4 The prerecession aggregate demand curve intersected the short-run aggregate supply curve at point a, with an equilibrium price level of P(0) and GNP at its full-employment level Y(0). The new aggregate demand curve intersects the short-run aggregate supply curve at point b, with a lower price level, P(1). The arrow numbered 2 shows the decline in the price level from P(0) to P(1). GNP is also lower during the recession, at Y(1). During the initial stages of the recession, workers are unwilling to accept lower nominal (money) wage rates because they believe that the price level will soon return to its older, higher value of P(0).

Figure 26.5 shows the macroeconomic adjustments that take place as the declining price level gradually brings about an end to the recession and a return to full employment. Part (a) of figure 26.5 is a copy of figure 26.4. It shows the beginning of the recession with a leftward shift of the aggregate demand curve. Part (b) of figure 26.5 introduces a new change in the macroeconomy. As the recession persists and the price level continues to fall, workers begin to adjust their belief about the future course of prices of the goods they buy. They no longer expect the price level to return to P(0). They realize that what is "normal" for the economy in the future is going to be different than in the past. Because their *expected* price level falls, workers are now willing to accept jobs at *lower* nominal wage rates. As nominal wage rates

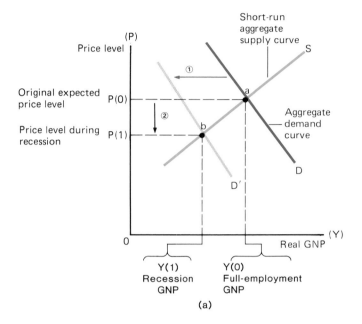

(a)

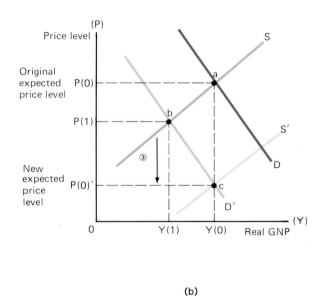

(b)

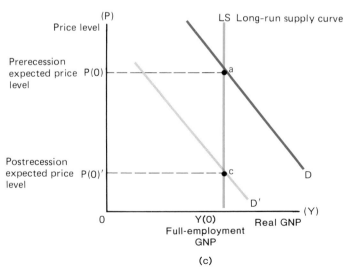

(c)

Figure 26.5 Aggregate demand and aggregate supply as the economy recovers from a recession with a lower price level

In part (a) the recession begins: (1) aggregate demand shifts to the left and (2) the price level and GNP decline.

In part (b), as the recession continues, (3) the aggregate supply curve shifts downward as the expected price level falls.

In part (c) the recession is over. The expected price level has fallen from P(0) to P(0)'. GNP has once again reached its full-employment level. Points a and c are on the *long-run aggregate supply curve.*

*The **theory of rational expectations** says that firms and households correctly incorporate available information in making decisions about their work effort, level of production, willingness to borrow and lend, and so forth; they are not fooled over and over by the effects of persistent or repeated economic events and government policy actions.*

fall, firms experience a decline in their costs. They are therefore willing to offer *every quantity* of goods and services for sale at lower prices than before. This change in firms' supply conditions is depicted by a *downward shift* in the aggregate supply curve, indicated by the arrow numbered 3 in part (b) of figure 26.5.

The downward shift in aggregate supply results in a further decline in the price level. During the recession, the intersection of the aggregate demand and aggregate supply curves initially shifted from point a to point b. Now, with the new aggregate supply curve, the intersection with aggregate demand occurs at point c. Point c in parts (b) and (c) of the figure shows where the recession has been brought to an end by the downward movement of the price level. Because a dollar now can purchase more goods, GNP has returned to its full-employment level, Y(0).

Since both points a and c correspond to the equilibrium values of the price level and of GNP when the economy is in full macroequilibrium, they both lie on the *long-run* aggregate supply curve. To illustrate the long-run aggregate supply curve, we have connected points a and c in part (c) of figure 26.5. The long-run aggregate supply curve is a vertical line that shows, in the long run, that the equilibrium level of GNP has only one value—its full-employment level—and that the price level adjusts so as to push the macroeconomy back to equilibrium when it enters a recession.

Our development of the long-run aggregate supply curve is based on the assumption that firms and households learn from their experience and adjust their expectations of future economic events accordingly. During the initial stages of a recession, it is difficult to tell whether the economy has actually entered a period of depressed business activity. Therefore, workers and firms are reluctant to accept lower prices for their services and products. However, when it becomes apparent that the only way to sell more output or to obtain desired employment is to accept lower prices and wages, these changes occur. Moreover, workers realize that with a lower price level, lower money wage rates do not represent proportionately lower purchasing power of their earnings. Firms realize that with lower money wages and lower prices for nonlabor inputs, they can accept lower prices for their output without incurring losses.

The idea that businesses and households use available information to forecast correctly the outcomes of economic events on prices and wages and to act accordingly in their own best interests is called the **theory of rational expectations.** This theory implies that while buyers and sellers of goods, services, labor, and loanable funds may initially be caught unaware by a sudden change in their economic environment, they learn to anticipate accurately the results of macroeconomic shocks that persist or occur repeatedly. Those who do not learn to adjust accurately to such changes in their economic environment lose out.

The basic idea imbedded in the long-run aggregate supply curve is that real GNP is determined in the long run by the capacity of the economy to produce goods and services (the aggregate production function) and by the willingness of workers to supply labor at various real wage rates (aggregate labor supply), not by the price level. The theory of rational expectations states that firms and workers adjust their behavior to their perception of "real" variables and are not fooled for long by changes in the level of money wage rates and prices. Therefore, in the long run, the quantity of GNP produced does not depend on the price level. An important implication of the theory of rational expectations is that recessions and inflationary episodes take place quickly. The return to full macroequilibrium will not be a prolonged process when firms and households learn to anticipate price level adjustments and react quickly. This implication of the rational expectations concept is still controversial among economists.

Aggregate Demand and Supply during an Inflationary Episode

The adjustments of aggregate demand and supply to determine the price level and equilibrium GNP during an inflationary episode are summarized in figure 26.6. In part (a), a macroeconomic "shock," such as a sudden improvement in investment opportunities, shifts the aggregate demand curve to the right. The preinflation aggregate demand curve intersected the short-run aggregate supply curve at point a, with an equilibrium price level of P(0) and GNP at its full-employment level, Y(0). The new aggregate demand curve intersects the short-run aggregate supply curve at point b, with a higher price level, P(1). This rightward shift in aggregate demand is indicated by the arrow numbered 1 in part (a) of figure 26.6. The increase in the price level is indicated by the arrow numbered 2. GNP has also risen to a higher level, Y(1). During the initial stages of the inflationary episode, employees feel they must honor their employers' request to work more and are glad to have the extra income. They may earn an agreed upon wage premium for overtime work, but they do not demand wage increases to compensate for a rising price level. If they see prices increasing, workers initially expect that the price level will soon return to "normal," which they believe to be P(0).

The events that take place as the inflationary episode continues are shown in part (b) of figure 26.6. As the inflation persists, workers gradually come to expect a permanent increase in the price level. Therefore, they demand increases in their nominal wage rates even when they are not working overtime, and employers find they can no longer hire all the labor they want unless they are willing to pay more for it. This increase in labor costs means that firms must receive a higher price at every level of production. That is, the aggregate supply curve *shifts upward* as indicated by the arrow numbered 3 in part (b) of figure 26.6. The upward shift in aggregate supply leads to further inflation as prices continue to rise. Finally, the new aggregate supply curve intersects the aggregate demand curve at point c. Point c shows where the inflationary episode has been brought to an end. As the price level has risen, the supply of loanable funds has moved to the left because of the increase in the denominator of $\Delta M/P$. The resulting rise in the interest rate has choked off investment, GNP, and the demand for labor. In general, the increase in prices has caused the purchasing power of a dollar to decline, and real GNP has fallen back to its full-employment level, Y(0).

Just as in the scenario traced during a recession, points a and c lie on the economy's *long-run* aggregate supply curve. The long-run aggregate supply curve is depicted in part (c) of figure 26.6, which shows that the inflationary episode has not caused a long-run increase in the level of real GNP. In the long run, real GNP is determined by the economy's available resources and technology. If the demand for goods and services increases when the economy is at full employment, the price level will rise so that real GNP cannot long remain above the initial level attained before the inflationary episode began.

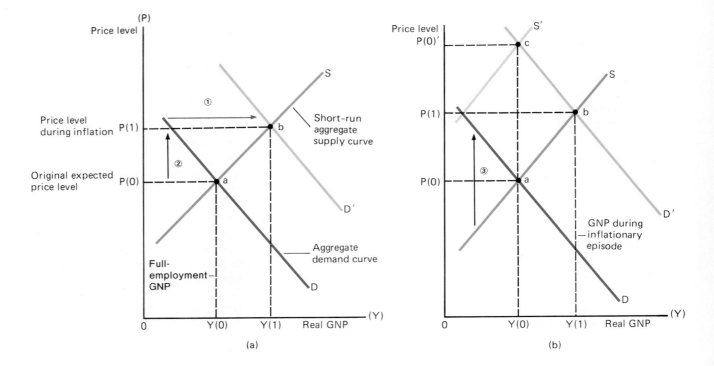

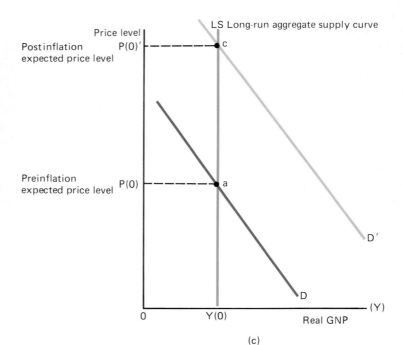

Figure 26.6   Aggregate demand and supply during an inflationary episode
In part (a) the inflation begins:
(1) aggregate demand shifts to the right, and (2) the price level and GNP increase.

In part (b), as the inflation continues, (3) the aggregate supply curve shifts upward as the expected price level rises.

In part (c) the inflationary episode is over. The expected price level has risen from P(0) to P(0)'. GNP has once again reached its full-employment level. Points a and c are on the *long-run aggregate supply curve*.

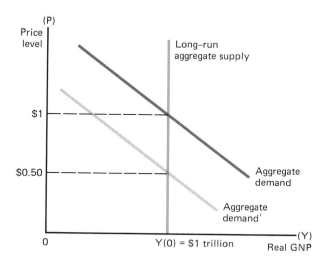

Figure 26.7   Money and prices
With full-employment real GNP equal to $1 trillion, a decrease in
the money supply from $250 billion to $125 billion, assuming V
= 4, will reduce the average commodity price from $1 to $0.50
and nominal GNP from $1 trillion to $500 billion. Real GNP
measured in terms of the prices prevailing before the money
supply contracted is unchanged.

Figures 26.5 and 26.6 can be used to follow up
our earlier numerical example of the relationship between the quantity of money and the price level. Referring to figure 26.7, which summarizes the stories
told in figures 26.5 and 26.6, suppose the economy is
at full employment with nominal and real GNP equal
to $1 trillion. Assume that one unit of a typical "good"
costs $1, that the quantity of money is $250 billion,
and that velocity equals 4. The quantity theory says
that if something should happen to reduce the quantity of money in circulation from $250 billion to $125
billion, then the resulting decline in the price of a typical good will be $0.50. The economy will return to
macroequilibrium with the price of a typical good only
half as great as before but with real GNP unchanged.
Nominal GNP will have declined from $1 trillion to
$500 billion, however. What will happen to the price
level and to real GNP if the quantity of money should
increase from $250 billion to $500 billion?*

We have shown how the aggregate demand and
supply curves summarize the relationship between the
quantity of money, the level of real GNP, and the price
level. Holding constant the economy's production
function, the supply of labor, the demand for investment goods, the level of government spending, taxes,
and the consumption function, the quantity of money
will determine a unique price level described by the
intersection of the aggregate demand curve and the
long-run aggregate supply curve. In the short run, the
aggregate supply curve slopes upward from left to
right, meaning that an increase in aggregate demand
will temporarily result in an increase in the price level,
GNP, and employment. A reduction in aggregate demand has the opposite effects. However, depending
on how quickly firms and workers anticipate the impact of raised or lowered prices, GNP and employment will return to their original levels as indicated
by the vertical, long-run aggregate supply curve.

We have also shown how changes in "real" variables, such as an increase or decrease in planned investment or in government spending, will cause the
aggregate demand curve to shift to the right or left
(with a given quantity of money). Again, a rightward
shift in aggregate demand leads to increasing prices
and in the short run increasing GNP and employment. In the long run, however, GNP is determined
by the (vertical) long-run aggregate supply curve, and
only the price level is determined by the position of
the aggregate demand curve. A leftward shift in aggregate demand causes a short-run reduction in GNP
and employment, but in the long run only the price
level declines, with GNP and employment determined by long-run aggregate supply conditions.

---

*The aggregate demand curves in figures 26.3 through 26.7 have
been drawn as straight lines for convenience. Actually, if the
quantity equation holds, the aggregate demand curve must get
flatter at lower price levels and steeper at higher price levels.
This is true because as long as real GNP and the quantity of
money are greater than zero, then the aggregate demand curve
cannot intersect either the vertical (price) or horizontal (real
GNP) axis.

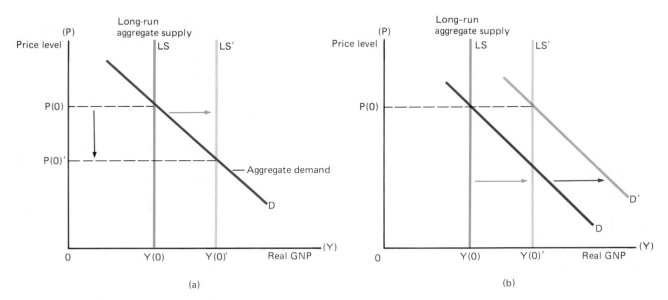

Figure 26.8   The equilibrium price level and GNP in a growth scenario
In part (a) economic growth is reflected in a rightward shift of the aggregate supply curve. Unless aggregate demand also shifts to the right, the equilibrium price level will fall.

As shown in part (b), if the Fed promotes a sufficient increase in the money supply, aggregate demand will shift to the right so as to maintain a stable price level.

▶ Macroequilibrium, Recession, and Inflation in a Growth Scenario

We have seen that in the long run, the equilibrium values of GNP and the price level depend on society's available resources, technology, and the quantity of money. When we discussed the relationship between the quantity of money and the price level, we assumed that resources and technology are unchanging. Now let us see what happens when we recognize that our capacity to produce real GNP may change over time. Specifically, if the stock of physical capital increases, labor becomes more productive. This is reflected in an upward shift in the aggregate production function, an increase in the marginal product of labor, and a rightward shift in the demand for labor. (Review figure 20.6 and see how these changes affect employment, GNP, and the real wage rate.) Since the full-employment level of GNP increases, the long-run aggregate supply curve will shift to the right.

It is important to recognize that as long as real investment expenditure is positive, the amount of physical capital is *constantly growing*. So the economy's full equilibrium value of GNP will also grow constantly. In figures 26.5, 26.6, and 26.7, we depicted the economy's long-run aggregate supply curve. The scenario for the economy we are describing now shows that in full macroequilibrium, economic growth occurs. This means that the long-run aggregate supply curve is constantly shifting to the right. This increase in long-run aggregate supply adds a new wrinkle to the problem of maintaining macroeconomic equilibrium, as figure 26.8 shows.

In part (a) of figure 26.8, we show the long-run aggregate supply curve shifting to the right, reflecting growth of the economy's capacity to produce GNP. With a *given* aggregate demand curve, this economic growth will result in a *decline* in the equilibrium price level from P(0) to P(0)'. Why does the equilibrium price *decline* when the economy is

Figure 26.9   The percentage growth of money supply (M1) and the percentage rate of inflation, 1963–1985
This chart compares the average annual rate of increase in M1 with the average annual rate of inflation. It shows that the money supply has grown more rapidly than the capacity to produce GNP. This has led to persistent inflation that has usually been greatest when the money supply has grown most rapidly.
From *Economic Report of the President*, 1986, p. 28.

growing in real terms? The quantity equation tells all. If the quantity of money, M, is constant but real GNP, Y, is growing and velocity, V, does not change, the price level must fall. Otherwise, the quantity of money available will not be able to sustain a level of nominal GNP, PY, corresponding to the new, higher level of real output. If you examine figure 26.11 on page 555, you will note that the years 1814–1857 and 1864–1900 were periods of rather prolonged *deflation*. A probable major cause of these periods of declining prices was a relatively slow growth in the money supply accompanying a rapidly growing capacity to produce goods and services. The United States was on the gold standard then, and there was no Fed. When monetary growth was slow relative to the growth of real GNP, the price level was pushed downward and recessions were relatively frequent and severe.

Figure 26.8, part (b), shows that if the Fed causes the money supply to grow as rapidly as the economy's capacity to produce goods and services, the aggregate demand curve will shift to the right by just the amount needed to keep the equilibrium price level from falling.

The quantity theory provides an explanation of one of the important causes of inflationary episodes and recessions in our economy. If the Fed allows the

money supply to grow more rapidly than the economy's capacity to produce goods and services grows, inflation is the inevitable long-run result. If monetary growth is too slow, the price level will eventually fall but the economy will be afflicted with persistent tendencies toward recession. A major reason for the recessions is that slow monetary growth leads in the short run to high real interest rates and reduced planned investment. During the last twenty-five years, the money supply has grown at a considerably greater rate than the economy's capacity has increased, and this has led to persistent inflation. That is why we have come to view a constantly rising price level as more or less normal. After the experience of the Great Depression and the lesson learned about the disastrous consequences of too little growth in the money supply (see chapter 28), it is perhaps understandable that the Fed has preferred to maintain too much rather than too little monetary growth.

Figure 26.9 shows the annual inflation rate from 1963 through 1985 and the annual rate of growth of M1 two years earlier in the United States. It is clear from this chart that inflation was closely associated with the rate of growth of the money supply, at least through 1982. In chapter 28, we will take a closer look at the causes of the inflation the United States

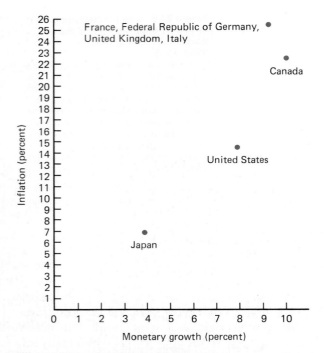

Figure 26.10   An international comparison of inflation and monetary growth, 1981–1985
The rate of inflation in several major industrial nations is positively related to the rate of monetary growth.
From International Monetary Fund, *World Economic Outlook*, 1985, Table 13, p. 218, and *Economic Report of the President*, 1986, Table B–108, p. 376.

economy has experienced over the past two and a half decades. We will also offer some speculation regarding the divergence between M1 growth and inflation that occurred after 1982.

The positive relationship between monetary growth and inflation is not confined to the United States. Figure 26.10 shows how increases in the money supply (M1) and inflation (as measured by the CPI) compare for some major industrial nations over the period 1981–85. It is clear that relatively high rates of monetary growth were positively related to high rates of inflation internationally, as well as within the United States.

A Brief Historical Note

Our economy has not always experienced inflation as the norm. Figure 26.11 illustrates that earlier in this century and on several occasions during the 1800s, deflation has occurred. Economists would probably disagree on whether and how rapidly falling prices and money wage rates would restore full employment in today's economic environment. There is little question, however, that they have done so more than once in the past. A particularly noteworthy adjustment occurred shortly after World War I.

In 1920, the United States economy entered a sharp recession. The unemployment rate was over three times as high in 1920 as it was in 1919.[1] Between 1919 and 1920, real GNP fell by 5 percent.[2] The price level fell sharply, however, so that by 1922 the consumer price index was one-sixth lower than in 1920. Wholesale prices dropped by over one-third. Recovery was rapid, so that by 1923 unemployment had fallen to a low level and real GNP stood above its 1919 level.

The Rate of Inflation and Unemployment during Recessions and Inflationary Episodes

Now that we have seen why our economy has typically experienced rising prices, even during recessions, over the period of the past twenty-five to thirty years, it would be a good idea to briefly review the macroeconomic events that occur during recessions and inflationary episodes. All of the events that we described as part of the macroeconomic adjustment process still represent a valid scenario provided that we make one minor adjustment. Instead of observing a *decline* in the price level during a recession, in recent years we have typically observed a *smaller* rate of inflation. When planned aggregate expenditure has exceeded aggregate production of goods and services, the price level has increased *more rapidly* than when full macroeconomic equilibrium prevails.

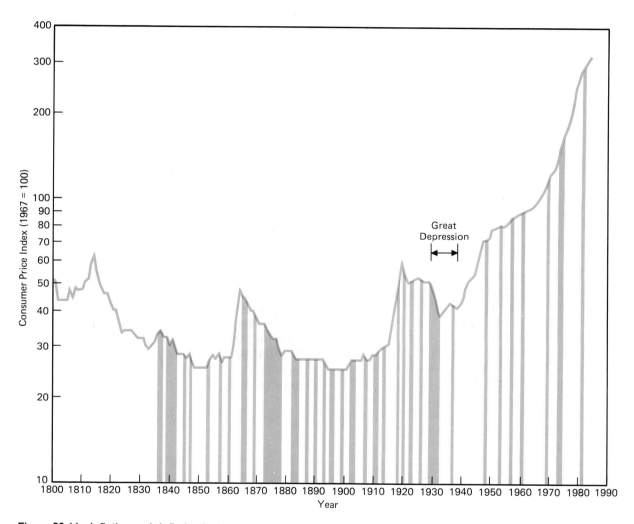

Figure 26.11   Inflation and deflation in the United States from colonial times to the present
This chart shows that deflations and inflationary episodes have alternated throughout the history of the United States. The period since World War II, however, has been characterized by rising prices.
From U.S. Bureau of the Census, *Economic Report of the President,* 1986, Table B-55, p. 315, and *Historical Statistics of the United States,* pp. 210, 211.

Stagflation is the coexistence of inflation and above-normal unemployment.

The *Phillips curve is a statistical relationship between the unemployment rate and the rate of inflation that is observed in the short run during inflationary episodes and recessions.*

Demand-induced inflation is caused by forces that shift the aggregate demand curve to the right.

Economists and policymakers have frequently focused attention on the parallel adjustments of the rate of inflation and the unemployment rate during recessions and inflationary episodes. We have seen that a basic feature of recessions is an increase in unemployment above its normal, "full-employment," level. During inflationary episodes, unemployment temporarily declines to abnormally low values. Does this mean that the inflation we have come to accept as normal for our economy has somehow been associated with a lower normal unemployment rate? Nothing could be further from the truth. When a certain rate of inflation has come to be *expected,* then our model of the macroeconomy predicts that unemployment will fall below its normal value only when inflation is *unexpectedly* high. During recessions, unemployment will rise above its normal level, even though inflation does not entirely disappear. The persistence of a growing price level and the appearance of recessionary unemployment has been named **stagflation.**

The relationship between unemployment and the rate of inflation that characterizes macroeconomic behavior during recessions and inflationary episodes is known as the **Phillips curve.**[3] Figure 26.12 shows Phillips curves for the United States over the years from 1965 to 1985. Notice that over short periods of time, it is possible to draw negatively sloped lines that more or less match the points marking the rate of inflation and unemployment rate. These lines are the Phillips curves for the years indicated. Except for the "outliers" of 1974, 1975, and 1982, all of the points plotted in figure 26.12 fall fairly close to one of the five Phillips curves.

The horizontal lines in figure 26.12 show how the average rate of inflation increased over the years from 1960 to 1981 and then decreased after 1981. As the inflation rate increased and then decreased, it is reasonable to assume that the public's expectation of future inflation changed in the same direction. Our macroeconomic model tells us that an upward trend

of expected inflation will result in an upward shift of the Phillips curve and a downward trend will result in downward shift of the Phillips curve. That is exactly what appears to have taken place. The Phillips curve for each successive time period through 1980–83 lies higher and higher in figure 26.12. The most recent Phillips curve (1983–85) has shifted down, showing that by the mid-1980s the public had come to expect lower inflation. In other words, as the rate of inflation rose over time, the average unemployment rate showed no long-run tendency to decline. Moreover, the unemployment rate fell back toward 7 percent as soon as the public realized that lower rates of inflation were likely to persist after 1982.

Notice that the average unemployment rate tended to rise over the period from 1965 to 1982, along with the rate of inflation. Our macromodel does not predict that the normal rate of unemployment will increase along with the rate of inflation. Evidently, some other forces in the economy were pushing up the normal unemployment rate over the period covered in figure 26.12. We will examine these forces in greater detail in chapter 28.

Can Workers or Other Suppliers Cause Inflation?

In our analysis of the economy's adjustments during an inflationary episode, we began with an *exogenous* increase in demand for investment goods. This exogenous increase in demand was the fundamental cause of the inflationary episode. We have also seen that too rapid an increase in the quantity of money is also inflationary. In chapter 28 we will find that still another cause of inflation can be an increase in government spending if it is not accompanied by an increase in taxes. All of these instances are examples of **demand-induced inflation,** which means that the initial macroeconomic shock shifts the aggregate demand curve to the right. Yet, when you read

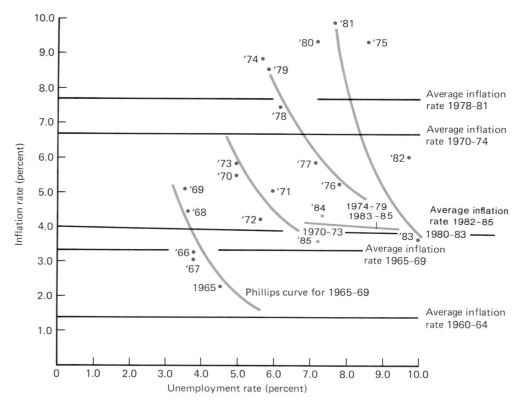

Figure 26.12   Phillips curves for the United States, 1965–1985
Over short periods of time, unemployment tends to be lower when the rate of inflation is greater than expected. This relationship is called the Phillips curve. This graph shows how the average inflation rate rose over the years after 1964. As expectations of inflation rose, the Phillips curves for the United States economy shifted upward, and as expectations of inflation declined, the Phillips curve shifted downward. Thus, a higher rate of inflation did not cause the unemployment rate to fall in the long run.
From *Economic Report of the President*, 1983, Federal Reserve Bank of St. Louis; *National Economic Trends*, October, 1983, *Economic Report of the President*, 1986, Table B-59, p. 320, Table B-35, p. 293.

newspaper accounts of inflation or watch the business news on television, you will often see or hear that inflation is "caused" by an increase in a specific price, such as the price of petroleum, construction, or wage rates. If you understand our discussion of inflation, you will view such "obvious" explanations with great skepticism.

In narrow sense, it is always true that inflation can be linked to a few prices in a price index. There are always some prices rising while some prices fall even during inflationary episodes. To "blame" inflation on those components of CPI or the GNP deflator is not only naive but it can also be dangerous if it leads to the wrong policies to combat rising prices.

*Cost-push inflation is caused by
increases in costs that shift the
aggregate supply curve to the left.*

If you recall our description of an inflationary episode, you will remember that prices begin to rise only *after* aggregate demand has increased. A likely scenario is that certain raw materials industries and some producers of manufactured goods develop shortages, which lead to price increases. Since these materials are inputs into further production, their price increases are *cost* increases in other industries. As these *costs* rise, the *prices* of goods these inputs are used to produce will increase. Therefore, to the casual observer, it will appear that *costs* are "pushing up" prices. As the CPI begins to rise, workers will demand increases in their wage rates to catch up with inflation. These wage increases will cause further cost increases for employers and will appear to push up prices even more. Hence we are often urged to believe that we are experiencing **cost-push inflation,** which results from a leftward shift in the aggregate supply curve, when the actual cause has been a rightward shift in aggregate demand.

It *is* possible for an exogenous increase in costs to cause inflation. Since the inflationary process is somewhat different than when an exogenous increase in aggregate demand results in a demand-induced inflation, the behavior of important macroeconomic variables will also be different. Consequently, the wrong macroeconomic policies may be chosen to cure what appears to ail the economy unless the causes of the symptoms are correctly diagnosed.

To understand the basic differences between cost-push and demand-induced inflation, we will use as an example an increase in the cost of labor. It is important to bear in mind, however, that an exogenous increase in the price of *any resource that accounts for a substantial fraction of production costs* will have a similar macroeconomic impact. For example, we could as easily discuss the cost-push effects of OPEC oil price increases in 1974 and again in 1979.

To see how a cost-push inflation might originate, refer to figure 25.1 on page 522. Suppose that a substantial majority of the labor force is unionized and that all the labor unions collaborate with one another to raise the real wage rates of their members. This would be represented in figure 25.1 by an *increase* in the real wage above its equilibrium value. Employment will fall as employers move back along their labor demand curves in response to the higher real wage they must pay. Since the aggregate labor supply curve has not shifted, however, *more* labor will be supplied just as the quantity of labor demanded declines. Thus, unemployment is likely to increase above its normal level.

When employment declines, so will real GNP. In other words, the economy's *aggregate supply curve* will shift to the left. This means that at every price level, the economy will now produce less GNP than before because labor costs have risen. An increase in costs shifts the aggregate supply curve to the left. To see what happens next, take a piece of paper and draw an aggregate demand and an aggregate supply curve. When you shift the aggregate supply curve to the left, what happens? The price level increases and GNP falls. This increase in the price level will be viewed as an inflationary episode by the public. At the same time, we have seen that the unemployment rate will have risen *above* its normal level. Thus, we have the seemingly paradoxical situation of a recession at the same time that the price level has increased. (When a certain amount of inflation is the norm, we observe an unexpected *increase* in the rate of inflation with unemployment rising above its normal level.) Notice that this relationship between inflation and unemployment is *exactly opposite* to that described by the Phillips curves in figure 26.12.

*An **accelerated inflation** is one in which the percentage rate of increase of prices increases from year to year.*

Unless labor unions demand and obtain a further increase in real wages, the inflation will stop at this point. The economy will remain at underemployment equilibrium with the price level higher than it was and GNP lower. However, the government will be under tremendous pressure to bring down the unemployment rate. In particular, political pressures on the Fed may lead it to *validate the cost-push inflation,* which means increasing the quantity of money more rapidly so that the aggregate demand curve shifts far enough to the right to return GNP (and unemployment) to its full-employment level.

Of course, if the Fed validates a cost-push inflation, the economy will end up with an even higher price level than before because the aggregate demand curve will shift to the right following a leftward shift in the aggregate supply curve. Unemployment will return to its normal level because the further increase in the price level, P, causes the *real wage rate,* W/P, to fall back to the level that brings about equilibrium in the labor market. This means, of course, that the initial increase in the real wage rate that began this inflationary episode will be wiped out by inflation. If workers try to regain their higher real wage rate and at the same time the Fed continues to validate the resulting cost-push inflation by increasing the quantity of money, a continuing inflation of wages and prices, called an **accelerated inflation** or an inflationary spiral, in which nominal wages and prices rise at faster and faster rates, will result. Take a moment to draw the aggregate demand and supply curves associated with cost-push inflation and for cost-push inflation with the Fed's support. It is important to note the higher equilibrium price level in the latter case and the fact that the price level does reach a new equilibrium in each case. Cost-push inflation can only persist for long periods of time if unions make repeated higher wage demands and/or the Fed continually pumps up the money supply more rapidly.

▶ Summary and Conclusions

In this chapter we explained how economic conditions can give rise to both rising inflation and unemployment rates and why price controls could not have cured the macroeconomic problems of the 1970s or early 1980s. We reviewed macroeconomic equilibrium and the adjustments made by the price level when disequilibrium prevails. The following points were emphasized.

The quantity theory of nominal GNP is a widely accepted explanation of the price level that prevails when the economy is in full-employment equilibrium.

Economists who accept the quantity theory tend to believe that velocity is relatively constant or changes slowly and predictably and that the full-employment level of GNP is determined by "real" variables. These economists are called monetarists.

A more elaborate view of the equilibrium price level and equilibrium GNP is given by the aggregate demand and aggregate supply curves.

Long-run aggregate supply is determined by the economy's available resources and its production function.

In a growth context, both the aggregate demand curve and the aggregate supply curve must shift rightward at the same rate to maintain a stable price level.

We have experienced inflation as the norm over the past twenty years because increases in the quantity of money have pushed the aggregate demand curve to the right faster than the aggregate supply curve has shifted.

In the long run, inflation does not cause GNP to be greater than its full-employment value or the unemployment rate to fall below the full-employment level.

It is possible for an exogenous increase in *costs* to cause inflation, but the behavior of major macroeconomic variables is different in cost-push inflation than in demand-pull inflation. In particular, cost-push inflation is associated with *above-normal* unemployment and a *lower* real GNP than the economy is capable of producing at full macroeconomic equilibrium.

▶ Key Terms

accelerated inflation
  559
aggregate demand and
  supply curves 543
cost-push inflation 558
demand-induced
  inflation 556
long-run aggregate
  supply curve 544
Phillips curve 556

quantity equation 539
short-run aggregate
  supply curve 544
stagflation 556
theory of rational
  expectations 548
velocity of money 539

▶ Questions for Discussion and Review

Are the statements in questions 1 through 5 true, false, or uncertain? Defend your answers.

1. An increase in the money supply will always lead to an increase in the price level assuming velocity is stable.

2. During periods of high inflation, the velocity of money will decline because rising prices will deter consumers from making purchases.

3. During periods of high inflation, people will want to hold more money so as to be able to afford the higher prices charged for goods and services.

4. Macroeconomic equilibrium can only occur at one particular level of prices in the long run.

5. In the long run, economic growth will cause the full-employment level of output to change.

6. Show by means of a graph what happens to aggregate demand and aggregate supply from a position of full-employment equilibrium in each of the following circumstances.
   a. The Fed sells government securities.
   b. Firms anticipate inflation in the near future.
   c. The UAW wins a large wage increase in contract negotiations, and the Fed increases the money supply to sustain it.
   d. The Fed raises the discount rate.
   e. The average number of years of schooling of the population increases.

7. What if any effect do innovations in banking such as credit cards, automated teller machines, and debit cards have on the price level?

8. Using the Phillips curve diagram, illustrate the following situations starting from the full-employment level of unemployment.
   a. The Fed buys government securities, short and long run.
   b. The expected price level rises.
   c. The price level rises unexpectedly.

9. Can the monetary authorities reduce inflation as easily as they can increase it through validation?

10. Considering the theory of rational expectations, what if anything could render government fiscal and monetary policies ineffective?

Chapter 27

Fiscal and Monetary Policies

Outline

I. Introduction *562*
II. Discretionary fiscal policy in a recession *564*
   A. Response of the fiscal authority to a decline in investment demand: An increase in expenditure *564*
      1. Reaction in the goods market *564*
      2. Reaction in the credit market *564*
   B. Why fiscal policy works *566*
   C. Discretionary fiscal policy when taxes are adjusted *566*
III. Discretionary fiscal policy to prevent an inflationary episode *569*
IV. Lags, politics, and fiscal policy *570*
V. Nondiscretionary fiscal policy *571*
VI. Recent fiscal policy developments *571*
VII. Discretionary monetary policy in a recession *572*
   A. The initial effect in the loanable funds market *574*
   B. The effect in the goods market *574*
   C. Why monetary policy works *574*
VIII. Discretionary monetary policy to prevent inflation *575*
   A. The politics of discretionary antiinflation monetary policy *576*
IX. Comparing the short-run and long-run effects of fiscal and monetary policies *577*
   A. Is discretionary policy useless? *577*
X. Summary and conclusions *578*
XI. Key terms *578*
XII. Questions for discussion and review *579*

Objectives

After reading this chapter, the student should be able to:

Describe how discretionary fiscal policy can be used to prevent a recession.

Describe how discretionary fiscal policy can be used to prevent an inflationary episode.

Discuss the problems with implementing discretionary fiscal policy.

Discuss the types of nondiscretionary fiscal policies that exist and how each is countercyclical.

Describe how discretionary monetary policy can be used to prevent a recession.

Describe how discretionary monetary policy can be used to prevent an inflationary episode.

Compare the short-run and long-run effects of fiscal and monetary policies.

▶ Introduction

During the period 1961–68 real GNP rose 5.7 percent per year from a value of $756.7 billion in 1972 to $1.058 trillion. The unemployment rate declined steadily from 6.7 percent to 3.6 percent, and consumer prices rose at a modest 1.7 percent annually. Economists announced the end of the business cycle and declared that with the prudent application of fiscal and monetary policy, the government could "fine-tune" the economy. Like a well-tuned automobile, the United States economy was expected to continue to move forward rapidly and smoothly. For many reasons, the overall performance of the United States economy

over the next two decades bore no resemblance either to actual economic experience during the 1961–68 period or to the almost unanimous predictions of economists. In chapters 28 and 29 we will have a great deal to say about what happened after 1968 and why. In this chapter we will focus on how fiscal and monetary policies affect the macroeconomy. Among other things, the discussion will provide some insight into why we could not fine-tune the United States economy in 1968 and why we cannot fine-tune the United States economy today.

In chapters 25 and 26 we paid little attention to the role of government in our model of the macroeconomy. In this chapter we emphasize the

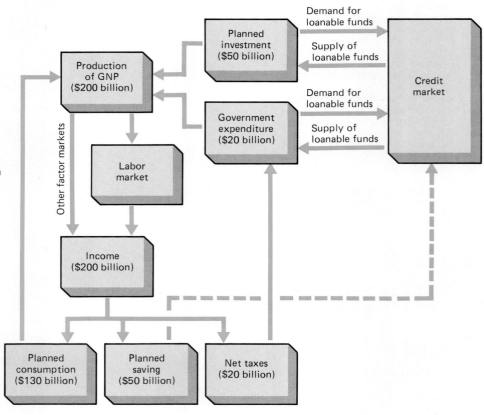

Figure 27.1   A quick review of full macroequilibrium
Part (a) shows the economy in full macroequilibrium.

In part (b) the economy is in full macroequilibrium because Ŝ = Î + (G − T) at Y(0), the full employment level of GNP, and because DLF = SLF at interest rate r(0).

In part (c) the aggregate demand and long-run aggregate supply curves intersect at the equilibrium price level P(0) and equilibrium level of GNP, Y(0).

(a)

Fiscal policy is the adjustment of taxes or government spending.

government's role in the goods market and the credit market. We will see how government expenditure and taxation policies, which are both included in the category of *fiscal policy,* can affect adjustments to short-run equilibrium in a recession or in an inflationary episode. In theory, fiscal policy can prevent recessions and inflationary episodes. We will also investigate how monetary policy might be used to eliminate cyclical unemployment and inflation.

Before describing how government might prevent recessions and inflationary episodes, we will illustrate full macroeconomic equilibrium once again. Figure 27.1 depicts a situation of full-employment macroeconomic equilibrium.

Part (a) of figure 27.1 recaps the numerical example of macroeconomic equilibrium presented in chapters 21 and 25. Gross national product is $200 billion, which is an equilibrium value because planned saving equals planned investment plus the government deficit. We have assumed that this is just the amount of GNP that satisfies the condition of no cyclical unemployment in the labor market. Parts (b) and (c) depict a more general view of macroeconomic equilibrium. The equilibrium interest rate, shown in part (b), is r(0), and the full-employment level of GNP, shown in part (c), is Y(0). The equilibrium price level, P(0), is indicated by the intersection of the aggregate demand and long-run aggregate supply curves in part (c) of figure 27.1.

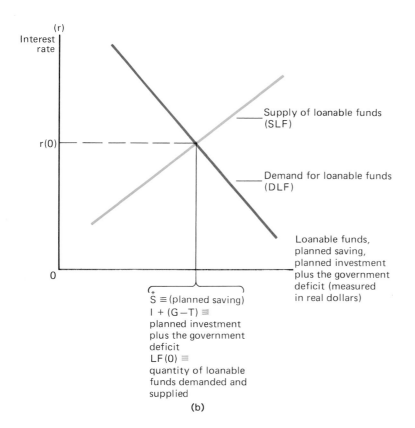

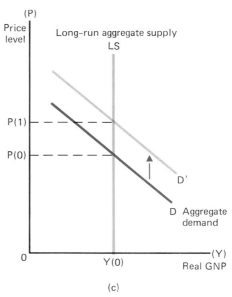

(b)

(c)

▶ Discretionary Fiscal Policy in a Recession

The economy will remain in equilibrium as long as no disturbances upset the balance between supply and demand in the goods, loanable funds, or labor market. Suppose, however, that planned investment declines by $10 billion. In part (a) of figure 27.1, this would involve a decline of planned investment to $40 billion, with no immediate change in any other macroeconomic magnitude except GNP. This recessionary tendency is indicated by the arrows pointing to the left in figure 27.2.

As we have seen, a decline in planned expenditure will create excess production of goods and services and lead to a recession. We learned in chapters 21 and 25 that the impact of a decline in planned investment on the goods market is given by the multiplier equation. (See page 453.) To make the arithmetic simple, suppose that the MPC is 0.8 and the MPS is 0.2. Then, the multiplier, which is 1/MPS, equals 5, and a decline in planned investment of $10 billion will lead to a potential short-run decline in equilibrium GNP of $10 billion $\times$ 5 = $50 billion. (Actually, the decline in planned investment and equilibrium GNP will be somewhat less to the extent that the interest rate declines and keeps planned investment from falling quite so far. See figure 25.5.)

Response of the Fiscal Authority to a Decline in Investment Demand: An Increase in Expenditure

Now suppose the government foresees the economy's coming recession. It is possible for the government to undertake discretionary fiscal policy, adjusting either its expenditure (G) or its taxes (T). The word *discretionary* means that the government agency responsible for setting the level of expenditure or taxes *uses its judgment* to adjust G or T to counteract the economy's recessionary tendency. Suppose the government decides to increase *immediately* its expenditure by an amount *exactly equal* to the decline in planned investment—$10 billion. Such an immediate increase in government expenditure on goods and services will prevent the recession from actually occurring. Neither aggregate demand nor the demand for loanable funds will shift leftward, and full macroeconomic equilibrium will continue.

Reaction in the Goods Market

The government's discretionary increase in its spending is just the right amount to prevent planned aggregate production in the goods market from exceeding planned aggregate expenditure at full-employment GNP. Planned saving at full employment is exactly equal to planned investment plus the government deficit because an increase in government spending has exactly offset the decline in planned investment. This means that the economy is no longer heading toward recession because the aggregate market for goods and services is once again in equilibrium.

Reaction in the Credit Market

The effect of an increase in government expenditure will also be felt in the credit market. Since the size of the government's tax revenue, T, has remained unchanged, an increase in G of $10 billion means that the budget deficit (G − T) also grows by $10 billion. In terms of figure 27.2, the larger budget deficit keeps the demand for loanable funds, DLF, exactly where it was before planned investment declined. Consequently, the real interest rate remains at its initial equilibrium value, r(0). However, DLF is now made up of a *smaller private demand* for loanable funds and a *larger government demand*. Government expenditure has replaced some private investment expenditure in GNP.

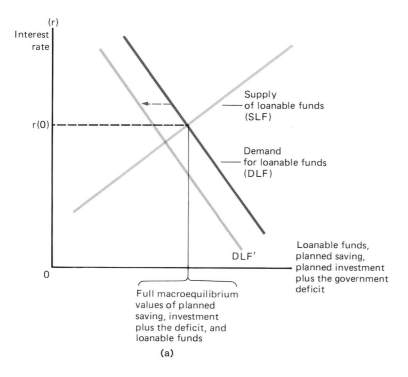

(r)
Interest
rate

Supply
— of loanable funds
(SLF)

r(0)

Demand
— for loanable funds
(DLF)

DLF'

Loanable funds,
planned saving,
planned investment
plus the government
deficit

0

Full macroequilibrium
values of planned
saving, investment
plus the deficit, and
loanable funds

(a)

**Figure 27.2   The government
increases spending to combat a
recession with fiscal policy**
The arrows show that planned
investment expenditure and aggregate
demand have declined. If planned
investment plus the government deficit [$\dot{I}$
+ (G − T)] declines, then the economy
will head toward a recession as indicated
by the leftward-pointing arrow. However,
if the government immediately increases
G, then [$\dot{I}$ + (G − T)] and aggregate
demand need not decline and the
recession can be avoided.
   In part (b) the recession begins:
aggregate demand shifts to the left and
the price level and GNP decline.

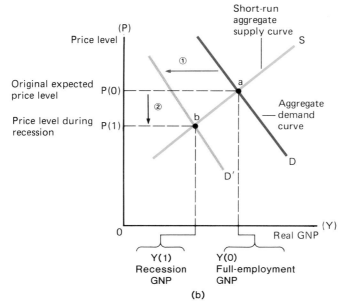

(P)
Price level

Short-run
aggregate
supply curve
S

①

Original expected
price level   P(0)

a

Aggregate
— demand
curve

Price level during   P(1)
recession

b

D

D'

(Y)

0

Real GNP

Y(1)
Recession
GNP

Y(0)
Full-employment
GNP

(b)

Why Fiscal Policy Works

Recall that we started out with a decline in planned investment, which of course led to a reduction in the amount of goods producers sold private investors in the economy. However, *assuming the government possesses perfect information about the economy,* it can enter the goods market and quickly increase its purchases of goods. The multiplier equation shows that fiscal policy works because it makes no difference to suppliers of goods and services whether exogenous expenditure, EX, is made up of government purchases or those of private investors. The private buyers of products such as steel and bricks who decide to reduce their purchases are replaced by government agents buying the same goods for the purpose of constructing schools, bridges, and so on. Any particular firm may be saddened by the loss of its private customers, but it will not change its prices or alter its production if, in the meantime, the government makes up the loss in sales by increasing its own purchases of goods and services.

Discretionary Fiscal Policy When Taxes Are Adjusted

If the government decides to reduce net taxes rather than increase its expenditures to carry out antirecessionary fiscal policy, it is relying on an increase in *private planned consumption* to offset the decline in planned investment. (It is important to recognize that an *increase in transfer expenditures*—payments to individuals or families to increase their incomes—will have an impact on the deficit and on consumption expenditures similar to a *reduction in taxes*.) In our macroeconomic analysis, reduced taxes and increased consumption work just as well to maintain full-employment equilibrium as does an increase in government expenditure. However, there are important

differences in the effects of a tax reduction and of a government expenditure increase that may lead to a preference of one form of fiscal policy action over the other.

To begin, there is the obvious difference that a tax reduction puts consumers in the driver's seat so to speak. They can choose which additional goods to purchase rather than delegate that authority to their representatives in Congress. Thus, those who favor a small rather than a large government tend to advocate tax reductions over expenditure increases in fiscal policy debates. Second, there are technical differences in the impact of decreases in taxes versus increases in government spending on macroeconomic equilibrium.

Remember that we showed in chapter 21 that the *initial* impact of a reduction in taxes on aggregate spending for goods and services is *smaller* than an equal increase in government spending. You may wish to review pages 453–54 to refresh your memory before going on. To summarize briefly, when taxes are lowered, consumers will allocate only *part* of their increased disposable income to consumption. Specifically, they will increase their planned consumption by the increase in their disposable income (the decline in taxes) multiplied by the marginal propensity to consume. In our numerical example, if taxes were to decline by $10 billion, consumers would increase their planned expenditure by 80 percent of this amount, or $8 billion. The remainder, $2 billion, goes to increased saving.

We showed in chapter 21 that the multiplier effect of a tax reduction is given by the equation

$$-(\Delta Y(0)/\Delta T) = b/(1 - b),$$

where b is the marginal propensity to consume and $1 - b$ is the marginal propensity to save. The multiplier effect of an increase in government expenditure, however, is $1/(1 - b)$. In our example, with an

Crowding out *means that an*
increase in the government deficit
raises the interest rate, leading to a
reduction in planned investment
expenditure.

MPC of 0.8, the multiplier effect of a tax reduction is only 80 percent as large as an equal increase in government expenditure. Therefore, the tax reduction required to maintain full employment is 1.25 (1/0.8) times as large as the required increase in government expenditure. If net taxes are reduced by $12.5 million, planned consumption will increase by 80 percent of this amount, or $10 million, which is precisely the decline in planned investment. Thus, full-employment equilibrium in the goods market will be maintained.

Our analysis of a reduction in taxes versus an increase in government spending has shown that discretionary fiscal policy reducing taxes requires a larger increase in the government deficit than a policy that raises expenditures—$2.5 billion more to be precise. Other things equal, this greater demand for loanable funds will result in an interest rate that is higher than otherwise. If an increase in the government deficit does raise the interest rate, it will lead to what is called **crowding out** of private investment because the quantity of investment goods demanded falls as the interest rate increases, *cet. par.* Does this mean that increasing government spending is a more desirable fiscal policy than reducing taxes? The answer to this question is not simple and leads to a great deal of economic and political debate. A fuller discussion of crowding out will follow, especially on pages 612–14.

Our macroeconomic model will help us sort out the issues. A tax reduction directly increases disposable income, which is GNP less taxes. Smaller taxes mean larger disposable income. Thus, when taxes fall, planned consumption and saving increase. In our example, planned saving will increase by the increased disposable income multiplied by the MPS of 0.2. If taxes are reduced $12.5 billion to prevent a recession, both disposable income and the deficit increase by

$12.5 billion. Increased saving amounts to $12.5 billion × 0.2 = $2.5 billion. Thus, the public's *increase in planned saving* when there is a tax reduction (as opposed to an increase in government expenditure) is *exactly* equal to the *additional* government deficit of $2.5 billion, *cet. par.* It is likely that this increase in planned saving will offset the additional government deficit by increasing the supply of loanable funds. Thus, the larger deficit caused by a tax reduction of $12.5 billion need not raise the rate of interest more than an increase in government expenditure of $10 billion would.

Moreover, other conditions in the economy may be affected by a tax reduction. *Additional* effects of the tax reduction may make reducing taxes *more* rather than *less* effective than an expenditure increase in combating the recession. The tax reduction, particularly if corporate income tax rates are reduced, will lead to an increase in the *after-tax* profitability of investment projects and the *after-tax* returns on loan contracts. It is what you "take home" *after* taxes that determines your willingness to invest or to purchase a loan contract. Therefore, this increase in after-tax returns on investments will lead to an increase in planned investment expenditure. At every rate of interest, planned private investment will be larger with a reduction in taxes than with an increase in government spending because after-tax returns to lenders and investors (borrowers) will be higher. To summarize, the *direct* effect of an increase in government spending may initially make it seem more effective in combating a recession. However, the *indirect* effects of tax reductions on planned saving and the supply of loanable funds and investment expenditures create powerful arguments in favor of reducing taxes.

Figure 27.3   The government reduces spending to combat an inflationary episode with fiscal policy
The arrows show that planned investment and aggregate demand have increased. If planned investment plus the government deficit $[\hat{I} + (G - T)]$ increases, then the economy will head toward an inflationary episode. However, if the government immediately reduces G or raises T, the inflationary episode can be avoided.

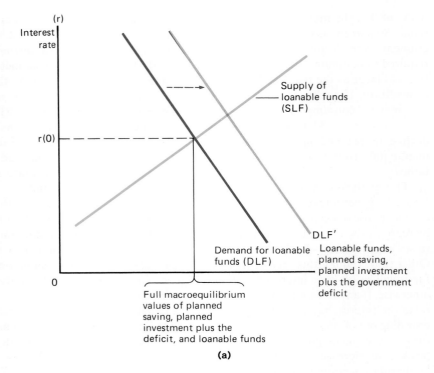

(a)

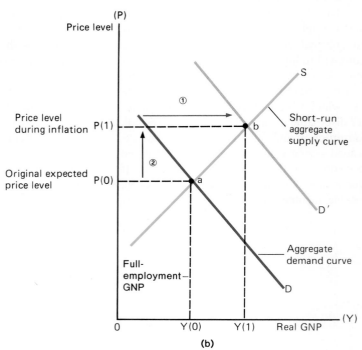

(b)

Discretionary Fiscal Policy to Prevent an Inflationary Episode

Theoretically, changes in government expenditures and taxes can be used to prevent an inflationary episode as well as a recession. The fiscal policy required is, of course, opposite in direction to the policies that would counteract a recessionary tendency in the economy.

Figure 27.3 depicts the economy in full macroequilibrium. Should investment demand increase as indicated by the arrows pointing to the right in part (a) of figure 27.3, an inflationary episode is imminent. As the arrows in part (b) show, (1) a rightward shift in aggregate demand will lead to (2) an increase in the price level. A discretionary *reduction* in government spending equal to the increase in planned investment can prevent the inflationary episode from occurring. Government will have reduced its expenditure in order to accommodate investors' desires to use more of the economy's resources. Planned investment will rise, but government spending will decline by just the right amount to prevent an excess demand for goods and services.

The government can also carry out its antiinflationary fiscal policy by increasing taxes. Either a reduction in spending or an increase in taxes will prevent inflation. However, the effects of these two alternative fiscal policies have different impacts on important macroeconomic variables, as we saw when analyzing the impact of antirecessionary government actions. The direct impact of a tax increase is to reduce private consumption expenditure and planned saving.

The resources for increased investment are taken from the production of consumers' goods and services. Moreover, taxes must be increased by a *greater* amount than government expenditures need be reduced to result in a decline in planned consumption equal to the increase in planned investment. The reason, of course, is that planned consumption will fall by *less* than the tax increase. To be sure that you fully understand why the increase in taxes must be greater than the reduction in government expenditure, work through the examples given for a reduction in taxes when planned investment falls. Now everything is reversed. Show *exactly* the *increase* in taxes when planned investment increases $10 billion that is required to maintain macroeconomic equilibrium.

As we have seen, there are additional effects of increasing taxes. The supply of loanable funds will fall because reduced disposable income will reduce saving. Moreover, an increase in tax *rates* reduces the after-tax return to holding loan contracts. On the demand for loanable funds side of the market, increased tax rates will reduce the after-tax returns on investment. This will reduce planned investment and shift the DLF curve to the left. The leftward shift will to some extent offset the initial increase in the demand for investment goods, causing planned investment to rise by less than it would if government expenditures were reduced instead of taxes increased. Table 27.1 summarizes the basic fiscal policy actions the government can take to fight inflationary episodes and recessions.

Table 27.1   Summary of fiscal policy to offset recessions or inflationary episodes

| To combat | The government can adjust either | | Effect on deficit |
	Taxes or Expenditure		
Recessions (expansionary fiscal policy needed)	Reduce	Increase	Increase
Inflationary episodes (contractionary fiscal policy needed)	Increase	Reduce	Reduce

*A **lag** is the time that elapses between the occurrence of an event and a reaction to the event.*

*A **recognition lag** is the time that elapses between the occurrence of an event and the observation that the event has occurred.*

▶ Lags, Politics, and Fiscal Policy

We have seen that as long as the government responds *quickly* and in the *appropriate direction,* changes in spending or taxes can offset any recessionary or inflationary tendencies that threaten the economy. Fiscal policy is *theoretically* sound; its basic problem is in *practice,* given the rapid pace of everyday changes in the economic life of a nation. Because of constitutional restraints and political realities, the government does not have the power to turn expenditures or taxes on or off at will. In the United States, congressional committees must meet and legislation must be passed before government agents can implement a policy calling for changing expenditures or taxes. Economists use the word **lag** to describe the delays inherent in fiscal policy. Whether these lags are sufficiently lengthy to destroy the effectiveness of fiscal policy is a matter that can be resolved only by careful empirical analysis of macroeconomic data. However, if lags are not too long, our analysis shows that discretionary fiscal policy can be a powerful stabilization tool.

An example from the severe recession of 1981–82 illustrates the difficulties in carrying out an increase in government spending to help cure a recession. In late 1982, Congress voted a substantial increase in federal funds allocated to state highway construction projects. One argument for the increased expenditure was that it would help reduce unemployment. In the state of Ohio, unemployment had risen to a higher level than in almost any other state. Therefore, the increased funds available for highway construction in 1983 should have been very welcome news. So they were, but paradoxically, expenditure on highway repair and construction actually *fell* during early 1983 compared to 1982.

This decline in highway expenditure was contrary to the intent of Congress and probably contributed to prolonged high unemployment in Ohio. One reason for the decline was, ironically, the existence of increased federal aid. To make sure that the state received full advantage from the available federal aid,

Ohio postponed signing contracts for highway construction until it was sure the contracts would be eligible for federal support. This delay contributed to a *50 percent decline* in authorized highway expenditures through April 1983 compared to the first four months of 1982.[1]

Even if the legislative process did not introduce lags in implementing fiscal policy, there are further problems in acting *quickly* enough for fiscal policy to be effective. As we have seen, preventing a recession requires that increases in government spending or reductions in taxes take place *before* planned investment actually declines. Unfortunately, it takes several months before the data that the government needs to recognize a recession or inflationary episode are available. This is called a **recognition lag.** Only then, when it may already be too late, will Congress *begin* the lengthy legislative process that precedes a discretionary tax or expenditure change. There may be further lags in starting up new projects if expenditures are to be increased. Implementing a change in tax policy, once the decision is made to do so, need not take as long.

The lags of *recognition* and *implementation* of fiscal policy are serious enough when recession threatens. However, fiscal policy is even less likely to be timed accurately enough to prevent an inflationary episode. The reason for this is the political danger to legislators in raising taxes or reducing government expenditures. While the public and its congressional representatives may strongly favor antirecessionary fiscal policy *in principle,* few people really believe that it is a good idea to increase *their* taxes or reduce allocations to *their* favorite projects.

Political realities as well as recognition and implementation lags lead many economists to believe that *discretionary* fiscal policy is unlikely to work well as an antiinflationary or antirecession macroeconomic tool. Fortunately, however, there are elements of fiscal policy that do not require new legislation every time an inflation or a recession threatens macroeconomic stability.

Countercyclical fiscal policy is fiscal policy designed explicitly to moderate fluctuations in GNP and employment.

Automatic fiscal stabilizers are fiscal policies that do not require new legislation or executive decisions to become effective because they are built into existing laws.

▶ Nondiscretionary Fiscal Policy

Various tax and expenditure programs serve as **countercyclical fiscal policy** (fiscal policy to offset recessions and inflationary episodes) that is relatively free of recognition and implementation lags.

Even without new legislation, changes in important aspects of the government's budget *automatically* come into play whenever the economy moves into a recessionary or inflationary phase. This is very important because market economies everywhere are characterized by business cycles that lead to alternating periods of excess expenditure and excess production in the goods market and to increases and decreases in unemployment in the labor market. The economy's **automatic fiscal stabilizers** are elements of fiscal policy that do not require new legislation each time they are used. They are valuable tools to reduce economic fluctuations, although they cannot be expected to prevent them. Automatic, or nondiscretionary, fiscal policy stems from the fact that our tax laws and certain government expenditures are programmed to increase or decrease *automatically* in the correct direction to offset recessions and inflations.

On the tax side, income and sales taxes automatically fall when incomes and the sales of goods and services decline. They rise as business conditions "heat up." Thus, such taxes *automatically* tend to slow down both the leftward shift of the aggregate demand curve during recessions and the rightward shift of aggregate demand during inflationary episodes. Beginning in 1984, the federal personal income tax brackets were adjusted for inflation. Through a process called *indexing,* increases in your income that are offset by inflation will not push you into a higher tax bracket under the changes implemented in 1984. The tax *rates* on individual incomes are not to increase just because of inflation. With indexing of tax brackets, income taxes will now rise less rapidly during inflationary episodes than they did in the past. Many economists favor indexing because it means that the tax rates we pay must be determined by legislation, not by inflation. However, indexing does reduce somewhat the effectiveness of the income tax as an automatic fiscal stabilizer during inflationary episodes.

Several categories of transfer expenditures increase when the economy heads into recessions and decline when incomes rise and unemployment falls. One program is unemployment insurance. During recessions, most laid-off workers become eligible for unemployment compensation. Thus, their lost wage income is partially replaced. Because their disposable income does not fall as much as their lost wage income, unemployed workers who receive unemployment compensation are able to maintain their consumption expenditures at a higher level than would be possible if they were completely on their own. The consumption expenditures supported by unemployment compensation payments help maintain the level of aggregate demand and thus reduce the severity of the recessions.

Other transfer expenditures that increase automatically during recessions and fall during movements toward inflationary episodes are all income maintenance programs, such as Aid to Families with Dependent Children (AFDC) and federal food stamps. When family incomes fall below legislatively determined levels, these programs provide additional income in the form of cash payments (AFDC) or stamps that can be traded in for food purchases. Under both programs, disposable income is maintained during recessions and reduced when earnings increase. Thus they act like unemployment compensation does: to offset declines in planned consumption during recessions and to reduce increases in planned consumption during inflationary episodes.

▶ Recent Fiscal Policy Developments

While it is useful to distinguish between countercyclical fiscal policy and long-term fiscal policy, the experience with changes in tax policy in the United States in the 1980s illustrates that distinctions are sometimes difficult to make. Federal income tax cuts in the early 1980s represented historic changes that could have positively affected long-term growth in the economy. Yet, as discussed more fully in chapter 29, more zealous advocates of the income tax changes argued that tax cuts would quickly stimulate the economy in countercyclical fashion.

In 1985, the Reagan administration proposed a "flat tax" that would drastically simplify and restructure the incentive effects of the personal and corporate income tax laws. Again, such efforts, if successful, could have a substantial long-term growth impact on the economy. Yet the surprisingly sluggish performance of the United States economy in 1985 was attributed in part to uncertainty by consumers and businesses about when and if tax law changes would take place and what those changes would look like. The more uncertain consumers and producers are about the rules of the game with respect to taxes, the more tentative they will be with respect to spending, saving, and investment decisions.

In short, the experience of the first half of the 1980s made it clear that long-term fiscal policy requiring changes in tax rates takes a long time to implement. The transition period was lengthy and the implications of the changes were uncertain. Increased uncertainty about where United States tax policy was going in the long run had significant and adverse short-run effects on the United States economy in the mid-1980s.

▶ Discretionary Monetary Policy in a Recession

As with fiscal policy, monetary policy can be a very potent weapon in forestalling macroeconomic disequilibrium. In fact, under present institutional arrangements, monetary policy may be more flexible and, hence, a more effective discretionary tool than fiscal policy. This is because the day-to-day conduct of monetary policy does not require the prior approval of the executive or congressional branches of government. It is conducted by the Fed, which is theoretically independent of Congress in deciding how to conduct monetary policies that affect the macroeconomy. In the sections that follow, we first see how discretionary monetary policy can prevent a recession and then how it can forestall an inflationary episode. Before going on you may wish to review the discussion of monetary policy and the role of the Fed in chapters 23 and 24.

In figure 27.4, parts (a) and (b), we illustrate the start of the same recession described in figure 27.2. Planned investment has declined as indicated by the leftward-pointing arrow in part (b) of figure 27.4. If no further changes occur, the economy is headed toward a recessionary equilibrium. In the recession, the interest rate will fall as indicated in part (b) of figure 27.4. GNP will decline as indicated by the arrow pointing leftward in part (a) of figure 27.4, and the price level will begin to fall (arrow pointing downward). However, if the Fed—the monetary authority—possesses this information about the coming recession, it can prevent it by engaging in an expansionary open market operation. If the Fed increases the banking system's reserves by a sufficient amount, the supply curve of loanable funds (SLF) and the aggregate demand curve (D) will shift far enough to the right to maintain planned investment and GNP at the full-employment level as shown in part (c) of figure 27.4.

The economy's supply of loanable funds consists of households' net supply of loanable funds plus the banking system's supply. The banking system's supply of loanable funds equals the rate of growth of real money balances, $\Delta M/P$. Therefore, the Fed's expansionary monetary policy must cause an *increase* in the *growth* of the real money supply large enough to keep planned investment at its initial level. Such an expansionary monetary policy is illustrated in part (c) of figure 27.4, where the arrow points to the right.

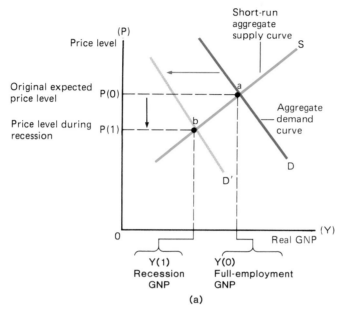

Short-run aggregate supply curve

(P)
Price level

Original expected price level   P(0)

Price level during recession   P(1)

Aggregate demand curve

S

a

b

D'

D

0   Real GNP   (Y)

Y(1)
Recession
GNP

Y(0)
Full-employment
GNP

(a)

Figure 27.4   The Fed adopts an expansionary monetary policy to prevent a recession
The arrows in parts (a) and (b) show that planned investment expenditure has declined and the economy will enter a recession unless immediate action is taken to prevent the recession.

As shown in part (c), if the Fed immediately buys government bonds to increase the reserves of the banking system, the supply of loanable funds will shift to the right (see arrow). The interest rate will fall, so that planned investment does not decline, avoiding the recession.

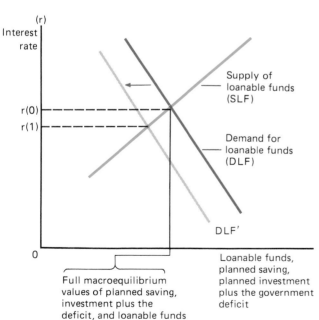

(r)
Interest rate

r(0)
r(1)

Supply of loanable funds (SLF)

Demand for loanable funds (DLF)

DLF'

0

Full macroequilibrium values of planned saving, investment plus the deficit, and loanable funds

Loanable funds, planned saving, planned investment plus the government deficit

(b)   The arrow shows that planned investment expenditures have declined and the economy will enter a recession unless immediate action is taken to prevent it.

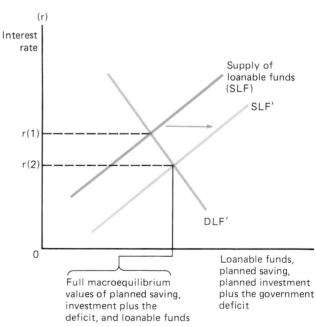

(r)
Interest rate

r(1)

r(2)

Supply of loanable funds (SLF)

SLF'

DLF'

0

Full macroequilibrium values of planned saving, investment plus the deficit, and loanable funds

Loanable funds, planned saving, planned investment plus the government deficit

(c)   If the Fed immediately buys government bonds to increase the reserves of the banking system, the supply of loanable funds will shift to the right as shown by the arrow. The interest rate will fall, so that planned investment does not decline, avoiding the recession.

The Initial Effect in the Loanable Funds Market

We will assume that the Fed has increased banking system reserves by the amount that leads to an increase in the rate of growth of the money supply *exactly* sufficient to offset the impending recession. This expansionary monetary policy shifts the supply curve of loanable funds rightward to SLF'. Given the new demand curve for loanable funds, DLF', there is now an excess supply of loanable funds at interest rate r(1). To eliminate this excess supply, lenders compete with one another to buy loan contracts. This competition forces the rate of interest all the way down to r(2), where SLF' intersects DLF'. At this interest rate, the loanable funds market is in equilibrium.

The Effect in the Goods Market

The success of the Fed's intervention in the macroeconomy results because the interest rate falls to the lower value of r(2). As a result of this decline, planned investment remains at the level that prevailed when the economy was in its initial state of full macroequilibrium. Therefore, at interest rate r(2), planned investment plus the government deficit equals planned saving with GNP at its full-employment level. Aggregate demand intersects aggregate supply at the original equilibrium price level, P(0).

With production and sales synchronized, firms have no incentive to lay off workers. The Fed's policy of expanding the banking system's reserves has removed the fundamental cause of the threatening recession, excess production in the goods market. Since equilibrium exists simultaneously in the goods, credit, and labor markets, full macroeconomic equilibrium has been maintained.

Why Monetary Policy Works

The Fed was able to counteract the recessionary threat resulting from the decline in the demand for investment goods by exerting a powerful influence on the rate of interest. By acting quickly to increase the supply of loanable funds, the Fed forced the rate of

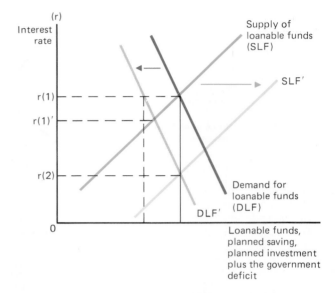

Figure 27.5   How monetary policy works to prevent a recession
Planned investment has declined, as indicated by the leftward-pointing arrow. However, the Fed can prevent a recession by an expansionary monetary policy that shifts the SLF sufficiently far to the right, as indicated by the rightward-pointing arrow, to force the interest rate down to r(2). This keeps planned investment and the quantity of loanable funds demanded and supplied at their full-employment levels.

interest down. In terms of the numerical example we used to illustrate the effects of fiscal policy, planned investment initially declined by $10 billion, as indicated by the leftward-pointing arrow in figure 27.5. Without any action by the Fed, the interest rate would have declined to r(1)', but this would not have been sufficient to boost planned investment back to its original level. The rightward-pointing arrow shows that the Fed's expansionary open market operation has shifted the SLF curve to the right, forcing the interest rate all the way down to r(2). This lower rate of interest reduced the cost of investment projects and thus stimulated the investment component of aggregate expenditure for goods and services. Recall that investors had initially planned to reduce their purchases of goods because of their pessimistic expectations about the future. At a sufficiently *lower* rate of interest, even these pessimistic investors wished to purchase the same quantity of investment goods as they had been buying *prior* to the decline in planned investment. Notice that at the lower rate of interest, r(2), both planned investment *and* the quantity of loanable funds demanded and supplied are exactly the same as before the initial decline in planned investment.

The mechanism by which monetary policy transmits its effects throughout the economy bears a striking resemblance to the way flexible prices automatically adjust the economy following a decline in planned investment. Monetary policy and flexible prices both affect the real value of the new money balances created when the banking system buys loan contracts. Remember that the real value of these new money balances is represented symbolically by the expression $\Delta M/P$, where ΔM is the change in *nominal* money balances and P is the price level. In the case of flexible prices, excess aggregate supply in the goods market produces a decline in prices, which makes the *denominator* of $\Delta M/P$ smaller and hence raises the value of the $\Delta M/P$ ratio. Monetary policy, on the other hand, works directly on the *numerator* of $\Delta M/P$ by making ΔM larger. The net effect in both cases is a rightward shift in SLF, the aggregate supply of loanable funds, and a resulting decline in the interest rate. Therefore, by using monetary policy, the Fed can achieve the same result that flexible prices do, without the economy's having to experience the undesirable symptoms of a recession—high unemployment and low production.

One reason that monetary policy can be such an effective weapon against recession should be clear. If the Fed wants to initiate a particular policy action, it can do so without going through a lengthy process of legislation. This potentially speedy response is a virtue as long as the Fed accurately anticipates changes in the goods market and takes the appropriate policy action to offset them. Remember, in this chapter we assumed that the Fed always chooses the correct policy because it is fully informed about the events unfolding in the real and financial sectors of the economy. The real world, unfortunately, is such a complicated place that the Fed often has to resort to educated

guesses about what is happening in the aggregate economy. Recognition lag affects monetary policy just as it does fiscal policy. For example, the Fed has to wait for three months or longer before it receives accurate data on the quantity of investment goods purchased in the goods market during any given period. In the meantime, it has to guess whether planned investment during that period has increased, decreased, or remained constant.

▶ Discretionary Monetary Policy
to Prevent Inflation

The Fed's ability to affect bank reserves can be used to prevent an inflationary episode as well as a recession. The monetary policy required is, of course, *restrictive,* or *contractionary,* just the opposite of the expansionary monetary policy needed to combat recession.

To make sure that you understand the theory of antiinflationary monetary policy, construct a diagram with the economy in macroequilibrium. Shift the demand curve for loanable funds to the right to indicate that investors' increased optimism about the future leads them to desire to invest *more* than previously. This will also result in a shift to the right of the aggregate demand curve, leading to the beginning of an inflationary episode. The Fed can prevent an inflationary episode from occurring, however, if it knows that planned investment is about to increase and takes immediate action to *reduce* bank reserves by just the amount needed to restore planned investment to its original level.

By *selling* government bonds in an open market operation, the Fed can accomplish its desired aim, and the supply of loanable funds will shift *leftward*. As a result of the ensuing *increase* in the rate of interest, investors see the cost of prospective investment projects increase. The Fed's restrictive monetary policy will offset the rightward shift in the demand for investment goods and prevent excess demand from occurring in the goods market. The Fed has achieved this goal by *reducing* the *numerator* of $\Delta M/P$.

Table 27.2   Comparison of monetary and fiscal policies

Policy needed to combat	The Fed should	Congress should	Impact of policy on DLF or SLF
Recession			
Expansionary monetary policy (open market operation)	Buy government bonds to increase bank reserves		Shifts SLF to the right
Expansionary fiscal policy		Increase expenditures or reduce taxes	Shifts DLF to the right
Inflationary episode			
Contractionary monetary policy (open market operation)	Sell government bonds to reduce bank reserves		Shifts SLF to the left
Contractionary fiscal policy		Reduce expenditures or increase taxes	Shifts DLF to the left

Table 27.2 summarizes and compares monetary and fiscal policies to offset recessions and inflationary episodes. The table also shows the impact of each type of policy on the supply of loanable funds (SLF) or the demand for loanable funds (DLF).

The Politics of Discretionary Antiinflation Monetary Policy

In our discussion of fiscal policy, we pointed out that in addition to the technical problems of recognizing when countercyclical fiscal policy is needed and of implementing the correct actions once their need is agreed upon, there is an additional problem when inflation threatens. It is simply that the cure for inflation always appears more painful than that for recession. Taking something away from borrowers or consumers is always going to be a less popular activity than giving something to them. We shall see in chapter 28 that this political reality has been an important factor contributing to the inflationary era in the United States that characterized the period from the late 1960s well into the 1980s.

The members of the Federal Open Market Committee (FOMC) do not stand for election as members of Congress must. Therefore, there is little question that they face less pressure when implementing antiinflationary policy than Congress does. However, the members of the Fed's Board of Governors are appointed by the President, and Congress has the power to pass laws that restrict the Fed's power to conduct monetary policy. Therefore, the Board of Governors and the FOMC cannot completely ignore public and congressional reaction to their monetary policies.

The principal problem faced by the Fed in its efforts to prevent inflationary episodes arises from the fact that an increase in investment demand is very unlikely to be spread uniformly over all industries. The expected returns on future investments may have increased much more in some areas (for example, computers or consumer electronics) than in others (for example, construction or automobile manufacturing). Therefore, when the Fed takes actions that raise the rate of interest, this will be seen as "choking off" investment in those areas of the economy where the investment demand schedule has *not* shifted to the right. Of course, this is simply a reflection of the need to reallocate resources from, say, the housing industry to the computer industry. The market is giving the correct signals to investors through the interest rate.

Unfortunately, the process of adjusting to the changed composition of investment goods demanded will not be painless for firms and workers who had been active in the sector of the economy not sharing in the growth of productivity or demand. The non-growing firms and their labor forces will experience reduced profits and increased unemployment as the needed adjustments occur. Their complaints to their elected representatives will lead to unpleasantness for the Fed as it tries to prevent inflation. This political pressure, then, represents an obstacle to the conduct of appropriate monetary policies to prevent inflation. Throughout the period 1980–83, the Fed committed itself to bringing inflation down from the double-digit levels of 1979 and 1980. The Reagan administration and many in Congress were highly critical of Fed Chairman Paul Volcker and blamed the Fed's restrictive monetary policy for the recession in 1981–82. By 1983 the economy began to expand rapidly and inflation appeared to be under control. Paul Volcker became popular in political circles for having arrested inflation. Although Volcker had originally been appointed by Democrat Jimmy Carter, the Republican incumbent reappointed him in 1983.

▶ Comparing the Short-run and Long-run Effects of Fiscal and Monetary Policies

Fiscal and monetary policies are the tools the government uses in influencing the aggregate economy. Both can correct a disequilibrium that will lead into a recession or a period of rising prices. *Fiscal policy* operates *directly* on the *goods market* because the government-spending component of fiscal policy is itself part of aggregate expenditure for goods and the tax component affects households' consumption demand for goods. *Monetary policy,* on the other hand, does not affect the goods market directly. The initial impact of *monetary policy* is felt in the *credit market,*

as *bank reserves* are affected. A change in the banks' supply of loanable funds in turn affects investment expenditure in the goods sector via changes in the interest rate.

Both fiscal and monetary policies can be used to offset business cycles. However, there are significant differences in the lags that occur before they are implemented and in their effects on various macroeconomic variables, such as government spending, taxes, saving, investment, consumption, and interest rates. Because of these differences, there is much political debate, and even some disagreement among economists, about the desirability of using one type of policy or the other. There is also disagreement regarding the form of fiscal policy—tax adjustments or expenditure changes—that should be used to promote aggregate economic health. We will survey the major features of these debates in chapter 29. Remember that *both* forms of policy can in theory restore or maintain full macroeconomic equilibrium. However, our concept of full equilibrium ignores the long-run impact of investment on the economy's capital stock and, hence, its capacity to produce goods and services. For example, fiscal policy to counteract a recession will in general result in a *lower level* of investment and a *higher level* of consumption or government spending than will monetary policy. Review figures 27.2 and 27.4 if you do not see why this is so. A great deal of political debate over the relative merits of alternative macroeconomic policies involves confusion over their immediate and long-run effects.

Is Discretionary Policy Useless?

In chapter 29 we will analyze a subtle issue hotly debated among economists called *monetarists* and *Keynesians,* but first we must introduce it here. The issue is twofold. First a number of empirical studies purport to show that because of the lags associated with implementing countercyclical monetary and fiscal policy, the timing for the use of each has been all wrong. In effect, the argument is that ill-timed countercyclical policies have actually made business cycles worse than they would have been without government discretionary actions. That evidence has led some economists (monetarists) to call for less use of discretionary monetary and fiscal policy until and unless we develop better methods for recognizing the need for policy action and for implementing policies in a timely fashion.

The second element of the debate is even more profound in its implications. Professor Robert Lucas of the University of Chicago and others view discretionary monetary and fiscal actions as attempts to smooth the growth process in a market economy by fooling consumers, savers, and investors into believing that the economy will not slow down or speed up despite evidence that such changes are taking place. As the public becomes more informed and sophisticated in its reading of economic variables indicating changes in the economy, they will become harder to fool with discretionary policies. This argument suggests that aggregate economic activity can only be smoothed by means of discretionary policy actions that surprise consumers, savers, and investors. The conclusion of these economists is that smoothing the rate of growth of the economy will only reduce long-run growth. If this view is correct, we would expect to observe that even well-timed fiscal and monetary policies would lose their effectiveness in modifying the short-run growth path of the macroeconomy.

These two positions—that recognition and implementation lags are at present insurmountable and that the public cannot continually be fooled by discretionary policies—present strong arguments against the use of discretionary monetary and/or fiscal policies. Keynesians, on the other hand, still favor the use of discretionary countercyclical monetary and fiscal policies.

▶ Summary and Conclusions

By now, you should be beginning to decide for yourself whether you believe that discretionary monetary and/or fiscal policies can help offset inflationary episodes or recessions. You will learn more about macroeconomic policies in practice in the next two chapters. Discretionary fiscal and monetary policies are, in *theory,* extraordinarily powerful weapons of macroeconomic control. By manipulating the dials of government expenditures, government taxation, and banks' reserves, government authorities can presumably ward off many of the destabilizing elements that affect the private sector of the economy. The following main points were emphasized.

Expansionary or restrictive fiscal and monetary policies can theoretically reduce the severity of business cycles.

Fiscal policy that operates through a change in taxes will have effects that differ from those of fiscal policy that operates through a change in government expenditures.

Monetary and fiscal policies have different impacts on major macroeconomic variables in both the short and the long run.

Both information lags and political considerations impede the effectiveness of discretionary countercyclical monetary and fiscal policies.

▶ Key Terms

automatic fiscal
    stabilizers *571*
countercyclical fiscal
    policy *571*
crowding out *567*

fiscal policy *563*
lag *570*
recognition lag *570*

▶ Questions for Discussion and Review

1. Are the following statements true, false, or uncertain? Defend your answers.
   a. Monetary and fiscal policies are equally effective in preventing inflationary episodes and recessions.
   b. One advantage of monetary over fiscal policy is that the Fed need not consider the political implications of its actions.
   c. One advantage of fiscal over monetary policy to combat inflationary episodes is that it promotes investment in physical capital to a greater extent.

2. Describe the differences between monetary and fiscal policies with regard to:
   a. the macroeconomic variables that are directly affected by the policies;
   b. the governmental authorities that are responsible for them.

3. Suppose you are in charge of discretionary fiscal policy and your computer model of the aggregate economy has just furnished you with the following information about the economy for the next twelve months:

Full-employment GNP	= $1,000
Consumption function	= $100 + .72(GNP − T)
Taxes (T)	= $100
Planned investment	= $100
Government spending	= $100

   Design a fiscal policy that will promote full employment without inflation for the next twelve months. Be sure to specify what changes (if any) will occur in
   a. Planned investment
   b. Planned saving
   c. Taxes
   d. Government spending
   e. The federal deficit
   f. The rate of interest

4. Using the data from question 3, suppose that you are the monetary authority and possess the following additional knowledge about the economy:

Money stock (M2)	= $600
Bank reserves	= $60
Required reserves	= $60
Elasticity of demand curve for investment goods with respect to the rate of interest	− 1.0
Current rate of interest	= 9%

   Design a monetary policy for the next twelve months to promote full employment without inflation. Be sure to specify what changes (if any) will occur in
   a. Open market operations
   b. Bank reserves
   c. The money supply
   d. All other variables (a through f in question 3).

5. Suppose the consumer price index has risen from 185 to 203 since last year and that this 9.7 percent rate of inflation is not spread evenly over all goods and services. The prices of housing and transportation have risen by 25 percent and 40 percent, respectively, while all other prices in the CPI "market basket" have remained unchanged. Prices are expected to behave this year as they did last year. Newspaper articles say that the inflation was caused by the price increases for housing and transportation. How would you recommend that the expected inflation be controlled? Should Congress pass a law setting a maximum price on these two commodities? Might such a law control inflation? Analyze the micro- and macroeconomic impacts of the law.

6. Discretionary monetary policy is often used to control or reduce inflation. Can you think of any economic reason for using discretionary monetary policy to reinflate the economy?

7. Find the latest employment rate figures for the United States and the rate of inflation over the past six months. Using the diagrammatic analysis developed in figures 25.4 through 25.5 describe the macroeconomic situation in the United States today. Which term best describes today's macroeconomy: recession, inflation, stagflation, or full macroequilibrium? Using the best data you can find on recent monetary and fiscal policies (try some back issues of the *New York Times* or the *Wall Street Journal*), determine whether they are appropriate, given your assessment of the policies needed at this time.

8. Indexing wages through cost-of-living adjustments protects wage earners from inflationary shocks to the economy.[2] Is this always optimal for the economy?

9. If government expenditures and taxes are increased by the same amount, will there be any effect on GNP? Explain.

10. A short-run solution to eliminating the government deficit, $(G - T)$, is to raise tax rates and the tax base. What are the long-run implications of this tactic?

Chapter 28

Monetary and Fiscal Policies in Action

Outline

    I. Introduction *582*
   II. The Great Depression *582*
       A. The United States economy in 1929 and 1930 *582*
          1. Appropriate fiscal and monetary policies in 1930 *583*
          2. Actual fiscal and monetary policies in 1930 *584*
       B. The United States economy in 1931 and 1932 *584*
          1. Monetary and fiscal policies in 1931 *584*
          2. Monetary policy in 1932 *585*
  III. The great inflation: 1965–? *585*
       A. The economic setting in late 1965 and early 1966 *585*
          1. The war and increased government expenditure *587*
          2. How monetary policy could have prevented inflation *587*
          3. Monetary policy in 1965 and 1966 *588*
          4. The reversal of the Fed's monetary policy *588*
          5. The effects of the Fed's expansionary monetary policy *589*
       B. Stagflation: The United States economy in the 1970s and early 1980s *589*
          1. Money growth, inflation, and unemployment *589*
          2. Money growth, inflation, and the interest rate *595*
   IV. Summary and conclusions *596*
    V. Questions for discussion and review *597*

Objectives

After reading this chapter, the student should be able to:

Describe the appropriate monetary and fiscal policy responses in 1930 and compare these with the actual policies used.

Describe the monetary and fiscal policies used in 1931 and their effects on the macroeconomy.

Explain how the monetary policy used in 1932 contributed to the Great Depression.

Explain how fiscal and monetary policies in 1966 led to the onset of an inflationary episode and what policies could have been used to combat the inflation.

Discuss the monetary policies used in the 1970s and early 1980s and explain the resulting stagflation.

▶ Introduction

Ask your grandparents or any other relatives old enough to have lived through the Great Depression of the 1930s how their lives and attitudes were changed by economic conditions then. Each story differs, but every one conveys a chilling picture of how mean and fearful the times were.

One relative tells us how he became a truck mechanic in 1933 with only one year of college behind him. He responded to an ad for the job by standing in line with about 600 other men. When he got to the front of the line, he was asked why he should be hired instead of one of the others. He recalls saying, "Because I have a wife and baby at home, and I'll do anything I have to to take care of them." He got the job, working eighty hours per week for $15.

In this chapter, we will explain the critical role that monetary and fiscal policy played in the depressed conditions of the 1930s, the accelerating inflation of the late 1960s, and the "stagflation" of the 1970s and early 1980s. In the process we will explain why our understanding of macroeconomic theory and policy leads us to believe that there is no reasonable expectation that we will experience a replay of the Great Depression in the future.

Our discussion will be "realistic" in that we take into account the fact that the government may not possess all of the information it needs— or the political will—to conduct effective macroeconomic policy. The specific questions we will answer are (1) What fiscal and monetary policies were followed by the government during these episodes? and (2) Did the government do everything possible to stabilize the economy at a position of macroeconomic equilibrium? We will specify the most effective policies that the government could have employed in combating recession and inflation and then compare them with the policies actually adopted.

▶ The Great Depression

During 1929 the United States economy was in a fairly prosperous position and, as table 28.1 shows, produced a real value of GNP equal to $316 billion (as measured in terms of 1972 dollars). Real GNP in 1929 was 6.7 percent higher than in 1928.[1] This is a fairly high rate of economic growth for the United States economy, based on historical experience in this century. Toward the end of 1929, however, world events adversely affected the expectations of United States citizens about the future of the economy.

The United States Economy in 1929 and 1930

The stock market crash in October 1929 was symptomatic of a collapse in confidence. Because stock ownership represents a claim on *future* profits, the present value of the *expected* stream of future profits is crucial in determining current stock prices. (This is also the case in determining the demand for investment goods.) A collapse in confidence about the future will lead investors to revise their estimate of future profits downward, and the net effect will be lower current prices for shares of common stock.

In terms of our macroeconomic model, this change in expectations in 1929 produced a decline in investment demand and, therefore, the demand curve for loanable funds. (You may wish to refer back to figure 27.2.) This meant that the economy was about to enter a period of falling production and declining prices, that is, a recession.

Table 28.1 shows that in 1930 the economy in fact displayed all of the characteristics associated with a recession. Real investment spending fell 33 percent, from $51.2 billion to $34.7 billion. Real GNP dropped 10 percent, to $284.4 billion. The consumer price index fell 2.5 percent from 40.9 to 39.9. Table 28.2 illustrates what was happening in the financial sector of the economy. The yield (nominal interest rate) on corporate bonds fell slightly, from 6.2 percent in 1929 to 5.9 percent in 1930.

Table 28.1   Real GNP, real investment, real government expenditures (federal, state, and local), and the consumer price index during 1929–1932

Year	Real GNP[a]	Real investment[a]	Real government expenditures[a]	Consumer Price index[b]
1929	315.7	51.2	41.0	40.9
1930	284.4	34.7	45.3	39.9
1931	262.4	21.3	47.3	36.3
1932	223.5	6.0	45.1	32.6

Source: From *Economic Report of the President, 1983.*
[a]Billions of 1972 dollars.
[b]1972 = 100.

Table 28.2   Money supply, commercial banks' reserves, and yield on corporate bonds for 1929–1932

Year	Money supply[a]	Banks' reserves[a]	Yield on corporate bonds[b]
1929	$26.3	$3.25	6.2%
1930	25.3	3.23	5.9
1931—first half	24.2	3.25	6.5
1931—second half	22.8	3.12	9.0
1932	20.5	2.91	9.3

Source: Milton Friedman and Anna Jacobson Schwartz, *A Monetary History of the United States, 1867–1960.* Copyright © 1963 by NBER. Table adapted with permission of Princeton University Press; and Federal Reserve System, *Banking and Monetary Statistics, 1914–1941* (bond yields).
[a]Billions of current dollars.
[b]Implicit interest rate received by lenders.

Appropriate Fiscal and Monetary Policies in 1930

Assuming that the government wanted to prevent or at least reduce the severity of the recession in 1930, appropriate policy responses would have been for the monetary authority to expand the reserves of the banking system and for the fiscal authority to increase government expenditure or reduce taxes. An expansion in banks' reserves produces a rightward shift in the supply curve for loanable funds, a lower real interest rate, and a narrowing of the gap between planned aggregate expenditure and production in the goods market. An increase in government expenditure is a direct addition to the planned aggregate expenditure for goods and also narrows the excess production in the goods market.

Actual Fiscal and Monetary Policies in 1930

Table 28.1 shows that real government spending rose slightly in 1930 as compared to 1929, but the increase was not large enough to offset the reduction in the investment component of planned aggregate expenditure.

Contrary to popular belief, the fiscal policy associated with the New Deal played only a minor role in the economy during the 1930s. Government spending on average rose only $1 billion per year over the decade. The federal government operated with a budget *surplus* in fiscal year 1930 that was almost as large (in current dollars) as in 1929.[2]

Turning to the monetary policy followed by the Fed in 1930, table 28.2 shows that banks' reserves *declined* slightly in 1930 from 1929. Accompanying this decline was a 4 percent *reduction* in the United States money supply from $26.3 billion in 1929 to $25.3 billion in 1930. While this policy is exactly the *opposite* of the one that our macromodel prescribes, it should be noted in fairness to the Fed that its policy error was not a major one. Rather, it appears as though the Fed maintained a hands-off attitude in 1930 with respect to the aggregate economy. Thus, we conclude that in 1930 fiscal policy was slightly expansionary but not large enough to be of major significance in stopping the recession. At the same time, monetary policy was basically playing a neutral role in influencing the United States economy, a role that amounted to an inappropriate contraction in the money supply.

The United States Economy in 1931 and 1932

Table 28.1 also shows us that during 1931 the United States economy experienced a continued reduction in real GNP, real investment, and the consumer price index. At first glance, these trends suggest that the private economy was incapable of returning to a position of full-employment macroeconomic equilibrium through its own devices. Before accepting this viewpoint, however, let us examine the course of monetary and fiscal policies in 1931.

Monetary and Fiscal Policies in 1931

As table 28.1 shows, fiscal policy was slightly stimulative during 1931, with real government expenditures rising by about 4.5 percent to $47.3 billion. Monetary policy, on the other hand, turned sharply *contractionary* in 1931. Commercial banks' reserves began to fall, especially in the second half of the year. As a result, the United States money supply declined by $3 billion from 1930 to the second half of 1931—this is roughly a 12 percent reduction in the United States money supply over the course of the year. Based on the smaller amount of reserves made available by the Fed, banks curtailed the number of new loan contracts they were willing to purchase. For the loanable funds market as a whole, this produced a *leftward* shift in the supply of loanable funds curve instead of the *rightward* shift called for in figure 27.4.

As a result of this leftward shift in the supply of loanable funds, the interest rate *increased*. Notice in table 28.2 that the yield on corporate bonds rose to 9 percent in the latter half of 1931. This increase in the interest rate probably explains much of the $13.4 billion drop in investment expenditures in 1931. Why? Because a higher interest rate induces investors to *move up* along their planned investment demand curve, thus lowering the quantity of investment goods purchased. One explanation for the behavior of the Fed in this period is that it thought a low interest rate might lead to an inflation. In order to prevent the inflation, the Fed decided to follow a contractionary monetary policy that ultimately contributed to the Great Depression. In addition, a number of banks experienced runs by nervous depositors. Between 1930 and 1933, 8,000 banks failed. No doubt those bank failures contributed to the sharp contraction in the money supply. Inaction by the Fed was sufficient to ensure a decline in the money supply.

The effect of this higher interest rate on the goods market, already in a state of disequilibrium, was disastrous. In 1931, producers' sales started to plummet dramatically as more and more investors reduced their purchases of goods in the face of a higher interest rate. The gap between supply and demand in the goods market widened after the Fed engineered a contraction in the banking system's reserves. Firms acquired still greater incentives to reduce prices and production as unsold inventories piled up.

If, at the end of 1931, the Fed had ceased interfering in the loan contract market, its mistake in 1931 would have been felt principally as a lengthening of the recessionary period. Even though the excess aggregate production of goods was large after the Fed's miscalculation, there is reason to believe that price reductions would have eventually produced a rightward shift in the supply curve of loanable funds. As this happened, the interest rate would have fallen, investment expenditure increased, and producers' sales risen. The aggregate economy would most likely have eventually returned to a position of macroeconomic equilibrium.

Monetary Policy in 1932

The severe depression persisted, however, because the Fed continued to follow a contractionary monetary policy. Table 28.2 shows that both banks' reserves and the money supply fell again in 1932. The reserves of the commercial banking system were 11 percent lower in 1932 than in 1931. (Fiscal policy was also contractionary.) Notice in table 28.1 that real government expenditures fell by more than 11 percent ($2 billion) in 1932. In terms of figure 27.4, the Fed's *contractionary* monetary policy prevented the loanable funds supply curve, SLF, and the aggregate demand curve from shifting to the right when prices fell in the early 1930s. The interest rate therefore stayed high, and firms observed little change in their total sales. The next step is obvious. To cut back on their inventories, firms began to lay off workers on a large scale and to contract sharply the aggregate amount of production.

In 1932, real GNP declined 15 percent to $223.5 billion. The entire economic system was in the grip of a gigantic collapse. The price level had fallen by over 20 percent since 1929, a price decline unequaled at any time since then. Over one-fourth of the labor force was unemployed, a human catastrophe that many

economists believe could have been made much less severe if not entirely avoided. If blame must be assigned for the Great Depression, should we place it on a collapse of the private economy or on the discretionary monetary policy used in the 1930s? On the basis of evidence, it appears that the Fed's mistakes contributed substantially to the Great Depression. In fairness, it must be pointed out that economists and policymakers simply did not know as much about macroeconomics and the appropriate monetary and fiscal policies as they do now.

The Great Inflation: 1965–?

The production of goods and services in the United States economy during 1965 was at or very close to the full-employment level. Late 1965 also marked a fundamental change in United States foreign policy—large-scale commitments of American troops and equipment were made to aid the South Vietnamese government in its fight against North Vietnam. For the United Sates economy, the decision to wage war in Southeast Asia was translated into a significant increase in the amount of goods and services purchased by the United States government, and this had a dramatic effect on the economy.

The Economic Setting in Late 1965 and Early 1966

Table 28.3 shows us that total government spending was nearly 10 percent higher in 1966 than in 1965, with most of the increase taking place in national defense. Figure 28.1 depicts the state of the United States economy both before and after the nation's entry into the Vietnam War. In part (a) of the figure, curve DLF represents the demand for loanable funds at the end of 1965—the sum of the government's budget deficit plus planned investment. DLF intersects SLF, the supply of loanable funds, at interest rate r(0). Hence, the loan contract market is in equilibrium. Since the planned saving equals planned investment plus the government deficit at the

Table 28.3   Total real government expenditures, federal expenditures, and defense expenditures for 1964–1966[a]

Year	Total government expenditures	Federal government expenditures	Defense expenditures
1964	$202.6	$100.2	$77.8
1965	209.8	100.3	70.3
1966	229.7	112.6	79.1

Source: From *Economic Report of the President, 1968 and 1983* and *Historical Statistics of the United States, Colonial Times to 1970.*
[a]All are in terms of billions of 1972 dollars.

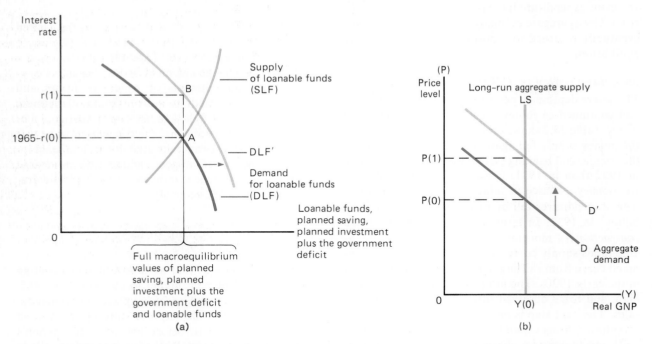

Figure 28.1   The initial impact of the Vietnam War on the United States economy and possible offsetting policy
The arrow in part (a) indicates that government expenditure increased because of the war in Vietnam. This is inflationary unless the government takes action through monetary or fiscal policy to offset the impact of increased expenditure. One possibility would have been to raise taxes, thus offsetting the effect of increased expenditures so as to keep the macroeconomy in full equilibrium at point A in part (a) and at

the price level P(0) in part (b). Another possibility would have been to sell government bonds to reduce the reserves of the banking system and thus restrict the money supply. This would have reduced the supply of loanable funds, raised the real interest rate, "choked off" some private investment, and returned the economy to a full macroeconomic equilibrium at point B. Under a restrictive monetary policy a new (reduced) SLF would intersect DLF' at point B and the price level would remain at P(0).

interest rate r(0), we have depicted a state of full-employment macroeconomic equilibrium as prevailing in the United States economy at the end of 1965. Part (b) of figure 28.1 restates the situation of full macroequilibrium, with full-employment GNP of Y(0) and a price level of P(0).

The War and Increased Government Expenditure

The government increased its expenditure in 1966 to acquire the military equipment and personnel needed for war. For the most part it chose not to increase taxes to finance this expenditure, although as figure 28.1 explains, increased taxes could have prevented inflation. Rather, the government took the alternative route of borrowing the necessary dollars in the loan contract market. It seems likely that this decision was made for political reasons. Higher taxes would have made the costs of the Vietnam War quite evident to the average United States citizen, and the war's unpopularity with the general public might have increased a good deal earlier than it did. As a result of this decision, the government's budget deficit rose. To finance this larger budget deficit, the government had to increase its demand for loanable funds.

When we add the larger government demand for loanable funds to the private investors' demand, we obtain the new, higher aggregate demand for loanable funds, curve DLF′ in part (a) of figure 28.1. Thus, at the beginning of 1966, the budget deficit due to the war in Vietnam led to a rightward shift in the demand curve for loanable funds, and the economy was at the beginning of an inflationary episode.

How Monetary Policy Could Have Prevented Inflation

Today it seems that the Fed's task in 1966 was clear-cut: to choose the monetary policy that would control the inflation stemming from the excess demand created by the increase in government wartime expenditure. Selling government bonds, which would have

reduced the reserves of the commercial banking system and thus money supply growth, would have shifted the supply of loanable funds through point B in part (a) of figure 28.1. If the Fed had taken such action, the resulting increase in the interest rate to r(1) would have raised the cost of all investment projects, thereby signaling investors to curtail their expenditures. Overall macroeconomic equilibrium would have been reattained without an inflationary episode had the interest rate increase caused a reduction in investment expenditure to offset the increase in the government's purchases of goods and services.

The function of a higher interest rate is to bring the message of scarcity to the private economy. Basically, participants in the private economy are being "told" by the marketplace that their share of goods must now fall because the government has decided that it wants more.

The point here is to clarify the macroeconomic repercussions of the Vietnam War. If society demands tanks and guns for the purpose of making war, it must be willing to reduce the demand for new homes, new buildings, and other new capital goods if inflation is to be avoided. If taxes had been increased to match the higher level of government expenditure, the inflation we experienced might not have occurred. The war, however, was deficit-financed.

Had the Fed taken action to prevent the onset of an inflationary episode, the new position of macroeconomic equilibrium would have been point B in part (a) of figure 28.1 with price level P(1) as shown in part (b) of figure 28.1. Therefore, aggregate expenditure on goods and services would have reflected more government goods and fewer private investment goods. This is somewhat similar to what would have happened had taxes been raised to pay for the war. (Can you explain how the composition of expenditure on GNP would have been different if taxes had been raised compared to what it would have been had the Fed engaged in contractionary monetary policy?)

Table 28.4   Money supply and commercial banks' reserves, December 1965 to December 1966[a]

Time period	Money supply	Banks' reserves
December 1965	$172	$22.7
January–September 1966	168	22.5
October–December 1966	173	23.4

Source: From *Economic Report of the President, 1968.*
[a]In billions of dollars.

Table 28.5   Yield on corporate bonds from December 1965 to March 1967

Time period	Yield
December 1965	4.68%
January–March 1966	4.81
April–June 1966	5.00
July–September 1966	5.32
October–December 1966	5.38
January–March 1967	5.08

Source: From *Economic Report of the President, 1968.*

Table 28.6   Housing starts and the consumer price index for 1965–1967

Year	Housing starts	CPI[a]
1965	1.5 million	75.4
1966	1.2 million	77.6
1967	1.3 million	79.8

Source: From *Economic Report of the President, 1968 and 1983.*
[a]1972 = 100.

Monetary Policy in 1965 and 1966

Table 28.4 shows that from January to September 1966, the Fed pursued a policy of restricting the reserves of the banking system. Along with the contraction in the banks' reserves, the United States money supply declined over the same period. A direct consequence of the Fed's policy was an increase in the rate of interest. Table 28.5 shows that the yield (the implicit interest rate paid to lenders) on corporate bonds rose from 4.81 percent at the beginning of 1966 to 5.32 percent during July through September of 1966. The higher interest rate caused investors to move up along the demand curve for investment goods.

This means that the supply of loanable funds in part (a) of figure 28.1 was beginning to shift to the left and move the economy toward point B. As table 28.6 suggests, the resulting reduction in investment expenditures narrowed the gap between demand and supply in the private goods market so that the consumer price index rose by nearly 3 percent over the course of 1966.

The Reversal of the Fed's Monetary Policy

The investors principally affected by the Fed's contractionary monetary policy were in the housing industry. In table 28.6, we can see that new housing starts fell by approximately *20 percent* between 1965 and 1966. This decline prompted both private citizens and government officials to complain about the high costs that the Fed's contractionary monetary policy imposed on the housing industry. However, as macroeconomic analysis indicates, the decline simply reflected the basic problem of scarcity. The economy was unable to produce more war goods without producing fewer goods of other types, such as housing. When the government demands more war goods, some people must lose out in the competitive struggle for the limited amount of full-employment production. In this instance, the housing industry was the principal loser.

In response to the outcry against its policy and fearing congressional investigation, the Fed decided to reverse its stand and pursue an *expansionary* monetary policy in late 1966. Table 28.4 shows us that increases in the reserves of the banking system and the United States money supply occurred from October to December 1966. Perhaps the Fed hoped, along with everyone else, that the problem of scarcity would suddenly disappear. It did not.

The Effects of the Fed's Expansionary Monetary Policy

As more reserves were created for the banking system, the market supply of loanable funds in figure 28.1, part (a), actually shifted *rightward* from SLF, instead of *leftward,* toward full equilibrium. Notice in table 28.5 that the yield on corporate bonds *declined* from a peak of 5.38 percent in October–December 1966 to 5.08 percent in the January–March period of 1967.

As far as the goods market was concerned, the Fed's expansionary monetary policy led to a larger amount of planned investment and thereby created an even larger excess of aggregate demand in the markets for goods and services. With investors placing more orders for goods and nobody curtailing demand in the private sector, firms found their sales growing by leaps and bounds. (As table 28.6 shows, the number of new housing starts rose in 1967 as compared to 1966.) Inventories fell drastically, and producers began to raise the prices of goods at faster rates. Of course, they attempted to acquire more factors of production, but since the economy was at a position of full employment, the price of resources—such as labor—also began to climb. Under the stimulus of the Fed's expansionary monetary policy, the United States economy in the mid-1960s entered a period during which the prices of its goods and services *continued* to rise at a rapid rate. In the next section we analyze the economy's behavior during the inflationary period of the late 1960s and 1970s.

Stagflation: The United States Economy in the 1970s and early 1980s

Under the impetus of the deficit-financed Vietnam War, the Fed instituted highly expansionary monetary policies. During 1967 and 1968 it permitted the nation's money supply to grow much faster than the economy's capacity to produce goods and services. As we have seen, if the money supply grows faster than is consistent with full macroeconomic equilibrium, an inflationary episode is inevitable. If the Fed continues to increase the ability of the banking system to create new money balances faster than they can be spent on output, when there already is full employment, the price level will continue to rise. A continuing increase in the price level is, of course, a full-blown inflation. The inflation will not stop until the Fed slows down money supply growth to a rate consistent with equilibrium in the goods market.

Money Growth, Inflation, and Unemployment

In the decade prior to 1965, real GNP grew at a rate of about 3.5 percent per year. The annual rate of growth of the money supply as measured by M2 was 4.5 percent, and the average annual rate of increase in the price level—the rate of inflation—was 2.0 percent, relatively low by standards of the 1970s and 1980s. There is no reason to believe that the productive capacity of the United States was growing more rapidly after 1965 than before. Therefore, a significant increase in the growth of the money supply was very likely to result in an increase in the rate of inflation. Between 1965 and 1980, the annual growth rate of M2 was about twice as high—8.9 percent—as it was during the period between 1955 and 1965. The rate of inflation rose dramatically to an average of 6 percent per year over the fifteen years between 1965 and 1980. The average annual growth of M2, annual inflation, and the average annual rate of unemployment from 1965 to 1982 are all shown in figure 28.2.

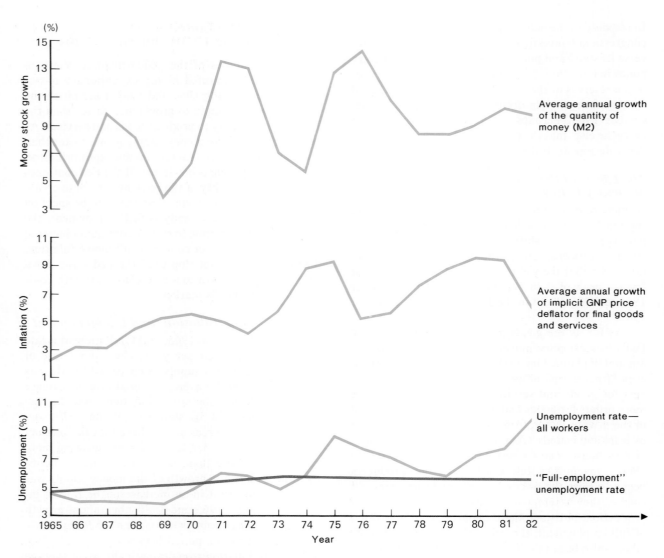

Figure 28.2   Money growth, inflation, and unemployment, 1965–1982

A high rate of monetary growth *temporarily* lowered unemployment while creating inflation. Source: *Economic Report of the President, 1983* and Michael L. Wachter, Personal Communication.

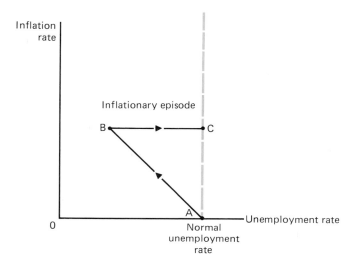

Figure 28.3 The short-run and long-run relationships between the inflation and unemployment rates: A period of inflation
When workers and firms come to expect inflation as the usual state of affairs, the unemployment rate returns to its normal level.

As our model of the macroeconomy predicts, the inflation caused by increased planned aggregate expenditure led to a *short-run* reduction in unemployment. In the late 1960s the unemployment rate was consistently *less* than the normal, or "full-employment" unemployment rate, which is also depicted in figure 28.2. The typical short-run and long-run behavior of the unemployment rate during an inflationary episode is summarized in figure 28.3. During the initial stages of an inflationary episode, unemployment falls to a level below the normal unemployment rate. However, workers eventually realize that an increase in the price level has reduced the real wage rate to a level below what they thought they were earning. As a result, unemployed workers take extra time to find jobs with acceptable wages. The outcome of these two events is that the unemployment rate eventually returns to its normal level as people become accustomed to inflation. In terms of the labor market and aggregate market for goods and services, as their expected real wage declines, workers move back along the aggregate labor supply curve. The economy's short-run aggregate supply curve begins to shift upward. As it crosses the aggregate demand curve at a higher price level, GNP begins to fall, paralleling the decline in the quantity of labor supplied.

This scenario begins with people accustomed to little or no inflation. As a result, they view an inflationary episode as unusual. In a period such as that beginning in 1965, however, business firms, workers, and consumers soon learn that a stable price level can no longer be expected. They then adjust their expectations to try to anticipate inflation in the future. Not to do so would result in economic losses to workers who commit themselves to work for money wages that buy less than expected and in losses to firms who fail to adjust the wages they pay and the prices they charge to the higher price level tomorrow is expected to bring.

In general, consumers, workers, and firms all have a strong incentive to learn from their past mistakes and forecast future events more accurately. They can do this by using available information to develop correct anticipations of the future course of inflation and other economic variables. In chapter 26 we pointed out that the idea that businesses and households do not waste information—that in their self-interest they use available information to correctly forecast the outcomes of economic events and government policy—is called the *theory of rational expectations*.

What does the theory of rational expectations imply concerning an inflationary episode that does not end itself because the Fed permits the money supply to grow at an inflationary rate over a prolonged period? It says that while inflation may *initially* be accompanied by a reduction in unemployment, if the inflation persists, unemployment will start to return to its normal level *without* a decline in inflation. Thus, in figure 28.3, the economy first moves from point A to point B and then to point C during an inflationary episode. The end result is inflation with no permanent reduction in the unemployment rate. Why? The answer was given in our analysis of labor markets in chapter 20. Specifically, the normal unemployment rate is a *real* phenomenon. As such, it can only be affected by policies and events that change the basic structure of labor markets. However, in the long run it will *not* be influenced by a general change in an economy wide *nominal* variable such as the aggregate price level. The upward adjustment of unemployment when inflation becomes the norm is illustrated by unemployment rate data for the United States in figure 28.2.

Periodically, the Fed temporarily decided to reverse its policy of "easy money." This further complicated the behavior of unemployment. The first sharp contraction in monetary growth after 1966 occurred in 1969. In that year the Fed decided to reverse its easy money policy by reducing the annual rate of growth of the money supply to 3.8 percent.

Our macroeconomic model predicts that such a rapid switch in monetary policy will lead to a recession. Why? Although a 3.8 percent annual growth rate of the money supply would have been the norm in the early 1960s, by 1969 the public had become accustomed to inflation and adjusted its behavior accordingly. Thus, slowing down the rate of the growth of money from 8 or 9 percent to only 3.8 percent had a macroeconomic impact similar to *reducing* the quantity of money (a negative growth rate) in the earlier period.

In terms of our macromodel, a contractionary monetary policy reduces the availability of loanable funds and shifts the supply curve of loanable funds (SLF) leftward. This reduction in the supply of loanable funds raises the interest rate and leads to reduced aggregate demand for goods and services and

to increased unemployment. As a result of the Fed's reduction of money growth in 1969, the unemployment rate began to rise. Such an increase in unemployment is shown in figure 28.4 as a movement from point C toward point D.

In 1970 the unemployment rate averaged 1.5 percentage points higher than in 1969—4.9 percent. Notice from the data in figure 28.2, however, that while the Fed's policy slowed inflation, it did not immediately halt it. In fact, for all of 1970 inflation averaged a little higher than in 1969. Because inflation had become a way of life, the Fed's 1969 actions took effect only with a considerable *lag in time*. Thus, it was not until 1971 that the twelve-month average rate of inflation actually declined. (If we were to examine the *monthly* rate of inflation during 1970, however, we would notice that the growth of prices began to slow down before the end of the year.)

In 1971, the unemployment rate continued to rise. This rise in unemployment is consistent with our generalizations concerning the short-run and long-run relationships between inflation and unemployment. In the short run, it takes time for firms, workers, and consumers to "unlearn" their inflationary anticipations. As *actual* inflation declines, the *expected* rate of inflation does not fall immediately. Consequently, unemployment rises above its full-employment, or normal, level. If the Fed were to *persist* in restraining inflation, then the public would eventually revise its expectations about the future, and the unemployment rate would eventually return to normal (from point D to point E in figure 28.4).

Two other influences on unemployment in the 1970s contributed to the simultaneous appearance of inflation and higher unemployment, which is labeled *stagflation*. One of them was not generally recognized at the time. As figure 28.2 shows, the normal or full-employment rate of unemployment had risen by about 0.7 percentage points since 1965. This was due primarily to the rapidly increasing fraction of young workers in the labor force. Thus, while the 5.9 percent average annual unemployment rate in 1971 was sharply higher than the previous year's rate, it was not much higher than the level to which the normal unemployment rate had grown.

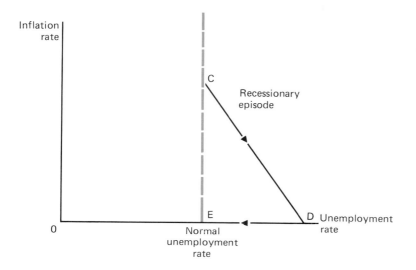

Inflation
rate

C

Recessionary
episode

E

0   Normal
unemployment
rate

D   Unemployment
rate

Figure 28.4   The short-run and long-run relationships between the inflation and unemployment rates: A recession following an inflationary episode
When workers and firms come to realize that inflation has ended and expect a stable price level, the unemployment rate returns to its normal level.

In the minds of many people, the appearance of stagflation seemed to contradict the basic laws of economics. This misunderstanding about the events unfolding in the economy during a period of simultaneously *decelerating* inflation and rising normal unemployment led to the establishment of a price control program in the summer of 1971. During that year, the rate of inflation declined to 4.1 percent. This slowing trend has sometimes been viewed as "proof" of the success of price controls in reducing the rate of inflation. The data indicate, however, that a substantial reduction in the inflation rate had occurred *prior* to the introduction of price controls in the summer of 1971. Price controls *appeared* to work because the economy was *already* approaching a position of macroeconomic equilibrium, with inflation proceeding at a more moderate rate. As figure 28.2 shows us, the average growth rate of the money supply from 1969 to 1971 was only about 5 percent, which was lower than any year since 1966. Notice also that the unemployment rate hit a peak of 5.9 percent in 1971 and then in 1972 declined to 5.6 percent, equal to its full-employment level.

In 1971, the Fed again sharply reversed its monetary policy, apparently "protected" from the evidence of its inflationary actions by the camouflage of price controls. As figure 28.2 shows, the money supply grew at the extremely high annual rate of 13.5 percent in 1971 and 13.0 percent in 1972, more than double the average growth rate of the previous two years. On the basis of high money supply growth rates, sharply increasing inflation in 1973, 1974, and 1975 should not have been surprising. The Fed's policy was predictably inflationary. Why did the Fed accelerate money growth in 1971 and 1972? Some observers have argued that Fed policy had become politicized. Arthur Burns, then chairman of the Fed, was a close friend of President Nixon. Expansionary monetary policy in 1971 and 1972 would assure that the president would be running for reelection without having to worry about a recession.

The Fed sharply reduced the growth rate of the money supply in 1973 and 1974, producing a recessionary trend similar to that which developed in 1969 after a contraction in the money supply growth rate. In 1975, the United States unemployment rate exceeded 8 percent. Inflation, however, persisted at a high rate well into the recession for reasons we have already discussed. It appeared to many that stagflation had become characteristic of the United States economy.

To be fair, we must mention the second factor other than monetary policy that may have contributed to stagflation in the United States in the mid-1970s and later. In 1973 and 1974, the Organization of Petroleum Exporting Countries (OPEC) sharply increased its power over world oil markets, and the price of imported oil in the United States began to rise sharply. The effect of OPEC on the United States economy is illustrated in figure 28.5.

Because of OPEC's actions, the United States had to make costly adjustments to use less oil and products made with oil. These adjustments required resources that had previously been used to produce other goods and services. This had an affect on full-employment GNP similar to what would have happened if we had suddenly lost some of our own capacity to produce petroleum. That is, the long-run aggregate supply curve shifted to the left. As figure 28.5 shows, the result of a leftward shift in the long-run aggregate supply curve is to lower GNP and raise the price level. In the aggregate labor market, unemployment increases, just as if the economy has entered a recession.

Economists disagree on the extent to which the increase in world oil prices contributed to stagflation in the United States. One fact that leads many economists to believe that its overall impact on inflation and unemployment was minor is the experience of other nations that import a much larger share of their petroleum than the United States does. In most Western European nations and in Japan, for example, stagflation was not the severe problem that the United States experienced. However, it is probably fair to conclude that events in the world oil market contributed to, if they did not dominate, the rising prices and high unemployment experienced during the middle to late 1970s in the United States.

As figure 28.2 illustrates, the monetary authority did not mend its ways after the recession of 1975. The cycle of high and accelerating monetary growth followed by "jamming on the brakes" continued. During the latter part of the Carter administration and the

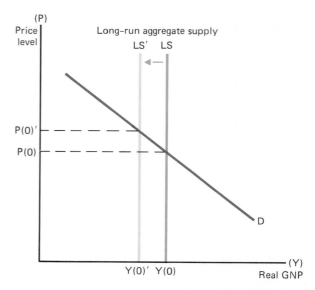

Figure 28.5   The effect of OPEC on aggregate supply and stagflation in the United States
OPEC's success in raising world oil prices had an effect on the United States similar to a leftward shift in the long-run aggregate supply curve. This contributed to stagflation by reducing GNP and raising unemployment and the price level.

early years of the Reagan administration, the Fed sharply curtailed monetary growth compared to its peak in 1976. The first result was an increase in the unemployment rate. In 1982, unemployment reached 10.8 percent, a level that was the highest of any period since the Great Depression. The second, later, result was a decline in the rate of inflation. By late 1982, inflation had been reduced dramatically.

Unfortunately, during 1982 and more so in 1983, the Fed claimed that its ability to determine the "correct" rate of monetary growth was harmed by the decontrol of the banking system (described in chapter 23). Whether banking deregulation actually did this by altering the quantity of money the public desired to hold remains a hotly debated issue. What is certain, however, is that the rate of growth of M1 and M2 sharply *increased* during 1983. Many economists

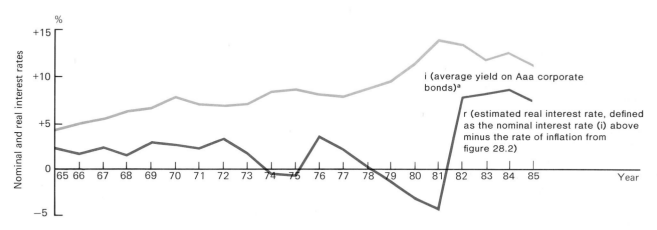

Figure 28.6   The real and nominal rates of interest in the United States, 1965–1985
From *Economic Report of the President,* 1983, 1986, B-59, p. 320 and B-68, p. 332.

and policymakers were very worried that this increase in the growth of the money supply would lead to a resurgence of inflation in 1984 and beyond if it were not curtailed.

It is interesting that inflation did *not* regain its force in 1984 and 1985, as many economists had predicted. The reasons are as yet unclear. One explanation is that the drastic weakening of OPEC and the resulting decline in world oil prices had the reverse effect of the increase of the 1970s. As we noted earlier, the inflation of the 1970s cannot be blamed entirely on OPEC, and not all oil-importing nations experienced the same degree of inflation that the United States did. Perhaps the United States inflation resulted in part from validation of cost-push inflation due to oil price increases, while other nations, such as Japan and Germany, refused to validate such cost-push inflation. It is not unlikely that oil price declines did help slow down inflation in the United States. That is, a rightward shift of the aggregate supply curve may have permitted a monetary growth rate in the United States that would have been more inflationary under "normal" circumstances.

Money Growth, Inflation, and the Interest Rate

As we emphasized in chapter 24, the interest rate that represents the cost of loanable funds to borrowers and the return to lenders is the *real* rate of interest. The real rate of interest is defined as the *nominal,* or market, rate of interest minus the expected rate of inflation. Remember, lenders and borrowers determine the value of loan contracts they wish to offer and purchase, respectively, on the basis of their *expected* rate of inflation. Thus, during a period in which inflation turns out to be greater than expected, lenders turn out to be losers. Once inflation is correctly anticipated, however, loan contracts will be negotiated to reflect fully the inflationary conditions that have prevailed in the recent past and that are expected to continue in the future.

In figure 28.6, the average interest rate on high-grade (low risk of default) corporate bonds in each year from 1965 through 1985 is labeled i. The period is characterized by a gradually rising trend through 1982. We can calculate an *estimate* of the real interest rate by assuming that the public's forecast of future inflation in any given year was equal to the actual rate of inflation for that year. When the rate of inflation from figure 28.2 is subtracted from i, we derive the estimated real interest rates (r). Note that during the severe inflations of 1974–75 and 1979–81, real interest rates in figure 28.6 were actually negative. Lenders were repaid in dollars so devalued by inflation that they did not even receive the full real value of their principal when they were paid back.

Notice that the highest real rates of interest occurred in 1976 and 1984. In 1976 inflationary *expectations* are likely to have been *sharply* increased by the inflation experienced in 1975. In 1984 the public was still forming expectations based on the inflationary experience of the late 1970s and early 1980s. Moreover, lenders who had recently been badly hurt by their underestimate of future inflation were less likely to lend at accustomed interest rates. In 1984, the real interest rate averaged 12.7 percent, one of the highest ever experienced in the economic history of the United States.

Phenomenally high real interest rates helped contribute to the unusually severe recession starting in 1982. This illustrates the heavy cost of the uncertainty created by the "jump on the gas, jam on the brakes" macroeconomic policies (especially monetary policy) in the United States during the period beginning in 1965. It is also important to point out that in addition to the effects of inflationary anticipations, high real interest rates may have also stemmed from the federal deficit. As discussed in chapter 27, our macroeconomic model indicates that an increase in the deficit, other factors unchanging, will probably raise the rate of interest.

▶ Summary and Conclusions

Will you ever experience as severe a recession as the Great Depression? Will you or your children ever go through an inflationary period as severe as that of the United States in the middle and late 1970s? No one can say for sure, although we understand what policy tools can prevent such unfortunate economic catastrophes. In this chapter we have seen that discretionary fiscal and monetary policies are, in practice, quite able to affect the macroeconomy. In pursuit of macroeconomic stabilization, government officials often make mistakes. These errors, especially in monetary policy, are made by people who are constrained both by political realities and by incomplete information about the complicated events that occur in an economy as large as that of the United States. *Theoretically,* monetary and fiscal policies can exert a *stabilizing* influence on the economy. Given our present state of knowledge about the macroeconomy, however, an important question that will continue to be debated is: Should society allow monetary and fiscal authorities to use these powers at their discretion as they see fit? The following main points were emphasized in this chapter.

Expansionary or restrictive monetary and fiscal policies can in practice have powerful effects on macroeconomic activity.

Incorrect discretionary monetary policy contributed to the Great Depression of the 1930s.

Discretionary fiscal policy had little effect on the Great Depression.

Monetary policy has been largely responsible for the great inflation that began in 1965.

The real interest rate has been quite high in recent years as lenders' expectations of inflation have fallen less rapidly than the actual rate of inflation.

▶ Questions for Discussion and Review

1. Are the following statements true, false, or uncertain? Defend your answers.
   a. The Great Depression was exacerbated by monetary policy.
   b. The Great Depression was exacerbated by fiscal policy.
   c. The great inflation was exacerbated by monetary policy.
   d. The great inflation was exacerbated by fiscal policy.

2. List four years during which the United States economy experienced high cyclical unemployment and four years during which the United States economy experienced rapid inflation. In which years, if any, did the economy experience both high unemployment and rapid inflation? Explain the macroeconomic causes of rapid inflation and high unemployment in these years. What type of monetary and fiscal policies could have reduced inflation and unemployment then?

3. Read chapter 1 of *The Economic Report of the President, 1983.* On the basis of this discussion, write a one-page essay on whether or not the recession of 1981–82 was "necessary." Be sure to include in your essay some mention of what caused the recession.

4. Society dislikes both inflation and unemployment. Concerning the long-term relationship between inflation and unemployment, what is society's optimal (preferred) combination of inflation and unemployment in the long term? Explain and support your answer graphically.

5. Write a three-page paper discussing whether or not the great inflation has ended.

6. During 1983 the interest rate on *three-month* Treasury securities averaged about 8 to 9 percent (on an annual basis). During the same period the inflation rate averaged 3 to 4 percent (on an annual basis). Were real interest rates low or high on the basis of historical experience? Explain. If high, why do you think they were?

Chapter 29

Summing Up
Macroeconomic Controversies

Outline

I. Introduction *600*
  A. Areas of agreement and disagreement among economists *600*
    1. Controversies over short-run macroeconomic policy: Is fine-tuning practical? *601*
  B. Monetarism and Keynesianism *601*
II. Different views of how the economy works *601*
  A. Keynesian and monetarist views about how monetary policy affects the economy *601*
  B. Monetarist and Keynesian explanations for the recession of the early 1980s and continued high interest rates through 1985 *602*
  C. Keynesian and monetarist differences of opinion about the need to try to control the macroeconomy and the ability to do so *603*
    1. Differences in Keynesian and monetarist policy recommendations *604*
      a. Monetary policy and interest rates *604*
      b. Fiscal policy *604*
      c. "Rules" versus discretionary policy *605*
III. Long-run considerations and the "supply side" *605*
  A. Supply-side economics *605*
    1. The Laffer curve *605*
  B. Supply-side, Keynesian, and monetarist views of government spending cuts during a recession *606*
IV. The government deficit: Does it matter? *606*
  A. Deficits and presidential politics *607*
  B. The sources of United States deficits in the 1980s *608*
    1. The recent debt experience of industrialized nations *610*
  C. The economic significance of the debt *610*
    1. Deficits and business cycles *610*
    2. Structural deficits *611*
    3. "Crowding out": The short-run and long-run effects of the deficit *612*
V. Summary and conclusions *614*
VI. Key terms *615*
VII. Questions for discussion and review *615*
VIII. Policy issue: You decide—Flat tax *616*
  A. The action-initiating event *616*
  B. The issue *616*
  C. Economic policy issues *616*
  D. Recommendations *616*

Objectives

After reading this chapter, the student should be able to:

Discuss how monetarists and Keynesians disagree on monetary and fiscal policies and their effectiveness in stabilizing the macroeconomy.

Explain the recession of the early 1980s and the continued high interest rates from both the monetarists' and the Keynesians' point of view.

Describe the supply-siders' view of the macroeconomy.

Discuss the history of the government deficit and reasons for its recent surge.

Compare the recent United States debt experience with that of other industrialized nations.

Discuss the economic significance of the budget deficit (including long-term crowding out).

► Introduction

When President Kennedy submitted his budget proposal to Congress for 1962, he and his political advisers were concerned about how the public would react to a federal budget in excess of $100 billion. The federal deficit that year was $4.2 billion. By 1974 federal expenditure had more than tripled to $356.6 billion, and the deficit of $69.36 billion was the largest this country had ever experienced. President Carter made a point of running against big government in 1976 and promised to balance the budget in 1980. The 1980 levels of federal government expenditures and deficit were $602.1 billion and $61.2 billion, respectively. Ronald Reagan promised to rein in big government and eliminate the deficit by 1984. Expenditures increased 46 percent to $879.9 billion in 1984, and the deficit nearly tripled to $176.4 billion. In the 1984 presidential campaign, Walter Mondale accused President Reagan of mortgaging the future of the nation by running high deficits.

We will return to a discussion of presidential campaigns and economic issues in the latter part of this chapter. However, this brief sketch of the politics of big federal budgets and deficits suggests several questions we will want to address. Are federal deficits bad for the economy, and if so, how do they hurt overall economic performance in the United States or other countries? If the federal deficit were to suddenly double relative to GNP, would we be twice as badly off? Why has it become so common for presidential contenders to promise to balance the federal budget and then fail to do so when they are elected? Is it really possible to mortgage the country's future?

Areas of Agreement and Disagreement among Economists

The United States economy has experienced wide fluctuations in unemployment and inflation. Matching the wide swings in economic performance, there is also wide disagreement among economists, politicians, and informed members of the public regarding the best course for macroeconomic policy to follow.[1] Before discussing and evaluating these controversies, however, we should emphasize that among the overwhelming majority of professional academic economists, there is a broad area of agreement on economic policy that we do not usually read about in the newspapers or see and hear on the television and radio.

In the *U.S. News & World Report* article in reference 1, you will find disagreement about such issues as the proper timing of monetary or fiscal policies and the degree to which our knowledge of the economic system, recognition and legislative lags, and political considerations permit effective "fine-tuning" of macroeconomic variables. These are factual issues about which opinions can change as knowledge and experience increase. Despite these differences in opinion— which are very strongly and emotionally held in many cases—there is also much common ground. For example, there is virtually unanimous agreement that the inflation we experienced after 1965 would not, and could not, have occurred without excessive money supply growth. Furthermore, there is no doubt expressed that over the long run, increases in our standard of living can result only from expansion of available resources or increases in productivity. What sparks disagreement are questions of *how* monetary control is to be implemented and *which* actions are most likely to promote productivity growth.

Monetarists and Keynesians are economists who hold different sets of views on monetary and fiscal policies.

Controversies over Short-run Macroeconomic Policy: Is Fine-tuning Practical?

Among professional economists, probably the most significant debate is over the possibility of fine-tuning macroeconomic policy in the short run by "twirling the knobs" of monetary and fiscal policy to assure a stable price level, full employment, and real output growth consistent with the economy's productive capacity. To a large extent these controversies have involved a division between the so-called **monetarists and Keynesians,** who are economists with different views about appropriate short-run macropolicy. The latter group takes its name from the famous economist John Maynard Keynes, whose publications in the 1930s revolutionized our understanding of macroeconomic relationships. (It is not at all clear that Keynes, were he still alive, would be a "Keynesian." However, we will use the terms *Keynesian* and *monetarist* because they represent useful distinctions today.)[2]

Monetarism and Keynesianism

There is no way to describe all of the differences between monetarism and Keynesianism in a brief space. Moreover, it would probably be impossible to differentiate the two groups in such a way that some members of each would not strongly disagree with our description of their beliefs. Therefore, our description of the monetarist versus Keynesian debate can only capture its major features.

The most distinctive principle of monetarism is probably that the money stock (M) and changes in the money supply (ΔM) are thought to be the most important variables influencing short-run fluctuations in the price level, output, and employment. The economist whose research and policy recommendations are most closely tied to the precepts of monetarism is Milton Friedman, who received the Nobel Prize in economic science in 1976.

Keynesians do not deny the importance of money's influence on macroeconomic performance. However, they differ—often markedly—from monetarists in their view of the way in which money affects the economy and, hence, on appropriate short-run policy. Keynesians represent a considerably broader spectrum of beliefs and policy recommendations than monetarists. Therefore, it is more difficult to name a typical Keynesian than a typical monetarist. Two prominent Keynesians, both of whom have also won Nobel Prizes, are Paul Samuelson (in 1970) and James Tobin (in 1981). Keynesians, as reflected in these two economists' policy recommendations, emphasize that the rate of interest is at least as important a guide to macroeconomic policy as the money stock or its rate of growth.

▶ Different Views of How the Economy Works

Keynesian and Monetarist Views about How Monetary Policy Affects the Economy

If one reviews textbook presentations of the Keynesian model, it is clear that monetary policy is viewed as primarily affecting the credit market. Expansion or contraction of the money supply shifts the supply of loanable funds to the right, lowers the real interest rate, and stimulates investment as investors move down the demand for loanable funds schedule in response to lower interest rates. If one believes that the real impact of monetary policy on the economy is through its impact on the real interest rate, then it is tempting to choose the interest rate as an appropriate target of monetary policy. Using the interest rate as a target can form the basis for one's judgment that monetary policy is "right" or "wrong." Generally, Keynesians judge monetary policy as too tight if interest rates seem high relative to where they would be at full macroeconomic equilibrium. For example, much of their pessimism about the economic recovery of 1983 and 1984 centered around the Keynesian notion that interest rates were too high and that tight monetary policy would choke off the recovery.

Monetarists disagree with Keynesians on both practical and theoretical grounds. As a practical matter, monetarists believe that we lack the detailed information that is needed to say, in the short run, whether a given interest rate is "too high," indicating excessive monetary restraint, or "too low," indicating an overly expansionary monetary policy. On theoretical grounds, they have an alternative explanation of the high interest rates that prevailed in 1983 and 1984 that is based on their view of the roles of money and inflationary expectations in the macroeconomy.

Basically, monetarists believe that monetary policy is neutral in the long run with respect to real economic changes. That is, they emphasize that full-employment GNP is determined by "real" events as opposed to monetary events. However, monetarists believe that monetary policy is unambiguously the basis for explaining the price level and inflation.

There is another, subtle distinction between monetarists and Keynesians that we have ignored until now in developing the macroeconomic model used in this text. While monetarists accept the impact of monetary policy in the credit market, they tend to believe that changes in the quantity of money also have a *direct* impact on consumption and investment spending. This direct impact does not depend upon, say, an expansionary monetary policy pushing down the interest rate. Rather, it acts *directly* to expand investment and consumption expenditures because with more money to spend, people tend to expand their purchases of all kinds of goods and services. An illustration of the possible direct impact of monetary policy is that an increase in the quantity of money may lead directly to expanded demand for both consumption and investment goods. This increase in expenditure may not, in other words, depend on a decline in the interest rate leading to greater incentives to purchase investment goods. If monetary policy affects expenditures directly, as well as through the interest rate, then the Keynesian view that the interest rate can tell us about the state of monetary policy may be incorrect.

Monetarists conclude that monetary expansion will promote recovery from a recession or, if the economy is at full employment, result in inflation. Monetary contraction (or too slow a rate of monetary growth) will depress aggregate demand and cause or worsen a recession if the economy is at or below full macroeconomic equilibrium. However, the current rate of interest is unlikely to convey much information about the impact of current monetary policy on GNP, employment, or the price level.

Monetarist and Keynesian Explanations for the Recession of the Early 1980s and Continued High Interest Rates through 1985

Monetarists explain the recession of 1981–82 as the result of too abrupt a reduction of the rate of monetary growth. They believe the expansion of the money supply during 1983–84 was in the right direction but too erratic. That is, the average rate of growth was acceptable over the period, but at times it was much too high and at other times, too low. Monetarists explain the relatively high real interest rates of 1983–85 as resulting from the continued persistence in the public's expectations that inflation would accelerate in the near future. From the monetarist standpoint, the federal deficit represented a problem only because the public anticipated that sooner or later the Fed would increase the money supply—monetizing the debt—in a vain effort to reduce interest rates. Then the monetarists held that although interest rates would not fall, the rate of inflation would increase.

To monetarists, then, the continuation of high real interest rates in 1984 and 1985 can be explained by the public's expectations that the rate of inflation would soon increase from 4 percent to about 7 percent. This was the average annual rate of inflation experienced from 1967 to 1981.

Keynesians view the recession of 1981–82 as primarily caused by the rapid run-up in oil prices in late 1979 and early 1980 in conjunction with the continued decline in the United States steel and automobile industries. Monetary policy contributed to the

A target of monetary policy is the variable(s), such as the rate of monetary growth or the rate of interest, that monetary policy attempts to influence for the purpose of smoothing out business cycles.

severity of the recession in their view by shifting the supply of loanable funds to the left, raising interest rates, and choking off investment demand for loanable funds.

A simple Keynesian explanation for continued high interest rates during the expansion of 1983–85 is that monetary policy was too tight. The rightward shift in the supply of loanable funds associated with expansion of the money supply was not rapid enough to offset the upward drift in interest rates associated with large federal deficits and the consequent rightward shift in the demand for loanable funds. From the Keynesian standpoint, the deficit represented a problem only because, in the presence of a relatively tight monetary policy, it kept interest rates high and discouraged private investment demand. A decline in private investment would tend to reduce the long-term growth potential of the economy. We will return to this point later in this chapter.

Keynesian and Monetarist Differences of Opinion about the Need to Try to Control the Macroeconomy and the Ability to Do So

Notice that both Keynesians and monetarists are very concerned with monetary policy. They differ intensely, however, over the appropriate **target of monetary policy,** which is the principal variable guiding the Fed's monetary policy decisions. The sources of this difference include scientific judgments about whether we possess the knowledge and ability to know what the appropriate interest rate target to shoot at is at any moment and whether it would be technically and politically possible to hit such a target if we knew what it was. The disagreements between monetarists and Keynesians probably also involve a difference in their tastes for government intervention in the economy. Generally, monetarists prefer to avoid government intervention and believe that we lack the knowledge to fine-tune such variables as interest rates in any event. Keynesians are less worried about the political and moral implications of government involvement in the economy and argue that we can control variables such as interest rates in order to improve macroeconomic performance.

This difference in approach is also related to fundamental difference in views these two groups have about how the economy works. The Keynesian presumption is that business cycles are basically due to "real" (nonmonetary) disturbances and are inherent in market economies. They are the result of imperfections in the linkages among the aggregate goods, credit, and labor markets in market economies as well as sluggish adjustments to change within these markets. The Keynesian remedy is the judicious application of fiscal policy to bolster aggregate demand when it is too low to sustain full employment and to restrain aggregate demand when it is too great to maintain full employment without accelerating inflation. Without such intervention, Keynesians believe, market economies will break down periodically. Fiscal policy is viewed as the instrument of choice to keep the economy on a smooth growth path. The traditional Keynesian perspective is that monetary policy affects the real economy only indirectly through credit markets and is therefore less predictable and effective than fiscal policy in controlling aggregate supply and demand.

The monetarist perspective is that discretionary monetary and fiscal policies both tend to accentuate rather than dampen business cycles. The presumption is that aggregate demand and supply shifts tend to be self-correcting and short-lived. Many monetarists bolster their pessimistic view of discretionary countercyclical policies by arguing that much of their impact on aggregate production and employment occurs only when the public is fooled into taking actions that it would not take if it had complete knowledge about the policies' timing and effects. They go on to argue that the public quickly learns what the effects of policies will be and adjusts accordingly. For example, an increase in the quantity of money during a period of nearly full employment may be targeted on the interest rate. However, if the public believes that inflation will result, interest rates will remain high. As noted in chapter 26, this idea—that the public cannot be repeatedly fooled by macroeconomic events—is called the theory of rational expectations. According to this theory, making the money supply grow faster would not reduce the rate of interest; rather, it would be more likely to raise it.

Monetarists believe that efforts to eliminate aggregate economic fluctuations with discretionary monetary and/or fiscal policies almost invariably make matters worse because of the timing problems (lags) we discussed in chapter 27. Since the obstacles to discretionary fiscal policy actions are greater than the obstacles to discretionary monetary policy, monetarists prefer discretionary monetary policy, if they must choose one or the other. However, the preferred position for monetarists would be to have a fixed money growth rate, beyond the discretion of the monetary authority, and no discretionary fiscal policy.

The distinction between Keynesians and monetarists regarding the proper size and role of government in the economy is directly related to their differences in perspectives about the primary causes of aggregate economic fluctuations. Keynesians view the aggregate economy as inherently prone to severe and perhaps prolonged fluctuations that necessitate discretionary intervention by the federal government. Monetarists view the aggregate economy as subject to moderate and short-term fluctuations and as inherently stable. Essentially, monetarists place their faith in the public's ability to anticipate the future course of prices quickly enough so that adjustment to full macroequilibrium will not be unacceptably slow. Attempts to smooth aggregate economic activity are viewed as irrelevant at best and often counterproductive. The extreme monetarist view is that discretionary monetary and fiscal policies only magnify business cycles.

Differences in Keynesian and Monetarist Policy Recommendations

We have developed our descriptions of the differences between Keynesian and monetarist views with frequent references to their diagnoses and prescriptions for macroeconomic problems in the United States during the early 1980s. It will help to crystallize the distinctions between Keynesians and monetarists if we summarize the distinct differences in their policy recommendations for stabilizing the macroeconomy.

Monetary Policy and Interest Rates   In late 1981, Keynesians agreed that the Fed and other government agencies should, above all, take steps to reduce the interest rate. It would be appropriate, they argued, to increase the quantity of money to whatever level would reduce the interest rate and speed recovery from recession. Monetarists argued, however, that as soon as the public perceived that the quantity of money was rising to higher and higher levels, fears of future inflation would keep interest rates high.

Fiscal Policy   As we have seen, monetarists place even less faith in discretionary fiscal policy than in discretionary monetary policy. Keynesians, on the other hand, view discretionary fiscal policy as an essential tool in stabilizing the business cycle. One of their frequent proposals aimed at lowering high interest rates in the early 1980s was to reduce the federal deficit by raising taxes. Notice that Keynesians have something of a difficulty here. Macroeconomic theory suggests that an increase in taxes has a negative multiplier effect on planned expenditure and aggregate demand. Thus, Keynesians' recommendation to raise taxes in order to lower interest rates and boost investment and GNP growth contains an element of self-contradiction. They evidently felt, however, that reducing the deficit by any means would be effective, on balance, in lowering interest rates, increasing investment, and raising GNP growth.

Monetarists viewed the Keynesians' arguments in favor of greater taxes as a subterfuge really aimed at maintaining or increasing the role of government in the economy. They argued that if the deficit was responsible for high interest rates (which they doubted), then the best way to reduce the deficit was to lower government expenditure, not to increase taxes. As you may have guessed, Keynesians argued that monetarists were disguising their distaste for "big government" in the cloak of their theory of the impact of the deficit.

Supply-side economics emphasizes the impact of monetary and fiscal policies on investment and real GNP in the long run.

The **Laffer curve** is a theory about the relationship between tax rates and tax revenues. It states that tax revenues fall when tax rates

increase to the levels that now exist in the United States and many other nations.

"Rules" versus Discretionary Policy   As we have seen, an appropriate monetary policy during the 1980s, in the monetarists' view, would have been to instigate a steady and gradual reduction of the rate of monetary growth. This reduction would continue until the money supply was growing at a rate about equal to the rate of growth of the economy's productive capacity, say, about 3 percent per year. Once a 3 percent monetary growth rate is achieved, monetarists would prefer to have it remain at that rate regardless of what may happen to interest rates.

In short, monetarists advocate a "rules" approach to monetary policy. Namely, they believe that the best we can hope for in the way of countercyclical monetary policy is to mandate through legislation that the Fed's monetary target should follow a prescribed rule. The rule would require a constant rate of monetary growth approximately equal to the long-run trend in our capacity to produce goods and services.

As a first approximation, monetarists would use the quantity theory of money and the quantity equation as a guide to selecting the appropriate rate of monetary growth. If velocity (V) is approximately constant, then the quantity theory tells us that the money supply ought to grow at the same rate as the economy's capacity to produce real GNP if there is to be no inflation. Monetarists admit that their proposed monetary policy would not eliminate business cycles. They argue, however, that macroeconomic stability would be greater than has been achieved under discretionary monetary policy.

Keynesians reject the monetarists' "rules" approach. They believe that with improvements in statistical models of the macroeconomy the monetary (and fiscal) authorities will be better able to exercise their "authority" over taxation, government expenditure, and interest rates to improve on past performance. The battle over "rules versus discretion" in macroeconomic policy debates will doubtless continue into the foreseeable future.

Long-run Considerations and the "Supply Side"

In recent years, there have been many discussions of another point of view on macropolicy called **supply-side economics.** Unfortunately, the issues involved with the supply side versus monetarism versus Keynesianism have been almost hopelessly confused in popular discussions of economic issues. It is probably fair to say that the overwhelming majority of professional academic economists are "supply siders" when it comes to appropriate economic policies for the long run. Problems arise, however, when long-run policies aimed at long-term economic growth are confused with strategies for smoothing out business cycles.

Supply-side Economics

The principal targets of supply-side economics are taxation and, depending on which supply sider is speaking, government spending. Supply-side economics emphasizes the effects of high tax rates on incentives to work, to save, and to invest. Lower tax rates, it is argued, will result in greater investment, more rapid capital accumulation, a greater supply of work effort, and hence a faster rate of real economic growth. Few economists disagree with this basic supply-side notion. However, there is profound disagreement on the quantitative impact of a tax reduction on economic growth.

The Laffer Curve

The best-known and most extreme form of supply-side economic policy is associated with the so-called **Laffer curve,** which is a theoretical relationship between tax rates and tax revenues. This concept is named after economist Arthur Laffer, who argues that tax rates in the United States have become so high that further increases in tax rates will reduce the amount of tax revenue. In his view, not only do higher tax rates discourage economic growth, but they also result in enlargement of the "underground economy," consisting of barter transactions and illicit businesses, which escape taxation. It follows, if one accepts extreme supply-side arguments, that a reduction in tax rates will not reduce government's actual tax collections. Real output and income will grow so much faster that tax collections will not fall. Consequently, a reduction in tax rates need not result in a greater government deficit.

Other economists who are sympathetic with supply-side arguments in favor of reduced tax rates favor them not because they accept the idea that lower tax rates will lead to no reduction in tax collections but because they believe that lower tax rates will lead to reduced government expenditure. Thinking in terms of the economy's production possibilities, these economists view much government spending as a "drag" on the economy whether it is financed through taxation or borrowing. They do not view supply-side reductions in government spending or tax rates as means of stimulating recovery from recessions or as tools for preventing inflation. Rather, they are policies to be pursued to achieve long-run goals at the same time that the monetary and fiscal authorities seek to achieve short-run macroeconomic stability.

Most economists are supply siders in the limited sense that they recognize the disincentive effects of taxation on investment and work decisions. This does not mean that there is general agreement that current rates of taxation and levels of government expenditure are too high. Some economists think they are probably about right, although there may be dissatisfaction with the allocation of government spending or the structure of some tax rates. As a rule of thumb, it is probably fair to categorize most monetarists as supply siders who favor reduced taxation because they hope it will accompany reduced government spending. Most Keynesians, on the other hand, are much less likely to advocate substantial reduction in taxation or government spending from their current levels.

Supply-side, Keynesian, and Monetarist Views of Government Spending Cuts during a Recession

The extreme supply siders, who are mainly responsible for recent popularization of the supply-side concept, do not adhere consistently to either Keynesian or monetarist positions on short-run macroeconomic policy. Short-run and long-run policy goals are not carefully distinguished in their arguments and hence cannot be separated for purposes of describing how extreme supply siders view the best way to mitigate the effects of business fluctuations on unemployment and inflation.

An example of this confusion can be seen in supply siders' advocacy of a reduced government deficit (as well as less restrictive monetary policy) in the 1981–82 recession in order to reduce unemployment. They argued that the relatively large deficit created high interest rates. Therefore, they advocated reduced government spending to lower interest rates and promote increased aggregate expenditure via an increase in investment. Our basic macroeconomic model indicates that lowering government spending would probably have reduced interest rates, but it would also have lowered GNP and employment in the short run. Neither Keynesians nor monetarists argue that an increase in government spending during a recession retards recovery toward full employment, although they disagree on whether a discretionary increase in government spending is the best policy.

▶ The Government Deficit: Does It Matter?

Concern over the size of the deficit in federal spending in the United States first appeared in the 1980 presidential campaign. Throughout the 1950s and well into the 1960s the annual deficit averaged around 1 percent of GNP. By the late 1970s federal deficits were averaging close to 2 percent of GNP in the United States. The prospect that federal deficits would continue to grow relative to GNP was viewed with some alarm.

Table 29.1   The national debt and the deficit

Fiscal year	(1)		(2)	
	(a)	**(b)**	**(a)**	**(b)**
	Annual budget deficit relative to GNP ([−] indicates budget deficit and [+] indicates budget surplus)		**Publicly held national debt**	
	($ billions)	*Relative to GNP (%)*	*($ billions)*	*Relative to GNP (%)*
1789	+0.000150	+0.09	0.00	0.00
1800	+0.000063	+0.01	.083	19.31
1860	−0.0071	−0.18	.064	1.63
1865	−0.963	−10.70	2.22	24.71
1900	+0.046	+0.25	1.023	5.47
1919	−13.36	−15.87	24.28	28.84
1933	−2.60	−4.66	55.80	39.70
1940	−3.10	−3.09	40.31	40.31
1945	−47.47	−22.40	213.39	100.45
1950	−3.11	−1.09	200.69	70.06
1955	−3.04	−0.80	203.01	53.34
1960	+0.269	+0.05	210.65	42.31
1965	−1.60	−0.24	222.51	33.74
1970	−2.85	−0.29	227.17	23.45
1971	−23.00	−2.23	238.81	23.15
1972	−23.37	−2.07	252.34	22.36
1973	−14.84	−1.19	267.86	21.39
1974	−4.69	−0.34	265.41	19.24
1975	−45.15	−3.05	311.91	21.08
1976	−66.41	−4.05	385.59	23.51
1977	−44.95	−2.41	446.84	23.97
1978	−48.81	−2.34	495.47	23.78
1979	−27.69	−1.18	529.00	22.48
1980	−59.56	−2.32	594.26	23.15
1981	−57.93	−2.03	669.97	23.44
1982	−110.61	−3.56	794.90	25.63
1983	−207.70	−6.20	929.40	27.30
1984	−185.3	−4.9	1,141.80	30.30
1985	−212.3	−5.3	1,312.60	32.90

Source: From James R. Barth and Stephen O. Morrell, "A Primer on Budget Deficits," *Economic Review of the Federal Reserve Bank of Atlanta*, 67 (August 1982), pp. 6–17 and Appendix; *Economic Report of the President*, 1986, Tables B–1 and B–73.
Phillip Cagan, "The Real Federal Debt and Financial Markets," *The AEI Economist* (November 1981), pp. 1–8.

Deficits and Presidential Politics

Apart from wartime emergencies, deficits have always been unpopular with voters. Jimmy Carter ran for president in 1976 promising to balance the federal budget by 1980. By early 1980 it was clear that the federal budget deficit would be close to $60 billion, or 2.3 percent of GNP, as indicated in table 29.1.

Ronald Reagan attacked the Democratic administration's inability to control the deficit and promised that if elected he would balance the federal budget by 1984.

As indicated in table 29.1, the deficit decreased slightly in dollar terms as well as relative to GNP in 1981. However, it increased dramatically in dollar amount and relative to GNP in both 1982 and 1983. While the deficit had declined to 5.3 percent of GNP by 1985, it had by no means vanished. The Council of Economic Advisers has projected that the deficit will not decline to as little as 2.3 percent of GNP again until 1989.[3]

During the presidential campaign of 1984, Walter Mondale promised to increase taxes in his acceptance speech at the Democratic convention. At the time, some political analysts suggested that Mondale may have taken a bold and positive position by speaking candidly about the debt issue. Throughout the fall campaign the challenger charged the Reagan administration with "mortgaging" America's future to support current spending.

Whatever other findings may emerge from analyses of the 1984 campaign, most observers agree that former Vice President Mondale's promise to raise taxes was a negative factor in his campaign. The American people elected the Reagan-Bush ticket. Evidently they were signaling that the deficit should be reduced through spending cuts and not through tax increases.

In 1985, Senators William P. Gramm and Warren Rudman of New Hampshire introduced a bill, known as the Gramm-Rudman Deficit-Reduction Act, that calls for Congress to achieve a balanced budget by 1990. Interestingly, Senator Gramm is a former professor of economics at Texas A & M University. The Gramm-Rudman bill sets specific declining deficit targets that reach zero in 1991. It requires the president to submit annual budgets containing deficits no greater than the specific target amount in each year. It also requires Congress to enact particular deficit-reduction measures in an attempt to reach these targets. If Congress fails to act in this manner, most federal programs would automatically be cut across the board by the Gramm-Rudman bill.

This bill won wide support from those favoring smaller government and caught many members of Congress, as well as the president, somewhat off guard

when it passed in December 1985. In the political atmosphere of the time, it seemed clear that the public would not support significant tax increases, so the Gramm-Rudman proposal was viewed as an attempt to force Congress to reduce expenditures. Along these lines, President Reagan agreed to submit a budget for fiscal year 1987 that would meet the legislation's required deficit target of $144 billion, even before the proposal was passed by Congress. Finally, while the Gramm-Rudman bill was the product of two Republican senators, President Reagan still had some objections to it. Specifically, he opposed the automatic cuts in certain segments of the budget, primarily defense. Despite his objections, the president signed the bill in December 1985. In July 1986, the Supreme Court ruled that the provision for *automatic* budget cuts, without congressional action in each case, is unconstitutional.

The Sources of United States Deficits in the 1980s

In order to understand the deficit and its economic pluses and minuses, we will first examine federal expenditures and receipts to see why the deficit has grown so much relative to GNP. We will also compare the United States experience with that of other industrialized countries over the same period. Federal government receipts and expenditures are listed in table 29.2 and illustrated in figure 29.1. Notice that in 1960, there was a federal budget surplus of one-tenth of 1 percent of GNP. This surplus was the result of tax revenues that amounted to 18.6 percent of GNP, while expenditures were only 18.5 percent. By 1985, the budget surplus had changed into a deficit of 5.3 percent of GNP. Table 29.2 and figure 29.1 show clearly that the deficit arose not because of plunging revenues but because of a surge in government expenditures. The principal source of this increase is the "other" category of government expenditure, which consists largely of government transfer and subsidy programs (not defense expenditures as is so often asserted).

Table 29.2   Budget outlays and receipts as a percentage of GNP, 1960–85

	1960	1970	1980	1982	1983	1984	1985
Total outlays	18.5	20.2	22.4	23.8	24.7	22.6	23.7
National defense	9.7	8.4	5.2	5.5	6.5	6.0	6.3
Net interest	1.4	1.5	2.0	2.8	2.8	2.9	3.2
Other	7.5	10.3	15.1	15.0	15.4	15.3	14.5
Total receipts	18.6	19.9	20.1	20.2	18.6	17.7	18.4

Source: From *Economic Report of the President,* 1986, Table B–1, p. 252, Table B–74, p. 341.

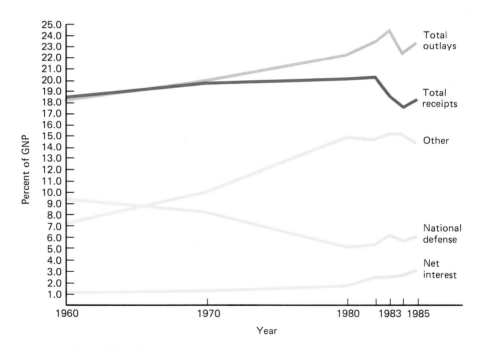

Figure 29.1   Sources of the federal deficit
The federal deficit is the difference between total government
outlays and government tax receipts. The deficit has grown
primarily because of an increase in outlays, while receipts have
remained more or less constant as a share of GNP. The main
source of increased outlays has been the category labeled
"other," which includes transfer expenditures, subsidies, and
related programs.
From *Economic Report of the President,* 1984, Table 1-1, p. 29.

President Reagan argued in 1980 and 1981 that his proposed tax cuts were intended to arrest the growth of the federal government—not dismantle it. The data in table 29.2 and figure 29.1 bear him out. They indicate that the deficit would be eliminated by a reduction in government expenditure as a share of GNP to the level that prevailed in 1960 or even in 1970. Furthermore, budget projections from the Reagan administration show anticipated tax revenue growing to about 19.8 percent of GNP—about the same as in 1970 but considerably less than the 1985 share of total federal expenditure.[4]

The source of the rapidly rising deficit during the early 1980s was primarily the continued rapid growth in federal spending. Total federal outlays rose steadily from 18.5 percent of GNP in 1960 to 20.2 percent in 1970, 22.4 percent in 1980, and 24.7 percent in 1983. Tax cuts proposed by the Reagan administration and approved by Congress resulted in a decline in receipts to 18.4 percent of GNP in 1985, which was not matched by a decline in outlays. The political debate for the next several years will revolve around whether or not federal spending can be cut enough to significantly reduce the deficit and without resorting to tax increases.

The Recent Debt Experience of Industrialized Nations

How does the United States deficit problem compare with deficit problems of other industrialized nations? As we have seen, the deficit in the United States has grown primarily because total expenditure has increased. The major source of this increase has been a doubling of transfer and subsidy programs and interest payments on the debt. United States experience in terms of changes in general government expenditure and the sources of change has been quite similar to the experiences of other major nations, including Canada, Japan, France, Italy, Germany, and the United Kingdom.[5] Indeed, even in 1984, the share of government expenditure in national income was greater in all of these nations except Japan than in the United States.

The rapid growth in transfer and subsidy programs in the United States in the last twenty years is similar to the pattern observed in other advanced economies. It has occurred both in rapidly expanding economies such as those of Germany and Japan and in slowly growing economies such as those of Italy and the United Kingdom. Similarly, these other nations have, on average, experienced budget deficits that have typically exceeded the deficit of the United States as a share of GNP.[6] Evidently, the existence of a large deficit relative to a country's national income does not tell us much about how healthy an economy is or how good its growth prospects are likely to be. This brings us to the economic issue of whether or not the large deficits of the 1980s are a serious obstacle for an economy to function properly and to grow at a healthy pace.

The Economic Significance of the Debt

In order to establish a framework for understanding the possible macroeconomic effects of the government deficit, we must first establish a standard against which we can measure whether the deficit is large or small. We have already done that to some extent by expressing a country's deficit as a ratio relative to its GNP. However, an important additional step involves recognizing that the economy's automatic fiscal stabilizers assure that the budget surplus will shrink or the deficit will grow during recessions.

Deficits and Business Cycles

When we are interested in the long-term effects of the deficit, we should consider what its size would be if the economy were at full employment; this is what economists call the **high employment deficit.** For example, we saw in table 29.1 that in 1983, the federal deficit was $207 billion. The President's Council of Economic Advisers has estimated that $95 billion of this deficit, or 48.7 percent, would have disappeared if the economy had experienced full employment in 1983. If the economy had been at full employment in 1982, it is estimated that the deficit would have been less than half as large.[7]

Monetization of the debt occurs when the Fed buys government bonds, particularly when the bonds are purchased directly from the Treasury.

*A **structural deficit** is a deficit that persists when the economy is at full employment.*

What has created growing concern over the deficit in recent years is that it has not disappeared, or turned into a surplus, during periods of full employment. As we have just seen, although the deficit would have been much smaller in recent years under full-employment conditions, it would still have been significant. Table 29.1 shows that until the 1970s, budget deficits were typically associated with wars and recessions. By far the largest deficits, relative to GNP, have been associated with wartime expenditures. Table 29.1 shows that the accumulated government debt held by the public rose from less than 2 percent of GNP in 1860 to almost 25 percent of GNP after the Civil War. By 1900, however, there had been enough years of budgetary surplus to reduce the publicly held debt to only 5.5 percent of GNP. World War I also was financed largely through deficit spending. The tandem effects of the Great Depression and World War II pushed the amount of publicly held government debt to over 100 percent of GNP.

Since creation of the Federal Reserve System, the public is not the only holder of the federal government's debt. When the government deficit is accompanied by an expansionary monetary policy (the Fed buying government bonds), we say that the Fed **monetizes the debt.** Monetization of the federal deficit has the same impact on the economy as printing dollar bills to finance an excess of government expenditure over tax collections. In 1982, the Fed held a little over 11 percent of the total outstanding federal debt.[8]

Structural Deficits

During the 1950s, the federal budget showed a surplus during three years, during the 1960s there were two years with surpluses, and since 1969 there has been a budget deficit every year. The federal government has become increasingly sensitive to the size and frequency of its deficits. In the thirty years from 1953 through 1982 there was a growing tendency to underestimate the size of the deficit when budgets were formulated.[9] The persistence of budget deficits even during periods of full employment has led to concern about the so-called **structural deficit,** the concept that even at full employment, government expenditure exceeds tax revenue.

Table 29.3	Estimates of the structural deficit as a percentage of GNP, 1980–89
1980	2.1
1981	1.3
1982	1.6
1983	3.2
1984	3.9
1985	4.2
1987	4.1
1989	3.7

The estimates and projections of the structural deficit suggest that even at full employment, the federal deficit will continue to be large relative to GNP, compared to historical standards.

Source: From *Economic Report of the President,* 1986, Table B–1, pp. 252–253.

The question we are concerned with is this: Has the deficit become so large that it harms the economy by raising real interest rates, thus slowing down investment and reducing the growth of productivity and real output? Even if we accept the idea that the federal government was operating with a structural deficit (that is, there would have been a deficit even at full-employment GNP) in the early 1980s, the deficit was not large by historical standards, at least not through 1982. Although 1982 was a recession year, the deficit as a fraction of GNP was lower than during the recession year of 1976. Table 29.1 shows that the deficit for 1983 was, however, rather large compared to previous deficits during times of peace.

Table 29.3 shows estimates of the structural deficit as a percentage of GNP, as estimated and projected by the President's Council of Economic Advisers, for the years 1980 through 1989. The table indicates a structural deficit in 1984 of 3.9 percent and in 1985 of 4.2 percent of GNP. This ratio is expected to remain quite high by historical standards for at least the rest of the 1980s. By contrast, table 29.1 shows that the *total value* of the publicly held national debt relative to GNP was far lower in 1982 than it was in 1960. What is the likely impact of the structural deficit on long-term economic prospects for the United States economy?

"Crowding Out": The Short-run and Long-run Effects of the Deficit

As noted in chapter 27, the process by which the federal deficit may harm prospects of long-run economic growth is referred to as *crowding out*, which means that the deficit, by increasing the total demand for loanable funds, raises interest rates and thus the cost of private investment projects. The quantity of investment goods demanded is then reduced. How likely is crowding out to deter private investment?

Once again, we refer to our macromodel. It tells us that in a recession an increase in the government deficit will reduce the quantity of private investment goods demanded relative to the amount of investment that would occur if the deficit were lower and expansionary monetary policy were used to stimulate economic recovery. However, an increase in the deficit will not lower investment relative to the amount that would occur during a recession if neither expansionary monetary nor expansionary fiscal policy were undertaken.

Under full-employment conditions, however, an increase in the deficit resulting from an increase in government spending will tend to crowd out private investment, at least in the short run, by causing an increase in the rate of interest. An increase in the deficit resulting from a reduction in taxes is more difficult to analyze. To the extent a reduction in tax revenue causes the deficit to increase, *cet. par.,* the rate of interest will rise and investment will be crowded out. However, a reduction in tax rates (particularly if slanted toward encouraging investment by raising depreciation allowances and so on) is likely to shift the investment demand schedule to the right. If reduced tax rates also lead to increased saving and the supply of loanable funds, a deficit caused by a reduction in taxes will result in less crowding out of investment than one caused by an increase in government spending. Thus, it could be that consumption is crowded out, rather than investment, if the deficit is increased by tax cuts that stimulate investment sufficiently.

If one accepts the crowding-out view, one has a pretty good grasp of the underlying economic assumptions in Walter Mondale's argument in the 1984 presidential campaign that the Reagan administration was mortgaging our future with large deficits in 1984 and beyond to stimulate the economy in the short run. The argument would be that deficit spending in 1984 and beyond would keep interest rates high, crowd out private investment expenditure, and reduce the economy's long-term growth prospects. Therefore, Mondale called for higher taxes and reduced government expenditure, at least for defense, in order to reduce the deficit and presumably the crowding-out effect. To the extent that voters rejected Mondale's proposals, they seem to have done so on the basis of favoring expenditure cuts, not tax increases—not because they were unconcerned about possible long-term crowding-out effects.

In contrast, President Reagan's position seemed to consist of three parts. First, he insisted that much of the deficit problem was cyclical and not structural. While that appears to be true for 1982 and 1983, the Council of Economic Advisers data in table 29.3 suggests that just the opposite is the case beyond 1984.

Second, the president insisted that the supply-side effects of the tax cuts of 1981–84 would raise the average full-employment rate of real economic growth in the United States well above the 3 to 3.5 percent rate of the last one hundred years or so. As we discussed earlier, the tax cuts of the early 1980s appear to have succeeded in putting a temporary lid on the federal tax bite out of GNP at a value near that of the early 1960s. While that may stand as a rather remarkable political accomplishment, it is difficult to see exactly how that change could induce supply-side effects large enough to raise the real full-employment growth rate by one full percentage point—almost a third of its historical average.

*The **Ricardian equivalence** **hypothesis** states that the method of financing government expenditure has no impact on private consumption or investment expenditures.*

Third, the president promised not to raise taxes and to cut federal expenditures enough to halve the projected deficit by 1988. Using the Council of Economic Advisers figures, that would reduce the projected deficit to about only 1.8 percent of GNP. The president's position did not deny the possibility of long-run crowding-out effects. Instead, Reagan forecast sufficient economic growth and expenditure cuts to render the crowding-out effect relatively inconsequential by 1988.

The impact of the government deficit on private investment expenditure is essentially a long-run problem. Moreover, the response of investment to the deficit depends on whether the deficit results from a reduction in taxes or an increase in government expenditure. Unfortunately, the question of whether or not government borrowing crowds out private borrowing cannot be answered completely by reference to our macromodel because the model cannot handle problems of what we shall now call the *very long run.*

In the very long run, the degree of crowding out depends on whether the public views the holding of government bonds as wealth. Why shouldn't government bonds held by the public be viewed as wealth? The answer lies in the theory of rational expectations. Suppose everyone in the economy were to purchase one dollar's worth of government bonds to finance the federal deficit. They would do so in return for the interest payments they expect to receive in the future. However, over the very long run, the public will learn that in order for the government to finance the interest payments, one of the following three events must occur: (1) taxes must be increased; (2) new bonds must be sold to the public (a further increase in government debt); or (3) the government can print the money, increasing the rate of monetary growth. Events 1 and 2 essentially take back the interest the public receives from its government debt holdings. Event 3 takes it back less directly, by using the "tax" of inflation.

The monetarist explanation for continued high interest rates throughout the mid-1980s turns on this third possibility. The argument is that nominal long-term interest rates remained above 10 percent despite inflation rates of 4 percent or less because the public was convinced that the debt would be monetized and that the rate of inflation would return to the 7 to 8 percent range experienced during the 1970s. Of course, if deficits were persistently monetized, the public would soon build inflationary expectations into all its economic behavior, and the government could not succeed in gaining additional resources through deception over the very long run. Persistent attempts to do so have led to hyperinflation in many nations.[10]

If event 1 or 2 occurs the public will eventually transfer back to the government the interest income received from the original debt purchases. By contrast, if each member of the public had purchased one dollar's worth of private debt from business firms, the interest would be paid with the revenues received for selling the additional production made possible by the investment goods financed through the debt issue. The private debt would be viewed as wealth "backed" by an addition to the economy's stock of physical capital.

If the public views a structural deficit as leading to an increase in future taxes, then in the very long run the effect on private investment will be equivalent to that of an equal increase in spending and taxes, with no change in the deficit. This view, that the method of *financing* government expenditure, either by borrowing or by taxation, has no effect on real economic variables, is called the **Ricardian equivalence hypothesis.**[11] It depends on the idea that deficit financing is a means of allowing the public to benefit from government expenditure in the present, while shifting the burden of taxes (payment of interest on the debt) to future generations. However, the Ricardian equivalence hypothesis maintains that the current generation cares about future generations. That is, the typical individual has a *bequest motive*. Thus, the public recognizes that today's deficit will raise future taxes, and it will increase its saving accordingly. This way future generations will be as well off as if current government expenditure were entirely financed through taxation. The increase in saving will shift the supply of loanable funds to the right, offsetting the impact of the government's demand for loanable funds.[12]

If the Ricardian equivalence hypothesis holds or if the public fully anticipates monetization of the debt, then the method of financing government expenditure does not affect the share of GNP that goes to private investment or consumption. It cannot be emphasized too strongly, however, that the level of government *expenditure* does affect private expenditure decisions. This is because, in the long run, whatever resources are used by the government are not available for use in the private sector. In other words, the real course of the economy is independent of the government's monetary and fiscal policies provided the public recognizes the effects of the deficit and the quantity of money on future taxes and the price level. Only "surprises" in the form of unexpected changes in monetary or fiscal policy will affect the allocation of the public's expenditures on consumption and investment goods.

There is considerable disagreement among economists on the existence and significance of long-term crowding-out effects of the public debt. This is because empirical evidence is scarce and subject to widely different interpretations. The political consensus appears to be that it is better to rein in government deficit spending than to wait around to discover what if any adverse effects the deficit may have if we do nothing.

▶ Summary and Conclusions

Now that you have surveyed the major macroeconomic controversies and know who the players are, can you identify them in the political debates leading up to the next congressional and presidential elections? Which side do you favor? In this chapter we discussed the basic differences between Keynesians' and monetarists' viewpoints about how the aggregate economy works. We also analyzed the controversy over the long-run effects of the national debt on the economy. The major points emphasized were these:

Keynesians tend to believe that monetary policy affects aggregate demand indirectly through its impact on the real interest rate and that the impact of fiscal policy on the economy is more significant and direct.

By contrast, monetarists believe that short-run economic impacts of monetary policy are more predictable than are the consequences of fiscal policy actions.

Monetarists also believe that monetary policy affects aggregate spending directly through its impact on consumption and investment expenditure as well as indirectly through its impact on the interest rate.

Monetarists tend to prefer monetary growth rules to either monetary or fiscal discretionary policies.

Keynesians generally believe that the economy can and should be induced to grow more smoothly through the use of discretionary policies.

Monetarists argue that the history of the use of discretionary policies is full of examples of mistakes that have increased the length and severity of recessions and inflations.

United States deficits during the early 1980s were made larger by the adverse cyclical effects of the recession in 1981–82.

United States experiences with respect to deficits, the size of interest payments on the debt, the growth of transfer and subsidy programs, and the size of general government expenditure relative to GNP have been similar to the experiences of other industrialized nations.

An international comparison of public debt shows no correlation with the rate of economic growth or the level of economic well-being.

The growth of the public debt in the United States has been dominated by the growth of expanding federal expenditure after 1965.

Monetarists and economists who accept the rational expectations view tend to view the size of the government debt as relatively unimportant to the long-run growth prospects for the United States economy.

The public debate over the size of the deficit is largely a debate over the appropriate size of government expenditure relative to GNP.

▶ Key Terms

high employment deficit *610*

Laffer curve *605*

monetarists and Keynesians *601*

monetization of the debt *611*

Ricardian equivalence hypothesis *613*

structural deficit *611*

supply-side economics *605*

target of monetary policy *603*

▶ Questions for Discussion and Review

1. Why would a Keynesian prefer the use of fiscal policy to the use of monetary policy to try to regulate the macroeconomy?

2. Why would a monetarist prefer the use of rules rather than discretion in the use of monetary and fiscal policy?

3. Why are we less concerned about the cyclical component of the deficit than we are about the structural component?

4. Explain the economic assumptions underlying the positions on the deficit taken by former Vice President Mondale and President Reagan in the 1984 presidential campaign.

5. How would monetarists and Keynesians explain the high interest rates of the mid-1980s?

6. Would you expect the income tax cuts of 1981–84 to generate substantial supply-side effects? Why?

7. What is the relationship between structural deficits and the possibility of long-run crowding out?

8. Explain the significance of the cyclical component of the deficit to the deficit/GNP ratio in the United States in 1982 and 1983.

9. Are there circumstances under which the public would view government bonds as wealth?

10. Will large deficits lead to long-run crowding out as long as the public views government bonds as a debt to be paid off?

11. Show by means of a graph how a change in the real value of money balances held by the public might *directly* influence consumption and aggregate demand.

Policy Issue: You Decide

Flat Tax

▶ The Action-Initiating Event

The president has decided that he wants to push for a single tax rate on personal income and to eliminate all corporate income taxes despite the problems that such legislation has faced in the past. The staff at the Council of Economic Advisers estimates that a flat tax of 25 percent on personal income will generate enough revenue to balance the current budget if all deductions are eliminated. The president wants to make a major televised address on this issue just before Congress recesses in order to get the public behind his proposal. He wants to be prepared to consider minor changes in his proposal and demonstrate publicly his command of facts regarding the implications with respect to his proposal and possible modifications.

▶ The Issue

Clearly, a single tax rate would substantially reduce marginal tax rates for middle- and upper-income families and individuals. The president is willing to consider a minimum income level below which there would be no tax in order to defuse the fairness issue. By themselves, the elimination of the corporate income tax and the lower income tax rate for many individuals should help to stimulate the economy. The elimination of all personal income tax deductions and business deductions will undoubtedly generate winners and losers with varying amounts of political clout. The president's chief of staff asked me to solicit your opinion on this entire matter. The concern within the inner circle is that the president could be committing political suicide on this issue.

▶ Economic Policy Issues

With respect to both personal and business activities, the president's initial proposal raises several concerns on which I would like to have your opinion. First, with respect to the treatment of personal income, how would the elimination of all deductions affect the housing industry, interest rates, charitable contributions, and any other areas that you might be concerned about? How would the elimination of corporation depreciation allowances and investment tax credits along with the corporate income tax itself affect the structure of industry in the long run? Who would be the big winners in the short run?

▶ Recommendations

If the political judgment is made that some personal deductions cannot be eliminated, we will need answers to the following questions from you: Would you recommend covering any increased deficit associated with retaining particular personal tax deductions by raising the personal tax rate, imposing a minimum corporate tax, or simply allowing the projected deficit to increase? Would a federal consumption tax or national sales tax be worth considering to reduce the deficit? Who would be the winners and losers from these various options? What would be the impact on the economy of the president's proposal as well as the other options? The White House wants the president to understand the implications of various alternatives before he goes public. While the mood in the country continues to favor tax reform, we do not want the president's position to seem unfair or impractical.

Part VIII

The International Economy

Chapter 30

Trade among Nations

Outline

I. Introduction 622
II. Import and export patterns in the United States economy and the world economy 623
III. Imports, exports, and the gains from trade 627
   A. The supply and demand for imports and exports 627
      1. The effect of the world price on domestic production and consumption 628
      2. The equilibrium world price and the flow of trade 630
      3. Supply, demand, and international trade patterns 633
   B. Winners and losers: The distribution of the gains from trade 634
      1. Winners and losers in the importing country 634
      2. Winners and losers in the exporting country 637
IV. Summary and conclusions 638
V. Key terms 639
VI. Questions for discussion and review 639

Objectives

After reading this chapter, the student should be able to:

Discuss the relative importance of international trade to the United States economy and the world economy.

Derive a nation's import and export curves for a commodity given the nation's supply and demand curves for that commodity.

Show how the world equilibrium price of a commodity is obtained.

Show the international effects of a shift in a nation's demand or supply of a commodity.

Discuss the winners and losers within the importing and exporting countries and the distribution of the gains from international trade.

Real aspects of international trade are concerned with the flows of commodities among nations.

Monetary aspects of international trade deal with currency flows, which are the financial counterpart of international commodity flows.

▶ Introduction

In a Detroit bar during the early 1980s, a young man of Chinese descent was drinking a beer. Two autoworkers started a fight with him, and when he left the bar, they chased him, attacked him, and killed him. Why? The autoworkers mistook their victim for Japanese, and they equated automobiles imported from Japan with lost jobs and reduced wages in the United States automobile industry. Not long afterward, a South Dakota banker drove to a local farm to discuss a loan that was in default. If the loan was not repaid soon, the bank would have to foreclose on the farm. A member of the farmer's family, hiding inside a barn, shot the banker dead as he started to get out of his car. This killing, too, was related to United States trade with other countries. During the early 1980s, farm exports declined because the dollar rose in price relative to foreign currencies, and this made American farm exports more expensive than those from other nations such as Canada, Argentina, and Australia. The resulting decline in the revenues of American farmers forced many of them into bankruptcy.

These two true stories illustrate the immense importance of international economic relationships in the lives of many individuals. They also reflect stupidly misplaced aggression based on ignorance about international and other economic issues. All of us depend on trade with other nations in many ways that may not be quite as obvious in our everyday lives. The American car you drive may have bumpers plated with chrome from South Africa; the gasoline it burns and the oil that lubricates its engine is almost as likely to

be imported as domestically produced; the pencil you use to take class notes is likely to contain tin, graphite, and rubber from three different nations.

Trade between nations occurs for exactly the same reason that individuals and firms within a nation specialize and deal with one another. Comparative advantage, specialization, and trade are crucial to maximizing the benefit we obtain from our scarce resources. In this and the next three chapters we explore how international trade affects the welfare and growth of advanced industrial nations as well as developing countries and examine some causes and effects of barriers to free trade. We will learn why the United States has experienced persistent international trade deficits (importing more than it exports) in recent years and what this means for the typical American citizen and worker. We will also examine the forces that determine the price of one country's currency in terms of another and the means by which inflations and recessions may be transmitted internationally through the international trade connection.

*The study of international trade is usually divided into two parts. Issues involving the trade of commodities are designated the **real aspects of international trade**, whereas matters relating to currency or exchange considerations are called the **monetary aspects of international trade**. In this chapter and chapter 31 most of our discussion deals with the real aspects of international trade. The monetary and macroeconomic aspects of international trade and how international currency flows relate to trade are treated* *in chapter 32. In this chapter, we show how supply and demand forces determine exchange rates, how exchange rates in turn affect the international flow of goods and services, and how international trade relates to aggregate employment and production. In chapter 33, we apply the lessons of the earlier chapters to help understand some current problems in today's international economy. We will see what problems led to the international debt crisis of the early 1980s and the way in which some nations have sought to use international trade as an engine of industrialization for their economies.*

▶ Import and Export Patterns in the United States Economy and the World Economy

Foreign trade's importance to the United States economy has grown in recent years. Figure 30.1 shows that using either the value of imports or exports as a measure, the share of foreign trade in GNP has doubled since 1950. Nevertheless, as measured by share of total production, other countries are more dependent on the foreign sector than is the United States. In few other countries do economic relations with foreign nations constitute a smaller proportion of gross

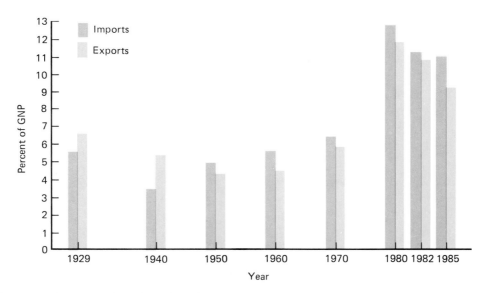

Figure 30.1   Imports and exports of goods and services as a share of GNP in the United States, 1929–1985
Both imports and exports have more than doubled as a percentage of GNP since 1950.
From *Economic Report of the President,* 1986, Table B-1, pp. 252–253.

Figure 30.2   Share of exports from the United States and other nations in total world exports (percent of dollar volume)
From *Economic Report of the President,* 1983, Table B-106, p. 282 and 1986, Table B-106, p. 374.

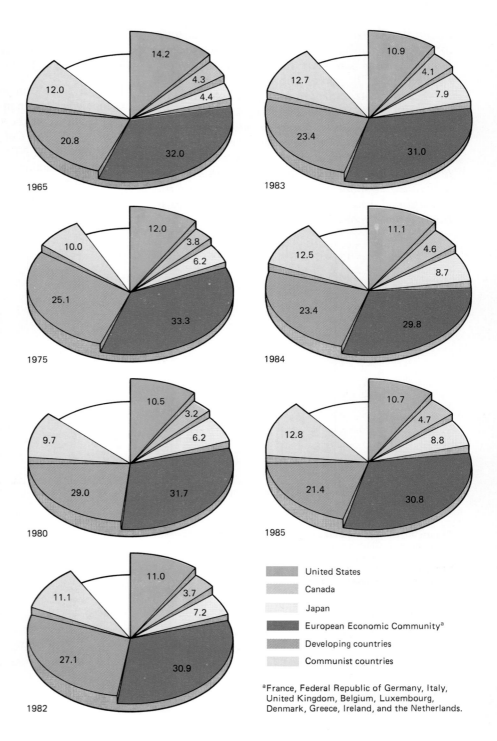

1965

1983

1975

1984

1980

1985

1982

United States

Canada

Japan

European Economic Community[a]

Developing countries

Communist countries

[a]France, Federal Republic of Germany, Italy, United Kingdom, Belgium, Luxembourg, Denmark, Greece, Ireland, and the Netherlands.

Table 30.1   Net United States imports of minerals and metals as a percentage of consumption, 1983

Mineral		Major foreign sources
Mica	100	India, Brazil, Madagascar
Manganese	99	South Africa, Gabon, Brazil, France
Bauxite	96	Jamaica, Australia, Guinea
Platinum	84	South Africa, Soviet Union, United Kingdom
Chromium	77	South Africa, Philippines, Soviet Union
Zinc	66	Canada, Spain, Mexico, Honduras
Petroleum	28	Saudi Arabia, Nigeria, Venezuela

Source: From *Statistical Abstract of the United States*, 1985, Table 1248, p. 703, Dept. of Commerce-Bureau of the Census.

product. All of the major industrialized market economies listed in figure 30.2 have export shares larger than the United States, and in most of them exports amount to 25 percent or more of their total output. In several of the world's less industrialized nations, exports account for over a third of gross product.[1] Obviously, export earnings are crucial to these nations' ability to import essential consumption goods and investment goods needed for economic growth.

In an important sense, the data in figure 30.1 grossly understate the relationship of the United States to the international economy. In terms of absolute size, the United States economy is so large relative to the rest of the world that even a small share of its GNP constitutes a large fraction of total commerce among nations. Figure 30.2 shows that United States exports constitute over 10 percent of total exports from all nations. Moreover, a number of raw materials essential to our economy are either unavailable within our borders or are much more costly to produce here than elsewhere. Some of these are listed in table 30.1. Even though we import far fewer than half of the petroleum products we use, events since 1973 clearly demonstrate how important trade can be even for a commodity for which we are largely self-sufficient. Table 30.1 shows that the United States

is currently almost totally dependent on imports for some important raw materials. What does Gabon have that United States citizens apparently cannot live without? Answer: a large share of the manganese for making high-quality steel. Do you use mica? Many of your electrical appliances probably do. Much of it comes from the remote island of Madagascar. The bauxite used to make your aluminum pots may have originated in the country of Guinea.

Despite the dominant role of the United States in world trade, the international marketplace has become more competitive in recent years. While the United States has been exporting an increasing share of its gross product and importing a larger fraction of the automobiles, steel, and petroleum used by American firms and consumers, other nations have expanded their role in the world economy even faster. For example, between 1965 and 1982, the United States share in total world exports declined by 3 percentage points (about 20 percent), while the share of Japan grew almost three percentage points (about a 60 percent increase in its export share). The share of the world's developing nations in total world exports grew by about six percentage points (about a 30 percent increase).

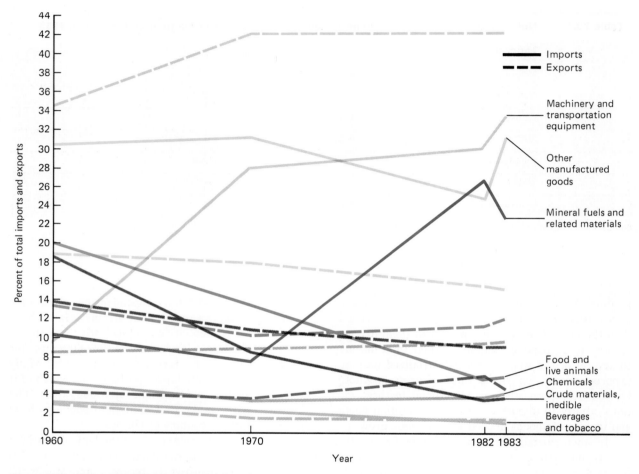

Figure 30.3   Percentage distribution of United States imports and exports by broad commodity groups, 1960–1983
From *Statistical Abstract of the United States,* 1984, Table 1474, p. 838 and 1985, Table 1447, p. 820.

Figure 30.3 shows the pattern of United States foreign trade according to broad categories of final product use. The data there indicate that in terms of dollar value, the United States is a net exporter of food, crude materials, chemicals, and machinery and transportation equipment. It is a net importer of mineral fuels (oil) and other manufactured goods. Figure 30.3 shows how United States imports and exports have changed over the years. The main shift in export patterns has been growth in the share of machinery and transportation equipment. Imports of this broad commodity group have also grown relative to total imports. As you might expect, the most striking change in United States foreign trade has been a

Table 30.2 **United States exports and imports, by country or region, 1984 (percent of total)**

Country or region	Exports	Imports
Canada	24.1	20.7
Japan	10.6	18.0
Western Europe	25.9	21.6
OPEC	6.3	8.0
Eastern Europe	1.9	0.7
Australia, New Zealand, and South Africa	3.6	1.7
Other (includes Latin America)	27.4	29.3

Source: From *Economic Report of the President*, 1983, Table B–103, p. 279.

roughly fourfold increase in the share of mineral fuels and related materials in total imports, from 7.7 percent in 1970 to 22.5 percent in 1983.

Table 30.2 indicates major trading partners of the United States. Measured in terms of either imports or exports, Canada is our single most important international trade partner. Mexico (not included in the table) accounted for 6.8 percent of United States exports and 5.2 percent of imports in 1980.[2] Western Europe accounts for over a quarter of United States exports and a little more than a fifth of imports, while trade with Eastern Europe constitutes a very small share of both United States exports and imports.

▶ Imports, Exports, and
the Gains from Trade

Before beginning our analysis of supply and demand in international commerce, it would be helpful for you to review the discussion of comparative advantage in chapter 1. The principle of the gains that arise when two individuals specialize and trade with each other according to their relative opportunity costs is universal. It applies equally to trade among nations when they specialize according to comparative advantage.

The Supply and Demand
for Imports and Exports

We will analyze the real aspects of international trade as if the world consisted of only two nations—the United States and Japan. While this is somewhat artificial, you should think of Japan as standing for "the rest of the world" relative to the United States. In other words, Japan stands for all of the other steel-manufacturing countries that export their product to the United States. In our illustration, Japan exports steel to the United States and receives dollars in return. Therefore, to keep everything straight, we will convert all Japanese prices into their dollar equivalents. As we develop the analysis of international trade in steel between Japan and the United States, you should bear in mind that trade essentially involves exchanging one set of *commodities* for another set of *commodities*. So even though we do not treat it explicitly, there is another *flow of currency from Japan* in exchange for *goods and services from the United States.*

*The **world price** is the price of
purchasing a given commodity or
service on the world market.*

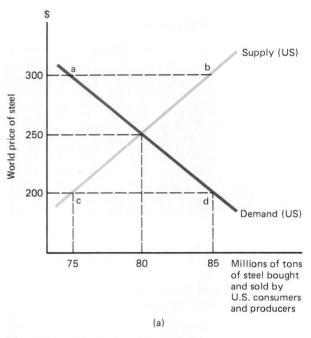

(a)

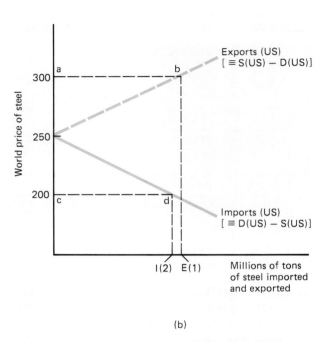

(b)

**Figure 30.4   Steel supply and demand in the United
States and its import and export curves**
The world price is the price that prevails in each country when
there are no restrictions on trade among nations. At a world
price of $200, for example, United States producers wish to
supply only 75 million tons of steel, while United States steel

users demand 85 million tons. Therefore, imports from Japan
will equal I(2) = 85 − 75 = 10 million tons at a world price of
$200. At a world price of $300, there will be an excess supply
of steel in the United States, which will be exported to Japan.
The quantity of steel exported at a world price of $300 is E(1)
tons.

The Effect of the World Price on Domestic Production and Consumption

In figure 30.4, part (a), we show the *long-run* supply
and demand for steel in the United States. The vertical axis measures the **world price** of steel, which is
the amount that it costs to purchase a ton of steel in
the worldwide market for it. Suppose the world price
of a ton of steel, measured in United States dollars,
equals $250. At $250, the United States demand curve
intersects the United States supply curve. This means
that steel producers in the United States can sell their
entire output of steel to United States citizens. At a
price of $250, United States steel buyers are willing
to purchase the total amount of steel that United
States producers wish to sell. Of course, this is the

same price that would prevail in the United States if
the possibility of international trade in steel did not
exist. If there were no international trade, a United
States price above $250 would create an excess supply
of steel, leading eventually to a reduction in price to
$250. At prices below $250, an excess demand would
exist and prices would rise to $250. However, with in-
ternational trade, the price of steel in the United
States need not converge to $250 as long as Japanese
and American citizens are willing to conduct trade in
steel with each another.

To see how trade works, refer to part (b) of figure
30.4. On the horizontal axis we measure the quantity
of steel the United States would export or import at
various world prices. Since the United States demand

result of the competition from Japanese manufacturers. The principal losers are American steel producers. Examining part (a) of figure 30.6, we observe that trade will ultimately curtail United States steel production from 80 million tons to 70 million tons. Trade with Japan will *eliminate* from the steel market those producers whose costs exceed $225 per ton. They will no longer be able to make and sell steel profitably because Japanese producers can do so at a lower cost. These producers, along with the workers they employ, are well aware of such effects and may attempt to prevent them by encouraging trade restrictions. In this way, they resist the competitive pressure on them to exit from the steel market to other industries making products that can be sold to United States buyers or exported.

In our example, the Japanese can produce steel at lower costs than *some* United States manufacturers. This cost advantage does *not* mean there will be *nothing* for *anyone* in the United States to produce. The United States *must* have something to sell to the Japanese or others in return for the dollars paid to import Japanese steel. In a world where people have varied talents, some can do certain tasks at lower opportunity costs than others. Thus, high-cost United States producers of steel will *always* be able to switch and compete effectively in other industries where the United States is *relatively* more efficient. The transition may be an unpleasant experience, but new jobs and industries *are* available to those forced to leave the steel industry.

It is important to remember that transferring resources to nonsteel-producing industries may be a painful process for the workers and the owners of other inputs used in steel manufacturing. During the transition period, they may experience unemployment and depressed incomes. In the long run, however, steel producers will be able to cover all their opportunity costs by shifting their efforts to other industries.

A second group that loses when steel trade with Japan is opened up are the low-cost United States manufacturers of steel. These producers are located in that segment of the United States supply curve lying to the left of 70 million tons in part (a) of figure 30.6. Costs for these producers remain unchanged, but

under the pressure of Japanese competition, the price they can charge—and hence the revenue they receive—declines.

Can we determine whether the net benefits associated with international trade are positive or negative? When most economists figure out the tally sheet for all society, the answer comes down unequivocally on the side of net positive benefits. The value of the gains received by buyers of steel outweighs the value of the losses experienced by the producers of steel. In other words, the gainers could *conceivably* compensate the losers and still have some positive gains left over. Instead of providing a complicated graphical proof of this assertion, let us use a simple numerical example. Suppose that in the pretrade situation a United States buyer purchased a ton of steel for $250. In manufacturing this ton of steel, the producer incurred $240 worth of cost, so that the producer received an economic profit of $10 per ton.

When the Japanese begin exporting steel to the United States the price of steel falls to, say, $225 per ton. The United States buyer, who was willing to pay $250 but who now need pay only $225, receives a benefit of $25 per ton. The United States producer must pay $240 for inputs that yield steel now selling for only $225. This results in a loss for the producer equal to $15 per ton of steel instead of the $10 profit the producer was accustomed to receiving. The producer can avoid the $15 loss by not purchasing the resources required to manufacture the ton of steel. These resources will no longer be used to produce steel in the United States and are now available to produce output in *another* industry. We would expect the $240 worth of inputs to yield output in another industry that can be sold for $240.

How do we know that $240 worth of resources will produce output in another industry that can be sold for $240? Assuming that the rest of the United States economy is in competitive equilibrium, we know (from chapter 20) that the cost of an additional extra unit of an input is equal to the value of its marginal product. Remember that when a price-taking firm maximizes its profit, its marginal cost equals the price of the good or service produced. Equivalently, the amount paid for a small additional amount of an input equals the value to the firm of the output it produces with that input. Thus, the $240 worth of resources that had been used to manufacture a ton of steel can be used elsewhere in the economy to produce output valued at $240.

In transferring out of the steel industry, the producer in our example will, of course, lose $10 in profit (or economic rent). That is, in the steel industry, the producer had been able to sell output for $250 that cost only $240 to produce before Japan began exporting steel to the United States. This may be because the producer had a "talent" for steel production. This talent is presumably not transferable to another industry. Yet, if you carefully examine the numbers involved, you will see that the steel buyers could give the producer, say, $20 as a more-than-sufficient compensation to cover the producer's loss in rent. The $20 comes from the benefit the buyer receives because it is now necessary to pay only $225 per ton of steel. The buyer would still be better off by $5 per ton of steel purchased. Trade creates net benefits in the sense that *all* United States citizens engaged in the buying and selling of steel *could* be better off by permitting Japanese firms to enter the United States market and compete with American manufacturers. It is important to note that in fact winners do not tend to compensate losers. The autoworkers in our introductory example were not compensated for their losses, and in their blind rage they killed an innocent young man.

There are additional gains in the United States. The United States demand curve in figure 30.6 shows how much Americans are willing to pay to purchase steel in excess of 80 million tons per year. Since $225 is less than this amount for all but the last ton purchased, American steel buyers are better off than they were. They have the opportunity to increase their steel purchases at a price lower than they were *willing* to pay for more steel.

It cannot be emphasized too strongly that the general principle of the gains from trade does not depend in any way on the particular numbers we have chosen. If consumption of steel in the United States remained at 80 million tons following the introduction of trade from Japan, each consumer would benefit from a reduction in the price of steel. At a

minimum, each consumer could be "taxed" an amount equivalent to his or her saving in expenditure on steel and steel products, and the proceeds could be given to steel producers who suffered lower revenues. However, steel users *voluntarily* increase their purchases of steel to 90 million tons at the new, lower price. They would not do this if it did not make them better off because they could, if they chose, continue to purchase the original quantity, 80 million tons. Steel consumption increases because the value of additional steel to steel users exceeds its cost. This additional benefit of steel consumption is represented by the shaded area under the United States steel demand curve to the right of 80 million tons in part (a) of figure 30.6. An additional net benefit to the United States comes from the fact that steel producers will not continue to produce 80 million tons of steel. The resources that had been used to manufacture 80 million less 70 million tons of steel, or 10 million tons of steel, will be transferred to other industries. The additional production in these industries represents a net gain to the United States economy because the steel that had been manufactured with these resources has been replaced by imports from Japan. This net gain is represented by the shaded area under the United States steel supply curve to the left of 80 million tons in part (a) of figure 30.6.

Before discussing the winners and losers in the exporting country, let us summarize what we have just found. In the importing country, the winners are primarily the consumers of steel and steel products who now either buy steel when before they did not or now buy steel for a lower price than before. The losers in the importing country include not only the high-cost firms who no longer produce steel but also the low-cost producers who now receive lower economic rents. Of course, it is really the workers and stockholders in these latter steel firms who are worse off because of their reduced profits and job opportunities. It is important for us to remember that the identity of the losers is a key political issue. Even though there is enough economic gain for the winners in the importing country to compensate the losers and have something left over, the politics of the situation are almost never going to make this happen. The losers from trade faced with little or no hope of compensation may simply try to block trade, thus making the country as a whole worse off.

This analysis of the gains and losses from trade is perhaps one of the most widely accepted principles of economics among economists. Nevertheless, it is surprising—indeed shocking—that occasionally an economist is found who claims that unrestricted international trade actually harms losers in an importing country more than it benefits winners. As far as we are aware, such arguments are based on a basic misunderstanding of the reasons countries trade with each other. In one fairly recent example, a well-known economist at a major university claimed that the analysis of international trade we have presented is in error because "There is little comparative advantage in today's manufacturing industries, since they produce the same goods in the same ways in all parts of the world."[3] In other words, this economist claims that the gains from trade depend on trading partners using different technologies. In fact, the entire analysis we have presented is based on the assumption that Japan and the United States (or any two trading partners) have access to exactly the same technology for producing traded goods. The advantage of trade comes from the fact that different countries have different resources and types of labor, as well as different demand curves for the traded goods. This is the reason that they can and do gain, on balance, from unrestricted trade.

Winners and Losers in the Exporting Country

A comparison of pretrade and posttrade positions in Japan reveals that the pattern of Japanese gains and losses is precisely the opposite of that in the United States steel market. Prior to trade, the Japanese equilibrium price equaled $175 in figure 30.6, part (c), while the quantity of steel bought and sold in Japan had been 40 million tons. With trade, the price of steel in Japan rises to the world equilibrium price of $225 per ton. This price increase leads to a reduction of Japanese consumption to 30 million tons and an expansion in steel production to 50 million tons. The losers, then, are the Japanese buyers of steel and steel products who now pay higher prices. Japanese steel

manufacturers receive benefits in the form of increased profit (or economic rent). Summing up the gains and losses within Japan will again produce a total positive net benefit for that country. The value of the Japanese steel buyers' losses is smaller than the value of the gains reaped by Japanese steel producers. Conceptually, we could redistribute the gains among all Japanese citizens so that each and every one is made to feel better off as a result of international trade.

How do we know that the value of Japanese steel buyers' losses is smaller than the value of the gains of Japanese steel producers? The analysis is similar to that of the distribution of gains and losses in the United States. To make the discussion simple, we will measure Japanese prices in terms of dollars. Suppose in the pretrade position a Japanese buyer purchased a ton of steel for $175 and in making this steel, the Japanese producer incurred $175 worth of opportunity cost so that economic rent was zero. When trade is opened with the United States, the price of steel rises to $225 per ton. The Japanese buyer now has to pay $225 for the same ton of steel that previously cost only $175.

Obviously, if $50 x 40 million tons of steel (the amount that would be produced in Japan without trade), or $2 billion, were taken from steel producers and distributed to Japanese steel consumers, consumers would be no worse off than before. Japanese steel producers, however, would still have an incentive to increase their production of steel to 50 million tons because the price of steel has risen to $225 per ton. The opportunity cost to the Japanese economy of this increased steel production is represented by the Japanese steel supply curve. Therefore, the shaded area in part (c) of figure 30.6 to the right of 40 million tons represents a gain to Japanese steel producers that does not correspond to a loss for Japanese steel users. They earn increased profit (or economic rent) by producing additional steel for the export market. The reason that Japanese producers can obtain the resources required to produce more steel without causing a loss to others is that producers must pay for the additional resources used. They are willing to pay because they can now sell the additional steel for more than the resources to produce it cost them.

There are additional net gains to the Japanese economy. Even if Japanese steel users were paid $50 for each ton of steel they used to purchase, they would no longer desire to purchase 40 million tons of steel. The Japanese demand curve indicates that at the new price of steel, $225, Japanese steel users prefer to substitute other goods for steel and therefore reduce the quantity of steel purchased to 30 million tons. Since they would have enough money to continue to purchase the amount of steel they used to but would choose to adjust their expenditures, they would be better off as a result of this adjustment. The shaded area above the Japanese steel demand curve to the left of 40 million tons represents an additional net gain from trade to the Japanese economy. It indicates that Japanese citizens can find goods other than steel to satisfy their needs when the price of steel increases. The source of this gain—as well as the gain described in the preceding paragraph—comes from the increase in the price Japanese producers receive for their steel. The higher price reflects the real value of the dollars earned by Japanese exporters when they sell steel to United States purchasers.

We have shown that no one *need* be worse off as a result of international trade. *From the viewpoint of both Japan and the United States, then, unimpeded trade in steel creates net benefits for the two countries.* Although there are likely to be winners and losers in both countries, the gains of the winners (consumers in the United States and producers in Japan) exceed the losses of the losers (producers in the United States and consumers in Japan).

To understand opposition to free trade it is important to realize that the losers from free trade within a country, particularly firms and workers producing goods that can be imported cheaply, are rarely compensated for their losses by the winners. Consequently, protectionist interests are not impressed by the efficiency arguments for free trade.

▶ Summary and Conclusions

Failure to understand the crucial importance of foreign trade to our economic well-being and the cruel hardships that changes in international trading patterns can inflict on citizens of both importing and exporting nations can lead only to tragic consequences for nations and the individuals who live in them. In this chapter we have explored the conditions determining patterns of world trade. The following major points were emphasized.

The United States is a major international trading partner, even though imports and exports make up only a relatively small share of its GNP compared to other nations.

The relative shares of broad commodity groups in United States imports and exports have changed in recent years, reflecting the changing pattern of comparative advantage.

Unrestricted trade benefits all trading nations.

The *distribution* of the gains from trade may result in some groups within each nation being worse off than they would be without trade, even though everyone can *potentially* be made better off through unrestricted international trade. Generally, losers know that they will not be compensated and therefore oppose free trade.

Because international trade involves an exchange of imports for exports and exports for imports, each trading partner has *both* winners and losers.

The major winners in importing countries are consumers, and the major losers are producers and their employees. The major winners in exporting countries are producers and their employees, and the major losers are consumers of the exported products.

▶ Key Terms

monetary aspects of
  international trade
  622

real aspects of
  international trade
  622

world price *628*

▶ Questions for Discussion and Review

In questions 1 through 4, judge whether the statements are true, false, or uncertain. Be sure to justify your answer graphically.

1. Even though every nation benefits from trade, some groups within each nation may lose.

2. A country always exports the good that its economy produces the most of.

3. The first country to be the low-cost producer of a good will always be the exporter of that good.

4. A wage increase among Japanese automobile producers will raise only the Japanese domestic price of cars and not the world price.

5. Figure 30.8 depicts international trade in wheat between Egypt and the United States. Which country will export wheat and which will import wheat? Why?

6. In the mid-1970s, a suggested cure for rising food prices in the United States was to restrict exports of United States agricultural output (wheat, corn, etc.). What effect would such a policy have had on domestic food prices, on world food prices, and on United States economic well-being? Illustrate your answer with a diagram.

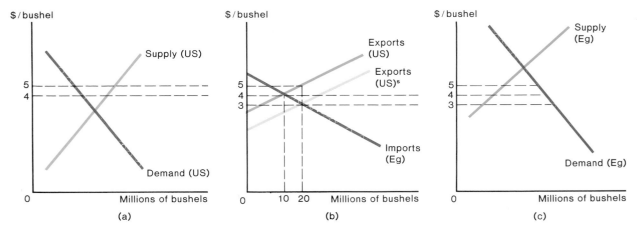

Figure 30.8 Effects of a United States subsidy on wheat exports to Egypt
If the United States subsidizes exports of wheat to Egypt, this is equivalent to lowering the United States export supply curve to (US)ˢ. The equilibrium price of wheat exports to Egypt falls, and exports of wheat to Egypt increase from ten million tons to twenty million tons.

7. True or false: Two countries that produce an identical commodity with identical technologies and labor costs will have no reason to trade. Defend your answer.

8. Draw the export and import functions for a commodity in two different countries. Show the effects of each of the following changes separately.
   a. An increase in demand for the exported good in the exporting country.
   b. A decrease in demand for the imported good in the importing country.
   c. A simultaneous decrease in demand in both countries for the good traded.

9. Suppose Japan exports steel to the United States at the world price of $\overset{*}{P}$. Suppose the Japanese domestic demand for steel increases to where the domestic equilibrium price is equal to $\overset{*}{P}$. Will steel exports cease? Explain.

10. Suppose a strike settlement in the United States steel industry raises domestic steel prices above Japanese domestic steel prices. Identify the posttrade winners and losers.

Chapter 31

The Regulation of
International Trade

Outline

I. Introduction *642*
II. Why interfere with a good thing? *643*
   A. Internal taxes as substitutes for tariffs: British and United States experiences *643*
   B. Income distribution considerations *643*
   C. Strategic goods and infant industries: Bases for import barriers? *644*
     1. Strategic supplies of steel *645*
     2. Infant industries and technology transfers *645*
     3. Import substitution *646*
III. Barriers to international trade *646*
   A. Tariffs *647*
     1. United States tariff history *647*
     2. A tariff on steel imports from Japan *648*
     3. Aggregate economic losses *649*
     4. Specific duties versus ad valorem tariffs *650*
       a. Protection of United States textile manufacturing *651*
       b. Protection of the United States steel industry *651*
   B. Quotas and other nontariff trade barriers (NTBs) *651*
     1. Revenue needs and the shift to NTBs *652*
     2. NTBs and the tariff revenue equivalent *652*
     3. "Voluntary" quotas *652*
       a. Imports and the United States auto industry *652*
       b. Quota rents to Japanese exporters *653*
       c. Estimates of gains and losses *654*
   C. The General Agreement on Tariffs and Trade (GATT), "fair" competition, and trade restrictions *654*
     1. The rules of the game and "unfair" trade practices *654*
   D. The Trade Expansion Act of 1962 *655*
   E. Customs Unions *656*
IV. Summary and conclusions *658*
V. Key terms *659*
VI. Questions for discussion and review *659*

Objectives

After reading this chapter, the student should be able to:

Explain why countries frequently restrict international trade flows.

Evaluate the national security and infant industry arguments for import restrictions.

Show the effects of a tariff on the price (in the importing and exporting countries) of a commodity and the quantity traded.

Discuss the losers and winners in each country from the imposition of a tariff.

Explain how the textile and steel industries used specific duties to protect low-quality goods.

Discuss the losers and winners in each country from a nontariff trade barrier such as a quota.

Discuss the effects of a voluntary quota on Japanese automobile exports to the United States.

Describe the provisions of the General Agreement on Tariffs and Trade (GATT) and the Trade Expansion Act of 1962.

Show the gains and losses associated with the formation of a customs union.

▶ Introduction

Textiles have been an important industry in the state of North Carolina and other states in the South. In 1985, a chain of grocery stores used bags carrying the following message: "If you and every other American shopper would redirect only $20 of your clothing purchases to American-made products rather than imports, you would immediately help create 100,000 American textile and apparel jobs. Think of what that would do for our textile-producing friends."

The grocery bag message recognizes the link between purchases of a product and job opportunities. It plays on our love of country and feelings of guilt at perhaps creating a job for a Korean instead of an American through our textile purchases. Such a campaign may fail to maintain job opportunities, however, if Americans basically prefer the quality and styling of foreign-made products. In 1985, a survey by the University of Detroit in cooperation with the Detroit News *found that people who live in Detroit, the heart of the American auto industry, felt that Japanese cars were better than American cars. In particular, 45 percent versus 15 percent of those polled felt Japanese cars were of higher quality than American cars. Lee Iacocca, the head of Chrysler Corporation, has often said that the government should do more to protect the American auto industry from "unfair" foreign competition. Recently, however, Chrysler bought a company airplane. The plane it chose was manufactured by a Canadian firm. When asked why a company that is such a proponent of "Buy American" would purchase a foreign-made airplane, the Chrysler Corporation's representative replied, "It was the best airplane available for what we*

wanted." In chapter 30, we saw that individual countries and the world as a whole benefit from free trade. Free trade permits each country to specialize in the production of goods and services that it can produce relatively most efficiently. These gains from trade increase the total amount of goods and services that the world has to distribute among countries and that countries have to distribute among their citizens. We also saw in chapter 30 that not all groups automatically benefit from international trade. Some groups, primarily workers and stockholders of firms in import-competing industries, would prefer to restrict trade in one form or another. We should not forget, however, that firms and workers in the export sector and consumers in general benefit from free trade. Thus, the regulation of international trade will also create winners and losers. An additional subtlety is that the government can profit in terms of political and financial power by paying attention to who the winners and losers from trade policy are and regulating trade to its (the government's) own best advantage.

A primary focus of this chapter will be on some of the more popular forms of trade restraints. We will also explain why trade restrictions are so pervasive when free trade is such a good economic idea. Third, we will explain how different forms of trade restriction work. Fourth, we will investigate why some forms of trade restriction are proliferating at the same time international negotiations are succeeding in reducing other forms of trade barriers. Finally, we will try to see why developing countries feel that international agreements to reduce trade restrictions have failed to address their particular concerns adequately.

▶ Why Interfere with a Good Thing?

One of the earliest motives for restricting international trade was to raise money for the government. When nation-states were first established, sovereigns had to secure their nations' borders from possible attack. Once armies have secured borders and therefore gained control of crossing points, much of the administrative structure necessary to collect taxes on anything going in or out is in place. Historically, border taxes—particularly taxes on imports—played a primary role in providing central governments with revenues with which to conduct their business. In case after case, one finds central governments moving toward freer trade only after alternative sources of revenue to import taxes have been found.

Internal Taxes as Substitutes for Tariffs: British and United States Experiences

Britain is often cited in textbooks as the historical leader in promoting freer trade in the nineteenth century. The dismantling of trade restrictions in Britain began in earnest in the mid-1820s. By the late 1830s the average tax rate on imports in Britain declined to 31 percent. However, the most dramatic steps in trade liberalization in Britain occurred along with the adoption of the income tax by the Peel government in 1841. When the income tax was renewed and made permanent in 1845, import taxes were eliminated on 450 items.

Throughout the post-World War II period, the United States has assumed a leadership role in the movement to deregulate international trade. Yet efforts to reduce or eliminate import taxes in the United States were largely frustrated after the Civil War until the income tax amendment was submitted to the states in 1909 and adopted in 1913.

Not surprisingly, today many developing countries that lack a well-developed system of internal taxes rely upon import and export taxes to provide revenue for their central governments. As governments develop alternative means of raising revenues, trade barriers generally decline.

Income Distribution Considerations

Following tax revenue, the most important reason for restrictions to international trade involves income distribution considerations. This is particularly true for restrictions on imports. While the aggregate gain from trade may be substantial, any individual buyer enjoys only a relatively small part of the total gain in his or her country. The total gain is widely diffused through the entire economy. Losers, however, are concentrated in one or several industries in importing nations. For example, in 1977 the value of all textiles (a United States industry that experiences severe foreign competition) shipped by United States manufacturers plus net imports (imports less exports) amounted to $173 for every member of the United States population.[1] The losers from import competition, on the other hand, lose big and are usually concentrated within particular regions, such as New England and the South in the case of textiles. In 1977, there were 876,000 textile workers in the United States, each earning an average of $9,000 per year.[2] Thus, in a very real sense, each worker's interest in the textile industry and in protecting it from foreign competition is about fifty times greater than that of a typical consumer. This is not to mention the *owners* of textile firms.

Textile workers and the firms that employ them fully recognize that the hypothetical compensation we discussed in the steel industry example of chapter 30 is unlikely to be translated into voluntary dollars and cents payments by those who gain from unrestricted trade. The losers see themselves as victims of unfair competition from exporting nations. Their strategy is quite simple: The losers must convince the government to limit the ability of foreigners to compete in domestic markets. Of course, this objective is seldom stated openly. Emotional appeals may be more effective—producers arguing about the unfair advantages of foreign manufacturers who exploit their workers by paying them sweat-shop wages. In conjunction with their employers, American workers will also complain that foreigners are stealing American jobs.[3] Textile production may even be labeled as vital to our national security and part of our cultural heritage. (We cannot have the United States Army depend on foreigners for boots and uniforms. Textile weaving dates back to the early colonial settlers of the Atlantic seaboard.) Congress, as a result, will be under great pressure to appease the parties who claim injury from foreign import competition.

The study of the politics and economics of international trade restrictions can be traced back to the eighteenth-century economist Adam Smith and his contemporaries. But the efforts to quantify the extent to which trade is regulated and to explain how political and economic forces combine to succeed in restricting trade have been the focus of an expanding body of research in the last fifteen years. Throughout our discussion in this chapter, we will refer to that literature for insights into the nature and scope of trade regulations today.

Strategic Goods and Infant Industries: Bases for Import Barriers?

Arguments other than those based on revenue needs of the central government or income distribution considerations can be used to support government restrictions on international trade. (1) It is dangerous to rely on foreign countries to supply goods that are indispensable for national defense; and (2) our country's relative price disadvantage in producing a good may change to an advantage once domestic firms gain sufficient experience to become internationally competitive.

There is doubtless merit in avoiding the risk of being deprived of some strategic resource such as steel or petroleum should international trade be restricted or cut off entirely by war. Even if the supplier of such a resource is not a military antagonist, air and sea transportation could become extremely difficult. There are sound reasons why a government, as part of overall defense strategy, should make sure that it is able to supply military needs in time of war. It does not follow, however, that restrictions on international trade in time of peace constitute the best policy. There are alternatives. One is simply to stockpile the materials that may be needed for military purposes. The United States government does, in fact, maintain strategic stockpiles of various metals and minerals, even of morphine, for military and civilian emergency use. There is also a strategic oil reserve of underground caverns designed to be filled with crude oil to be used in the event of a national emergency.

It may be argued that, in addition to material stockpiles, it is also necessary to preserve production capability of items such as steel and other key manufactured goods. This may require barriers to foreign competition in order to keep strategically needed firms from going out of business. Carried to its extreme, however, the strategic industry argument can be used to justify protecting almost every industry. After all, soldiers need all of the consumer items that civilians do, in addition to military goods. Thus, why not protect the industries that produce shoes, soap, movies to relieve boredom, rice for a varied diet, and sugar for desserts to maintain morale? As with any other defense strategy, protecting domestic industries has costs that must be weighed against the strategy's prospective benefits. Most economists are generally skeptical of arguments in favor of restricting trade for strategic purposes. Generally, there are less costly means of insuring military preparedness than protecting high-cost industries from international competition.

*The **infant industry argument** for trade restriction states that if an industry is protected in its early years of development, when it is unable to compete on the world market, it will be saved in the long term because the production experience it gains will ultimately make it competitive.*

Strategic Supplies of Steel

The United States steel industry has used national security as an argument to bolster its frequent demand for restrictions on imported steel. From the mid-1970s until today, United States producers of steel have faced stiff competition in the form of imports from Japan and Europe, particularly West Germany, and more recently from South Korea and Brazil. Capacity utilization has remained at or below 60 percent in the United States steel industry throughout this period and fell to a low of 38 percent during the 1982–83 recession. The national security argument has been a significant part of the steel industry's successful battle for systematic restrictions on steel imports into the United States. Yet actual military needs for steel require no more than 10 percent of the economy's existing capacity. Contrary to industry claims, when stiff import competition started the process of shaking out inefficient firms that use outdated production technologies, our ability to satisfy strategic demand for steel was never threatened.

Infant Industries and Technology Transfers

A second reason sometimes stated by engineers and economists to support foreign trade restrictions is based on technical considerations. It is generally recognized that firms learn to be more efficient as they gain experience with new products or production techniques. The **infant industry argument** for trade restrictions states that the reduction in costs that occurs with accumulated production of a good can ultimately reverse a nation's relative price disadvantage in world trade. It does not follow, however, that trade restriction is the best means of securing these cost reductions. By definition, if a nation has a comparative disadvantage in international trade because its firms lack experience in production, there are firms in other nations that do have this expertise. Unless there are legal restrictions on exporting their technology or knowledge, it should be possible to purchase it or to pay foreign firms for their assistance in developing domestic capabilities. If this is possible, then the cost of purchasing foreign technology outright must be weighed against the costs of restricting trade. While the cost of outright purchase is confined to the industries directly involved, the cost of trade restrictions can be much broader. This is especially true if economic warfare results in barriers that affect trade in a wide variety of unrelated goods and services.

Historically, some international restrictions on the transfer of technology might have justified the infant industry argument as a valid reason for international trade restrictions. For example, during the late eighteenth and early nineteenth centuries, England attempted to prohibit the international transfer of information on modern textile production technology. Originally, China was the only country in which knowledge of silk production from silkworms was known, and China guarded its knowledge zealously. (It is said that among Marco Polo's acquisitions on his legendary journey to China were knowledge of silk technology and of the noodle. Both industries, of course, have greatly benefited the Italian economy.) Today, the United States and other nations protect many trade secrets through patents and other means. Moreover, restrictions are imposed on transfer of strategically valuable technology to potentially unfriendly nations. Nevertheless, international transfer of technology and expertise does occur, and it is generally an efficient substitute for trade barriers. One example is the attempt by General Motors to gain knowledge of Japanese methods for producing relatively inexpensive small cars by forming a joint venture with Toyota in the United States.[4]

Just as with the strategic goods and industries argument, the infant industry argument can easily be used as an excuse to support government protection for high-cost industries. This protection cannot typically be justified on efficiency grounds, however. Again, most economists tend to believe that unless exceptional circumstances can be documented, the domestic firms directly involved can arrange to acquire improved technology by purchasing it from foreign firms or negotiating joint ventures whereby both

Import substitution is the use of trade restrictions to promote domestic production of manufactured goods that are currently imported.

sides benefit. If such arrangements are expected to prove unprofitable, this is evidence that protection from foreign competition would also provide benefits that are smaller than the costs to society at large.

Import Substitution

One of the broadest applications of the idea that trade restrictions can be useful in promoting new industries has been the adoption by developing countries in the post-World War II period of a strategy for industrialization referred to as **import substitution.** Import substitution is based on the idea that by restricting imports of manufactured goods a government can provide an incentive for domestic industrial firms to produce substitutes for imports. The desire to promote more rapid industrialization in developing countries was based on two general beliefs. First, throughout much of the 1950s and 1960s, policymakers in developing countries believed that long-term changes in international prices favored manufactured goods rather than the kinds of agricultural and natural resource based products exported by developing countries. This perception led to the belief that developing countries could not benefit much from expanding their role in international commerce.

The second major reason used to support the import substitution policies in developing countries has been the belief that agricultural and natural resource based product prices and output are subject to wide variations in international demand—more so than are the prices and output of manufactured goods. To the extent that production could be diversified by promoting domestic manufacturing industries capable of competing in world markets, policymakers believed that export earnings could be stabilized. This would presumably provide stable foreign currency earnings needed to continue imports of critical products needed for further industrialization.

The behavior of the relative prices of imports and exports for developing nations is analyzed in chapter 33. Briefly, the data reveal that both developing nations and major industrial nations that do not export oil suffered during the period from 1975 through the early 1980s as a result of the rising world prices for petroleum. However, even if one believes that developing nations have a sensible desire to try to speed up the industrialization process, the case for trade restrictions is by no means obvious. If government intervention should be required because of incomplete or underdeveloped internal capital markets, then investment tax credits, direct subsidies, accelerated depreciation laws, and so on would all seem to be more direct and efficient ways of promoting domestic industrialization than the use of import taxes or other import restrictions. Unfortunately, many developing countries currently find themselves in much the same circumstances as Britain in the early nineteenth century and the United States in the early twentieth century; they lack well-developed internal tax and income redistribution mechanisms. Therefore, as crude as import taxes or other trade restrictions may be for the purpose of promoting particular domestic industries, they may in fact represent the best that domestic policymakers can do at the moment.

▶ Barriers to International Trade

We have looked at the many reasons why nations have traditionally imposed restrictions on international trade, even though free trade potentially provides benefits for everyone. In the remainder of this chapter we will analyze the most common forms taken by trade barriers and examine who wins and loses when they are imposed. We will also look at efforts toward international economic cooperation to promote free trade and evaluate what they have accomplished.

*A **tariff** is a tax on imported goods that is collected by the government of an importing country.*

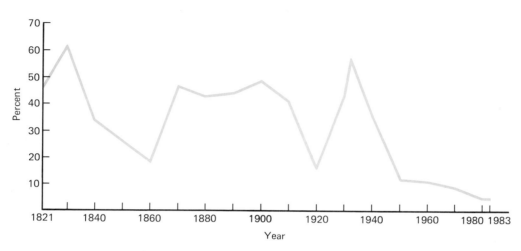

Figure 31.1   Tariffs as a percentage of the value of imports: United States, 1821–1983
Tariffs as a percentage of the value of imports are much less important today than they were prior to World War II. Throughout the nineteenth century tariff revenues constituted a major source of income for the United States government. From *Historical Statistics of the United States Colonial Times to 1970* Series U211 and U212, and *Statistical Abstract of the United States:* 1982/83, Table 1482, p. 833, and 1985, Table 1450, p. 823.

Tariffs

Probably the most common response by the United States Congress to the demand for international trade protection has been to legislate a **tariff** on imported goods, which is a tax that must be paid to the government of the importing country. Its effect is to raise the cost of selling imported goods in the nation with the tariff. This shields domestic industry from foreign competition.

United States Tariff History

As you can see in figure 31.1, tariffs in the United States currently average about 5 percent of the value of imported goods on which tariffs have been imposed. (Imports on which there are no tariffs currently constitute about half of the value of all United States imports.) While these tariffs raise the prices of goods to United States consumers, they are currently lower than at other times in our history. The peak of protectionism occurred before the Civil War, when tariffs were imposed on most imports and amounted to about 60 percent of their value. (Tariff revenues, as we have discussed, were also the major source of federal government revenue at that time.) Since the Civil War, our willingness to tax imports has fallen gradually and very irregularly. As figure 31.1 illustrates, tariff rates also reached peaks around 1870 and again during the Great Depression.

To some extent, the high post-Civil War tariffs were part of the spoils of war for the winning North. The North, with emerging industries, had been losing the battle for protection in Congress before the war. With the conclusion of the Civil War and the exclusion of southern states from congressional votes, the

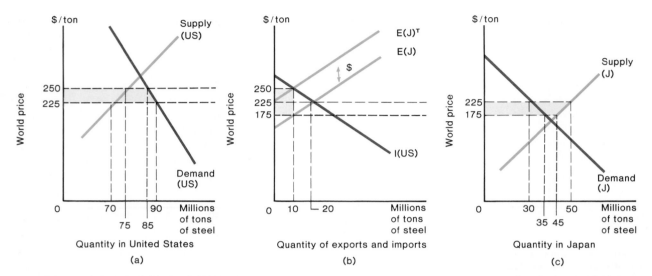

Figure 31.2   Effects of a United States tariff on steel imports
When the United States imposes a tariff on steel imported from Japan, the supply of Japanese exports is shifted upward to $E(J)^T$. As a result, the price of steel to United States buyers rises to $250 while the price received by Japanese producers falls to $175 per ton. Both Japanese producers and United States consumers lose some of their gains from trade as shown by the shaded areas in parts (a) and (c). The United States does gain tariff revenues (customs duties), however, as shown by the shaded area in part (b).

northern states obtained the tariff protection they wanted. The Smoot-Hawley tariff of 1930 raised the average tariff to 59 percent. This tariff was a hysterical attempt to shield the United States from a worldwide depression. Instead, the domestic and international economies were adversely affected by the increase in protection for United States import-competing industries.

A Tariff on Steel Imports from Japan
Figure 31.2 illustrates the effects of a tariff on the price, quantity demanded, and production of steel.[5] If there were no tariff, international trade between Japan and the United States would occur at the equilibrium price of $225 per ton. (You may wish to review the discussion of the gains from trade on pages 634–38 before going on.) Suppose that the United States government levies a tariff of, say, $75 per ton of steel, which must be paid by Japanese exporters for every ton they sell to the United States. As a result, the Japanese export supply curve in part (b) of figure 31.2 will shift to the line $E(J)^T$. At any given quantity of steel exports, the difference between the line $E(J)^T$ and the initial export supply curve $E(J)$ equals the fixed dollar amount of the United States tariff. This shift occurs because the price of steel must reflect its production costs plus the tariff if exporters are to avoid losses. Given the upward shift of Japan's export supply curve, the price of $225 per ton no longer equates United States imports and Japanese exports. The tariff

has increased the selling costs of Japanese firms whenever they ship goods to United States buyers. As a result, the volume of steel that Japanese producers wish to export to the United States at each price will decline. This is illustrated by the shift from E(J) to E(J)^T.

The tariff raises the price of Japanese steel in the United States. As a result, United States consumers will switch expenditures from high-priced Japanese steel to domestic steel. The switch in consumer demand to United States products will induce United States firms to expand production in response to higher prices. The excess demand pressure within the United States market increases the United States price of steel until it finally reaches $250 per ton. At this price, E(J)^T crosses I(US), and the sum of United States production plus Japanese exports again equals the total quantity of steel demanded by United States buyers.

Equivalently, United States steel importers must pay enough for the steel they purchase from Japan to cover Japanese producers' opportunity costs plus the tariff now imposed by the United States government. Thus, it makes no difference to our analysis whether we show Japan's export supply curve shifting upward by $75 per ton or the United States' import demand curve shifting downward by the same amount. To make sure you understand that it makes no difference whether United States importers or Japanese exporters actually write the check paying the United States government's tariff bill, redraw part (b) of figure 31.2, shifting I(US) down by $75 instead of shifting E(J) up. Show that exactly the same effects on the price in the United States and the level of production in the United States occur.

The price effects of the United States tariff on imported steel are precisely the opposite in the Japanese steel market. Notice in part (b) of figure 31.2 that the volume of Japanese exports has declined from 20 million tons to 10 million tons. (Remember that the price Japanese producers now actually receive for their steel is $175 per ton, which is less than the domestic United States price of $250 per ton by the amount of the tariff that has to be paid.) Since Japanese exports equal the difference between Japan's supply and demand curves for steel, the tariff induced decline in United States exports will make this difference smaller. The gap between supply and demand in Japan will close only if the Japanese price of steel falls. In other words, at the initial world price of $225 per ton, the tariff creates a state of excess supply in the Japanese market that can only be eliminated by a reduction in the Japanese price of steel. In part (c) of figure 31.2, the price of steel prevailing in Japan after the introduction of the United States tariff is $175.

The tariff, then, raises United States prices and lowers Japanese steel prices. In Japan, the lower price induces a reduction in the quantity of steel produced by Japanese firms and an increase in the quantity purchased by Japanese buyers. As part (c) of figure 31.2 shows, Japanese production now equals 45 million tons, while consumption is 35 million tons. In the United States, on the other hand, the higher price stimulates United States production of steel and reduces the quantity purchased by United States steel users. In part (a) of figure 31.2, the new quantity of steel supplied by United States firms equals 75 million tons, while purchases fall to 85 million tons.

Aggregate Economic Losses

We will now evaluate the tariff in terms of benefits and losses for United States citizens. For the same reasons that introducing free trade leads to an aggregate gain for society, reducing the amount of trade by means of a tariff results in an aggregate economic loss. Needless to say, the principal victims of the tariff are United States buyers, who now pay a higher price and

*A **specific duty** is a tariff equal to a specified amount per unit of an imported item.*

*An **ad valorem tariff** is defined in percentage terms rather than a specific amount.*

purchase a smaller quantity of steel. Because of the tariff, fewer goods requiring steel will be bought by United States citizens over a given period of time. The winners are United States steel producers, who had been threatened with elimination from the steel market by Japanese competitors or who would have remained in the market, receiving lower economic rents than they do with a tariff. Another group of winners are those who benefit from the tariff revenues (customs duties) collected by the United States government.

We can see the extent to which the tariff on steel imports into the United States would reduce economic efficiency in the United States by again referring to part (a) of figure 31.2. The total shaded area represents the total losses to United States steel users from tariffs on steel imports from Japan. The shaded area bounded by the price axis and the United States supply curve is redistributed from consumers to producers in the form of increased sales revenues above and beyond the costs of expanding United States production from 70 million tons to 75 million tons. The part of the shaded area below the United States supply curve between an output of 70 million tons and 75 million tons is the increased expenditure by steel users needed to cover increased United States production costs. That part of the shaded area is called the *deadweight loss* associated with having the additional 5 million tons of steel produced in the United States when Japanese steel producers could have supplied that same steel at a price of $225 per ton rather than $250 per ton. It represents a net loss to society, resulting from reduced economic efficiency. A deadweight loss simply means that the decreased economic well-being of steel users is not offset by increased income for steel producers. This deadweight loss arises even though producers receive additional revenue from steel users. The additional revenue is just sufficient, however, to cover their costs, which are higher than the costs of Japanese steel producers.

The shaded area between 75 million tons and 85 million tons is equal to the consumer loss that is transferred from steel users to the government in the form of tariff revenue. Finally, the loss equal to the shaded area under the United States demand curve bounded by 85 million tons and 90 million tons is also called *deadweight loss.* That area represents lost economic well-being resulting from the artificial rise in the price of steel, which reduces total domestic consumption of steel from 90 million tons to 85 million. By artificially raising the price of steel in the United States from $225 per ton to $250 per ton the tariff induces consumers to reduce their consumption of steel. Remember that the area under the demand curve and above the price paid for steel represents the value steel users receive over the price they pay. Therefore, reducing consumption of steel artificially by imposing a tariff eliminates a portion of the value that steel users had received from their purchases.

To summarize, the tariff reduces total economic well-being by diverting steel production from efficient Japanese producers to more expensive domestic producers in the United States and by inducing United States purchasers to reduce their consumption of steel. The benefits they receive from the goods they substitute for the steel they no longer purchase are not perfect substitutes for the steel. Thus, consumers cannot completely offset the increased cost of steel by switching to other goods.

Specific Duties versus ad Valorem Tariffs

In discussing the effects of tariffs, we have taken the simplest possible example, in which the government imposes a specific dollar tax, called a **specific duty,** on a particular good, such as steel. Most countries today impose tariffs in percentage terms (for example a 5 percent tariff or a 10 percent tariff) rather than in specific duty form. A tariff defined as a percentage import tax is called an **ad valorem tariff,** which means that the tariff depends on the value of the imported item.

Nontariff trade barriers (NTBs) are nonprice trade restrictions.

*A **quota** is an NTB that limits the quantity of an imported good that may be sold in a country.*

Prior to the twentieth century, almost all tariffs were in the form of specific duties. Unlike ad valorem tariffs, which tend to raise the relative price of all grades of a particular product to the same extent, specific duties represent a higher *percentage* tax on relatively cheap varieties of a product than on the more expensive ones. A specific duty of $75 per ton on imported steel would represent a 50 percent tariff on low-quality steel costing only $150 per ton but only a 25 percent tax on high-quality steel that costs $300 per ton. Therefore, a specific duty is more protective of domestic production of low-quality brands than high-quality brands of products. By contrast, an ad valorem tariff is neutral in its protective effect on the various grades of a product.

We will now discuss two historical examples of the use of specific duties in the United States that did promote the production of low-quality goods rather than high-quality goods within given product lines.

Protection of United States Textile Manufacturing In the period preceding the Civil War, the United States was struggling to become competitive with Britain in textile production. The British had an overwhelming comparative advantage in the production of fine fabrics of all kinds and a modest advantage in the production of coarse fabrics of various types. The tariff of 1828 included a specific duty on cotton textiles. All imported cloth that cost $0.35 per yard or more was taxed at the ad valorem rate of 25 percent. However, all imported cloth costing less than $0.35 would be treated as if it cost $0.35 and taxed $0.0875 per yard. Thus, the United States tariff schedule indicated a tariff rate of about 25 percent on imported cotton textiles. However, the actual price of plain cotton sheeting imports in 1830 was close to $0.11 per yard. Therefore, the actual average percentage tariff in 1830 was close to 80 percent (0.0875/0.11), with the rate higher for low-quality than high-quality imports.[6] The United States produced mostly low-quality cotton sheeting at a price of $0.13 per yard. Obviously, then, the specific duty of $0.0875 per yard favored United States production of low-quality cotton textiles while not prohibiting imports of high-quality fabrics from Britain.

Protection of the United States Steel Industry In the last part of the nineteenth century—particularly prior to 1896—the United States developed a strong domestic pig iron industry. At the same time it remained highly dependent on Scotland and England to provide imports of high-quality alloy steels. Throughout the period 1870–99 the specific duty averaged $6.43 per ton. Empirical evidence suggests that the specific duty directly induced a shift of imports away from the low-price steels, which competed directly with emerging United States production. Imports shifted toward high-quality iron and steel products needed but not yet produced in the United States.[7]

In each of the cases described here, there was a definite preference on the part of domestic producers to have protection skewed toward low-quality goods that they produced without needlessly raising the price of high-quality imports substantially. Specific duties work quite well in such cases.

Quotas and Other Nontariff Trade Barriers (NTBs)

Nontariff trade barriers (NTBs) are simply nonprice forms of international trade restrictions. Probably the most common form of NTB is the **quota,** which assigns a definite limit to the amount of goods that can be imported into a country. In our example of the steel market, the United States government can establish a quota on steel by arbitrarily declaring the maximum quantity of steel that it will permit Japan to ship to the United States market.[8] The basic effects of a quota are parallel to those of a tariff, and similar winners and losers emerge from quota intervention as from tariff legislation. When a quota is applied to imports from a specific country like Japan, the main issue is the selection of the lucky exporters from among the entire set of Japanese firms and whether the United States government will collect any revenue from the quota arrangement. One can envision many possibilities, ranging from a lottery system to a collection of license fees by the United States government.

Revenue Needs and the Shift to NTBs

Unless the government can conduct a competitive auction for licenses to purchase quota-restricted imports, government revenues will be less with a quota or other NTB than with an equally restrictive tariff. Therefore, until a government finds suitable alternatives to tariffs to meet its revenue needs, policymakers will have a natural preference for tariffs over quotas. The general shift in protectionism away from tariffs in the last fifty years may partially reflect the decline in government preferences for tariffs relative to other forms of trade restrictions. For many developing countries, tariff revenue is critical as a source of government funding. Ad valorem tariffs have the advantage that during periods of general inflation and resulting increased government expenses, tariff revenues increase automatically.

NTBs and the Tariff Revenue Equivalent

NTBs result in price increases that must be paid by buyers who can no longer obtain imports, just as tariffs do. However, the shaded area in part (a) of figure 31.2 that represents tariff revenue is no longer received by the government of the importing country because there is no tariff. Different NTBs will result in different distributions of the increased amount paid for imported items that might have ended up as tariff revenue. The government of the importing nation can direct the price increase benefits to either domestic or to foreign producers or their government. This added element of flexibility associated with NTBs may make it possible for domestic industry pressure groups to lobby successfully for nontariff barriers to trade when it might prove impossible to gain tariff protection.

The most common NTB is a quota. However, there are other devices. One is a "domestic content" requirement that a certain proportion of the value of imported items be made with parts manufactured in the importing nation. Another is "minimum quality" requirements for imported items, such as a minimum size for tomatoes imported from Mexico. If Mexican farmers' comparative advantage is in producing small tomatoes, a minimum-size requirement makes it more difficult for them to export tomatoes to the United States and thus protects United States tomato growers.

"Voluntary" Quotas

International trade currently operates under a set of rules governing what are "fair" and "unfair" trade practices. We will have more to say about the generally accepted rules governing appropriate and inappropriate barriers to trade later in this chapter. When it cannot be established that an exporting country has engaged in an unfair international trade practice, it violates international rules to increase a tariff or to impose a quota to protect domestic producers. However, another tactic that produces the same effect as a quota is to negotiate a "voluntary" export restraint with the exporting country. Clearly, any act, "voluntary" or not, that reduces imports below the level that would prevail in unimpeded international trade has many of the effects discussed for mandatory quotas.

Imports and the United States Auto Industry   "Voluntary" quotas on Japanese auto exports to the United States have been used to protect United States automobile manufacturers in recent years. Japanese automobile producers have developed a significant cost advantage over United States producers of small cars. One analysis comparing the Toyota Corolla and the Chevrolet Chevette in 1983 found that the Japanese could deliver a car to the United States at a cost of $1,718 less than the cost of a comparable vehicle produced within the United States. None of this cost differential was attributable to a Japanese government subsidy. Over half was due to better Japanese management systems and less than a third to lower Japanese labor compensation.[9] Quotas of any kind, of course, limit the degree to which this Japanese cost advantage is passed on to United States consumers. In 1983, the Japanese government announced the intention to end its voluntary quotas on auto exports to the United States.[10]

In fact, however, the Japanese extended their voluntary restriction on total exports of automobiles to the United States market into 1986. When President Reagan indicated in March 1985 that the United States would not ask Japan to continue to limit its automobile exports to the United States, the Japanese themselves indicated that they would continue to limit exports anyway. Why do you suppose the Japanese would voluntarily restrict their own sales of automobiles in the United States?

Imports were a fairly small share of the total automobile market in the United States until the late 1960s.[11] Rising imports were probably stimulated by rapidly rising United States automobile prices and increasing skepticism about the United States automobile industry's ability to meet federally mandated emission control standards and still produce high-quality automobiles. Between 1973 and 1974–75, a recession sharply reduced automobile purchases. Total new registrations fell by almost 30 percent, and most of this represented reduced purchases of domestically produced cars. Import sales were buoyed during the recession by rapidly rising gasoline prices as consumers switched to fuel-efficient foreign cars. By 1978, both total and domestic automobile sales were close to their 1973 levels. The rapid rise in the price of oil following the Iranian revolution in 1979 depressed total car sales and promoted an even larger shift of consumer demand toward fuel-efficient imports. The one-third drop in domestically produced new car sales between 1978 and 1981 led to considerable pressure on the United States government to limit foreign automobile imports into the United States.

By 1981, Japanese imports were judged by consumers to be much better than cars made in the United States.[12] Chrysler's financial woes in the early 1980s were surely related to the low-quality ratings given to Chrysler cars by consumers. At the same time, the hourly wage in automobile production in the United States remained more than 50 percent above the hourly wage rate in United States manufacturing in general and, as recently as 1983, 140 percent higher than the hourly wage rate in automobile production in Japan.[13]

In response to the disaster rapidly approaching for the United States automobile industry, Congress threatened to impose severe barriers on Japanese car exports to the United States. To avoid what might have been a worse outcome for them, the Japanese "volunteered" to restrict their exports to an agreed quota.

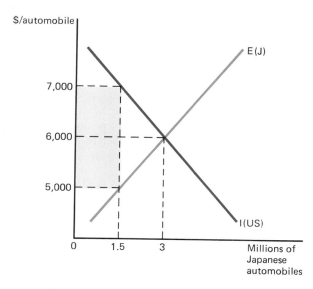

Figure 31.3   A "voluntary" quota on Japanese automobile exports to the United States
I(US) is the United States import demand for Japanese automobiles, and E(J) is the Japanese export supply. Without voluntary quotas, the United States price of Japanese automobiles would be $6,000, and 3 million cars would be sold to the United States. The voluntary quota system reduces Japanese cars exported to the United States to 1.5 million. The actual marginal cost of supplying cars to the United States falls to $5,000. Japanese automobile producers benefit to an extent indicated by the shaded area, which is equal to $3 billion.

Quota Rents to Japanese Exporters   Figure 31.3 illustrates the United States import demand for Japanese automobiles and the Japanese export supply curve. The curves I(US) and E(J) represent the United States import demand for Japanese automobiles and the export supply curve for automobiles from Japan. Unrestricted trade would result in imports equal to 3 million automobiles at a price of $6,000 each. With imports from Japan artificially restricted by an export quota of 1.5 million automobiles, the United States price of Japanese automobiles will rise to $7,000. The shaded area in figure 31.3 would have amounted to tariff revenues if a tariff had been used to restrict imports to 1.5 million automobiles. This area now represents additional profits of $3 billion to Japanese producers who are lucky enough to gain government permission to export automobiles to the United States.

*The **General Agreement on Tariffs and Trade (GATT)** is an agreement that was reached by most nations after World War II to reduce trade barriers, such as tariffs and quotas, and to discourage "unfair" competition on the world market through the use of export subsidies.*

Recall that even when President Reagan indicated in March 1985 that the United States would not ask Japan to continue to voluntarily restrict exports, the Japanese indicated they would do so anyway. Clearly, existing major producers in Japan who have obtained export licenses and are able to export autos to the United States will lobby the Japanese government to keep the quotas in order to protect their monopoly rents and protect themselves from other Japanese manufacturers trying to gain access to the United States market.

Estimates of Gains and Losses   Our discussion of quotas and tariffs has indicated that producers in the United States gain and consumers lose when imports are restricted. Through early 1985, the accumulated cost of restricting Japanese automobile imports to the United States economy was $3.6 billion. This resulted from a loss of $4 billion to consumers and a gain of only $0.4 billion to domestic producers. The cost of each dollar of automobile workers' earnings protected in the United States was estimated to be $23.90 to consumers and $21.41 to the economy at large. The accumulated deadweight loss of quotas on Japanese auto imports was estimated to be approximately $3 billion. This is an indication that the deadweight loss to the United States of restrictions on imports of Japanese cars was quite high.[14]

The General Agreement on Tariffs and Trade (GATT), "Fair" Competition, and Trade Restrictions

Following World War II, the vast majority of nations signed the **General Agreement on Tariffs and Trade (GATT),** which is intended to promote trade among the nations of the world by lowering tariffs, quotas, and other barriers. As a result of several conferences, the nations participating in GATT have greatly reduced trade barriers since the late 1940s. This is reflected in the decline in average tariff rates shown in figure 31.1.

The Rules of the Game and "Unfair" Trade Practices

The GATT also defines a number of "unfair" trade practices. If a nation engages in certain proscribed behavior, such as subsidizing its exports so that they compete "unfairly" with those of other nations, the countries whose exports are affected can retaliate with countervailing measures. Export subsidies can occur through various channels besides direct payments to companies that export goods or services. A government may provide low-interest loans, remit taxes, or take any action that lowers the cost of exported goods relative to those sold domestically. If a country thinks it is harmed by such subsidies, it can impose import duties (tariffs) to offset the subsidies of a nation that violates GATT, or it can impose quotas on imports from that nation.

It is an open question whether a nation is well advised to retaliate against "unfair" trade practices that lower the costs of its imports. If Great Britain uses its taxpayers' money to subsidize exports to the United States, it is essentially taxing its citizens to raise the standard of living of American citizens. Producers in Great Britain do benefit, of course, but not as much as British consumers lose. To see this, review figure 31.2 and the discussion of the winners and losers when a tariff is imposed. If Japan were to subsidize steel exports to the United States by, say, $75 per ton, this would lower the E(J) curve in part (b) of figure 31.2 by $75. You may wish to redraw figure 31.2 to show the impact of an export subsidy by Japan. You will see that the effects are opposite those of the $75 tariff. The subsidy-distorted export supply curve will be shifted downward to the right of E(J). Steel trade will increase, the price of steel in Japan will rise, and Japanese consumers will be worse off. Moreover, the difference between the marginal cost of steel and the new, lower export price is paid by Japan's taxpayers. This amounts to a gift from Japan to the United States. In the United States, the price of steel will fall, consumers will be better off, and producers will suffer, along with their employees.

Following the analysis in our discussion of the distribution of the gains from trade in chapter 30, it is fairly easy to show that the subsidy will benefit American consumers more than it harms American producers and workers. However, the same pressures that might lead the United States government to restrict any trade with Japan will also tempt it to retaliate against Japan's export subsidy. It is a question of the distribution of the gains within the United States. Furthermore, retaliation against real or alleged unfair trade practices may spill over into other markets, resulting in a general increase in trade barriers. Probably the most forceful argument against one country's subsidizing its exports to another, then, is that such practices increase the political pressure by producer groups for general protection from imports. To the extent that the rules of the game seem unfair to some, it is more difficult for governments to resist the ever present pressure to erect international trade barriers.

As you might expect, domestic firms frequently charge that foreign governments unfairly subsidize exports to obtain protection from import competition. Sometimes these charges are well founded, but it is often very difficult to document the exact amount of such subsidies. Domestic firms and their employees naturally tend to see the main problem they face as unfair foreign export tactics rather than their own high costs, less advanced technology, or poorer management techniques.

Two industries in which import competition has been particularly severe in the United States are steel and automobiles. We have already discussed the use of "voluntary" quotas to protect the United States automobile industry.

When the United States had rich iron ore deposits, it had a comparative advantage in the production of many forms of steel. Over the years, the richest United States iron ore deposits were exhausted. As a result, this advantage began to shift to other countries that do not necessarily have access to rich iron ore but that do have lower cost labor. In addition, some of these steel exporters have subsidized steel exports. This underlies why steel producers in the United States petitioned the United States Department of Commerce and International Trade Commission to impose countervailing tariffs on steel imports from countries violating GATT.[15]

The principal reason for growing steel imports into the United States, however, is not export subsidies but rather lower manufacturing costs in exporting nations. For example, in 1981 almost one-third of United States steel imports came from Japan, which was not found to subsidize its exports.[16] Moreover, the most rapid growth in world steel production capacity is occurring in several "advanced developing countries" (ADCs). Among ADCs, only Brazil was found to subsidize its steel exports. In the United States, average total hourly compensation (wages plus fringe benefits) of steelworkers in 1981 was $19.42 compared to $12.18 in petroleum refining, $11.89 in coal mining, and $11.01 in motor vehicles.[17] Even in Canada, where wage rates are frequently as high as those of the United States, steelworkers' hourly compensation was only $12.63 in 1981. (Canada supplied about 15 percent of United States steel imports in 1981.) In Japan, the average steelworker received $10.15 per hour.[18] In ADCs, compensation was still lower. It is evident that significant wage adjustments must occur if the United States steel industry is to retain a significant share of the domestic market for steel. The collective bargaining agreement signed in 1983 between the United Steelworkers' Union and the major United States steel producers reflected an attempt to bring labor costs more in line with those of steelworkers in other countries.[19]

The Trade Expansion Act of 1962

Despite all of the pressures for protection from industries harmed by import competition, Congress also responds to the desires of consumer groups and export industries, which benefit from free trade. To reduce political pressure for tariffs and quotas, Congress

The **Trade Expansion Act of 1962** authorized government financial assistance to workers who were designated as displaced and firms that went out of business because of foreign competition.

A **customs union** is a group of nations that impose a common set of trade barriers against the rest of the world but none among themselves.

A **common market** is a customs union that also allows the free movement of labor and capital among its member countries.

passed the **Trade Expansion Act of 1962,** which provided trade adjustment assistance (TAA) in the form of financial aid to workers and firms judged to have been displaced by international competition. Other countries have passed similar legislation. Under TAA, financial aid was paid for retraining and relocation into industries less threatened by imports. By 1981, the costs of adjustment assistance in the United States had become much larger than anticipated, and most forms were eliminated. One reason the costs became so large is that firms and workers increasingly sought compensation for harm from all forms of competition—international and domestic. Moreover, a majority of workers who received TAA either returned to jobs in their original industries or retired when their TAA benefits ran out. It is often difficult to discover why a company is failing when others in the same industry survive. It seemed to many observers that it was no fairer to protect workers and firms from the effects of foreign than of domestic competition. This weakened support for adjustment assistance in principle.

Customs Unions

The GATT agreement and the successive rounds of tariff reductions to liberalize international trade are examples of attempts to coordinate trade policies to the mutual benefit of participating nations.

Another example of an attempt to coordinate trade policies with a view toward mutual benefit is the establishment of a **customs union,** which is a group of nations that remove international trade restrictions among themselves while maintaining common external barriers with nonmember nations. Such arrangements are permitted under GATT even though they clearly discriminate against trade with some nations and in favor of trade with other nations. The simple argument for the GATT exception is that any move toward free trade, even among a few nations, is a step in the "right" direction.

Clearly, the best-known example of a customs union is the *European Economic Community (EEC),* which was established in 1957–58 by the Treaty of Rome. France, West Germany, Italy, Belgium, the

Netherlands, and Luxembourg agreed to eliminate trade barriers among themselves and to develop common external trade barriers over time between 1958 and mid-1968. Only a few years earlier, Belgium, the Netherlands, and Luxembourg integrated their economies in the form of Benelux. The Stockholm convention of 1960 created the European Free Trade Association, EFTA, as a rival trade agreement. The seven original members Austria, Denmark, Norway, Portugal, Sweden, Switzerland, and the United Kingdom agreed to remove trade barriers among themselves in stages over the period from 1960 to 1965. Finland and Iceland joined EFTA in 1961 and 1970, respectively.

Denmark, Ireland, and the United Kingdom joined the EEC in 1972–73, Greece in 1981, and Spain and Portugal in 1985. In the interim, trade barriers were removed among the nine (prior to the addition of Greece) and with the remaining EFTA countries during the mid-1970s. Trade preference agreements have also been reached with most nonmember Mediterranean countries similar to those reached earlier with developing countries (most of which were former colonies of EEC countries). The earliest agreements included those with Greece in 1961, Turkey in 1964, and Spain and Malta in 1970. In fact, Turkey is likely to become the next full member of the EEC.

Before turning to an assessment of the gains and losses associated with forming a customs union, we should note that beginning in late 1968, the members of the EEC agreed to form the Common Market. A **common market** differs from a customs union by permitting labor and capital to move freely among member nations. That process of further integration was fairly complete by the late 1970s. The next step is to form an **economic union,** which is an integrated community in which monetary and fiscal policy are fully coordinated. The European community has been wrestling with this next step for more than ten years.

Figure 31.4 illustrates the potential short-term gains and losses associated with the formation of a customs union. The demand and supply curves are domestic demand and supply for computer terminals. With no trade, the domestic price would be $400 per

*An **economic union** is a common market in which the member countries coordinate their monetary and fiscal policies.*

*The **trade creation effects of a customs union** are the increased gains from trade resulting from expanded imports and exports within the union.*

*The **trade diversion effects of a customs union** are the reduced gains from trade resulting from diminished imports from countries outside the union.*

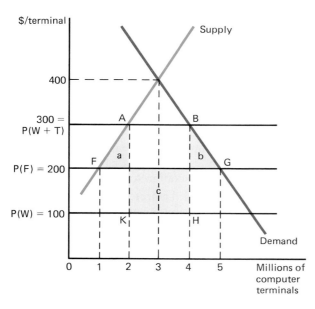

Figure 31.4   The effect of a customs union on the gains from trade
This diagram shows the domestic demand and supply for computer terminals. P(W) = $100 is the world supply curve for computer terminals, and P(F) = $200 is the foreign trade partner's supply curve. The curve P(W + T) = $300 is the world supply curve facing domestic consumers when a tariff, T = $200, is imposed. Before the customs union is formed, imports are from the world market at price P(W) = $100. At the domestic price of P(W + T) = $300, imports equal two million, and tariff revenue equals the area ABHK, or $400 million. A customs union expands trade by lowering the domestic price to $200. Imports expand to 5 million. The expansion of trade leads to trade creation gains equal to the shaded areas a and b, or $150 million. Tariff revenue is zero, and area c represents the trade diversion losses associated with the increased cost of the original two million imports from a less-efficient trade partner. The diversion losses in this case equal $200 million.

these supply curves are completely elastic because the country depicted in figure 31.4 is small relative to the world market for traded goods. Hence, it is a price taker in international trade.) Initially, the home country imposes a specific duty of T = $200 per unit of imports on all its trading partners. Imports will come exclusively from the world market—that is, there is no trade with the potential trading partner. The domestic price of imports is therefore equal to P(W + T) = $300, and imports equal 2 million terminals. Domestic production equals 2 million terminals, and tariff revenue equals the area ABHK, or $400 million.

If a customs union is formed with a potential trading partner, the domestic price of imports from that partner will fall to P(F) = $200, while the domestic price of the same product from the rest of the world will still be P(W + T) = $300. Imports will shift entirely from the world market to the new trading partner. Since the domestic price falls, domestic production, which is relatively inefficient, falls to 1 million terminals. The decline in price benefits consumers who can now buy more imported goods at lower prices. Imports expand from 2 million terminals to 5 million terminals. Areas a and b represent the net improvement in economic well-being arising from the gains from increased trade and are called the **trade creation effects of a customs union.** In the case illustrated, areas a and b are equal in total value to $150 million.

Once the customs union is formed, all of the imports are purchased from the trading partner within the customs union rather than from the more efficient world market. Therefore, tariff revenue falls to zero. Some of the income that had gone to the government before the customs union was formed has been redistributed to consumers through cheaper import prices. However, the shaded area c, representng income that had been collected as tariff revenue, now goes to the trading partner to pay for imports. The cost of the initial level of imports of 2 million terminals has increased by an amount equal to area c, or $200 million because trade has been diverted from the lowest-cost world producers to a less efficient customs union partner. That loss of gains from trade is referred to as a **trade diversion effect of a customs union.**

terminal and the domestic output would be 3 million units. If we assume that the country depicted in figure 31.4 would benefit from trade with another country in a customs union or with the world as a whole, we would expect trade to lower the price of traded goods and lead to gains from trade as discussed in chapter 30.

The horizontal line P(W) = $100 represents the world supply curve of traded goods facing this country, and P(F) = $200 is the supply curve of a potential trading partner within a customs union. (We assume

If you study figure 31.4 carefully, you will see that the more inelastic the domestic demand and supply curves are, the smaller the trade creation effects of a customs union will be. The less efficient are trading partners within the union relative to the world market—that is, the higher is P(F) relative to P(W)—the greater will be the trade-diverting effects of a customs union. Demand and supply curves for agricultural products tend to be fairly inelastic, and European agricultural production is not very efficient relative to the rest of the world. Therefore, it is not surprising that one of the most divisive issues within the EEC has been the structure of its common agricultural plan, which includes import restrictions on agricultural exports from nonpartner countries. This protection against non-EEC agricultural products is the source of some estrangement between the EEC and the United States because the United States is a lower-cost producer of agricultural products than the EEC countries. Note in the simple case of the computer terminals that the trade diversion costs actually exceed the trade creation effects by $50 million.

It is hoped that in the long run the benefits associated with access to a larger and freer market will offset any short-term negative effects of a customs union. However, clear-cut evidence on whether the gains from trade creation exceed the costs of trade diversion does not yet exist in the case of the EEC.

▶ Summary and Conclusions

What do you now think of the message on the grocery bag that illustrated our introductory discussion? In this chapter we explored the reasons why most nations have erected some barriers to free international trade and the means chosen to do it. The following major points were emphasized.

Tariffs have been important revenue sources for governments of countries that have not developed effective internal taxation schemes.

National security and the protection of infant industries are two arguments used by proponents of import restrictions.

Tariffs and quotas reduce international economic efficiency and create winners and losers that were among the groups of losers and winners from unrestricted trade.

Specific duties protect relatively cheap varieties of products, whereas ad valorem tariffs are financially neutral in this regard.

Legal and voluntary quotas are the primary forms of nontariff barriers to international trade. Quotas typically create economic rents for the holder of the import license.

The General Agreement on Tariffs and Trade (GATT) has led to reduced trade barriers and defines a number of "unfair" trade practices.

Customs unions exhibit both trade creation and trade diversion effects by encouraging trade between member nations and discouraging trade with countries outside the customs union.

▶ Key Terms

ad valorem tariff *650*

common market *656*

customs union *656*

economic union *657*

General Agreement on Tariffs and Trade (GATT) *654*

import substitution *646*

infant industry argument *645*

nontariff trade barriers (NTBs) *651*

quota *651*

specific duty *650*

tariff *647*

trade creation effects of a customs union *657*

trade diversion effects of a customs union *657*

Trade Expansion Act of 1962 *656*

▶ Questions for Discussion and Review

1. Why might a developing country use a tariff rather than subsidized loans or tax credits to promote industrialization?

2. Why do developing countries want to develop export markets for manufactured goods?

3. Illustrate and explain the net production and consumption losses from a tariff.

4. Illustrate and explain the distribution of quota rents to exporters when voluntary export restrictions are imposed on a product.

5. Illustrate and explain government revenue gains from the competitive auction of import licenses for a quota-restricted commodity.

6. Explain why a specific duty tends to limit imports of low-quality goods more than high-quality goods.

7. Explain why governments in developed countries might have a relative preference for NTBs to restrict trade while governments in developing countries might have a relative preference for tariffs to restrict trade.

8. What is the infant industry argument for import restrictions?

9. What factors help to explain the rapid rise of the import share in United States automobile sales between 1965 and 1985?

10. Illustrate and explain the welfare effects of trade creation.

Chapter 32

Monetary and Macroeconomic Aspects of International Trade

Outline

I. Introduction *662*
II. Paying for foreign trade: Currency's role *663*
   A. The supply and demand for foreign currency *664*
      1. Fixed exchange rates *666*
      2. Flexible exchange rates *667*
III. The balance of payments and the balance of trade *669*
   A. Equilibrium and disequilibrium *672*
IV. The international transmission mechanism *674*
V. Macroeconomic influences on the United States balance of trade and international financial flows *675*
   A. Inflation and the trade balance *675*
   B. Macroeconomic policy, interest rates, and international financial flows *675*
VI. Summary and conclusions *678*
VII. Key terms *678*
VIII. Questions for discussion and review *678*
IX. Appendix: International financial cooperation *680*
   A. The International Monetary Fund and the World Bank *680*
   B. Eurodollars and Eurocurrency banking *681*
   C. Key terms *681*

Objectives

After reading this chapter, the student should be able to:

Explain how systems of fixed and flexible exchange rates operate in terms of the supply and demand for foreign currency.

Discuss the balance of trade and its significance compared to the balance of payments.

Analyze the effects of foreign exchange intervention.

Show how a macroeconomic disturbance in one nation can be transferred to another nation.

Explain the trade deficit of the United States during the 1970s and early 1980s and why it was not eliminated by changes in exchange rates.

Discuss the past and present roles of the International Monetary Fund and the World Bank.

Discuss the role of Eurodollars and Eurocurrency banks in the international economy.

▶ Introduction

In early 1980 two young business people founded promising international firms. One was Rick, a whiz-kid computer technician in Dallas, Texas. The other was Helga, a bright computer scientist in West Germany. Each began producing and selling what are called dumb computer terminals (used with minicomputers for word processing and scientific computing) for sale in Germany. Both Rick and Helga are capable business people who produced quality products. Nevertheless, by February 1985 their businesses had failed. The common link between them was the rapid rise in the value of the United States dollar relative to the West German deutsche mark (DM). This was the primary cause of their financial ruin. The change was something that neither of them had anticipated or understood. Between the beginning of 1980 and February 1985 the deutsche mark price of United States dollars rose 55 percent, from DM 2.1 to DM 3.25. Let us briefly consider what happened to each business.

Rick began selling his terminals in West Germany for $200 each and found that he could hardly produce enough of them to meet his customers' needs. By early 1985, Rick had managed to keep producing his terminals for $200 each but could find no one to buy them.

Helga borrowed $2 million from a large New York bank to finance her business. She sold her terminals in West Germany for DM 210 each and paid about DM 50 on each terminal she sold to meet her loan payments. By early 1985, it was clear that to maintain the 1980 level of sales she would have to recover DM 77.4 for loan payments. Since none of her other costs of production had changed, she could not cover all of her costs unless she charged DM 237.4 for each of her computers. Unfortunately, at that price she could not find many buyers and had to discontinue production.

In this chapter we will explain how changes in the price of one currency in terms of another can occur and how such changes interact with the flow of goods and services among nations. This will explain how the changes in the deutsche mark price of the United States dollar between 1980 and 1985 caused Rick's and Helga's businesses to fail. We will then extend our analysis of international economic relationships to show how the macroeconomic performances of the world's economies are related by trade. We will use the macroeconomic model developed in chapters 19 through 29 to explain how the United States and other economies have performed in the recent past and how their macroeconomies have been affected by international trade and finance.

A foreign exchange rate is the amount of one country's currency (money) that it takes to buy one unit of another country's currency.

▶ Paying for Foreign Trade: Currency's Role

In chapters 30 and 31 we analyzed international trade in terms of the exchange of exports for imports. An example would be the United States exporting wheat to Japan in exchange for Japanese automobiles. Although treating trade between two nations as though it involved *bartering* one set of goods for another emphasizes many important aspects of international markets, it is incomplete. After all, a Kansas wheat farmer may prefer American cars to Japanese imports. More important, if the farmer did accept a Japanese car as payment, how would he find an American car dealer who would accept the Japanese car in exchange? What if the farmer did not want an automobile at all but preferred to use the income received from selling wheat to Japan to buy clothes or pay college tuition for the children? These problems do not usually arise as a result of international transactions for the same reason that they do not plague trade among domestic firms and consumers: *Money is used as a medium of exchange in international transactions just as within every market economy.* The farmer does not receive automobiles for the wheat sold to Japan; the farmer receives dollars that the Japanese importers purchased with yen. Similarly, the Japanese auto exporters receive yen that American importers purchased with dollars.

Trade among nations requires the use of *money* for the same reasons that trade among individuals in the same country does. Money greatly facilitates *specialization* in international trade just as it does at home. If means did not exist to exchange one nation's currency for another's, the production possibilities of the world's economy would be much smaller. Money is also used for international transactions that do not directly involve the exchange of one nation's goods for another's. It is used, for example, when a United States citizen wishes to purchase financial assets in another country, such as foreign government bonds or common stock of a firm in Japan, Great Britain, or Italy. Money is used when the United States government grants foreign aid to another nation to assist in

its economic development. Money is used when a United States bank lends funds to, say, the Mexican or Brazilian government, and it is required when these debts are repaid. The complication that arises in international trade is that each country uses its own currency so that foreign sales and purchases will inevitably involve exchanges of the currencies of the countries involved. This fact quickly gives rise to questions like how many Japanese yen can I buy with one United States dollar.

Because of the multiple uses for international currencies, the price of one nation's money in terms of another's, which is called the **foreign exchange rate,** can have an important influence on the quantity and type of goods traded among nations. For example, in 1984 and early 1985 the price of many European currencies—the British pound, the West German deutsche mark, the French franc, and others—fell abruptly in relation to the United States dollar. United States citizens found that they could purchase cashmere sweaters in Britain, luxury automobiles in Germany, and fancy dinners in Paris at bargain rates. Foreign travel accelerated as many Americans decided to take vacations abroad rather than at home. European firms catering to travelers were delighted; many United States firms lost sales and suffered lower profits.

Governments recognize the effect of foreign exchange rates on the volume and direction of trade. They frequently buy and sell their own currencies and those of other nations to influence exchange rates and thus control international trade. We will explore the impact of such actions in this chapter and chapter 33.

There are almost as many different currencies as there are nations—dollars for the United States, yen for Japan, pesos for Mexico, cruzeiros for Brazil, zlotis for Poland, and so on. To find out how the existence of different currencies affects the international economy, we must explore how foreign exchange rates are determined. We must also examine how countries settle their financial accounts with one another through the international balance of payments.

The foreign exchange market is where currencies are bought and sold; it is where foreign exchange rates are determined.

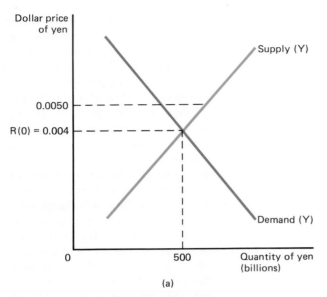

(a)

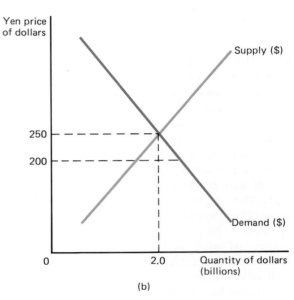

(b)

Figure 32.1   The supply and demand for foreign exchange
The exchange rate equates the quantity of yen demanded by United States citizens with the quantity of yen supplied by Japanese citizens. At the same time the quantity of dollars supplied by the United States is equated with the quantity demanded in Japan. If the price of yen in terms of dollars is

above equilibrium, say, $0.005, then there will be an excess supply of yen. If the exchange rate falls below R(0), there will be an excess demand for yen. If the equilibrium price of yen in terms of dollars is $0.004, then the equilibrium price of dollars in terms of yen is 1/$0.004 = 250 yen. The equilibrium quantities of yen and dollars are 500 billion yen and $2 billion, respectively.

The Supply and Demand for Foreign Currency

Suppose a United States exporter sells computer equipment to, say, a Japanese importer. The United States exporter, being a United States citizen and employing United States factors of production, will demand payment not in yen but in dollars. How, then, does the Japanese importer *convert* yen into dollars? The importer goes to a financial dealer in the **foreign exchange market,** where yen can be sold in return for dollars. The price determined in this foreign exchange market is the foreign exchange rate measuring the dollar price of yen and the yen price of dollars. For example, suppose the Japanese importer wants to purchase 5,000 yen worth of dollars and the exchange rate of dollars for yen is $0.004. (That is, the price of one yen is 4/1000 United States dollars.) Given this exchange rate, our importer could exchange 5,000 yen for $20.

The key question, of course, is what determines the exchange rate? Before answering this question, let us construct the demand and supply for foreign exchange (yen and dollars, for example). Figure 32.1 illustrates the foreign exchange market in which dollars and yen are traded. Because two currencies are involved, two sets of supply and demand curves are required. Part (a) of figure 32.1 illustrates the supply and demand for yen in terms of dollars, and part (b) depicts the supply and demand for dollars in terms of yen. On the horizontal axes we measure the quantities of yen and dollars, respectively; the vertical axes measure the dollar price of yen and the yen price of dollars. The supplies of yen and dollars to the foreign exchange market are drawn with a positive slope.

The main reason the supply curves are positively sloped is that as their respective exchange rates rise, Japanese citizens are able to acquire more dollars for each of their yen and Americans can purchase more yen with each dollar. That is, American products (expressed in dollar prices) become cheaper to Japanese citizens as the dollar price of yen increases, and Japanese goods (expressed in yen prices) become cheaper to United States citizens as the yen price of the dollar increases. For example, suppose an American-made microcomputer has a $100 price tag and the exchange rate is $0.004 per yen. This means that the computer costs 100/.004 = 25,000 yen. If the dollar price of the yen rises to $0.008 per yen, you can see that the Japanese price of the computer has fallen to 12,500 yen. Given an increase in the exchange rate of dollars for yen, Japanese citizens would have an incentive to buy larger quantities of American items. As Japanese importers expressed this desire in various United States markets, United States exports of many different items would rise. Japanese importers would need dollars, and they in turn would obtain them by supplying yen to the foreign exchange market. In other words, the supply of yen in figure 32.1, part (a), represents the demand for United States dollars by Japanese citizens depicted in part (b). Everything we have said about the supply of yen and the demand for dollars applies, of course, to the supply of dollars in part (a) of figure 32.1 and the demand for yen in part (b).

Suppose Japanese consumers demand ten American microcomputers with price tags of $100 each when the exchange rate is $0.004 per yen. Thus, Japan imports 250,000 yen worth ($1,000) of computers from the United States. If the value of the yen rises to $0.008 per yen, from the Japanese perspective this is equivalent to a decline in the unit price of microcomputers from 25,000 yen to 12,500 yen. The quantity of yen supplied will increase if Japanese consumers decide to spend *more* than 250,000 yen on United States computers now that their price (in terms of yen) has fallen. For example, if the Japanese now want to purchase twelve microcomputers, they will cost only 150,000 yen, and the quantity of yen supplied to the foreign exchange market *may fall, not rise.* But if the Japanese decide to buy 25 microcomputers at the lower yen price of 12,500 yen, the quantity of yen supplied to the foreign exchange market will rise to 312,500 yen.

Under what conditions would an increase in the dollar price of yen lead to an increase in the quantity of yen supplied? Suppose that in response to the *50 percent reduction* in the yen price of United States computers, Japanese importers wish to *more than double* their purchases of United States microcomputers. As indicated above, if Japan now imports, say, twenty-five microcomputers, it will take 312,500 yen to purchase them. This would imply that the Japanese demand for United States microcomputers is elastic—that is, greater than one. The more elastic is a country's demand for imports, the more elastic is its supply of currency to the foreign exchange market, *ceteris paribus.* If the elasticity of demand for imports is less than one, as in our first example—when a 50 percent price decline increased the quantity of microcomputers demanded from ten to twelve, or 20 percent—the supply of yen will actually decline.

What we have just seen is that Japan's supply curve of yen will be upward sloping if its *elasticity of demand* for United States goods *is greater than one* in absolute value. Is this likely? As long as we think of the supply of yen with respect to the dollar-yen exchange rate, *holding constant* the exchange rate of yen for other currencies, the answer is yes. The reason is that as the *yen* price of United States goods falls, *ceteris paribus,* United States imports become cheaper relative to those that might be bought in Japan or purchased from countries other than the United States. Because United States computers, wine, and wheat are close substitutes for similar goods produced elsewhere, Japan's elasticity of demand for them is likely to be quite high. The same logic applies to the United States supply of dollars to the yen-dollar foreign exchange market.

The demand curve for yen in part (a) of figure 32.1 is drawn with a negative slope. This demand curve ultimately represents the desires of American citizens for Japanese items ranging from steel to digital watches to the common stock of Japanese companies. As the dollar price of yen falls, the dollar cost of Japanese exports (whose prices are expressed in yen) falls. For example, suppose a Japanese television costs 120,000 yen and the dollar price of yen is $0.004 per yen. Translated into dollars, the television's price

Fixed exchange rates are exchange
rates that governments arbitrarily
set between their countries'
currencies.

Devaluation occurs when a country
makes its currency cheaper in terms
of other countries' currencies under
a system of fixed exchange rates.

Revaluation occurs when a country
increases the value of its currency
in terms of other countries'
currencies under a system of fixed
exchange rates. (Revaluation is the
opposite of devaluation.)

is 120,000 × .004 = \$480. If the dollar price of yen
fell to \$0.002 per yen, the television's dollar price
would decline to \$240. A reduction in the dollar price
of yen gives Americans a greater incentive to purchase Japanese imports. Since Americans need yen to
pay Japanese exporters, the demand for foreign exchange (yen) reflects the desire of American citizens
to purchase Japanese products. The demand curve for
yen will be downward sloping as long as the United
States demand for Japanese imports is downward
sloping. The same analysis applies, of course, to the
Japanese demand for dollars in part (b) of figure 32.1.

It is important to emphasize the symmetry involved in transactions in the foreign exchange market.
In figure 32.1, the American demand for yen is also
the American supply of dollars to the Japanese. Japan's supply of yen to the United States is also Japan's demand for dollars. Similarly, a *change* in the
demand for yen is also a change in the supply of dollars, and a change in the demand for dollars is also a
change in the supply of yen. Finally, also remember
that an exchange rate can be expressed in either of
two ways. In our example, it can be dollars per yen
or yen per dollar.

Fixed Exchange Rates

Given the supply and demand for foreign exchange,
what determines the exchange rate? After World War
II and prior to 1971, there was a system of **fixed exchange rates** whereby governments maintained exchange rates at predetermined levels. The fixed
exchange rate system caused problems for the international economy whenever the fixed exchange rate
differed from the one equating demand and supply in
the foreign exchange market. To see how these problems developed, suppose the United States and Japan
agreed at some point in the past to fix the exchange
rate of yen for dollars at 200 yen per dollar (equivalent to \$0.005 per yen). Presumably, this exchange
rate at one time represented the intersection of the
supply and demand curves—that is, the equilibrium

exchange rate. Suppose that today, as figure 32.1 indicates, conditions in the United States and Japan
have changed so that the agreed-upon dollar price of
yen is too high and the agreed-upon yen price of dollars is too low.

With the quantity of yen supplied exceeding the
quantity demanded, Japanese importers who want
dollars cannot obtain all they would like from people
who want to sell dollars. They must therefore go to
the Japanese central bank, the Bank of Japan, and
hand over yen. In exchange, they receive dollars. As
long as the Bank of Japan has a sufficient quantity of
dollars in reserve, it can maintain the exchange rate
at \$0.005. The United States might also be willing to
cooperate in maintaining the artificially low value of
the dollar by printing dollars and supplying them to
Japanese importers on demand.

It is also possible that under a fixed exchange rate
system economic forces would be set in motion to correct the excess supply of yen at \$0.005. For example,
as the Bank of Japan accepted larger quantities of yen
from its citizens, the amount of yen in circulation
would be reduced. This would reduce the Japanese
money supply and lead to a recession. The end result
would be lower prices for Japanese goods and services. Japanese products would then become more attractive to American buyers. The demand for yen
would shift rightward, thus narrowing the excess
supply gap in the foreign exchange market. Alternately, if the United States government supported the
\$0.005 price of yen by printing dollars, inflation might
result in the United States, leading to a reduction in
the demand for United States exports and an increase
in demand for Japanese imports within the United
States.

Recessions and inflations are a high price to pay
for equilibrium under a fixed exchange rate system.
What happens if the United States is unwilling to risk
inflation to support the price of the yen? Then Japan
is left with the task of financing the demand from its
dollar reserves. What may well happen before a

recession in Japan restores equality between demand and supply in the foreign exchange market is that the Bank of Japan exhausts its supply of dollars. When that happens, Japan will be forced to lower its exchange rate, a process known as **devaluation.** To restore equilibrium, it must lower the dollar value of the yen to $0.004, where the demand and supply for yen exchange are equal. In the opposite case, in which Japan increased the dollar value of the yen officially, we refer to the change as **revaluation.**

Historically, countries have used tariffs, quotas, subsidies, and other trade restrictions to try to maintain fixed exchange rates. Such policies can induce severe distortions in resource allocation throughout an economy.

Flexible Exchange Rates

Foreign exchange crises during which substantial devaluations occur with little warning can be avoided with a **flexible exchange rate system,** a system in which exchange rates are allowed to fluctuate freely in response to changes in demand and supply in the foreign exchange market. In this case the exchange rate of yen for dollars would have moved of its own accord from $0.005, which equated demand and supply at some point in the past, to $0.0042, the current equilibrium exchange rate. Under a flexible exchange rate system, a decline in the equilibrium price of a currency is called **depreciation,** and an increase in the equilibrium price is called **appreciation.** The presumption in favor of flexible exchange rates is based on the idea that allowing currency prices to vary moderately from day to day as international demand and supply conditions change is less disruptive than sudden and often large changes that occur under a fixed exchange rate system. There is now some concern that the post-1971 flexible exchange rate system has been characterized by large swings in currency prices. In this chapter and the next we will investigate why exchange rates have fluctuated so much in recent years.

The need for government intervention—and the occasions for media descriptions of international monetary crises—prior to 1971 would have been less under flexible exchange rates. In a flexible system, buyers and sellers can *always* buy and sell all the foreign exchange they want at the current equilibrium exchange rate.

Since 1971, the governments of most non-Communist countries have allowed their exchange rates to increase and decrease with the forces of supply and demand with only modest amounts of intervention. (While the central banks of some countries have occasionally voluntarily intervened to dampen swings in their exchange rates, such intervention is not required by international banking rules.) So far, the system of flexible exchange rates has worked well. International monetary crises like those that occurred under the fixed exchange rate standard have been avoided. As you will see in the next section, the supply and demand for foreign currencies depends not only on the flow of exports and imports but also on the desire of one country's citizens to invest in another country. Basically, however, exchange rates are determined by the costs of trading partners' goods and services and the trading patterns that result. Thus, we would expect a shift in United States consumers' demand in favor of British rock records to lead to an appreciation of the pound and a depreciation of the dollar, *ceteris paribus,* while an increase in the popularity of American-made movies in Britain would lead to an appreciation of the dollar and a simultaneous depreciation of the pound.

The demand for another country's currency is also affected by *speculation* that its value (exchange rate) will change in the future. Most economists agree that speculation does not alter the main effects of the forces we have outlined so far. Although we will not look at the complicating effects of speculation on foreign exchange markets, a brief word is in order. In our example, if United States citizens expect the price of

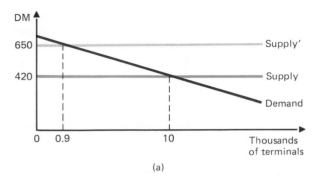

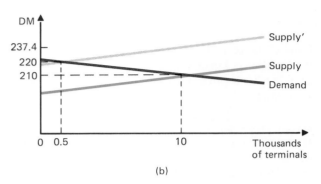

(a)   (b)

Figure 32.2   The effect of a change in foreign exchange rates on exports and imports of computer terminals
Part (a): initially, Rick sold 10,000 terminals for 420 deutsche marks (DM) each. The rise in the deutsche mark price of the United States dollar from DM 2.10 to DM 3.25 between 1980 and 1985 shifted the supply curve to Supply'. Even though demand was unchanged, the price of terminals rose to DM 650 and sales fell to 900 units.

Part (b): initially, Helga sold 10,000 terminals for DM 210 each. The rise in the deutsche mark value of the United States dollar had the effect of shifting Helga's supply curve to Supply' as the deutsche mark cost of her loan payments rose from DM 500,000 to DM 773,809. Despite the fact that Demand did not change, sales dropped to 500 units as the price rose to DM 220 and Helga defaulted on the loan by mid-year.

yen in terms of dollars to rise over time, it may be profitable for them to buy yen now. Suppose they expect the price of yen to rise from $0.004 to $0.005. An American can withdraw, say, $10,000 dollars from a United States bank account and purchase 2.5 million yen. Then, if the yen actually appreciates as expected, these yen can be used to purchase $12,500— a profit of $2,500. Notice that speculation that the yen will appreciate shifts the demand for yen to the right in part (a) of figure 32.1, causing the *expected* exchange rate increase to occur in the present. Since the speculation is carried out in terms of United States dollars, the supply of dollars shifts to the right, causing a simultaneous depreciation of the United States dollar in part (b) of figure 32.1.

Returning to our introductory example, part (a) of figure 32.2 illustrates what happened to Rick's computer business. The diagram shows Rick's supply curve for terminals and the demand for his terminals in West Germany in 1980. Equilibrium price is DM 420 or $200, and equilibrium sales are 10,000 terminals. By 1985, the demand for Rick's terminals was unchanged, but because the deutsche mark price of the United States dollar had risen from 2.10 to 3.25 the West German price of $200 per terminal had risen to DM 650. The effect was the same as if Rick's costs

of production had risen 55 percent or as if his supply curve had shifted up to Supply'. As illustrated, sales fell to less than 1,000 terminals. In effect, the rise in the deutsche mark price of the dollar raised the delivered price of Rick's terminals to the West German market by 55 percent, and he was no longer competitive. By late 1985, Rick had stopped production and was looking for a new job.

Part (b) of figure 32.2 shows the initial demand and supply curves for Helga's terminals in West Germany. Initial sales were equal to 10,000 and the price for her somewhat less fancy terminals was DM 210. The fifty deutsche marks she had to pay for each sale to cover her loan payments amounted to total payments of DM 500,000, or $238,095. With the rise in the deutsche mark value of the dollar from 2.1 to 3.25, that same loan payment of $238,095 each year increased from DM 500,000 to DM 773,809. As a result, Helga could not continue to sell 10,000 terminals for DM 210 each. Instead, to earn the same profit in 1985 that she earned in 1980, she would have to have charged DM 237.4, with sales unchanged. As illustrated in figure 32.2, part (b), the higher cost of the United States loan in terms of deutsche marks had the effect of shifting up the supply curve to Supply'. As shown, the result was a dramatic loss of sales. Helga declared bankruptcy in mid-1985.

*The **balance of payments** is the accounting for the flow of goods and services and the means of paying for them among international trading partners.*

Table 32.1   United States balance of payments (millions of dollars)

Current account (international flows of goods, services, and gifts)	1970			1980			1983		
	Credits less debits[a]	Credits	Debits	Credits less debits[a]	Credits	Debits	Credits less debits[a]	Credits	Debits
Merchandise (except military) "balance of trade"	+2,603	42,469	39,866	−25,342	223,966	249,308	−61,055	200,257	261,312
Military goods and services	−3,354	1,501	4,855	−2,515	8,231	10,746	515	12,737	12,222
Services (investment income, foreign travel)	+6,375	21,704	15,329	+38,636	112,470	73,834	27,628	119,208	91,580
Gifts (foreign aid, private gifts; includes government pensions to persons living abroad)	−3,294			−7,056			−8,651		
Current account balance	+2,330			+3,723			−41,563		
Capital account (international currency flows, borrowing and lending, changes in foreign assets in the U.S. and U.S. assets abroad, and special drawing rights[b]) (will be negative when current account is positive)	−2,111	7,226	9,337	−33,363	51,415	84,776	32,232	81,722	49,490
Statistical discrepancy **Balance of payments[c]**	−219 −0−			29,640 −0−			9,331 −0−		

Source: From *Statistical Abstract of the United States*, 1985, Table 1425, pp. 800–801.

[a]Positive balance indicates credits exceed debits. In the current account, a credit refers to goods and services exported to other countries. A debit in the current account refers to goods and services imported from other countries. When credits exceed debits, the United States exports more than it imports.

In the capital account, a credit refers to dollars or other currencies sent from the United States to other countries or an increase in the amount owed to other countries by the United States. A debit refers to dollars or other currencies received by the United States from other countries or an increase in the amount owed to the United States by other countries. When credits exceed debits, the United States has sent more dollars or other currencies abroad than it has received, or it has increased the amount it owes to (has borrowed from) other countries. This shows how the United States has paid for its net imports or was paid for its net exports.

[b]See the appendix to this chapter.

[c]Statistical discrepancy is a balancing item that assures that the balance of payments will equal zero.

▶ The Balance of Payments and the Balance of Trade

To see how the international flows of goods and services and currencies mesh, it is necessary to understand the international **balance of payments,** which is a set of accounts that keeps track of the flows of currencies in international transactions. A country's balance of payments records all of the economic transactions between residents of that country and the residents of foreign countries during a given period. To understand the information contained in balance of payments accounts, we will analyze data for the United States' balance of international payments in three different years. These data appear in table 32.1.

The flow of international payments is recorded, accounting-style, in credit and debit columns. In the balance of payments accounting system, a *debit* is a

*The **balance of trade** is equal to a country's merchandise exports minus its merchandise imports.*

transaction that is recorded in a right-hand column, and *credit* is a transaction recorded in a left-hand column. In the international payment accounts, a credit entry records an export of some valuable item from the United States. A debit entry records a flow in the opposite direction, an import. For example, if a business firm in Italy purchases a computer from IBM for $1 million, this will appear as a $1 million credit entry in the row labeled "merchandise" in table 32.1. Another entry records the payment for the computer. For example, the payment might consist of IBM's increasing its holding of lira worth $1 million. In this case, the second entry will be a debit to United States holdings of Italian currency. Another possibility, however, is that IBM executives and other United States citizens purchase $1 million worth of Ferraris during the same year and pay for them with lira purchased on the foreign exchange market. The exchange of dollars and lira in these transactions would cancel each other. Therefore, at the end of the year all that would appear in the balance of payments accounts would be a credit for $1 million worth of computers exported from the United States to Italy, and a debit for $1 million worth of automobiles imported by the United States from Italy.

All international transactions must be accounted for as either purchases or gifts, and all purchases must be paid for either in cash or by issuing a promise to pay (an IOU). Thus, *the flow of payments among nations must always balance.* It is *impossible* for a country to be out of balance in its foreign transactions because of this accounting definition. That is why the bottom line of table 32.1 contains *only* zeros. Unfortunately for an accountant's peace of mind, the documents from which the international payments statistics are gathered are imperfect and incomplete. Many transactions are represented by inaccurate or missing sales slips, so to speak. Therefore, it is necessary that the next-to-bottom line in the balance of payments accounts be something called "statistical discrepancy." Statistical discrepancy is the same type of entry that many of us use in our checkbooks each month to reconcile our balance with that shown on our bank statements. If we (and our banks) never

made addition or subtraction errors and always remembered to record each check, charge, and deposit, then the statistical discrepancy in our checkbooks would be zero.

Let us examine the balance of payments accounts of the United States for 1970, 1980, and 1983, starting in 1970 at the top of table 32.1. During 1970, the United States exported merchandise valued at $42,469 million ($42.5 billion). This flow of value from the United States is recorded as a *credit* in the merchandise row. During 1970, merchandise valued at $39,866 million ($39.9 billion) also flowed *into* the United States. This is recorded as a *debit* in the merchandise row of the balance of payments accounts. The difference between merchandise exports and imports is called the **balance of trade** and is sometimes given quite a bit of attention in the media.

The United States balance of trade in 1970 was $2,603 million, meaning that the United States exported about $2.6 billion more merchandise than it imported. The United States balance of trade was also positive in 1975. But it was negative in 1980, when the United States imported $25,342 million ($25.3 billion) more merchandise than it exported. If we were to accept the news media evaluations, we would usually conclude that a positive balance of trade is "good" and a negative balance is "bad." However, such an interpretation generally has no basis in economic analysis. In a fundamental sense, if other countries were willing to accumulate claims on the United States indefinitely, by holding its dollars or IOU's (both claims on the production of the United States), would it not be better always to have a *negative* trade balance? A country's citizens can consume *more* goods to the extent that their country imports *more,* not *less,* than it exports. The same logic applies to our relationship with nations that have a heavy debt to us. How can we ever expect this debt to be repaid if we are unwilling to import more goods and services from our debtors than we export to them? Such a negative balance of trade for the United States provides developing countries that have large loans from United States banks with the dollars to pay off their financial obligations to the United States.[1]

*The **balance of payments on current account** is equal to the exports of merchandise, military items, and services plus gifts to the United States less imports of merchandise, military items and services, and gifts to other countries.*

*The **capital account** is the section of the balance of payments accounts that indicates how the current account balance has been financed; it indicates international currency flows plus borrowing and lending.*

Another reason why the news media emphasis on the balance of trade is generally misplaced is that *merchandise* is not the only flow generating payments or IOUs among nations. Services are imported and exported, also. Service exports include services bought by foreigners when they visit the United States on business or vacation and payments to United States shipowners for carrying freight to other countries. Service exports also include interest and dividend payments on United States investments abroad. For example, Americans buy securities in foreign countries or accept foreign IOUs in exchange for United States exports. Their investments generate returns that flow back to the United States over time in the form of interest and dividends. These flows back to the United States have the same effect on the United States balance of payments as exports of goods, which also generate payment flows from foreign countries. In 1970 and 1980, the United States was a net *exporter* of services, which generated a net flow of claims on foreign countries ranging from $6.4 billion in 1970 to $38.6 billion in 1980. In 1983, the United States imported $41.6 billion more in total goods and services than it exported.

During the decade from 1970 to 1980, the United States spent more on military purchases in foreign countries than the value of military goods it exported to them. This was largely the result of the goods and services purchased to maintain American military personnel stationed around the world. By 1983, however, the balance of military goods and services had reversed itself. Between 1970 and 1983, private gifts and foreign aid generated a net flow of claims from the United States. To the extent the United States government or its individual citizens send benefits abroad, foreigners do not have to pay for the merchandise, services, or military goods the United States exports to them.

When all of the *net* flows (shown in the "credits less debits" column) are added up, we obtain the **balance of payments on the current account.** (Exports of merchandise, military items, and services less imports are what comprised *net exports* in our discussion of GNP in chapters 19 and 20.) Notice that the United States' current account balance was positive in both 1970 and 1980, despite a substantial negative balance of trade in 1980.

The **capital account** shows how the current account balance is financed. Consider the +$3,723 million ($3.72 billion) current account balance in 1980. This means that despite the fact the United States imported $25,342 million ($25.3 billion) more merchandise than it exported, money claims *by* the United States on foreigners exceeded their claims on the United States by $3.7 billion. How were these claims settled? Since the current account balance indicates a net flow of value *from* the United States (positive net exports of goods and services), the capital account must represent a flow of payments or IOUs equal in value *to* the United States. The capital account summarizes these settlements. It includes increases in United States investments in foreign countries whereby United States investors, on net, accept stock in foreign companies as payments for United States exports to them. It also includes increases in foreign IOUs held by the United States government, exporters, and banks. Finally, it reflects increases in United States holdings of foreign currency relative to foreign holdings of United States currency. If there were no statistical discrepancy, the entry in the *capital account* would be equal, and opposite in sign, to the *current account balance*.

One way to settle a positive balance of payments on the current account is for foreigners to draw down their dollar balances and pay United States banks and exporters. However, foreigners may not keep dollar balances, or if they do, they may not want to use them up. Then what foreigners can do is simply to purchase dollars on the foreign exchange market. Thus, if foreigners owe the United States more than the United States owes them, this will tend to push up the price of dollars in terms of foreign currencies. However, to the extent foreigners offer Americans investment opportunities or IOUs with attractive rates of return or interest rates, United States citizens might prefer to accept these claims on future payments from foreigners instead of currency. Thus, relatively high real interest rates or returns on investments in foreign

Foreign exchange intervention *means that the government of a country (through its central bank) buys or sells foreign exchange for the purpose of affecting the exchange rates for its currency in a particular way.*

countries will tend to cause the dollar to increase in value less rapidly or to decrease in value more rapidly relative to other currencies than it otherwise would, given the balance of payments on current account. The reverse situation partly explains the strength of the United States dollar relative to other major currencies between 1980 and 1985. Relatively high real interest rates in the United States caused the dollar to increase in value more rapidly relative to other currencies than it otherwise would have, given the balance of payments on current account.

Before proceeding, make sure you are clear on the difference between the balance of payments and the balance of trade. Moreover, be sure that you can give some examples of a credit as opposed to a debit item in each. Suppose the United States were to get foreign aid. Where would it appear in the balance of payments? How do purchases of United States corporate bonds by foreigners (loans to United States businesses) appear? You will find the answers to questions such as these in table 32.1. If you can answer them, you are ready to proceed to the issues in the rest of this chapter.

Equilibrium and Disequilibrium

In concluding our discussion of the balance of payments, we cannot emphasize too strongly that there is *no economic meaning to the concept of balance of payments disequilibrium* under a system of flexible exchange rates. Every transaction reflected in the balance of payments accounts represents a choice among alternatives, given the price of imported and exported goods and services, exchange rates, and interest rates in the countries of the world. If residents of the United States need to pay West Germans for *any* reason, to finance imports, to purchase West German IOUs, or to invest directly in West German business firms, they can *always* purchase West German deutsche marks in the foreign exchange market. Any tendency to develop an excess demand for deutsche marks will be quickly eliminated by an

increase in the value of deutsche marks relative to United States dollars. The United States dollar price of deutsche marks will rise. This will make it more expensive for Americans to import goods and services or to invest in West Germany. Thus, United States citizens will not be as eager to purchase deutsche marks. As a result, the potential balance of payments deficit in the United States that would have resulted from, say, an increased demand in the United States for West German automobiles—the potential excess demand for deutsche marks and excess supply of United States dollars—is offset by the appreciation of West Germany currency (and depreciation of United States dollars). This adjustment of exchange rates automatically eliminates the deficit. Figure 32.3 illustrates the shift in the United States demand for West German goods from Demand(1) to Demand(2) and the subsequent appreciation of West German deutsche marks, which eliminates the excess demand for West German currency in the United States.

Persistent, long-term disequilibrium in the balance of payments has economic meaning only if one country's government desires to maintain a particular value of its currency in terms of other currencies at some fixed value regardless of the forces of supply and demand. For example, suppose that the Canadian government wishes to promote exports to the United States to maintain the political support of workers in its export industries. To do this, the government may choose to try to keep the Canadian dollar cheap relative to the United States dollar by intervening in the foreign exchange market. In this case, **foreign exchange intervention** requires that the Canadian government *buy* United States dollars with Canadian dollars.

One way to obtain these Canadian dollars is for the Canadian government to tax its citizens. This amounts to a gift from Canadian taxpayers to the United States. The reason is that it allows United States citizens to purchase Canadian goods with Canadian dollars that would otherwise have been available for Canadian citizens to purchase Canadian

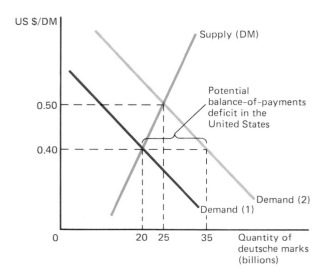

Figure 32.3 The effect of a shift in demand for West German goods on the price of West German deutsche marks in the United States
A shift in demand for West German goods in the United States will shift the United States demand for deutsche marks to Demand(2). At the initial price of deutsche marks in America, $0.40, an excess demand for deutsche marks equal to DM 15 billion would emerge. This excess demand represents America's balance-of-payments deficit and West Germany's balance-of-payments surplus. The appreciation of the deutsche mark represented by the price rise from $0.40 to $0.50 eliminates the United States' potential balance-of-payments deficit and West Germany's potential surplus.

goods. The flow of Canadian dollars to the United States is something like an international payments disequilibrium. It occurs only because the Canadian government is unhappy with the exchange rate that would be determined by the forces of supply and demand without intervention. The international payments account will still balance, however. When Canada buys United States dollars, this will appear as a *credit* in the United States balance of payments capital account with Canada, because the United States is exporting dollars to Canada. If Canada is successful in its strategy, the offsetting entry will be an equivalent *debit* reflecting United States imports of goods or services from Canada.

To see how arbitrary it is to think of this scenario as representing balance of payments disequilibrium, suppose that the Canadian government decided to be more forthright and explicitly stated it was granting foreign aid to the United States. (We ignore the absurdity of trying to defend such an action to Canadian voters.) Then, the "gifts" row in the credit less debits column for the United States in table 32.1 would show a positive entry with respect to Canada, and United States citizens would need fewer Canadian dollars to pay for Canadian imports. The Canadian government would use taxes collected from Canadian citizens to pay Canadian producers for exports to the United States. The effect on the United States-Canadian exchange rate would be the same as an equivalent intervention in the foreign exchange market, but we would be less likely to define this set of transactions as reflecting a balance of payments disequilibrium.

Some news media interpretations and political discussions of balance of payments disequilibrium either reflect ignorance or are disguises for promoting the special interests of groups that see themselves as being harmed by some aspect of international trade. More likely than not, such groups will consist of firms (and their employees) who see themselves as being harmed by import competition. They will shout with horror at a negative balance of trade or balance of payments on current account, perhaps defining a negative balance as "disequilibrium." Since "disequilibrium" sounds like a rather uncomfortable situation that might cause harm unless "equilibrium" is restored, use of the term may bolster calls for import protection. Why a positive balance is not also a "disequilibrium" is not usually spelled out. The use of rhetoric to make one's position look more reasonable is not new. In our discussions of trade regulations, you could easily imagine United States autoworkers and steelworkers calling for fair, rather than free, trade. During the 1950s and 1960s these same groups were quite happy with our strong export sales and never suggested that perhaps we were being unfair to Europe or Japan.

► The International Transmission Mechanism

The macromodel developed in chapters 19 through 29 tells us how macroeconomic disturbances are transferred from one country to another. The key relationship is that one country's imports are exports from the point of view of other nations. Figure 32.4 shows, for example, how a recession that begins in the United States is transmitted to Canada. Exports to the United States constitute a significant component of Canada's GNP—about 20 percent in 1984.[2]

A nation's exports make up part of *exogenous expenditure* on GNP. Therefore, a change in exports exerts an impact on equilibrium GNP through the *exogenous expenditure multiplier*. The effect of a change in exports can be illustrated by using the aggregate demand and supply curves. When the United States enters a recession, production and income fall. Consequently, consumption and imports decline. Because exports from Canada make up a large share of United States imports, Canada experiences a reduction in its exports and, hence, aggregate demand. The leftward shift in Canada's aggregate demand indicates that Canada is entering a recession. The recession in the United States has been transmitted to Canada through their international economic relationship.

The aggregate demand and supply curves also illustrate that an inflationary episode in the United States will lead to a rightward shift in Canada's aggregate demand curve. If Canada happens to be in a recessionary phase of the business cycle, then the international transmission mechanism will lead to a faster recovery for Canada. However, if Canada's macroeconomy is at full employment, then an inflationary episode in the United States will be transmitted to Canada, leading its economy into an inflationary period, too.

In general, economic disturbances in the United States are transmitted to any nation whose exports to the United States make up a significant fraction of that nation's GNP. By contrast, it is much less likely that a macroeconomic disturbance in any *individual* foreign nation will have a dramatic impact on the United States economy. The reason is that most other

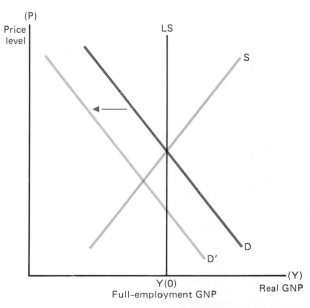

Figure 32.4   The international transmission of a recession from the United States to Canada
This diagram depicts the macroeconomic situation in Canada when the United States experiences a recession. When the United States enters a recession, production and income fall. Consequently, consumption and imports decline. Because exports from Canada to the United States make up a large share of Canadian GNP, Canada experiences a reduction in aggregate demand. The leftward shift in Canada's aggregate demand indicates that Canada is entering a recession. The recession in the United States has been transmitted to Canada through their international economic relationship.

nations' GNPs are much smaller than the GNP of the United States. Consequently, a given change in their imports constitutes a fairly small fraction of United States GNP. Consider the United States-Canada relationship for example. Canada's GNP is only about one-tenth the size of that of the United States.[3] Therefore, so long as Canada's imports from the United States roughly equal its exports to the United States, United States exports to Canada amount to only about 0.1 × 0.2, or 2 percent of United States GNP. The point is not that Canadian economic changes have no impact on the United States economy but rather that on balance the net transmission of economic disturbances across international borders is generally from the United States to Canada and its other trading partners.

Macroeconomic Influences on the United States Balance of Trade and International Financial Flows

We have seen how international financial flows, exchange rates, and features of the *monetary* aspects of international trade interact with the *real* flows of goods and services to determine the balance of trade and balance of payments. In this section we will relate this knowledge to our discussion in this chapter of international macroeconomic relationships. Throughout much of the post-World War II period the United States had a positive merchandise, or commodity, balance of trade. By 1973, however, merchandise exports barely exceeded imports. Thereafter, the United States commodity balance of trade turned negative, and in 1985 the trade deficit exceeded $120 billion. In chapter 33 we shall see that one reason for this trade deficit was our growing dependence on imported oil. Related to increasing oil prices was a shift in demand for small foreign-made cars—especially from Japan. Indeed, our balance of trade deficit with Japan was particularly worrisome to many United States citizens and policymakers. In 1983, for example, United States merchandise exports to Japan were only half as large as its imports.[4] By 1985, the United States trade deficit with Japan exceeded $40 billion.

Inflation and the Trade Balance

In addition to the shift in demand for Japanese cars, another important reason for the Japanese trade imbalance with the United States was the lower rate of inflation in Japan. Throughout the 1970s and the first half of the 1980s, Japan had a much lower inflation rate than the United States. (The reasons for this are discussed in chapter 33.) We would expect that a tendency to import more from Japan than the United States exports to Japan would lead to an increase in the demand for yen to pay for these imports. Moreover, inflation in the United States would lead Japanese producers to export less to the United States as the purchasing power of the dollars they receive fell; Japanese importers would find it less attractive to

purchase American-made goods as their price rose. These two effects of United States inflation would *reduce* the supply of yen to the foreign exchange market.

We have seen that the combined impact of the increased demand for yen and reduced supply would be expected to lead to *appreciation of the yen in terms of the dollar* (that is, an increase in the dollar price of yen). If no other changes occurred in the Japanese-United States trading relationship, the equilibrium price of yen in terms of the dollar would rise sufficiently to restore equilibrium in the balance of trade between the two countries.

The reason the United States experienced a *continuing* negative balance of trade with Japan and other industrial countries is that the price of foreign exchange did *not* rise sufficiently to increase the cost of imports to United States citizens and reduce the cost of United States exports to foreigners. Between 1978 and 1980 the dollar *appreciated* in value by over 20 percent, after adjusting for the degree of inflation in the United States and in countries with which it traded.[5] Between 1980 and early 1985 the dollar appreciated another 30 percent. In the next section we will explore why changes in the foreign exchange markets did not eliminate the United States trade imbalance.

Macroeconomic Policy, Interest Rates, and International Financial Flows

In chapters 28 and 29 we saw how monetary restraint to control inflation led to higher real interest rates in the United States during the early 1980s. We also discussed how federal deficits relative to GNP increased during the same period. Between 1977 and 1979 United States deficits relative to GNP averaged 2.0 percent. Between 1980 and 1984 the deficit-GNP ratio averaged 4.1 percent. That increase in the United States deficit required immense increases in United States Treasury bond sales. This was a new situation for the United States economy, except in time of war. The combined shocks of unanticipated monetary restraint and the accelerated pace of federal borrowing increased both short-term and long-term real interest

^aFrance, Federal Republic of Germany, Italy, and United Kingdom

Figure 32.5   Average annual short-term interest rates in the United States and other major industrial countries, 1976–1984
This figure shows the average interest rates for short-term loans corrected for the rate of inflation in the United States and other major industrial nations.
From International Monetary Fund, *World Economic Outlook*, 1984, Table 2.6, p. 120, and 1985, Table 2.7, p. 121.

rates. Figures 32.5 and 32.6 show how real interest rates on short-term and long-term bonds changed over the period 1976–84 in the United States and several of the countries with which it traded.

Remember that *real* interest rates are nominal interest rates adjusted for the rate of inflation. Thus, it is possible for real interest rates to be negative— less than zero—when unanticipated inflation leads to lenders' being repaid in amounts insufficient to maintain their purchasing power. Over the period 1976–79, the average real short-term interest rate in the United States was −0.6 percent and −0.4 percent in the four major European countries shown in figure 32.5. Japanese credit markets are relatively closed to the West, and short-term interest rates there did not closely

parallel those in the United States and Western Europe. Later on, over the five-year period 1980–84, average real short-term interest rates in the United States had risen to 4.4 percent, compared to 3.1 percent in the four major European countries.

In the United States, long-term real interest rates increased from an average of 1.4 percent over the 1976–79 period to 5.0 percent in 1980–84. In the four major European nations, long-term real interest rates averaged 0.5 percent and 3.5 percent, respectively. Figures 32.5 and 32.6 show that monetary restraint and deficit financing in the United States helped raise the differential real interest rates on both short-term and long-term bonds between the United States and European countries. This made the United States an

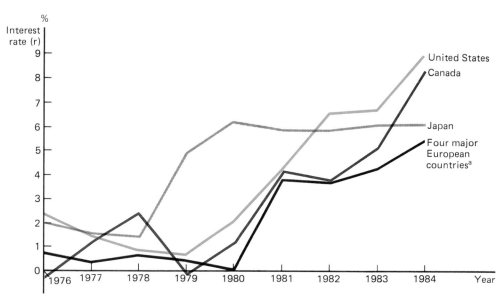

ᵃFrance, Federal Republic of Germany, Italy, and United Kingdom

Figure 32.6   Average annual long-term interest rates in the United States and other major industrial countries, 1976–1984
This figure shows the average interest rates for long-term loans corrected for the rate of inflation in the United States and other major industrial nations.
From International Monetary Fund, *World Economic Outlook*, 1984, Table 2.2, p. 121, and 1985, Table 2.7, p. 121.

attractive place for foreign lenders, not only European but also OPEC nations and other major trading partners of the United States, to send their loanable funds. Still another factor influencing foreigners' desire to hold United States financial assets was a high level of political uncertainty in many nations. Particularly after the fall of the Shah of Iran, with the growing political anarchy in Lebanon and the state of unrest among other nations in the eastern Mediterranean, North Africa, and Persian Gulf regions, the United States became a "safe haven" for foreign investments. Economic and political crises in the early 1980s in countries like Chile, Argentina, Brazil,

Mexico, Nicaragua, and El Salvador have added to the "safe haven" demand for United States-financed assets and to Miami's development into an international financial center.

To the extent that foreigners were willing to lend the United States money, or simply accumulate dollars as the dollar tended to appreciate in terms of foreign currency, they did not spend their dollars on United States exports. This is what balanced the excess demand for foreign commodities by the United States and allowed the United States to run a prolonged balance of trade deficit.

▶ Summary and Conclusions

Foreign exchange rates and our international economic relations affect all of us daily in our personal
and professional lives and will continue to do so in the
foreseeable future. That is why it is important to learn
about the markets that determine how nations pay for
trade with one another. The following major points
were emphasized in this chapter.

Under a system of fixed exchange rates, equilibrium
    in foreign trade occurs through changes in the
    levels of national income and/or prices of trading
    partners rather than in their currencies'
    exchange rate.

In a system of flexible exchange rates, the price of
    one country's currency in terms of other
    currencies is determined by the supply of the
    currency and the demand for it.

In a system of flexible exchange rates, there is no
    economic meaning to the concept of balance of
    payments disequilibrium.

When a nation keeps the price of its currency
    artificially low in terms of the currency of
    another nation, the result is the same as if it
    granted foreign aid to that nation.

The shock of monetary restraint and high
    government deficits in the early 1980s raised
    interest rates and allowed the United States to
    maintain a balance of trade deficit that was not
    offset by depreciation of the dollar.

▶ Key Terms

appreciation 667
balance of payments
    669
balance of payments on
    current account 671
balance of trade 670
capital account 671
depreciation 667
devaluation 667
fixed exchange rates
    666
flexible exchange rate
    system 667
foreign exchange
    intervention 672
foreign exchange
    market 664
foreign exchange rate
    663
revaluation 667

▶ Questions for Discussion and Review

In questions 1 through 4, judge whether the statements are true, false, or uncertain. Be sure to justify
your answer.

1. Under flexible exchange rates a domestic
    currency's appreciation will make imports more
    expensive.

2. A negative balance of trade denotes
    disequilibrium in the international currency
    market.

3. An increase in the United States money supply
    at the full-employment level of GNP will cause
    the exchange rate to fall.

4. Under fixed exchange rates an excess supply of dollars in France can be eliminated by devaluing the franc.

5. A reduction in domestic income taxes at full employment could decrease the demand for imports through an appreciation in the exchange rate.

6. Under flexible exchange rates an increase in demand for Japanese goods in the United States will raise the price of United States exports to Japan.

7. Why would an exporting nation ever accept increased holdings of another country's currency or its IOUs instead of imports in return for its exports? When an exporter does not demand imports of goods or services as payment, what is the effect on the price of the exporter's currency in terms of the importing country's currency?

8. Use a diagram such as figure 32.1 to show the effects of the following events on the value of the United States dollar in terms of the currencies of other nations.
   a. Inflation in the United States and in other countries.
   b. An increase in interest rates in the United States and in other countries.
   c. A recession in the United States.
   d. Vastly improved investment opportunities abroad.

9. Between 1970 and 1982, the world's major oil-exporting nations experienced the following *cumulative* (total) current account balances with respect to their international payments (in billions of United States dollars).[6]

Saudi Arabia	$165.3	Gabon	1.2 (1970–81)
Kuwait	85.2	Nigeria	−3.3
United Arab		Algeria	−16.5
Emirates	48.8	Venezuela	6.8
Qatar	16.9	Indonesia	2.7 (1970–81)
Omon	4.9	Ecuador	−3.8 (1970–81)
Iran	31.2	Mexico	45.4
Iraq	22.9		
Libya	21.2		

Use the format of table 32.1 to show how these countries might have balanced their payments with the rest of the world. Which countries were exporting more goods and services than they were importing? What would be the major difference between the balancing entries of the countries with positive current balances and those with negative balances?

10. Suppose you are a foreign exchange trader for a major United States bank. Assume the theory of rational expectations holds. There is a fully anticipated increase in the United States money supply with the money supply of Japan remaining constant. Would you make more profit by buying or selling yen now?

Appendix to Chapter 32

International Financial Cooperation

We have already mentioned that prior to 1971 governments established fixed exchange rates among their currencies. This type of government intervention was called the *gold or gold exchange standard* prior to World War II. According to this standard, each country would define its money in terms of gold. For example, if one ounce of gold cost $30 in the United States and £10 in Great Britain, then the exchange rate was $3 per British pound. Private citizens could, if they wished, *require* payment in gold rather than the currency of a particular country. This system was officially replaced by the dollar exchange standard following the *Bretton Woods Agreement* of 1944. In the Bretton Woods system, each country's money was still defined in terms of gold, but private citizens could no longer require payment in gold. If they did not want a particular country's money, the only other form of payment permitted was in dollars. In effect, the United States dollar price of gold was held constant at $35 per ounce of gold. Other countries then set a fixed price for their currencies in terms of the United States dollar.

▶ The International Monetary Fund and the World Bank

To help implement the change from the gold standard to the dollar exchange standard, the Bretton Woods Agreement provided for the creation of the *International Monetary Fund (IMF)*, which began operating in 1946. One of the principal architects of the new system was John Maynard Keynes, senior representative of Great Britain to the Bretton Woods Conference.

The IMF was intended to serve as a kind of international bank. Member countries deposit currency with the IMF and were able to draw on these accounts either in their own currencies or in other currencies in order to finance imports on a temporary basis while maintaining a fixed United States dollar price for their currencies. As already noted, the United States dollar was used to define a fixed price of $35 per ounce of gold. That fixed price was maintained until 1968, when the "official" price of gold among central banks remained $35 per ounce but the private market price of gold was allowed to fluctuate. The United States abandoned the fixed price of gold in August 1971. The collapse of the Bretton Woods Agreement was the direct result of rapid inflation in the United States associated with financing the Vietnam War. The money supply in the United States grew too fast to maintain either a fixed world gold price or fixed prices of other currencies in terms of United States dollars. In particular, there was considerable pressure in currency markets to allow the dollar price of West German deutsche marks and Japanese yen to rise substantially.

Between 1946 and 1971 countries borrowed from the IMF with the objective of maintaining fixed exchange rates for their currencies relative to the dollar. Until 1971 international trade was financed predominantly in United States dollars, and even during the 1970s, after the fixed currency price system ended, three-fourths of all international transactions were made in dollars. However, the relatively rapid rate of inflation in the United States that occurred after the mid-1960s created difficulties with this system. Attempts to reestablish the fixed exchange rate system have not been seriously considered since 1974. Even today, there are occasional discussions among international bankers to try to return to a relatively fixed exchange rate system, but there is no agreement on how that could be done without recreating the problems of the Bretton Woods system. The first serious effort to coordinate monetary policy among industrial nations to influence the value of the United States dollar abroad was initiated by the United States Secretary of the Treasury in late 1985 and early 1986.

Special drawing rights (SDRs) are a kind of international money created by the International Monetary Fund.

*The **Eurodollar market** is a financial market in which Eurodollars are borrowed and lent.*

***Eurodollars** are dollar deposits in European banks.*

In order to reduce reliance on the United States dollar as the principal monetary unit of international trade transactions in the late 1960s, the IMF developed a kind of international paper money called **special drawing rights (SDRs)** in 1970. The value of SDRs was originally defined as a weighted average of sixteen currencies but that was streamlined to five currencies in 1981 (the United States dollar, West German deutsche mark, French franc, Japanese yen, and British pound).

The creation of SDRs extended the international central bank nature of the IMF. Member votes to expand allocations of SDRs are qualitatively similar to money creation by, say, the Fed in the United States. Suppose, for example, members of the IMF vote to expand the quantity of SDRs by one billion units. These SDRs then become available for any participating nation to borrow in order to finance imports from other participating nations. Thus, the demand for an exporting country's goods will increase as a result of importing nations' borrowing SDRs from the IMF.

The *World Bank* was created in conjunction with the IMF and serves to provide countries that have international financial problems with low-interest loans to assist in improving their domestic and international competitiveness over time. The World Bank was intended to help countries finance long-term internal changes that would eliminate their recurring short-term international financial problems.

▶ Eurodollars and Eurocurrency Banking

The final international link among countries that we want to introduce here is the **Eurodollar market,** which is not a particular geographic place but rather the sum of transactions outside the United States dealing in United States dollar-denominated assets. Elements of the Eurodollar market can be found in such major financial centers as London, Paris, Zurich, and the Cayman Islands. About 70 to 75 percent of the transactions in banks dealing with currencies of other nations in Europe involve United States dollars.

Eurodollars are dollar deposits in European banks. They are the creation of Eurocurrency banks. *Eurocurrency banks* are banks that simultaneously deal in the currencies of many nations and are exempt from many national banking regulations. Eurocurrency banks exist primarily for the convenience of large international business transactions and usually maintain multimillion dollar minimum amounts for deposits and loans. The Eurodollar market began to develop when these banks needed to find a means for providing United States dollars to finance East-West trade during the 1950s. At that time, the "cold war" between East and West prevented direct trade between the United States and eastern-bloc countries.

The Eurodollar market grew quickly for several reasons. First, by maintaining high minimum balance requirements on deposits and dealing exclusively with large loans, the interest rate spread between deposit and loan rates at Eurocurrency banks could be kept low, which permitted the banks to offer high deposit rates and low loan rates compared to other banks. Since Eurocurrency banks are not subject to many national regulations on banks, they tend to hold lower reserve balances and to pay higher deposit interest than other banks. Another reason for the rapid expansion of the Eurodollar market was that between 1965 and 1974, there was a shortage of dollars to finance international transactions. This shortage resulted from efforts by the United States and a number of other countries to limit international capital flows and to maintain the fixed price currency system that eventually collapsed in 1971. As the central banks limited the availability of United States dollars for international transactions, traders and currency dealers relied more and more on Eurodollar banks to obtain the United States dollars they wanted despite central bank controls.

▶ Key Terms

Eurodollar market *681*
Eurodollars *681*

special drawing rights (SDRs) *681*

Chapter 33

Current Issues in
International Trade

Outline

I. Introduction *684*
II. Recent United States economic performance relative
to that of other major industrial countries *685*
  A. Growth, inflation, and employment *685*
  B. Inflation rates in industrial countries *687*
  C. Employment and unemployment in advanced
economies *688*
  D. Monetary and fiscal policies in industrial countries
689
    1. Central government deficits relative to GNP
690
    2. Monetary policy in major industrial countries
691
III. The impact of changes in the world oil market *693*
IV. Export problems of small, developing economies
694
  A. Export prices *694*
    1. Trends and variations in prices of primary
products other than oil *695*
V. Trade imbalance in developing economies *696*
  A. The expansion of external debt in the 1970s and
1980s *697*
    1. Monetary expansion *698*
  B. The Mexican experience: Domestic inflation,
balance of trade deficit, and overvaluation of the
peso *699*
    1. Mexican inflation and the dollar value of the
peso *699*
    2. Overvaluation of the Mexican peso *700*
      a. Winners and losers from overvaluation
700
      b. The value of existing and potential loans
701
      c. Overvaluation and speculation against the
domestic currency *702*
      d. Terminology: Devaluation or depreciation?
703
  C. The external debt of developing nations *703*
    1. What caused the world debt crisis? *704*
VI. Summary and conclusions *705*
VII. Key terms *706*
VIII. Questions for discussion and review *706*
IX. Policy issue: You decide—Will encouraging workers
to cut their wages save many jobs lost to foreign
exports? *707*

Objectives

After reading this chapter, the student should be able to:

*Discuss the role of monetary policy and central government
deficits in explaining international differences in
macroeconomic performance in the United States
compared to other major industrial nations.*

*Explain how the world oil market in the middle and late
1970s contributed to recessionary episodes and stagflation
among major oil-importing nations.*

*Explain why developing nations often face a highly variable
commodity terms of trade and the impact of this on their
economies.*

*Explain why excessive external debt in many developing
nations is often accompanied by high domestic inflation
rates.*

*Discuss the recent Mexican experience with overvaluation
of the peso.*

*Discuss the external debt crisis that developed in the late
1970s and early 1980s.*

▶ Introduction

In chapters 28 and 29 we discussed actual experience with the use of monetary and fiscal policies in the United States. The problems of defining and assessing policy actions in an international setting are at least as complex. We will begin this chapter with a comparison of economic conditions in the United States and other major industrial nations in recent years. Apart from providing a better perspective on United States policy, that comparison will demonstrate how the effectiveness of domestic monetary and fiscal policy can be influenced by international trade. Economic conditions in the advanced industrial nations as a group strongly influence the macroeconomic options available to the less developed countries. Moreover, in many of the world's developing nations, policy difficulties are often made worse by problems of implementation. For example, while visiting Cairo, Egypt, one of the authors of this book was told about what is mockingly referred to as the "season of fires." It is contended that in the month prior to the deadline for filing income tax statements many businesses are burned to the ground along with all of their financial records. The government official telling us the story said that the practice at times has been so popular that during that month an uninformed observer would think that the night sky was quite beautiful with all the red glow throughout the city. Obviously, forecasting national government revenues can be quite difficult under such circumstances.

In Bolivia the rate of inflation in mid-1985 was estimated to be at least 1,000 percent per year. By that time national elections had become a regular occurrence as each successive regime willingly offered the opposition the opportunity to try to make sense out of a national economic nightmare. No one seemed to know what money growth rates should be over time or to worry much about attaining them.

Chile seemed to be on the road to economic growth and stability in the late 1970s. But by the early 1980s, the unemployment rate was soaring, the economy was in a tailspin, and foreign debt was rapidly expanding. The government of President Pinochet tried to maintain a fixed exchange rate relative to the United States dollar despite the fact that the world price of copper, Chile's major export, had collapsed with no hope for a quick rebound. In retrospect, it was clear that the Pinochet government had erred badly in maintaining the fixed rate vis-à-vis the dollar. But no one could offer any simple remedy to the economic crisis accompanying the rapid fall in copper prices. What could Chile have done to soften the adverse impact of the declining world price of copper, and how much good would it have done?

This chapter explores some of the major international economic problems of the 1970s and 1980s and devotes considerable attention to those facing the world's developing economies. The problems of the world's developing nations are not that much different from those of the United States. However, they are of a much greater order of magnitude relative to these nations' limited productive capacities. We will pay particular attention to the experience of those countries that compete with many others in world export markets. Such countries are essentially price takers—

competitive suppliers of their exports and competitive buyers of imports on the world market. (By contrast, a major exporter of petroleum, such as Saudi Arabia, can and does have a major impact on the world price of oil through its decisions to export more or less oil.)

Small, developing nations often see themselves as subject to domination by wealthier, industrial nations in ways that limit their growth. In this chapter we shall briefly look at evidence bearing on this claim. We will see how some developing nations have borrowed from the industrialized countries to finance imports of desired capital and consumer goods and explore factors underlying the international debt problems that have resulted. We will also see how a strategy of trying to manipulate the value of a country's currency in foreign exchange markets by its own government ties in with alternative approaches to industrialization.

It should be clear by now that the economic prospects of the United States are tied through international trade and finance to the ability of developing nations to deal effectively with their own economic problems. Nowhere is this clearer than in the ramifications of the sharp increase in world oil prices that occurred during the middle and late 1970s. Because the United States is such a dominant force in world trade, due to the sheer size of its economy, we begin this chapter by analyzing recent United States economic performance relative to that of other major industrial nations. We then study the impact of the oil "crisis" before going on to look in more detail at the problems of smaller, less industrialized countries.

► Recent United States Economic Performance Relative to that of Other Major Industrial Countries

In chapters 28 and 29 we reviewed some major macroeconomic events in the United States. We will now relate these periods of inflation and recession to the experience of other nations. This comparison will help us to see the strengths and weaknesses of the United States economy in broader perspective. It will also show how changes in aggregate economic conditions in the United States have often caused similar changes in other advanced economies.

Growth, Inflation, and Employment

Figures 33.1 and 33.2 contain data on annual changes in real GNP and the aggregate price level for the United States, Canada, Japan, and four major European countries (France, the Federal Republic of Germany, Italy, and the United Kingdom) between 1967 and 1985. During the nine-year period 1967–76, the United States experienced a rate of economic growth of 2.8 percent annually. Although this was well below the 3.5 percent growth rate the United States enjoyed during the preceding nine years, 1958–67, it was not much below the hundred-year average of 3 percent. During the 1967–76 time span, the United States experienced economic growth that was slower than that of Canada, Japan, or the four major European countries represented in figure 33.1. During the 1967–76 period, the United States initially improved its rate of GNP growth relative to the other countries shown. Between 1978 and 1982, however, the rate of economic growth in the United States fell sharply, and this pattern was matched elsewhere, except in Japan, where economic growth declined but

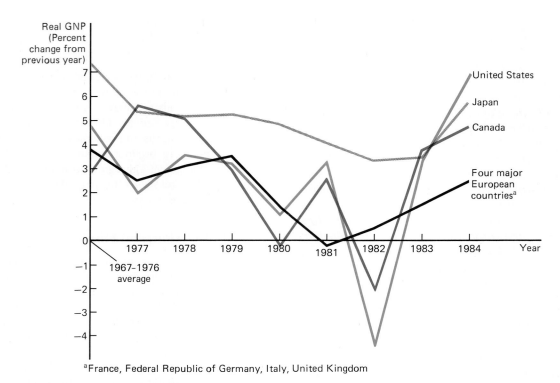

Real GNP
(Percent
change from
previous year)

United States
Japan
Canada
Four major
European
countriesᵃ

1967–1976
average

Year

ᵃFrance, Federal Republic of Germany, Italy, United Kingdom

Figure 33.1   Economic growth in several major industrial economies, 1967–1984
This figure illustrates the annual percentage rates of real GNP growth for the United States and a number of other advanced economies.
From International Monetary Fund, *World Economic Outlook*, 1985, Table 2, p. 206.

not as severely. During the expansion of 1983 through 1985 United States economic growth was as vigorous as that of most of the other major industrial countries. The Japanese economy exhibited a relatively high but declining rate of economic growth throughout the entire period covered in figure 33.1. Japan appears to be moving toward matching, rather than exceeding, the economic growth rates of Canada, the United States, and Western Europe.

Japan is the only major industrial country that sustained substantial economic growth in the 1980–82 time period. No doubt the oil price shock of 1979 contributed to the economic downturn that followed in most of the developed and developing countries by doubling the price of crude oil. But Japan's experience indicates that such an explanation is too simple. Japan imports about 95 percent of the oil that it uses, and most of that oil comes from the Persian Gulf—the heart of OPEC.

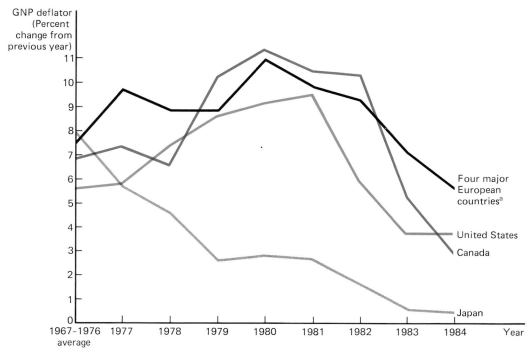

ᵃFrance, Federal Republic of Germany, Italy, United Kingdom

Figure 33.2   Inflation rates in several major industrial economies, 1967–1986
This figure illustrates the annual percentage rates of inflation as measured by the GNP deflator for the United States and a number of other advanced economies.
From International Monetary Fund, *World Economic Outlook*, 1985, Table 8, p. 213.

Inflation Rates in Industrial Countries

Figure 33.2 indicates the annual percentage change in a broad measure of domestic prices—the GNP deflator. Inflation increased substantially in the United States after 1967 as a consequence of the monetary and fiscal policies associated with the Vietnam War, as we saw in chapter 28. However, inflation in the United States remained below that in most other industrial countries. During the period of rapidly accelerating inflation (1978–81), the GNP deflator in the United States rose less rapidly than in Canada, or most of Western Europe. (Inflation in the Federal Republic of Germany was less than in the United States.) In 1983 and 1984, only Japan and the Federal Republic of Germany achieved inflation rates lower than that in the United States.

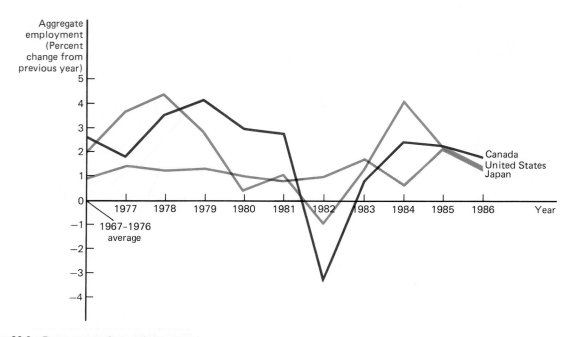

**Figure 33.3   Percentage change in aggregate
employment in the United States, Canada, and Japan,
1967–1986**
From International Monetary Fund, *World Economic Outlook,*
Table 6, p. 173, and 1985, Table 4, p. 209.

Employment and Unemployment in Advanced Economies

Figures 33.3 and 33.4 summarize changes in total employment and the unemployment rate for the United States, Canada, Japan, and the Federal Republic of Germany (unemployment only), whose unemployment has been typical of other Western European nations. We saw in chapter 28 how United States unemployment increased during the 1970s and early 1980s. From an average annual unemployment rate of 5.4 percent for 1967–76, the United States unemployment rate rose to 7.5 percent on average during the 1977–85 period, reaching a peak of 9.7 percent in 1982. Unemployment increased less dramatically in Western Europe until the 1980s. One reason was that these countries employed "guest workers" from the Mediterranean region, who were allowed to work when unemployment was low but who were shipped back to their home countries when employment opportunities diminished during the 1970s. However, by the 1980s, a continued decline in new employment opportunities began to raise unemployment rates in Western Europe to levels as high or higher than those in the United States. In Japan, stable economic conditions, along with a tradition of long-term job attachment, helped maintain exceptionally low unemployment rates despite slow employment growth.

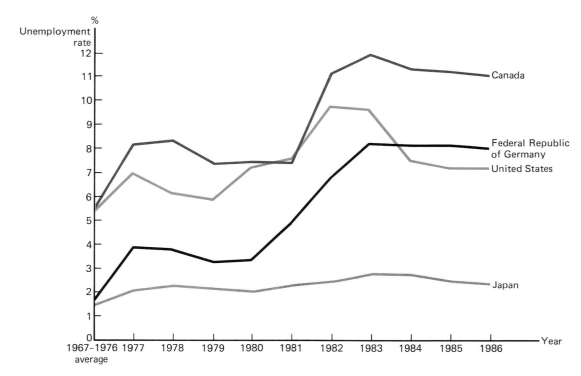

Figure 33.4   Average unemployment rates in the United States and other major industrial countries, 1967–1986
From International Monetary Fund, *World Economic Outlook,* 1985, Table 4, p. 209.

Employment growth in Japan during the 1967–84 period was little more than half that in the United States. In fact, although figure 33.3 does not show it, employment growth in the United States exceeded the average for all of Western Europe and Canada during these years. One of the best-kept secrets about United States economic performance between 1967 and 1985 is the dramatic expansion in employment that took place in comparison to most of the other industrialized countries.

Monetary and Fiscal Policies in Industrial Countries

One issue concerning policymakers around the world has been the apparent common pattern of business cycles in the industrialized countries. Politicians in Europe and Canada were quick to argue that the stagflation they experienced during 1979–82 resulted from monetary and fiscal mismanagement in the

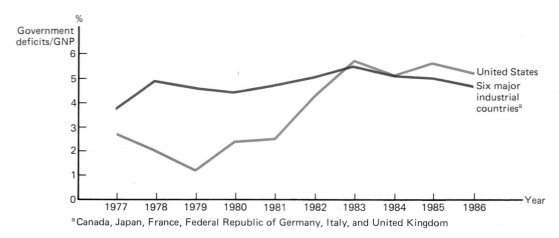

Figure 33.5   Government deficits as a percentage of GNP in the United States and other major industrial countries, 1967–1986
From International Monetary Fund, *World Economic Outlook*, 1984, Table 8, p. 174, and 1985, Table 15, p. 220.

United States. (However, we have seen that an increase in the world price of oil in 1979 and 1980 may have played a part in affecting the fortunes of all oil-importing nations, including Japan and the countries of Western Europe.) It is clear that as a result of its sheer size alone, conditions in the United States would tend to affect its industrial trading partners. Yet both Japan and Germany managed to avoid the pattern of inflation observed in the United States during the late 1970s and early 1980s. Moreover, Japan sustained positive and significant economic growth throughout the period 1977–84. Clearly, the economic ups and downs of the world's economy cannot be explained simply as the result of United States fiscal and monetary policies. Nor can they be explained solely in terms of a common response to OPEC's success in raising world oil prices. In this chapter, we will explore in some detail how macroeconomic policies in the United States have influenced economic conditions around the world.

Central Government Deficits Relative to GNP

One of the issues that has most concerned major trading partners of the United States has been the immense quantity of borrowing on the part of the United States Treasury to finance government expenditure. What evidence is there that deficit spending in the United States or elsewhere has harmed or helped the economies of major industrial countries?

Figure 33.5 shows the size of central (federal) government deficits relative to GNP in the United States and six other major industrial countries. Our first observation is that the much publicized United States deficit to GNP ratio was actually *below* that of other major industrial countries throughout much of the period following 1976. If we were to look at the deficits of the six individual countries other than the United States represented in figure 33.5, we would see that there is no relationship between the size of the deficit relative to GNP and the degree of inflation or economic growth in each country.

Researchers at the International Monetary Fund have calculated the deficits for these countries relative to their full-employment GNP levels, and the results still indicate little relationship between deficits and various measures of aggregate economic performance.[1] The size of the deficit in the United States does not appear to be associated with changes in other countries' GNP, rate of inflation, employment, or unemployment. Moreover, these measures of economic "health" in each country appear unrelated to their own deficits. Within individual countries, the tax structure, marginal tax rates, patterns of government spending, and other details of fiscal policy may help explain the varying macroeconomic patterns exhibited in figures 33.1 through 33.5. The sheer size of the deficits relative to GNP, however, does not stand out as an important variable, at least for the range of values observed in recent years across industrial countries.

Monetary Policy in Major Industrial Countries

In earlier chapters, we have repeatedly stressed the long-run link between monetary growth and nominal GNP. The rationale underlying this relationship is our macromodel. In particular, the *quantity theory of money* implies a close relationship between the quantity of money (M) and nominal GNP (PY), given velocity (V). The quantity theory tells us that relatively rapid monetary growth will be associated with a relatively rapid rate of increase in either real GNP (Y) or the price level (P), or both, depending upon whether the economy is at full employment or in a recessionary phase of the business cycle. Either way, *nominal* GNP is expected to be closely associated with monetary growth. However, our macromodel also tells us that macroeconomic disturbances are transmitted from one nation to another via imports, exports, and currency flows. What evidence can we find to shed light on the relative importance of these two major determinants of macroeconomic fluctuations in major industrial countries?

Figure 33.6 illustrates the relationship between the annual percentage growth rates of the money stock and nominal GNP in the United States, Canada, Japan, and four major Western European countries. Perhaps the most obvious relationship is that on average, over the entire 1977–84 time span, monetary growth rates and nominal GNP growth rates are closely matched. The graphs of monetary growth and nominal GNP growth are very close together for all of the countries shown. In the United States and Canada, the monetary growth lines tend to lie a little above the nominal GNP growth lines, while in Japan and Western Europe, the lines cross each other, indicating that average monetary and nominal GNP growth are approximately equal over the period.

The second obvious feature of figure 33.6 is that the major trends and turning points of monetary and nominal GNP growth in the United States are reflected closely in these series for Canada. They are reflected somewhat less clearly in the Western European nations and still less in Japan. Evidently, the international linkage of macroeconomic performance discussed in chapter 32 is an important force determining the economic experiences of our international trading partners. The closer the partnership, the more closely linked are other nations' macroeconomies with that of the United States. Nevertheless, as the experience of Japan and Western Europe indicates, other nations can and do exert considerable independent control over their aggregate economies.

Figure 33.6　Percentage rates of monetary and GNP growth in the United States and other major countries, 1977–1984

This figure illustrates the rate of M1 growth in major industrial nations and compares it to the rate of growth of nominal GNP. This comparison is based on the quantity theory of money, which relates the stock of money (M) to nominal GNP (PY). In these charts, the rate of GNP growth in one year is compared to the rate of monetary growth in the preceding year.

From International Monetary Fund, *World Economic Outlook,* 1985, Tables 2, 8, pp. 206, 213.

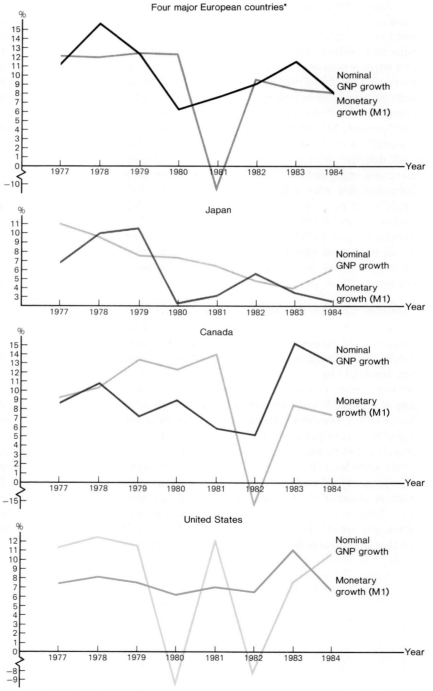

*France, Federal Republic of Germany, Italy, United Kingdom

▶ The Impact of Changes in the World Oil Market

The United States experienced two major recessions after 1970. The first recession occurred in 1974–75 following the consolidation of the OPEC cartel in the autumn of 1973. Between the autumn of 1973 and mid-1974, Saudi Arabian crude oil rose in price from $2 to $3 per barrel up to $12. During the 1970s, the oil-exporting countries were successful in limiting the world supply of oil by restricting their own production. In 1979, their total production was no greater than it had been in 1973.[2] Because of this restriction in supply, given the growth of world demand for oil, the price of oil rose to over $30 per barrel ($20 in terms of 1974 prices) by the early 1980s.

Figure 33.7 depicts the major shifts in demand and supply that accounted for major disruptions in the world oil market in the 1970s and early 1980s. D(1) and S(1) represent the demand and supply of oil in 1973. Equilibrium occurs at point E(1) with a price of $3 per barrel. The consolidation of the OPEC cartel is illustrated by the shift in supply from S(1) to S(2), leading to the equilibrium indicated by point E(2). Because world demand was relatively inelastic, the rapid increase in price to $12 per barrel was accompanied by only a small production cutback.

A recession occurred in the United States during 1974 and 1975. As we discussed in chapter 28, this recession was probably linked to the quadrupling of world oil prices. United States auto sales slumped in part because American firms lost sales to manufacturers of fuel-efficient foreign cars. The most dramatic impact was on the steel industry and on manufacturing in general. Relative to other industrialized nations, the United States had previously been able to count on cheap energy to produce goods and services. Differences in the impact of the oil price hike among industrial nations arose because (1) other countries already imposed heavy taxes on oil, most of which was imported, and were accustomed to high

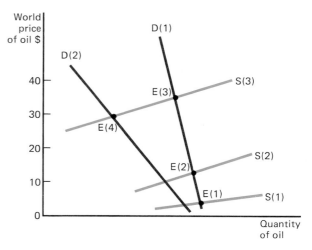

Figure 33.7   Shifts in world demand and supply for oil
D(1) and S(1) are the world demand and supply for oil in 1973. Equilibrium is at point E(1) with a price of $3 per barrel. S(2) represents the world oil supply in 1974 after OPEC established production quotas. Equilibrium shifts to point E(2) with an equilibrium price of $12 per barrel. S(3) represents the world oil supply in late 1979 after the Shah of Iran was deposed and Iranian oil production fell from 6.5 to 0.5 million barrels per day. Equilibrium shifts to E(3) with an equilibrium price of $34 per barrel. The world economic recession of 1981–82 plus conservation efforts shifted demand from D(1) to D(2). Equilibrium price fell to $29 per barrel.

energy prices; (2) the United States had traditionally imported relatively little oil, even though it had been quite cheap; and (3) in the 1970s, the United States began to rely more on oil imports because its own oil fields were becoming less productive. Thus, the impact of OPEC on manufacturers in the United States was *relatively* more severe than on manufacturers in other major industrial nations, who had already learned to adapt to high fuel costs.

The United States experienced another major recession in 1980–82. As figure 33.1 shows, real GNP growth was near zero during this period. Unemployment rose from 5.7 percent of the labor force in 1979 to 7.2 percent in 1980, reaching 9.7 percent in 1982.

The **commodity terms of trade**
measures the quantity of imports
that a country can obtain for a
given quantity of the goods it
exports. It is the ratio of the price of
exports divided by the price of
imports.

Contributing to the recession were the events following the Iranian revolution. After the Shah was deposed, Iranian oil production fell from 5.4 million barrels per day in 1978 to 1.7 million barrels per day by 1980. Total OPEC production fell from 31.5 million barrels per day in 1979 to 27.8 million barrels per day in 1980. This is illustrated by the leftward shift in the world oil supply curve in figure 33.7 to S(3). The new equilibrium is represented by the point E(3), with the price of oil rising to $34 per barrel. Neither the automobile nor steel industry in the United States had made substantial gains since 1974 in cutting production costs or in competing more successfully with imported products. Thus both industries were once again severely affected by events in the world oil market.

By 1984, the sharp increase in oil prices had finally led to significant conservation efforts, and the 1980–82 recession reduced oil demand worldwide. Conservation and production innovations meant that world oil demand had become more elastic, and the recession also pushed demand leftward, to D(2) in figure 33.7.

The world price of oil began to fall as OPEC found it increasingly difficult to restrict its production enough to maintain its market power. Even though OPEC oil output fell from 31.5 million barrels per day in 1979 to 19.5 million barrels per day by 1984, the world price of oil fell by $5 per barrel. One of the probable consequences of this drop in the cost of fuel was that real GNP growth in the industrialized nations rose to an average of 3.6 percent in 1984. Thus, we have seen how demand and supply shifts in a single important market were linked to aggregate economic activity in the United States and, partially through the United States, to the economies of other countries.

In the remainder of this chapter, we will focus on problems that are especially important to small countries, particularly those that are in the process of developing a modern, industrialized sector.

▶ Export Problems of Small, Developing Economies

Export Prices

For years, policymakers in countries whose principal exports are crops and raw materials (primary products), manufactured foods, and light manufactured consumer products have complained that as price takers in world markets, they are subject to wide fluctuations as well as long-term trends in market prices that they cannot control. Compounding their sense of being victimized is the perception that other participants in world markets, such as the industrialized countries of the United States, Western Europe, and Japan, exercise substantial market power in markets for their manufactured goods. Indeed, one defense offered by the OPEC nations for the dramatic increase in crude oil prices in 1973–74 was that such increases were necessary to maintain their purchasing power over western manufactured goods, whose prices had been rising rapidly.

In short, many small nations, which often must rely on only one or two primary products to earn foreign currency, perceive that the rules of the international trade game favor the major industrial nations. In fact, prices of primary products have traditionally fluctuated severely over short periods, as the complaints of farmers in the United States attest. Thus, small, developing nations' export earnings, which are critical for food and capital imports, are often quite unpredictable from year to year. There is a separate issue from that of how predictable export earnings are from one year to the next—one that is of paramount concern to policymakers in developing countries. This issue is how the purchasing power of exports, which is called the **commodity terms of trade,** is likely to change in the long run. For example, if a small country exports sugar and the world price of sugar declines steadily over time, imports that are critical to that country's economic development will be increasingly difficult to finance.

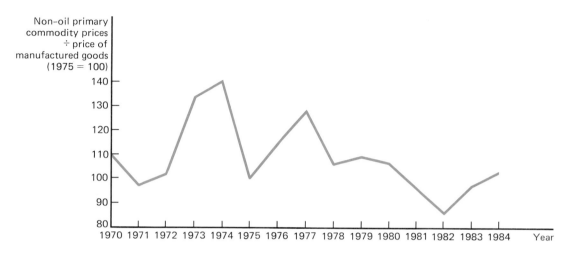

Figure 33.8 Index of the commodity terms of trade for nations that do not export oil, 1970–1984
This figure illustrates the commodity terms of trade for exporters of primary products other than oil. The commodity terms of trade measures the purchasing power of these exports in terms of the manufactured goods exported by the industrial countries. The commodity terms of trade is expressed in index-number form, with the index taking on the value of 100 in 1975.
From International Monetary Fund, *World Economic Outlook,* 1985, Table 3-1, p. 131.

Countries care how their commodity terms of trade change over time because a deterioration in the commodity terms of trade means they have to devote more of their resources to purchase a given quantity of imported goods and services. When this occurs, their economic well-being is reduced or, at best, grows less rapidly than it would have if the purchasing power of their exports had remained higher.

Trends and Variations in Prices of Primary Products Other than Oil

Figure 33.8 indicates what happened to the commodity terms of trade for exporters of primary products other than oil from 1970 to 1984. From 1970 to 1974, the trend in the price of primary products such as food, beverages, agricultural raw materials, and metals tended to favor their exporters when measured against the prices of imported manufactured goods. We mentioned that the OPEC nations defended their price increases in part as an effort to maintain the purchasing power of their oil exports relative to goods manufactured in the West. Ironically, the increases in oil prices in 1974 and again in 1979 caused an acceleration in the rate of price increases for manufactured goods. The linkage between oil prices and manufactured goods prices is easier to understand once we realize that increased oil and energy prices in general will directly increase the costs of producing manufactured goods. This is why the index in figure 33.8 peaks in 1974 and trends downward to a low of only 60 percent of its 1974 peak by 1982. Since OPEC's control over world oil prices has weakened the commodity terms of trade for these nonoil primary product exporters has begun to increase again.

Industrialized countries, too, suffered from the increase in the OPEC-dominated world price of oil. Between 1967 and 1976, the terms of trade for the world's industrialized nations declined by approximately 1 percent per year. From 1977 through 1983, this downward trend accelerated to 1.4 percent annually. For the entire period 1967 through 1983, the industrialized countries of the world experienced an 18.8 percent decline in their commodity terms of trade.[3] One of the principal effects of OPEC's actions, then, was to seriously lower the purchasing power of the developing nations that do not produce oil in terms of their imports of manufactured goods and also to lower the terms of trade of the industrialized countries somewhat.

Policymakers in developing nations were correct if they viewed the decade after 1974 as unfavorable for their terms of trade. However, they seem to have shared this fate with many highly industrialized countries. Figure 33.8 also shows the year-to-year variability of the commodity terms of trade for exporters of primary products. For example, the highest value reached, in 1974, is about 30 percent higher than the mean value, 40 percent higher than the index value reached only two years earlier, and 40 percent higher than the level to which it fell over the following twelve months. One can imagine the difficulty that buyers and sellers of these commodities have in planning purchases and sales over time. Moreover, governments in many developing countries find that the year-to-year variability in the prices they face for their exports makes it difficult to plan for the use of export revenues to help finance food and capital imports or to pay off government loans from abroad. Many governments have been led to seek industrial diversification by developing domestic manufacturing industries as a means of avoiding the uncertainties they face in the markets for their exports.

One cause of variability of the commodity terms of trade is the business cycle. In the short term, each country's supply curve of, say, a crop or some mineral is relatively inelastic, as indicated in figure 33.9. This means that when there is a recession or an inflationary episode, the shifts in demand for these products tend to cause relatively large changes in their prices. Additional factors affecting primary product prices include weather, national disasters, discoveries of new sources of supplies of minerals, and the development of substitutes for them.

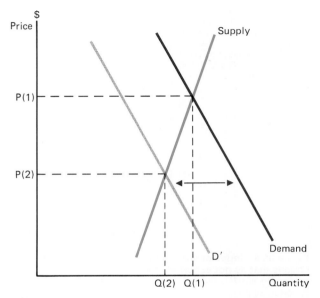

Figure 33.9   The supply and demand for primary products over the business cycle
The supply curves for primary products tend to be relatively inelastic. Therefore, during business cycles leftward and rightward shifts in the demand for these goods lead to relatively large changes in their prices.

▶ Trade Imbalance in Developing Economies

Trade problems in developing countries are frequently linked to their governments' attempts to alter the outcomes of domestic markets. Some frequent forms of government intervention in the markets of developing countries include subsidization of cheap food imports, low-income housing, and investment in industrialization. All too often these commitments are not matched by the financial resources necessary to import the required goods and services. Four sources are available to governments wishing to engage in massive social projects: (1) taxing the general public, (2) borrowing from domestic lenders, (3) borrowing from foreign lenders in order to pay for imports that exceed the value of exports, and (4) printing the money to purchase the goods and services desired.

*The **debt-service ratio** is a country's payments of principal and interest on its external debt divided by the value of its exports.*

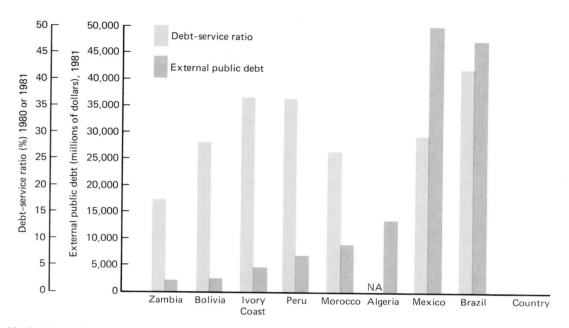

Figure 33.10   External public debt and debt-service ratios for some developing countries
From *Statistical Abstract of the United States,* 1985, Table 1510, p. 864.

Since developing countries are usually not wealthy, foreign borrowing and inflationary monetary growth have been extremely tempting choices.

By contrast, governments of some developing countries have successfully managed to export more than they import, which has led to economic growth stimulated by expanding export industries. In this case, government intervention has been required to maintain a persistent balance of trade surplus.

To summarize, balance of trade deficits and surpluses have been common in many smaller nations. They have resulted from government efforts to attain a wide range of social goals. In the remainder of this chapter, we will explore the successes and limitations experienced by nations that have used international trade surpluses and deficits as means of attaining their economic and political goals. We will also examine policies that some nations have adopted when they have failed to accomplish their goals despite the maintenance of persistent trade imbalances.

The Expansion of External Debt in the 1970s and 1980s

Figure 33.10 contains information on the external debt of several developing nations in the 1970s and 1980s. The first column of figure 33.10 reports the **debt-service ratio,** which measures annual payments on foreign debt relative to export earnings. The debt-service ratio is important because it measures a country's ability to repay its debts to foreign lenders while maintaining a level of imports sufficient to meet its internal economic and political demands. Contrast, for example, the debt-service situations of Zambia and Brazil in 1982. In the former case, $0.17 of every dollar in export sales (foreign exchange earnings) must be spent to pay off debt. In Brazil, $0.42 of every dollar of foreign exchange earned from exports is earmarked for debt repayment. To the extent that countries continually rely upon foreign loans to finance domestic public projects, they often experience rapidly rising debt-service ratios. This not only reduces

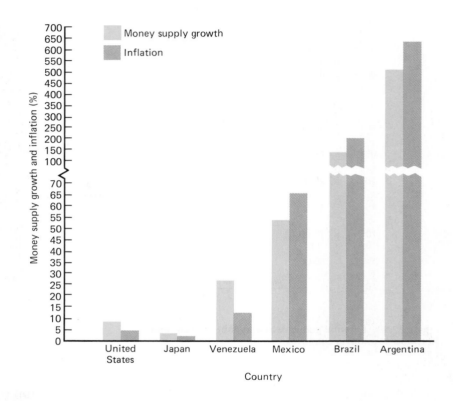

Figure 33.11   Average annual money supply growth and inflation rates in developed and developing countries, 1983–1984
From *Statistical Abstract of the United States,* 1984, Table 1535, p. 886, and 1985, Table 1508, p. 863.

the share of export earnings available to buy imports, but it also makes foreign lenders reluctant to extend further loans.

Figure 33.10 lists countries that have acquired particularly high debt-service ratios in recent years. Brazil and Mexico have been frequently noted trouble spots because the sheer size of their foreign debt is a threat to the solvency of many of the banks that lent money to them. Between 1973 and 1982 the foreign debt of these nations increased from about $20 billion to $566 billion, and in 1982 their combined debt service amounted to over a third of their export earnings.

Developing countries with rising debt-service ratios and a declining willingness of foreign banks and others to provide additional loans to them face a difficult dilemma. Their problem is that they must choose between reducing imports and finding other means of financing the projects that the imports support. Internal political pressures almost always point in the direction of continued imports rather than austerity.

Monetary Expansion

The simplest means of financing desired social projects when external borrowing becomes difficult is to speed up the pace at which money is printed. Figure 33.11 indicates rates of monetary growth for some developed and developing countries. Monetary growth between 1983 and 1984 is used to illustrate the immense differences among these nations in the impact of their monetary policies in recent years. Money supply growth averaged only 6.9 percent annually in the United States and 2.9 percent in Japan. By contrast, money supply growth was 506 percent in Argentina, 138 percent in Brazil, 53 percent in Mexico, and 27 percent in Venezuela.

Excessive monetary expansion leads to inflation in developing nations as well as in industrialized countries. Therefore, we should not be surprised to learn that Argentina, Brazil, Mexico, and Venezuela all experienced inflation rates that exceeded those in the United States and Japan. Whereas inflation in the United States and Japan was 4.3 percent and 2.3 percent per year, respectively, in the other four nations prices rose at a rate of 627 percent for Argentina, 197 percent for Brazil, 66 percent for Mexico, and 13 percent for Venezuela. The simple quantity theory, discussed in chapter 26, tells us that the inevitable result of unrestrained monetary growth is inflation. Therefore, you should not be surprised at the rates of inflation that resulted in the countries shown in figure 33.11.

The Mexican Experience: Domestic Inflation, Balance of Trade Deficit, and Overvaluation of the Peso

We have seen that in the late 1970s and early 1980s Mexico experienced more rapid inflation than the United States and that this was associated with a rate of monetary growth in Mexico several times greater than the rate maintained in the United States. In chapter 32 we saw how inflation in the United States—a major trading partner of Mexico—could be transmitted to other nations. Can we be sure that Mexico's inflation wasn't merely the tail being wagged by the United States dog?

The answer to this question lies in what happens in the foreign exchange market when inflation in the United States increases. As the prices of goods in the United States rise relative to those in Mexico, imports from Mexico increase as does the demand for pesos by United States importers. The increase in Mexican exports to the United States will shift aggregate demand for Mexican goods to the right and may lead to an increase in the Mexican price level. However, the increased demand for pesos will be accompanied by a reduced supply as Mexicans find imports from the United States becoming more expensive. The resulting *appreciation* of the peso will make United States goods cheaper to Mexicans and Mexican goods more expensive to United States citizens.

Thus, under a system of flexible foreign exchange rates, there need not be a prolonged increase in exports from Mexico to the United States or a prolonged decline in imports by Mexico from the United States in response to United States inflation. In short, flexible foreign exchange rates will severely limit the impact of United States inflation on the Mexican economy. We must therefore conclude that the rapid monetary growth and high inflation experienced by Mexico resulted from actions taken by the Mexican government and did not result from transmission of United States inflation abroad. We will now see how Mexican inflation fit in with the political strategies of the Mexican government and how it affected the price of the peso in terms of the dollar.

Mexican Inflation and the Dollar Value of the Peso

Figure 33.12 illustrates the impact of rapid monetary growth and inflation in Mexico on the demand and supply of pesos in terms of United States dollars. The demand and supply curves D and S represent the conditions in the market for Mexican pesos before the Mexican government adopted a policy of rapid monetary growth. The equilibrium dollar price of pesos

*An **overvalued currency** is one whose price relative to some other currency is kept artificially above the price that would clear the foreign exchange market without government intervention.*

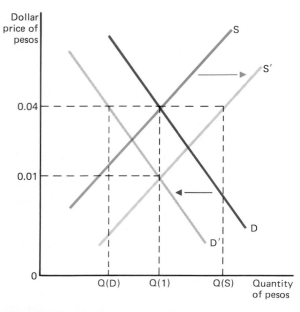

Figure 33.12   Maintaining an overvalued Mexican peso
The curves D and S are the initial demand and supply curves for Mexican pesos in terms of United States dollars. Inflation in Mexico that is greater than in the United States results in a rightward shift in the supply of pesos and a leftward shift in demand. With flexible exchange rates, the equilibrium price of the peso in terms of dollars will fall from $0.04 to $0.01—a depreciation of the peso. However, if the Mexican government desires to maintain the peso at an overvalued price, $0.04, there will be an excess supply of pesos equal to Q(S) − Q(D). The Mexican government must therefore be prepared to purchase these pesos. If the government has sufficient dollar reserves, it can achieve its goal, or as long as the Mexican government can borrow dollars, it may also be able to maintain an overvalued peso.

was about $0.04 (23.3 pesos per dollar) in the mid-1970s. In figure 33.12, the quantity of pesos exchanged for dollars was Q(1). When Mexico began to experience rapid inflation relative to that in the United States, the demand curve for pesos shifted leftward and the supply curve of pesos shifted to the right. If there had been no other changes in factors influencing foreign trade between the United States and Mexico, the market for pesos would have reached a new equilibrium with a depreciated peso selling for about $0.01.[4]

Overvaluation of the Mexican Peso

If the Mexican government wants to prevent the peso from depreciating in order to maintain low-priced imports for its citizens, it must deal with the laws of supply and demand. If the desired price of the peso is $0.04, given demand and supply curves D′ and S′ and an equilibrium price of $0.01, the government must be prepared to deal with an excess supply equal to Q(S) − Q(D) pesos. This excess supply of pesos represented the financial side of a balance of trade deficit with the United States. At the artificially high price of the peso (low price of the dollar), the quantity of imports demanded from the United States remained high and the quantity of exports demanded from Mexico remained low. One means that the Mexican government used to deal with this problem was to borrow dollars from the United States to pay for the excess of Mexican imports over its exports.

Mexico succeeded in maintaining a very high value for the peso compared to the dollar only by means of Mexican government loans from large United States banks. The dollar loans that the government obtained were sufficient to buy up the excess supply of pesos illustrated in figure 33.12. The peso is **overvalued** in this position in the sense that the high price of the peso—$0.04—is maintained by government borrowing from abroad. It is an artificially high price for the peso compared to the free market price of $0.01 that would exist without government action as illustrated in figure 33.12.

Winners and Losers from Overvaluation   Why did the Mexican government insist on maintaining an artificially high price for the peso rather than let it depreciate? Why did the government allow its foreign debt and the debt-service ratio rise to levels that wiped out its ability to borrow additional foreign currency? To answer these questions, we need to look more closely at who wins and who loses when a currency is overvalued. One group who may win consists of those who successfully speculate against an overvalued currency. In the case of the peso, it became obvious in the early 1980s that its price in terms of dollars was being kept artificially high and that the Mexican government could not continue to support the peso much longer. If a speculator can purchase dollars with pesos before depreciation of the peso and then, after depreciation, use the dollars to purchase a much larger quantity of pesos than were originally used to buy the dollars, he or she can gain a great deal of wealth.

In every case in which a currency is overvalued, there is an effort by individuals to sell their domestic currency holdings at the overvalued price. The more obvious the overvaluation, the greater the pressure for people to get their money out of the country. Therefore, it is not surprising that in late 1981, just before the Mexican government allowed the dollar price of the peso to fall dramatically, it nationalized the banks and froze private accounts to stem the rapid flow of currency out of the country. One can only guess at the profits captured by corrupt government officials and black market money traders after this strong signal by the Mexican authorities that depreciation relative to the dollar was imminent. The point is that government officials and political insiders may have much to gain personally by interfering with free exchange rates.

The second major group that benefited from an overvalued peso consisted of anyone who desired imported goods. If the peso had been allowed to depreciate to its equilibrium value, it is clear that the price of imported goods would have increased. For example, suppose a United States product costs $1. With the peso valued at $0.04, the product would cost twenty-five pesos. When, in 1982, the peso was devalued to $0.01, the same United States product quadrupled in price to one hundred pesos. Mexican imports included food and other basic items that were used to support the poor in both urban and rural areas. It is not difficult to imagine that the Mexican government found the prospect of rapidly rising imported food prices to be politically unacceptable in 1981, on the eve of the national elections.

Depreciation of the peso would have stimulated exports by making them cheaper in terms of the dollar. Thus, exporters should have welcomed depreciation. However, one of Mexico's major exports is oil, and the OPEC price of oil is set in terms of dollars, not the currency of the exporting country. Throughout the late 1970s and early 1980s, Mexico and other oil-exporting countries were under great pressure not to lower their United States dollar price of oil. In addition, the United States and other industrialized countries were increasingly inclined to limit imports by imposing quotas. A sharp depreciation of the peso might have increased such restrictions and thus offset any gains to Mexican exporters.

To the extent that currency depreciation would have expanded export sales, the domestic prices of exported goods would have increased, too. In Mexico, a large fraction of domestically produced goods is exported, and therefore Mexican consumers would have faced increasing inflation for both imports and domestically produced goods. If the Mexican government had not initially tried to maintain an overvalued peso, it would have depreciated gradually, and the additional impact of depreciation on domestic inflation would not have been as noticeable. However, given the significant overvaluation that had occurred by the early 1980s, any attempt to restore equilibrium in the foreign exchange market was bound to have a large inflationary impact on the Mexican economy.

The Value of Existing and Potential Loans   Another effect of peso depreciation was on the value of Mexico's foreign debt. Most of Mexico's external debt is owed to United States lenders and is denominated in dollars, not pesos. So if Mexico has an external debt of $50 billion and the peso depreciates from $0.04 to $0.01, the value of the debt in terms of domestic currency would automatically increase from 1.25 trillion pesos to 5 trillion pesos. For both political and payment purposes, the Mexican government would prefer to keep the value of its external debt denominated in pesos as small as possible. That can be done—but only for a while—by keeping the peso overvalued.

Not only does depreciation of the peso increase the peso value of Mexico's foreign debt, it also makes it more difficult to attract foreign investment into Mexico. Suppose, for example, that a United States company desires to invest $1 billion in a factory to be built in Mexico City. With the peso valued at $0.04, the peso cost of the factory would be 25 billion pesos. Suppose that the United States investor expects to be able to sell the factory for 50 billion pesos one year later. This would amount to a profit of 25 billion pesos, or $1 billion—an attractive return on the initial investment. Now suppose instead that during the year, the value of the peso falls from $0.04 to $0.01. Then, the same sale of the factory for 50 billion pesos would only yield $500 million, or 50 percent of the original investment. Clearly, that would be a very unattractive investment.

The government has every reason to fear that a depreciation of the domestic currency will discourage foreign private investment. Therefore, there is a temptation to delay depreciation as long as possible. Unfortunately, potential foreign investors are well able to read the foreign exchange statistics and will soon anticipate an inevitable official depreciation. Therefore, maintaining an overvalued currency relative to the United States dollar is unlikely to encourage continued foreign investment when the state of disequilibrium becomes apparent to all who care to look.

Overvaluation and Speculation Against the Domestic Currency   Earlier we mentioned that one set of gainers from overvaluation consists of "insiders" who manage to purchase dollars at just the right time to reap substantial gains in terms of the domestic currency upon depreciation. As a general rule, when a currency becomes obviously overvalued and market conditions do not change in favor of supporting that value, a depreciation will have to take place sooner or later. This result of the laws of supply and demand encourages speculation against the overvalued currency. For example, if I withdraw 1 million pesos from my bank account in Mexico and transfer them into

dollar deposits in the United States, I will receive $40,000 when the peso is worth $0.04. Once the peso has declined in value to $0.01, I can transfer my $40,000 back into 4 million pesos. The potential profit of 3 million pesos is a very attractive return to speculating against the peso. Of course, it increases the excess supply of pesos and adds further pressure toward eventual depreciation.

A government trying to support an overvalued currency will, at least officially, tend to look with extreme disfavor on speculators, who are viewed as troublemakers and profiteers. Because these "undesirables" benefit when depreciation actually occurs, governments tend to find this consequence of ultimate, forced depreciation of the domestic currency particularly galling.

To summarize, currency overvaluation and external borrowing are opposite sides of the same coin when a government is trying to support consumption or investment expenditures beyond the capacity of its economy to produce. Borrowing from abroad acts as a buffer between the demand for foreign currency and currency depreciation. By building up an external debt, the government merely postpones the date at which imported goods must be paid for. If the government ultimately defaults or if the debt is renegotiated with lower interest or stretched out repayments, the result is equivalent to foreign aid granted by the lenders, which are usually privately owned banks. Eventually, countries reach the limit of their capacity to borrow because foreign lenders do not wish to grant aid; they desire to earn a profit in their banking activities. Thus, countries like Mexico with relatively high rates of inflation compared to their major trading partners invariably experience currency depreciation.

We indicated earlier that Argentina and Brazil experienced much more rapid inflation than the United States during the late 1970s and early 1980s. Therefore, it is not surprising that the Argentine peso fell from $5 in 1980 to $0.21 in 1982 and the value of the cruzeiro fell from $0.015 in 1980 to $0.004 in 1982.

Terminology: Devaluation or Depreciation?   Unfortunately, much of the press coverage of currency crises in Mexico, Argentina, and elsewhere has contributed to sloppy use of terminology. We indicated earlier that a devaluation (revaluation) consists of a decrease (increase) in the value of one currency relative to all other traded currencies under a fixed exchange rate system such as that prevailing from 1945 to 1971. During that period, all currencies had a fixed price relative to (were "pegged to") the dollar, and the dollar had a fixed price in terms of gold. Since 1971, many countries, like Mexico, continue to peg the value of their currency to the United States dollar. But not all currencies remain pegged to the dollar, and the United States dollar is no longer fixed in terms of the price of gold. When Mexico or another country depreciates relative to the United States dollar, the press often calls it a devaluation. This is not strictly correct, since all currencies are no longer pegged to the United States dollar. However, since nearly 75 percent of all international trade is defined in United States dollar terms, a depreciation of a currency relative to the United States dollar is in effect very much like a devaluation.

The External Debt of Developing Nations

In our discussion of persistent balance of trade deficits that characterize many developing nations, we saw that many governments have tried to postpone the inevitable need to pay for their imports by accumulating more and more foreign debt. Any discussion of worldwide international trade problems requires some assessment of the significance of the external debt of the world's developing nations. Between 1977 and 1984, the ratio of external debt to GNP in the world's developing countries that are not major oil exporters rose by 50 percent.[5] The rapid increase in external debt for many developing countries that do not export oil arose in response to the oil price shocks of 1974 and 1979. Moreover, the interest rates on most of these loans were not fixed. As global inflation accelerated, countries that were paying only 6 percent interest in 1976 were paying as much as 15 percent in 1982.

By 1983, developing and Eastern European countries had $700 billion in debt to the West and more than forty countries could not meet their schedules for debt repayments. The problems of debt repayment for developing countries became a matter of serious concern for the United States and other industrialized nations. Between the beginning and the end of the 1970s, private banks came to be the principal lenders to developing countries. Although by 1983 most developing countries' debt was still owed to other governments, the nine largest United States banks had loans outstanding to Argentina, Brazil, and Mexico alone that totaled more than the combined net worth of the banks! To the extent that such loans might go into default, there was concern that it would lead to a global financial panic. To avoid financial crises the banks began to revise and lengthen the schedule for loan payments from developing countries. The issue remained open, however, as to whether substantial numbers of bank failures could be avoided.

In order to help avoid what many feared would be an international financial catastrophe, the International Monetary Fund (IMF) took an active role in assisting debtor nations. By 1983, the IMF had conditional loans with forty-seven countries. The word *conditional* means that countries receiving these loans had to agree to take steps to reduce domestic government expenditures, deficits, imports, and inflation. Countries were also encouraged to reduce trade restrictions and to move toward free market exchange rates. The loans were financed by increased contributions to the IMF from major industrial nations. These nations—mainly the United States—have contributed their taxpayers' money to subsidize developing country loans. Thus, the developing countries benefit at the expense of taxpayers elsewhere. Perhaps the biggest gainers, however, have been private banks and their stockholders who have been able to rely on international lending agency assistance to make their bad debts good. Again, the primary losers are taxpayers in the countries that support the IMF, who must ultimately pick up the tab for misjudgments of major private banks that overextended their international loans.

What Caused the World Debt Crisis?

Before moving on to other issues, we want to briefly review some of the conditions that contributed to the world debt problem. The debt crisis was not simply the outcome of bad bank practices and irresponsible government borrowing. World economic conditions made several dramatic and unanticipated changes in direction between 1973 and 1983, with OPEC and the United States playing central roles.

World inflation was moderate in 1973, and world trade was expanding at a healthy pace, continuing a twenty-five-year trend. Shortly after OPEC consolidated its position in the world petroleum market in late 1973 and early 1974, the price of crude oil increased fourfold. The United States economy slipped into what at that time was the worst recession in the postwar period, with unemployment rising rapidly from 5.5 percent to over 9 percent. The higher price of oil and the United States economic slowdown both had strong influences on economic conditions in developing countries. First, the oil price increase caused import prices of crude oil to developing countries that do not produce oil to skyrocket. Without either the hard currency (currencies traded in major foreign exchange markets) earnings needed to finance the higher priced imports or popular support for rapid domestic gasoline price increases, governments looked to foreign banks for loans. At the same time, OPEC revenues soared and vast amounts of "petrodollars" flowed into banks of the United States and other industrial countries. With vast amounts of cash on hand, banks lent heavily to developing countries. Other developing countries, like Mexico and Venezuela, found that the price their oil sold for rose rapidly, too. They used their oil export earnings to press on with ambitious public works and industrialization schemes.

The United States economic slowdown in 1974 contributed to a slowdown in other developed countries, too. As a result, the developing nations that do not produce oil found their exports earnings stagnating or declining, while oil prices continued to rise. The demand for international loans by developing countries accelerated in line with the flow of petrodollars to banks, which were happy to have customers willing to borrow at higher and higher interest rates.

Throughout the late 1970s, oil prices continued to rise, the Fed and other central banks allowed domestic money supplies to grow rapidly to avoid another recession, and both inflation and interest rates consequently continued to rise. Debtor nations expanded their debts at higher and higher rates, and it seemed that the spiral of rising prices and nominal interest rates would never end. Oil-producing developing nations such as Mexico and Nigeria continued to enjoy high oil export earnings and to plow the money into public programs with no end in sight.

The Iranian revolution in 1979 led to a rapid decline in Iran's oil exports and additional dramatic increases in oil prices. The pace of public spending in oil-producing countries accelerated, along with the international borrowing by developing countries that produce no oil.

Tight monetary policy in the United States to reduce inflation led to a decline in inflation and, in 1981–82, to the worst recession in the United States since World War II. Export earnings for all developing countries took an unexpected downturn, but interest rates remained high because lenders and borrowers remained skeptical that inflation had been arrested in the United States and other industrial countries. Quite suddenly, it became apparent that countries producing oil, such as Mexico, had over-committed themselves to public works programs and many countries (including those who produce oil and those who do not) had borrowed too much relative to their now less certain ability to sell exports. Large banks that had committed huge sums of money to these countries quickly became less certain that the loans could ever be repaid. All of these elements of the debt crisis story were in place by 1982.

Beginning in 1983 and continuing into 1985, rapid economic growth in the United States played a key role in stimulating world growth and renewed growth of export earnings for the developing countries. During that period, the financial risks to the large banks were reduced by renegotiating loans with developing countries to spread them out over more realistic time periods. Furthermore, moderating inflation in the United States helped to bring nominal interest rates down substantially. By mid-1985 it was clear that very little new money was flowing to developing countries and that many of those countries continued to have serious debt problems. The major banks had weathered the storm, but the verdict was still out for many developing countries.

In July 1985, the newly elected government of Peru announced that it would not repudiate its debts but that it would not pay them as scheduled. This announcement was expected to be repeated by governments of other debtor nations. While such actions may seem to resolve the immediate problem, they also create concern. How will developing countries so desperate for financial resources convince banks to lend them money in the future? How will such countries convince private investors to lend them funds if they cannot be trusted to repay their loans as promised?

▶ Summary and Conclusions

The example that introduced this chapter described some severe economic anomalies in developing economies. We have shown in this chapter how the economic systems of the world's industrialized nations are linked to one another and to those of the developing countries. We have also shown that the economic problems in developing nations are often more severe than in the more advanced industrialized nations and described how they interact with the developing nations' dependence on foreign trade. The following major points were emphasized.

The slowdown in GNP growth in the United States that began in the 1970s was more severe than the slowdown in other advanced economies.

Inflation accelerated in the United States during the 1970s but not by more than in other major industrial countries.

By the mid-1980s, unemployment rates in Japan, Canada, and Western Europe were not, on average, lower than those in the United States.

Record deficits relative to GNP in the United States in the early 1980s were similar to the relative deficits in other major industrial countries and appear unrelated to international differences in the growth of GNP or inflation.

International trade linkages apparently have led to a similar pattern of monetary and nominal GNP growth in the major industrial nations.

The oil price shocks of the middle and late 1970s contributed to a common pattern of recessions and stagflation among major oil-importing nations, primarily through their impact on the United States.

The oil price increase in 1974 and 1979 led to declines in the commodity terms of trade for developing countries that do not export oil and for major industrial nations.

Many developing nations have financed imports by increasing their external debt beyond the level at which they can comfortably repay principal and interest with their export earnings.

Excessive monetary growth and inflation have often accompanied growth of the external debt of developing nations. Mexico is an example of a country that has encouraged domestic inflation and a large external debt and has accompanied these policies with actions to maintain an overvalued currency.

▶ Key Terms

commodity terms of
  trade *694*

debt-service ratio *697*

overvalued currency
  700

▶ Questions for Discussion and Review

1. What evidence can you point to in this chapter to suggest that a comparison of unemployment rates across industrialized countries in the 1970s understates how well the United States economy performed relative to other advanced industrial countries.

2. Did inflation in the 1970s cause high rates of inflation in other industrialized nations? Support your answer with evidence presented in this chapter.

3. Explain why the oil price shocks of 1974 and 1979 did not have as negative aggregate economic effects on the Japanese economy as they did on the United States economy.

4. Illustrate and explain who wins and who loses if the British pound depreciates relative to the United States dollar.

5. Illustrate and explain conditions under which inflation in the United States can cause inflation in France.

6. Explain why some Mexican citizens tried to transfer their deposits from Mexican banks to United States banks just prior to the collapse in the value of the peso in 1982.

7. What impact would a currency appreciation have on the willingness of foreigners to invest in a country and on the burden of foreign debt?

8. Why do you suppose United States commercial banks became so heavily involved in loans to financially risky countries like Argentina, Brazil, and Mexico?

9. Why does there seem to be a greater bias toward rapid growth in the money supply and domestic inflation in developing countries than in developed countries?

10. Who wins and who loses when a currency is overvalued?

Will Encouraging Workers to Cut Their Wages Save Many Jobs Lost to Foreign Exports?

In early 1983, the United Steelworkers Union signed an agreement to reduce wages in an attempt to restore some employment opportunities for steelworkers. At the same time, approximately 40 percent of workers in the union were on layoff. Here is the issue. When one of your authors was on the staff of the President's Council of Economic Advisers, he was asked to estimate how many job opportunities would be created by the wage cut the steelworkers accepted. How would you do it? After you think about this and sketch your answer, proceed to the following paragraph to find out how your author came up with an estimate.

At the time of the assignment, the following facts were known: (1) the steelworkers took approximately a 5 percent wage cut, (2) labor costs are about 35 percent of total production costs in the steel industry in the United States, and (3) a 1 percent increase in the price of steel is typically associated with about a 1.5 percent reduction in the quantity of steel demanded. Assuming that in the short run a wage reduction does not affect the technology used to make steel, a 5 percent cut in wages will lead to a 1.75 percent (0.35 $\times$ 5 percent) cut in the cost of steel production by domestic steel firms. In light of what we have said about the demand for steel, this should generate about a 2.6 percent increase in the quantity of steel demanded. A simple assumption is that the steel industry will use 2.6 percent more of all of its inputs, including labor. Thus, a 5 percent wage cut will probably lead to at least a 2 to 3 percent increase in job opportunities in the steel industry. With 159,000 members of the steelworkers union employed and working at the time of the wage cut, a 2 to 3 percent increase amounted to about 4,000 additional jobs.

There is more to the story, though. In response to a wage cut, manufacturers are likely to use a greater proportion of labor in each ton of steel compared to the amount of machinery and other capital used. Your author estimated that this change in the steel industry's input mix would double the estimate of additional jobs created—to about 8,000.

Unfortunately, 8,000 jobs amounted to only about 8 percent of the 106,000 steelworkers who were out of work in 1983. The moral of the story seems to be that the wage cuts for steelworkers were not likely to go very far in offsetting the previous employment loss due to reduced domestic sales. One reason for this disappointing conclusion is that steel, as currently produced in the United States, uses relatively little labor per ton of steel produced. Thus, a 5 percent wage cut leads to a fairly small cut in production costs because only 35 percent of total costs are labor costs. Another reason is that hourly pay in the steel industry in 1982 was approximately $26. This was at least twice as high as steelworkers in other steel-exporting countries were earning. A much larger wage cut than 5 percent would have been necessary to return a substantial number of the 106,000 laid-off steelworkers to their old jobs.

Part IX

Economic Growth and Comparative Systems

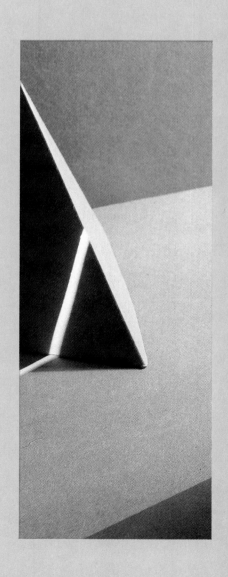

Chapter 34

Economic Growth and Change

Outline

I. Introduction *712*
II. A review of scarcity and the production possibilities frontier (PPF) *712*
   A. Factors that shift the PPF *713*
      1. Labor productivity in the United States *714*
   B. Forces behind recent productivity growth in the United States and other industrial nations *714*
III. Adjusting to economic change *718*
   A. Has the United States been deindustrializing? *718*
   B. A critical look at industrial policy *720*
      1. Japanese industrial policy *720*
IV. Summary and conclusions *722*
V. Key terms *722*
VI. Questions for discussion and review *722*

Objectives

After reading this chapter, the student should be able to:

Define productivity and describe how it affects economic growth.

Demonstrate economic growth as a shift in the production possibilities frontier.

List possible reasons for the recent slowdown in productivity growth in the United States.

Compare economic growth rates in the United States and other industrial nations.

Discuss major economic changes that have affected economic growth in the United States in recent decades.

Discuss how Japanese industrial policy works and to what degree it has been successful.

> *Economic growth is an increase in the economy's capacity to produce real GNP and can be represented by an outward shift in the production possibilities frontier.*

▶ Introduction

The first thing we learned in this book was that scarcity is the basic economic problem. Mick Jagger of the Rolling Stones almost got it right when he said you can't always get what you want. Had Mick finished his studies at the London School of Economics, he would probably have refined his statement to you can't always get enough of all the things you want. This is especially true for society as a whole. Scarcity constantly affects our everyday lives because it forces us to choose among alternatives as individuals and as a society. In terms of these choices, every economic system decides what things get produced.

During the middle 1960s, the United States was engaged in two activities that would leave permanent marks on our country. One was the war in Vietnam, and the other was the establishment of the social programs that comprised what was to become known as the Great Society. During this period, Lyndon Johnson promised us that we could have both guns and butter. By this he meant that the United States could both wage the Vietnam War and generously spend for social welfare programs. To the casual observer it seemed as though President Johnson was right. After all we were doing both at the time. The subtlety here, however, is that although we were waging a war against poverty and a war in Vietnam at the same time, this does not mean that President Johnson found a way to avoid the concept of opportunity costs. While we were fighting the war in Vietnam, we used resources that could have been used on programs in the domestic economy (or vice versa). Even President Johnson could not truly avoid the problem of scarcity.

▶ A Review of Scarcity and the Production Possibilities Frontier (PPF)

The issue of scarcity and how it forces us to make choices is nicely represented by the concept of a production possibilities frontier (PPF). The production possibilities frontier in figure 34.1 is a general representation of how society must choose among goods (such as automobiles, clothing, and housing) and services (such as education, entertainment, and dry cleaning) at any point in time.

It is important to remember a number of the properties of the production possibilities frontier. First, the graphical representation of PPF is basically limited to two (or at most three) dimensions. This means that even though society produces a myriad of items, we can only represent two general categories of production in our diagram. This does not mean, however, that we are ignorant of the great diversity of production within society. Second, the production possibilities frontier reminds us that when an economy is operating efficiently, it is at a point on its PPF, such as A or B in figure 34.1. Points *inside* the PPF are economically inefficient; society is wasting resources in the sense that it is foregoing both goods and services. In particular, at point C society can have more goods and more services. Finally, combinations of goods and services outside the PPF are currently unattainable. Does this mean that society can *never* get the combination described by point D in figure 34.1?

The answer to this question is that at any moment in time, the economy's PPF defines the limits on what can be produced and consumed. How is it, then, that the typical individual consumed about three times more goods and services in 1984 than fifty years earlier?[1] The answer is that the PPF is not necessarily fixed in one position. Rather, it can shift outward over time; this is known as **economic growth**.

Labor productivity measures the quantity of goods or services produced by a typical worker during a particular period of time.

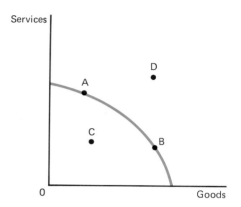

Figure 34.1   Society's production possibilities frontier (PPF) for goods and services
Society's production possibilities frontier for goods and services indicates the options society has for answering the What question of economics. Points inside the PPF indicate wasted resources or economic inefficiency. Points outside the PPF are unattainable in light of current resources and technology.

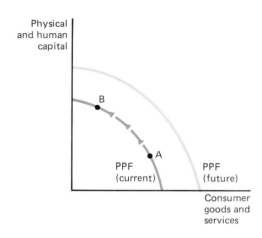

Figure 34.2   Greater investment in physical and human capital leads to expansion of the production possibilities frontier in the future, or economic growth
If society invests more in physical and human capital, there is a movement from a point such as A to a point such as B that occurs along the current PPF. This increased stock of capital allows society to produce more consumer goods and services (and capital) in the future. The increased potential to consume goods and services is known as economic growth.

Figure 34.2 illustrates the key issues involved in economic growth. At any point in time, say, now, society chooses how many consumer goods and services it wants as opposed to using its resources to produce physical and human capital. By definition, producing capital uses up resources that could be available for consumer goods and services but expands production possibilities in the future. Thus, if society chooses to forego some consumer goods and services today and increases its production of physical or human capital, this would be illustrated by a movement from point A to point B in figure 34.2. Ultimately, the physical and human capital that is accumulated expands production possibilities in the future, including the ability to produce physical and human capital itself. Improved and increased amounts of machinery and a more educated population are the key elements in explaining why society can have more in the future. We might also add that economic growth can occur if new, more effective production techniques (such as the assembly line) are developed or if an inefficient economy, such as one at point C in figure 34.1, becomes more efficient, moving toward its PPF.

Factors that Shift the PPF

Suppose there is an outward shift of the PPF, with no additional work effort or employment required. A typical individual can consume more goods and services because of this economic growth. What are some additional details involved in how an increase in physical and human capital ultimately leads to the outward shift in the PPF described in figure 34.2? In the situation we have been describing, economic growth means that more is produced with each hour of work, and this is called an increase in **labor productivity.** Economists are in general agreement that increases in the productivity of labor have been the principal cause of increases in consumption per capita in the United States and most other nations. Thus, the answer to our question requires that we identify a few more details of how investment in human and physical capital causes labor productivity to grow over time. In the process, we will discover additional factors that are related to labor productivity growth.

Figure 34.3   Output per hour of all persons in the business economy, 1909–1985
From Bureau of Labor Statistics, U.S. Department of Labor, June 1983, Bulletin 2172, *Productivity and the Economy: A Chartbook* and *Economic Report of the President*, 1985, 1986.

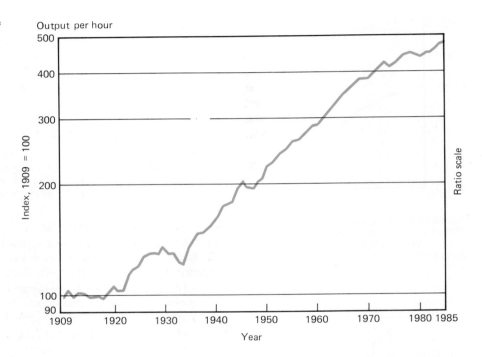

Labor Productivity in the United States

Figure 34.3 illustrates how productivity has grown in the United States since 1909. The measure of productivity used is output per hour of all workers in the business (nongovernment) sector of the economy. One important fact about productivity is immediately evident. Productivity has grown substantially over time. The average American worker was over 4.7 times as productive in the middle 1980s as in 1909.

Table 34.1 tells us that labor productivity has grown about 2.4 percent per year in the United States since 1947. The table also shows that the rate of productivity growth has fluctuated considerably. For example, during 1947 to 1965, labor productivity grew relatively rapidly. In more recent years, productivity growth slowed dramatically. For example, annual productivity growth between 1973 and 1982 was less than 1 percent, and between 1984 and 1985 it was only 0.3 percent. Only during the recovery from severe recession, 1982–84, did productivity growth rise

above 1 percent per year. This slowdown is sometimes misinterpreted in the mass media as a decline in the *level* of productivity of United States workers. This is clearly incorrect, as indicated by the fact that the line in figure 34.3 has not sloped downward in recent years. Put differently, the data of table 34.1 and figure 34.3 show us that the production possibilities frontier of the United States has continued to shift outward in recent years, although at a relatively slow rate.

Forces Behind Recent Productivity Growth in the United States and Other Industrial Nations

Figure 34.4 compares labor productivity in the United States to that of some other industrial nations. Notice that only the Federal Republic of Germany, France, and Canada approached the United States in terms of labor productivity in 1981. Despite what you may have thought, labor productivity in Japan was only about two-thirds of that in the United States. This is

Table 34.1   Productivity growth in the United States, 1947–85

Period	Output per hour of all persons in the business economy (average annual percentage change)
1947–85	2.4
1947–65	3.4
1965–73	2.4
1973–82	0.9
1982–84	2.1
1984–85	0.3

Rates of growth in the productivity of the business economy have slowed significantly since 1965. Explanations for the slowdown have included the effects of change in the composition of the labor force as the proportion of younger and less experienced workers has increased; a slower rise in the capital-labor ratio, resulting from lessened investment in equipment and structures at the same time that employment and hours rose strongly; a leveling off in research and development expenditures; diversion of investment funds to pollution abatement; the maturation of some industries with little new technology; and changes in attitudes toward work. No simple explanation for the decline exists; nor is there general agreement on the quantitative impact of the various factors.

Source: From Bureau of Labor Statistics, U.S. Department of Labor, June 1983, Bulletin 2172, *Productivity and the Economy: A Chartbook* and *Economic Report of the President,* 1985, 1986.

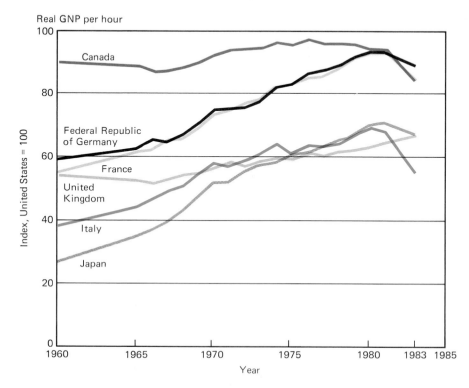

Figure 34.4   Relative levels of real gross domestic product per employed person, selected countries and years, 1960–1983
From Bureau of Labor Statistics, U.S. Department of Labor, June 1983, Bulletin 2172, *Productivity and the Economy: A Chartbook and Economic Report of the President,* 1985; and *Statistical Abstract of the United States,* 1986.

Table 34.2   United States productivity growth compared to that of other major industrial countries, 1950–81

Country	Real gross domestic product per employed person (average annual percentage change)		
	1950–81	**1965–73**	**1973–81**
United States	1.6	1.6	0.2
Canada	1.9	2.4	0.1
France	4.1	4.6	2.4
Federal Republic of Germany	4.5	4.3	2.5
Japan	6.3	8.2	2.9
United Kingdom	2.2	3.2	1.3

Between 1950 and 1981, real gross domestic product (GDP) per employed person increased at substantially different rates among the six major industrial countries compared here. It grew about 1.5 percent per year in the United States and 2 percent per year in Canada and the United Kingdom compared to 6 percent per year in Japan and 4 and 4.5 percent per year in France and the Federal Republic of Germany.

Each country experienced a slower rate of growth in real GDP per employed person in the period 1973 to 1981 than in previous periods. The slowdown was greatest in the United States and Canada and least in France and the Federal Republic of Germany.

Source: From Bureau of Labor Statistics, U.S. Department of Labor, June 1983, Bulletin 2172, *Productivity and the Economy: A Chartbook* and *Economic Report of the President*, 1985.

not to say that we should ignore the fact that the *rate of growth* in our ability to consume goods and services has slowed recently. Economists have studied the reasons for this slowdown and have reached agreement on some, but not all, of the factors responsible. One of the interesting facts they have discovered is that the decline in productivity growth in the the late 1970s and the beginning of the 1980s was not confined to the United States economy. Others shared this experience. This is documented by the data in table 34.2. In every country in this table, labor productivity grew on an average much more slowly between 1973 and 1981 than during 1965–73.

Probably the most important factor behind this slowdown was a decline in the rate at which business firms purchased or invested in new buildings and equipment for their employees. Workers produce goods and services with the aid of machinery, tools, buildings, trucks, computers, and myriad other forms of investment (capital) goods. The larger the amount of annual investment per worker, the higher is the rate of productivity growth.

One of the principal concerns of economic policy in recent years has been to encourage more investment spending, which is expected to foster more rapid productivity growth. This concern is especially acute because of recent slowdowns in the rate of capital accumulation in the United States and other industrial nations. For example, data indicate that the rate of net (after depreciation) nonresidential fixed investment as a fraction of GNP declined by over one-fourth between the late 1960s and the late 1970s. In particular, the rate was 4 percent of GNP during 1966–70 and just under 3 percent during 1976–80. This reduction in the rate of investment contributed, in part, to a noticeable deceleration in the accumulation of capital per worker in the United States. Net capital stock per worker grew at about 4 percent per year during 1966–70 but only about 0.4 percent (one-tenth as much) during the latter half of the 1970s.[2] Among the possible explanations for this reduced rate of investment are government regulation, increasing energy costs, high real interest rates, and a possible change in the time horizons of businesses toward a more short-term versus long-term profit orientation.[3]

The importance of the rate of investment to productivity growth is evident when we look at table 34.3, where we see that those nations investing the greatest percentages of their gross domestic products tended to have the highest rates of growth of output per hour of work.

Table 34.3   Comparison of capital formation in six countries, 1971–80 (percent)

Country	Gross investment as a percentage of gross domestic product	Growth rate of output per hour in manufacturing
France	24.2	4.8%
Federal Republic of Germany	23.7	4.9
Italy	22.4	4.9
Japan	34.0	7.4
United Kingdom	19.2	2.9
United States	19.1	2.5

Source: From *Economic Report of the President*, 1983, p. 81.

Another important influence on productivity growth—one that rivals investment in new plant and equipment—has been changes in the *quality* of labor. The American labor force is better educated today than at any time in the past. Increased schooling was an important contributor to productivity growth during the first half of this century in the United States. However, now that the vast majority of United States workers are high school graduates, the contribution of increased education to productivity growth is not as dramatic as it used to be. Moreover, some people argue that the quality of education in the United States has actually fallen in recent years. This issue will probably continue to be hotly debated.

Schooling is only one determinant of labor quality, however. Other determinants are experience and training. Two changes in the composition of the United States labor force affected the average level of worker experience and training during the 1960s and 1970s. One of these was the decline in the average age of the labor force. As people born in the late 1940s through the early 1960s (the "baby boom" generation) entered the labor force, the proportion of workers with no prior labor market experience increased. Not only were those new jobholders less productive than their older counterparts already in the labor force, but providing them with training also used up some effort of other workers that could have otherwise been devoted to current production of more goods and services. Of course, training young workers contributes to productivity growth in the future. Another change in the labor force was a sharp increase in the fraction of

married women working. Newly hired women typically had less prior job experience than previously hired men. More than half of all married women now work in the labor force, and it seems unlikely that this fraction will continue to grow in the future as rapidly as it did in the past. Thus, this cause of decline in productivity growth should be much less important in the near future than it was in the last three decades.

In preceding paragraphs we have discussed the forces impinging upon productivity growth about which there is general agreement. However, they are not the only factors that have been suggested for the slowdown in output per worker that characterized the United States during the late 1970s and early 1980s except for the 1982–84 recovery period. The others are more speculative, and we will mention them with little discussion. One is the difficulty in measuring productivity itself. Some evidence suggests that workers are now using less of their time on the job actually working than they did twenty years ago and that if this were taken into account, much of the reported slowdown in productivity growth would disappear.[4] Other factors that have been cited include the slight slowdown in expenditures for research and technology development, the rising divorce rate (which presumably makes people less happy and therefore less productive), increases in drug abuse among workers, greater white-collar crime (which reduces industrial output), and a general malaise.[5] Some have even gone so far as to blame the slowdown in productivity growth on the sexual revolution.[6]

Economic change, or structural shifts, refers to changes in the pattern of economic activity, such as the level and distribution of output or employment, in any economy over time.

It is important to recognize that even if greater government regulation in the form of safety requirements and antipollution devices is responsible for the slowdown of measured productivity growth, this is not necessarily bad. It simply means that society has made a choice to trade greater productivity growth for increased job safety and a cleaner environment. Remember that economic decisions such as these must always be phrased in terms of their trade-offs or the opportunity costs involved. Specifically, what are the costs of the productivity slowdown, and what are the benefits that go with it?

It is also important to realize that while the slowdown in labor productivity growth is disturbing to many people, it is impossible to conclude on the basis of economic analysis that this slowdown is "bad." After all, this is what conservationists and proponents of slow growth want when they argue that "small is beautiful." Preserving our nation's natural and scenic resources will certainly slow the rate of industrial development and growth of labor productivity. Some people view this as a desirable outcome and others do not. Economists find it extremely difficult to say whether more or less productivity growth is a good thing. The reason is rooted in problems of market deficiencies in the form of externalities and the public-good nature of some forms of conservation. These difficulties make measuring the growth of economic well-being much more difficult than measuring productivity growth as it is usually defined.

Productivity growth started to rebound in the United States after 1982. In particular, output per hour of all persons in the business sector grew at an annual rate of 4 percent during the first quarter of 1983 and at an annual rate of almost 5 percent during the second three months of 1984.[7] Although it seemed reasonable, there is reason to believe that higher productivity growth would continue into the future,[8] these hopes have evidently not materialized because productivity growth slowed down to 0.3 percent per year after 1984.

▶ Adjusting to Economic Change

Economic growth is only one of many aspects of a dynamic economy. In recent years policymakers have also been greatly concerned with the issue of **economic change,** or **structural shifts,** which means an alteration of the distribution of economic activity within the economy. During periods of economic change, some industries grow and others shrink; similarly, new jobs are created in some areas and disappear in others. The policy issue involves who will reap the benefits and who will pay the costs of economic change.

Has the United States Been Deindustrializing?

Some observers of the United States economy feel that it has been "deindustrializing" in recent years. What do they mean by this? Is so-called deindustrialization a cause for alarm? It is not easy to give a precise definition of deindustrialization. However, it generally refers to a situation in which manufacturing's share of the economy has been eroding because markets have allocated capital and other resources away from heavy manufacturing industries (automobiles, steel, and anything with a smokestack) and toward service industries (such as fast-food restaurants and boutiques). Thus, deindustrialization could also be called "servicization." The concern over possible deindustrialization is that it may lead to the elimination of high-paying blue-collar jobs, which will be replaced by lower-paying service-sector jobs.

The facts suggest that if the United States *has* been deindustrializing, it has not been doing so very rapidly. During the period 1950–80, for example, production, capital stock, and employment all grew in manufacturing. This is shown in table 34.4. While the rate of growth was somewhat slower in the 1970s than during the 1960s, the growth was still there.

*The **industrial policy debate** concerns the proper role of government in fostering economic change and helping the losers from economic change.*

Table 34.4   Size and share of the United States manufacturing sector, selected years 1950–84

| Year | Manufacturing | | | Share of total | | |
	Output (billions of 1972 dollars)	Employment (millions)	Capital stock (billions of 1972 dollars)	Output	Employment	Capital stock
				Percent		
1950	131.1	15.2	106.4	24.5	33.7	28.4
1960	171.8	16.8	140.4	23.3	31.0	25.8
1970	261.2	19.4	202.2	24.1	27.3	23.5
1980	351.0	20.3	287.0	23.8	22.4	23.4
1984	471.0	19.4	306.0	21.8	20.6	22.1

Source: From *Economic Report of the President, 1986*, pp. 264, 298, and *Statistical Abstract of the United States, 1986*, p. 527.

The data in table 34.4 also indicate the share of total output, capital stock, and employment in the manufacturing sector of the United States economy. Notice that total output and capital as shares of the United States total remained roughly the same between 1960 and 1980. While manufacturing output as a share of total GNP declined somewhat between 1980 and 1984, only manufacturing's share of total employment has not fallen to any great extent in the period of time covered by this table. Thus, the data in table 34.4 suggest that manufacturing productivity increased rather than that the manufacturing sector experienced a decline. The pattern of relative slowdown in the growth of manufacturing production and employment also occurred in other industrialized countries, including France, Germany, Japan, and the United Kingdom.[9]

There have been some important shifts *within* the manufacturing sector of the United States economy since 1960. In particular, there has been a trend toward more high-tech manufacturing. High-tech industries have relatively large components of research and development expenditures as proportions of their total production costs. The importance of research and development expenditures in these industries can be measured by examining *value added,* which is industry revenue minus the cost of inputs purchased from other industries. Between 1960 and 1980, value added increased by 40 percent and employment increased by more than 20 percent in high-tech manufacturing.[10] The United States is switching from being the world's producer of steel and automobiles to being the world's engineering consultant and banker. Whether this is good or bad, there are winners and losers from this change. An important issue is how the costs and benefits are shared within the United States economy. Do the beneficiaries of economic change—the stockholders and employees of growing industries—owe anything to the losers in declining industries? What, if anything, do the members of society who are not affected directly owe the losers? These important economic policy issues form the core of what has been called the **industrial policy debate.**

A Critical Look at Industrial Policy

Suggestions for a formal industrial policy (that is, one explicitly recognized through the establishment of a bureau, commission, or cabinet post) in the United States and existing industrial policy in Japan and Western Europe have several common elements. First, there is a central planning body to make the government's industrial policy decisions. This agency is typically advised by a group of representatives from business, labor, and the government itself and seeks to gather information on the problems and growing pains of particular industries. It then tries to form a consensus for action. In keeping with the stated goal of industrial policy, there is also some form of development bank, which invests money in industries that are selected as targets for relatively high growth. The justification for such a bank is that the targeted industries supposedly receive inadequate capital from private financial markets. We will examine this argument in more depth shortly. Finally, industrial policy typically contains some form of government aid for declining industries coupled with import protection while they adjust to changing economic conditions. With these ideas in mind let us examine Japanese industrial policy. Our goal is to discover whether industrial policy appears to be a cost effective way to smooth an economy's adjustment to economic change.

Japanese Industrial Policy

At the center of Japanese industrial policy is the Ministry of International Trade and Industry (MITI). One function of the MITI is to identify those industries likely to have relatively high growth in the future. The MITI seeks information from leaders in the major industrial centers around the world, as well as Japanese bankers, industrialists, traders, and academics.[11] Once the MITI feels it has determined those industries offering the most promise for future growth, plans are

made to foster that growth. The plans are formulated in councils including representatives of banks, the news media, academic institutions, trade unions, and the firms involved. One of the key purposes of these councils is to create a consensus among the "key players" so that MITI's plans will not be opposed once they are begun.[12]

On the basis of the information it has gathered and the consensus it has built concerning the likely emerging industries, the MITI utilizes a number of tools to try to stimulate economic growth in the targeted industries. First, it provides subsidies for research to develop new technology. It has done this, for example, in the computer, semiconductor, and commercial aircraft industries. The MITI has also encouraged joint research among firms where competition might otherwise have prevented them from cooperating. Another way the MITI has encouraged certain emerging industries economically is by providing low-interest loans from the government-owned Japan Development Bank (JDB).[13]

Finally, the MITI has tried to provide emerging industries protection from competition or excess capacity caused by recessions and possible overly rapid expansion. During periods of excess capacity, the MITI has organized "recession cartels." These cartels are designed to restrict output and thus prevent prices and profits from falling as far as they would during a competitive industry's typical adjustment to a recession. The MITI has also organized production quotas when foreign governments put pressure on the Japanese government to restrain Japanese exports.[14]

We have seen what Japanese industrial policy has done for new industries. What are the key components of Japanese industrial policy for declining industries? In this case, the basic goal has been to facilitate the flow of resources out of such industries. The MITI has tied its help to declining industries to an agreement on an explicit plan by the industry for reducing production. After an agreement has been reached, the MITI has approved subsidized loans and recession cartels to restrict production and keep profits and prices from falling as much as they might normally. Aid to declining industries has also included formal protection from foreign trade, although such protection has not always been used. However, informal trade barriers must still be present to protect the domestic Japanese cartels from foreign competition.[15]

Recently, there has been some in-depth examination of how important Japanese industrial policy has been to the country's relatively rapid economic growth. In an extremely insightful and clearly written discussion, Charles Schultze, head of President Carter's Council of Economic Advisers, took a close look at Japan's success.[16] Schultze argued that reasons other than the MITI have contributed most to Japan's rapid economic growth. Among other things, Japan saved 30 to 35 percent of its GNP versus 17 to 20 percent for the United States during the past two decades or more. Japan also had less capital stock to begin with. This is likely to have contributed to a relatively large proportionate payoff to investment. Schultze also cited the unique set of employer-employee relations in Japan that makes labor-management strife relatively infrequent.

However, risk taking by entrepreneurs, rather than by the JDB, has probably played the most important role in Japan's economic development. Schultze noted that about three-fourths of the Japan Development Bank's funds went to merchant shipping, electric utilities, and regional and urban development. These are hardly high-growth industries. Moreover, JDB loans to the electrical machinery sector, which includes computers and semiconductors, were only 0.6 to 0.8 percent of total bank lending to those industries during the 1960s and 1970s.[17] Since the 1970s, public investment in Japan, as in the United States, has emphasized energy and pollution control. Very little money has been devoted to developing new technology. He concluded that public funds have been divided up according to political criteria rather than directed to industries targeted for economic growth. This is no different from the ordinary practice in the United States, which does not have a formal industrial policy.

Finally, Schultze pointed out that the MITI has tried (and fortunately for Japan has failed) to implement some incredibly bad decisions. These include an attempt to keep Honda out of automobile production and Sony out of the development of transistors. Schultze argued that the government cannot regularly predict the winners involved in economic change. Who would have predicted Japan's dominance in motorcycles, Sweden's in ball bearings, or that of the United States in pharmaceuticals and design? In any case, the private market has an incentive to move resources in the economically "right" direction. In particular, rates of return to investment in capital and wages will be high in growth sectors; this will draw resources away from the rest of the economy. As declining sectors shrink, the removal of resources will tend to make the remaining firms profitable and the remaining capital and labor more productive and remunerative.

Even though most economists would agree that Japanese industrial policy has influenced Japan's industrial structure, it is clearly debatable whether it has enhanced or slowed down economic growth.[18] While the MITI has chosen to support some industries that have turned out to be winners, it has also backed losers. The MITI has tried to help industries that would have become successful without any help at all. The most objective thing to say about the Japanese industrial policy is that its net contribution to rapid Japanese economic growth is unclear.[19]

▶ Summary and Conclusions

We will never be able to get *all* that we want, but the way an economic system promotes economic growth is crucial in helping us to obtain *more* of what we would like than we would get in a stationary economy. In this chapter we have examined economic growth and change. The following major points were emphasized.

Economic growth refers to an increase in the economy's ability to produce and is represented graphically by an outward shift of the production possibilities frontier.

A common measure of economic growth is the proportionate change over time in labor productivity (output per employee hour).

Economic growth stems from an increase in the resources available to society or from an increased capacity to produce output from those resources due, say, to technological innovation.

Although the level of labor productivity in the United States has remained the highest of all countries in recent years, productivity growth has slowed relative to earlier periods and relative to some other industrialized countries.

Factors underlying the slowdown in productivity growth in the United States include comparatively low capital formation and a change in the compositon of the labor force toward greater numbers of less-experienced workers.

Economic change produces winners and losers. A crucial policy issue is how the losers will be helped to ease their situations and who will pay for that help. A second policy issue is whether the government should take an active role in selecting winners and attempting to accelerate economic change.

Industrial policy in Japan is a conscious effort by the government to help the winners and losers involved in economic change. On the basis of available evidence, it is difficult to conclude that Japanese industrial policy has fostered economic growth, although it has undoubtedly influenced the pattern of economic activity in Japan.

▶ Key Terms

economic change or structural shifts *718*

economic growth *712*

industrial policy debate *719*

labor productivity *713*

▶ Questions for Discussion and Review

Are the statements in questions 1 through 5 true, false, or uncertain? Defend your answers.

1. A decline in the average education level of the population causes the production possibilities curve to shift inward.

2. Low real interest rates today could encourage economic growth in the future.

3. Society can provide unlimited medical care to all who want it.

4. A decline in the growth rate of labor productivity indicates that output per worker hour in all sectors of the economy has fallen.

5. An important reason for owning your own home is to increase the level of domestic investment and thus ensure future economic growth.

6. Illustrate the following situations with respect to the production possibilities frontier.
   a. The Great Depression
   b. The Vietnam War era
   c. Devoting all resources to medical care
   d. The innovation of a 32-bit microchip

7. Would expectations of future inflation have any effect on an entrepreneur's risk taking?

8. Compare the recession cartels concept with the infant industry argument regarding international trade.

9. Who would benefit if research and development costs were disallowed as ordinary business expenses on corporate income taxes?

10. Is there any possibility that a country can consume more of a commodity than its production possibilities frontier shows it can produce? Explain.

Chapter 35

Alternative Economic Systems

Outline

I. Introduction 724
II. Basic issues to be addressed by every economic system 725
   A. The relative importance of market forces and state planning in capitalist and planned, socialist economies 726
   B. Differences in performance criteria for capitalist and planned economies 727
III. Characteristics of a planned, socialist economy 729
   A. How annual output plans are developed in the Soviet Union 729
   B. Incentives 729
   C. Market-clearing mechanisms 730
      1. Product markets under price controls 730
      2. Factor price determination and the allocation of factor inputs 731
IV. Economic performance of capitalist and socialist economic systems 733
   A. General measures of health and literacy 735
      1. Health and health services 735
      2. Communication and education services 735
   B. Military spending and military presence 738
V. Summary and conclusions 739
VI. Key terms 740
VII. Questions for discussion and review 740
VIII. Appendix: The government's role in mixed, capitalist economies 741
   A. Voting behavior in a democracy 741
      1. Self-interest, rational ignorance, and voting behavior 741
   B. Social choices in a democracy: Outcomes of the political process 742
      1. Special interests and logrolling 742
      2. Shortsightedness and obfuscation 742
      3. The budgetary process: Separation of taxes from expenditures 743
      4. Bureaucratic behavior and the cost in output of government services 744
         a. Labor costs in government 745
      5. Some illustrations of public choice 745
         a. Government and private costs compared 745
   C. Key terms 745
IX. Policy issue: You decide—An industrialization plan 746
   A. The action-initiating event 746
   B. The issue 746
   C. Economic policy issues 747
   D. Recommendations 747

Objectives

After reading this chapter, the student should be able to:

Describe the primary differences between capitalist and socialist economies.

Describe how output decisions are made in a centrally planned economy such as the Soviet Union.

Illustrate graphically how shortages and surpluses are eliminated in a centrally planned, socialist economy.

Compare economic performance in capitalist and socialist economies.

Discuss the economic approach to government activity in a mixed economy.

Explain why government intervention in a mixed economy frequently sacrifices economic efficiency to alter the distribution of economic gains and losses.

Cite examples of government economic activity in a mixed economy that are substitutes for production by privately held firms.

*An **economic system** is the set of institutions, such as free markets or planning agencies, rules, and laws that determines the answers to the basic economic questions in a country.*

▶ Introduction

When you think about it, it is really quite difficult to imagine everyday life in another country's economy. It takes some facts and figures to get any kind of feel for life there. Here are some numbers for China that you may find surprising. The China Daily *reports that there are only about sixteen washing machines per 100 families in Beijin. There are only two refrigerators for every 100 families.*

In China, a bicycle is a very prized possession. It is like a car in the United States in terms of how it is used for an individual's transportation needs. However, bicycles have been quite difficult to obtain in China and thus have been rationed. Those who are lucky enough to get a ration coupon are allowed one month to find a shop that has a bicycle in stock. Those who pass this hurdle must then raise $82.50, the equivalent of about two months' wages in China.

The purpose of this chapter is to paint a picture of the various economic systems in effect around the world and to compare and contrast their goals and performance. In earlier chapters we discussed the relative economic performance of different industrialized economies and of developing economies. We also touched on the causes and consequences of varying degrees of government involvement in those market-oriented economies. In contrast with earlier chapters, this chapter focuses on market versus centrally planned economies. As we shall see, market and planned economies are generally quite different in terms of their expressed goals, the mechanisms for achieving those goals, and the incentive schemes they use.

*An **economic system** is a set of mechanisms and institutions that determines the methods by which a country's production, consumption, and income distribution decisions are made and implemented. In this chapter we will focus on the two most important types of economic systems: capitalist systems such as those found in the United States, Japan, and many nations of Western Europe and planned, socialist systems such as those of the Soviet Union, China, and many of their allies.*

*A **capitalist economic system** is one in which private property and free markets are the principal institutions determining the answers to the basic economic questions.*

▶ Basic Issues to Be Addressed by Every Economic System

In chapter 1 we discussed three basic economic questions that every economic system must address. We can sharpen our focus on the essential characteristics of capitalist and socialist systems by discussing how they generally address these basic issues. The three basic questions are (1) What gets produced? (2) How are goods and services produced? and (3) For whom are goods and services produced? To these three questions, we will now add a fourth: (4) What are the incentives within a system that make it work? Question 3 will help us understand the essential differences between capitalist and socialist systems and see the crucial importance of the fourth question when we also consider the question of who owns or controls property.

Throughout this book we have discussed the characteristics of individual product markets and the aggregate markets of industrialized and developing countries. The term **capitalist economic system** is applied to all countries in which the market is the primary instrument with which the four basic economic questions are answered. Almost all capitalist economies are mixed economies in the sense that some industries may be nationalized, as is the case with basic industries like steel and coal in some European nations, or heavily dependent on government contracts as opposed to private expenditures, as is the case with the defense industry in the United States. What binds capitalist economies like the United States, the United Kingdom, and Japan together is not that markets alone determine *what* is to be produced but that markets play the dominant role in answering this question.

Similarly, *how* goods are produced is not determined solely by market forces even in the United States. Regulations exist with respect to health and safety conditions in the workplace. Environmental regulations affect both the location of various kinds of production facilities and production techniques. Zoning laws are the most obvious example of the former kind of restriction, while limitations on strip-mining of coal and the use of high-sulfur coal (through emission controls) in electricity generation are examples of the latter type of limitation. Nevertheless, among the varied mechanisms that do determine how goods and services are produced, markets are of primary importance in capitalist economic systems.

The question of who owns property is critical in determining how wealth is distributed and, therefore, *for whom* goods and services are provided. Capitalist economic systems have the common characteristic that property is primarily privately owned. Thus, private demands for goods and services are the major ingredients on the demand side of each market. Private demands tend to determine what is produced and for whom. All capitalist countries have some nationalized industries that amount to state property, not private property (such as the United States Postal Service, federal land holdings, and some public transportation systems in the United States). Moreover, virtually all capitalistic economic systems use their taxing powers to redistribute income and wealth. Nevertheless, most property is privately owned in capitalist societies.

Table 35.1   Attributes and examples of capitalist and planned, socialist economies

Questions	Answers	
	Capitalism	Socialism
What gets produced?	Market determined (decentralized)	Centrally planned
How are goods produced?	Primarily market determined	Primarily planned
Who owns property?	Primarily private property	Primarily state property
What motivates productive effort?	Primarily material gain	Both private and collective material gains
	Examples	
	United States	Bulgaria
	Canada	China
	Federal Republic of Germany	Czechoslovakia
	Greece	Democratic Republic of Germany
	Japan	Hungary
	Spain	Poland
	Turkey	Romania
	United Kingdom	Soviet Union

The final basic question is this: *What is the incentive mechanism in the society that motivates the production of goods and services?* Clearly, if individual and household incomes depend largely on how we supply productive factors, such as our labor, to the production process and if individuals and households own these resources, private material gain will be the dominant incentive mechanism of our economic system. Even in capitalist economies, tax collections amount to between one-fourth and one-half of national income.[1] An important use of tax revenues is to provide income maintenance and welfare services to various groups in society. Private charitable contributions are also substantial in capitalist countries. For example, in 1984, total contributions by private philanthropy funds amounted to $74.3 billion, which was more than total outlays under all major federal and state income maintenance programs.[2] While it is clear that collective social welfare is of considerable concern and therefore does motivate economic activity in capitalist societies, the primary motivation is private material gain.

Table 35.1 contains a summary of the attributes of capitalist and planned, socialist economic systems and gives examples of specific countries that can be classified as mainly either capitalist or socialist.

The Relative Importance of Market Forces and State Planning in Capitalist and Planned, Socialist Economies

None of the countries listed in table 35.1 is either a "pure" capitalist or socialist system. In the world's socialist economies the answer to the question of what gets produced is determined primarily by central plans rather than market signals. However, free markets exist in certain areas. For example, in the Soviet Union, private plots within agricultural cooperatives yield an important part of total farm output. Planned, socialist economies often use the term *second market* to describe the mix of goods and services that is market determined. These markets are not limited to agriculture, even in the Soviet Union. In recent years, Eastern European countries including Hungary and Czechoslovakia have preferred to be thought of as modified centrally planned economies in which market forces are important in determining what gets produced. Although it would be theoretically possible for a country's government to own all property but to allow market forces to guide what is produced and how, the primary mechanism for deciding what gets produced in socialist countries is primarily central planning and not the forces of market demand and supply.

In capitalist countries the primary source of information on the appropriate methods for producing goods and services is the market-determined profits and losses of enterprises. In planned economies market signals are largely bypassed or at least heavily filtered out. Thus, historical experience and the technical know-how of central planners will be the primary determinants of how to produce goods and services. In the controlled sectors of planned economies the forces of demand and supply will not signal how goods can be produced most efficiently. Planners may use information gleaned from unregulated markets to guide decisions in methods of production in centrally planned sectors. Observations on how capitalist countries produce goods whose production is controlled in centrally planned economies may encourage planners to adopt techniques of production that are not dramatically different from those signaled by unconstrained market forces. Thus, we tend to observe the same basic production methods used to produce steel, automobiles, and other items in the Soviet Union as in capitalist countries, even if many inefficiencies plague socialist firms.[3]

In contrast to capitalist economic systems, in which property is primarily owned by private individuals, in planned, socialist economies property is primarily owned by the "state." As indicated earlier, small plots of land and the output produced on them by workers in agricultural cooperatives in the Soviet Union are privately owned. Recognizing the power of private incentives in promoting effort, China has recently permitted small businesses to be run as private enterprises.[4] A number of East European countries have permitted limited private ownership of land, farm animals, and so forth, in recent years.[5] Evidently, the Soviet Union will not risk the efficiency of its arms production program to satisfy socialist incentive norms. One analyst believes that incentives for productive efficiency in arms production are more effectively harnessed in the Soviet system than in the United States because the Soviets in this case have used the capitalist incentive system more effectively than has the United States government.[6]

On a more cynical note, one might ask how the "state" can be defined as anything other than a particular set of private individuals with the political power to obtain the property rights to the means of production. Presumably, the "state" is different from private property owners in that its expressed goal—in socialist economies—is to create a more even distribution of wealth among workers and households. Theoretical models of socialism certainly spell out equality as a major justification for doing away with private property. If income or wealth inequality is comparable in capitalist and planned, socialist economies, it can be argued that this principal justification for socialism is a facade for a more basic motivation. One of the major issues on which we will focus in this chapter is the extent to which capitalism and planned socialism *as actually practiced* in specific countries lead to consistent differences in the quality of life and distribution of wealth.

Differences in Performance Criteria for Capitalist and Planned Economies

To the extent that there are real differences between capitalist and planned, socialist economies with respect to their methods of operation and their institutions, there are likely to be differences in their overall economic goals. Therefore, simple comparisons of economic data across capitalist and planned, socialist economies may tell us little about how effective countries are in achieving their aims. A rather extreme example may help to illustrate our point. Suppose you were to visit a very strict religious monastery in a remote country to study its economic and social organization. You might find that the members of the monastery eke out a perilous standard of living by using archaic production methods. If you suggested that the monastery should resort to private ownership of the means of production and a capitalist incentive system in order to increase its output per person and its level of material well-being, you would probably be misunderstanding the principal reason for the monastery's existence—the renunciation of material welfare in order to promote spiritual welfare.

Table 35.2   Gross national product in constant (1981) dollars and rates of growth, 1975–82

	GNP (billions of dollars)			Per capita GNP (dollars)			Per capita growth rate 1975–82 (percent)
	1975	1980	1982	1975	1980	1982	
Capitalist economies							
United States	2,416.1	2,883.0	2,897.2	11,290	12,661	12,482	10.6
Canada	230.5	264.6	261.0	10,153	11,026	10,610	4.5
Federal Republic of Germany	576.1	686.7	679.6	9,321	11,148	11,032	18.36
Greece	30.9	38.3	37.9	3,438	3,992	3,870	12.57
Japan	857.7	1,094.7	1,157.3	7,685	9,372	9,774	27.18
Spain	166.4	183.1	186.0	4,700	4,894	4,894	4.13
Turkey	49.8	56.6	61.6	1,229	1,230	1,279	4.07
United Kingdom	467.3	508.9	501.4	8,344	9,087	8,954	7.31
Socialist economies							
Bulgaria	31.8	33.4	35.3	3,659	3,747	3,969	8.47
China	420.8	603.5	658.4	446	595	630	41.26
Czechoslovakia	125.6	139.5	138.7	8,485	9,115	9,007	6.15
Democratic Republic of Germany	143.1	160.7	165.6	8,469	9,622	9,914	17.06
Hungary	57.8	63.8	65.2	5,500	5,962	6,092	10.76
Poland	187.2	193.8	176.2	5,504	5,444	4,868	−11.56
Romania	78.8	95.6	98.9	3,717	4,308	4,394	18.21
Soviet Union	1,382.0	1,556.6	1,617.7	5,430	5,863	5,991	10.33

Source: From *Statistical Abstract of the United States, 1985*, Table 1481, p. 846.

Although the different values and aims of socialist and capitalist societies make comparisons of how effectively they achieve the goals of high average material well-being and equality somewhat difficult, such comparisons are still meaningful. Both economic growth and equity are stated goals of most societies today. To the extent that one form of economic and social organization achieves more in one direction and no less in the other, it probably is possible to draw positive conclusions about the effectiveness of one system over the other.

A common goal in both capitalist and socialist economies is to have a high and stable real rate of economic growth. Most planned, socialist economies are not highly industrialized. Because of the strong drive to develop heavy industry, they have frequently emphasized high rates of growth, even if this has meant severely limiting the production of consumer goods. Table 35.2 indicates real aggregate output, output per capita, and growth in output per capita for

the same countries listed in table 35.1. Except for the Democratic Republic of Germany and Czechoslovakia, the levels of per capita output in the socialist economies are quite low by western industrial standards. For most of the socialist economies, including the Soviet Union, this measure of the standard of living suggests that they are at a level comparable to that of countries like Greece, Spain, and Turkey rather than the United States, the Federal Republic of Germany, and Canada. Despite the high priority claimed for growth in these semideveloped economies, only China, the poorest of the lot, has achieved a degree of expansion that is remarkable by the standards of capitalist countries.

One rationale given for planning is to avoid the "chaos" of capitalist societies as reflected in their recurring business cycles. Therefore, the socialist economies also tend to emphasize stable economic growth as part of a central plan. With respect to inflation and employment, socialist economies tend to use more price controls to keep "necessities" affordable and to

*The **materials balance approach** is a planning device in which a set of accounts is formulated by a central planning agency and used to coordinate the quantities of inputs and outputs needed to achieve production goals for an economy.*

guarantee jobs for workers to a greater extent than is the case in capitalist economies. Both price controls and job guarantees create economic waste and resource misallocations, but they are viewed as effective means of protecting the standard of living of working people and avoiding unemployment. After all, socialist planning is advertised as a means of avoiding the deterioration of living standards and growing unemployment of the working classes that Karl Marx viewed as an inevitable by-product of capitalist economic development.

If we take the popular socialist statement "to each according to his needs" as a goal of socialist economies, then there should be a commitment to a substantially more equal distribution of income across households in socialist economies, in which property is mainly owned by the state, than in capitalist economies, which are characterized by private property arrangements. The argument for nationalizing property in the socialist economies has been to avoid the rich-poor contrast with which the socialist governments characterize capitalist societies.

▶ Characteristics of a Planned, Socialist Economy

We can learn a great deal about differences between socialist and capitalist economies by discussing specific examples. Our examples will be the two archetypes of their respective economic systems, the Soviet Union and the United States. We have already devoted most of this book to examining the United States economy. Now we will look at how the economic system of the Soviet Union works. This will represent our benchmark of the level of economic performance in socialist economies. The Soviet Union is the oldest continuously planned socialist economic system in the world. It has served as a model for Eastern Europe, China, and other socialist states. In a way, different planned, socialist economies can be usefully described as variants of the Soviet centrally planned economy. The relative importance of the Soviet Union in world affairs and the relative ignorance among westerners of how its economic system works makes it an important case to analyze.

How Annual Output Plans Are Developed in the Soviet Union

In terms of general command structure, the Communist party of the Soviet Union (CPSU) is the principle organ of control and supervision in the Soviet Union. The CPSU decides what the overall objectives of the economy ought to be in terms of a plan and prepares directives that eventually filter down through the economy to local plant managers. The state planning agency is called Gosplan. It has the tasks of providing the CPSU with information that can be used to determine future plans. It also must establish the instructions that tell each industry and firm what should be done to put the plan into effect. The major organizing unit for each industry is called the ministry of that industry. In the early stages of planning, the ministry transmits the tentative output targets and other instructions to individual enterprises for comments and informational input. Then the proposed targets, along with proposed modifications, work their way back up through the system to Gosplan.

To complete the plan, a **materials balance approach** is used, which means that physical units of inputs and outputs are added up to ensure that quantities demanded and supplied are all equal to each other. In principle, the questions of what to produce and how to produce it are answered simultaneously during this last round of planning. Finally, Gosplan directives are sent out in the *techprominplan* (technical industrial financial plan). These disaggregated unit enterprise targets are legally binding. Only a few thousand basic commodities are centrally planned this way. Most products are subject to planning at the regional or local level, and many are not subject to planning at all. Plans are revised annually.

Incentives

Individual enterprises are run by managers who are on fixed base salaries. In addition to their base salaries, managers receive bonuses for achieving or exceeding planned output targets. These bonuses can be as much as 35 percent of base salaries. There are two interesting negative side effects of the bonus system. First, in the early stages of formulating the plan, managers have an incentive to convince Gosplan to set low targets. Often, fraudulent information is provided in efforts to deceive Gosplan into setting lower targets than originally proposed. The more successful the deception, the more certain and substantial will be the bonus a manager receives. Second, if targets are expressed in terms of quantities only, without specification of quality standards, there is an obvious incentive to produce large quantities of shoddy output in order to exceed target and qualify for bonuses.

Market-Clearing Mechanisms

As we have seen, the complexity of planning production of all commodities and coordinating inputs is too great a task for Gosplan. Much coordination is left to regional and local subunits of the CPSU and planning agency. The materials balance approach is simply insufficient to assure a balance of supply and demand in all markets. Consequently, other mechanisms must be used to help eliminate shortages and surpluses of various goods and services.

Product Markets Under Price Controls

Each planned enterprise in the Soviet Union has a budget. Budgets go through the state bank, which is called Gosbank. Included in the budgets are investment funds, subsidies, profits, and all sales and purchases. Prices are usually set by administrative authority to equal estimated average cost plus a small profit. Prices at the wholesale level were set in 1955 and remained fixed until 1966. The last general reform of wholesale prices occurred in 1966–1967. At the retail level, prices are adjusted to equate demand and supply by using a system of taxes and subsidies. Figures 35.1 and 35.2 illustrate how taxes and subsidies are used to clear markets in the Soviet Union.

In figure 35.1, the demand and supply curves, D and S, would determine an equilibrium market-clearing price of P(0) and a quantity of Q(0) in a market economy. Suppose, however, that historical precedent has determined that the controlled price is P(C). At this price, there is an excess demand for the

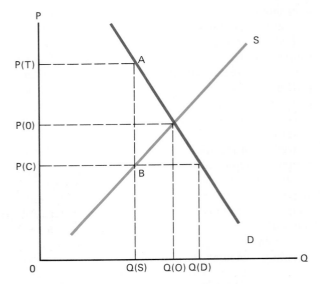

Figure 35.1   Setting prices in the Soviet Union
D and S are the demand and supply curves for some commodity. Since prices are centrally planned and seldom revised, the price is not likely to be the market-clearing (equilibrium) price P(0), associated with the equilibrium output Q(0). If the controlled price is set at P(C), output Q(S) will be less than the quantity demanded Q(D). A "turnover" tax is added to P(C) to reach price P(T) and clear the market. Turnover tax revenue equals the area of the rectangle P(C)P(T)AB.

product equal to Q(D) − Q(S). In order to eliminate this shortage, a "turnover" tax is imposed, equal to P(T) − P(0). This tax, when added to the controlled price, results in a market price of P(T). Notice that the new price, including the tax, clears the market in the sense that the quantity Q(S) also becomes the quantity demanded. The government then collects turnover tax revenue represented by the rectangle P(T) A B P(C). If the turnover tax is paid out to the enterprise producing this good, it may increase its output. However, if the government retains the tax revenue, consumers end up paying a higher price for less output than they would in a market economy. Given the inertia inherent in bureaucratic systems and the absence of a profit incentive to meet consumer (as opposed to Gosplan) demands, controlled prices and targeted output levels are not likely to respond quickly or fully to market signals.

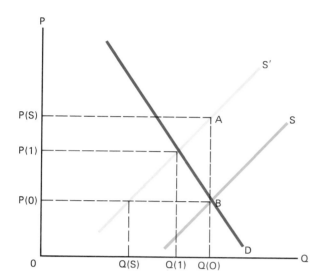

Figure 35.2   Price adjustments in the Soviet Union
D and S are initial demand and supply conditions for some
commodity, and P(0) and Q(0) are equilibrium price and
quantity. An adverse supply shift to S′ will shift equilibrium
price and quantity to P(1) and Q(1) in a market economy. In the
Soviet Union an excess demand of Q(0) − Q(S) results at the
old price. A production subsidy of P(S) − P(0) causes the
quantity supplied to equal the quantity demanded.

Figure 35.2 illustrates what happens when there
is a change in the initial demand and supply conditions. Suppose the production of some good is reduced
because a supplier fails to provide a necessary input
or because of a weather-related shortfall of some raw
material. The supply curve shifts from S to S′, reflecting the changed condition. At the controlled price
of P(0), a shortage of Q(0) − Q(S) will result where
none had existed before. The free market response
would be an increase in the equilibrium price from
P(0) to P(1). However, in a controlled economy, a
consumer price of P(0) might be maintained and the
market cleared by providing producers with a payment, or subsidy, equal to P(1) − P(0). The monetary cost of this program to the government is
represented by the area of the rectangle
P(S) A B P(0). In this response to an excess demand,
the government has encouraged more output than a
free market would.

Setting controlled prices and then adjusting them
with taxes and subsidies to eliminate shortages (or
gluts) may appear to lead to relatively smoothly
working "markets" under the best of circumstances.
However, this practice is almost certain to result in
overproduction of some goods and underproduction
of others when judged against the criterion of economic efficiency. Even though consumers can purchase all they want in figures 35.1 and 35.2 at the
posttax and postsubsidy prices, they would prefer to
have more of the good in figure 35.1 and less of the
good in figure 35.2 than Gosplan has chosen to provide. Moreover, as we previously noted, product
quality often suffers as a result of the planning emphasis on meeting quotas, which are set in quantity
terms.

Factor Price Determination and the Allocation
of Factor Inputs
Factor prices in the Soviet Union are not designed to
signal firms to economize on relatively scarce inputs
or to direct labor, machinery, and raw materials toward their most productive uses. Land and buildings
are primarily owned by the state. Land is allocated
to enterprises and farms administratively, and no rent
is charged. Private saving decisions have virtually
nothing to do with the allocation of aggregate production between consumption and investment. The
Soviet Union has a strong desire for economic growth
as reflected in a ratio of investment to GNP of between 35 and 40 percent. Note that even though this
is more than double the ratio in the United States, the
GNP growth rate in the Soviet Union has tended to
be less, not more, than in its major capitalist competitor.

We indicated earlier that in the Soviet Union the
choice of production technique is generally made by
a planning agency. The expressed goal of planning is
to minimize cost, that is, to satisfy the plan efficiently.
However, without market-determined wage rates,
capital costs, interest rates, and so on to guide them,
planners are often wide of the mark when it comes to
cost minimization. Furthermore, planners often have
political goals that may lead to decisions that are non-
cost minimizing. For example, heavy industries such

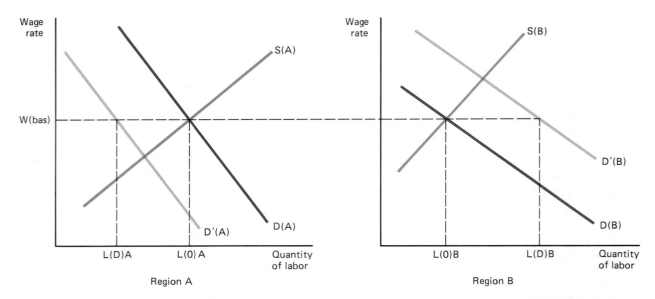

Figure 35.3   Shortages and underemployment of labor in the Soviet Union

D(A), D(B), S(A), and S(B) are the initial labor demand and supply curves in regions A and B, respectively. The equilibrium wage rate in each region is initially W(bas), the basic wage rate. Equilibrium employment is initially L(0)A and L(0)B, respectively. A leftward shift in the demand for labor in region A creates underemployment equal to L(0)A − L(D)A, while an increase in demand in region B creates a shortage equal to L(D)B − L(0)B.

as steel production and armament manufacturing may be promoted to lend an appearance of military strength to the nation. Some national regions may be favored with new facilities in order to please local political leaders even though other locations would be less costly. Finally, the immense discretion and power in the hands of strategically located planning officials opens the door to personal gain through bribery and corruption.

Once we recognize the maze of administrative levels, directives, plans, and individuals that directs the allocation of resources, it becomes easy to understand the immense possibilities for distortions and misallocations, to understand why all recent Soviet administrations have been plagued by widespread corruption.

Workers in the Soviet Union have some discretion in their choice of job and where they work. Nevertheless, basic wage rates and differentials associated with different skills are set administratively rather than in the marketplace. The government manipulates wage differentials to adjust labor supplies.

Figure 35.3 illustrates how the manipulation of wage rates can generate shortages of labor in some areas simultaneously with a glut, or unemployment, of labor in other regions. The curves D(A), D(B), S(A), and S(B) represent labor demand and supply in regions A and B, respectively. The planning authority has set a basic wage rate for both regions, W(bas), that initially equates the quantity of labor demanded and supplied. Suppose now that the demand for output from region A declines while that in region B increases. Labor demand in region A falls to D'(A), while that in region B rises to D'(B). In a free labor market we would expect the wage rate in region A to fall and the wage rate in region B to rise, leading to a shift of labor to region B from region A. This migration of labor would cause the labor supply curve in region A to shift leftward and the labor supply curve in region B to shift rightward. This shift of the labor force would continue until wage rates in the two regions were once again equal.

With administratively set wage rates, a labor shortage equal to $L(D)B - L(0)B$ will appear in region B. In the Soviet system, any evidence of unemployment is looked upon with great disfavor. Therefore, enterprise managers in region A would be risking their reputations if they laid off the workers no longer desired. Thus, the excess supply of labor in region A—$L(0)A - L(D)A$—takes the form of disguised unemployment. *Disguised unemployment* amounts to making work for employees who are no longer required in order to avoid direct evidence of more workers than jobs. This problem of simultaneous disguised unemployment and labor shortages across occupations and geographic regions is common in the Soviet Union. When shortages become particularly acute, planners will adjust wage rates and working conditions to attract workers. However, as in administration of the turnover tax and subsidy schemes described above, the adjustments are too few and too slow to avoid substantial misallocation of labor.

The Soviet system of administered prices and wages creates unfilled demands for goods and workers in many areas. This creates numerous opportunities for workers to increase their incomes substantially if they can help fill these demands either legally or illegally.[7] One interesting result has occurred in agriculture. In addition to guaranteed wages earned on state-owned or collectively owned farms, families are allowed to own small (half acre) plots and to sell their produce on the open market. Since the end of World War II the private agricultural sector has provided a very large share of the fresh meat, fruit, and vegetables in Soviet markets and is estimated to have provided about 40 percent of all farm income. The second way in which workers can enhance their incomes is to provide services to the underground economy of illegal activities. This does not necessarily involve dealing in illicit commodities, but perhaps providing services such as auto repair, plumbing, and so on, outside the system. The amount of production carried on in this fashion can only be guessed at.

Economic Performance of Capitalist and Socialist Economic Systems

The bottom line in evaluating comparative economic systems is how well they perform in meeting general social goals. We will now briefly examine the success that a sample of socialist economies and capitalist economies have had in providing their citizens with some broad measures of economic well-being. In evaluating these performance measures we should also bear in mind that in addition to material measures, many individuals would also include political and economic freedom as desired characteristics of economic and social organization. While measures of freedom cannot be made as precisely as measures of production and consumption, it is generally agreed that citizens in planned, socialist economies have less than do those of most capitalist economies. If the two economic systems turned out to perform equally well on purely economic criteria, then, a case could be made that greater freedom of choice and action makes capitalism the preferred system. This is a consideration that each reader should bear in mind when comparing capitalist and socialist economic performance.

Another point that should be considered when comparing the relative performance of capitalist and socialist economies is that the *level* of economic development (as measured by per capita income) is also an important determinant of various performance measures. For example, the proportion of total production devoted to health and welfare services, or to education, depends on per capita wealth as well as on the political-economic system of a country. The process of economic development itself has historically been associated with increased equality of the relative income distribution and increased quality of social services. We can suggest two explanations for this observation. One explanation, as Adam Smith observed, is that rapid economic growth often provides benefits for even the poorest elements of society. The second explanation is that advanced capitalist societies have had at least one or two centuries to observe the social and political stresses that emerge in market economies. They have had the time and experience to develop systems that reduce poverty, social alienation,

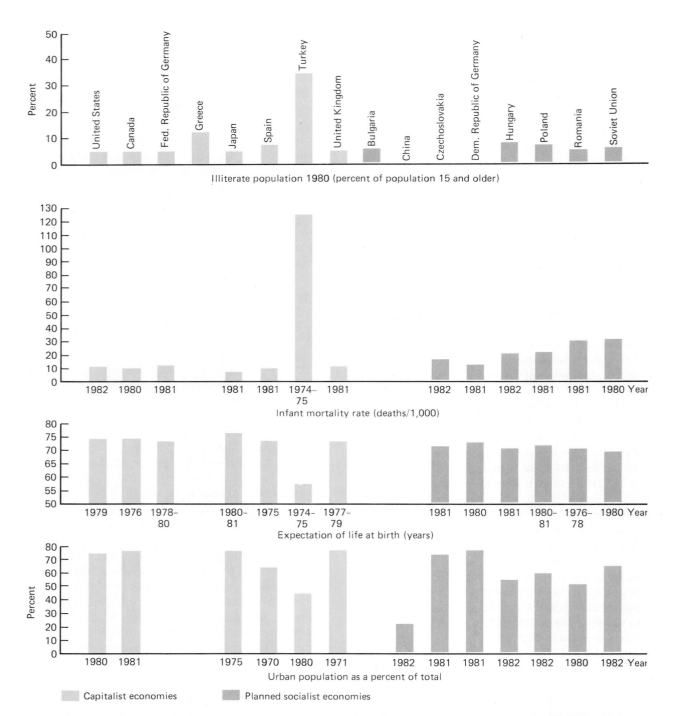

Figure 35.4   Population characteristics in capitalist and planned, socialist economies

From *Statistical Abstract of the United States,* Table 1505, p. 861, Table 1506, p. 862, and Table 1508, pp. 863–64.

and political unrest. To avoid confusing the effects of a country's economic system with its level of economic development, remember that countries such as Greece and Spain are at about the same level of economic development as most planned, socialist economies. In our evaluation of relative performance, we will examine several different characteristics of countries that are related to the quality of everyday life.

General Measures of Health and Literacy

Figure 35.4 contains data on several measures of the welfare of the population of capitalist and socialist countries. First, we see that the proportion of the population that is urban in the socialist countries (with the exception of Czechoslovakia and the Democratic Republic of Germany) is similar to that of Spain. The least developed capitalist and socialist economies in our sample, Turkey and China, respectively, are predominantly agrarian societies.

Estimates of life expectancy at birth in the socialist economies are generally less than in the advanced capitalist economies and even less than in Spain. Surprisingly, life expectancy at birth in the Soviet Union (69 years) is less than in all of the other Eastern European countries for which we have data. The relatively low life expectancy at birth in the socialist countries is partly attributable to their high infant mortality rates. The infant mortality rate reflects live births that result in death by age one per 1,000 live births. The worst figure (125) is for Turkey, the poorest country for which we have data. The infant mortality rate among socialist economies for which we have data is highest in the Soviet Union (28–30), and it is three times the infant mortality rate in Spain. Mothers' health, the quality of prenatal care, and the availability and quality of infant medical care all affect the infant mortality rates. These figures raise some doubts about the quality of health care provided under planned socialism.

On the other hand, if literacy is important to the quality of life, the planned economies fare well relative to Greece and Spain. In fact, for several planned economies, including the Soviet Union, the illiteracy rates compare favorably with those of the most advanced capitalist economies.

Health and Health Services

Figure 35.5 provides information on the commitment of material resources and personnel to health care services in capitalist and socialist economies. As one might expect, the least developed capitalist and socialist economies, Turkey and China, have the highest ratios of population per hospital bed and per physician. In terms of the availability of hospital beds, physicians, and dentists, the socialist economies fare well in comparison with the most advanced capitalist economies. It is of course important to bear in mind that the data in figure 35.5 reflect the quantity of health care facilities and personnel available but do not inform us about the quality of those facilities or the skills of the health care personnel.

Communication and Education Services

Figure 35.6 contains data on various communication and education services. The first four sections report on the relative availability of telephones, newspapers, televisions, and radios in our sample countries. The relative availability of televisions and radios in the socialist countries is comparable to availability in Spain and Greece. Daily newspapers are as readily available in socialist economies as in the more advanced capitalist economies and more available than in Spain. In contrast, telephones are much more readily available in Greece and Spain than in any of the socialist economies. Since telephones permit private individuals to send and receive information from one another, the relative scarcity of telephones in socialist states may have more to do with the security of the government than with the ability of planned economies to provide telephone services. Try to imagine how different United States society would be if eight out of every nine telephones were removed to replicate the relative scarcity of telephones in the Soviet Union. The failure of the trade union movement in Poland to prevent martial law through more effective coordination of strikes and work slowdowns in 1980 may be easier to understand when one realizes that there is one telephone for every ten people in Poland compared to almost eight telephones for every ten people in the United States.

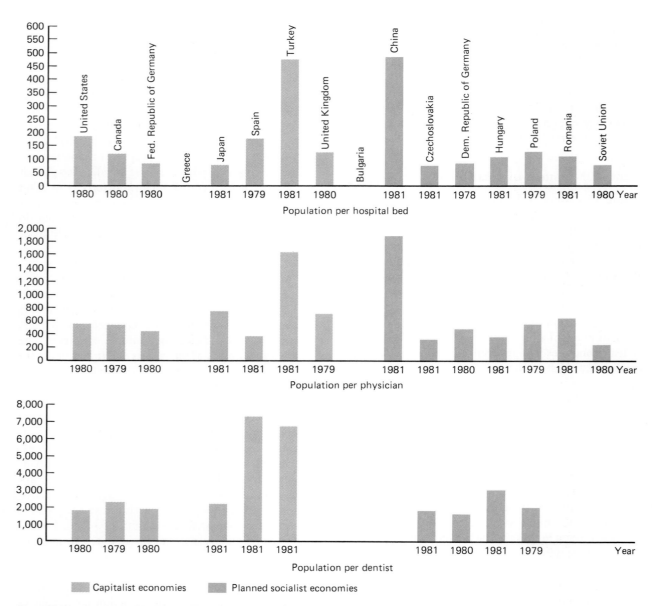

Figure 35.5   Provision of health services in capitalist and planned, socialist economies

From *Statistical Abstract of the United States,* Table 1506, p. 862, Table 1508, pp. 863–64, and Table 1531, pp. 881–82.

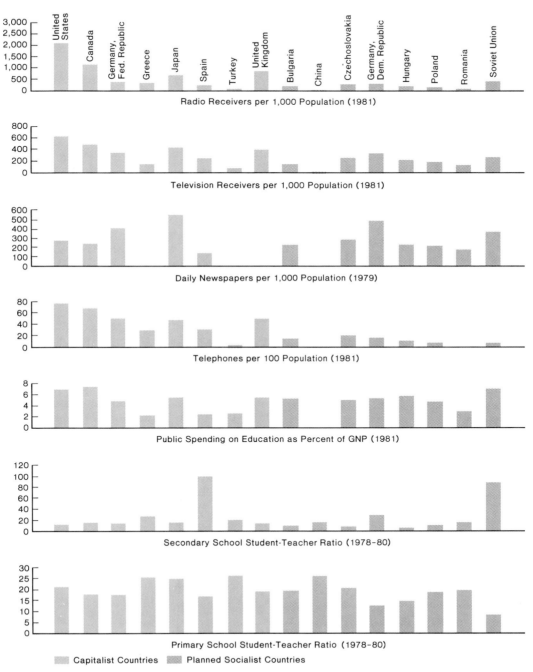

Figure 35.6   Education and communication services in capitalist and socialist economies

From *Statistical Abstract of the United States,* Table 1508, pp. 863–64, Table 1531, pp. 881–82, 1985, Table 1480, p. 845, and Table 1487, p. 849.

Figure 35.6 also illustrates public expenditures on education relative to GNP and student-teacher ratios. Student-teacher ratios for primary and secondary schools are similar across capitalist and planned economies. Spain and the Soviet Union seem to have extremely high student-teacher ratios in their secondary schools. Spain and Greece have lower shares of GNP going to public education than any of the socialist economies for which we have data. Public expenditures on education relative to aggregate income in the socialist economies compare favorably to the corresponding shares observed in the most advanced capitalist economies. Adding in private school expenditures relative to GNP would no doubt raise the aggregate educational expenditure-GNP ratios in capitalist economies above those for the socialist countries.

Military Spending and Military Presence

Americans have traditionally been concerned about the role of the military in society. There are frequent expressions of concern about the potential diversion of economic resources to wasteful military projects that benefit only the "military-industrial complex." Opposition to maintaining a large standing army during peacetime and arguments for the draft in wartime have often rested on the belief that a substantial professional military force is always a threat to democracy.

The first four columns of table 35.3 contain data on military spending in several economies. Not surprisingly, the United States and the Soviet Union are the capitalist and socialist economies that spend the highest share of GNP on the military. It is surprising, however, that even at the height of the Vietnam War in 1971, military spending relative to GNP in the United States was only 7 percent, less than half of the 14.9 percent GNP share going to the military in the Soviet Union. By 1982, United States military expenditure relative to GNP was 6.4 percent, whereas the Soviet Union's share of GNP going to the military increased to 15.0 percent. Soviet military expenditures were equivalent to $242.4 billion in 1982 compared to $185.2 billion in the United States. It is interesting to note that in his biography, deposed Soviet Premier Nikita Khrushchev echoed President Eisenhower's warning about the danger to society of a growing military-industrial complex.[8] Even apart from the United States and the Soviet Union, the share of GNP going to the military tends to be higher in planned, socialist economies than in capitalist economies.

The last two columns of table 35.3 indicate the relative presence of the military among the population. In 1975, the number of armed forces personnel was lower in the United States than in the Soviet Union, 0.99 percent compared to 1.61 percent. By 1982, the presence of military personnel had declined to 0.91 in the United States. However, it had risen to 1.63 percent in the Soviet Union.

Other socialist economies also tend to have more military personnel relative to their populations than do other capitalist countries. Whatever the explanation for that difference may be, to many people it reflects a relatively unattractive characteristic of the planned economies.

Table 35.3   Military spending and armed forces personnel in capitalist and socialist economies

Capitalist countries	Military expenditures in constant 1981 dollars (millions)		Percent of GNP		Armed Forces (thousands) (1982)	Armed forces per 1,000 population	
	1975	1982	1975	1982		1975	1982
United States	141,213	185,205	5.8	6.4	2,108	9.9	9.1
Canada	4,392	5,790	1.9	2.2	82	3.4	3.3
Federal Republic of Germany	20,924	22,970	3.6	3.4	480	8.0	7.9
United Kingdom	23,068	25,815	4.9	5.1	322	6.2	5.8
Planned socialist countries							
China	48,909	46,691	11.6	7.1	4,490	4.6	4.3
Democratic Republic of Germany	8,060	9,655	5.6	5.8	233	13.0	14.0
Soviet Union	206,351	242,419	14.9	15.0	4,400	16.1	16.3

Source: From *Statistical Abstract of the United States, 1985,* table 1513, p. 866.

▶ Summary and Conclusions

Having completed an extensive introduction to how capitalist economies allocate resources and a comparison with socialist allocation mechanisms, you should now be able to form your own opinion about which system forms the best basis for society to deal with the ever present problem of scarcity. This chapter has focused on the ways in which planned, socialist economies find answers to the basic economic questions that must be answered by all economic systems. The following major points were emphasized.

The questions of what to produce, how to produce it, and for whom to produce it are determined primarily by market forces in capitalist economies and by central planning in socialist economies.

Except for the Democratic Republic of Germany and Czechoslovakia, the levels of per capita output in socialist countries are quite low by western industrial standards. By this measure, the standard of living in the Soviet Union and most socialist countries is at a level comparable to that of countries like Greece, Spain, and Turkey.

Real economic growth during the 1970s was no greater among the socialist economies than among capitalist economies.

While basic commodities are produced subject to central plans in the Soviet Union, most products are subject to planning at the regional or local level. Plans are revised annually.

Prices at the wholesale level in the Soviet Union were last set in 1966/1967. Government taxes are used to eliminate excess demands, and government subsidies are used to eliminate excess supplies of goods subject to controlled prices.

Wage rates and wage differentials associated with different skills are set administratively rather than by market forces in the Soviet Union. Consequently, there tend to be persistent labor shortages in some regions and occupations, while at the same time there are labor surpluses in other regions and occupations.

Estimates of life expectancy at birth in the socialist economies are generally less than in the advanced capitalist economies.

The infant mortality rate in the Soviet Union is three times as high as it is in Spain. Life expectancy at birth is sixty-nine years in the Soviet Union, which is less than in the socialist countries of Eastern Europe in general.

The relative availability of hospital resources, doctors, and dentists in the socialist countries compares favorably with the availability of such resources in the advanced capitalist economies.

Public expenditures on education relative to aggregate income in the socialist economies compares favorably to the corresponding shares observed in advanced capitalist economies.

Television sets and radios are about as available in the socialist countries as they are in Greece and Spain. Telephones are much less available in socialist economies than in Spain and Greece.

Military spending relative to GNP is twice as high in the Soviet Union as it is in the United States. In 1982, military expenditures equaled $242.4 billion in the Soviet Union and $185.2 billion in the United States.

Military personnel are almost twice as large a share of the population in the Soviet Union as in the United States.

▶ Key Terms

capitalist economic system *725*

economic system *724*

materials balance approach *729*

▶ Questions for Discussion and Review

1. What are the four basic issues confronting any economic system, and how are they generally dealt with in capitalist and socialist economies?

2. Give specific examples of production techniques in capitalist countries that are not primarily market determined and explain them.

3. Give specific examples in which the answer to the question "what gets produced" is not primarily market determined in capitalist economies and explain your examples.

4. Explain how final annual production targets are established by the state planning agency in the Soviet Union.

5. Explain the positive and negative effects of bonus incentives for enterprise managers in the Soviet Union.

6. Illustrate and explain how a poor wheat harvest would be reflected in the Soviet Union if the price of wheat is fixed at P(W).

7. Illustrate and explain how a shortage of skilled labor could develop in the Soviet Union.

8. What, if any, incentive problems could arise if the United States tried to use taxes to reduce income inequality to equal that in the Soviet Union?

9. What political, social, and economic forces do you suppose could explain why income is as evenly distributed across households in a capitalist country like the United Kingdom as in the Soviet Union?

10. Explain how the size of the military-industrial complex could slow real economic growth in socialist economies and why they commit relatively more resources including personnel to the military than is generally true in capitalist economies.

*The **economic approach to government activity** uses the tools of modern economic analysis to study government behavior.*

11. Are the following statements true, false, or uncertain? Be sure to justify your answers.
   a. Government's primary economic role is to enforce property rights in a market economy.
   b. Government facilitates voluntary exchange in a market economy by protecting workers and consumers from exploitation.
   c. Individual self-interest is likely to lead to more ignorance in political decisions than in market decisions.
   d. The profit motive leads bureaucrats to supply public needs at the lowest possible cost to society.
   e. The principal difference between the behavior of politicians and that of business leaders is that business firms are operated solely to achieve the self-interest of their owners, while politicians cannot win elections if they do not strive for maximum social welfare.

12. A number of states and localities have passed legislation in the past few years limiting the power of their legislators to raise taxes without explicit voter approval. However, these restrictions do not govern which tax-expenditure issues will be placed on the ballot and which will be financed from general funds. Given this legislator discretion, which of the following activities are most likely to be submitted to the electorate for approval or rejection and which reserved for control of the legislative bodies? Defend your answers in terms of the analysis of government behavior developed in this chapter.
   a. Financing an ambulance and emergency squad.
   b. Subsidizing local bus transportation.
   c. Funding day-care centers for the children of working mothers.
   d. Supporting a local junior college.
   e. Urban redevelopment.

Appendix to Chapter 35

The Government's Role in Mixed, Capitalist Economies

Capitalist economies are mixed economies in that government plays a role in many branches of economic activity. In this section we will analyze government's goals, its means of achieving its ends, and the important behavioral characteristics of governments in mixed, capitalist economies. The **economic approach to government activity** is a theory of government activity in the same spirit that theory guides the economist's analysis of the behavior of households and business firms. Capitalist economies, as opposed to socialist economies, generally have representative governments, such as in the United States. In representative governments individual citizens affect government policies indirectly through their elected representatives. It is this process of indirect representation via the voting process that leads to different governmental behavior in capitalist systems than in most socialist systems, where the democratic process is much less well-developed, if it exists at all.

Bear in mind that a politician cannot work toward any desired goals without being elected. In other words, political survival is necessary, just as economic survival is necessary for a firm. Recall that in a competitive environment, surviving firms are forced to maximize profits. Similarly, the need to win elections serves as an effective constraint on politicians' desires to work toward "good government" when achieving that goal conflicts with the expressed goals of certain groups of voters in a democracy.

▶ Voting Behavior in a Democracy

We will now develop a simple analysis of voting behavior in a representative democracy. Then we will explore the actions of politicians, the voters' elected representatives. Finally, we will use the concepts of the "demand" and "supply" of government activities to derive some implications for government behavior in a mixed economy.

Self-Interest, Rational Ignorance, and Voting Behavior

The problems of financing public goods also affect citizens' voting behavior. By voting behavior, we mean the activities leading up to the act of voting, whether or not a citizen actually votes in an election, and the choice expressed if a vote

Logrolling is the mutual exchange of political support among special-interest groups.

is cast. To what extent does it make sense for an individual voter to gather information about the choices offered in an election or even to vote? When the voting population is large, say, 1,000 voters or more, the probability is extremely low that any single vote will determine which candidate or which proposition wins. However, the cost to an individual of acquiring information and casting a vote can be significant. Moreover, an individual citizen will benefit or be harmed by an election's results independently of whether or not he or she participates in the election.

These considerations imply that in public choices involving issues not likely to affect individuals, either significantly or directly, voters are likely to be free riders. They have a tendency to spend very little time becoming informed about, or even voting in, those elections where their own special interests are not involved. Suppose for the purpose of discussion that you would prefer an election outcome that transfers income to people below the median level of income in society. How much time and money would you be willing to spend to discover the probable effect of law X or candidate Y on this aspect of the income distribution? Probably not very much if you do not expect your vote to matter.

By contrast, if you are a member of the United Auto Workers Union, you are much more likely to learn about each candidate's position on tariffs on imported automobiles and other import restrictions. While you may fully understand that an increase in the tariff on Japanese autos will harm your fellow citizens, your relatively large gain compared to their relatively small individual losses is likely to influence you to vote against free trade in automobiles. The payoff to acquiring information and voting is relatively greater where private choices are involved. Thus, it is much more likely for ignorance to be rational in a public choice situation than when deciding whether to buy a particular item and how much of it to buy. An implication of this "principle of rational ignorance" is that public choice outcomes are likely to reflect individual preferences much less accurately than private choices.

► Social Choices in a Democracy: Outcomes of the Political Process

The behavior of voters and politicians can be thought of as roughly equivalent to the demand for and supply of public choices that determine government behavior in a democracy. Let us now examine how the interactions between voters and politicians affect government's role in a mixed economy.

Special Interests and Logrolling

Those of you who are budding politicians may have already developed some strategies to win elections when you run for office. One strategy is probably that you will align your platform to appeal to the strongly held feelings of certain important special-interest groups. One of the implications of our analysis of voters' and politicians' behavior is that voters with special interests will have a much stronger impact on legislation than one would expect on the basis of their proportion of the electorate. Anyone who doubts this need only reflect on agricultural policy in the United States and other industrial democracies of the world. Farmers account for only about 3 percent of the United States labor force and less than 10 percent of the Japanese and Western European labor forces. Yet their influence on public policy is immense in those nations.[1]

A second strategy to win elections is **logrolling,** whereby a politician convinces various special-interest groups to support him or her and vice versa. In this way certain minority held, but strongly felt, views may prevail in public choices. For example, votes from the arid South for flood control in the North may be exchanged for New England's support for massive irrigation projects in the South. Legislators who are not willing to make deals are not likely to get very far in promoting constituents' interests.

Frequently, logrolling has a negative connotation in the mass media and other public forums. On the one hand, it can serve as a means whereby citizens engage in mutually beneficial exchange of their votes in a manner similar to voluntary exchange in goods markets. On the other hand, it can also lead to expenditures on projects that cost more than the value to their beneficiaries. This is economically inefficient. For example, if southwesterners and New Englanders logroll at the expense of residents of the Midwest, then midwesterners may pay for part of projects in other regions that do not benefit them and that New Englanders and southwesterners would be unwilling to pay for in full. Why would midwesterners pay? They may be in a minority, or more importantly, their lack of a special interest in the projects that benefit other regions may lead to their ignorance of the relatively small amounts they pay per individual.

Shortsightedness and Obfuscation

Surviving politicians may emphasize the present relative to the future and obfuscate (confuse) rather than clarify issues. Forming an opinion about the future requires close attention and a willingness by voters to spend time weighing the facts and hypotheses involved in forecasting. The principle of rational voter ignorance works against politicians' supplying citizens with information they do not want to use, and this is likely to lead to rational shortsightedness on the part of voters. That is, voters are not likely to take the time or devote much effort to evaluating the effects of policies that they do not expect to have a major impact on their well-being.

It is difficult to test the hypothesis that people are often shortsighted when it comes to political issues. Concrete data on this topic are not available. Still, informal observations lend support. One example is in the area of national defense. Military preparedness involves substantial current cost in return for uncertain future benefits. Moreover, the information required to make informed decisions is extensive and costly to acquire and evaluate. Who knows whether we will really need a larger air force or more nuclear missiles in Europe to protect us and our allies from the Soviet Union? The costs are borne now and are readily perceived. The benefits—costly and difficult to evaluate—are at best uncertain. Thus, there would appear to be a tendency in societies with representative, democratic governments to allocate fewer resources to defense than do countries with totalitarian governments. As table 35.3 indicates, reality apparently bears out this tendency. In evaluating this comparison, it is important to keep in mind that the cost of a given amount of military protection is likely to be inflated by government decisions, and this will also influence the amount of protection chosen in a democratic process. We will deal with the costs of government activities shortly.

Another example of shortsightedness is "government by crisis." Immediate solutions to severe problems are more appealing than preventing problems over the long term. For example, the long-term impacts of price controls on quantities supplied are frequently less persuasive than their immediate and short-lived effects on the amount that must be paid for a good. Excessively accelerating the money supply is known to be ultimately inflationary, but it may yield short-term political gains by temporarily increasing the pace of economic activity. Another example of the tendency to put off dealing with problems until they reach the critical stage is Social Security funding. Only when there is imminent danger of exhausting funds for current payments has Congress been willing to address the problems of financing Social Security and determining benefits. Even then, there is a strong bias toward quick and temporary fixes rather than long-term solutions.

Because of rational ignorance, present benefits or costs are more readily apparent to an average citizen than benefits or costs that will occur in the future. Thus, present benefits or costs are more likely to influence public choices in a democracy. At the same time, politicians who want to pool the support of special-interest groups through logrolling will do well to exploit the principle of rational ignorance. It will in general be harmful to a politician's political survival to clarify and emphasize project costs to the general public. Special-interest groups will be willing to learn about the benefits and costs of projects that concern them directly. However, as far as members of the general public are concerned, the politician will be inclined to act as if what they don't know won't hurt them. It may even pay to cloud the issues with extraneous facts and misleading arguments. For example, the average voter is unlikely to take the time to learn why it is *fallacious* to argue that lowering dairy industry price supports will lead to milk shortages and higher prices. Thus, this is a popular argument used by supporters of minimum prices for fresh milk.

Another example of obfuscation is government's eagerness to use conscription in obtaining military personnel, especially in time of war. Many people sincerely believe that a military draft is necessary to preserve civilian control over the military in a democracy and to share defense burdens fairly. However, when military forces are staffed through conscription rather than by paying wages high enough to attract voluntary armed forces, much of the cost is borne by draftees in foregone earnings and other lost opportunities in the private sector of the economy. If the costs were more obvious to nondrafted citizens through increases in their taxes or reductions in nonmilitary government expenditures, it would be more difficult to maintain armed forces of a given size, and popular support for military activities in wartime would probably be reduced. Thus, whatever the moral arguments in favor of a draft may be, they are reinforced by conscription's appeal as a cost-hiding way to finance military expenditures.

The Budgetary Process: Separation of Taxes from Expenditures

Logrolling and obfuscation of costs are more difficult in situations where taxpayers are presented with a tax bill for each individual government project. If each dam, income-maintenance program, and change in agricultural price supports were accompanied by the need to vote on the taxes to finance them, politicians would probably find it more difficult to commit government to expenditures from which many voters receive little or no benefit. State constitutions and local charters often specify that certain types of expenditures, such as public schools, libraries, and public transportation, must be linked to specific property tax levies or sales taxes or to other earmarked tax receipts. However, financing from a general fund appears to be politicians' method of choice when possible because it makes it easier to benefit special-interest groups at the expense of all taxpayers.

Bureaucratic Behavior and the Cost in Output of Government Services

How does government provide the services politicians or voters decide upon in a democracy? In the private sector the firm provides goods and services. Government also purchases the output of private firms, however. These government purchases are usually inputs into the process by which governments produce the services they ultimately furnish to their constituents. Within governments, *agencies* or *bureaus* correspond to private-sector firms in their role of producing government services from purchased inputs. Knowing how bureaus function in comparison to private-sector firms is crucial to understanding government's economic role in the mixed economy.

The key to understanding the difference between bureaucratic and firm behavior is profit and how it is affected by revenue and cost. Competitive firms must minimize costs if they are to survive. While monopoly power reduces survival pressures as a motive to lower costs, monopolists still benefit directly if they act to reduce their costs. This is not so with bureaucrats. A government official's salary is not in general linked, even indirectly, to success in reducing costs or increasing the value of government services to citizens. Because a bureau's services are not sold in the marketplace, its revenues are derived from legislative appropriations. A bureaucrat who reduces his or her agency's costs may actually receive a smaller appropriation next year rather than earn a promotion or salary increase.

If, through diligence, an agency's costs are reduced, the official in charge may receive a letter of commendation or possibly a promotion. However, the opposite may occur insofar as salary and prestige depend upon the number of employees supervised or the size of the agency's budget. Thus, the direct gain from cost saving is likely to be far less than

to a private firm. Moreover, reducing costs may involve laying off workers who are friends or political supporters. Cost savings that arise from cutting down office space, reducing the quality of the office environment, or moving to a cheaper location are likely to reduce bureaucrats' satisfaction on the job. And they are unlikely to receive monetary compensation for such sacrifices. We conclude, then, that bureaucratic costs per unit of service provided are likely to be higher than the costs of a private firm.

How is the output of a government bureau likely to differ from that of a private firm? First, consider the demand for a government agency's services. Most government activities involve goods or services that are not 100 percent "public." There is a private component, for example, to police protection insofar as individual citizens may ask a patrol car to drive through their neighborhood to quiet a rowdy party. Therefore, individual users' demands can affect government agencies' output directly in many cases. Generally, these services are not priced on a fee-per-use basis. This means that a user will typically face a zero marginal money cost and will demand a greater quantity of the service than if he or she were directly confronted with the true marginal cost of providing it. If an agency meets all demands, rather than engaging in formal or informal rationing, the tendency to charge users less than marginal cost will cause bureaucratic output to be larger than that of a private firm.

Bureaucrats' goals and constraints affect their willingness to meet individual citizens' demands for government services. We assume that government employees, like politicians, act in their own self-interest. Of course, they may wish to satisfy altruistic motives, and they may place a high value on the services their particular agencies provide to the public. Nevertheless, their behavior will be affected by the constraints they face in government employment, just as employees of private firms must function within the constraints imposed by the marketplace.

How, then, will bureaucrats respond to the demand for their output? There is no certain answer to this question. Remember that the management of a government agency is unlikely to do anything to reduce an agency's budget. We have shown that the quantity of government services demanded is likely to be larger than the quantity of comparable services demanded from the private sector because government is likely to charge less than the marginal cost of providing those services. A bureau will meet demand if its budget is large enough, but there is little incentive to avoid a shortage if to do so would require reducing its costs per unit of service. A shortage, after all, will create political pressure to increase the agency's budget. Thus, it is uncertain whether a government agency will supply more or less output than would a private firm providing the same good or service.

Labor Costs in Government

Our analysis of government costs is difficult to test against the facts because there are few data comparing government and private costs of producing similar products or providing similar services. (We do report some interesting empirical cost comparisons in the next subsection, however.) Bear in mind that government costs are likely to be higher than private costs *even if government pays the same price for its inputs as private employers do.* As we pointed out, a government official who lays off workers in order to reduce costs may well reduce political support in a democracy. The same line of reasoning suggests that government employers will not seek to hire workers of given skills at the lowest possible wage rates.

The principle of rational ignorance implies that if governments pay their employees more than market wage rates, a typical voter will not know. However, government employees have an intense interest in making sure their employee organizations and unions exert political pressure for high wages. In addition, it may hurt a politician's popularity with many voters to acquire a reputation of being hard on labor. There is evidence that government employees do earn more than workers in the private sector who are similar in such wage-related characteristics as experience, schooling, and health. This differential is most apparent at the federal government level, where workers have earned about 20 to 30 percent more than their private-sector counterparts in recent years.[2]

Some Illustrations of Public Choice

It is difficult to be precise in assessing the degree to which the democratic political process influences economic decisions made in the public sector. The reason is that for many important government functions, similar choices are not made in the private sector of a mixed economy. National defense is typically a government activity, for example. In those nations where mercenary armies are used, data on costs and effectiveness are virtually nonexistent. As we have already seen in chapter 35, another interesting comparison is with the government provision of military activities and national defense in planned, socialist economies, where government operates under a different set of constraints than in democracies.

Despite difficulties of little or no data, it is possible to gain some factual insights into the costs and quality of government services in a mixed economy, and we will now summarize information available on some areas of economic behavior at the local and national levels of government in the United States.

Government and Private Costs Compared

Government does not often compete directly with private industry in the United States, but there are some cases in which comparisons between government and private industry costs and quality can be made. Even without precise data, casual impressions of the success of United Parcel Service, Federal Express, Purolator, and other private package delivery services suggest that they outperform the United States Postal Service in certain instances. Some detailed analyses provide evidence that government's cost, and perhaps quality of service, disadvantages are by no means confined to package delivery. One study compared the efficiency of private and public provision of services in five industries.[3] One of these comparisons is for another country—between a government and a privately owned airline in Australia. The other comparisons involve the provision of fire protection, electricity, hospital services, and garbage collection in the United States. Each study was designed to compare the government and private costs of providing services of approximately equal quality. In every case, the government spent at least as much—and usually significantly more—to furnish a given quantity of service as did suppliers from the private sector.

The fire protection study is particularly interesting because it involved a government service that is traditionally organized and provided by the public sector. Scottsdale, Arizona, elected to hire a private firm to provide fire protection.[4] Payments to the private firm were financed from tax revenues, so this is an excellent illustration of the distinction between government's financing and government's providing a public service. Using detailed data on the production of fire protection, the study predicted that if Scottsdale had used a traditional government-operated fire department, its annual costs would have been 88 percent higher than what it actually paid the private firm.

▶ Key Terms

economic approach to   logrolling *742*
  government activity *741*

An Industrialization Plan

▶ The Action-Initiating Event

The opposition have been claiming that the country will never approach real economic growth rates like those experienced during the mid-1960s in the United States without systematic planning at the federal level. This is not a new presidential campaign issue. In fact, the opposition have been playing the same tune since the last presidential election campaign. However, our pollsters reported at last weekend's high-level campaign strategy meeting that the public is starting to take the opposition seriously. Apparently, voters have lost patience with the rate of economic growth in the country under the free market policies popularized by the government forces in the early 1980s. The leadership is afraid that the campaign could be hurt if we appear to have no position on the issue of federally directed growth programs. Obviously, the government cannot embrace the opposition proposals. The issue is whether we should offer a less government-directed program of our own or oppose any such program. We need some hard-headed analysis of the pros and cons of getting involved in the business of industrial planning at the national level.

▶ The Issue

There are three sets of issues to be addressed. First, there is the simple question of whether the slow rate of economic expansion in the United States in the last few years has in any way been attributable to a lack of economic planning that could have been undertaken at the national level. If recent economic performance in the United States could not have been improved upon by national planning, what could have been done that was not done? Other countries such as France, West Germany, the Soviet Union, and all of the Eastern bloc countries use some degree of central planning. How well have those countries performed in terms of economic growth compared to the United States in recent years? We all know that Japan has continued to experience rapid economic growth and that the Ministry for International Trade and Industry (MITI), is somehow involved in planning or making loans or conducting other activities related to economic development. The opposition are running all over the country claiming that MITI did this and MITI did that. How does MITI operate, and what if any evidence is there that MITI was at all responsible for Japan's rapid economic expansion in recent years?

A second set of issues that our political people will focus on involves the consequences for a democracy of moving toward central planning. Any philosophical thoughts you may have would be appreciated. However, we really would prefer that you concentrate on the economic issues.

The final set of issues we must consider is also economic rather than political. Suppose we opted not to endorse some form of national industrial planning. What economic reasons can we give for rejecting it? We know that the people at the top of the government's ticket lean in that direction philosophically. If we suppose for the sake of argument that voters are getting more sophisticated in their thinking on economic issues, we cannot simply wave the flag and say that planning is un-American. We will have to explain the kinds of economic nightmares that could emerge from federal industrial planning.

► Economic Policy Issues

To treat all of the foregoing systematically, you must pull together answers to the following set of economic questions: What have been some of the major reasons for slower than promised economic growth in the United States in recent years? Have countries that rely somewhat on central planning of industrial activities done as well or better than the United States in terms of economic growth in recent years? What is the planning role of MITI in Japan, and is it all that the opposition makes it out it to be? Can you give us some examples of how economic planning works in other countries? To the extent that we come down on the side of opposing federal industrial planning, can you provide some specific examples of how such planning creates more problems than it solves?

► Recommendations

We all know that the final decision on which direction the campaign takes will be made at the next level up in the election committee. However, there may be some second thoughts as election day gets closer—especially if it looks like a close race. For the moment, I want your best judgments regarding the specific questions that have been raised in this memorandum. However, I would appreciate your taking a litle extra time to pull together your own thoughts after responding to the questions posed above to provide me with your opinion on whether there is any role for federal industrial planning in our economy. If you think there could be such a role, what form would it have to take? I need that deeper insight from you in case we are ever faced with one of those eleventh hour strategy sessions and someone asks, "Now, what the hell do we do?"

Appendix A

Graphs

The economic models throughout this text are illustrated in diagrams called *graphs*. Graphing skills are essential for the analysis of economic problems, and this appendix is intended to outline the techniques and mechanics of graphing so that you may better understand and interpret these graphs. The following sections will familiarize you with the tools you will need. The best approach is to work through all of the examples in this appendix until you are satisfied that you can use the material confidently. A major mistake some beginning students of economics make is to try to memorize the graphs and then reproduce them for exams. You will find that this approach has a low probability of success. You should view the material presented here as essential not only for this course but any future courses in economics or other subjects in which graphs are important.

▶ What Is a Graph?

By illustrating economic relationships instead of merely talking about them, we can be much more precise, thus reinforcing your understanding of the subject matter. We depict many economic relationships by borrowing graphing techniques from mathematics. The basic idea of graphing is to illustrate the relationship between two measurable quantities that vary. These quantities are called *variables*. The basic layout of a graph is depicted in figure 1. Since we are going to examine the relationship between two variables, the graph is called a two-dimensional graph. We measure the two variables by means of two perpendicular lines called *axes*. Each axis represents the values of one of our two variables. The point of intersection for the axes is called the *origin* of the graph and is usually zero on both axes.

The next step is to assign values to our variables and then represent the values on the graph. This process is called *plotting* and begins with some representative values of the variables arranged in a table called a *schedule*. The schedule

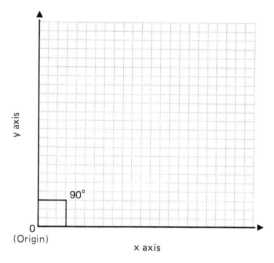

Figure 1

of values in table 1 will be used to plot the relationship between the two variables. The variables in this table represent the expected score on an economics midterm exam and the hours spent watching television the night before the exam. The two variables form associations called *ordered pairs*, which can be plotted on the graph. The first element of the ordered pair is associated with the horizontal or *x* axis on the graph. The second element of the ordered pair is associated with the vertical or *y axis* on the graph. In figure 2, the hours spent watching television the night before the exam are plotted on the x axis, and the expected scores on the exam are plotted on the y axis. After we plot the points from the schedule, we then connect the points to form a line. Notice that this straight line exhibits a downhill tilt from left to right. We call such a straight-line graph a *linear* graph that illustrates an *inverse* or *negative relationship* between the two variables. In other words, when one of the variables increases the other variable decreases. In this example, we say that your exam score is inversely or negatively related to the number of hours you spend watching television.

Some schedules of variables exhibit a *direct* or *positive relationship*. This means that as one variable becomes larger, the other variable also increases. Such a schedule is shown in table 2. We illustrate this data in figure 3 by plotting the number of hours spent studying for an economics exam on the x axis and the expected exam scores on the y axis. The

Table 1

Exam scores	Hours spent watching television
100	0
90	2
80	4
70	6

Table 2

Expected exam scores	Hours spent studying
60	1
70	2
80	3
90	4

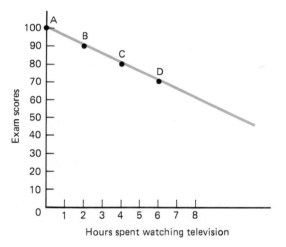

Figure 2

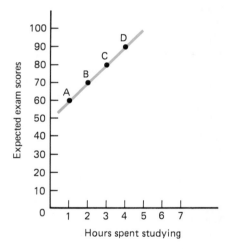

Figure 3

interpretation of this graph is that the more hours you spend studying for the exam, the higher you can expect your exam score to be. Notice that this linear graph tilts uphill from left to right. This indicates a positive or direct relationship between two variables. You should be able to see by now that one of the key advantages of using and understanding graphs is to be able to tell at a glance whether two variables are positively or negatively related without examining every line of a schedule.

A third type of relationship is frequently encountered in economics. Certain variables exhibit no relationship between each other. This situation is graphed in figure 4. The number of hours in a week (168) is constant and therefore is not influenced by the value of the other variable on the graph, the scores on the exam. We represent the fixed number of hours in a week by drawing a horizontal line parallel to the x axis at 168 on the y axis. This illustration indicates that no matter what the score on the economics exam, the number of hours in a week is still 168.

Not all relationships between variables in economics are linear. Variables sometimes exhibit a *nonlinear* or *curvilinear relationship* with each other. In general, a nonlinear relationship between two variables indicates that the relationship changes as the variables change value. (In the previous examples, the variables exhibited the same relationship regardless of their size.) We illustrate a curvilinear relationship between two variables in figure 5. The y axis shows the number of pages typed per hour, and the x axis shows the number of hours spent typing. The hill-shaped curve that shows the relationship between the two variables indicates that as the typist begins to type, typing speed accelerates as the typist becomes familiar with the typewriter and the material being typed. The maximum number of pages typed per hour occurs at six hours. After that, the number of pages typed per hour begins to fall, probably because the typist is tired and makes more mistakes. The curvilinear graph in figure 5 exhibits both uphill and downhill tilt.

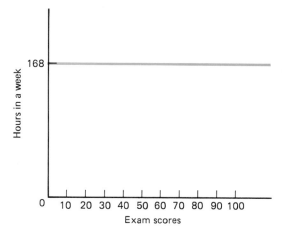

Figure 4

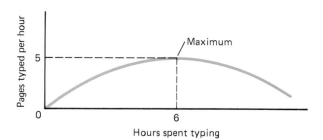

Figure 5

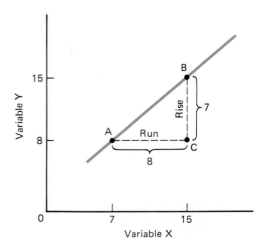

Figure 6

► Slope

Until now, we have referred to the tilt of the line as being either uphill or downhill. The tilt of the line can be measured more precisely with a concept known as *slope*. The slope of a straight line measures the relative change in the two variables that are graphed. Specifically, the formula for slope is the ratio of the difference between two values of the y-axis variable to the difference between the corresponding values of the x-axis variable. In the language we previously used, the slope measures the degree of the tilt of the line. In figure 6, a positive linear relationship is illustrated between two variables called X and Y. Notice the triangle ABC. The height of this triangle, CB, measures the amount of *rise* in the line between points A and B. The base of the triangle, AC, measures the horizontal distance between A and B. This distance is referred to as the *run* between two points. Therefore, a good way to remember the formula for the slope of a line is "rise over run," or in our figure, the distance BC divided by the distance AC. Having an intuitive feel for what slope is, we can measure precisely the slope of a line with the following formula:

$$\text{Slope} = \frac{Y_2 - Y_1}{X_2 - X_1},$$

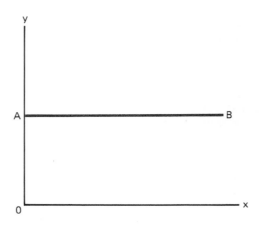

Figure 7

where Y_2 and X_2 represent the ordered pair associated with point B, and Y_1 and X_1 represent the ordered pair associated with point A. In the text, we usually use the symbol Δ to indicate a change in a variable, such as the change in Y between Y_1 and Y_2 or in X between X_1 and X_2. Using this symbol, the formula for slope becomes

$$\text{slope} = \frac{\Delta Y}{\Delta X},$$

where ΔY represents $Y_2 - Y_1$ and ΔX represents $X_2 - X_1$. Substituting for the variables in the slope formula, the slope of this line is $+\frac{7}{8}$. The slope of a straight line is always the same everywhere on the line so it does not matter which pair of points we choose to calculate the slope. If the sign of the slope is positive, the line exhibits a positive or direct relationship. If the sign of the slope is negative, the line exhibits an inverse or negative relationship. Go back to figure 2 and prove to yourself that the slope of the line shown there is negative. (Hint: What value of $X_2 - X_1$ is required to increase your score by ten points?)

Figures 7 and 8 illustrate two special cases of slope. In figure 7, the horizontal line drawn parallel to the x axis has a slope equal to zero. This line has zero slope because there is no rise to the line regardless of the length of the run. Figure 8 depicts a line drawn parallel to the y axis. This line has infinite slope because the rise is infinite and the run is zero.

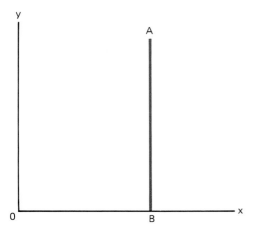

Figure 8

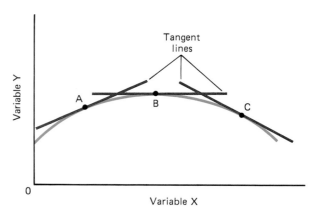

Figure 9

These special cases are used frequently in economics, and it is therefore necessary to recognize and understand them.

How do you measure the slope of a curvilinear relationship? We can see by inspection that the slope of a curve such as that in figure 5 is not always the same. It continually changes at each point along the curve. The answer to the question is surprisingly simple because we can apply the previous method for measuring the slope of a straight line. Figure 9 depicts a curvilinear relationship between the variables X and Y. Since the curve does not have a constant slope, we have to measure the slope at particular points along the curve. The procedure is to draw straight lines that touch the curve only at the points at which we want to measure the curve's slope. Such lines are called *tangent lines* and are illustrated in figure 9. The next step is to calculate the slopes of the tangent lines using the previous formula. In figure 9, the curve has a positive slope at point A. At point B, the maximum, the curve has zero slope, and at point C, the curve has a negative slope.

An important but often ignored problem with slope measurements is that they are sensitive to the units of measurement used for plotting the variables on the graph. This problem often leads to misinterpretations of the graph. For example, suppose that you want to measure the altitude of an airplane at various points in time after the airplane leaves the ground. You can measure the altitude in feet or miles. But when you plot your results with altitude on the y axis and time on the x axis, the slope of the graph measured in miles will be much smaller than the slope of the graph measured in feet. With slope interpreted as the rate of change of altitude with respect to time, the graph measured in miles will give the impression of a slowly climbing airplane. The graph measured in feet will give the impression of a rapidly climbing airplane. Since data in economics are often measured in different units, economists frequently avoid this problem with slope by emphasizing *percentage changes* for the variables. In this example, when the altitude of the airplane increases from 500 feet to 1,000 feet, there is a percentage change of 100 percent. If you measured the same altitude change in miles, you would still have a 100 percent change in altitude. This approach to plotting data avoids the pitfalls in the interpretation of the slope. Chapter 3 uses the idea of percentage changes in developing the important economic concept of *elasticity.*

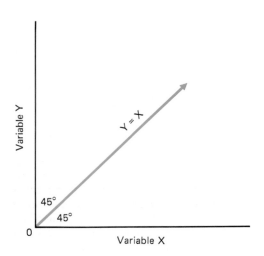

Figure 10

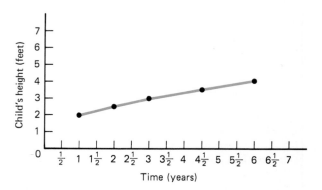

Figure 11

▶ Special Graphs

Certain graphs in this text are designed for special situations in which measuring the sign or magnitude of the slope is not the focus of the analysis. This section explains these graphs and their purpose.

A linear graph starting at the origin is called a *ray*. A particular ray that makes a 45-degree angle with the x and y axes has the slope of $+1$. It has the special feature that for every point on the ray, the variables X and Y are equal as in figure 10. In other words, this ray is a plotting of the points $Y = X$. The ordered pairs on this ray would be (1,1), (2,2), (10,10), and so on. This line is used as a reference line in economics to illuminate other economic relationships.

A *time-series graph* is useful in illustrating certain economic variables. Such graphs are characterized by the variable time's being plotted on the horizontal axis. The basic idea is to show how some variable changes over time. In figure 11, a child's height is plotted against time. We can see that as the child ages, his or her height increases. Not all economic variables change smoothly over time and are illustrated by time-series graphs that resemble the teeth of a handsaw.

Another graph that is frequently used to illustrate changes in a variable over time is the *bar chart*. The focus here is not on the rate of change on the variable as much as on comparing the levels of the variable over time or among different groups of people. Figure 12 shows hypothetical data on average income among different age-groups in the form of a bar graph. Notice that the bar graph emphasizes the difference in the levels of income among the age-groups.

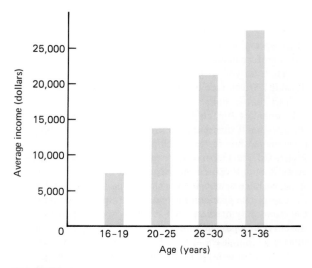

Figure 12

▶ Conclusion

The purpose of this appendix is to illustrate and explain various graphing techniques and the uses of special graphs in economics. Remember these two key points: (1) This material should be well understood now so that graphs will become a useful tool for economic analysis and not an obstacle. (2) It is not sound strategy to memorize various graphs in the text and try to reproduce them for an exam. Instead, try to understand how the graphs are drawn so that you can use them yourself to illustrate various topics in economics.

Appendix B

How to Solve the Policy Issues

You will find a policy issue at the end of each major section of this book. These issues represent puzzles to help you apply basic economics to important social decisions. The purpose of these puzzles is to give you a chance to use the information you have learned to analyze important economic issues. Most puzzles assume that you are a staff economist for a government agency and require you to provide input into a decision that will be made by your boss, who holds a major political office. We want to get you off to a good start by listing the steps you should follow for solving the policy issues, which all have some common major features. We will use the puzzle following section 1 to illustrate a basic approach to the policy issues that follow later sections.

▶ Steps for Solving the Policy Issues

1. *Identify the problem*
   Identify the main issue or problem to be addressed. List any subproblems that may exist. Be able to distinguish between the main problem and the subproblems.

2. *Sort out the issues*
   What groups are involved? What are their objectives/priorities? What concerns do they have regarding the main problem? What discrepancies and overlaps exist between the objectives of the various groups?

3. *List and evaluate alternative solutions*
   Develop various solutions to the main problem identified in step 1. Analyze how the solutions affect the groups identified in step 2. Who are the winners and losers? Do the "wins" offset the "losses"? Are the priorities of some groups more significant than those of others? If you cannot develop a priority list of the objectives of the various groups, is a compromise possible? What are the benefits and drawbacks of a compromise?

4. *Recommend a solution to the problem*
   Given your analysis in step 3, select and defend a solution to the problem.

Now, together, let's work through the policy issue that follows Part I, "Who Should Pay for Clean Air?"

▶ Identifying the Problem

The first thing you may have noticed is that the policy issue asks you to address several related questions at the same time. The puzzle embraces a number of economic policy issues that vary in difficulty and clarity. Each member of the city council will have his or her own idea regarding which issues are more important than others. One member may decide whether or not to support the ordinance primarily on the basis of its potential effects on business owners. Another may feel that the impact on workers deserves more consideration, while still another member of the council may view the interests of taxpayers as a group as most important. You will also need to consider whether the council has asked you all of the important questions. If not, what other questions do you think the council should consider in deciding how to vote?

As an economic analyst you will often have to make your own decisions about the relative importance of the questions asked of you and whether or not to try to convince your employer to consider other questions that you think are important but have not been asked explicitly. Moreover, since those who ask you the questions will not usually have your expertise, you will have to figure out how to provide an answer that will clearly sort out the issues but without too much technical jargon.

Any social policy issue will involve both objective, or positive, questions about how a particular policy will work and value, or normative, questions about what should be done. Since your value judgments may be different from those of some council members, you will want to provide the council with as clear an indication as possible of the positive and normative elements of your analysis.

▶ Getting Started

Recall that in chapter 1 we introduced the idea of developing a model in order to focus on the key elements of an economic issue. What economic models and concepts have you learned about in chapter 1 that you can use to discuss the pros and cons of providing the city with clean air? What kinds of data will you need to give council members quantitative measures of the opportunity costs of different amounts of improved air quality? What sources of statistical information do you know of that will enable you to obtain these data? (Hint: Look in the source notes to various tables and figures in the text and in the reference section for each chapter at the end of the text for some suggestions.)

With respect to affected parties, can you think of conditions that would increase the likelihood that clean air legislation would actually cause some manufacturing enterprises to leave the city? Under what circumstances would you expect the ordinance to lower wages and/or create serious unemployment problems? Are there conditions under which the tax burden would be so severe that taxpayers would rebel and vote council members out of office? Are there circumstances under which you would recommend that compliance with the new clean air standards be required immediately? Would you ever recommend that firms be allowed several years to comply with the new standards?

In summary, you will be most successful in providing council members with the information they need if you can help them identify the important issues. Each question you have been asked can be broken down into several related questions that help to clarify the pros and cons of the proposed ordinance. Furthermore, your judgments about what will happen if the law is passed will be clearer if you can provide facts instead of mere guesses about the consequences of the clean air legislation.

Now go ahead and draft your memo for the city council. Later, after you have studied additional chapters and added to the simple tools of analysis now at your command, take another look at the clean air issue. We guarantee that your added study of economics will have changed some of your judgments about the likely impact of the ordinance. You will have a clearer idea of what the relevant issues are and how to present them to the council members for consideration.

References

Chapter 1

1. "Economics of Life and Death Arises in Debate over Kidney Therapy," *New York Times,* 25 May 1982.
2. This discussion is based on Charles Lave, "The Cost of Going 55," *Newsweek,* 23 Oct. 1978.

Chapter 2

1. For data on consumer expenditures prior to 1950, see U.S. Bureau of the Census, *Historical Statistics of the United States, Colonial Times to 1970,* Bicentennial Editon, Part 1 (Washington, D.C., 1975), Series G416–469. This is available at most college and big-city libraries and is probably the most complete collection of aggregate data for the United States throughout its history.
2. *Live at St. Douglas Convent,* Warner Bros. Records, Inc., 1980, #BSK 3440.

Chapter 3

1. Thomas F. Hogarty and Kenneth G. Elzinga, "The Demand for Beer," *Review of Economics and Statistics,* May 1972, pp. 195–198.
2. "Average Price of New Home Tops $100,000 for First Time," *New York Times,* 30 June 1984.
3. See, for example, John M. Quigley, "What Have We Learned about Urban Housing Markets?" in *Current Issues in Urban Economics,* ed. Peter Mieszkowski and Mahlon Straszheim (Baltimore: Johns Hopkins University Press, 1979). We are grateful to John C. Weicher of the American Enterprise Institute for helpful information on this topic.
4. "Gas Demand: How Elastic?" *New York Times,* 4 June 1979, p. D1.

5. W. Wold and L. Jureen, *Demand Analysis* (New York: John Wiley & Sons, 1953); R. Andersen and L. Benham, "Factors Affecting the Relationship Between Family Income and Medical Care Consumption," in *Empiricial Studies in Health Economics,* ed. Herbert Klarman (Baltimore: Johns Hopkins University Press, 1970); Gregory C. Chow, *Demand for Automobiles in the United States* (Amsterdam: North-Holland Publishing Co., 1957); T. F. Hogarty and K. G. Elzinga, "The Demand for Beer," *Review of Economics and Statistics,* May 1972, pp. 195–198; and C. Misket and F. Vakil, "Some Estimates of Price and Expenditure Elasticities among UCLA Students," *Review of Economics and Statistics,* November 1982.

Appendix to Chapter 4

1. For a real-world example of the importance of variable costs in supply decisions, see "Harvester Is Selling Trucks Below Cost in Dismal Market," *Wall Street Journal,* 20 Apr. 1983.
2. See, for example, Hans Fantel, "Money Still Buys Audio Value," *New York Times,* 26 Sept. 1982.
3. For an analysis of the long-term economic impact of the sharp increase in energy prices, see Michael Bruno, "World Shocks, Macroeconomic Response, and the Productivity Puzzle," *National Bureau of Economic Research Working Paper,* No. 942 (Cambridge, Mass: National Bureau of Economic Research, Inc., 1982). For a summary of Bruno's study, see *The NBER Digest* (Cambridge, Mass.: National Bureau of Economic Research, Inc., Nov. 1982).

4. See Bill Richards, "Boom Times Again in Oil City," *The Guardian* (U.S. edition), 23 Nov. 1975, p. 20; reprinted from the *Washington Post.*
5. For a summary of price controls and their effects on domestic petroleum (and natural gas) production, see the *Economic Report of the President, 1982* (Washington, D.C.: U.S. Government Printing Office, 1982).

Chapter 5

1. The average price of all grain crops was 41 percent higher in 1973 than in 1972. See Department of Commerce, Bureau of Economic Analysis, *National Income and Product Accounts of the United States 1929–74,* (Washington, D.C.: U.S. Government Printing Office), table 7.10.
2. David Ignatius, "West Beirut Plagued by Seige Economics: Food Prices Double," the *Wall Street Journal,* 19 July 1982.
3. William Wong, "Sugar Industry Revels in Record Prices," the *Wall Street Journal,* 26 Sept. 1974, p. 30.
4. Marilyn Chase, "City of Doctors," the *Wall Street Journal,* 13 Mar. 1980, p. 1.

Chapter 6

1. *Economic Report of the President, 1984,* chapter 4.
2. *Statistical Abstract of the United States 1985,* table 1130, p. 642.
3. Ibid., table 1323, p. 738.
4. Ibid., table 1049, p. 602.
5. Ibid., table 1047, p. 601.
6. *Statistical Abstract of the United States 1986,* tables 1152 and 1153, pp. 649, 650.
7. Ibid., table 1130, p. 639.
8. Ibid.

9. James Bovard, "Free Food Bankrupts Foreign Farmers," *Wall Street Journal*, 2 July 1984, p. 18.
10. James Bovard, "A Subsidy Both Woolly-Headed and Mammoth," *Wall Street Journal*, 17 Apr. 1985, p. 32.
11. *Statistical Abstract of the United States 1985*, table 1146, p. 650.
12. See also Virginia Inman, "Poultry Farms Feel Betrayed by PIK Plan," *Wall Street Journal*, 29 June 1983, p. 37.
13. For more discussion see Marj Charlier, "Cropland Erosion Is a Growing Problem," *Wall Street Journal*, 26 Apr. 1985, p. 6.
14. See James Bovard, "Free Food."
15. *Statistical Abstract of the United States 1986*, table 200, p. 122.
16. Ibid., table 154, p. 100.
17. Ibid., table 1039, p. 596.

Chapter 7

1. United Press International, "Fewer Clothes Sold; Antifreeze Abundant," *Columbus Dispatch*, n.d.; and Associated Press, "Oil Drilling Gets Boost from Auto Sales Drop," *Columbus Dispatch*, 9 Apr. 1980.
2. Readers who wish to study this subject in greater depth may want to read William M. Wardell and Louis Lasagna, *Regulation and Drug Development* (Washington, D.C.: American Enterprise Institute for Public Policy Research, 1975); and Sam Peltzman, *Regulation of Pharmaceutical Innovations* (Washington, D.C.: American Enterprise Institute for Public Policy Research, 1974).
3. For an excellent discussion, see "Russian Economy Gives Andropov Huge Problems," *New York Times*, 12 June 1983.
4. "Hungary Builds Lively Economy on West's Ideas," *New York Times*, 3 Dec. 1981.
5. Bruno Koeppl, "Tricks of the Arms Trade," *Newsweek*, 21 Apr. 1980, p. 21.
6. Martin Feldstein, "An Economist Looks at China's New Economy," *Wall Street Journal*, 8 July 1982.
7. "In Mosaic of Southeast Asia, Capitalist Lands Are Thriving," *New York Times*, 1 Nov. 1981.

Chapter 8

1. If you would like to learn more about the legal foundations of agricultural cooperatives in the United States, a readable reference is Alan M. Anderson, "The Agricultural Cooperative Antitrust Exemption," *Cornell Law Review* 67 (1981): 396–414.
2. See Doug Bandow, "White House Hasn't Soured on Marketing Orders," *Wall Street Journal*, 10 Jan. 1984.
3. See "Milk, Fruit, Feel the Stirrings of Antitrust," *New York Times*, 5 Oct. 1975.
4. "Price Should Cover Cost, Says Farm Chief," *Columbus Dispatch*, 10 Sept. 1982.
5. See Donald O. Parsons and Edward John Ray, "The United States Steel Consolidation: The Creation of Market Control," *Journal of Law and Economics*, April 1975, pp. 181–219.
6. See Reuben A. Kessel, "Price Discrimination in Medicine," *Journal of Law and Economics*, October 1958, pp. 20–53.
7. For additional discussion of price discrimination, see Edwin Mansfield, *Microeconomics, Theory and Applications*, 5th ed. (New York: W. W. Norton, 1985), pp. 296–302.

Chapter 9

1. See Margaret Yao, "Three Grocery Stores in Cleveland Face Trial on Charges of Price-Fixing Plot," *Wall Street Journal*, 13 Aug. 1981.
2. F. M. Scherer, *Industrial Pricing: Theory and Evidence* (Chicago: Rand McNally & Company, 1970), p. 38.
3. "OPEC Members Expressing Doubt about Wisdom of Raising Oil Prices," *Wall Street Journal*, 13 Apr. 1981. For a discussion of OPEC's pricing strategy see "Cartel's Revival," *Wall Street Journal*, 20 Jan. 1983.
4. "Gas Demand: How Elastic?" *New York Times*, 4 June 1979.
5. After having several years to adjust, the elasticity of demand for gasoline is about four times larger than after only one year. Ibid.

6. This discussion is based on Donald O. Parsons and Edward John Ray, "The United States Steel Consolidation: The Creation of Market Control," *Journal of Law and Economics*, April 1975, pp. 181–219.
7. The original work on this subject is Oscar Morgenstern and John von Neumann, *Theory of Games and Economic Behavior*, (Princeton, N.J.: Princeton University Press, 1944).
8. See Tibor Scitovsky, *Welfare and Competition* (Chicago: Richard D. Irwin, 1951), pp. 384–391.
9. George J. Stigler and James K. Kindahl, *The Behavior of Industrial Prices* (New York: National Bureau of Economic Research, 1970).

Chapter 10

1. F. M. Scherer, *Industrial Market Structure and Economic Performance*, 2d ed. (Chicago: Rand McNally & Company, 1980), chapter 3.
2. For an interesting discussion of the role played by the local grocery store, see Teri Agiris, "Latin Oases, To Hispanics in the U.S. a Bodega, or Grocery, Is a Vital Part of Life," *Wall Street Journal*, 15 Mar. 1985, p. 1.
3. See Ed Bean, "Doctors Find a Dose of Marketing Can Cure Pain of Sluggish Practice," *Wall Street Journal*, 15 Mar. 1985, p. 27.
4. For a discussion of a particular case, see Michael Waldholz, "Pillbox War, Drug Battle Heats Up Between Brand-Name and Generic Makers," *Wall Street Journal*, 13 Aug. 1984, p. 1.
5. See Steve Weiner, "Want a Rolex for $25? Want a Trip to Jail?" *Wall Street Journal*, 15 Mar. 1985, p. 27.
6. For a discussion, see Douglas F. Greer, *Industrial Organization and Public Policy*, 2d ed. (New York: Macmillan Publishing Company, 1984), chapter 16.
7. See "A Curious Push to Weaken FTC Advertising Rules," *New York Times*, 14 Nov. 1982.
8. Greer, *Industrial Organization*, p. 358.
9. Phillip Nelson, "The Economic Consequences of Advertising," *Journal of Business*, April 1975, p. 237.

10. Kenneth D. Boyer, "Information and Goodwill Advertising," *Review of Economics and Statistics,* November 1974, pp. 541–548.
11. Lee Benham, "The Effect of Advertising on the Price of Eyeglasses," *Journal of Law and Economics,* October 1972, pp. 337–352.
12. Greer, *Industrial Organization,* p. 362.

Chapter 11

1. Douglas F. Greer, *Industrial Organization and Public Policy,* 2d ed. (New York: Macmillan Publishing Company, 1984), p. 201.
2. For a good discussion of the opposing viewpoints in the IBM case, see Alan K. McAdams, "The Price of Dropping the Antitrust Suit," and Franklin M. Fisher, "A Case for Keeping IBM Big," *New York Times,* 13 May 1984.
3. Greer, *Industrial Organization,* pp. 201–202.
4. Ibid., pp. 416–17.
5. Ibid., p. 181.
6. Ibid.
7. Ibid., p. 183.
8. Ibid., p. 265.
9. Ibid., p. 268.
10. For additional discussion of the AT&T breakup, see the following issues of *Newsweek:* 1982 (18 Jan., 25 Jan., 5 Apr., 23 Aug., 27 Sept., 25 Oct.); 1983 (24 Jan., 4 Apr., 20 June, 17 Oct., 28 Nov.); and 1984 (9 Apr.).
11. Greer, *Industrial Organization,* p. 272.
12. Ibid., pp. 451–452.
13. *Economic Report of the President, 1983,* chapter 5.
14. Ibid.
15. *Economic Report of the President, 1983,* p. 109.
16. Greer, *Industrial Organization,* pp. 451–52.
17. The data in the paragraph are from the *Economic Report of the President, 1983,* p. 109.
18. See Victo S. Zonana, "Turbulent Times—End of Glamorous Life Looms for U.S. Pilots as Competition Grows," *Wall Street Journal,* 2 Nov. 1983, p. 1.

Chapter 13

1. Mary Williams, "Ten Minutes' Work for 12 Hours' Pay? What's the Catch?" *Wall Street Journal,* 12 Oct. 1983.
2. For a description of a recent shortage of teenage labor, see "Youth Labor Scarcity Forcing Up Low-Level Pay in New York Area," *New York Times,* 17 Mar. 1986.
3. See "Income Differences Between Regions Narrow as a Result of Mobility, More Women at Work," *Wall Street Journal,* 4 Mar. 1982. For a more technical discussion of regional wage differentials, see Don Bellante, "The North-South Differential and the Migration of Homogeneous Labor," *American Economic Review,* March 1979, pp. 166–175.
4. See, for instance, Richard Thaler and Sherwin Rosen, "The Value of Saving a Life: Evidence from the Labor Market," in *Household Production and Consumption,* ed. Nestor E. Terleckyj (New York: Columbia University Press for the National Bureau of Economic Research, 1975).
5. For an illustration of such employer mobility, see "As the Nation Ages, Utah Gets Younger, Thanks to Mormons," *Wall Street Journal,* 7 Nov. 1984.
6. For an analysis of monopsony in the professional baseball players' market, see Belton M. Fleisher and Thomas J. Kniesner, *Labor Economics: Theory, Evidence, and Policy* (Englewood Cliffs, N.J.: Prentice-Hall, 1984), pp. 213–217; and Gerald W. Scully, "Pay and Performance in Professional Baseball," *American Economic Review,* December 1974.
7. For example, in 1984, President Reagan proposed cutting the salaries of all federal employees by 5 percent. He probably would not have done this had it been likely that most government offices would have had to close their doors because of insufficient staff if wages were reduced somewhat. See "Reagan Proposes $34 billion Saving and Pay Cut of 5%," *New York Times,* 6 Dec. 1984.

8. *Statistical Abstract of the United States 1984,* table 730, p. 441.
9. See, for example, "Chavez Seeks a Halt to Nation's 'Worst' Influx of Illegal Aliens," *New York Times,* 23 July 1974. Although the newspaper reference is old, it still applies today. See also, "Coast Jobs Disappear through 'Gateway to Pacific,'" *New York Times,* 26 Nov. 1982.
10. See Fleisher and Kniesner, *Labor Economics,* pp. 266–275.
11. Albert Rees, *The Economics of Trade Unions,* rev. ed. (Chicago: The University of Chicago Press, 1977), p. 182; and *Statistical Abstract of the United States 1984,* table 731, p. 442.

Chapter 14

1. See Belton M. Fleisher and Thomas J. Kniesner, *Labor Economics: Theory, Evidence, and Policy* (Englewood Cliffs, N.J.: Prentice-Hall, 1984), chapter 9.
2. *Statistical Abstract of the United States 1981,* table 236, p. 145.
3. Richard Freeman, *The Overeducated American* (New York: Academic Press, 1976).
4. Judy L. Ward, "Firms Forcing Employees to Repay Some Costs If They Quit Too Soon," *Wall Street Journal,* 16 July 1985, p. 35.
5. See, for example, Robert Hanley, "Jersey Judge Rules That an Ex-Wife Should Share in Doctor's Income," *New York Times,* 7 Dec. 1980; and Judith Cummings, "A Share in Spouse's Future Earnings Suggested by Coast Court in Divorce," *New York Times,* 24 Jan. 1982, p. A12.
6. See, for example, Donald O. Parsons, "Specific Human Capital: An Application to Quit Rates and to Layoff Rates," *Journal of Political Economy,* November–December 1972, pp. 120–143.
7. Gary S. Becker, Elisabeth M. Landes, and Robert J. Michael, "An Economic Analysis of Marital Instability," *Journal of Political Economy,* December 1977, pp. 1141–1189.

8. The data in this paragraph are from *Economic Indicators* (Washington, D.C.: U.S. Government Printing Office). This monthly publication is prepared for the Joint Economic Committee by the Council of Economic Advisers.
9. For a study of firms' investment decisions, see David Schwartzman, *The Expected Return from Pharmaceutical Research* (Washington, D.C.: American Enterprise Institute for Public Policy Research, 1975).
10. See, for example, Robert H. Haveman, *The Economic Performance of Public Investments: An Ex Post Evaluation of Water Resources Investments.* (Baltimore: The Johns Hopkins University Press for Resources for the Future, 1972).
11. Edward M. Gramlich, *Benefit-Cost Analysis of Government Programs* (Englewood Cliffs, N.J.: Prentice-Hall, 1981); and Edith Stokey and Richard Zeckhauser, *A Primer for Policy Analysis* (New York: W. W. Norton & Co., 1978), chapter 9.
12. Stokey and Zeckhauser, *Policy Analysis,* chapter 9.
13. Gramlich, *Cost-Benefit Analysis,* chapter 8.
14. Ibid.

Chapter 15
1. See, for example, "Census Says 3 Plans Would Raise Many Above Poverty Line," and "Measuring Poverty," *New York Times,* 15 Apr. 1982; and "Redefining Poverty: Some Interesting but Loaded Choices," *New York Times,* 18 Apr. 1982.
2. This aspect of unions has been advocated by Richard B. Freeman and James Medoff in *What Do Unions Do?* (New York: Basic Books, 1984).
3. See, for example, "Louisville Frets Over Labor Strike Record as Companies Depart and Jobs Disappear," *Wall Street Journal,* 16 Aug. 1982.

4. For more discussion, see Richard B. Freeman, "Unionism and the Dispersion of Wages," *Industrial and Labor Relations Review,* October 1980, pp. 3–23.
5. For a survey, see Belton M. Fleisher, *Minimum Wage Regulation in the United States* (Washington, D.C.: National Chamber Foundation, 1983).
6. See, for example, "Higher Pay's Price: Rise in Minimum Wage Spurs Some Firms to Cut Work Hours and Hiring of Youths," *Wall Street Journal,* 15 Aug. 1978.
7. See Thomas J. Kniesner, "The Low-Wage Workers: Who Are They?" in *The Economics of Legal Minimum Wages,* ed. Simon Rottenberg (Washington, D.C.: American Enterprise Institute for Public Policy Research, 1981).
8. *Report of the Minimum Wage Study Commission,* Vol. 1, (Washington, D.C.: U.S. Government Printing Office, 1981), p. 103.
9. "Economic Rigidity Hampers Western Europe," *New York Times,* 1 Dec. 1982.
10. For a discussion of one recent experiment of this sort, see "Paring the Rolls? Reagan's Plan to Put Welfare Clients in Jobs Stirs Much Opposition," *Wall Street Journal,* 4 June 1981.
11. For a discussion of taxes, transfers, and the incentives to work in another country, see "How Britain's Workers Are Penalized for Working," *Wall Street Journal,* 20 Jan. 1982.

Chapter 16
1. Data on black-white earnings differences and other labor market variables are taken from Richard B. Freeman, "Black Economic Progress after 1964: Who Has Gained and Why?" in *Studies in Labor Markets,* ed. Sherwin Rosen. A Conference Report of the Universities-National Bureau Committee for Economic Research, no. 31 (Chicago: University of Chicago Press, 1981), pp. 247–294; and James B. Smith and F. R. Welch, *Closing the Gap: Forty Years of Economic Progress for Blacks* (Santa Monica, Calif.: The Rand Corporation, 1986).

2. For one view of the answer, see Freeman, "Black Economic Progress."
3. For more discussion, see Belton M. Fleisher and Thomas J. Kniesner, *Labor Economics: Theory, Evidence, and Policy,* 3d ed. (Englewood Cliffs, N.J.: Prentice-Hall, 1984), pp. 399–405.
4. *Job Tenure Declines as Work Force Changes,* United States Department of Labor, Washington, D.C., Special Labor Force Report 235.
5. *Statistical Abstract of the United States 1986,* table 703, p. 419.
6. United States Department of Labor, Women's Bureau, *Fact Sheet on the Earnings Gap* (Washington, D.C.: United States Department of Labor).
7. Ibid.
8. *Statistical Abstract of the United States 1986,* table 764, p. 456.
9. This view is summarized in Cynthia B. Lloyd and Beth T. Niemi, *The Economics of Sex Differentials* (New York: Columbia University Press, 1979). See in particular pp. 1286–1308.
10. For background information and more details, see *The Comparable Worth Issue,* DLR no. 208, Bureau of National Affairs, Inc., Washington, D.C., 28 Oct. 1961; and June O'Neill, "The 'Comparable Worth' Trap," *Wall Street Journal,* 20 Jan. 1984.
11. Two studies are A. Thomas King and Peter Mieskowski, "Racial Discrimination, Segregation, and the Price of Housing," *Journal of Political Economy,* May/June 1973, pp. 590–606; and Martin J. Bailey, "Effects of Race and Other Demographic Factors on the Values of Single-Family Homes, *Land Economics,* May 1966, pp. 215–222.

Chapter 17
1. *Statistical Abstract of the United States 1983,* table 360, p. 208.
2. Steven N. S. Cheung, "The Fable of the Bees: An Economic Investigation," *Journal of Law and Economics,* April 1973, pp. 11–33.

Chapter 18

1. For further information on the problems of economic development, see Charles Kindleberger and B. Herrick, *Economic Development*, 4th ed. (New York: McGraw-Hill, 1983).
2. Population data for years prior to 1980 are from *Statistical Abstract of the United States 1986*, tables 1463 and 1466, pp. 834–835.
3. Data on income per capita are derived from *Statistical Abstract of the United States 1984*, table 1509, p. 865.
4. For example, in 1980, the proportion of population living in cities of more than 500,000 people in the thirty-six lowest-income countries of the world was 55 percent, exactly the same as in the world's highest-income industrial market economies. On the other hand, the proportion of the labor force in manufacturing in the low-income countries was 13 percent, while that in the advanced economies was 39 percent, nearly three times as large. These data are from *World Development Report 1984* (New York: Oxford University Press 1984), tables 21 and 22, pp. 258–261. This report was published for the World Bank.

Chapter 19

1. *Economic Report of the President* (Washington, D.C.: U.S. Government Printing Office). Copies may be obtained from the Superintendent of Documents, U.S. Government Printing Office, Washington, D.C. 20402.
2. See, for example, *Economic Report of the President, 1983* (Washington, D.C.: U.S. Government Printing Office), Tables B–76, B–77, and B–78.
3. See Organization for Economic Cooperation and Development (OECD), *The Hidden Economy in the Context of National Accounts* (Paris: OECD, 1981); John W. Kendrick, "Expanding Imputed Values in the National Income and Product Accounts," *Review of Income and Wealth*, Dec. 1979, pp. 349–63; Edward F. Denison, "Is U.S. Growth Underrated Because of the Underground Economy? Employment Ratios Suggest Not." *Review of Income and Wealth*, 1982.
4. *Economic Report of the President, 1983*, Table B–34, p. 202.
5. *Economic Report of the President, 1983*, p. 30.
6. See, for instance, Belton M. Fleisher, *The Economics of Delinquency* (Chicago: Quadrangle Books, 1966).

Chapter 20

1. For more discussion, see the *Economic Report of the President, 1983* (Washington, D.C.: U.S. Government Printing Office), pp. 46–49.
2. If your local library has a collection of videotapes of television documentaries, view the NBC White Paper, "America Works When America Works," originally broadcast 25 June 1981. This program deals with structural unemployment, and it contains interviews with steelworkers who refused to move from their hometown of Youngstown, Ohio, despite tremendously reduced job opportunities in the steel industry. The interviews are a chilling reminder of the substantial emotional upheaval that can accompany the thought of leaving home for a job in another part of the country.
3. See the *Economic Report of the President, 1983*, p. 44.
4. Ibid., pp. 46–47.
5. See "Labor Seeks Less," *Business Week*, 21 Dec. 1981, pp. 82–88.
6. See *Economic Report of the President, 1983*, p. 29.

Chapter 21

1. "Socking It Away, Drop in Inflation Spurs Many to Cut Spending and Increase Saving," *Wall Street Journal*, 9 Dec. 1982, p. 1.
2. *The Economic Report of the President, 1983* (Washington, D.C.: U.S. Government Printing Office), Table B–24.
3. "Taking a Chance, Accent Is on Growth as Tax Law Changes Many Investors' Ways," *Wall Street Journal*, 13 Jan. 1982.

Chapter 22

1. Milton and Rose Friedman, *Free to Choose* (New York: Harcourt Brace Jovanovich, 1980), p. 252.
2. See J. Huston McCulloch, *Money and Inflation*, 2d ed. (New York: Academic Press, 1982). For those who would like to study money and inflation in greater depth, McCulloch's book is an excellent and highly readable source.
3. See *Federal Reserve Bulletin*, Feb. 1983, p. A18.
4. For a fascinating, easy-to-read history of money in the United States, see Arthur Nussbaum, *A History of the Dollar* (New York: Columbia University Press, 1957).
5. For more precise definitions of M1, M2, and M3, see a recent issue of the *Federal Reserve Bulletin*, which is published by the Board of Governors of the Federal Reserve System and is available in most libraries.

Chapter 23

1. *American Banker*, 6 Jan. 1986, p. 10.
2. See two opposing articles by Jeffrey E. Garten and William M. Isaac under the title "Dealing with a Changed Banking System," *Wall Street Journal*, 29 May 1984; Michael J. Boskin, "Going Overboard on Bank Bailouts," *Wall Street Journal*, 23 Aug. 1984; and George J. Benston, "Why the Government Can't Run a Bank," *New York Times*, 29 July 1984.
3. See "Extra Duty: Fed's Chief Took on Big Role in Attacking World's Financial Ills," *Wall Street Journal*, 14 Mar. 1983; "FDIC Surprise," *Wall Street Journal*, 15 Apr. 1983; "U.S. Will Invest $4.5 Billion in Rescue of Chicago Bank, Vowing More if Needed," *New York Times*, 27 July 1984; and George A. Benston, "Why the Government Can't Run a Bank," *New York Times*, 29 July 1984.

Chapter 24

1. For example, between 1940 and 1959, the federal government had budget surpluses during eight years. See *Economic Report of the President, 1983* (Washington, D.C.: U.S. Government Printing Office, 1983), table B-75.
2. *Statistical Abstract of the United States 1986,* table 781.

Chapter 25

1. Victor Zarnowitz, "Recent Work on Business Cycles in Historical Perspective: A Review of Theories and Evidence," *Journal of Economic Literature,* June 1985, pp. 523–580, tables 2 and 3.

Chapter 26

1. All data are taken from *Historical Statistics of the United States, Colonial Times to 1970.*
2. Ibid., Series F125.
3. The Phillips curve is so-named because of research reported by an Australian economist, A. S. H. Phillips, "The Relationship Between Unemployment and the Rate of Change of Money Wage Rates in the United Kingdom, 1861–1967," *Economica,* Nov. 1958. However, it would have been fairer to name it the Fisher curve, after the famous American economist Irving Fisher, who pointed out the relationship between unemployment and inflation over thirty years earlier in an article entitled "A Statistical Relation Between Unemployment and Price Changes," *International Labour Review,* June 1926; reprinted in *Journal of Political Economy,* Mar./ Apr. 1973.

Chapter 27

1. "State Highway Work on Hold," *Columbus Dispatch,* 29 Apr. 1983. Further examples of the implementation lag of government expenditures are contained in the *Economic Report of the President, 1983,* pp. 39–41.
2. Holland, Stephen A., "The Impact of Inflation Uncertainty on the Labor Market," *Federal Reserve Bank of St. Louis Review,* Aug./ Sept. 1984, pp. 26–27.

Chapter 28

1. *Historical Statistics of the United States, Colonial Times to 1970,* p. 226.
2. James R. Barth and Stephen O. Morrell, "A Primer on Budget Deficits," Federal Reserve Bank of Atlanta *Review,* Aug. 1982, pp. 6–17.

Chapter 29

1. For an informative overview of the areas of agreement and disagreement among economists, see "How to Get the Country Moving Again: Advice from Six Nobel Prize Economists," *U.S. News & World Report,* 31 Jan. 1983, pp. 66–71.
2. For an interesting discussion of Keynes' impact on economics, see Paul A. Samuelson, "The House That Keynes Built," *New York Times,* 29 May 1983. See also the four articles by Nobel Laureates Sir John Hicks, Paul Samuelson, Friedrich Hayek, and Milton Friedman entitled "The Keynes Centenary," *The Economist,* 4, 11, 18, and 25 June 1983.
3. *Economic Report of the President, 1984,* table 1.1, p. 29.
4. Ibid.

5. For detailed statistics on the government budgets of other nations, see International Monetary Fund, *World Economic Outlook* (Washington, D.C.: International Monetary Fund, 1984), table 1.1, p. 100.
6. Ibid.
7. *Economic Report of the President, 1984,* table 1.2, p. 36.
8. *Economic Report of the President, 1983.* See also Alan S. Blinder, "Monetization of Deficits," Working Paper No. 1052 (Cambridge, Mass.: National Bureau of Economic Research, Inc., 1983).
9. "Budget Estimates and Realities," *New York Times,* 9 Feb. 1982.
10. See "When Inflation Rate Is 116,200%, Prices Change by the Hour," *Wall Street Journal,* 7 Feb. 1985.
11. The Ricardian equivalence hypothesis, or theorem, is named after the famous nineteenth-century economist David Ricardo. See Robert J. Barro, *Macroeconomics* (New York: John Wiley & Sons, 1984), chap. 15.
12. See Robert J. Barro, "A Deficit Nearly on Target," *Wall Street Journal,* 19 Jan. 1985.

Chapter 30

1. *Statistical Abstract of the United States 1981,* table 1551.
2. *Statistical Abstract of the United States 1981,* table 1514, p. 846.
3. John M. Culbertson, " 'Free Trade' Is Impoverishing the West," *New York Times,* 28 July 1985. For a view that is much more widely accepted among economists, see Herbert Stein, "Best-Selling Fiction: 3 Million Jobs," *Wall Street Journal,* 29 July 1985.

Chapter 31

1. *Statistical Abstract of the United States 1981.*
2. Ibid.
3. See, for instance, "Coast Jobs Disappear through 'Gateway to Pacific,' " *New York Times,* 26 Nov. 1982.
4. See "GM Needs Toyota Efficiency," *New York Times,* 16 Feb. 1983.
5. This example is especially relevant because the United States imposed a new set of tariffs on so-called *specialty* steel, which is a low-volume, high-value product considered vital for national defense, telecommunications, aerospace, and oil refining. In 1982, specialty steel accounted for about 2 percent of tonnage but about 10 percent of the value of total steel production in the United States. See "U.S. Places Tough Curbs on Imports of Specialty Steel," *Washington Post,* 6 July 1983, p. A1.
6. Bennett D. Baack and Edward J. Ray, "Tariff Policy and Income Distribution: The Case of the United States 1830–1860," *Explorations in Economic History,* Winter 1974, pp. 103–121.
7. Bennett D. Baack and Edward J. Ray, "Tariff Policy and Comparative Advantage in the Iron and Steel Industry: 1870–1929," *Explorations in Economic History,* Fall 1973, pp. 3–24.
8. Recent United States trade restrictions on specialty steel also include quotas; see "The Fight Over Steel Quotas," *New York Times,* 22 Aug. 1984.
9. For data on United States automobile imports, see *The Brookings Review,* Summer 1984, table 1, p. 9.
10. Ibid., table 4, p. 11.
11. Ibid., table 5, p. 11.
12. David G. Tarr and Morris E. Morkre, "Aggregate Costs to the United States of Tariffs and Quotas on Imports," Bureau of Economics Staff Report to the Federal Trade Commission, Dec. 1984, table 4, p. 4.
13. Ibid.
14. Ibid.
15. See John M. Starrels, "Steel's Stiff Competition," *Wall Street Journal,* 9 July 1982.
16. Ibid.
17. United States Department of Labor, reported in "Steel's Elusive Search for a New Deal," *New York Times,* 18 Nov. 1982.
18. Ibid.
19. For details, see "Steel Union Leaders Ratify Concessions," *New York Times,* 1 Mar. 1983.

Chapter 32

1. See David Glasner, "The Much-Maligned U.S. Trade Gap," *New York Times,* 21 Oct. 1984.
2. *Statistical Abstract of the United States 1986,* tables 1433 and 1472.
3. *Statistical Abstract of the United States 1982/83,* tables 693 and 1524.
4. *Economic Report of the President, 1984,* table B101, p. 335.
5. International Monetary Fund, "Exchange Rate Volatility and World Trade," *Occasional Paper No. 28.* (Washington, D. C.: International Monetary Fund, 1984), p. 43.
6. "Oil Cut to Hurt Poorer Nations," *New York Times,* 7 Mar. 1983.

Chapter 33

1. International Monetary Fund, *World Economic Outlook, 1984* (Washington, D.C.: International Monetary Fund), table 3.2, p. 130.
2. Ibid., table 8, p. 174.
3. Ibid., table 10, p. 176.
4. For values of foreign exchange rates, see *Statistical Abstract of the United States 1984,* table 1538, p. 887.
5. International Monetary Fund, *World Economic Outlook, 1984,* table 36, p. 206.

Chapter 34

1. *Economic Report of the President, 1985,* table B-24.
2. *Economic Report of the President, 1983,* chapter 4.
3. See Ibid.; Ralph E. Winter, "Multiple Choice, Many Culprits Named in National Slowdown of Productivity Gains," *Wall Street Journal,* 21 Oct. 1981, p. 1; and Ralph E. Winter, "Paper Weight, Many Businesses Blame Governmental Policies for Productivity Lag," *Wall Street Journal,* 28 Oct. 1981, p. 1.
4. Ralph E. Winter, "Gauging Growth, Productivity Debate Is Clouded by Problem of Measuring Its Lag," *Wall Street Journal,* 14 Oct. 1981, p. 1.
5. Ralph E. Winter, "Multiple Choice."
6. Barbara Toohey, "Sexual Revolution Wrecks U.S. Productivity," *Wall Street Journal,* 8 May 1981, p. 26. Ms. Toohey is a librarian who formulates economic theories for pleasure in her spare time.
7. *Economic Indicators, December 1984* (Washington, D.C.: United States Government Printing Office), p. 16.
8. John Kendrick, "Productivity Gains Will Continue," *Wall Street Journal,* 29 Aug. 1984, p. 22.
9. *Economic Report of the President, 1984,* p. 90.
10. Ibid., p. 89.

11. Geoffrey Carliner, "Japanese Industrial Policy and U.S. Trade Policy," memorandum to the Council of Economic Advisers, Executive Office of the President, Washington, D.C., 25 July 1983.
12. Ibid.
13. Ibid.
14. Ibid.
15. Ibid.
16. Charles L. Schultze, "Industrial Policy: A Dissent," *The Brookings Review*, Fall 1983, pp. 3–12.
17. *Economic Report of the President, 1984*, p. 97.
18. For such a debate, see "Do We Need Industrial Policy? The True Cost of Economic Change," *Harper's*, Feb. 1985, pp. 35–48. See also, Kim Kiwhan "A Case Study in the Perils of Industrial Policy," *Wall Street Journal*, 22 June 1983; and "Helping Business, Japanese Style." *New York Times*, 17 Nov. 1981.
19. For discussion of an attempt to introduce industrial policy into the United States, see Tamar Lewin, "Putting Industrial Policy to a Vote," *New York Times*, 10 June 1984; and Howard Kurtz, "A 'New Idea' Fizzles on Launch, Skeptical Rhode Islanders Wouldn't Go for 'Industrial Policy,'" *Washington Post*, 15 July 1984, p. B5.

Chapter 35

1. *Statistical Abstract of the United States 1982/83*, table 1530, p. 870.
2. *Statistical Abstract of the United States 1986*, table 655, p. 385.
3. See, for example, "Russian Economy Gives Andropov Huge Problems," *New York Times*, 12 June 1983.
4. See Martin Feldstein, "An Economist Looks at China's New Economy," *Wall Street Journal*, 8 July 1982; and D. Gale Johnson, *Progress of Economic Reform in the People's Republic of China* (Washington, D.C., American Enterprise Institute, 1982).
5. "Hungary Builds Lively Economy on West's Ideas," *New York Times*, 3 Dec. 1981.
6. Bruno Koeppl, "Tricks of the Arms Trade," *Newsweek*, 21 Apr. 1980, p. 21.
7. See, for instance, Gregory Grossman, "Notes on the Illegal Private Economy and Corruption," in Joint Economic Committee, *Soviet Economy in a Time of Change*, vol. 1 (Washington, D.C.: U.S. Government Printing Office, 1979).
8. N. Khrushchev, *Khrushchev Remembers*, ed. and trans. Strobe Talbott (Boston: Little, Brown, 1970), pp. 519–520.

Appendix to Chapter 35

1. See, for example, "Trade War Feared Over Food Export Issue," *New York Times*, 22 Feb. 1983.
2. See "VA May Face Crisis as Veterans Turn 65 and Seek Free Care," *New York Times*, 26 Feb. 1983.
3. Sharon P. Smith, "Pay Differentials between Federal Government and Private Sector Workers," *Industrial and Labor Relations Review*, (Jan. 1976), pp. 179–199.
4. Robert M. Spann, "Public Versus Private Provision of Government Services," in *Budgets and Bureaucrats*, ed. Thomas E. Borcherding (Durham, N.C.: Duke University Press, 1977), pp. 71–89.

Glossary

accelerated inflation An accelerated inflation is one in which the percentage rate of increase of prices increases from year to year.

ad valorem tariff An ad valorem tariff is defined in percentage terms rather than a specific amount.

aggregate demand and supply curves The aggregate demand and supply curves describe the relationship between the price level and the quantities of GNP demanded and supplied, respectively.

aggregate demand for labor [D(L)] The aggregate demand curve for labor [D(L)] illustrates the total number of workers that society's firms wish to hire at various real wage rates.

aggregate demand for loanable funds (DLF) The aggregate demand for loanable funds (DLF) is a schedule illustrating the total amount of loanable funds borrowers seek to borrow at various real interest rates.

aggregate economics Aggregate economics is a synonym for macroeconomics that reminds us that in order to be manageable, macroeconomic analysis must summarize the workings of an entire economy as the behavior of a few aggregate measures of economic performance including the inflation and unemployment rates.

aggregate supply curve of labor [S(L)] The aggregate supply of labor [S(L)] illustrates the total number of people in society who want employment at the various real wage rates that might exist.

aggregate supply of loanable funds (SLF) The aggregate supply of loanable funds (SLF) is a schedule illustrating the total amount of loanable funds lenders offer at various real interest rates.

antitrust laws Antitrust laws permit the government to sue, and thus penalize, firms that try to prevent other firms from competing in the production and sale of a product or service.

appreciation Appreciation refers to an increase in an exchange rate under a flexible exchange rate system.

assumptions Assumptions are statements about the nature of the world that are taken to be true for purposes of developing a model, or theory, such as the theory or model of demand.

automatic fiscal stabilizers Automatic fiscal stabilizers are fiscal policies that do not require new legislation or executive decisions to become effective because they are built into existing laws.

average cost Average cost is the cost a firm incurs per unit of output.

average total cost (ATC) Average total cost (ATC) is total cost divided by the quantity of output.

average variable cost (AVC) Average variable cost (AVC) is variable cost divided by the quantity of output.

balance of payments The balance of payments is the accounting for the flow of goods and services and the means of paying for them among international trading partners.

balance of payments on current account The balance of payments on current account is equal to the exports of merchandise, military items, and services plus gifts to the United States less imports of merchandise, military items and services, and gifts to other countries.

balance of trade The balance of trade is equal to a country's merchandise exports minus its merchandise imports.

bank A bank is a financial institution that accepts deposits and makes loans.

bank run A bank run occurs when a large proportion of a bank's depositors want to withdraw their funds all at once.

barriers to entry A barrier to entry is a financial, legal, or technological restriction faced by firms that are outside an industry that did not or do not affect the firm(s) already in the industry.

barter economy A barter economy is one in which money plays an unimportant role and in which goods and services are traded directly.

base year The base year is the date at which a cost of living index is set equal to 100 for the purpose of comparison with other years.

basic accounting identity   The basic accounting identity describes the structure of all balance sheets; it says that net worth is defined as the difference between assets and liabilities.

black market   A black market is an illegal arrangement for buying and selling a good or service or ration coupons when a legal maximum price or some other market interference creates an excess demand.

break-even point   The break-even point occurs at that price that allows the firm to cover all of its costs exactly but to earn no profit in the short run.

budget constraint   A budget constraint is a mathematical description (either algebraic or geometric) of the choices a consumer is able to make in light of his or her available time and income and the prices of goods and services.

business cycle   The business cycle is the pattern of recession followed by recovery that characterizes the United States and other market economies.

▶ **capital**   The term capital is often used as a short expression for physical capital and for the services of physical capital used in production.

capital account   The capital account is the section of the balance of payments accounts that indicates how the current account balance has been financed; it indicates international currency flows plus borrowing and lending.

capitalist economic system   A capitalist economic system is one in which private property and free markets are the principal institutions determining the answers to the basic economic questions.

cartel   A cartel is a group of firms that collude.

cash drain   Cash drain is the flow of money into the public's holding of currency when there is an increase in the total money stock.

categorical welfare program   A categorical welfare program uses personal and family characteristics to determine who in the low-income population is eligible for financial support.

central bank   The central bank is a nation's monetary authority and is responsible for determining the quantity of money under a paper monetary standard.

ceteris paribus   *Ceteris paribus* means that all but one factor influencing some form of economic behavior (such as demand) are assumed not to change.

change in demand   A change in demand or a change (shift) in the demand curve is a movement of the demand curve to the right (an increase in demand) or left (a decrease in demand). A change in the quantity demanded at every price results when the demand curve shifts to the right or left. Such a shift occurs when there is a change in a factor that affects the demand for a good or service other than the good's or the service's own price.

change in the quantity demanded   A change in the quantity demanded is an increase or decrease in the desired purchases of a good or service because of a change in its price, *cet. par.*

change in the quantity supplied   A change in the quantity supplied is a change in the quantity of a good or service a firm desires to sell that results when its price changes along a given supply curve.

change in supply   A change in supply or a change (shift) in the supply curve is a movement of the supply curve to the right (an increase in supply) or left (a decrease or reduction in supply). A change in the quantity supplied at every price results when the supply curve shifts to the right or left. Such a shift occurs when there is a change in a factor that affects the supply of a good or service other than the good's or the service's own price.

circular flow of GNP   The circular flow of GNP refers to the flow of money back and forth between the buyers and sellers of society's output and means that GNP can be calculated in either of two ways—as the flow of payments for the products of society or as the payments for the inputs used to make society's output.

Civil Rights Act of 1964   The Civil Rights Act of 1964 attempts to increase minority and female employment in sectors where they are severely underrepresented by setting legal standards for hiring and promoting workers.

collective bargaining   Collective bargaining is the process by which a union represents the interests of its members as a group in negotiating pay and working conditions with an employer or group of employers.

collusion   Collusion is cooperation by the firms in an industry in order to create or exert monopoly power.

commodity standard of money   Under a commodity standard of money, the quantity of money is determined by the amount of a specific commodity, such as gold.

commodity terms of trade   The commodity terms of trade measures the quantity of imports that a country can obtain for a given quantity of the goods it exports. It is the ratio of the price of exports divided by the price of imports.

common market A common market is a customs union that also allows the free movement of labor and capital among its member countries.

comparable worth legislation Comparable worth legislation refers to laws that would require a firm to pay equal wages for jobs that have been determined by the government to have equal value to the firm.

comparative advantage Comparative advantage is determined by which producer has the lowest opportunity cost of producing a good or service. Since opportunity cost is measured in terms of the quantity of one good or service that must be sacrificed to produce one more unit of another good or service, *everyone* has a *comparative* advantage in producing *something*.

compensating wage differentials Compensating wage differentials are pay differences that offset unequal working conditions in jobs held by identical workers.

competition Competition defines a type of market that individual firms can enter or leave at will and in which individual firms have no direct control over the price at which they sell their output.

competitive firms Competitive firms are price takers in the market for the good or service they produce and in the markets for the inputs that they use.

complement Two goods are complements if when the price of one good changes, *cet. par.*, the demand curve for the other good shifts in the *opposite* direction.

compound interest Compound interest is the interest paid on interest payments that have been accumulated in the past.

concentration ratio A concentration ratio measures the share of total industry sales accounted for by a specific number of firms—usually the largest four or largest eight firms in the industry.

constant-cost industry A constant-cost industry is one in which production costs per unit of output neither increase nor decrease as industry output changes in the long run, *cet. par.*

constant returns to scale Constant returns to scale for a firm means that the firm's long-run average total cost curve and long-run marginal cost curve are horizontal. Alternatively, increasing (decreasing) all factor inputs by a constant percentage will cause output to increase (decrease) by the same percentage.

consumer price index (CPI) The consumer price index (CPI) for the United States is a number that represents the cost of purchasing a representative group of goods and services relative to some time in the past.

consumers' surplus Consumers' surplus is the maximum amount consumers are willing to pay for a good or service less the amount they have to pay.

consumption Consumption refers to households' expenditures on goods and services to be used primarily during the year in question.

consumption function The consumption function is a schedule, or equation, indicating society's total intended consumption expenditures at various levels of aggregate real income.

controlled economies Controlled economies are characterized by controlled markets, in which prices, and sometimes quantities bought and sold, are mandated by law or government decree. Some transactions may occur in uncontrolled markets.

corporate profits Corporate profits represent the income people receive from dividends paid to them on the stocks they own and earnings retained by the corporation for reinvestment.

cost-benefit analysis Cost-benefit analysis is a quantitative comparison of the present values of economic costs and benefits associated with an investment decision.

cost-effectiveness analysis Cost-effectiveness analysis is a quantitative comparison of the present value of benefits associated with a set of investment projects each having identical costs, or a quantitative comparison of the present values of costs associated with a set of investment projects each having identical benefits.

cost-push inflation Cost-push inflation is caused by increases in costs that shift the aggregate supply curve to the left.

countercyclical fiscal policy Countercyclical fiscal policy is fiscal policy designed explicitly to moderate fluctuations in GNP and employment.

credit markets Credit markets are markets in which loans of various time lengths are arranged between borrowers and lenders.

cross price elasticity of demand The cross price elasticity of demand is the percentage change in the quantity demanded of one good that results when there is a 1 percent change in the price of another good, *cet. par.*

crowding out Crowding out means that an increase in the government deficit raises the interest rate, leading to a reduction in planned private investment expenditure.

Current Population Survey (CPS) The Current Population Survey (CPS) is a monthly survey of approximately 60,000 households in the United States for the purpose of gathering up-to-date data on personal characteristics and the labor force behavior of the U.S. population.

current prices Current prices are the prices of goods and services actually in effect during the year in question.

customs union A customs union is a group of nations that impose a common set of trade barriers against the rest of the world but none among themselves.

cyclical unemployment Cyclical unemployment results when workers are laid off because the aggregate demand for output declines and firms cut back on production.

▶ **deadweight loss** The deadweight loss of monopoly is the consumers' surplus that is lost in excess of the consumers' surplus that becomes monopoly profits.

debt-service ratio The debt-service ratio is a country's payments of principal and interest on its external debt divided by the value of its exports.

decreasing returns to scale Decreasing returns to scale for a firm means that the firm's long-run marginal cost curve is upward sloping. Alternatively, increasing (decreasing) all factor inputs by a constant percentage will increase (decrease) output by a smaller percentage.

decreasing returns to variable factors (inputs) Decreasing returns to variable factors (inputs) means that as output increases, with a given set of fixed inputs, marginal cost increases.

demand Demand is the relationship between the desire to buy various quantities of a good or service and its price.

demand curve A demand curve for a good or service is a geometric representation of demand.

demand deposits Demand deposits include any bank account from which the owner may demand immediate payment to the owner or to a third party by means of a check, telephone call, or telegram.

demand for labor The demand for labor is the relationship that defines the quantity of labor a firm would like to hire at various real wage rates.

demand-induced inflation Demand-induced inflation is caused by forces that shift the aggregate demand curve to the right.

depository institution A depository institution accepts deposits from the general public and from other banks.

Depository Institutions Deregulation and Monetary Control Act of 1980 The Depository Institutions Deregulation and Monetary Control Act of 1980 extends control of the Fed to all depository institutions and provides for greater competition among banks and for eventual decontrol of most interest rates they charge and pay.

depreciation Depreciation refers to a decline in a currency's exchange rate under a flexible exchange rate system.

depression A depression is a very severe recession, a period of time when a very severe decline in real GNP is occurring.

derived demands Derived demands for inputs are so called because they depend on the demand for the goods and services the inputs are used to produce.

devaluation Devaluation occurs when a country makes its currency cheaper in terms of other countries' currencies under a system of fixed exchange rates.

diminishing marginal utility Diminishing marginal utility means that the extra satisfaction obtained from additional consumption, while positive, is smaller the more of the item already consumed.

direct credit controls Direct credit controls allow the Fed to tell banks how much they can lend and to whom.

discount rate The discount rate is the interest rate banks must pay when they borrow from the Fed. The term discount refers to the payment of the interest charge in advance so the actual loan is the net of the total interest payment.

discrimination Discrimination occurs when an individual or a group of individuals must pay or receive a price for a good or service that differs from the price paid or received by others who are alike in every respect except some personal characteristic unrelated to the cost or productivity of the good or service provided.

disposable income (YD) Disposable income (YD) is the total income consumers have to spend after their taxes (T) are paid, so that $YD \equiv Y - T$.

dissaving Dissaving occurs when people consume more than their disposable income.

durable consumer goods Durable consumer goods are equipment that provide services to a household over a number of years.

▶ **economic approach to government activity** The economic approach to government activity uses the tools of modern economic analysis to study government behavior.

economic change, structural shifts Economic change, or structural shifts, refers to changes in the pattern of economic activity, such as the level and distribution of output or employment, in any economy over time.

economic growth Economic growth is an increase in the economy's capacity to produce real GNP and can be represented by an outward shift in the production possibilities frontier.

economic profit Economic profit is the excess of a firm's revenue over *all* its costs of production.

economic rent Economic rent arises from the difference between the price of a good or service and its opportunity cost.

economic system An economic system is the set of institutions, such as free markets or planning agencies, rules, and laws that determines the answers to the basic economic questions in a country.

economic union An economic union is a common market in which the member countries coordinate their monetary and fiscal policies.

economies of scale Economies of scale define a situation in which a firm's average total cost decreases as output increases.

effective maximum price An effective maximum price is a ceiling price that is less than the equilibrium price.

effective minimum price An effective minimum price is a price floor that is set above the equilibrium price.

efficient economy An efficient economy derives as much benefit as possible from its available resources; in this sense it wastes no resources.

elasticity of supply The elasticity of supply is the percentage change in the quantity supplied divided by the percentage change in price along a given supply curve.

endogenous An endogenous change in an economic variable is caused by a change from within an industry (or an economy). An endogenous change in an input price is caused by a shift in the demand for the input by the industry experiencing the price change.

endogenous consumption Endogenous consumption is that part of planned consumption that depends on GNP.

Equal Employment Opportunities Commission (EEOC) The Equal Employment Opportunities Commission (EEOC) enforces the fairness provisions of the Civil Rights Act of 1964 by mediating complaints by workers against firms and by bringing suits against employers who it believes have violated the law.

equilibrium interest rate The equilibrium interest rate is the real interest rate that equates the aggregate supply and demand for loanable funds; at the equilibrium interest rate borrowers want to borrow exactly the amount of funds that lenders want to lend.

equilibrium in the aggregate labor market Equilibrium in the aggregate labor market occurs when an employment–real wage combination is found that leaves no buyer or seller of labor unsatisfied.

equilibrium price The equilibrium price is the price at which the quantity of a good or service demanded equals the quantity supplied.

equilibrium quantity The equilibrium quantity is the quantity that results from the equilibrium price. It is both a quantity demanded and supplied.

equilibrium real GNP Equilibrium real GNP occurs when the aggregate real quantity of goods and services produced exactly equals planned aggregate expenditure.

equity Equity, when describing the way in which society's income or wealth is divided among society's members, refers to the fairness of the division when judged against an ethical standard.

equity-efficiency quandary The equity-efficiency quandary occurs when a society must choose between promoting an efficient economy and improving the fairness with which income or wealth is divided among its members.

eurodollar market The eurodollar market is a financial market in which eurodollars are borrowed and lent.

eurodollars Eurodollars are dollar deposits in European banks.

excess demand An excess demand, or shortage, is the amount by which the quantity demanded exceeds the quantity supplied.

excess reserves Excess reserves are banks' deposits at the Fed and other reserves in excess of their required amount.

excess supply, or glut An excess supply, or glut, is the excess of the quantity supplied over the quantity demanded.

exclusion principle The exclusion principle refers to the possibility, at a reasonable cost, of preventing people from using a good or service if they do not pay for it.

exogenous An exogenous change in an economic variable is caused by a change from outside an industry (or an economy). An exogenous change in an input price is caused by a shift in the supply of the input to the industry experiencing the price change.

exogenous consumption Exogenous consumption is that part of planned consumption that depends on factors other than GNP.

expected real wage (W/P^e) The expected real wage (W/P^e) is the nominal (paycheck) wage in terms of its purchasing power expected in the near future.

external diseconomy, external cost, or negative externality An external diseconomy, external cost, or negative externality results when part of the cost of producing or consuming a good or service is paid for by a firm or household other than the one that produces or consumes it.

external economy, external benefit, or positive externality An external economy, external benefit, or positive externality results when part of the benefit of producing or consuming a good or service accrues to a firm or household other than that which produces or consumes it.

▶ **factor demand curve** A factor demand curve relates the quantity of the factor demanded to its price.

factor payments Factor payments are the amounts firms spend to purchase the services of productive factors.

factors of production, productive factors Factors of production, or productive factors, include the services of labor and capital.

featherbedding Featherbedding refers to a practice, usually provided in a contract with a union, that forces an employer to pay for more labor than the employer would like to hire.

Federal Deposit Insurance Corporation (FDIC) The Federal Deposit Insurance Corporation (FDIC) insures "small" bank deposits (those not exceeding $100,000) against losses if a bank fails.

Federal Open Market Committee (FOMC) The Federal Open Market Committee (FOMC) is the part of the Fed that controls bank reserves.

Federal Reserve notes Federal Reserve notes are our paper currency.

Federal Reserve System (Fed) The Federal Reserve Bank, or Fed for short, is the central bank of the United States.

fiat money Fiat money is money because the government has declared it to be so.

financial instrument A financial instrument is an asset for one party and a liability for another party.

financial sector The financial sector consists of the economy's money and credit markets.

firm A firm is the basic economic unit that makes production decisions in a market economy, just as the household is the basic unit that makes consumption decisions.

firm's labor demand curve [d(l)] A firm's labor demand curve [d(l)] is a graph illustrating the firm's desired labor force at various possible real wage rates.

firm's long run A firm's long run refers to a period of time over which the firm can alter all of its inputs.

firm's short run A firm's short run refers to a period of time over which the firm cannot alter some of its inputs.

fiscal policy Fiscal policy is the adjustment of taxes or government spending.

fixed costs Fixed costs are those costs that do not change when a firm adjusts its output.

fixed exchange rates Fixed exchange rates are exchange rates that governments set between their countries' currencies.

flat tax A flat tax would tax all eligible income at the same rate.

flexible exchange rate system In a flexible exchange rate system the forces of supply and demand in foreign exchange markets determine exchange rates for currencies.

foreign exchange intervention Foreign exchange intervention means that the government of a country (through its central bank) buys or sells foreign exchange for the purpose of affecting the exchange rates for its currency in a particular way.

foreign exchange market The foreign exchange market is where currencies are bought and sold; it is where foreign exchange rates are determined.

foreign exchange rate A foreign exchange rate is the amount of one country's currency (money) that it takes to buy one unit of another country's currency.

45° line The 45° line exactly divides the right angle created by the two axes of the consumption function graph. Along this line, whatever expenditure components are measured along the vertical axis exactly equal GNP, which is measured along the horizontal axis.

fractional reserve system In a fractional reserve system, required reserves are less than the banks' deposit liabilities.

free market economies Free market economies are those that operate with the least amount of government control over the prices and quantities of goods and services bought and sold; few such economies operate with absolutely no government influence, however.

free-rider problem The free-rider problem occurs because of the ability of a user of a good or service to avoid paying for it when the user cannot easily be excluded from the benefits.

frictional unemployment Frictional unemployment occurs because it takes time for newly unemployed workers to find jobs even though there are enough jobs to go around.

full employment Full employment occurs when there is no cyclical unemployment.

full-employment GNP Full-employment GNP requires that there is equilibrium in the aggregate market for goods and services and full employment in the aggregate labor market at the same time.

full macroeconomic equilibrium Full macroeconomic equilibrium occurs when equilibrium exists in the labor, goods, and credit markets simultaneously.

functional distribution of income The functional distribution of income is a quantitative summary of the percentage of society's total income paid to the owners of various inputs that are used to produce goods and services.

game theoretic approach The game theoretic approach to price setting in oligopoly analyzes firm behavior in terms of achieving the best outcome in a game played against the other firms in the industry.

General Agreement on Tariffs and Trade (GATT)   The General Agreement on Tariffs and Trade (GATT) is an agreement that was reached by most nations after World War II to reduce trade barriers, such as tariffs and quotas, and to discourage "unfair" competition on the world market through the use of export subsidies.

general training   General training increases a worker's labor market productivity by the same amount in a large number of jobs and firms.

GNP deflator   The GNP deflator is a special index number that expresses the average price of current GNP in terms of prices that prevailed in a base year.

government spending   Government spending is the total dollar value of the purchases of goods and services by all government units—federal, state, and local.

gross national product (GNP)   Gross national product (GNP) measures the total value of all final goods and services the economy produces during a year.

▶ **high employment deficit**   The high employment deficit is the excess of government spending over tax revenues when full employment prevails.

human capital   Human capital describes society's labor resources.

hyperinflation   Hyperinflation is an *extremely* rapid and continuous increase in the price level.

▶ **import substitution**   Import substitution is the use of trade restrictions to promote domestic production of manufactured goods that are currently imported.

income distribution   Income distribution is a quantitative summary of how society's total income (production) is divided among the members of society.

income effect   The income effect refers to the tendency of people to demand more of most goods and services when their purchasing power rises and to demand less when their purchasing power falls.

income elasticity of demand   The income elasticity of demand is the percentage change in the quantity of a good demanded divided by the percentage change in the real income of purchasers of the good.

increasing returns to scale   Increasing returns to scale for a firm means that the firm's long-run marginal cost curve is downward sloping. Alternatively, increasing (decreasing) all factor inputs by a constant percentage will increase (decrease) output by a greater percentage.

increasing returns to variable factors (inputs)   Increasing returns to variable factors (inputs) means that as output increases, with a given set of fixed inputs, marginal cost declines.

indexing   Indexing is a means of adjusting nominal payments by referring to a price index so that their real value is unaffected by the rate of inflation.

indifference curve   An indifference curve illustrates combinations of consumption activities to which the individual attaches equal levels of utility.

indifference curve map   An indifference curve map is a collection of indifference curves and is a geometric description of a consumer's tastes and preferences (the utility function).

indirect business taxes   Indirect business taxes are those taxes paid by firms on the basis of the value of production taking place.

industrial policy debate   The industrial policy debate concerns the proper role of government in fostering economic change and helping the losers from economic change.

infant industry argument   The infant industry argument for trade restriction states that if an industry is protected in its early years of development, when it is unable to compete on the world market, it will be saved in the long term because the production experience it gains will ultimately make it competitive.

inferior goods   An inferior good is one for which the demand curve shifts to the left as purchasers' real incomes rise.

innovation   An innovation is the application of a new production technique or the development of a new product by a firm.

instruments of monetary policy   The Fed's instruments of monetary policy are the different types of actions it can take to control the money supply.

interest rate   The interest rate is the percentage of a dollar that a borrower must pay a lender per year for each $1 borrowed.

intermediate goods   Intermediate goods are goods purchased by a firm to use in further production.

investment   Investment occurs when businesses add to their collection of physical capital (plant and equipment) and inventories. It also includes the purchases of new dwellings, even if by individuals or families.

▶ **kinked demand curve**   The kinked demand curve is a description of oligopoly behavior that says that if a firm raises its price, it will lose a large amount of sales but that if it lowers its price, it will gain very few sales.

labor   The term labor is frequently used to refer to the services of human capital used in production.

labor force   The labor force is the sum of employed plus unemployed people in the population.

labor force participation   Labor force participation refers to whether a person desires to work or not. Someone who is willing to work at a given wage rate is a labor force participant.

labor market discrimination   Labor market discrimination occurs when members of a particular race, sex, or other group receive lower pay even though they have the same investment in human capital as others do.

labor productivity   Labor productivity measures the quantity of goods or services produced by a typical worker during a particular period of time.

Laffer curve   The Laffer curve is a theoretical relationship between tax rates and tax revenues. It illustrates tax revenues falling when tax rates increase to the levels that now exist in the United States and many other nations.

lag   A lag is the time that elapses between the occurrence of an event and a reaction to the event.

law of demand   The law of demand states that there is a negative relationship between desired purchases and the price of a good or service, *cet. par.*

law of supply   The law of supply states that the quantity of a good or service firms desire to sell is greater the higher the price of the good or service, *cet. par.*

less-developed countries (LDCs), developing countries   Less-developed countries (LDCs), also known as developing countries, are characterized by economies that generate low per capita incomes and generally have not achieved a high level of industrialization that is typical of the world's developed nations.

loanable funds   Loanable funds consist of money borrowed and lent in the credit market.

loan contract   A loan contract is an agreement created when one party borrows from another. It is a financial instrument specifying a repayment schedule along with interest owed to the lender.

loan contract, financial, or credit market   The loan contract, financial, or credit market is where borrowers and lenders of money arrange the terms of loans.

lockout   A lockout is the employer's counterpart to a strike whereby workers are not allowed inside an establishment without a valid contract with a union.

logrolling   Logrolling is the mutual exchange of political support among special-interest groups.

long-run aggregate supply curve   The long-run aggregate supply curve is a vertical line relating the price level to the full macroeconomic equilibrium value of real GNP.

long-run average total cost (LATC) curve   The long-run average total cost (LATC) curve for a firm refers to its average total cost curve when the firm can alter all of its inputs.

long-run equilibrium   Long-run equilibrium for an industry means that no firm in the industry has an incentive to change its output and that no firm desires to enter or leave the industry.

long-run supply (LRS)   The long-run supply (LRS) of a competitive industry is the relationship between the price of a good or service and the quantity offered for sale when the industry is in long-run equilibrium.

luxury good   A luxury good is one with an income elasticity of demand that exceeds 1.0.

M1   M1 includes all deposits (except those of the United States Treasury) in the banking system's consolidated balance sheet on which checks can be written plus currency and traveler's checks in the hands of the nonbank public.

M2   M2 includes M1 plus "small" certificates of deposit, savings accounts, money market mutual fund accounts, and certain other bank obligations that banks' depositors treat as readily available to carry out transactions.

M3   M3 includes M2 plus "large" CD's and other deposits that are relatively liquid but are inconvenient to use in day-to-day transactions.

macroeconomics   Macroeconomics analyzes the behavior of an entire economy.

marginal cost, incremental cost   Marginal, or incremental, cost is the change in costs that occurs when a firm produces more or less output.

marginal firm   A marginal firm is one that generates no economic rent for its owners in the long run.

marginal private cost, internal cost   The marginal private cost, or internal cost, of a good or service is the opportunity cost that the producer or user must pay to produce or use one more unit.

marginal product of labor (mpl)   The marginal product of labor (mpl) measures the additional output a firm produces when it hires an additional unit of labor all other inputs such as machinery held constant. (The marginal product of capital is defined as the additional output obtained from using one more unit of capital with a given amount of labor.)

marginal propensity to consume (MPC)   The marginal propensity to consume (MPC) is the additional aggregate consumption spending that occurs out of each additional dollar of disposable income; MPC is a fraction (b) between 0 and 1.

marginal propensity to save (MPS) The marginal propensity to save (MPS) is the extra aggregate saving that occurs out of each additional dollar of disposable income; $MPS \equiv 1 - MPC \equiv 1 - b$ and is therefore a fraction between 0 and 1.

marginal revenue, incremental revenue Marginal, or incremental, revenue is the change in revenue that a firm receives when it produces (and sells) more or less output.

marginal social cost The marginal social cost of a good or service includes both the private and external costs (if any) of producing one more unit.

marginal tax rate The marginal tax rate is the percentage of an additional dollar of taxable income that must be paid in taxes.

marginal utility Marginal utility is the increment in satisfaction obtained from greater consumption of a given good, service, or leisure activity, all other consumption held constant.

marginal value The marginal value of a good or service is the maximum amount that someone is willing to pay for one more unit.

market A market may be an actual location, but in economics it is best thought of as an idealized concept that describes how buyers and sellers of a particular good or service come together.

market deficiencies Market deficiencies are situations in which equilibrium prices do not reflect all of the opportunity costs (or all of the benefits) of producing a good or service.

market economy A market economy is one in which most goods and services are bought and sold in markets rather than each good and service being produced by each person or family that uses it.

market failure Market failure is the provision of a good or service in a quantity that is not economically efficient.

materials balance approach The materials balance approach is a planning device in which a set of accounts is formulated by a central planning agency and used to coordinate the quantities of inputs and outputs needed to achieve production goals for an economy.

medium of exchange A medium of exchange is something that is widely accepted by people in return for the sale of commodities or services or as payment for a loan.

minimax strategy The minimax strategy is one rule that a firm may follow in pursuing a game theoretic approach to setting its price; it means choosing a price that minimizes the probability of a very bad outcome in terms of profit.

mixed economies Mixed economies contain many government-owned industries that are typically privately owned in free market systems.

model An economic model is an abstract, simplified representation of how decision makers interact, how their decisions are affected by the economic environment, and the behavior that results from these decisions.

monetarists and Keynesians Monetarists and Keynesians are economists who hold different sets of views on monetary and fiscal policies.

monetary aspects of international trade Monetary aspects of international trade deal with currency flows, which are the financial counterpart of international commodity flows.

monetary authority A nation's monetary authority is usually its central bank, which is responsible for determining the quantity of money under a paper monetary standard.

monetary base The monetary base is the raw material from which banks create deposit liabilities and is equal to the sum of banks' reserves, currency in their vaults, and currency in the hands of the public.

monetary policy The Fed's monetary policy determines how much money circulates in the United States economy.

monetary standard A monetary standard defines the basis of an economy's money.

monetization of the debt Monetization of the debt occurs when the Fed buys government bonds, particularly when the bonds are purchased directly from the Treasury.

money Money consists mainly of checking account balances owned by business firms and individuals (not those owned by banks and the government) plus paper money and coins (currency) outside banks' vaults.

money multiplier The money multiplier is the ratio of the change in the quantity of money that results from a change in banks' reserves.

monopolistic competition Monopolistic competition is a market form in which firms produce differentiated products and therefore are not price takers. However, there are also few or no barriers preventing firms from producing quite similar products in a monopolistically competitive industry.

monopoly Monopoly is a market form in which only one seller provides an industry's total production.

monopoly power Monopoly power is the ability of a firm or group of firms to charge more than the competitive price for the goods or services they sell.

monopsony Monopsony means "one buyer" and usually refers to an employer with market power over the wage rates paid to its workers.

moral suasion Moral suasion is one of the Fed's methods of encouraging banks to lend more or less than they would like or to favor certain classes of customers.

multiple deposit expansion   Multiple deposit expansion means that when the banking system's reserves increase, the quantity of checking account liabilities can be increased by a larger amount.

multiplier, exogenous expenditure multiplier   The multiplier (also called the exogenous expenditure multiplier) is the ratio $1/(1 - b)$, where b is the marginal propensity to consume, which shows how changes in exogenous expenditure (planned investment, government spending, or exogenous consumption) are related to changes in equilibrium GNP.

mutual interdependence of price and output decisions   Mutual interdependence of price and output decisions means that each firm must consider the reactions of other firms in the industry when deciding how much to produce and what to charge for it.

▶ **necessity**   A necessity is a good or service with an income elasticity of demand that exceeds 0 but is 1.0 or less. (Both necessities and luxury goods are also normal goods.)

net exports   Net exports represent the dollar value of a country's exports minus the dollar value of its imports.

nominal, or paycheck, wage (W)   The nominal, or paycheck, wage (W) is the pay a worker receives measured in dollars per hour.

nominal GNP   Nominal GNP is the observed value of GNP during a given time period, say, a year, with goods and services evaluated at current prices.

nominal interest rate   A nominal interest rate is sometimes referred to as the market rate of interest; it is the interest rate borrowers and banks agree to and is unadjusted for the rate of inflation.

nondurable consumer goods   Nondurable consumer goods are goods used up by households in the year they are purchased.

nonlabor income   Nonlabor income is income someone receives that is independent of the amount worked.

nonmarket activities   Nonmarket activities are the production of goods and services at home that are not sold for a price on a market.

nontariff trade barriers (NTBs)   Nontariff trade barriers (NTBs) are nonprice trade restrictions.

normal employment (L^n)   Normal employment (L^n) is the amount of employment denoted by the aggregate labor supply curve at a given real wage.

normal goods   A normal good is one for which the demand curve shifts to the right as purchasers' real incomes rise.

normal unemployment rate (u^n)   The normal unemployment rate (u^n) is the unemployment rate when the labor market is in equilibrium; it is the percentage of the labor force that is frictionally or structurally unemployed.

normative view   A normative view concerns the ethics of an issue or what is "right" or "just" versus "wrong" or "unjust."

▶ **oligopoly**   Oligopoly is a market form in which only a small number of firms participate.

open market operations   Open market operations are the purchases and sales of government bonds by the Fed on the open market (the market for government bonds).

opportunity cost   Opportunity cost is the amount of one good or service that must be given in order to produce a unit of another good or service.

overvalued   An overvalued currency is one whose price relative to some other currency is kept artificially above the price that would clear the foreign exchange market without government intervention.

▶ **paper standard of money**   Under a paper standard, the quantity of money is determined by a monetary authority and is unrelated to any commodity.

peak load problem   The peak load problem is the difficulty a local public utility can have in attempting to serve customers who may demand a relatively large quantity of its service at certain times of the day and a relatively small quantity at other times.

perfect price discrimination   Perfect price discrimination exists when a firm is able to charge the most consumers will pay (all the traffic will bear) for each unit of output separately.

permanent shift in demand or supply   A permanent shift in demand or supply is one that is not expected to reverse itself during the period over which buyers and sellers formulate their plans.

Phillips curve   The Phillips curve is a statistical relationship between the unemployment rate and the rate of inflation that is observed in the short run during inflationary episodes and recessions.

physical capital   Physical capital consists of society's nonlabor resources.

planned aggregate expenditure ($\dot{E}$)   Planned aggregate expenditure ($\dot{E}$) is the sum of aggregate planned consumption by households ($\dot{C}$), investment planned by firms ($\dot{I}$), and government spending (G)—as well as net exports (X).

positive economics   Positive economics is the study of how economic variables are related to one another.

poverty level of income   The poverty level of income is the official government figure used to determine whether or not a particular family is poor.

present value (PV) Present value (PV) is a single number that measures the economic value of a financial asset or capital good yielding a stream of returns (benefits) over its lifetime.

price ceiling A price ceiling is the highest price at which it is legal to buy or sell a good or service.

price discrimination Price discrimination occurs when a firm is able to charge different prices to different buyers who purchase the identical good or service.

price elasticity of demand The price elasticity of demand is the percentage change in the quantity of a good demanded divided by the percentage change in its price, from one point to another along a given demand curve. It measures the sensitivity of quantity demanded to a change in price.

price floor A price floor is the lowest price at which it is legal to buy or sell a good or service.

price index A price index is a number that indicates the ratio of the cost of purchasing or producing a given bundle of goods and services relative to some base year, multiplied by 100.

price leadership Price leadership is a form of collusion, usually informal, in which one firm assumes the responsibility for setting the industry price; other firms follow.

price searchers Price searchers are firms that seek the profit-maximizing price for the goods or services they sell.

price subsidy A price subsidy is a government payment to producers or consumers per unit of the good or service sold or purchased.

price taker A price taker is a buyer or seller that has no direct control over the market price of a good or service. All competitive firms are price takers.

prime interest rate The prime interest rate is the standard or base rate of interest that banks charge borrowers for one-year loans.

principle of increasing cost The principle of increasing cost is the assumption that a firm's production costs increase proportionately more rapidly than its output does. This means that marginal cost increases as output increases in the short run.

product differentiation Product differentiation is the creation of brand names or superficial distinctions among products that are either identical or very similar.

production function A production function quantifies the relationship between a firm's output and its inputs.

production possibilities frontier (PPF) A production possibilities frontier (PPF) illustrates the alternative output levels for an economy that gets the most it can from its given set of resources and available technology. It shows the maximum production possible for each good or service, given the output of all other goods and services.

progressive income tax A progressive income tax has a rate schedule whereby the higher one's taxable income, the higher is the percentage of an additional dollar of taxable income that must be paid in taxes.

property right A property right is the legal entitlement to use or sell an asset, such as land, a good or service, or an invention.

proprietors' income Proprietors' income is the income earned by the self-employed from their business activities.

public goods A public good (or service), if provided for one user, is, by its nature, provided for many users at no additional cost.

quantity demanded The quantity demanded of a good or service is the particular amount people desire to buy, given its price and other factors influencing demand.

quantity equation The quantity equation expresses the quantity of money as proportional to nominal GNP.

quota A quota is a nontariff trade barrier (NTB) that limits the quantity of an imported good that may be sold in a country.

rate of inflation The rate of inflation is the percentage change in the general price level and is typically measured by the percentage change in the CPI between two years.

rate regulation Rate regulation is the general term for the situation in which a government agency has the power to approve or disapprove a firm's price and output (profit) decisions.

rationing Rationing a good or service means that the right to consume it is allocated by an authority, such as a government, on grounds other than consumers' willingness to pay.

real aspects of international trade Real aspects of international trade are concerned with the flows of commodities among nations.

real GNP Real GNP is the value of the economy's total production adjusted to ignore changes in the prices of goods and services over time.

real income Real income measures the quantity of goods and services that can be purchased by a consumer.

real interest rate The real interest rate is the nominal (market) interest rate minus the expected rate of inflation.

real wage (W/P) The real wage (W/P) is equal to the nominal (or paycheck) wage (W) divided by the aggregate price level (P); the real wage expresses a worker's pay in terms of its ability to purchase goods and services.

recession A recession is a period of time when real GNP declines for two or more consecutive quarters.

recognition lag A recognition lag is the time that elapses between the occurrence of an event and the observation that the event has occurred.

rental income   Rental income is the income produced by renting out machinery or buildings for use in production or consumption.

required reserve ratio   The required reserve ratio is the amount of reserves that banks must keep with the Fed or on hand, expressed as a fraction of the banks' deposit liabilities.

reserves   Reserves consist of assets banks retain to pay their depositors when they wish to withdraw from their accounts. In today's banking system, reserves include a bank's cash on hand and demand deposits it holds in other banks. The most important component of commercial banks' reserves are deposits they hold with the central bank—the Fed in the United States.

revaluation   Revaluation occurs when a country increases the value of its currency in terms of other countries' currencies under a system of fixed exchange rates. (Revaluation is the opposite of devaluation.)

Ricardian equivalence hypothesis
The Ricardian equivalence hypothesis states that the method of financing government expenditure has no impact on private consumption or investment expenditures.

▶ **saving**   Saving is the difference between total income and the amount spent on the consumption of goods and services or paid to the government in taxes.

saving function   The saving function is a schedule, or equation, indicating how much society plans to save at various possible levels of aggregate real income.

scarcity   Scarcity means that human wants or desires far exceed the capacity of the world's limited resources to satisfy those wants or desires.

secondary discrimination   Secondary discrimination occurs when members of a particular race, sex, or other group are discouraged from investing in human capital because of labor market discrimination.

shared monopoly   A shared monopoly is an industry in which a group of firms establish the monopoly price and share the monopoly rents.

shortage, or excess demand   A shortage, or excess demand, is the amount by which the quantity demanded exceeds the quantity supplied.

short run   The short run is the period of time in which firms adjust their output by using more or less inputs but not by entering or leaving the market for a good or service. Over the short run, some of a firm's costs are fixed costs.

short-run aggregate supply curve
The short-run aggregate supply curve shows what happens to the price level and real GNP during inflationary episodes and recessions.

short-run macroeconomic equilibrium
Short-run macroeconomic equilibrium occurs when equilibrium occurs in the aggregate market for goods and services but not all aggregate markets.

shutdown point   The shutdown point is a firm's minimum (lowest) average variable cost; if the price falls lower than the shutdown point, the firm will not produce anything.

size distribution of income   The size distribution of income is a quantitative summary of the percentage of society's income received by various groups of individuals.

societal discrimination   Societal discrimination occurs when members of a particular race, sex, or other group receive less favorable treatment from government, firms, or their families regarding opportunities for investing in human capital.

special drawing rights (SDRs)
Special drawing rights (SDRs) are a kind of international money created by the International Monetary Fund.

specialization   Specialization occurs when people produce a good or service to trade or sell to others, not because they may wish to use the good or service they are producing.

specific duty   A specific duty is a tariff equal to a specified amount per unit of an imported item.

specific training   Specific training increases a worker's labor market productivity primarily in the job and firm where he or she is currently employed.

stagflation   Stagflation is the coexistence of inflation and above-normal unemployment.

store of value   A store of value is any means of keeping wealth over time.

structural deficit   A structural deficit is a deficit that persists when the economy is at full employment.

structural unemployment   Structural unemployment arises from the job losses people suffer when firms move out of a region, the skill requirements of the work force change, or when there is a minimum wage rate.

structure of interest rates   The structure of interest rates refers to the variation in interest rates across loans by the type of borrower and the term of the loan (loan period).

substitute   Two goods are substitutes if when the price of one good changes, *cet. par.*, the demand for the other good shifts in the *same* direction.

substitution effect   The substitution effect refers to the tendency for desired purchases of a good or service to rise when its price falls and to fall when its price rises relative to the price of others goods and services, *cet. par.*

supply   Supply is the quantity offered for sale at each possible price.

supply of labor   The supply of labor is the relationship that defines the amount of labor offered to firms by individuals.

supply-side economics   Supply-side economics emphasizes the impact of monetary and fiscal policies on investment and real GNP in the long run.

▶ **target of monetary policy**   A target of monetary policy is the variable(s), such as the rate of monetary growth or the rate of interest, that monetary policy attempts to influence for the purpose of smoothing out business cycles.

tariff   A tariff is a tax on imported goods that is collected by the government of an importing country.

technical monopoly   A technical monopoly (sometimes called a *natural monopoly*) is a market form in which one firm can provide a good or service at a lower cost than a larger number of firms.

temporary, or transitory, shift in demand or supply   A temporary, or transitory, shift in demand or supply is one that is expected to reverse itself during the period over which buyers and sellers formulate their plans.

theory of rational expectations   The theory of rational expectations says that firms and households correctly incorporate available information in making decisions about their work effort, level of production, willingness to borrow and lend, and so forth; they are not fooled over and over by the effects of persistent or repeated economic events and government policy actions.

the three fundamental economic questions   Every economic system must answer the three fundamental economic questions: What? How? For whom?

threat effect   A threat effect is the effect of unions on the pay received by nonunion workers whose employers pay them more than the competitive wage to forestall their joining a union.

time-of-day pricing   Time-of-day pricing is a price structure in which a service costs the consumer more at times of peak use than at other times of the day.

total revenue (TR)   Total revenue (TR) equals a commodity's price multiplied by the quantity sold; i.e., $TR \equiv PQ$.

trade creation effects   The trade creation effects of a customs union are the increased gains from trade resulting from expanded imports and exports within the union.

trade diversion effects   The trade diversion effects of a customs union are the reduced gains from trade resulting from diminished imports from countries outside the union.

Trade Expansion Act of 1962   The Trade Expansion Act of 1962 authorized government financial assistance to workers who were designated as displaced and firms that went out of business because of foreign competition.

transaction costs   Transaction costs are expenditures of time, money, and other resources required for a buyer or seller to arrange a transaction.

transfer payments   Transfer payments are the opposite of taxes: payments from government to individuals or firms to raise their incomes.

▶ **unemployed**   The unemployed are people who did not work during the week before the CPS, but were available for work that week *and* (1) made specific efforts to find a job within the four weeks prior to the survey, (2) were waiting to be called back to jobs from which they had been laid off, or (3) were waiting to report to a new job within the next month.

unemployment rate   The unemployment rate is the percentage of the labor force classified as unemployed.

unfair labor practices   An unfair labor practice is an illegal action on the part of labor or management to frustrate the opposition in an organizing or collective-bargaining dispute.

unit of account   A unit of account is the way in which an economy's prices are expressed (such as in dollars or yen).

unrestricted entry   Unrestricted entry means that no factors other than production costs hinder a firm from deciding to produce a good or service.

utility   Utility refers to the amount of satisfaction, happiness, or well-being an individual experiences from spending his or her income.

utility function   A utility function is a mathematical description, either geometric or algebraic, of the link between an individual's utility and his or her consumption of goods and services.

▶ **value of the marginal product of labor (vmpl)**   The value of the marginal product of labor (vmpl) is the increase in a competitive firm's sales revenue resulting from the sale of the extra output produced when an additional worker is hired.

variable costs   Variable costs are those costs that change when a firm adjusts its output.

velocity of money (V)   Velocity (V) tells us the constant of proportionality in the quantity equation: 1/V is the constant of proportionality between nominal GNP and the quantity of money required to sustain it.

▶ **white market**   A white market is a legal arrangement for buying and selling ration coupons when a legal maximum price or some other market interference creates an excess demand for a good or service.

world price   The world price is the price of purchasing a given commodity or service on the world market.

Index

Abortions, supply/demand for, 134
Accelerated inflation, 559
Accounting, profit from viewpoint of, 84
Acid rain, 354, 374
Ad valorem tariffs, vs. specific duties, 650–51
Advanced developing countries, 655
Advertising, 206, 212, 214–20
  and consumer protection, 219–20
  informative, and prices, 214–17
  product differentiation, monopoly power and, 219
  profits, prices and, 220
AFDC. *See* Aid to Families of Dependent Children
Aggregate demand curve, 543, 544–45
  during inflationary episodes, 549–51
  during a recession, 545–49
  equilibrium with supply, 545
Aggregate demand for labor [D(L)], 420–22
Aggregate demand for loanable funds (DLF), 504–5
Aggregate economic losses, and tariffs, 649–50
Aggregate economics, 380, 381
Aggregate expenditures on goods and services, 439–40
  analysis of, 440–56
  and disposable income, 446 (fig.)
Aggregate labor market, equilibrium in, 424–25, 521
Aggregate production,
  expenditure and equilibrium GNP, 449–56
  and price levels, 543–51
Aggregate supply curve, 543, 545
  during inflationary episodes, 549–51
  during a recession, 545–49
  equilibrium with demand, 545
  long-run/short-run, 544
Aggregate supply of labor [S(L)], 423
Aggregate supply of loanable funds (SLF), 510
Agricultural allotments, 177

Agricultural marketing organizations, 180–81, 192
Agricultural technology, 62
Agriculture, 380, 622
  government programs for, 122
    credit, 371, 372 (fig.)
    payment in kind (PIK), 134–36
    price subsidies, 132–33
    price supports, 129–32, 162–63
    ripple effect of, 136
Aid to Families with Dependent Children (AFDC), 306, 307, 311, 423, 441, 571
Airline Deregulation Act, 236
Airline industry, 186
  deregulation, 235–37
Airline Pilots' Association, 237
Air traffic controllers' union, 276
American Association of Advertising Agencies, 216
American Tobacco Company, 192
Antitrust laws, 173, 193, 198, 227–28
  defined, 225
Appreciation of currency, 667
Arc elasticity, 65
Argentina, 699, 703
Arms supplies, in Lebanon, 111
AT&T, antitrust case against, 228–29
Australian National Bank, 480
Automatic fiscal stabilizers, 571
Automation, 254, 283
Automobiles, 353–54, 622, 642
  diffusion of Japanese, into U.S. market, 50–51
  import quotas on, 652–53
  market for small, 139–40
Average cost,
  defined, 86
  marginal cost, supply and, 85–89
  relationship to marginal cost, 88–89
Average fixed cost (AFC), 101
Average total cost (ATC), 100–101
  defined, 86
Average variable cost (AVC), 101
  defined, 86
  shutdown point, 88

Baby boom generation, 362, 717
Balance of payments, 669–73
  on current account, 671
  equilibrium/disequilibrium in, 672–73
  U.S., 669 (table)
Balance of trade, 669–73
  imbalances in developing countries, 696–705
Balance sheet, banks, 469–71
  consolidated, 474
  of the Federal Reserve, 481 (table), 482
Bank(s),
  assets of U.S. commercial, 475 (fig.)
  bailouts of, 489, 490
  balance sheet of, 469–71
  creation of money by, 470–73
  definition of, 464
  failures, 584–85
  loan operations of, 508 (table)
  reserves. *See* Reserves
  as suppliers of loanable funds, 507–9
Banking system, 468–76
  consolidated balance sheet of, 474–75
  deregulation of, 490–91, 515, 594
Bank of England, 480
Bank of Japan, 480, 666
Bank runs, 489
Barriers to entry, into industries, 170
Barter economy, 21–22
  advantage of monetary economy over, 465
Base year, 390
Basic accounting identity, 469, 470
Beer, supply/demand for, 115–16
Benefits, external, 341
Benham, Lee, 220
Bequest motive, 614
Bethlehem Steel, 198
Black Lung disability program, 310
Black market(s),
  defined, 127
  and food policies, 367
Black-white wage differences, 325–26
Bolivia, 684
Brand names, 206, 655

Brazil, 354, 697, 698, 699, 703
Breakeven point, 102
Bretton Woods Agreement of 1944, 680
Brewing industry, 190
Brink's Incorporated, 192
Budgetary process in democracies,
        743–44
Budget constraints,
    and consumer choice, 57, 59
    and price elasticities, 71
Bureaucratic behavior, government, vs.
        firm's behavior, 744–45
Business cycle, 395
    and government deficits, 610–11

▶ California, market for Japanese cars in,
        50–51
Canada, 22, 194, 374, 610, 655, 672, 673
    size distribution of income in,
        299–301
    transmission of U.S. recession to, 674
Capital, 246
    effect of changes in, on demand for
        labor, 253–55
    fixed, and labor, 249 (fig.)
    formation, 717 (table)
    measuring the value of, 283–86
    opportunity cost of, 231
    See also Human capital; Physical
        capital
Capital account, 671
Capitalist economic system, 725
    government role in, 741–45
    market forces and state planning in,
        726–27
    vs. socialist, 726 (fig.)
        economic performance in, 733–39
        GNP, 728 (fig.)
        performance criteria, 727–29
Capital services, 268
Capper-Volstead Act of 1922, 173, 192
Career-ladder employment, 429
Careers in economics, 25, 26
Carnegie Steel Company, 198
Cartel(s), defined, 192
Carter, Jimmy, 600, 607
Carter administration, 295, 354, 498, 594,
        721
Cash drain, and multiple deposit
        expansion, 473
Categorical welfare program, 310
Central bank, 468. See also Federal
        Reserve System
Ceteris paribus, defined, 36
Change in quantity demanded, 45
Change in quantity supplied, 89–90
Chernobyl nuclear disaster, 354
Childrearing, 326

Chile, 684
China. See People's Republic of China
Chrysler Corporation, 642, 653
Cigarette industry, 192
Circular flow of GNP, 388
Civil Aeronautics Board (CAB), 229,
        235–36
Civil Rights Act of 1964, 326
Clayton Antitrust Act of 1914, 173, 192
Coal, 351, 354
Coca-Cola Company, 47, 206
Collective bargaining, 276
Collusion, 191–93
    defined, 192
    pricing with, 192–97
    pricing without, 197–202
Commodity(ies),
    imports/exports of, 626 (fig.)
    price supports/subsidies for producers
        of, 129–33
Commodity standard of money, 467
Commodity terms of trade, 694, 696
Common Market. See European
        Economic Community (EEC)
Comparable worth issue, 328–29
Comparative advantage,
    defined, 20
    specialization, and opportunity cost,
        19–20
Compensating wage differentials, 269–70
Competition,
    defined, 80
    differences among monopoly,
        oligopoly, and monopolistic
        competition, 209 (table)
    differences between monopoly and,
        173 (table)
    and economic efficiency, 156–59
    monopolistic, 207–12
    vs. monopoly, 225 (fig.), 272
    price differences in, 213
Competitive firms and industries,
    application of theory of, 154–59
    demand for labor and other inputs,
        255–56, 416–17
    long run supply/demand in, 145–54
    output/input decisions, labor and
        profit maximizing, 247–48
    rate regulation in potentially, 233–35
Compliments of goods/services, 47
Compound interest, 284
Computer software industry, 144
    and property rights, 348
Computer terminals, effect of foreign
        exchange rate on imports/
        exports of, 662, 668 (fig.)
Concentration of production, 191–93
Concentration ratio, 191

Conceptual market, 21
Consolidated balance sheet, 474
Constant cost industry, 148–50, 170
Constant return to scale, 102, 103
Consumer choice,
    geometry and economics of, 58–59
    theory of, 54–59
    See also Demand; Product
        differentiation
Consumer cooperatives, 213
Consumer expenditures, 33, 34 (fig.)
    aggregate, 439–57
    and price elasticity of demand, 66,
        67–69 (fig.)
Consumer goods and services,
    aggregate expenditure on, 439–57
    aggregate quantity supplied, 424–25
    comparative advantage, opportunity
        costs and, 20
    compliments of, 47
    effect of monetary policy on, 574
    equilibrium in aggregate market for,
        521–22
    and government spending, 564
    luxury vs. necessities, 72
    prices of related, 47–48
    recession and, 529–30
    substitutes of, 47
    total production and, 21
    See also Durable consumer goods;
        Intermediate goods;
        Nondurable consumer goods
Consumer Price Index (CPI), 390, 392,
        417, 588 (fig.)
Consumer protection, and advertising,
        219–20
Consumers,
    goals of, 33, 35, 402
    limitations on choices of, 35–36,
        402–3
    one-time, and demand shifts, 116–17
    tastes and preferences of, 47
    theory of choice in, 54–59
    well-being, and choices, 40
Consumers' surplus, 175
    and price discrimination, 183
    and perfect price discrimination, 185
Consumption (C),
    efficiency in, 157
    and nominal GNP, 382
    time required for, and demand, 48
Consumption function, 441–45
    expressed graphically, 444–45
    expressed quantitatively, 441–44
Continental Illinois National Bank of
        Chicago, 490
Controlled economies, 22, 159
    See also Socialist economies

Cooperatives, 117, 180, 213
Copyright, 219, 348
Corporate bonds, yield on, 1965–1967, 588 (fig.)
Corporate profits, 389
Cost(s),
    external, 341
    government vs. private, 745
    of labor, 252–53, 418, 558, 745
    long run increasing, 150–51
    of maintaining inventories, 117
    and price differences, 212–13
    principle of increasing, 82–83
    private and social, of pollution, 341–43
    relationship to production, 81, 82
    See also Average cost; Average fixed cost; Average total cost; Average variable cost; Constant cost industry; Fixed cost; Marginal cost; Opportunity cost; Transaction cost; Variable cost
Cost-benefit analysis, 294
Cost-effectiveness analysis, 294
Cost-push inflation, 558, 595
Council of Economic Advisors, 608, 610, 611, 721
Credit,
    cheap, in developing countries, 371–72
    direct controls on, 488–89
    money, national income and, 491–93
Credit cards, as money, 476
Credit markets, 464, 500, 533
    equilibrium in, 522–23
    and government spending, 564
    See also Loan contract market
Credit unions, 464, 469
Cross price elasticity of demand, 72
Crowding out, 567, 612–14
Currency, 644, 662
    appreciation/depreciation, 666
    devaluation/revaluation, 666
    overvalued, 700, 702
    role in paying for trade, 663–69
    See also Foreign exchange rate; Money
Currency drain, and open market operations, 486–87
Current Population Survey (CPS), 397–98, 426
Current prices, 381
Customs unions, 656–57
Cyclical unemployment, 429–30
    vs. normal, 433
Czechoslovakia, 726

Dairy industry, 162–63, 180, 181
Deadweight loss, 226, 650
Debt. *See* External debt; National debt
Debt-service ratio, 697
Decreasing returns to scale, 104
Decreasing returns to variable factors (inputs), 101
Deficit. *See* Government deficit
Deflation, 553
    periods of inflation and, 555 (fig.)
Delta Air Lines, 236
Demand, 31–59, 401–6
    analysis method of, 36, 403
    basic assumptions of theory of, 33–36, 401–2
    change in, 45, 404–6
    competitive industry and long run, 145–54
    defined, 32
    derived. *See* Derived demands
    effect of shift in, on equilibrium price/ quantity, 110–17, 410–11
    excess. *See* Excess demand
    government policies that shift, 136–40
    income elasticity of, 71–72
    and international trade patterns, 633–34
    for labor inputs, 247–56, 282, 415–22
    law of, 36–44, 403–44
        applications of, 50–51
    permanent shifts in, 110–11
        with supply, 112–14
    price and production levels determined by supply and, 107–9
    price elasticity. *See* Price elasticity of demand
    relationships of, 33–44
    temporary shifts in, 115–17
    and utility, 41
    vs. quantity demanded, 45–50
Demand curve, 36–44, 61–75, 403–4
    change in, 45, 404–6
        factors effecting, 46–50
    defined, 37
    hypothesis of kinked, 201–2
    industry's, and monopoly, 170
    quantity demanded, price and, 62–71
    value, and marginal utility, 38–44
Demand deposits, 469, 470
Demand-induced inflation, 556–57
Demand schedule, 37
Democracies, 741–45
Democratic Party, 372
Denmark, 301
Deposit insurance, 489
Depository institutions, 464

Depository Institutions Deregulation and Monetary Control Act of 1980, 481, 490
Depreciation, 83, 441
Depreciation of currency, 667
    vs. devaluation, 703
Depression, defined, 394, 395
Deregulation,
    airline, 235–37
    of banking system, 490–91, 515, 594
    case for, 235
Derived demands, 247, 256, 277, 415, 419, 431
Devaluation of currency, 666
    vs. depreciation, 703
Developing countries, 361–73
    cheap food policies in, 366–67
    cheap housing policies in, 368–69
    economic conditions in, 362–65
    export problems of, 694–96
    external debt of, 703–5
    minimum wage and price controls in, 369–71
    shift of industry to, 354
    trade imbalances in, 696–705
Diminishing marginal utility, 43–44
    defined, 43
    and utility function, 54–55
Direct credit controls, 488
Discount rates, 488
Discount window, 489
Discrimination,
    defined, 322
    in housing markets, 329–33
    in labor markets, 322–29
    secondary, 323
    in selling, 124
Disposable income (YD), 441
    and aggregate consumption, 446 (fig.)
Dissaving, 443. *See also* Saving
Drug diversion, 240
Drugs, illegal,
    supply/demand for, 114, 134
Drugs, medicinal,
    complications/effects of regulating, 154–56
    regulating resales of, 240
Duopoly, 199
Durable consumer goods, 293, 382
Duties, specific, 650–51

Earning power, and training, 289–92
Eastern Europe, economies of, 22
Eastman Kodak Co., 179
Economic analysis, 8–9
Economic approach to government activity, 741

Economic change, 718–21
  critical look at industrial policy and,
    720–21
  deindustrialization and, 718–19
Economic data, 438
Economic development, criteria for, 361
Economic efficiency, 11, 340
  competition and, 156–59
  in labor markets and other factors of
    production, 270–71
  and monopoly, 174–75
  production possibilities frontier,
    opportunity cost and, 13–16
  and property rights, 349
Economic Equity Act, 327
Economic growth, 712–13
  defined, 13
  internationally, 685–86
  macroequilibrium, recession, inflation
    and, 552–59
Economic models, 10
  assumptions of, 33
  graphs and, 749–54
Economic profit, 78, 407. *See also* Profit
Economic questions, three fundamental,
    6–8, 725
Economic Recovery Tax Act of 1981
    (ERTA), 447
Economic Report of the President, 382,
    384, 392
Economic rent,
  defined, 96
  and profit in the long run, 153–54
  and wages, 261
Economics,
  agreement/disagreement in, 600–601
  careers in, 25, 26
  profit from point of view of, 84
  See also Keynesian economists;
    Monetarist economists
Economic system,
  basic issues to be addressed by,
    725–29
  capitalist vs. socialist, 726
    economic performance of, 733–39
    performance criteria, 727–29
  characteristics of socialist, 729–33
  defined, 724
Economic union, 656
Economic waste, government promotion
    of, 129
Economies of scale, 178

Education,
  and communications in capitalist and
    socialist economies, 735,
    737 (fig.), 738
  investment in, 287–93, 717
    deciding for, 288
    and functional income distribution,
      303–4
  social benefits of, 343, 344–45
  years of school completed in U.S.,
    287 (fig.)
Effective maximum price, 123
Effective minimum price, 130
Efficiency and equity in human capital
    investment, 293
Efficient economy, 11, 14
  competition and, 156–59
Egypt, 193, 684
Elastic demand curve, 64
Elasticity, prices and total consumer
    spending, 66–68
Elasticity of demand, 66
  for oil, 195, 196
  See also Cross price elasticity of
    demand; Income elasticity of
    demand; Price elasticity of
    demand
Elasticity of labor demand curve, 256
Elasticity of supply, 89–90, 112
Electricity,
  demand for, 32, 46–47
  rate structure of, 231–32
Employees, as cause of inflation, 556–59
Employer discrimination and profit, 324
Employment,
  full. *See* Full employment
  international, 688–89
  normal, 424
  See also Labor; Labor market
Employment Service, 427
Employment stability,
  training, earning power and, 291–92
Endangered Species Act, 294
Endogenous change in variables, 151
Endogenous consumption, 441–43
Environmental Protection Agency (EPA),
    353
Equal Employment Opportunity
    Commission (EEOC), 326
Equality,
  and inequality in income distribution,
    298
  of opportunity or results, 307
  relationship of, 81, 86, 253

Equilibrium, in labor market, 266–71,
    424–25
Equilibrium interest rate, 510–13, 563
Equilibrium price, 107
  effects of supply/demand shifts on,
    110–17, 410
  forces working to establish, 108–9
  levels of, and the quantity theory,
    539–43
  and output, 248 (fig.)
Equilibrium quantity, 107
  effects of supply/demand shifts on,
    110–17, 410
  forces working to establish, 108–9
Equilibrium real GNP, 449–56
  numerical example of, 450 (fig.)
  saving, investment, and government
    deficit, 451–55
Equity, 156
  efficiency, marginal cost and, 158–59
Equity-efficiency quandary in human
    capital investment, 293
Ethical issues, 8
Eurodollar markets, 681
European Economic Community (EEC),
    656
European Free Trade Association
    (EFTA), 656
Excess demand, 108, 410
  and price ceilings, 123, 124 (fig.)
Excess reserves, 483
Excess supply, 109
Exchange rates, 664–68
Exogenous change in variables, 151
Exogenous consumption, 441–43, 454
Exogenous expenditure multiplier. *See*
    Multiplier concept
Expectations,
  and demand curve, 48, 406
  and normal employment, 424
Expected real wage, 424, 425
Exports. *See* Imports/exports; Net
    exports
External benefits, 341, 343–45
  reassessing, 345
External cost, 341, 355
External debt,
  of developing nations, 703–5
  expansion of, 697–99
  Mexican case, 699–703
  world crisis in, 704–5
External economies and diseconomies,
    341–45
  government response to, 346–56
External principle, 345

▶ Factor demand curve, 247
Factor markets, 265–80
    concept of, 266
    equilibrium in labor,
        interconnected competitive,
            268–71
        single competitive, 266–68
    and income distribution, 246–47
    noncompetitive influences in, 271–79
Factor payments, 247
Factors of production, 246
    economic efficiency of, 270–71
    marginal product of, 249–51
    in socialist economies, 731–33
Fair housing legislation, 330
    imperfectly enforced, 332–33
    perfectly enforced, 331–32
Farm Aid, 122
Farmer cooperative associations, 180, 192
Farm issues. See Agriculture
Featherbedding, 277
Federal Communications Commission
    (FCC), 229, 233
Federal Deposit Insurance Corporation
    (FDIC), 480, 489
Federal Open Market Committee
    (FOMC), 483, 576
Federal Reserve Bank. See Federal
    Reserve System
Federal Reserve notes, 469, 476
Federal Reserve System, 468, 480,
    483 (fig.), 611
    monetary policies of, 576–77
        during the Great Depression,
            584–85
        during post-1965 inflation, 587–89
    role of, 481–91, 572
Federal Savings and Loan Insurance
    Corporation (FSLIC), 489
Federal Steel Corporation, 198
Federal Trade Commission, 190, 220, 229
Fiat money, 467
Financial flows, 675–77
Financial instruments, 468, 499
    held by households, 499 (fig.)
Financial market. See Loan contract
    market
Finland, 301
Firm(s),
    behavior of, vs. government's
        bureaucratic behavior, 744–45
    defined, 78, 407
    demand for labor, 247–56, 416–20
        production, output and, 420
    demand for loanable funds, 501–3

    example of monopolistically
        competitive, 208–9
    labor supply to, 260–61
    long and shortrun costs, 100–104
    marginal, 154
    price leadership and dominant,
        198–99
    survival and monopoly, 173–74
    theory of surviving, 152–54. See also
        Profit maximization
    See also Competitive firms and
        industries
Fiscal policy,
    compared to monetary policy,
        576 (table), 577–78
    defined, 563
    discretionary,
        to prevent inflationary episodes,
            568 (fig.), 569
        in a recession, 564–68, 569 (table)
        value of, 577–78
        when taxes are adjusted, 566–67
    during the Great Depression,
        actual, 584, 585
        appropriate, 583
    in industrial countries, 689–92
    Keynesians vs. monetarists on, 604
    lags, politics and, 570
    nondiscretionary, 571
    recent developments in, 571–72
    why it works, 566
Fixed cost,
    defined, 80, 81
    long run variable cost, profit and,
        145–51
    price discrimination and, 186–87
Fixed exchange rates, 666–68
Flat tax, 312 (fig.), 572, 616
Flexible exchange rates, 667–68
Food,
    as consumer expenditure, 33, 34 (fig.),
        62
    policies on, in developing countries,
        366–67
    supply of, in Lebanon, 111
Food and Drug Administration, 154, 207
Food co-ops, 117
Food, Drug, and Cosmetic Act, 154
Food for Peace, 132
Food Stamp program, 137–38, 310, 423,
    571
Foreign exchange intervention, 672
Foreign exchange market, 664
    supply/demand for, 664–68
Foreign exchange rate, 663

Fractional reserve system, 482
France, 22, 610
Free market economy, 22
Free-rider problem, 342, 355–56
    international, 356
Free trade, 642
Frictional unemployment, 427–28
Friedman, Milton, 466, 601
Fruit growers, 181
Full employment, 430
    GNP, 440, 521, 523, 525, 541
Full macroeconomic equilibrium, 520,
    521–26, 562–63 (fig.)
    adjustment toward, with flexible
        prices, 530–32
Functional distribution of income, 301–3
Future prices, effect on supply, 92–93

▶ Game theoretic approach to pricing,
    199–200
"Gary diners," 198
Gary, Elbert, 198
Gasoline. See Oil and gas
General Agreement on Tariffs and Trade
    (GATT), 654–55
General Motors, 246, 645
General training, 289
    and lifetime earnings, 289–91
German Federal Bank, 480
Glut. See Excess supply
GNP. See Gross national product (GNP)
GNP deflator, 391, 392, 417, 420
Gold standard in currency, 467, 680
Goods and services. See Consumer goods
    and services
Gosplan, 729
Government,
    bureaucratic behavior in, 744–45
    demand for loanable funds, 503–4
    investment of,
        in human capital, 293
        in physical capital, 294–95
    labor costs in, 745
    role in capitalist and mixed economies,
        741–45
    See also Politics
Government bonds, 487, 575
Government deficit, 600, 606–14
    economic significance of, 610–14
    and equilibrium GNP, 451–55
    financing in the loan contract market,
        503
    monetizing, 503
    and the national debt, 607 (table)
    vs. other nations, 610

planned savings, planned investment
    and, 458–61
and presidential politics, 607–8
relative to GNP, 690–91
short and long term effects of, 612–14
sources of, 608–10
structural, 611
See also National debt
Government intervention,
    in developing countries,
        cheap credit, 371–72
        food policies, 366–67
        housing policies, 368–69
        minimum wage/price controls,
            369–71
    and foreign exchange, 672
    and social welfare, 122–23
Government policies,
    and agriculture, 122, 129–36
    and economic waste, 129
    fiscal. *See* Fiscal policy
    impact on medical care, 9
    limitations on implementing, 351–52
    monetary. *See* Monetary policy
    and regulation. *See* Government
        regulation
    to restrain market forces, 123–33
    that work through supply/demand,
        134–40
    and theory of demand, 51
    toward pollution, 353–54
    toward unemployment, 427–28, 429,
        433
    toward wage differences in race,
        325–26
    toward wage differences in sex,
        326–29
Government regulation, 223–40
    antitrust laws, 173, 193, 198, 225–29
    and deregulation, 235–37
    of medicinal drugs, 154–56, 240
    rate regulation, 229–35
Government spending (G), 384, 614
    and aggregate investment, 448
    decreased, as response to inflation,
        568 (fig.), 569
    increased, as response to investment
        decline, 564–65
    view on cutting, during recessions, 606
    See also Government deficit
Gramlich, Edward, 295
Gramm-Rudman Deficit-Reduction Act,
    608
Gramm, William P., 608
Graphs, 747–52
Great Britain. *See* United Kingdom

Great Depression, 278, 380, 395, 397,
    480, 489, 553
    monetary and fiscal policy during,
        582–85
Great Society, 712
Greer, Douglas, 233
Gross national product (GNP), 227, 380
    circular flow of, 388
    deflator, 391, 392, 417, 420
    equilibrium real, 449
    full employment, 440
    as measure of total income, 388–89,
        439–40
    as measure of total production,
        381–87
    and national income accounts, 456
    nominal value of, 381, 382–85, 691
    quantity theory of, 539–43
    real, 381, 414
        calculating, 390–95
        estimates of, 394–95
    relative to deficits, 690–91
Growth recession, 394

Hall, Robert, 312
Health,
    in capitalist and socialist economies,
        735, 736 (fig.)
    as human capital, 282
High employment deficit, 610
High tech industries, 719
Hotel prices, and temporary demand
        shifts, 116–17
Households as suppliers of loanable funds,
    505–7
Housing,
    as consumer expenditure, 33, 34 (fig.)
    discrimination in, 320–33
    effect of Fed's policies on, 588
    income elasticity of, 72
    policies toward, in developing
        countries, 368–69
    price ceilings on, 123
    price elasticity of, 68
    quality decline in, 369
    starts, 1965–1967, 588 (fig.)
Houthakker, Hendrik S., 69
Human capital, 246, 326, 713
    education/training as investment in,
        287–93
    and functional income distribution,
        303–4
    good health as, 282
    productivity, income and, 282–83
    See also Labor
Hungary, 159, 299, 726
Hyperinflation, 466, 613

Iacocca, Lee, 642
IBM Corporation, 224
Identity, relationship of, 81, 86, 415
Illegal aliens, 246
Illegal transactions, and GNP, 387
Imports/exports,
    of commodity groups, 626 (fig.)
    and gains from trade, 627–38
    patterns in U.S. and world economies,
        623–27
    supply/demand for, 627–34
    trading partners in, 627 (table)
    See also Net exports; Net imports
Import substitution, 646
Incentives in socialist economies, 729–30
Income,
    disposable. *See* Disposable income
        (YD)
    effect on demand curve, 46–47
    GNP as measure of total, 388–89,
        439–40
    GNP as source of, 388–89
    measurement of national, 390–95
    nonlabor, 257, 267
    uses of total, 439–40
Income distribution, 298–304
    and demand curve, 48–49
    and factor markets, 246–47
    human capital and functional, 303–4
    measurements of, 299–303
    and monopoly, 176–77
    redistribution, 304–17
    and trade regulations, 643–44
Income effect,
    defined, 37, 403
    and demand curve shifts, 46–49
Income elasticity of demand, 71–72
Income maintenance programs, 305,
    310–11
Income transfer programs, 306, 310–17,
    423, 441, 571
    and government spending, 384
Increasing cost, principle of, 82–83,
    87 (fig.)
Increasing returns to scale, 104
Increasing returns to variable factors
    (inputs), 101
Incremental cost. *See* Marginal cost
    (MC)
Incremental revenue. *See* Marginal
    revenue (MR)
Indexing, 571
    and inflation, 394
Indifference curve map, 56
Indifference curves, and consumer choice,
    55–57, 59
Indirect business taxes, 389

Industrial policy,
    developing, 746–47
    in Japan, 720–21, 746
Industry,
    barriers to entry into, 170
    government regulation of, 223–40
    infant, 645–46
    labor supply to, 260–61
    short-run supply, 146
    See also Competitive firms and
        industries
Inelastic demand curve, 64
Infant industries, and import barriers,
        645–46
Inferior goods, 46
Inflation, 286, 390, 466
    accelerated, 559
    aggregate supply/demand in, 549–51
    cost-push, 558, 595
    demand-induced, 556–57
    discretionary monetary policy to
        prevent, 575–77
    due to increase in planned investment,
        533–35
    and economic growth, 552–59
    in industrial countries, 687
    and money supply, 553 (fig.)
    in 1970's, 520, 538
    periods of deflation and, 555 (fig.)
    post-1965, 585–96
    and price indexes, 393–94
    rate of, 393
    reasons for concerns about, 394
    and stagflation, 589–96
    and trade balance, 675
    and unemployment, 554–56
    workers as cause of, 556–59
Information, 591
    advertising, product differentiation,
        214–20
    and externalities, 344 (fig.)
    and limitations on government policy
        implementation, 351–52
    quality of economic, 360, 364
Injecting funds, 452
Innovations, 179
Input(s), 154
    demand for labor, 247–56
    supply of labor, 257–61
    supply of nonhuman, 262
    See also Factor markets; Labor
Interest rates, 284, 395–97
    decline in, and recession, 527–29, 532
    and demand for loanable funds, 502,
        505

equilibrium, 510–12, 563
    and international trade, 675–77
    and investment, 447, 502
    Keynesians vs. monetarists on high,
        602–3, 604
    nominal, 1960–1986, 512 (table)
    real vs. nominal, 396–97, 595
    regulation of, 488–89
    selecting, in present value calculations,
        286
    in stagflation, 595–96
    structure of, 512–13
    and supply of loanable funds, 506–7,
        508–9
Intermediate goods, 381
Intermediate transactions, and GNP, 387
Internal cost, 342
International financial cooperation in
        monetary policy, 680–81
International Monetary Fund, 680–81,
        703
International trade,
    balance of payments and balance of,
        669–73
    changes in oil market and, 693–94
    currency's role in, 663–69
    developing countries' problems and,
        694–96
    distribution of gains from, 634–38
        exporting country, 637–38
        importing country, 634–37
    economic performance and, 685–92
    imbalances in, 696–705
    imports/exports,
        and gains from trade, 627–38
        patterns of, 623–27
    macroeconomic influences on, 675–77
    monetary aspects of, 622
    real aspects of, 622
    regulations on, 646–58
        reasons for, 643–46
    supply/demand and patterns of,
        633–34
    transmission mechanism, 674
International Trade Commission, 655
International transmission mechanisms,
        674
Interstate Commerce Commission (ICC),
        229, 233
Inventories, 115, 456
    and temporary shifts in supply/
        demand of, 116, 117

Investment (I),
    aggregate, 445–48
    and credit in developing countries,
        371–72
    crowding out, 567, 612–14
    defined, 383
    and equilibrium GNP, 451–55
    equilibrium relationship between
        planned savings and planned,
        458–61
    in human capital, 287–93, 713
    increased government spending as
        response to decline in, 564–65
    and national income accounts, 456
    and nominal GNP, 383–84
    in physical capital, 293–95, 713
    planned, and declining interest rates,
        527–29
    planned, and inflation, 533–35
    theory, 283–86
Investor optimism, and recessions, 527,
        545
Iran, 194, 196, 677, 694, 704
Israel, 111, 193
Italy, 610

▶ Japan, 22, 199, 348, 353, 594, 610
    currency, 665–67
    economic growth in, 686
    industrial policy in, 720–21, 746
    trade in automobiles, 50, 51, 139, 622,
        652–53
    trade in steel with U.S., 627–38,
        648–49
Japan Development Bank, 720
Job Training and Partnership Act,
        (JTPA), 293, 429
Johnson, Lyndon, 712

▶ Kennedy, John F., 520, 600
Key money payments, 368–69
Keynes, John Maynard, 538, 680
Keynesian economists, 542, 577–78
    on controlling the macroeconomy,
        603–5
    defined, 601
    on 1980's recession/interest rates,
        602–3
    policy recommendations, 604–5
    on role of monetary policy, 601–2
Kidney dialysis, 9
Kindahl, James K., 202
Kinked demand curve hypothesis, 201–2

Labor, 246
   aggregate demand for, 420–22
   aggregate supply of, 423
   cost of, 252–53, 418, 558, 745
   demand for, 247–56, 282, 415–22
      shifts in, 267–68, 419–20
   influence of unions on demand/supply
      of, 277
   marginal product of. *See* Marginal
      product of labor (mpl)
   mobility of, and wages, 268–70
   productivity, 713–14
      growth in, 714–18
   shortages/underemployment in Soviet
      Union, 732 (fig.)
   supply of, 257–61, 422–23
      shifts in, 267–68
Labor force, 398, 426 (fig.)
   participation, 259
Labor market, 266, 414–25
   in developing countries'
      manufacturing, 370–71
   discrimination in, 322–29
   economic efficiency in, 270–71
   equilibrium in, 521
      interconnected competitive,
         268–71
      single competitive, 266–68
   and recession, 529–30, 534
   teenage, 429
Labor skills, changes in, effect on supply,
   92
Labor unions, 192, 275–79
   membership, 278, 279 (fig.)
   role in income redistribution, 307–8
   tasks of, 275–77
   wages and, 278, 432
Laffer, Arthur, 605
Laffer curve, 605–6
Lag, 570
Law of demand, 36–44, 403–4
   applications, 50–51
Law of supply, 80, 407–8
   applications, 95–97
Laws of society, price ceilings and
   damages to, 125
Leakages of income, 452, 486
Lebanon, 111, 677
Leisure,
   and GNP, 386
   individual supply of, and demand for,
      257–59, 267
Less-developed countries. *See* Developing
   countries
Liggett and Myers, 192
Living conditions, in developed and
   developing countries, 364–65

Loanable funds, 500
   aggregate demand for, 504–5
   aggregate supply of, 510
   demand for, 500–505
      recession and shift in, 527
   effect of monetary policy on, 574
   and money supply, 541 (fig.)
   supply of, 505–10
Loan contract, 468, 499
   decision to hold money vs., 500
   details of, 500–501
Loan contract market, 500–513
   equilibrium in, 510–13
   model of, 501
Lockouts, 276
Logrolling, 742
Long-run economic events,
   aggregate supply curve, 544
   average total cost (LATC) curve, 102,
      103 (fig.)
   costs, firm's, 102
   fixed cost, 145–51
   labor supply, 269
   marginal cost, 103 (fig.), 104
   monopolistic competition in, 210–12
   profit in the, 145–51
   supply and demand, in competitive
      firms and industries, 145–54
   and the "Supply Side," 605–6
   variable cost, 145–51
Long-run equilibrium, 148
Long-run supply (LRS), 150, 154
Lucas, Robert, 578
Luxury goods, 72

M1, 474, 475, 542
M2, 475, 542
M3, 475
Macroeconomics, 439, 464, 474
   and balance of trade, 675–77
   controversies in, 599–616
   introduction to, 380–81
   See also Full macroeconomic
      equilibrium
Macroeconomy, 519–36
   in a growth scenario, 552–59
   Keynesians vs. monetarists on
      controlling the, 603–5
   measuring performance of, 392 (fig.)
Malaysia, 134
Male-female wage differences, 326–29
Manufacturing sector, U.S., 719 (table)
Marginal cost (MC),
   defined, 82
   efficiency, equity, and, 158–59
   profit, law of supply and, 80–90
   relationship to average cost, 88–89

Marginal firm, 154
Marginal private cost, 342
Marginal product of labor (mpl), 250,
   251 (fig.), 282, 415
   value of, 251–52, 416–20
Marginal propensity to consume (MPC),
   444
Marginal propensity to save (MPS), 453
Marginal revenue (MR), 81, 82, 272
   demand, and monopoly price, 195
Marginal social cost, 342
Marginal tax rate, 311
Marginal utility,
   defined, 41
   and demand, 41–44
   See also Diminishing marginal utility
Marginal value,
   defined, 40
   vs. marginal utility, 44
   and monopoly, 174
Market(s), 105–19
   creating, for pollution rights, 352–53
   defined, 21
   government policies to restrain forces
      of, 123–33
   See also Demand; Supply
Market-clearing mechanisms in socialist
   economies, 730–33
Market deficiencies, 157, 339–58
   causes of, 346–49
   external economies/diseconomies,
      341–45
   government response to, 346–56
   and public goods, 345–46
Market demand curve, 37–38
Market economy, 21–22
Market equilibrium, 107, 409–11
   forces working to establish, 108–9
Market failure, 340
Marketing order, 181
Market price, 81
   above equilibrium, 109
   below equilibrium, 108–9
Marshall, Alfred, 256
Marshall's rules, 256, 276, 279
Materials balance approach, 729
Maximum production, opportunity costs
      and comparative advantage, 20
Media, advertising by, 217 (fig.)
Medicaid, 9, 138
Medical care, 11, 14
   impact of government policy on, 9,
      138
   price discrimination in, 186
   social benefits of, 343
   supply and demand for, 112–13
   See also Drugs, medicinal

Medicare, 9, 138
Medium of exchange, 465
Mexico, 22, 196, 698, 699–703, 704
    inflation and dollar value of the peso,
        699–700
    overvaluation of peso, 700–703
Military spending/military presence, in
        capitalist and socialist
        economies, 738, 739 (fig.)
Minimax strategy, 200
Minimum wages,
    in developing countries, 369–71
    legislation for, 308–10
Ministry of International Trade and
        Industry (MITI), Japan, 720,
        746
Mixed economies, 22
    government's role in, 741–45
Mobility among labor markets, 268–70
Models. *See* Economic models
Mondale, Walter, 600, 612
Monetarist economists, 539, 577–78
    on controlling the macroeconomy,
        603–5
    defined, 601
    on 1980's recession/interest rates,
        602–3
    policy recommendations, 604–5
    on role of monetary policy, 601–2
    See also Quantity theory
Monetary authority, 480. *See also* Federal
        Reserve System
Monetary base, 487
Monetary economy,
    advantage over barter, 465
Monetary policy, 481
    compared to fiscal policies,
        576 (table), 577–78
    discretionary,
        to prevent inflation, 575–77
        in a recession, 572–75
        "rules" approach vs., 605
        value of, 577–78
    during the Great Depression,
        actual, 584, 585
        appropriate, 583
    in industrial countries, 691–92
    instruments of, 482–91
    Keynesians vs. monetarists on, 601–2,
        604, 605
    1979 change in, 498
    target of, 603
    why it works, 575

Monetary standards, 467–68
Monetization of the debt, 611
Money, 14, 464
    and the banking system, 468–76
    credit, national income and, 491–93
    decision to hold, vs. loan contracts,
        500
    definition of, in U.S. economy, 475–76
    and post-1965 inflation, 587–89
    quantity of, and prices, 539–43,
        551 (fig.)
    role of, 465–68
    velocity of, 539, 540, 542–43
    See also Currency
Money multiplier, 472
Money supply,
    controls on, 481–91, 493 (table)
    and external debt, 698–99
    growth of, in stagflation, 589–96
    and inflation, 553 (fig.)
    and loanable funds market, 541 (fig.)
    1965–1966, 588 (fig.)
Monopolistic competition, 207
    and advertising, 215
    long-run, 210–12
    price differences in, 213
    short-run, 207–10
Monopoly, 169–82, 224
    application of, 180–81
    vs. competition, 225 (fig.), 272
    control. *See* Government regulation
    deadweight loss of, 226
    defined, 169
    differences among competition,
        oligopoly, and monopolistic
        competition, 209 (table)
    differences between competition and,
        173 (table)
    economic evaluation of, 173–80
    output decisions of, 169–73
    price differences in, 213
    rents, 176–77, 372
    shared, 192
    social costs of, 225–27
    technical, 178–80
    See also Price discrimination
Monopoly power, 169
    and advertising, 218 (fig.), 219
    sources of, 182
Monopsony, 272–75
    equilibrium wage and employment
        and, 274 (fig.)
    labor supply/marginal labor cost and,
        273 (fig.)

Moral suasion of Federal Reserve, 488,
        489
Moscow on the Hudson (film), 124
Multiple deposit expansion, 471 (table),
        472
    and cash drain, 473
    open market operations and,
        484 (fig.), 485 (fig.)
Multiplier concept, 452, 453–54, 566
    and graphical analysis, 458–61

National Bureau of Economic Research,
        394
National debt, 607 (table)
    monetarizing, 611
National defense, 345, 355–56, 374–75,
        644, 743
National Environment Policy Act, 294,
        352
National income, 390
    accounts of, 456
    credit, money and, 491
National Labor Relations Board, 279
National Wool Act, 133
Natural gas, 78
Necessities, 72
Negative externality. *See* External cost
Negotiable order of withdrawal (NOW),
        490–91
Net exports (X), 671
    and aggregate investment, 448
    and GNP, 385
    See also Imports/exports
Net imports, of minerals and metals,
        625 (table)
New Deal, 584
Nigeria, 704
Nixon administration, 97, 126, 520, 538
Nominal interest rate, 396
Nominal (paycheck) wage (W), 418
Nondurable consumer goods, 382
Nonlabor income, 257, 267, 423
Nonmarket activities, 257, 385–86, 422
Nontariff trade barriers (NTB), 651–54
Normal employment, 424
Normal goods, 46
Normal unemployment rate, 431, 592–93
    vs. cyclical, 433
Normative views, 8, 156, 298
Norris-LaGuardia Act of 1932, 278–79
NOW. *See* Negotiable order of
        withdrawal (NOW)

▶ Oil and gas, 151
  conflicting government policies about, 129
  crude oil imports into U.S., 194
  demand for, 47, 50, 66–67, 70–71
  impact of changes in world market for, 693–94, 704
  1970's price increase in, 126, 197, 529, 594, 653, 695, 704
  price ceilings and 1973–74 crisis, 126–29
  supply of, 92
  See also Organization of Petroleum Exporting Countries (OPEC)
Oligopoly, 189–203
  defined, 190
  differences among competition, monopoly, and monopolistic competition, 209 (table)
  economic evaluation of, 202
  price and output decisions in, 191–202
Olympic Games, 116
OPEC. *See* Organization of Petroleum Exporting Countries
Open market operations, 483–87
  and currency drain, 486
  and multiple deposit expansion, 484 (fig.), 485 (fig.)
Opportunity cost, 388
  and air pollution, 27
  applications of, 16–20
  of capital, 231
  case of 55-mph speed limit, 17–19
  comparative advantage, specialization and, 19–20
  defined, 6–7
  law of increasing, 15
  production possibilities frontier, economic efficiency and, 13–16
  and supply, 80
Organization of Petroleum Exporting Countries (OPEC), 67, 70, 92, 95–97, 139, 182, 594, 695
  rise of a cartel, 193–97
Output,
  monopolist's decisions on, 169–73
  and price in oligopolies, 191–202
  profit maximizing input and, 247–48
  and rate regulation, 230
  and shortrun monopolistic competition, 209–10
Overvalued currency, 700, 702

▶ Palestine Liberation Organization (PLO), 111
Paper standard of money, 467, 480
Pastoral Letter on Catholic Social Teaching and the United States Economy, 298
Patent system, 179
Payment in Kind (PIK) program, 134
Payoff matrix, 199
Peak load problem, 232
People's Republic of China, economy of, 22, 159, 724, 727
Pepsi Company, 47, 206
Perfect price discrimination, 184–86
Permanent shifts in supply or demand, 110–14
  effecting other markets, 114
Personal computers, price of, 62
Peru, 705
Pharmaceutical industry, regulating, 154–56
Philippines, demand shift in, 106
Phillips curve, 556
  for the U.S., 557 (fig.)
Physical capital, 246, 713
  input to firms and industries, 262
  investment in, 293–95
  productivity, income and, 282
Pizza restaurants, 190
Planned aggregate expenditure, aggregate production, equilibrium GNP and, 449–56
Plywood industry, antitrust case against, 229
Poland, 299
Polaroid Corporation, 179
Policy Issues,
  air pollution, 27
  banking industry deregulation, 515
  cutting labor costs to save jobs, 335
  cutting wages to save jobs lost to foreign exports, 707
  flat tax, 616
  how to solve, 755–56
  industrialization plan, 746–47
  international cooperation on pollution and defense, 374–75
  medicinal drug resales, 240
  price supports for dairy industry, 162–63
  See also Government policies
Politics,
  and fiscal policy, 570
  and free-market policies in developing countries, 372

  government deficit and presidential, 607–8
  and international pollution, 354–55
  and monetary policy, 576–77
  and property rights, 349
  See also Government
Pollution, 27, 157, 340
  expenditures on, 341 (fig.)
  international cooperation on, 374–75
  possible solutions to, 350–55
  private/social costs of, 341–43
Population,
  characteristics in capitalist and socialist economies, 734 (fig.)
  and demand curve, 48–49
  growth/density of, in developing countries, 362–63
Positive economics, 8
Positive externality. *See* External benefits
Poverty, 274, 298
  measuring, 305–6
  by race and sex, 323 (fig.)
Poverty level of income, 306
PPF. *See* Production possibilities frontier (PPF)
Present value (PV) of assets, 284–85
Price(s),
  advertising, profits and, 220
  changes in, and demand for labor, 254 (fig.)
  changes in expected future, and effect on supply, 92–93, 409
  changes in input, and effect on supply, 92, 409
  controls on, 538
  in developing countries, 369–71
  in socialist economies, 730–31
  See also Rate regulation
  current, 381
  declining, and supply of loanable funds, 531–32
  effective maximum, 123
  effective minimum, 130
  effect of supply and demand on, 107–9, 409–11
  equilibrium level of, 539–43
  flexible, and full macroeconomic equilibrium, 530–32
  and informative advertising, 214–17
  and inventory costs, 117
  and output in oligopolies, 191–202
  relationship to quantity demanded, 62–71
  and short-run monopolistic competition, 209–10
  world, 628–33

Price ceiling, 78, 97, 123–29
  alternatives to, 127–29
  case study of 1973–74 gasoline crisis,
      126–29
Price differentiation,
  vs. price discrimination, 187
  within markets, 212–13
Price discrimination, 182–87
  in medicine, 186
  perfect, 184–86
  in practice, 183–84
  vs. price differentiation, 187
  with substantial fixed costs, 186–87
Price elasticity of demand, 64–69, 112,
      126
  calculating, 64–66
  cross, 72
  defined, 64
  estimates of, for the U.S., 68–69
  reasons for variations in, 70–71
  and total consumer spending, 66–68
Price fixing, 228
Price floor, 129–33
Price index, 390
  and inflation, 393–94
  method of calculating, 391 (fig.)
  need for, 390–92
Price leadership, 192–93
  with a dominant firm, 198–99
Price searchers, 169
Price subsidies, agricultural, 132–33
Price supports, agricultural, 129–32
Price taker, 80, 169
  in the labor market, 260, 416
Pricing policies,
  and collusion, 191–97
  and interdependence, 197–202
  time-of-day, 232
Primary products, 695–96
Prime interest rate, 395
Producers, 388
  goals of, 78–79
  limits on, 80
Product(s),
  effect of demand for, on demand for
      labor, 253–55
  efficiency and variety in, 211–12
  price ceilings and quality of, 124
  safety, 155
Product differentiation,
  tastes, preferences and, 217–19

Production,
  aggregate expenditure, equilibrium
      GNP and aggregate, 449–56
  economically efficient, 157
  measures of, 390–95. See also Gross
      national product (GNP)
  price level, and aggregate, 543–51
Production function, 255
  defined, 249
  and demand for labor, 420
  and marginal product of labor, 249–51
Production levels,
  effect of supply and demand on,
      107–9, 409–11
Production possibilities frontier (PPF),
      11–13, 712–18
  applications of, 16–20
  and efficient economies, 156, 157
  factors behind productivity growth,
      714–18
  factors that shift, 713–14
  opportunity cost, economic efficiency
      and, 13–16
  shape of, 14–16
Productive factors. See Factors of
      production
Productivity, labor, 713–14
  reasons behind growth in, 714–18
Product market, monopoly in, 272
Profit(s),
  accountant's vs. economist's view of,
      84
  advertising, prices and, 220
  and discrimination, 324
  and economic rent in long run, 153–54
  long run fixed cost, variable cost and,
      145–51
  marginal cost, law of supply and,
      80–90
  monopoly, 176–77
  and perfect price discrimination, 185
Profit maximization, 79, 407
  with incomplete knowledge, 152–54
  output/input and labor, 247–48
Progressive income taxation, 311–17
Property rights, 179, 347–49
  and economic efficiency, 349
  political economy of, 349
Proprietors' income, 389
Public goods and services, 345–46
  government response to, 346–56

Quality of products, 651
  and price ceilings, 124
Quantity equation, 539
Quantity of goods and services demanded,
      44, 45, 404–6
  relationship to price, 62–71
  vs. demand, 45–50
Quantity of goods and services supplied,
      424–25
Quantity theory, 539–43, 553, 691
Quotas, 651–54
  voluntary, 652–54

Rabushka, Alvin, 312
Race, discrimination based on, 322–23
  and wage differences, 325–26
Rate regulation, 229–35
  defined, 229
  and deregulation, 235–37
  effect on prices, 233
  in potentially competitive industries,
      233–35
  in practice, 231–33
  and technical monopoly, 229–30
  in theory, 231
Rate structure, 231–32
Rational expectations, theory of, 548, 591
Rationing, 127–28
Reagan, Ronald, 372, 600, 607
Reagan administration, 135, 572, 577,
      594, 608, 612–13
Real income, defined, 37
Real interest rate, 396
Real wage rate (W/P), 418
  expected, 424, 425
Recession, 520–21, 526–33, 541, 602–3
  aggregate demand/supply in, 545–49
  defined, 394
  discretionary fiscal policy in, 564–68
  and economic growth, 552–59
  unemployment in, 430–33
      and inflation rate, 554–56
Recognition lag, 570
Redistribution effects, 122–23
Redistribution of income, 304–17
  policies for, 307–17
  reasons for, 304–7
Rent, 96, 299. See also Economic rent
  controls on, 368–69
  monopoly, 176–77, 372
Rental income, 389

Required reserve ratio, 482, 487–88
Reserves, 468, 507
    excess, 483
    1965–1966, 588 (fig.)
Revaluation of currency, 666
Reynolds Company, R. J., 192
Ricardian equivalence hypothesis, 613–14
Robots, 254, 283, 382
Roosevelt, Franklin, 480

St. Laurent, Yves, 154
Samuelson, Paul, 601
Saudia Arabia, 193, 194, 196, 197
Saving(s), 439, 440. *See also* Dissaving
    decline in, and recessions, 530
    and equilibrium GNP, 451–55
    equilibrium relationship between
        planned investment and
        planned, 458–61
    households' decision for, 505–6
    and national income accounts, 456
    planned, and government deficit,
        455 (fig.)
Saving function, 454
Savings and loan associations, 464, 469
    failures of, 480
Scarcity, 57, 712–18
    defined, 6
    and opportunity costs, 16
    in small economies, 11–13
Scherer, F. M., 207
Schultz, Charles, 721
Secondary discrimination, 323
Segregation, 324
Seller, effect of price ceilings on, 124
Sex, discrimination based on, 322–23
    and wage differences, 326–29
Shared monopoly, 192
Sherman Antitrust Act of 1890, 173, 192,
    198, 227–28
Shortage. *See* Excess demand
Short-run economic events,
    aggregate supply curve, 544
    average cost and supply in the,
        87 (fig.)
    defined, 80, 81
    and fine-tuning policy, 601
    firm's, 101 (fig.), 102
    labor supply, 266–68, 269
    marginal cost, profit and supply in the,
        83–85
    monopolistic competition, 207–10
    revenue, cost and profit in, 146,
        147 (fig.)

Short-run macroeconomic equilibrium,
    520, 530
Short term, 115
Short term supply curve, 116
Shutdown point, on average variable cost
    curve, 88, 102
Size distribution of income, 299–301
Small economies, and scarcity, 11–13
Smith, Adam, 158, 349, 644, 733
Smoot-Hawley tariff, 648
Social choice in a democracy, 742–45
Socialist economies,
    vs. capitalist, 726 (fig.)
    characteristics of, 729–33
    market forces and state planning in,
        726–27
        economic performance of, 733–39
        GNP and, 728 (fig.)
        performance criteria, 727
Social Security, 9, 138, 306, 310, 423,
    441
Social welfare, and government
    intervention, 122–23
Societal discrimination, 323, 324–25
Southeast Asia, economies of, 159
South Korea, 22, 354
Soviet Union, 22, 159, 348, 354, 726–33
Special drawing rights (SDR), 681
Special interests, 742
Specialization,
    defined, 19
    opportunity costs, comparative
        advantage and, 19–20
Specific duties vs. ad valorem tariffs,
    650–51
Specific training, 289
    lifetime earning, employment stability
        and, 292
Speculation in currency, 667–68, 702
Speed limit, and opportunity costs, 17
Stagflation, 498, 520
    defined, 556
    during 1970's, 1980's, 589–96
Statistical Abstract of the United States,
    33, 34 (fig.), 298, 382
Steel industry, 182, 198–99, 246, 380,
    432, 693
    and pollution, 350 (fig.), 351–54
    private/social costs of, 343 (fig.)
    protection of, 651
    strategic supplies of, 645
    and U.S./Japanese trade, 627–38,
        648–49

Stigler, George J., 202
Stocks. *See* Inventories
Store of value, 466
Strategic goods, and import barriers,
    644–46
Strikes, 276
Structural deficit, 611
Structural shifts. *See* Economic change
Structural unemployment, 428–29
    policies to reduce, 429
Substitutes of goods/services, 47, 55–57,
    403
    and price elasticities, 70
Substitution effect, defined, 36–37
Sugar, supply/demand for, 114
Suppliers, goals of, 407
Supply, 77–104, 401, 406–9
    basic assumptions on theory of, 78–80,
        406–7
    competitive industries and long run,
        145–54
    defined, 32
    effect of shifts in, on equilibrium
        price/quantity, 110–17,
        410–11
    elasticity. *See* Elasticity of supply
    excess. *See* Excess supply
    factors that shift, 90–95
    government policies that shift,
        134–36, 138–40
    and international trade patterns,
        633–34
    of labor inputs, 257–61, 415, 422–23
    law of, 80, 407–8
        applications of, 95–97
    marginal cost, profit and, 80–90
    permanent shifts in, 111
        with supply, 112–14
    of physical capital inputs, 262
    price and production levels determined
        by demand and, 107–9
    price elasticities of, 90
    relationships of, 78–94
    temporary shifts in, 115–17
Supply curve,
    constant costs, and industry's long run,
        148–50
    shifts in, 90–95, 408
Supply Side economics, 605–6
Surplus. *See* Excess supply
Sweden, 22, 301

Taft-Hartley Act of 1947, 279
Taiwan, 354
Targeted Jobs Tax Credit (TJTC), 429
Target of monetary policy, 603
Tariffs, 647–51
    aggregate economic losses and,
        649–50
    internal taxes instead of, 643
    on Japanese steel, 648–49
    specific duties vs. ad valorem, 650–51
    U.S. history of, 647–48
    U.S. steel industry, 651
    U.S. textile industry, 651
Tastes and preferences, consumer,
    and demand curve, 47
    and product differentiation, 217–19
Taxes, 439
    as alternative to price ceiling, 128
    and consumption function, 442
    fiscal policy and, 571–72
        and adjusted, 566–67
    flat, 312 (fig.), 572, 616
    indexing, 571
    and pollution, 351
    progressive income, 311–17, 571–72
    as substitutes for tariffs, 643
    and Supply Side economics, 605–6
Taxi cab industry and monopoly, 168
Taylor, Lester D., 69
Technical monopoly, 178–79
    as a category of public goods, 346
    and rate regulation, 229–30
Technology,
    changes in, and demand for labor, 255,
        268
    changes in, effect on supply, 91–92,
        408–9
    transfers of, in international trade,
        645–46
Telephone company, rate structure of,
    231–32
Telico Dam project, 294–95
Temporary shifts in supply and demand,
    115–17
Tennessee Valley Authority, 295
Textile industry, 642
    protection of, 651
Third World. *See* Developing countries
Threat effect, 278
Time horizons,
    effect on demand curve, 48
    effect on price elasticities, 70–71
    effect on supply, 93–94

Time-of-day pricing, 232
Tobin, James, 601
Total consumer spending, 437–61
    relationship to price elasticities, 66,
        67 (fig.)
Total revenue (TR), 66
Total utility, 54
Toyota, 645, 652
Trade. *See* International trade
Trade creation effects, 657
Trade diversion effects, 657
Trade Expansion Act of 1962, 655–56
Trademarks, 206
Training, investment in, 287–93, 717
    and earning power, 289–92
Transaction cost, 115
    and market deficiencies, 346–47, 348
Transfer payments, 384, 441
Transfers of income. *See* Income transfer
    programs
Transitory shift. *See* Temporary shifts in
    supply and demand

Unemployment, 16, 246, 414, 426–33
    cyclical, 429–30
    definition/measurement of, 397–98,
        426
    distribution of, 429, 430 (fig.)
    frictional, 426–27
    full, 430
    importance of, 398
    and inflation rate, 554–56
    international, 688–89
    normal rate of, 431, 433, 592–93
    and stagflation, 589–95
    structural, 428–29
    varieties/causes of, 426–34
Unemployment insurance, 311, 427, 571
Unemployment rate, 398
Unfair labor practices, 279
Unfair trade practices, 654–55
Unions. *See* Labor unions
Unitary elastic demand curve, 64
United Kingdom, 22, 466, 610, 654, 680
    taxes as substitutes for tariffs in,
        643–46
U.S. Bureau of Labor Statistics, 398
U.S. Congress, 295, 312, 570
U.S. Department of Commerce, 655
U.S. Department of Justice, 192, 224, 228

United States economy, 21–22, 151
    definitions of money in, 475–76
    deindustrialization of, 718–19
    economic performance relative to
        other countries, 685–92
    impact of Vietnam War on, 586 (fig.),
        587, 712
    import/export patterns, 623–27
    industries with few firms, 191
    inflation/deflation in, 555 (fig.)
    in 1929–1930, 582–84
    in 1931–1932, 584–85
    1970's, 1980's stagflation, 589–96,
        602–3
    post-1965 inflation, 585–96
    size distribution of income in,
        299–301
    and trade with Japan, 627–38
    views on workings of, 601–5
U.S. Steel Corporation, 182, 246, 432
    price leadership of, 198–99
U.S. Supreme Court, 327
U.S. Treasury, 476, 503
    securities of, 512–13
United Steelworkers Union, 707
Unit of account, 465–66
Unrestricted entry, defined, 80
Utilities, public, 32, 46–47
    and rate structure, 231–32
Utility,
    defined, 41
    and demand, 41, 42 (fig.)
    maximizing, 58
    total, 54
Utility function,
    defined, 54

Value,
    demand curve, marginal utility and,
        38–44
Value of marginal product of labor
    (vmpl), 251–52
Variable cost, 84
    defined, 81
    long run fixed cost, profit and, 145–51
Velocity of money, 539, 540, 542–43
Venezuela, 699
Vietnam War, 344, 680
    impact on U.S. economy, 586 (fig.),
        587, 712
Volker, Paul, 577
Voting behavior in democracies, 741–42

▶ Wages, 255, 261, 267, 298–304
  compensating differentials in, 269–70
  controls on, 538
  and labor mobility, 268–70
  and labor unions, 278
  minimum. *See* Minimum wages
  nominal. *See* Nominal (paycheck)
        wage (W)
  race, and differences in, 325–26
  real. *See* Real wage rate (W/P)
  sex, and differences in, 326–29
  and training, 289–92
  two-tiered structure, 335
  See also Income distribution
Wagner Act of 1935, 279, 307
Wall Street Journal, 112–13

Washington Public Power Commission,
        (WHOOPS), 32, 46–47
Wealth of Nations, 158
Welfare of society,
    capitalist vs. socialist, 733–39
    in developing vs. developed nations,
        364–65
    and GNP, 385–87
    and government intervention, 122–23
    loss to, due to monopoly, 226–27
Welfare programs. *See* Income transfer
        programs
Well-being. *See* Welfare of society
Wells Fargo Armored Service
        Corporation, 192
West Germany, 22, 199, 354, 610, 673
Westinghouse Corporation, 192

Whaling industry, and property rights,
        348–49
White market, defined, 127
Women,
    discrimination against, 322–23,
        326–29
    labor force participation of, 386
Workfare, 311
World Bank, 680
World prices,
    effect on domestic consumption,
        628–30
    equilibrium, and flow of trade, 630–33

▶ Yellow-dog contract, 278–79
Yugoslavia, 301

▶ Zambia, 697